Signs of Life in the U.S.A.

Fifth Edition

Signs of Life in the U.S.A.

Readings on Popular Culture for Writers

Sonia Maasik
University of California, Los Angeles

Jack Solomon
California State University, Northridge

BEDFORD/ST. MARTIN'S   Boston ◆ New York

For All Our Creatures, Great and Small

For Bedford/St. Martin's

Developmental Editor: John E. Sullivan III
Production Editor: Ryan Sullivan
Production Supervisor: Joe Ford
Senior Marketing Manager: Rachel Falk
Art Director: Lucy Krikorian
Text Design: Anna Palchik
Copy Editor: Wendy Polhemus-Annibell
Photo Research: Linda Finigan
Cover Design: Donna Lee Dennison
Cover Art: Pair of old sneakers. Image: © Royalty-Free/Corbis; Movie popcorn. Image: © Royalty-Free/Corbis; Basketball. Image: © Royalty-Free/Corbis; Kaiser roll hamburger. Image: © Royalty-Free/Corbis; Close-up of a green backpack. Image: © Royalty-Free/Corbis; Two cups of coffee, and biscotti. Image: © Royalty-Free/Corbis; Sign warning of "Blind Hill." Image: © Royalty-Free/Corbis; Personal computer with peripherals. Image: © Royalty-Free/Corbis; Browning automatic pistol. Image: © Peter Russell, The Military Picture Library/CORBIS; Still life of a new wireless Internet and camera cell phone. © Rubberball/Getty; Black and white cow with bell. Photographer: Don Mason Brand X Pictures/Creatas; Skateboard. Photodisc/Creatas; Two white dice. IT Stock Free/Creatas; Cell phone. Rubberball Productions/Getty.
Composition: Macmillan India Ltd
Printing and Binding: R.R. Donnelley & Sons Company

President: Joan E. Feinberg
Editorial Director: Denise B. Wydra
Editor in Chief: Karen S. Henry
Director of Marketing: Karen Melton Soeltz
Director of Editing, Design, and Production: Marcia Cohen
Managing Editor: Erica T. Appel

Preface for Instructors

For a few weeks after that terrible day in September 2001, it really did appear that maybe, this time, things were going to change, that the direction of American culture, especially popular culture, was destined to move into a more serious, less entertainment-obsessed social channel. Reality TV, which in 2001 was the emergent new upstart of network and cable programming, appeared set for a comeuppance; the ever-growing number of entertainment awards ceremonies and their attendant displays of unabashed celebrity worship seemed poised for a decline after the cancellation and postponement of the Grammys and the Latin Grammys. And the sudden emergence of a whole new group of cultural icons, led by the personnel of the New York City Fire and Police Departments, looked to eclipse the entertainment icons whose images cast such shadows across the cultural landscape.

But now, scarcely four years later, it is evident that the portents of 2001 were short-lived indeed. Though the country is embroiled in two separate overseas conflicts and the color code of daily terror-alert warnings is an established part of our lives, America's obsession with entertainment is more intense than ever. Reality TV has reemerged with a vengeance, virtually engulfing the airwaves; entertainment awards ceremonies continue to proliferate; and celebrity worship has swept back into fashion with all of its glittering glory. Americans got back to normal very quickly, it appears, and "normalcy" in America now embraces a potent popular culture that has become an essential part of our lives.

Which means that it can't be ignored. American popular culture is not simply an embellishment on our lives, a superficial ornament that can be put on or taken off at will. Popular culture has virtually *become* our culture, permeating almost everything that we do. So if we wish to understand ourselves as a culture, we must learn to think critically about the vast panoply of what was once condescendingly regarded as "mass culture." Indeed, with apologies to a large retail toy chain, "popular culture is us."

Then and Now

This, of course, has not always been apparent to the academic world. When the first edition of *Signs of Life in the U.S.A.* appeared, the study of popular culture was still embroiled in the "culture wars" of the late 1980s and early 1990s, a struggle for academic legitimacy in which the adherents of popular cultural studies ultimately prevailed. Since then, more and more scholars and teachers have come to recognize the importance of understanding what Michel de Certeau has called "the practice of everyday life" and the value of using popular culture as a thematic ground for educating students in critical thinking and writing. Once excluded from academic study on the basis of a naturalized distinction between "high" and "low" culture, which contemporary cultural analysis has shown to be historically contingent, popular culture has come to be an accepted part of the curriculum, widely studied in freshman composition classrooms, as well as in upper-division undergraduate courses and graduate seminars. But recognition of the importance that popular culture has assumed in our society has not been restricted to the academy. Increasingly, Americans are realizing that American culture and popular culture are virtually one and the same, and that whether we are looking at our political system, our economy, or simply our national consciousness, the power of popular culture to shape our lives is strikingly apparent. Sometimes this realization has been fraught with controversy, as when after a spate of schoolyard shootings in the late 1990s a host of politicians and pundits pointed their fingers at violent entertainment as the culprit behind the violence. At other times, the growing influence of popular culture has been received more enthusiastically, as in the widespread belief in the Internet as a medium of economic and educational reform and revival. But whether the recognition is tinged with controversy or splashed with enthusiasm, at no time in our history have Americans been more aware of the place of popular culture in their lives.

For this reason, we believe that learning to think and write critically about popular culture is even more important today than it was when we published the first edition of this book. As the boundary between "culture" and popular culture blurs and even disappears, it is all the more essential that our students understand how popular culture works and how it generates meaning. This is why we continue to make semiotics, the study of signs, the guiding methodology behind *Signs of Life in the U.S.A.* For semiotics leads us, and our students, to take an analytic stance toward popular culture, one that avoids the common pitfalls of uncritical celebration or simple scapegoating.

The reception of the first four editions of this text has demonstrated that the semiotic approach to popular culture has indeed found a place in America's composition classrooms. Composition instructors have seen that students feel a certain sense of ownership toward the products of popular culture — and that using popular culture as a focus can help students overcome the sometimes alienating effects of traditional academic subject matter. At the same time, the semiotic method has helped instructors lead their students to analyze critically the popular cultural phenomena that they enjoy writing about, and so learn the critical thinking and writing skills that their composition classes are designed to impart.

The Critical Method: Semiotics

Reflecting the broad academic interest in cultural studies, we've assumed an inclusive definition of popular culture. The nine chapters in *Signs of Life in the U.S.A.* embrace everything from the marketing and consumption of the products of mass production to the racial and sexual ideologies that inform the content of our entertainment. Unlike other popular culture texts, *Signs of Life in the U.S.A.* adopts an interpretive approach — semiotics — that is explicitly designed to analyze that intersection of ideology and entertainment that we call popular culture. We have chosen semiotics because it has struck us that while students enjoy assignments that ask them to look at popular cultural phenomena, they often have trouble distinguishing between an argued interpretive analysis and the simple expression of an opinion. Some textbooks, for example, suggest assignments that involve analyzing a TV program or film, but they don't always tell a student how to do that. The semiotic method provides that guidance.

At the same time, semiotics reveals that there's no such thing as a pure, ideologically neutral analysis. Anthologies typically present analysis as a "pure" category: They present readings that students are asked to analyze, but articulate no conceptual framework and neither explore nor define theoretical assumptions and ideological positions. Being self-conscious about one's point of view, however, is an essential part of academic writing, and we can think of no better place for students to learn that lesson than in a writing class.

We've found through experience that a semiotic approach is especially well suited to this purpose. As a conceptual framework, semiotics teaches students to formulate cogent, well-supported interpretations. It emphasizes the examination of assumptions and the way language shapes our apprehension of the world. And, because it focuses on *how* beliefs are formulated within a social and political context (rather than just judging or evaluating those beliefs), it's ideal for discussing sensitive or politically charged issues. As an approach used in literature, media studies, anthropology, art and design coursework, sociology, law, and market research (to name only some of its more prominent field applications), semiotics has a cross-disciplinary appeal that makes it ideal for a writing class of students from a variety of majors and disciplines. We recognize that semiotics has a reputation for being highly technical or theoretical; rest assured that *Signs of Life in the U.S.A.* does not require students or instructors to have a technical knowledge of semiotics.

We've provided clear and accessible introductions that explain what students need to know.

We also recognize that adopting a theoretical approach may be new to some instructors, so we've designed the book to allow instructors to be as semiotic with their students as they wish. The book does not obligate instructors or students to spend a lot of time with semiotics — although we do hope you'll find the approach intriguing and provocative.

The Editorial Apparatus

With its emphasis on popular culture, *Signs of Life in the U.S.A.* should generate lively class discussion and inspire many kinds of writing and thinking activities. The general introduction provides an overall framework for the book, acquainting students with the semiotic method they can use to interpret the topics raised in each chapter. It is followed by a section on Writing about Popular Culture that not only provides a brief introduction to writing about popular culture but additionally features three sample student essays that demonstrate different approaches to writing critical essays on pop culture topics. A Citing Sources section that follows will help your students document their writing assignments properly.

The chapters start with a frontispiece, a provocative visual image related to the chapter's topic, and an introduction that suggests ways to "read" the topic, provides model interpretations, and links the issues raised by the reading selections. Every chapter introduction contains three types of boxed questions designed to stimulate student thinking on the topic. The Exploring the Signs questions invite students to reflect on an issue in a journal entry or other prewriting activity, whereas the Discussing the Signs questions trigger class activities such as debates, discussions, or small group work. Reading the Net questions invite students to explore the chapter's topic on the Internet, both for research purposes and for texts to analyze.

The readings themselves are followed by two sorts of assignments. The Reading the Text questions help students comprehend the selections, asking them to identify important concepts and arguments, explain key terms, and relate main ideas to each other and to the evidence presented. The Reading the Signs questions are writing and activity prompts designed to produce clear analytic thinking and strong persuasive writing; they often make connections among reading selections from different chapters. Most assignments call for analytic essays, while some invite journal responses, in-class debates, group work, or other creative activities. Complementing the readings in each chapter are images that serve as visual texts that can be discussed. We've also included a glossary of semiotic terms, which can serve as a ready reference of key terms and concepts used in the chapter introductions. Finally, the instructor's manual (*Editors' Notes to Accompany* SIGNS OF LIFE IN THE U.S.A.) provides suggestions for organizing your syllabus, encouraging student responses to the readings, and using popular culture and semiotics in the writing class.

What's New in the Fifth Edition

Few subjects change so quickly as popular culture, and the fifth edition of *Signs of Life in the U.S.A.* reflects this essential mutability through its substantial revision of the fourth edition. First, we have updated our readings, adding 26 selections that focus on issues and trends important in the new millennium. We have also updated many of the exemplary topics in our introductions used to model the critical assignments that follow and have adjusted the focus of some chapters to reflect changing conditions. A new chapter ("American Paradox: Culture and Contradiction in the U.S.A.") introduces students to fundamental contradictions in the American mythology. On close examination, these contradictions explain so many of the odd things that we do.

From the beginning, *Signs of Life in the U.S.A.* was predicated on the premise that in a postindustrial, McCluhanesque world, the image has been coming to supplant the printed word in American, and global, culture. That is yet another of the reasons we chose semiotics, which provides a rational basis for the critical analysis of images, as the guiding methodology for every edition of our book. Each edition of *Signs of Life in the U.S.A.* has accordingly included images for critical analysis. In the fifth edition, a new design updates the look of the book, and new color ads in Chapter Two and photographs in each chapter help students learn to think critically about visual popular culture. We have also added a new image portfolio that works as a kind of photo essay on the past half-century of American popular culture that asks students to analyze the cultural significance of the exemplary images (from Lucille Ball to Britney Spears) that are displayed. Each chapter includes special images with discussion and writing questions. The images supplement the readings, offering a visual perspective designed to enhance the critical understanding modeled by the texts, not to replace them. We strongly believe that, while the interpretation of images can help students in the honing of their writing skills, it should not be a substitute for learning critical thinking through the analysis of written texts.

Even as we revise this text to reflect current trends, popular culture continues to evolve. The inevitable gap between the pace of editing and publishing, on the one hand, and the flow of popular culture, on the other, need not affect its use in the classroom, however. The readings in the text, and the semiotic method we propose, are designed to show students how to analyze and write critical essays about any topic they choose. They can, as one of our student writers does, choose a topic that appeared before they were born, or they can turn to the latest box office or prime-time hit to appear after the publication of this edition of *Signs of Life in the U.S.A.* To put it another way, the practice of everyday life may itself be filled with evanescent fads and trends, but it is not itself a fad. As the vital texture of our lived experience, popular culture provides a stable background against which students of every generation can test their critical skills.

If we have not included something you'd like to work on, you may still direct your students to it, using this text as a guide, not as a set of absolute prescriptions. The practice of everyday life includes the conduct of a classroom, and we want all users of the fifth edition of *Signs of Life in the U.S.A.* to feel free to pursue that practice in whatever way best suits their interests and aims.

Acknowledgments

The vastness of the terrain of popular culture has enabled many users of the fourth edition of this text to make valuable suggestions for the fifth edition. We have incorporated many such suggestions and thank all for their comments on our text. We are grateful for the help of those who completed an in-depth review of the fourth edition: Judith Ashton, San Bernardino Valley College; Keith Gumery, Temple University; Jennifer Jett, Bakersfield College; Marsha Kruger, University of Nebraska at Omaha; Cory A. Lund, Southwestern Illinois College; Jason McEntee, South Dakota State University; Frank Napolitano, University of Connecticut; Marva Nelson, Southern Illinois University at Carbondale; Lindee Owens, University of Central Florida; Peggy L. Richards, The University of Akron; and John Warnock, University of Arizona. We would also like to acknowledge those who filled out questionnaires on the fourth edition: LynnDianne Beene, University of New Mexico; Lacey Benns, Columbia State University College; Gina Claywell, Murray State University; Theresa Conway, University of Central Florida; Jim Dail, University of California, Riverside; Nicolette de Csipkay, SUNY, Buffalo; Carolyn Embree, University of Akron; Stacy Floyd, University of Kentucky; Stephen Fuller, University of Southern Mississippi; Karl Lisovsky, University of California, Los Angeles; Tim Melnarik, California State University, San Bernardino; Michael Moreno, University of California, Riverside; Andrew Morse, University of Oregon; Terry Nienhuis, Western Carolina University; Manuel Perea, Pasadena City College; Jean Petrolle, Columbia College; Joshua Reid, University of Kentucky; John Schilb, Indiana University; Janet Selitto, University of Central Florida; Phillip Serrato, California State University, Fullerton; Andrew Stracuzzi, Fanshawe College; Mary Strunk, Syracuse University; Wilbur Tietsort, Bowling Green State University; and Jeremy Wallach, Bowling Green State University.

Once again, we wish to thank heartily the people at Bedford/St. Martin's who have enabled us to make this fifth edition a reality, particularly Joan Feinberg, who has now been at the helm through eight of our textbook projects. We cannot say enough about our editor, John Sullivan, who, having been compared to Maxwell Perkins twice already in our last two acknowledgments, might be compared as well to Sir George Martin, who was, in essence, the fifth Beatle. We only wish we could arrange a knighthood for John. Erica Appel and Ryan Sullivan ably guided our manuscript through the rigors of production, while Kaitlin Hannon handled the innumerable questions and details that arise during textbook development. Wendy Polhemus-Annibell expertly copyedited the manuscript. Linda Finigan researched and obtained permission for art, and Sandy Schechter and Sue Brekka cleared text permissions. We are grateful for their help.

Contents

"It's unsettling, if not downright depressing, to go through life embarrassed about the identity of one's childhood idols."

Introduction

POPULAR SIGNS

*Or, Everything You Always
Knew about American Culture
(but Nobody Asked)*

Scene 1: A Backlot Hollywood Studio Office

Okay, so here's the pitch: Donald Trump, Jessica Simpson, and Paris Hilton will lead an all-star cast of *Survivor All Stars* on a quest to the Hawaiian Islands, where the last remaining member of the team will drop a goblet of fire into the cauldron of Mauna Loa. Assisting the team will be a green ogre, a white wizard, and Spider-Man. Midway through the series Paris Hilton will undergo plastic surgery to make her look like Nicole Richie, and Nicole Richie (in a network exclusive) will be made over to look like Paris Hilton. Donald Trump and the ogre will be similarly made over into each other (without plastic surgery), at which point Ryan Seacrest, in a special guest appearance, will interview and then fire one of them. A million-dollar prize, along with a contract to appear on *The Letterman Show*, will be awarded to the winner (who will have been chosen before the series begins according to the results of an Internet poll on what sort of person 18- to 29-year-old Americans would most like to see win a major reality TV contest). And the series will be called *Lord of the Things*.

Scene 2: The General Introduction to *Signs of Life in the U.S.A.*

So all right, this is just a fantasy. You won't be seeing *Lord of the Things* anytime soon on a television screen near you. But just as, once upon a time, wags noted that the key to writing a best-selling story would be to write about Abraham Lincoln's doctor's dog, current popular culture would seem to be especially

1

fixated upon the stars and situations of reality TV and the fantasies of J.R.R. Tolkien, J. K. Rowling, and Pixar Studios.

The question is, what does such a fascination tell us?

At first glance, the simultaneous popularity of *reality* television programming and *fantasy* films might appear to present a cultural contradiction (and American culture, as Chapter 5 of this book explores, is filled with such contradictions). But consider the nature of reality programming: Shows like *Survivor* invite their viewers to imagine themselves in exotic and adventurous surroundings where they compete for million-dollar prizes while becoming instant TV stars, while those in the tradition of *Who Wants to Marry a Millionaire?* invite a vicarious experience of instant romance and riches. *The Apprentice* lets you imagine that you, too, might be able to work for the glamorous Donald Trump, while at the same time experiencing the thrill of seeing the sort of people you compete with in the real workplace put down, rejected, and humiliated. Plastic surgery–based makeover shows let you imagine that looking like your favorite celebrity is just a surgeon's slice away, while programs starring the offspring of the rich and famous (like Nicole Richie, Paris Hilton, and the Ozzy Osbournes) can make you feel like you are sharing the lives of the postmodern jet set.

In short, what reality TV has to offer is actually a broad range of fantasies, escapes from the humdrum banalities of actual life that are barely more realistic than tales of wizards, quests, and cartoon superheroes. This transformation of reality into fantasy suggests that Americans, especially younger ones, have become profoundly bored by, even dissatisfied with, their ordinary lives. Turning to a world of entertainment where the line between fantasy and reality has been blurred, they can find a compensation for the lack of excitement in everyday life. Indeed, it could be said that Americans today, failing to be adequately stimulated by their actual lives in a world of office cubicles and sterile classrooms, demand entertainments of all sorts to give their lives the pizzazz that they desire but cannot find in ordinary reality. This demand is producing a new kind of culture — call it an "entertainment culture" — in which the traditional lines between "high culture" and "low culture," along with the line between reality and fantasy, are being erased, leaving a culture in which just about everything is expected to be entertaining. So now the question is, how did we get to such a state?

From Folk to Fab

Until the nineteenth century, "low," as opposed to "high" or elite culture, constituted the culture of the masses. A genuinely "popular" culture, in the etymological sense of being of the people, often overlapped with what we now call "folk" culture. Quietly existing alongside elite culture, folk culture expressed the experience of the masses in the form of ballads, songs, agricultural festivals, fairy tales, feasts, folk art, and so on. Self-produced by amateur performers, folk culture can be best envisioned by thinking of neighbors gathering

Traditional examples of "high" and "low" culture: the symphony and the circus.

on a modest Appalachian front porch to play their guitars, dulcimers, zithers, mandolins, fiddles, and whatnot to perform, for their own entertainment, ballads and songs passed down from generation to generation. Folk culture, of course, still exists. But it has been dwindling, with increasing rapidity, for the past two hundred years, coming to be overwhelmed by a new kind of popular culture that, while still associated with low culture, is quite different from the self-produced culture of the folk. This popular culture, the popular culture that is most familiar today and that is the topic of this book, is a professional, for-profit culture aimed at providing entertainment to a mass audience. Corporate rather than communal, it is creative rather than conservative, but its creativity is tied to commodification, turning entertainment into a commodity to be marketed alongside all the other products in a consumer society.

The forces that transformed folk culture into contemporary popular culture arose in the industrial revolution of the late eighteenth century and its accompanying urbanization of European and American society. Along with the rise of corporate capitalism and the advent of electronic technologies, these historical forces shaped the emergence of the mass cultural marketplace of entertainments that we know today. To see how this happened, let's begin with the industrial revolution. Prior to the industrial revolution, most Europeans and Americans lived in scattered agricultural settlements. While traveling entertainers in theatrical troupes and circuses might come to visit the larger of these settlements, most people, especially those with little money, had to produce their own entertainment. But with the industrial revolution, masses of people who had made their living through agriculture were compelled to leave their rural communities and move to the cities where employment increasingly was to be had. A concentration of population began to appear in urban centers as the rural countryside emptied. This concentration helped lead to the development of mass societies in which more and more people lived in fewer and fewer places.

With the emergence of mass society came the development of mass culture. For just as mass societies are governed by centralized systems of governance (consider how the huge expanse of the United States is governed by a federal government concentrated in Washington, D.C.), so too are mass cultures entertained by culture industries concentrated in a few locations (as the film and TV industry is concentrated in Hollywood and its immediate environs). Thanks to the invention of such electronic technologies as the cinema, the phonograph, and the radio at the turn of the nineteenth to twentieth century, and of television and digital technology in the twentieth century, the means to disseminate centrally produced mass entertainments to a mass society became possible. Thus, whether you live in Boston or Boise, New York or Nebraska, the entertainment you enjoy is produced in the same few locations and is the same entertainment (TV programs, movies, CDs, what-have-you) no matter where you consume it. The growth of mass culture has been conditioned as well by the growth of a capitalist economic system in America.

It is American capitalism that has ensured that American mass culture would develop as a for-profit industry. Indeed, capitalism has been the ideological linchpin of the entire process by which traditional folk culture evolved into contemporary popular culture.

To get a better idea of how the whole process unfolded, let's go back to that Appalachian front porch. Before electricity and urbanization, folks living in the backwoods of rural America needed to make their music themselves if they wanted music. No one could turn on a radio, a phonograph, a CD player, or an iPod without electricity, and theaters with live performers were hard to get to and too expensive for poor folk. Under such conditions, the Appalachian region developed a vibrant folk music culture. But as people began to move to places like Pittsburgh and Detroit, where the steel and auto industries began to offer employment in the late nineteenth and early twentieth centuries, the conditions under which neighbors could produce their own music decayed, for the communal conditions under which folk culture thrives were broken down by the mass migration to the cities. At the same time, the need to produce one's own music declined as folks who once plucked their own guitars and banjos could simply turn on their radios or purchase records to listen to professional musicians perform for them. Those musicians were themselves recorded in the first place by companies in business to turn a profit, and their music, in turn, could be heard on the radio because corporate sponsors provided the advertising that made (and still makes) radio broadcasting possible.

So what had once been an amateur, do-it-yourself activity (the production of folk music) became a professional, for-profit industry with passive consumers paying for their entertainment either through the direct purchase of a

Devices such as the iPod promote the purchase and consumption of mass-produced music.

commodity (for example, a record) or by having to listen to the advertising that encouraged them to purchase the products that sponsored the radio programs. It was and is still possible, of course, to make one's own music (or, more generally, one's own entertainment), but not only is it just easier and perhaps aesthetically more pleasing to listen to a professional recording, but in the kind of mass consumer society in which live, we are, in effect, constantly being trained to be the sort of passive consumers that keep the whole consumer-capitalist system going. If everyone stopped buying CDs, or stopped watching television or movies, the economy would probably collapse. A constant bombardment of advertising and public relations work, accordingly, keeps us in line as consumers, rather than producers, of entertainment. This bombardment has been so successful that American popular culture now shows signs of a new evolutionary development in which the high and low cultures of the past are melting into each other in a cultural synthesis that could be called an "entertainment culture" — a culture, that is to say, in which all aspects of society are linked by a common imperative to entertain.

Pop Goes the Culture

Thus, far from being a mere frivolity that we could do without, our popular culture, in effect, *is* our culture, constituting the essential fiber of our everyday lives. From the way we entertain ourselves to the goods and services that we consume, we are enveloped in a popular cultural environment that we can no longer do without. To see this, just try to imagine a world without television, or movies, or sports, or music, or shopping malls, or advertising, or DVD, MTV, or MP3. Given the importance of popular culture in our lives and the life of our country, it may seem surprising that until recently its study was largely excluded from university curricula. Not until the advent of "cultural studies," which was first pioneered in British universities and which came to America in the late 1980s, did the study of popular culture become a common, and accepted, topic for university study. But as the barrier between high and low culture, privileged and popular, continues to erode in a world where the Three Tenors perform Pink Floyd–like stadium gigs and Mel Gibson plays Hamlet, where *Romeo and Juliet* is a rap opera and string quartets have been part of the rock scene ever since the Beatles' "Yesterday," the study of pop culture is emerging as a mainstay of contemporary education.

This has been especially true in American composition classrooms, which have taken the lead in incorporating popular culture into academic study, both because of the inherent interest value of the subject and because of its profound familiarity to most students. Your own expertise in popular culture means not only that you may know more about a given topic than your instructor but that you may use that knowledge as a basis for learning the critical thinking and writing skills that your composition class is charged to teach you. This book is designed to show you how to do that — how to write about American popular culture as you would write about any other academic subject.

We have prepared *Signs of Life in the U.S.A.*, in other words, because we believe that you are already a sophisticated student of American culture. Think of all you already know. Just list all the performers you can name. Or television series. Or movies. Do you always pick the green M&Ms — especially when in mixed company — or know the difference between Tupac and Wu Long? Face it, you're an expert. So isn't that a good place to start learning how to write college essays, with what you know already? We all write best when we can write from our strengths, and this book is intended to let you tap into your own storehouse of information and experience as you learn to write college essays.

Signs of Life in the U.S.A., then, is designed to let you exploit your knowledge of popular culture so that you may grow into a better writer about any subject. You can interpret the popularity of programs like *CSI: Las Vegas*, for example, in the same manner as you would interpret, say, a short story, because *CSI*, too, constitutes a kind of sign. A sign is something, anything, that carries a meaning. A stop sign, for instance, means exactly what it says: "Stop when you approach this intersection," while carrying the implied message "or risk getting a ticket." Words, too, are signs: You read them to figure out what they mean. You were trained to read such signs, but that training began so long ago that you may well take your ability to read for granted. But all your life you have been encountering, and interpreting, other sorts of signs that you were never formally taught to read. You know what they mean anyway. Take the way you wear your hair. When you get your hair cut, you are not simply removing hair: You are making a statement, sending a message about yourself. It's the same for both men and women. For men, think of the different messages you'd send if you got a buzz cut to match a goatee, or grew your hair out long, or shaved your head. What does a woman communicate when she chooses beaded braids rather than the sleek Avril Lavigne look? Why was your hair short last year and long this year (or long last year and short this year)? Aren't you saying something with the scissors? In this way, you make your hairstyle into a sign that sends a message about your identity. You are surrounded by such signs. Just look at your classmates.

The world of signs could be called a kind of text, the text of America's popular culture. We want you to think of *Signs of Life in the U.S.A.* as a window onto that text. What you read in this book's essays and introductions should lead you to study and analyze the world around you for yourself. Let the readings guide you to your own interpretations, your own readings, of the text of America.

We have chosen nine "windows" in this edition of *Signs of Life in the U.S.A.*, each of which looks out onto a separate, but often interrelated, segment of the American scene. We have put some of the scenery directly into this book, as when we include actual ads in our chapter on advertising or cartoons that can be directly interpreted. Where it is impossible to put something directly into a textbook, like a TV show or a movie, we have included essays that help you think about specific programs and films, and assignments that invite you to go out and interpret a TV show or movie of your own choosing. Each chapter also includes an introduction written to alert you to the kinds of signs you will find there, along with advice on how to go about interpreting them.

We have designed *Signs of Life in the U.S.A.* to reflect the many ways in which culture shapes our sense of reality and of ourselves, from the things that we buy to the way that culture, through such media as television and the movies, constructs our ethnic and gender identities. This text thus introduces you to both the entertainment and the ideological sides of popular culture — and shows how the two sides are mutually interdependent. Indeed, one of the major lessons you can learn from this book is how to find the ideological underpinnings of some of the most apparently innocent entertainments and consumer goods.

Signs of Life in the U.S.A. accordingly begins with a chapter on "Consuming Passions," because America is a consumer culture, and so the environment within which the galaxy of popular signs functions is, more often than not, a consumerist one. This is true not only for obvious consumer products like blue jeans and sport utility vehicles but for such traditionally nonconsumer items as political candidates and college campuses as well, both of which are often marketed like any other consumer product. It is difficult to find anything in contemporary America that is not affected in one way or another by our consumerist ethos or by consumerism's leading promoter, the advertiser. Thus, the second chapter, "Brought to You B(u)y," explores the world of advertising, for advertising provides the grease, so to speak, that lubricates the engine of America's consumer culture. Because television (including MTV) and film are the sources of many of our most significant cultural products, we include a chapter on each. Chapters on American contradictions, gender, race, public space, and popular icons round out our survey of everyday life.

Throughout, the book invites you to go out and select your own "texts" for analysis (an advertisement, a film, a fashion fad, a political opinion, a building, and so on). Here's where your own experience is particularly valuable, because it has made you familiar with many different kinds of popular signs and their backgrounds, with the particular popular cultural system or environment to which they belong.

The nine "windows" you will find in *Signs of Life in the U.S.A.* are all intended to reveal the common intersections of entertainment and ideology that can be found in contemporary American life. Often what seems to be simply entertainment, like a TV show, is actually quite political, while what seems purely political, like a gender conflict, can be cast as entertainment as well — as in movies like *Thelma and Louise*. The point is to see that little in American life is "merely" entertainment; indeed, just about everything we do has a meaning, often a profound one.

The Semiotic Method

To find this meaning, to interpret and write effectively about the signs of popular culture, you need a method, and it is part of the purpose of this book to introduce such a method to you. Without a methodology for interpreting signs, writing about them could become little more than descriptive reviews or opinion pieces. There is nothing wrong with writing descriptions and opinions, but one of your tasks in your writing class is to learn how to write academic essays — that is, analytical essays that present theses or arguments that are well supported by evidence. The method we draw upon in this book — a method that is known as *semiotics* — is especially well-suited for analyzing popular culture. Whether or not you're familiar with this word, you are already practicing sophisticated semiotic analyses every day of your life. Reading this page is an act of semiotic decoding (words and even letters are signs that must be interpreted), but so is figuring out just what your classmate means by wearing a particular shirt or dress. For a semiotician (one who practices semiotic analysis), a shirt, a haircut, a television image, anything at all, can be taken as a sign, as a message to be decoded and analyzed to discover its meaning. Every cultural activity for the semiotician leaves a trace of meaning, a kind of blip on the semiotic Richter scale, that remains for us to read, just as a geologist "reads" the earth for signs of earthquakes, volcanoes, and other geological phenomena.

Many who hear the word *semiotics* for the first time assume that it is the name of a new, and forbidding, subject. But in truth, the study of signs is neither very new nor forbidding. Its modern form took shape in the late nineteenth and early twentieth centuries through the writings and lectures of two men. Charles Sanders Peirce (1839–1914) was an American philosopher who first coined the word *semiotics*, while Ferdinand de Saussure (1857–1913) was a Swiss linguist whose lectures became the foundation for what he called *semiology*. Without knowing of each other's work, Peirce and Saussure established the fundamental principles that modern semioticians or semiologists — the terms are essentially interchangeable — have developed into the contemporary study of semiotics.

The application of semiotics to the interpretation of popular culture was pioneered in the 1950s by the French semiologist Roland Barthes (1915–1980) in a book entitled *Mythologies* (1957). The basic principles of semiotics had already been explored by linguists and anthropologists, but Barthes took the matter to the heart of his own contemporary France, analyzing the cultural significance of everything from professional wrestling to striptease, toys, and plastics. It was Barthes, too, who established the political dimensions of semiotic analysis. Often, the subject of a semiotic analysis — a movie, say, or a TV program — doesn't look political at all; it simply looks like entertainment. In our society (especially in the aftermath of the Watergate and Monicagate scandals), *politics* has become something of a dirty word, and to *politicize* something seems somehow to contaminate it. So you shouldn't feel alarmed if at first it feels a little odd to search for a political meaning in an apparently neutral topic. You may even think that to do so is to read too much into that topic. But Barthes's point — and the point of semiotics in general — is that all social behavior is political in the sense that it reflects some personal or group interest. Such interests are encoded in what are called *ideologies*, or world-views that express the values and opinions of those who hold them. Politics, then, is just another name for the clash of ideologies that takes place in any complex society where the interests of all those who belong to it constantly compete with one another.

Take, for example, the way people responded to Michael Moore's *Fahrenheit 9/11* in 2004. Those viewers who liked the film shared its anti-administration political values. Conservative viewers, on the other hand, loathed *Fahrenheit 9/11*, complaining about the "liberal bias" of the media while flocking to see Mel Gibson's *The Passion of the Christ*. In each case, the viewers' responses were shaped in part by their ideological and political interests, not simply by their taste in the style of a movie.

While not all movies are as manifestly political as *Fahrenheit 9/11*, careful analysis can usually uncover some set of political values at the heart of a film, although those values may be subtly concealed behind an apparently apolitical facade. Indeed, the political values that guide our social behavior are often concealed behind images that don't look political at all. Consider, for example, the depiction of the "typical" American family in the classic TV sitcoms of the fifties and sixties, particularly all those images of happy, docile housewives. To most contemporary viewers, those images looked "normal" or natural at the time that they were first broadcast — the way families and women

The popular television show *Leave It to Beaver* exemplified traditional family values of the 1950s.

were supposed to be. The shows didn't seem at all ideological. To the contrary, they seemed a retreat from political rancor to domestic harmony. But to a feminist semiotician, the old sitcoms were in fact highly political, because the happy housewives they presented were really images designed to convince women that their place was in the home, not in the workplace competing with men. Such images — or signs — did not reflect reality; they reflected, rather, the interests of a patriarchal, male-centered society. If you think not, then ask yourself why there were shows called *Father Knows Best, Bachelor Father*, and *My Three Sons*, but no *My Three Daughters*? And why did few of the women in the shows have jobs or ever seem to leave the house? Of course, there was always *I Love Lucy*, but wasn't Lucy the screwball character that her husband Ricky had to rescue from one crisis after another?

Such are the kinds of questions that semiotics invites us to ask. They may be put more generally. When analyzing any popular cultural phenomenon, always ask yourself questions like these: Why does this thing look the way it does? Why are they saying this? Why am I doing this? What are they really saying? What am I really doing? In short, take nothing for granted when analyzing any image or activity.

Interpreting Popular Signs

Signs, in short, often conceal some interest or other, whether political, or commercial, or whatever. And the proliferation of signs and images in an era of electronic technology has simply made it all the more important that we learn to decode the interests behind them. Semiotics, accordingly, is not just about signs and symbols: It is equally about ideology and power. This makes semiotics sound rather serious, and often the seriousness of a semiotic analysis is quite real. But reading the text of modern life can also be fun, for it is a text that is at once popular and accessible, a "book" that is intimately in touch with the pulse of American life. As such, it is constantly changing. The same sign can change meaning if something else comes along to change the environment in which it originally appeared. Take the return of the VW Beetle.

In 1998, after a hiatus of some twenty-five years, the Volkswagen Beetle returned to the American automotive marketplace. But the return of the Beetle was not only a consumer event; it was also a sign, an indicator of a broader trend within American popular culture. The question is, of what? To answer that question, we need to look at some history. This is especially important in analyzing the cultural significance of the VW Beetle because of the dramatic changes that have occurred within its history. Originally conceived as a kind of propagandistic challenge to America's ability to provide automotive transport to the common person, the Volkswagen, or "people's wagon," was Adolf Hitler's answer to the Model T. It was expressly designed to connote the superiority of the Third Reich and to be a symbol of Germany's triumphant entry to the center of world power and prosperity.

Drive my car: the new VW Beetle.

The defeat of Nazi Germany put a swift end to that significance, and when the VW Beetle first appeared in American showrooms in the 1950s, its meaning changed accordingly. During an era of postwar prosperity when U.S. automobiles, the biggest and gaudiest on earth, were signifiers of American affluence, the humble Beetle was a car for the prudent and the penny-pinching. One of the first subcompact "economy cars," the VW Beetle, with its under-one-thousand-dollar price tag, served as a kind of reverse status symbol, identifying its owner as someone who didn't have a lot of money to spend. Realizing this, the advertisers for the VW decided to make a virtue of necessity, and so used humor to market their product as a homely but sensible alternative in a marketplace of tail-finned extravagance and status sedans.

This humor, and the low cost of the Beetle, contributed to the next stage of the VW's semiotic history, which intersected with the rise of the sixties youth culture. For then the Beetle, along with its wildly popular Microbus cousin, became the car of the counterculture, a cheap set of wheels for free-wheeling hippies who disdained the muscle cars, luxury chariots, and ordinary autos of the rest of America. Indeed, original Beetles and Microbuses — preferably plastered with Grateful Dead stickers — retain something of that significance to this day, mixing memory and nostalgia for many an aging baby boomer.

The Beetle disappeared from the American road in the seventies as the hippie scene turned yuppie and a host of more fuel-efficient Japanese subcompacts (in those days they were known simply as "Toyotas" and "Datsuns") provided a more functional alternative in the wake of an exponential increase in gas prices. Volkswagen scrapped the Beetle and turned to the Rabbit, which has never had much cultural significance at all. But, as they say, that was then, and this is now. The question for our semiotic analysis is what does the Beetle signify today? It certainly isn't a sign of Nazi prosperity, nor is it simply a perky economy car (it's a bit too expensive for that). It's no signifier of the counterculture either. But it is a sign, a signifier of current popular cultural preoccupations. To see what it is a signifier of, we need to look at the current system in which the Beetle functions as a sign.

To establish the system in which a sign functions and gets its meaning, we need to look at some things with which the sign can be associated, or related, for from a semiotic perspective, the meaning of a sign largely lies in its relations to other signs, both in its similarities to them and in its differences. In other words, when looking at a popular cultural sign, you want to ask "what is this thing like?" as well as "how is it different from some of the things that it resembles?" By asking such questions, by establishing a set of associations and differences, you can approach the semiotic significance of your topic.

Let's return to the Beetle to see how this works. Ask yourself, with what things can the return of the Beetle be associated? It would be useful to begin with those products that are closest to it: other automobiles. But this association, while essential to our analysis, only takes us so far, because every year witnesses the introduction of new automobile lines as manufacturers seek to stimulate consumption through the introduction of new models and styles. The Beetle's return, in other words, is part of the system of automobile production and consumption, but without any way of distinguishing the Beetle from other cars within the system, its meaning would be limited to "new car offering in a marketplace that continually offers new models in order to stimulate consumption." This *is* a part of the Beetle's meaning, but there is a lot more to it than that.

Here is where we can consider the role of *difference* in a semiotic analysis. Among the new model car offerings of the new millenium were a host of SUVs, sedans, pickups, sports cars, subcompacts — in short, the whole array of automotive lines. What made the Beetle different was, in large part, the fact that it was a revival (with some modifications) of a popular, and culturally acclaimed, auto from the golden age of American motoring: the fifties and the sixties. What ended this era was the Arab oil embargo of 1973, which sent gas prices on an irreversible skyrocket and prompted carmakers to search for more functional and fuel-efficient automotive designs (Chrysler's bland K Car might represent the epitome of this chapter in automotive history). The Beetle, which was not as fuel efficient as the new subcompacts from Japan, was a casualty of the gasoline spike, and it can be argued that the flair of automotive design was as well.

The return of the Beetle, then, marked a return to an earlier era of car design. So, what significance can we find in this? To answer this question, we can look back to the primary system in which the Beetle figures — the system of new car offerings at the turn of the millenium — and look for some more associations or similarities. And what we find are a number of other automobiles that represent the revival of earlier, largely abandoned styles from the golden age of American motoring. These include the return of the sporty two-seater, inaugurated by the Mazda Miata, whose success led to the reintroduction of many such cars, including the two-seated Thunderbird. There are also the revival of the Mini, the creation of Chrysler's PT Cruiser, which, while a new design, was intended to suggest the styling of a fifties hot-rod jalopy, the Chevrolet SSR, and in 2005 the splashy and eagerly awaited revival of the original Ford Mustang.

So, there has been a pattern of what might be called nostalgic revivals in the automotive marketplace. This pattern already provides a clue to the cultural significance of the return of the Beetle, but before describing that meaning it would be useful to broaden our perspective a bit to see whether the pattern we have found within the system of car production can be found within the broader system of American consumer behavior. And, sure enough, it can. Indeed, the last five or ten years have seen quite a number of revivals from the fifties and sixties. In 2001, for example, S&H Greenstamps, an icon of fifties and sixties consumer culture that disappeared years ago along with such relatives as Blue Chip Stamps and Plaid Stamps, staged a digitalized comeback as Greenpoints. In the realm of entertainment, movies such as *Ocean's 11* and *The Rat Pack*, along with the emergence of a lounge music scene, represented a revival of the Sinatra/Martin/Davis/Lewis/Bishop era. Then there has been the long-playing revival of retro clothing styles, especially as drawn from the 1970s, as well as any number of retro wristwatch designs from the 1920s and 1930s (not to mention the return of the pocket watch and chain).

We could continue searching for related revivals, but the outline of a significant pattern is already emerging. Clearly, the turn of the century witnessed a number of popular cultural retro revivals. Such revivals arguably signify a certain nostalgia for a bygone era, a desire to return to the products and images of the past. This raises yet another question: Why should Americans desire to return to the past?

Here you need to look at a much broader context in your semiotic analysis: the overall mood and state of American consciousness. By the end of the millenium, that mood was at once jaunty — in the wake of the huge stock market run-up of the nineties — and uncertain, as Americans worried about what Y2K would bring. At times of uncertainty, we tend to cling to what we know, the old verities as it were. In a consumer culture, those things include tried-and-true consumer goods, like, well, VW Beetles or Ford Thunderbirds. The return of such vehicles reflects a calculated gamble on the part of their manufacturers that Americans would embrace them as signifiers of a more certain and comforting past.

But wouldn't you interpret the owner of a Chevrolet SSR differently from the owner of a VW Beetle? Or what about a Thunderbird buyer? Or a Mini purchaser? All these cars can be associated together and all bear a similar meaning in one context, but there are also their differences to consider. These differences help to establish an even more precise significance for the Beetle, and so, to conclude our analysis, we must turn to them.

What differences can you note between the image of a Beetle owner and, say, a Chevrolet SSR driver? Though there may be a number of differences to note, gender difference is especially striking here, for the Beetle, with its bright green and yellow color options, as well as its low-octane cuteness, has especially become the choice of women consumers. With its relatively low, but not bargain basement, price tag, the Beetle has become a favorite choice for better-off young people, particularly women in their early careers. While not being nearly as connotative as the Beetle of the sixties, then, the current model has already assumed a certain significance, sending an identifiable image. Since Americans have always used their automobiles to make statements about themselves and to construct a personal image, we can interpret just what sort of person is likely to drive what sort of car. Indeed we do this all the time, as do market researchers, who, as you will see in Chapter 2 on advertising, commonly construct consumer profiles on the basis of the products that they buy. And after all, don't you interpret others on the basis of the cars they drive? Isn't your own car a lifestyle signifier?

The Classroom Connection

The interpretive analysis we have sketched out here is intended to illustrate the kind of thought process that goes into a semiotic analysis. The historical surveying and contextualization, the comparative associations and analytic distinctions, and the drawing of interpretive conclusions, are what come first in the writing process. Once you have done that, you will have your thesis, or argument, which will then form the structural backbone of your written analysis. Your paper will present that thesis and defend it with the evidence that your semiotic thinking produced. This process is, in essence, no different from the more conventional interpretive analyses you will be asked to perform in your college writing career. It is in the nature of all interpretations to make connections and mark differences in order to go beyond the surface of a text or issue toward a meaning. The skills you already have as an interpreter of the popular signs around you — of images, objects, and forms of behavior — are the same skills that you develop as a writer of critical essays that present an argued point of view and the evidence to defend it.

Because most of us tend to identify closely with our favorite popular cultural phenomena and have strong opinions about them, it can be more difficult to adopt the same sort of analytic perspective toward popular culture that we do toward, say, texts assigned in a literature class. Still, that is what you should do in a semiotic interpretation: You need to set your opinions aside in order to pursue an interpretive argument with evidence to support it. Note how in our interpretation of the VW Beetle we didn't say whether we like the car: Our concern was what it might mean within a larger cultural context. It is not difficult to express an opinion, but that isn't the goal of analytic writing. Analytic writing requires the martialing of supporting evidence, just like a lawyer needs evidence to argue a case. So by learning to write analyses of our culture, by searching for supporting evidence to underpin your interpretive take on modern life, you are also learning to write critical arguments.

"But how," you (and perhaps your instructor) may ask, "can I know that a semiotic interpretation is right?" Good question — it is commonly asked by those who fear that a semiotic analysis might read too much into a subject. But then, it can be asked of the writer of any interpretive essay, and the answer in each case is the same. No one can absolutely *prove* the truth of an argument in the human sciences; what you do is *persuade* your audience through the use of pertinent evidence. In writing analyses about popular culture, that evidence comes from your knowledge of the system to which the object you are interpreting belongs. The more you know about the system, the more convincing your interpretations will be. And that is true whether you are writing about popular culture or about more traditional academic subjects.

But often our interpretations of popular culture involve issues that are larger than those involved in music or entertainment. How, for instance, are we to analyze fully the widespread belief — as reflected in the classic sitcoms mentioned earlier — that it is more natural for women to stay at home and take care of the kids than it is for men to do so? Why, in other words, is the concept of housewife so easy to accept, while the idea of a househusband may seem ridiculous? How, in short, can we interpret some of our most basic values semiotically? To see how, we need to look at those value systems that semioticians call *cultural mythologies*.

Of Myths and Men

As we have seen, in a semiotic analysis we do not search for the meanings of things in the things themselves. Rather, we find meaning in the way we can relate things together, either through association or differentiation. We've done this with the Volkswagen Beetle, but what about with beliefs? This book asks you to explore the implications of social issues like gender norms that involve a great many personal beliefs and values that we do not always recognize as beliefs and values. Rather, we think of them as truths ("Of course it's odd for a man to stay home and take care of the house!"). But from a semiotic perspective, our values too belong to systems from which they take their meaning. Semioticians call these systems of belief *cultural mythologies*.

A cultural mythology, or *myth* for short, is not some fanciful story from the past; indeed, if this word seems confusing because of its traditional association with such stories, you may prefer to use the term *value system*. Consider the value system that governs our traditional thinking about gender roles. Have you ever noticed how our society presumes that it is primarily the role of women — adult daughters — to take care of aging and infirm parents? If you want to look at the matter from a physiological perspective, it might seem that men would be better suited to the task: In a state of nature, men are physically stronger and so would seem to be the natural protectors of the aged. And yet, though our cultural mythology holds that men should protect the nuclear family, it tends to assign to women the care of extended families. It is culture that decides here, not nature.

But while cultural myths guide our behavior, they are subject to change. You may have already experienced a transitional phase in the myths surrounding courtship behavior. In the past, the gender myths that formed the rules of the American dating game held that it is the role of the male to initiate proceedings (he calls) and for the female to react (she waits by the phone). Similarly, the rules once held that it is invariably the responsibility of the male to plan the evening and pay the tab. These rules are changing, aren't they? Can you describe the rules that now govern courtship behavior?

A cultural mythology, or value system, then, is a kind of lens that governs the way we view our world. Think of it this way: Say you were born with rose-tinted eyeglasses permanently attached over your eyes, but you didn't know they were there. Because the world would look rose-colored to you, you would presume that it is rose-colored. You wouldn't wonder whether the world might look otherwise through different lenses. But in the world there are other kinds of eyeglasses with different lenses, and reality does look different to those who wear them. Those lenses are cultural mythologies, and no culture can claim to have the one set of glasses that sees things as they really are.

The profound effect our cultural mythologies have on the way we view reality, on our most basic values, is especially apparent today when the myths of European culture are being challenged by the worldviews of the many other cultures that have taken root in American soil. European American culture, for example, upholds a profoundly individualistic social mythology, valuing individual rights before those of the group, but traditional Chinese culture believes in the primacy of the family and the community over the individual. Maxine Hong Kingston's short story "No Name Woman" poignantly demonstrates how such opposing ideologies can collide with painful results in its tale of a Chinese woman who is more or less sacrificed to preserve the interests of her village. The story, from *The Woman Warrior* (1976), tells of a young woman who gives birth to a baby too many months after her husband's departure to America with most of her village's other young men for it to be her husband's child. The men had left in order to earn the money in America that keeps the impoverished villagers from starving. They may be away for years and so need to be assured that their wives will remain faithful to them in their absence lest they refuse to go at all. The unfortunate heroine of the tale — who, to sharpen the agony, had probably been more the victim of rape than the instigator of adultery — is horribly punished by the entire village as an example to any other wives who might disturb the system.

That Kingston wrote "No Name Woman" as a self-conscious Asian American, as one whose identity fuses both Chinese and Euro-American values, reveals the fault lines between conflicting mythologies. As an Asian, Kingston understands the communal values behind the horrific sacrifice of the No Name Woman, and her story makes sure that her Euro-American readers understand this too. But, as an American and as a feminist, she is outraged by the violation of an individual woman's rights on behalf of the group (or mob, which is as the village behaves in the story). Kingston's own sense of personal conflict in this clash of mythologies — Asian, American, and feminist — offers a striking example of the inevitable conflicts that America itself will face as it changes from a monocultural to a multicultural society.

To put this another way, from the semiotic perspective, how you interpret something is very much a product of who you are, for culture is just another name for the frames that shape our values and perceptions. Traditionally, American education has presumed a monocultural perspective, a melting-pot view that no matter what one's cultural background, truth is culture-blind. Langston Hughes took on this assumption many years ago in his classic poem "Theme for English B," where he observes, "I guess I'm what / I feel and see and hear," and wonders whether "my page will be colored" when he writes. "Being me, it will not be white," the poet suggests, but while he struggles to find what he holds in common with his white instructor, he can't suppress the differences. In essence, that is the challenge of multicultural education itself: to identify the different cultural codes that inform the mythic frameworks of the many cultures that share America while searching for what holds the whole thing together.

That meaning is not culture-blind, that it is conditioned by systems of ideology and belief that are codified differently by different cultures, is a foundational semiotic judgment. Human beings, in other words, construct their own social realities, and so who gets to do the constructing becomes very important. Every contest over a cultural code is, accordingly, a contest for power, but the contest is usually masked because the winner generally defines its mythology as the truth, as what is most natural or reasonable. Losers in the contest become objects of scorn and are quickly marginalized, declared unnatural, or deviant, or even insane. The stakes are high as myth battles myth, with truth itself as the highest prize.

This does not mean that you must abandon your own beliefs when conducting a semiotic analysis, only that you cannot take them for granted and must be prepared to argue for them. We want to assure you that semiotics will not tell you what to think and believe. It *does* assume that what you believe reflects some cultural system or other and that no cultural system can claim absolute validity or superiority. The readings and chapter introductions in this book contain their own values and ideologies, and if you wish to challenge those values you can begin by exposing the myths that they may take for granted.

To put this another way, everything in this book reflects a political point of view, and if you hold a different one it is not enough to simply presuppose the innate superiority of your own point of view — to claim that one writer is being political while you are simply telling the truth. This may sound heretical precisely because human beings operate within value systems whose political invisibility is guaranteed by the system. No mythology, that is to say, begins by saying, "this is just a political construct or interpretation." Every myth begins, "this is the truth." It is very difficult to imagine, from within the myth, any alternatives. Indeed, as you read this book, you may find it upsetting to see that some traditional beliefs — such as the "proper" roles of men and women in society — are socially constructed and not absolute. But the outlines of the myth, the bounding (and binding) frame, best appear when challenged by another myth, and this challenge is probably nowhere more insistent than in America, where so many of us are really "hyphenated" Americans, citizens combining in our own persons two (or more) cultural traditions.

Getting Started

Mythology, like culture, is not static, however, and so the semiotician must always keep his or her eye on the clock, so to speak. History, time itself, is a constant factor in a constantly changing world. Since the earlier editions of this book, American popular culture has moved on. In this edition, we have tried to reflect those changes, but inevitably, further changes will occur in the time it takes for this book to appear on your class syllabus. That such changes occur is part of the excitement of the semiotic enterprise: There is always something new to consider and interpret. What does not change is the nature of semiotic interpretation: Whatever you choose to analyze in the realm of American popular culture, the semiotic approach will help you understand it.

It's your turn now. Start asking questions, pushing, probing. That's what critical writing is all about, but this time you're part of the question. Arriving at answers, conclusions, is the fun part here, but answers aren't the basis of analytic thinking: Questions are. You always begin with a question, a query, a hypothesis, something to explore. If you already knew the answer, there would be no point in conducting the analysis. We leave you to it to explore the almost infinite variety of questions that the readings in this book raise. Many come equipped with their own "answers," but you may (indeed will and should) find such answers raise further questions. To help you ask those questions, keep in mind the two elemental principles of semiotics that we have explored so far:

1. The meaning of a sign can be found not in itself but in its *relationships* (both differences and similarities) with other signs within a *system*. To interpret an individual sign, then, you must determine the general system in which it belongs.
2. What we call social "reality" is a human construct, the product of a *cultural mythology* or *value system* that intervenes between our minds and the world we experience. Such cultural myths reflect the values and ideological interests of its builders, not the laws of nature or logic.

Perhaps our first principle could be more succinctly phrased, "everything is connected," and our second simply summarized as "question authority." Think of them that way if it helps. Or just ask yourself whenever you are interpreting something, "what's going on here?" In short, question *everything*. And one more reminder: Signs are like weather vanes; they point in response to invisible historical winds. We invite you now to start looking at the weather.

PORTFOLIO
Images from the History
of Popular Culture

READING THE SIGNS

1. Identify each of the images in the portfolio. To what decade does each belong? Is your class as a whole more familiar with some images than others?

2. In what ways do these images represent American popular culture? What, in your opinion, makes for a lasting mark on popular culture?

3. Does the portfolio of images suggest something about the changing nature of popular culture? Explain your answer.

4. If you were asked to select an image not included in the portfolio that represents some key aspect of popular culture, what image would you choose? Why?

WRITING ABOUT POPULAR CULTURE

Throughout this book, you will find readings on popular culture that you can use as models for your own writing or as subjects to which you may respond, assignments for writing critical essays on popular culture, and semiotic tips to help you analyze a wide variety of cultural phenomena. As you approach these readings and assignments, you may find it helpful to review the following suggestions for writing critical essays — whether on popular culture or on any subject — as well as some examples of student essays written in response to assignments based on *Signs of Life in the U.S.A.* Mastering the skills summarized and exemplified here should prepare you for writing the kinds of papers you will be assigned through the rest of your college career.

As you prepare to write a critical essay on popular culture, remember that you are already an expert in your subject. Being an expert doesn't necessarily mean spending years of study in a library; simply by actively participating in everyday life, you have accumulated a vast store of knowledge about what makes our culture tick. Just think about all you know about movies, or the thousands on thousands of ads you've seen, or even the many unwritten "rules" governing courtship behavior among your circle of friends. All of these help form the fabric of contemporary American culture — and, if you've ever had to explain to a younger sibling why her latest outfit was inappropriate for work or why his comment to a blind date struck the wrong chord, you've already played the role of expert.

Because popular culture is part of everyday life, however, you may take for granted this knowledge: It might not seem that it can "count" as material for a college-level assignment, and you might not think to include it in an essay.

Thus, it can be useful to spend some time, before you start writing, to generate your ideas freely and openly: Your goal at this point is to develop as many ideas as possible, even ones that you might not actually use in your essay. Writing instructors call this process *prewriting*, and it's a step you should take when writing on any subject in any class, not just in your writing class. This textbook includes many suggestions for how you can develop your ideas; even if your instructor doesn't require you to use all of them, you can try them on your own.

Developing Ideas about Popular Culture

The first step in developing your ideas for an essay about any topic is to make sure you understand accurately the reading selections that your instructor has assigned. You want to engage in *active* reading — that is, you want not simply to get the "drift" of a passage but to understand the nuances of how the author constructs his or her argument. With any selection, it can be helpful to read at least twice: first, to gain a general sense of the author's ideas and, second, to study more specifically how those ideas are put together to form an argument. Ask yourself questions, such as the following, that enable you to evaluate the selection:

- What is the author's primary argument? Can you identify a thesis statement, or is the thesis implied?
- What words or key terms are fundamental to that argument? If the fundamental vocabulary of the selection is unfamiliar to you, be sure to check a dictionary or encyclopedia for the word's meaning.
- What evidence does the author provide to support the argument?
- What underlying assumptions shape the author's position? Does the author consider alternative points of view (counterarguments)?
- What style and tone does the author adopt?
- What is the genre of the piece? You need to take into account what kind of writing you are responding to, for different kinds have different purposes and goals. A personal narrative, for instance, expresses the writer's experiences and beliefs, but you shouldn't expect it to present a fully demonstrated argument.
- Who is the intended readership of this selection, and does it affect the author's reasoning or evidence?

As you read, take notes in your book. Doing so will help you both remember and analyze what you read. A pencil or pen is probably the best memory aid ever invented. No one, not even the most experienced and perceptive reader, remembers everything — and let's face it, not everything that you read is worth remembering. Writing annotations as you read will lead you back to important points. And annotating helps you start analyzing a reading — long before you have to start writing an essay — rather than uncritically accepting what's on the page.

Learning to read actively means *interacting* with what you read by responding: You should question, summarize, agree with, refute what the author says. It means that you're having a kind of conversation with the author rather than simply listening to a lecture by an expert. Studies have shown that such interactive learning simply works better than passive learning; if you read actively, you'll gain knowledge at a higher rate and retain it longer.

There's another reason to annotate what you read: You can use the material you've identified as the starting point for your journal notes and essays; and since it doesn't take long to circle a word or jot a note in the margin, you can save a great deal of time in the long run. Note that we suggest using a pencil or pen, not a highlighter. While using a highlighter is better than using nothing — it will at least help you identify key points — writing *words* in your book goes an important step further in helping you analyze what you read. We've seen entire pages bathed in fluorescent yellow highlighter, and that's of doubtful use in finding the important stuff. Of course, if you simply can't bring yourself to mark up your book, you can write on sticky notes instead, and put those in the margins.

So as you read, circle key words, note transitions between ideas, jot definitions of unfamiliar terms (you can likely guess their meaning from the context or look them up later), underline phrases or terms to research on a search engine such as Google, write short summaries of important points, or simply note where you're confused or lost with a question mark or a *huh?!* In fact, figuring out exactly what parts you do and don't understand is one of the best ways to tackle a difficult reading. Frequently, the confusing bits turn out to be the most interesting — and sometimes the most important. We're not suggesting that you cover your pages with notes; often a few words get the job done. Responding to what you read *as* you read will help you become a more active reader — and that will ultimately help you become a stronger writer.

To illustrate what we mean, let's look at the first two paragraphs of an essay that appears in Chapter 9, along with a reader's annotations of it.

Emily Prager

Our Bodies, Ourselves, very funny

Our Barbies, Ourselves

I read an astounding obituary in the *New York Times* not too long ago. It concerned the death of one *Jack Ryan.*

Who is Zsa Zsa?

A former husband of Zsa Zsa Gabor, it said, Mr. Ryan had been an inventor and designer during his lifetime. A man of eclectic creativity, he designed Sparrow and Hawk missiles when he worked for the Raytheon Company, and, the notice said, when he consulted for Mattel he designed Barbie.

eclectic = widely varied

a guy designed B.

If Barbie was designed by a man, *suddenly a lot of things made sense* to me, things I'd wondered about for years. I used to look at Barbie and wonder, What's wrong

I never wonder who designed B.

with this picture? What kind of woman designed this doll? Let's be honest: Barbie looks like someone who got her start at the Playboy Mansion. She could be a regular guest on *The*

Yeah!

Howard Stern Show. It is a fact of Barbie's design that her breasts are so out of proportion to the rest of her body that if she were a human woman, she'd fall flat on her face.

Here, the title reminds the reader of a book title he recalls (*Our Bodies, Ourselves*); he knows it addresses women, and he thinks the allusion is funny. Then he wonders who the woman with the funny name is (Zsa Zsa Gabor), defines an unfamiliar word (*eclectic*), and notes an important point (that a man, and not a woman, designed the Barbie doll). These comments are brief and were made quickly, but they can help the reader remember details for class discussion and journal entries.

Signs of Life in the U.S.A. frequently asks you to respond to a reading selection in your journal, sometimes directly and sometimes indirectly, as in suggestions that you write a letter to the author of a selection. In doing so, you're taking an important step in articulating your response to the issues and to the author's presentation of them. In asking you to keep a journal or a reading log, your instructor will probably be less concerned with your writing style than with your comprehension of assigned readings and your thoughtful responses to them. Let's say you're asked to write your response to Emily Prager. You should first think through exactly what Prager is saying — what her point is — by using the questions listed and by reviewing your annotations. Then consider how you feel about it. If you agree with Prager's belief that the Barbie doll perpetuates outmoded ideas about women, why do you feel that way? Can you think of other objects (or even people) that seem to exemplify those same ideas? What alternative ways of designing a doll can you imagine? Note that the purpose of imagining your own doll is not so you'll actually produce one; it's so you think through alternatives and explore the implications of Prager's and your own thoughts. Or say you're irritated by Prager's argument: Again, why do you feel that way? What would you say to her in response? What, perhaps in your own experience as a child, might show that she's wrong? Your aim in jotting all this down is not to produce a draft of an essay. It's to play with your own ideas, see where they lead, and even just help you decide what your ideas are in the first place.

Signs of Life in the U.S.A. includes many visual images, along with accompanying questions for analysis in many cases. The semiotic method lends itself especially well to visual analysis. Here are some questions to consider as you look at images:

- What is the **format of the image**? Is it black and white? Color? Glossy? Consider how the form in which the image is expressed affects its message. If an image is composed of primary colors, does it look fun and lively, for instance?

- What **kind of image** is it? Is it abstract, does it represent an actual person or place, or is it a combination of the two? If there are people, who are they?

- Who is the intended **audience** for the image? Is it an artistic photograph or a commercial work, such as an advertisement? If it is an ad, to what kind of person is it directed? Where is the ad placed? If it is in a magazine, consider the audience for the publication.

- What **emotions** does the image convey? Overall, is it serious, sad, funny, boring? Is that expression, in your opinion, intentional? What associations do you make with the image?

- If the image includes more than one element, what is the most prominent element in the **composition**? A particular section? A logo? A section of writing?

- How does the **layout** of the image lead your eye? Are you drawn to any specific part? What is the order in which you look at the various parts? Does any particular section immediately jump out?

- Does the image include **text**? If so, how do the image and the text relate to one another?

- Does the image suggest that you act in some way? For instance, does it suggest that you purchase a product? If so, what claims does it make?

Let's look at a sample analysis of an advertisement using the preceding questions (see image on p. 36).

Format: Although this image is reproduced here in black and white, it originally appeared in color. The colors are muted, however, almost sepia-toned, and thus suggest an old-fashioned look.

Kind of image: This is a fairly realistic image, with a patina of rural nostalgia. A solitary woman, probably in her twenties or thirties, but perhaps older, is set against an empty natural expanse. She has a traditional hairstyle evocative of the 1950s or early 1960s and leads an old-fashioned bicycle with a wicker basket attached.

Audience: This image is an advertisement for Lee Jeans. The intended audience is likely a woman in her late twenties or older. We see only the model's back, and so she is faceless. That allows the viewer to project herself into the scene, and the nostalgic look suggests that the viewer could imagine herself at a younger time in her life. Note that the product is "stretch" jeans. There's no suggestion, often made, that the jeans will enhance a woman's

The things that give a woman substance will never appear on any "what's in/what's out" list.

Straight Leg STRETCH **Lee**

sexual appeal; rather, the claim is that the jeans are practical — and will fit a body beyond the teen years. Note the sensible hairstyle and shoes. For an interesting contrast you might compare this ad to one for Guess? Jeans. (Mentally substitute Paris Hilton — the effect is absurd.)

Emotion: The woman's body language suggests individuality and determination; she's literally "going it alone." She's neither posing for nor aware of the viewer, suggesting that "what you see is what you get." And, perhaps, she doesn't particularly care what you think.

Composition and layout: The layout of the ad is carefully designed to lead your eye: The hill slopes down from top right toward middle left, and the bike draws your eye from bottom right to mid-left, with both lines converging on the product, the jeans. For easy readability, the text is included at the top against the blank sky.

Text: The message, "The things that give a woman substance will never appear on any 'what's in/what's out' list," suggests that Lee Jeans is a product for those women who aren't interested in following trends, but rather want a good, old-fashioned value — "substance," not frivolity.

In sum, most fashion ads stress the friends (and often, mates) you will attract if you buy the product, but this ad presents "a road not taken," suggesting the American ideology of marching to the beat of a different drummer, the kind of old-fashioned individualism that brings to mind Robert Frost and Henry David Thoreau. The pastoral surroundings and the "old painting" effect echo artists such as Andrew Wyeth and Norman Rockwell. All of these impressions suggest lasting American values (rural, solid, middle American) that are meant to be associated with anti-trendiness and enduring qualities, such as individualism and practicality. And these impressions suggest the advertisers carefully and effectively kept the ad's semiotic messages in mind as they designed it.

These strategies will work when you are asked to respond to a particular reading or image. Sometimes, though, you may be asked to write about a more general subject. Often your instructor may ask you to brainstorm ideas or to freewrite in response to an issue. These are both strategies you can use in your journal or on your own as you start working on an essay. Brainstorming is simply amassing as many relevant (and even some irrelevant) ideas as possible. Let's say your instructor asks you to brainstorm a list of popular toys used by girls and boys in preparation for an essay about the gendered designs of children's toys. Try to list your thoughts freely, jotting down whatever comes to mind. Don't censor yourself at this point. That is, don't worry if something is really a toy or a game, or if it is used by both boys and girls, or if it really is an adult toy. Later on you can throw out ideas that don't fit. What you'll be left with is a rich list of examples that you can then study and analyze. Freewriting works much the same way and is particularly useful when you're not sure of how you feel about an issue. Sit down and just start writing or typing, and don't stop until you've written for at least ten or fifteen minutes. Let your ideas wander around your subject, working associatively, following their own path. As with brainstorming, you may produce some irrelevant ideas, but you may also come to a closer understanding of how you really feel about an issue.

Sometimes your instructor may invite you to create your own topic. Where should you start? Let's say you decide to analyze an aspect of the film industry but can't decide on a focus. Here, the Internet might help. You could explore a search engine such as Yahoo!, specifically its Movies and Films index. There you'll find dozens of subcategories, such as History, Theory and Criticism, Cultures and Groups, and Trivia. Each of these subcategories has many sites to explore: History, for instance, includes the Archives of Early Lindy Hop as well as the Bill Douglas Centre for the History of Cinema and Popular Culture, a wonderful compendium of 25,000 books, posters, and other movie-related memorabilia. With so many sites to choose from, you're bound to find something that interests you. The Net, in effect, allows you to engage in electronic brainstorming and so arrive at your topic.

One cautionary note: In using the Internet to brainstorm, be sure to evaluate the appropriateness of your sources. Many sites are commercial and therefore are intended more to sell a product or image than to provide reliable information. In addition, since anyone with the technological know-how can set up a Web site, some sites (especially personal home pages) amount to little more than personal expression and need to be evaluated for their reliability, accuracy, and authenticity. Scrutinize the sites you use carefully: Is the author an authority in the field? Does the site identify the author, at least by name and e-mail address (be wary of fully anonymous sites)? Does the site contain interesting and relevant links? If you find an advocacy site, one that openly advances a special interest, does the site's bias interfere with the accuracy of its information? Asking such questions can help ensure that your electronic brainstorming is fruitful and productive. If you are not sure of the validity of a Web site, you might want to check with your instructor.

Not all prewriting activities need be solitary, of course. In fact, *Signs of Life* includes lots of suggestions that ask you to work with other students, either in your class or from across campus. We do that because much academic work really is collaborative and collegial. When a scientist is conducting research, for instance, he or she often works with a team, may present preliminary findings to colloquia or conferences, and may call or e-mail a colleague at another school to try out some ideas. There's no reason you can't benefit from the social nature of academic thinking as well. But be aware that such in-class group work is by no means "busy work." The goal, rather, is to help you to develop and shape your understanding of the issues and your attitudes toward them. If you're asked to study how a product is packaged with three classmates, for instance, you're starting to test Thomas Hine's thesis in "What's in a Package" (Chapter 1), seeing how it applies or doesn't apply and benefiting from your peers' insights.

Let's say you're asked to present to the class a semiotic reading of a childhood toy. By discussing a favorite toy with your class, you are articulating, perhaps for the first time, what it meant (or means) to you and so are taking the first step toward writing a more formal analysis of it in an essay (especially if you receive feedback and comments from your class). Similarly, if you stage an in-class debate over whether Batman is a gay character, you're amassing a wonderful storehouse of arguments, counterarguments, and evidence to consider when you write your own essay that either supports or refutes Andy Medhurst's thesis in "Batman, Deviance, and Camp" (Chapter 9). As with other strategies to develop your ideas, you may not use directly every idea generated in conversation with your classmates, but that's okay. You should find yourself better able to sort through and articulate the ideas that you do find valuable.

Developing Strong Arguments about Popular Culture

We expect that students will write many different sorts of papers in response to the selections in this book. You may write personal experience narratives, opinion pieces, research papers, formal pro-con arguments, and many others. We'd like here to focus on writing analytic essays because the experience of analyzing popular culture may seem different from that of analyzing other subjects. Occasionally we've had students who feel reluctant to analyze popular culture because they think that analysis requires them to trash their subject, and they don't want to write a "negative" essay about what may be their favorite film or TV program. Or a few students may feel uncertain because "it's all subjective." Since most people have opinions about popular culture, they say, how can any one essay be stronger than another?

While these concerns are understandable, they needn't be an obstacle in writing a strong analytic paper — whether on popular culture or any other topic. First, we often suggest that you set aside your own personal tastes when writing an analysis. We do so not because your preferences are not important; recall that we often ask you to explore your beliefs in your journal, and we want you to be aware of your own attitudes and observations about your topic. Rather, we do so because an analysis of, say, *The Aviator* is not the same as a paper that explains "why I like (or dislike) this movie." Instead, an analysis would explain how it works, what cultural beliefs and viewpoints underlie it, what its significance is, and so forth. And such a paper would not necessarily be positive or negative; it would seek to explain how the elements of the film work together to have a particular effect on its audience. If your instructor asks you to write a critical analysis or a critical argument, he or she is requesting neither a hit job nor a celebration of your topic.

As a result, the second concern, about subjectivity, becomes less of a problem. That's because your analysis should center around a clear argument about that movie. You're not simply presenting a personal opinion about it; rather, you're presenting a central insight about how the movie works, and you need to demonstrate it with logical, specific evidence. It's that evidence that will take your essay out of the category of being "merely subjective." You should start with your own opinion, but you want to add to it lots of proof that shows the legitimacy of that opinion. Does that sound familiar? It should, because that's what you need to do in any analytic essay, no matter what your subject matter happens to be.

When writing about popular culture, students sometimes wonder what sort of evidence they can use to support their points. Your instructor will probably give you guidelines for each assignment, but we'll provide some general suggestions here. Start with your subject itself. You'll find it's useful to view your subject — whether it's an ad, a film, or anything else — as a text that you can "read" closely. That's what you would do if you were asked to analyze a poem: You would read it carefully, studying individual words, images, rhythm, and so forth, and those details would support whatever point you wanted to make about the poem. Read your pop culture subject with the same care. Let's say your instructor asks you to analyze a photograph. Look at the details: Who appears in the photo, and what are their expressions? What props are used, and what is the "story" that the photo tells? Is there anything missing from this scene that you would expect to find? Your answers to such questions could form the basis of the evidence that you use in your essay.

If your instructor has asked you to write a semiotic analysis, you can develop evidence as well by locating your subject within a larger system. Recall that a system is the larger network of related signs to which your subject belongs and that identifying it helps to reveal the significance of your subject. This may sound hard to do, but it is through identifying a system that you can draw on your own vast knowledge of popular culture. And that may sound abstract, but it becomes very specific when applied to a particular example. If you were to analyze platform shoes, for instance, it would help to locate them within the larger fashion system — specifically, other choices of footwear. How do the signals sent by wearing a pair of platforms differ from those sent by wearing, say, a pair of Doc Martens? How does the history of platform shoes, specifically their popularity in the 1970s, affect their current appeal? Can you associate the retro look of platforms with any other fashion and popular cultural trends? Teasing out such differences and associations can help you explain the shoes' social and cultural significance.

You can strengthen your argument as well if you know and use the history of your subject. That might sound like you have to do a lot of library research, but often you don't have to: You may already be familiar with the social and cultural history of your subject. If you know, for instance, that the baggy pants so popular among teens in the mid-1990s were a few years before ubiquitous among street gang members, you know an important historical detail that goes a long way toward explaining their significance. Depending on your assignment, you might want to expand on your own historical knowledge and collect other data about your topic, perhaps through surveys and interviews. If you're analyzing gendered patterns of courtship rituals, for instance, you could interview some people from different age groups, as well as both genders, to get a sense of how such patterns have evolved over time.

The material you gather through such an interview will be raw data, and you'll want to do more than just "dump" the information into your essay. See this material instead as an original body of evidence that you'll sort through (you probably won't use every scrap of information), study, and interpret in its own right.

Reading Essays about Popular Culture

In your writing course, it's likely that your instructor will ask you to work in groups with other students, perhaps reviewing each other's rough drafts. You'll find many benefits to this activity. Not only will you receive more feedback on your own in-progress work, but you will see other students' ideas and approaches to an assignment and develop an ability to evaluate academic writing. For the same reasons, we're including three sample student essays that satisfy assignments about popular culture. You may agree or disagree with the authors' views, and you might think you'd respond to the assigned topics differently: That's fine. We've selected these essays because they differ in style, focus, and purpose and thus suggest different approaches to their assignments — approaches that might help you as you write your own essays about popular culture. We've annotated the essays to point out argumentative, organizational, and rhetorical strategies that we found effective. As you read the essays and the annotations, ask why the authors chose these strategies and how you might incorporate some of the same strategies in your own writing.

Essay 1: Personal Experience Essay

Some assignments may allow you to respond to a topic by discussing your own personal experiences and observations. Such assignments enable you to draw on a wealth of details and specific evidence that you have close to hand, and they also enable you to develop your own voice as a writer (because the subject is your own experience, you will want to use the first-person form of address). Dana Mariano, a student at Lehigh University in Bethlehem, Pennsylvania, wrote the following essay, "Patrons of the Arts," about a recent trend that many young people have embraced despite their parents' disapproval: tattooing and body piercing. Mariano was not required to base her discussion on a close reading of the selections. But notice that she combines her own tale of visiting a tattoo parlor with a full and rich consideration of the system into which her visit can be interpreted — thus fulfilling one of the central tenets of the semiotic approach.

Patrons of the Arts

Dana begins with a catchy narrative introduction that establishes her focus on the motivations behind tattooing and body piercing.

The glow from Tattoo 46's neon sign reflected onto the dashboard of my car and attracted most of the flies from the surrounding area. As I walked into Tattoo 46, I asked myself a very logical question: "What the hell am I doing here?" I was not a biker, a World War II veteran, or a criminal; I was simply an eighteen-year-old girl who wanted a tattoo. Actually, I had wanted a tattoo since I was in the eighth grade, and now I was finally old enough to get one.

I looked around the waiting room of Tattoo 46 and saw plastered on the walls a potpourri of tattoos that ranged from fire-breathing dragons to roses to cartoon characters. I could hear a faint buzz coming from a room in the back that was shut off with a curtain that looked like a bedspread from the sixties. Luckily, I already knew exactly what tattoo I wanted, so I did not have to search for the perfect one from the plethora of tattoos on the walls. I planned to get my tattoo of a Hawaiian flower and get it tattooed onto my lower stomach.

Dialogue adds drama to the narrative.

A burly, gray-haired man, who reminded me so much of Jerry Garcia, walked out from another back room and asked, "So, let me guess. You are here to get your belly-button pierced."

"Actually, I would like it if you could do a tattoo of this," I said as I handed him the picture of the tiny narcissus flower my friend Samantha had drawn for me.

"Yeah, I can do this," he said. "Do you have any ID?"

"Sure, here it is," I said triumphantly as I showed him my driver's license.

"Well, well, well. Happy Birthday. So, are you ready to roll?" he asked.

"As ready as I'll ever be," I replied with a voice that lacked any semblance of confidence.

As I walked into the small room, I saw all over the walls pictures of tattooed and pierced people. Most of these people had body piercings in regions where I had only heard people could get them, but I never thought it was truly physically possible. I heard a man scream from the other room, and once again I asked myself, "What the hell am I doing here?" I was a medium-height, blonde, Abercrombie-wearing, sorority type of girl. Why would I get a tattoo or anything other than my ears pierced?

Looking at society today, one realizes that a variety of people are now getting tattoos and body piercings. These body adornments, which were once an accessory for rebels, punks, bikers, and freaks, are now commonly seen on models, actors, people in the business world, and even teachers. Today, one cannot walk down the street without seeing someone sporting a tattoo, eyebrow ring, tongue ring, or labret (pierced lower lip).

Dana broadens her focus to a general cultural trend.

These people are proud to show off their personal artwork. Tattooing and body piercing were once symbols of nonconformity in society; now they almost seem to be a form of conformity. The question is, why have so many decided to pierce their bodies in weird areas and adorn their bodies with tattoos? What exactly has happened to polite society?

Celebrities and rock stars have always influenced the way people believe they should look. With many models, rock icons, sports figures, actors, and actresses getting their bodies tattooed and pierced, the public wants to follow in their footsteps. Even the most feminine and revered actresses and models are tattooing themselves with small flowers and butterflies or getting their belly-buttons pierced as a symbol of sexuality. Sports figures such as Dennis Rodman cannot stop with just one tattoo and body piercing. For many, body piercing and tattooing become a strange addiction. Society has always looked at these types of people as role models. If they can pierce and tattoo, why shouldn't the public?

She analyzes her subject, drawing on popular culture to describe the semiotic system in which tattoos and body piercing exist.

If one looks at the type of people who are piercing themselves, one sees that many are in their thirties and forties, the baby boomers who are in the midlife-crisis age range. Many baby boomers have reached the midlife-crisis age and need something to show a sense of rebellion against society. Also, many baby boomers did not feel that having a tattoo or body piercing was appropriate until now because of its new appeal in polite society and the mainstream.

My mother is one of the people in this category. She got a tattoo five years ago. One could say that she was going through a midlife crisis. She lost one hundred pounds, grew her once-short hair rather long, and bought a very cute red convertible. The last thing on her agenda of making a new woman was to get a tattoo of a butterfly on her lower stomach. Now she is through her midlife crisis, and she feels a sense of youth from her tattoo. She has even said when she dies she wants there to be a hole in her dress where her tattoo is. She wants everyone to be able to see her personal work of art.

Dana provides an alternative explanation, which adds depth to her analysis.

Another explanation for this trend is the *National Geographic* syndrome. In other parts of the world, tattooing and piercing have been common practices for thousands of years. In many non-Western cultures and societies, body art is an indicator of nobility and the upper class. In India, when a woman gets married, she is covered with patterns in henna, a type of dye. This body art is considered a sacred symbol of beauty for an Indian woman. Since the world is becoming more and more aware of other cultures, we can see other cultures' ways and are far more accepting of them. The globalization of the world has truly opened up society to be more accepting of one another's cultures, views, and even body adornments.

She offers a third explanation and follows it with an extended example.

A compelling reason for the act seems to be to establish identity. This is why many people my age get body piercings and tattoos. Many teenagers are scared of getting lost in the crowd, and that is why they resort to such measures. It is so hard to stand out in a diverse society; teenagers today go to any measure they can to get more attention. My friend Deanna, who is the valedictorian of my class, recently got her eyebrow pierced. She is one of the people who did this as a form of rebellion and to make a departure from her girly, brainy persona. She did this a few days before graduating high school.

"So, do you think all the parents will be thrilled to see my beautiful eyebrow ring?" Deanna asked with a sly grin.

Dialogue dramatizes the point and makes it personal and immediate.

"Oh, you know they are going to love it. I am sure that you will make the school so proud sporting your eyebrow ring," I said in one of my more sarcastic tones.

"Do you know that the principal already asked me to take it out for graduation? He said he doesn't want me to give the school a bad look," Deanna said with a hint of pride.

"You aren't going to take it out, are you?" I asked.

"Are you kidding me? Of course not. I refuse to allow people to remember me as perfect little Deanna. I would look like I was the principal's pet, even though I was at one time. I have worked so hard to move away from the old Deanna. This eyebrow ring represents a new, more independent Deanna," she firmly stated.

Whatever the reason, many people have decided to adorn their bodies with tattoos and piercings. Today's diverse society makes it harder and harder for a person to get noticed, so many have changed their appearance so they can stand out in the crowd. The abundance of body piercing and tattooing has also changed the way society looks at beauty. It was once considered ugly and manly for a woman to have a tattoo. Today, it is considered sexy and erotic if a woman has a small, feminine tattoo on her body. The abundance of tattooing and body piercing has certainly changed the way that society views these things that were once considered proper only for freaks.

    As I lay on the cold metal table, I tried to decide whether I truly wanted this tattoo or not. I pulled down my pants and watched my tattoo artist get out a new needle. I was going to do this. I had no idea why, but I was going to get the tattoo I always wanted. There is no rational explanation for why I wanted a tattoo; I just did.

Dana returns to the introduction's dramatic scene, signaling closure to the narrative.

    "So why are you getting a tattoo?" my tattoo artist asked.

    "I don't know," I said. "I just want one."

Essay 2: Critical Reading of a Film

Your instructor may ask you to read one of the selections in this text and then to apply the author's general ideas to a new example, either one provided by the assignment or one that you select. Such an assignment asks you to work closely with two "texts" — the reading selection and a pop cultural example — and requires you to articulate the relationship you see between the two. In essence, such an assignment asks you to use the reading selection as a critical framework for analyzing the particular example. In this essay, William Martin-Doyle of Harvard University applies Robert B. Ray's theory of heroic archetypes in American cinema ("The Thematic Paradigm," p. 308) to a film of his own choice, *Cool Hand Luke*. His instructor explained to his class, "A really good essay will not simply say *why* Ray's theory does or does not apply but will go further and speculate what that relevance or irrelevance *means*." As you read Martin-Doyle's essay, look for how the student fulfills both tasks.

Cool Hand Luke: The Exclusion of the Official Hero in American Cinema

William sums up Ray's definition of hero and presents his argument that Cool Hand Luke *(CHL) departs from Ray's archetypal pattern.*

In his article "The Thematic Paradigm," Robert B. Ray contends that the two heroic types of outlaw and official are the stock figures of American cinema. The author implies that by the acceptance of the two characters' juxtaposition in popular culture, Americans are revealing a type of immaturity: "The parallel existence of these two contradictory traditions evinced the general pattern of American mythology: the denial of the necessity for choice" (para. 15). This contention is well rooted: movies such as *Shane*, for example, illustrate Ray's point quite effectively, presenting the viewer with the story of a gunslinger and a farmer joining forces to combat evil and defend the American way. Movies have come a long way since *Shane*, though. Films display their coming-of-age by making choices far more often than they used to. This new decisiveness does not necessarily reflect a responsible adulthood, however; when a choice is made, it is now frequently for the outlaw hero. This trend is easily seen in the movie *Cool Hand Luke* (1967).

The paragraph doesn't just give a plot summary but explains plot details in terms of the ideologies Ray describes.

The movie tells the story of an individualist who is sentenced to two years working on a chain gang for his rebellion against authority. To avoid alienating the viewer with the story of an inhuman criminal, the makers of the movie choose a crime that panders to the audience, in the form of "malicious destruction of municipal property": cutting the heads off parking meters while bored and drunk. In this way, lawbreaking is romanticized as the vice of a man who refuses to conform. Luke's individualism and powerful personality initially alienate the other prisoners, but he soon becomes their idol; through him they live vicariously. After attempting to live in the suffocating atmosphere of the prison camp, Luke begins his escape efforts. He is repeatedly recaptured, with mounting consequences for each attempt. The authorities, as symbolized by the nameless man who supervises the chain gang's work from behind the mask of his sunglasses, attempt to break Luke's spirit. They degrade and beat him for every attempt, and they finally kill him after his third try, but Luke's refusal to conform, expressed through his escapes, is made into a victory for individuality.

Cool Hand Luke's unreserved depiction of the legal system as a brutally unjust entity signals a definite departure from movies that contain both of Ray's stock hero types. Ray asserts that "by customarily portraying the law as the tool of villains . . . this mythology betrayed a profound pessimism about the individual's access to the legal system" (para. 11). The law, confusingly, is also the tool of the official hero. This is a puzzling situation in many movies, as order is the very basis for the character of the official hero. That the support for the "Good Good Boys" (para. 3) should come from an insti-tution that the audience for some reason views with suspicion sug-gests that the official hero character is only a substitute for the out-law hero in most people's minds: the renegade is the ideal. The presence of both types in a film might indicate a certain confusion in the viewer about what he or she really values. Ray, however, indi-cates that American cinema is typified by the presence of the two. *Cool Hand Luke* represents a departure from that "duplicity" (para. 23). There is no confused romanticizing of two conflicting ideals: instead, the clear choice is Newman's outlaw. Everywhere in the movie, the forces of law and order are portrayed as a tool for oppres-sion rather than for the protection of everyday citizens, a group to which one might assume the average audience member belongs.

William pre-sents more fully Ray's definition of heroes and moves to the essay's asser-tion that CHL fails to fulfill this pattern.

Ray writes of the pervasive theme of the reluctant hero, the man who is eventually forced by outside pressures into promoting the greater good; he is "the private man attempting to keep from being drawn into action on any but his own terms. In this story, the reluctant hero's ultimate willingness to help the community satisfied the official values" (para. 18). In this way, the reluctant hero repre-sents a synthesis of the official and the outlaw hero, rendering a somewhat contradictory picture, almost of a man with a split person-ality. Once again, *Shane* epitomizes this concept, as the mysterious stranger is drawn into aiding the brave settlers in their struggle against the ranchers, despite his initial desire to lay aside his guns and lead a peaceful life. In contrast, *Cool Hand Luke* presents no such capitulation to the moral pressure of helping others. Luke's only priority is to live his life his own way, not to aid the other pris-oners. There is no plot device of the hero righteously leading a rebel-lion against the armed guards for subjecting them to life in the chain gang. Luke never consciously tries to become a leader, and the other prisoners' admiration for him never fosters a sense of responsi-bility in him for their well-being. His strong personality induces oth-ers to become attached to him, yet he never feels any reciprocal ties. Indeed, the only strong emotional bond that he has during the

Here and in the next two paragraphs, William ana-lyzes specific cinematic de-tails that demonstrate the kind of hero Luke is.

entire movie is the one to his sickly mother, who comes to visit him
at one point. Later in the movie, word of her death arrives, and Luke
is cut off from any emotional tie, making him a complete loner. Even
this instance is used as an example of the cruelty of the established
authority, as Luke is confined in a wooden box the size of a closet
for several days just so that he won't get any ideas about escaping to
go to the funeral. This measure does force Luke to the edge, but his
response is not that of Ray's stereotypical hero, who exhibits traits of
both the official and the outlaw hero. His response is straightforward,
in keeping with his character. He doesn't combat injustice in general,
helping the greater good of the other prisoners; instead, he makes his
first attempt at escape (a perfectly understandable, yet hardly selfless
action). In this way, the character of Luke remains consistent: he
begins as an outlaw, and he never strays from that image.

William doesn't limit his analysis to Luke; he studies other characters as well.

The conspicuous lack of an official hero is accented by George
Kennedy's character Dragune, who at first seems like he might play
that role. A prisoner who has been serving time for several years, he
has become a sort of leader among the prisoners, who listen to him
because of his strength and his outspokenness. A bit of a blowhard,
he defends the status quo, holding forth on the value of order in the
prisoners' lives: "We got rules here. In order to learn 'em, you gotta
do more work with your ears than with your mouth." Ray states that
the official hero's motto is "You cannot take the law into your own
hands" (para. 12), and this is clearly Dragune's own personal opinion. Luke, on the other hand, obviously has no use for society's
impositions; during his first night, he says, "I ain't heard that much
worth listening to. Just a lot of guys laying down a lot of rules and
regulations." When conflict arises between Dragune and Luke, it first
appears that the viewpoint of the authority will triumph over Luke's
championing of the individual. They box, as is the custom for two
prisoners with irreconcilable differences, and Dragune easily beats
Luke senseless. This physical triumph of authority quickly turns into
a moral victory for Luke, however, as Dragune is forced to leave the
ring when he realizes that the only way that Luke will ever stay on
the ground after a knockdown is if Dragune kills him. After this
turning point, Dragune soon becomes Luke's friend and eventually
his disciple.

Luke's tenacity is simultaneously the strong point of his personality, the very trait that makes him worthy of admiration, and

his fatal flaw. This character will never give up, no matter the pain he must endure, whether the situation is in the boxing ring against a man who heavily outweighs him, in a bet that he can eat fifty eggs in an hour, or in his repeated attempts at escape, for which he is punished with escalating viciousness. These escape attempts are the main outlet for his rebellion, and they are always initially successful. Despite the fact that he is always later apprehended, he always makes his escapes in grand fashion, confounding the authorities who attempt to chase him. The escapes are therefore victories of a kind against the establishment, symbolic of his death grip on his own identity. After the first recapture, the captain of the camp debases Luke and reflects to the other prisoners: "What we've got here is failure to communicate. Some men, you just can't reach." In this world of polar extremes, there can be no communication between the outlaw hero and the forces of conformity that would normally be wielded by an official hero. It is officialdom's failure to reach Luke, to "get his mind right," that gives the outlaw his victory. His death is imbued with nobility as the car that takes him away, dying, crushes the supervisor's sunglasses that have come to be the recurring metaphor for the rule of the law.

Cool Hand Luke represents a shift away from the standards presented in Ray's article, as illustrated by *Shane*, in which American movies have a conflicting duality of protagonists. *Cool Hand Luke* has instead made the choice for the outlaw hero. This is a definite shift away from earlier movies that emphasized the official hero, such as Jimmy Stewart films, and war movies, which celebrated the triumph of the ultimate official body, the United States government. Despite the fact that the movie was a product of the late 1960s, a time of political and social unrest, *Cool Hand Luke*'s decision still has relevance in this decade. The rejection of society in its present form, as represented by the official hero, is still visible in the progression to modern hits like *Natural Born Killers* and *Pulp Fiction*, which glorify serial killers and organized crime hit men. Ray implies that Americans' failure to make a choice when it comes to their movies is a societal problem. In *Cool Hand Luke*, the choice has been made, but a new problem is reflected in that choice. Any country is based on the idea that there must be rules to govern acceptable and unacceptable behavior; the constant deprecation of those rules therefore signals an extreme dissatisfaction with present society. Such

William locates CHL in the context of American film history, including films that both predate and postdate CHL.

The essay moves toward its conclusion by suggesting the social implications of the ideology presented in CHL.

dissatisfaction is a normal reaction against the perceived failure of authority, as exemplified by problems such as the Vietnam War, Watergate, and the national economy. Dissatisfaction isn't necessarily a bad thing, but expressing discontent without hinting at the possibility of a real solution is troubling.

William con-
cludes with a
sharp state-
ment of his
view of those
implications.

The problem with the choice of the outlaw hero lies in the fact that the outlaw doesn't confront issues and deal with them in a mature fashion. Instead, he runs away as Luke did or uses force until there is nothing left to face. In short, the choice of the outlaw hero exposes the fact that Americans are indulging in a form of moral escapism: they dislike their present circumstances, yet are too scared to face up to them.

Work Cited

Ray, Robert B. "The Thematic Paradigm." *Signs of Life in the U.S.A.: Readings on Popular Culture for Writers.* 5th ed. Ed. Sonia Maasik and Jack Solomon. Boston: Bedford/St. Martin's, 2006. 308–15.

Essay 3: Open-Ended Analytic Assignment

Your instructor may assign an open-ended topic, one that gives you certain guidelines but that allows you to pick your own object for analysis. If you receive such an assignment, first brainstorm possible topics that interest you, for you'll produce the best writing if you're excited about your subject. And be sure you understand if your instructor wants you to use specific reading selections as a framework for your analysis, or if you have the latitude to select your own essays that can buttress your interpretation. The following essay, by Joshua Keim of California State University, Northridge, is entitled "Nostalgia Mongering at City Walk"; his assignment asked him to write a semiotic analysis of the social and cultural values implicit in a retail store of his own choosing. In this essay, Keim lets his interpretation unfold as he narrates the process of walking around City Walk.

Nostalgia Mongering at City Walk

I knew I had arrived. I was standing at the west end of City
Walk, in Universal City, California, an avenue of glittering billboards
and myriad neon signs, towering effigies of King Kong, Fender Stra-
tocasters, and other pop culture icons, each one like a giant animus
floating out of some vast collective unconscious. This was it. From
the Metro Link that dropped me off in Universal City to the tram
that conveniently shuttled me up to the top, all signs seemed to
point toward here. This was the virtual mecca of post-industrial consumerism.

City Walk. Is it some evil genius' vision for the future of "retail
therapy" and homage to Manifest Destiny? Or a unique hybrid of
strip mall, expo, and theme park — indeed, since it's adjacent to one
of Los Angeles' most frequented theme parks, Universal Studios?
Designed and built in 1993 by architect Jon Jerde — whose firm the
Jerde Partnership, Inc. is also responsible for that other bastion of
supra-capitalism, the Mall of America in Bloomington, Minnesota —
City Walk was conceived to give the appearance of just that: a virtual "streetscape," a metropolis unto itself, isolated safely atop the
Universal City hillside, and offering, as M. L. Bierman put it, "*risk-
free* consumption in a private dream world" (qtd. in Giacconia,
emphasis added). That's right: "risk-free." In other words, City Walk
was designed to give the appearance of an urban setting without the
influx of certain "undesirable" urban elements, namely street punks,
prostitutes, and bums who might otherwise spoil the illusion (Giacconia). That way you and your family can get down to the business
of buying things.

Of course, City Walk is not just food courts, gift shops, and
megaplex movie theaters; it's a *fantastic* shopping experience. The
question is, "what is the fantasy?" How are All-Star Collectibles,
Hard Rock Café, and Retro Rad each connected? I needed an answer —
some sign — so I headed east into that pulsing artery of dreamworks,
until I came to it.

You'd almost miss it if weren't for the looming six-foot face of
Sparky the Cat about to knock you over the head or the sixteen-
year-old salesgirl greeting you just outside the door and demonstrating the quantum mechanics of Slinkies with a lollipop in her mouth.
Sparky's Candy and Other Swell Stuff! Located just off the Fountain

*Joshua grabs
the reader's
attention with
a catchy nar-
rative opener.*

*He provides
a brief his-
tory of the
creation of
City Walk.*

*Next he asks
a question
that focuses
the essay's
subsequent
discussion.*

Court (or food court) next to a smoothie shop and across from Cama-
cho's Mexican restaurant, Sparky's is the perfect post-dining pit stop
to grab a little something for the sweet tooth and of course to get a
little browsing in — indeed, since the much advertised candy is at
the back of the store, you're forced to pass all the merchandise to
get to it — while you chomp away on caramels and salt-water taffy
at $2.00 per ¼ lb. since it's part candy store, part *vintage* retailer.

Joshua sug-
gests an ini-
tial interpreta-
tion of one
store.

As I gazed in awe at over seven hundred types of Pez dispensers
and Wacky Wobblers on display in the store windows, it suddenly
occurred to me that Sparky's — along with a number of other City
Walk stores — was aggressively selling nostalgia to the masses. As
the store's on-line advertisement suggests,

> Sparky's is a unique fun store that takes you on a joyride
> through your favorite childhood memories. Whether [the]
> Fabulous Forties or Generation X, Sparky's uncovers the kid in
> all of us. Celebrating classic ideas by mixing fun new products
> with original vintage items, Sparky's is chock full of "Really
> Swell Stuff." ("Sparky's")

Swell. Even that word smacked of 1950s slang. But before I figured
out whose dream they were selling, I wanted to know how they
sold it.

In the 1990s, the large proliferation of vintage stores had a lot
to do with the Generation Xers who were disenchanted with the
American dream — which they believed didn't include them —
disillusioned by where they thought the system was heading, and
tended to look at the world with a lot of postmodern irony. As a
counterculture movement, they were unique in that they were the
first generation of American youths who didn't see themselves suc-

He adds
depth to that
interpretation
by drawing
on Shames
to explain the
cultural
mythology
underlying
the popularity
of vintage
stores.

ceeding more than their parents. As Laurence Shames suggests in "The
More Factor," a lot of this skepticism is linked to the fact that Americans, as a result of our frontier myth, have always believed in social
mobility and the idea that there would always be "more" of whatever
we needed to progress (57). But, as Shames also points out, since 1949
and up through the 1980s, we saw a steady decrease in "income
expansion" and thus expectations, and in the early nineties we were
still "running out of more" (60, 59). Often, when the future looks dry,
people look to the symbols of the past for comfort and guidance, and
so vintage fashions (for example, bell-bottoms), vintage furnishings

(lava lamps), and vintage modes of music (the rockabilly-swing fusion of Brian Setzer) all made a brief return to the pop culture scene, although each with a slight difference — hence, compact disc players made-up to look like Victrola record players for $249.99. Of course, their parents, the baby boomers who were entering one mass mid-life crisis, were equally frustrated with their progeny and the glass ceiling, and so they too tried to recapture their innocence by buying it, usually from one of these pop culture appreciation expos. Sparky's is a testament to this cultural phenomenon and is pandering it to both generations.

But with all the vintage item stores still in full swing, what sets Sparky's apart?

As I looked at the right window display with all the Wacky Wobblers — you know, those plastic dolls with bobbing heads you usually see on car dashboards — I noticed a sign reading "Photo Spot" and an arrow pointing to a colorful box, which was really a human-sized replica of the Wacky Wobbler packaging. To take advantage of this photo opportunity, you have to *walk into the store* while someone photographs you from outside, thereby attracting the attention of other bystanders — excuse me, consumers. Surely enough, some tourists were snapping away while one of their friends was making miming gestures inside the box. As I looked on I thought, "what an ingenious device to get people to buy these useless baubles." "See yourself in this package, identify with the brand-name, now see yourself buying the product," it seemed to say. In fact, each Wacky Wobbler featured the familiar image of some popular cartoon character (Dick Tracy and Jughead) or product mascot (the Starkist Tuna and the Jolly Green Giant), which implies that they're selling brand-name identification once more to you.

"Do you have to pay to take a photo in the box?" I asked the clerk.

The dialogue adds drama to the discussion.

"Nope," she replied, removing the lollipop from her mouth.

"I wish I had a camera. My professor would appreciate this."

"Well, we sell disposable cameras inside," she grinned.

How convenient. It was time I saw the inside of the store.

Just inside the entry, at the center, as the sounds of (yep!) Brian Setzer oozed out the store, there stood some contraption that looked like it was straight off the pier at Coney Island called a "Super Squisher." You've probably seen these things in theme parks before. Basically, you stick a penny in the slot and, through some marvel of science, in less than a minute your penny is transformed into a useless token with the City Walk logo on it. I found this to be a particularly significant form of "behavior modification" (Solomon 161). On the one hand, the machine gets you to take your money out of your pocket to start spending it — and when your kids start clamoring for a penny, you will spend it. On the other hand, it gets you used to the idea of not getting anything of material value for your money, just souvenirs . . . like so many memories. Not having any children, I safely moved on.

Joshua makes use of Underhill's terminology as found in Gladwell's essay.

By this point I was in what Paco Underhill refers to as the "Decompression Zone," the area in a store that allows consumers to enter a shopping mode, but Sparky's wasn't allowing anyone to decompress (qtd. in Gladwell 404). They were taking the customer right into the time warp. In fact, as I walked in I was suddenly inundated with old-fashioned Coca-Cola machines circa 1955 ($4,800), two racks of Pioneer Roadster go-carts ($399.99), and one of those compact disc Victrolas. These were high-ticket items, and they were just six feet inside the store. Contrary to Underhill's advice, Sparky's didn't seem to be wasting time promoting their most expensive products. Once more, as I looked at the Pioneer Roadster go-carts, I saw not only a reiteration of the frontier myth, but because they were originally conceived as a child's toy, I also imagined neighborhood streets filled with kids racing them and started to associate the go-carts with families and community. So I looked around to see if the store wasn't exploiting this image further.

To the right of the store were the rows of Wacky Wobblers; to the left, the rows of Pez dispensers, each portraying again some cartoon figure and hanging on the rack like a pop culture apotheosis. Over each display was a sign that read "Collect them all!" Why? How many Pez dispensers does one person need? It was obvious that Sparky's was promoting the kind of "pathological buying" that John De Graaff, David Wann, and Thomas H. Naylor warn about in "The Addictive Virus," and that we were stuck in "more mode," or shopping to fill a void (74). In fact, if you check out the Pez Web site (www.pezco.securesites.com), you'll find a whole subculture that's been collecting and auctioning these "interactive cand[ies]" for over fifty years — they've even got a newsletter. So if you buy Homer, you better get Marge, the whole family, and the rest of the population of

Springfield so your collection will be complete, because you're not just buying Pez now, you're buying the Pez sense of community: social belonging and family values. I could start to see the attraction of these products, not just to children, but to Gen Xers and baby boomers — since as Sparky's ad suggests, they are the collectors. Now I wanted to know what belonging meant.

Joshua complicates his analysis by articulating another set of social values.

At the back of the store, G.I. Joes and Barbies stood side by side. These have been two of the largest wardens of gender coding in children's toys for the last forty-plus years, and they were in tandem, on display together at Sparky's. But again, they weren't being sold merely as children's toys but as collector's items. So why would Gen Xers and baby boomers identify with these?

G.I. Joe was first introduced in 1964 as "the first boy's 'Action Figure' in the world," according to Hasbro's Web site ("G.I. Joe"). After the Kennedy assassination, the then-dubious new Johnson administration, and the looming conflict in Vietnam, Joe was a paragon of conventional masculinity with his buff, martial posturing, John Wayne swagger, and patriotic self-righteousness. He remained a sort of stronghold against the feminist movement, which threatened to subvert the code. Originally, as Gary Cross argues, the doll "began as a celebration of an *all-male* world of realistic combat" (emphasis added, 774). In fact, G.I. Joe has always reflected politicized gender coding — usually the conservative right's. As a Gen Xer myself, I remember the cartoon series of the 1980s in which Cobra, a fascist dictator, was G.I. Joe's sworn enemy, illustrating Hasbro's attempt to capitalize on the cold war paranoia and anti-Communist sentiment that were still strong during the Reagan administration. As the product box so accurately puts it, Joe's a "real American hero."

He locates G.I. Joe in its historical context.

However, the collector's edition on display at Sparky's signaled something slightly different. It was the "Pearl Harbor 60th Anniversary series," released in 2001. Joe still represented that John Wayne brand of patriotism like the Joes of old, but the fact that this series was still being sold had a lot to with September 11, 2001. Though the toy company might claim the series was released in conjunction with the December 7 anniversary of the attacks on Pearl Harbor of that year, if the series was still bankable it was for another reason. In the first few weeks after the September 11 attacks, every politician and political commentator, including the president himself, was

Then he contrasts that context, and the meaning it suggests, with the toy's significance today.

associating the attack on the World Trade Center with the bombing of Pearl Harbor, since it was the first strike on American soil since December 7, 1941 — that "day that [would] live in infamy in the minds of all Americans," as Roosevelt declared. In this new age of "terror" and uncertainty, of both dissent and nationalism, Hasbro promises you that G.I. Joe will be there as a role model of both "heroic" masculinity and patriotism. And with Operation Iraqi Freedom already begun, it will be interesting to see how these dolls fare.

And then there's Joe's girlfriend. You'd think that after years of feminist indignation over Barbie's image problems that this doll would have been boycotted or Mattel would have canceled her by now. You'd be wrong. Albeit, she's undergone some confusing wardrobe changes over the last forty-four years, but Barbie is still the perennial favorite of little girls all over the world. But it's this year's collector's edition Barbies that should get more than a few *Joshua inter-* genderologists' trigger-fingers twitching. In the series on display at *prets the gen-* Sparky's, "Maria Therese," for example, is the very image of Marian *der roles as-* purity and patriarchal co-dependency in her flowing, starched-white *signed to* bridal gown and veil. "Movie Star Barbie," on the other hand, with *Barbie.* her swanky, leopard-print bathing suit, Jackie-O sunglasses, and Brigitte Bardot feyness harks back to the Hollywood starlets of the late fifties and early sixties, to signify the American cult of celebrity worship. And then there's "Fashion Model Barbie," scantily clad in a pink teddy and negligee, but no sign of "Dr. Barbie" or "Supreme Court Justice Barbie," if such existed. (Interestingly enough, the African American version of the same design is in a *black* teddy and negligee, signifying that colorism is still alive.) The message that these dolls seem to be sending women is that they are nothing if not sex objects. Emily Prager remarks in "Our Barbies, Ourselves" that Barbie "looks like someone who got her start at the Playboy Mansion" (para. 2). Thus, each Barbie at Sparky's can only recommend women for their breeding ability or their sex appeal. So why is it that baby boomers are gushing nostalgically over Maria Therese? "Oh! I use to have one like this," she tells her friend as she picks up the box. A divorcee, perhaps?

Considering the sexual confusion and evolving gender codes that Americans have witnessed since the feminist movement and sexual revolution of the 1960s, it is easy to see why Generation Xers and baby boomers alike look to Barbie and G.I. Joe for guidance from "simpler times." Barbie has reflected many of these shifts — from patriarchal to feminist to postfeminist ideals. She has never failed to represent the promise of empowerment, but only through sexual fidelity, no matter how many careers she's had. And at the core, she's always remained the Anglophilic, blond bombshell[1] who many feminists accuse of inciting such social diseases as domestication and anorexia, to mention a few. But with Barbie, you will always know what type of woman she is because the doll beneath the clothing doesn't change. The same goes for G.I. Joe and masculinity. He will always be a representation of muscular patriotism — what with his overtly phallic .30 caliber machine. And with the two side by side, the message is even clearer: "In times of war, ladies, stand by your man." I noticed that "G.I. Jane," released by Hasbro in 1997, was nowhere to be found — at least not at Sparky's.

He concludes by seeing Kit-Kat clocks as emblematic of Americans' desire for security.

And then I saw the ultimate sign of the times . . . of any time: the Kit-Kat clock, with its bulging cat eyes and circular clock-face, was "just like the one in grandma's kitchen," or so the box read. And it was hanging over the Barbies and G.I. Joes, telling me that whenever Americans get confused or feel uncertain, they will in- evitably return to those signs representing the mythologies that the nation was built on for security in their insecure world. Like the pendulum swing of the Kit-Kat clock's tail, the codes and myths mentioned — these old standbys — will eventually come back to us from time to time. And retailers will always count on it because to them, like the tourist in the Wacky Wobbler box, we are predictable, prepackaged consumers — predictable because they shape us.

I had to get out of there; I was feeling dizzy. But as I made my way to the tram stop, I could now connect Sparky's to the other stores at City Walk. Hard Rock Café: cheeseburgers and fries (comfort food) and good old rock 'n' roll (comfort music). All-Star Collectibles: baseballs autographed by Joe DiMaggio in 1956 (when men knew how to be men, and damn it, that Joltin' Joe was a man's man).

[1]Although in 1968, Mattel did release Christie, Barbie's first African American friend, and other ethnically representative dolls since, to reflect changes in multicultural awareness (Zumhagen). However, the point is that these dolls have never been "Barbie," the central character of the Barbie storyline, but remained her peripheral counterparts — her *other* friends.

Retro Rad clothiers: ladies, get your sexy disco platform shoes (the men will love you for it).

As I boarded the tram, I noticed a U.S. marine and his girlfriend a few rows in front of me, holding hands. Her fingers were stroking his neck and sort of sending him off somewhere.

Works Cited

Cross, Gary. "Barbie, G.I. Joe, and Play in the 1960s." *Signs of Life in the U.S.A.* 5th ed. Ed. Sonia Maasik and Jack Solomon. Boston: Bedford/St. Martin's, 2006. 772–78.

De Graaff, John, David Wann, and Thomas H. Naylor. "The Addictive Virus." *Signs of Life in the U.S.A.* 4th ed. Ed. Sonia Maasik and Jack Solomon. Boston: Bedford/St. Martin's, 2003. 71–76.

Giacconia, Paolo. "Universal City Walk: Displacement of Heterotopia." 29 Nov. 2002 <http://www.architettura.supereva.it/files/200211291>.

"G.I. Joe — Authentic Military History." 25 Nov. 2002 <http://www.gijoe.com/ . . . tic/pl/page.history>.

Gladwell, Malcolm. "The Science of Shopping." *Signs of Life in the U.S.A.* 5th ed. Sonia Maasik and Jack Solomon. Boston: Bedford/St. Martin's, 2006. 642–48.

"Sparky's." *City Walk Hollywood*. 2002. Universal Studios. 25 Nov. 2002 <http://www.citywalkhollywood.com/shopping.html>.

"Stuff About Pez." *Pez.com*. Pez Candy, Inc. 25 Nov. 2002 <http://www.pezco.securesites.com/stuff/about.php>.

Prager, Emily. "Our Barbies, Ourselves." *Signs of Life in the U.S.A.* 5th ed. Ed. Sonia Maasik and Jack Solomon. Boston: Bedford/St. Martin's, 2006. 769–71.

Shames, Laurence. "The More Factor." *Signs of Life in the U.S.A.* 5th ed. Ed. Sonia Maasik and Jack Solomon. Boston: Bedford/St. Martin's, 2006. 76–82.

Solomon, Jack. "Masters of Desire: The Culture of American Advertising." *Signs of Life in the U.S.A.* 5th ed. Ed. Sonia Maasik and Jack Solomon. Boston: Bedford/St. Martin's, 2006. 409–19.

Zumhagen, Brian. "A Timeline of Barbie's History." 25 Nov. 2002 <http://www.adiosbarbie.com/bology/bology_timeline.htm>.

CITING SOURCES

When you write an essay and use another author's work — whether you use the author's exact words or his or her ideas — you need to cite that source for your readers. In most humanities courses, writers use the system of documentation developed by the Modern Language Association (MLA). This system indicates a source in two ways: (1) notations that briefly identify the sources in the body of your essay and (2) notations that give fuller bibliographic information about the sources at the end of your essay. The notations for some commonly used types of sources are illustrated in this chapter. For documenting other sources, consult a writing handbook or Joseph Gibaldi's *MLA Handbook for Writers of Research Papers*, Sixth edition (New York: Modern Language Association of America, 2003).

In-Text Citations

In the body of your essay, you should signal to your reader that you've used a source and indicate, in parentheses, where your reader can find the source in your list of works cited. You don't need to repeat the author's name in both your writing and in the parenthetical note.

SOURCE WITH ONE AUTHOR

Patrick Goldstein asserts that "Talk radio has pumped up the volume of our public discourse and created a whole new political language — perhaps the prevailing political language" (16).

SOURCE WITH TWO OR THREE AUTHORS

Researchers have found it difficult to study biker subcultures because, as one team describes the problem, "it was too dangerous to take issue with outlaws on their own turf" (Hooper and Moore 368).

INDIRECT SOURCE

In discussing the baby mania trend, *Time* claimed that "Career women are opting for pregnancy and they are doing it in style" (qtd. in Faludi 106).

List of Works Cited

At the end of your essay, include a list of all the sources you have cited in parenthetical notations. This list, alphabetized by author, should provide full publication information for each source; you should indicate the date you accessed any online sources.

The first line of each entry should begin flush left. Subsequent lines should be indented half an inch (or five spaces) from the left margin. Double-space the entire list, both between and within entries.

Nonelectronic Sources

BOOK BY ONE AUTHOR

Faludi, Susan. *Backlash: The Undeclared War against American Women*. New York: Crown, 1991.

BOOK BY TWO OR MORE AUTHORS

Collins, Ronald K. L., and David M. Skover. *The Death of Discourse*. New York: Westview Press, 1996.

(Note that only the first author's name is reversed.)

WORK IN AN ANTHOLOGY

Prager, Emily. "Our Barbies, Ourselves." *Signs of Life in the U.S.A.: Readings on Popular Culture for Writers*. 5th ed. Ed. Sonia Maasik and Jack Solomon. Boston: Bedford/St. Martin's, 2006. 769–71.

ARTICLE IN A WEEKLY MAGAZINE

Lacayo, Richard. "How Does '80s Art Look Now?" *Time* 28 March 2005: 58+.

(A plus sign is used to indicate that the article is not printed on consecutive pages; otherwise, a page range should be given: *16–25*, for example.)

ARTICLE IN A MONTHLY MAGAZINE

Judd, Elizabeth. "After School." *The Atlantic* June 2005: 118.

ARTICLE IN A JOURNAL

Hooper, Columbus B., and Johnny Moore. "Women in Outlaw Motorcycle Gangs." *Journal of Contemporary Ethnography* 18 (1990): 363–87.

PERSONAL INTERVIEW

Chese, Charlie. Personal interview. 28 Sept. 2005.

Electronic Sources

FILM OR VIDEOTAPE

Cinderella Man. Dir. Ron Howard. Perf. Russell Crowe, Renée Zellweger. Miramax, 2005.

TELEVISION PROGRAM

CSI: Miami. Perf. David Caruso. KBAK, Bakersfield. 18 April 2005.

COMPACT DISC

Adams, Ryan. *Cold Roses*. Lost Highway, 2005.

E-MAIL

Katt, Susie. "Interpreting the Mall." E-mail to the author. 29 Sept. 2005.

ARTICLE IN AN ONLINE REFERENCE BOOK

"Gender." *Britannica Online*. 31 July 2004. Encyclopaedia Britannica. 30 May 2006 <http://www.britannica.com/eb/article?eu=37051>.

(Note that the first date indicates when the information was posted; the second indicates the date of access.)

ARTICLE IN AN ONLINE JOURNAL

Schaffer, Scott. "Disney and the Imagineering of History." *Postmodern Culture* 6.3 (1996): 62 pars. 12 Aug. 2005 <http://jefferson.village.virginia.edu/pmc/backissues/contents .596.html>.

ARTICLE IN AN ONLINE MAGAZINE

Rosenberg, Scott. "Don't Link or I'll Sue!" *Salon* 12 Aug. 1999. 13 Aug. 2005 <http://
www. salon.com/tech/col/rose/1999/08/12/deep_links/index.html>.

ONLINE BOOK

James, Henry. *The Bostonians*. London and New York, 1886. *The Henry James Scholar's
Guide to Web Sites*. Ed. Richard Hathaway. Aug. 1999. SUNY New Paltz. 13 Aug. 2005
<http://www.newpaltz.edu/~hathaway/bostonians1.html>.

ONLINE POEM

Frost, Robert. "The Road Not Taken." *Mountain Interval*. New York, 1915. *Project Bartleby
Archive*. Ed. Steven van Leeuwen. Mar. 1995. 13 Aug. 2005 <http://www.bartleby
.com/119/1.html>.

PROFESSIONAL WEB SITE

National Council of Teachers of English. Jan. 2002. 1 May 2005 <http://www.ncte.org>.

PERSONAL HOME PAGE

Rochelle, James. Home page. May 2006. 13 Aug. 2006 <http://www.homestead.com/
jamestheviking>.

POSTING TO A DISCUSSION LIST

Diaz, Joanne. "Poetic Expressions." Online posting. 29 Apr. 2006. Conference on College
Composition and Communication. 4 Jul. 2006 <http://www.ncte.org/cccc/06>.

ONLINE SCHOLARLY PROJECT

Corpus Linguistics. Ed. Michael Barlow. Apr. 1998. Rice U. 13 Aug. 2005 <http//www
.ruf.rice.edu/~barlow/corpus.html>.

WORK FROM AN ONLINE SUBSCRIPTION SERVICE

"Race." *Compton's Encyclopedia Online*. Vers. 3.5. 1999. America Online. 30 Jul. 2005.
Keyword: Compton's.

CONSUMING PASSIONS

*The Culture of
American Consumption*

You Are What You Buy

If you were given a blank check to purchase anything — and everything — you wanted, what would you buy? Try making a list, and then annotate that list with brief explanations for why you want each item. Do your choices say something about yourself that you want others to know? Do they project an image?

Now consider the things you do own. Make another list and annotate it too. Why did you buy this item or that? Which were presents that reflect someone else's tastes and desires? What compromises did you have to make in choosing one item over another? How often did price or quality affect your decisions? How often did style or image? Do the images sent by your actual possessions differ from the ones sent by your ideal ones? Why? Or why not?

Such questions are a good place to begin a semiotic analysis of American consumer culture, for every choice you make in the products you buy, from clothing to furniture to cars to electronics and beyond, is a sign, a signal you are sending to the world about yourself. Those aren't just a pair of shoes you're wearing: They're a statement about your identity. That's not just an iPod playlist: It's a message about your worldview.

To read the signs of American consumption, it is best to start with yourself, because you've already got an angle on the answers. But be careful and be honest. Remember, a cultural sign gets its meaning from the *system*, or *code*, in which it appears. Its significance does not lie in its usefulness but rather in its symbolism, in the image it projects, and that image is socially constructed.

You didn't make it by yourself. To decode your own possessions, you've got to ask yourself what you are trying to say with them and what you want other people to think about you. And you've got to remember the difference between fashion and function.

To give you an idea of how to go about analyzing consumer objects and behavior, let's look at a product that on the surface seems completely functional — a tool, not a sign. Let's look at cell phones.

Interpreting the Culture of American Consumption

As you read in the Introduction to this book, the semiotic interpretation of a cultural sign can usefully begin with a historical survey of the object you are interpreting. Such a survey can reveal how the meaning of an object can change depending on the circumstance in which it is found. This is strikingly true in the case of cell phones, which, while practically ubiquitous today, were once rare and expensive. They first appeared for public use in 1982 and were originally hard-wired into automobiles (often limousines), which is why many people who remember that time still call them "car phones." In such a context, cell phones were potent status symbols, sending an image of unusual wealth and prestige, the exclusive equipment of VIPs.

But in an era when cell phones can be acquired for free (provided that the consumer also signs up for an activation contract, of course), and when even the latest digitized and video-screened models cost only a fraction of what the original models cost, the cell phone is so common that it can't send a status message anymore. Everyone seems to have one. But that doesn't mean that cell phones no longer have a semiotic significance. It simply means that the significance of the cell phone has changed as its history has changed.

Discussing the Signs of Consumer Culture

On the board, list in categories the fashion styles worn by members of the class. Be sure to note details, such as styles of shoes, jewelry, watches, or sunglasses, as well as broader trends. Then discuss what the clothing choices say about individuals. What messages are people sending about their personal identity? Do individual students agree with the class's interpretations of their clothing choices? Can any distinctions be made by gender, age, or ethnicity? Then discuss what the fashion styles worn by the whole class say: Is a group identity projected by class members?

To interpret the current significance of the cell phone, we need to situate it in its immediate system of related signs and products. One product that is extremely similar to the cell phone, and which thus belongs to the same system, is the pager. The history of the pager is quite similar to that of the cell phone. Once pagers were carried almost exclusively by high-status professionals who needed to be in constant contact with their places of business. This was particularly true for physicians, who commonly carried pagers when they were "on call" (this was before the advent of even the earliest cell phones), and so pagers acquired something of the status of their professional users. The image sent by pagers changed radically, however, when they came to be the standard equipment of drug dealers, who would use them to set up clandestine drug deals. The former status image declined as a new one emerged: To carry a pager was to send an image of gangster toughness, and, for many American teens, gangster coolness. Once a signifier of professional prestige and responsibility, the pager shifted systems and became part of the code of a bad-assed youth culture.

But now pagers might be carried by little children whose parents haven't gotten them cell phones yet, and so they too have changed significance. In fact, as cell phones become more and more common, pagers seem to be dwindling in significance and number. Not too long ago, pagers were hot stuff; now, cell phones enjoy that status.

With almost everyone owning a cell phone these days, one might expect them to have a more or less neutral image. After all, they are genuinely useful and so could well be viewed in solely a functional light. But that doesn't appear to be the case. Think of those bumper stickers that read HANG UP AND DRIVE or the fact that many people over forty years of age may apologize for owning one, as in "I own a cell phone, but I only use it for emergencies." People wouldn't make such apologies, or post such messages on their cars, if there weren't a lingering sense that, somehow, something is wrong with cell phones. And what is wrong lies in their cultural significance, not in the objects themselves.

To see what this significance is, let's look further into the system in which cell phones appear. What often comes to mind when we think of cell phones today is their association with a certain kind of consumer, especially people driving SUVs and luxury sedans like the Lexus. There is a functional reason for this: Cell phones have become necessary equipment for the sorts of businesspeople, such as real estate professionals, who must spend a great deal of time in their cars and whose business activities make it important (as well as pleasurable) to drive status automobiles. At the same time, many middle-class parents find that cell phones are very good ways of keeping track of their children, and SUVs have become the automotive choice of the middle- and upper-middle-class American mom these days. Indeed, all you need to do is utter the phrase *soccer mom*, and immediately an image of a woman driving a Cadillac Escalade while chatting on a cell phone may come to mind.

Now, part of the negativity in this image has to do with the history of the cell phone, particularly that intermediate era when cell phones were no longer the prerogative of the extremely powerful and wealthy but were still expensive enough to be out of ordinary consumers' reach. At that time, roughly the late 1980s, cell phones were the common possession of the notorious yuppies (an image reinforced by a 1980s song called "Car Phone," a parody of the seventies hit "Convoy"), and were widely despised accordingly. Ironically, even when millions of non-yuppies and anti-yuppies carry cell phones today, the old taint lingers.

But only lingers. For, with the cell phone being so common, its significance is now less a matter of who owns one as how it is used. Here we can look at the behavioral component of the system to which the cell phone belongs. And what we find are not only people who drive dangerously while gabbing on their phones but also compulsive users who chat away in restaurants (causing some eateries to ban cell phone use) and theaters. Then there all those phones that start ringing in classrooms and other public places, disrupting the business at hand while someone fumbles in a purse or backpack to turn the thing off.

What all such behaviors share is the way that they reflect a certain privatization of public space — the way, that is, that cell phone users perform in public what was once a highly private act: talking on the telephone. Once telephone conversations were conducted in the privacy of one's home or office — or, if in public, with the door to the phone booth shut. Now such conversations, whether for business or for pleasure, take place on the road, in the restaurant or theater, in shops, on the sidewalk, indeed just about everywhere. And here lies a good part of the current negative image of the cell phone, though most people are probably not conscious of it.

For to treat publicly shared space as if it were one's private preserve, annoying or endangering others for one's personal pleasure or convenience, is, in essence, antisocial behavior. No one minds when people use their own private space privately, but when public space is treated as if it were private, something is taken away. The sense of a shared, common environment with its own set of rules to govern the social interactions that take place there is lost. And while we may not always be conscious of it, this is one of the reasons we resent cell phone users, even when we use cell phones ourselves.

At this point, as is often the case with a semiotic analysis, we can broaden the scope of our investigation to see what other current cultural phenomena can be associated with the cell phone's privatization of public space. We've already considered one such phenomenon: the SUV. For SUVs are not simply a mode of transportation, or even just status vehicles. Many who purchase them say that they would have preferred another car but feel safer in an SUV. Whether they put it explicitly or not, what they mean is that if they get into an accident, they want to be in the car that "wins." This may seem like perfectly rational behavior, and according to a highly individualistic (perhaps *selfish* would be the better word) code of conduct, it is. But looked at from a more communitarian perspective, the desire to prevail in a car accident, the unconscious decision to kill rather than be killed, is less than social behavior.

Similarly, the increasing number of Americans who withdraw behind the literal gates and figurative moats of gated communities also can be seen to represent a mode of antisocial behavior (it's no accident that they often drive SUVs). In a dangerous world, this behavior too is perfectly rational, but what it signifies is a society that is becoming so mistrustful that it is becoming atomized into suspicious individuals whose homes and cars are becoming fortresses against everyone else. The cell phone fits neatly into this system insofar as many of its users own them for safety purposes, whether it be to keep in touch with children who no longer seem safe in the public realm or with family members. Many women carry them because the streets aren't such a safe place for women anymore.

The September 11 attacks augmented this significance in an especially grim way. Stories of final conversations from passengers and crew on doomed airlines and employees in the World Trade Center lent a new dimension to the image of the cell phone as a safety device. In this sense, it became a signifier within an American system threatened by terrorism, a shift in meaning that undermined, at least for a while, the negative image of the cell phone as the frivolous instrument of inconsiderate people. Once again, we can see from this semiotic adjustment how ordinary objects can be signifiers of changing historical conditions.

The cell phone is such a rich source of semiotic significance that its analysis could go on considerably further, investigating, for instance, the way that it can be seen to reflect a workaholic world in which people feel the need to conduct their business anywhere and anytime, or the way that it has contributed to a new consciousness that demands constant communication (do you flip on your phone for a chat the moment you get out of class?). In both cases, the e-mail revolution is a part of the same cultural system and reflects a similar cultural significance. But before leaving any further analysis to your own exploration, there is a new entrant in the cultural system to which the cell phone belongs that bears mentioning here: the iPod.

The Invasion of the Music Snatchers

They're everywhere, those sleek little gizmos that enable you to carry an entire personal library of music around with you wherever you go. Like cell phones, they enable their users to take what was once a private activity (listening to music) into the public realm. The iPod, of course, was not the first device to make this possible: Its historical system would include the first portable radios, boom boxes, and, perhaps most importantly, the Sony Walkman, which also featured an earphone-equipped personal concert hall. Indeed, between the iPod and the Walkman there lies a difference more in scale and convenience than in cultural significance, for both devices reflect an entertainment-driven society where people demand, and expect, to be able to take their own personalized entertainment with them everywhere. Throw in the recent TiVO technology, which enables consumers to construct their own private television playlists, as it were, and you have the growing outlines of a culture in which individualized entertainment is introducing a new wrinkle in the history of mass culture. What was once a kind of one-size-fits-all entertainment system, with top-forty radio play and three major television networks, is atomizing not only into niche markets constructed by the culture industry but also into one-size-fits-me personal entertainment units that consumers themselves construct. Paradoxically, the emerging entertainment system is at once more democratic (consumers make their own choices) and privatized — a new American contradiction that we are living simultaneously without even realizing it. (See Chapter 5 for more on American contradictions.)

Disposable Decades

When analyzing a consumer sign, you will often find yourself referring to particular decades in which certain popular fads and trends were prominent, for the decade in which a given style appears may be an essential key to the system that explains it. Have you ever wondered why American cultural trends seem to change with every decade, why it is so easy to speak of the sixties or the seventies or the eighties and immediately recognize the popular styles that dominated each decade? Have you ever looked at the style of a friend and thought, "Oh, she's so seventies"? Can you place an Earth Shoe, or a Nehru jacket, at the drop of a hat? A change in the calendar always seems to herald a change in style in a consuming culture. But why?

The decade-to-decade shift in America's pop cultural identity goes back a good number of years. It is still easy, for example, to distinguish F. Scott Fitzgerald's Jazz Age twenties from John Steinbeck's wrathful thirties. The fifties, an especially connotative decade, raise images of ducktail haircuts and poodle skirts, drive-in culture and Elvis, family sitcoms and white-bread innocence, while the sixties are remembered for acid rock, hippies, the student

---

Exploring the Signs of Consumer Culture

"You are what you buy." In your journal, freewrite on the importance of consumer products in your life. How do you respond to being told your identity is equivalent to the products you buy? Do you resist the notion? Do you recall any instances when you have felt lost without a favorite object? How do you communicate your sense of self to others through objects, whether clothing, books, food, home decor, cars, or something else?

revolution, and back-to-the-land communes. We remember the seventies as a pop cultural era divided between disco, Nashville, and preppiedom, with John Travolta, truckers, and Skippy and Muffy as dominant pop icons. The boom-boom eighties gave us Wall Street glitz and the yuppie invasion. Indeed, each decade since World War I — which, not accidentally, happens to coincide roughly with the rise of modern advertising and mass production — seems to carry its own consumerist style.

It's no accident that the decade-to-decade shift in consumer styles coincides with the advent of modern advertising and mass production because it was mass production that created a need for constant consumer turnover in the first place. Mass production, that is, promotes stylistic change because with so many products being produced, a market must be created to consume all of them, and this means constantly consuming more. To get consumers to keep buying all the new stuff, you have to convince them that the stuff they already have is passé. Why else do fashion designers completely redesign their lines each year? Why else do car manufacturers annually change their color schemes and body shapes when the old model year seemed good enough? The new designs aren't simply functional improvements (though they are marketed as such); they are inducements to go out and replace what you already have to avoid appearing out of fashion. Just think: If you could afford to buy any car that you wanted, what would it be? Would your choice a few years ago have been the same?

Mass production, then, creates consumer societies based on the constant production of new products that are intended to be disposed of with the next product year. But something happened along the way to the establishment of our consumer culture: We began to value consumption more than production.

Shoppers storm the doors as the post–Thanksgiving rush begins early in Lincoln, Nebraska, on Friday, November 26, 2004.

Listen to the economic news: Consumption, not production, is relied upon to carry America out of its economic downturns. When Americans stop buying, our economy grinds to a halt. Consumption lies at the center of our economic system now, and the result has been a transformation in the very way we view ourselves.

A Tale of Two Cities

It has not always been thus in America, however. Once, Americans prided themselves on their productivity. In 1914, for example, the poet Carl Sandburg boasted of a Chicago that was "Hog butcher for the world, Tool maker, Stacker of Wheat, Player with Railroads and the Nation's Freight Handler." One wonders what Sandburg would think of the place today. From the south shore east to the industrial suburb of Gary, Indiana, Chicago's once-proud mills and factories rust in the winter wind. The broken windows of countless tenements stare blindly at the Amtrak commuter lines that transport the white-collared brokers of the Chicago Mercantile Exchange to the city center, where trade today is in commodity futures, not commodities. Even Michael Jackson, Gary's most famous export, rarely goes home.

Meanwhile, a few hundred miles to the northwest, Bloomington, Minnesota, buzzes with excitement. For there stands the Mall of America, a colossus of consumption so large that it contains within its walls a seven-acre Knott's Berry Farm theme park, with lots of room to spare. You can find almost anything you want in the Mall of America, but most of what you will find won't have been manufactured in America. The proud tag "Made in the USA" is an increasingly rare item.

It's a long way from Sandburg's Chicago to the Mall of America, a trip that traverses America's shift from a producer to a consumer economy. This shift is not simply economic; it is behind a cultural transformation that is shaping a new mythology within which we define ourselves, our hopes, and our desires.

Ask yourself right now what your own goals are in going to college. Do you envision a career in law, or medicine, or banking and finance? Do you want to be a teacher, an advertising executive, or a civil servant? Or maybe you are preparing for a career in an Internet-related field. If you've considered any of these career examples, you are contemplating what are known as service jobs. While essential to a society, none of them actually produces anything. If you've given thought to going into some facet of manufacturing, on the other hand, you are unusual because America offers increasingly fewer opportunities in that area and little prestige. The prestige jobs are in law and medicine, and, increasingly, in high-tech marketing operations like Amazon.com, a fact that it is easy to take for granted. But ask yourself: Does it have to be so?

Simply to ask such questions is to begin to reveal the outline of a cultural mythology based in consumption rather than production. For one thing, while law and medicine require specialized training available to only a few, doctors and lawyers also make a lot of money and so are higher up on the scale of consumption. Quite simply, they can buy more than others can. It is easy to presume that this would be the case anywhere, but in the former Soviet Union physicians — most of whom were women — were relatively low on the social scale. Male engineers, on the other hand, were highly valued for their role in facilitating military production. In what was a producer rather than a consumer culture, it was the producers who roosted high on the social ladder.

And as for the Internet, though the road has been a good deal rockier than was originally anticipated, there are still high hopes for the retail potential of the Web. Computer makers and chip manufacturers, who, after all, do produce something, are rivaled by such firms as eBay and America Online, companies that do not produce anything but, rather, are efficient media for consumption.

To live in a consumer culture is not simply a matter of shopping, however; it is also a matter of *being*. For in a consumer society, you are what you consume, and the entire social and economic order is maintained by the constant encouragement to buy. The ubiquity of television and advertising in America is a direct reflection of this system, for these media deliver the constant stimulus to buy through avalanches of consuming images. Consider how difficult it is to escape the arm of the advertiser. You may turn off your TV set, but a screen awaits you at the checkout counter of your supermarket, displaying incentives to spend your money. If you rush to the restroom to hide, you may find advertisements tacked to the stalls. If you log onto the Internet, advertisements greet you on your monitor. Resistance is useless. Weren't you planning to do some shopping this weekend anyway?

Reading Consumer Culture on the Net

Log onto one of the many home shopping networks or auction sites. You might try the Internet Shopping Network (www.isn.com), Shop at Home (www.shopathome.com), or e-Bay (www.ebay.com). Analyze both the products sold and the way they are marketed. Who is the target audience for the network you're studying, and what images and values are used to attract this market? How does the marketing compare with nonelectronic sales pitches, such as displays in shopping malls and magazines or TV advertising? Does the electronic medium affect your own behavior as a consumer? Does the time pressure of an electronic auction affect your behavior as a consumer? How do you account for any differences in electronic and traditional marketing strategies?

When the Going Gets Tough, the Tough Go Shopping

In a cultural system where our identities are displayed in the products we buy, it accordingly behooves us to pay close attention to what we consume and why. From the cars we drive to the clothes we wear, we are enmeshed in a web of consuming images. As students, you are probably freer to choose the particular images you wish to project through the products you consume than most other demographic groups in America. This claim may sound paradoxical: After all, don't working adults have more money than starving students? Yes, generally. But the working world places severe restrictions on the choices employees can make in their clothing and grooming styles, and even automobile choice may be restricted (real estate agents, for example, can't escort their clients around town in VW Beetles). Corporate business wear, for all its variations, still revolves around a central core of necktied and dark-hued sobriety, regardless of the gender of the wearer. And even with the return of long hair for men into fashion in the nineties, few professions outside the entertainment industry allow it on the job. On campus, on the other hand, you can be pretty much whatever you want to be, which is why your own daily lives provide you with a particularly rich field of consumer signs to read and decode.

So go to it. By the time you read this book, a lot will have changed. A new decade is more than half over without yet having achieved a distinctive identity, not to mention a name. What will the "00s" be the decade of? Look around yourself. Start reading the signs.

The Readings

As this chapter's lead essay, Laurence Shames's "The More Factor" provides a mythological background for the discussions of America's consuming behavior that follow. Shames takes a historical approach to American consumerism, relating our frontier history to our ever-expanding desire for more goods and services. Anne Norton follows with a semiotic analysis of shopping malls, mail-order catalogues, and the Home Shopping Network, focusing on the ways in which they construct a language of consumption tailored to specific consumer groups. Then "Credit Card Barbie" appears, offering an opportunity for direct analysis. Thomas Hine's interpretation of the packaging that contains America's most commonly consumed products shows how packages constitute complex sign systems intended for consumer "readings," and Fred Davis surveys the history of blue jeans and how they have been transformed from an emblem of labor to one of leisure. Joan Kron follows with a study of the way we use home furnishings to reflect our sense of personal identity, while David Goewey turns to automotive signs in his semiotic analysis of the SUV trend. Next, Thomas L. Friedman offers prescient insights into the global dimensions of American consumer culture and the cultural conflicts behind the September 11 terrorist attacks. Thomas Frank concludes the chapter with his musings on how marketers exploit 1960s countercultural values as a means to improve their clients' bottom lines.

LAURENCE SHAMES
The More Factor

A bumper sticker popular in the 1980s read, "Whoever dies with the most toys wins." In this selection from The Hunger for More: Searching for Values in an Age of Greed *(1989), Laurence Shames shows how the great American hunger for more — more toys, more land, more opportunities — is an essential part of our history and character, stemming from the frontier era when the horizon alone seemed the only limit to American desire. The author of* The Big Time: The Harvard Business School's Most Successful Class and How It Shaped America *(1986) and the holder of a Harvard M.B.A., Shames is a journalist who has contributed to such publications as* Playboy, Vanity Fair, Manhattan, inc., *and* Esquire. *He currently is working full-time on writing fiction and screen plays, with his most recent publications including* Florida Straits *(1992),* Sunburn *(1995),* Welcome to Paradise *(1999),* The Naked Detective *(2000), and, with Peter Barton,* Not Fade Away *(2003).*

1

Americans have always been optimists, and optimists have always liked to speculate. In Texas in the 1880s, the speculative instrument of choice was towns, and there is no tale more American than this.

What people would do was buy up enormous tracts of parched and vacant land, lay out a Main Street, nail together some wooden sidewalks, and start slapping up buildings. One of these buildings would be called the Grand Hotel and would have a saloon complete with swinging doors. Another might be dubbed the New Academy or the Opera House. The developers would erect a flagpole and name a church, and once the workmen had packed up and moved on, the towns would be as empty as the sky.

But no matter. The speculators, next, would hire people to pass out handbills in the Eastern and Midwestern cities, tracts limning the advantages of relocation to "the Athens of the South" or "the new plains Jerusalem." When persuasion failed, the builders might resort to bribery, paying people's moving costs and giving them houses, in exchange for nothing but a pledge to stay until a certain census was taken or a certain inspection made. Once the nose count was completed, people were free to move on, and there was in fact a contingent of folks who made their living by keeping a cabin on skids and dragging it for pay from one town to another.

The speculators' idea, of course, was to lure the railroad. If one could create a convincing semblance of a town, the railroad might come through it, and a real town would develop, making the speculators staggeringly rich. By these devices a man named Sanborn once owned Amarillo.[1]

But railroad tracks are narrow and the state of Texas is very, very wide.   5 For every Wichita Falls or Lubbock there were a dozen College Mounds or Belchervilles,[2] bleached, unpeopled burgs that receded quietly into the dust, taking with them large amounts of speculators' money.

Still, the speculators kept right on bucking the odds and depositing empty towns in the middle of nowhere. Why did they do it? Two reasons — reasons that might be said to summarize the central fact of American economic history and that go a fair way toward explaining what is perhaps the central strand of the national character.

The first reason was simply that the possible returns were so enormous as to partake of the surreal, to create a climate in which ordinary logic and prudence did not seem to apply. In a boom like that of real estate when the railroad barreled through, long shots that might pay one hundred thousand to one seemed worth a bet.

The second reason, more pertinent here, is that there was a presumption that America would *keep on* booming — if not forever, then at least longer than it made sense to worry about. There would always be another gold rush, another Homestead Act, another oil strike. The next generation would always ferret out opportunities that would be still more lavish than any that had gone before. America *was* those opportunities. This was an article not just of faith, but of strategy. You banked on the next windfall, you staked your hopes and even your self-esteem on it, and this led to a national turn of mind that might usefully be thought of as the habit of more.

A century, maybe two centuries, before anyone had heard the term *baby boomer*, much less *yuppie*, the habit of more had been instilled as the operative truth among the economically ambitious. The habit of more seemed to suggest that there was no such thing as getting wiped out in America. A fortune lost in Texas might be recouped in Colorado. Funds frittered away on grazing land where nothing grew might flood back in as silver. There was always a second chance, or always seemed to be, in this land where growth was destiny and where expansion and purpose were the same.

The key was the frontier, not just as a matter of acreage, but as idea. Vast,   10 varied, rough as rocks, America was the place where one never quite came to the end. Ben Franklin explained it to Europe even before the Revolutionary War had finished: America offered new chances to those "who, in their own

---

[1] For a fuller account of railroad-related land speculation in Texas, see F. Stanley, *Story of the Texas Panhandle Railroads* (Borger, Tex.: Hess Publishing Co., 1976).

[2] T. Lindsay Baker, *Ghost Towns of Texas* (Norman, Okla.: University of Oklahoma Press, 1986).

Countries, where all the Lands [were] fully occupied . . . could never [emerge] from the poor Condition wherein they were born."[3]

So central was this awareness of vacant space and its link to economic promise that Frederick Jackson Turner, the historian who set the tone for much of the twentieth century's understanding of the American past, would write that it was "not the constitution, but free land . . . [that] made the democratic type of society in America."[4] Good laws mattered; an accountable government mattered; ingenuity and hard work mattered. But those things were, so to speak, an overlay on the natural, geographic America that was simply *there*, and whose vast and beckoning possibilities seemed to generate the ambition and the sometimes reckless liberty that would fill it. First and foremost, it was open space that provided "the freedom of the individual to rise under conditions of social mobility."[5]

Open space generated not just ambition, but metaphor. As early as 1835, Tocqueville was extrapolating from the fact of America's emptiness to the observation that "no natural boundary seems to be set to the efforts of man."[6] Nor was any limit placed on what he might accomplish, since, in that heyday of the Protestant ethic, a person's rewards were taken to be quite strictly proportionate to his labors.

Frontier; opportunity; more. This has been the American trinity from the very start. The frontier was the backdrop and also the raw material for the streak of economic booms. The booms became the goad and also the justification for the myriad gambles and for Americans' famous optimism. The optimism, in turn, shaped the schemes and visions that were sometimes noble, sometimes appalling, always bold. The frontier, as reality and as symbol, is what has shaped the American way of doing things and the American sense of what's worth doing.

But there has been one further corollary to the legacy of the frontier, with its promise of ever-expanding opportunities: Given that the goal — a realistic goal for most of our history — was *more*, Americans have been somewhat backward in adopting values, hopes, ambitions that have to do with things *other than* more. In America, a sense of quality has lagged far behind a sense of scale. An ideal of contentment has yet to take root in soil traditionally more hospitable to an ideal of restless striving. The ethic of decency has been upstaged by the ethic of success. The concept of growth has been applied almost exclusively to things that can be measured, counted, weighed. And the hunger for those things that are unmeasurable but fine — the sorts of accomplishment that cannot be undone by circumstance or a shift in social fashion, the kind of

---

[3]Benjamin Franklin, "Information to Those Who Would Remove to America," in *The Autobiography and Other Writings* (New York: Penguin Books, 1986), 242.

[4]Frederick Jackson Turner, *The Frontier in American History* (Melbourne, Fla.: Krieger, 1976 [reprint of 1920 edition]), 293.

[5]Ibid., 266.

[6]Tocqueville, *Democracy in America*.

serenity that cannot be shattered by tomorrow's headline — has gone largely unfulfilled, and even unacknowledged.

2

If the supply of more went on forever, perhaps that wouldn't matter very much. Expansion could remain a goal unto itself, and would continue to generate a value system based on bulk rather than on nuance, on quantities of money rather than on quality of life, on "progress" itself rather than on a sense of what the progress was for. But what if, over time, there was less more to be had?

That is the essential situation of America today.

Let's keep things in proportion: The country is not running out of wealth, drive, savvy, or opportunities. We are not facing imminent ruin, and neither panic nor gloom is called for. But there have been ample indications over the past two decades that we are running out of more.

Consider productivity growth — according to many economists, the single most telling and least distortable gauge of changes in real wealth. From 1947 to 1965, productivity in the private sector (adjusted, as are all the following figures, for inflation) was advancing, on average, by an annual 3.3 percent. This means, simply, that each hour of work performed by a specimen American worker contributed 3.3 cents worth or more to every American dollar every year; whether we saved it or spent it, that increment went into a national kitty of ever-enlarging aggregate wealth. Between 1965 and 1972, however, the "more-factor" decreased to 2.4 percent a year, and from 1972 to 1977 it slipped further, to 1.6 percent. By the early 1980s, productivity growth was at a virtual standstill, crawling along at 0.2 percent for the five years ending in 1982.[7] Through the middle years of the 1980s, the numbers rebounded somewhat — but by then the gains were being neutralized by the gargantuan carrying costs on the national debt.[8]

Inevitably, this decline in the national stockpile of more held consequences for the individual wallet.[9] During the 1950s, Americans' average hourly earnings were humping ahead at a gratifying 2.5 percent each year. By the late seventies, that figure stood just where productivity growth had come to stand, at a dispiriting 0.2 cents on the dollar. By the first half of the

[7]These figures are taken from the Council of Economic Advisers, *Economic Report of the President*, February 1984, 267.

[8]For a lucid and readable account of the meaning and implications of our reservoir of red ink, see Lawrence Malkin, *The National Debt* (New York: Henry Holt and Co., 1987). Through no fault of Malkin's, many of his numbers are already obsolete, but his explanation of who owes what to whom, and what it means, remains sound and even entertaining in a bleak sort of way.

[9]The figures in this paragraph and the next are from "The Average Guy Takes It on the Chin," *New York Times*, 13 July 1986, sec. 3.

eighties, the Reagan "recovery" notwithstanding, real hourly wages were actually moving backwards — declining at an average annual rate of 0.3 percent.

Compounding the shortage of more was an unfortunate but crucial demo- 20 graphic fact. Real wealth was nearly ceasing to expand just at the moment when the members of that unprecedented population bulge known as the baby boom were entering what should have been their peak years of income expansion. A working man or woman who was thirty years old in 1949 could expect to see his or her real earnings burgeon by 63 percent by age forty. In 1959, a thirty-year-old could still look forward to a gain of 49 percent by his or her fortieth birthday.

But what about the person who turned thirty in 1973? By the time that worker turned forty, his or her real earnings had shrunk by a percentage point. For all the blather about yuppies with their beach houses, BMWs, and radicchio salads, and even factoring in those isolated tens of thousands making ludicrous sums in consulting firms or on Wall Street, the fact is that between 1979 and 1983 real earnings of all Americans between the ages of twenty-five and thirty-four actually declined by 14 percent.[10] The *New York Times*, well before the stock market crash put the kibosh on eighties confidence, summed up the implications of this downturn by observing that "for millions of breadwinners, the American dream is becoming the impossible dream."[11]

Now, it is not our main purpose here to detail the ups and downs of the American economy. Our aim, rather, is to consider the effects of those ups and downs on people's goals, values, sense of their place in the world. What happens at that shadowy juncture where economic prospects meld with personal choice? What sorts of insights and adjustments are called for so that economic ups and downs can be dealt with gracefully?

Fact one in this connection is that, if America's supply of more is in fact diminishing, American values will have to shift and broaden to fill the gap where the expectation of almost automatic gains used to be. Something more durable will have to replace the fat but fragile bubble that had been getting frailer these past two decades and that finally popped — a tentative, partial pop — on October 19, 1987. A different sort of growth — ultimately, a growth in responsibility and happiness — will have to fulfill our need to believe that our possibilities are still expanding.

The transition to that new view of progress will take some fancy stepping, because, at least since the end of World War II, simple economic growth has stood, in the American psyche, as the best available substitute for the literal frontier. The economy has *been* the frontier. Instead of more space, we have had more money. Rather than measuring progress in terms of geographical expansion, we have measured it by expansion in our standard of living.

[10]See, for example, "The Year of the Yuppie," *Newsweek*, 31 December 1984, 16.
[11]"The Average Guy."

Economics has become the metaphor on which we pin our hopes of open space and second chances.

The poignant part is that the literal frontier did not pass yesterday: it has not existed for a hundred years. But the frontier's promise has become so much a part of us that we have not been willing to let the concept die. We have kept the frontier mythology going by invocation, by allusion, by hype.

It is not a coincidence that John F. Kennedy dubbed his political program the New Frontier. It is not mere linguistic accident that makes us speak of Frontiers of Science or of psychedelic drugs as carrying one to Frontiers of Perception. We glorify fads and fashions by calling them Frontiers of Taste. Nuclear energy has been called the Last Frontier; solar energy has been called the Last Frontier. Outer space has been called the Last Frontier; the oceans have been called the Last Frontier. Even the suburbs, those blandest and least adventurous of places, have been wryly described as the crabgrass frontier.[12]

What made all these usages plausible was their being linked to the image of the American economy as an endlessly fertile continent whose boundaries never need be reached, a domain that could expand in perpetuity, a gigantic playing field that would never run out of room and on which the game would get forever bigger and more filled with action. This was the frontier that would not vanish.

It is worth noting that people in other countries (with the possible exception of that other America, Australia) do not talk about frontier this way. In Europe, and in most of Africa and Asia, "frontier" connotes, at worst, a place of barbed wire and men with rifles, and at best, a neutral junction where one changes currency while passing from one fixed system into another. Frontier, for most of the world's people, does not suggest growth, expanse, or opportunity.

For Americans, it does, and always has. This is one of the things that sets America apart from other places and makes American attitudes different from those of other people. It is why, from *Bonanza* to the Sierra Club, the notion or even the fantasy of empty horizons and untapped resources has always evoked in the American heart both passion and wistfulness. And it is why the fear that the economic frontier — our last, best version of the Wild West — may finally be passing creates in us not only money worries but also a crisis of morale and even of purpose.

3

It might seem strange to call the 1980s an era of nostalgia. The decade, after all, has been more usually described in terms of coolness, pragmatism, and a blithe innocence of history. But the eighties, unawares, were nostalgic for

---

[12]With the suburbs again taking on a sort of fascination, this phrase was resurrected as the title of a 1985 book — *Crabgrass Frontier: The Suburbanization of America*, by Kenneth T. Jackson (Oxford University Press).

frontiers; and the disappointment of that nostalgia had much to do with the time's greed, narrowness, and strange want of joy. The fear that the world may not be a big enough playground for the full exercise of one's energies and yearnings, and worse, the fear that the playground is being fenced off and will no longer expand — these are real worries and they have had consequences. The eighties were an object lesson in how people play the game when there is an awful and unspoken suspicion that the game is winding down.

It was ironic that the yuppies came to be so reviled for their vaunting ambition and outsized expectations, as if they'd invented the habit of more, when in fact they'd only inherited it the way a fetus picks up an addiction in the womb. The craving was there in the national bloodstream, a remnant of the frontier, and the baby boomers, described in childhood as "the luckiest generation,"[13] found themselves, as young adults, in the melancholy position of wrestling with a two-hundred-year dependency on a drug that was now in short supply.

True, the 1980s raised the clamor for more to new heights of shrillness, insistence, and general obnoxiousness, but this, it can be argued, was in the nature of a final binge, the storm before the calm. America, though fighting the perception every inch of the way, was coming to realize that it was not a preordained part of the natural order that one should be richer every year. If it happened, that was nice. But who had started the flimsy and pernicious rumor that it was normal?

READING THE TEXT

1. Summarize in a paragraph how, according to Shames, the frontier functions as a symbol of American consciousness.

2. What connections does Shames make between America's frontier history and consumer behavior?

3. Why does Shames term the 1980s "an era of nostalgia" (para. 30)?

READING THE SIGNS

1. Shames asserts that Americans have been influenced by the frontier belief "that America would *keep on* booming" (para. 8). Do you feel that this belief continues to be influential into the twenty-first century? Write an essay arguing for your position. To develop your ideas, consult Gregg Easterbrook's "The Progress Paradox" (p. 400).

2. Shames claims that, because of the desire for more, "the ethic of decency has been upstaged by the ethic of success" (para. 14) in America. In class, form teams and debate the validity of Shames's claim.

3. Read or review Joan Kron's "The Semiotics of Home Decor" (p. 109). How is Martin J. Davidson influenced by the frontier myth that Shames describes?

[13]Thomas Hine, *Populuxe* (New York: Alfred A. Knopf, 1986), 15.

4. In an essay, argue for or refute the proposition that the "hunger for more" that Shames describes is a universal human trait, not simply American. To develop your ideas, consult Joan Kron, "The Semiotics of Home Decor" (p. 109), and Thomas L. Friedman, "Revolution Is U.S." (p. 130).

ANNE NORTON
The Signs of Shopping

Shopping malls are more than places to shop, just as mail-order cata-logues are more than simple lists of goods. Both malls and catalogues are coded systems that not only encourage us to buy but, more pro-foundly, help us to construct our very sense of identity, as in the J. Peter-man catalogue that "constructs the reader as a man of rugged outdoor interests, taste, and money." In this selection from Republic of Signs *(1993), Anne Norton (b. 1954), a professor of political science at the Uni-versity of Pennsylvania, analyzes the many ways in which malls, cata-logues, and home shopping networks sell you what they want by telling you who you are. Norton's other books include* Alternative Americas *(1986),* Reflections on Political Identity *(1988),* Ninety-five Theses on Politics, Culture, and Method *(2003), and* Leo Strauss and the Politics of American Empire *(2004).*

Shopping at the Mall

The mall has been the subject of innumerable debates. Created out of the modernist impulse for planning and the centralization of public activity, the mall has become the distinguishing sign of suburban decentralization, spring-ing up in unplanned profusion. Intended to restore something of the lost unity of city life to the suburbs, the mall has come to export styles and strategies to stores at the urban center. Deplored by modernists, it is regarded with affec-tion only by their postmodern foes. Ruled more by their content than by their creators' avowed intent, the once sleek futurist shells have taken on a certain aura of postmodern playfulness and popular glitz.

The mall is a favorite subject for the laments of cultural conservatives and others critical of the culture of consumption. It is indisputably the cultural locus of commodity fetishism. It has been noticed, however, by others of a less condemnatory disposition that the mall has something of the mercado, or the agora, about it. It is both a place of meeting for the young and one of the rare places where young and old go together. People of different races and classes, different occupations, different levels of education meet there. As M. Pressdee and John Fiske note, however, though the mall appears to be a public place, it is not. Neither freedom of speech nor freedom of assembly is permitted there. Those who own and manage malls restrict what comes within their confines. Controversial displays, by stores or customers or the plethora of organizations and agencies that present themselves in the open spaces of the mall, are not permitted. These seemingly public spaces conceal a pervasive private authority.

The mall exercises its thorough and discreet authority not only in the regulation of behavior but in the constitution of our visible, inaudible, public discourse. It is the source of those commodities through which we speak of our identities, our opinions, our desires. It is a focus for the discussion of style among peripheral consumers. Adolescents, particularly female adolescents, are inclined to spend a good deal of time at the mall. They spend, indeed, more time than money. They acquire not simple commodities (they may come home with many, few, or none) but a well-developed sense of the significance of those commodities. In prowling the mall they embed themselves in a lexicon of American culture. They find themselves walking through a dictionary. Stores hang a variety of identities on their racks and mannequins. Their window displays provide elaborate scenarios conveying not only what the garment is but what the garment means.

A display in the window of Polo provides an embarrassment of semiotic riches. Everyone, from the architecture critic at the *New York Times* to kids in the hall of a Montana high school, knows what *Ralph Lauren* means. The polo mallet and the saddle, horses and dogs, the broad lawns of Newport, Kennebunkport, old photographs in silver frames, the evocation of age, of ancestry and Anglophilia, of indolence and the Ivy League, evoke the upper class. Indian blankets and buffalo plaids, cowboy hats and Western saddles, evoke a past distinct from England but nevertheless determinedly Anglo. The supposedly arcane and suspect arts of deconstruction are deployed easily, effortlessly, by the readers of these cultural texts.

Walking from one window to another, observing one another, shoppers, especially the astute and observant adolescents, acquire a facility with the language of commodities. They learn not only words but a grammar. Shop windows employ elements of sarcasm and irony, strategies of inversion and allusion. They provide models of elegant, economical, florid, and prosaic expression. They teach composition.   5

The practice of shopping is, however, more than instructive. It has long been the occasion for women to escape the confines of their homes and enjoy the companionship of other women. The construction of woman's role as one of provision for the needs of the family legitimated her exit. It provided an occasion for women to spend long stretches of time in the company of their friends, without the presence of their husbands. They could exchange information and reflections, ask advice, and receive support. As their daughters grew, they would be brought increasingly within this circle, included in shopping trips and lunches with their mothers. These would form, reproduce, and restructure communities of taste.

The construction of identity and the enjoyment of friendship outside the presence of men was thus effected through a practice that constructed women as consumers and subjected them to the conventions of the marketplace. Insofar as they were dependent on their husbands for money, they were dependent on their husbands for the means to the construction of their identities. They could not represent themselves through commodities without the funds men provided, nor could they, without money, participate in the community of women that was realized in "going shopping." Their identities were made contingent not only on the possession of property but on the recognition of dependence.

Insofar as shopping obliges dependent women to recognize their dependence, it also opens up the possibility of subversion.[1] The housewife who shops for pleasure takes time away from her husband, her family, and her house and claims it for herself. Constantly taught that social order and her private happiness depend on intercourse between men and women, she chooses the company of women instead. She engages with women in an activity marked as feminine, and she enjoys it. When she spends money, she exercises an authority over property that law and custom may deny her. If she has no resources independent of her husband, this may be the only authority over property she is able to exercise. When she buys things her husband does not approve — or does not know of — she further subverts an order that leaves control over property in her husband's hands.[2]

Her choice of feminine company and a feminine pursuit may involve additional subversions. As Fiske and Pressdee recognize, shopping without buying and shopping for bargains have a subversive quality. This is revealed, in a form that gives it additional significance, when a saleswoman leans forward and tells a shopper, "Don't buy that today, it will be on sale on Thursday." Here solidarity of gender (and often of class) overcome, however partially and briefly, the imperatives of the economic order.

Shoppers who look, as most shoppers do, for bargains, and salespeople 10 who warn shoppers of impending sales, see choices between commodities as something other than the evidence and the exercise of freedom. They see covert direction and exploitation; they see the withholding of information and

---

[1] Nuanced and amusing accounts of shopping as subversion are provided in John Fiske's analyses of popular culture, particularly *Reading the Popular* (Boston: Unwin Hyman [now Routledge], 1989), pp. 13–42.

[2] See R. Bowlby, *Just Looking: Consumer Culture in Dreiser, Gissing, and Zola* (London: Methuen, 1985), p. 22, for another discussion and for an example of the recommendation of this strategy by Elizabeth Cady Stanton in the 1850s.

the manipulation of knowledge. They recognize that they are on enemy terrain and that their shopping can be, in Michel de Certeau's[3] term, a "guerrilla raid." This recognition in practice of the presence of coercion in choice challenges the liberal conflation of choice and consent.

Shopping at Home

Shopping is an activity that has overcome its geographic limits. One need no longer go to the store to shop. Direct mail catalogues, with their twenty-four-hour phone numbers for ordering, permit people to shop where and when they please. An activity that once obliged one to go out into the public sphere, with its diverse array of semiotic messages, can now be done at home. An activity that once obliged one to be in company, if not in conversation, with one's compatriots can now be conducted in solitude.

The activity of catalogue shopping, and the pursuit of individuality, are not, however, wholly solitary. The catalogues invest their commodities with vivid historical and social references. The J. Peterman catalogue, for example, constructs the reader as a man of rugged outdoor interests, taste, and money.[4] He wears "The Owner's Hat" or "Hemingway's Cap," a leather flight jacket or the classic "Horseman's Duster," and various other garments identified with the military, athletes, and European imperialism. The copy for "The Owner's Hat" naturalizes class distinctions and, covertly, racism:

> Some of us work on the plantation.
> Some of us own the plantation.
> Facts are facts.
> This hat is for those who own the plantation.[5]

Gender roles are strictly delineated. The copy for a skirt captioned "Women's Legs" provides a striking instance of the construction of the gaze as male, of women as the object of the gaze:

> just when you think you see something, a shape you think you recognize,
> it's gone and then it begins to return and then it's gone and of course you
> can't take your eyes off it.

---

[3]**Michel de Certeau** (1925–1986) French social scientist and semiologist who played an important role in the development of contemporary cultural studies. –Eds.

[4]I have read several of these. I cite *The J. Peterman Company Owner's Manual No. 5*, from the J. Peterman Company, 2444 Palumbo Drive, Lexington, Ky. 40509.

[5]Ibid., p. 5. The hat is also identified with the Canal Zone, "successfully bidding at Beaulieu," intimidation, and LBOs. Quite a hat. It might be argued against my reading that the J. Peterman Company also offers the "Coal Miner's Bag" and a mailbag. However, since the descriptive points of reference on color and texture and experience for these bags are such things as the leather seats of Jaguars, and driving home in a Bentley, I feel fairly confident in my reading.

> Yes, the long slow motion of women's legs. Whatever happened to those things at carnivals that blew air up into girls' skirts and you could spend hours watching.[6]

"You," of course, are male. There is also the lace blouse captioned "Mystery": "lace says yes at the same time it says no."[7] Finally, there are notes of imperialist nostalgia: the Sheapherd's Hotel (Cairo) bathrobe and white pants for "the bush" and "the humid hell-holes of Bombay and Calcutta."[8]

> It may no longer be unforgivable to say that the British left a few good things behind in India and in Kenya, Singapore, Borneo, etc., not the least of which was their Englishness.[9]

As Paul Smith observes, in his reading of their catalogues, the *Banana Republic* has also made capital out of imperial nostalgia.[10]

The communities catalogues create are reinforced by shared mailing lists. The constructed identities are reified and elaborated in an array of semiotically related catalogues. One who orders a spade or a packet of seeds will be constructed as a gardener and receive a deluge of catalogues from plant and garden companies. The companies themselves may expand their commodities to appeal to different manifestations of the identities they respond to and construct. Smith and Hawken, a company that sells gardening supplies with an emphasis on aesthetics and environmental concern, puts out a catalogue in which a group of people diverse in age and in their ethnicity wear the marketed clothes while gardening, painting, or throwing pots. Williams-Sonoma presents its catalogue not as a catalogue of things for cooking but as "A Catalog for Cooks." The catalogue speaks not to need but to the construction of identity.

The Nature Company dedicates its spring 1990 catalogue "to trees," endorses Earth Day, and continues to link itself to the Nature Conservancy through posters and a program in which you buy a tree for a forest restoration project. Here, a not-for-profit agency is itself commodified, adding to the value of the commodities offered in the catalogue.[11] In this catalogue, consumption is not merely a means for the construction and representation of the self, it is also a means for political action. Several commodities are offered as "A Few Things You Can Do" to save the earth: a string shopping bag, a solar battery recharger, a home newspaper recycler. Socially conscious shopping

[6]Ibid., p. 3. See also pp. 15 and 17 for instances of women as the object of the male gaze. The identification of the gaze with male sexuality is unambiguous here as well.

[7]Ibid., p. 17.

[8]Ibid., pp. 7, 16, 20, 21, 37, and 50.

[9]Ibid., p. 20.

[10]Paul Smith, "Visiting the Banana Republic," in *Universal Abandon?* ed. Andrew Ross for *Social Text* (Minneapolis: University of Minnesota Press, 1988), pp. 128–48.

[11]*The Nature Company Catalog*, The Nature Company, P.O. Box 2310, Berkeley, Calif. 94702, Spring 1990. See pp. 1–2 and order form insert between pp. 18 and 19. Note also the entailed donation to Designs for Conservation on p. 18.

is a liberal practice in every sense. It construes shopping as a form of election, in which one votes for good commodities or refuses one's vote to candidates whose practices are ethically suspect. In this respect, it reveals its adherence to the same ideological presuppositions that structure television's Home Shopping Network and other cable television sales shows.

Both politically informed purchasing and television sales conflate the free market and the electoral process. Dollars are identified with votes, purchases with endorsements. Both offer those who engage in them the possibility to "talk back" to manufacturers. In television sales shows this ability to talk back is both more thoroughly elaborated and more thoroughly exploited. Like the "elections" on MTV that invite viewers to vote for their favorite video by calling a number on their telephones, they permit those who watch to respond, to speak, and to be heard by the television. Their votes, of course, cost money. On MTV, as in the stores, you can buy as much speech as you can afford. On the Home Shopping Network, the purchase of speech becomes complicated by multiple layers and inversions.

Each commodity is introduced. It is invested by the announcer with a number of desirable qualities. The value of these descriptions of the commodities is enhanced by the construction of the announcer as a mediator not only between the commodity and the consumer but between the salespeople and the consumer. The announcer is not, the format suggests, a salesperson (though of course the announcer is). He or she is an announcer, describing goods that others have offered for sale. Television claims to distinguish itself by making objects visible to the eyes, but it is largely through the ears that these commodities are constructed. The consumer, in purchasing the commodity, purchases the commodity, what the commodity signifies, and, as we say, "buys the salesperson's line." The consumer may also acquire the ability to speak on television. Each purchase is recorded and figures as a vote in a rough plebiscite, confirming the desirability of the object. Although the purchase figures are announced as if they were confirming votes, it is, of course, impossible to register one's rejection of the commodity. Certain consumers get a little more (or rather less) for their money. They are invited to explain the virtue of the commodity — and their purchase — to the announcer and the audience. The process of production, of both the consumers and that which they consume, continues in this apology for consumption.

The semiotic identification of consumption as an American activity, indeed, a patriotic one, is made with crude enthusiasm on the Home Shopping Network and other video sales shows. Red, white, and blue figure prominently in set designs and borders framing the television screen. The Home Shopping Network presents its authorities in an office conspicuously adorned with a picture of the Statue of Liberty.[12] Yet the messages that the Home

---

[12]This moment from the Home Shopping Network was generously brought to my attention, on videotape, by Peter Bregman, a student in my American Studies class of fall 1988, at Princeton University.

Shopping Network sends its customers — that you can buy as much speech as you can afford, that you are recognized by others in accordance with your capacity to consume — do much to subvert the connection between capitalism and democracy on which this semiotic identification depends.

READING THE TEXT

1. What does Norton mean when she claims that the suburban shopping mall appears to be a public place but in fact is not?
2. What is Norton's interpretation of Ralph Lauren's Polo line?
3. How is shopping a subversive activity for women, according to Norton?
4. How do mail-order catalogues create communities of shoppers, in Norton's view?
5. What are the political messages sent by the Home Shopping Network, as Norton sees them, and how are they communicated?

READING THE SIGNS

1. Visit a local shopping mall, and study the window displays, focusing on stores intended for one group of consumers (teenagers, for example, or children). Then write an essay in which you analyze how the displays convey what the stores' products "mean."
2. Bring a few product catalogues to class, and in small groups compare the kind of consumer "constructed" by the catalogues' cultural images and allusions. Do you note any patterns associated with gender, ethnicity, or age group? Report your group's conclusions to the whole class.
3. Interview five women of different age groups about their motivations and activities when they shop in a mall. Then use the results of your interviews as evidence in an essay in which you support, refute, or complicate Norton's assertion that shopping constitutes a subversive activity for women.
4. Watch an episode of the Home Shopping Network or a similar program, and write a semiotic analysis of the ways in which products are presented to consumers.
5. Select a single mail-order catalogue, and write a detailed semiotic interpretation of the identity it constructs for its market.
6. Visit the Web site for a major store chain (for instance, **www.gap.com**), and study how it "moves" the consumer through it. How does the site induce you to consume?

Credit Card Barbie

READING THE SIGNS

1. Why might girls enjoy playing with a Barbie who shops rather than engaging her in some other kind of activity?

2. Do you think that having Barbie use a credit card to purchase cosmetics has an effect on the girls who play with the doll? If so, what are those effects?

THOMAS HINE
What's in a Package

What's in a package? According to Thomas Hine (b. 1947), a great deal, perhaps even more than what is actually inside the package. From the cereal boxes you find in the supermarket to the perfume bottles sold at Tiffany's, the shape and design of the packages that contain just about every product we consume have been carefully calculated to stimulate consumption. Indeed, as Hine explains in this excerpt from The Total Package: The Evolution and Secret Meanings of Boxes, Bottles, Cans, and Tubes *(1995), "for manufacturers, packaging is the crucial final pay-off to a marketing campaign." A former architecture and design critic for the* Philadelphia Inquirer, *Hine has also published* Populuxe *(1986), on American design and culture;* Facing Tomorrow *(1991), on past and current attitudes toward the future; and* The Rise and Fall of the American Teenager: A New History of the American Adolescent Experience *(1999).*

When you put yourself behind a shopping cart, the world changes. You become an active consumer, and you are moving through environments — the supermarket, the discount store, the warehouse club, the home center — that have been made for you.

During the thirty minutes you spend on an average trip to the supermarket, about thirty thousand different products vie to win your attention and ultimately to make you believe in their promise. When the door opens, automatically, before you, you enter an arena where your emotions and your appetites are in play, and a walk down the aisle is an exercise in self-definition. Are you a good parent, a good provider? Do you have time to do all you think you should, and would you be interested in a shortcut? Are you worried about your health and that of those you love? Do you care about the environment? Do you appreciate the finer things in life? Is your life what you would like it to be? Are you enjoying what you've accomplished? Wouldn't you really like something chocolate?

Few experiences in contemporary life offer the visual intensity of a Safeway, a Krogers, a Pathmark, or a Piggly Wiggly. No marketplace in the world — not Marrakesh or Calcutta or Hong Kong — offers so many different goods with such focused salesmanship as your neighborhood supermarket, where you're exposed to a thousand different products a minute. No wonder it's tiring to shop.

There are, however, some major differences between the supermarket and a traditional marketplace. The cacophony of a traditional market has given way to programmed, innocuous music, punctuated by enthusiastically intoned commercials. A stroll through a traditional market offers an array of sensuous aromas; if you are conscious of smelling something in a supermarket, there is a problem. The life and death matter of eating, expressed in traditional markets by the sale of vegetables with stems and roots and by hanging animal carcasses, is purged from the supermarket, where food is processed somewhere else, or at least trimmed out of sight.

But the most fundamental difference between a traditional market and   5
the places through which you push your cart is that in a modern retail setting nearly all the selling is done without people. The product is totally dissociated from the personality of any particular person selling it — with the possible exception of those who appear in its advertising. The supermarket purges sociability, which slows down sales. It allows manufacturers to control the way they present their products to the world. It replaces people with packages.

Packages are an inescapable part of modern life. They are omnipresent and invisible, deplored and ignored. During most of your waking moments, there are one or more packages within your field of vision. Packages are so ubiquitous that they slip beneath conscious notice, though many packages are designed so that people will respond to them even if they're not paying attention.

Once you begin pushing the shopping cart, it matters little whether you are in a supermarket, a discount store, or a warehouse club. The important thing is that you are among packages: expressive packages intended to engage your emotions, ingenious packages that make a product useful, informative packages that help you understand what you want and what you're getting. Historically, packages are what made self-service retailing possible, and in turn such stores increased the number and variety of items people buy. Now a world without packages is unimaginable.

Packages lead multiple lives. They preserve and protect, allowing people to make use of things that were produced far away, or a while ago. And they are potently expressive. They assure that an item arrives unspoiled, and they help those who use the item feel good about it.

We share our homes with hundreds of packages, mostly in the bathroom and kitchen, the most intimate, body-centered rooms of the house. Some packages — a perfume flacon, a ketchup bottle, a candy wrapper, a beer can — serve as permanent landmarks in people's lives that outlast homes, careers, or spouses. But packages embody change, not just in their age-old promise that their contents are new and improved, but in their attempt to respond to changing tastes and achieve new standards of convenience. Packages record changing hairstyles and changing life-styles. Even social policy issues are reflected. Nearly unopenable tamperproof seals and other forms of closures testify to the fragility of the social contract, and the susceptibility of the great mass of people to the destructive acts of a very few. It was a mark of rising environmental consciousness when containers recently began to make a novel promise: "less packaging."

For manufacturers, packaging is the crucial final payoff to a marketing 10 campaign. Sophisticated packaging is one of the chief ways people find the confidence to buy. It can also give a powerful image to products and commodities that are in themselves characterless. In many cases, the shopper has been prepared for the shopping experience by lush, colorful print advertisements, thirty-second television minidramas, radio jingles, and coupon promotions. But the package makes the final sales pitch, seals the commitment, and gets itself placed in the shopping cart. Advertising leads consumers into temptation. Packaging is the temptation. In many cases it is what makes the product possible.

But the package is also useful to the shopper. It is a tool for simplifying and speeding decisions. Packages promise, and usually deliver, predictability. One reason you don't think about packages is that you don't need to. The candy bar, the aspirin, the baking powder, or the beer in the old familiar package may, at times, be touted as new and improved, but it will rarely be very different.

You put the package into your cart, or not, usually without really having focused on the particular product or its many alternatives. But sometimes you do examine the package. You read the label carefully, looking at what the product promises, what it contains, what it warns. You might even look at the package itself and judge whether it will, for example, reseal to keep a product fresh. You might consider how a cosmetic container will look on your dressing table, or you might think about whether someone might have tampered with it or whether it can be easily recycled. The possibility of such scrutiny is one of the things that make each detail of the package so important.

The environment through which you push your shopping cart is extraordinary because of the amount of attention that has been paid to the packages that line the shelves. Most contemporary environments are landscapes of inattention. In housing developments, malls, highways, office buildings, even furniture, design ideas are few and spread very thin. At the supermarket, each box and jar, stand-up pouch and squeeze bottle, each can and bag and tube and spray has been very carefully considered. Designers have worked and reworked the design on their computers and tested mock-ups on the store shelves. Refinements are measured in millimeters.

All sorts of retail establishments have been redefined by packaging. Drugs and cosmetics were among the earliest packaged products, and most drugstores now resemble small supermarkets. Liquor makers use packaging to add a veneer of style to the intrinsic allure of intoxication, and some sell their bottle rather than the drink. It is no accident that vodka, the most characterless of spirits, has the highest-profile packages. The local gas station sells sandwiches and soft drinks rather than tires and motor oil, and in turn, automotive products have been attractively repackaged for sales at supermarkets, warehouse clubs, and home centers.

With its thousands of images and messages, the supermarket is as visu- 15 ally dense, if not as beautiful, as a Gothic cathedral. It is as complex and as predatory as a tropical rain forest. It is more than a person can possibly take in during an ordinary half-hour shopping trip. No wonder a significant percentage of people who need to wear eyeglasses don't wear them when they're shopping, and some researchers have spoken of the trancelike state that pushing a cart through this environment induces. The paradox here is that the visual intensity that overwhelms shoppers is precisely the thing that makes the design of packages so crucial. Just because you're not looking at a package doesn't mean you don't see it. Most of the time, you see far more than a container and a label. You see a personality, an attitude toward life, perhaps even a set of beliefs.

The shopper's encounter with the product on the shelf is, however, only the beginning of the emotional life cycle of the package. The package is very important in the moment when the shopper recognizes it either as an old friend or a new temptation. Once the product is brought home, the package seems to disappear, as the quality or usefulness of the product it contains becomes paramount. But in fact, many packages are still selling even at home, enticing those who have bought them to take them out of the cupboard, the closet, or the refrigerator and consume their contents. Then once the product has been used up, and the package is empty, it becomes suddenly visible once more. This time, though, it is trash that must be discarded or recycled. This instant of disposal is the time when people are most aware of packages. It is a negative moment, like the end of a love affair, and what's left seems to be a horrid waste.

The forces driving package design are not primarily aesthetic. Market researchers have conducted surveys of consumer wants and needs, and consultants have studied photographs of families' kitchen cupboards and medicine chests to get a sense of how products are used. Test subjects have been tied into pieces of heavy apparatus that measure their eye movement, their blood pressure or body temperature, when subjected to different packages. Psychologists get people to talk about the packages in order to get a sense of their innermost feelings about what they want. Government regulators and private health and safety advocates worry over package design and try to make it truthful. Stock-market analysts worry about how companies are managing their "brand equity," that combination of perceived value and consumer loyalty that is expressed in advertising but embodied in packaging. The retailer is paying attention to the packages in order to weed out the ones that don't sell or aren't sufficiently profitable. The use of supermarket scanners generates information on the profitability of every cubic inch of the store. Space on the supermarket shelf is some of the most valuable real estate in the world, and there are always plenty of new packaged products vying for display.

Packaging performs a series of disparate tasks. It protects its contents from contamination and spoilage. It makes it easier to transport and store goods. It provides uniform measuring of contents. By allowing brands to be created and standardized, it makes advertising meaningful and large-scale distribution possible. Special kinds of packages, with dispensing caps, sprays, and other convenience features, make products more usable. Packages serve as symbols both of their contents and of a way of life. And just as they can very powerfully communicate the satisfaction a product offers, they are equally potent symbols of wastefulness once the product is gone.

Most people use dozens of packages each day and discard hundreds of them each year. The growth of mandatory recycling programs has made people increasingly aware of packages, which account in the United States for about forty-three million tons, or just under 30 percent of all refuse discarded. While forty-three million tons of stuff is hardly insignificant, repeated surveys have shown that the public perceives that far more than 30 percent — indeed, nearly all — their garbage consists of packaging. This perception creates a political problem for the packaging industry, but it also demonstrates the power of packaging. It is symbolic. It creates an emotional relationship. Bones and wasted food (13 million tons), grass clippings and yard waste (thirty-one million tons), or even magazines and newspapers (fourteen million tons) do not feel as wasteful as empty vessels that once contained so much promise.

Packaging is a cultural phenomenon, which means that it works differently in 20 different cultures. The United States has been a good market for packages since it was first settled and has been an important innovator of packaging technology and culture. Moreover, American packaging is part of an international culture of modernity and consumption. At its deepest level, the culture of American packaging deals with the issue of surviving among strangers in a new world. This is an emotion with which anyone who has been touched by modernity can identify. In lives buffeted by change, people seek the safety and reassurance that packaged products offer. American packaging, which has always sought to appeal to large numbers of diverse people, travels better than that of most other cultures.

But the similar appearance of supermarkets throughout the world should not be interpreted as the evidence of a single, global consumer culture. In fact, most companies that do business internationally redesign their packages for each market. This is done partly to satisfy local regulations and adapt to available products and technologies. But the principal reason is that people in different places have different expectations and make different uses of packaging.

The United States and Japan, the world's two leading industrial powers, have almost opposite approaches to packaging. Japan's is far more elaborate than America's, and it is shaped by rituals of respect and centuries-old traditions of wrapping and presentation. Packaging is explicitly recognized as an expression of culture in Japan and largely ignored in America. Japanese packaging is designed to be appreciated; American packaging is calculated to be unthinkingly accepted.

Foods that only Japanese eat — even relatively humble ones like refrigerated prepared fish cakes — have wrappings that resemble handmade paper or leaves. Even modestly priced refrigerated fish cakes have beautiful wrappings in which traditional design accommodates a scannable bar code. Such products look Japanese and are unambiguously intended to do so. Products that are foreign, such as coffee, look foreign, even to the point of having only Roman lettering and no Japanese lettering on the can. American and European companies are sometimes able to sell their packages in Japan virtually unchanged, because their foreignness is part of their selling power. But Japanese exporters hire designers in each country to repackage their products. Americans — whose culture is defined not by refinements and distinctions but by inclusiveness — want to think about the product itself, not its cultural origins.

We speak glibly about global villages and international markets, but problems with packages reveal some unexpected cultural boundaries. Why are Canadians willing to drink milk out of flexible plastic pouches that fit into reusable plastic holders, while residents of the United States are believed to be so resistant to the idea that they have not even been given the opportunity to do so? Why do Japanese consumers prefer packages that contain two tennis balls and view the standard U.S. pack of three to be cheap and undesirable? Why do Germans insist on highly detailed technical specifications on packages of videotape, while Americans don't? Why do Swedes think that blue is masculine, while the Dutch see the color as feminine? The answers lie in unquestioned habits and deep-seated imagery, a culture of containing, adorning, and understanding that no sharp marketer can change overnight.

There is probably no other field in which designs that are almost a century 25 old — Wrigley's gum, Campbell's soup, Hershey's chocolate bar — remain in production only subtly changed and are understood to be extremely valuable corporate assets. Yet the culture of packaging, defined by what people are buying and selling every day, keeps evolving, and the role nostalgia plays is very small.

For example, the tall, glass Heinz ketchup bottle has helped define the American refrigerator skyline for most of the twentieth century (even though it is generally unnecessary to refrigerate ketchup). Moreover, it provides the tables of diners and coffee shops with a vertical accent and a token of hospitality, the same qualities projected by candles and vases of flowers in more upscale eateries. The bottle has remained a fixture of American life, even though it has always been a nuisance to pour the thick ketchup through the little hole. It seemed not to matter that you have to shake and shake the bottle, impotently, until far too much ketchup comes out in one great scarlet plop. Heinz experimented for years with wide-necked jars and other sorts of bottles, but they never caught on.

Then in 1992 a survey of consumers indicated that more Americans believed that the plastic squeeze bottle is a better package for ketchup than the glass bottle. The survey did not offer any explanations for this change of preference, which has been evolving for many years as older people for whom the tall bottle is an icon became a less important part of the sample. Could it be that the difficulty of using the tall bottle suddenly became evident to those born after 1960? Perhaps the tall bottle holds too little ketchup. There is a clear trend toward buying things in larger containers, in part because lightweight plastics have made them less costly for manufacturers to ship and easier for consumers to use. This has happened even as the number of people in an average American household has been getting smaller. But houses, like packages, have been getting larger. Culture moves in mysterious ways.

The tall ketchup bottle is still preferred by almost half of consumers, so it is not going to disappear anytime soon. And the squeeze bottle does contain visual echoes of the old bottle. It is certainly not a radical departure. In Japan, ketchup and mayonnaise are sold in cellophane-wrapped plastic bladders that would certainly send Americans into severe culture shock. Still, the tall bottle's loss of absolute authority is a significant change. And its ultimate disappearance would represent a larger change in most people's visual environment than would the razing of nearly any landmark building.

But although some package designs are pleasantly evocative of another time, and a few appear to be unchanging icons in a turbulent world, the reason they still exist is because they still work. Inertia has historically played a role in creating commercial icons. Until quite recently, it was time-consuming and expensive to make new printing plates or to vary the shape or material of a container. Now computerized graphics and rapidly developing technology in the package-manufacturing industries make a packaging change easier than in the past, and a lot cheaper to change than advertising, which seems a far more evanescent medium. There is no constituency of curators or preservationists to protect the endangered package. If a gum wrapper manages to survive nearly unchanged for ninety years, it's not because any expert has determined that it is an important cultural expression. Rather, it's because it still helps sell a lot of gum.

So far, we've been discussing packaging in its most literal sense: designed 30 containers that protect and promote products. Such containers have served as the models for larger types of packaging, such as chain restaurants, supermarkets, theme parks, and festival marketplaces. . . . Still, it is impossible to ignore a broader conception of packaging that is one of the preoccupations of our time. This concerns the ways in which people construct and present their personalities, the ways in which ideas are presented and diffused, the ways in which political candidates are selected and public policies formulated. We must all worry about packaging ourselves and everything we do, because we believe that nobody has time to really pay attention.

Packaging strives at once to offer excitement and reassurance. It promises something newer and better, but not necessarily different. When we talk about a tourist destination, or even a presidential contender, being packaged, that's not really a metaphor. The same projection of intensified ordinariness, the same combination of titillation and reassurance, are used for laundry detergents, theme parks, and candidates alike.

The imperative to package is unavoidable in a society in which people have been encouraged to see themselves as consumers not merely of toothpaste and automobiles, but of such imponderables as lifestyle, government, and health. The marketplace of ideas is not an agora, where people haggle, posture, clash, and come to terms with one another. Rather, it has become a supermarket, where values, aspirations, dreams, and predictions are presented with great sophistication. The individual can choose to buy them, or leave them on the shelf.

In such a packaged culture, the consumer seems to be king. But people cannot be consumers all the time. If nothing else, they must do something to earn the money that allows them to consume. This, in turn, pressures people to package themselves in order to survive. The early 1990s brought economic recession and shrinking opportunities to all the countries of the developed world. Like products fighting for their space on the shelf, individuals have had to re-create, or at least represent, themselves in order to seem both desirable and safe. Moreover, many jobs have been reconceived to depersonalize individuals and to make them part of a packaged service experience.

These phenomena have their own history. For decades, people have spoken of writing resumes in order to package themselves for a specific opportunity. Thomas J. Watson Jr., longtime chairman of IBM, justified his company's famously conservative and inflexible dress code — dark suits, white shirts, and rep ties for all male employees — as "self-packaging," analogous to the celebrated product design, corporate imagery, and packaging done for the company by Elliot Noyes and Paul Rand. You can question whether IBM's employees were packaging themselves or forced into a box by their employer. Still, anyone who has ever dressed for success was doing a packaging job.

Since the 1950s, there have been discussions of packaging a candidate [35] to respond to what voters are telling the pollsters who perform the same tasks as market researchers do for soap or shampoo. More recently, such discussions have dominated American political journalism. The packaged candidate, so he and his handlers hope, projects a message that, like a Diet Pepsi, is stimulating without being threatening. Like a Weight Watchers frozen dessert bar, the candidate's contradictions must be glazed over and, ultimately, comforting. Aspects of the candidate that are confusing or viewed as extraneous are removed, just as stems and sinew are removed from packaged foods. The package is intended to protect the candidate; dirt won't stick. The candidate is uncontaminated, though at a slight remove from the consumer-voter.

People profess to be troubled by this sort of packaging. When we say a person or an experience is "packaged," we are complaining of a sense of excessive calculation and a lack of authenticity. Such a fear of unreality is at least a century old; it arose along with industrialization and rapid communication. Now that the world is more competitive, and we all believe we have less time to consider things, the craft of being instantaneously appealing has taken on more and more importance. We might say, cynically, that the person who appears "packaged" simply doesn't have good packaging.

Still, the sense of uneasiness about encountering packaged people in a packaged world is real, and it shouldn't be dismissed. Indeed, it is a theme of contemporary life, equally evident in politics, entertainment, and the supermarket. Moreover, public uneasiness about the phenomenon of packaging is compounded by confusion over a loss of iconic packages and personalities.

Producers of packaged products have probably never been as nervous as they became during the first half of the 1990s. Many of the world's most famous brands were involved in the merger mania of the 1980s, which produced debt-ridden companies that couldn't afford to wait for results either from their managers or their marketing strategies. At the same time, the feeling was that it was far too risky to produce something really new. The characteristic response was the line extension — "dry" beer, "lite" mayonnaise, "ultra" detergent. New packages have been appearing at a rapid pace, only to be changed whenever a manager gets nervous or a retailer loses patience.

The same skittishness is evident in the projection of public personalities as the clear, if synthetic, images of a few decades ago have lost their sharpness and broken into a spectrum of weaker, reflected apparitions. Marilyn Monroe, for example, had an image that was, Jayne Mansfield notwithstanding, unique and well defined. She was luscious as a Hershey's bar, shapely as a Coke bottle. But in a world where Coke can be sugar free, caffeine free, and cherry flavored (and Pepsi can be clear!), just one image isn't enough for a superstar. Madonna is available as Marilyn or as a brunette, a Catholic schoolgirl, or a bondage devotee. Who knows what brand extension will come next? Likewise, John F. Kennedy and Elvis Presley had clear, carefully projected images. But Bill Clinton is defined largely by evoking memories of both. As our commercial civilization seems to have lost the power to amuse or convince us in new and exciting ways, formerly potent packages are recycled and devalued. That has left the door open for such phenomena as generic cigarettes, President's Choice cola, and H. Ross Perot.

This cultural and personal packaging both fascinates and infuriates. There 40 is something liberating in its promise of aggressive self-creation, and something terrifying in its implication that everything must be subject to the ruthless discipline of the marketplace. People are at once passive consumers of their culture and aggressive packagers of themselves, which can be a stressful and lonely combination.

READING THE TEXT

1. How does Hine compare a supermarket with a traditional marketplace?

2. What does Hine mean when he asserts that modern retailing "replaces people with packages" (para. 5)?

3. How does packaging stimulate the desire to buy, according to Hine?

4. How do American attitudes toward packaging compare with those of the Japanese, according to Hine?

READING THE SIGNS

1. Bring one product package to class, preferably with all students bringing items from the same product category (personal hygiene, say, or bottled water). Give a brief presentation to the class in which you interpret your own package. After all the students have presented, compare the different messages the packages send to consumers.

2. Visit a popular clothing store, such as Urban Outfitters or the Gap, and study the ways the store uses packaging to create, as Hine puts it, "a personality, an attitude toward life" (para. 15). Be thorough in your observations, studying everything from the store's shopping bags to perfume or cologne packages to clothing labels. Use your findings as evidence for an essay in which you analyze the image the store creates for itself and its customers.

3. In your journal, write an entry in which you explore your motives for purchasing a product only because you liked the package. What did you like about the package, and how did it contribute to your sense of identity?

4. Visit a store with an explicit political theme, such as the Body Shop or Whole Foods, and write a semiotic analysis of some of the packaging you see in the store.

5. Study the packages that are visible to a visitor to your home, and write an analysis of the messages those packages might send to a visitor. To develop your ideas, consult Joan Kron's "The Semiotics of Home Decor" (p. 109).

FRED DAVIS
Blue Jeans

Blue jeans are almost certainly America's greatest contribution to fashion history, and in this analysis, which originally appeared in his book Fashion Culture and Identity *(1992), Fred Davis (1925–1992) shows how this staple of the American wardrobe has become a symbol of many of our most enduring, and contradictory, cultural values. At once an emblem of democratic populism and an elite status symbol, blue jeans are part of an American dialectic, Davis argues, in which "status and antistatus, democracy and distinction," are in a constant flux, moving with the tides of history itself. A former professor of sociology at the University of California at San Diego, Davis authored such books as* Yearning for Yesterday: A Sociology of Nostalgia *(1979) and* Illness, Interaction, and the Self *(1972).*

The new clothes [jeans] express profoundly democratic values. There are no distinctions of wealth or status, no elitism; people confront one another shorn of these distinctions.

> — CHARLES A. REICH,
> *The Greening of America*

Throughout the world, the young and their allies are drawn hypnotically to denim's code of hope and solidarity — to an undefined vision of the energetic and fraternal Americanness inherent in them all.

> — KENNEDY FRASER,
> "That Missing Button"

Karl Lagerfeld for Chanel shapes a classic suit from blue and white denim, $960, with denim bustier, $360, . . . and denim hat, $400. All at Chanel Boutique, Beverly Hills.

> — Photograph caption in *Los Angeles Times Magazine*
> for article "Dressed-Up Denims," April 19, 1987

Since the dawn of fashion in the West some seven hundred years ago, probably no other article of clothing has in the course of its evolution more fully served as a vehicle for the expression of status ambivalences and ambiguities than blue jeans. Some of the social history supporting this statement is by now generally well known.[1] First fashioned in the mid-nineteenth-century American West by Morris Levi Strauss, a Bavarian Jewish peddler newly arrived in San Francisco, the trousers then as now were made from a sturdy, indigo-dyed cotton cloth said to have originated in Nimes, France. (Hence the

---

[1] Excellent, sociologically informed accounts of the origins and social history of blue jeans are to be found in Belasco (n.d.) and Friedmann (1987).

anglicized contraction to *denim* from the French *de Nimes*.) A garment similar to that manufactured by Levi Strauss for goldminers and outdoor laborers is said to have been worn earlier in France by sailors and dockworkers from Genoa, Italy, who were referred to as "genes"; hence the term *jeans*. The distinctive copper riveting at the pants pockets and other stress points were the invention of Jacob Davis, a tailor from Carson City, Nevada, who joined the Levi Strauss firm in 1873, some twenty years after the garment's introduction.

More than a century went by, however, before this workingman's garment attained the prominence and near-universal recognition it possesses today. For it was not until the late 1960s that blue jeans, after several failed moves in previous decades into a broader mass market, strikingly crossed over nearly all class, gender, age, regional, national, and ideological lines to become the universally worn and widely accepted item of apparel they are today. And since the crossover, enthusiasm for them has by no means been confined to North America and Western Europe. In former Soviet bloc countries and much of the Third World, too, where they have generally been in short supply, they remain highly sought after and hotly bargained over.

A critical feature of this cultural breakthrough is, of course, blue jeans' identity change from a garment associated exclusively with work (and hard work, at that) to one invested with many of the symbolic attributes of leisure: ease, comfort, casualness, sociability, and the outdoors. Or, as the costume historians Jasper and Roach-Higgins (1987) might put it, the garment underwent a process of cultural authentication that led to its acquiring meanings quite different from that with which it began. In bridging the work/leisure divide when it did, it tapped into the new, consumer-goods-oriented, postindustrial affluence of the West on a massive scale. Soon thereafter it penetrated those many other parts of the world that emulate the West.

But this still fails to answer the questions of why so rough-hewn, drably hued, and crudely tailored a piece of clothing should come to exercise the fascination it has for so many diverse societies and peoples, or why within a relatively short time of breaking out of its narrow occupational locus it spread so quickly throughout the world. Even if wholly satisfactory answers elude us, these questions touch intimately on the twists and turns of status symbolism. . . .

To begin with, considering its origins and longtime association with work- 5 ingmen, hard physical labor, the outdoors, and the American West, much of the blue jeans' fundamental mystique seems to emanate from populist sentiments of democracy, independence, equality, freedom, and fraternity. This makes for a sartorial symbolic complex at war, even if rather indifferently for nearly a century following its introduction, with class distinctions, elitism, and snobbism, dispositions extant nearly as much in jeans-originating America as in the Old World. It is not surprising, therefore, that the first non–"working stiffs" to become attached to blue jeans and associated denim wear were painters and other artists, mainly in the southwest United States, in the late 1930s and 1940s (Friedmann 1987). These were soon followed by "hoodlum" motorcycle gangs ("bikers") in the 1950s and by New Left activists and hippies in the 1960s (Belasco n.d.). All these groups (each in its own way, of course) stood strongly in opposition to the dominant conservative, middle-class, consumer-oriented culture of American society. Blue jeans, given their origins and historic associations, offered a visible means for announcing such antiestablishment sentiments. Besides, jeans were cheap, and, at least at first, good fit hardly mattered.

Whereas by the late 1950s one could in some places see jeans worn in outdoor play by middle-class boys, until well into the 1960s a truly ecumenical acceptance of them was inhibited precisely because of their association with (more, perhaps, through media attention than from firsthand experience) such disreputable and deviant groups as bikers and hippies. Major sales and public relations campaigns would be undertaken by jeans manufacturers to break the symbolic linkage with disreputability and to convince consumers that jeans and denim were suitable for one and all and for a wide range of occasions (Belasco n.d.). Apparently such efforts helped; by the late 1960s blue jeans had achieved worldwide popularity and, of greater relevance here, had fully crossed over the occupation, class, gender, and age boundaries that had circumscribed them for over a century.

What was it — and, perhaps, what is it still — about blue jeans? Notwithstanding the symbolic elaborations and revisions (some would say perversions) to which fashion and the mass market have in the intervening years subjected the garment, there can be little doubt that at its crossover phase its underlying symbolic appeal derived from its antifashion significations: its visually persuasive historic allusions to rural democracy, the common man, simplicity, unpretentiousness, and, for many, especially Europeans long captivated by it, the romance of the American West with its figure of the free-spirited, self-reliant cowboy.[2]

But as the history of fashion has demonstrated time and again, no vestmental symbol is inviolable. All can, and usually will be, subjected to the whims of those who wish to convey more or different things about their person than the "pure" symbol in its initial state of signification communicates. Democratic, egalitarian sentiments notwithstanding, social status still counts for too much in Western society to permanently suffer the proletarianization that an unmodified blue-jean declaration of equality and fraternity projected. No sooner, then, had jeans made their way into the mass marketplace than myriad devices were employed for muting and mixing messages, readmitting evicted symbolic allusions, and, in general, promoting invidious distinctions among classes and coteries of jean wearers. Indeed, to the extent that their very acceptance was propelled by fashion as such, it can be said an element

---

[2]This is not to put forward some absurd claim to the effect that everyone who donned a pair of jeans was swept up by this imagery. Rather, it is to suggest that it was such imagery that came culturally to be encoded in the wearing of blue jeans (Berger 1984, 80–82), so that whether one wore them indifferently or with calculated symbolic intent, imitatively or in a highly individual manner, they would "on average" be viewed in this light.

of invidiousness was already at play. For, other things being equal and regardless of the "message" a new fashion sends, merely to be "in fashion" is to be one up on those who are not as yet.[3]

Elite vs. Populist Status Markers

Beyond this metacommunicative function, however, the twists, inversions, contradictions, and paradoxes of status symbolism to which blue jeans subsequently lent themselves underscore the subtle identity ambivalences plaguing many of their wearers. In a 1973 piece titled "Denim and the New Conservatives," Kennedy Fraser (1981, 92) noted several such, perhaps the most ironic being this:

> Some of the most expensive versions of the All-American denim theme have come bouncing into our stores from European manufacturers. The irresistible pull of both European fashion and denim means that American customers will pay large sums for, say, French blue jeans despite the galling knowledge that fashionable young people in Saint-Tropez are only imitating young people in America, a country that can and does produce better and cheaper blue jeans than France.

By 1990 a nearly parallel inversion seemed about to occur in regard to the garment's post-1950s image as leisure wear, although for destination other than fields and factories. With the introduction of men's fall fashions for the year featuring "urban denim," a spokesman for the Men's Fashion Association said (Hofmann 1990): "It's not just about cowboys and country and western anymore. It used to be that denim meant play clothes; now men want to wear it to the office the next day."

Framing the garment's status dialectic was the contest of polarities, one pole continuing to emphasize and extend blue jeans' "base-line" symbolism of democracy, utility, and classlessness, the other seeking to reintroduce traditional claims to taste, distinction, and hierarchical division. (Any individual wearer, and often the garment itself, might try to meld motifs from both sides in the hope of registering a balanced, yet appropriately ambivalent, statement.)

---

[3]From this perspective, assumed by such important French critics as Barthes (1983) and Baudrillard (1984), all fashion, irrespective of the symbolic content that animates one or another manifestation of it, gravitates toward "designification" or the destruction of meaning. That is to say, because it feeds on itself (on its ability to induce others to follow the fashion "regardless"), it soon neutralizes or sterilizes whatever significance its signifiers had before becoming objects of fashion. Sheer display displaces signification; to take the example of blue jeans, even people hostile to their underlying egalitarian message can via fashion's mandate wear them with ease and impunity and, contrary to the garment's symbolic anti-invidious origins, score "status points" by doing so. This argument is powerful but in my view posits, in a manner similar to the claim that fashion is nothing more than change for the sake of change, too complete a break between the symbolic content of culture and the communication processes that embody and reshape it.

Conspicuous Poverty: Fading and Fringing

From the "left" symbolic (and not altogether apolitical) pole came the practice of jean fading and fringing. Evocative of a kind of conspicuous poverty, faded blue jeans and those worn to the point of exposing some of the garment's warp and woof were soon more highly prized, particularly by the young, than new, well-blued jeans. Indeed, in some circles worn jeans commanded a higher price than new ones. As with Chanel's little black dress, it cost more to look "truly poor" than just ordinarily so, which new jeans by themselves could easily accomplish. But given the vogue that fading and fringing attained, what ensued in the marketplace was predictable: Jeans manufacturers started producing prefaded, worn-looking, stone- or acid-washed jeans.[4] These obviated, for the average consumer if not for the jeans connoisseur disdainful of such subterfuge, the need for a long break-in period.

Labeling, Ornamentation, and Eroticization

From the "right" symbolic pole emerged a host of stratagems and devices, all of which sought in effect to de-democratize jeans while capitalizing on the ecumenical appeal they had attained: designer jeans, which prominently displayed the label of the designer; jeans bearing factory sewn-in embroidering, nailheads, rhinestones, and other decorative additions; specially cut and sized jeans for women, children, and older persons; in general, jeans combined (with fashion's sanction) with items of clothing standing in sharp symbolic contradiction of them, e.g., sports jackets, furs, dress shoes, spiked heels, ruffled shirts, or silk blouses.

Paralleling the de-democratization of the jean, by the 1970s strong currents toward its eroticization were also evident. These, of course, contravened the unisex, de-gendered associations the garment initially held for many: the relative unconcern for fit and emphasis on comfort; the fly front for both male and female; the coarse denim material, which, though it chafed some, particularly women, was still suffered willingly. Numerous means were found to invest the jean and its associated wear with gender-specific, eroticized meaning. In the instance of women—and this is more salient sociologically since it was they who had been de-feminized by donning the blatantly masculine blue jeans in the first place—these included the fashioning of denim material into skirts, the "jeans for gals" sales pitches of manufacturers, the use of softer materials, cutting jeans so short as to expose the buttocks, and, in general, the transmogrification of jeans from loose-fitting, baggy trousers into pants so snugly pulled over the posterior as to require some women to lie

[4]A yet later variation on the same theme was "shotgun washed" jeans manufactured by a Tennessee company that blasted its garments with a twelve-gauge shotgun (Hochswender 1991).

down to get into them. So much for comfort, so much for unisexuality! Interestingly, in the never-ending vestmental dialectic on these matters baggy jeans for women again became fashionable in the mid-1980s.

Designer Jeans

Of all of the modifications wrought upon it, the phenomenon of designer jeans speaks most directly to the garment's encoding of status ambivalences. The very act of affixing a well-known designer's label — and some of the world's leading hautes couturiers in time did so — to the back side of a pair of jeans has to be interpreted, however else it may be seen, along Veblenian lines, as an instance of conspicuous consumption; in effect, a muting of the underlying rough-hewn proletarian connotation of the garment through the introduction of a prominent status marker.[5] True, sewing an exterior designer label onto jeans — a practice designers never resort to with other garments — was facilitated psychologically by the prominent Levi Strauss & Co. label, which had from the beginning been sewn above the right hip pocket of that firm's denim jeans and had over the years become an inseparable part of the garment's image. It could then be argued, as it sometimes was, that the outside sewing of a designer label was consistent with the traditional image of blue jeans. Still, Yves Saint Laurent, Oscar de la Renta, or Gloria Vanderbilt, for that matter, are not names to assimilate easily with Levi Strauss, Lee, or Wrangler, a distinction hardly lost on most consumers.

But as is so characteristic of fashion, every action elicits its reaction. No sooner had the snoblike, status-conscious symbolism of designer jeans made its impact on the market than dress coteries emerged whose sartorial stock-in-trade was a display of disdain for the invidious distinctions registered by so obvious a status ploy. This was accomplished mainly through a demonstration of hyperloyalty to the original, underlying egalitarian message of denim blue jeans. As Kennedy Fraser (1981, 93) was to observe of these countercyclicists in 1973:

> The denim style of the more sensitive enclaves of the Village, the West Side, and SoHo is the style of the purist and neo-ascetic. Unlike the "chic" devotee of blue jeans, this loyalist often wears positively baggy denims,

[5]Everyone, without exception, whom I interviewed and spoke with in the course of my research on fashion (designers, apparel manufacturers, buyers, persons from the fashion press, fashion-conscious laypersons) interpreted designer jeans in this light. Most felt that status distinctions were the *only* reason for designer jeans because, except for the display of the designer label, they could detect no significant difference between designer and nondesigner jeans. Not all commentators, however, are of the opinion that the prominent display of an outside label can be attributed solely to invidious status distinctions. Some (Back 1985) find in the phenomenon overtones of a modernist aesthetic akin, for example, to Bauhaus design, exoskeletal building construction, action painting, and certain directions in pop art wherein the identity of the creator and the processual markings of his/her creation are visibly fused with the art work itself.

and scorns such travesties as embroideries and nailheads. To underline their association with honesty and toil, the denims of choice are often overalls.

Not long after, the "positively baggy denims" of which Fraser speaks — this antifashion riposte to fashion's prior corruption of denim's 1960s-inspired rejection of status distinctions — were themselves, with that double reflexive irony at which fashion is so adept, assimilated into the fashion cycle. Then those "into" denim styles could by "dressing down" stay ahead of — as had their older, first-time-around denim-clad siblings of the sixties — their more conformist, "properly dressed" alters.

Conclusion

And so . . . do the dialectics of status and antistatus, democracy and distinction, inclusiveness and exclusiveness pervade fashion's twists and turns; as much, or even more, with the workingman's humble blue jeans as with formal dinner wear and the evening gown.

But such is fashion's way. If it is to thrive it can only feed off the ambiguities and ambivalences we endure in our daily lives and concourse, not only over those marks of social status considered here but equally over such other key identity pegs as age, gender, and sexuality, to mention but the most obvious. Were it the case, as some scholars have maintained, that fashion's sole symbolic end was registering and re-registering invidious distinctions of higher and lower, or better and lesser — that is, distinctions of class and social status — it would hardly have enough "to talk about"; certainly not enough to account for its having thrived in Western society for as long as it has. But, as we have already seen . . . , it does have more to say: about our masculinity and femininity, our youth and age, our sexual scruples or lack thereof, our work and play, our politics, national identity, and religion. This said, one need not take leave of what has engaged us here, that rich symbolic domain that treats of the deference and respect we accord and receive from others (what Max Weber meant by *status*), in order to appreciate that fashion is capable of much greater subtlety, more surprises, more anxious backward glances and searching forward gazes than we credit it with.

WORKS CITED

Back, Kurt W. 1985. "Modernism and Fashion: A Social Psychological Interpretation," in Michael R. Solomon, ed., *The Psychology of Fashion*. Lexington, Mass.: Heath.

Barthes, Roland. 1983. *The Fashion System*. Translated by Matthew Ward and Richard Howard. New York: Hill and Wang.

Baudrillard, Jean. 1984. "La Mode ou la féerie du code." *Traverses* 3 (October): 7–19.

Belasco, Warren A. n.d. "Mainstreaming Blue Jeans: The Ideological Process, 1945–1980." Unpublished.

Berger, Arthur Asa. 1984. *Signs in Contemporary Culture*. New York: Longman.

Fraser, Kennedy. 1981. *The Fashionable Mind*. New York: Knopf.

Friedmann, Daniel. 1987. *Une Histoire du blue jean*. Paris: Ramsay.

Hochswender, Woody. 1991. "Patterns." *New York Times*, Jan. 8.

Hofmann, Deborah. 1990. "New Urbanity for Denim and Chambray." *New York Times*, Sept. 24.

Jasper, Cynthia R., and Mary Ellen Roach-Higgins. 1987. "History of Costume: Theory and Instruction." *Clothing and Textile Research Journal* 5, no. 4 (Summer): 1–6.

Reich, Charles A. 1970. *The Greening of America*. New York: Crown.

READING THE TEXT

1. Why, according to Davis, were jeans linked with "disreputability" (para. 6) until the mid-1960s?

2. In Davis's view, what enabled jeans to "crossover" (para. 2) from being disreputable to fashionable?

3. Summarize in your own words the ambivalence between "democracy and distinction" (para. 17) and "left" (para. 12) and "right" (para. 13) that Davis ascribes to jeans since the 1960s.

4. How does Davis interpret the advent of designer jeans?

READING THE SIGNS

1. Bring to class a current fashion magazine for men or women (such as *Details* or *Glamour*) and study the jeans ads in small groups. Do you find that today's jeans ads use the democratizing or de-democratizing symbolism that Davis describes? To develop your ideas, consult Jack Solomon's "Masters of Desire: The Culture of American Advertising" (p. 409).

2. This selection, originally published in 1992, takes its analysis through the 1980s. Using Davis's categories of democracy and distinction, write your own analysis of jeans that are popular today. For evidence of the system in which jeans operate, you can rely on advertisements, videos, film, Web sites of jeans manufacturers, and other popular media.

3. Write an argumentative essay in response to the contention that, rather than having a social or cultural significance as Davis presumes, jeans are worn simply for comfort and budgetary reasons.

4. In your journal, brainstorm a list of brands of jeans, and then note which you currently wear, would like to wear, or would never consider wearing. Reflect on the image associated with each brand. How does image affect your taste in attire?

5. Observe students at your school congregating in a public place (say, the student union building), and note the predominant fashion styles. Then write a semiotic interpretation of the fashion trends you observe.

JOAN KRON

The Semiotics of Home Decor

Just when you thought it was safe to go back into your living room, here comes Joan Kron with a reminder that your home is a signaling system just as much as your clothing is. In Home-Psych: The Social Psychology of Home and Decoration *(1983), from which this selection is taken, Kron takes a broad look at the significance of interior decoration, showing how home design can reflect both an individual and a group identity. Ranging from a New York entrepreneur to Kwakiutl Indian chiefs, Kron further discusses how different cultures use possessions as a rich symbol system. The author of* High Tech: The Industrial Style and Source Book for the Home *(1978) and of some five hundred articles for American magazines, she is particularly interested in fashion, design, and the social psychology of consumption. Currently an editor-at-large at* Allure *magazine, Kron has also published* Lift: Wanting, Fearing, and Having a Face-Lift *(1998).*

On June 7, 1979, Martin J. Davidson entered the materialism hall of fame. That morning the thirty-four-year-old New York graphic design entrepreneur went to his local newsstand and bought fifty copies of the *New York Times* expecting to read an article about himself in the Home section that would portray him as a man of taste and discrimination. Instead, his loft and his life-style, which he shared with singer Dawn Bennett, were given the tongue-in-cheek treatment under the headline: "When Nothing but the Best Will Do."[1]

Davidson, who spent no more money renovating his living quarters than many of the well-to-do folks whose homes are lionized in the *Times*'s Thursday and Sunday design pages — the running ethnographic record of contemporary upper-middle-class life-style — made the unpardonable error of telling reporter Jane Geniesse how much he had paid for his stereo system, among other things. Like many people who have not been on intimate terms with affluence for very long, Davidson is in the habit of price-tagging his possessions. His 69-cent-per-bottle bargain Perrier, his $700 Armani suits from Barney's, his $27,000 cooperative loft and its $150,000 renovation, his sixteen $350-per-section sectionals, and his $11,000 best-of-class stereo. Martin J. Davidson wants the world to know how well he's done. "I live the American dream," he told Mrs. Geniesse, which includes, "being known as one of Barney's best customers."[2]

---

[1]Jane Geniesse, "When Nothing but the Best Will Do," *New York Times*, June 7, 1979, p. C1ff.

[2]Ibid.

Davidson even wants the U.S. Census Bureau's computer to know how well he has done. He is furious, in fact, that the 1980 census form did not have a box to check for people who live in cooperatives. "If someone looks at my census form they'll think I must be at the poverty level or lower."[3] No one who read the *Times* article about Martin Davidson would surmise that.

It is hard to remember when a "design" story provoked more outrage. Letters to the editor poured in. Andy Warhol once said that in our fast-paced media world no one could count on being a celebrity for more than fifteen minutes. Martin Davidson was notorious for weeks. "All the Martin Davidsons in New York," wrote one irate reader, "will sit home listening to their $11,000 stereos, while downtown, people go to jail because they ate a meal they couldn't pay for."[4] "How can one man embody so many of the ills afflicting our society today?"[5] asked another offended reader. "Thank you for your clever spoof," wrote a third reader. "I was almost convinced that two people as crass as Martin Davidson and Dawn Bennett could exist."[6] Davidson's consumption largesse was even memorialized by Russell Baker, the *Times*'s Pulitzer Prize–winning humorist, who devoted a whole column to him: "While simultaneously consuming yesterday's newspaper," wrote Baker, "I consumed an article about one Martin Davidson, a veritable Ajax of consumption. A man who wants to consume nothing but the best and does."[7] Counting, as usual, Davidson would later tell people, "I was mentioned in the *Times* on three different days."

Davidson, a self-made man whose motto is "I'm not taking it with me and while I'm here I'm going to spend every stinking penny I make," couldn't understand why the *Times* had chosen to make fun of him rather than to glorify his 4,000-square-foot loft complete with bidet, Jacuzzi, professional exercise gear, pool table, pinball machine, sauna, two black-tile bathrooms, circular white Formica cooking island, status-stuffed collections of Steiff animals, pop art (including eleven Warhols), a sound system that could weaken the building's foundations if turned up full blast, and an air-conditioning system that can turn cigarette smoke, which both Davidson and Bennett abhor, into mountain dew — a loft that has everything Martin Davidson ever wanted in a home except a swimming pool and a squash court.

"People were objecting to my life-style," said Davidson. "It's almost as if there were a correlation between the fact that we spend so much on ourselves and other people are starving. No one yells when someone spends $250,000 for a chest of drawers at an auction," he complained. "I just read in the paper

---

[3]Author's interview with Martin Davidson.

[4]Richard Moseson, "Letters: Crossroads of Decadence and Destitution," *New York Times*, June 14, 1979, p. A28.

[5]Letter to the Editor, *New York Times*, June 14, 1979, p. C9.

[6]Letter to the Editor, ibid.

[7]Russell Baker, "Observer: Incompleat Consumer," *New York Times*, June 9, 1979, p. 25.

that someone paid $650,000 for a stupid stamp. Now it'll be put away in a vault and no one will ever see it."[8]

But Dawn Bennett understood what made Davidson's consumption different. "It's not very fashionable to be an overt consumer and admit it,"[9] she said.

What Are Things For?

As anyone knows who has seen a house turned inside out at a yard sale, furnishing a home entails the acquisition of more objects than there are in a spring housewares catalog. With all the time, money, and space we devote to the acquisition, arrangement, and maintenance of these household possessions, it is curious that we know so little about our relationships to our possessions.

"It is extraordinary to discover that no one knows why people want goods," wrote British anthropologist Mary Douglas in *The World of Goods*.[10] Although no proven or agreed-upon theory of possessiveness in human beings has been arrived at, social scientists are coming up with new insights on our complicated relationships to things. Whether or not it is human nature to be acquisitive, it appears that our household goods have a more meaningful place in our lives than they have been given credit for. What comes across in a wide variety of research is that things matter enormously.

Our possessions give us a sense of security and stability. They make us feel in control. And the more we control an object, the more it is a part of us. If it's *not mine*, it's *not me*.[11] It would probably make sense for everyone on the block to share a lawn mower, but then no one would have control of it. If people are reluctant to share lawn mowers, it should not surprise us that family members are not willing to share TV sets. They want their own sets so they can watch what they please. Apparently, that was why a Chicago woman, furious with her boyfriend for switching from *The Thorn Birds* to basketball, stabbed him to death with a paring knife.[12]

---

[8]Author's interview with Martin Davidson.

[9]Author's interview with Dawn Bennett.

[10]Mary Douglas and Baron Isherwood, *The World of Goods* (New York: Basic Books, 1979), p. 15. A number of other social scientists have mentioned in recent works the lack of attention paid to the human relationship to possessions: See Coleman and Rainwater, *Social Standing*, p. 310. The authors observed that "the role of income in providing a wide range of rewards — consumption — has not received sufficient attention from sociologists." See Carl F. Graumann, "Psychology and the World of Things," *Journal of Phenomenological Psychology*, Vol. 4, 1974–75, pp. 389–404. Graumann accused the field of sociology of being thing-blind.

[11]Lita Furby, "Possessions: Toward a Theory of Their Meaning and Function Throughout the Life Cycle," in Paul B. Baltes (ed.), *Life-Span Development and Behavior*, Vol. 1 (New York: Academic Press, 1978), pp. 297–336.

[12]"'Touch That Dial and You're Dead,'" *New York Post*, March 30, 1983, p. 5.

Besides control, we use things to compete. In the late nineteenth century the Kwakiutl Indian chiefs of the Pacific Northwest made war with possessions.[13] Their culture was built on an extravagant festival called the "potlatch," a word that means, roughly, to flatten with gifts. It was not the possession of riches that brought prestige, it was the distribution and destruction of goods. At winter ceremonials that took years to prepare for, rival chiefs would strive to outdo one another with displays of conspicuous waste, heaping on their guests thousands of spoons and blankets, hundreds of gold and silver bracelets, their precious dance masks and coppers (large shields that were their most valuable medium of exchange), and almost impoverishing themselves in the process.

Today our means of competition is the accumulation and display of symbols of status. Perhaps in Utopia there will be no status, but in this world, every human being is a status seeker on one level or another — and a status reader. "Every member of society," said French anthropologist Claude Lévi-Strauss, "must learn to distinguish his fellow men according to their mutual social status."[14] This discrimination satisfies human needs and has definite survival value. "Status symbols provide the cue that is used in order to discover the status of others, and, from this, the way in which others are to be treated," wrote Erving Goffman in his classic paper, "Symbols of Class Status."[15] Status affects who is invited to share "bed, board, and cult,"[16] said Mary Douglas. Whom we invite to dinner affects who marries whom, which then affects who inherits what, which affects whose children get a head start.

Today what counts is what you eat (gourmet is better than greasy spoon), what you fly (private jet is better than common carrier), what sports you play (sailing is better than bowling), where you matriculate, shop, and vacation, whom you associate with, how you eat (manners count), and most important, where you live. Blue Blood Estates or Hard Scrabble zip codes as one wizard of demographics calls them. He has figured out that "people tend to roost on the same branch as birds of a feather."[17] People also use status symbols to play net worth hide-and-seek. When *Forbes* profiled the 400 richest Americans,[18] its own in-house millionaire Malcolm Forbes refused to

---

[13]Ruth Benedict, *Patterns of Culture* (Boston: Houghton Mifflin [1934], 1959); Frederick V. Grunfeld, "Homecoming: The Story of Cultural Outrage," *Connoisseur*, February 1983, pp. 100–106; and Lewis Hyde, *The Gift* (New York: Vintage Books, [1979, 1980], 1983), pp. 25–39.

[14]Edmund Leach, *Claude Lévi-Strauss* (New York: Penguin Books, 1980), p. 39.

[15]Erving Goffman, "Symbols of Class Status," *British Journal of Sociology*, Vol. 2, December 1951, pp. 294–304.

[16]Douglas and Isherwood, *World of Goods*, p. 88.

[17]Michael J. Weiss, "By Their Numbers Ye Shall Know Them," *American Way*, February 1983, pp. 102–106 ff. "You tell me someone's zip code," said Jonathan Robbin, "and I can predict what they eat, drink, drive, buy, even think."

[18]"The Forbes 400," *Forbes*, September 13, 1982, pp. 99–186.

disclose his net worth but was delighted to drop clues telling about his status entertainments — his ballooning, his Fabergé egg hunts, his châteaux, and his high life-style. It is up to others to translate those obviously costly perks into dollars.

A high price tag isn't the only attribute that endows an object with status. Status can accrue to something because it's scarce — a one-of-a-kind artwork or a limited edition object. The latest hard-to-get item is Steuben's $27,500 bowl etched with tulips that will be produced in an edition of five — one per year for five years. "Only one bowl will bloom this year,"[19] is the headline on the ad for it. Status is also found in objects made from naturally scarce materials: Hawaii's rare koa wood, lapis lazuli, or moon rock. And even if an object is neither expensive nor rare, status can rub off on something if it is favored by the right people, which explains why celebrities are used to promote coffee, cars, casinos, and credit cards.

If you've been associated with an object long enough you don't even have to retain ownership. Its glory will shine on you retroactively. Perhaps that is why a member of Swiss nobility is having two copies made of each of the Old Master paintings in his collection. This way, when he turns his castle into a museum, both his children can still have, so to speak, the complete collection, mnemonics of the pictures that have been in the family for centuries. And the most potent status symbol of all is not the object per se, but the *expertise* that is cultivated over time, such as the appreciation of food, wine, design, or art.

If an object reflects a person *accurately*, it's an index of status. But *symbols* of status are not always good indices of status. They are not official proof of rank in the same way a general's stars are. So clusters of symbols are better than isolated ones. Anyone with $525 to spare can buy one yard of the tiger-patterned silk velvet that Lee Radziwill used to cover her dining chair seats.[20] But one status yard does not a princess make. A taxi driver in Los Angeles gets a superior feeling from owning the same status-initialed luggage that many of her Beverly Hills fares own. "I have the same luggage you have," she tells them. "It blows their minds," she brags. But two status valises do not a glitterati make. Misrepresenting your social status isn't a crime, just "a presumption," said Goffman. Like wearing a $69 copy of a $1,000 watch that the mail-order catalog promises will make you "look like a count or countess on a commoner's salary."[21]

"Signs of status are important ingredients of self. But they do not exhaust all the meanings of objects for people," wrote sociologists Mihaly Csikszentmihalyi and Eugene Rochberg-Halton in *The Meaning of Things: Domestic Symbols*

[19]Steuben Glass advertisement, *The New Yorker*, April 4, 1983, p. 3.
[20]Paige Rense, "Lee Radziwill," *Celebrity Homes* (New York: Penguin Books, 1979), pp. 172–81.
[21]*Synchronics* catalogue, Hanover, Pennsylvania, Fall 1982.

of the Self.[22] The study on which the book was based found that people cherished household objects not for their status-giving properties but especially because they were symbols of the self and one's connections to others.

The idea that possessions are symbols of self is not new. Many people have noticed that *having* is intricately tied up with *being*. "It is clear that between what a man calls *me* and what he simply calls *mine*, the line is difficult to draw," wrote William James in 1890.[23] "Every possession is an extension of the self," said Georg Simmel in 1900.[24] "Humans tend to integrate their selves with objects," observed psychologist Ernest Beaglehole some thirty years later.[25] Eskimos used to *lick* new acquisitions to cement the person/object relationship.[26] We stamp our visual taste on our things making the totality resemble us. Indeed, theatrical scenic designers would be out of work if Blanche DuBois's boudoir could be furnished with the same props as Hedda Gabler's.

Csikszentmihalyi and Rochberg-Halton discovered that "things are cherished not because of the material comfort they provide but for the information they convey about the owner and his or her ties to others."[27] People didn't value things for their monetary worth, either. A battered toy, a musical instrument, a homemade quilt, they said, provide more meaning than expensive appliances which the respondents had plenty of. "What's amazing is how few of these things really make a difference when you get to the level of what is important in life,"[28] said Csikszentmihalyi. All those expensive furnishings "are required just to keep up with the neighbors or to keep up with what you expect your standard of living should be."

"How else should one relate to the Joneses if not by keeping up with them," asked Mary Douglas provocatively.[29] The principle of reciprocity requires people to consume at the same level as one's friends.[30] If we accept hospitality, we have to offer it in return. And that takes the right equipment and the right setting. But we need things for more than "keeping level" with our friends.

20

---

[22]Mihaly Csikszentmihalyi and Eugene Rochberg-Halton, *The Meaning of Things: Domestic Symbols of the Self* (New York: Cambridge University Press, 1981), p. 18.

[23]William James, *Principles of Psychology*, Vol. 1 (New York: Macmillan, 1890), p. 291.

[24]Georg Simmel, *The Philosophy of Money*, trans. Tom Bottomore and David Frisby (Boston: Routledge & Kegan Paul, 1978), p. 331.

[25]Ernest Beaglehole, *Property: A Study in Social Psychology* (New York: Macmillan, 1932).

[26]Ibid., p. 134.

[27]Csikszentmihalyi and Rochberg-Halton, p. 239.

[28]Author's interview with Mihaly Csikszentmihalyi.

[29]Douglas and Isherwood, *World of Goods*, p. 125. Also see Jean Baudrillard, *For a Critique of the Political Economy of the Sign*, trans. Charles Levin (St. Louis, MO: Telos Press, 1981), p. 81. Said Baudrillard: "No one is free to live on raw roots and fresh water. . . . The vital minimum today . . . is the standard package. Beneath this level, you are an outcast." Two classic novels on consumption are (1) Georges Perec, *Les Choses* (New York: Grove Press, [1965], 1967). (2) J. K. Huysmans, *Against the Grain (A Rebours)* (New York: Dover Publications, [1931], 1969).

[30]Douglas and Isherwood, *World of Goods*, p. 124.

We human beings are not only toolmakers but symbol makers as well, and we use our possessions in the same way we use language — the quintessential symbol — to *communicate* with one another. According to Douglas, goods make the universe "more intelligible." They are more than messages to ourselves and others, they are "the hardware and the software . . . of an information system."[31] Possessions speak a language we all understand, and we pay close attention to the inflections, vernacular, and exclamations.

The young husband in the film *Diner* takes his things very seriously. How could his wife be so stupid as to file the Charlie Parker records with his rock 'n' roll records, he wants to know. What's the difference, she wants to know. What's the difference? How will he find them otherwise? Every record is sacred. Different ones remind him of different times in his life. His things *take* him back. Things can also *hold* you back. Perhaps that's why Bing Crosby's widow auctioned off 14,000 of her husband's possessions — including his bed. " 'I think my father's belongings have somehow affected her progress in life,' " said one of Bing's sons.[32] And things can tell you where you stand. Different goods are used to rank occasions and our guests. Costly sets of goods, especially china and porcelain, are "pure rank markers. . . . There will always be luxuries because rank must be marked," said Douglas.[33]

One of the pleasures of goods is "sharing names."[34] We size up people by their expertise in names — sports buffs can converse endlessly about hitters' batting averages, and design buffs want to know whether you speak spongeware, Palladio, Dansk, or Poggenpohl. All names are not equal. We use our special knowledge of them to show solidarity and exclude people.

In fact, the social function of possessions is like the social function of food. Variations in the quality of goods define situations as well as different times of day and seasons. We could survive on a minimum daily allotment of powdered protein mix or grains and berries. But we much prefer going marketing, making choices, learning new recipes. "Next to actually eating food, what devout gastronomes seem to enjoy most is talking about it, planning menus, and remembering meals past," observed food critic Mimi Sheraton.[35] But it's not only experts who thrive on variety. Menu monotony recently drove a Carlsbad, New Mexico, man to shoot the woman he was living with. She served him green beans once too often. "Wouldn't you be mad if you had to eat green beans all the time?" he said.[36] If every meal were the same, and if everyone dressed alike and furnished alike, all meanings in the culture would be wiped out.[37]

[31] Ibid., p. 72.

[32] Maria Wilhelm, "Things Aren't Rosy in the Crosby Clan as Kathryn Sells Bing's Things (and not for a Song)," *People*, May 31, 1982, pp. 31–33.

[33] Douglas and Isherwood, *World of Goods*, p. 118.

[34] Ibid., p. 75.

[35] Mimi Sheraton, "More on Joys of Dining Past," *New York Times*, April 9, 1983, p. 48.

[36] "Green Beans Stir Bad Blood," *New York Times*, March 26, 1983, p. 6.

[37] Douglas and Isherwood, *World of Goods*, p. 66.

The furnishings of a home, the style of a house, and its landscape are all part of a system — a system of symbols. And every item in the system has meaning. Some objects have personal meanings, some have social meanings which change over time. People understand this instinctively and they desire things, not from some mindless greed, but because things are necessary to communicate with. They are the vocabulary of a sign language. To be without things is to be left out of the conversation. When we are "listening" to others we may not necessarily agree with what this person or that "says" with his or her decor, or we may misunderstand what is being said; and when we are doing the "talking" we may not be able to express ourselves as eloquently as we would like. But where there are possessions, there is always a discourse.

And what is truly remarkable is that we are able to comprehend and ma- 25 nipulate all the elements in this rich symbol system as well as we do — for surely the language of the home and its decor is one of the most complex languages in the world. But because of that it is also one of the richest and most expressive means of communication.

Decor as Symbol of Self

One aspect of personalization is the big I — Identity. Making distinctions between ourselves and others. "The self can only be known by the signs it gives off in communication," said Eugene Rochberg-Halton.[38] And the language of ornament and decoration communicates particularly well. Perhaps in the future we will be known by our computer communiqués or exotic brainwaves, but until then our rock gardens, tabletop compositions, refrigerator door collages, and other design language will have to do. The Nubian family in Africa with a steamship painted over the front door to indicate that someone in the house works in shipbuilding, and the Shotte family on Long Island who make a visual pun on their name with a rifle for a nameplate, are both decorating their homes to communicate "this is where our territory begins and this is who we are."

Even the most selfless people need a minimum package of identity equipment. One of Pope John Paul I's first acts as pontiff was to send for his own bed. "He didn't like sleeping in strange beds," explained a friend.[39] It hadn't arrived from Venice when he died suddenly.

Without familiar things we feel disoriented. Our identities flicker and fade like ailing light bulbs. "Returning each night to my silent, pictureless apartment, I would look in the bathroom mirror and wonder who I was," wrote D. M. Thomas, author of *The White Hotel*, recalling the sense of detachment he felt while living in a furnished apartment during a stint as author-in-residence at a

---

[38]Eugene Rochberg-Halton, "Where Is the Self: A Semiotic and Pragmatic Theory of Self and the Environment." Paper presented at the 1980 American Sociological Meeting, New York City, 1980, p. 3.

[39]Dora Jane Hamblin, "Brief Record of a Gentle Pope," *Life*, November 1978, p. 103.

Washington, D.C., university. "I missed familiar things, familiar ground that would have confirmed my identity."[40]

Wallpaper dealers wouldn't need fifty or sixty sample books filled with assorted geometrics, supergraphics, and peach clamshells on foil backgrounds if everyone were content to have the same roses climbing their walls. Chintz wouldn't come in forty flavors from strawberry to licorice, and Robert Kennedy Jr.'s bride Emily wouldn't have trotted him around from store to store "for ten hours" looking for a china pattern[41] if the home wasn't an elaborate symbol system — as important for the messages it sends to residents and outsiders as for the functions it serves.

In the five-year-long University of Chicago study[42] into how modern Americans relate to their things, investigators Mihaly Csikszentmihalyi and Rochberg-Halton found that we all use possessions to stand for ourselves. "I learned that things can embody self," said Rochberg-Halton. "We create environments that are extensions of ourselves, that serve to tell us who we are, and act as role models for what we can become."[43] But what we cherish and what we use to stand for ourselves, the researchers admitted, seemed to be "scripted by the culture."[44] Even though the roles of men and women are no longer so tightly circumscribed, "it is remarkable how influential sex-stereotyped goals still remain."[45] Men and women "pay attention to different things in the same environment and value the same things for different reasons," said the authors.[46] Men and children cared for action things and tools; women and grandparents cared for objects of contemplation and things that reminded them of family. It was also found that meaning systems are passed down in families from mothers to daughters — not to sons.

Only children and old people cared for a piece of furniture because it was useful. For adults, a specific piece of furniture embodied experiences and memories, or was a symbol of self or family. Photographs which had the power to arouse emotions and preserve memories meant the most to grandparents and the least to children. Stereos were most important to the younger generation, because they provide for the most human and emotional of our needs — release, escape, and venting of emotion. And since music "seems to act as a modulator of emotions," it is particularly important in adolescence "when daily

[40]D. M. Thomas, "On Literary Celebrity," *The New York Times Magazine*, June 13, 1982, pp. 24–38, citation p. 27.

[41]"Back Home Again in Indiana Emily Black Picks Up a Freighted Name: Mrs. Robert F. Kennedy, Jr.," *People*, April 12, 1982, pp. 121–23, citation p. 123.

[42]Eugene Rochberg-Halton, "Cultural Signs and Urban Adaptation: The Meaning of Cherished Household Possessions." Ph.D. dissertation, Department of Behavioral Science, Committee on Human Development, University of Chicago, August 1979; and Mihaly Csikszentmihalyi and Eugene Rochberg-Halton, *The Meaning of Things: Domestic Symbols of the Self* (New York: Cambridge University Press, 1981).

[43]Author's interview with Eugene Rochberg-Halton.

[44]Csikszentmihalyi and Rochberg-Halton, *Meaning of Things*, p. 105.

[45]Ibid., p. 112.

[46]Ibid., p. 106.

swings of mood are significantly greater than in the middle years and . . . later life."[47] Television sets were cherished more by men than women, more by children than grandparents, more by grandparents than parents. Plants had greater meaning for the lower middle class, and for women, standing for values, especially nurturance and "ecological consciousness."[48] "Plateware," the term used in the study to cover all eating and drinking utensils, was mentioned mostly by women. Of course, "plates" are the tools of the housewife's trade. In many cultures they are the legal possession of the women of the house.

The home is such an important vehicle for the expression of identity that one anthropologist believes "built environments" — houses and settlements — were originally developed to *"identify a group* — rather than to provide shelter."[49] But in contemporary Western society, the house more often identifies a person or a family instead of a group. To put no personal stamp on a home is almost pathological in our culture. Fear of attracting attention to themselves constrains people in crime-ridden areas from personalizing, lack of commitment restrains others, and insecurity about decorating skill inhibits still others. But for most people, painting some sort of self-portrait, decoratively, is doing what comes naturally.

All communications, of course, are transactions. The identity we express is subject to interpretation by others. Will it be positive or negative? David Berkowitz, the "Son of Sam" murderer, didn't win any points when it was discovered he had drawn a circle around a hole in the wall in his apartment and written "This is where I live."[50] A person who fails to keep up appearances is stigmatized.

READING THE TEXT

1. Summarize how, according to Kron, our possessions act as signs of our identity.

2. How do our living places work to create group identity?

3. Why did *New York Times* readers object to the consumption habits of Martin J. Davidson?

4. In your own words, explain how possessions give one a sense of "stability" (para. 10).

READING THE SIGNS

1. In a small group, discuss the brand names of possessions that each of you owns. Then interpret the significance of each brand. What do the brands say about each of you? About the group?

[47]Ibid., p. 72.
[48]Ibid., p. 79.
[49]Amos Rapoport, "Identity and Environment," in James S. Duncan (ed.), *Housing and Identity: Cross-Cultural Perspectives* (London: Croom Helm, 1981), pp. 6–35, citation p. 18.
[50]Leonard Buder, "Berkowitz Is Described as 'Quiet' and as a Loner," *New York Times*, August 12, 1977, p. 10.

2. With your class, brainstorm factors other than possessions that can communicate a person's identity. Then write an essay in which you compare the relative value of possessions to your own sense of identity with the additional factors your class brainstormed.

3. Write an essay in which you argue for or against Kron's claim that "to put no personal stamp on a home is almost pathological in our culture" (para. 32).

4. Analyze semiotically your own apartment or a room in your house, using Kron's essay as a critical framework. How do your possessions and furnishings act as signs of your identity?

5. Using Kron's essay as a critical framework, analyze the semiotic significance of possessions in Karen Karbo's "The Dining Room" (p. 663).

DAVID GOEWEY

"Careful, You May Run Out of Planet":
SUVs and the Exploitation of the American Myth

If you think that a car is just a car and that a sport utility vehicle is just a bigger car, then David Goewey's (b. 1955) semiotic analysis of the SUV craze could be something of an eyeopener for you. Situating America's love affair with the automobile, in general, and the SUV, in particular, within a historical context, Goewey reveals how the sport utility vehicle is a full-fledged myth machine, symbolically incorporating many of America's ideological values and contradictions within its several tons of heavy metal. And with the explosive popularity of the Cadillac Escalade and GM's Hummer, Goewey's 1999 essay is still on target. An actor and teacher, Goewey wrote this essay, which won the Oliver Evans Undergraduate Essay Prize at California State University, Northridge, as a term paper in a class on popular culture. He recently published Crash Out *(2005), about an escape from Sing Sing prison.*

"For centuries man had fantasized about the glories of independent travel," wrote the thirteenth-century scientist and philosopher Roger Bacon. Although writing during the Middle Ages, Bacon predicted, with uncanny accuracy, that humanity "shall endow chariots with incredible speed, without the aid of any animal" (Pettifer and Turner 9). Bacon's prescient forecast conjured a vision that became a twentieth-century American fact of life: the ubiquitous automobile. By 1872, French inventor Amédée Bollée had developed steam-powered demonstration models (Flink 6), and within the next thirty-five years the United

States dominated the world market for gasoline-powered automobiles (Pettifer and Turner 15). In the new century America itself — with a vast geography, scattered settlements, and relatively low population density — seemed best suited to the spread of a romanticized car culture (Flink 43). America, in short, took to the roads with relish.

The automobile quickly entered American popular culture. Tin Pan Alley devoted no fewer than six hundred songs to the pleasures of motoring (Pettifer and Turner 17). The futurist art movement, furthermore, appropriated the automobile as a specific symbol of modernity itself (Wernick 80), representative of speed, progress, and technology. As a token, the car embodied escapist fantasy (Pettifer and Turner 239), allowing the individual to conquer time and space. But it was America's unique values of freedom, individualism, and the pursuit of happiness that became manifested in the automobile — values that imbued the car with definitive mythic significance (Robertson 191).

Now, at the end of the twentieth century, the vehicle that combines the most potent mix of American mythologies is the sport utility vehicle (SUV) — hybrid passenger cars/light trucks with four-wheel drive. With sales expected to exceed one million units in 1998, the SUV is the fastest-growing segment of the automobile market (Storck 79). However, as a social phenomenon, SUVs contain both practical and mythic contradictions. For example, these vehicles are designed for rugged, off-road motoring, yet a mere 10 percent of drivers ever leave surface streets or highways (Storck 99). With their muscular styling and dominant height and weight, SUVs are almost ludicrously masculine in design, yet women account for 40 percent of sales (Storck 79). Furthermore, while SUV advertising campaigns often pose the vehicle in rural settings of woodlands or along lakesides, the SUV is anything but nature-friendly with its thirsty gasoline tank and lower emission standards (Pope 14). In short, the modern SUV represents a preeminent symbol of American popular culture.

A semiotic analysis of the contradictions inherent in the SUV phenomenon, as well as its historical and socioeconomic significance, therefore, reveals the intriguing ironies that underscore America's predominant ideology. American culture's faddish preoccupation with the SUV may be seen as deeply embedded in a national identity. Furthermore, a close look at the SUV trend also reveals America's understanding of reality and fantasy and its conflicting attitude toward human survival and environmental protection. As a cultural signifier, the SUV both reveals and reflects the principal components of America's popular mythology.

The most obvious ironies are perhaps best observed in the SUV model names chosen by the manufacturers. Many vehicle names are directly evocative of America's western frontier mythology, such as the Jeep Wrangler or the Isuzu Rodeo. Others are linked to the Western European tradition of the exploration and settlement of foreign lands, such as the Ford Explorer or the Land Rover Discovery. Indeed, the GMC Yukon blends both American western imagery and the European exploratory drive and thus embodies the American notion of a frontier: remote, extremely wild, and to the average person unknown.

"I'm changing the climate! Ask me how!" Robert Lind tags a Lincoln Navigator SUV with a bumper sticker in a parking lot in Corte Madera, California. Lind tags oversized SUVs with bumper stickers because he believes they harm the environment.

The fascination with the American frontier, which today's automakers so effectively exploit, is directly tied to America's historical beginnings. The idea of the frontier as both sacred and menacing is a principal tenet in the nation's mythology. The first Europeans, after all, encountered a daunting wilderness. *Mayflower* passenger William Bradford described a "hideous and desolate wilderness . . . represent[ing] a wild and savage hue" (Robertson 45). The Europeans, steeped in fairy-tale traditions of the forest as the dark dwelling place of witches and cannibals, therefore considered the woods intrinsically evil (Robertson 49). The forests were godless and had to be tamed before they could be inhabitable, leveled before they could be considered usable. The Native Americans, likewise, were viewed as the personification of this savage wasteland and therefore had to be subjugated along with the wilderness to ensure the spread of civilization (Robertson 50). And the early Americans' religious convictions justified this expansion.

The notion that Americans were on a God-given mission to subdue this newfound jungle and expand Western civilization "into the limitless wilderness" (Robertson 44) became institutionalized in American mythology by the Jacksonian policy of Manifest Destiny. Americans were believed to be ordained by God to carry the noble virtues of democracy, freedom, and civilization westward across the continent (Robertson 72). This relentless expansionism, then, was suffused with religious significance and mission. The frontier was seen as the demarcation between order and disorder, between goodness and evil. To challenge the frontier, therefore, took supreme courage and zeal, and men like Daniel Boone, George Rogers Clark, and Andrew Jackson became outstanding western heroes (Robertson 80).

Corollary to this idea of an expansive frontier was the belief in the ever-abundant opportunities and riches available to whoever was brave and ambitious enough to pursue them. This idea of "more" was contingent on the belief in a limitless frontier and served as a motivating factor in the pursuit of happiness and the drive to succeed. Expansion, in a sense, became an end in itself (Shames 33–34). However, in late-twentieth-century America, the concept of more has suffered a practical setback. Diminishing economic expectations from the 1960s through the 1980s, including a shrinking productivity rate, a decrease in real earnings, and a growing national debt, all contributed to challenge the mythic notion of the frontier as fruitful with economic possibilities (Shames 34–36).

It is perhaps not coincidental, then, that the sport utility vehicle craze began in earnest in the early 1980s (Storck 79). In reaction to "the fear that the world may not be . . . big enough" (Shames 37), the decade's penchant for conspicuous consumption can be seen as a challenge to that anxiety. And the introduction of large, powerful vehicles into the mass market, with names like the Ford Bronco and the Chevy Blazer, may represent the reassertion of a courageous American defiance in response to threatened frontiers.

Furthermore, the growth of the SUV market through the 1990s, with this 10 segment comprising 23 percent of total auto sales (Storck 79), suggests the adaptability of the SUV's mythic significance. The expanding economy of the Clinton years — based on the globalization of economic interests and the consequent resurrection of expanding frontiers — recasts the SUV as a celebratory metaphor for power and control. The SUV, in this context, represents the resurgence of the conquering American.

The GMC Yukon, named for a region far from the American mainstream, can be seen to embody the cultural notion of the wild frontier as fearsome and therefore in need of civilization. And the vehicle is certainly well designed for the rugged task of settlement. Weighing in at over 5,300 pounds (with passengers), measuring over 16½ feet in length and just under 6 feet in height, the GMC Yukon is among the largest SUVs on the market (Storck 27). Its massive size arguably manifests the expansive idea of America's western frontier.

However, the GMC Yukon's heftiness necessarily affects its miles-per-gallon ratio. The average rounds off at a measly 13 miles per gallon (Storck 27), less than half what the U.S. government requires for passenger cars. And with a fuel tank capacity of 30 gallons and an estimated full tank mileage of under 400 miles, the GMC Yukon can be seen vehemently to declare the concept of more. Furthermore, juxtaposing the GMC Yukon with its namesake suggests an egregious symmetry. The Yukon Territory, north of British Columbia, Canada, abuts Prudhoe Bay. Exploratory oil drilling there in 1967 uncovered the largest oilfield in North America, with an estimated capacity of about 10 billion barrels (Yergin 571). The American myth of an ever-expansive frontier, then, is powerfully manifested in the heavyweight GMC Yukon, which locates and justifies its own mass production in the fact of a naturally oil-abundant Yukon Territory.

Another popular SUV that contains a doubly potent signifier within the manufacturer's title is the Jeep Cherokee. Considered the original SUV, the Jeep Cherokee dates all the way back to 1948. As a result, owners take a measure of purist's pride, believing their SUV is the one that started it all (Storck 41). But a closer look at this SUV's mythohistorical connections may provide the owners' pride with a deeper significance.

The Jeep Cherokee prototype — the General Purpose Vehicle, which was shortened to Jeep — was introduced during World War II in response to a U.S. Army–sponsored competition among automakers. It was first developed by the Bantam Motor Company, and the design was then completed by the Willys-Overland Company. The Ford Motor Company also assisted in the mass production of what was soon considered the "backbone of all Allied military transport" and the "crowning success of the war" (Flink 276). No doubt drawing on their heroic wartime performance, surplus military jeeps were sold stateside and helped to introduce a market for four-wheel drive recreational vehicles (Flink 276).

The usefulness and durability of four-wheel-drive vehicles, however, was recognized even earlier during World War I, and many automakers, including Packard, Peerless, and Nash motor companies, vied for government contracts. Manufacturers found that luxury car chassis were easily converted to 2 or 3 ton truck bodies (Flink 78) — a literal blending of automobiles and trucks that clearly prefigures the modern SUV. Along with the Jeep's victorious wartime service, then, the SUV conveys such powerful militaristic connotations as morally righteous patriotism, overwhelming industrial ingenuity and might, and the imperative conquest of evil.

An interesting link between automobility and the American frontier was provided approximately forty years earlier by a Civil War hero. On his retirement in 1903, Civil War veteran General Nelson A. Miles, who had successfully hunted Chief Joseph and the Nez Perce to ground in 1877 and to whom the Apache war leader Geronimo surrendered in 1886 (Josephy 416, 429), foresaw the military promise of motor vehicles. He urged Secretary of War Elihu Root to "replace five regiments of calvary" with troops on bicycles and in motor vehicles (Flink 74), believing that the horse was now obsolete. General Miles's foresight was ironic in light of the Jeep Cherokee's double significance.

The Jeep Cherokee's militaristic connotations become oppressive when considering the grotesquely racist misapplication of a Native American tribal name to a motor vehicle. Although the word *Cherokee* is a misnomer derived from the Choctaw definition for cave dwellers and actually has no meaning in the language of those to whom it is applied, it is nevertheless used to designate at least one group of Native Americans, the United Keetoowah Band of Cherokee, in Oklahoma (Josephy 323). This original misnaming indicates the indeterminability of language, especially in the traumatic context of Native American history. And while it may be argued that such indeterminacy freely

15

allows a manufacturer's use of the name to sell a product, the word *Cherokee* nevertheless denotes a group of people still thriving today despite oppression.

In the 1820s, despite the fierce allegiance to tradition held by many Cherokee, a large number of them succumbed to the ongoing proselytizing efforts of Moravian missionaries to become the "most acculturated of southern tribes" (Josephy 320). The Cherokee learned the English alphabet and even innovated a Cherokee alphabet based on the English model. In 1828, this led to the remarkable publication, in English and Cherokee, of a native newspaper (Josephy 320). Cherokee efforts to assimilate into what could be seen even then as a dominant culture, in other words, were vigorous.

Nevertheless, also in 1828, President Andrew Jackson undertook an aggressive campaign of ethnic cleansing against the Cherokee. Capitalizing on white racism to pass anti-Cherokee legislation, and with the discovery of gold on Cherokee territory, Jackson made physical removal of the tribe a national issue (Josephy 325). This culminated in the infamous and tragic Trail of Tears, the forced march west to Oklahoma of eighteen thousand Cherokee men, women, and children under the armed escort of General Winfield Scott and seven thousand U.S. Army troops (Josephy 331).

The manufacturers of the Jeep Cherokee clearly ignore this dismal chapter [20] in U.S. history and instead evoke superficially positive components of a mythic American past. Drawing on traditional viewpoints of the western frontier as the border between civilization and wilderness (Robertson 92) and oblivious to the fact that the Cherokee were an enforced western tribe, the Jeep Cherokee manufacturer exploits mythic identifications of Native Americans with the fearsome and violent "imagery and logic of the frontier" (Robertson 106).

The Jeep Cherokee manufacturer also mines the symbol of the quintessential American hero, the cowboy. Pitted against the frontier, the cowboy was directly descended from the backwoodsmen and pathfinders who pioneered west to the Ohio River Valley and beyond to the Northwest Passage. As the frontier pushed on, the continent's western plains and mountains became the wilderness that was next in need of subjugation and control. The cowboy, and his close companions in the American mythic imagination of the Wild West, the U.S. Cavalry, became the defenders of civilization and the champions of progress (Robertson 161–62). As such, they symbolized law and order in a lawless land. Both the cowboy and the U.S. Cavalry were the good guys risking themselves to save civilization from the bad guys, most notably the wildly violent Indians (Robertson 162).

The Jeep Cherokee, then, is a multilayered symbol indeed. This SUV appropriates the token of a victorious American struggle over the frontier, won by American cowboys and cavalrymen, and combines it with the morally righteous conquest over evil achieved during World War II. The modern driver who slips behind the wheel of a Jeep Cherokee assumes the militaristically heroic mantle that is suffused within the vehicle's legend and manifested in the control available in the "tight and precise steering, easy maneuverability . . . and taut overall feel from the firm suspension" (Storck 41). Detached from historical truths, however, the SUV's "excellent visibility all around" and "superior driving position" (Storck 41), qualities essential to success in battle, capitalize on these military/frontier connotations and at the same time sublimate factual battlefield horrors into an aggressive game of on-the-road cowboys and Indians.

The SUV, with its rugged militaristic symbolism, magnifies the traditional association of the automobile as a masculine token. Yet women account for a sizable share of the SUV market (Storck 79). This appeal, in fact, extends and amplifies a traditional relationship between women and motor vehicles. The introduction of the automobile may well have affected the scope of women's societal role more than that of men. Unlike the horse and buggy, for instance, the automobile demanded skill over physical strength to operate, and so women were offered mobility and parity that driving a team of horses denied them (Flink 162).

However, middle-class women by the 1920s were still traditionally tied to the home, for the most part, although electrical household appliances had nevertheless increased leisure time. The refrigerator, for example, permitted the bulk buying of a week's worth of perishable food at one stop, leaving time for socializing or an afternoon movie matinee (Flink 164). The added spare time, combined with automobility's enhanced sense of individual freedom (Robertson 191), afforded women at least temporary escape from the confines of the home that defined their routine (Flink 163).

As the automobile helped to change women's role from that of home- 25 based providers of food and clothing into consumers of mass-produced goods, car designers soon recognized the potential of the female market. Such comfort features as plush upholstery, heaters, and automatic transmissions were planned with women in mind (Flink 163). And advertising executives, quick to determine that women were disproportionately the nation's consumers (Marchand 66), began to target automobile ads at them. One of the most famous advertisements, for the Jordan Motor Company's Playboy automobile, began "Somewhere west of Laramie there's a broncho-busting, steer-roping girl" (Pettifer and Turner 130), clearly utilizing the familiar western imagery of freedom and control.

This relationship between women and their automobiles has grown even more complex in recent years. First, the car didn't so much redefine women's fundamental domestic role as increase the scope of its domain. Also, it is reasonable to assume that the automobile facilitated women's introduction into the workplace by easing transportation between the home and job. And yet in 1997, economic equality still eludes the American workforce: Working women earn less than 75 percent of men's average income (Jones et al. 49). A woman's job, furthermore, may include not only doing outside work but ferrying children to and from school and activities and shopping for the family. A subsequent feeling of disempowerment, then, may find relief behind the wheel of a physically powerful and symbolically potent SUV.

Advertisers evidently think so. They still acknowledge a woman's buying power and capitalize on the appeal SUVs hold for many female drivers. One current SUV advertisement aimed at women, promoting the Subaru Forester, both stresses its inherent power and rugged potential and notes the female-friendly design of this smaller vehicle. The larger photo in a . . . two-page spread in *Time* shows the Forester kicking up a dust trail as it barrels down a dirt track. The accompanying smaller picture presents a casually dressed young woman easily tying a kayak to the SUV's roof. The ad's dominant image is a rough and careless strength. And while the woman in the ad is proportionally submissive, she is capably preparing for an exciting outdoor adventure. The double message suggests a sense of diminishment that is compensated for with images of ability, ease, and the casual transference of power.

Perhaps the most logical and disarming association carmakers and advertisers exploit when designing and promoting an SUV is the vehicle's connection to nature. As previously noted, implicit within the SUV's frontier imagery is a confrontational attitude toward the wilderness. Accordingly, automakers design — and advertisers sell — SUVs capable of handling the roughest terrain. And indeed, much of the appeal of SUVs is their promise of providing access to the farthest reaches of the globe. As a marketing gimmick, for instance, Land Rover cosponsors and participates in the annual Camel Trophy relay, pitting various SUVs against the jungle wilds of Borneo and South America. Besides the obvious British imperialistic connotations such a race implies, the challenge of maneuvering a Land Rover Discovery "over garbage can sized rocks" or "through streams where the entire vehicle is submerged" (Storck 6) positions the competitor in a naturally inharmonious contest.

Advertisers take a dual approach when exploiting the adversarial relationship between SUVs and nature. In some print ads this relationship is clothed in benign natural imagery, often with a warning text. The Mitsubishi Montero Sport, for example, pictures a gleaming silver vehicle perched prominently on the rocky shoreline of a wooded lakesite. The tall stand of evergreen trees are at a safe distance; the water surface is without a ripple. The bold black headline proclaims, "It Came to Comfort Earth," and the text goes on to inform the reader that "the planet wasn't exactly designed for your comfort."

So the Montero Sport offers a wondrous solution to an uncomfortable 30 world. The proximity of nature to the vehicle in the photo is remote, suggesting that the mere presence of the Montero Sport is enough to keep nature at bay. Furthermore, the SUV's silver color combines with the headline to imply that the Montero Sport carries an otherworldly salvation. Nature and its uncomfortability, therefore, are controlled by the SUV's omnipresence, and the driver is safe due to the vehicle's "car-like . . . civility."

Ads for the luxury Infiniti QX4 portray a similar oppositional message but with a more active approach. A silver SUV is pictured once again, but this time bolting through the shallow water of a black-rock lakeshore. The landpoint jutting into the water directly behind the QX4, as though in pursuit, is in silhouette and resembles a large black serpent lagging just behind. The text's message cautions: "careful, you may run out of planet." Although the threat is clear, the presentation is nevertheless one of SUV power in opposition to nature. Indeed, the QX4 appears to be riding atop the water, and the text ends with the admonishment, "resist the urge to circumnavigate the globe."

So while the Infiniti ad sells the promise of adventure, at the same time it positions the SUV's representational power as necessary and inevitable. The QX4 is vigorously slashing through the water on its way to points unknown because it has to; the natural environment is dangerous, hostile to civilization, and quite capable of destroying it if not met with even more superior power. And as if to drive home the point, both the Montero Sport and the Infiniti QX4 ads present a silver SUV as the symbol of modernity, thereby drawing on the traditional American mythology of progress in opposition to a hostile wilderness.

The design and marketing of SUVs are based on traditional American attitudes toward nature and the wilderness. The vehicles are at the same time built for access to the natural world and yet sold by exploiting that relationship as confrontational. The SUV, in other words, makes easily available a world that is threatening to the driver and its occupants. And yet underlying these contradictions, and compounding them, is the very real impact that SUVs make on the environment.

The GMC Suburban, big sister to the aforementioned GMC Yukon, asserts itself with a 42 gallon capacity fuel tank. With a curb-side weight pushing five thousand pounds and amenities like air conditioning, the Suburban's gas mileage is generously estimated at about 16 miles to the gallon (Storck 29). While the GMC Suburban is admittedly the largest SUV model on the market, poor gas mileage ratios are the norm for these vehicles. Where the Environmental Protection Agency has determined that automobiles must meet a fuel economy standard of 27.5 miles a gallon, light trucks, which include all SUVs, currently need only to clear 20.7 miles a gallon. And many don't even achieve that (Bradsher).

The world oil industry may keep billions of barrels in their inventories on 35 any given day (Yergin 686), leading to the understandable public perception that supplies are unlimited. But fossil fuels are still a nonrenewable resource. Moreover, American gasoline use is expected to rise by 33 percent within the next fifteen years, indicating that fuel conservation is not much of an issue with consumers (Bradsher).

But perhaps the more pressing problem, and one that is directly exacerbated by the SUV craze, is the threat of global warming from the increased burning of fossil fuels. Carbon dioxide levels in the atmosphere have risen by about 25 percent in the last century and appear to coincide with a worldwide increase in the use of petroleum. Various cataclysmic effects are predicted as a result, including rising sea levels from melting ice caps, the spread of tropical diseases to normally temperate regions, and extreme weather fluctuations (McKibben 9, 18). Yet the booming SUV market belies any overwhelming concern on the part of American consumers. In fact, the vehicle's popularity in the face of such dire predictions seems the latest manifestation of an established confrontational relationship to nature.

As the world does indeed become more dangerous, the apparent protection that SUVs afford becomes more desirable, and the need to control the uncontrollable becomes more acute. Driving a five thousand pound, resource-devouring behemoth not only justifies the impact on the environment, as a means of revenge against an enemy, but it acts as a means of celebration — the exultation of victory over the savage beast of nature. The SUV, in its design and presentation, seeks to make safely available what it can ultimately dominate; as such, it attempts to reduce the entire world to the state of a drive-through wildlife nature preserve. At the end of the twentieth century, the SUV perfectly embodies an American mythology of conquest and control.

America's love affair with the sport utility vehicle shows the abiding power of traditional beliefs. The expansion of the frontiers continues despite facts that suggest there is nowhere left to go. This joyful faith in "more" feeds on the challenge of less. Indeed, a sport utility vehicle is the triumphant representation of denial — denial of the past, the present, and the future. American mythology is continuously reinvented and thereby endures in this pop cultural symbol.

WORKS CITED

Bradsher, Keith. "Light Trucks Increase Profits but Foul Air More Than Cars." *New York Times* 30 Nov. 1997, national ed., sec. 1:1+.

Flink, James J. *The Automobile Age*. Cambridge: MIT, 1988.

Jones, Barbara, Anita Blair, Barbara Ehrenreich, Arlie Russell Hochschild, Jeanne Lewis, and Elizabeth Perle McKenna. "Giving Women the Business." *Harper's* Dec. 1997: 47–58.

Josephy, Alvin M., Jr. *Five Hundred Nations: An Illustrated History of North American Indians*. New York: Knopf, 1994.

Marchand, Roland. *Advertising the American Dream: Making Way for Modernity 1920–1940*. Berkeley: University of California Press, 1985.

McKibben, Bill. *The End of Nature*. New York: Anchor, 1989.

Pettifer, Julian, and Nigel Turner. *Automania: Man and the Motorcar*. Boston: Little, Brown, 1984.

Pope, Carl. "Car Talks — Motown Walks." *Sierra Magazine* Mar./Apr. 1996: 14+.

Robertson, James Oliver. *American Myth, American Reality*. New York: Hill & Wang, 1980.

Shames, Laurence. "The More Factor." *Signs of Life in the USA: Readings on Popular Culture for Writers*. Ed. Sonia Maasik and Jack Solomon. Boston: Bedford, 1994.

Storck, Bob. *Sport Utility Buyer's Guide '98*. Milwaukee: Pace, 1998.

Wernick, Andrew. "Vehicles for Myth." *Signs of Life in the USA: Readings on Popular Culture for Writers*. Ed. Sonia Maasik and Jack Solomon. Boston: Bedford, 1994.

Yergin, Daniel. *The Prize: The Epic Quest for Oil, Money and Power*. New York: Simon & Schuster, 1991.

READING THE TEXT

1. What significance does Goewey see in the names automakers give to SUVs?

2. In your own words, explain why Goewey considers the popularity of SUVs to be full of "ironies" (para. 5) and "contradictions" (para. 4).

3. How does Goewey account for the SUV's appeal to women?

4. In Goewey's view, why does the imagery associated with SUVs have an adversarial relationship with nature?

5. Chart how Goewey uses the semiotic method. How does he explicate the system to which SUVs belong and the cultural mythologies that such vehicles evoke?

READING THE SIGNS

1. Write a journal entry in which you interpret how your own car (or that of a friend or relative) acts as a sign. What messages does it send about your identity?

2. Using Goewey's approach as a model, interpret a different category of automobile, such as pickup trucks or small two-seaters.

3. Collect automobile advertising from several popular magazines, and analyze how the cars are promoted as signs. What slogans are used to catch your attention? What values and ideologies are linked to particular makes and models?

4. Since Goewey wrote this article in 1999, many models of SUV have entered the market, including smaller makes such as the Saturn Vue and larger ones like the Cadillac Escalade and the Hummer line. Study the imagery associated with these newer models in print advertising and on the manufacturers' Web sites. Then write an essay in which you argue whether Goewey's position — that SUVs are linked with American frontier mythology — applies to SUVs today.

5. Adopting the perspective of Gregg Easterbrook in "The Progress Paradox" (p. 400), write an analysis of the popularity of SUVs. To what extent is this trend an instance of the "runaway materialism" that Easterbrook describes?

THOMAS L. FRIEDMAN
Revolution Is U.S.

With the downfall of the Soviet Union and the end of the cold war, a new historical era emerged that replaced superpower competition with a consumer-driven politico-economic dynamic generally referred to as globalization. And though America is not the sole player in this new global system, its domination of the world's consumer and entertainment markets, as Thomas L. Friedman (b. 1953) points out in this selection, is often taken by the rest of the world as a kind of conspiracy to dominate, or Americanize, the world itself. But whether globalization equals Americanization, Friedman suggests, we seem to want a world in which there is "a Web site in every pot, a Pepsi on every lip, [and] Microsoft Windows in every computer," for in the end, "globalization is us." The winner of two Pulitzer Prizes for reporting and the winner of a National Book Award for From Beirut to Jerusalem *(1989), Friedman is the foreign affairs columnist for the* New York Times *and the author of* The Lexus and the Olive Tree *(2000), from which this reading is taken. His most recent book is* The World Is Flat: A Brief History of the Twenty-first Century *(2005).*

I believe in the five gas stations theory of the world.

That's right: I believe you can reduce the world's economies today to basically five different gas stations. First there is the Japanese gas station. Gas is $5 a gallon. Four men in uniforms and white gloves, with lifetime employment contracts, wait on you. They pump your gas. They change your oil. They wash your windows, and they wave at you with a friendly smile as you drive away in peace. Second is the American gas station. Gas costs only $1 a gallon, but you pump it yourself. You wash your own windows. You fill your own tires. And when you drive around the corner four homeless people try to steal your hubcaps. Third is the Western European gas station. Gas there also costs $5 a gallon. There is only one man on duty. He grudgingly pumps your gas and unsmilingly changes your oil, reminding you all the time that his union contract says he only has to pump gas and change oil. He doesn't do windows. He works only thirty-five hours a week, with ninety minutes off each day for lunch, during which time the gas station is closed. He also has six weeks' vacation every summer in the south of France. Across the street, his two brothers and uncle, who have not worked in ten years because their state unemployment insurance pays more than their last job, are playing boccie ball. Fourth is the developing-country gas station. Fifteen people work there and they are all cousins. When you drive in, no one pays any attention to you because they are all too busy talking to each other. Gas is only 35 cents a gallon because it is subsidized by the government, but only one of the six pumps actually works. The others are broken and they are waiting for the replacement parts to be flown in from Europe. The gas station is rather run-down because the absentee owner lives in Zurich and takes all the profits out of the country. The owner doesn't know that half his employees actually sleep in the repair shop at night and use the car wash equipment to shower. Most of the customers at the developing-country gas station either drive the latest-model Mercedes or a motor scooter — nothing in between. The place is always busy, though, because so many people stop in to use the air pump to fill their bicycle tires. Lastly there is the communist gas station. Gas there is only 50 cents a gallon — but there is none, because the four guys working there have sold it all on the black market for $5 a gallon. Just one of the four guys who is employed at the communist gas station is actually there. The other three are working at second jobs in the underground economy and only come around once a week to collect their paychecks.

What is going on in the world today, in the very broadest sense, is that through the process of globalization everyone is being forced toward America's gas station. If you are not an American and don't know how to pump your own gas, I suggest you learn. With the end of the Cold War, globalization is globalizing Anglo-American-style capitalism and the Golden Straitjacket. It is globalizing American culture and cultural icons. It is globalizing the best of America and the worst of America. It is globalizing the American Revolution and it is globalizing the American gas station.

But not everyone likes the American gas station and what it stands for, and you can understand why. Embedded in the Japanese, Western European, and communist gas stations are social contracts very different from the American one, as well as very different attitudes about how markets should operate and be controlled. The Europeans and the Japanese believe in the state exercising power over the people and over markets, while Americans tend to believe more in empowering the people and letting markets be as free as possible to sort out who wins and who loses.

Because the Japanese, Western Europeans, and communists are uncomfort- 5
able with totally unfettered markets and the unequal benefits and punishments they distribute, their gas stations are designed to cushion such inequalities and to equalize rewards. Their gas stations also pay more attention to the distinctive traditions and value preferences of their communities. The Western Europeans do this by employing fewer people, but paying them higher wages and collecting higher taxes to generously support the unemployed and to underwrite a goody bag of other welfare-state handouts. The Japanese do it by paying people a little less but guaranteeing them lifetime employment, and then protecting those lifetime jobs and benefits by restricting foreign competitors from entering the Japanese market. The American gas station, by contrast, is a much more efficient place to drive through: The customer is king; the gas station has no social function; its only purpose is to provide the most gas at the cheapest price. If that can be done with no employees at all — well, all the

better. A flexible labor market will find them work somewhere else. Too cruel, you say? Maybe so. But, ready or not, this is the model that the rest of the world is increasingly being pressured to emulate.

America is blamed for this because, in so many ways, globalization is us — or is at least perceived that way by a lot of the world. The three democratizations were mostly nurtured in America. The Golden Straitjacket was made in America and Great Britain. The Electronic Herd is led by American Wall Street bulls. The most powerful agent pressuring other countries to open their markets for free trade and free investment is Uncle Sam, and America's global armed forces keep these markets and sea lanes open for this era of globalization, just as the British navy did for the era of globalization in the nineteenth century. Joseph Nye Jr., dean of the Harvard University Kennedy School, summarized this reality well when he noted: "In its recent incarnation, globalization can be traced in part back to American strategy after World War II and the desire to create an open international economy to forestall another depression and to balance Soviet power and contain communism. The institutional framework and political pressures for opening markets were a product of American power and policy. But they were reinforced by developments in the technology of transportation and communications which made it increasingly costly for states to turn away from global market forces." In other words, even within the Cold War system America was hard at work building out a global economy for its own economic and strategic reasons. As

A street in Lahore, Pakistan.

a result, when the information revolution, and the three democratizations, came together at the end of the 1980s, there was a power structure already in place that was very receptive to these trends and technologies and greatly enhanced their spread around the world. As noted earlier, it was this combination of American power and strategic interests, combined with the made-in-America information revolution, that really made this second era of globalization possible, and gave it its distinctly American face.

Today, globalization often wears Mickey Mouse ears, eats Big Macs, drinks Coke or Pepsi, and does its computing on an IBM PC, using Windows 98, with an Intel Pentium II processor, and a network link from Cisco Systems. Therefore, while the distinction between what is globalization and what is Americanization may be clear to most Americans, it is not — unfortunately — to many others around the world. In most societies people cannot distinguish anymore among American power, American exports, American cultural assaults, American cultural exports, and plain vanilla globalization. They are now all wrapped into one. I am not advocating that globalization should be Americanization — but pointing out that that is how it is perceived in many quarters. No wonder the Japanese newspaper *Nihon Keizai Shimbun* carried a headline on June 4, 1999, about a conference in Tokyo on globalization that referred to the phenomenon as "The American-Instigated Globalization." When many people in the developing world look out into this globalization system what they see first is a recruiting poster that reads: UNCLE SAM WANTS YOU (for the Electronic Herd).

Martin Indyk, the former U.S. ambassador to Israel, told me a story that illustrates this point perfectly. As ambassador, he was called upon to open the first McDonald's in Jerusalem. I asked him what he said on the occasion of McDonald's opening in that holy city, and he said, "Fast food for a fast nation." But the best part, he told me later, was that McDonald's gave him a colorful baseball hat with the McDonald's logo on it to wear as he was invited to eat the first ceremonial Big Mac in Jerusalem's first McDonald's — with Israeli television filming every bite for the evening news. The restaurant was packed with young Israelis eager to be on hand for this historic event. While Ambassador Indyk was preparing to eat Jerusalem's first official Big Mac, a young Israeli teenager worked his way through the crowd and walked up to him. The teenager was carrying his own McDonald's hat and he handed it to Ambassador Indyk with a pen and asked, "Are you the ambassador? Can I have your autograph?"

Somewhat sheepishly, Ambassador Indyk replied, "Sure. I've never been asked for my autograph before."

As Ambassador Indyk took the hat and prepared to sign his name on the bill, the teenager said to him, "Wow, what's it like to be the ambassador from McDonald's, going around the world opening McDonald's restaurants everywhere?"

Stunned, Ambassador Indyk looked at the Israeli youth and said, "No, no. I'm the *American* ambassador — not the ambassador from McDonald's!"

The Israeli youth looked totally crestfallen. Ambassador Indyk described what happened next: "I said to him, 'Does this mean you don't want my autograph?' And the kid said, no, I don't want your autograph, and he took his hat back and walked away."

No wonder that the love-hate relationship that has long existed between America and the rest of the world seems to be taking on an even sharper edge these days. For some people Americanization-globalization feels more than ever like a highly attractive, empowering, incredibly tempting pathway to rising living standards. For many others, though, this Americanization-globalization can breed a deep sense of envy and resentment toward the United States — envy because America seems so much better at riding this tiger and resentment because Americanization-globalization so often feels like the United States whipping everyone else to speed up, Web up, downsize, standardize, and march to America's cultural tunes into the Fast World. While I am sure there are still more lovers of America than haters out there, this [essay] is about the haters. It is about the *other* backlash against globalization — the rising resentment of the United States that has been triggered as we move into a globalization system that is so heavily influenced today by American icons, markets, and military might.

As the historian Ronald Steel once pointed out: "It was never the Soviet Union but the United States itself that is the true revolutionary power. We believe that our institutions must confine all others to the ash heap of history. We lead an economic system that has effectively buried every other form of production and distribution — leaving great wealth and sometimes great ruin in its wake. The cultural messages we transmit through Hollywood and McDonald's go out across the world to capture and also undermine other societies. Unlike more traditional conquerors, we are not content merely to subdue others: We insist that they be like us. And of course for their own good. We are the world's most relentless proselytizers. The world must be democratic. It must be capitalistic. It must be tied into the subversive messages of the World Wide Web. No wonder many feel threatened by what we represent."

The classic American self-portrait is Grant Wood's *American Gothic*, the straitlaced couple, pitchfork in hand, expressions controlled, stoically standing watch outside the barn. But to the rest of the world, American Gothic is actually two twentysomething American software engineers who come into your country wearing long hair, beads, and sandals, with rings in their noses and paint on their toes. They kick down your front door, overturn everything in the house, stick a Big Mac in your mouth, fill your kids' heads with ideas you've never had or can't understand, slam a cable box onto your television, lock the channel to MTV, plug an Internet connection into your computer, and tell you: "Download or die." 15

That's us. We Americans are the apostles of the Fast World, the enemies of tradition, the prophets of the free market, and the high priests of high tech. We want "enlargement" of both our values and our Pizza Huts. We want the world to follow our lead and become democratic, capitalistic, with a Web site in every pot, a Pepsi on every lip, Microsoft Windows in every computer and most of all — most of all — with everyone, everywhere, pumping their own gas.

READING THE TEXT

1. Summarize in your own words Friedman's five-gas-stations theory of the world (para. 2). What cultural values are implicit in each variety of station?

2. What did historian Ronald Steel mean when he argued that "it was never the Soviet Union but the United States itself that is the true revolutionary power" (para. 14)?

3. What, to the rest of the world, is the image of "American Gothic" (para. 15), according to Friedman?

4. Characterize Friedman's tone in outlining the five types of gas station. How does his tone affect your response to his piece?

READING THE SIGNS

1. To much of the rest of the world, the United States is responsible for globalization. Conduct an in-class debate arguing whether this assessment is accurate. To develop support for your team's position, you might interview some international students about the attitudes toward the United States that prevail in their countries.

2. In America there is a great deal of resentment, especially from labor unions, of international trade agreements like the North American Free Trade Agreement (NAFTA) that America has signed in the name of globalization. In light of this resentment, write an essay arguing for or against the proposition that globalization is beneficial for America. To enhance your argument, research the economic effects of such treaties as NAFTA on the American economy.

3. Evaluate the validity of Friedman's assertion that "we Americans are the apostles of the Fast World, the enemies of tradition, the prophets of the free market, and the high priests of high tech" (para. 16).

4. Write an argumentative essay that analyzes the validity of Friedman's five-gas-stations theory of the world. To what extent could Friedman be accused of stereotyping cultural patterns? To what extent could his discussion be considered serious or tongue-in-cheek?

THOMAS FRANK
Countercultural Consumerism

Since the 1960s, the image of the hipster consumer as a kind of rebel without a cause has been a favorite of American marketers, especially those with something to sell to the young. Every mass-produced product that promises that its purchase will affirm its consumer as a certified individualist who can't be fooled into buying into mass consumerism is, in effect, "commodifying dissent" — that is, turning anticapitalist dissent itself into a capitalist commodity. In this selection, Thomas Frank (b. 1965) explores the history of this potent marketing phenomenon, calling it, in a highly significant oxymoron, "countercultural consumerism." Frank, who helped coin the phrase "commodify your dissent," is the cofounder of The Baffler, *which critically analyzes contemporary popular culture, and is coeditor, with Matt Wieland, of* Commodify Your Dissent: Salvos from the Baffler *(1997). Frank is also the author of* The Conquest of Cool *(1997), from which this selection is taken;* One Market Under God *(2000); and* What's the Matter with Kansas? *(2004).*

In contemporary American public culture the legacy of the consumer revolution of the 1960s is unmistakable. Today there are few things more beloved of our mass media than the figure of the cultural rebel, the defiant individualist resisting the mandates of the machine civilization. Whether he is an athlete decked out in mohawk and multiple-pierced ears, a policeman who plays by his own rules, an actor on a motorcycle, a movie fratboy wreaking havoc on the townies' parade, a soldier of fortune with explosive bow and arrow, a long-haired alienated cowboy gunning down square cowboys, or a rock star in leather jacket and sunglasses, he has become the paramount cliché of our popular entertainment, the preeminent symbol of the system he is supposed to be subverting. In advertising, especially, he rules supreme.

The language of menswear remains particularly beholden to talk of style subversion, now routinely supercharged with academic-sounding phrases and suffixes. Even when it became clear that the tastes of the various prominent menswear designers for fall 1997 were veering ever so slightly toward more traditional looks (tweed, pinstripes, gray flannel, camel hair), the *New York Times*, while freely acknowledging that the "clothes reeked of currency," still insisted on describing them in the language of revolution. These are clothes, *Times* writer Amy Spindler asserts, about "turning cash into the ultimate tool for rebellion. . . ." Even the most "transgressive" designers agree about affluence's subversiveness, Spindler points out. She also notes that designer Tommy Hilfiger had an alternative rock band and a rap group performing at his show and quotes the editor of *Details* asking himself, "how is a man rebelling today?"

On the other side of the coin, of course, are the central-casting prudes and squares (police, Southerners, old folks, etc.) against whom contemporary advertising, rock stars, and artists routinely cast themselves. "By now it should be obvious," writes historian Rochelle Gurstein, "that there is something fraudulent, if not perverse, in the endless rehearsal of arguments that were developed to destroy nineteenth-century Victorians in a world where Victorians have been long extinct."[1] But the clichés persist nonetheless, thriving on some cultural logic of their own: rebellion is both the high- and mass-cultural motif of the age; order is its great bogeyman.

And in many ways, our standard binary understanding of the 1960s revolt as the negation of the "conformity" of the 1950s is but the historical rendering of this nonstop pageant of rebellion against order, a PBS version of one of those commercials in which the individualistic Red Dog defies the martinet dog. We believe in the rebel sixties, in the uprising against the humorless "establishment," like we believe in World War II as "the good war."

Yet, through it all, capital remained firmly in the national saddle, its economic and cultural projects unimpeded even though the years of conformity had given way to those of cultural radicalism. What changed during the sixties, it now seems, were the strategies of consumerism, the ideology by which business explained its domination of the national life. Now products existed to facilitate our rebellion against the soul-deadening world of products, to put us in touch with our authentic selves, to distinguish us from the mass-produced herd, to express our outrage at the stifling world of economic necessity.

The counterculture came out of its brush with hip consumerism changed as well. While its symbols, music, and lingo were transformed safely into mass culture, many of its participants turned to a more adversarial understanding of their experiences. Abbie Hoffman's *Steal This Book* is a handbook of politicized theft. Appearing in 1971, after events like the Chicago police riot, Kent State, and the various Weatherman bombings had polarized the movement, the book had no place for the softer, gentler counterculture of 1967. Lifestyle was most definitely *not* revolution, and the epiphany of Charles Reich was not what Hoffman was aiming for.

> Smoking dope and hanging up Che's picture is no more a committment [*sic*] than drinking milk and collecting postage stamps. A revolution in consciousness is an empty high without a revolution in the distribution of power. We are not interested in the greening of Amerika except for the grass that will cover its grave.[2]

The book is profoundly hostile to the consumer order: the majority of its content describes various ways to steal the things one needs to live, and a host of publishers rejected it because the title, emblazoned in enormous white letters on a black cover, promised to subvert the fundamental operation of book

---

[1] Rochelle Gurstein, *The Repeal of Reticence* (New York: Hill and Wang, 1996), p. 6.
[2] Abbie Hoffman, *Steal This Book* (New York: Pirate Editions, 1971), p. v.

publishing (Hoffman ultimately had to have it printed by himself). Its cover blurb, "Everything You Always Wanted for FREE," mocked the slogans and material dreams of the mass society, and the author's photograph depicted him stealing from a bookstore. Years later, Hoffman wrote of this call to theft as a sort of consumerism in reverse, a politicized anti-shopping:

> It's universally wrong to steal from your neighbor, but once you get beyond the one-to-one level and pit the individual against the multinational conglomerate, the federal bureaucracy, the modern plantation of agrobusiness, or the utility company, it becomes strictly a value judgment to decide exactly who is stealing from whom. One person's crime is another person's profit. Capitalism *is* license to steal; the government simply regulates who steals and how much.[3]

Abbie Hoffman's counterculture of thieves may have prefigured certain characteristics of later varieties of American consumerism — its exaggerated hedonism, for example — but he clearly conceived of it as a direct subversion of the affluent society. This ambivalence informs much of the counterculture's larger self-understanding as well. Even as it provided business with a cultural vehicle for its new understanding of consumption, even as it introduced a new array of mores appropriate to new modes of accumulation, many of its participants understood it as a diametrical opponent of the commodity fetishism in which consumerism is grounded. Feminist writing from the 1960s was particularly conscious of consumerism's power to create the narrow boundaries within which American women were forced to live. A 1970 essay by Alice Embree specifically confronts . . . various "feminist" campaigns . . . in observing that

> the mass media molds everyone into more passive roles, into roles of more frantic consuming, into human beings with fragmented views of society. But what it does to everyone, it does to women even more. The traditional societal role for women is already a passive one, already one of a consumer, already one of an emotional non-intellectual who isn't supposed to think or act beyond the confines of her home.[4]

The counterculture as envisioned by people like Hoffman and Embree grew from an instinctive revulsion toward the fundamental assumptions of consumerism. Money was not the measure of all things; under no conditions could products (even drugs) bring happiness; culture and government should not be the exclusive provinces of business; ownership of goods was a chump's game. This revulsion, appearing in different, more or less sophisticated forms, has informed American writing on consumerism from Veblen's day to the present. Hoffman believed that the counterculture represented a real-life acting-out

---

[3]Abbie Hoffman, *The Best of Abbie Hoffman* (New York: Four Walls Eight Windows, 1989), p. 180.

[4]Alice Embree, "Madison Avenue Brainwashing — The Facts," in *Sisterhood Is Powerful: An Anthology of Writings from the Women's Liberation Movement*, edited by Robin Morgan (New York: Vintage, 1970), p. 201.

of this impulse, and in certain of its manifestations it clearly did. Regardless of its usefulness to business, the counterculture gave rise to an enormous corpus of works that seek to understand the nation's mass-cultural operations without succumbing to the platitudes of affirmation or elitism.

READING THE TEXT

1. In your own words, summarize the influence that the 1960s counterculture has had on consumerism to this day.

2. What relationship does Frank see between "rebellion" and "order" (para. 3)?

3. What does Frank mean when he writes that "products existed to facilitate our rebellion against the soul-deadening world of products" (para. 5)?

4. What does Abbie Hoffman mean by "anti-shopping" (para. 6)?

READING THE SIGNS

1. Analyze a current men's magazine, such as *Details* or *Maxim*, and write an essay in which you assess the extent to which the "cultural rebel" remains a marketing motif.

2. In class, brainstorm a list of today's cultural rebels, either marketing characters or real people such as actors or musicians, and discuss why these rebels are considered attractive to their intended audience. Use the class discussion as a springboard for your own essay analyzing how the status of cultural rebels is a sign of the mood of modern American culture.

3. Write an essay in which you agree with, disagree with, or modify Alice Embree's contention that "the traditional societal role for women is already a passive one, already one of a consumer, already one of an emotional non-intellectual who isn't supposed to think or act beyond the confines of her home" (para. 7). To develop your ideas, consult Anne Norton's "The Signs of Shopping" (p. 83).

4. Visit a youth-oriented store such as Urban Outfitters and analyze its advertising, product displays, and both exterior design and interior decor. Write an essay in which you gauge the extent to which the store uses anti-shopping motifs as a marketing strategy.

BROUGHT TO YOU B(U)Y

The Signs of Advertising

Advertising on the Edge

An attractive young woman runs frantically down a suburban street pursued by a ferocious pit bull. She leaps upward into the branches of a tree, but the dog leaps right after her and sinks his teeth into the pant leg of her jeans. With a wrench of his jaws, he peels the jeans right off her, then, abruptly, leaves her alone, running down the street with the jeans in his teeth. The woman follows him into a house where, clad only in bikini briefs, she sees the dog carry the jeans to a young man who puts them on and gives the girl a scolding glance as she shamefacedly watches him.

Sounds rather like the narrative for some especially nasty porno flick, doesn't it? But it's not. As you've probably already recognized, this is a summary of a television advertisement for Levi's jeans that could have been seen on prime-time network television in 2004.

You might have seen the following ad in 2004 as well: Two men stand in front of a rustic cabin with their dogs. One of the men is pale, slender, and expensively dressed in a fishing outfit that could have come from L.L. Bean. His dog is a purebred, highly trained terrier. The other man is husky, rugged looking, dressed in jeans and a plaid shirt. His dog is an unusually scruffy-looking mutt. The first man, in a supercilious tone of voice, tells the second that his dog has been trained to fetch beer for him. With exaggerated self-confidence, he tells his dog to fetch, and the dog obediently runs to a cooler, pulls out a bottle of beer, and neatly brings it to his master. The second man looks on gruffly for a moment, then tells his dog to fetch. The dog rushes right at the other man and leaps straight for his crotch. The man screams and, backing away, flings his beer to the scruffy dog's master, who catches it with a rough gesture of victory.

This second ad, for Budweiser beer, was chosen by a viewers' poll as the best ad of Super Bowl XXXVII. And like the Levi's ad, it bears a cultural message.

To analyze these ads we need, as with all cultural signs, to establish the system that they belong to. Since both ads were made for television and feature dogs, we could begin with TV advertisements that feature animals, especially dogs. Of course there are a slew of such ads, especially for pet foods (remember Morris the Nine Lives cat, or that pooch that chases the chuckwagon across a kitchen floor?), but animals have been used to advertise a great many products, usually with the intention of lending a cute and cuddly image to the product (like the Charmin teddy bear). Budweiser itself began to use animal mascots in the 1980s with its Spuds Mackenzie campaign, which featured an anthropomorphic English pit bull who surfed, partied, and hung out with his own crew of bikini-clad Spudettes as he laid claim to be the world's supreme "party animal." Shortly before the Spuds campaign appeared, the Strohs Beer Company had a dog named Alex who, while behaving like an ordinary dog in most ways, seemed to have a taste for Strohs himself.

Both Spuds and Alex were funny figures (as were the ants, frogs, lizards, and ferrets that succeeded Spuds in the Budweiser campaigns of the 1990s) and, like many such advertising animals, were designed to confer upon the products they fronted an aura of humorous fun through the sheer incongruity of their behavior. The Levi's and Budweiser ads we are analyzing here are also trying to be funny, and so can be associated with the system of humorous animal-themed advertisements. But the source of their humor is quite different, and it is in that difference that we can find the significance of the ads.

In both ads the behavior of the animals is not incongruous nor, in itself, funny. The Levi's pit bull engages in the kind of aggressive behavior that, all

---

Discussing the Signs of Advertising

Bring to class a print ad from a newspaper or magazine, and in small groups discuss your semiotic reading of it. Be sure to ask, "Why am I being shown this or being told that?" How do the characters in the ad function as signs? What sort of people don't appear as characters? What cultural myths are invoked in this ad? What relationship do you see between those myths and the intended audience of the publication? Which ads do your group members respond to positively and why? Which ads doesn't your group like?

too often, compels animal control authorities to put dogs down; the Budweiser mutt makes the kind of sudden attack out of which personal injury lawsuits are made. What makes their attacks funny (or at least intended to be funny) is whom they attack. In the one ad, it is an attractive young woman; in the other, a caricature of a yuppie. And the ads assume that their target audience will take pleasure in seeing such victims attacked and discomfited.

You've probably already guessed who that audience might be, but let's work through it semiotically. In determining the audience for a particular advertisement, it can be very useful to pick out the character or characters within the ad with whom its viewers are expected to identify. Since no one wishes to be chased into a tree by a dog and have one's clothing torn off, and because no one wants to be bitten in the crotch, we can assume that viewers are meant to identify with neither the young woman in the Levi's ad nor the yuppie in the Budweiser ad. But the matter goes deeper than that. In the case of the Budweiser ad, the yuppie is carefully coded to appeal to a populist class resentment of supercilious wealth. It is no accident that the hero of the ad is coded to appear as a kind of rural workingman's hero, an ordinary Joe, with his ordinary dog, who is revenged upon the upper-class snob who crosses him. The ad works very much like a carefully staged professional wrestling match in which a populist warrior beats up a wrestler who is coded to symbolize elite wealth or privilege. Playing to a traditional American mythology that celebrates the common man, the Budweiser ad, with its testosterone-driven vision of appropriate class vengeance, thus can be seen as appealing to male viewers who can identify not only with the ordinary Joe in the ad but with his resentment of wealth and privilege as well.

The Levi's ad also appeals to men, but not at all in the same way. For one thing, class resentment has nothing to do with this ad. But there is another kind of resentment — and it isn't of people who borrow your jeans without permission. That the ad is intended to appeal to male viewers is evident in the entire point of view embodied in the ad, beginning with what film critics call the "male gaze" of the camera. The camera watches the woman flee, and then records her being stripped, carefully revealing her sexy underwear. When she limps back after the dog to the house where the dog's owner is putting on his restored jeans, his gaze, along with the camera's, rests upon her, in her humiliation, and her underwear. It is hardly likely that any woman would identify with the woman in this ad. But males (especially young males, given the relative youth of both characters) are expected to identify with the man in the ad, who, instead of being featured heroically rescuing the damsel in distress (as might have happened in an ad in the 1950s), smugly gives the woman a look that says, more or less, "don't do that again." One wonders if another version of the ad will feature music from the Rolling Stones' hit "Under My Thumb."

The Levi's ad signifies a profound misogyny that can be found throughout contemporary American popular culture, from women-despising pop and hip-hop lyrics (see Andre Mayer's "The New Sexual Stone Age" in Chapter 3) to fashion magazine spreads that feature women who look like they're about to be raped (or have already been raped). Such signifiers point to a profound resentment of, even hostility toward, young women on the part of young men, a resentment whose origins are not easy to identify. Whether caused by the advances women have made through the women's movement, or by a growing feeling of helplessness in a corporate capitalist society that causes men to lash out at women as scapegoats for the powerlessness they feel in a world that has made them expendable, or by whatever social causes that one might discover, the brutal humor presented in the Levi's ad is a sign of a new kind of gender gap in which women, once placed on a kind of pedestal in sexual relations, have been cast into the dirt.

The fact that both ads feature violence is a sign of a further social disaffection that is by no means confined to the United States. Does someone bother you? Sic your dog on him (it's no accident that attack dog breeds like Rottweilers and pit bulls have become massively popular). Your girlfriend borrows your jeans again? Send Bowser after her. Someone cut you off on the freeway? Don't just give him the finger, shoot the sucker. In short, if you've got a problem, let violence solve it. There's a lot of rage loose in the land — and the world. And if this doesn't sound very serious to you, consider that it is just this kind of thinking that led to the destruction of the World Trade Center on September 11, 2001.

And Here's the Pitch

The preceding analysis was brought to you by the advertising industry and was intended to illustrate how advertisements too are signs of cultural desire and consciousness. Indeed, advertising is not just show and tell. In effect, it's a form of behavior modification, a psychological strategy designed not only to inform you about products but also to persuade you to buy them by making associations between the product and certain pleasurable experiences or emotions that may have nothing to do with the product at all — like sex, or a promise of social superiority, or a simple laugh. No one knows for sure just how effective a given ad campaign might be in inducing consumer spending, but no one is taking any chances either, as you can see by the annual increase in advertising costs for the Super Bowl: At last count it was some $2.25 million for a thirty-second spot.

With all the advertising out there, it is getting harder and harder for advertisers to get our attention, or keep it, so they are constantly experimenting with new ways of getting us to listen. In recent years, for example, advertisers who are out to snag the youth market have taken to staging their television ads as if they were MTV videos — complete with rapid jump-cut filming techniques, rap or rock background music, and dizzying montage effects — in order to grab the attention of their target audience and to cause their viewers to associate the product with the pleasures of MTV. Self-conscious irony has also

---

Exploring the Signs of Advertising

Select one of the products advertised in the "Portfolio of Advertisements" (in this chapter), and design in your journal an alternative ad for that product. Consider what different images or cast of characters you could include. What different myths — and thus different values — could you use to pitch this product? Then freewrite on the significance of your alternative ad. If you have any difficulty imagining an alternative image for the product, what does that say about the power of advertising to control our view of the world? What does your choice of imagery and cultural myths say about you?

---

been a popular advertising technique as advertisers strive to overcome the ad-savvy sophistication of generations of consumers who have become skeptical of the claims and techniques of advertising.

More recently, a marketing strategy known as "stealth advertising" has appeared in selected locations. For example, companies pay people to do things like sit in Starbucks and play computer games; when someone takes an interest, they talk about how cool it is and ask passersby on the street to take their photo with a really cool new camera — and by the way, they say, isn't this a really cool new camera?! The trick here is to advertise without having people actually know they're being marketed to — just what the ad doctor ordered for advertising-sick consumers.

As the years pass and the national mood shifts with the tides of history, new advertising techniques will emerge. So look around you and ask yourself, as you're bombarded with advertising, "Why am I being shown *that*, or being told *this*?" Or cast yourself as the director of an ad, asking yourself what you would do to pitch a product; then look at what the advertiser has done. Pay attention to the way an ad's imagery is organized. Every detail counts. Why are these colors used, or why is the ad in black and white? Why are cute stuffed animals chosen to pitch toilet paper? What are those people *doing* in that perfume commercial? Why the cowboy hat in an ad for jeans? Look too for what the ad *doesn't* include: Is it missing a clear view of the product itself or an ethnically diverse cast of characters? In short, when interpreting an ad, transform it into a text and read it as you would an editorial or any piece of rhetoric, for in its mandate to persuade, advertising constitutes the most potent rhetoric of our times.

The Semiotic Foundation

There is perhaps no better field for semiotic analysis than advertising, for ads work characteristically by substituting signs for things, and by reading those signs you can discover the values and desires that advertisers seek to exploit. It has long been recognized that advertisements substitute images of desire for the actual products, that Coca-Cola ads, for example, don't really sell soda: They sell images of fun, or popularity, or sheer celebrity, promising a gratifying association with the likes of Paula Abdul or Whitney Houston if you'll only drink "the Real Thing." Automobile commercials, for their part, are notorious for selling not transportation but fantasies of power, prestige, and sexual potency.

By substituting desirable images for concrete needs, modern advertising seeks to transform desire into necessity. You need food, for example, but it takes an ad campaign to convince you through attractive images that you need a Big Mac. Your job may require you to have a car, but it's an ad that persuades you that a Lexus is necessary for your happiness. If advertising worked otherwise, it would simply present you with a functional profile of a product and let you decide whether it will do the job.

From the early twentieth century, advertisers have seen their task as the transformation of desire into necessity. In the twenties and thirties, for example, voluminously printed advertisements created elaborate story lines designed to convince readers that they needed this mouthwash to attract a spouse or that caffeine-free breakfast drink to avoid trouble on the job or in the home. In such ads, products were made to appear not only desirable but absolutely necessary. Without them, your very survival as a socially competent being would be in question.

Many ads still work this way, particularly "guilt" ads that prey on your insecurities and fears. Deodorants are typically pitched in such a fashion, playing on our fear of smelling bad in public. Can you think of any other products whose ads play on guilt or shame? Do you find them to be effective?

The Commodification of Desire

Associating a logically unrelated desire with an actual product (as in pitching beer through sexual come-ons) can be called the "commodification" of desire. In other words, desire itself becomes the product that the advertiser is selling. This marketing of desire was recognized as early as the 1950s in Vance Packard's *The Hidden Persuaders*. In that book, Packard points out how by the 1950s America was well along in its historic shift from a producing to a consuming economy. The implications for advertisers were enormous. Since the American economy was increasingly dependent on the constant growth of consumption, as the introduction to Chapter 1 of this text discusses, manufacturers had to find ways to convince people to consume ever more goods. So they turned to the advertising mavens on Madison Avenue, who responded with advertisements that persuaded consumers to replace perfectly serviceable products with "new and improved" substitutions within an overall economy of planned design obsolescence.

Today's Special: The Home Shopping Network.

America's transformation from a producer to a consumer economy also explains that while advertising is a worldwide phenomenon, it is nowhere so prevalent as it is here. Open a copy of the popular French picture magazine *Paris Match*. You'll find plenty of paparazzi photos of international celebrities but almost no advertisements. Then open a copy of *Vogue*. It is essentially a catalogue, where scarcely a page is without an ad. Indeed, advertisers themselves call this plethora of advertising "clutter" that they must creatively "cut through" each time they design a new ad campaign. The ubiquity of advertising in our lives points to a society in which people are constantly pushed to buy, as opposed to economies like Japan's that emphasize constant increases in production. And desire is what loosens the pocketbook strings.

While the basic logic of advertising may be similar from era to era, the content of an ad, and hence its significance, differs as popular culture changes. Looking at ads from different eras tells the tale. Advertising in the 1920s, for instance, focused especially on its market's desires for improved social status. Ads for elocution and vocabulary lessons, for example, appealed to working- and lower-middle-class consumers who were invited to fantasize that buying the product or service could help them enter the middle class. Meanwhile, middle-class consumers were invited to compare their enjoyment of the sponsor's product with that of the upper-class models shown happily slurping this coffee or purchasing that vacuum cleaner in the ad. Of course, things

---

Reading Advertising on the Net

Many viewers watch the Super Bowl as much for the commercials as for the football game; indeed, the Super Bowl ads now have their own pregame public-relations hype and, in many a media outlet, their own postgame analysis and ratings. Visit *Advertising Age*'s report on the most recent Super Bowl (http://www.adage.com/reports.cms), and study the ads and their commentary about them. What images and styles predominate, and what do the dominant patterns say about popular taste? What does the public's avid interest in Super Bowl ads say about the power of advertising and its role in American culture?

---

haven't changed *that* much since the twenties. Can you think of any ads that use this strategy today? How often are glamorous celebrities called in to make you identify with their "enjoyment" of a product? Have you heard ads for vocabulary-building programs that promise you a "verbal advantage" in the corporate struggle?

One particularly amusing ad from the twenties played on America's fear of communism in the wake of the Bolshevik Revolution in Russia. "Is your washroom breeding Bolsheviks?" asks a print ad from the Scott paper towel company. The ad's lengthy copy explains how it might be doing so: If your company restroom is stocked with inferior paper towels, it says, discontent will proliferate among your employees and lead to subversive activities. RCA Victor and Campbell's Soup, we are assured, are no such breeding grounds of subversion, thanks to their contracts with Scott. You, too, can fight the good fight against communism by buying Scott Towels, the ad suggests. To whom do you think this ad was directed? What did they fear?

Populism vs. Elitism

American advertising tends to swing in a pendulum motion between the status-conscious ads that dominated the twenties and the more populist approach of decades like the seventies, when *The Waltons* was a top TV series and country music and truck-driving cowboys lent their popular appeal to Madison Avenue. This swing between elitist and populist approaches in advertising reflects a basic division within the American dream itself, a mythic promise that at once celebrates democratic equality *and* encourages you to rise above the crowd, to be better than anyone else. Sometimes Americans are more attracted to one side than to the other, but there is bound to be a shift back to the other side when the thrill wears off. Thus, the populist appeal of the seventies (even disco had a distinct working-class flavor: recall John Travolta's character in *Saturday Night Fever*) gave way to the elitist eighties, and advertising followed. Products such as Gallo's varietal wines, once considered barely a step up from jug wine, courted an upscale market through ads that featured classy yuppies serving it along with their salmon and asparagus, while Michelob light beer promised its fans that they "could have it all." Status advertising was all the rage in that glitzy, go-for-the-gold decade.

The nineties brought in a different kind of advertising that was neither populist nor elitist but was characterized by a cutting, edgy sort of humor. This humor was especially common in dot.com ads that typically addressed the sort of young, irreverent, and rather cocky souls who were the backbone of the so-called New Economy. More broadly, edgy advertising appealed to twentysomething consumers who were particularly coveted by the marketers who made possible such youth-oriented television networks as Fox and WB. Raised in the *Saturday Night Live* era, such consumers were accustomed to cutting humor and particularly receptive to anything that smacked of attitude, and in the race to get their attention, advertisers followed with attitude-laden advertising.

The Levi's and Budweiser ads discussed earlier indicate that this sort of advertising and attitude is still very much alive in the first decade of the twenty-first century. Although there is, as we've seen, a touch of populism in the Budweiser commercial, the emphases are attitude and schadenfreude; that is, taking pleasure in the suffering or misfortune of others (look for a fuller analysis of this current trait in popular culture in the analysis of reality TV in the introduction to Chapter 3). Look at the ads around you (they're impossible to miss): What moods, what desires can you detect? Are Americans drawing together, or are we splintering into niche market groups and atomizing into single units of competitive consumption? The ads will tell.

The Readings

Our selections in this chapter include interpretations and analyses of the world of advertising, as well as advertisements for you to interpret yourselves. The chapter begins with a historical perspective: Roland Marchand's "The Parable of the Democracy of Goods" shows how advertisers in the 1920s played on the unconscious desires of their market by exploiting the fundamental myths of middle-class American culture. Steve Craig follows with four practical analyses of the ways in which television advertisers code their advertisements to appeal to men or women consumers. Warren St. John is next with a report on the ways in which marketers are cashing in on the recent "metrosexual" phenomenon, while Eric Schlosser looks at the world of children's advertising in which kids are manipulated to manipulate their parents. Gloria Steinem's insider's view of what goes on behind the scenes at women's magazines offers an exposé of the often cozy relationship between magazine content and advertisers' desires. James B. Twitchell concludes the chapter's readings with a detailed description of the way that market researchers categorize consumers according to tidy lifestyle stereotypes. This chapter also includes a "Portfolio of Advertisements" for you to decode for yourself.

ROLAND MARCHAND
The Parable of the Democracy of Goods

Advertisements do not simply reflect American myths; they create them, as Roland Marchand (1933–1997) shows in this selection from Advertising the American Dream *(1985). Focusing on elaborate advertising narratives, he describes "The Parable of the Democracy of Goods," which pitches a product by convincing middle-class consumers that, by buying this toilet seat or that brand of coffee, they can share an experience with the very richest Americans. The advertising strategies Marchand analyzes date from the 1920s to 1940s, and new "parables" have since appeared that reflect more modern times, but even the oldest are still in use today. A former professor of history at the University of California, Davis, Marchand also published* The American Peace Movement and Social Reform, 1898–1918 *(1973) and* Creating the Corporate Soul: The Rise of Public Relations and Corporate Imagery in American Big Business *(1998).*

As they opened their September 1929 issue, readers of the *Ladies' Home Journal* were treated to an account of the care and feeding of young Livingston Ludlow Biddle III, scion of the wealthy Biddles of Philadelphia, whose family coat-of-arms graced the upper right-hand corner of the page. Young Master Biddle, mounted on his tricycle, fixed a serious, slightly pouting gaze upon the reader, while the Cream of Wheat Corporation rapturously explained his constant care, his carefully regulated play and exercise, and the diet prescribed for him by "famous specialists." As master of Sunny Ridge Farm, the Biddles's winter estate in North Carolina, young Livingston III had "enjoyed every luxury of social position and wealth, since the day he was born." Yet, by the grace of a modern providence, it happened that Livingston's health was protected by a "simple plan every mother can use." Mrs. Biddle gave Cream of Wheat to the young heir for both breakfast and supper. The world's foremost child experts knew of no better diet; great wealth could procure no finer nourishment. As Cream of Wheat's advertising agency summarized the central point of the campaign that young Master Biddle initiated, "every mother can give her youngsters the fun and benefits of a Cream of Wheat breakfast just as do the parents of these boys and girls who have the best that wealth can command."[1]

While enjoying this glimpse of childrearing among the socially distinguished, *Ladies' Home Journal* readers found themselves schooled in one of

[1] *Ladies' Home Journal*, Sept. 1929, second cover; *JWT News Letter*, Oct. 1, 1929, p. 1, J. Walter Thompson Company (JWT) Archives, New York City.

the most pervasive of all advertising tableaux of the 1920s — the parable of the Democracy of Goods. According to this parable, the wonders of modern mass production and distribution enabled every person to enjoy the society's most significant pleasure, convenience, or benefit. The definition of the particular benefit fluctuated, of course, with each client who employed the parable. But the cumulative effect of the constant reminders that "any woman can" and "every home can afford" was to publicize an image of American society in which concentrated wealth at the top of a hierarchy of social classes restricted no family's opportunity to acquire the most significant products.[2] By implicitly defining "democracy" in terms of equal access to consumer products, and then by depicting the everyday functioning of that "democracy" with regard to one product at a time, these tableaux offered Americans an inviting vision of their society as one of incontestable equality.

In its most common advertising formula, the concept of the Democracy of Goods asserted that although the rich enjoyed a great variety of luxuries, the acquisition of their *one* most significant luxury would provide anyone with the ultimate in satisfaction. For instance, a Chase and Sanborn's Coffee tableau, with an elegant butler serving a family in a dining room with a sixteen-foot ceiling, reminded Chicago families that although "compared with the riches of the more fortunate, your way of life may seem modest indeed," yet no one — "king, prince, statesman, or capitalist" — could enjoy better coffee.[3] The Association of Soap and Glycerine Producers proclaimed that the charm of cleanliness was as readily available to the poor as to the rich, and Ivory Soap reassuringly related how one young housewife, who couldn't afford a $780-a-year maid like her neighbor, still maintained a significant equality in "nice hands" by using Ivory.[4] The C. F. Church Manufacturing Company epitomized this version of the parable of the Democracy of Goods in an ad entitled "a bathroom luxury everyone can afford": "If you lived in one of those palatial apartments on Park Avenue, in New York City, where you have to pay $2,000 to $7,500 a year rent, you still couldn't have a better toilet seat in your bathroom than they have — the Church Sani-white Toilet Seat which you can afford to have right now."[5]

Thus, according to the parable, no discrepancies in wealth could prevent the humblest citizens, provided they chose their purchases wisely, from retiring to a setting in which they could contemplate their essential equality, through possession of an identical product, with the nation's millionaires. In 1929, Howard Dickinson, a contributor to *Printers' Ink*, concisely expressed the social psychology behind Democracy of Goods advertisements: " 'With

[2]*Saturday Evening Post*, Apr. 3, 1926, pp. 182–83; Nov. 6, 1926, p. 104; Apr. 16, 1927, p. 199; Scrapbook 54 (Brunswick-Balke-Collender), Lord and Thomas Archives, at Foote, Cone and Belding Communications, Inc., Chicago.

[3]*Chicago Tribune*, Nov. 21, 1926, picture section, p. 2.

[4]*Los Angeles Times*, July 14, 1929, part VI, p. 3; *Tide*, July 1928, p. 10; *Photoplay Magazine*, Mar. 1930, p. 1.

[5]*American Magazine*, Mar. 1926, p. 112.

whom do the mass of people think they want to foregather?' asks the psychologist in advertising. 'Why, with the wealthy and socially distinguished, of course!' If we can't get an invitation to tea for our millions of customers, we can at least present the fellowship of using the same brand of merchandise. And it works."[6]

Some advertisers found it more efficacious to employ the parable's negative counterpart — the Democracy of Afflictions. Listerine contributed significantly to this approach. Most of the unsuspecting victims of halitosis in the mid-1920s possessed wealth and high social position. Other discoverers of new social afflictions soon took up the battle cry of "nobody's immune." "Body Odor plays no favorites," warned Lifebuoy Soap: No one, "banker, baker, or society woman," could count himself safe from B.O.[7] The boss, as well as the employees, might find himself "caught off guard" with dirty hands or cuffs, the Soap and Glycerine Producers assured readers of *True Story*. By 1930, Absorbine Jr. was beginning to document the democratic advance of "athlete's foot" into those rarefied social circles occupied by the "daintiest member of the junior set" and the noted yachtsman who owned "a railroad or two" (Fig. 1).[8]

The central purpose of the Democracy of Afflictions tableaux was to remind careless or unsuspecting readers of the universality of the threat from which the product offered protection or relief. Only occasionally did such ads address those of the upper classes who might think that their status and "fastidious" attention to personal care made them immune from common social offenses. In 1929 Listerine provided newspaper readers an opportunity to listen while a doctor, whose clientele included those of "the better class," confided "what I know about *nice* women."[9] One might have thought that Listerine was warning complacent, upper-class women that they were not immune from halitosis — except that the ad appeared in the *Los Angeles Times*, not *Harper's Bazaar*. Similarly, Forhan's toothpaste and the Soap Producers did not place their Democracy of Afflictions ads in *True Story* in order to reach the social elite. Rather, these tableaux provided enticing glimpses into the lives of the wealthy while suggesting an equalizing "fellowship" in shared susceptibilities to debilitating ailments. The parable of the Democracy of Goods always remained implicit in its negative counterpart. It assured readers that they could be as healthy, as charming, as free from social offense as the very "nicest" (richest) people, simply by using a product that anyone could afford.

---

[6]*Printers' Ink*, Oct. 10, 1929, p. 138.

[7]*Tide*, Sept. 15, 1927, p. 5; *American Magazine*, Aug. 1929, p. 93; *True Story*, June 1929, p. 133; *Chicago Tribune*, Jan. 11, 1928, p. 16; Jan. 18, 1928, p. 15; Jan. 28, 1928, p. 7; *Photoplay Magazine*, Feb. 1929, p. 111.

[8]*True Story*, May 1928, p. 83; June 1929, p. 133; *American Magazine*, Feb. 1930, p. 110; *Saturday Evening Post*, Aug. 23, 1930, p. 124.

[9]*Los Angeles Times*, July 6, 1929, p. 3.

FIGURE 1   A negative appeal transformed the Democracy of Goods into the Democracy of Afflictions. Common folk learned from this parable that they could inexpensively avoid afflictions that beset even the yachting set.

Another variation of the parable of the Democracy of Goods employed historical comparisons to celebrate even the humblest of contemporary Americans as "kings in cottages." "No monarch in all history ever saw the day he could have half as much as you," proclaimed Paramount Pictures. Even reigning sovereigns of the present, Paramount continued, would envy readers for their "luxurious freedom and opportunity" to enter a magnificent, bedazzling "palace for a night," be greeted with fawning bows by liveried attendants, and enjoy modern entertainment for a modest price (Fig. 2). The Fisher Body Corporation coined the phrase "For Kings in Cottages" to compliment ordinary Americans on their freedom from "hardships" that even kings had been forced to endure in the past. Because of a lack of technology, monarchs who traveled in the past had "never enjoyed luxury which even approached that of the present-day automobile." The "American idea," epitomized by the Fisher Body Corporation, was destined to carry the comforts

FIGURE 2   Of course, real kings had never shared their status with crowds of other "kings." But the parable of the Democracy of Goods offered a brief, "packaged experience" of luxury and preference.

and luxuries conducive to human happiness into "the life of even the humblest cottager."[10]

Even so, many copywriters perceived that equality with past monarchs might not rival the vision of joining the fabled "Four Hundred" that Ward McAllister had marked as America's social elite at the end of the nineteenth century. Americans, in an ostensibly conformist age, hungered for exclusivity. So

[10] *Saturday Evening Post*, May 8, 1926, p. 59; *American Magazine*, May 1932, pp. 76–77. See also *Saturday Evening Post*, July 18, 1931, pp. 36–37; Aug. 1, 1931, pp. 30–31; *Better Homes and Gardens*, Mar. 1930, p. 77.

advertising tableaux celebrated their ascension into this fabled and exclusive American elite. Through mass production and the resulting lower prices, the tableaux explained, the readers could purchase goods formerly available only to the rich — and thus gain admission to a "400" that now numbered millions.

The Simmons Company confessed that inner-coil mattresses had once been a luxury possessed only by the very wealthy. But now (in 1930) they were "priced so everybody in the United States can have one at $19.95." Woodbury's Soap advised the "working girl" readers of *True Story* of their arrival within a select circle. "Yesterday," it recalled, "the skin you love to touch" had been "the privilege of one woman in 65," but today it had become "the beauty right of every woman."[11] If the Democracy of Goods could establish an equal consumer right to beauty, then perhaps even the ancient religious promise of equality in death might be realized, at least to the extent that material provisions sufficed. In 1927 the Clark Grave Vault Company defined this unique promise: "Not so many years ago the use of a burial vault was confined largely to the rich. . . . Now every family, regardless of its means, may provide absolute protection against the elements of the ground."[12] If it seemed that the residents of Clark vaults had gained equality with the "400" too belatedly for maximum satisfaction, still their loving survivors could now share the same sense of comfort in the "absolute protection" of former loved ones as did the most privileged elites.

The social message of the parable of the Democracy of Goods was clear. 10 Antagonistic envy of the rich was unseemly; programs to redistribute wealth were unnecessary. The best things in life were already available to all at reasonable prices. But the prevalence of the parable of the Democracy of Goods in advertising tableaux did not necessarily betray a concerted conspiracy on the part of advertisers and their agencies to impose a social ideology on the American people. Most advertisers employed the parable of the Democracy of Goods primarily as a narrow, nonideological merchandising tactic. Listerine and Lifebuoy found the parable an obvious, attention-getting strategy for persuading readers that if even society women and bankers were unconsciously guilty of social offenses, the readers themselves were not immune. Simmons Mattresses, Chevrolet, and Clark Grave Vaults chose the parable in an attempt to broaden their market to include lower-income groups. The parable emphasized the affordability of the product to families of modest income while attempting to maintain a "class" image of the product as the preferred choice of their social betters.

Most advertisers found the social message of the parable of the Democracy of Goods a congenial and unexceptionable truism. They also saw it, like the other parables prevalent in advertising tableaux, as an epigrammatic

[11] *Saturday Evening Post*, Nov. 10, 1928, p. 90; *True Story*, Aug. 1934, p. 57. See also *Chicago Tribune*, Oct. 8, 1930, p. 17; *American Magazine*, Aug. 1930, p. 77; *Woman's Home Companion*, May 1927, p. 96.

[12] *American Magazine*, Feb. 1927, p. 130.

statement of a conventional popular belief. Real income was rising for nearly all Americans during the 1920s, except for some farmers and farmworkers and those in a few depressed industries. Citizens seemed eager for confirmation that they were now driving the same make of car as the wealthy elites and serving their children the same cereal enjoyed by Livingston Ludlow Biddle III. Advertisers did not have to impose the parable of the Democracy of Goods on a contrary-minded public. Theirs was the easier task of subtly substituting this vision of equality, which was certainly satisfying *as a vision*, for broader and more traditional hopes and expectations of an equality of self-sufficiency, personal independence, and social interaction.

Perhaps the most attractive aspect of this parable to advertisers was that it preached the coming of an equalizing democracy without sacrificing those fascinating contrasts of social condition that had long been the touchstone of high drama. Henry James, writing of Hawthorne, had once lamented the obstacles facing the novelist who wrote of an America that lacked such tradition-laden institutions as a sovereign, a court, an aristocracy, or even a class of country gentlemen. Without castles, manors, and thatched cottages, America lacked those stark juxtapositions of pomp and squalor, nobility and peasantry, wealth and poverty that made Europe so rich a source of social drama.[13] But many versions of the parable of the Democracy of Goods sought to offset that disadvantage without gaining James's desired "complexity of manners." They dressed up America's wealthy as dazzling aristocrats, and then reassured readers that they could easily enjoy an essential equality with such elites in the things that really mattered. The rich were decorative and fun to look at, but in their access to those products most important to comfort and satisfaction, as the magazine *Delineator* put it, "The Four Hundred" had become "the four million."[14] Advertisers left readers to assume that they could gain the same satisfactions of exclusiveness from belonging to the four million as had once been savored by the four hundred.

While parables of consumer democracy frequently used terms like "everyone," "anyone," "any home," or "every woman," these categories were mainly intended to comprise the audience of "consumer-citizens" envisioned by the advertising trade, or families economically among the nation's top 50 percent. Thus the *Delineator* had more in mind than mere alliteration when it chose to contrast the old "400" with the new "four million" rather than a new "one hundred and twenty million." The standard antitheses of the Democracy of Goods parables were "mansion" and "bungalow." Advertising writers rarely took notice of the many millions of Americans whose standard of living fell below that of the cozy bungalow of the advertising tableaux. These millions might overhear the promises of consumer democracy in the newspapers or magazines, but advertising leaders felt no obligation to show how their promises to "everyone" would bring equality to those who lived in the nation's

[13]Henry James, *Hawthorne*, rev. ed. (New York, 1967 [c. 1879]), p. 55.
[14]*Printers' Ink*, Nov. 24, 1927, p. 52.

apartment houses and farmhouses without plumbing, let alone those who lived in rural shacks and urban tenements.

In the broadest sense, the parable of the Democracy of Goods may be interpreted as a secularized version of the traditional Christian assurances of ultimate human equality. "Body Odor plays no favorites" might be considered a secular translation of the idea that God "sends rain on the just and on the unjust" (Matt. 5:45). Promises of the essential equality of those possessing the advertised brand recalled the promise of equality of access to God's mercy. Thus the parable recapitulated a familiar, cherished expectation. Far more significant, however, was the parable's insinuation of the capacity of a Democracy of Goods to redeem the already secularized American promise of political equality.

Incessantly and enticingly repeated, advertising visions of fellowship in a Democracy of Goods encouraged Americans to look to similarities in consumption styles rather than to political power or control of wealth for evidence

FIGURE 3   Advertising such as this encouraged Americans to pursue consumption-oriented lifestyles.

of significant equality. Francesco Nicosia and Robert Mayer describe the result as a "deflection of the success ethic from the sphere of production to that of consumption." Freedom of choice came to be perceived as a freedom more significantly exercised in the marketplace than in the political arena. This process gained momentum in the 1920s; it gained maturity during the 1950s as a sense of class differences was nearly eclipsed by a fascination with the equalities suggested by shared consumption patterns and "freely chosen" consumer "lifestyles."[15]

READING THE TEXT

1. Summarize in your own words what Marchand means by the "parable of the Democracy of Goods" (para. 2).
2. What is the "Democracy of Afflictions" (para. 5), in your own words?
3. In class, brainstorm examples of current ads that illustrate the parable of the democracy of goods and the democracy of afflictions.

READING THE SIGNS

1. Does the parable of the democracy of goods work to make society more egalitarian, or does it reinforce existing power structures? Write an essay arguing for one position or the other, focusing on particular ads for support.
2. Bring to class a popular magazine of your own choosing. In groups, study your selections. In which magazines is the myth of the democracy of goods most common? Do you find any relationship between the use of this myth and the magazines' intended readership?
3. Obtain from your college library an issue of *Time* magazine dating from the 1920s, and compare it with a current issue. In what ways, if any, have the social messages communicated in the advertising changed? Try to account for any changes you identify.
4. Compare and contrast the myth of the democracy of goods with the frontier myth that Laurence Shames describes in "The More Factor" (p. 76). Consider how the two myths shape our consuming behavior; you may also want to show how the myths appear in some current ads.

[15]Francesco M. Nicosia and Robert N. Mayer, "Toward a Sociology of Consumption," *The Journal of Consumer Research* 3 (1976): 73; Roland Marchand, "Visions of Classlessness; Quests for Dominion: American Popular Culture, 1945–1960," in *Reshaping America: Society and Institutions, 1945–1960*, ed. Robert H. Bremner and Gary W. Reichard (Columbus, Ohio, 1982), pp. 165–70.

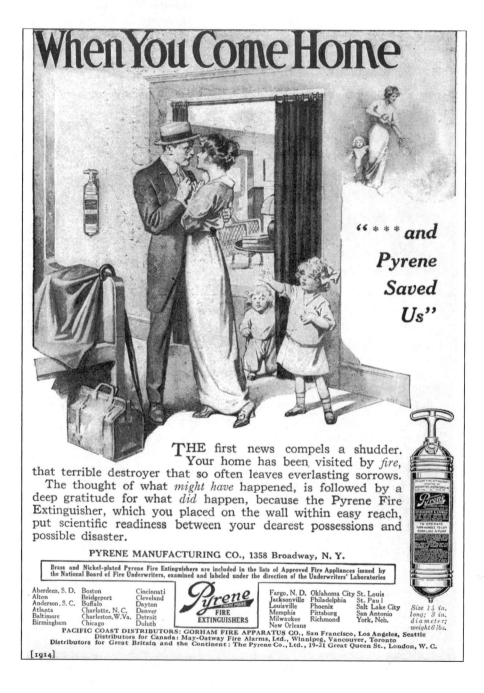

When You Come Home

"*** *and*
Pyrene
Saved
Us"

T**HE** first news compels a shudder. Your home has been visited by *fire*, that terrible destroyer that so often leaves everlasting sorrows. The thought of what *might have* happened, is followed by a deep gratitude for what *did* happen, because the Pyrene Fire Extinguisher, which you placed on the wall within easy reach, put scientific readiness between your dearest possessions and possible disaster.

PYRENE MANUFACTURING CO., 1358 Broadway, N. Y.

Brass and Nickel-plated Pyrene Fire Extinguishers are included in the lists of Approved Fire Appliances issued by the National Board of Fire Underwriters, examined and labeled under the direction of the Underwriters' Laboratories

Aberdeen, S. D.	Boston	Cincinnati		Fargo, N. D.	Oklahoma City	St. Louis
Alton	Bridgeport	Cleveland		Jacksonville	Philadelphia	St. Paul
Anderson, S. C.	Buffalo	Dayton		Louisville	Phoenix	Salt Lake City
Atlanta	Charlotte, N. C.	Denver		Memphis	Pittsburg	San Antonio
Baltimore	Charleston, W. Va.	Detroit		Milwaukee	Richmond	York, Neb.
Birmingham	Chicago	Duluth		New Orleans		

Pyrene
TRADE MARK
FIRE
EXTINGUISHERS

*Size 14 in.
long; 3 in.
diameter;
weight 6 lbs.*

PACIFIC COAST DISTRIBUTORS: GORHAM FIRE APPARATUS CO., San Francisco, Los Angeles, Seattle
Distributors for Canada: May-Oatway Fire Alarms, Ltd., Winnipeg, Vancouver, Toronto
Distributors for Great Britain and the Continent: The Pyrene Co., Ltd., 19-21 Great Queen St., London, W. C.

[1914]

READING THE SIGNS

1. The advertisement on page 160 tells a story. What is it? You might start with the title of the ad.

2. To whom is the ad directed? What emotions does it play on? Be sure to provide evidence for your answers. What are the "dearest possessions" the ad refers to?

3. This ad originally appeared in 1914. If you were to update it for a magazine today, what changes would you make? Why?

STEVE CRAIG

Men's Men and Women's Women

Men and women both drink beer, but you wouldn't guess that from the television ads that pitch beer as a guy beverage and associate beer drinking with such guy things as fishing trips, bars, and babes. Conversely, both men and women can find themselves a few pounds overweight, but you wouldn't know that from the ads, which almost always feature women intended to appeal to women dieters. In this selection, Steve Craig (b. 1947) provides a step-by-step analysis of four TV commercials, showing how advertisers carefully craft their ads to appeal, respectively, to male and female consumers. A professor in the department of radio, television, and film at the University of North Texas, Craig has written widely on television, radio history, and gender and media.

Gender and the Economics of Television Advertising

The economic structure of the television industry has a direct effect on the placement and content of all television programs and commercials. Large advertisers and their agencies have evolved the pseudo-scientific method of time purchasing based on demographics, with the age and sex of the consumer generally considered to be the most important predictors of purchasing behavior. Computers make it easy to match market research on product buying patterns with audience research on television viewing habits. Experience, research, and intuition thus yield a demographic (and even psychographic) profile of the "target audience." Advertisers can then concentrate their budgets on those programs which the target audience is most likely to view. The most economical advertising buys are those in which the target audience is most concentrated (thus, the less "waste" audience the advertiser must purchase) (Barnouw, 1978; Gitlin, 1983; Jhally, 1987).

Good examples of this demographic targeting can be seen by contrasting the ads seen on daytime television, aimed at women at home, with those on weekend sports telecasts. Ads for disposable diapers are virtually never seen during a football game any more than commercials for beer are seen during soap operas. True, advertisers of some products simply wish to have their commercials seen by the largest number of consumers at the lowest cost without regard to age, sex, or other demographic descriptors, but most consider this approach far too inefficient for the majority of products.

A general rule of thumb in television advertising, then, is that daytime is the best time to reach the woman who works at home. Especially important to advertisers among this group is the young mother with children. Older women, who also make up a significant proportion of the daytime audience, are generally considered less important by many advertisers in the belief that they spend far less money on consumer goods than young mothers.

Prime time (the evening hours) is considered a good time to reach women who work away from home, but since large numbers of men are also in the audience, it can also be a good time to advertise products with wider target audiences. Weekend sports periods (and, in season, "Monday Night Football") are the only time of the week when men outnumber women in the television audience, and therefore, become the optimum time for advertising products and services aimed at men.

Gendered Television, Gendered Commercials

In his book *Television Culture* (1987, Chs. 10, 11), John Fiske discusses "gendered television," explaining that the television industry successfully designs some programs for men and others for women. Clearly, program producers and schedulers must consider the target audience needs of their clients (the advertisers) in creating a television program line up. The gendering of programming allows the industry to provide the proper audience for advertisers by constructing shows pleasurable for the target audience to watch, and one aspect of this construction is in the gender portrayals of characters.

Fiske provides the following example:

> Women's view of masculinity, as evidenced in soap operas, differs markedly from that produced from the masculine audience. The "good" male in the daytime soaps is caring, nurturing, and verbal. He is prone to making comments like "I don't care about material wealth or professional success, all I care about is us and our relationship." He will talk about feelings and people and rarely express his masculinity in direct action. Of course, he is still decisive, he still has masculine power, but that power is given a "feminine" inflection. . . . The "macho" characteristics

of goal centeredness, assertiveness, and the morality of the strongest that identify the hero in masculine television, tend here to be characteristics of the villain. (p. 186)

But if the programming manipulates gender portrayals to please the audience, then surely so must the commercials that are the programs' reason for being. My previous research (Craig, 1990) supports the argument that advertisers also structure the gender images in their commercials to match the expectations and fantasies of their intended audience. Thus, commercials portraying adult women with children were nearly four times more likely to appear during daytime soap operas than during weekend sports (p. 50). Daytime advertisers exploit the image of women as mothers to sell products to mothers. Likewise, during the weekend sports broadcasts, only 18% of the primary male characters were shown at home, while during the daytime ads, 40% of them were (p. 42). For the woman at home, men are far more likely to be portrayed as being around the house than they are in commercials aimed at men on weekends.

Gendered commercials, like gendered programs, are designed to give pleasure to the target audience, since it is the association of the product with a pleasurable experience that forms the basis for much American television advertising. Yet patriarchy conditions males and females to seek their pleasure differently. Advertisers therefore portray different images to men and women in order to exploit the different deep-seated motivations and anxieties connected to gender identity. I would now like to turn to a close analysis of four television commercials to illustrate some of these differing portrayals. Variations in how men and women are portrayed are especially apparent when comparing weekend and daytime commercials, since ads during these day parts almost completely focus on a target audience of men or women respectively.

Analysis of Four Commercials

In order to illustrate the variation of gender portrayal, I have chosen four commercials. Each was selected to provide an example of how men and women are portrayed to themselves and to the other sex. The image of men and women in commercials aired during weekend sports telecasts I call "Men's Men" and "Men's Women." The portrayals of men and women in commercials aimed at women at home during the daytime hours I call "Women's Men" and "Women's Women." Although there are certainly commercials aired during these day parts which do not fit neatly into these categories, and even a few which might be considered to be counter-stereotypical in their gender portrayals, the commercials and images I have chosen to analyze are fairly typical and were chosen to permit a closer look at the practices revealed in my earlier content analysis. Further, I acknowledge that the readings of these commercials are my own. Others may well read them differently.

Men's Men

I would first like to consider two commercials originally broadcast during 10
weekend sports and clearly aimed at men. (These and the other commercials
I will discuss were broadcast on at least one of the three major networks. I
recorded them for analysis during January, 1990.)

COMMERCIAL 1: ACURA INTEGRA (:30)

MUSIC: Light rock guitar music runs throughout. Tropical elements (e.g., a
steel drum) are added later.

A young, white, blond, bespectacled male wearing a plain sweatshirt is
shown cleaning out the interior of a car. He finds an old photograph of
himself and two male companions (all are young, slender, and white)
posing with a trophy-sized sailfish. He smiles. Dissolve to what appears
to be a flashback of the fishing trip. The three men are now seen driving
down the highway in the car (we now see that it is a new black Acura Integra) in a Florida-like landscape. We see a montage of close-ups of the
three men inside the car, then a view out the car window of what looks
to be the Miami skyline.

ANNOUNCER (male): "When you think about all the satisfaction you get out
of going places. . . . Why would you want to take anything less . . ."

Dissolve to a silhouette shot of a young woman in a bathing suit walking
along the beach at sunset.

ANNOUNCER: ". . . than America's most satisfying car?"

On this last line, the three young men are seen in silhouette knee-deep in
the water at the same beach, apparently watching the woman pass. One
of the men drops to his knees and throws his arms up in mock supplica-
tion. A montage of shots of the three men follows, shots of a deep-sea
fishing boat intercut with shots of the first man washing the car. The
montage ends with the three posing with the trophy sailfish. The screen
flashes and freezes and becomes the still photo seen at the first of the
commercial. The final shot shows a long shot of the car, freshly washed.
The first man, dressed as in the first shot, gives the car a final polish and
walks away. The words "Acura" and "Precision Crafted Performance" are
superimposed over the final shot.

ANNOUNCER: "The Acura Integra."

This ad, which ran during a weekend sports telecast, has a number of features that makes it typical of many other commercials aimed at men. First, it
is for an automobile. My previous research found that 29% of the network
commercials telecast in the weekend time period were for cars and other automotive products (compared to only 1% during the daytime sample) (Craig,

1990, p. 36). In our culture, automobiles are largely the male's province, and men are seen by the automotive industry as the primary decision makers when it comes to purchases. Further, cars are frequently offered as a means of freedom (literally so in this ad), and escapism is an important component in many weekend ads (only 16% of weekend ads are set at home compared to 41% of daytime ads) (p. 43).

Second, with the exception of a brief silhouette of the woman on the beach, there are no women in this commercial. Camaraderie in all-male or nearly all-male groupings is a staple of weekend commercials, especially those for automobiles and beer. Again, my earlier research indicates that fully one-third of weekend commercials have an all-adult male cast (but only 20% of daytime commercials have an all-adult female cast) (p. 36).

The escapism and male camaraderie promised in this commercial are simply an extension of the escapism and camaraderie men enjoy when they watch (and vicariously participate in) weekend sports on television. Messner (1987) suggests that one reason for the popularity of sports with men is that it offers them a chance to escape from the growing ambiguity of masculinity in daily life.

> Both on a personal/existential level for athletes and on a symbolic/ideological level for spectators and fans, sport has become one of the "last bastions" of male power and superiority over — and separation from — the "feminization" of society. The rise of football as "America's number-one game" is likely the result of the comforting *clarity* it provides between the polarities of traditional male power, strength, and violence and the contemporary fears of social feminization. (p. 54)

The Acura commercial acts to reinforce male fantasies in an environment of clear masculinity and male domination. Men's men are frequently portrayed as men without women. The presence of women in the commercials might serve to threaten men's men with confusing uncertainty about the nature of masculinity in a sexist, but changing, society (Fiske, 1987, pp. 202–209, offers an extended psychoanalytic explanation of the absence of women in masculine television). On the other hand, the absence of women must *not* suggest homosexuality. Men's men are clearly heterosexual. To discourage any suspicions, the Acura ad portrays three (rather than two) men vacationing together.

It is also at least partly for this reason that the single quick shot in which 15 the woman *does* appear in this commercial is important. She is nothing more than an anonymous object of desire (indeed, in silhouette, we cannot even see her face), but her presence both affirms the heterosexuality of the group while at the same time hinting that attaining sexual fulfillment will be made easier by the possession of the car. Men's men have the unchallenged freedom of a fantasized masculinity — to travel, to be free from commitment, to seek adventure.

Men's Women

COMMERCIAL 2: MILLER BEER (:30)

We see the interior of a cheap roadside cafe. It is lit with an almost blinding sunlight streaming in the windows. A young couple sits in a far booth holding hands. A young, blond waitress is crossing the room. A silent jukebox sits in the foreground. At first we hear only natural sounds. We cut to a close-up from a low angle from outside the cafe of male legs as they enter the cafe. The legs are clad in blue jeans and cowboy boots. As the man enters, we cut to a close-up of the blond waitress looking up to see the man. We see a close-up of the man's body as he passes the silent jukebox. As if by magic, the jukebox begins to play the rhythm and blues number "I Put a Spell on You." We see the couple that was holding hands turn in surprise. The man in the booth's face is unlit and we can see no features, but the woman is young with long blond hair. She looks surprised and pulls her hand away from the man's. We cut to an extreme close-up of the waitress's face. It is covered with sweat. As she watches the man pass, a smile appears on her face. She comes over to take the man's order. The camera takes the man's point of view.

MAN: "Miller Genuine Draft."
WAITRESS: "I was hopin' you'd say that."

We see a shot of a refrigerator door opening. The refrigerator is filled with sweating, backlit bottles of Miller beer. We then see a close-up of the man holding a bottle and opening it magically with a flick of his thumb (no opener). A montage of shots of the product amid blowing snow follows this. The sounds of a blizzard are heard.

ANNOUNCER: "Cold filtered. Never heat pasteurized. Miller Genuine Draft. For those who discover this real draft taste . . . the world is a *very* cool place."

On this last line we see close-ups of the woman in the booth and the waitress. Wind is blowing snow in their faces and they are luxuriating in the coolness. The waitress suddenly looks at the camera with shocked disappointment. We cut to an empty seat with the man's empty beer bottle rocking on the table. The music, snow, and wind end abruptly. We see the man's back as he exits the cafe. The final shot is of the waitress, elbow propped on the counter, looking after the man. The words "Tap into the Cold" are superimposed.

When women do appear in men's commercials, they seldom challenge the primary masculine fantasy. Men's women are portrayed as physically attractive, slim, and usually young and white, frequently blond, and almost always dressed in revealing clothing. Since most men's commercials are set in locations away from home, most men's women appear outside the home, and only infrequently are they portrayed as wives. There are almost always hints of sexual availability in men's women, but this is seldom played out explicitly. Although the sexual objectification of women characters in these ads is often quite subtle, my previous content analysis suggests that it is far more common in weekend than in daytime ads (Craig, 1990, p. 34). Men's women are also frequently portrayed as admirers (and at times, almost voyeurs), generally approving of some aspect of product use (the car he drives, the beer he drinks, the credit card he uses).

In these respects, the Miller ad is quite typical. What might have been a simple commercial about a man ordering and drinking a beer becomes an elaborate sexual fantasy, in many respects constructed like a porn film. The attractive, eager waitress is mystically drawn to the man who relieves her bored frustrations with an orgasmic chug-a-lug. She is "hot" while he (and the beer) is "*very* cool." But once he's satisfied, he's gone. He's too cool for conversation or commitment. We never see the man's face, but rather are invited, through the use of the point-of-view shot, to become a participant in the mystic fantasy.

There is, of course, considerable tongue-in-cheek intent in this ad. Males know that the idea of anonymous women lusting after them, eager for sex without commitment, is fantasy. But for many men, it is pleasurable fantasy, and common enough in weekend commercials. The main point is that the product has been connected, however briefly, with the pleasure of this fantasy. The physical pleasure of consuming alcohol (and specifically cold Miller beer) is tied to the pleasurable imaginings of a narrative extended beyond that which is explicitly seen.

One industry executive has explained this advertising technique. Noting the need for "an imaginary and motivating value" in ads, Nicolas (1988) argues that:

> Beyond the principle of utility, it becomes more and more important to associate a principle of pleasure to the value. The useful must be linked to the beautiful, the rational to the imaginary, the indispensable to the superfluous. . . . It is imperative that the image be seductive. (p. 7)

Although some research has documented changes in gender portrayals in television advertising over the past few years (e.g., Bretl & Cantor, 1988; Ferrante, et al., 1988), such conclusions are based on across-the-schedule studies or of prime time rather than of specifically gendered day parts. While avoiding portraying women as blatant sex objects is doubtless good business in daytime or prime time, it would almost certainly inhibit male fantasies such as this one, commonly seen during weekend sports. The man's woman continues to be portrayed according to the rules of the patriarchy.

The next two commercials were originally aired during daytime soap operas. They represent Madison Avenue's portrayal of women and men designed for women.

Women's Women

COMMERCIAL 3: WEIGHT WATCHERS (:30)

The opening shot is a quick pan from toe to head of a young, thin, white woman with dark hair. She is dressed in a revealing red bathing suit and appears to be reclining on the edge of a pool. Her head is propped up with a pillow. She is wearing sunglasses and smiling.

ANNOUNCER (woman, voice-over): "I hate diets . . . but I lost weight fast with Weight Watchers' new program."

We see the same woman sitting at a dining table in a home kitchen eating a meal. She is wearing a red dress. The camera weaves, and we briefly glimpse a man and two small children also at the table. Another close-up of the woman's body at the pool. This time the camera frames her waist.

ANNOUNCER: "And I *hate* starving myself."

We see the same family group eating pizza at a restaurant. More close-ups of the woman's body at poolside.

ANNOUNCER: "But with their new 'fast and flexible' program I don't have to."

Shot of the woman dancing with the man, followed by a montage of more shots of the family at dinner and close-ups of the woman at poolside.

ANNOUNCER: "A new food plan lets me live the way I want . . . eat with my family and friends, still have fun."

Close-up shot of balance scales. A woman's hand is moving the balance weight downward.

ANNOUNCER: "And in no time . . . *here I am!*"

Shot of the woman on the scales. She raises her hands as if in triumph. The identical shot is repeated three times.

ANNOUNCER: "Now there's only one thing I hate . . . not joining Weight Watchers sooner."

As this last line is spoken, we see a close-up of the woman at the pool. She removes her sunglasses. The man's head comes into the frame from the side and kisses her on the forehead.

This commercial portrays the woman's woman. Her need is a common one in women's commercials produced by a patriarchal society — the desire to attain and maintain her physical attractiveness. Indeed, my previous research indicates that fully 44% of the daytime ads sampled were for products relating to the body (compared with only 15% of the ads during weekend sports). In this ad, her desire for an attractive body is explicitly tied to her family. She is portrayed with a husband, small children, and a nice home. It is her husband with whom she dances and who expresses approval with a kiss. Her need for an attractive body is her need to maintain her husband's interest and maintain her family's unity and security. As Coward (1985) has written:

> Most women know to their cost that appearance is perhaps the crucial way by which men form opinions of women. For that reason, feelings about self-image get mixed up with feelings about security and comfort. . . . It sometimes appears to women that the whole possibility of being loved and comforted hangs on how their appearance will be received. (p. 78)

But dieting is a difficult form of self-deprivation, and she "hates" doing it. Implicit also is her hatred of her own "overweight" body — a body that no longer measures up to the idealized woman promoted by the patriarchy (and seen in the commercial). As Coward explains:

> . . . advertisements, health and beauty advice, fashion tips are effective precisely because somewhere, perhaps even subconsciously, an anxiety, rather than a pleasurable identification [with the idealized body] is awakened. (p. 80)

Weight Watchers promises to alleviate the pain of dieting at the same time it relieves (or perhaps delays) the anxiety of being "overweight." She can diet and "still have fun."

A related aspect is this ad's use of a female announcer. The copy is written in the first person, but we never see the model speaking in direct address. We get the impression that we are eavesdropping on her thoughts — being invited to identify with her — rather than hearing a sales pitch from a third person. My earlier research confirmed the findings of other content analyses that female voice-overs are relatively uncommon in commercials. My findings, however, indicated that while only 3% of the voice-overs during weekend sports were by women announcers, 16% of those during daytime were. Further, 60% of the women announcers during daytime were heard in commercials for body-related products (Craig, 1990, p. 52). 25

Women's Men

COMMERCIAL 4: SECRET DEODORANT (:30)

> We open on a wide shot of a sailing yacht at anchor. It is sunrise and a women is on deck. She descends into the cabin. Cut to a close-up of the woman as she enters the cabin.
>
> WOMAN: "Four bells. Rise and shine!"

A man is seen in a bunk inside the cabin. He has just awakened. Both he and the woman are now seen to be young and white. She is thin and has bobbed hair. He is muscular and unshaven (and a Bruce Willis look-alike).

MUSIC: Fusion jazz instrumental (UNDER).
MAN (painfully): "Ohhhh . . . I can't move."
WOMAN: "Ohhhhh. I took a swim — breakfast is on — I had a shower. Now it's *your turn*."

As she says this, she crosses the cabin and places a container of Secret deodorant on a shelf above the man. The man leans up on one elbow then falls back into bed with a groan.

MAN: "Ahhh, I can't."

She pulls him back to a sitting position then sits down herself, cradling him in her arms.

WOMAN: "Come onnn. You only changed *one* sail yesterday."
MAN (playfully): "Yeah, but it was a *big* sail."

Close-up of the couple. He is now positioned in the bed sitting with his back to her. He leans his head back on her shoulder.

WOMAN: "Didn't you know sailing's a sport? You know . . . an active thing."
MAN: "I just don't get it. . . . You're *so* together already. . . . Um. You smell great."
WOMAN: "Must be my Secret."

She looks at the container of Secret on the shelf. The man reaches over and picks it up. Close-up of the Secret with the words "Sporty Clean Scent" visible on the container.

MAN: "Sporty clean?"
WOMAN: "It's new."
MAN: "Sounds like something I could use."
WOMAN: "Unnnnn . . . I don't think so. I got it for me."

She takes the container from him and stands up and moves away. He stands up behind her and holds her from behind.

WOMAN: "For these close quarters . . . ?"
MAN: "Well close is good."

He begins to kiss her cheek.

WOMAN: "I thought you said you couldn't move."

She turns to face him.

MAN: "I was saving my strength?"
WOMAN: "Mmmm."

We dissolve to a close-up of the product on the shelf.

ANNOUNCER (woman): "New Sporty Clean Secret. Strong enough for a man, but pH-balanced for an active woman."

This commercial portrays the woman's man. He's good looking, sensitive, and romantic, and he appreciates her. What's more, they are alone in an exotic location where he proceeds to seduce her. In short, this commercial is a 30-second romance novel. She may be today's woman, be "so together," and she may be in control, but she still wants him to initiate the love-making. Her man is strong, active, and probably wealthy enough to own or rent a yacht. (Of course, a more liberated reading would have her as the owner of the yacht, or at least sharing expenses.) Yet he is also vulnerable. At first she mothers him, holding him in a Pietà-like embrace and cooing over his sore muscles. Then he catches her scent — her Secret — and the chase is on.

As in the Weight Watchers commercial, it is the woman's body that is portrayed as the source of the man's attraction, and it is only through maintaining that attraction that she can successfully negotiate the relationship. Although at one level the Secret woman is portrayed as a "new woman" — active, "sporty," self-assured, worthy of her own deodorant — she still must rely on special (even "Secret") products to make her body attractive. More to the point, she still must rely on her body to attract a man and fulfill the fantasy of security and family. After all, she is still mothering and cooking breakfast.

Once again, the product is the source of promised fantasy fulfillment — not only sexual fulfillment, but also the security of a caring relationship, one that allows her to be liberated, but not too liberated. Unlike the women of the Acura and Miller's commercials who remained anonymous objects of desire, the men of the Weight Watchers and Secret commercials are intimates who are clearly portrayed as having relationships that will exist long after the commercial is over.

Conclusion

Gender images in television commercials provide an especially intriguing field of study. The ads are carefully crafted bundles of images, frequently designed to associate the product with feelings of pleasure stemming from deep-seated fantasies and anxieties. Advertisers seem quite willing to manipulate these fantasies and exploit our anxieties, especially those concerning our gender identities, to sell products. What's more, they seem to have no compunction about capitalizing on dehumanizing gender stereotypes to seek these ends.

A threat to patriarchy is an economic threat, not only to men who may 30 fear they will have their jobs taken by women, but also in a more fundamental way. Entire industries (automotive, cosmetics, fashion) are predicated on the assumption that men and women will continue behaving according to their stereotypes. Commercials for women therefore act to reinforce patriarchy and to co-opt any reactionary ideology into it. Commercials for men need only reinforce masculinity under patriarchy and, at most, offer men help in coping with a life plagued by women of raised conscience. Betty Friedan's comments of 1963 are still valid. Those "deceptively simple, clever, outrageous ads and commercials" she wrote of are still with us. If anything, they have become more subtle and insidious. The escape from their snare is through a better understanding of gender and the role of mass culture in defining it.

WORKS CITED

Barnouw, E. (1978). *The sponsor*. NY: Oxford.
Bretl, D. J. & Cantor, J. (1988). The portrayal of men and women in U.S. television commercials: A recent content analysis and trends over 15 years. *Sex Roles, 18*(9/10), 595–609.
Coward, R. (1985). *Female desires: How they are sought, bought and packaged*. New York: Grove.
Craig, S. (1990, December). *A content analysis comparing gender images in network television commercials aired in daytime, evening, and weekend telecasts*. (ERIC Document Reproduction Service Number ED 329 217.)
Ferrante, C., Haynes, A., & Kingsley, S. (1988). Image of women in television advertising. *Journal of Broadcasting & Electronic Media, 32*(2), 231–37.
Fiske, J. (1987). *Television culture*. New York: Methuen.
Friedan, B. (1963). *The feminine mystique*. New York: Dell.
Gitlin, T. (1983). *Inside prime time*. New York: Pantheon.
Jhally, S. (1987). *The codes of advertising: Fetishism and the political economy of meaning in the consumer society*. NY: St. Martin's.
Messner, M. (1987). Male identity in the life course of the jock. In M. Kimmel (Ed.), *Changing men* (pp. 53–67). Newbury Park, CA: Sage.
Nicolas, P. (1988). From value to love. *Journal of Advertising Research, 28*, 7–8.

READING THE TEXT

1. How, according to John Fiske, is television programming gendered?

2. Why is male camaraderie such a common motif in "men's men" advertising, according to Craig?

3. What roles do women tend to play in the two types of commercials aimed at men? And what roles do men tend to play in the two types aimed at women?

4. Why does Craig believe that "a threat to patriarchy is an economic threat" (para. 30)?

READING THE SIGNS

1. In class, discuss whether you agree with Craig's interpretations of the four commercials. If you disagree, what alternative analysis do you propose?

2. The four commercials Craig analyzes were aired in 1990. View some current commercials broadcast during daytime and sports programs. Use your observations as the basis for an argument about whether the gendered patterns in advertising that Craig outlines still exist today. If the pattern persists, what implications does that have for the tenacity of gender codes? If you see differences, how can you account for them?

3. Write an essay in which you support, refute, or modify Craig's belief that gendered advertising of the sort he describes is "dehumanizing" (para. 29).

4. Do metrosexuals fit any of the four patterns that Craig describes (see Warren St. John's "Metrosexuals Come Out," p. 174)? If so, explain your reasoning; if not, create your own fifth pattern to fit this type of consumer.

5. Watch TV programs that are not overtly geared toward one gender, such as prime-time drama or network news programs. To what extent does the advertising that accompanies these shows fit Craig's four categories of gender portrayal? How do you account for your findings?

6. Enter the debate over the origins of gender identity: Is it primarily biological or largely socially constructed? Write an essay in which you advance your position. You can develop your ideas by consulting Andre Mayer's "The New Sexual Stone Age" (p. 284), Aaron Devor's "Gender Role Behaviors and Attitudes" (p. 458), Deborah Blum's "The Gender Blur: Where Does Biology End and Society Take Over?" (p. 475), or Mariah Burton Nelson's "I Won. I'm Sorry." (p. 446).

WARREN ST. JOHN
Metrosexuals Come Out

They've been lampooned on The Simpsons *and pampered on* Queer Eye for the Straight Guy — *and Madison Avenue is taking notice. "They" are that category of consumers popularly known as "metrosexuals": straight young men whose fashion and grooming tastes have crossed over into areas once reserved for feminine consumption. As Warren St. John (b. 1969) reports in this analysis of the metrosexual phenomenon on the eve of* Queer Eye's *debut in 2003, the metrosexual is a tempting target for marketers, offering a growing market for goods traditionally coded for women. St. John is a reporter for the* New York Times, *where this selection was first published, and the author of* Rammer, Jammer, Yellow Hammer *(2004).*

By his own admission, 30-year-old Karru Martinson is not what you'd call a manly man. He uses a $40 face cream, wears Bruno Magli shoes and custom-tailored shirts. His hair is always just so, thanks to three brands of shampoo and the precise application of three hair grooming products: Textureline Smoothing Serum, got2b styling glue and Suave Rave hairspray. Mr. Martinson likes wine bars and enjoys shopping with his gal pals, who have come to trust his eye for color, his knack for seeing when a bag clashes with an outfit, and his understanding of why some women have 47 pairs of black shoes. ("Because they can!" he said.) He said his guy friends have long thought his consumer and grooming habits a little . . . different. But Mr. Martinson, who lives in Manhattan and works in finance, said he's not that different. "From a personal perspective there was never any doubt what my sexual orientation was," he said. "I'm straight as an arrow."

So it was with a mixture of relief and mild embarrassment that Mr. Martinson was recently asked by a friend in marketing to be part of a focus group of "metrosexuals" — straight urban men willing, even eager, to embrace their feminine sides. Convinced that these open-minded young men hold the secrets of tomorrow's consumer trends, the advertising giant Euro RSCG, with 233 offices worldwide, wanted to better understand their buying habits. So in a private room at the Manhattan restaurant Eleven Madison Park recently, Mr. Martinson answered the marketers' questions and schmoozed with 11 like-minded straight guys who were into Diesel jeans, interior design, yoga and Mini Coopers, and who would never think of ordering a vodka tonic without specifying Grey Goose or Ketel One. Before the focus group met, Mr. Martinson said he was suspicious that such a thing as a metrosexual existed. Afterward, he said, "I'm fully aware that I have those characteristics."

America may be on the verge of a metrosexual moment. On July 15, Bravo will present a makeover show, *Queer Eye for the Straight Guy*, in which a team of five gay men "transform a style-deficient and culture-deprived straight man from drab to fab," according to the network. Condé Nast is developing a shopping magazine for men, modeled after *Lucky*, its successful women's magazine, which is largely a text-free catalog of clothes and shoes. There is no end to the curious new vanity products for young men, from a *Maxim*-magazine-branded hair coloring system to Axe, Unilever's all-over body deodorant for guys. And men are going in for self-improvement strategies traditionally associated with women. For example, the number of plastic surgery procedures on men in the United States has increased threefold since 1997, to 807,000, according to the American Society for Aesthetic Plastic Surgery.

"Their heightened sense of aesthetics is very, very pronounced," Marian Salzman, chief strategy officer at Euro RSCG, who organized the gathering at Eleven Madison Park, said of metrosexuals. "They're the style makers. It doesn't mean your average Joe American is going to copy everything they do," she added. "But unless you study these guys you don't know where Joe American is heading."

Paradoxically, the term metrosexual, which is now being embraced by 5 marketers, was coined in the mid-90's to mock everything marketers stand for. The gay writer Mark Simpson used the word to satirize what he saw as consumerism's toll on traditional masculinity. Men didn't go to shopping malls, buy glossy magazines or load up on grooming products, Mr. Simpson argued, so consumer culture promoted the idea of a sensitive guy — who went to malls, bought magazines and spent freely to improve his personal appearance.

Within a few years, the term was picked up by British advertisers and newspapers. In 2001, Britain's Channel Four brought out a show about sensitive guys called *Metrosexuality*. And in recent years the European media found a metrosexual icon in David Beckham, the English soccer star, who paints his fingernails, braids his hair and poses for gay magazines, all while maintaining a manly profile on the pitch. Along with terms like "PoMosexual," "just gay enough" and "flaming heterosexuals," the word metrosexual is now gaining currency among American marketers who are fumbling for a term to describe this new type of feminized man.

America has a long tradition of sensitive guys. Alan Alda, John Lennon, even Al Gore all heard the arguments of the feminist movement and empathized. Likewise, there's a history of dashing men like Cary Grant and Humphrey Bogart who managed to affect a personal style with plenty of hair goop but without compromising their virility. Even Harrison Ford, whose favorite accessory was once a hammer, now poses proudly wearing an earring. But what separates the modern-day metrosexual from his touchy-feely forebears is a care-free attitude toward the inevitable suspicion that a man who dresses well, has good manners, understands thread counts or has opinions on women's fashion is gay.

"If someone's going to judge me on what kind of moisturizer I have on my shelf, whatever," said Marc d'Avignon, 28, a graduate student living in the East Village, who describes himself as "horrendously addicted to Diesel jeans" and living amid a chemistry lab's worth of Kiehl's lotions. "It doesn't bother me at all. Call it homosexual, feminine, hip, not hip — I don't care. I like drawing from all sorts of sources to create my own persona."

While some metrosexuals may simply be indulging in pursuits they had avoided for fear of being suspected as gay — like getting a pedicure or wearing brighter colors — others consciously appropriate tropes of gay culture the way white suburban teenagers have long cribbed from hip-hop culture, as a way of distinguishing themselves from the pack. Having others question their sexuality is all part of the game. "Wanting them to wonder and having them wonder is a wonderful thing," said Daniel Peres, the editor in chief of *Details*, a kind of metrosexual bible. "It gives you an air of mystery: could he be? It makes you stand out."

Standing out requires staying on top of which products are hip and which   10
are not. Marketers refer to such style-obsessed shoppers as prosumers, or urban influentials — educated customers who are picky or just vain enough to spend more money or to make an extra effort in pursuit of their personal look. A man who wants to buy Clinique for Men, for example, has to want the stuff so badly that he will walk up to the women's cosmetics counter in a department store, where Clinique for Men is sold. A man who wants Diesel jeans has to be willing to pay $135 a pair. A man who insists on Grey Goose has to get comfortable with paying $14 for a martini. "The guy who drinks Grey Goose is willing to pay extra," said Lee Einsidler, executive vice president of Sydney Frank Importing, which owns Grey Goose. "He does it in all things in his life. He doesn't buy green beans, he buys haricots verts."

Other retailers hope to entice the man on the fence to get in touch with his metrosexual side. Oliver Sweatman, the chief executive of Sharps, a new line of grooming products aimed at young urban men, said that to lure manly men to buy his new-age shaving gels — which contain Roman chamomile, gotu kola and green tea — the packaging is a careful mixture of old and new imagery. The fonts recall the masculinity of an old barber shop, but a funny picture of a goat on the label implies, he said, something out of the ordinary.

In an effort to out closeted metrosexuals, Ms. Salzman and her marketing team at Euro RSCG are working at perfecting polling methods that will identify "metrosexual markers." One, she noted, is that metrosexuals like telling their friends about their new finds. Mr. Martinson, the Bruno Magli–wearing metrosexual, agreed. "I'm not in marketing," he said. "But when you take a step back, and say, 'Hey, I e-mailed my friends about a great vodka or a great Off Broadway show,' in essence I am a marketer and I'm doing it for free."

Most metrosexuals, though, see their approach to life as serving their own interests in the most important marketing contest of all: the battle for babes. Their pitch to women: you're getting the best of both worlds.

Some women seem to buy it. Alycia Oaklander, a 29-year-old fashion publicist from Manhattan, fell for John Kilpatrick, a Washington Redskins season ticket holder who loves Budweiser and grilling hot dogs, in part because of his passion for shopping and women's fashion shows. On their first dates, Mr. Kilpatrick brought champagne, cooked elaborate meals and talked the talk about Ms. Oaklander's shoes. They were married yesterday. "He loves sports and all the guy stuff," Ms. Oaklander said. "But on the other hand he loves to cook and he loves design. It balances out."

The proliferation of metrosexuals is even having an impact in gay circles. 15
Peter Paige, a gay actor who plays the character Emmett on the Showtime series *Queer as Folk*, frequently complains in interviews that he's having a harder time than ever telling straight men from gays. "They're all low-slung jeans and working out with six packs and more hair product than I've ever used in my life, and they smell better than your mother on Easter," he said. Mr. Paige said there was at least one significant difference between hitting on metrosexuals and their less evolved predecessors. "Before, you used to get punched," he said. "Now it's all, 'Gee thanks, I'm straight but I'm really flattered.'"

READING THE TEXT

1. Write your own definition of the term *metrosexual*.
2. Summarize the typical buying habits that marketers ascribe to metrosexuals.
3. How, according to St. John, do metrosexuals compare with such "sensitive" men as Alan Alda and John Lennon (para. 7)?
4. In St. John's view, how do women and gay men typically view metrosexuals?

READING THE SIGNS

1. Analyze an issue of the magazine *Details*, studying both the advertising and the articles. To what extent does it fit St. John's description as "a kind of metrosexual bible" (para. 9)?
2. Write an essay in which you support, refute, or complicate St. John's claim that "America may be on the verge of a metrosexual moment" (para. 3). To support your position, study men's magazines or the advertising that accompanies TV programs with substantial male viewership; you might research as well grooming products available in drug or department stores and the strategies used to market them.
3. Read or review Nell Bernstein's "Goin' Gangsta, Choosin' Cholita" (p. 604), and write an essay in which you assess the phenomenon of "trying on" a different identity, whether it be ethnic, as in Bernstein's essay, or gender, as St. John discusses. What explanation can you give for its popularity?
4. Read or review James B. Twitchell's "What We Are to Advertisers" (p. 203). Where in the "psychographic" "VALS2+" system would you locate metrosexuals, and why? If you do not see this group fitting in this system, how would you alter the system to include metrosexuals?

ERIC SCHLOSSER
Kid Kustomers

Children rarely have much money of their own to spend, but they have a great deal of "pester power," along with the "leverage" to get their parents to buy them what they want. And so, as Eric Schlosser reports in this reading, Madison Avenue has been paying a great deal of attention to "kid kustomers" in recent years, pitching them everything from toys and candy to cell phones and automobiles. With more and more working couples spending more money on their kids to compensate for spending less time with them, Schlosser suggests, we are likely to see only an increase in such advertising in the years to come. Hmmm . . . are preteen dating services next? A correspondent for The Atlantic, *Schlosser is the author of* Fast Food Nation *(2001), from which this selection is taken, and* Reefer Madness: Sex, Drugs, and Cheap Labor in the American Black Market *(2003).*

Twenty-five years ago, only a handful of American companies directed their marketing at children — Disney, McDonald's, candy makers, toy makers, manufacturers of breakfast cereal. Today children are being targeted by phone companies, oil companies, and automobile companies as well as clothing stores and restaurant chains. The explosion in children's advertising occurred during the 1980s. Many working parents, feeling guilty about spending less time with their kids, started spending more money on them. One marketing expert has called the 1980s "the decade of the child consumer." After largely ignoring children for years, Madison Avenue began to scrutinize and pursue them. Major ad agencies now have children's divisions, and a variety of marketing firms focus solely on kids. These groups tend to have sweet-sounding names: Small Talk, Kid Connection, Kid2Kid, the Gepetto Group, Just Kids, Inc. At least three industry publications — *Youth Market Alert, Selling to Kids*, and *Marketing to Kids Report* — cover the latest ad campaigns and market research. The growth in children's advertising has been driven by efforts to increase not just current, but also future, consumption. Hoping that nostalgic childhood memories of a brand will lead to a lifetime of purchases, companies now plan "cradle-to-grave" advertising strategies. They have come to believe what Ray Kroc and Walt Disney realized long ago — a person's "brand loyalty" may begin as early as the age of two. Indeed, market research has found that children often recognize a brand logo before they can recognize their own name.

The discontinued Joe Camel ad campaign, which used a hip cartoon character to sell cigarettes, showed how easily children can be influenced by the right corporate mascot. A 1991 study published in the *Journal of the American*

Medical Association found that nearly all of America's six-year-olds could identify Joe Camel, who was just as familiar to them as Mickey Mouse. Another study found that one-third of the cigarettes illegally sold to minors were Camels. More recently, a marketing firm conducted a survey in shopping malls across the country, asking children to describe their favorite TV ads. According to the CME KidCom Ad Traction Study II, released at the 1999 Kids' Marketing Conference in San Antonio, Texas, the Taco Bell commercials featuring a talking chihuahua were the most popular fast food ads. The kids in the survey also like Pepsi and Nike commercials, but their favorite television ad was for Budweiser.

The bulk of the advertising directed at children today has an immediate goal. "It's not just getting kids to whine," one marketer explained in *Selling to Kids*, "it's giving them a specific reason to ask for the product." Years ago sociologist Vance Packard described children as "surrogate salesmen" who had to persuade other people, usually their parents, to buy what they wanted. Marketers now use different terms to explain the intended response to their ads — such as "leverage," "the nudge factor," "pester power." The aim of most children's advertising is straightforward: Get kids to nag their parents and nag them well.

James U. McNeal, a professor of marketing at Texas A&M University, is considered America's leading authority on marketing to children. In his book *Kids As Customers* (1992), McNeal provides marketers with a thorough analysis of "children's requesting styles and appeals." He classifies juvenile nagging tactics into seven major categories. A *pleading* nag is one accompanied by repetitions of words like "please" or "mom, mom, mom." A *persistent* nag involves constant requests for the coveted product and may include the phrase "I'm gonna ask just one more time." *Forceful* nags are extremely pushy and

Do Frosted Flakes plus Yoda equal a "sugar-coated nag"?

may include subtle threats, like "Well, then, I'll go and ask Dad." *Demonstrative* nags are the most high-risk, often characterized by full-blown tantrums in public places, breath-holding, tears, a refusal to leave the store. *Sugar-coated* nags promise affection in return for a purchase and may rely on seemingly heartfelt declarations like "You're the best dad in the world." *Threatening* nags are youthful forms of blackmail, vows of eternal hatred and of running away if something isn't bought. *Pity* nags claim the child will be heartbroken, teased, or socially stunted if the parent refuses to buy a certain item. "All of these appeals and styles may be used in combination," McNeal's research has discovered, "but kids tend to stick to one or two of each that proved most effective . . . for their own parents."

McNeal never advocates turning children into screaming, breath-holding   5
monsters. He has been studying "Kid Kustomers" for more than thirty years and believes in a more traditional marketing approach. "The key is getting children to see a firm . . . in much the same way as [they see] mom or dad, grandma or grandpa," McNeal argues. "Likewise, if a company can ally itself with universal values such as patriotism, national defense, and good health, it is likely to nurture belief in it among children."

Before trying to affect children's behavior, advertisers have to learn about their tastes. Today's market researchers not only conduct surveys of children in shopping malls, they also organize focus groups for kids as young as two or three. They analyze children's artwork, hire children to run focus groups, stage slumber parties and then question children into the night. They send cultural anthropologists into homes, stores, fast food restaurants, and other places where kids like to gather, quietly and surreptitiously observing the behavior of prospective customers. They study the academic literature on child development, seeking insights from the work of theorists such as Erik Erikson and Jean Piaget. They study the fantasy lives of young children, they apply the findings in advertisements and product designs.

Dan S. Acuff — the president of Youth Market System Consulting and the author of *What Kids Buy and Why* (1997) — stresses the importance of dream research. Studies suggest that until the age of six, roughly 80 percent of children's dreams are about animals. Rounded, soft creatures like Barney, Disney's animated characters, and the Teletubbies therefore have an obvious appeal to young children. The Character Lab, a division of Youth Market System Consulting, uses a proprietary technique called Character Appeal Quadrant Analysis to help companies develop new mascots. The technique purports to create imaginary characters who perfectly fit the targeted age group's level of cognitive and neurological development.

Children's clubs have for years been considered an effective means of targeting ads and collecting demographic information; the clubs appeal to a child's fundamental need for status and belonging. Disney's Mickey Mouse Club, formed in 1930, was one of the trailblazers. During the 1980s and 1990s, children's clubs proliferated, as corporations used them to solicit the names, addresses, zip codes, and personal comments of young customers.

"Marketing messages sent through a club not only can be personalized," James McNeal advises, "they can be tailored for a certain age or geographical group." A well-designed and well-run children's club can be extremely good for business. According to one Burger King executive, the creation of a Burger King Kids Club in 1991 increased the sales of children's meals as much as 300 percent.

The Internet has become another powerful tool for assembling data about children. In 1998 a federal investigation of Web sites aimed at children found that 89 percent requested personal information from kids; only 1 percent required that children obtain parental approval before supplying the information. A character on the McDonald's Web site told children that Ronald McDonald was "the ultimate authority in everything." The site encouraged kids to send Ronald an e-mail revealing their favorite menu item at McDonald's, their favorite book, their favorite sports team — and their name. Fast food Web sites no longer ask children to provide personal information without first gaining parental approval; to do so is now a violation of federal law, thanks to the Children's Online Privacy Protection Act, which took effect in April of 2000.

Despite the growing importance of the Internet, television remains the 10 primary medium for children's advertising. The effects of these TV ads have long been a subject of controversy. In 1978, the Federal Trade Commission (FTC) tried to ban all television ads directed at children seven years old or younger. Many studies had found that young children often could not tell the difference between television programming and television advertising. They also could not comprehend the real purpose of commercials and trusted that advertising claims were true. Michael Pertschuk, the head of the FTC, argued that children need to be shielded from advertising that preys upon their immaturity. "They cannot protect themselves," he said, "against adults who exploit their present-mindedness."

The FTC's proposed ban was supported by the American Academy of Pediatrics, the National Congress of Parents and Teachers, the Consumers Union, and the Child Welfare League, among others. But it was attacked by the National Association of Broadcasters, the Toy Manufacturers of America, and the Association of National Advertisers. The industry groups lobbied Congress to prevent any restrictions on children's ads and sued in federal court to block Pertschuk from participating in future FTC meetings on the subject. In April of 1981, three months after the inauguration of President Ronald Reagan, an FTC staff report argued that a ban on ads aimed at children would be impractical, effectively killing the proposal. "We are delighted by the FTC's reasonable recommendation," said the head of the National Association of Broadcasters.

The Saturday-morning children's ads that caused angry debates twenty years ago now seem almost quaint. Far from being banned, TV advertising aimed at kids is now broadcast twenty-four hours a day, closed-captioned and in stereo. Nickelodeon, the Disney Channel, the Cartoon Network, and the other children's cable networks are now responsible for about 80 percent of all television viewing by kids. None of these networks existed before 1979. The typical American child now spends about twenty-one hours a week watching television — roughly one and a half months of TV every year. That does not include the time children spend in front of a screen watching videos, playing video games, or using the computer. Outside of school, the typical American child spends more time watching television than doing any other activity except sleeping. During the course of a year, he or she watches more than thirty thousand TV commercials. Even the nation's youngest children are watching a great deal of television. About one-quarter of American children between the ages of two and five have a TV in their room.

READING THE TEXT

1. Why, according to Schlosser, did an "explosion in children's advertising" (para. 1) occur during the 1980s?
2. What is "pester power" (para. 3), and how is it used as a marketing strategy?
3. How has the Internet contributed to the expansion in advertising directed toward children, according to Schlosser?
4. What strategies does Schlosser say marketers use to determine children's tastes in products?

READING THE SIGNS

1. Watch a morning of Saturday cartoon shows on TV, and make a list of all the products that are advertised. What products are directly tied in to the show? Use your observations as the basis for an essay in which you analyze the relationship between children's programming and the advertising that supports it.
2. Perform a semiotic analysis of an advertisement from any medium directed at children. What signifiers in the ad are especially addressed to children? Consider such details as the implied narrative of the ad, its characters and their appearance, colors, music, and voice track.
3. Conduct an in-class debate over whether children's advertising should be more strictly regulated. To develop support for your team's position, watch some TV programs aimed at children and the advertising that accompanies them.
4. Read or review James Twitchell's "What We Are to Advertisers" (p. 203), and write an essay in which you analyze whether Twitchell's assertion that "mass marketing means the creation of mass stereotypes" (para. 1) applies to child consumers.

GLORIA STEINEM
Sex, Lies, and Advertising

One of the best-known icons of the women's movement, Gloria Steinem (b. 1934) has been a leader in transforming the image of women in America. As a cofounder of Ms. *magazine, in which this selection first appeared, Steinem has provided a forum for women's voices for more than thirty years, but as her article explains, it has not been easy to keep this forum going. A commercial publication requires commercials, and the needs of advertisers do not always mesh nicely with the goals of a magazine like* Ms. *Steinem ruefully reveals the compromises* Ms. *magazine had to make over the years to satisfy its advertising clients, compromises that came to an end only when* Ms. *ceased to take ads. Steinem's publications include* Revolution from Within *(1992), a personal exploration of the power of self-esteem;* Moving Beyond Words *(1994); and* Outrageous Acts and Everyday Rebellions *(2nd ed., 1995). Currently the president of Voters for Choice and a consulting editor for* Ms., *Steinem continues to combine her passion for writing and activism as an unflagging voice in American feminism.*

Goodbye to cigarette ads where poems should be.
Goodbye to celebrity covers and too little space.
Goodbye to cleaning up language so *Ms.* advertisers won't be boycotted by
    the Moral Majority.
In fact, goodbye to advertisers *and* the Moral Majority.
Goodbye to short articles and short thinking.
Goodbye to "post-feminism" from people who never say "post-
    democracy."
Goodbye to national boundaries and hello to the world.
Welcome to the magazine of the post-patriarchal age.
The turn of the century is *our turn!*

That was my celebratory mood in the summer of 1990 when I finished the original version of the exposé you are about to read. I felt as if I'd been released from a personal, portable Bastille. At least I'd put on paper the ad policies that had been punishing *Ms.* for all the years of its nonconforming life and still were turning more conventional media, especially (but not only) those directed at women, into a dumping ground for fluff.

    Those goodbyes were part of a letter inviting readers to try a new, ad-free version of *Ms.* and were also a homage to "Goodbye to All That," a witty and lethal essay in which Robin Morgan bade farewell to the pre-feminist male Left of twenty years before. It seemed the right tone for the birth of a brand-new, reader-supported, more international form of *Ms.*, which Robin was heading as editor-in-chief, and I was serving as consulting editor. Besides,

I had a very personal kind of mantra running through my head: *I'll never have to sell another ad as long as I live.*

So I sent the letter off, watched the premiere issue containing my exposé go to press, and then began to have second thoughts: Were ad policies too much of an "inside" concern? Did women readers already know that magazines directed at them were filled with editorial extensions of ads — and not care? Had this deceptive system been in place too long for anyone to have faith in changing it? In other words: Would anybody give a damn?

After almost four years of listening to responses and watching the ripples spread out from this pebble cast upon the waters, I can tell you that, yes, readers do care; and no, most of them were not aware of advertising's control over the words and images around it. Though most people in the publishing industry think this is a practice too deeply embedded ever to be uprooted, a lot of readers are willing to give it a try — even though that's likely to mean paying more for their publications. In any case, as they point out, understanding the nitty-gritty of ad influence has two immediate uses. It strengthens healthy skepticism about what we read, and it keeps us from assuming that other women must want this glamorous, saccharine, unrealistic stuff.

Perhaps that's the worst punishment ad influence has inflicted upon us.   5
It's made us feel contemptuous of other women. We know we don't need those endless little editorial diagrams of where to put our lipstick or blush — we don't identify with all those airbrushed photos of skeletal women with everything about them credited, *even their perfume* (can you imagine a man's photo airbrushed to perfection, with his shaving lotion credited?) — but we assume there must be women out there somewhere who *do* love it; otherwise, why would it be there?

Well, many don't. Given the sameness of women's magazines resulting from the demands made by makers of women's products that advertise in all of them, we probably don't know yet what a wide variety of women readers want. In any case, we do know it's the advertisers who are determining what women are getting now.

The first wave of response to this exposé came not from readers but from writers and editors for other women's magazines. They phoned to say the pall cast by anticipated or real advertising demands was even more widespread than rebellious *Ms.* had been allowed to know. They told me how brave I was to "burn my bridges" (no critic of advertising would ever be hired as an editor of any of the women's magazines, they said) and generally treated me as if I'd written about organized crime instead of practices that may be unethical but are perfectly legal. After making me promise not to use their names, they offered enough additional horror stories to fill a book, a movie, and maybe a television series. Here is a typical one: when the freelance author of an article on moisturizers observed in print that such products might be less necessary for young women — whose skin tends to be not dry but oily — the article's editor was called on the carpet and denounced by her bosses as "anti-moisturizer." Or how about this: the film critic for a women's magazine asked its top editor, a woman who makes millions for her parent company, whether movies could finally be reviewed critically, since she had so much clout. No, said the editor; if you can't praise a movie, just don't include it; otherwise we'll jeopardize our movie ads. This may sound like surrealism in everyday life, or like our grandmothers advising, "If you can't say something nice, don't say anything," but such are the forces that control much of our information.

I got few negative responses from insiders, but the ones I did get were bitter. Two editors at women's magazines felt I had demeaned them by writing the article. They loved their work, they said, and didn't feel restricted by ads at all. So I would like to make clear in advance that my purpose was and is to change the system, not to blame the people struggling within it. As someone who has written for most women's magazines, I know that many editors work hard to get worthwhile articles into the few pages left over after providing all the "complementary copy" (that is, articles related to and supportive of advertised products). I also know there are editors who sincerely want exactly what the advertisers want, which is why they're so good at their jobs. Nonetheless, criticizing this ad-dominant system is no different from criticizing male-dominant marriage. Both institutions make some people happy, and both seem free as long as your wishes happen to fall within their traditional boundaries. But just as making more equal marital laws alleviates the suffering of many, breaking the link between editorial and advertising will help all media become more honest and diverse.

A second wave of reaction came from advertising executives who were asked to respond by reporters. They attributed all problems to *Ms.* We must have been too controversial or otherwise inappropriate for ads. I saw no stories that asked the next questions: Why had non-women's companies from Johnson & Johnson to IBM found our "controversial" pages fine for their ads? Why did desirable and otherwise unreachable customers read something so "inappropriate"? What were ad policies doing to *other* women's media? To continue my marriage parallel, however, I should note that these executives seemed only mildly annoyed. Just as many women are more dependent than men on the institution of marriage and so are more threatened and angry when it's questioned, editors of women's magazines tended to be more upset than advertisers when questioned about their alliance. . . .

Then came the third wave — reader letters which were smart, thoughtful, 10 innovative, and numbered in the hundreds. Their dominant themes were anger and relief: relief because those vast uncritical oceans of food/fashion/ beauty articles in other women's magazines weren't necessarily what women wanted after all, and also relief because *Ms.* wasn't going to take ads anymore, even those that were accompanied by fewer editorial demands; anger because consumer information, diverse articles, essays, fiction, and poetry could have used the space instead of all those oceans of articles about ad categories that had taken up most of women's magazines for years. . . .

Last and most rewarding was the response that started in the fall. Teachers of journalism, advertising, communications, women's studies, and other contemporary courses asked permission to reprint the exposé as a supplementary text. That's another reason why I've restored cuts, updated information, and added new examples — including this introduction. Getting subversive ideas into classrooms could change the next generation running the media.

The following pages are mostly about women's magazines, but that doesn't mean other media are immune.

Sex, Lies, and Advertising

Toward the end of the 1980s, when glasnost was beginning and *Ms.* magazine seemed to be ending, I was invited to a press lunch for a Soviet official. He entertained us with anecdotes about the new problems of democracy in his country; for instance, local Communist leaders who were being criticized by their own media for the first time, and were angry.

"So I'll have to ask my American friends," he finished pointedly, "how more subtly to control the press."

In the silence that followed, I said: "Advertising." 15

The reporters laughed, but later one of them took me aside angrily: How dare I suggest that freedom of the press was limited in this country? How dare I imply that *his* newsmagazine could be influenced by ads?

I explained that I wasn't trying to lay blame, but to point out advertising's media-wide influence. We can all recite examples of "soft" cover stories that newsmagazines use to sell ads, and self-censorship in articles that should have taken advertised products to task for, say, safety or pollution. Even television news goes "soft" in ratings wars, and other TV shows don't get on the air without advertiser support. But I really had been thinking about women's magazines. There, it isn't just a little content that's designed to attract ads; it's almost all of it. That's why advertisers — not readers — had always been the problem for *Ms.* As the only women's magazine that didn't offer what the ad world euphemistically describes as "supportive editorial atmosphere" or "complementary copy" (for instance, articles that praise food/fashion/beauty subjects in order to "support" and "complement" food/fashion/beauty ads), *Ms.* could never attract enough ads to break even.

"Oh, *women's* magazines," the journalist said with contempt. "Everybody knows they're catalogs — but who cares? They have nothing to do with journalism."

I can't tell you how many times I've had this argument since I started writing for magazines in the early 1960s, and especially since the current women's movement began. Except as moneymaking machines — "cash cows," as they are so elegantly called in the trade — women's magazines are usually placed beyond the realm of serious consideration. Though societal changes being forged by women have been called more far-reaching than the industrial revolution by such nonfeminist sources as the *Wall Street Journal* — and though women's magazine editors often try hard to reflect these changes in the few pages left after all the ad-related subjects are covered — the magazines serving the female half of this country are still far below the journalistic and ethical standards of news and general-interest counterparts. Most depressing of all, this fact is so taken for granted that it doesn't even rate an exposé.

For instance: If *Time* and *Newsweek*, in order to get automotive and GM 20 ads, had to lavish editorial praise on cars and credit photographs in which newsmakers were driving, say, a Buick from General Motors, there would be a scandal — maybe even a criminal investigation. When women's magazines from *Seventeen* to *Lear's* publish articles lavishing praise on beauty and fashion products, and credit in text, the cover, and other supposedly editorial photographs a particular makeup from Revlon or a dress from Calvin Klein because those companies also advertise, it's just business as usual.

When *Ms.* began, we didn't consider *not* taking ads. The most important reason was to keep the price of a feminist magazine low enough for most women to afford. But the second and almost equal reason was to provide a forum where women and advertisers could talk to each other and experiment with nonstereotyped, informative, imaginative ads. After all, advertising was (and is) as potent a source of information in this country as news or TV or movies. It's where we get not only a big part of our information but also images that shape our dreams.

We decided to proceed in two stages. First, we would convince makers of "people products" that their ads should be placed in a women's magazine: cars, credit cards, insurance, sound equipment, financial services — everything that's used by both men and women but was then advertised only to men. Since those advertisers were accustomed to the division between editorial pages and ads that news and general-interest magazines at least try to maintain, such products would allow our editorial content to be free and diverse. Furthermore, if *Ms.* could prove that women were important purchasers of "people products," just as men were, those advertisers would support other women's magazines, too, and subsidize some pages for articles about something other than the hothouse worlds of food/fashion/beauty. Only in the second phase would we add examples of the best ads for whatever traditional "women's products" (clothes, shampoo, fragrance, food, and so on) that subscriber surveys showed *Ms.* readers actually used. But we would ask those advertisers to come in *without* the usual quid pro quo of editorial features praising their product area; that is, the dreaded "complementary copy."

From the beginning, we knew the second step might be even harder than the first. Clothing advertisers like to be surrounded by editorial fashion spreads (preferably ones that credit their particular labels and designers); food advertisers have always expected women's magazines to publish recipes and articles on entertaining (preferably ones that require their products); and shampoo, fragrance, and beauty products in general insist on positive editorial coverage of beauty aids — a "beauty atmosphere," as they put it — plus photo credits for particular products and nothing too depressing; no bad news. That's why women's magazines look the way they do: saccharine, smiley-faced and product-heavy, with even serious articles presented in a slick and sanitized way.

But if *Ms.* could break this link between ads and editorial content, then we should add "women's products" too. For one thing, publishing ads only for gender-neutral products would give the impression that women have to become "like men" in order to succeed (an impression that *Ms.* ad pages sometimes *did* give when we were still in the first stage). For another, presenting a full circle of products that readers actually need and use would allow us to select the best examples of each category and keep ads from being lost in a sea of similar products. By being part of this realistic but unprecedented mix, products formerly advertised only to men would reach a growth market of women, and good ads for women's products would have a new visibility.

Given the intelligence and leadership of *Ms.* readers, both kinds of products 25 would have unique access to a universe of smart consultants whose response would help them create more effective ads for other media too. Aside from the advertisers themselves, there's nobody who cares as much about the imagery in advertising as those who find themselves stereotyped or rendered invisible by it. And they often have great suggestions for making it better.

As you can see, we had all our energy, optimism, and arguments in good working order.

I thought at the time that our main problem would be getting ads with good "creative," as the imagery and text are collectively known. That was where the women's movement had been focusing its efforts, for instance, the National Organization for Women's awards to the best ads, and its "Barefoot and Pregnant" awards for the worst. Needless to say, there were plenty of candidates for the second group. Carmakers were still draping blondes in evening gowns over the hoods like ornaments that could be bought with the car (thus also making clear that car ads weren't directed at women). Even in ads for products that only women used, the authority figures were almost always male, and voice-overs for women's products on television were usually male too. Sadistic, he-man campaigns were winning industry praise; for example, *Advertising Age* hailed the infamous Silva Thin cigarette theme, "How to Get a Woman's Attention: Ignore Her," as "brilliant." Even in medical journals, ads for tranquilizers showed depressed housewives standing next to piles of dirty dishes and promised to get them back to work. As for women's magazines, they seemed to have few guidelines; at least none that excluded even the ads for the fraudulent breast-enlargement or thigh-thinning products for which their back pages were famous.

Obviously, *Ms.* would have to avoid such offensive imagery and seek out the best ads, but this didn't seem impossible. The *New Yorker* had been screening ads for aesthetic reasons for years, a practice that advertisers accepted at the time. *Ebony* and *Essence* were asking for ads with positive black images, and though their struggle was hard, their requests weren't seen as unreasonable. . . .

Let me take you through some of our experiences — greatly condensed, but just as they happened. In fact, if you poured water on any one of these, it would become a novel:

- Cheered on by early support from Volkswagen and one or two other car 30 companies, we finally scrape together time and money to put on a major reception in Detroit. U.S. carmakers firmly believe that women choose the upholstery color, not the car, but we are armed with statistics and reader mail to prove the contrary: A car is an important purchase for women, one that is such a symbol of mobility and freedom that many women will spend a greater percentage of income for a car than will counterpart men.

But almost nobody comes. We are left with many pounds of shrimp on the table, and quite a lot of egg on our face. Assuming this near-total boycott is partly because there was a baseball pennant play-off the same day, we blame ourselves for not foreseeing the problem. Executives go out of their way to explain that they wouldn't have come anyway. It's a dramatic beginning for ten years of knocking on resistant or hostile doors, presenting endless documentation of women as car buyers, and hiring a full-time saleswoman in Detroit — all necessary before *Ms.* gets any real results.

This long saga has a semi-happy ending: Foreign carmakers understood better than Detroit that women buy cars, and advertised in *Ms.*; also years of research on the women's market plus door-knocking began to pay off. Eventually, cars became one of our top sources of ad revenue. Even Detroit began to take the women's market seriously enough to put car ads in other women's magazines too, thus freeing a few more of their pages from the food/fashion/beauty hothouse.

But long after figures showed that a third, even half, of many car models were being bought by women, U.S. makers continued to be uncomfortable addressing female buyers. Unlike many foreign carmakers, Detroit never quite learned the secret of creating intelligent ads that exclude no one and then placing them in media that overcome past exclusion. Just as an African American reader may feel more invited by a resort that placed an ad in *Ebony* or *Essence*, even though the same ad appeared in *Newsweek*, women of all races may need to see ads for cars, computers, and other historically "masculine" products in media that are clearly directed at them. Once inclusive ads are well placed, however, there's interest and even gratitude from women. *Ms.* readers were so delighted to be addressed as intelligent consumers by a routine Honda ad with text about rack-and-pinion steering, for example, that they sent fan mail. But even now, Detroit continues to ask: "Should we make special ads for women?" That's probably one reason why foreign cars still have a greater share of the women's market in the United States than of the men's.

• In the *Ms.* Gazette, we do a brief report on a congressional hearing into coal tar derivatives used in hair dyes that are absorbed through the skin and may be carcinogenic. This seems like news of importance: Newspapers and newsmagazines are reporting it too. But Clairol, a Bristol-Myers subsidiary that makes dozens of products, a few of which have just come into our pages as ads *without* the usual quid pro quo of articles on hair and beauty, is outraged. Not at newspapers or newsmagazines, just at us. It's bad enough that *Ms.* is the only women's magazine refusing to provide "supportive editorial" praising beauty products, but to criticize one of their product categories on top of it, however generically or even accurately — well, *that* is going too far.

We offer to publish a letter from Clairol telling its side of the story. In an 35
excess of solicitousness, we even put this letter in the Gazette, not in Letters to the Editors, where it belongs. Eventually, Clairol even changes its hair-coloring formula, apparently in response to those same hearings. But in spite of surveys that show *Ms.* readers to be active women who use more of almost everything Clairol makes than do the readers of other women's magazines, *Ms.* gets almost no ads for those dozens of products for the rest of its natural life.

• Women of color read *Ms.* in disproportionate numbers. This is a source of pride to *Ms.* staffers, who are also more racially representative than the editors of other women's magazines (which may include some beautiful black models but almost no black decisionmakers; Pat Carbine hired the first black editor at *McCall's,* but she left when Pat did). Nonetheless, the reality of *Ms.*'s staff and readership is obscured by ads filled with enough white women to make the casual reader assume *Ms.* is directed at only one part of the population, no matter what the editorial content is.

In fact, those few ads we are able to get that feature women of color — for instance, one made by Max Factor for *Essence* and *Ebony* that Linda Wachner gives us while she is president of Max Factor — are greeted with praise and relief by white readers, too, and make us feel that more inclusive ads should win out in the long run. But there are pathetically few such images. Advertising "creative" also excludes women who are not young, not thin, not conventionally pretty, well-to-do, able-bodied, or heterosexual — which is a hell of a lot of women.

• Our intrepid saleswomen set out early to attract ads for the product category known as consumer electronics: sound equipment, computers, calculators, VCRs, and the like. We know that *Ms.* readers are determined to be part of this technological revolution, not to be left out as women have been in the past. We also know from surveys that readers are buying this kind of stuff in numbers as high as those of readers of magazines like *Playboy* and the "male 18 to 34" market, prime targets of the industry. Moreover, unlike traditional women's products that our readers buy but don't want to read articles about, these are subjects they like to see demystified in our pages. There actually *is* a supportive editorial atmosphere.

"But women don't understand technology," say ad and electronics executives at the end of our presentations. "Maybe not," we respond, "but neither do men — and we all buy it."

"If women *do* buy it," counter the decisionmakers, "it's because they're 40 asking their husbands and boyfriends what to buy first." We produce letters from *Ms.* readers saying how turned off they are when salesmen say things like "Let me know when your husband can come in."

Then the argument turns to why there aren't more women's names sent back on warranties (those much-contested certificates promising repair or replacement if anything goes wrong). We explain that the husband's name may be on the warranty, even if the wife made the purchase. But it's also true that women are experienced enough as consumers to know that such promises are valid only if the item is returned in its original box at midnight in Hong Kong. Sure enough, when we check out hair dryers, curling irons, and other stuff women clearly buy, women don't return those warranties very often either. It isn't the women who are the problem, it's the meaningless warranties.

After several years of this, we get a few ads from companies like JVC and Pioneer for compact sound systems — on the grounds that women can understand compacts, but not sophisticated components. Harry Elias, vice president of JVC, is actually trying to convince his Japanese bosses that there is something called a woman's market. At his invitation, I find myself speaking at trade shows in Chicago and Las Vegas trying to persuade JVC dealers that electronics showrooms don't have to be locker rooms. But as becomes apparent, however, the trade shows are part of the problem. In Las Vegas, the only women working at technology displays are seminude models serving champagne. In Chicago, the big attraction is Marilyn Chambers, a porn star who followed Linda Lovelace of *Deep Throat* fame as Chuck Traynor's captive and/or employee, whose pornographic movies are being used to demonstrate VCRs.

In the end, we get ads for a car stereo now and then, but no VCRs; a welcome breakthrough of some IBM personal computers, but no Apple or no Japanese-made ones. Furthermore, we notice that *Working Woman* and *Savvy*, which are focused on office work, don't benefit as much as they should from ads for office equipment either. . . .

• Then there is the great toy train adventure. Because *Ms.* gets letters from little girls who love toy trains and ask our help in changing ads and box-top photos that show only little boys, we try to talk to Lionel and to get their ads. It turns out that Lionel executives *have* been concerned about little girls. They made a pink train and couldn't understand why it didn't sell.

Eventually, Lionel bows to this consumer pressure by switching to a pho- 45 tograph of a boy *and* a girl — but only on some box tops. If trains are associated with little girls, Lionel executives believe, they will be devalued in the eyes of little boys. Needless to say, *Ms.* gets no train ads. If even 20 percent of little girls wanted trains, they would be a huge growth market, but this remains unexplored. In the many toy stores where displays are still gender divided, the "soft" stuff, even modeling clay, stays on the girls' side, while the "hard" stuff, especially rockets and trains, is displayed for boys — thus depriving both. By 1986, Lionel is put up for sale.

We don't have much luck with other kinds of toys either. A *Ms.* department, Stories for Free Children, edited by Letty Cottin Pogrebin, makes us one of the very few magazines with a regular feature for children. A larger proportion of *Ms.* readers have preschool children than do the readers of any other women's magazine. Nonetheless, the industry can't seem to believe that feminists care about children — much less have them.

- When *Ms.* began, the staff decided not to accept ads for feminine hygiene sprays and cigarettes on the same basis: They are damaging to many women's health but carry no appropriate warnings. We don't think we should tell our readers what to do — if marijuana were legal, for instance, we would carry ads for it along with those for beer and wine — but we should provide facts so readers can decide for themselves. Since we've received letters saying that feminine sprays actually kill cockroaches and take the rust off metal, we give up on those. But antismoking groups have been pressuring for health warnings on cigarette ads as well as packages, so we decide we will accept advertising if the tobacco industry complies.

Philip Morris is among the first to do so. One of its brands, Virginia Slims, is also sponsoring women's tennis tournaments and women's public opinion polls that are historic "firsts." On the other hand, the Virginia Slims theme, "You've come a long way, baby," has more than a "baby" problem. It gives the impression that for women, smoking is a sign of progress.

We explain to the Philip Morris people that this slogan won't do well in our pages. They are convinced that its success with *some* women means it will work with *all* women. No amount of saying that we, like men, are a segmented market, that we don't all think alike, does any good. Finally, we agree to publish a small ad for a Virginia Slims calendar as a test, and to abide by the response of our readers.

The letters from readers are both critical and smart. For instance: 50 Would you show a photo of a black man picking cotton next to one of an African American man in a Cardin suit, and symbolize progress from slavery to civil rights by smoking? Of course not. So why do it for women? But instead of honoring test results, the executives seem angry to have been proved wrong. We refuse Virginia Slims ads, thus annoying tennis players like Billie Jean King as well as incurring a new level of wrath: Philip Morris takes away ads for *all* its many products, costing *Ms.* about $250,000 in the first year. After five years, the damage is so great we can no longer keep track.

Occasionally, a new set of Philip Morris executives listens to *Ms.* saleswomen, or laughs when Pat Carbine points out that even Nixon got pardoned. I also appeal directly to the chairman of the board, who agrees it is unfair, sends me to another executive — and *he* says no. Because we won't take

Virginia Slims, not one other Philip Morris product returns to our pages for the next sixteen years.

Gradually, we also realize our naïveté in thinking we could refuse all cigarette ads, with or without a health warning. They became a disproportionate source of revenue for print media the moment television banned them, and few magazines can compete or survive without them; certainly not *Ms.*, which lacks the support of so many other categories. Though cigarette ads actually inhibit editorial freedom less than ads for food, fashion, and the like — cigarette companies want only to be distant from coverage on the dangers of smoking, and don't require affirmative praise or photo credits of their product — it is still a growing source of sorrow that they are there at all. By the 1980s, when statistics show that women's rate of lung cancer is approaching men's, the necessity of taking cigarette ads has become a kind of prison.

Though I never manage to feel kindly toward groups that protest our ads and pay no attention to magazines and newspapers that can turn them down and still keep their doors open — and though *Ms.* continues to publish new facts about smoking, such as its dangers during pregnancy — I long for the demise of the whole tobacco-related industry. . . .

• General Mills, Pillsbury, Carnation, Del Monte, Dole, Kraft, Stouffer, Hormel, Nabisco: You name the food giant, we try to get its ads. But no matter how desirable the *Ms.* readership, our lack of editorial recipes and traditional homemaking articles proves lethal.

We explain that women flooding into the paid labor force have changed 55 the way this country eats; certainly, the boom in convenience foods proves that. We also explain that placing food ads *only* next to recipes and how-to-entertain articles is actually a negative for many women. It associates food with work — in a way that says only women have to cook — or with guilt over *not* cooking and entertaining. Why not advertise food in diverse media that don't always include recipes (thus reaching more men, who have become a third of all supermarket shoppers anyway) and add the recipe interest with specialty magazines like *Gourmet* (a third of whose readers are men)?

These arguments elicit intellectual interest but no ads. No advertising executive wants to be the first to say to a powerful client, "Guess what, I *didn't* get you complementary copy." Except for an occasional hard-won ad for instant coffee, diet drinks, yogurt, or such extras as avocados and almonds, the whole category of food, a mainstay of the publishing industry, remains unavailable to us. Period. . . .

• By the end of 1986, magazine production costs have skyrocketed and postal rates have increased 400 percent. Ad income is flat for the whole magazine industry. The result is more competition, with other magazines offering such "extras" as free golf trips for advertisers or programs for "sampling" their products at parties and other events arranged by the magazine for desirable consumers. We try to compete with the latter by "sampling" at what we certainly have enough of: movement benefits. Thus, little fragrance bottles turn up next to the dinner plates of California women lawyers (who are delighted), or wine samples lower the costs at a reception for political women. A good organizing tactic comes out of this. We hold feminist seminars in shopping centers. They may be to the women's movement what churches were to the civil rights movement in the South — that is, *where people are*. Anyway, shopping center seminars are a great success. Too great. We have to stop doing them in Bloomingdale's up and down the East Coast, because meeting space in the stores is too limited, and too many women are left lined up outside stores. We go on giving out fancy little liquor bottles at store openings, which makes the advertisers happy — but not us.

Mostly, however, we can't compete in this game of "value-added" (the code word for giving the advertisers extras in return for their ads). Neither can many of the other independent magazines. Deep-pocketed corporate parents can offer such extras as reduced rates for ad schedules in a group of magazines, free tie-in spots on radio stations they also own, or vacation junkets on corporate planes.

Meanwhile, higher costs and lowered income have caused the *Ms.* 60/40 preponderance of edit over ads — something we promised to readers — to become 50/50: still a lot better than most women's magazines' goals of 30/70, but not good enough. Children's stories, most poetry, and some fiction are casualties of reduced space. In order to get variety into more limited pages, the length (and sometimes the depth) of articles suffers. Though we don't solicit or accept ads that would look like a parody in our pages, we get so worn down that some slip through. Moreover, we always have the problem of working just as hard to get a single ad as another magazine might for a whole year's schedule of ads.

Still, readers keep right on performing miracles. Though we haven't been 60
able to afford a subscription mailing in two years, they maintain our guaranteed circulation of 450,000 by word of mouth. Some of them also help to make up the advertising deficit by giving *Ms.* a birthday present of $15 on its fifteen anniversary, or contributing $1,000 for a lifetime subscription — even those who can ill afford it.

What's almost as angering as these struggles, however, is the way the media report them. Our financial problems are attributed to lack of reader interest, not an advertising double standard. In the Reagan-Bush era, when "feminism-is-dead" becomes one key on the typewriter, our problems are used to prepare a grave for the whole movement. Clearly, the myth that advertisers go where the readers are — thus, if we had readers, we would have advertisers — is deeply embedded. Even industry reporters rarely mention the editorial demands made by ads for women's products, and if they do, they assume advertisers must be right and *Ms.* must be wrong; we must be too controversial, outrageous, even scatalogical to support. In fact, there's nothing in our pages that couldn't be published in *Time, Esquire,* or *Rolling Stone* — providing those magazines devoted major space to women — but the media myth often wins out. Though comparable magazines our size (say, *Vanity Fair* or the *Atlantic*) are losing more money in a single year than *Ms.* has lost in sixteen years, *Ms.* is held to a different standard. No matter how much never-to-be-recovered cash is poured into starting a magazine or keeping it going, appearances seem to be all that matter. (Which is why we haven't been able to explain our fragile state in public. Nothing causes ad flight like the smell of nonsuccess.)

My healthy response is anger, but my not-so-healthy one is depression, worry, and an obsession with finding one more rescue. There is hardly a night when I don't wake up with sweaty palms and pounding heart, scared that we won't be able to pay the printer or the post office; scared most of all that closing our doors will be blamed on a lack of readers and thus the movement, instead of the real cause. ("Feminism couldn't even support one magazine," I can hear them saying.)

We're all being flattened by a velvet steamroller. The only difference is that at *Ms.,* we keep standing up again.

Do you think, as I once did, that advertisers make decisions based on rational and uniform criteria? Well, think again. There is clearly a double standard. The same food companies that insist on recipes in women's magazines place ads in *People* where there are no recipes. Cosmetics companies support the *New Yorker*, which has no regular beauty columns, and newspaper pages that have no "beauty atmosphere."

Meanwhile, advertisers' control over the editorial content of women's 65 magazines has become so institutionalized that it is sometimes written into "insertion orders" or dictated to ad salespeople as official policy — whether by the agency, the client, or both. The following are orders given to women's magazines effective in 1990. Try to imagine them being applied to *Time* or *Newsweek.*

- Dow's Cleaning Products stipulated that ads for its Vivid and Spray 'n Wash products should be adjacent to "children or fashion editorial"; ads for Bathroom Cleaner should be next to "home furnishing/family" features; with similar requirements for other brands. "If a magazine fails for ½ the brands or more," the Dow order warned, "it will be omitted from further consideration."

- Bristol-Myers, the parent of Clairol, Windex, Drano, Bufferin, and much more, stipulated that ads be placed next to "a full page of compatible editorial."

- S. C. Johnson & Son, makers of Johnson Wax, lawn and laundry products, insect sprays, hair sprays, and so on, insisted that its ads "*should not be opposite extremely controversial features or material antithetical to the nature/copy of the advertised product.*" (Italics theirs.)

- Maidenform, manufacturer of bras and other women's apparel, left a blank for the particular product and stated in its instructions: "The creative concept of the _____ campaign, and the very nature of the product itself, appeal to the positive emotions of the reader/consumer. Therefore, it is imperative that all editorial adjacencies reflect that same positive tone. The editorial must not be negative in content or lend itself contrary to the _____ product imagery/message (e.g., *editorial relating to illness, disillusionment, large size fashion, etc.*)." (Italics mine.)

- The De Beers diamond company, a big seller of engagement rings, pro- 70 hibited magazines from placing its ads with "adjacencies to hard news or anti-love/romance themed editorial." . . .

- Kraft/General Foods, a giant with many brands, sent this message with an Instant Pudding ad: "urgently request upbeat parent/child activity editorial, mandatory positioning requirements — opposite full page of positive editorial — right hand page essential for creative — minimum 6 page competitive separation (i.e., all sugar based or sugar free gelatins, puddings, mousses, creames [sic] and pie filling) — Do not back with clippable material. Avoid: controversial/negative topics and any narrow targeted subjects."

- An American Tobacco Company order for a Misty Slims ad noted that the U.S. government warning must be included, but also that there must be: "no adjacency to editorial relating to health, medicine, religion, or death."

- Lorillard's Newport cigarette ad came with similar instructions, plus: "Please be aware that the Nicotine Patch products are competitors. The minimum six page separation is required."

Quite apart from anything else, you can imagine the logistical nightmare this creates when putting a women's magazine together, but the greatest casualty is editorial freedom. Though the ratio of advertising to editorial pages in women's magazines is only about 5 percent more than in *Time* or *Newsweek*, that nothing-to-read feeling comes from all the supposedly editorial pages that are extensions of ads. To find out what we're really getting when we pay our money, I picked up a variety of women's magazines for February 1994, and counted the number of pages in each one (even including table of contents, letters to the editors, horoscopes, and the like) that were not ads and/or copy complementary to ads. Then I compared that number to the total pages. Out of 184 pages, *McCall's* had 49 that were nonad or ad-related. Of 202, *Elle* gave readers 48. *Seventeen* provided its young readers with only 51 nonad or ad-related pages out of 226. *Vogue* had 62 out of 292. *Mirabella* offered readers 45 pages out of a total of 158. *Good Housekeeping* came out on top, though only at about a third, with 60 out of 176 pages. *Martha Stewart Living* offered the least. Even counting her letter to readers, a page devoted to her personal calendar, and another one to a turnip, only seven out of 136 pages had no ads, products, or product mentions. . . .

Within the supposedly editorial text itself, praise for advertisers' products 75 has become so ritualized that fields like "beauty writing" have been invented. One of its practitioners explained to me seriously that "It's a difficult art. How many new adjectives can you find? How much greater can you make a lipstick sound? The FDA restricts what companies can say on labels, but we create illusion. And ad agencies are on the phone all the time pushing you to get their product in. A lot of them keep the business based on how many editorial clippings they produce every month. The worst are products [whose manufacturers have] their own name involved. It's all ego."

Often, editorial becomes one giant ad. An issue of *Lear's* featured an elegant woman executive on the cover. On the contents page, we learn she is wearing Guerlain makeup and Samsara, a new fragrance by Guerlain. Inside, there just happen to be full-page ads for Samsara, plus a Guerlain antiwrinkle skin cream. In the article about the cover subject, we discover she is Guerlain's director of public relations and is responsible for launching, you guessed it, the new Samsara. . . .

When the *Columbia Journalism Review* cited this example in one of the few articles to include women's magazines in a critique of ad influence, Frances Lear, editor of *Lear's*, was quoted at first saying this was a mistake, and then shifting to the defense that "this kind of thing is done all the time."

She's right. Here's an example with a few more turns of the screw. Martha Stewart, *Family Circle*'s contributing editor, was also "lifestyle and entertaining consultant" for Kmart, the retail chain, which helped to underwrite the renovation of Stewart's country house, using Kmart products; *Family Circle* covered the process in three articles not marked as ads; Kmart bought $4 million worth of ad pages in *Family Circle*, including "advertorials" to introduce a line of Martha Stewart products to be distributed by Kmart; and finally, the "advertorials," which at least are marked and only *look* like editorial pages, were reproduced and distributed in Kmart stores, thus publicizing *Family Circle* (owned by the New York Times Company, which would be unlikely to do this kind of thing in its own news pages) to Kmart customers. This was so lucrative that Martha Stewart now has her own magazine, *Martha Stewart Living* (owned by Time Warner), complete with a television version. Both offer a happy world of cooking, entertaining, and decorating in which nothing critical or negative ever seems to happen.

I don't mean to be a spoilsport, but there are many articles we're very unlikely to get from that or any other women's magazine dependent on food ads. According to Senator Howard Metzenbaum of Ohio, more than half of the chickens we eat (from ConAgra, Tyson, Perdue, and other companies) are contaminated with dangerous bacteria; yet labels haven't yet begun to tell us to scrub the meat and everything it touches — which is our best chance of not getting sick. Nor are we likely to learn about the frequent working conditions of this mostly female work force, standing in water, cutting chickens apart with such repetitive speed that carpal tunnel syndrome is an occupational hazard. Then there's Dole Food, often cited as a company that keeps women in low-level jobs and a target of a lawsuit by Costa Rican workers who were sterilized by contact with pesticides used by Dole — even though Dole must have known these pesticides had been banned in the United States.

The consumerist reporting we're missing sometimes sounds familiar.   80
Remember the *Ms.* episode with Clairol and the article about potential car-
cinogens in hair dye? Well, a similar saga took place with L'Oréal and *Made-
moiselle* in 1992, according to an editor at Condé Nast. Now, editors there are
supposed to warn publishers of any criticism in advance, a requirement that
might well have a chilling effect.

Other penalties are increasing. As older readers will remember, women's
magazines used to be a place where new young poets and short story
writers could be published. Now, that's very rare. It isn't that advertisers of
women's products dislike poetry or fiction, it's just that they pay to be adjacent to articles and features more directly compatible with their products.

Sometimes, advertisers invade editorial pages — literally — by plunging
odd-shaped ads into the text, no matter how that increases the difficulty of
reading. When Ellen Levine was editor of *Woman's Day*, for instance, a magazine originally founded by a supermarket chain, she admitted, "The day the
copy had to rag around a chicken leg was not a happy one."

The question of ad positioning is also decided by important advertisers, a
rule that's ignored at a magazine's peril. When Revlon wasn't given the place of
the first beauty ad in one Hearst magazine, for instance, it pulled its ads from *all*
Hearst magazines. In 1990 Ruth Whitney, editor in chief of *Glamour*, attributed
some of this pushiness to "ad agencies wanting to prove to a client that they've
squeezed the last drop of blood out of a magazine." She was also "sick and tired
of hearing that women's magazines are controlled by cigarette ads." Relatively
speaking, she was right. To be as controlling as most advertisers of women's
products, tobacco companies would have to demand articles in flat-out praise of
smoking, and editorial photos of models smoking a credited brand. As it is, they
ask only to be forewarned so they don't advertise in the same issue with an
article about the dangers of smoking. But for a magazine like *Essence*, the only
national magazine for African American women, even taking them out of one
issue may be financially difficult, because other advertisers might neglect its
readers. In 1993, a group called Women and Girls Against Tobacco, funded by
the California Department of Health Services, prepared an ad headlined "Cigarettes Made Them History." It pictured three black singers — Mary Wells, Eddie
Kendricks, and Sarah Vaughan — who died of tobacco-related diseases. *Essence*
president Clarence Smith didn't turn the ad down, but he didn't accept it either.
When I talked with him in 1994, he said with pain, "the black female market
just isn't considered at parity with the white female market; there are too many
other categories we don't get." That's in spite of the fact that *Essence* does all
the traditional food-fashion-beauty editorial expected by advertisers. According
to California statistics, African American women are more addicted to smoking
than the female population at large, with all the attendant health problems.

Alexandra Penney, editor of *Self* magazine, feels she has been able to include smoking facts in health articles by warning cigarette advertisers in advance (though smoking is still being advertised in this fitness magazine). On
the other hand, up to this writing in 1994, no advertiser has been willing to

appear opposite a single-page feature called "Outrage," which is reserved for important controversies, and is very popular with readers. Another women's magazine publisher told me that to this day Campbell's Soup refuses to advertise because of an article that unfavorably compared the nutritional value of canned food to that of fresh food — fifteen years ago.

I don't mean to imply that the editors I quote here share my objections to   85
ad demands and/or expectations. Many assume that the women's magazines at which they work have to be the way they are. Others are justifiably proud of getting an independent article in under the advertising radar, for instance, articles on family violence in *Family Circle* or a series on child sexual abuse and the family courts in *McCall's*. A few insist they would publish exactly the same editorial, even if there were no ads. But it's also true that it's hard to be honest while you're still in the job. "Most of the pressure came in the form of direct product mentions," explained Sey Chassler, who was editor in chief of *Redbook* from the sixties to the eighties and is now out of the game. "We got threats from the big guys, the Revlons, blackmail threats. They wouldn't run ads unless we credited them."

What could women's magazines be like if they were as editorially free as good books? as realistic as the best newspaper articles? as creative as poetry and films? as diverse as women's lives? What if we as women — who are psychic immigrants in a public world rarely constructed by or for us — had the same kind of watchful, smart, supportive publications on our side that other immigrant groups have often had?

We'll find out only if we take the media directed at us seriously. If readers were to act in concert in large numbers for a few years to change the traditional practices of *all* women's magazines and the marketing of *all* women's products, we could do it. After all, they depend on our consumer dollars — money we now are more likely to control. If we include all the shopping we do for families and spouses, women make 85 percent of purchases at point of sale. You and I could:

- refuse to buy products whose ads have clearly dictated their surroundings, and write to tell the manufacturers why;

- write to editors and publishers (with copies to advertisers) to tell them that we're willing to pay *more* for magazines with editorial independence, but will *not* continue to pay for those that are editorial extensions of ads;

- write to advertisers (with copies to editors and publishers) to tell them that we want fiction, political reporting, consumer reporting, strong opinion, humor, and health coverage that doesn't pull punches, praising them when their ads support this, and criticizing them when they don't;

- put as much energy and protest into breaking advertising's control over what's around it as we put into changing the images within it or protesting harmful products like cigarettes;

- support only those women's magazines and products that take us seriously as readers and consumers;

- investigate new laws and regulations to support freedom from advertising influence. The Center for the Study of Commercialism, a group founded in 1990 to educate and advocate against "ubiquitous product marketing," recommends whistle-blower laws that protect any members of the media who disclose advertiser and other commercial conflicts of interest, laws that require advertiser influence to be disclosed, Federal Trade Commission involvement, and denial of income tax exemptions for advertising that isn't clearly identified — as well as conferences, citizen watchdog groups, and a national clearinghouse where examples of private censorship can be reported.

Those of us in the magazine world can also use this carrot-and-stick technique. The stick: If magazines were a regulated medium like television, the editorial quid pro quo demanded by advertising would be against the rules of the FCC, and payola and extortion would be penalized. As it is, there are potential illegalities to pursue. For example: A magazine's postal rates are determined by the ratio of ad pages to editorial pages, with the ads being charged at a higher rate than the editorial. Counting up all the pages that are *really* ads could make an interesting legal action. There could be consumer fraud cases lurking in subscriptions that are solicited for a magazine but deliver a catalog.

The carrot is just as important. In twenty years, for instance, I've found no independent, nonproprietary research showing that an ad for, say, fragrance is any more effective placed next to an article about fragrance than it would be when placed next to a good piece of fiction or reporting. As we've seen, there are studies showing that the greatest factor in determining an ad's effectiveness is the credibility and independence of its surroundings. An airtight wall between ads and edit would also shield corporations and agencies from pressures from both ends of the political spectrum and from dozens of pressure groups. Editors would be the only ones responsible for editorial content — which is exactly as it should be.

Unfortunately, few agencies or clients hear such arguments. Editors often 90 maintain the artificial purity of refusing to talk to the people who actually control their lives. Instead, advertisers see salespeople who know little about editorial, are trained in business as usual, and are usually paid on commission. To take on special controversy editors might also band together. That happened once when all the major women's magazines did articles in the same month on the Equal Rights Amendment. It could happen again — and regularly.

Meanwhile, we seem to have a system in which everybody is losing. The reader loses diversity, strong opinion, honest information, access to the arts, and much more. The editor loses pride of work, independence, and freedom from worry about what brand names or other critical words some sincere freelancer is going to come up with. The advertiser loses credibility right along with the ad's surroundings, and gets more and more lost in a sea of similar ads and interchangeable media.

But that's also the good news. Because where there is mutual interest, there is the beginning of change.

If you need one more motive for making it, consider the impact of U.S. media on the rest of the world. The ad policies we tolerate here are invading the lives of women in other cultures — through both the content of U.S. media and the ad practices of multinational corporations imposed on other countries. Look at our women's magazines. Is this what we want to export?

Should *Ms.* have started out with no advertising in the first place? The odd thing is that, in retrospect, I think the struggle was worth it. For all those years, dozens of feminist organizers disguised as *Ms.* ad saleswomen took their courage, research, slide shows, humor, ingenuity, and fresh point of view into every advertising agency, client office, and lion's den in cities where advertising is sold. Not only were sixteen years of *Ms.* sustained in this way, with all the changeful words on those thousands of pages, but some of the advertising industry was affected in its imagery, its practices, and its understanding of the female half of the country. Those dozens of women themselves were affected, for they learned the art of changing a structure from both within and without, and are now rising in crucial publishing positions where women have never been. *Ms.* also helped to open nontraditional categories of ads for women's magazines, thus giving them a little more freedom — not to mention making their changes look reasonable by comparison.

But the world of advertising has a way of reminding us how far there is 95 to go.

Three years ago, as I was finishing this exposé in its first version, I got a call from a writer for *Elle*. She was doing an article on where women parted their hair: Why, she wanted to know, did I part mine in the middle?

It was all so familiar. I could imagine this writer trying to make something out of a nothing assignment. A long-suffering editor laboring to think of new ways to attract ads for shampoo, conditioner, hairdryers, and the like. Readers assuming that other women must want this stuff.

As I was working on this version, I got a letter from Revlon of the sort we disregarded when we took ads. Now, I could appreciate it as a reminder of how much we had to disregard:

> We are delighted to confirm that Lauren Hutton is now under contract to Revlon.
>
> We are very much in favor of her appearing in as much editorial as possible, but it's important that your publication avoid any mention of competitive color cosmetics, beauty treatment, hair care or sun care products in editorial or editorial credits in which she appears.
>
> We would be very appreciative if all concerned are made aware of this.

I could imagine the whole chain of women — Lauren Hutton, preferring to be in the Africa that is her passion; the ad executive who signed the letter, only doing her job; the millions of women readers who would see the resulting artificial images; all of us missing sources of information, insight, creativity, humor, anger, investigation, poetry, confession, outrage, learning, and perhaps most important, a sense of connection to each other; and a gloriously diverse world being flattened by a velvet steamroller.

I ask you: Can't we do better than this?   100

READING THE TEXT

1. What does Steinem mean by "complementary copy" (para. 17) and "advertorial" (para. 78)?

2. Summarize the relationship Steinem sees between editorial content and advertising in women's magazines.

3. In Steinem's view, what messages about gender roles does complementary copy send readers of women's magazines?

4. What is the history of response to this article since its initial publication in 1990, according to Steinem?

READING THE SIGNS

1. Steinem asserts that virtually all content in women's magazines is a disguised form of advertising. Test her hypothesis by writing a detailed analysis of a single issue of a magazine such as *Cosmopolitan*, *Jane*, or *Elle*. Do you find instances of complementary copy and advertorials? How do you react as a potential reader of such a magazine?

2. Explore whether Steinem's argument holds for men's magazines such as *Maxim* or *GQ*. If you identify differences, how might they be based on different assumptions about gender roles?

3. Have each member of the class bring in a favorite magazine. In small groups, study the relationship between ads and articles. Which magazines have the most complementary copy? How can you account for your findings?

4. In your journal, explore whether you believe advertisers infringe on the freedom of the press.

Portfolio of Advertisements

READING THE SIGNS

Consider these questions as you analyze the advertisements on the following pages.

1. Study the gender roles that are implicit in the narrative depicted in the OnStar ad. Do you think the ad is intended to appeal to men, women, or both, and why?

2. Why do you think the Sub-Zero ad uses Danny Shanahan, a famous *New Yorker* cartoonist, to create an ad that resembles a *New Yorker* cartoon?

3. Wine advertisements commonly associate their product with romance or sophistication, but the Redwood Creek ad uses instead a nostalgic, retro design. How does that design work to attract consumers to this brand of wine? To whom does this advertisement most appeal?

4. The Phoenix Wealth Management ad clearly appeals to female consumers. Study the image of the models in the ad. What image of the target market is created in the ad, and to what attitudes toward gender roles and class is the ad appealing?

5. Do a semiotic interpretation of the Symantec ad, which promotes Internet security products. How do the details—the room's decor, the shopping bags, the model's appearance and her actions, even the company's name, bag design, and logo—create an image that potential new customers might find attractive?

6. As a tourist destination, Nevada is best known as the home of Las Vegas. How does this ad seek to expand Nevada's appeal without reducing the importance of Las Vegas on a travel itinerary? To what kind of tourist are the ad's images and copy addressed?

7. This ad for Cooper Tires presents a humorous pastiche of a typical country music performance. What knowledge of country music does this ad presuppose? How does this knowledge create the ad's humorous effect? And why does it feature a vintage microphone rather than a modern one?

Always the gentleman, Charles Willis opens the car door for his wife.

Even when she's 250 miles away.

Charles always opens the car door for his wife. Always. So when she locked her keys in her car 250 miles away from home, that didn't stop him. He simply called OnStar* to send a signal to unlock her doors,* proving that chivalry is indeed not dead. Make sure you're never without the valuable assistance of OnStar. If your current vehicle has OnStar, press the blue button to make sure your service is active. Visit your dealer or onstar.com to learn more.

by **GM**

visit onstar.com

The first year of service is included on all new OnStar-equipped vehicles.

CHEVROLET • BUICK • PONTIAC • GMC • Cadillac • HUMMER • SAAB • SATURN

"A longer, healthier life? I'm prescribing Sub-Zero."

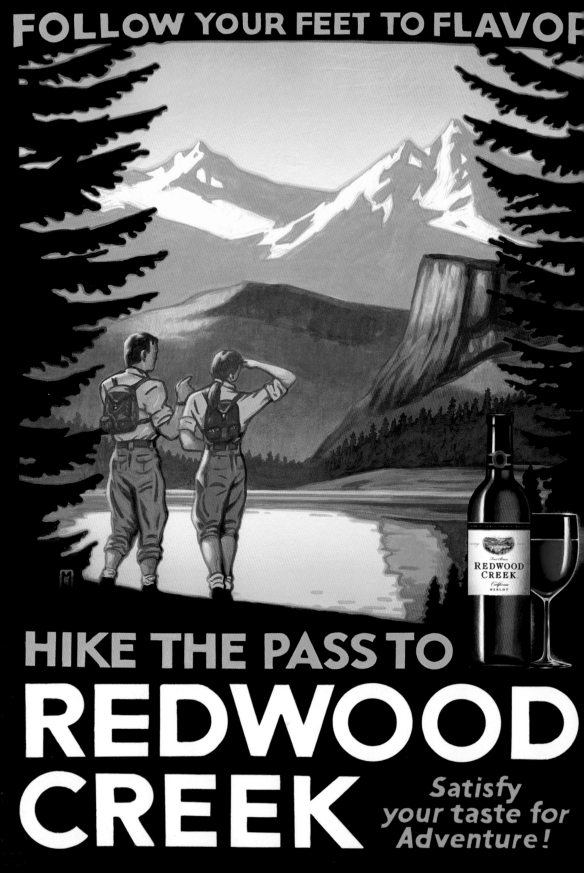

Gives her broker investment ideas.

Is taking her company public.

Earns more than her CEO husband.

Wonders why anyone would be surprised.

Today, more women are making more money in more ways than ever before.

That's why our wealth management products and

Money. It's just not what it used to be.

services help meet the accumulation, preservation and transfer needs of today's most successful people.

Talk to your financial advisor about Phoenix.

◇ **PHOENIX** WEALTH MANAGEMENT®
LIFE • ANNUITIES • INVESTMENTS

PhoenixWealthManagement.com

WHILE YOU WERE OUT HACKERS TRIED TO BREAK IN

symantec™

Antivirus
Personal Firewall
Privacy Protection
Parental Control
Spam Filtering

Norton
Internet Security

Protect your personal information from hackers.

Find out if you're secure. **www.symantec.com/freesecuritycheck**

His wife left him. His dog ran away.
Then things got really bad.

He bought the wrong tires.

JAMES B. TWITCHELL
What We Are to Advertisers

Are you a "believer" or a "striver," an "achiever" or a "struggler," an "experiencer" or a "maker"? Or do you have no idea what we're talking about? If you don't, James Twitchell (b. 1943) explains it all to you in this selection in which the psychological profiling schemes of American advertising are laid bare. For like it or not, advertisers have, or think they have, your number, and they will pitch their products according to the personality profile they have concocted for you. And the really spooky thing is that they're often right. A prolific writer on American advertising and culture, Twitchell's books include Adult USA: The Triumph of Advertising in American Culture *(1996),* Twenty Ads That Shook the World *(2000),* Living It Up: Our Love Affair with Luxury *(2002), and* Lead Us into Temptation: The Triumph of American Materialism *(1999), from which this selection is taken. His most recent book is* Branded Nation *(2004).*

Mass production means mass marketing, and mass marketing means the creation of mass stereotypes. Like objects on shelves, we too cluster in groups. We find meaning together. As we mature, we move from shelf to shelf, from aisle to aisle, zip code to zip code, from lifestyle to lifestyle, between what the historian Daniel Boorstin calls "consumption communities." Finally, as full-grown consumers, we stabilize in our buying, and hence meaning-making, patterns. Advertisers soon lose interest in us not just because we stop buying but because we have stopped changing brands.

The object of advertising is not just to brand parity objects but also to brand consumers as they move through these various communities. To explain his job, Rosser Reeves, the master of hard-sell advertising like the old Anacin ads, used to hold up two quarters and claim his job was to make you believe they were different, and, more importantly, that one was better than the other. Hence, at the macro level the task of advertising is to convince different sets of consumers — target groups — that the quarter they observe is somehow different in meaning and value than the same quarter seen by their across-the-tracks neighbors.

In adspeak, this is called *positioning.* "I could have positioned Dove as a detergent bar for men with dirty hands," David Ogilvy famously said, "but I chose to position it as a toilet bar for women with dry skin." Easy to say, hard to do. But if Anheuser-Busch wants to maximize its sales, the soccer mom driving the shiny Chevy Suburban must feel she drinks a different Budweiser than the roustabout in the rusted-out Chevy pickup.[1]

The study of audiences goes by any number of names: psychographics, ethnographics, macrosegmentation, to name a few, but they are all based on the ineluctable principle that birds of a feather flock together. The object of much consumer research is not to try to twist their feathers so that they will flock to your product, but to position your product in such a place that they will have to fly by it and perhaps stop to roost. After roosting, they will eventually think that this is a part of their flyway and return to it again and again.

Since different products have different meanings to different audiences, segmentation studies are crucial. Although agencies have their own systems for naming these groups and their lifestyles, the current supplier of much raw data about them is a not-for-profit organization, the Stanford Research Institute (SRI). 5

The "psychographic" system of SRI is called acronomically VALS (now VALS2 +), short for Values and Lifestyle System. Essentially this schematic is based on the common-sense view that consumers are motivated "to acquire products, services, and experiences that provide satisfaction and give shape, substance, and character to their identities" in bundles. The more "resources" (namely money, but also health, self-confidence, and energy) each group has, the more likely they will buy "products, services, and experiences" of the group they associate with. But resources are not the only determinant. Customers are also motivated by such ineffables as principles, status, and action. When SRI describes these various audiences they peel apart like this (I have provided them an appropriate car to show their differences):

- Actualizers: These people at the top of the pyramid are the ideal of everyone but advertisers. They have "it" already, or will soon. They are sophisticated, take-charge people interested in independence and character. They don't need new things; in fact, they already have their things. If not,

---

[1]Cigarette companies were the first to find this out in the 1930s, much to their amazement. Blindfolded smokers couldn't tell what brand they were smoking. Instead of making cigarettes with different tastes, it was easier to make different advertising claims to different audiences. Cigarettes are hardly unique. Ask beer drinkers why they prefer a particular brand and invariably they tell you: "It's the taste," "This goes down well," "This is light and refreshing," "This is rich and smooth." They will say this about a beer that has been described as their brand, but is not. Anheuser-Busch, for instance, spent three dollars per barrel in 1980 to market a barrel of beer; now they spend nine dollars. Since the cost to reach a thousand television households has doubled at the same time the audience has segmented (thanks to cable), why not go after a particular market segment by tailoring ads emphasizing, in different degrees, the Clydesdales, Ed McMahon, Beechwood aging, the red and white can, dates certifying freshness, the spotted dog, the Eagle, as well as "the crisp, clean taste." While you cannot be all things to all people, the object of advertising is to be as many things to as many segments as possible. The ultimate object is to convince as many segments as possible that "This Bud's for you" is a sincere statement.

THE VALS2 NETWORK

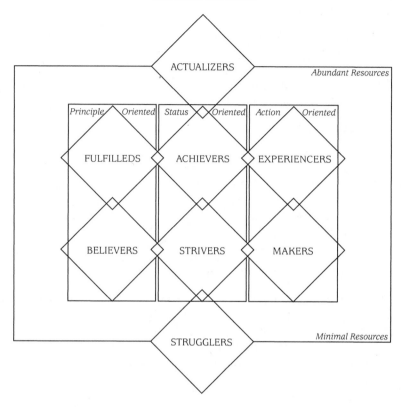

The VALS2 paradigm. Lifestyle styled: a taxonomy of taste and disposable income. (Stanford Research Institute)

they already know what "the finer things" are and won't be told. They don't need a new car, but if they do they'll read *Consumer Reports*. They do not need a hood ornament on their car.

- Fulfilled: Here are mature, satisfied, comfortable souls who support the status quo in almost every way. Often they are literally or figuratively retired. They value functionality, durability, and practicality. They drive something called a "town car," which is made by all the big three automakers.

- Believers: As the word expresses, these people support traditional codes of family, church, and community, wearing good Republican cloth coats. As consumers they are predictable, favoring American products and recognizable brands. They regularly attend church and Wal-Mart, and they are transported there in their mid-range automobile like an Oldsmobile. Whether Oldsmobile likes it or not, they do indeed drive "your father's Oldsmobile."

Moving from principle-oriented consumers who look inside to status-driven consumers who look out to others, we find the Achievers and Strivers.

- Achievers: If consumerism has an ideal, here it is. Bingo! Wedded to job as a source of duty, reward, and prestige, these are the people who not only favor the establishment but *are* the establishment. They like the concept of prestige. Not only are they successful, they demonstrate their success by buying such objects as prestigious cars to show it. They like hood ornaments. They see no contradiction in driving a Land Rover in Manhattan.

- Strivers: A young Striver is fine; he will possibly mature into an Achiever. But an old Striver can be nasty; he may well be bitter. Since they are unsure of themselves, they are eager to be branded as long as the brand is elevating. Money defines success and they don't have enough of it. Being a yuppie is fine as long as the prospect of upward mobility is possible. Strivers like foreign cars even if it means only leasing a BMW.

Again, moving to the right are those driven less by the outside world but by their desire to participate, to be part of a wider world.

- Experiencers: Here is life on the edge — enthusiastic, impulsive, and even reckless. Their energy finds expression in sports, social events, and "doing something." Politically and personally uncommitted, experiencers are an advertiser's dream come true as they see consumption as fulfillment and are willing to spend a high percent of their disposable income to attain it. When you wonder about who could possibly care how fast a car will accelerate from zero to sixty m.p.h., they care.

- Makers: Here is the practical side of Experiencers; they like to build things and they experience the world by working on it. Conservative, suspicious, respectful, they like to do things in and to their homes, like adding a room, canning vegetables, or changing the oil in their pickup trucks.

- Strugglers: Like Actualizers, these people are outside the pale of materialism not by choice, but by low income. Strugglers are chronically poor. Their repertoire of things is limited not because they already have it all, but because they have so little. Although they clip coupons like Actualizers, theirs are from the newspaper. Their transportation is usually public, if any. They are the invisible millions.

As one might imagine, these are very fluid categories, and we may move through as many as three of them in our lifetimes. For instance, between ages 18–24 most people (61 percent) are Experiencers in desire or deed, while less than 1 percent are Fulfilled. Between ages 55 to 64, however, the Actualizers, Fulfilled, and Strugglers claim about 15 percent of the population each, while the Believers have settled out at about a fifth. The Achievers, Strivers, and Makers fill about 10 percent apiece, and the remaining 2 percent are Experiencers. The numbers can be broken down at every stage allowing for marital status, education, household size, dependent children, home ownership, household income, and occupation. More interesting still is the ability to accurately predict the appearance of certain goods in each grouping. SRI sells data on precisely who buys single-lens reflex cameras, who owns a laptop computer, who drinks herbal tea, who phones before five o'clock, who reads the *Reader's Digest*, and who watches *Beavis and Butthead*.

When one realizes the fabulous expense of communicating meaning for a product, the simple-mindedness of a system like VALS2+ becomes less risible. When you are spending millions of dollars for a few points of market share for your otherwise indistinguishable product, the idea that you might be able to attract the owners of socket wrenches by shifting ad content around just a bit makes sense. Once you realize that in taste tests consumers cannot tell one brand of cigarettes from another — including their own — nor distinguish such products as soap, gasoline, cola, beer, or what-have-you, it is clear that the product must be overlooked and the audience isolated and sold.

READING THE TEXT

1. What do marketers mean by *positioning* (para. 3), and why is it an important strategy to them?

2. What does the acronym *VALS* stand for, and what is the logic behind this system?

3. Why do marketers believe that the "product must be overlooked and the audience isolated and sold" (para. 8), according to Twitchell?

READING THE SIGNS

1. Consult the VALS2 network chart on page 205, and write a journal entry in which you place yourself on the chart. How neatly do you fit the VALS2 paradigm? What is your attitude toward being stereotyped by marketers?

2. In class, discuss whether the categories of consumers defined by the VALS2 paradigm are an accurate predictor of consumer behavior. Use the discussion as the basis of an essay in which you argue for or against the proposition that stereotyping consumer lifestyles is an effective way of marketing goods and services.

3. Study the VALS2 paradigm in terms of the values it presumes. To what extent does it presume traditionally American values such as individualism? Use your analysis to formulate an argument about whether this marketing tool is an essentially American phenomenon.

4. Twitchell, Eric Schlosser ("Kid Kustomers," p. 178), and Malcolm Gladwell ("The Science of Shopping," p. 642) all describe marketing research strategies. Read the three selections, and write an argument that supports, opposes, or modifies the proposition that marketers have misappropriated academic research techniques for manipulative and therefore ethically questionable purposes.

VIDEO DREAMS

Television, Music, and Cultural Forms

Interpreting the Televising of America

Even before the advent of cultural studies, writing about television was a common assignment in American classrooms, so this chapter's topic might be quite familiar to you. Indeed, in high school you may have been asked to write about a favorite TV program or music video, perhaps in a summary writing exercise, a descriptive essay, or an opinion piece on why such-and-such a program is your favorite show, or why you don't like another show. But in college you will be asked to write critical interpretations of television, a somewhat different task than expressing an opinion about how entertaining a program is. In interpreting TV, you still need to rely on your skills in description and summary, because you need to describe the show for your reader, but your purpose will be to go beyond these writing tasks toward the construction of interpretive arguments about the cultural significance of your topic.

Television offers an especially rich field of possible writing topics, ranging from a historical analysis of a whole category of TV programming (such as the sitcom or detective show) to an interpretation of a single episode or video. Some topics, especially if you choose a historical approach, will require research. Let's say, for example, that you want to analyze the roles of women in situation comedies over the years. Comparing the women in *I Love Lucy*, *Father Knows Best*, *The Mary Tyler Moore Show*, *Murphy Brown*, *Roseanne*, and *Everyone Loves Raymond* will reveal a great deal about the cultural contexts in which those programs appeared and so enable you to construct a thesis about American gender roles over the past fifty years. Such an analysis lends itself particularly well to the semiotic method of establishing a system of related, or associated, signs, and then noting the differences that distinguish your subject. All of the shows from *I Love Lucy* to *Everyone Loves Raymond*, for example, feature comic female leads, but their characters are presented in very different ways. By analyzing those differences and situating each show within its cultural context, you can discover how the cultural perspective on women's roles in society has changed dramatically over the years. Indeed, such shows are particularly striking cultural barometers.

The interpretation of a single television episode is much like interpreting a short story. You should consider every potentially significant detail in the episode and subject it to a close reading. As with all semiotic analyses, your first step when preparing to write an analysis of a TV program is to suspend your aesthetic opinions — that is, whether you like a show or not. What you are working toward is a critical analysis, what you think a program's underlying cultural significance may be. This process also differs from describing what you think the show's *explicit* message is. Many programs have clearly presented messages, but what you are looking for is the message beyond the message, so to speak, the *implicit* signals the show is sending. An episode of *Las Vegas* that aired in 2004, for example, began with a scene of two of the show's stars coaching a Pee Wee League football game. Throughout the episode, the staff of the casino in which *Las Vegas* is set earnestly follows the football team's progress toward a league championship, and even rescuing from a kidnapper the father of the team quarterback. By portraying the personnel of a Las Vegas casino as such warm and fuzzy, family-friendly guys and gals, the episode was implicitly acting as a kind of advertisement for the city of Las Vegas itself, sending the message that Vegas is *the* place to take the family on your next vacation (the many family-oriented advertisements that accompanied this episode reinforced this message). It was good PR, but oddly contradictory to the fact that the primary purpose of the casino staff, from the security department to the hostesses, is to make certain that the casino guests are separated from as much of their money as possible.

Discussing the Signs of Television

In class, choose a current television program, and have the entire class watch one episode (either watch the episode as "homework" or ask someone to tape it and then watch it in class). Interpret the episode semiotically. What values and cultural myths does the show project? What do the commercials broadcast during the show say about the presumed audience for it? Go beyond the episode's surface appeal or "message" to look at the particular images it uses to tell its story, always asking, "What is this program *really* saying?"

Whatever show you choose to analyze, remember why it is on TV in the first place: Television, whether network or cable, is there to make money. It is a major part of our consumer culture, and most of what appears on TV is there because advertisers who want to reach their intended markets sponsor it. The shows that command the highest share of viewers, accordingly, command the highest advertising rates, and so producers are keen to have their viewers emotionally connect with their programs—and a main strategy involves satisfying viewer fantasies. This is especially striking in teen-address TV shows that feature fashion-model-glamorous actors and actresses (often in their twenties) playing adolescents in the awkward years, but it is also true for adult-address shows, which invite their viewers to identify with high-status professionals like doctors (*ER*) and lawyers (*The Practice*). Identifying with their favorite characters, viewers—or so television sponsors hope—will identify with the products they see associated with the shows. And buy them.

This is why one of the most revealing features in a TV episode analysis includes the advertising that accompanies the show. Be sure to catalog the advertising to see what it says about the intended audience. Why, for example, is the nightly news so often sponsored by over-the-counter pain killers? Why is daytime TV, especially in the morning, so often accompanied by cheesy ads for vocational training schools? Why are youth-oriented prime-time shows filled with fast-food commercials, while family programs like *Malcolm in the Middle* have a lot of car ads?

Your analysis of a single episode of a television program can also usefully include a survey of where the show fits within what cultural studies pioneer Raymond Williams called the "flow" of an evening's TV schedule. Flow refers to the sequence of TV programs and advertisements, from, say, the five o'clock news, through the pre-prime time 7:00 to 8:00 slot, through prime time and on through to the 11:00 news and the late-night talk shows. What precedes your program? What follows? Can you determine the strategy behind your show's scheduling?

Reality Bites

One kind of programming that you simply cannot miss anymore in the evening's flow is reality TV, a genre that seems to be on the verge of supplanting every other kind of television show. With its relatively low production costs and lack of superstar salary demands, reality TV was a producer's dream come true from the first, but audiences, especially in the coveted eighteen- to thirty-year-olds market niche, have absolutely adored it. In spite of its popularity, RTV is not without its critics, however, and there is certainly something about the whole matter that begs for cultural analysis. Let's conduct one here.

As with any semiotic analysis, a little history is helpful. One might say that reality television began in 1948 with Alan Funt's *Candid Camera*, which featured the filming of real people (who didn't know that they were on camera, unlike today's reality contestants) as they reacted to annoying situations con-cocted by the show's creators. The show's attraction lay in the humor viewers could enjoy in watching other people get into minor jams. There is a name for this kind of humor that comes from psychoanalytic theory: *schadenfreude*, or taking pleasure in the misfortunes of others. As we shall see, this early appeal from the history of reality TV is very much a part of the current popularity of the genre.

After *Candid Camera* came the 1970s PBS series *An American Family*. In this program a camera crew moved in with a suburban family named the Louds and filmed them in their day-to-day lives. The Louds were not contes-tants and there were no prizes to be won. The program was conceived as an experiment to see if it was possible for television to be authentically realistic. The experiment was a bit of a failure, however, as the Loud family members began to act out for the camera. The result was the eventual dissolution of the Louds as a family unit and a general sense of unease about such experiments. There were no sequels. (It might be said that MTV's 2002 hit *The Osbournes* reintroduced the basic concept in a celebrity format.)

The next, and probably most crucial step, was when MTV launched its *Real World* in 1992. More like a "real world" anticipation of *Friends* than like its reality predecessors, *Real World* was at once realistic, with its constant camera recording of the lives of a group of people living together in the same house, and a fantasy, insofar as the noncontestant protagonists could offer their viewers the vicarious experience of becoming instant TV stars. That the protagonists of *Real World* are also young and attractive is another part of the show's vicarious fantasy, which enables its viewers to imagine themselves as having the opportunity to live for a while under unusually glamorous and ro-mantic conditions. The fact that, at least in principle, the "characters" on the show are selected from "ordinary" life is a key part of this appeal.

Which takes us to the dawn of the reality revolution. The astounding suc-cess of the first versions of *Who Wants to Marry a Millionaire?* and *Survivor* constituted reality TV's coming-of-age. In both programs we can see strong traces of what made their pioneering predecessors popular, especially *Real World*. But through their introduction of a game show element into the genre, complete with contestants competing for huge cash prizes, a whole new di-mension was added that ultimately differentiates the new reality shows from those of the past and helps establish their significance.

The game show elements of programs like *Who Wants to Marry a Million-aire?* are obvious enough, and so part of their appeal is just that of the game show: the vicarious chance to imagine oneself as being in the shoes of the contestants (after all, anyone in principle can get on a game show) and win-ning lots of money. There is also an element of schadenfreude here, if one takes pleasure in watching the losers in game show competitions. But by adding the real-life element of actual marriage to the mix, *Who Wants to Marry a Millionaire?* brought a whole new dimension of humiliation to the genre. It's one thing to be caught on camera during the emotional upheaval of competing for large cash prizes; it's another to be seen competing erotically but losing. The humiliation of not being chosen on the basis of one's erotic power is all the more extreme.

Of course, shows like *Who Wants to Marry a Millionaire?* and all its progeny (*The Bachelor*, *The Bachelorette*, *Hot Tub Date*, and on and on) have their origins, in part, in the system of television programming that began with *The Dating Game* in the 1960s, and the many dating programs that followed in its wake. But *The Dating Game* tried to reduce the inherent humiliation factor through a split-screen effect that allowed the audience to see a single contestant, say, on the left, and three other contestants on the right, who would be concealed from the one on the left. That contestant would ask questions of the three concealed contestants (men if the questioner was a woman, women if it was a man), and pick one out for a date. This sort of nicety looks rather quaint today in the aftermath of another pioneering RTV program, *Temptation Island*, a show that made the sexual humiliation of its protagonists the main attraction. In *Temptation Island* voyeurism linked up with schadenfreude in a formula that is now common on all sex-themed RTV programs.

Survivor, for its part, combines a game show element with an action-adventure theme that invites viewers to imagine themselves in exciting outdoor situations that are exaggerated versions of the sort of adventure-safari vacations that had become very popular in the 1990s. With people spending $75,000 and upward to be guided to the top of Mount Everest, a show like *Survivor* is very much a reflection of the fantasies of its viewers. Indeed, it presents the ultimate fantasy of enjoying an extreme vacation while becoming a television star overnight as contestants reemerge in civilization on the talkshow circuit and in milk commercials.

Survivor also includes both voyeurism and schadenfreude in its formula for success, as viewers can watch the weekly humiliation of contestants struggling to stay in the game. But it adds yet another dimension to the mix by inviting viewers to identify with some contestants and to despise others (though the creators of the show deny this, there is evidence that contestants are directed to play out specified roles). One need only look at the weekly Internet commentary to see just how much the ordinary folk on *Survivor* can be hated, and the experience of watching contestants be voted off the show thus brings in a dimension of sadism as viewers take pleasure in the disappointments of the contestants they despise (indeed, some reality programs, like Holland's *Big Brother*, take this element a step further by allowing viewers to participate in voting contestants off).

Finally, while game shows usually feature some sort of competition among the contestants, the *Survivor* series takes such competition to a new level in the way it compels its contestants to engage in back-stabbing conspiracies in order to claw their way toward a million-dollar payoff. It isn't enough for tribe to compete against tribe; there has to be intratribal backbiting and betrayal as well. Such a subtext constitutes a kind of grotesque parody of American capitalism itself, in which the cutthroat competition of the workplace is moved to the wilderness. Not to miss out on a good thing, RTV soon brought it all back to the office with *The Apprentice*, a show that makes capitalist competition its major theme, while echoing the talent show elements of *American Idol*. Indeed, so successful was the formula that *The Apprentice* would be joined by *My Big Fat Obnoxious Boss*, which really turned the evils of life under capitalism into schadenfreude-laden entertainment.

Then there are all the makeover shows, from *Queer Eye for the Straight Guy* to *Extreme Makeover*, and every clone and spinoff that you can think of. Though there are significant differences among such shows (not all, for example, feature the freak show overtones of *The Swan* and its pathetic contestants), they all share the message that something is wrong with us that needs to be corrected by experts. Our houses aren't decorated properly; our clothes aren't right; our nose is all wrong; we're not beautiful enough. There doesn't seem to be anything that the makeover shows can't offer to improve. In effect, all such shows send the message that a well-lived life is a matter of proper consumption, that spending money can make you the kind of person you've always wanted to be — or the kind of person that you think others want you to be. Indeed, makeover TV is the perfect companion to a consumer culture: No wonder advertisers love it.

Voyeurism. Schadenfreude. Sadism. Dog-eat-dog capitalist competitiveness. Conspicuous consumption. RTV's formula seems to appeal to some of the most primitive and socially disruptive of human instincts, violating taboos in

Fantasia Barrino (L) and Diana DeGarmo appear on stage during the finals of the *American Idol* competition, May 26, 2004.

the name of profits. Indeed, in the aftermath of an actual injury suffered by one of the *Survivor: Outback* contestants (he got burned by a fire), commentators wondered whether future installments would have to include the death of a contestant to satisfy their viewers' ever-greater desires for mayhem. But while there has been no such event (to date), reality TV continues to grow, covering every imaginable possible topic (spouse swapping, anyone?). Sound far-fetched? What about Fox's *Trading Spouses*? Combining disdain with desire, RTV invites its viewers to fantasize that they too can be celebrities, or rich, or beautiful, while sneering at those who, by becoming contestants or characters on such shows, actually pursue the fantasy. We've come a long way from the "I'm OK. You're OK" era. Today, it's more like "I'm not OK. You're an idiot."

Crime Scene Imaginations

A fairly recent spinoff of the reality TV fervor has been the criminal mystery series in which the techniques of crime solving have been more important than the plot. Led by such shows as *CSI: Las Vegas*, the new crime dramas share with their predecessors a story line centered on a murder mystery and the investigators who solve it. But in a crucial difference, the new shows feature crime solvers who aren't cops or detectives: They're forensic laboratory technicians (as in *CSI: Las Vegas*) or casino security employees (as in *Las Vegas*). These programs combine a scripted fictional story line with (presumably) realistic views into the world of the forensic scientist, or whoever the crime-solving team happens to be. The clinical realism of a show like *CSI: Las Vegas* suggests an audience interest in reality-based programming even when the program is a fiction. Part of this interest may well have been stimulated in the days of the O. J. Simpson murder trial, during which, for a year or so, audiences could witness daily the testimony of forensic technicians and scientists — rather nerdy sorts, actually, when compared with the dashing detectives of murder mystery tradition, but they seem to have struck a chord, if all the spinoffs from *CSI: Las Vegas* are any indicator.

A second source for the interest in reality-oriented crime dramas can probably be found in the aftermath of the September 11 attacks. With brutal suddenness, Americans became aware of the complex array of otherwise ordinary people who are responsible for maintaining national security. In the past, the threat from abroad lay in intercontinental ballistic missiles, weapons wielded by governments whom only the U.S. military could challenge. But after 9/11, the military has been joined by hosts of nonmilitary personnel whose mission is to prevent another catastrophe. The new crime dramas, without even having to refer directly to national security and terrorism, show us these ordinary people and their equipment (think of all those surveillance devices available to the casino security crew in *Las Vegas*), and subtly reassure their audiences that ordinary people like them are at work keeping track of the bad guys.

Altered States

Our point is that whether you are considering a show like *Friends* or one like *Survivor*, or any other sort, you can find a cultural message behind the entertaining facade shown on the screen. The facade is the fantasy that distracts its viewers from the ways in which television programmers use their programs to achieve their primary ends — which are, in effect, to get us to go out and buy the products that sponsor the shows. That is why TV shows reflect the attitudes and desires of their core audiences and why interpreting TV reveals what those attitudes and desires are.

Interpreting television programming is especially valuable at a time when TV is blurring the line between fantasy and reality in an ever-more-profound manner. Just think of the 1992 presidential election, when Dan Quayle made Murphy Brown a campaign issue because she chose to become a single mother. For months the fictional protagonist of the show, played by Candice Bergen, sparred with the real vice president over the rights of single mothers in a public battle whose most interesting significance was that everyone acted as if Murphy Brown was as real as Dan Quayle.

Such blurring of the line between fiction and reality (a process accelerated by the advent of docudrama-style shows like *America's Most Wanted* and skewered in a film like *Natural Born Killers*) reflects television's profound effect on the very way that we perceive our world. If television were to vanish today — no more shows, no more prime time — its effects would live on in the way it has altered our sense of reality. We expect instant visual access to every corner of the earth because of TV, and we want to get to the point quickly. It is often claimed that our attention spans have been shortened in a universe of televised sound bites, but at the same time our desire for information has expanded (inquiring minds want to know). Indeed, the television age has equally been an information age.

In semiotic terms, the ubiquity of television and video in our lives represents a shift from one kind of sign system to another. As Marshall McLuhan pointed out over forty years ago in *The Gutenberg Galaxy* (1962), Western culture since the fifteenth century has defined itself around the printed word — the linear text that reads from left to right and top to bottom. The printed word, in the terminology of the American founder of semiotics, Charles Sanders Peirce, is a *symbolic* sign, one whose meaning is entirely arbitrary or conventional. A symbolic sign means what it does because those who use it have decided so. Words don't look like what they mean. Their significance is entirely abstract.

Not so with a visual image like a photograph or TV picture, which does resemble its object and is not entirely arbitrary. Though a photograph is not literally the thing it depicts and often reflects a good deal of staging and manipulation by the photographer, we often respond to it as if it were an innocent reflection of the world. Peirce called such signs *icons*, referring by this term to any sign that resembles what it means. The way you interpret an icon, then, differs from the way you interpret a symbol or word. The interpretation of words involves your cognitive capabilities; the interpretation and reception of icons is far more sensuous, more a matter of vision than cognition. The shift from a civilization governed by the paradigm of the book to one dominated by television accordingly involves a shift in the way we "read" our world, as the symbolic field of the printed page yields to the iconic field of the video screen.

The shift from a symbolic, or word-centered, world to an iconic universe filled with visual images carries profound cultural implications. Such implications are not necessarily negative. The relative accessibility of video technology, for example, has created opportunities for personal expression that have never existed before. It is very difficult to publish a book, but anyone can create a widely reproducible video simply by possessing a camcorder. The rapid transmissibility of video images speeds up communication and can bond groups of linguistically and culturally diverse people together, as MTV speaks to millions of people around the nation and world at once in the language of dance and music.

At the same time, video images may be used to stimulate political action. Rappers and their audiences particularly view rap and rap videos as subversions of the dominant society, just as baby boomers in the sixties used rock-and-roll in challenging the Establishment. Indeed, while many critics of TV deplore the passivity of its viewers, the medium is not inherently passive. Look at it this way: TV has a visceral power that print does not. Words abstractly describe things; television shows concrete images. The world pretty much ignored the famine in sub-Saharan Africa in the early 1980s, for example, until the TV cameras arrived to broadcast its images of starvation. Television, in short, bears the potential to awaken the apathetic as written texts cannot.

But there is a price to be paid for the new modes of perception that the iconic world of TV stimulates. For while one can read the signs of TV and video actively and creatively, and one can be moved to action by a video image, the sheer visibility of icons tempts one to receive them uncritically. Icons look so much like the realities they refer to that it is easy to forget that icons, too, are signs: Images that people construct that carry ideological meanings.

Just think of all those iconic images of the classic fifties-era sitcoms. *Leave It to Beaver*, *Father Knows Best*, *The Ozzie and Harriet Show*, and so on have established an American mythology of an idyllic era by the sheer persuasiveness of their images. In fact, the 1950s were not such idyllic years. Along with the McCarthyite hysteria of the cold war and the looming specter of nuclear war and contamination from open-air nuclear testing, there were economic downturns, the Korean War, and a growing sense that American life was becoming sterile, conformist, and materialistic — though it wasn't until the sixties that this uneasiness broke into the open. Few fathers in the fifties had the kind of leisure that the sitcom dads had, and the feminist resurgence in the late sixties demonstrated that not all women were satisfied with the housewifely roles assigned them in every screenplay. And yet, those constructed images of white middle-class contentment and security have become so real in the American imagination that they can be called on in quite concrete ways. *Leave It to Beaver* doesn't simply show up in Trivial Pursuit games: The image of the show has become a potent political weapon. Conservative campaigners point to the classic sitcoms as exemplars of the "family values" that America is losing, but while family dysfunctionality rather than solidarity seems to be the focus of such contemporary sitcoms as *The Simpsons* and *Malcolm in the Middle*, there are still plenty of programs, like *Everyone Loves Raymond* and *The Bernie Mac Show*, in which the old values may still be found, albeit in a culturally updated form.

Niche Marketing

One thing has changed in the relatively brief history of television: the emergence of cable TV. The proliferation of cable channels has fostered a more finely targeted programming schedule by which producers can focus on narrowly defined audiences, from nature lovers to home shoppers. This is referred to as *niche marketing*, and television today is far more divided into special niches than it was in the early days. For this reason today's Nielsen leaders, which have been designed to appeal to special niche markets, don't get nearly the numbers that sixties hits like *The Beverly Hillbillies* enjoyed, but they don't need to either. When there was less viewer choice, everyone watched the same shows, but where there is more choice, television producers target the most desirable audiences — that is, those who are perceived as commanding the most disposable income. Thus most prime-time television is aimed at middle- to upper-middle-class viewers between the ages of eighteen and forty-nine.

The fine-tuning of audiences, then, simply reflects a fine-tuning of marketing: Specially defined audiences can be targeted for specially defined marketing campaigns. In this sense, the advent of cable TV repeats the same history as that of traditional commercial television, which became a medium primarily for the pitching of goods and services. But the proliferation of channels bears the potential to upset television's commercial monopoly. When NBC, CBS, ABC, and their affiliates ruled the airways, programming decisions for an entire nation were made by a tiny group of executives. Aside from the Nielsen ratings, viewers had little chance to let programmers know what they wanted to see. While certainly no revolution has occurred in the wake of cable, there has been some movement toward audience participation in viewing.

The phenomenal success of MTV provides a good example of the increasing power of the television audience. In its early years, rock music appeared on

---

Exploring the Signs of Music Videos

In your journal, explore the impact music videos have had on you. How have videos shaped your desires and expectations about life? How were your actions and behavior influenced by MTV? What videos were especially meaningful to you? What did you think about them when you were younger, and how do you see them now? (If you didn't watch MTV, you might focus instead on other types of television programs.)

TV in such programs as *American Bandstand*, *Shindig*, and *Hullabaloo*. In each case, a rock act had to be toned down considerably before it could be televised (Elvis was ordered not to bump and grind lest he be banned from the TV screens of the fifties). What amounted to censorship worked because the venues for the televising of rock were often adult-oriented (consider how the Beatles first appeared to American audiences on the adult variety program *The Ed Sullivan Show*). MTV, on the other hand, is an entirely youth-oriented station. Though it too exists to promote products — through both the videos it displays and the commercials it runs — MTV must conform to the tastes of its audience to succeed, rather than simply dictate to that audience what it will broadcast.

Hey Hey, Oh My, Will Rock 'n' Roll Ever Die?

Rock performers from The Who to Neil Young have written songs about the enduring destiny of rock 'n' roll, but while news of the death of rock is certainly premature, it has certainly been surpassed in recent years by rap and rhythm and blues as the most popular youth music in America. Once an authentic urban street phenomenon culturally coded as the music of African Americans (which is why early white rappers like Vanilla Ice and Marky Mark were regarded as something of a joke), rap has fully crossed over to be the preferred pop entertainment of teens of all ethnicities, making it possible for white rappers like Eminem to succeed — though his act is carefully designed to appear as authentically "black."

Eminem's success repeats, in its own fashion, the rise of Elvis Presley in the 1950s, for once rock 'n' roll, too, was perceived as being an African American musical form — though, of course, fans of rock pioneers like Carl Perkins and Jerry Lee Lewis might want to have a word about that. Indeed, disc jockeys in the still segregated South refused to include black musicians on their playlists, and the success of Elvis was attributed at the time to the fact that he was "a white boy who sounded black." Eventually, such early rock innovators as Chuck Berry, Bo Diddley, and Little Richard were reclassified as rhythm

Reading Music on the Net

Many popular musicians and groups boast their own Web site or host special "concert" events on the Internet. Find the site of a favorite artist by using a search engine such as Yahoo! (**www.yahoo.com/ Entertainment/Music/Artists**) or trying a commercial site, **artistdirect .com**. Then study your artist's site, and analyze the images created for him or her. How is the artist "packaged" on the Net, and does that packaging differ from that used in other media? What sort of relationship is established between the artist and you, the fan, and how does the electronic medium affect that relationship?

and blues performers (just as even today urban music is a code word for black) and were largely exiled to marginal radio stations, while white-bread performers like Pat Boone and Ricky Nelson became, at least for a while, rock stars.

There is an interesting cultural question involved in the early co-optation of "black" rock 'n' roll, and the contemporary co-optation of rap by such performers as Eminem. That question is why mainstream white middle-class youths continue to turn to the music of marginalized black America to express and entertain themselves. The simplest answer is that in the last fifty years or so, white teens have identified with the African American subculture, viewing the music of black America as an authentic medium for the expression of their own resentments and desires. In the 1950s, Beat hipsters like Jack Kerouac turned to the cultural forms of black America (especially hot jazz and bebop) as an alternative to a society that they found repressive and sterile, while young white audiences found in the more sexually expressive music of rhythm and blues an outlet for their own sexual desires in a sexually repressed era. Today, the carefully scripted anger and hostility that can be found in many hip-hop numbers is embraced by white teens as an expression of their own anger — against their parents, against rules and restrictions, against any form of authority at all, not to mention hostility against women for many a male rap fan.

Indeed, no cultural form in America today is more identified with youth than the rock-to-rap continuum. Wedded to television through the auspices of MTV, such music (now consumed via a legion of iPods) embodies the collective consciousness of generation after generation of young consumers, forming lasting bonds of generational identity. Today's cutting edge top-ten single will be on tomorrow's "classic rap" playlist, prompting future young listeners to smile in mild derision as they contemplate the musical taste of their elders (that is, *you*), while enjoying their own forms of musical rebellion.

The Readings

We begin the readings in this chapter with a trio of essays devoted to television's now-dominant genre: reality TV. Francine Prose starts with a provocative piece arguing that the ruthless Machiavellian behavior we can watch every night on such shows as *Survivor* and *The Apprentice* is really no different from — in fact, is a reflection of — the behavior of America's current corporate and political leadership. In a more lighthearted vein, Anita Creamer takes on the radical makeover craze — à la plastic surgery — while Rick Pieto and Kelly Otter tackle *The Osbournes*. James Harold follows with a philosophical meditation on the guilty pleasures of *The Sopranos*. Carl Matheson looks at *The Simpsons* — one of TV's longest-running institutions — and explores what happens when self-conscious irony overrides just about everything else. Steven Stark's analysis of *The Oprah Winfrey Show* suggests that Oprah, and talk-show hosts like her, provide a kind of "group therapy for the masses," while Susan Douglas argues that behind the progressive surfaces of *NYPD Blue* and *ER* lies a less-than-enlightened ideology. Two pieces follow on popular music, with Gwendolyn Pough providing a definition of the hip-hop concept of "wreck" — as in "wrecking it" — and Andre Mayer offering a scathing critique of the misogynistic tendencies in contemporary pop. Marissa Connolly concludes the chapter with an analysis of how *Will and Grace* makes gay-themed television "safe" for network viewing.

FRANCINE PROSE

Voting Democracy off the Island: Reality TV and the Republican Ethos

It is an essential semiotic principle that, one way or another, everything connects up in a society. In this provocative analysis of the underlying ideology of reality television (RTV), Francine Prose (b. 1947) discovers what may seem a surprising connection between the RTV craze and current trends in American politics. When millions of Americans tune in to watch Donald Trump dump, one by one, the frantic contenders for a dazzling corporate job, or cheer as the quasi-democracies of Survivor *vote each other out until only one "winner" is left, we can see the Social Darwinism that seems to guide, as Prose argues, the current crop of national leaders at work. The author of twelve novels—including* A Peaceable Kingdom *(1993),* Hunters and Gatherers *(1996),* Guided Tours of Hell: Novellas *(1997), and* A Changed Man *(2005)—Prose is a contributing editor at* Harper's *and a writer on art for the* Wall Street Journal. *This article originally appeared in* Harper's *in 2004.*

Not even Melana can believe it's real. As the "former NFL cheerleader and beauty queen looking to fall in love with the perfect guy" swans a bit dazedly through the Palm Springs mansion in which she will soon undertake the task of selecting Mr. Right from among sixteen eligible bachelors, she coos about the thrill of living a "dream come true."

It's the premiere episode of NBC's *Average Joe*, one of the extremely popular and profitable "reality-based" television shows that, in recent years, have proliferated to claim a significant share of major-network prime time. Featuring ordinary people who have agreed to be filmed in dangerous, challenging, or embarrassing situations in return for the promise of money, romance, or fame, these offerings range from *Who Wants to Marry a Millionaire?* to *Who Wants to Marry My Dad?*, from long-run hits such as *Survivor* and *The Real World* to the short-lived *Are You Hot?* and *Boy Meets Boy*.

The title *Average Joe* has evidently alerted Melana to the possibility that her bachelor pool may not be stocked with the same species of dazzling hunks, those walking miracles of body sculpting, cosmetic dentistry, and hair-gel expertise who courted *The Bachelorette*. Clearly, she's expecting to meet the more routinely, unself-consciously attractive sort of guy one might spot on the street or at the water cooler.

But, as frequently happens, the audience is privy to an essential truth— or, in the argot of reality programming, a "reveal"—concealed from the hapless participants. Now, as the cameras whisk us to the bachelors' quarters, we instantly get the visual joke that is, even by the standards of reality TV, sadistic.

The men about to compete for Melana's affections are not merely Joe   5
Well Below Average but Joe Out of the Question. Several are obese; others have tics, dermatological or dental problems, or are short, bespectacled, balding, stooped. Racial and cultural diversity is provided by a diminutive "university professor" from Zimbabwe with a penchant for intellectual boasting and grave fashion miscalculations.

Although the sight of Melana's suitors is intended to amuse and titillate rather than to touch us, it would (to paraphrase Dickens amid this Dickensian crowd) take a heart of stone not to be moved by the moment when the men take a look at one another and realize that their inclusion in this confraternity of nerds is probably not a mistake.

Meanwhile, night has fallen on the desert, and the lovely Melana, all dressed up and as starry-eyed as a kid on Christmas morning, comes out to meet the guys. A white limousine pulls up. A male model emerges, and Melana's face brightens, only to darken seconds later when he announces that, sadly, he is not one of her bachelors.

The white limo carries the tease away. Presently a bus arrives.

The bus doors open. They send the fat guys out first. And by the time a half-dozen sorry specimens are lined up, grinning their hearts out, even Melana gets it. Her shock and dismay are genuine. The men cannot help but notice. "This is *bad*," she whispers, and we can read her lips. "Someone's messing with my head."

What lends the scene its special poignancy is that Melana knows, as do   10
we, that what has befallen her is not some cruel accident of fate. Rather, she has brought misfortune on herself. In filling out the questionnaire that led to her being selected as the heroine of *Average Joe*, she indicated that "a good personality" mattered more to her than did appearance. And in doing so, she violated one of the cardinal rules, a basic article of faith, one of the values that this new version of reality pumps out, hour after hour, night after night, into the culture. Had Melana watched more reality-based TV, she would have learned that surface beauty (preferably in concert with a strong manipulative instinct, a cunning ability to play the game, and vast quantities of money) is all that counts. Melana has transgressed. And now, as we sit back and watch, she is about to be punished.

If this — a dash of casual brutality, a soupçon of voyeurism — is your recipe for entertainment, it's a taste you can satisfy, in the privacy of your living room, nearly every evening. In fact, unless you own one of those televisions that allow you to watch two programs at once, you may be forced to make some hard choices.

On a typical night — Thanksgiving Eve, November 26, 2003 — you could, at eight, watch a contestant on CBS's *Survivor Pearl Islands* secure himself some sympathy by misleading his fellow tribe members into thinking that his

Landing the big one: a scene from the début of the RTV hit
Survivor.

grandmother has just died. But witnessing the "biggest lie ever told on *Sur-vivor*" would mean missing the episode of NBC's *Queer Eye for the Straight Guy* in which a quintet of homosexual fashion and lifestyle advisers convince a balding lawyer to lose his unflattering hairpiece. At nine, you could shop along with ABC's Trista for *Trista and Ryan's Wedding*, an account of the big-ticket ceremony that would solemnize the love affair spawned, as America watched, on *The Bachelorette*. And at ten, on *Extreme Makeover*, the most liter-ally invasive series so far, two lucky souls (chosen from more than 10,000 ap-plicants) have their lives transformed by plastic surgery. On this night a man whose 200-pound weight loss has left him looking like a shar-pei, and a rather pretty grade-school teacher — who believes that she is only a rhinoplasty and a chin implant away from rivaling her beautiful sisters — will go under the knife.

In the event that three hours of watching your fellow humans suffer and squirm and endure surgical procedures has left you feeling uneasy about how you have spent your time, or what you have found amusing, you can be reassured — as are the network executives, it would seem — by the fact that you are not alone. In January 2003 the premiere of Fox Network's *Joe Million-aire*, in which a construction worker courted women tricked into believing that he possessed a vast personal fortune, attracted 18.6 million viewers; 40 million tuned in for its conclusion. *American Idol*, the talent show that asks fans to vote for their favorite contestants by telephone, received 110 million calls in its first season and 15.5 million calls during the final show alone. By contrast, the most popular national news program — NBC's *Nightly News* — averages around 11 million viewers per night.

Like Melana, network accountants were quick to see reality shows as a dream come true. For although production values and costs have risen, reality-based programs are still relatively cheap to produce, mostly because they avoid the expense of hiring actors whose salary demands can rise astronomically if the show becomes a hit. One consequence is that television actors have seen a radical reduction in the number and range of available roles.

Despite the fact that journalists periodically hail the death of reality TV, it 15 has proved remarkably long-lived. MTV's *The Real World*, which sends seven attractive young strangers to spend six months turning their luxury housing into a Petri dish of sexual, racial, and interpersonal tension, has been running since 1992. Now in its eighth season, *Survivor* has airlifted a succession of warring "tribes" from the Amazon to the jungles of Thailand. During the week of November 17–23, 2003, the only shows more popular than *Survivor Pearl Islands* (which drew 19.9 million viewers) were *CSI, ER*, and *Friends*.

On aesthetic grounds alone, it's arguable that reality-based shows are no better or worse than *CSI, ER*, and *Friends*. But the most obvious difference is the most crucial one. Fans of *Friends* understand that they are watching a sitcom, cast with celebrity actors. Watching *Survivor* and *The Real World*, they believe that they are observing *real* men and women.

Viewers do, of course, realize that some of what they're seeing has been instigated or exacerbated by the show's producers. Yet the fact is that viewers *are* watching people who, regardless of their career ambitions or masochistic exhibitionism, are amateurs who may have been chosen *for* their fragility and instability. Many of the "Average Joes" could never get hired as character actors. And observing their response to stress and humiliation generates a gladiatorial, bread-and-circus atmosphere that simply does not exist when we see movie stars in scrubs sail a gurney down the halls of *ER*.

Reality-based TV, then, is not a scripted fiction but an improvisation, an apparently instructive improvisation that doles out consistent and frequently reinforced lessons about human nature and, yes, reality. These programs also generate a jittery, adrenalized buzz that produces a paradoxically tranquilized numbness in which our defenses relax and leave us more receptive to the "information" we are receiving. For this reason alone, even those who take pride in never looking at TV, except for the occasional peek at PBS, might want to tune in and see what reality their fellow citizens have been witnessing.

What might future anthropologists (or, for that matter, contemporary TV-addicted children and adults) conclude about our world if these programs constituted their primary source of information? The most obvious lesson to be drawn from reality TV, the single philosophical pole around which everything else revolves, is that the laws of natural selection are even more brutal, inflexible, and *sensible* than one might suppose from reading *Origin of Species*. Reality is a Darwinian battlefield on which only the fittest survive, and it's not merely logical but admirable to marshal all our skills and resources to succeed in a struggle that only one person can win.

Compelling its testy, frequently neurotic castaways to operate as if they 20 were several rungs down the evolutionary ladder, grubbing roots and berries and forced to earn such basic necessities as blankets by performing acrobatic stunts, *Survivor* is the prototype. The show urges its participants to labor for their tribe but always, ultimately, for themselves. Because at the end of the day — in this case, the final episode — only one person will walk away with a million dollars. And in case we lose sight of first principles, the show's motto, which appears in its logo, is "Outwit. Outplay. Outlast."

Survivor is the younger American cousin of the 1997 Swedish *Expedition Robinson*, a title judged too literary for the U.S. market. It's probably just as well that the series wasn't called *Expedition Robinson*. *Robinson Crusoe* and *Swiss Family Robinson* extol the virtues and advantages of fellowship and cooperation, whereas on *Survivor* such considerations are useful only to a point. *Survivor* could be Defoe's masterpiece rewritten by Ayn Rand. And for all its Darwinian trappings, the series offers a skewed view of the *purpose* of the struggle for dominance. Propagating the species is the last thing on these people's minds.

And so the steps that lead toward that goal aren't determined by physical combat or brilliant displays of plumage. Rather, contestants are eliminated by a democratic process; every few days, tribe members vote on which of their fellows will be forced to leave the island. As we watch, the loser trudges across a rope bridge or rock ledge and off to a dismal future without a million dollars.

Observant readers may already have noted that the guiding principles to which I've alluded — flinty individualism, the vision of a zero-sum society in which no one can win unless someone else loses, the conviction that altruism and compassion are signs of folly and weakness, the exaltation of solitary striving above the illusory benefits of cooperative mutual aid, the belief that certain circumstances justify secrecy and deception, the invocation of a reviled common enemy to solidify group loyalty — are the exact same themes that underlie the rhetoric we have been hearing and continue to hear from the Republican Congress and our current administration.

Of course, no sensible person would imagine that Donald Rumsfeld is sitting down with the producers of reality-based TV to discuss the possibility that watching the contestants sweat and strain to bring civilization to the jungle will help us accept the sacrifices we have been and are still being asked to make in Iraq. On the other hand, there is the unsettling precedent set by *Profiles from the Front Line*, a series that aired around the time of the war in Iraq and was produced for ABC Entertainment by Jerry Bruckheimer, whose credits include *Black Hawk Down*.

According to an advance release from the network, [25]

the Pentagon and the Department of Defense lent their full support and cooperation to this unique production. . . . As America prepares for a possible war with Iraq, the country continues to wage a perilous war on terrorism. ABC will transport viewers to actual battlefields in Central Asia with a six-episode series that will feature actual footage of the elite U.S. Special Operations forces apprehending possible terrorists, as well as compelling, personal stories of the U.S. military men and women who bear the burden and risks of this fighting.

Indeed, ABC News complained that — in order to film the soldiers arresting a "big-time" Taliban leader, disarming rockets, providing medical care to Afghan civilians, capturing fuel-truck hijackers, and accepting the love and gratitude of the Afghan people — the show's producers were being granted a level of access to the troops that Pentagon officials denied the network's actual reporters.

But even when the collaboration between the military, the government, and the entertainment industry is not nearly so overt, these shows continue to transmit a perpetual, low-frequency hum of agitprop. The ethics (if one can call them that) and the ideals that permeate these programs at once reflect and reinforce the basest, most mindless and ruthless aspects of the current political zeitgeist. If the interests of the corporate culture that controls our television stations are at heart the same as those that fund and support lobbyists and politicians, it stands to reason that — when network executives do meet to determine what is appropriate, entertaining, profitable, what people want and need to see — they are unlikely to flinch at portraying stylized versions of the same behavior we read about in the press, or can observe on the Senate floor.

If reality TV does turn out to be not only the present but also the future of prime-time television, it seems more than likely that a steady, high-intake, long-term diet of *Survivor* and *The Bachelorette* will subtly, or not so subtly, affect the views and values of the audiences that tune in week after week. Watching a nightly Darwinian free-for-all cannot help but have a desensitizing effect. Once you've absorbed and assimilated the idea that civility is, at best, a frill, you may find yourself less inclined to suppress an eruption of road rage or the urge to ridicule the homely Average Joe who dares to approach a pretty girl. If the lesson of reality TV is that anyone will do anything for money, that every human interaction necessarily involves the swift, calculated formation and dissolution of dishonest, amoral alliances, it seems naive to be appalled by the fact that our government has been robbing us to pay off its supporters in the pharmaceutical industry and among the corporations profiting from the rebuilding of Iraq. After you've seen a "real person" lie about his grandmother's death, you may be slightly less shocked to learn that our leaders failed to come clean about the weapons of mass destruction.

After all, it's the way the world works; it's how people behave. We can't have witnessed all that reality without having figured that out by now. How foolish it would be to object to the billing practices of companies such as Halliburton, or to the evidence that our government has been working behind the scenes to dismantle the social security system and to increase (in the guise of reducing) what the elderly will have to pay for health care. *Everybody* acts like that, given half the chance. And we all admire a winner, regardless of how the game was won.

Which is the message we get, and are meant to be getting, every time a bachelor outsmarts his rivals, every time the castaways vote a contender off the island and inch one rung up the ladder. Indeed, those weekly tribal councils at which the voting occurs, held in a cavern or cave decorated to evoke the palm-fringed exotica of the tiki lounge or the Bugs Bunny cartoon, are arguably the most disturbing and pernicious moments in the reality-TV lineup. They're a travesty of democracy so painfully familiar, so much like what our political reality is actually becoming, that it's far more unnerving than watching Donald Trump brutally fire each week's losers, or ugly single guys made to feel even more unattractive than they are.

The castaways vote, as we do, but it's a democracy that might have been 30 conceived if the spirit of Machiavelli had briefly possessed the mind of Thomas Jefferson; indeed, the reasons behind the survivors' ballots might puzzle our Founding Fathers. Because this fun-house version of the electoral process seeks to dismantle civilization rather than to improve it, the goal is neither a common good nor the furthering of life, liberty, or the pursuit of happiness. It's a parody of democracy, robbed of its heart and soul, a democracy in which everyone always votes, for himself.

READING THE TEXT

1. What explanations does Prose provide for the recent dramatic increase in the number of reality TV programs?
2. How does Prose contrast reality TV with other sorts of programming, such as sitcoms and dramas?
3. Summarize in your own words the guiding social and philosophical principles that underlie reality television.
4. What relationship does Prose see between reality TV and Republican politics?
5. What effect does Prose believe a long-term diet of reality TV will have on the American consciousness?

READING THE SIGNS

1. In an argumentative essay, support, refute, or modify Prose's proposition that the same guiding principles underlying reality TV shape the policies of the current Republican administration.
2. Interview several fans of reality TV about their attraction to such programs. Do they like all reality TV shows, or do they discriminate among them? If the latter, what is their pattern of preference? Then use your findings as the basis of an argumentative essay about why this genre has developed a loyal following in early twenty-first-century America.

3. Read or review the Introduction to this chapter, and then write an essay in which you analyze whether the appeal of the episode of *Average Joe* that Prose describes is based on schadenfreude.

4. In class, brainstorm responses to Prose's question: "What might future anthropologists . . . conclude about our world if [reality] programs constituted their primary source of information?" (para. 19). Then write an essay proposing your own response to this question.

5. Write an essay in which you support, challenge, or complicate Prose's claim that the contestant voting ritual that occurs on many reality TV programs is "a parody of democracy, robbed of its heart and soul, a democracy in which everyone always votes, for himself" (para. 30).

ANITA CREAMER

Reality TV Meets Plastic Surgery: An Ugly Shame

Perhaps the first reality TV makeover show was PBS's This Old House, *in which Bob Vila spent a season carefully transforming a dilapidated house into a showplace. We've come a long way since then, with extreme makeover programs like* The Swan *featuring "ugly" people in need of cosmetic enhancement and* I Want a Famous Face *propelling ordinary people into plastic surgery in the hopes of looking like this or that celebrity's forgotten twin. For Anita Creamer, this whole assault on human dignity is "an ugly shame" that is likely to backfire not only on the contestants themselves but on the society that has fostered it as well. Creamer is lifestyle columnist for the* Sacramento Bee, *where this article originally appeared in 2004.*

On MTV, a baby-faced blonde named Sha is talking about her life's ambition, which is to look like Pamela Anderson and become a *Playboy* centerfold. Sha — pronounced Shay — already looks cute, but that's not enough. She's collected stacks of old *Playboys*, and she pores over them as if they're how-to manuals.

She's 19, but the older you get, the younger that sounds. So: Should Sha really make such an important decision, to undergo major surgery and have her double chin suctioned and her lips and breasts augmented, when she's so deluded in her aspirations?

Ethics aren't MTV's deal.

But the moral of *I Want a Famous Face* seems to be that tragically insecure people make bad decisions about their lives — and not surprisingly, their families, who should've raised them with better values and bigger ambitions, aren't any help at all. The eternal American habit of reinvention has come to this — remaking our faces and bodies instead of our lives; the annihilation of the self in the name of self-improvement. And all for TV ratings.

Surgery has become entertainment. Making a name for yourself — once the product of education, achievement and providing something of worth in the world — now involves allowing a voyeuristic nation to watch the transformation of your looks.

Your inner life doesn't matter.

"The new wave of plastic surgery reality television" — now there's a fabulous phrase — "is a serious cause for concern," Dr. Rod Rohrich, president of the American Society of Plastic Surgeons, has said in a press release. "Some patients on these shows have unrealistic and frankly unhealthy expectations about what plastic surgery can do for them."

What gave it away, *Famous Face*'s seriously misguided 20-year-old twins who underwent surgery to look like Brad Pitt? Telling them to grow up, grow into their faces and appreciate their uniqueness doesn't exactly make for good TV.

While plastic surgeons may be alarmed about cosmetic surgery reality TV, they're still taking advantage of the trend. Americans are spending more money than ever on Botox injections and brow lifts, according to ASPS, with 8.7 million cosmetic procedures performed in 2003. That number represents a 33 percent jump over 2002 figures. Elective plastic surgery has become routine.

Yet the reality TV programs showcasing it could just as easily serve as cautionary tales instead of success stories. The fact is, for example, that many of the folks on *Extreme Makeover*, ABC's entry in the genre, end up looking nothing at all like themselves. At best, they look attractive in a bland and homogenous way; at worst, they look like transvestites with orange makeup and badly styled hair. Now *The Swan* — Fox's appalling new show, in which 17 so-called ugly ducklings undergo an array of cosmetic surgery procedures, then compete in a beauty contest — is drawing mediocre ratings.

It would be nice to think this lack of audience enthusiasm is proof that we find a TV show that takes advantage of women's body dysmorphia to be cruel beyond words. But the problem with *The Swan*, according to critics, is less its utter lack of sensitivity than its lack of TV-friendly dramatic moments.

So. Perhaps enlightenment remains on hold.

By the end of Sha's *I Want a Famous Face* episode, a *Playboy* scout is telling her that the magazine prefers a more natural look, instead of the obviously phony va-voom of those Andersonesque implants. Sha doesn't look like a cute little blonde any more. She has duck lips, and her breast augmentation makes her look overstuffed instead of sexy. But she got her wish. She's on TV, a flash-in-the-pan star, just like Pamela Anderson.

And for the impressionable and unassured, that may be all that matters.

READING THE TEXT

1. What conclusions does Creamer draw about the motives and experiences of Sha, the *I Want a Famous Face* contestant?

2. What effect does Creamer believe reality TV shows focused on plastic surgery have on the "American habit of reinvention" (para. 4)?

3. What response do plastic surgeons — and their clients — have to the sorts of programs Creamer describes, and what is Creamer's attitude toward that response?

READING THE SIGNS

1. Read or review Francine Prose's "Voting Democracy off the Island: Reality TV and the Republican Ethos" (p. 222). Using Prose's claim that the ingredients of reality TV involve "a dash of casual brutality, a soupçon of voyeurism" (para. 11), analyze one of the shows that Creamer discusses.

2. Using Naomi Wolf's "The Beauty Myth" (p. 486) as your critical framework, write an essay in which you analyze the cultural values that underlie such programs as *I Want a Famous Face* and *The Swan*.

3. Compare and contrast the style and tone of Creamer's essay and of Francine Prose's "Voting Democracy off the Island: Reality TV and the Republican Ethos" (p. 222). Which do you find more effective, and why? Keep in mind that Creamer's article was first published in the *Sacramento Bee* and that Prose's appeared first in *Harper's*.

4. Write an essay in which you explore further Creamer's observation that "surgery has become entertainment" (para. 5). Can you relate this form of reality TV to other pop cultural phenomena?

RICK PIETO AND KELLY OTTER

The Osbournes: *Genre, Reality TV, and the Domestication of Rock 'n' Roll*

Once upon a time, Ozzy Osbourne was a parental nightmare: a satanic heavy metalist who threatened children with images of depravity and sacrilege. Now, thanks to reality TV, he is one of America's favorite TV parents, almost, but not quite, joining such predecessors as Ozzie Nelson and Robert Young. As Rick Pieto and Kelly Otter argue in this in-depth analysis of the precise television genre to which The Osbournes *belongs, this TV transformation of a rock 'n' roll rebel into a lovably aging rock star constitutes a whole new myth of pop music stardom, in effect domesticating what was once a subversive rock mythology. Rick Pieto (b. 1954) is an instructor in the department of culture and communication at New York University. Kelly Otter (b. 1965) is assistant dean of the School of Arts and Sciences at the College of New Rochelle, where she also teaches as an adjunct professor in the graduate school.*

The latest trend of television programming is reality TV, a genre that finds its most valuable content in the unabashed display of individuals willing to be put on display as they part with their privacy, dignity, and composure. The genre is clear, yet the formula varies so as to keep it fresh and increasingly bizarre to maintain its audience. Young women compete for a husband on camera by attempting to win the affection of a bachelor in six weeks; individuals compete for money by conquering their fears and consume live insects or allow themselves to be submerged under water for as long as possible; and couples test the strength of their relationships by subjecting themselves to the temptation of desirable strangers. Love, fear, and conflict provide the substance of a good story, and television producers have found a context in which drama is manufactured before a camera crew. But given the absence of a constructed context and specific roles to play, how do we define *The Osbournes*? How should we generically define this program about an aging heavy metal rock star and his "dysfunctional family"?

One way to begin to place *The Osbournes* within an appropriate genre is to look at MTV's presentation of the show. MTV sells *The Osbournes* as a reality TV sitcom and indeed its narrative structure is loosely similar to the sitcom formula, with real-life segments edited and sequenced to be reminiscent of a scripted program. More specifically, the show is framed within the genre of 1950s sitcoms. The opening credits have a self-consciously retro look to them. The theme song replays a lounge music aesthetic both in its melody and in the voice of the male singer. The title of the show, *The Osbournes*, connotes early sitcom family names such as the Cramdens, the Cleavers and, of course, the Nelsons. Indeed a visit to *The Osbournes*' Web site explicitly draws this connection between the archetypal '50s father Ozzie Nelson and MTV's incarnation Ozzy Osbourne. *The Osbournes* is obviously too dark and "dysfunctional" to fall within the boundaries of '50s sitcoms; however, the ironic '50s signifiers in the show's opening credits contradict the typically straightforward use of generic signals, especially as they are used in movie and television credits. Traditionally, with television and films, genre is clearly signaled for and marketed to the target audience. The correct packaging of movies and television programs according to genre is meticulously researched so as to appeal to the appropriate audience. The tongue-in-cheek opening credits of *The Osbournes* do something more than signal an audience or define a genre: they suggest to the audience a possible intertextual reading of the show. The opening credits do not say to the audience "This is a fifties style sitcom"; rather they say, "This is *not* a fifties style sitcom but you can read it as though it were one." By ignoring the typical conventions of generic signaling, MTV invites the audience to perform an intertextual reading, juxtaposing the heavy metal rock star dad within markers of a genre in which the signifiers of "dad" connote Ward Cleaver as opposed to Ozzy, creating an appropriate amount of added-value irony.

The Osbournes seems to be more closely aligned intertextually to another more recent subgenre of sitcoms, the anti-fifties sitcoms such as *Roseanne* and *Married with Children*. *The Osbournes* shares with these sitcoms a cynical and dysfunctional view of modern family life, a self-conscious denial of the optimism and mutual appreciation associated with fifties sitcoms. However, what distinguishes *The Osbournes* from *Roseanne* and *Married with Children* is not so much the difference between fiction and nonfiction (reality TV), but the way highly visible markers of class operate within each show. Whereas these sitcoms present membership in the working class as an insurmountable given (particularly *Roseanne*'s final season with the revelation that the Conners's lottery win was a fantasy), *The Osbournes* proves that even a working-class kid from Britain (whose "class" was tantamount to poverty) can realize the American dream of upward mobility and wealth, especially when paired with an ambitious upper-middle-class wife/manager. There is a reversal here that reveals problems with the basic generic distinctions of fact and fiction: the *fictional* narratives of *Roseanne* and *Married with Children* present a more "realistic" portrayal of the experience of working-class families and the minimal probability that they could attain financial success at the level of the Osbournes. The Osbournes, on the other hand, through their reality-based show, exemplify the American ideology of upward mobility. The reality of the Osbournes' affluence is an ideological fiction for most working-class Americans.

This brings us to a more pertinent genre for classifying *The Osbournes*: reality TV. As a popular term, reality TV denotes a variety of shows from *Cops* to *Survivor*, from the *The Bachelor* to *The Osbournes*. The term reality TV implies the documentation of the "reality" of an event or "referent" that somehow, in some way, exists independently of the recording machines that capture the event. Not only does MTV bend the conventions of the fictional genre with its ironic use of opening credits, but it also bends the codes, conventions, and ethics of documentary filmmaking so as to capture a segment of the youth market. This practice efficiently produces an ironic brand of media for a presumed media-savvy (read: young) audience. The footage of police pullovers that are recorded by dashboard-mounted cameras for the reality show *Cops*, however problematic, more accurately fit the description of *reality* TV. Programs such as *Survivor*, *The Bachelor*, *The Real World*, and even *The Osbournes* do not document or observe an independent reality through a camera, as documentary films purport to do; they record the behaviors and activities appropriate to self-consciously constructed situations. As Erica Goode stated in a *New York Times* article, shows like *Survivor*, *Big Brother*, and *The Bachelor* are direct descendants of the social psychology experiments of the sixties and seventies.[1] The film version of Stanley Milgram's infamous study *Obedience to Authority* and Philip Zimbardo's 1971 Stanford study provide the generic roots of reality TV. What these texts have in common, from Milgram's study to *Big Brother*, is the construction of an all-encompassing social situation with compelling rules and rigidly defined roles that influence, in often highly predictable ways, the social actions of the people who are in the situations. What reality TV presents is not the unobtrusive observations of an event that would have existed independently of the camera, but a highly controlled situation that produces a social drama constructed specifically for the camera (or experimenter).

What is key here is that the type of manipulation and control which television shows like *Survivor*, *Big Brother*, or *The Bachelor* perform regularly with impunity would never be allowed in any kind of legitimate social science experiment, at least not without rigorous and strict oversight by a Human Subjects Review board. 5

As the institutional representation of the formalized code of the rights of participants in experiments or research, it is the principles of Human Subjects Review that suggest the deeper problems of the reality TV genre. Two of the fundamental principles of subjects' rights are the right to confidentiality and the right of voluntary participation.[2] The first right does not apply to the landscape of reality TV; indeed the participants of *Big Brother* or *Survivor*, we assume, gladly waive the right of confidentiality for their 15 minutes of fame. However, the right to participate voluntarily and to be free from coercion carries with it

[1]Goode, Erica. "Hey, What if Contestants Give Each Other Shocks?" *The New York Times*, August 27, 2000, in Ideas and Trends, p. 3.

[2]*The Belmont Report*, Office of the Secretary, Ethical Principles and Guidelines for the Protection of Human Subjects of Research, The National Commission for the Protection of Human Subjects of Biomedical and Behavioral Research, Department of Health, Education and Welfare, April 18, 1979.

some interesting corollaries that directly affect the manipulation and control that go into the production of reality TV. Included in the notion of voluntary participation is the right of participants to review any and all materials that are derived from their participation (e.g., audio or video recording) and even to have them destroyed if they wish. It is the goal of this rule to shelter the participant from any embarrassment or discomfort (just think of Milgram's "teachers" and their extreme unease as they believed they administered electrical shocks to the "learners"). This right of participants, which is a given in legitimate social science research, would completely transform the nature of production of reality TV. To give the participants or contestants of a reality TV show the right and power to destroy any part of the record would shift the power from the producers of the show to the participants. We see within this set of issues the coercion that goes into the making of reality TV; the contestants have no rights to the final text, which they have had a real hand in producing. The participants have only two choices: they can submit to the wishes of the producers or walk off the show. This lack of control on the part of the participants of reality TV mirrors the more subtle lack of choice of television viewers. Just as reality TV show participants have no say in the day-to-day production of the shows they take part in, so television viewers have no control over what appears on their television screens. Viewers, like reality TV participants, have only one limited choice of any consequence: submit to the wishes of the broadcasters or turn off the show.

What seems to give reality TV its feeling of reality, its "reality effect," is the consolidation within the reality TV text of two powerful social discourses: surveillance and therapy. We can easily see a version of Foucault's panopticon at work in this genre.[3] For example, the total surveillance imposed on the Osbourne family, with 50 cameras following them continually, is an attempt to capture and display to the viewing audience the intimate elements in the lives of the Osbournes, much in the same way the observation tower of the panopticon aims to place the prisoners under constant inspection (or at least make them feel that way). However, the surveillance of reality shows differs from Bentham's and Foucault's formulation in a fundamental way: Bentham's panopticon disciplines the prisoner by inhibiting and thus curtailing behavior, but reality TV's panopticon sanctions (and disciplines) the participant to exhibit all types of behavior. Bentham's panopticon implants in the incarcerated a controlling gaze; a gaze once internalized within the incarcerated produces a self-disciplining, self-regulating subject. This discipline works through the interaction of the panoptic architecture and the subject's visible body to limit and reduce any unwanted behavior. Reality television works differently, as it imposes on the participants a visual regime that requires the exhibition of all kinds of behavior. For reality TV, behavior of all sorts must be rooted out, not for the sake of limiting it, but for the sake of multiplying it, for expanding it

[3]Foucault, Michel. *Discipline and Punish: The Birth of the Prison*, Vintage Books: New York, 1979.

and permitting it to play itself out. This can be seen in *The Osbournes* as we witness the family dealing with not only small domestic problems but with the major crises of alcoholism, drug use, and cancer. We have a kind of discipline (because the participants of reality TV are pressured to deliver the goods) through the *dis*inhibition and exhibition of what we believe is private behavior for television cameras. This surveillance does not stop at presenting the participants' actions, but must penetrate to the interior of the participant and expose for the spectacle his or her inner thoughts and emotions. This is the point at which mass media surveillance easily slides into the therapeutic realm.

Scholars such as T. J. Jackson Lears[4] and Mimi White[5] have pointed to the prevalence of the therapeutic ethos in modern culture, from advertising to talk shows. Reality TV has adopted the techniques of therapy, the use of the confession, the interview and the intimate disclosure, to extend its surveillance of the participants from their behavior to their emotions, desires, and thoughts. Surveillance must penetrate the exterior behavior of subjects and reveal the contents of their consciousness, and conscience. What was once the strict and private domain of therapists, psychotherapists, and counselors and their clients, is now open to public inspection. At one time it was enough for an individual to privately disclose to a professional their secret traumas, but within the mediatized therapeutic ethos, individuals must confess to the listener/camera and its audience, and we must listen and watch. In a society of total surveillance, therapy is no longer a means of helping people with their problems, but has become a technique of rendering us visible and transparent in all aspects of our lives.

So what about *The Osbournes*? Each member of the Osbournes has a developed performance persona in contrast to the anonymous celebrity wannabes who participate in reality shows. Unlike the participants in most reality shows, the Osbournes have a considerable amount of control over the conditions of production of the show. They negotiate a contract for an amount of money to which they agree, and cameras are not permitted in Ozzy and Sharon's bedroom; in most shows there is no guarantee participants will get the prize and they have no say as to the ground rules.

Furthermore, performance plays too much of a central role in *The* 10 *Osbournes* for the show to be categorized within the traditional definition of documentary, according to which any hint of self-conscious performance is an example of artifice or artificiality which then negates any claims to truth or reality. Their lives, up to the point of the show, were intertwined in the music and entertainment industries. Kelly and Jack's careers grew out of Ozzy's

[4]Lears, T. J. Jackson. "From Salvation to Self-Realization: Advertising and the Therapeutic Roots of the Consumer Culture, 1880–1930," in *The Culture of Consumption: Critical Essays in American History 1880–1980*, Richard Wightman Fox and T. J. Jackson Lears, ed., Pantheon Books: New York, 1983.

[5]White, Mimi. *Tele-Advising: Therapeutic Discourse in American Television*, The University of North Carolina Press: Chapel Hill, 1992.

career: family life was often "on the road" and contextualized by his perfor-mance career. To support this value, . . . the Osbourne children dropped out of school, with Sharon's blessing, to pursue their careers. To separate the Osbournes' real lives from performance seems impossible.

The Osbournes may more accurately be defined as a performative docu-mentary, which records the highly reflexive exhibitions of its participants. This subgenre records the presentations of performers from drag queens to rock stars, as exemplified by the film Paris Is Burning. As Stella Bruzzi states, "Performance has always been at the heart of documentary filmmaking and yet it has been treated with suspicion because it carries connotations of falsi-fication and fictionalization, traits that inherently destabilize the nonfiction pursuit."[6] The question that remains, then, is what are the Osbournes per-forming?

One level of performance is that of the rock star playing "dad." The Osbournes is an example of ethnographic programming, which instead of pro-viding a representation of an obscure tribe in a mountain village to a Western viewer, brings to mainstream middle-class America this "other" in our midst: a heavy metal rock star and his family in Beverly Hills, a remote community of extreme wealth and fame inaccessible to most Americans other than via television. But Ozzy's perennial working-class features reveal that he is not so "other" to most of us as he putters around the house taking out garbage, scooping up dog waste, and admonishing (with great irony) his kids not to use drugs. There is no otherness evident in these domestic scenes. We're amazed to see this celebrity functioning very much the way we do; we find the famil-iarity bizarre. Another level of performance is that because real families are so unlike any television portrayal of the family, the Osbournes may flaunt the other end of the TV family/real family dichotomy. They are aware of the pre-cedent and the irony they provide.

The better answer is that The Osbournes, as a performative documentary, is performing a new myth of rock 'n' roll: the myth of the aging rock star as doting father and the rock star as domesticated family man. Up to this point we have had only two myths for aging rock stars: old Mick and dead Janis. Rock stars either rust or fade away. Ozzy provides us the intimate details of an older rock star as he lives his life outside of his rock 'n' roll image: it is an image of an exasperated father and a homebody.

Also, it is important that we realize that MTV was the producer of this new myth. It is now a truism to say that MTV changed rock 'n' roll by making it more image-conscious. As the theory goes, rockers themselves were less image-conscious before MTV, less ruled by the laws of photogenic selection, and listeners were free to imagine their own stories and images along with the music. Critics of the music video phenomenon argue that MTV somehow dominated the listener's imagination with a cultural imperialism of the image,

[6]Bruzzi, Stella. New Documentary: A Critical Introduction, Routledge: London, 2000, p. 125.

though their theory is unfounded because whether or not listeners create their own little narratives or what they do is never discussed or proven. MTV did not make rock 'n' roll image-conscious; the image was a key component of the performance of rock 'n' roll from the beginning, as evidenced by the visuality of live concerts with the youthful male body as the focus. Only think about the pouring over of album covers, magazines, and rock stars appearing in movies and making TV appearances. MTV may have intensified it, but the importance of images for rock 'n' roll was always there. What MTV did to transform rock 'n' roll was to domesticate the image of rock stars: MTV turned rock stars into TV stars. The image transformed them from rare and luminous to mundane and pixeled. Just as the image of a movie star is elusive in contrast to the pedestrian television star accessible in every home, the presence of rock stars became a standard feature of the home, as ever present as soap operas, commercials, and sitcoms. It is a logical extension of MTV's televisual domestication of rock 'n' roll that a rocker's family would star in his own show about home life on MTV.

Yet, is it really a myth if we see their lives in such intimate detail? The   15 myths of rock 'n' roll are very distant to real lives. The myths of the lives of Jim Morrison, Janis Joplin, and Elvis were about living fast and dying young, something most of us don't do. The aging rock stars are still rock stars, of sorts, but we don't have the kind of knowledge of their lives as we have about Ozzy's life. In fact, aging rock stars are really caricatures of their former selves, sans their sex and physical appeal and their connection to youth culture. Rock 'n' roll was never about the home; it was about people who lived outside the conventions of patriarchy, the nuclear family, and the traditional home, which was marked by monogamy, sobriety, heterosexuality. The myth of rock 'n' roll rebellion offered youth a means of subverting the hearth and home, and the associated drug culture represented a means of escape from those boundaries and rebellion to family and rules. What makes this new myth resonate is that Ozzy is an established icon of the rock 'n' roll-as-rebellion myth. Looking at Ozzy as the doting husband, bat-head biter.

MTV had prepared the way for a performative documentary about a rock star "performing" in his home by continually broadcasting into the home images of rock stars performing. Furthermore, Ozzy was the perfect person for this. He has all the characteristics of rock 'n' roll excess, but is unusually grounded in his family life. The reason the show was so popular is that, unbeknownst to MTV, by sheer luck all these elements came together in *The Osbournes*.

READING THE TEXT

1. According to Pieto and Otter, how does *The Osbournes* allude both to classic sitcoms and anti-1950s sitcoms?

2. Why do the authors believe that most reality TV programs do not represent reality?

3. How do reality TV shows use "coercion" with participants, and what attitude do Pieto and Otter have toward this practice?

4. Define in your own words the roles that survellience and therapy play in reality television.

5. What do the authors mean by "performative documentary" (paras. 11, 13)?

READING THE SIGNS

1. Watch an episode of *The Osbournes*, and write an essay that supports, challenges, or modifies Pieto and Otter's position that the program is "performing a new myth of rock 'n' roll" (para. 13).

2. Drawing on the authors' comments about reality TV's coercive control of contestants, write an analysis of the episode of *Average Joe* that Francine Prose describes in the opening to "Voting Democracy off the Island: Reality TV and the Republican Ethos" (p. 222).

3. Watch an episode of another supposedly unscripted program such as *Real World,* and analyze its "reality effect" (para. 7). Does the program display the same use of surveillance and therapy that Pieto and Otter find in *The Osbournes*, or is the reality effect achieved through different means?

4. In class, discuss the implications of Pieto and Otter's claim that "the type of manipulation and control which television shows like *Survivor*, *Big Brother*, or *The Bachelor* perform regularly with impunity would never be allowed in any kind of legitimate social science experiment, at least not without rigorous and strict oversight by a Human Subjects Review board" (para. 5). Use the discussion as a springboard for your own argumentative essay that considers the social and ethical implications of reality TV. To develop your ideas further, consult Francine Prose's "Voting Democracy off the Island: Reality TV and the Republican Ethos" (p. 222) and Anita Creamer's "Reality TV Meets Plastic Surgery: An Ugly Shame" (p. 229).

5. Pieto and Otter argue that *The Osbournes* presents a domesticated version of a formerly rebellious cultural figure, the rock star. Considering their position, write an argument that supports, challenges, or complicates the proposition that, even when considered "trailblazing," TV programming nonetheless tends to preserve traditional cultural values. Develop your ideas by consulting Marisa Connolly's "Homosexuality on Television: The Heterosexualization of *Will and Grace*" (p. 287), Andre Mayer's "The New Sexual Stone Age" (p. 284), and Susan Douglas's "Signs of Intelligent Life on TV" (p. 270).

"You're Fired."

Reading the Signs

1. What is *The Apprentice*? To what does "You're Fired" refer? Provide reasons why this expression has become a popular catchphrase.

2. What is the purpose of this banner? What does it promote? Is it, in your opinion, effective?

JAMES HAROLD

A Moral Never-Never Land: Identifying with Tony Soprano

Tony Soprano kills people. He breaks their legs and threatens to castrate them. Yet, somehow, James Harold likes Tony Soprano. He knows this might seem odd, and he wonders whether there is anything morally wrong with it. Since Harold (b. 1971) is also a philosopher, he is well equipped to reflect on the matter, as he does in this philosophical exploration, which first appeared in The Sopranos and Philosophy *(2004), of the moral effect of* The Sopranos. *Arguing that* The Sopranos *offers a multifaceted view of gangster life that combines both sympathetic and repulsive elements, Harold concludes that it is indeed beneficial for such a TV show to stimulate viewers to think deeply about the nature of good and evil. An assistant professor of philosophy at Mount Holyoke College, Harold's essays have been published in the* Journal of Aesthetics and Art Criticism, Philosophical Investigations, *and the* British Journal of Aesthetics.

I like Tony Soprano; I can't help it. I like him despite the fact that I recognize that he's a vicious and dangerous criminal. I don't particularly *want* to like him, and I certainly don't think I would like him if he were a real person who lived down the street from me. If he were really my neighbor, I think I'd feel for him what the Cusamanos do: a mixture of fear, fascination, and disgust. Nonetheless, recognizing that he is fictional, I like him. I find myself sympathizing with him: when he is depressed, I pity him; when he is wronged, I feel anger towards those who have betrayed him; and when he is successful, I share in his happiness. I want him to do well. I root for him to defeat his opponents, and, at the end of Season Four, for him to win back his wife Carmela.

Is there anything *morally* wrong with caring about Tony Soprano in this way? If Tony Soprano were a real person, then most people would agree that liking him is at least a little bit morally unsavory. This is Charmaine Bucco's opinion, for example, especially with regard to her husband Artie's friendship with Tony, and it's also the view of most of the other non-Mafia related characters on the show, such as Dr. Melfi's friends and family, the Cusamanos, and so on. But Tony Soprano isn't real — he's fictional, and I know that even if the Cusamanos don't. So what could be wrong with my liking Tony Soprano, given that I know that *The Sopranos* is a work of fiction?

From time to time, as political winds change, politicians, including, for example, Tipper Gore, Joseph Lieberman, and Bob Dole, have weighed in against various artworks in popular culture on the grounds that these artworks are morally dangerous. *The Sopranos* has attracted its fair share of this kind of criticism. Usually these criticisms are answered by proponents of freedom of expression, and the discussion turns to censorship and the necessity of toleration and diversity of viewpoints. What often gets left behind in these debates is the crucial issue of whether or not there really is any reason to think that a series like *The Sopranos* can be morally corrupting. It is often unclear exactly how artworks like *The Sopranos* are supposed to be bad for us. One of the things that worries some of us is that television shows like *The Sopranos* make very bad people seem, well, likeable.

When Is Art Dangerous?

The first Western philosopher to worry seriously about the moral effects of fiction on its audience was Plato. Plato worried about the way that the dramatic poets like Homer played on the emotions of audience members in ways that could be dangerous and manipulative. Poetry, Plato believed, evokes strong emotion in ways that could undermine social stability. In Plato's time, a dramatic poem like *The Odyssey* would be read aloud or sung in a public performance, and so poetry, for Plato, is more like theater for us. An ideal society, Plato thought, would be governed by principles of reason, and our willingness to follow through on these rational principles could be weakened by desires arising from strong emotion — the province of poetry. Poetry was supposed to be dangerous because it can lead us to sympathize with fictional characters, and thus the feelings of the fictional characters come to infect the audience. Plato wrote:

> When even the best of us hear Homer or one of the other tragedians imitating one of the heroes sorrowing and making a long lamenting speech or singing and beating his breast, you know that we enjoy it, give ourselves up to following it, sympathize with the hero, take his sufferings seriously, and praise as a good poet the one who affects us most in this way.[1]

In the end, the feelings of the audience and the feelings of the character are the same, and the audience may feel pity, or grief, even when it's not appropriate to do so. Further, we may carry these inappropriate emotions home with us, and they can become part of our character, and affect the way we act. Plato recognized how strongly we can feel about poetry, and the power that this passion can have: sympathetic attention to art, he said, "nurtures and waters them and establishes them as rulers in us."[2] These passions can become so strong that we can no longer control them in our everyday lives. Plato's example is of a man who enjoys comic plays and who then comes to act like a buffoon at

---

[1]Plato, *Republic* (605c–d), translated by G.M.A. Grube and C.D.C. Reeve. (Indianapolis: Hackett, 1992).
[2]Plato, 606d.

home; but someone who enjoyed a show like *The Sopranos* could well be possessed by more dangerous emotions, like rage, revenge, or contempt for ordinary people. If you are inclined to think that Plato's arguments don't apply to modern audiences, consider the following quote, taken from a fan Web site discussion of "University," which speaks to just this kind of worry.

> When my boyfriend and I watch *The Sopranos*, he gets so caught up, you would think it was happening to him. This gentle man, who wouldn't harm a fly. It's strange phenomena [*sic*], and not unlike soap addicts who confuse TV with reality.[3]

In the nineteenth century, Leo Tolstoy expressed similar concerns about art (including much of his own writing) in his book *What Is Art?* Tolstoy had undergone a deep religious experience late in his life, and he came to believe that most art was morally corrupt. Like Plato, he held that art evoked strong emotions in its audience, and he believed that many such emotions are, in his view, morally corrupting. Only art motivated by true Christian feeling, according to Tolstoy, could be morally acceptable. Tolstoy therefore rejected virtually all art, except popular Christian peasant art, which, he believed, conveyed only simple Christian love. Other artworks transmitted corrupt feelings to their audiences — feelings of unjust pride or lust, for example.[4] These feelings make people worse morally, because the feelings are selfish, and they alienate people from one another.

Plato and Tolstoy are separated by thousands of years, but their views share certain features in common: they both hold that art corrupts its audience by playing on emotion; they both hold that some art is worse than others in doing so; they believe that the emotional impact of art is great enough to influence how we act and what kind of people we become, so that art can make us bad people; they were both particularly critical of the most popular artists of their day. There is little doubt that both of them would have disapproved of *The Sopranos*. Should we, like Plato and Tolstoy, be worried that we might be infected by watching *The Sopranos*, and caring about the immoral protagonists?

Plato and Tolstoy have their present-day counterparts, too. Some cognitive scientists believe that when we watch a television show like *The Sopranos*, we simulate the feelings of the characters portrayed on screen. That is, we use our own minds to imitate what we imagine is going on in the minds of characters, and we feel an emotion that is in some ways like the emotion that the character feels. This emotion can then affect us in a number of ways. We sometimes call this "sympathizing" or "identifying" with a character onscreen. Though in many cases we are able to separate the character's emotion from

---

[3]<http://www.the-sopranos.com/db/ep32_review.htm>. The post was anonymous.
[4]One important difference between Plato and Tolstoy is that Tolstoy thought that the feelings transmitted were the feelings of the artist or author, whereas Plato thought that they were the feelings of the character.

our own feelings, sometimes our imaginings of the fictional character's emotions infect and affect our own.[5]

Tony Soprano does this himself in "Proshai, Livushka." After the death of his mother, Tony watches his favorite film, *Public Enemy*. In this movie, Jimmy Cagney's character is a gangster with a gentle, loving mother. As Tony watches, he sympathizes with the Cagney character, and imagines having a loving, trusting relationship with his mother. This makes him smile, at first, and then cry, as he compares this imagined mother-son relationship with his own experience. We understand why Tony is so deeply affected by this film, because we can also be affected by works of fiction. Tony is moved by identifying with the Cagney character, and we are moved by identifying with Tony.

A key feature of this view is that we pick out a character to identify with, and we focus on that person's feelings and emotions. It is this character that we identify with; he or she is the one that we know the best, and often, he or she is the one that we like the most. In the case of *The Sopranos*, despite a large, strong ensemble cast, the primary character with whom audiences identify is Tony himself. This is how I come to care about Tony, and why I feel relief when he is successful, even when his "success" consists in murder, as when he strangles the mob informant Febby Petrulio in "College."

The problem with this sympathetic identification is that sometimes the character with whom we identify has thoughts and feelings which are morally reprehensible, and by identifying with that character, we risk being infected by these vicious sentiments. We might start to think that Tony's views about violence and vengeance are reasonable, or we might come to share his propensity for anger, jealousy, rage, and suspicion. If imagining these feelings leads us to share them (even to a small extent), then liking Tony could make a person morally worse.

Why *The Sopranos*?

There are so many works of popular art that feature gangsters — not to mention other kinds of vicious people — as protagonists that it hardly seems fair to pick on *The Sopranos*. *Godfather Parts I, II, and III*, *Goodfellas*, *Carlito's Way*, *Scarface*, *Casino*, and *Public Enemy* are just a few examples of films that feature gangsters as main characters. (Most of these movies are referenced and discussed by the characters in *The Sopranos*, especially by Silvio Dante, who loves to imitate Al Pacino's character from *The Godfather*.) But *The Sopranos* distinguishes itself from these other works in three ways. First, *The Sopranos* is an ongoing television series, not a two-hour movie. As of this writing, four seasons comprising fifty-two episodes have been shown, and at least two more

[5]This phenomenon is discussed by Robert Gordon in his "Sympathy, Simulation, and the Impartial Spectator," in *Mind and Morals: Essays on Ethics and Cognitive Science*, edited by Larry May, Marilyn Friedman, and Andy Clark (Boston: MIT Press, 1996), pp. 165–80.

seasons are planned. That will make more than three *days* worth of material if one were to sit down and watch them all back-to-back. By contrast, all the films of the *Godfather* series, taken together, would take fewer than ten hours to watch. So loyal viewers of *The Sopranos* spend a long time with these characters, getting to know much more about them, and potentially, to care much more about them than viewers ever could with a film character. Not surprisingly, we are more deeply affected by characters we spend more time with and get to know better, and we get to spend a lot of time with Tony and friends.

Second, the gangsters in *The Sopranos*, especially Tony, are portrayed in deeply psychological and often quite intimate ways. We often get to see Tony's dreams (occasionally we see other characters' dreams, such as Christopher's and Dr. Melfi's, but not often). Through Tony's sessions with Dr. Melfi, we get to know Tony's feelings much better than we could otherwise. In those sessions, we get to understand his childhood (through flashbacks), his hopes and concerns, and his fears. We get a very strong picture of Tony as a complete human being. The character himself is a rich and complex one. In addition to being a gangster (with all that implies) we also learn that Tony tries, in his own way, to be a good father and husband, that he cares deeply about his children and wants them to do well. We learn that he loves his friends deeply, even those (like Big Pussy) that he ends up killing. He has a strong sense of responsibility, and when he says he will do something, he feels bound to do it. Despite (perhaps because of) his evil, vicious qualities, Tony has some good features, as well. Tony Soprano is a more fully developed character than any other fictional gangster ever created, and we get to know him intimately.

Third, *The Sopranos* strives for verisimilitude. It does not have the ironic stylishness of *Goodfellas*, nor is it an idealized period piece like *The Godfather*. With one major exception — the number of gang killings[6] — the show is strikingly realistic. Virtually every element, including the psychoanalysis, the New Jersey settings, the language used by the characters, Tony and Carmela's family dynamics, the FBI surveillance techniques, and the mob structure and organization is very close to what is found in the real world. The show is set in our own time and many of the phenomena that the characters deal with — for example, Prozac, 9/11, Attention Deficit Disorder, coaches sexually assaulting student athletes, the competitiveness of college acceptance, teen drug use — are phenomena that we deal with as well. The characters on *The Sopranos* are aware of the fictional portrayals of gangsters and they discuss these. In "Christopher," Carmela and her friends attend a lecture about the portrayal of Italian-American women as mob wives; Dr. Melfi's ex-husband Richard complains over and over again about the stereotyped portrayal of Italian-Americans

---

[6]One fan Web site counts thirty-nine deaths over the first four seasons (http://www.the-sopranos.com/db/bodycount.htm). The number of killings on the show far exceeds the number in real life for similar mobs.

in gangster films. The psychiatrist who Tony consults when Dr. Melfi won't see him makes a reference to the Robert DeNiro comedy *Analyze This*. *The Sopranos* thus continues the tradition of gangster fictions, but in a deeper, more reflective way than most do: like us, the characters on *The Sopranos* know that these other stories are fictional.

All of these features conspire to make Tony Soprano a very sympathetic character. When Plato says, "We enjoy it, give ourselves up to following it, sympathize with the hero, take his sufferings seriously," the hero he describes could be Tony. But sympathizing with Tony is not like sympathizing with Artie Bucco; Tony is a terribly vicious and violent man. Tony personally commits five murders that we see on screen: he strangles Febby Petrulio in "College"; he shoots one of Junior's hired killers in "I Dream of Jeanie Cusamano" (this one, at least, is self-defense); in "From Where to Eternity," he kills Matt Bevilaqua with Big Pussy; and then he, Paulie, and Silvio turn around and shoot Big Pussy in "Funhouse"; finally, he kills Ralph Cifaretto in "Whoever Did This." On top of these five, he orders many, many other killings which are carried out by other members of his gang (some shown onscreen and some off). He loses his temper continually, administering beatings to girlfriends (Irina, Gloria) and business associates (Mikey Palmice, Georgie the bartender, Ralphie Cifaretto, Assemblyman Zellman). He doesn't ever hit Dr. Melfi, but he comes quite close. On top of his propensity for personal violence, we have his virulent racism and homophobia, his profiting from corruption, gambling, drugs, and other enterprises that presumably ruin the lives of people we never see on screen. There is no doubt that Tony Soprano is evil, vicious, and morally bankrupt. Yet we like him.

Is It Morally Wrong to Watch *The Sopranos*?

The Sopranos leads its audience to identify with a terrible person. Is it then wrong to watch the show? Could identifying with Tony make us worse people too? In the end, I doubt it. There are a number of reasons why *The Sopranos* as a whole does more than just make bad people look good. First, although Tony Soprano is the main character on the show, some of the main characters of *The Sopranos* who are quite sympathetic are not gangsters and are pretty good people, particularly Dr. Melfi and Meadow Soprano. Many other characters, if not good, at least suffer pangs of conscience for the evil they do (or the evil men they love), and they try to do good from time to time: Carmela, Artie Bucco,[7] and Adriana, for example. These characters struggle continually with their moral positions, and their complicity in the crimes

---

[7]Artie is a very interesting character, morally speaking. For the most part, he is not involved in Tony's activities. Artie did have a brief fling with loan sharking in season four, but it didn't work out, and he wasn't really up to the nasty side of it. But he does indirectly profit from Tony's business, and he keeps silent about some of his wrongdoings.

being committed all around them. Even some thoroughly bad characters like Christopher and Paulie are forced from time to time to reflect on the moral consequences of what they do ("From Where to Eternity").

But the primary moral center of the show, which serves to balance out 15 the immoral facets of these attractive characters, is Jennifer Melfi's psychiatrist's office. It is here that the viewer is most often led to identify not just with Tony, but with his victims, and to see Tony's life in a richer, more morally sophisticated way. In a long-running series like *The Sopranos*, we see things from more than just one point of view. Tony's psychoanalysis sessions with Dr. Melfi afford us an opportunity to see Tony from the outside as well as from the inside, and to remind us of the self-deception and flimsy justifications that Tony uses in order to continue his life of crime and violence. Tony likes to compare himself to a soldier at war, or a "captain of industry," but he doesn't convince anyone with these analogies (perhaps not even himself). Dr. Melfi's facial expressions make clear her contempt for these facile attempts at justification.

Consider the episode entitled "House Arrest." In this episode, on the advice of his lawyer, Tony has decided to distance himself from criminal activity and spend his time with his legitimate businesses. He grows increasingly restless and agitated; he develops a serious rash; he becomes irritable and frustrated, and he complains of this to Dr. Melfi. Dr. Melfi asks him: "Do you know why a shark keeps moving? . . . There's a psychological condition known as alexithymia,[8] common in certain personalities. The individual craves almost ceaseless action, which enables them to avoid acknowledging the abhorrent things they do." When Tony asks what happens when such people are forced to stop and reflect, she answers, "They have time to think about their behavior. How what they do affects other people. About feelings of emptiness and self-loathing, haunting them since childhood. And they crash." Tony gets her point, but he chooses to respond to this lesson not by reflecting, but by returning to Satriale's with the other mobsters and getting back into action — thus, the shark gets back in motion rather than think about the ethical consequences of how he lives.

Jennifer Melfi continually reminds us as an audience of the dangers of seeing things exclusively from Tony's point of view, and her character provides an alternative point of view on Tony's life and actions. When she complains to her psychiatrist, Elliot Kupferberg, that she is in a "moral never-never land" with Tony Soprano, "Not wanting to judge but to treat," we know exactly how she feels ("From Where to Eternity"). Dr. Melfi, and sometimes other characters such as the Buccos, Meadow, or even Carmela, provide us with an alternative moral center that allows us to see Tony and his actions from the outside, and

[8]Alexithymia, strictly speaking, is somewhat different than Jennifer Melfi's account of it here. Ordinarily, alexithymia refers to a condition wherein the patient has difficulty in recognizing her or his own emotions. Melfi is describing how alexithymia manifests itself in sociopathic personalities like Tony's.

they remind us of the moral consequences of what Tony does. After Dr. Melfi's rapist goes free, she realizes that she could tell Tony about her rapist, and be revenged on him, but she does not do so ("Employee of the Month"). During this sequence, we sympathize with Melfi, and her moral choice, not with Tony. The finale of the second season ("Funhouse") concludes with one of the few montage sequences ever used in the series.[9] We see alternating shots of the Soprano family celebrating Meadow's graduation, and various shots of the criminal activities that will be paying Meadow's tuition. By juxtaposing these two scenes, the producers of *The Sopranos* remind us that what we like about Tony cannot be separated from the evil he does.

The problem with Plato's and Tolstoy's moral criticism of art is that their emotional theories of artistic identification are simplistic. We do not just take on one character or one point of view, and we do not respond emotionally in only one way. *The Sopranos* provides us with many different ways of seeing the life of a gangster, and it also invites us to feel in a variety of ways about it. Sometimes the show does make Tony and his crew look quite sympathetic; but it also provides us with other perspectives, and permits us, if we try, to formulate a complex and sophisticated personal moral response to gangster life, and not merely to imitate Tony.

This does not mean that Plato's and Tolstoy's concerns about art should be dismissed lightly. They are right that artworks can affect us deeply, and sometimes cause audiences to identify with immoral characters. But whether or not these artworks are morally corrupting depends on other factors as well. Television shows like *The Sopranos* which provide multiple moral perspectives on evil characters, and which offer room for moral reflection, might even be good for us, rather than evil.

READING THE TEXT

1. Explain in your own words why Plato and Tolstoy believed that art could be "dangerous."

2. How, according to Harold, does the depiction of the mob in *The Sopranos* compare with other cinematic portrayals of gangsters?

3. Why does Harold believe that Dr. Melfi is the "moral center" (para. 15) of the program?

4. In class, discuss the effect of Harold's first-person opener: "I like Tony Soprano; I can't help it" (para. 1). Why do you think he begins with this confession?

---

[9]The second season has more of these moments of moral reflection and serious moral examination than any other season: from the very beginning of the season, when Dr. Melfi has to decide whether she has a moral responsibility to take Tony back as a patient, to this final sequence, the characters and the creators grapple with right and wrong in a very direct way. None of the other seasons has as much sustained, direct attention to morality.

READING THE SIGNS

1. Write an essay supporting, opposing, or modifying Harold's contention that *The Sopranos* has a moral center and that it is Dr. Melfi.

2. Watch an episode of *The Sopranos*, and assess the validity of Harold's claim that programs like it "might even be good for us, rather than evil" (para. 19).

3. Read or review Vivian C. Sobchack's "The Postmorbid Condition" (p. 372), and then write an essay in which you argue whether *The Sopranos* displays the "carelessness toward violence" trend that Sobchack believes dominates contemporary cinema.

4. Compare and contrast *The Sopranos* with one of the gangster films that Harold lists in paragraph 10. How is the mob represented in each work, and what does that representation suggest about the values and interests of the era in which it was created?

5. Read or review Robert B. Ray's "The Thematic Paradigm" (p. 308), and write an essay in which you argue whether Tony Soprano can be considered a hero. If so, what kind of hero is he? If not, why not?

CARL MATHESON

The Simpsons, *Hyper-Irony, and the Meaning of Life*

Don't have a cow or anything, but most comedy, as Carl Matheson (b. 1957) points out in this analysis of The Simpsons, *which first appeared in* The Simpsons and Philosophy *(2001), is based in cruelty. And while Matheson doesn't "mean to argue that the makers of* The Simpsons *intended the show primarily as a theater of cruelty," he does "imagine that they did." At any rate, Matheson suggests, the pervasive irony that makes the program funny should serve as a warning to anyone who believes that this ever-popular cartoon sitcom is a warm endorser of family values. Carl Matheson is a professor in, and chair of, the department of philosophy at the University of Manitoba. He has published essays in the* British Journal of Aesthetics, *the* Journal of Aesthetics and Art Criticism, *and* Philosophy and Literature.

DISAFFECTED YOUTH #1: Here comes that cannonball guy. He's cool.
DISAFFECTED YOUTH #2: Are you being sarcastic, dude?
DISAFFECTED YOUTH #1: I don't even know anymore.

— "Homerpalooza," Season 7

What separates the comedies that were shown on television fifty, forty, or even twenty-five years ago from those of today? First, we may notice technological differences, the difference between black-and-white and color, the difference between film stock (or even kinescope) and video. Then there are the numerous social differences. For instance, the myth of the universal traditional two-parent family is not as secure as it was in the 1950s and 1960s, and the comedies of the different eras reflect changes in its status — although even early comedies of the widow/widower happy fifties, sixties, and seventies were full of nontraditional families, such as are found in *The Partridge Family, The Ghost and Mrs. Muir, Julia, The Jerry van Dyke Show, Family Affair, The Courtship of Eddie's Father, The Andy Griffith Show, The Brady Bunch, Bachelor Father*, and *My Little Margie*. Also, one may note the ways in which issues such as race have received different treatments over the decades.

But I would like to concentrate on a deeper transformation: today's comedies, at least most of them, are funny in different ways from those of decades past. In both texture and substance the comedy of *The Simpsons* and *Seinfeld* is worlds apart from the comedy of *Leave It to Beaver* and *The Jack Benny Show*, and is even vastly different from much more recent comedies, such as *MASH* and *Maude*. First, today's comedies tend to be highly *quotational*: many of today's comedies essentially depend on the device of referring to or quoting other works of popular culture. Second, they are *hyper-ironic*: the flavor of humor offered by today's comedies is colder, based less on a shared sense of humanity than on a sense of world-weary cleverer-than-thouness. In this essay I would like to explore the way in which *The Simpsons* uses both quotational-ism and hyper-ironism and relate these devices to currents in the contempo-rary history of ideas.

Quotationalism

Television comedy has never completely foregone the pleasure of using pop culture as a straight man. However, early instances of quotation tended to be opportunistic; they did not comprise the substance of the genre. Hence, in sketch comedy, one would find occasional references to popular culture in *Wayne and Shuster* and *Johnny Carson*, but these references were really treated as just one more source of material. The roots of quotationalism as a main source of material can be found in the early seventies with the two visionary comedies, *Mary Hartman Mary Hartman*, which lampooned soap operas by be-ing an ongoing soap opera, and *Fernwood 2Night*, which, as a small-budget talk show, took on small-budget talk shows. Quotationalism then came much more to the attention of the general public between the mid-seventies and early eight-ies through *Saturday Night Live, Late Night with David Letterman*, and *SCTV*. Given the mimical abilities of its cast and its need for weekly material, the chief comedic device of *SNL* was parody — of genres (the nightly news, television de-bates), of particular television shows (*I Love Lucy, Star Trek*) and of movies (*Star Wars*). The type of quotationalism employed by Letterman was more abstract and less based on particular shows. Influenced by the much earlier absurdism of such hosts as Dave Garroway, Letterman immediately took the formulas of television and cinema beyond their logical conclusions (*The Equalizer Guy*, chimp cam, and spokesperson Larry "Bud" Melman).

However, it was *SCTV* that gathered together the various strains of quota-tionalism and synthesized them into a deeper, more complex, and more mys-terious whole. Like *Mary Hartman*, and unlike *SNL*, it was an ongoing series with recurring characters such as Johnny Larue, Lola Heatherton, and Bobby Bittman. However, unlike *Mary Hartman*, the ongoing series was about the workings of a television station. *SCTV* was a television show about the pro-cess of television. Through the years, the models upon which characters like Heatherton and Bittman were based vanished somewhat into the background, as Heatherton and Bittman started to breathe on their own, and therefore, came to occupy a shadowy space between real (fictional) characters and simu-lacra. Furthermore, *SCTV*'s world came to intersect the real world as some of the archetypes portrayed (such as Jerry Lewis) were people in real life. Thus, *SCTV* eventually produced and depended upon patterns of inter-textuality and cross-referencing that were much more thoroughgoing and subtle than those of any program that preceded it.

The Simpsons was born, therefore, just as the use of quotationalism was ma-   5
turing. However, *The Simpsons* was not the same sort of show as *SNL* and *SCTV*.
One major difference, of course, was that *The Simpsons* was animated while the
others were (largely) not, but this difference does not greatly affect the relevant
potential for quotationalism — although it may be easier to draw the bridge of
the *U.S.S. Enterprise* than to rebuild it and re-enlist the entire original cast of *Star
Trek*. The main difference is that as an ostensibly ongoing family comedy, *The
Simpsons* was both plot and character driven, where the other shows, even those
that contained ongoing characters, were largely sketch driven. Furthermore,
unlike *Mary Hartman Mary Hartman*, which existed to parody soap operas, *The
Simpsons* did not have the *raison d'être* of parodying the family-based comedies
of which it was an instance. The problem then was this: how does one transform
an essentially non-quotational format into an essentially quotational show?

The answer to the above question lies in the form of quotationalism
employed by *The Simpsons*. By way of contrast, let me outline what it was de-
finitively not. Take, for instance, a *Wayne and Shuster* parody of Wilde's *The
Picture of Dorian Gray*. In the parody, instead of Gray's sins being reflected in
an artwork, while he remains pure and young in appearance, the effects of
Gray's overeating are reflected in the artwork, while he remains thin. The situation's permissions and combinations are squeezed and coaxed to produce
the relevant gags and ensuing yuks. End of story. Here the quotationalism is
very direct; it is the source both of the story line and of the supposedly humorous contrast between the skit and the original novel. Now, compare this
linear and one-dimensional use of quotation for the purposes of parody with
the pattern of quotation used in a very short passage from an episode from
The Simpsons entitled "A Streetcar Named Marge." In the episode, Marge is
playing Blanche Dubois opposite Ned Flanders's Stanley in *Streetcar!*, her
community theatre's musical version of the Tennessee Williams play. In need
of day care for little Maggie, she sends Maggie to the Ayn Rand School for
Tots, which is run by the director's sister. Headmistress Sinclair, a strict discipli-
narian and believer in infant self-reliance, confiscates all of the tots' pacifiers
which causes an enraged Maggie to lead her classmates in a highly organized
reclamation mission, during which the theme from *The Great Escape* plays in
the background. Having re-acquired the pacifiers the group sits, arrayed in rows,
making little sucking sounds, so that when Homer arrives to pick up Maggie,
he is confronted with a scene from Hitchcock's *The Birds*.

The first thing that one can say about these quotations is that they are
very funny. . . . To see that these quotations are funny just watch the show
again. Second, we note that these quotations are not used for the purpose of
parody.[1] Rather, they are allusions, designed to provide unspoken meta-
phorical elaboration and commentary about what is going on in the scene.

---

[1] I don't mean to say that *The Simpsons* does not make use of parody. The episode currently under discussion contains a brilliant parody of Broadway adaptations, from its title to
the show-stopping tune "A Stranger Is Just a Friend You Haven't Met!"

The allusion to Ayn Rand underscores the ideology and personal rigidity of Headmistress Sinclair. The theme music from *The Great Escape* stresses the determination of Maggie and her cohort. The allusion to *The Birds* communicates the threat of the hive-mind posed by many small beings working as one. By going outside of the text via these nearly instantaneous references, *The Simpsons* manages to convey a great deal of extra information extremely economically. Third, the most impressive feature of this pattern of allusion is its pace and density, where this feature has grown more common as the series has matured. Early episodes, for instance the one in which Bart saws the head off the town's statue of Jebediah Springfield, are surprisingly free of quotation. Later episodes derive much of their manic comic energy from their rapid-fire sequence of allusions. This density of allusion is perhaps what sets *The Simpsons* most apart from any show that has preceded it.

However, the extent to which *The Simpsons* depends on other elements of pop culture is not without cost. Just as those readers who are unfamiliar with Frazer's *Golden Bough* will be hindered in their attempt to understand Eliot's "The Waste Land," and just as many modern-day readers will be baffled by many of the Biblical and classical allusions that play important roles in the history of literature, many of today's viewers won't fully understand much of what goes on in *The Simpsons* due to an unfamiliarity with the popular culture that forms the basis for the show's references. Having missed the references, these people may interpret *The Simpsons* as nothing more than a slightly off-base family comedy populated with characters who are neither very bright nor very interesting. From these propositions they will probably derive the theorem that the show is neither substantial nor funny, and also the lemma that the people who like the show are deficient in taste, intelligence, or standards of personal mental hygiene. However, not only do the detractors of the show miss a great deal of its humor, they also fail to realize that its pattern of quotations is an absolutely essential vehicle for developing character and for setting a tone. And, since these people are usually not huge fans of popular culture to begin with, they will be reluctant to admit that they are missing something significant. Oh well. It is difficult to explain color to a blind man, especially if he won't listen. On the other hand, those who enjoy connecting the quotational dots will enjoy their task all the more for its exclusivity. There is no joke like an in-joke: the fact that many people don't get *The Simpsons* might very well make the show both funnier and better to those who do.

Hyper-Ironism and the Moral Agenda

Without the smart-ass, comedy itself would be impossible. Whether one subscribes, as I do, to the thesis that all comedy is fundamentally cruel, or merely to the relatively spineless position that only the vast majority of comedy is fundamentally cruel, one has to admit that comedy has always relied upon the joys to be derived from making fun of others. However, usually the cruelty has been employed for a positive social purpose. In the sanctimonious *MASH*, Hawkeye and the gang were simply joking to "dull the pain of a world gone mad," and the butts of their jokes, such as Major Frank Burns, symbolized threats to the liberal values that the show perpetually attempted to reinforce in the souls of its late-twentieth-century viewers. In *Leave It to Beaver*, the link between humor and the instillation of family values is didactically obvious. A very few shows, most notably *Seinfeld*, totally eschewed a moral agenda.[2] *Seinfeld*'s ability to maintain a devoted audience in spite of a cast of shallow and petty characters engaged in equally petty and shallow acts is miraculous. So, as I approach *The Simpsons*, I would like to resolve the following questions. Does *The Simpsons* use its humor to promote a moral agenda? Does it use its humor to promote the claim that there is no justifiable moral agenda? Or, does it stay out of the moral agenda game altogether?

These are tricky questions, because data can be found to affirm each of them. To support the claim that *The Simpsons* promotes a moral agenda, one usually need look no further than Lisa and Marge. Just consider Lisa's speeches in favor of integrity, freedom from censorship, or any variety of touchy-feely social causes, and you will come away with the opinion that *The Simpsons* is just another liberal show underneath a somewhat thin but tasty crust of nastiness. One can even expect Bart to show humanity when it counts, as when, at military school, he defies sexist peer-pressure to cheer Lisa on in her attempt to complete an obstacle course. The show also seems to engage in self-righteous condemnation of various institutional soft targets. The political system of Springfield is corrupt, its police chief lazy and self-serving, and its Reverend Lovejoy ineffectual at best. Property developers stage a fake religious miracle in order to promote the opening of a mall. Mr. Burns tries to increase business at the power plant by blocking out the sun. Taken together, these examples seem to advocate a moral position of caring at the level of the individual, one which favors the family over any institution.

However, one can find examples from the show that seem to be denied accommodation within any plausible moral stance. In one episode, Frank Grimes (who hates being called "Grimey") is a constantly unappreciated model worker, while Homer is a much beloved careless slacker. Eventually, Grimes breaks down and decides to act just like Homer Simpson. While "acting like Homer" Grimes touches a transformer and is killed instantly. During the funeral oration by Reverend Lovejoy (for "Gri-yuh-mee, as he liked to be called") a snoozing Homer shouts out "Change the channel, Marge!" The rest of the service breaks into spontaneous and appreciative laughter, with Lenny saying "That's our Homer!" End of episode. In another episode, Homer is unintentionally responsible for the death of Maude Flanders, Ned's wife. In the crowd at a football game, Homer is eager to catch a T-shirt being shot

---

[2]For a different view, see Robert A. Epperson, "Seinfeld and the Moral Life," in William Irwin, ed., *Seinfeld and Philosophy: A Book about Everything and Nothing* (Chicago: Open Court, 2000), pp. 163–74.

from little launchers on the field. Just as one is shot his way, he bends over to pick up a peanut. The T-shirt sails over him and hits the devout Maude, knocking her out of the stands to her death. These episodes are difficult to locate on a moral map; they certainly do not conform to the standard trajectory of virtue rewarded.

Given that we have various data, some of which lead us towards and others away from the claim that *The Simpsons* is committed to caring, liberal family values, what should we conclude? Before attempting to reach a conclusion, I would like to go beyond details from various episodes of the show to introduce another form of possibly relevant evidence. Perhaps, we can better resolve the issue of *The Simpsons*' moral commitments by examining the way it relates to current intellectual trends. The reader should be warned that, although I think that my comments on the current state of the history of ideas are more or less accurate, they are greatly oversimplified. In particular, the positions that I will outline are by no means unanimously accepted.

Let's start with painting. The influential critic, Clement Greenberg, held that the goal of all painting was to work with flatness as the nature of its medium and he reconstructed the history of painting so that it was seen to culminate in the dissolution of pictorial three-dimensional space and the acceptance of total flatness by the painters of the mid-twentieth century. Painters were taken to be like scientific researchers whose work furthered the progress of their medium, where the idea of artistic progress was to be taken as literally as that of scientific progress. Because they were fundamentally unjustifiable and because they put painters into a straitjacket, Greenberg's positions gradually lost their hold, and no other well-supported candidates for the essence of painting could be found to take their place. As a result painting (and the other arts) entered a phase that the philosopher of art, Arthur Danto, has called "the end of art." By this Danto did not mean that art could no longer be produced, but rather that art could no longer be subsumed under a history of progress towards some given end.[3] By the end of the 1970s, many painters had turned to earlier, more representational styles, and their paintings were as much commentaries on movements from the past, like expressionism, and about the current vacuum in the history of art, as they were about their subject matter. Instead of being about the essence of painting, much of painting came to be about the history of painting. Similar events unfolded in the other artistic media as architects, filmmakers, and writers returned to the history of their disciplines.

However, painting was not the only area in which long-held convictions concerning the nature and inevitability of progress were aggressively challenged. Science, the very icon of progressiveness, was under attack from a number of quarters. Kuhn held (depending on which interpreter of him you agree with) either that there was no such thing as scientific progress, or that if there was, there were no rules for determining what progress and scientific rationality

---

[3]See Arthur Danto, *After the End of Art* (Princeton: Princeton University Press, 1996).

were. Feyerabend argued that people who held substantially different theories couldn't even understand what each other was saying, and hence that there was no hope of a rational consensus; instead he extolled the anarchistic virtues of "anything goes." Early sociological workers in the field of science studies tried to show that, instead of being an inspirational narrative of the disinterested pursuit of truth, the history of science was essentially a story of office-politics writ large, because every transition in the history of science could be explained by appeal to the personal interests and allegiances of the participants.[4] And, of course, the idea of philosophical progress has continued to be challenged. Writing on Derrida, the American philosopher Richard Rorty argues that anything like *the* philosophical truth is either unattainable, nonexistent, or uninteresting, that philosophy itself is a literary genre, and that philosophers should reconstrue themselves as writers who elaborate and reinterpret the writings of other philosophers. In other words, Rorty's version of Derrida recommends that philosophers view themselves as historically aware participants in a conversation, as opposed to quasi-scientific researchers.[5] Derrida himself favored a method known as deconstruction, which was popular several years ago, and which consisted of a highly technical method for undercutting texts by revealing hidden contradictions and unconscious ulterior motives. Rorty questions whether, given Derrida's take on the possibility of philosophical progress, deconstruction could be used only for negative purposes, that is, whether it could be used for anything more than making philosophical fun of other writings.

Let me repeat that these claims about the nature of art, science, and philosophy are highly controversial. However, all that I need for my purposes is the relatively uncontroversial claim that views such as these are now in circulation to an unprecedented extent. We are surrounded by a pervasive crisis of authority, be it artistic, scientific or philosophical, religious or moral, in a way that previous generations weren't. Now, as we slowly come back to earth and *The Simpsons*, we should ask this: if the crisis I described were as pervasive as I believe it to be, how might it be reflected generally in popular culture, and specifically in comedy?

We have already discussed one phenomenon that may be viewed as a consequence of the crisis of authority. When faced with the death of the idea of progress in their field, thinkers and artists have often turned to a reconsideration of the history of their discipline. Hence artists turn to art history, architects to the history of design, and so on. The motivation for this turn is natural; once one has given up on the idea that the past is merely the inferior pathway to a

15

---

[4]Thomas Kuhn, *The Structure of Scientific Revolutions*, second edition (Chicago: University of Chicago Press, 1970). Paul Feyerabend, *Against Method* (London: NLB, 1975). For a lively debate on the limits of the sociology of knowledge, see James Robert Brown (ed.), *Scientific Rationality: The Sociological Turn* (Dordrecht: Reidel, 1984).

[5]Richard Rorty, "Philosophy as a Kind of Writing," pp. 90–109 in *Consequences of Pragmatism* (Minneapolis: University of Minnesota Press, 1982).

better today and a still better tomorrow, one may try to approach the past on its own terms as an equal partner. Additionally, if the topic of progress is off the list of things to talk about, an awareness of history may be one of the few things left to fill the disciplinary conversational void. Hence, one may think that quotationalism is a natural offshoot of the crisis of authority, and that the prevalence of quotationalism in *The Simpsons* results from that crisis.

The idea that quotationalism in *The Simpsons* is the result of "something in the air" is confirmed by the stunning everpresence of historical appropriation throughout popular culture. Cars like the new Volkswagen Beetle and the PT Cruiser quote bygone days, and factories simply can't make enough of them. In architecture, New Urbanist housing developments try to re-create the feel of small towns of decades ago, and they have proven so popular that only the very wealthy can buy homes in them. The musical world is a hodgepodge of quotations of styles, where often the original music being quoted is simply sampled and re-processed.

To be fair, not every instance of historical quotationalism should be seen as the result of some widespread crisis of authority. For instance, the New Urbanist movement in architecture was a direct response to a perceived erosion of community caused by the deadening combination of economically segregated suburbs and faceless shopping malls; the movement used history in order to make the world a better place for people to live with other people. Hence the degree of quotationalism in *The Simpsons* could point towards a crisis in authority, but it could also stem from a strategy for making the world better, like the New Urbanism, or it could merely be a fashion accessory, like retro-khaki at the Gap.

No, if we want to plumb the depths of *The Simpsons'* connection with the crisis in authority we will have to look to something else, and it is at this point that I return to the original question of this section: does *The Simpsons* use its humor to promote a moral agenda? My answer is this: *The Simpsons* does not promote anything, because its humor works by putting forward positions only in order to undercut them. Furthermore, this process of undercutting runs so deeply that we cannot regard the show as merely cynical; it manages to undercut its cynicism too. This constant process of undercutting is what I mean by "hyper-ironism."

To see what I mean, consider "Scenes from the Class Struggle in Spring- [20] field," an episode from the show's seventh season. In this episode Marge buys a Coco Chanel suit for $90 at the Outlet Mall. While wearing the suit, she runs into an old high-school classmate. Seeing the designer suit and taking Marge to be one of her kind, the classmate invites Marge to the posh Springfield Glen Country Club. Awed by the gentility at the Club, and in spite of sniping from club members that she always wears the same suit, Marge becomes bent on social climbing. Initially alienated, Homer and Lisa fall in love with the club for its golf-course and stables. However, just as they are about to be inducted into the club, Marge realizes that her newfound obsession with social standing has taken precedence over her family. Thinking that the club also probably doesn't want them anyway, she and the family walk away. However, unbeknownst to the Simpsons, the club has prepared a lavish welcome party for them, and is terribly put out that they haven't arrived — Mr. Burns even "pickled the figs for the cake" himself.

At first glance, this episode may seem like another case of the show's reaffirmation of family values: after all, Marge chooses family over status. Furthermore, what could be more hollow than status among a bunch of shallow inhuman snobs? However, the people in the club turn out to be inclusive and fairly affectionate, from golfer Tom Kite who gives Homer advice on his swing despite that fact that Homer has stolen his golf clubs — and shoes — to Mr. Burns, who thanks Homer for exposing his dishonesty at golf. The jaded cynicism that seems to pervade the club is gradually shown to be a mere conversational trope; the club is prepared to welcome the working-class Simpsons with open arms — or has it realized yet that they are working class? Further complicating matters are Marge's reasons for walking away. First, there is the false dilemma between caring for her family and being welcomed by the club. Why should one choice exclude the other? Second is her belief that the Simpsons just don't belong to such a club. This belief seems to be based on a classism that the club itself doesn't have. This episode leaves no stable ground upon which the viewer can rest. It feints at the sanctity of family values and swerves closely to class determinism, but it doesn't stay anywhere. Furthermore, upon reflection, none of the "solutions" that it momentarily holds is satisfactory. In its own way, this episode is as cruel and cold-blooded as the Grimey episode. However, where the Grimey episode wears its heartlessness upon its sleeve, this episode conjures up illusions of satisfactory heart-warming resolution only to undercut them immediately. In my view, it stands as a paradigm of the real *Simpsons*.

I think that, given a crisis of authority, hyper-ironism is the most suitable form of comedy. Recall that many painters and architects turned to a consideration of the history of painting and architecture once they gave up on the idea of fundamental trans-historical goal for their media. Recall also that once Rorty's version of Derrida became convinced of the non-existence of transcendent philosophical truth, he reconstructed philosophy as an historically aware conversation which largely consisted of the deconstruction of past works. One way of looking at all of these transitions is that, with the abandonment of *knowledge* came the cult of *knowingness*. That is, even if there is no ultimate truth (or method for arriving at it) I can still show that I understand the intellectual rules by which you operate better than you do. I can show my superiority over you by demonstrating my awareness of what makes you tick. In the end, none of our positions is ultimately superior, but I can at least show myself to be in a superior position for now on the shifting sands of the game we are currently playing. Hyper-irony is the comedic instantiation of the cult of knowingness. Given the crisis of authority, there are no higher purposes to which comedy can be put, such as moral instruction, theological revelation, or showing how the world is. However, comedy can be used to attack anybody at all who thinks that he or she has any sort of handle on the answer to any major question, not to replace the object of the attack with a better way of looking at things, but merely for the pleasure of the attack, or perhaps for the sense of momentary superiority mentioned earlier. *The Simpsons* revels in the attack. It treats nearly everything as a target, every stereotypical character, every foible, and every institution. It plays games of one-upmanship with its audience members by challenging them to identify the avalanche of allusions it throws down to them. And, as "Scenes from the Class Struggle in Springfield" illustrates, it refrains from taking a position of its own.

However, to be fair to those who believe *The Simpsons* takes a stable moral stance, there are episodes which seem not to undercut themselves at all. Consider, for instance, the previously mentioned episode in which Bart helps Lisa at military school. In that episode, many things are ridiculed, but the fundamental goodness of the relationship between Bart and Lisa is left unquestioned. In another episode, when Lisa discovers that Jebediah Springfield, the legendary town founder, was a sham, she refrains from announcing her finding to the town when she notices the social value of the myth of Jebediah Springfield. And, of course, we must mention the episode in which jazzman Bleeding Gums Murphy dies, which truly deserves the Simpsonian epithet "worst episode ever." This episode combines an uncritical sentimentality with a naive adoration of art-making, and tops everything off with some unintentionally horrible pseudo-jazz which would serve better as the theme music for a cable-access talk show. Lisa's song "Jazzman" simultaneously embodies all three of these faults, and must count as the worst moment of the worst episode ever. Given these episodes and others like them, which occur too frequently to be dismissed as blips, we are still left with the conflicting data with which we started. . . . Is *The Simpsons* hyper-ironic or not? One could argue that the hyper-ironism is a trendy fashion accessory, irony from the Gap, which does not reflect the ethos of the show. Another critically well-received program, *Buffy the Vampire Slayer* is as strongly committed to a black and white distinction between right and wrong as only teenagers can be. Its dependence on wisecracks and subversive irony is only skin deep. Underneath the surface, one will find angst-ridden teens fighting a solemn battle against evil demons who want to destroy the world. Perhaps, one could argue, beneath the surface irony of *The Simpsons* one will find a strong commitment to family values.

I would like to argue that *Simpsonian* hyper-ironism is not a mask for an underlying moral commitment. Here are three reasons, the first two of which are plausible but probably insufficient. First, *The Simpsons* does not consist of a single episode, but of over two hundred episodes spread out over more than ten seasons. There is good reason to think that apparent resolutions in one episode are usually undercut by others.[6] In other words, we are cued to respond

---

[6]Thanks to my colleague and co-contributor, Jason Holt, for first suggesting this to me.

ironically to one episode, given the cues provided by many other episodes. However, one could argue, that this inter-episodic undercutting is itself undercut by the show's frequent use of happy family endings.

Second, as a self-consciously hip show, *The Simpsons* can be taken to be aware of and to embrace what is current. Family values are hardly trendy, so there is little reason to believe that *The Simpsons* would adopt them wholeheartedly. However, this is weak confirmation at best. As a trendy show, *The Simpsons* could merely flirt with hyper-irony without fully adopting it. After all, it is hardly hyper-ironic to pledge allegiance to any flag, including the flag of hyper-ironism. Also, in addition to being a self-consciously hip show, it is also a show that must live within the constraints of prime-time American network television. One could argue that these constraints would force *The Simpsons* towards a commitment to some sort of palatable moral stance. Therefore, we cannot infer that the show is hyper-ironic from the lone premise that it is self-consciously hip.

The third and strongest reason for a pervasive hyper-ironism and against the claim that *The Simpsons* takes a stand in favor of family values is based on the perception that the comedic energy of the show dips significantly whenever moral closure or didacticism rise above the surface (as in the Bleeding Gums Murphy episodes). Unlike *Buffy the Vampire Slayer, The Simpsons* is fundamentally a comedy. *Buffy* can get away with dropping its ironic stance, because it is an adventure focused on the timeless battle between good and evil. *The Simpsons* has nowhere else to go when it stops being funny. Thus, it's very funny when it celebrates physical cruelty in any given *Itchy and Scratchy Show*. It's very funny when it ridicules Krusty and the marketing geniuses who broadcast *Itchy and Scratchy*. It's banal, flat, and not funny when it tries to deal seriously with the issue of censorship arising from *Itchy and Scratchy*. The lifeblood of *The Simpsons*, and its astonishing achievement, is the pace of cruelty and ridicule that it has managed to sustain for over a decade. The prevalence of quotationalism helps to sustain this pace, because the show can look beyond itself for a constant stream of targets. When the target-shooting slows down for a wholesome message or a heart-warming family moment, the program slows to an embarrassing crawl with nary a quiver from the laughmeter.

I don't mean to argue that the makers of *The Simpsons* intended the show primarily as a theater of cruelty, although I imagine that they did. Rather, I want to argue that, as a comedy, its goal is to be funny, and we should read it in a way that maximizes its capability to be funny. When we interpret it as a wacky but earnest endorsement of family values, we read it in a way that hamstrings its comedic potential. When we read it as a show built upon the twin pillars of misanthropic humor and oh-so-clever intellectual one-upmanship, we maximize its comedic potential by paying attention to the features of the show that make us laugh. We also provide a vital function for the degree of quotationalism in the show, and as a bonus, we tie the show into a dominant trend of thought in the twentieth century.

But, if the heart-warming family moments don't contribute to the show's comedic potential, why are they there at all? One possible explanation is that they are simply mistakes; they were meant to be funny but they aren't. This hypothesis is implausible. Another is that the show is not exclusively a comedy, but rather a family comedy — something wholesome and not very funny that the whole family can pretend to enjoy. This is equally implausible. Alternatively, we can try to look for a function for the heart-warming moments. I think there is such a function. For the sake of argument, suppose that the engine driving *The Simpsons* is fueled by cruelty and one-upmanship. Its viewers, although appreciative of its humor, might not want to come back week after week to such a bleak message, especially if the message is centered on a family with children. *Seinfeld* never really offered any hope; its heart was as cold as ice. However, *Seinfeld* was about disaffected adults. A similarly bleak show containing children would resemble the parody of a sitcom in Oliver Stone's *Natural Born Killers*, in which Rodney Dangerfield plays an alcoholic child-abuser. Over the years, such a series would lose a grip on its viewers, to say the least. I think that the thirty seconds or so of apparent redemption in each episode of *The Simpsons* is there mainly to allow us to soldier on for twenty-one and a half minutes of maniacal cruelty at the beginning of the next episode. In other words, the heart-warming family moments help *The Simpsons* to live on as a series. The comedy does not exist for the sake of a message; the occasional illusion of a positive message exists to enable us to tolerate more comedy. Philosophers and critics have often talked of the paradox of horror and the paradox of tragedy. Why do we eagerly seek out art forms that arouse unpleasant emotions in us like pity, sadness, and fear? I think that, for at least certain forms of comedy, there is an equally important paradox of comedy. Why do we seek out art that makes us laugh at the plight of unfortunate people in a world without redemption? The laughter here seems to come at a high price. *The Simpsons'* use of heart-warming family endings should be seen as its attempt to paper over the paradox of comedy that it exemplifies so well.

I hope to have shown that quotationalism and hyper-ironism are prevalent, inter-dependent, and jointly responsible for the way in which the humor in *The Simpsons* works. The picture I have painted of *The Simpsons* is a bleak one, because I have characterized its humor as negative, a humor of cruelty and condescension — but really funny cruelty and condescension. I have left out a very important part of the picture however. *The Simpsons*, consisting of a not-as-bright version of the Freudian id for a father, a sociopathic son, a prissy daughter, and a fairly dull but innocuous mother, is a family whose members love each other. And, we love them. Despite the fact that the show strips away any semblance of value, despite the fact that week after week it offers us little comfort, it still manages to convey the raw power of the irrational (or nonrational) love of human beings for other human beings, and it makes us play along by loving these flickering bits of paint on celluloid who live in a flickering hollow world. Now *that's* comedy entertainment.

READING THE TEXT

1. Write an outline of Matheson's essay, being sure to note how the writer establishes differences and similarities with other pop cultural phenonema. Compare your outline with those produced by the rest of the class.

2. Explain in your own words what Matheson means by "quotationalism" and "hyper-irony" (para. 2).

3. What does Matheson mean by "historical appropriation" (para. 17)?

4. Matheson outlines recent intellectual trends in the study of art, science, and philosophy. What are those trends, and what relationship does Matheseon find between them and a TV program such as *The Simpsons*?

5. What connection does Matheson see between the "crisis of authority" (para. 15) and hyper-irony?

READING THE SIGNS

1. Write an argumentative essay that supports, challenges, or complicates Matheson's position that "heart-warming family moments" appear in *The Simpsons* "mainly to allow us to soldier on for twenty-one and a half minutes of maniacal cruelty" (para. 28).

2. In class, brainstorm other TV shows and films that are hyper-ironic, and use the list as the basis for your own essay in which you argue whether their popularity is a barometer of the current cultural mood in America or whether it is an aberration of that mood.

3. Watch an episode of *The Simpsons*, and analyze the extent to which it supports Matheson's belief that, rather than promoting a moral stance, the show "does not promote anything" (para. 19).

4. Visit a Web site devoted to *The Simpsons*, such as **www.thesimpsons.com**. To what extent does the Web site display the hyper-ironic style that Matheson attributes to the show? How can you explain any differences you might observe?

5. Compare and contrast the humor in *The Simpsons* with that of another TV show such as *SpongeBob SquarePants*. Do the shows appeal to different audiences, and if so, why? To develop your discussion, you might interview viewers of both programs about their responses to each show.

STEVEN D. STARK

The Oprah Winfrey Show *and the Talk-Show Furor*

Oprah Winfrey just might be the most powerful woman in America, and if not, certainly the most influential literary critic. In this selection from Glued to the Set: The Sixty Television Shows and Events That Made Us What We Are Today *(1997), Steven D. Stark (b. 1951) explains how she got that way. Tracing the evolution of daytime talk from Donahue to Jenny Jones, Stark analyzes the social forces behind this much vilified television genre in which Oprah is the reigning monarch. Finding in television a mirror image not of American realities but of American needs and desires, Stark thus provides a model for understanding the cultural significance of the tube. A contributor to such publications as the* Atlantic Monthly *and the* New York Times Magazine, *Stark is also a commentator for National Public Radio.*

Start with these two basic premises:

1. Oprah Winfrey is probably the most celebrated and powerful black woman in U.S. history.
2. Oprah Winfrey is the undisputed leader of a television genre which has been more vehemently attacked by the Establishment than any other in television history.

You don't have to be an Albert Einstein to recognize that these two propositions are related.

The modern daytime talk show — created by Phil Donahue in the late 1960s, revolutionized by Oprah in the 1980s, and then transmogrified in the 1990s by everyone from Ricki Lake to Jenny Jones — is the newest genre to sweep television. On an average mid-nineties weekday, *The Oprah Winfrey Show* was watched by ten million Americans, mostly women, and the 20 or so other daytime talk shows in 1995 had a combined daily audience of around 50 million viewers — though many people undoubtedly watched a whole slew of these shows each day. Though these numbers were high, they pale when compared to those of the combined audiences that watch the violence of prime-time action shows or the local news.

Yet the talk-show genre was absolutely vilified by critics — blamed for everything from the culture's preoccupation with victimization to the general decline of civic discourse. Daytime talk generated a well-publicized crusade (led by two U.S. senators and former Secretary of Education William Bennett) to purify the medium, not to mention a dozen or so critical books and hundreds of negative articles which joined these Washington officials in calling the new genre a "case study of rot" and "the pollution of the human environment."

Admittedly daytime talk shows are not for the squeamish or children — ⁵
though one hopes that Bennett and his minions were as concerned about
the millions who live full-time in economic and social surroundings far more
squalid than anything on *The Maury Povich Show*. The shows typically involve
from two to six guests talking about their personal experiences, followed by
boos, applause, tears, questions, and shouts from a studio audience modeled
roughly on Howdy Doody's Peanut Gallery. A typical week of mid-nineties
programming on these shows was likely to include such topics as:

Leathermen Love Triangles
Bisexuals
Abusive Boyfriends
Men Engaged to Three Pregnant Women
Clueless Men
Women Who Marry Their Rapists
Runaway Teens
Secret Crushes

This was the genre where a man was surprisingly "confronted" with a secret
admirer on *Jenny Jones*, found the admirer was a man, and killed him after the
show for humiliating him on national television. (The show was never broadcast due to the shooting.) "Rather than being mortified, ashamed, or trying to
hide their stigma," two sociologists wrote of this genre, "guests willingly and
eagerly discuss their child-molesting, sexual quirks, and criminal records in
an effort to seek 'understanding' for their particular disease."

These shows obviously offer a distorted vision of America, thrive on feeling rather than thought, and worship the sound-bite rather than the art of
conversation. Yet it's not like television hasn't been walking down these same
paths in other forms every day for the past 50 years. If daytime talk has been
preoccupied with sex, race, and family dysfunction, it may be because there
is still so little discussion of those rather significant topics elsewhere on television, even in the nineties. All movements have their crazies. Yet when Oprah
Winfrey can rank in a poll as the celebrity Americans believe to be most qualified to be president (far more than Bill Bennett, by the way), something significant is going on.

Just as vaudeville was the root of much early American television, the circus and carnival with their freak shows influenced talk shows. Like any new
television genre, these talk shows were a mixture of old programming types —
many of which once dominated the daytime. Morning and afternoon talk,
geared mostly to women, has a long TV history, beginning with Arthur Godfrey
and with Art Linkletter's *People Are Funny*. From the soap opera, these new
shows borrowed a feminine style of disclosure and a focus on issues considered to be of particular relevance to women, like family and relationships.
Game shows were a rich source: From programs like *The Price Is Right* the new
talk shows learned how to involve an audience of ordinary people. From games
like *Strike It Rich* and *Queen for a Day* they learned about the entertainment

Oprah Winfrey.

value of debasing "contestants" who will tell their sob story for money or fleeting fame. And from *Family Feud* they learned that conflict sells in the daytime. Throw in a smattering of TV religion (the televised confession and revelation so prominent on these shows), melodrama (Will the runaway teenager's father take her back?), and the news sensibility of Barbara Walters, once an early-morning mainstay on *Today*, and the pieces were in place for a profitable genre — especially because daytime talk shows are so inexpensive to stage.

Like other popular forms of programming, these shows also mirrored their times. Phil Donahue created the genre because network television wasn't reflecting the serious concerns of many of its women viewers. It began in 1967, at the dawn of the women's movement, when this Midwestern Catholic started a new type of daytime talk show in Dayton, Ohio, hosting for that first show atheist Madalyn Murray O'Hair. Donahue's story was simple: "The average housewife is bright and inquisitive," he said, "but television treats her like a mental midget." His approach was to take TV talk out of its preoccupation with entertainment celebrities, and tackled instead (often with only one guest an hour) "difficult" women's issues that television wasn't addressing — sexism, artificial insemination, impotence, and homosexuality — combined with more-traditional topics, like bathroom fixtures. "He flies in the face of TV tradition, which used to be that you didn't risk offending anyone," Steve Allen, former host of *The Tonight Show*, said. Donahue also brilliantly added an active studio audience, usually composed almost entirely of women (though not by design — they're just the ones who showed up), which not only served as a kind of Greek chorus for the guests, but also asked many of the show's most penetrating questions.

For his part, Donahue the rebel frequently bounced about the crowd, microphone in hand, smashing the barrier between host and audience. It didn't hurt the show's populist appeal that it came to stations independently through syndication, rather than from a paternalistic network. In its heyday, *Donahue* also originated from Chicago — in the nation's heartland — rather than among the elites in New York. The more the women's movement progressed, however, the more well-educated women left home for the workplace, and found other outlets for their interests. That left Donahue and his imitators with a growing audience of less-affluent, homebound women who often were full of anger and confusion, ignored as they were by more elite media. The women's movement first made Donahue, and then took away the cream of his audience who were interested in more serious topics.

Still, for over a decade he had the field to himself before along came a certain Oprah Winfrey in 1984. She was an empathetic black woman and former coanchor of the local news in Baltimore. Oprah's advantage over Donahue was that, seeming to resemble her audience, she used that similarity to create a talk show which made the political more personal. Her program was infused with a therapeutic sensibility: Though Oprah did some politics, like her celebrated show in Forsyth County, Georgia, in 1987 (when white racists were on the march), she was more likely to do a show on abusive boyfriends, recovering alcoholics, or competitive sisters. The cause of many of the problems discussed on her show was not so much men, but the so-called rigid confines of traditional family. "What we are witnessing with the proliferating talk show is a social revolution which has at its core the demystification of the family," Michael Arlen, former TV critic for *The New Yorker*, would tell a reporter much later. Say good-bye to Ozzie and Harriet!

Oprah's style was different, too. If Donahue was, at heart, a journalist exposing issues, Oprah ran what she called a "ministry" — the "church" being a branch of pop psychology which held that revealing problems, improving self-esteem, and receiving empathy could cure just about anything, and empower women besides. Oprah hugged her guests, wept openly, and personally said good-bye to each member of the studio audience after a show. Even in 1996, Oprah spoke far more often on her shows than other hosts did. She confessed on the air that she had been sexually abused by relatives as a child, and in later years that she had smoked cocaine. On a show about dieting, she told the audience about the night she ate hot-dog buns drowned in syrup.

Oprah's race and street sass ("Hey, Girl!") also made her more authentically hip, at least to her audience, than almost anyone else on television. Oprah would call her success an alternative to the "Twinkies and Barbie and Ken dolls" that make up so much of television. "Racism remains the most difficult subject in America, and it is only really on the talk show that the raw hatred and suspicion that the races feel for each other is vented," Arlen had told that reporter. As a host who could walk the narrow line between the races, Oprah offered reassurance which others couldn't hope to match. That cultural bilingualism also allowed her to put together an audience coalition of the sort that Jesse Jackson could only dream about.

With rock-and-roll in the 1950s, black artists had been swept aside so that more-acceptable white singers could "cover" their songs. With daytime talk, the opposite occurred: Oprah's show soon wiped out *Donahue* in the ratings — and everyone else, too. By 1994, *Working Woman* put Oprah's net worth at over $250 million. By then the show itself was grossing almost $200 million a year, had 55 percent more viewers than *Donahue* (its closest competitor), and enjoyed higher ratings on many days than *Today, Good Morning America*, and the *CBS Morning News* combined.

Understandably, Oprah's success bred imitators. Since other hosts couldn't hope to match her in identifying with the audience personally (Ricki Lake was a notable exception, as she went after younger viewers), they tried to win viewers by topping her with their list of sensationalistic topics and revelations. As TV news became ever more tabloid, these shows pushed the envelope even further. By 1992, even Donahue was tackling topics like "Safe Sex Orgies" and "What Happens When Strippers Get Old?" Other shows borrowed from the confrontational style of talk shows once run by Mort Downey Jr. and turned Oprah's group hug into a daily talk riot with topics like "Wives Confront the Other Woman."

By the mid-1990s, an average day on these other shows revealed subjects 15 like "Married Men Who Have Relationships with Their Next-Door Neighbors," "Mothers Who Ran Off with Their Daughter's Fiancé," and "Drag Queens Who Got Makeovers." A 1995 study of these programs, done by a team of researchers at Michigan State University, found that a typical one-hour show had:

> four sexual-activity disclosures, one sexual-orientation disclosure, three abuse disclosures, two embarrassing-situation disclosures, two criminal-activity disclosures and four personal-attribute disclosures, for a total of 16 personal disclosures. . . .

These entertainment programs were selling more, however, than just their guests' disclosures or the "hot" topics which seemed to come straight out of the supermarket tabloids. They also purported to offer group therapy for the masses, at a price everyone could afford. As psychotherapist Murray Nossel once told a reporter, America is "the country that popularized psychoanalysis. Freud's theory of the psyche is that repression brings depression, whereas expression is liberating. Emotionally to cathart in America, to reveal one's darkest secrets, is a desired social good in and of itself." Critics would have a field day pointing out the dangers of trying to provide such "therapy" on television, but that played right into the notion that elites were trying to keep the masses away from something that had once exclusively been available only to the well-to-do. After all, if daytime talk shows thrived on the violation of taboos, that was, in part, to stick a finger in the eye of those members of the Establishment who looked down on a television pursuit favored by the downscale.

The supporters of these shows also felt that they regularly received too little credit for tackling issues which mainstream television had traditionally ignored, like race and family dysfunction. "If people didn't get up there and talk about incest," Lee Fryd, director of media relations for the *Sally Jessy Raphael* show once told a reporter, "it would never come to light." If these shows often presented what many considered a freak parade, others would argue that they had helped bring nonconformists further into the mainstream. Joshua Gamson, a cultural critic, once wrote:

> The story here is not about commercial exploitation but just about how effective the prohibition on asking and telling is in the United States, how stiff the penalties are, how unsafe this place is for people of atypical sexual and gender identities. You know you're in trouble when Sally Jessy Raphael (strained smile and forced tear behind red glasses) seems your best bet for being heard, understood, respected, and protected. That for some of us the loopy, hollow light of talk shows seems a safe, shielding haven should give us all pause.

On the other hand, the values of these talk shows were oddly traditional — one reason why they posted such strong ratings with Bible Belt females who considered themselves conservative. The parade of guests was almost always hooted down by the studio audience, which embodied a rather conventional view of morality (albeit one heavily tempered by empathy for victims). The parade of "trash," to use one critic's words, was also a way for those at home to feel better about themselves, since their lives were rarely as hopeless as what they could find here on the screen. Like so much else on TV, what these shows offered was a form of reassurance.

If these talk shows had a larger political consequence, it came with the administration of Bill Clinton, who accomplished little but empathized with everybody. He ran a kind of talk-show presidency — forged in the 1992 campaign with his appearance on *Donahue*, and continuing in that year into a second debate with George Bush and H. Ross Perot which did away with journalist-questioners and substituted an inquiring studio audience like Oprah's. One of Clinton's principal contributions to our culture was to take the language and zeitgeist of the talk show and bring it into mainstream politics. After all, the "I feel your pain" trademark of his presidency first gained cultural prominence as a talk-show staple: The whole point of talk shows like Oprah's is to encourage "audience-victims" to "feel their pain" as a way of empowering themselves to strike back against those who seem more powerful.

Such a stance was undoubtedly a big reason why women, over time, sup- 20 ported Clinton so strongly. In fact, by 1996, the talk-show style and its celebration of victims was on display throughout both political conventions: There was Liddy Dole's Winfreyesque "among the delegates" talk to the Republican convention, Al Gore's speech recounting his dying sister's final moments, and the endless parade of the disease-afflicted. Our politics had been Opracized.

Yet if the nineties has been a decade tending to elevate feeling over thought and encourage a no-fault approach to behavior, the talk shows were hardly the only culprit, no matter what Bill Bennett thought. Few cultural movements of this magnitude proceed from the bottom up rather than the other way around. As Michiko Kakutani would point out in another context in the *New York Times*, the cult of subjectivity enveloping America came as much from Oliver Stone, with his fantasies about JFK, and from "inventive" biographers like Joe McGinniss, as they came from Ricki Lake. Invective was as much a calling card of CNN's *Crossfire* as it was of Montel and Jerry Springer.

By late 1995, however, in response to criticisms by Bennett and others (and as ratings for the "confrontational" shows dropped by as much as a third), Oprah changed her mix of guests and topics too, moving away from tabloid psychology and toward less-conventional, more "educational" subjects like anorexia and planning for old age. "She said to us that after 10 years and 2,000 shows of mostly dysfunctional people, she felt it was time to start focusing on solutions," said Tim Bennett, Oprah's production-company president. At the same time, *The Rosie O'Donnell Show* rose to daytime prominence by essentially taking the old fifties' upbeat variety formula, popularized by Arthur Godfrey, and repackaging it with a likable female host, celebrity guests, and a nineties' zeitgeist.

But were even these small shifts something of a betrayal of a large portion of the talk show audience? What was always most striking about this form of "entertainment" — and what made it so different from anything else on television — was its never-ending portrait of despair and alienation. If the downtrodden who populated these shows popularized deviancy or celebrated the cheap confessional, they did it mostly as a plaintive cry for help. Yet Oprah had been there to bless them at the end of every weekday. "They are the people you'd ignore if you saw them in line at the supermarket instead of on TV," Wendy Kaminer, a cultural analyst, once wrote, but that was precisely the point. Talk television was yet another step in the 1990s' trend to democratization of the medium — this time to include the real have-nots. That may be why the elites responded with their usual rejoinder to let them eat cake.

READING THE TEXT

1. What does Stark mean when he says that *The Oprah Winfrey Show* and its imitators "offer group therapy for the masses" (para. 16)?

2. What evidence does Stark provide to support his view that talk shows have a special appeal to women?

3. Why does Stark say that talk shows are "oddly traditional" (para. 18), despite their often lurid content?

4. Explain what Stark means by saying that Bill Clinton "ran a kind of talk-show presidency" (para. 19).

READING THE SIGNS

1. In your journal, reflect on your responses to talk shows. If you enjoy sensationalized programming, explore why; if you avoid it, discuss the reasons for your distaste.

2. Write an argumentative essay supporting, refuting, or complicating Stark's assertion that talk shows have helped to bring about the "democratization" (para. 23) of television.

3. Watch an episode of *The Oprah Winfrey Show*, and write an essay in which you offer your own analysis of its appeal. To develop your support, you might interview some avid fans of the program.

4. Write a letter to talk-show critics such as William Bennett, supporting or refuting their desire to "purify" television.

5. Another television genre that relies on sensationalism is reality TV. Write an essay in which you compare and contrast talk shows with RTV programs, examining their content, the claims made by marketers about their appeal, and your own reading of why they attract their viewers. Be sure to base your argument on a study of specific programs of both genres. To develop your ideas, consult Francine Prose's "Voting Democracy off the Island: Reality TV and the Republican Ethos" (p. 222), Anita Creamer's "Reality TV Meets Plastic Surgery: An Ugly Shame" (p. 229), and Rick Pieto and Kelly Otter's "*The Osbournes*: Genre, Reality TV, and the Domestication of Rock 'n' Roll" (p. 232).

SUSAN DOUGLAS
Signs of Intelligent Life on TV

Do you look for television programming that reflects an enlightened view of American women? Susan Douglas (b. 1950) does, and in this essay that originally appeared in Ms. *in 1995, she reports her findings, which are mixed, at best. Although popular TV dramas like* ER *and* NYPD Blue *appear to present characters and plotlines that defy gender stereotypes, Douglas still finds the telltale signs of cultural bias against women in such programs — especially a bias against strong professional women. When not watching TV, Douglas is chair of the department of communication studies at the University of Michigan and media critic for* The Progressive. *She is the author of* Where the Girls Are: Growing Up Female with the Mass Media *(1994),* Inventing American Broadcasting, 1899–1922 *(1987), and* Listening In: Radio and the American Imagination *(1999).*

When the hospital show *ER* became a surprise hit, the pundits who had declared dramatic television "dead" were shocked. But one group wasn't surprised at all.

Those of us with jobs, kids, older parents to tend to, backed-up toilets, dog barf on the rug, and friends/partners/husbands we'd like to say more than "hi" to during any diurnal cycle don't have much time to watch television. And when we do — usually after 9:38 P.M. — we have in recent years been forced to choose between Diane Sawyer interviewing Charles Manson or Connie Chung chasing after Tonya [Harding] and Nancy [Kerrigan]. People like me, who felt that watching the newsmagazines was like exposing yourself to ideological smallpox, were starved for some good escapist drama that takes you somewhere else yet resonates with real life and has ongoing characters you care about.

When *NYPD Blue* premiered in the fall of 1993 with the tough-but-sensitive John Kelly, and featuring strong, accomplished women, great lighting, bongo drums in the sound track, and male nudity, millions sighed with relief. When *ER* hit the air, we made it one of the tube's highest rated shows. Tagging farther behind, but still cause for hope, is another hospital drama, *Chicago Hope*.

All three shows acknowledge the importance of the adult female audience by featuring women as ongoing characters who work for a living and by focusing on contemporary problems in heterosexual relationships (no, we haven't yet achieved everyday homosexual couples on TV). More to the point, hound-dog-eyed, emotionally wounded yet eager-to-talk-it-through guys are center stage. So what are we getting when we kick back and submerge ourselves in these dramas? And what do they have to say about the ongoing project of feminism?

For those of you who don't watch these shows regularly, here's a brief précis: *NYPD Blue* is a cop show set in New York City and has producer Steven Bochco's signature style — lots of shaky, hand-held camera work, fast-paced editing (supported by the driving, phallic backbeat in the sound track), and multiple, intersecting plots about various crimes and the personal lives of those who work in the precinct. Last season there were more women in the show; and last season there was John Kelly.

This year, the show is more masculinized. Watching Bobby Simone, played by Jimmy Smits, earn his right to replace Kelly was like witnessing a territorial peeing contest between weimaraners. Bobby had to be as sensitive and emotionally ravaged as Johnny, so in an act of New Age male one-upmanship, the scriptwriters made him a widower who had lost his wife to breast cancer. But Bobby had to be one tough customer too, so soon after we learn of his wife's death, we see him throwing some punks up against a fence, warning them that he will be their personal terminator unless they stop dealing drugs.

ER has the same kind of simultaneous, intersecting story lines, served up with fast-tracking cameras that sprint down hospital corridors and swirl around operating tables like hawks on speed. And there are the same bongo drums and other percussive sounds when patients are rushed in for treatment. *Chicago Hope* is *ER* on Valium: stationary cameras, slower pace, R&B instead of drumbeats. It's also *ER* on helium or ether, kind of a *Northern Exposure* goes to the hospital, with more offbeat plots and characters, like a patient who eats his hair or a kid whose ear has fallen off.

Whenever I like a show a lot—meaning I am there week in and week out—I figure I have once again embraced a media offering with my best and worst interests at heart. Dramatic TV shows, which seek a big chunk of the middle- and upper-income folks between 18 and 49, need to suck in those women whose lives have been transformed by the women's movement (especially women who work outside the home and have disposable income) while keeping the guys from grabbing the remote. What we get out of these twin desires is a blend of feminism and antifeminism in the plots and in the female characters. And for the male characters we have an updated hybrid of masculinity that crossbreeds decisiveness, technical expertise, and the ability to throw a punch or a basketball, with a soft spot for children and a willingness to cry.

On the surface, these shows seem good for women. We see female cops, lawyers, doctors, and administrators, who are smart, efficient, and successful. But in too many ways, the women take a backseat to the boys. In *NYPD Blue*, for example, we rarely see the women actually doing their jobs. The overall message in the three shows is that, yes, women can be as competent as men, but their entrance into the workforce has wrecked the family and made women so independent and hard-hearted that dealing with them and understanding them is impossible. Despite this, they're still the weaker sex.

In *ER* it is Carol Hathaway (Julianna Margulies), the charge nurse, who 10 tried to commit suicide. It is Dr. Susan Lewis (Sherry Stringfield) who is taken in by an imposter who claims to be a hospital administrator. Dr. Lewis is also the only resident who has trouble standing up to white, male authority figures: She is unable to operate while the head cardiologist watches her. In *Chicago Hope*, a psychiatrist prevails upon a female nurse to dress up like Dorothy (ruby slippers, pigtails, and all) because a patient refusing surgery is a *Wizard of Oz* junkie. Even though she points out that no male doctor would be asked to do anything like it, the shrink insists she continue the masquerade because the patient's life is at stake. Here's the crucial guilt-shifting we've all come to know and love—this patient's illness is somehow more her responsibility than anyone else's. Her humiliation is necessary to save him.

The Ariel Syndrome—Ariel was the name of Walt Disney's little mermaid, who traded her voice for a pair of legs so that she could be with a human prince she'd seen from afar for all of ten seconds—grips many of the women, who have recurring voice problems. Watch out for female characters who "don't want to talk about it," who can't say no, who don't speak up. They make it even harder for the women who do speak their minds, who are, of course, depicted as "bitches."

One major "bitch" is the wife of *ER*'s Dr. Mark Greene (Anthony Edwards). He's a doctor who's barely ever home, she's a lawyer who lands a great job two hours away, and they have a seven-year-old. Those of us constantly negotiating about who will pick up the kids or stay late at work can relate to this. The problem is that *ER* is about *his* efforts to juggle, *his* dreams and ambitions. We know this guy, we like him, we know he's a great doctor who adores his wife and child. Her, we don't know, and there's no comparable female doctor to show the woman's side of this equation. As a result, when conflicts emerge, the audience is primed to want her to compromise (which she's already done, so he can stay at the job he loves). When she insists he quit his job and relocate, she sounds like a spoiled child more wedded to a rigid quid pro quo than to flexibility, love, the family. It's the conservative view of what feminism has turned women into — unfeeling, demanding blocks of granite.

One of the major themes of all three shows is that heterosexual relationships are a national disaster area. And it's the women's fault. Take *NYPD Blue*. Yes, there's the fantasy relationship between Andy Sipowicz (Dennis Franz) and Sylvia Costas (Sharon Lawrence), in which an accomplished woman helps a foul-mouthed, brutality-prone cop with really bad shirts get in touch with his feelings and learn the pleasures of coed showering. While this affair has become the emotional anchor of the show, it is also the lone survivor in the ongoing gender wars.

It looks like splitsville for most of the show's other couples. Greg Medavoy (Gordon Clapp) infuriates Donna Abandando (Gail O'Grady) by his behavior, which includes following her to see whom she's having lunch with. She's absolutely right. But after all the shots of Greg looking at her longingly across the office (again, we're inside his head, not hers), the audience is encouraged to think that she should give the guy a break. By contrast, her explanations of why she's so angry and what she wants have all the depth and emotional warmth of a Morse code message tapped out by an iguana. Of course Greg doesn't understand. She won't help him.

In this world, female friendships are nonexistent or venomous. And there is 15 still worse ideological sludge gumming up these shows. Asian and Latina women are rarely seen, and African American women are also generally absent except as prostitutes, bad welfare moms, and unidentified nurses. In the *ER* emergency room, the black women who are the conscience and much-needed drill sergeants of the show don't get top billing, and are rarely addressed by name. There is also an overabundance of bad mothers of all races: adoptive ones who desert their kids, abusive ones who burn their kids, and hooker ones (ipso facto bad). Since the major female characters — all upper-middle-class — don't have kids, we don't see their struggles to manage motherhood and work. And we certainly don't see less privileged moms (the real majority in the United States), like the nurses or office workers, deal with these struggles on a lot less money.

One of the worst things these shows do, under a veneer of liberalism and feminism, is justify the new conservatism in the United States. The suspects brought in for questioning on *NYPD Blue* are frequently threatened and sometimes beaten, but it's O.K. because they all turn out to be guilty, anyway. Legal representation for these witnesses is an unspeakable evil because it hides the truth. After a steady diet of this, one might assume the Fourth Amendment, which prohibits unreasonable search and seizure, is hardly worth preserving.

So why are so many women devoted to these shows? First off, the women we do see are more successful, gutsy, more fully realized than most female TV characters. But as for me, I'm a sucker for the men. I want to believe, despite all the hideous evidence to the contrary, that some men have been human-ized by the women's movement, that they have become more nurturing, sen-sitive, and emotionally responsible. I want to believe that patriarchy is being altered by feminism. Since I get zero evidence of this on the nightly news, I want a few hours a week when I can escape into this fantasy.

Of course, we pay a price for this fantasy. TV depicts "real men" being feminized for the better and women masculinized for the worse. The message from the guys is, "We became the kind of men you feminists said that you wanted, and now you can't appreciate us because you've forgotten how to be a 'real' woman." It's a bizarre twist on the real world, where many women have changed, but too many men have not. Nevertheless, in TV land femi-nism continues to hoist itself with its own petard. Big surprise.

READING THE TEXT

1. What does Douglas mean by saying that "watching the newsmagazines was like exposing yourself to ideological smallpox" (para. 2), and what attitude to-ward the media does this comment reveal?

2. Why, in Douglas's view, are professional women attracted to programs such as *ER* and *NYPD Blue*?

3. What, according to Douglas, is the overt message about gender roles commu-nicated by the TV shows she discusses? What is the hidden message?

4. How are non-Caucasian women presented in *ER* and *NYPD Blue*, according to Douglas, and what is her opinion about their presentation?

5. How does Douglas view the "new conservatism in the United States" (para. 16)?

READING THE SIGNS

1. Watch an episode of *ER* or *NYPD Blue*, and write an argumentative essay in which you support, refute, or modify Douglas's belief that the show, despite superficial nods at feminism, perpetuates traditional gender roles.

2. In class, brainstorm TV shows that portray women as professionals or in other responsible, intelligent roles. Then, using Douglas's argument as your starting point, discuss whether the shows adopt a feminist or an antifeminist stance in portraying female characters.

3. In your journal, discuss your favorite prime-time TV show, exploring exactly what you find attractive about the program.

4. Watch a TV show that focuses on young adult characters. Do you see evidence of the covert antifeminism that Douglas describes? What does the treatment of female characters say about the show's presumed audience? Use your find-ings as evidence in an analytical essay about the show's portrayal of women.

5. Do you see evidence of covert antifeminism in advertising? Write an essay in which you explore the depiction of women in advertising, focusing per-haps on ads in a woman's magazine such as *Elle* or *Jane*. To develop your ar-gument, consult Steve Craig's "Men's Men and Women's Women" (p. 161).

GWENDOLYN POUGH
Women, Rap, Wreck

You won't find the operative hip-hop definition of wreck *in your standard dictionary, but for Gwendolyn Pough (b. 1970) it is the guiding principle of contemporary women's rap music. Both as a noun and a verb,* wreck *is a way of at once disrupting the status quo and gaining attention. In this survey of the history of female rappers, Pough shows how black women have brought wreck to the male-dominated hip-hop scene as well as to the larger dominant white society. An assistant professor in the department of women's studies at the University of Minnesota, Pough is the author of* Check It While I Wreck It: Black Womanhood, Hip-Hop Culture, and the Public Sphere *(2004), from which this selection is taken.*

Most examinations of rap music and Hip-Hop culture critique rap as a masculine discursive space and seldom look at Black women's experiences within this space. With the exception of critiques of misogyny and sexism in rap music and Hip-Hop culture, how rap music and Hip-Hop culture influence Black womanhood goes unexplored. Several Hip-Hop scholars have begun to take on the task of writing women into the history of Hip-Hop and validating the creative contributions of women to the field. They have written revisionist histories that document the women who were involved during the early days of Hip-Hop culture. And they are giving critical attention and consideration to women rap lyricists and the interventions their lyrics and presence have made in the counter–public sphere that is Hip-Hop culture.

The work of Nancy Guevara and Cristina Veran can best be classified as revisionist histories. They find that women have always been a part of the culture, even in the early days. Guevara finds that while women's participation has been distorted, women have been involved creatively in Hip-Hop culture via rap, graffiti writing, and break dancing. She reinserts these women by using the personal stories of women participants: graffiti artist Lady Pink, female rap group US Girls, female rapper Roxanne Shante, and break-dancer Baby Love. She finds that the dismissal of women in historical accounts of the development of minority cultures is quite deliberate and "serves to impede any progressive artistic or social development by women that might threaten male hegemony in the sphere of cultural production."[1]

Likewise, Cristina Veran traces women's early histories in rap by documenting the women rappers of the 1970s and 1980s. She notes the early vision of

---

[1] Nancy Guevara, "Women Writin' Rappin' Breakin'," in William Eric Perkins, ed., *Droppin' Science: Critical Essays on Rap Music and Hip-Hop Culture* (Philadelphia: Temple University Press, 1996), p. 51.

women such as Sugar Hill Records label owner Sylvia Robinson, who had the foresight to sign up-and-coming young rappers and produce many of the early rap albums. Veran notes that there were many women actively involved in the shaping of Hip-Hop culture in the early days — women who started their own businesses, organized parties, and created new styles from dance to music.[2] It would be too easy to ask why we do not hear more about these early women Hip-Hop innovators. They have no doubt fallen victim to the same erasure that provokes us to reenvision history in all aspects of society. Veran notes that a love for the culture of Hip-Hop motivated many of the women involved in the early days. And I would add that a simple love for the culture — not a desire to become rich and famous — could be the reason that many of the early women in Hip-Hop were more inclined to play the background, much like the Black women who wanted simply to improve the Black community and not become race spokespeople.

The women rappers — the female MCs — that Guevara and Veran uncover are all women that I remember hearing as a young Hip-Hop head. I remember seeing and hearing US Girls in the movie *Beat Street* (1984). Even then, their refrain "US Girls can boogie too" let me know that there could potentially be a space for me in the culture that I loved. The group consisted of Lisa Lee, Sha Rock, and Debbi Dee, and they held it down for women in Hip-Hop in the film. But before I ever heard of US Girls, I was already jamming to the Sugar Hill Records female group Sequence. I knew all their lyrics, and I even bit some of Cheryl the Pearl's rhymes in my own burgeoning baby raps. These early women could rap just as well as the men who were rapping during that time. More female MCs, such as the Mercedes Ladies, who boasted of being the first all-female crew with a woman DJ and MC, followed them, as would female rap groups such as Finesse and Sequence, Salt-N-Pepa, BWP, JJ Fad, and Sweet Tee and Jazzy Joyce; solo artists such as Dimples Dee, Sparky D, Roxanne Shante, the Real Roxanne, Pebblee Poo, Sweet Tee, MC Lyte, Queen Latifah, Yo Yo, Boss, and Da Brat; and the Trinas, Eves, Lil' Kims, Foxy Browns, and Missy Elliotts that grace the airwaves today. While the number of recorded women rappers in no way surpasses that of men, their presence in the rap game speaks volumes. As the most visible element of Hip-Hop culture currently, rap sets the tone for a lot of what the dominant society recognizes as Hip-Hop culture. Having women's voices represented via Hip-Hop in the larger public sphere opens the door for a wealth of possibilities in terms of the validation of the Black female voice and Black women's agency.

Scholars such as Venise T. Berry, Yvonne Bynoe, Cheryl Keyes, Murray   5 Forman, Kyra D. Gaunt, Wanda Renee Porter, Robin Roberts, Tricia Rose, and Eric King Watts have all explored the various aspects of Black women's

---

[2]Christina Veran, "First Ladies: Fly Females Who Racked the Mike in the 70s and 80s," in *Vibe Magazine, Hip-Hop Divas* (New York: Three Rivers, 2001), p. 6.

Salt 'N' Pepa.

agency via rap music. They address the ways Black women use Hip-Hop culture to grapple with and create images.[3] They discuss the ways Black women use rap to negotiate body politics and sexual politics.[4] They explore the Black feminist aspects of some Black women rappers.[5] They link lineages

---

[3]For more detailed examinations, see V. Berry, "Feminine or Masculine: The Conflicting Nature of Female Images in Rap Music," in S. Cook and J. Tsou, eds., *Cecilia Reclaimed: Feminist Perspectives on Gender and Music* (Champaign: University of Illinois Press, 1994); Y. Bynoe, "Defining the Female Image Through Rap Music and Hip-Hop Culture," *Doula: The Journal of Rap Music and Hip Hop Culture* 1:2 (2001).

[4]For more detailed examinations, see W. Porter, "Salt-N-Pepa, Lil' Kim, Foxy Brown, and Eve: The Politics of the Black Female Body," *Doula: The Journal of Rap Music and Hip Hop Culture* 1:1 (2000); T. Rose, "Bad Sistas: Black Women Rappers and Sexual Politics in Rap Music," in *Black Noise: Rap Music and Pop Culture in America* (Hanover: Wesleyan University Press, 1994); E. Watts, "The Female Voice in Hip Hop: An Exploration into the Potential of Erotic Appeal," in Marsha Houston, ed., *Centering Ourselves: African American Feminist and Womanist Studies of Discourse* (Cresskill: Hampton, 2002).

[5]For more detailed discussion, see M. Forman, " 'Movin' Closer to an Independent Funk': Black Feminist Theory, Standpoint, and Women in Rap," *Women's Studies* 23 (1994); R. Roberts, " 'Ladies First': Queen Latifah's Afrocentric Feminist Music Video," *African American Review* 28 (1994).

of Black women's expressive cultures, from double dutch to girls' games to Hip-Hop.[6] And they also examine issues of Black female empowerment via Hip-Hop.[7] The growing body of scholarship on women and rap music provides a rich starting ground for explorations into the ways Black women use the whole of Hip-Hop culture to not only assert agency, claim voice, grapple with and create images, negotiate sexual and body politics, evoke Black feminism, continue lineages, and empower themselves, but also lay claim to the public sphere and subvert stereotypes and domination by bringing wreck.

Cheryl Keyes argues strongly for the centrality of women's voices in rap music, noting that they are not incidental and have added significantly to the genre of music. Her essays " 'We're More Than a Novelty, Boys': Strategies of Female Rappers in the Rap Music Tradition" and "Empowering Self, Making Choices, Creating Spaces: Black Female Identity Via Rap Music Performance" place the artistry of female rappers on the map and lend credence to their skills. She notes that early women rappers, while shedding light on the female perspective of life in urban America, often employed strategies such as appropriating male performance behavior and directly contradicting male standards as a way to gain recognition.[8] And she shows that their co-opting of b-boy stances did not stop them from borrowing from foremothers such as comedienne Jackie "Moms" Mabley and song stylist Millie Jackson.[9] Like the revisionist historians discussed earlier, Keyes firmly locates women in the rap continuum. She also places female rappers in four categories: the queen mother, the fly girl, the sista with attitude, and the lesbian.[10] For my own purposes, categorization of women rappers is not beneficial, since lines blur and identities constantly intersect. I am more interested in the ways women rappers resist easy categorization in defining their own identity and negotiating representations of Black womanhood. Therefore, the way they grapple with images and deal with sexual politics becomes crucial.

Venise T. Berry, Tricia Rose, Eric King Watts, and Kyra Gaunt have begun to think about the ways women rappers deal with conflicting female images and sexual politics in Hip-Hop. Berry explores the development of a Black feminist voice in rap music via a struggle for positive images and Black female identity construction.[11] She also examines the way women rappers resist

---

[6]See K. Gaunt, "Translating Double-Dutch to Hip-Hop: The Musical Vernacular of Black Girls' Play," in J. Adjaye and A. Andrews, eds., *Languages, Rhythm, and Sound: Black Popular Cultures into the Twenty-first Century* (Pittsburgh: University of Pittsburgh Press, 1997).

[7]See C. Keyes, "Empowering Self, Making Choices, Creating Spaces: Black Female Identity via Rap Music Performance," *Journal of American Folklore* 113 (2000); C. Keyes, " 'We're More Than a Novelty, Boys': Strategies of Female Rappers in the Rap Music Tradition," in J. Radner, ed., *Feminist Messages: Coding in Women's Folk Culture* (Urbana: University of Illinois Press, 1993).

[8]Keyes, " 'We're More than a Novelty, Boys,' " p. 204.

[9]Ibid., p. 205.

[10]Keyes, "Empowering Self, Making Choices, Creating Spaces," p. 256.

[11]Berry, "Feminine or Masculine," p. 184.

stereotypes. Rose sees women rappers as a part of the dialogic process in rap and notes that there are three dominant themes in women's rap songs: "heterosexual courtship, the importance of female voice and mastery in women's rap and black female public displays of physical and sexual freedom."[12] Watts notes the potential for an empowering eroticism of the female voice in Hip-Hop. He examines the power of the erotic to lend women control over their own representation and by extension the entire rap game itself.[13] And Gaunt finds that there is a direct lineage between the games that Black women grow up playing and their contributions to Black expressive cultures.[14] All of the research that has been completed on Black women in rap is crucial and sets the foundation for further study. Frankly, compared to what has been written about men, there has not been enough of a focus on women and rap. Therefore, what currently exists becomes crucial for further studies. I find that these early works formulate not only a history of women in rap but also the beginnings of a theoretical body of work aimed at understanding women's participation and the societal elements that influence and/or inhibit that participation.

Rap music and Hip-Hop culture, as an example of a youth movement that crosses gender, sexuality, race, and class, becomes an excellent example of public displays of intersections and contact zones, providing an ideal space to examine the way difference is simultaneously constructed and navigated. The ways Black women find a voice and establish a presence in this arena further nuances the ways difference is negotiated in this particular youth movement. What happens when Black womanhood enters Hip-Hop culture? How does that presence bring wreck to commonly held ideas about gender and difference? And what impact does this wreck have on the larger societal public sphere?

I believe that Black women participants in Hip-Hop culture have developed key survival skills and formulated various ways to bring wreck to the stereotypes and marginalization that inhibit their interaction in the larger public sphere. Through Hip-Hop culture, a generation of Black women is coming to voice and bringing wreck. These women are attacking the stereotypes and misconceptions that influenced their lives and the lives of their foremothers. And they are maintaining a public presence while they counter the negative representations of Black womanhood that exist within Hip-Hop culture. Usually when they are able to grab public attention by bringing wreck, these moments become instances when everyone pays attention. Queen Latifah's "U.N.I.T.Y." presents one such instance.

[12]Tricia Rose, *Black Noise: Rap Music and Black Culture in Contemporary America* (Hanover: Wesleyan University Press, 1994), p. 147.

[13]Eric King Watts, "The Female Voice in Hip-Hop: An Exploration into the Potential of Erotic Appeal," in Marsha Houston and Olga I. Davis, eds., *Centering Ourselves: African American Feminist and Womanist Studies of Discourse* (Cresskill: Hampton, 2002).

[14]Kyra Gaunt, "The Musical Vernacular of Black Girls' Play," in Joseph Adjaye and Adrianne Andrews, eds., *Language, Rhythm, and Sound: Black Popular Cultures into the Twenty-first Century* (Pittsburgh: University of Pittsburgh Press, 1997).

"U.N.I.T.Y.," which won a Grammy in 1993, presents the perfect starting 10
example of a Black woman bringing wreck in Hip-Hop in a way that has implications for change both within the counter–public sphere of Hip-Hop and the
society at large. In this song, Queen Latifah builds on the legacy of promoting
and fostering community and vindicating Black womanhood left by her Black
womanist foremothers by calling for unity. Love of the Black community is evident in the song's refrains: she chants that Black men and women should be
loved "from infinity to infinity." The song is also an instance of outspokenness
in that she calls attention to sexual harassment, domestic violence, and the influence negative images of Black womanhood have on young Black women.

The first verse of the song is a critique of society that calls into question beliefs about "proper" dress and being able to walk on the streets free from harassment. Queen Latifah's story of walking down the street in cutoff shorts on a hot
day and being groped by an unknown man carries with it the experiences of
millions of women who walk down the street and receive catcalls from strangers
and the millions of women who suffer more than verbal abuse, the women who
are attacked or raped. Queen Latifah's story is the in-between, in that she is not
raped but she is touched in addition to the verbal harassment of being called a
bitch. Because it is in-between, it serves as a pedagogical moment in the diva
sense of bringing wreck. It has the power to call into question not only what
happened to Queen Latifah but also all of the variations, such as what could
have happened to her and what has happened to many women. As we listen to
Queen Latifah, we realize that no matter how short the pun-pun shorts a woman
is wearing, it is not okay for a man to make lewd comments. And it is definitely
not okay for a man to touch, fondle, rape, or otherwise invade the sanctity of her
body and her personal space. Queen Latifah's lyrics make us call into question a
variety of acts that occur daily in the objectification of women, from catcalls to
physical harassment and rape. And by doing so she brings wreck not only to
"those who disrespect [her] like a dame," but also to notions of what is acceptable in our society in regard to women and their bodies. While this form of
wreck does not go past the initial moment when the song was released and constantly played on the airwaves, it does represent a moment when the masses of
people were thinking about these issues collectively.

Queen Latifah's strong message has feminist undertones, even if Queen
Latifah herself does not identify as a feminist. When asked if she was a feminist, Queen Latifah balked: "I don't even adhere to that shit. All that shit is
bullshit! I know that at the end of the day, I'm a Black woman in this world
and I gotta get mine. I want to see the rise of the Black male in personal
strength and power. I wanna see the creation of a new Black community for
ourselves and respect from others."[15] Queen Latifah, then, appears to be a
Hip-Hop embodiment — minus the cursing of course — of the Black clubwomen

---

[15]Bonz Malone, "Queen Latifah: Original Flavor," *The Source: The Magazine of Hip-Hop Music, Culture and Politics*, May 1994, p. 66.

who went before her. She has definite goals that do not include the label "feminist," but her agenda, because she is a Black woman, certainly overlaps with feminist causes such as harassment and domestic violence. However, the vindication of Black womanhood is a trait she shares most strongly with the Black women who went before her.

Queen Latifah also tackles the impact that negative representations of Black womanhood found in rap lyrics have on the young Black women who listen to it. In addition to letting the listener know that she is neither a bitch nor a ho, she also challenges the image of the gangsta bitch popularized in the rap lyrics of some men rappers and questions the usefulness of this image to young Black women. This critique is important because often young women listen to these lyrics minus any real critique, and they emulate the kind of woman that the men rap about. The gangsta bitch, in an era of gangsta rap, becomes the epitome of Black womanhood; she is what young women strive to be in order to gain acceptance from the men. Queen Latifah brings the reality of this kind of lifestyle into focus when she cautions young would-be gangster girls about the possibilities of being shot or having their face sliced with a knife by another gangster girl.[16] Her words of advice are an example of bringing wreck because she actively seeks to uplift and create change. Queen Latifah is reaching out to a younger generation of Black women in order to teach them the reality of trying to emulate the kind of woman some rappers — in this instance her own friend rapper Apache — rap about as the ideal woman. The reality for the gangsta bitch is she could be shot and killed, or she can be scarred for life with one slice of the knife. This image is a very different image than the "ride or die chicks" that most men rappers paint in their lyrics, the down-for-whatever, hard-core shortys who will do anything for their men. Queen Latifah offers the reality, and by doing so she brings wreck.

In the second stanza, Queen Latifah calls attention to domestic violence and represents a woman who has had enough and finally leaves the abuser. She paints the picture of a woman who has come to the realization that love does not come with physical pain. Queen Latifah's lyrics are forceful and empowering. She lays out the facts and suggests actions that the woman can take. Even though she tells the story in the first person, the message, the pedagogical moment, comes as a stated fact that is directed at the listener: "A man don't really love you if he hits ya." This well-placed statement broadens the implication of bringing wreck further. It makes the story bigger than the teller and includes the millions of abused women suffering around the world. Queen Latifah brings wreck by bringing the issue of women's abuse into focus for the society at large and causing us to question both the abuse against women and our own action or inaction against it.

Similarly, Eve's "Love Is Blind" brings the issue of domestic violence into both the counter–public sphere of Hip-Hop and the larger public sphere. Eve, 15

---

[16]Queen Latifah, "U.N.I.T.Y.," *Black Reign*, Motown, 1993.

however, does not take on the persona of the battered woman, as Queen Latifah does in "U.N.I.T.Y." She instead takes on the persona of the vengeful best friend. She threatens the abuser with murder throughout the song, which ends with her killing the abuser. Similar to Queen Latifah's "U.N.I.T.Y.," Eve uses the song as a pedagogical moment. However, it is a lesson aimed not only at the women who suffer abuse but also at the men who abuse. For the men, the message is clear: keep beating up on women and you might catch a bullet and die. For the women, the message is similar to the one found in Queen Latifah's lyrics: men who really love you do not hit you. Eve makes use of rhetorical questions throughout the song to highlight her point by essentially asking if a man who really loves a woman would give her a black eye, make her cry every night, and ultimately cause her to wish for his death.[17] Eve is bringing wreck not only by rapping the lyrics and posing these questions. She also expands on the activist elements of bringing wreck by building institutions aimed at combating the problem. She started the Love Is Blind foundation to address domestic violence issues in more significant ways than a song could.[18] She too has a mission of uplift similar to that of her Black foremothers, and she would like to see a collective effort of women in the Hip-Hop generation uplifting each other. She notes, "A lot of women tell me I uplift them. . . . We gotta do it collectively. . . . I see how a lot of women disrespect themselves. When we change our actions, men will change their minds. I think a lot of women get tired of hearing that shit. I'm glad that women feel like I can uplift them."[19] While Eve's words may seem a bit naive in terms of the exact amount of influence women's actions have on the men rappers who use the words *bitch* and *ho*, she is on to something in her desire for the collective action of Black women. This collective action could take the form of the collective niggerbitchfit that Jill Nelson encourages. Or it could be as simple as Black women collectively deciding not to deal with men who do not respect Black womanhood, as Rebecca Walker recommends in "Becoming the Third Wave."[20] The important point is that songs such as "Love Is Blind" and "U.N.I.T.Y." inspire the desire for collective action. Eve's "Love Is Blind" and the second stanza of Queen Latifah's "U.N.I.T.Y." build on the diva qualities of bringing wreck in that they offer testimonies aimed at changing the world, or at least the way we think about women's place in it.

Within each rapper's delivery and style of rap there are other elements of bringing wreck. These are most evident in the music videos of these songs. In the "U.N.I.T.Y." video, for example, Queen Latifah raps the lyrics from a

[17]Eve, "Love Is Blind," *Ruff Ryders' First Lady*, Ruff Ryders, 1999.

[18]Margeaux Watson, "Eve Blows Our Mind," *Honey*, August 2002, p. 85.

[19]Ryan Ford, "Eve: Material Girl," *The Source: The Magazine of Hip-Hop Music, Culture and Politics*, August 2002, p. 146.

[20]Rebecca Walker, "Becoming the Third Wave," in Amy Kesselman, Lily D. McNair, and Nancy Schniedwind, eds., *Women, Images and Realities: A Multicultural Anthology* (Mountain View: Mayfield, 1999).

telephone booth, and she is yelling into the phone in a manner that can best be classified as turning it out or going off. In the video for "Love Is Blind" Eve represents the calculated and thought-out stance of a woman ready to turn it out or, better yet, navigate a niggerbitchfit. She studies the situation; throughout the video, she is on the side examining the scene. The video, unlike the lyrics, does not end with her killing the abuser. She does use the gun to threaten him, but the event culminates in a bright beam of lights and doves flying into the air and him on the ground alive. The video version, more than the song alone, serves as a pedagogical moment. Both songs' lyrics and videos offer examples of the ways Black women have used rap music to bring wreck.

READING THE TEXT

1. Why, in Pough's view, do historical accounts of hip-hop culture tend to neglect the contributions of women?

2. Why does Pough see Queen Latifah as aligned with feminism, despite the rapper's dismissal of it?

3. How are women typically portrayed in male rap songs, according to Pough, and how does Queen Latifah subvert that portrayal?

4. How is Eve's "Love Is Blind" a "pedagogical moment" (para. 15)?

READING THE SIGNS

1. In your journal, brainstorm a list of attributes that you would like to give your gender in a video of your own design. Then write a "screen play" for your own rap video, being sure to incorporate your preferred attributes. Share your screen play with the class.

2. Write an argumentative essay supporting, refuting, or complicating Pough's claim that " 'U.N.I.T.Y.' . . . has implications for change both within the counter–public sphere of Hip-Hop and the society at large" (para. 10).

3. Study the work of a contemporary female rapper, and write an essay in which you analyze the extent to which her work "bring[s] wreck to the stereotypes and marginalization that inhibit [black women's] interaction in the larger public sphere" (para. 9).

4. Using Pough's article as your critical framework, compare and contrast a male rap video and a female rap video. What gender roles do you see in each video, and what is the viewer's likely response? To develop your ideas, read or review Aaron Devor's "Gender Role Behaviors and Attitudes" (p. 458) and Joan Morgan's "Sex, Lies, and Videos" (p. 496).

ANDRE MAYER
The New Sexual Stone Age

More than thirty years after the beginning of the modern women's movement, the traditional codes that govern gender behavior and identity are being replaced by new notions of what it means to be a man or woman. But you wouldn't know it by listening to contemporary pop music, especially rap-metallists like Kid Rock and Limp Bizkit, who, Andre Mayer argues in this selection from the online magazine Shift.com, have returned "to an age of rampant chauvinism, where men swagger about in a testosterone rage and women are reduced to sexual ornaments." Suddenly, it's "pimp culture" time on the pop airwaves, where men are men and women are, well—maybe you should watch a videotape of the Britney Spears Pepsi commercial run during Super Bowl XXXVI. Mayer is a columnist for Shift.com magazine, where this piece first appeared in 2001.

Everywhere you look, people are taking a more open-minded stance on gender roles. In October 2000, the Dutch parliament implemented legislation that would make it the first country in the world to recognize gay marriages. Ohio University announced it would designate thirty campus bathrooms "unisex" to accommodate transgendered students. The number of male nurses is rising, as is the overall viewership of women's sports. Outmoded notions about the roles of men and women are relaxing; except, that is, in pop music, where quite the opposite is true. Glance at magazine covers, at videos, at lyric sheets: We've returned to an age of rampant chauvinism, where men swagger about in a testosterone rage and women are reduced to sexual ornaments.

The most visible advocates are artists like Kid Rock, Limp Bizkit, and Crazy Town, who not only resemble eighties hair metal in their thudding guitar assault, but in their celebration of male debauchery and female subservience. In song, females are oppugned; in videos, they're totted up like bimbos and objectified. Limp Bizkit's "Nookie" does both: The track is a misogynistic kiss-off to a girlfriend, and when singer Fred Durst shouts "I did it all for the nookie," he's blatantly admitting that he exploited her for sex. Critics have long reproved hip hop for its too-enthusiastic use of words like "bitches" and "hos," but rappers could always deflect accountability for claiming that their lyrics were a stark reflection of ghetto reality. With the advent of rap-metal, however, artists like Kid Rock and Limp Bizkit have taken the gritty argot of their hip hop heroes and are passing it off as their own. With widespread use, such hateful language becomes more accepted.

The same can be said for the current prevalence of pimp iconography. Echoing rappers like the Notorious B.I.G. and Too $hort, Kid Rock fancies himself an "American pimp," but he's part of a greater trend that includes apparel (Phat Pimp Clothing, Pimpdaddy.com), movies (the Hughes brothers' documentary *American Pimp* and the upcoming comedy *Lil' Pimp*, about a nine-year-old procurer), and staged events, like Boston's annual "Pimps and Hos Ball." It stems from the general nostalgia for blaxploitation flicks like *Cleopatra Jones* and *The Mack*, in which pimps are the pinnacle of camp, dressing in garish attire and spouting comical jive. Real pimps are far less cuddly — as we know, they insult, abuse, and unscrupulously lord over their female charges. Most people would agree that pimping is abhorrent, but the image has become so widespread — and in many cases, sentimentalized — that a new generation of pop culture consumers blithely embraces it.

Unfortunately, the current contingent of female stars is doing little to correct these primitive attitudes. Many of them — the Britneys, the Christinas, the Jessicas — dress like prostitutes, or at the very least, extras in a Van Halen video. When these chirpy, vacuous singers swept into vogue, they knocked more intelligent and progressive gals like Tori Amos and Alanis Morissette off the charts. Every new video or awards show is an opportunity for immodest types like Mariah Carey and Toni Braxton to set new standards for libidinous spectacle, and while they pay lip service to positive messages, the only thing they offer their distaff fans is an unattainable image of female sexuality.

So what's the cause of this retrograde sexism? Many critics have pointed   5
to the feelings described by Susan Faludi in her book *Stiffed: The Betrayal of the American Man*, in which she claims that feelings of emasculation (due to a number of factors, including joblessness and feminism) have spurred many men to reassert their manhood. The most glaring consequence of this may be the popularity of so-called "lad mags," of which *Maxim* was arguably the catalyst. Started in the mid-nineties, *Maxim* captured an immense demographic of horny males by offering *Playboy*-type titillation (stopping just short of pornography) and insolent commentary. The effect inevitably snowballed into other media — while pop has always used sex to help sell albums, record executives undoubtedly felt that increasing the T&A in the marketing of female artists would also satisfy the booming *Maxim* niche.

The music press seems eerily complicit with the problem. While some writers have commented on the inherent virgin-whore complex in Britney Spears's image, for example, many seem only too happy to defend it, or at the very least excuse it. The Spears profile in the September 13th issue of *Rolling Stone* typifies the music press's soft treatment of gender. The cover features Spears with trademark bared midriff and salacious leer and carries the kicker "Britney talks back: Don't treat me like a little girl." Like most Spears interviews, it's a shameless red herring. The story is punctuated with Spears's cheerily oblivious musings on the nature of her appeal, and in lieu of any remotely revealing quotes, writer Jenny Eliscu comes to the shrugging conclusion that "Britney and her image are one and the same — she is as much of a delightful contradiction as she seems." The title of Spears's single, "I'm a Slave 4 U," suggests that her provocative image shows no signs of flagging.

Meanwhile, those females who assert their strength often seem misguided. The catchphrase "independent women" is as hollow as the shrieks of "girl power!" back in 1997.

Destiny's Child equate self-sufficiency with having the wherewithal to buy their own clothes, shoes, and cars. Then again, any assertion of dignity seems practical at a time when Eminem protégés D12 spout, "Independent women in the house / Show us your tits and shut your motherfucking mouth" ("Ain't Nuttin' But Music").

This prevailing machismo not only denigrates women, but inherently scorns anyone whom it deems less than "manly" (i.e., impervious to sensitivity and militantly hetero). Barring gender benders like Marilyn Manson and Placebo's Brian Molko, few artists seem interested in exploring the androgyny of David Bowie and Freddie Mercury. And why would they? Right now, pop seems not only unreceptive but hostile to such liberalism.

The easiest qualification of music's current homophobia is taking a tally 10 of the number of openly gay stars. There are few beyond Elton John, k.d. lang, Melissa Etheridge, and Rufus Wainwright. Has anyone heard from George Michael lately? He's probably wary of returning to this increasingly homophobic milieu. Given the current indication for close-mindedness, sitting out until pop emerges from the Stone Age seems like a sound idea.

READING THE TEXT

1. What contradiction does Mayer see in the evolution of gender roles and the content and style of contemporary pop music?
2. What does Mayer mean by "pimp iconography" (para. 3)?
3. Characterize Mayer's tone in this essay. How does it affect your response to his argument?
4. According to Mayer, what is the significance of the relative dearth of gay performers in today's pop music world?

READING THE SIGNS

1. Write an essay defending, refuting, or modifying Mayer's contention that much of popular music reinforces outmoded notions about gender roles.
2. Mayer describes a trend he sees in popular music, but he does not offer his own explanation for it. Write an essay in which you present your thesis for why so much modern pop music is sexist. To develop support for your stance, you might analyze current videos on MTV, paying attention to both lyrics and the personal style of the artists you watch. You might also consult Gwendolyn Pough's "Women, Rap, Wreck" (p. 275) and Joan Morgan's "Sex, Lies, and Videos" (p. 496).
3. Mayer cites *Maxim* as a current magazine that exploits the desire of "many men to reassert their manhood" (para. 5). Analyze an issue of *Maxim*, and write an essay that disputes or supports Mayer's characterization of it. To

develop your ideas, you might interview some men who are regular readers of the magazine and some men who find no interest in it.

4. Write an essay in which you analyze the style of female rappers. To what extent do they share the "primitive" (para. 4) attitudes that Mayer ascribes to such stars as Britney Spears and Mariah Carey? How do you account for any differences that you may observe? To develop your ideas, consult Gwendolyn Pough's "Women, Rap, Wreck" (p. 275).

5. Form teams and conduct an in-class debate on whether the patterns Mayer sees in pop music are indeed chauvinistic and dangerous or, instead, a sign of liberation. Use the debate to generate ideas for an essay in which you formulate your own argument about this question.

MARISA CONNOLLY

Homosexuality on Television:
The Heterosexualization of Will and Grace

Network TV is on the cutting edge of social change, right? Courageously challenging long-standing prejudices on behalf of progressive new viewpoints? After all, it has brought us Will and Grace, *a perennial hit sitcom featuring gay characters that shatter the homophobic history of popular culture. So why, Marisa Connolly asks, is the relationship between gay Will and straight Grace so, well, romantic? Why does the show maintain an erotic tension between the two that continues from season to season? Why hasn't Will yet had an onscreen gay relationship? Could it be that* Will and Grace *isn't really so very courageous after all? Connolly (b. 1979), who is the media director for* Science and Theology News, *thinks not.*

He's single, successful and good-looking. She's independent, strong-willed and attractive. They'd make the perfect couple, except for one teensy problem — he's gay, she's straight.

Such is the premise of NBC's *Will and Grace*, a half-hour situation comedy in its fifth season that serves two purposes. First, the show attempts to explore a totally platonic relationship between two best friends of opposite sexes. Secondly, the show features two gay male leads with polar-opposite personalities in order to destigmatize the representation of the homosexual man. The show has been one of NBC's most successful since its debut, garnering both critical and public praise for its portrayal of homosexuality as just another aspect of the lives of the four main characters.

However, in order to make a show with such controversial subject matter palatable for the masses, both scriptwriters and the mainstream media have taken to talking about the show's two leads more like a romantic couple rather than a pair of best friends. For the purposes of this analysis, "couple" will refer specifically to a romantic pairing. This metaphor, which plays out on screen in both word and action, also carries over into the language used to describe the show and its characters in mainstream print media. Metaphors that misclassify this relationship can make a television show with a gay male lead easier to digest for the viewing audience, but it can also have negative effects on the inroads the show has made in making homosexuality more acceptable on mainstream television.

This analysis will explore the extent to which reviews in mainstream print media reflect the heterosexual undercurrent apparent in *Will and Grace*. Common representations of homosexuality on television will be explained, followed by an examination of how *Will and Grace* heterosexualizes the relationship between the two lead characters. Finally, the paper will examine how those metaphors translate into print media, and how that translation affects the viewing public.

None of this discussion is meant to demean the accomplishments of *Will and Grace* as the first vehicle to tackle homosexuality naturally in prime time. However, it is important to evaluate the discourse about an important program such as this one, in order to understand how the public uses old metaphors to make sense of new representations that push the envelope of what has been previously accepted.

Background

During television's 1997–1998 season, viewers watched as ABC's *Ellen* became the first television show ever to feature an openly gay lead character — Ellen Morgan, played by actress/comedienne Ellen DeGeneres. The actress timed her personal coming out with the coming out of her character amidst an onslaught of controversy, protest, and criticism from right-wing conservatives such as Jerry Falwell. Initial viewer and public reaction to Ellen's revealed sexuality was positive. But as the season continued and the episodes continued to delve into Ellen's self-discovery and the hardships she faced as a lesbian in today's society, the audience slipped away while criticism continued, forcing ABC to cancel the program at the end of the season.

TV critics and reviewers attributed the failure of *Ellen* not to the public's inability to embrace an openly gay character, but more to the show's almost preachy overtones in the episodes following Ellen's initial coming out. The consensus among scholars was that *Ellen* was too political and didactic, containing "veritable lessons in queer socio-politics."[1] As a result of the negative

---

[1]James R. Keller. "*Will and Grace*: The Politics of Inversion." *Queer (Un)Friendly Film and Television* (London: McFarland & Company, 2002): 122.

feedback and criticism with which ABC had to deal, it seemed unlikely that any network would be willing to take a risk with a homosexual character again anytime soon.

Will and Grace: More Accessible Homosexuality

However, in September 1998, NBC launched *Will and Grace*. Created by writers Max Mutchnick and David Kohan and directed by James Burrows (of *Cheers*, *Friends*, and *Frasier* fame), the program featured the first openly gay male character in a lead role on prime-time television. The move was risky — airing a program like *Will and Grace* so soon after *Ellen* crashed and burned could have plunged the show and the network into boundless controversy.

But NBC was confident that *Will and Grace* would be a more successful vehicle for an openly gay character for a few reasons. First, the show did not focus around a homosexual man's coming out, but rather homosexuality as a way of life. There was no pilot episode that depicted Will coming to terms with his sexuality, although flashback episodes have explored this moment in Will's life. Will's homosexuality has been a given from the very beginning of the series. Additionally, the character of Will was not portrayed with any common stereotypical "gay" behavior. The final reason NBC could be more confident in the show's success was that the producers threw a heterosexual woman into the mix.

The show revolves around Will Truman (Eric McCormack), a young 10 lawyer living in New York City who just ended a seven-year relationship with another man. His best friend, Grace Adler (Debra Messing), is an interior designer who, in the pilot episode, leaves her fiancé at the altar. The two friends had dated in college, until Will revealed his sexuality to Grace, and they'd been the best of friends ever since.

The relationship between Will and Grace was based on the real-life friendship between Mutchnick, who is himself openly gay, and his friend Janet, who is straight. Mutchnick and Kohan wanted to explore the male-female relationship dynamic "when sex doesn't get in the way," but they also wanted to present a more true-to-life representation of a gay man in Will, who is good-looking, successful, and less effeminate than most stereotypes.

They balanced that representation with the addition of Will's friend Jack McFarland (Sean Hayes), who is flamboyantly gay and serves as comic relief along with Grace's assistant, Karen Walker (Megan Mullally). The combination of all four players created an aesthetically pleasing representation of single life in New York City, and resulted in a much less controversial success for NBC.

The show debuted in a Monday night timeslot, moved to Tuesdays after it showed promise, and ended up in the coveted "Must See TV" line-up on Thursday night before its first season had even ended. It garnered critical praise from both mainstream sources and homosexual interest groups. GLAAD (the Gay and Lesbian Alliance Against Defamation) hailed the show for its portrayal of two different representations of gay men. The show even found itself competing for the same advertising dollars as ABC's *Dharma and Greg*, a program based on the lives of a heterosexual couple. It seemed that mainstream society had grown to accept the gay community on its television programs.[2]

Criticism from Other Sources

In the years since *Will and Grace* premiered to great success on NBC, so soon after the negativity swirled around *Ellen*, media critics have tried to understand why the show did not come under the fire of public outcry. The overwhelming consensus is that though *Will and Grace* has been monumental in bringing homosexuality as a reality into the living rooms of houses around the world, it "negotiates with the dominant culture by making the most important relationships between the two gay characters heterosocial and quasi-heterosexual."[3] It has been clear since the show's first season that the most important relationship has been the friendship between Will and Grace. Though the program is about a homosexual male and his heterosexual best friend, scripts and comic devices have often made it seem that Will and Grace were the perfect heterosexual couple, separated only by sexual orientation. Battles and Hilton-Morrow present this situation as yet another example of delayed consummation — a plot line that puts off the matchup of the leading male and female characters in order to keep the audience tuning in on a weekly basis. Will and Grace are often positioned as a couple, as well as subject to the barbs of Karen, who often chides their bickering or displays of affection with lines like "Oh, just climb on top of each other and get it over with already!"[4]

It is this placement of Will and Grace as a heterosexual couple almost 15 destined to be together that seems to be the reason for its widespread appeal and lack of criticism from right-wing groups. Even though the show contains openly gay and sometimes raunchy humor, provided by Jack and Karen, according to Battles and Hilton-Morrow, this behavior is shown as almost infantile, playing to a familial relationship among the four characters. Karen and Jack are the children to Will and Grace's parental figures.[5] That fact alone plays into the inherent heterosexual relationship between gay Will and straight Grace.

---

[2]Kathleen Battles and Wendy Hilton-Morrow. "Gay Characters in Conventional Spaces: *Will and Grace* and the Situation Comedy Genre." *Critical Studies in Media Communication*. 19 (2002): 89.

[3]Keller, 123.

[4]Battles and Hilton-Morrow, 93.

[5]Battles and Hilton-Morrow, 97.

Media Representation

Since *Will and Grace*'s first season, print media and other forums have run many reviews, criticisms and praises for the program. In looking at the representation of homosexuals in this program, it became clear that these reviews may look at the relationship between Will and Grace similarly to the way the relationship is portrayed on the program itself. Specifically, to what extent does the print media heterosexualize the characters? Focusing specifically on the language used to describe their friendship, does the print media use words like "couple," "romance" and "sexual tension" when they comment on Will and Grace? Do they use any metaphors or comparisons to past television couples that carry a heterosexual connotation?

Television reviews in print media sources play a large role in creating the general buzz around a show, as well as contribute to the total viewership of a program. If these reviews are presenting the relationship between Will and Grace as heterosexual, they could be responsible for detracting from the audience's understanding of the show as an exploration of a homosexual lifestyle.

Of course, the media would not be entirely to blame for any misrepresentations of the relationship between Will and Grace — the writers of the program have come under some degree of fire for keeping Will out of any real romantic relationship with another man. The media can only comment on what is presented to them in a weekly episode. This paper explores how much of that veiled metaphor of heterosexuality translated itself into the print media.

Methodology

In order to analyze the extent to which the print media perpetuates the idea that *Will and Grace* depicts a successful homosexual television vehicle because it masquerades Will and Grace as a quasi-heterosexual couple, this study examined certain metaphors and phraseology used in various articles and reviews in newspapers during the show's lifetime. Because the show has been on the air for five seasons at the writing of this paper, it has accumulated quite a bit of press. Therefore, in order to make the research more manageable the search was limited to two time periods: articles written in U.S. newspapers and magazines during the show's first season — 1998–1999 — and articles written to commemorate the show's fifth season and 100th episode — September 2002–December 9, 2002. A new television program always receives much media attention in its early days in order for producers to introduce the show, its characters, and its premise, but also so television critics can make their opinions known on whether the program will be a success or a flop. *Will and Grace* was a product of NBC — whose "Must See TV" line-ups are among television's most successful — and it featured the first homosexual male lead on American television; therefore print media pieces filled with character description and analysis were easy to find during this time period.

In addition, looking at articles written around a commemorative event [20] like a sitcom's 100th episode is a helpful way to monitor the changes in media perception of the show between its first season and its current one. Have the metaphors changed with the show's writing as the years have gone by?

The articles used in the analysis were located using two different news index sources: Lexis-Nexis and EBSCO Host through Academic Search Premier. Searches for "will and grace" in Arts and Sports News/Entertainment News from September 1998 through June 1999 turned up over 200 matches. A search from September 2002 through December 2002 turned up about 124 articles. Filtering out the one-sentence blurbs and weekly ratings reports, the data set included 27 articles that could be classified as reviews, trend stories, and actor interviews, each of which used in some way the metaphors and phraseology discovered in the analysis. These articles also came from all over the country, in papers as large as the *Washington Post* to smaller papers such as the *Bergen County Record* (New Jersey).

In the analysis of these articles, it is important to note that many articles written during the first season of *Will and Grace* highlighted and discussed the same criticisms of the show explored in this analysis. The metaphors and language used as examples here are separate examples of metaphors or language used by the media to describe the relationship between lead characters Will and Grace, and have nothing to do with articles or sections of articles that use this language to further discussion about the show's interpretation of homosexuality. To do so would obviously have skewed the analysis in one direction.

Findings

Research has uncovered a few common metaphors used by print media to describe the relationship between Will and Grace as heterosexual. In each instance the form the metaphor takes is different. Sometimes the metaphor appears in one sentence as a one-time comparison or description; in other examples it permeates the entire paragraph like a literary device, perhaps repeating one word or playing off the creation of a mental image earlier in the paragraph. The metaphor use also differs between simple word choice and the writer's personal opinion. Word choice tends to reflect what the writer has seen in that evening's particular episode. A review that carries the writer's opinion of the show as a whole, and not simply one specific episode, tends to tie everything it critiques to the larger picture of the show as a whole. When the writer's opinion colors the review, the metaphor can set a tone for the entire article, focusing on Grace, for example, "still harboring hopes for a man who has his eye on other men."[6]

Specifically, three metaphors occurred frequently within the data set. Two focus explicitly on making Will and Grace's relationship heterosexual, while

---

[6]Matthew Gilbert. "Will Success Ruin NBC's *Will & Grace*?" *Boston Globe* 8 Apr. 1999: El.

the third is a more general classification of relationships between gay men and straight women and how print media relates to them. Following are several examples from the data set where each metaphor demonstrates how these metaphors are used in each article.

THE "ROMANCE" METAPHOR

Many reviews during the first season have classified Will and Grace's relation- 25 ship as a "romantic" one, using words like "love," "lovers" and "romance" when describing what these characters mean to each other. The use of a metaphor involving "love" in some way is not out of the ordinary to describe these characters. After all, the show is meant to explore a strong platonic love between a man and a woman. Similarly, most writers are quick to point out, subsequently, that it is "not that kind of love."[7] However, the reader is often set up from the beginning of the review to think that Will and Grace are just another couple. For example, the first part of the previous example reads, "Will (Eric McCormack) and Grace (Debra Messing), they're in love."[8]

The problem with using such romance-heavy terminology in describing Will and Grace is that it cements the characters into a position of physical, romantic love. There have been too many sitcoms to count that have focused on a pair or group of friends that did not hinge on this idea of subliminal love. In a program that is trying to make the relationship between these four people seem as mainstream as possible, it takes away from that idea to continuously refer to the obvious love Will and Grace share for one another.

The "romance" metaphor also tends to make much more of the physical nature of Will and Grace's relationship. For example, an article in *The Nation* makes this reference: "Grace has already moved in, at his insistence, as his new roommate, which will give them many opportunities to hug each other after they've resolved whatever antics come between them. . . ."[9] This quote is a good example of how the author's opinion colors the metaphor used. Here, the writer is clearly making the hugs between Will and Grace more romantic than they are perhaps intended to be, labeling certain experiences "excuses" to hug.

Entering into the fifth season, the "romance" metaphor has not disappeared. Another article in the *Boston Globe* compared Will and Grace's gay-straight relationship as "a sexless love affair."[10] This metaphor takes "romance" to another level by marking it as forbidden love, and brings even more complex connotations to the relationship.

Another example of the romance metaphor was paired with the second major metaphor, which will be described in the next section: "Do Will and

[7]Drew Jubera. "Ready or Not, It's Time for Fall Season to Open." *Atlanta Journal and Constitution* 21 Sept. 1998: 01C.

[8]Jubera, 01C.

[9]Alyssa Katz. "Beyond Ellen." *The Nation* 2 Nov. 1998: 32–34.

[10]Matthew Gilbert. "Pop Music: More Than Friends. Forget the Naysayers, with Its Unique Wit and Style, *Will and Grace* Remains One of TV's Elite Comedies." *Boston Globe* 17 Nov. 2002: Nl.

Grace love each other? Clearly. They live together; they depend on and bicker with each other; they share their hopes, desires and neuroses; they praise, criticize and tease each other relentlessly."[11] Each one of these behaviors is associated with the state of being in love. Again, there are many kinds of love that can be described in this way, but the writer of this review makes it clear he is referring to only romantic love between a man and a woman.

THE "COUPLE" METAPHOR

The example above segues nicely into the "couple" metaphor. The review 30 follows that quote with a segment from that week's episode in which Will and Grace are fighting in public and a stranger mistakes them for a married couple:

> "We're not married!" Grace fires back. "And I'm gay!" Will snaps.
> "Well, if you're not married, and you're gay," the man says, nodding toward Will, "what the hell's all this about?"
> What, indeed.[12]

It is obvious, from the last line of this quote, that the writer of this review has a clear opinion that Will and Grace should be a classical heterosexual couple. Many times, Will and Grace are described as "the perfect couple," with only one major barrier keeping them apart: "Will's gayness is the only thing that stands between the devoted pair and lifelong happiness."[13]

A second example of this insinuation: "They are the perfect couple. But they aren't lovers, nor will they be."[14] With no real label for a platonic relationship between a heterosexual woman and a homosexual man, it seems as though writers can only refer to the characters by the strongly marked word "couple," risking the romantic connotation. The only label writers seem to be able to come up with is "perfect," idealizing to some extent the relationship between these two characters as something that neither homosexuality nor heterosexuality can completely emulate: "the perfectly committed no-commit couple,"[15] and "the boy and the girl are too perfect for each other to ever get it on."[16] This kind of idealization leads to the ultimate end in coupledom, that Will and Grace belong together: "Naturally, the show puts them together. More importantly, it makes us believe they belong together."[17]

---

[11]Eric Mink. "*Will and Grace* Top of Class of '99: Bright Season Finale Proves It's Not Just Another Sitcom." *New York Daily News* 13 May 1999: 106.

[12]Ibid, 106.

[13]Katz, 32–34.

[14]Tom Walter. "New-Season Shopping? Start with *Will and Grace*." *Commercial Appeal (TN)* 21 Sept. 1998, C2.

[15]Jubera, 01C.

[16]Katz, 34.

[17]Robert Bianco. "16 New Series Premiere This Week, NBC's *Will & Grace* Leads the Lineup." *USA Today* 21 Sept. 1998: 1D.

Some uses of the metaphor even go as far to suggest that Will's gayness is something that he can "get over," in order to bring Will and Grace together in the end:

> They are, in short, a perfect match except that they are sexually incompatible and there is a strange but unmistakably romantic tone to the show. Is it possible that the producers actually want viewers to hope, unconsciously, that these two terrific and very good-looking people will, eventually, somehow, overcome that little sexual, uh, glitch?[18]

THE "ODD COUPLE" METAPHOR

Some writers, however, have made an attempt to put a different label on the relationship — a new spin on the term "couple" which works well for developing a trend in popular culture that seems to enjoy pairing homosexual men with heterosexual women. Just before *Will and Grace* hit television airwaves, Hollywood had made a few movies following this formula. First coined in an article appearing in *Entertainment Weekly*, the "Odd Couple" metaphor relates Will and Grace, and other gay man–straight woman relationships to the opposites attract relationship between the characters on the original *Odd Couple* television show: "Gay men and straight women are to the '90s what Oscar and Felix were to the '70s."[19] In the first season, this metaphor does not exactly speak to the heterosexual nature of Will and Grace's relationship, because Oscar and Felix were two same-sex friends, but it does seem to make the idea of homosexuality friendlier to the viewing audience, which is, again, one of the major criticisms of *Will and Grace* as a groundbreaking television program. Another example of the "Odd Couple" metaphor: "If only she'd had a pal like Will Truman, half of television's latest odd couple in *Will and Grace. . . .*"[20]

The motivation behind the word "odd" in this metaphor, however, raises 35 a few questions, and begins to mark where the mainstream media has stopped feeling the influence of the show's scripts and intentions. From the beginning, Mutchnick and Kohan were trying to create a show about homosexuality that made it more mainstream, blending homosexual and heterosexual life into one seamless world. Marking Will and Grace's relationship as "odd" is not something one could believe Mutchnick would find acceptable. The "odd" can only really refer to the neuroses and behaviors of the "bickering, superficial, relationship-impaired foursome,"[21] and not to the social status of their relationship.

[18]Eric Mink. "Peacock's Got the 'Will'." *New York Daily News* 21 Sept. 1998: 71.

[19]A. Jacobs. "When Gay Men Happen to Straight Women." *Entertainment Weekly*. Retrieved November 14, 2002 from www.ew.com.

[20]Stephen McCauley. "He's Gay, She's Straight, They're a Trend." *New York Times* 20 Sept. 1998, 31.

[21]Gilbert, 2002, Nl.

But later repetition of the metaphor makes a few changes. Rather than specifically relating Will and Grace to same-sex friends Oscar and Felix, the "couple" part of "Odd Couple" starts to take on comparisons to other television pairings: "They rank with some of TVs classic couples, including Sam and Diane [*Cheers*], and Oscar and Felix."[22] The most interesting aspect of this morphing of the "Odd Couple" metaphor is now we have Will and Grace paired with one of television's most well-known pairs of frustrated lovers — Sam and Diane from James Burrows's *Cheers*. In season five, Will and Grace are not considered "odd" as much as they are considered "fated" never to be together, yet always to be together, as good friends.

Conclusion

The consequences of metaphors like the ones discussed above still carry heavily on the future of *Will and Grace*. To date, the show is still one of NBC's most popular, holding down the 9 p.m. timeslot in the "Must-See TV" lineup. Megan Mullally, Sean Hayes, and Eric McCormack have each gone on to win supporting and lead acting trophies, respectively, and the show itself earned the Emmy for Outstanding Comedy Series in 2000. However, Will's character has yet to have a serious on-screen romantic relationship with another man comparable to those of Grace, and a more recent plot line has revolved around Will and Grace's attempts to have a child together.

If the program continues to push Will and Grace together with pseudo-romantic overtones, then the print media will most likely continue to discuss the characters' exploits with heterosexual metaphors. The media can only represent the images, words and storylines a television program shows them. Perhaps a look at the metaphors used to describe the relationship between supporting players Karen and Jack would turn more favorably towards a platonic gay man–straight woman relationship, but until the show changes its name to *Karen and Jack*, the emphasis will be on Will, Grace, and the love that almost constantly seems to speak its name.

READING THE TEXT

1. Why, according to Connolly, did *Ellen* fail?
2. How did *Will and Grace*'s creators work to defuse the controversy over the show's focus on gay characters?
3. In Connolly's view, how are Will and Grace made to appear like a heterosexual couple?
4. What is Connolly's methodology in her research of the media's response to *Will and Grace*?

[22]Gilbert, 2002, Nl.

READING THE SIGNS

1. Watch an episode of *Will and Grace*, and analyze the relationship between the two lead characters. To what extent does the episode encourage viewers to imagine the characters as a heterosexual couple?

2. Adopt Susan Douglas's ("Signs of Intelligent Life on TV," p. 270) perspective of TV's treatment of gender roles, and analyze *Will and Grace*'s tendency to present the lead characters as a heterosexual couple.

3. Analyze another TV program that features gay characters, such as *Queer Eye for the Straight Guy* or *Queer as Folk*. Do you see evidence of the soft-peddling of homosexuality?

4. Write an argumentative essay in response to the proposition that, despite the heterosexualization of the two lead characters, *Will and Grace* still represents a milestone in the media's depiction of gay characters and culture. To develop your ideas, consult Andy Medhurst's "Batman, Deviance, and Camp" (p. 753) and Sean Cahill's "The Case for Marriage Equality" (p. 469).

THE HOLLYWOOD SIGN

The Culture of American Film

The Prequel

Let's play Jeopardy. Category: Hollywood movies for $250. Buzzers ready? "In recent years the following movies all shared something in common: *Shrek 2, Spider-Man 2, Princess Diaries 2, Scooby Doo 2, Ocean's 11, Ocean's 12, Meet the Fockers, War of the Worlds, The Bourne Supremacy, Exorcist: The Beginning, The Longest Yard, The Lion King, The Stepford Wives, Starsky and Hutch, Fat Albert, Son of the Mask,* and *Miss Congeniality 2.*"

Time's up. And the correct response is: "What are some recent Hollywood sequels, prequels, remakes, and adaptations?"

And now a daily double for $500. "He said, 'It looks like déjà vu all over again.'"

Time's up. And the correct response is: "Who was Yogi Berra?"

You can say that again. And again.

The Sequel: Or, How the Grinch Rehashed Christmas

Now, seriously, do you ever get the impression that Hollywood is stuck on replay? That there's nothing on except for reruns? That the creative departments of America's movie industry are all on summer vacation? It's true that not everything on the silver screen is a rehash of an old warhorse, but certainly a lot of duplication has been coming out of Hollywood these days. And, as is usually the case when a pattern appears in popular culture, we can find a semiotic message behind it.

Once again, the first step in conducting a semiotic analysis is to establish the system within which the sign to be analyzed may be associated with other similar signs. Such systems are frequently historical in nature, and in the case of the Hollywood remake, the system is quite venerable. Film classics like *Wuthering Heights, Hamlet, Rebecca, Moby Dick*, and any film based on a Jane Austen novel have all been made and remade in years past. Such remakes may signify nothing more than a given director's desire to pay homage to a revered predecessor or to appeal to audiences' desire to see a favorite story retold with more modern faces. And in the case of Gus Van Sant's 1998 remake of Alfred Hitchcock's *Psycho* (1960), which put Anne Heche in Janet Leigh's shoes (or, one should say, shower), both motivations are apparent.

But the sheer number of Hollywood remakes, sequels, prequels, and adaptations in recent years suggests an intensification of the phenomenon that is not easily explained in such terms. This difference within the system points to at least two semiotic meanings, the first of which involves the postmodern context in which the contemporary Hollywood remake appears.

Flashback: The Postmodern System

Postmodernism is, in effect, both a historical period and an attitude. As a historical period, *postmodernism* refers to the culture that has emerged in the wake of the media age, one obsessed with electronic imagery and the products of mass culture. As an attitude, postmodernism rejects the values of the past, not in favor of new values but only to ironize value systems as such. Thus, in the postmodern worldview, our traditional hierarchical distinctions — valuing high culture over low culture, say, or creativity over imitation — tend to get flattened out. What was once viewed in terms of an oppositional hierarchy (origination is opposed to emulation and is superior to it) is reconceived and deconstructed. Postmodern artists, accordingly, tend to reproduce, with an ironic or parodic twist, already existing cultural images in their work, especially if they can be drawn from mass culture and mass society — as Roy Lichtenstein's cartoon canvasses parody mass cultural cartoon books and Andy Warhol's tomato soup cans repeat the familiar labels of the Campbell's corporation — thus mixing high culture and mass culture in a new, non-oppositional, relation.

Similarly, postmodern filmmakers frequently allude to existing films in their work, as in the final scene of Tim Burton's *Batman*, which directly alludes to Alfred Hitchcock's *Vertigo*, or Oliver Stone's and Quentin Tarantino's *Natural Born Killers*, which recalls *Bonnie and Clyde*. Such allusions to, and repetitions of, existing cultural images in postmodern cinema are called double-coding, because of the way that the postmodern artifact simultaneously refers to existing cultural codes and recasts them in new contexts. The conclusion of *Batman*, for example, while echoing *Vertigo*'s climactic scene, differs dramatically in its significance (turning in this case from tragedy to farce).

To put this another way, the postmodern-style worldview holds that it is no longer possible or desirable to create new images; rather, one surveys the vast range of available images that mass culture has to offer, and repeats them, but with a difference. Such a formula would seem to explain the age of the remake rather nicely, and certainly some of today's remakes reflect post-modern sophistication in their creation. But, somehow, too often such productions lack that ironic wink of self-consciousness that identifies postmodern artistry, that sense of parody that begs you not to take it too seriously, which leads to a second interpretation.

Segue Back to the Grinch

Take Ron Howard's *The Grinch* (2000), a remake of Chuck Jones's animated television special *How the Grinch Stole Christmas* (1966). Jones's movie, of course, was itself an adaptation of Dr. Seuss's classic tale, which itself was, in effect, a remake of sorts of Charles Dickens's *A Christmas Carol* (1843), with the furry Grinch taking the place of Ebenezer Scrooge. But even Dickens's story is a sort of remake, not in the postmodern vein but in an archetypal sense, reprising an ancient tale of sin and redemption in which the lost protagonist finds salvation in the end. Dr. Seuss's version is equally archetypal, adapting the ancient pattern for a modern children's Christmas story. For his part, Chuck Jones translated the beloved Dr. Seuss tale into a different medium, thus offering a new way of experiencing the original text — as cinematic versions of novels always do by definition. But Ron Howard's version? What did it do?

In effect, *The Grinch* simply rehashed Chuck Jones's version, but with live actors and special effects rather than animation, and a newly concocted back-story for the Grinch to flesh out the tale into a feature-length movie. And why? Was there anything missing from the original animated version? Did Chuck Jones leave anything out?

No, Jones's cartoon is a classic. Remaking it with a popular comic star (Jim Carrey) was simply a safe way of guaranteeing a big box-office haul. And that's what the spate of recent remakes and whatnot signifies: that the movie industry has become so beholden to the profit motive that risk taking and imagination take a back seat to bottom line imperatives, with Accounting calling the shots instead of Creative. Why come up with something new when you can be sure of a hit by rehashing an existing hit? Indeed, wherever one looks in popular culture today, one can read the same semiotic message, with music companies and television producers (especially reality TV producers), alongside their cinematic brethren, all producing clones of what has already worked (more Britneys, more *Makeovers*, more *Fockers*), making money if not art along a yellow brick road paved with gold.

The Culture Industry

Of course, no one walks down that road without an audience eager to pay the price of admission, be it in a theater ticket, a DVD, or what have you. And 2004, with its raft of remakes, set another record at the box office, even in the face of increasing competition from DVD sales. So it doesn't look like anyone is complaining. And it isn't difficult to explain why, because Hollywood moviemakers have been providing American, and world, audiences with entertainments that have both reflected and shaped audience desires for roughly a century. Long before the advent of TV, movies were providing their viewers with the glamour, romance, and sheer excitement that modern life seems to deny. So effective have movies been in molding audience desire that such early culture critics as Theodor Adorno and Max Horkheimer[1] have accused them of being part of a vast, Hollywood-centered "culture industry" whose products have successfully distracted their audiences from the inequities of modern life, and so have effectively maintained the social status quo by drawing everyone's attention away from it.

More recent analysts, however, are far less pessimistic. Indeed, for many cultural studies "populists," films, along with the rest of popular culture, can represent a kind of mass resistance to the political dominance — or what is often called the "hegemony" — of the social and economic powers-that-be. For such critics, films can provide utopian visions of a better world, stimulating their viewers to imagine how their society might be improved, and so, perhaps, inspiring them to go out and do something about it.

Whether you believe that films distract us from the real world or inspire us to imagine a better one, their central place in contemporary American culture demands interpretation. For their impact goes well beyond the movie theater or video screen. Far from being mere entertainments, the movies constitute a profound part of our everyday lives, with every film festival and award becoming major news, and each major release becoming the talk of the country, splashed across the entire terrain of American media from newspapers to television to the Internet. Just think of the pressure you feel to be able to discuss the latest film sensation among your friends. How, if you decide to save a few bucks and wait for the DVD release, you would lose face and be seriously on the social outs. No, there is nothing frivolous about the movies. You've been watching them all your life: Now's the time to start thinking about them semiotically.

Interpreting the Signs of American Film

Interpreting a movie or a group of movies is not unlike interpreting a television program or group of programs. Here too you must suspend your personal

---

[1]Theodor Adorno and Max Horkheimer   Theodor Adorno (1903–1969) and Max Horkheimer (1895–1973), authors of *Dialectic of Enlightenment* (1947), a book whose analyses included a scathing indictment of the culture industry. –Eds.

Exploring the Signs of Film

In your journal, list your favorite movies. Then consider your list: What does it say about you? What cultural myths do the movies tend to reflect, and why do you think those myths appeal to you? What signs particularly appeal to your emotions? What sort of stories about human life do you most respond to?

---

feelings or aesthetic judgments about your subject. As with any semiotic analysis, your goal is to interpret the cultural significance of your topic, not to give it a thumbs up or a thumbs down. Thus, you may find it more rewarding to interpret those films that promise to be culturally meaningful rather than simply choosing your favorite flick. Determining whether a movie is culturally meaningful in the prewriting stage, of course, may be a hit-or-miss affair; you may find that your first choice does not present any particularly interesting grounds for interpretation. That's why it can be helpful to consider factors — such as enormous popularity or widespread critical attention — that seem to set off a particular movie as being special. Of course, cult favorites, while often lacking in critical or popular attention, can also be signs pointing toward their more self-selected audiences and so are perfectly good candidates for analysis. Academy Award candidates are also reliable as cultural signs.

As demonstrated in the preceding analysis of the Hollywood remake, your interpretation of a movie or group of movies should begin with a construction of the system in which it belongs — that is, those movies, past and present, with which it can be associated. While tracing those associations, be on the lookout for striking differences from what is otherwise like what you are analyzing — in the case of our analysis above, a significant increase in the sheer volume of Hollywood remakes — because those differences are what often identify the significance of your subject.

Archetypes, as we also saw in our analysis of the remake, are useful features for film analysis as well. An archetype is anything that has been repeated in storytelling from ancient times to the present. There are character archetypes, such as the ugly duckling, which is behind part of the *Harry Potter* appeal, and plot archetypes, as in the heroic quest, which is the archetypal backbone of films like *The Lord of the Rings* trilogy. All those male buddy films — from *Butch Cassidy and the Sundance Kid* to *Lethal Weapon* to *Men in Black* — hark back to archetypal male bonding stories as old as *Gilgamesh* (from the third millennium B.C.) and the *Iliad*; while Cruella de Vil from *101 Dalmatians* is sister to the Wicked Witch of the West, Snow White's evil stepmother, and every other witch or crone dreamed up by the patriarchal imagination. All those sea monsters, from Jonah's "whale" to *Moby Dick* to *Jaws,* are part of the same archetypal phylum, and every time a movie hero struggles to return home after

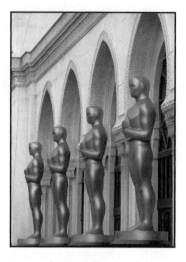

A row of Oscar statues. Oscar award–winning films are often good subjects for semiotic analysis.

a long journey — Dorothy to Kansas, Lassie to Timmie — a story as old as *Exodus* and the *Odyssey* is retold.

Hollywood is well aware of the enduring appeal of archetypes (see Linda Seger's selection in this chapter for a how-to description of archetypal script writing), and George Lucas's reliance on Joseph Campbell in his creation of the *Star Wars* saga is widely known. But it is not always the case that either creators or consumers are consciously aware of the archetypes before them. Part of a culture's collective unconscious, archetypal stories can send messages that are only subliminally understood by their audiences. A heavy dosage of male bonding films in a given Hollywood season, for instance, can send the unspoken cultural message that a man can't really make friends with a woman, that women are simply the sexual reward for manly men. Similarly, too many

Discussing the Signs of Film

In any given year, one film may dominate the Hollywood box office, becoming a blockbuster that captures that public's cinematic imagination. In class, discuss which film would be your choice as this year's top hit. Then analyze the film semiotically. Why has *this* film so successfully appealed to so many moviegoers?

witches in a given Hollywood season can send the message that there are too many bitches (think of *Fatal Attraction* and *Basic Instinct*).

Movies as Metaphors

Sometimes movies can also be seen as metaphors for larger cultural concerns. Consider the grade-B horror flicks of the 1950s—for instance, the original *Godzilla*. If we study only its plot, we would see little more than a cheesy horror story featuring a reptilian monster that is related archetypally to the dragons of medieval literature. But Godzilla was no mere dragon transported to the modern world. The dragons that populated the world of medieval storytelling were themselves often used as metaphors for the Satanic serpent in the Garden of Eden, but Godzilla was a wholly different sort of metaphor. Created by Japanese filmmakers, Godzilla was originally a metaphor for the nuclear era. A female mutant creation of nuclear poisoning, Godzilla rose over her Japanese audiences like a mushroom cloud, symbolizing the potential for future mushroom clouds both in Japan and around the world in the cold war era.

For their part, American filmmakers in the 1950s had their own metaphors for the nuclear era. Whenever some "blob" threatened to consume New York or some especially toxic slime escaped from a laboratory, the suggestion that science — especially nuclear science — was threatening to destroy the world filled the theater along with the popcorn fumes. And if it wasn't science that was the threat, cold war filmmakers could scare us with communists, as films like *Invasion of the Body Snatchers* metaphorically suggested through its depiction of a town in which everyone looked the same but had really been taken over by aliens. "Beware of your neighbors," the movie warned, "they could be communists."

Reading Film on the Net

Most major films now released in the United States receive their own Web site. You can find them listed in print ads for the film (check your local newspaper). Select a current film, find the Web address, log on, and analyze the film's site semiotically. What images are used to attract your interest in the film? What interactive strategies, if any, are used to increase your commitment to the film? If you've seen the movie, how does the Net presentation of it compare with your experience viewing it either in a theater or on video? Alternatively, analyze the posters designed to attract attention to a particular film; a useful resource is the Movie Poster Page (www.musicman.com/mp/mp.html).

In such ways, an entire film can be a kind of metaphor, but you can find many smaller metaphors at work in the details of a movie as well. Early film-makers, for example, used to put a tablecloth on the table in dining scenes to signify that the characters at the table were good, decent people (you can find such a metaphor in Charlie Chaplin's *The Kid*, where an impoverished tramp who can't afford socks or a bathrobe still has a nice tablecloth on the break-fast table). Sometimes a director's metaphors have a broad political signifi-cance, as at the end of the James Dean classic *Giant*, where the parting shot presents a tableau of a white baby goat standing next to a black baby goat, which is juxtaposed with the image of a white baby standing in a crib side by side with a brown baby. Since the human babies are both the grandchildren of the film's protagonist (one of whose sons has married a Mexican woman, the other an Anglo), the goats are added to underscore metaphorically the message of racial reconciliation that the director wanted to send.

Reading a film, then, is much like reading a novel. Both are texts filled with intentional and unintentional signs, metaphors, and archetypes, and both are cultural signifiers. The major difference is in their medium of expres-sion. Literary texts are cast entirely in written words; films combine verbal language, visual imagery, and sound effects. Thus, we perceive literary and cinematic texts differently, for the written sign is perceived in a linear fashion that relies on one's cognitive and imaginative powers, while a film primarily targets the senses: One sees and hears (and sometimes even smells!). That film is such a sensory experience often conceals its textuality. One is tempted to sit back and go with the flow, to say that it's only entertainment and doesn't have to "mean" anything at all. But as cinematic forms of storytelling overtake written forms of expression, the study of movies as complex texts bearing cultural messages and values is becoming more and more important. Our "libraries" are increasingly to be found in theaters and mini-malls, where the texts of Hollywood can be read for eight dollars (or so) a view or rented for three dollars a night. There's a lot to read out there.

The Readings

The readings in this chapter address the various myths that pervade Hollywood films, starting with Robert B. Ray's analysis of the ways in which America's "official" and "outlaw" heroes appear both in the cinema and in American his-tory and culture. Linda Seger and Charles Ealy follow with a pair of readings focusing on the *Star Wars* franchise, with Seger offering a screenwriter's how-to guide for the creation of the kind of archetypal characters that make *Star Wars* one of the most popular movies of all time, and Ealy presenting a jour-nalistic survey of the academic reception of this much-interpreted film. Todd Boyd is next with an analysis that situates the "gangsta" film within a history of gangster movies, focusing on the politics of such films as *Boyz N the Hood*. David Denby's "High-School Confidential" explains why generations of teenagers flock to all those jocks-and-cheerleaders-versus-the nerds movies, while Vicki L. Eaklor analyzes the gender codes, and their subtle subversion, behind *Gone with the Wind*. Jessica Hagedorn then surveys a tradition of American filmmaking in which Asian women are presented as either tragic or trivial, and Michael Parenti provides a class-based approach to the codes of American cinema, noting the social biases inherent in such popular hits as *Pretty Woman*. Finally, Vivian C. Sobchack concludes the chapter with an almost-unflinching analysis of screen violence.

ROBERT B. RAY
The Thematic Paradigm

Usually we consider movies to be merely entertainment, but as Robert Ray (b. 1943) demonstrates in this selection from his book A Certain Tendency of the Hollywood Cinema *(1985), American films have long reflected fundamental patterns and contradictions in our society's myths and values. Whether in real life or on the silver screen, Ray explains, Americans have always been ambivalent about the value of civilization, celebrating it through official heroes like George Washington and Jimmy Stewart, while at the same time questioning it through outlaw heroes like Davy Crockett and Jesse James. Especially when presented together in the same film, these two hero types help mediate America's ambivalence, providing a mythic solution. Ray's analyses show how the movies are rich sources for cultural interpretation; they provide a framework for decoding movies as different as* Lethal Weapon *and* Malcolm X. *Ray is a professor and director of film and media studies at the University of Florida at Gainesville. His publications include* The Avant Garde Finds Andy Hardy *(1995) and* How a Film Theory Got Lost and Other Mysteries in Cultural Studies *(2001).*

The dominant tradition of American cinema consistently found ways to overcome dichotomies. Often, the movies' reconciliatory pattern concentrated on a single character magically embodying diametrically opposite traits. A sensitive violinist was also a tough boxer (*Golden Boy*); a boxer was a gentle man who cared for pigeons (*On the Waterfront*). A gangster became a coward because he was brave (*Angels with Dirty Faces*); a soldier became brave because he was a coward (*Lives of a Bengal Lancer*). A war hero was a former pacifist (*Sergeant York*); a pacifist was a former war hero (*Billy Jack*). The ideal was a kind of inclusiveness that would permit all decisions to be undertaken with the knowledge that the alternative was equally available. The attractiveness of Destry's refusal to use guns (*Destry Rides Again*) depended on the tacit understanding that he could shoot with the best of them, Katharine Hepburn's and Claudette Colbert's revolts against conventionality (*Holiday, It Happened One Night*) on their status as aristocrats.

Such two-sided characters seemed particularly designed to appeal to a collective American imagination steeped in myths of inclusiveness. Indeed, in creating such characters, classic Hollywood had connected with what Erik Erikson has described as the fundamental American psychological pattern:

> The functioning American, as the heir of a history of extreme contrasts and abrupt changes, bases his final ego identity on some tentative

combination of dynamic polarities such as migratory and sedentary, individualistic and standardized, competitive and co-operative, pious and free-thinking, responsible and cynical, etc. . . .

To leave his choices open, the American, on the whole, lives with two sets of "truths."[1]

The movies traded on one opposition in particular, American culture's traditional dichotomy of individual and community that had generated the most significant pair of competing myths: the outlaw hero and the official hero.[2] Embodied in the adventurer, explorer, gunfighter, wanderer, and loner, the outlaw hero stood for that part of the American imagination valuing self-determination and freedom from entanglements. By contrast, the official hero, normally portrayed as a teacher, lawyer, politician, farmer, or family man, represented the American belief in collective action, and the objective legal process that superseded private notions of right and wrong. While the outlaw hero found incarnations in the mythic figures of Davy Crockett, Jesse James, Huck Finn, and all of Leslie Fiedler's "Good Bad Boys" and Daniel Boorstin's "ring-tailed roarers," the official hero developed around legends associated with Washington, Jefferson, Lincoln, Lee, and other "Good Good Boys."

An extraordinary amount of the traditional American mythology adopted by Classic Hollywood derived from the variations worked by American ideology around this opposition of natural man versus civilized man. To the extent that these variations constituted the main tendency of American literature and legends, Hollywood, in relying on this mythology, committed itself to becoming what Robert Bresson has called "the Cinema."[3] A brief description of the competing values associated with this outlaw hero–official hero opposition will begin to suggest its pervasiveness in traditional American culture.

1. *Aging:* The attractiveness of the outlaw hero's childishness and propensity to whims, tantrums, and emotional decisions derived from America's cult of childhood. Fiedler observed that American literature celebrated "the notion that a mere falling short of adulthood is a guarantee of insight and even innocence." From Huck to Holden Caulfield, children in American literature were privileged, existing beyond society's confining rules. Often, they set the plot in motion (e.g., *Intruder in the Dust, To Kill a Mockingbird*), acting for the adults encumbered by daily affairs. As Fiedler also pointed out, this image of

[1] Erik H. Erikson, *Childhood and Society* (New York: Norton, 1963), p. 286.

[2] Leading discussions of the individual-community polarity in American culture can be found in *The Contrapuntal Civilization: Essays Toward a New Understanding of the American Experience,* ed. Michael Kammen (New York: Crowell, 1971). The most prominent analyses of American literature's use of this opposition remain Leslie A. Fiedler's *Love and Death in the American Novel* (New York: Stein and Day, 1966) and A. N. Kaul's *The American Vision* (New Haven: Yale University Press, 1963).

[3] Robert Bresson, *Notes on Cinematography,* trans. Jonathan Griffin (New York: Urizen Books, 1977), p. 12.

childhood has impinged upon adult life itself, has become a 'career' like every-thing else in America,"[4] generating stories like *On the Road* or *Easy Rider* in which adults try desperately to postpone responsibilities by clinging to adolescent lifestyles.

While the outlaw heroes represented a flight from maturity, the official heroes embodied the best attributes of adulthood: sound reasoning and judgment, wisdom and sympathy based on experience. Franklin's *Autobiography* and *Poor Richard's Almanack* constituted this opposing tradition's basic texts, persuasive enough to appeal even to outsiders (*The Great Gatsby*). Despite the legends surrounding Franklin and the other Founding Fathers, however, the scarcity of mature heroes in American literature and mythology indicated American ideology's fundamental preference for youth, a quality that came to be associated with the country itself. Indeed, American stories often distorted the stock figure of the Wise Old Man, portraying him as mad (Ahab), useless (Rip Van Winkle), or evil (the Godfather).

2. *Society and Women:* The outlaw hero's distrust of civilization, typically represented by women and marriage, constituted a stock motif in American mythology. In his *Studies in Classic American Literature,* D. H. Lawrence detected the recurring pattern of flight, observing that the Founding Fathers had come to America "largely to get *away*. . . . Away from what? In the long run, away from themselves. Away from everything."[5] Sometimes, these heroes undertook this flight alone (Thoreau, *Catcher in the Rye*); more often, they joined ranks with other men: Huck with Jim, Ishmael with Queequeg, Jake Barnes with Bill Gorton. Women were avoided as representing the very entanglements this tradition sought to escape: society, the "settled life," confining responsibilities. The outlaw hero sought only uncompromising relationships, involving either a "bad" woman (whose morals deprived her of all rights to entangling domesticity) or other males (who themselves remained independent). Even the "bad" woman posed a threat, since marriage often uncovered the clinging "good" girl underneath. Typically, therefore, American stories avoided this problem by killing off the "bad" woman before the marriage could transpire (*Destry Rides Again, The Big Heat, The Far Country*). Subsequently, within the all-male group, women became taboo, except as the objects of lust.

The exceptional extent of American outlaw legends suggests an ideological anxiety about civilized life. Often, that anxiety took shape as a romanticizing of the dispossessed, as in the Beat Generation's cult of the bum, or the characters of Huck and "Thoreau," who worked to remain idle, unemployed, and unattached. A passage from Jerzy Kosinski's *Steps* demonstrated the extreme modern version of this romanticizing:

[4]Leslie A. Fiedler, *No! In Thunder* (New York: Stein and Day, 1972), pp. 253, 275.

[5]D. H. Lawrence, *Studies in Classic American Literature* (New York: Viking/Compass, 1961), p. 3. See also Fiedler's *Love and Death in the American Novel* and Sam Bluefarb's *The Escape Motif in the American Novel: Mark Twain to Richard Wright* (Columbus: Ohio State University Press, 1972).

> I envied those [the poor and the criminals] who lived here and seemed so free, having nothing to regret and nothing to look forward to. In the world of birth certificates, medical examinations, punch cards, and computers, in the world of telephone books, passports, bank accounts, insurance plans, wills, credit cards, pensions, mortgages and loans, they lived unattached.[6]

In contrast to the outlaw heroes, the official heroes were preeminently worldly, comfortable in society, and willing to undertake even those public duties demanding personal sacrifice. Political figures, particularly Washington and Lincoln, provided the principal examples of this tradition, but images of family also persisted in popular literature from *Little Women* to *Life with Father* and *Cheaper by the Dozen*. The most crucial figure in this tradition, however, was Horatio Alger, whose heroes' ambition provided the complement to Huck's disinterest. Alger's characters subscribed fully to the codes of civilization, devoting themselves to proper dress, manners, and behavior, and the attainment of the very things despised by the opposing tradition: the settled life and respectability.[7]

3. *Politics and the Law:* Writing about "The Philosophical Approach of the 10 Americans," Tocqueville noted "a general distaste for accepting any man's word as proof of anything." That distaste took shape as a traditional distrust of politics as collective activity, and of ideology as that activity's rationale. Such a disavowal of ideology was, of course, itself ideological, a tactic for discouraging systematic political intervention in a nineteenth-century America whose political and economic power remained in the hands of a privileged few. Tocqueville himself noted the results of this mythology of individualism which "disposes each citizen to isolate himself from the mass of his fellows and withdraw into the circle of family and friends; with this little society formed to his taste, he gladly leaves the greater society to look after itself."[8]

This hostility toward political solutions manifested itself further in an ambivalence about the law. The outlaw mythology portrayed the law, the sum of society's standards, as a collective, impersonal ideology imposed on the individual from without. Thus, the law represented the very thing this mythology sought to avoid. In its place, this tradition offered a natural law discovered intuitively by each man. As Tocqueville observed, Americans wanted "To escape from imposed systems . . . to seek by themselves and in themselves for the only reason for things . . . in most mental operations each American relies on individual effort and judgment" (p. 429). This sense of the law's inadequacy to needs detectable only by the heart generated a rich tradition of

---

[6]Jerzy Kosinski, *Steps* (New York: Random House, 1968), p. 133.

[7]See John G. Cawelti, *Apostles of the Self-Made Man: Changing Concepts of Success in America* (Chicago: University of Chicago Press, 1965), pp. 101–23.

[8]Alexis de Tocqueville, *Democracy in America*, ed. J. P. Mayer, trans. George Lawrence (Garden City, N.Y.: Anchor/Doubleday, 1969), pp. 430, 506. Irving Howe has confirmed Tocqueville's point, observing that Americans "make the suspicion of ideology into something approaching a national creed." *Politics and the Novel* (New York: Avon, 1970), p. 337.

legends celebrating legal defiance in the name of some "natural" standard: Thoreau went to jail rather than pay taxes, Huck helped Jim (legally a slave) to escape, Billy the Kid murdered the sheriff's posse that had ambushed his boss, Hester Prynne resisted the community's sexual mores. This mythology transformed all outlaws into Robin Hoods, who "correct" socially unjust laws (Jesse James, Bonnie and Clyde, John Wesley Harding). Furthermore, by customarily portraying the law as the tool of villains (who used it to revoke mining claims, foreclose on mortgages, and disallow election results — all on legal technicalities), this mythology betrayed a profound pessimism about the individual's access to the legal system.

If the outlaw hero's motto was "I don't know what the law says, but I do know what's right and wrong," the official hero's was "We are a nation of laws, not of men," or "No man can place himself above the law." To the outlaw hero's insistence on private standards of right and wrong, the official hero offered the admonition, "You cannot take the law into your own hands." Often, these official heroes were lawyers or politicians, at times (as with Washington and Lincoln), even the executors of the legal system itself. The values accompanying such heroes modified the assurance of Crockett's advice, "Be sure you're right, then go ahead."

In sum, the values associated with these two different sets of heroes contrasted markedly. Clearly, too, each tradition had its good and bad points. If the extreme individualism of the outlaw hero always verged on selfishness, the respectability of the official hero always threatened to involve either blandness or repression. If the outlaw tradition promised adventure and freedom, it also offered danger and loneliness. If the official tradition promised safety and comfort, it also offered entanglements and boredom.

The evident contradiction between these heroes provoked Daniel Boorstin's observation that "Never did a more incongruous pair than Davy Crockett and George Washington live together in a national Valhalla." And yet, as Boorstin admits, "both Crockett and Washington were popular heroes, and both emerged into legendary fame during the first half of the nineteenth century."[9]

The parallel existence of these two contradictory traditions evinced the 15 general pattern of American mythology: the denial of the necessity for choice. In fact, this mythology often portrayed situations requiring decision as temporary aberrations from American life's normal course. By discouraging commitment to any single set of values, this mythology fostered an ideology of improvisation, individualism, and ad hoc solutions for problems depicted as crises. American writers have repeatedly attempted to justify this mythology in terms of material sources. Hence, Irving Howe's "explanation":

> It is when men no longer feel that they have adequate choices in their styles of life, when they conclude that there are no longer possibilities of

---

[9]Daniel J. Boorstin, *The Americans: The National Experience* (New York: Random House, 1965), p. 337.

honorable maneuver and compromise, when they decide that the time has come for "ultimate" social loyalties and political decisions — it is then that ideology begins to flourish. Ideology reflects a hardening of commitment, the freezing of opinion into system. . . . The uniqueness of our history, the freshness of our land, the plenitude of our resources — all these have made possible, and rendered plausible, a style of political improvisation and intellectual free-wheeling.[10]

Despite such an account's pretext of objectivity, its language betrays an acceptance of the mythology it purports to describe: "honorable maneuver and compromise," "hardening," "freezing," "uniqueness," "freshness," and "plenitude" are all assumptive words from an ideology that denies its own status. Furthermore, even granting the legitimacy of the historians' authenticating causes, we are left with a persisting mythology increasingly discredited by historical developments. (In fact, such invalidation began in the early nineteenth century, and perhaps even before.)

The American mythology's refusal to choose between its two heroes went beyond the normal reconciliatory function attributed to myth by Lévi-Strauss. For the American tradition not only overcame binary oppositions; it systematically mythologized the certainty of being able to do so. Part of this process involved blurring the lines between the two sets of heroes. First, legends often brought the solemn official heroes back down to earth, providing the sober Washington with the cherry tree, the prudent Franklin with illegitimate children, and even the upright Jefferson with a slave mistress. On the other side, stories modified the outlaw hero's most potentially damaging quality, his tendency to selfish isolationism, by demonstrating that, however reluctantly, he would act for causes beyond himself. Thus, Huck grudgingly helped Jim escape, and Davy Crockett left the woods for three terms in Congress before dying in the Alamo for Texas independence. In this blurring process, Lincoln, a composite of opposing traits, emerged as the great American figure. His status as president made him an ex officio official hero. But his Western origins, melancholy solitude, and unaided decision-making all qualified him as a member of the other side. Finally, his ambivalent attitude toward the law played the most crucial role in his complex legend. As the chief executive, he inevitably stood for the principle that "we are a nation of laws and not men"; as the Great Emancipator, on the other hand, he provided the prime example of taking the law into one's own hands in the name of some higher standard.

Classic Hollywood's gallery of composite heroes (boxing musicians, rebellious aristocrats, pacifist soldiers) clearly derived from this mythology's rejection of final choices, a tendency whose traces Erikson detected in American psychology:

The process of American identity formation seems to support an individual's ego identity as long as he can preserve a certain element of deliberate

---

[10]*Politics and the Novel*, p. 164.

tentativeness of autonomous choice. The individual must be able to convince himself that the next step is up to him and that no matter where he is staying or going he always had the choice of leaving or turning in the opposite direction if he chooses to do so. In this country the migrant does not want to be told to move on, nor the sedentary man to stay where he is; for the life style (and the family history) of each contains the opposite element as a potential alternative which he wishes to consider his most private and individual decision.[11]

The reconciliatory pattern found its most typical incarnation, however, in one particular narrative: the story of the private man attempting to keep from being drawn into action on any but his own terms. In this story, the reluctant hero's ultimate willingness to help the community satisfied the official values. But by portraying this aid as demanding only a temporary involvement, the story preserved the values of individualism as well.

Like the contrasting heroes' epitomization of basic American dichotomies, the reluctant hero story provided a locus for displacement. Its most famous version, for example, *Adventures of Huckleberry Finn*, offered a typically individualistic solution to the nation's unresolved racial and sectional anxieties, thereby helping to forestall more systematic governmental measures. In adopting this story, Classic Hollywood retained its censoring power, using it, for example, in *Casablanca* to conceal the realistic threats to American self-determination posed by World War II.

Because the reluctant hero story was clearly the basis of the Western, American literature's repeated use of it prompted Leslie Fiedler to call the classic American novels "disguised westerns."[12] In the movies, too, this story appeared in every genre: in Westerns, of course (with *Shane* its most schematic articulation), but also in gangster movies (*Angels with Dirty Faces, Key Largo*), musicals (*Swing Time*), detective stories (*The Thin Man*), war films (*Air Force*), screwball comedy (*The Philadelphia Story*), "problem pictures" (*On the Waterfront*), and even science fiction (the Han Solo character in *Star Wars*). *Gone with the Wind,* in fact, had two selfish heroes who came around at the last moment, Scarlett (taking care of Melanie) and Rhett (running the Union blockade), incompatible only because they were so much alike. The natural culmination of this pattern, perfected by Hollywood in the 1930s and early 1940s, was *Casablanca*. Its version of the outlaw hero–official hero struggle (Rick versus Laszlo) proved stunningly effective, its resolution (their collaboration on the war effort) the prototypical Hollywood ending.

The reluctant hero story's tendency to minimize the official hero's role (by making him dependent on the outsider's intervention) suggested an imbalance basic to the American mythology: Despite the existence of both heroes, the national ideology clearly preferred the outlaw. This ideology strove to make that figure's origins seem spontaneous, concealing the calculated, commercial

[11]*Childhood and Society*, p. 286.
[12]*Love and Death in the American Novel*, p. 355.

efforts behind the mythologizing of typical examples like Billy the Kid and Davy Crockett. Its willingness, on the other hand, to allow the official hero's traces to show enables Daniel Boorstin to observe of one such myth, "There were elements of spontaneity, of course, in the Washington legend, too, but it was, for the most part, a self-conscious product."[13]

The apparent spontaneity of the outlaw heroes assured their popularity. By contrast, the official values had to rely on a rational allegiance that often wavered. These heroes' different statuses accounted for a structure fundamental to American literature, and assumed by Classic Hollywood: a split between the moral center and the interest center of a story. Thus, while the typical Western contained warnings against violence as a solution, taking the law into one's own hands, and moral isolationism, it simultaneously glamorized the outlaw hero's intense self-possession and willingness to use force to settle what the law could not. In other circumstances, Ishmael's evenhanded philosophy paled beside Ahab's moral vehemence, consciously recognizable as destructive.

D. H. Lawrence called this split the profound "duplicity" at the heart of nineteenth-century American fiction, charging that the classic novels evinced "a tight mental allegiance to a morality which all [the author's] passion goes to destroy." Certainly, too, this "duplicity" involved the mythology's pattern of obscuring the necessity for choosing between contrasting values. Richard Chase has put the matter less pejoratively in an account that applies equally to the American cinema:

> The American novel tends to rest in contradictions and among extreme ranges of experience. When it attempts to resolve contradictions, it does so in oblique, morally equivocal ways. As a general rule it does so either in melodramatic actions or in pastoral idylls, although intermixed with both one may find the stirring instabilities of "American humor."[14]

Or, in other words, when faced with a difficult choice, American stories resolved it either simplistically (by refusing to acknowledge that a choice is necessary), sentimentally (by blurring the differences between the two sides), or by laughing the whole thing off.

Reading the Text

1. What are the two basic hero types that Ray describes in American cinema?
2. How do these two hero types relate to America's "psychological pattern" (para. 2)?
3. Explain why, according to Ray, the outlaw hero typically mistrusts women.

[13]*The Americans: The National Experience*, p. 337.
[14]Richard Chase, *The American Novel and Its Tradition* (Garden City, N.Y.: Anchor/Doubleday, 1957), p. 1.

READING THE SIGNS

1. Read Gary Engle's "What Makes Superman So Darned American?" (p. 744) and Andy Medhurst's "Batman, Deviance, and Camp" (p. 753), and write an essay in which you explain which type of heroes Superman and Batman are to their audiences.

2. What sort of hero is Arnold Schwarzenegger in the *Terminator* films? Write an essay in which you apply Ray's categories of hero to the Schwarzenegger character, supporting your argument with specific references to one or more films.

3. In class, brainstorm on the blackboard official and outlaw heroes you've seen in movies. Then categorize these heroes according to characteristics they share (such as race, gender, profession, or social class). What patterns emerge in your categories, and what is the significance of those patterns?

4. Watch one of the *Alien* films, and discuss whether Sigourney Weaver fits either of Ray's two categories of hero.

5. Cartoon television series like *The Simpsons* and *South Park* feature characters that don't readily fit Ray's categories of hero. Invent a third type of hero to accommodate such characters.

LINDA SEGER
Creating the Myth

To be a successful screenwriter, Linda Seger suggests in this selection from Making a Good Script Great *(1987), you've got to know your archetypes. Seger reveals the secret behind the success of such Hollywood creations as* Star Wars' *Luke Skywalker and tells you how you can create such heroes yourself. In this how-to approach to the cinema, Seger echoes the more academic judgments of such semioticians of film as Umberto Eco — the road to popular success in mass culture is paved with cultural myths and clichés. A script consultant and author who has given professional seminars on filmmaking around the world, Seger has also published* Creating Unforgettable Characters *(1990) and* When Women Call the Shots: The Developing Power and Influence of Women in Television and Film *(1996).*

All of us have similar experiences. We share in the life journey of growth, development, and transformation. We live the same stories, whether they involve the search for a perfect mate, coming home, the search for fulfillment, going after an ideal, achieving the dream, or hunting for a precious treasure. Whatever our culture, there are universal stories that form the basis for all our particular stories. The trappings might be different, the twists and turns that create suspense might change from culture to culture, the particular characters may take different forms, but underneath it all, it's the same story, drawn from the same experiences.

Many of the most successful films are based on these universal stories. They deal with the basic journey we take in life. We identify with the heroes because we were once heroic (descriptive) or because we wish we could do what the hero does (prescriptive). When Joan Wilder finds the jewel and saves her sister, or James Bond saves the world, or Shane saves the family from the evil ranchers, we identify with the character, and subconsciously recognize the story as having some connection with our own lives. It's the same story as the fairy tales about getting the three golden hairs from the devil, or finding the treasure and winning the princess. And it's not all that different a story from the caveman killing the woolly beast or the Roman slave gaining his freedom through skill and courage. These are our stories — personally and collectively — and the most successful films contain these universal experiences.

Some of these stories are "search" stories. They address our desire to find some kind of rare and wonderful treasure. This might include the search for outer values such as job, relationship, or success; or for inner values such as respect, security, self-expression, love, or home. But it's all a similar search.

317

Some of these stories are "hero" stories. They come from our own experiences of overcoming adversity, as well as our desire to do great and special acts. We root for the hero and celebrate when he or she achieves the goal because we know that the hero's journey is in many ways similar to our own.

We call these stories *myths*. Myths are the common stories at the root of our universal existence. They're found in all cultures and in all literature, ranging from the Greek myths to fairy tales, legends, and stories drawn from all of the world's religions.

A myth is a story that is "more than true." Many stories are true because one person, somewhere, at some time, lived it. It is based on fact. But a myth is more than true because it is lived by all of us, at some level. It's a story that connects and speaks to us all.

Some myths are true stories that attain mythic significance because the people involved seem larger than life, and seem to live their lives more intensely than common folk. Martin Luther King, Jr., Gandhi, Sir Edmund Hillary, and Lord Mountbatten personify the types of journeys we identify with, because we've taken similar journeys — even if only in a very small way.

Other myths revolve around make-believe characters who might capsulize for us the sum total of many of our journeys. Some of these make-believe characters might seem similar to the characters we meet in our dreams. Or they might be a composite of types of characters we've met.

In both cases, the myth is the "story beneath the story." It's the universal pattern that shows us that Gandhi's journey toward independence and Sir Edmund Hillary's journey to the top of Mount Everest contain many of the same dramatic beats. And these beats are the same beats that Rambo takes to set free the MIAs, that Indiana Jones takes to find the Lost Ark, and that Luke Skywalker takes to defeat the Evil Empire.

In *Hero with a Thousand Faces*, Joseph Campbell traces the elements that form the hero myth. "In their own work with myth, writer Chris Vogler and seminar leader Thomas Schlesinger have applied this criteria to *Star Wars*. The myth within the story helps explain why millions went to see this film again and again."

The hero myth has specific story beats that occur in all hero stories. They show who the hero is, what the hero needs, and how the story and character interact in order to create a transformation. The journey toward heroism is a process. This universal process forms the spine of all the particular stories, such as the *Star Wars* trilogy.

The Hero Myth

1. In most hero stories, the hero is introduced in ordinary surroundings, in a mundane world, doing mundane things. Generally, the hero begins as a nonhero; innocent, young, simple, or humble. In *Star Wars*, the first time we see Luke Skywalker, he's unhappy about having to do his chores, which consists of picking out

Star Wars, 1977.

some new droids for work. He wants to go out and have fun. He wants to leave his planet and go to the Academy, but he's stuck. This is the setup of most myths. This is how we meet the hero before the call to adventure.

2. Then something new enters the hero's life. It's a catalyst that sets the story into motion. It might be a telephone call, as in *Romancing the Stone*, or the German attack in *The African Queen*, or the holograph of Princess Leia in *Star Wars*. Whatever form it takes, it's a new ingredient that pushes the hero into an extraordinary adventure. With this call, the stakes are established, and a problem is introduced that demands a solution.

3. Many times, however, the hero doesn't want to leave. He or she is a reluctant hero, afraid of the unknown, uncertain, perhaps, if he or she is up to the challenge. In *Star Wars*, Luke receives a double call to adventure. First, from Princess Leia in the holograph, and then through Obi-Wan Kenobi, who says he needs Luke's help. But Luke is not ready to go. He returns home, only to find that the Imperial Stormtroopers have burned his farmhouse and slaughtered his family. Now he is personally motivated, ready to enter into the adventure.

4. In any journey, the hero usually receives help, and the help often comes 15 from unusual sources. In many fairy tales, an old woman, a dwarf, a witch, or a wizard helps the hero. The hero achieves the goal because of this help, and because the hero is receptive to what this person has to give.

There are a number of fairy tales where the first and second son are sent to complete a task, but they ignore the helpers, often scorning them. Many times they are severely punished for their lack of humility and unwillingness to accept help. Then the third son, the hero, comes along. He receives the help, accomplishes the task, and often wins the princess.

In *Star Wars*, Obi-Wan Kenobi is a perfect example of the "helper" character. He is a kind of mentor to Luke, one who teaches him the Way of the Force and whose teachings continue even after his death. This mentor character appears in most hero stories. He is the person who has special knowledge, special information, and special skills. This might be the prospector in *The Treasure of the Sierra Madre*, or the psychiatrist in *Ordinary People*, or Quint in *Jaws*, who knows all about sharks, or the Good Witch of the North who gives Dorothy the ruby slippers in *The Wizard of Oz*. In *Star Wars*, Obi-Wan gives Luke the light saber that was the special weapon of the Jedi Knight. With this, Luke is ready to move forward and do his training and meet adventure.

5. The hero is now ready to move into the special world where he or she will change from the ordinary into the extraordinary. This starts the hero's transformation, and sets up the obstacles that must be surmounted to reach the goal. Usually, this happens at the first Turning Point of the story, and leads into Act Two development. In *Star Wars*, Obi-Wan and Luke search for a pilot to take them to the planet of Alderaan, so that Obi-Wan can deliver the plans to Princess Leia's father. These plans are essential to the survival of the Rebel Forces. With this action, the adventure is ready to begin.

6. Now begin all the tests and obstacles necessary to overcome the enemy and accomplish the hero's goals. In fairy tales, this often means getting past witches, outwitting the devil, avoiding robbers, or confronting evil. In Homer's *Odyssey*, it means blinding the Cyclops, escaping from the island of the Lotus-Eaters, resisting the temptation of the singing Sirens, and surviving a shipwreck. In *Star Wars*, innumerable adventures confront Luke. He and his cohorts must run to the *Millennium Falcon*, narrowly escaping the Stormtroopers before jumping into hyperspace. They must make it through the meteor shower after Alderaan has been destroyed. They must evade capture on the Death Star, rescue the Princess, and even survive a garbage crusher.

7. At some point in the story, the hero often hits rock bottom. He often 20 has a "death experience," leading to a type of rebirth. In *Star Wars*, Luke seems to have died when the serpent in the garbage-masher pulls him under, but he's saved just in time to ask R2D2 to stop the masher before they're crushed. This is often the "black moment" at the second turning point, the point when the worst is confronted, and the action now moves toward the exciting conclusion.

8. Now, the hero seizes the sword and takes possession of the treasure. He is now in charge, but he still has not completed the journey. Here Luke has the Princess and the plans, but the final confrontation is yet to begin. This starts the third-act escape scene, leading to the final climax.

9. The road back is often the chase scene. In many fairy tales, this is the point where the devil chases the hero and the hero has the last obstacles to overcome before really being free and safe. His challenge is to take what he has learned and integrate it into his daily life. He *must* return to renew the mundane world. In *Star Wars*, Darth Vader is in hot pursuit, planning to blow up the Rebel Planet.

10. Since every hero story is essentially a transformation story, we need to see the hero changed at the end, resurrected into a new type of life. He must face the final ordeal before being "reborn" as the hero, proving his courage and becoming transformed. This is the point, in many fairy tales, where the Miller's Son becomes the Prince or the King and marries the Princess. In *Star Wars*, Luke has survived, becoming quite a different person from the innocent young man he was in Act One.

At this point, the hero returns and is reintegrated into his society. In *Star Wars*, Luke has destroyed the Death Star, and he receives his great reward.

This is the classic "Hero Story." We might call this example a *mission* or *task* 25 *myth*, where the person has to complete a task, but the task itself is not the real treasure. The real reward for Luke is the love of the Princess and the safe, new world he had helped create.

A myth can have many variations. We see variations on this myth in James Bond films (although they lack much of the depth because the hero is not transformed), and in *The African Queen*, where Rose and Allnutt must blow up the *Louisa,* or in *Places in the Heart*, where Edna overcomes obstacles to achieve family stability.

The *treasure myth* is another variation on this theme, as seen in *Romancing the Stone*. In this story, Joan receives a map and a phone call which forces her into the adventure. She is helped by an American birdcatcher and a Mexican pickup truck driver. She overcomes the obstacles of snakes, the jungle, waterfalls, shootouts, and finally receives the treasure, along with the "prince."

Whether the hero's journey is for a treasure or to complete a task, the elements remain the same. The humble, reluctant hero is called to an adventure. The hero is helped by a variety of unique characters. S/he must overcome a series of obstacles that transform him or her in the process, and then faces the final challenge that draws on inner and outer resources.

The Healing Myth

Although the hero myth is the most popular story, many myths involve healing. In these stories, some character is "broken" and must leave home to become whole again.

The universal experience behind these healing stories is our psychological 30 need for rejuvenation, for balance. The journey of the hero into exile is not all that different from the weekend in Palm Springs, or the trip to Hawaii to get away from it all, or lying still in a hospital bed for some weeks to heal. In all cases, something is out of balance and the mythic journey moves toward wholeness.

Being broken can take several forms. It can be physical, emotional, or psychological. Usually, it's all three. In the process of being exiled or hiding out in the forest, the desert, or even the Amish farm in *Witness,* the person becomes whole, balanced, and receptive to love. Love in these stories is both a healing force and a reward.

Think of John Book in *Witness.* In Act One, we see a frenetic, insensitive man, afraid of commitment, critical and unreceptive to the feminine influences in his life. John is suffering from an "inner wound" which he doesn't know about. When he receives an "outer wound" from a gunshot, it forces him into exile, which begins his process of transformation.

At the beginning of Act Two, we see John delirious and close to death. This is a movement into the unconscious, a movement from the rational, active police life of Act One into a mysterious, feminine, more intuitive world. Since John's "inner problem" is the lack of balance with his feminine side, this delirium begins the process of transformation.

Later in Act Two, we see John beginning to change. He moves from his highly independent life-style toward the collective, communal life of his Amish hosts. John now gets up early to milk the cows and to assist with the chores. He uses his carpentry skills to help with the barn building and to complete the birdhouse. Gradually, he begins to develop relationships with Rachel and her son, Samuel. John's life slows down and he becomes more receptive, learning important lessons about love. In Act Three, John finally sees that the feminine is worth saving, and throws down his gun to save Rachel's life. A few beats later, when he has the opportunity to kill Paul, he chooses a nonviolent response instead. Although John doesn't "win" the Princess, he has nevertheless "won" love and wholeness. By the end of the film, we can see that the John Book of Act Three is a different kind of person from the John Book of Act One. He has a different kind of comradeship with his fellow police officers, he's more relaxed, and we can sense that somehow, this experience has formed a more integrated John Book.

Combination Myths

Many stories are combinations of several different myths. Think of *Ghostbusters,* 35 a simple and rather outrageous comedy about three men saving the city of New York from ghosts. Now think of the story of "Pandora's Box." It's about the woman who let loose all manner of evil upon the earth by opening a box she was told not to touch. In *Ghostbusters,* the EPA man is a Pandora figure. By shutting off the power to the containment center, he inadvertently unleashes all the ghosts upon New York City. Combine the story of "Pandora's Box" with a hero story, and notice that we have our three heroes battling the Marshmallow Man. One of them also "gets the Princess" when Dr. Peter Venkman finally receives the affections of Dana Barrett. By looking at these combinations, it is apparent that even *Ghostbusters* is more than "just a comedy."

Tootsie is a type of reworking of many Shakespearean stories where a woman has to dress as a man in order to accomplish a certain task. These

Shakespearean stories are reminiscent of many fairy tales where the hero becomes invisible or takes on another persona, or wears a specific disguise to hide his or her real qualities. In the stories of "The Twelve Dancing Princesses" or "The Man in the Bearskin," disguise is necessary to achieve a goal. Combine these elements with the transformation themes of the hero myth where a hero (such as Michael) must overcome many obstacles to his success as an actor and a human being. It's not difficult to understand why the *Tootsie* story hooks us.

Archetypes

A myth includes certain characters that we see in many stories. These characters are called *archetypes*. They can be thought of as the original "pattern" or "character type" that will be found on the hero's journey. Archetypes take many forms, but they tend to fall within specific categories.

Earlier, we discussed some of the helpers who give advice to help the hero — such as the *wise old man* who possesses special knowledge and often serves as a mentor to the hero.

The female counterpart of the wise old man is the *good mother*. Whereas the wise old man has superior knowledge, the good mother is known for her nurturing qualities, and for her intuition. This figure often gives the hero particular objects to help on the journey. It might be a protective amulet, or the ruby slippers that Dorothy receives in *The Wizard of Oz* from the Good Witch of the North. Sometimes in fairy tales it's a cloak to make the person invisible, or ordinary objects that become extraordinary, as in "The Girl of Courage," an Afghan fairy tale about a maiden who receives a comb, a whetstone, and a mirror to help defeat the devil.

Many myths contain a *shadow figure*. This is a character who is the opposite 40 of the hero. Sometimes this figure helps the hero on the journey; other times this figure opposes the hero. The shadow figure can be the negative side of the hero which could be the dark and hostile brother in "Cain and Abel," the stepsisters in "Cinderella," or the Robber Girl in "The Snow Queen." The shadow figure can also help the hero, as the whore with the heart of gold who saves the hero's life, or provides balance to his idealization of woman.

Many myths contain *animal archetypes* that can be positive or negative figures. In "St. George and the Dragon," the dragon is the negative force which is a violent and ravaging animal, not unlike the shark in *Jaws*. But in many stories, animals help the hero. Sometimes there are talking donkeys, or a dolphin which saves the hero, or magical horses or dogs.

The *trickster* is a mischievous archetypical figure who is always causing chaos, disturbing the peace, and generally being an anarchist. The trickster uses wit and cunning to achieve his or her ends. Sometimes the trickster is a harmless prankster or a "bad boy" who is funny and enjoyable. More often, the trickster is a con man, as in *The Sting,* or the devil, as in *The Exorcist,* who demanded all the skills of the priest to outwit him. The "Till Eulenspiegel" stories revolve around the trickster, as do the Spanish picaresque novels. Even the tales of Tom Sawyer have a trickster motif. In all countries, there are stories that revolve around this figure, whose job it is to outwit.

"Mythic" Problems and Solutions

We all grew up with myths. Most of us heard or read fairy tales when we were young. Some of us may have read Bible stories, or stories from other religions or other cultures. These stories are part of us. And the best way to work with them is to let them come out naturally as you write the script.

Of course, some filmmakers are better at this than others. George Lucas and Steven Spielberg have a strong sense of myth and incorporate it into their films. They both have spoken about their love of the stories from childhood, and of their desire to bring these types of stories to audiences. Their stories create some of the same sense of wonder and excitement as myths. Many of the necessary psychological beats are part of their stories, deepening the story beyond the ordinary action-adventure.

Myths bring depth to a hero story. If a filmmaker is thinking only about the action and excitement of a story, audiences might fail to connect with the hero's journey. But if the basic beats of the hero's journey are evident, a film will often inexplicably draw audiences, in spite of critics' responses to the film.

Take *Rambo,* for instance. Why was this violent, simple story so popular with audiences? I don't think it was because everyone agreed with its politics. I do think Sylvester Stallone is a master at incorporating the American myth into his filmmaking. That doesn't mean it's done consciously. Somehow he is naturally in sync with the myth, and the myth becomes integrated into his stories.

Clint Eastwood also does hero stories, and gives us the adventure of the myth and the transformation of the myth. . . . Eastwood's films have given more attention to the transformation of the hero, and have been receiving more serious critical attention as a result.

All of these filmmakers—Lucas, Spielberg, Stallone, and Eastwood—dramatize the hero myth in their own particular ways. And all of them prove that myths are marketable.

Application

It is an important part of the writer's or producer's work to continually find opportunities for deepening the themes within a script. Finding the myth beneath the modern story is part of that process.

To find these myths, it's not a bad idea to reread some of Grimm's fairy tales or fairy tales from around the world to begin to get acquainted with various myths. You'll start to see patterns and elements that connect with our own human experience.

Also, read Joseph Campbell and Greek mythology. If you're interested in Jungian psychology, you'll find many rich resources within a number of books on the subject. Since Jungian psychology deals with archetypes, you'll find many new characters to draw on for your own work.

With all of these resources to incorporate, it's important to remember that the myth is not a story to force upon a script. It's more a pattern which you can bring out in your own stories when they seem to be heading in the direction of a myth.

As you work, ask yourself:

Do I have a myth working in my script? If so, what beats am I using of the hero's journey? Which ones seem to be missing?

Am I missing characters? Do I need a mentor type? A wise old man? A wizard? Would one of these characters help dimensionalize the hero's journey?

Could I create new emotional dimensions to the myth by starting my character as reluctant, naive, simple, or decidedly "unheroic"?

Does my character get transformed in the process of the journey?

Have I used a strong three-act structure to support the myth, using the first turning point to move into the adventure and the second turning point to create a dark moment, or a reversal, or even a "near-death" experience?

Don't be afraid to create variations on the myth, but don't start with the myth itself. Let the myth grow naturally from your story. Developing myths are part of the rewriting process. If you begin with the myth, you'll find your writing becomes rigid, uncreative, and predictable. Working with the myth in the rewriting process will deepen your script, giving it new life as you find the story within the story.

READING THE TEXT

1. How does Seger define the "hero myth" (para. 11)?
2. In your own words, explain what Seger means by the "healing myth" (para. 29).
3. What is an "archetype" (para. 37) in film?

READING THE SIGNS

1. Seger is writing to aspiring screenwriters. How does her status as an industry insider affect her description of heroic archetypes?
2. Compare Seger's formulation of heroes with Robert B. Ray's in "The Thematic Paradigm" (p. 308). To what extent do Seger and Ray adequately explain the role of women in movies?

3. Review Michael Parenti's "Class and Virtue" (p. 368), and then write an essay identifying the myths behind the modern stories *Pretty Woman* and *Indecent Proposal*.

4. Rent a DVD of *Titanic,* and write an essay explaining the myths and archetypal characters the film includes. How might archetypal and mythic patterns explain the film's success?

5. Seger recommends that aspiring screenwriters reacquaint themselves with Grimm's fairy tales for inspiration (para. 50). Read some of Grimm's tales, and then write an argument for or against the suitability of such tales as inspiration for films today.

6. What myths about American history, race, and gender do you see in *Gone with the Wind*? Brainstorm a list of these myths in class, and then use your list to write an essay in which you explain why the film has become an American classic. To develop your ideas, consult Vicki L. Eaklor's "Myth and Gender in *Gone with the Wind*" (p. 349).

CHARLES EALY

Understanding Star Wars

A lot has changed since the days when literary scholarship meant studying the likes of Milton and Shakespeare; with the advent of cultural studies, scholars are now tackling such subjects as, well, Star Wars. *In this journalistic feature written in 1999 for the* Dallas Morning News, *Charles Ealy (b. 1953) surveys academic opinion about George Lucas's epic fantasy, finding wide-ranging interpretations — from one that sees the film as an attack on the Nixon presidency to another that equates it with* Birth of a Nation's *racist defense of the Confederacy. And there's a lot more opinion in between. Charles Ealy is an entertainment writer for the* Dallas Morning News.

You wouldn't think a movie like *Star Wars* would cause controversy in the hallowed halls of academia. After all, it was initially intended for kids. But for the last two decades, scholars have carried on an argument that matches, and sometimes exceeds, the passion of those odd adults who dress up in Darth Vader helmets and occasionally pop up on the evening news.

It's not that the scholars think the movie is particularly important artistically. . . . Rather, they're trying to understand the cultural significance of the *Star Wars* saga, and in turn, discover clues about how a story captures the imagination of a society. It's too easy to dismiss *Star Wars* as unworthy of critical attention, they say. It's quite another matter to attempt to understand its resonance.

Do the *Star Wars* movies represent a cultural conservatism that encourages viewing the world as good vs. evil — a development that liberal scholars belittle? Are the films tapping into a hunger for meaning in a world that seems devoid of clear answers? Or are the childlike films stifling the intellectual development of an art form and infantilizing the movie-going public's tastes? "Politically, blockbuster movies [like *Star Wars*] embrace both the right and the left, so there's a wide range of opinion about them," says Peter Biskind, author of the . . . history of Hollywood in the '60s and '70s, *Easy Riders, Raging Bulls.* "By their very nature, blockbusters can't antagonize any segment of the audience." Scholars, however, can and do revel in antagonizing the public. Yet, even they appear to have reached a tentative consensus on the following:

- The *Star Wars* phenomenon, which began in 1977, was far more significant than first suspected, helping set the tone for the Reagan-era view that the Soviet Union was the "evil empire" and making arguments for building a Star Wars missile defense system sound more realistic;

- The movie signaled a dramatic shift from the morally ambiguous films of the '60s and '70s and heralded the return of the popular Hollywood formula of good vs. evil;

- And the impact of the George Lucas films will only increase with the opening of *The Phantom Menace*.

Sounds simple, but it's not. Some scholars, primarily defenders of *Star Wars*, see the movies as tapping into long-held myths about the coming of age of a young hero who must go through a series of trials before saving civilization. Others see the saga as a political commentary, with the "evil emperor" representing former President Richard Nixon and the dark lieutenant, Darth Vader, representing Henry Kissinger. (Creator George Lucas, having grown up in the Vietnam era, has given credence to this interpretation in various interviews.) Another group sees it in a darker light — as a remake of the racist *Birth of a Nation*, D. W. Griffith's early Hollywood blockbuster about the Civil War, with Luke Skywalker as the noble Southern cavalier and R2-D2 and C-3PO as the "sassy but loyal slaves."

Critical interpretations differ dramatically because "the characters in *Star Wars* are basically flat; they have no depth," says Dr. Andrew Gordon, a professor of English at the University of Florida in Gainesville. "The fact that the characters are flat means that they're like people in a fairy tale. Anyone can identify with them. They're kind of a template." Dr. Gordon, however, makes it clear that he has his own views. He sees the cultural significance — and the notions of renewal and hope in *Star Wars* — as a key to the trilogy. "Like soap operas or cliffhanging serials, the *Star Wars* movies generate the audience desire to see the next episode," he says. "But unlike those episodic forms, which are loosely structured and can be spun out forever, *Star Wars* has the unifying structure of the monomyth."

What's a monomyth, you might ask?   5

In the case of *Star Wars*, "The hero of the monomyth undergoes a rite of passage, is tested and tried as he stands in for the entire culture," Dr. Gordon says, referring to the theories of myth expert Joseph Campbell. "What he brings back from his adventure helps restore the civilization. It's the presence of the mythic hero, the stages of the hero's journey and the archetypal characters — the wise old man, the beautiful princess, the animal helpers, the gnomes and dwarves, the Black Knight — that account for the fundamental appeal of *Star Wars*." Dr. Gordon dismisses the notion that high-tech special effects are the most important source of the public's fascination. *Star Wars* "is a throwback: old-fashioned and reassuringly conservative," he says. "It has a gleaming post-modern surface but a premodern core, like a starship run on steam. It has a clear-cut theme of good and evil. People respond to that, because life is often messy and lacks a meaningful pattern. People hunger for moral simplicity."

Dr. Gordon acknowledges that *Star Wars* "coincided with a right-wing turn in America, and that it preceded by a few years the Reagan revolution." And, yes, he says, the simple moral view of the *Star Wars* world parallels that of the Reagan administration, with the Soviet Union representing the "evil empire," as the former president put it. "But I don't think that was Lucas's intention," Dr. Gordon says. "And I don't think he would be happy with the purposes to which his movies have been put," such as giving Mr. Reagan's Strategic Defense Initiative a nickname. "Authors are not necessarily responsible for the uses to which their work is put," he says. "Can you blame [writer J. D.] Salinger because *Catcher in the Rye* is a favorite of crazed killers?"

Other scholars say it's not a matter of blaming the artist, and they defend the right of Mr. Lucas to create whatever kind of movie he wishes. But they do argue that the *Star Wars* saga has to be considered in a cultural context. Sometimes, that context isn't too flattering.

Take the controversial arguments of Clyde Taylor, an English professor at Tufts University in Massachusetts. Writing in the academic journal *Screen,* Dr. Taylor proposes that "the narrative homologies between *Birth of a Nation* and *Star Wars* click beyond the possibility of accident.

"The historical setting is a futuristic version of post–Civil War Reconstruc-   10
tion. Princess Leia is divinely inspiring, pure white Victorian womanhood, Lillian Gish reincarnated, the symbolic pawn that must be rescued and protected from Darth Vader and his evil designs," Dr. Taylor writes. "Darth Vader (dark invader?) is the upstart commander of 'black' political forces, threatening a weakened, but spiritual, refined, and honor-bound version of the 'South.' . . . [R2-D2 and C-3PO] take the place of those sassy, back-talking darky house servants, of equally mechanical loyalty to their betters." Dr. Taylor also expresses dismay about the "racist undertones of the light/good versus dark/evil" social fantasy, supported by the feudal notion that "the Force can only be transmitted by blood, a notion that is noted as 'very unAmerican' by Pauline Kael," the former *New Yorker* critic.

All of this is important, Dr. Taylor argues, because it shows that North American popular culture is obsessed with recycling what he sees as a "master narrative." He acknowledges that Mr. Lucas may argue that he was controlling or even subverting U.S. political culture by making *Star Wars*, but Dr. Taylor adds that the 1977 movie was successful because it tapped into "a moment when the utopian lustre of the American dream was dulled; not lost, but more vibrant as nostalgia than prospect." In essence, Dr. Taylor writes, *Star Wars* tapped into the public's sense of needing an evil adversary, just as *Birth of a Nation* exploited racial anxieties, and just as Ronald Reagan offered grandfatherly reassurance in the face of worries about the United States' future.

Mr. Biskind, the author of *Easy Riders, Raging Bulls*, strikes a middle ground between Dr. Gordon (*Star Wars* as mythologically cool) and Dr. Taylor (*Star Wars* as ideologically corrupt). Mr. Biskind calls himself a fan of the *Star Wars* saga, but he regrets that the films heralded the end of the morally ambiguous, personal and intellectually complex films of the late '60s and early '70s. "You always have to view films in context, in certain historical periods," he says. "Films can't help but carry social and historical baggage. It's an integral part of viewing movies. And in the case of *Star Wars*, there's a lot of baggage."

Mr. Lucas and fellow blockbuster director Steven Spielberg helped create a moral vision — and a vision of childhood — that changed radically as we entered the Reagan era, Mr. Biskind says. "One vehicle for this change, however unwitting, were Lucas's and Spielberg's films. By attacking irony, critical thinking, self-consciousness, by pitting heart against head, they did their share in helping to reduce an entire culture to childishness, and in so doing helped prepare the ground for the growth of the right. The kids prevailed, but the ideals they stood for had been drained of content."

Defenders of *Star Wars* say it offers our culture a reassuring mythic tale, Mr. Biskind says. But he also thinks we can't ignore the timing of *Star Wars* — coming after a wave of U.S. self-doubt. "It was in reaction to our growing awareness of European-like complexity in the '70s, where people were more ambiguous and there were no simple narratives. *Star Wars* was definitely a reaction to that, and Lucas says specifically that people were tired of that and longed for pre-Vietnam myths. "Lucas wanted to restore notions of good and evil, the idea of heroes and villains," he says. "Vietnam had complicated those notions, but Lucas wanted to revive them." Mr. Biskind says this trend can be seen as good or bad, depending upon your political perspective — and upon your views about culture and art. "One problem for films and U.S. culture was that *Star Wars* made so much money that it created a bloodlust," he says. "The studios lost interest in the more complicated films of [Martin] Scorsese and [Francis Ford] Coppola. *Star Wars* legitimized comic-book movies, where the endings are happy. It took serial formulas, B-movie formulas of the 1930s, and used modern technology to pump up those formulas and reinvent them. I call it the gentrification of the B movie. . . . It paved the way for the blockbuster syndrome of the '80s."

Mr. Biskind notes that Mr. Lucas has a good defense of such criticism. "He says that movies like *Star Wars* subsidize movies that don't make money. It's   15 the trickle-down theory, and there is some truth to that. Only a handful of studio movies make money, and those that do help subsidize the others. But what's going to happen in many cases with *The Phantom Menace* is that eight of the 10 multiplex screens will have it, and there won't be any independent films showing at all." Mr. Biskind says he doesn't expect *The Phantom Menace* to stray much from the *Star Wars* formula. Mr. Lucas "has reasserted the pleasures of straightforward, unironic storytelling, along with accessible two-dimensional characters whose adventures end happily," Mr. Biskind says. *Star Wars* tells people that it's OK to become wrapped up in a movie again, that it's fine "to yell and scream and really roll with it." Or, as Mr. Lucas himself says, "I'm very much a visual filmmaker, and very much of a filmmaker who is going for emotions over ideas."

For better or worse, that's the message of *Star Wars* — and its implications for our culture.

READING THE TEXT

1. Why, in Ealy's view, does *Star Wars* invite such a broad array of interpretations by academics?
2. Define "monomyth" (para. 5) in your own words.
3. What myths underlie the *Star Wars* films, according to Ealy?
4. Why is Clyde Taylor's interpretation of *Star Wars* controversial?

READING THE SIGNS

1. Watch one of the *Star Wars* films, and then propose your own thesis about the cultural significance of the saga. As you develop your argument, be sure to situate it in the spectrum of scholarly interpretations that Ealy outlines. How does your position compare with them?
2. In an essay, support, refute, or complicate Peter Biskind's assertion that "*Star Wars* legitimized comic-book movies, where the endings are happy" (para. 14).
3. Adopting the perspective of Linda Seger in "Creating the Myth" (p. 317), evaluate the various academic explanations of *Star Wars*' popularity that Ealy presents. Which positions do you think Seger would support, and which would she dismiss?
4. Ealy explains that blockbuster films typically employ fundamental cultural myths. Watch a segment of the recent blockbuster *The Lord of the Rings*, and analyze the myths that underlie the film. Do you see it as qualifying as a monomyth, and why?

TODD BOYD

So You Wanna Be a Gangsta?

Before there were "gangstas" there were gangsters, and as Todd Boyd points out in this selection from Am I Black Enough for You? Popular Culture from the 'Hood and Beyond *(1997), both have played their part in American and cinematic history. From the Italian gangsters of* Scarface *and the* Godfather *films to the Latino and African American gangstas of* American Me *and* Boyz N the Hood, *the gang movie has provided a dramatic setting for an ongoing contest in which the American underclass both resists and embraces the values of mainstream society. A professor of critical studies in the School of Cinema-Television at the University of Southern California, Boyd is coeditor (with Aaron Baker) of* Out of Bounds: Sports, Media, and the Politics of Identity *(1997) and (with Kenneth Shropshire) of* Basketball Jones: America above the Rim *(2000). He has written for such journals as* Wide Angle, Cinéaste, Film-forum, *and* Public Culture. *His most recent books are* New H.N.I.C: The Death of Civil Rights and the Reign of Hip Hop *(2002) and* Young, Black, Rich, and Famous: The Rise of the NBA, the Hip Hop Invasion, and the Transformation of American Culture *(2003).*

The gangster film and the Western are two of the most important genres in the history of Hollywood, especially with respect to articulation of the discourse of American history and masculinity. Whereas the Western concentrated on the mythic settling of the West and a perceived notion of progression, it was primarily concerned with the frontier mentality of the eighteenth through the late nineteenth century. The gangster genre, on the other hand, is about the evolution of American society in the twentieth century into a legitimate entity in the world economy.

Though the Western covertly articulated the politics of oppression against Native Americans during the settling of the West, the gangster genre focused on questions of ethnicity — e.g., Italian, Irish — and how these are transformed over time into questions of race — Black, Latino, etc. This ideological shift provided an interesting representation of the significant position that race has come to occupy in the discourse of American society. We must look at the transformation of the linguistic sign "gangster" and its slow transition to its most recent embodiment as "gangsta" as an instructive historical metaphor. . . .

Americans have always had a fascination with the underworld society populated by those who openly resisted the laws of dominant society and instead created their own world, living by their own rules. Gangsters have in many ways been our version of revolutionaries throughout history. Whereas Europe has always had real-life political revolutionaries, twentieth-century American discourse, upheld by police and government activity, seems to have found ways of perverting for the public the political voices that exist outside the narrow traditions of allowed political expression.

The displacement of these political voices by the forces of oppression has created a renegade space within American culture that allows for the expression of gangster culture. Gangsters indeed function as somewhat revolutionary in comparison to the rest of society, as demonstrated by their open defiance of accepted societal norms and laws, existence in their own environment, and circulation of their own alternative capital. This allows them to remain part of the larger society but to fully exist in their own communities at the same time. This lifestyle has been a consistent media staple throughout the twentieth century, particularly in film.

From as early as D. W. Griffith's *Musketeers of Pig Alley* (1912) and the   5
celebrated studio films of the 1930s — e.g., *Little Caesar* (1930), *Public Enemy* (1931), and *Scarface* (1932) — through the epic treatment rendered in the first two *Godfather* films (1972, 1974), the gangster has enjoyed a vivid screen life. What is important here is that these criminals, as they are deemed by the dominant society, are defined as deviant primarily because of issues of ethnicity, as opposed to issues of race, though to some extent all definitions of ethnicity in this context are inevitably influenced by a subtle definition of race.

This emphasis on ethnicity as it functions in opposition to the standard "white Anglo-Saxon Protestant" is summarized in the first two *Godfather* films. As the United States, both at and immediately after the turn of the century, increasingly became a nation of European immigrants, incoming Italians were consigned to the bottom of the social ladder. In the opening segment of *Godfather II*, Michael Corleone is berated and verbally abused by Senator Geery of Nevada because of his Italian heritage. The word "Italian" is set in opposition to "American" constantly in this segment so as to highlight the ethnic hierarchy which remains a foundational issue in this film. Corleone's ascension to power is complicated by his inability to fully surmount this societal obstacle, at least at this point in the film, and by extension that point in American history — the early 1950s.

It is Francis Ford Coppola's argument that such oppression forced these Italian immigrants into a subversive lifestyle and economy much like that practiced throughout southern Italy, especially in Sicily. Borrowing from their own cultural tradition, some of these new Americans used the underground economy as a vital means of sustenance in the face of ethnic, religious, and cultural oppression. And though their desire, being heavily influenced by the discourse of an "American dream," was to ultimately be fully assimilated into American society, the achievement of this desire was revealed to be at the cost of losing their ethnic and cultural heritage. . . .

At a larger level, the film's historical themes indicate the assimilation of ethnicity into a homogeneous American society, yet foreground the continued rejection of race as a component of the metaphoric "melting pot" — because it is the challenge of race that accelerates the assimilative process of ethnicity.

In the first *Godfather* film, we see this same social dynamic at play regarding ethnicity over race. Near the film's conclusion, we witness the memorable meeting of the "heads of the five families," where the dilemmas of drug trafficking are being discussed by the various Mafia leaders. Vito Corleone is characterized as opposing this potentially lucrative venture for moral reasons, while many of the other members are excited about the possible financial benefits. The chieftain from Kansas City suggests that the Mafia should engage in selling drugs, but only at a distance, leaving the underside of this environment to be experienced by what he describes as the "dark people" because, as he adds, "they're animals anyway, let them lose their souls." His use of the phrase "dark people" and his labeling of them as "animals" clearly reference African Americans, and by extension racialized others in general. This line of dialogue is viewed by many African Americans as prophetic, seeing that the release of *The Godfather* in the early 1970s closely paralleled the upsurge in underworld drug activity throughout African American ghetto communities.

In relation to the assimilation of ethnicity at the expense of race, this line 10 also signifies the way in which the previously mentioned structural hierarchy exists aside from the racial hierarchy, which many African Americans have been unable to transcend because of the difference in skin color. Though Italians through this perverted formulation could be considered inferior to "wasps," those traits that make them different can be easily subsumed when contrasted with the obvious difference of skin color and the history that goes along with being darker. It is in this context that the thematic progression of the *Godfather* films signals the end of the public fascination with the Italian gangster and his ethnically rich underworld.

Furthermore, this line indicates that the drug culture would be an important turning point in the historical discourse specific to the question of race as time moved forward. This line of reasoning has been pursued in numerous texts, most recently through Bill Duke's film *Deep Cover* (1992), which comments on the conspiracy involved in both furnishing and addicting segments of the Black community with drugs as a political maneuver by the government to keep these individuals sedated and oppressed so as to quell any potential political resistance. Mario Van Peebles's film *Panther* (1995) asserts the same theory in connection with the attempted destruction of the Black Panther Party by J. Edgar Hoover and the FBI. In both cases, crime can be seen as affirming capitalism, yet in specifically racial terms.

With this assimilation of ethnicity as signified through the Coppola films, America finds the need to fulfill this otherwise empty space with the next logical descending step on the social ladder, that being race.[1] Two other films from the 1980s effectively mark the shift away from the ethnic gangster to the racialized gangsta. Brian De Palma's remake of *Scarface* (1983) is an obvious rewriting of the genre from the perspective of race. Whereas the main character in the 1932 film was an Italian, in the De Palma version we deal with a racialized Cuban.

Drawing from real political events, De Palma's film begins with the Mariel boat lift of Cuban refugees into south Florida during the latter part of the 1970s, an event which many still consider a lingering legacy of Jimmy Carter's presidency. The film's main character, Tony Montana, is clearly foregrounded as a racialized other. His Cuban identity, broken accent, penchant for garishness, and overall ruthless approach to wealth and human life served as the basis for the popular media representation of Latin American drug dealers that came to dominate the 1980s.

With an increase in drug paranoia from the conservative Reagan and Bush administrations, this form of representation would nearly erase past images of Italian mob figures from the popular memory. While John Gotti was a celebrated folk hero for his stylish media-friendly disposition, individuals such as Carlos Lader Rivas, Pablo Escobar, and Manuel Noriega, who became common sights on the evening news and network news magazine programs, were depicted as threats to the very fabric of our society. To add to this popular form of representation, NBC's series *Miami Vice* drew many of its story lines and criminal figures from this newly accepted version of racialized representation.[2] . . .

The other major filmic event that reflected this obsession with the drug   15
culture and the question of race was Dennis Hopper's *Colors* (1988). Hopper's film offered an intricate look at the gang culture that existed in both South Central and East Los Angeles. Its main characters were two white Los

---

[1]The popular 1990 Martin Scorsese film *Goodfellas* is different from the gangster films which preceded it. At the conclusion of this film, the main character, Henry Hill, turns state's evidence on his former colleagues, thus violating one of the most stringent codes of the gangster lifestyle. And though some would argue that this film is a revisionist gangster film, it is sufficiently separated from other examples of the genre so as not to be confused. Scorsese's *Casino* (1995) continues this move to a contemporary gangster epic.

Another example of this revisionist trend would be Barry Levinson's fictional account of the life of Benjamin "Bugsy" Siegel, with its emphasis on Siegel's mistress, Virginia Hill, and the way in which her influence can be read as substantial, though detrimental, to Siegel in the financial decisions that he makes. *Bugsy* (1991) presents a sentimental underworld figure who has been "softened" by this female presence, which goes against the masculinist approach normally associated with the gangster. This rereading of the central character, with an emphasis on the female, adds to my notion of a revisionist trend in the genre, though in this case it is gender, not race, that is the point of transition.

[2]For a detailed discussion of the drug trade in Los Angeles, see Mike Davis, "The Political Economy of Crack," in *City of Quartz* (New York: Verso, 1990), and for a larger discussion of the role played by the media, the politics of Reagan/Bush, and the drug culture of the 1980s, see Jimmie Reeves and Richard Campbell, *Cracked Coverage* (Durham: Duke Univ. Press, 1994).

Angeles police officers who were commissioned with the monumental task of eliminating the urban crime being perpetrated by African American and Latino youth. This film tied in neatly with the increasing commentary presented by national news programs about what had begun as a regional situation and was later argued to have spread throughout the country. Using the police, and by extension the rest of white society, as its victims, the film endorsed the racial paranoia concerning criminality that at this time was in full swing.

Colors, for all intents and purposes, made the gangbanger America's contemporary criminal of choice, turning a localized problem into a national epidemic that once again linked crime with specific notions of race. In many ways, *Colors* served the same function for gangsta culture that *Birth of a Nation* served for the early stages of African American cinema. Both films, through their overt racial paranoia, and in both cases using armed militia as an answer to the perceived Black threat — in one case the Ku Klux Klan, in the other a racist police department — inspired a series of African American cinematic responses. This regressive film engendered a public fascination with the newly defined "gangsta."

With the traditional white ethnic gangster film having all but disappeared, the way was clear for the entrance of a new popular villain to be screened across the mind of American society. The ideological link between crime and race would be made worse, and the image of the African American gangbanger would become not only popular in the sense of repeated representation, but financially lucrative as well. In addition to the changing history of the Hollywood gangster film, several other historical factors specific to African American culture would contribute to the emergence and eventual proliferation of the African American "gangsta."

From the Black Godfather to the Black Guerrilla Family

The late 1960s and early 1970s saw an increase in underworld activity, especially involving drugs, throughout many lower-class Black communities. In many ways more important than the drugs themselves was the culture that accompanied this underworld lifestyle and the way in which it was represented visually. The garish fashions popularized by Eleganza and Flag Brothers, heavily adorned, ornament-laden Cadillacs, and other materialistic excesses helped to define this cultural terrain as "cool" during this period. . . .

In several of the films that define this period, eventually known as the "Blaxploitation" era of Hollywood (1970–73), the Black protagonist was presented in opposition to a stereotypical white menace who was bent on destroying the African American community, primarily through the influx of drugs and the accompanying culture of violence. For the most part, evil in the films was personified in the form of a corrupt police or mafia figure, if not both at the same time. Thus much of the narrative action appeared in battles

between some faction of the white mafia, who had traditionally been in control of the ghetto, albeit from a distance, and the emerging Black underworld
figures who were striving to wrest control of this alternative economy from
their white counterparts.

It was as if the loosening of societal restrictions gained during the civil 20
rights movement permitted exploitation of the community through control of
underworld vices, though the actual control was in the hands of manipulative
outsiders, who used the Black gangster as their foil. The Black gangster,
whether he was a pimp, dope dealer, or hustler, through these films became
a prominent example of what it meant to be an entrepreneur. The tension
between outside influence and inside control is represented in many of the
films of the period, most notably *Cotton Comes to Harlem*, *Across 110th Street*,
Superfly, and *The Mack*. The African American gangster had become a media
staple by the mid-1970s. . . .

Many of the films of this period were based on the dynamics of an
African American underworld existence (e.g., *Sweetsweetback's Badass Song*,
The Mack, *Willie Dynamite*, *Coffy*, *Cleopatra Jones*), and in conjunction with the
popular ghetto literature of Iceberg Slim and Donald Goines, as well as the
more esoteric works of author Chester Himes and playwright Charles Gor-
done, this form of representation remained viable long after this period had
passed. In line with Nelson George's argument that "Blaxploitation movies are
crucial to the current '70's retro-nuevo phase" (149), this historical period left
a series of low-budget films which would eventually be perfect for transfer to
the home video format. The "Blaxploitation" films would leave an indelible
imprint on African American popular culture as the "gangsta" continued to
rise in prominence and position.

A Small Introduction to the "G" Funk Era

With the historical antecedents of the Hollywood gangster film and 1970s
Blaxploitation films, along with popular African American literature that
explored the culture, the stage was set for the flowering of gangsta culture in
the late 1980s and early 1990s. The contemporary manifestation continued to
appear in the form of cinema, but also gained increasing visibility in the world
of rap music, to the point of establishing its own genre and forming a solid cultural movement. This transition from genre to cultural movement included
representations in film, music, and literature, and involved multiple layers of
society: communal, political, and corporate. From the regular individuals whose
personal narratives drew heavily from gangster culture, to rap artists whose
real-life antics coincided with the fictional rhetoric of their lyrics, and finally to
the highest levels of government, where questions of moral integrity, community debasement, and freedom of speech were constantly being posed, this
cultural movement had a great deal of currency with respect to African Americans in society, especially the African American male. . . .

Though there are glimpses of the gangster lifestyle in a number of films that appeared throughout the late 1980s and especially in the early 1990s, the two films most relevant to an understanding of gangsta culture are John Singleton's *Boyz N the Hood* (1991) and Allen and Albert Hughes's *Menace II Society* (1993). Not to ignore such a popular film as Mario Van Peebles's *New Jack City* (1991) or Abel Ferrera's cult video classic *The King of New York* (1990), but these texts are more directly influenced by the traditional gangster paradigm, in addition to being set in New York City. The filmic representation of gangsta culture draws many of its influences from rap music, and in turn rap music assumes a great deal of identity with the work of Singleton and the Hughes brothers. Contemporary gangsta culture is undoubtedly a West Coast phenomenon.

The other film that holds a vital position in the representation of gangsta culture is Edward James Olmos's *American Me* (1992). This film addresses the culture from a Latino perspective as opposed to an African American one. This is of utmost importance, for while gangsta culture is publicly regarded as an African American entity, much of the culture derives from the close proximity in which African Americans and Latinos coexist in racialized Los Angeles. . . .

Hispanics Causin' Panic

American Me demonstrates that aspects of African American gangsta life and   25
Mexican American gangsta culture are in dialogue with one another, though it can at times be a highly contested dialogue. There are two distinct instances in the film where a potential clash between the races is openly criticized as being counterproductive to someone's coming to consciousness and ultimate cultural empowerment. As the Mexican mafia (La Eme) smuggles drugs into the prison, we witness a Black inmate who steals the cocaine intended for another inmate. Upon revelation of the culprit, Santana, the leader of La Eme, instructs his soldiers to burn the man as an act of punishment. This triggers a cell-block confrontation that borders on a riot between La Eme and the Black Guerrilla Family (BGF). As the prison guards descend, the riot is aborted, but not without critical commentary. Santana informs the leader of the BGF that the situation was not racially motivated, but simply an action of retribution to forestall any future attempts at hindering their drug-trafficking efforts in prison. In other words, "business, never personal." This is a case in which the interest of underground capitalism supersedes any specific racial agenda.

Yet this scene is important as the setup for a similar situation that occurs later in the film. When La Eme attempts to sever its tie with the traditional Italian Mafia, the move is met with much resistance. Scagnelli, the mob boss, refuses to relinquish his end of the drug business in East L.A. As a result, several members of La Eme rape and murder Scagnelli's son while he is in prison. In response, Scagnelli sends uncut heroin into the barrio, causing several overdoses. This creates a chain reaction of retribution, which eventually culminates in Santana's death at the hands of his own men. At a certain point during this series of events, J.D., the only white member of La Eme, who slowly attempts to wrest control of the gang from Santana, orders a hit on the BGF by using the Aryan Brotherhood, the white gang represented in the film. Santana objects to this action and criticizes J.D. for "sending out the wrong message."

Santana's objection is based on his increasing awareness of racial and so-cial consciousness, which has been facilitated by the politically empowered female character Julie. Julie, like the female character of Ronnie in *Menace*, helps Santana to realize the error of his misguided ways. On several occasions she criticizes his violent philosophy in ways that other characters cannot for fear of death. In a pivotal scene late in the film, Julie exposes Santana's posi-tion in all its limitations. After a series of extremely critical remarks about Santana's hypocritical use of crime as a way of arguing for *la raza*, he tells her, "If you were a man, I'd . . ." His incomplete sentence is cut short by Julie's own completion of it: "You'd kill me; no, you'd fuck me in the ass." Having witnessed several scenes in which men were raped because of Santana's power over them, in addition to his rape of Julie, we can feel the magnitude of her statement. She not only criticizes his politics, she has criticized his mas-culinity by alluding to the latent homosexuality of his supposed gestures of power.

Ultimately, she forces Santana to understand that the power struggles which often take place between those who are marginalized permit the con-tinued oppression of their voices by those in power. Santana even says to J.D., "We spend all our time dealing with the miatas [their slang term for Blacks], and the Aryan Brotherhood, only to be dealing with ourselves." In other words, ideological distractions ultimately leave us in the same place, with no advance-ment in consciousness or power.

These ideas eventually separate Santana's newfound political conscious-ness from J.D.'s "business as usual" approach to crime and the underlying destruction of the community. It is not coincidental that J.D.'s whiteness, which is endorsed by Santana early in the film, looms as the final authority once he has ordered the killing of Santana and presumably taken control of the gang. At the beginning of the film, as expressed through the American military oppression of the Mexican American citizens, and at the conclusion, with J.D.'s murdering of Santana, thus destroying any possibility for an overall group consciousness, we can see that racism and white supremacy are the root causes of the chaos that permeates much of the present-day urban land-scape. It is this fundamental understanding of race, racism, and complicity in one's own oppression that substantiates the importance of *American Me*. *American Me* engages history and politics to subtly yet convincingly argue that the real root of evil in American society as it relates to oppressed minorities is the bondage of systemic and institutionalized racism. This understanding also distinguishes it as a political statement from the rather limited bourgeois poli-tics of *Boyz N the Hood* and the nihilistically apolitical *Menace II Society*. . . .

Boyz Will Be Boyz

> Either they don't know, won't show, or don't care what's going on in the
> hood.
>
> —DOUGHBOY, *Boyz N the Hood*

While *American Me* serves as an "objective third party" against which to eval-   30
uate *Boyz* and *Menace*, the similarities notwithstanding, to engage the culturally specific tenets of Black popular culture we must look at texts which are
firmly situated in the domain of African American cinema in order to study
the class politics of each film. In this regard, the political position of *Boyz N the
Hood* can be defined as either a bourgeois Black nationalist or an Afrocentric
model that focuses on the "disappearing" Black male, yet also fits easily into
the perceived pathology of the culture in a modernized version of the legendary Moynihan report of the late 1960s. This report regarded the typically
broken African American family as a cause of societal dysfunction at the highest level.

Singleton's film was integral to the politically charged period of resurgent
Black nationalism in the late 1980s and early 1990s. This cultural resurgence
of Black nationalism, most closely associated with the work of Public Enemy,
KRS-One, and Sister Souljah, also set the tone for the discourse that informed
Do the Right Thing, as well as many of the debates that emerged after the film's
release.

From the outset it is obvious that Singleton's film is conversant with the
Afrocentric discourse that permeates much of Black intellectual and cultural
life. The film opens by establishing South Central Los Angeles as its geographical, cultural, and political center. Yet the landscape of Los Angeles is a
historically specific one. The film begins in 1984, as we quickly spot several
campaign posters that support the re-election of President Ronald Reagan —
the obvious contradiction of this image being seen in a community such as
South Central, which is the type of community most victimized by the racial
and class politics of Reagan's first term. Another contradiction is signaled as a
young Black male, while looking at an abandoned dead body lying in an alley,
gives this political image "the finger." This young character is identified as
being closely associated with gang culture. He declares that both of his brothers have been shot, and in turn they are heroic in his mind because they have
yet to be killed. His marginal status allows him to recognize at some level that
this supreme image of white male authority is in stark contrast to his own
existence.

As we enter the classroom, we are presented with another contradiction.
The camera pans the student drawings that cover the wall. These pictures
contain images of people being shot, police brutality, and other acts that
emphasize the daily violence that defines many of the lives in this poor Black
community. These images are contradicted by the speech being delivered by the
white teacher about the historical importance of the first European "settlers" or

"pilgrims" on American soil. Her lecture is on the reasons this country celebrates the Thanksgiving holiday, yet by implication it also articulates the
exploitation of America and Native Americans and the ensuing colonization,
which was a helpful instrument in establishing the societal hierarchy that we
inhabit today.

The ideology that is being discussed is being put into practice through the
attitudes and policies of Ronald Reagan. Reagan clearly felt the need to return
to some form of these earlier examples of oppression in the course of his
presidential career, as his repeated attacks on affirmative action, his support
of states' rights, and his overall embrace of positions consistent with right-
wing conservatism about race clearly indicated. In a sense, the actions of those
who are being celebrated by the teacher, the "pilgrims," have contributed to
the conditions of the people depicted in the children's drawings. The film sets
up a binary opposition between the conservative politics of America and
African Americans' rejection of these oppressive policies. This scene is one
of the few in the film in which racism and white supremacy are directly cri-
tiqued.

As the scene develops, Tre, the film's main character, confronts his ele- 35
mentary school teacher, asserting that humankind originated in Africa and
not in Europe. Yet in his presentation, Tre is criticized not only by his teacher,
but by other students as well. The same student who gave Reagan "the finger" completely dissociates himself from Tre's Afrocentric assertion, "We're
all from Africa." In response, this child declares, "I ain't from Africa, I'm from
Crenshaw Mafia," further linking himself to gang culture through his identification with the set known as "Crenshaw Mafia." The obvious irony of this
scene is that gang affiliation is set in direct conflict with one's racial and cultural

American Me, 1992.

identity. It is as if being a gangsta supersedes race, as opposed to being a result of racial and class hierarchies in America.

In this same exchange, we can also hear echoes of Tre's father, Furious, and his lessons on life that recur throughout the film. This is once again set in opposition to the words of the aspiring gangsta's older brothers. This exchange leads to a fight between the two children, underscoring the incompatibility of progressive politics and existence in gangsta culture. Yet through the setting of gangsta culture in opposition to nationalist politics, it becomes clear that this bourgeois understanding ignores the fact that gangsters historically are easily transformed into revolutionaries because of their marginal status in society.

Remarks about the plight of the "Black man" dominate much of Furious's commentary in the film. As critic Michael Dyson has alluded, these comments fit well with the male-centered Afrocentric ideals of thinkers such as Jawanza Kanjufu, Haki Madhabuti, and Molefi Asante. *Boyz* uses gangsta culture as an alluring spectacle, which is underscored by the film's exaggeratedly violent trailer, but this spectacle is used to engage an Afrocentric critique that denounces the routine slaying of Black men, whether by other gang members or by the police. *Boyz* makes interesting use of many of the icons of gangsta culture while conducting its Black nationalist critique. The film straddles both areas, opening the door to the ensuing onslaught of gangsta imagery.

In this sense, *Boyz* is much like the imagery connected with one of its co-stars, Ice Cube. As a rapper, Ice Cube has consistently combined signs of gangsta culture with an ideological perspective that emphasizes a perverted Black nationalist agenda, borrowed primarily from the Nation of Islam. Similarly, *Boyz* combines gangsta icons with Afrocentrism, ultimately privileging the ideological critique over the iconography. This strain of political discourse was popular during the late 1980s and early 1990s, with *Boyz* providing a cinematic counterpart to rap music. Singleton's film, though visualizing gangsta culture on a mass scale, is really more acceptable as a political text than as a thesis on the complex gangsta mentality. In many ways, *Boyz* represents the culmination of this politically resurgent period, as the theme of Black nationalism slowly disappeared from most popular forms shortly thereafter.

Though the film is overtly political, it reflects a bourgeois sense of politics. At the conclusion of the film we see a didactic scroll which tells us that Tre and Brandi, the one utopic Black male/female relationship presented in the film, have ventured off to Morehouse and Spelman College in Atlanta, respectively, to pursue their middle-class dreams far away from South Central L.A. Morehouse and Spelman have often been thought of as the Black equivalent of Harvard or Yale, the historical breeding ground for bourgeois Blackness. The fact that the two colleges are located in Atlanta, the current "mecca" of Black America, underscores the film's flimsy political position. *Boyz N the Hood* demonizes the landscape of Los Angeles while uncritically offering middle-class Atlanta as a metaphoric space where future generations of African Americans can exist free of the obstacles that are depicted in this film.

READING THE TEXT

1. What, according to Boyd, has been the cultural and political significance of the gangster underworld in American history and popular culture?

2. How did Hollywood in the late 1960s and early 1970s respond to the emergence of a drug culture in impoverished black communities, in Boyd's analysis?

3. Why does Boyd believe that *Boyz N the Hood* reflects both black nationalist and conventional bourgeois values?

4. How did *American Me* reflect the conflicts between Mexican American and African American gang subcultures?

5. What is the difference, according to Boyd, between race and ethnicity?

READING THE SIGNS

1. Write an essay supporting, complicating, or refuting the proposition that Hollywood's depiction of gangstas glorifies criminal behavior.

2. Rent a film like *Scarface* or *The Godfather,* and write an analysis comparing its treatment of ethnic "others" with the treatment of black gang members in a movie like *Boyz N the Hood.*

3. Write an essay in which you explore the reasons gangsta films and culture are so popular among middle-class white teens. To develop your ideas, consult Nell Bernstein's "Goin' Gangsta, Choosin' Cholita" (p. 604).

4. In class, form teams and debate the proposition that Hollywood exploits the black community in making gang films.

5. Rent a film focusing on African Americans that Boyd does not discuss — *Waiting to Exhale.* Then write a response to Boyd in which you address the importance of gender in film analysis.

DAVID DENBY

High-School Confidential: Notes on Teen Movies

Face it: High school for most of us is one extended nightmare, a long-playing drama starring cheerleaders and football players who sneer at the mere mortals who must endure their haughty reign. So it's little wonder that, as David Denby (b. 1943) argues in this New Yorker *essay from 1999, teen movies so often feature loathsome cheerleaders and football stars who, one way or another, get theirs in this ever-popular movie genre. Indeed, Denby asks, "Who can doubt where Hollywood's twitchy, nearsighted writers and directors ranked—or feared they ranked—on the high-school totem pole?" Nerds at the bottom, where else, like the millions of suffering kids who flock to their films. A contributing editor for the* New Yorker, *Denby is the author of* The Great Books: My Adventures with Homer, Rousseau, Woolf, and Other Indestructible Writers of the Western World *(1996) and* American Sucker *(2003).*

The most hated young woman in America is a blonde—well, sometimes a redhead or a brunette, but usually a blonde. She has big hair flipped into a swirl of gold at one side of her face or arrayed in a sultry mane, like the magnificent pile of a forties movie star. She's tall and slender, with a waist as supple as a willow, but she's dressed in awful, spangled taste: her outfits could have been put together by warring catalogues. And she has a mouth on her, a low, slatternly tongue that devastates other kids with such insults as "You're vapor, you're Spam!" and "Do I look like Mother Teresa? If I did, I probably wouldn't mind talking to the geek squad." She has two or three friends exactly like her, and together they dominate their realm—the American high school as it appears in recent teen movies. They are like wicked princesses, who enjoy the misery of their subjects. Her coronation, of course, is the senior prom, when she expects to be voted "most popular" by her class. But, though she may be popular, she is certainly not liked, so her power is something of a mystery. She is beautiful and rich, yet in the end she is preëminent because . . . she is preëminent, a position she works to maintain with Joan Crawford-like tenacity. Everyone is afraid of her; that's why she's popular.

She has a male counterpart. He's usually a football player, muscular but dumb, with a face like a beer mug and only two ways of speaking—in a conspiratorial whisper, to a friend; or in a drill sergeant's sudden bellow. If her weapon is the snub, his is the lame but infuriating prank—the can of Sprite emptied into a knapsack, or something sticky, creamy, or adhesive deposited in a locker. Sprawling and dull in class, he comes alive in the halls and in the cafeteria. He hurls people against lockers; he spits, pours, and sprays; he has a projectile relationship with food. As the crown prince, he claims the

343

best-looking girl for himself, though in a perverse display of power he may invite an outsider or an awkward girl — a "dog" — to the prom, setting her up for some special humiliation. When we first see him, he is riding high, and virtually the entire school colludes in his tyranny. No authority figure — no teacher or administrator — dares correct him.

Thus the villains of the recent high-school movies. Not every American teen movie has these two characters, and not every social queen or jock shares all the attributes I've mentioned. (Occasionally, a handsome, dark-haired athlete can be converted to sweetness and light.) But as genre figures these two types are hugely familiar; that is, they are a common memory, a collective trauma, or at least a social and erotic fantasy. Such movies of the past year [1999] as *Disturbing Behavior*, *She's All That*, *Ten Things I Hate about You*, and *Never Been Kissed* depend on them as stock figures. And they may have been figures in the minds of the Littleton shooters, Eric Harris and Dylan Klebold, who imagined they were living in a school like the one in so many of these movies — a poisonous system of status, snobbery, and exclusion.

Do genre films reflect reality? Or are they merely a set of conventions that refer to other films? Obviously, they wouldn't survive if they didn't provide emotional satisfaction to the people who make them and to the audiences who watch them. A half century ago, we didn't need to see ten Westerns a year in order to learn that the West got settled. We needed to see it settled ten times a year in order to provide ourselves with the emotional gratifications of righteous violence. By drawing his gun only when he was provoked, and in the service of the good, the classic Western hero transformed the gross tangibles of the expansionist drive (land, cattle, gold) into a principle of moral order. The gangster, by contrast, is a figure of chaos, a modern, urban person, and in the critic Robert Warshow's formulation he functions as a discordant element in an American society devoted to a compulsively "positive" outlook. When the gangster dies, he cleanses viewers of their own negative feelings.

High-school movies are also full of unease and odd, mixed-up emotions. 5 They may be flimsy in conception; they may be shot in lollipop colors, garlanded with mediocre pop scores, and cast with goofy young actors trying to make an impression. Yet this most commercial and frivolous of genres harbors a grievance against the world. It's a very specific grievance, quite different from the restless anger of such fifties adolescent-rebellion movies as *The Wild One*, in which someone asks Marlon Brando's biker "What are you rebelling against?" and the biker replies "What have you got?" The fifties teen outlaw was against anything that adults considered sacred. But no movie teenager now revolts against adult authority, for the simple reason that adults have no authority. Teachers are rarely more than a minimal, exasperated presence, administrators get turned into a joke, and parents are either absent or distantly benevolent. It's a teen world, bounded by school, mall, and car, with occasional moments set in the fast-food outlets where the kids work, or in the kids' upstairs bedrooms, with their pinups and rack stereo systems. The enemy is not authority; the enemy is other teens and the social system that they impose on one another.

The bad feeling in these movies may strike grownups as peculiar. After all, from a distance American kids appear to be having it easy these days. The teen audience is facing a healthy job market; at home, their parents are stuffing the den with computers and the garage with a bulky S.U.V. But most teens aren't thinking about the future job market. Lost in the eternal swoon of late adolescence, they're thinking about their identity, their friends, and their clothes. Adolescence is the present-tense moment in American life. Identity and status are fluid: abrupt, devastating reversals are always possible. (In a teen movie, a guy who swallows a bucket of cafeteria coleslaw can make himself a hero in an instant.) In these movies, accordingly, the senior prom is the equivalent of the shoot-out at the O.K. Corral; it's the moment when one's worth as a human being is settled at last. In the rather pedestrian new comedy *Never Been Kissed*, Drew Barrymore, as a twenty-five-year-old newspaper reporter, goes back to high school pretending to be a student, and immediately falls into her old, humiliating pattern of trying to impress the good-looking rich kids. Helplessly, she pushes for approval, and even gets herself chosen prom queen before finally coming to her senses. She finds it nearly impossible to let go.

Genre films dramatize not what happens but how things feel — the emotional coloring of memory. They fix subjectivity into fable. At actual schools, there is no unitary system of status; there are many groups to be a part of, many places to excel (or fail to excel), many avenues of escape and self-definition. And often the movies, too, revel in the arcana of high-school cliques. In last summer's *Disturbing Behavior*, a veteran student lays out the cafeteria ethnography for a newcomer: Motorheads, Blue Ribbons, Skaters, Micro-geeks ("drug of choice: Stephen Hawking's *A Brief History of Time* and a cup of jasmine tea on Saturday night"). Subjectively, though, the social system in *Disturbing Behavior* (a high-school version of *The Stepford Wives*) and in the other movies still feels coercive and claustrophobic: humiliation is the most vivid emotion of youth, so in memory it becomes the norm.

The movies try to turn the tables. The kids who cannot be the beautiful ones, or make out with them, or avoid being insulted by them — these are the heroes of the teen movies, the third in the trio of character types. The female outsider is usually an intellectual or an artist. (She scribbles in a diary, she draws or paints.) Physically awkward, she walks like a seal crossing a beach, and is prone to drop her books and dither in terror when she stands before a handsome boy. Her clothes, which ignore mall fashion, scandalize the social queens. Like them, she has a tongue, but she's tart and grammatical, tending toward feminist pungency and precise diction. She may mask her sense of vulnerability with sarcasm or with Plathian rue (she's stuck in the bell jar), but even when she lashes out she can't hide her craving for acceptance.

The male outsider, her friend, is usually a mass of stuttering or giggling sexual gloom: he wears shapeless clothes; he has an undeveloped body, either stringy or shrimpy; he's sometimes a Jew (in these movies, still the generic outsider). He's also brilliant, but in a morose, preoccupied way that suggests masturbatory absorption in some arcane system of knowledge. In a few special cases, the outsider is not a loser but a disengaged hipster, either saintly or satanic. (Christian Slater has played this role a couple of times.) This outsider wears black and keeps his hair long, and he knows how to please women. He sees through everything, so he's ironic by temperament and genuinely indifferent to the opinion of others—a natural aristocrat, who transcends the school's contemptible status system. There are whimsical variations on the outsider figure, too. In the recent *Rushmore*, an obnoxious teen hero, Max Fischer (Jason Schwartzman), runs the entire school: he can't pass his courses but he's a dynamo at extracurricular activities, with a knack for staging extraordinary events. He's a con man, a fund-raiser, an entrepreneur—in other words, a contemporary artist.

In fact, the entire genre, which combines self-pity and ultimate vindica-   10
tion, might be called "Portrait of the Filmmaker as a Young Nerd." Who can doubt where Hollywood's twitchy, nearsighted writers and directors ranked—or feared they ranked—on the high-school totem pole? They are still angry, though occasionally the target of their resentment goes beyond the jocks and cheerleaders of their youth. Consider this anomaly: the young actors and models on the covers of half the magazines published in this country, the shirtless men with chests like burnished shields, the girls smiling, glowing, tweezed, full-lipped, full-breasted (but not too full), and with skin so honeyed that it seems lacquered—these are the physical ideals embodied by the villains of the teen movies. The social queens and jocks, using their looks to dominate others, represent an American barbarism of beauty. Isn't it possible that the detestation of them in teen movies is a veiled strike at the entire abs-hair advertising culture, with its unobtainable glories of perfection? A critic of consumerism might even see a spark of revolt in these movies. But only a spark.

My guess is that these films arise from remembered hurts which then get recast in symbolic form. For instance, a surprising number of the outsider heroes have no mother. Mom has died or run off with another man; her child, only half loved, is ill equipped for the emotional pressures of school. The motherless child, of course, is a shrewd commercial ploy that makes a direct appeal to the members of the audience, many of whom may feel like outsiders, too, and unloved, or not loved enough, or victims of some prejudice or exclusion. But the motherless child also has powers, and will someday be a success, an artist, a screenwriter. It's the wound and the bow all over again, in cargo pants.

As the female nerd attracts the attention of the handsomest boy in the senior class, the teen movie turns into a myth of social reversal—a Cinderella fantasy. Initially, his interest in her may be part of a stunt or a trick: he is leading her on, perhaps at the urging of his queenly girlfriend. But his gaze lights her up, and we see how attractive she really is. Will she fulfill the eternal American fantasy that you can vault up the class system by removing your specs? She wants her prince, and by degrees she wins him over, not just with her looks but with her superior nature, her essential goodness. In the male version of the Cinderella trip, a few years go by, and a pale little nerd (we see him at a reunion) has become rich. All that poking around with chemicals paid off. Max Fischer, of *Rushmore*, can't miss being richer than Warhol.

So the teen movie is wildly ambivalent. It may attack the consumerist ethos that produces winners and losers, but in the end it confirms what it is attacking. The girls need the seal of approval conferred by the converted jocks; the nerds need money and a girl. Perhaps it's no surprise that the outsiders can be validated only by the people who ostracized them. But let's not be too schematic: the outsider who joins the system also modifies it, opens it up to the creative power of social mobility, makes it bend and laugh, and perhaps this turn of events is not so different from the way things work in the real world, where merit and achievement stand a good chance of trumping appearance. The irony of the Littleton shootings is that Klebold and Harris, who were both proficient computer heads, seemed to have forgotten how the plot turns out. If they had held on for a few years they might have been working at a hip software company, or have started their own business, while the jocks who oppressed them would probably have wound up selling insurance or used cars. That's the one unquestionable social truth the teen movies reflect: geeks rule.

There is, of course, a menacing subgenre, in which the desire for revenge turns bloody. Thirty-one years ago, Lindsay Anderson's semi-surrealistic *If . . .* was set in an oppressive, class-ridden English boarding school, where a group of rebellious students drive the school population out into a courtyard and open fire on them with machine guns. In Brian De Palma's 1976 masterpiece *Carrie*, the pale, repressed heroine, played by Sissy Spacek, is courted at last by a handsome boy but gets violated — doused with pig's blood — just as she is named prom queen. Stunned but far from powerless, Carrie uses her telekinetic powers to set the room afire and burn down the school. *Carrie* is the primal school movie, so wildly lurid and funny that it exploded the clichés of the genre before the genre was quite set: the heroine may be a wrathful avenger, but the movie, based on a Stephen King book, was clearly a grinning-gargoyle fantasy. So, at first, was *Heathers*, in which Christian Slater's satanic outsider turns out to be a true devil. He and his girlfriend (played by a very young Winona Ryder) begin gleefully knocking off the rich, nasty girls and the jocks, in ways so patently absurd that their revenge seems a mere wicked dream. I think it's unlikely that these movies had a direct effect on the actions of the Littleton shooters, but the two boys would surely have recognized the emotional world of *Heathers* and *Disturbing Behavior* as their own. It's a place where feelings of victimization join fantasy, and you experience the social élites as so powerful that you must either become them or kill them.

But enough. It's possible to make teen movies that go beyond these fixed polarities — insider and outsider, blond-bitch queen and hunch-shouldered nerd.

In Amy Heckerling's 1995 comedy *Clueless*, the big blonde played by Alicia Silverstone is a Rodeo Drive clotheshorse who is nonetheless possessed of extraordinary virtue. Freely dispensing advice and help, she's almost ironically good—a designing goddess with a cell phone. The movie offers a sun-shiny satire of Beverly Hills affluence, which it sees as both absurdly swollen and generous in spirit. The most original of the teen comedies, *Clueless* casts away self-pity. So does *Romy and Michele's High School Reunion* (1997), in which two gabby, lovable friends, played by Mira Sorvino and Lisa Kudrow, review the banalities of their high-school experience so knowingly that they might be criticizing the teen-movie genre itself. And easily the best American film of the year so far is Alexander Payne's *Election*, a high-school movie that inhabits a different aesthetic and moral world altogether from the rest of these pictures. *Election* shreds everyone's fantasies and illusions in a vision of high school that is bleak but supremely just. The movie's villain, an over-achieving girl (Reese Witherspoon) who runs for class president, turns out to be its covert heroine, or, at least, its most poignant character. A cross between Pat and Dick Nixon, she's a lower-middle-class striver who works like crazy and never wins anyone's love. Even when she's on top, she feels excluded. Her loneliness is produced not by malicious cliques but by her own implacable will, a condition of the spirit that may be as comical and tragic as it is mysterious. *Election* escapes all the clichés; it graduates into art.

READING THE TEXT

1. Describe in your own words the stereotypical male and female villains common in teen movies.
2. What does Denby mean by the comment, "Adolescence is the present-tense moment in American life" (para. 6)?
3. What sort of characters are typically the heroes in teen films, in Denby's view?
4. In what ways does a Cinderella fantasy inform teen films?
5. What is the "menacing subgenre" (para. 14) of teen movies?

READING THE SIGNS

1. Using Denby's description of stock character types in teen movies as your critical framework, analyze the characters in a current teen TV program, such as *The O.C.* Do you see the same conventions at work? How do you account for any differences you might see?
2. In class, brainstorm a list of current teen films. Then, using the list as evidence, write an essay in which you assess the validity of Denby's claim: "The enemy [in teen films] is not authority; the enemy is other teens and the social system that they impose on one another" (para. 5).
3. Rent a video or DVD of *American Beauty*, and write an essay in which you argue whether it can be categorized as a teen film, at least as Denby defines the genre.

4. Denby asks, "Do genre films reflect reality? Or are they merely a set of conventions that refer to other films?" (para. 4). Write an essay in which you propose your own response to these questions, using as evidence your high
school experience and specific teen films.

VICKI L. EAKLOR
Myth and Gender in Gone with the Wind

*One of the most famous movie posters of all time features Clark Gable,
as the masterful Rhett Butler, clasping in a passionate embrace a bent-
backward Vivian Leigh as Scarlett O'Hara. But as Vicki L. Eaklor points
out in this detailed analysis of gender roles in* Gone with the Wind, *the
poster's image of unqualified male dominance is dramatically undercut
by Scarlett's actual behavior — that is, her "inability and/or unwillingness to do more than feign the role of submissive wife." This complex
dynamic between the representation and the subversion of traditional
gender roles, Eaklor believes, lies at the heart of the film's enduring popularity. Eaklor (b. 1954) is a professor of history and chair of the division
of human studies at Alfred University.*

Scarlett's O'Hara's final words in *Gone with the Wind* may be the most recognizable, and quoted, in film history. Even those who haven't seen the film
know the reference, a phenomenon evidently assumed by art critic Robert
Hughes when he closed his recent eight-part video history of American art and
architecture, *American Visions*, with this of all lines.[1] That the film is "popular"
and has been literally since its premiere in December 1939 may be all too
obvious, but less clear is the meaning and sources of this popularity. My claims
are, first, that America's relationship to *Gone with the Wind* is more complex
than "popularity" suggests and might be characterized as one of love/hate —
for the subject matter, the characters, even for the film's notoriety. Second, this
love/hate relationship is rooted, I believe, in the ways in which American
myths, particularly those related to sex and gender, are both referenced and
then violated in this film, particularly in the character of Scarlett O'Hara.

What seems to bother many viewers, including critics, is that *Gone with
the Wind* is *Scarlett's* story. Typical was film critic Otis Ferguson, who wrote,
"Scarlett is too many things in too rapid succession; the exact point of her

[1] *American Visions: The History of American Art and Architecture*, volume 8: *The Age of
Anxiety*. PBS HomeVideo, 1996.

aspirations is confused; there is so much sobbing and color and DeMille display, such a mudbath of theme music, that a clean realization of character or events is out of the question."[2]

The seeming inability to understand Scarlett's character is at the heart of both the dynamics of *Gone with the Wind* and responses to it. Scarlett makes viewers uncomfortable because she exposes the underside of regional and gender myths while embodying basic American (male) values transformed (but not transplanted) during an era of drastic economic change. The central, consistent, and apparently disturbing, theme of Scarlett's ambiguous gender identity can be seen in . . . her relation to gender roles and other people. . . .

Rhett holds Scarlett, her face upturned and upper body partly exposed, in a classic pose and poster from the film. The message is clear: male dominance and female passivity, the model for heterosexual romantic love in America (and elsewhere). In Rhett's dreams, maybe, but never completely in reality, and this is precisely the point: Scarlett loses Rhett because of her inability and/or unwillingness to do more than feign the role of submissive wife. While Scarlett at times denies reality, or at least puts off thinking about it, she is the most real character in the story. Caught in America's powerful masculine/feminine gender myth, she also exposes its fallacies by violating it throughout.

Scarlett paradoxically highlights prescribed feminine virtues by serving as   5 counterpoint to them, both through her own failures in virtually every female role and in her relations with other women. Scarlett is a " 'bad' daughter, sister, wife, mother, friend, and lover" in Helen Taylor's words, while Anne Jones adds "belle" and "widow" to the list.[3] "Nurse" also comes to mind, though not then a completely feminized profession. Still, she does aspire to these roles, knowing no others, and through her shortcomings in each she is the embodiment of a strong tension not only within herself but also evident within the culture at large. This tension is manifest when messages of collective American values (career success, self-expression, and especially independence) are juxtaposed with their opposites (domesticity, self-denial, dependence) as expressed in idealized femininity.

Models of American womanhood appear in Scarlett's mother, Ellen O'Hara, and her sister-in-law, Melanie Hamilton Wilkes. Despite fine performances by Barbara O'Neill and Olivia de Havilland (respectively), neither character transcends stereotype because each is consistent with the myth, though in different ways. Ellen's two-dimensional character results from her relatively brief appearance in the film as compared to her extended treatment in the novel; in fact, the film conveys largely Scarlett's idealization of her mother

---

[2]Robert Wilson, ed., *The Film Criticism of Otis Ferguson* (Philadelphia, 1971), 297–98.

[3]Helen Taylor, *Scarlett's Women: Gone with the Wind and Its Female Fans* (New Brunswick, 1989), 106; Anne Jones, " 'The Bad Little Girl of the Good Old Days': Gender, Sex, and the Southern Social Order," in Darden Asbury Pyron, ed., *Recasting:* Gone with the Wind *in American Culture* (Miami, 1983), 107.

(not necessarily a cinematic weakness since Scarlett is the central character). Ellen dies at a crucial moment — at the war's end and before Scarlett's return to Tara — the timing of which can be interpreted as both emphasizing the necessity of Scarlett's self-sufficiency upon her homecoming and conveying the message that the ideals symbolized by Ellen, including those feminine, have become anachronistic in postbellum America.

Although Melanie, like Ellen, is stereotypically feminine, Melanie's relationship to Scarlett is more complicated, for Scarlett merely idolizes her mother but believes she hates Melanie. Typically, we see Melanie from Scarlett's perspective, which emphasizes her unconditional devotion to her loved ones (including Scarlett) and leaves viewers feeling that she is too cloyingly sweet to be credible. This is unfortunate but significant. Read another way, Melanie's goodness is a source of genuine and potentially radical sisterhood (remember, only Melanie defends prostitute Belle against other women's disdain and rejection). Perhaps her ability to love and identify with other women is too dangerous to be portrayed as believable. At any rate Melanie, like Ellen, must die, and each death serves importantly as a catalyst for change in Scarlett. Dying while pregnant, Melanie represents the ultimate Woman, while her death forces Scarlett to face psychological reality just as Scarlett's mother's death forced Scarlett to face material reality: Immediately upon Melanie's death, Scarlett recognizes Ashley's love for his wife and her own love for both Rhett and Melanie.[4]

Scarlett's inability to bond with Melanie, or with any woman in the story, reinforces the central conflict, the feminine/masculine opposition. On the one hand, this may be the only sense in which she becomes archetypically female, and as such acceptable to the culture at large: one woman against other women in competition for men. On the other hand, her total lack of female friendships places Scarlett more on the masculine than the feminine side of the indelible gender line in the culture.

If Scarlett's isolation from women is typical, though problematic in its extremity, her relations with men do not redeem her as comfortably female/feminine. Curiously, gender bending is as rampant among her men as within Scarlett herself. Her first two husbands are obvious "sissies" in the masculine/feminine lexicon: Charles Hamilton dying of pneumonia rather than like a "real" man on the battlefield . . . and that "old maid in britches" (as Scarlett says of him), Frank Kennedy.[5] She plays the dominant (presumed male) role with each of these men, reversing the culturally prescribed gender relations within marriage and rendering herself objectionable to many viewers.

[4]These relationships in the novel are also noted in Charles Rowan, "Gone with the Wind, and Good Riddance," *Southwest Review*, vol. 78, no. 3 (1993), 377, e.g. (published two years after my original draft was written), and discussed in Freudian terms in Elizabeth Fox-Genovese, "Scarlett O'Hara: The Southern Lady as New Woman," *American Quarterly*, 33 (Fall, 1981), especially 405–6.

[5]A broader and relevant discussion of male types in film is the chapter, "Who's a Sissy?" in Vito Russo, *The Celluloid Closet: Homosexuality in the Movies*, rev. ed. (New York, 1987), 3–59.

Rhett and Scarlett.

The most interesting character in this context is Ashley. While Scarlett is   10
a masculine woman, he is a feminine man. His relationship with Melanie,
despite her two pregnancies, appears more cerebral than sexual; they are
kindred spirits who "understand each other," in Ashley's words. Luckily, they
produce a male heir, relieving both of the duty to procreate, and the film
implies that Melanie's second pregnancy results more from her impulses
toward motherhood than Ashley's toward her. Ashley, in fact, personifies what
American society has understood, in a stereotypical way, as latent homosexuality.[6]

This possible reading underscores my theme. *Gone with the Wind*, I am
arguing, not only strikes chords with its viewers but also touches some nerves,
particularly those of gender. Homosexuality, particularly in its perceived challenge to gender conformity, is apparently the rawest nerve of all in our culture, perhaps because it represents the ultimate violation of comfortable and
orderly identity in a heterosexist society. I agree, therefore, with Theodore
Roszak's concise summary of thirty years ago, and I emphasize the relevance
of his observation for understanding both the film and discomfort with it:
"Deeper down than we are rich or poor, black or white, we are he or she. This
is the last ditch of our socially prescribed identity . . . the one line of our psychic defense we dare not surrender."[7]

[6]Interestingly, Anne Edwards noted that a possible model for Ashley in Margaret
Mitchell's life, Clifford Henry, may have had "homosexual tendencies." Anne Edwards, *Road to
Tara: The Life of Margaret Mitchell* (New York, 1983), 54.

[7]Theodore Roszak, "The Hard and the Soft: The Force of Feminism in Modern Times," in
Betty Roszak and Theodore Roszak, eds., *Masculine/Feminine Readings in Sexual Mythology and
the Liberation of Women* (New York, 1969), 94.

What Scarlett sees in Ashley remains a mystery throughout, especially because she despises stereotypically feminine traits in everyone else, including other women. This mystery is encouraged by the film's dynamics because it offers Rhett as the perfect match for Scarlett and suggests that her inability to reconcile herself to this match underscores her failures as a woman. Further, Rhett and Ashley are not merely different: they represent opposite ends of the masculinity continuum as our society defines it (Taylor called them "the king and the wimp"[8]). The most vivid image of this antithesis is Rhett carrying the wounded Ashley to bed to receive treatment. It is tempting to suggest the encoding of a pseudo-Freudian message: Scarlett the girl fell in love with Ashley and Scarlett the woman supposedly loved Rhett, implying that as she reached maturity she recognized and desired him who could dominate her "properly." Perhaps this reading stretches the point (although Rhett himself tells her he's waiting for her to "grow up" and get Ashley out of her mind), but the film's equation throughout is that *masculinity =ability* and *willingness to dominate a woman =sexual attractiveness.* Correspondingly, the stronger or more independent (read masculine) the woman, the more masculine the man required to conquer her. Clearly Ashley (and Charles and Frank) will not do.

However, a parallel reading complicates the picture while making a certain kind of sense. If, as I assert, Scarlett embodies masculine ideals housed in a female form, her desire for both Rhett and Ashley achieves a balance. Scarlett mediates between Rhett (the masculine) and Ashley (the feminine). Similarly, Ashley mediates between Melanie (the feminine) and Scarlett (the masculine). This dualistic pattern produces two gender balances among the four characters, but only in two groups of three, and notably with Scarlett and Ashley, the most ambivalent sexually, at the center of each opposition.

Such a configuration suggests that the coupling of Ashley and Scarlett would achieve a balance after all. This violates the myth in two related ways, however. First, it would imply that we should have trusted Scarlett's instincts over those of everyone around her, including Ashley's; that women just might be capable of discerning what they want or need. Second and more important, that pairing would have completely disrupted the male-dominant/female-submissive dynamic at the very core of the myth of "right" heterosexual relations in our culture. When Scarlett discovers at the movie's end both her love for Rhett and her illusionary concept of Ashley, she finally validates the only masculine-feminine paradigm considered acceptable.

The epitome of the myth is the romance of Scarlett and Rhett, the central 15 relationship that exposes the seams tenuously holding the fabric of the myth together. The more one looks at their interactions, the more predictable is Rhett's departure — even a relief — and the more apparent is the fact that the roots of their differences lay as much in institutionalized gender roles as in the characters' specific personalities. As it turns out, each tragically wants

[8]Taylor, *Scarlett's Women,* 109–39.

from the union precisely that which s/he cannot have: for Rhett, complete control; for Scarlett, independence with security.

If Rhett failed to achieve his goals, at least his more nearly correspond to both the myth of romance and the reality of nineteenth-century marriage. From the moment he sees Scarlett at the Twelve Oaks barbecue, she becomes his quarry; thereafter, themes of pursuit, dominance, and force characterize their entire history. After their first unfortunate encounter in the Wilkes's library, Rhett appears in Atlanta as a swashbuckling blockade-runner, and successfully bids for Scarlett at a benefit dance. She accepts, of course, but Rhett wields the power (and money!) to control their situation. This control, not to mention its relation to economics and gender, underlies their ups and downs. Visiting Scarlett a bit later, for example, Rhett refuses to kiss her, saying, "No, I don't think I will kiss you, although you need kissing badly. That's what's wrong with you. You should be kissed and often, by someone who knows how." Clearly we are now meant to see Scarlett through Rhett's eyes, and agree that the cure for her or any other woman's presumed maladjustment is the right man to dominate her. After the death of Scarlett's second husband, Scarlett visits Rhett and they kiss. He says, "This is what you were meant for. None of the fools you've ever known has kissed you like this, has he? Not Charles or your Frank or your stupid Ashley." Consistently, even Rhett's marriage proposal reeks of coercion, as he tells the drunken Scarlett to "Say yes, say yes" amid more kissing.

Once one realizes that Rhett's need to dominate Scarlett pervades their every encounter, the infamous (apparent) rape scene, potentially so offensive from a feminist perspective, becomes less eventful though no less disturbing. Initially having asked myself if what occurred upstairs was really a rape, I now believe this question to be less relevant than two related observations. First, the entire relationship, modeled on rape as it is, renders that one scene more symbolic than offensive reality. Second, this Rhett/Scarlett relationship, with rape as its dynamic model, portrays for viewers the prototypical romance, leading to the logical and dangerous conclusion that romance and rape are indistinguishable. Scarlett's high spirits in the morning-after scene, apparently denoting satisfaction, reinforce both this view of romance/rape and the corresponding myth that women, despite their protests, want and need to be conquered.[9]

[9]The results of this mythology are very much apparent in the seeming epidemics of date rape and domestic violence which, like the film, demand a more sophisticated approach to understanding heterosexual dynamics than simply attempting to fix blame. Scarlett's ambivalent reactions to Rhett's aggression are all too believable, though still objectionable from a feminist standpoint; that she might even think she had to be forced into sex or generally dominated by a man is part of the overall tension here and accurately reflects attitudes consistent with her time, class, and religion (that "virtue" and sexual desire were mutually exclusive, for example). My reading, of this scene and the issue, has been influenced in particular by the view summarized by Dianne F. Herman, "The Rape Culture," in Jo Freeman, ed., *Women: A Feminist Perspective*, 4th ed. (Mountain View, CA, 1989), 20–44 (and see her sources also, especially Brownmiller). It parallels that of Ellen Willis, " 'War!' Said Scarlett. 'Don't You Men Think about Anything Important?' " in Philip Nobile, ed., *Favorite Movies: Critics' Choice* (New York, 1973), 194, and those cited by Taylor, *Scarlett's Women*, 131–32; see also Taylor, 129–37, for her correspondents' reactions, and Molly Haskell, *From Reverence to Rape: The Treatment of Women in the Movies* (New York, 1973), 166–67.

Ultimately, the scene epitomizes the difference between male and female power as manifested in the traditional American marriage. On the one hand, so-called female power is paradoxical. Whatever control Scarlett has over Rhett is sexual in origin and passive in implementation; one of the few ways she can wield her power is to deny him. Rhett's power, on the other hand, is institutionalized, particularly through his complete legal right to Scarlett's body as well as her property. Besides the previous examples, after their daughter Bonnie's birth, Scarlett informs Rhett (albeit euphemistically) that she won't be risking pregnancy with him anymore. In quick succession, he names the options his power provides: He asks, "and do you know I can divorce you for this?"; tells her "I'll find comfort elsewhere"; and finally, when she threatens to lock the door, he kicks it in, saying, "If I wanted to come in, no lock could keep me out."

This male power, so integral to the romantic myth, extends conveniently over other women as well (Belle, the local prostitute, is also at Rhett's disposal, also for a price) but within strictly drawn class and racial lines (the male always must be of the dominant class/race, doubling his power). Thus, when Rhett uses force, he is viewed as romantic, but when males outside the ruling class threaten the same (a Yankee scavenger at Tara and later the Shantytown drunks who challenge Scarlett), the picture changes. And of course, protecting the honor of "their women" supposedly justified the racist/classist terrorism visited on Shantytown which got Frank Kennedy killed and Ashley wounded.[10]

Importantly, Rhett's power derives from wealth (and race) as well as gender, rendering the Butler marriage prototypical also in an economic sense. This power configuration leads to two notions of marriage as entirely different as the power behind them: his (sex, fun, control) and hers (romance, economic security). Scarlett's concept of the institution is all too practical for many viewers, perhaps, as she woos Frank Kennedy for the taxes on Tara after failing to get them from Rhett. Later, after the death of Frank, she agrees to marry Rhett because of his wealth:

RHETT: Did you say yes because of my money?
SCARLETT: Well . . . yes, partly.
RHETT: Partly?
SCARLETT: Well, you know, Rhett, money does help, and, of course, I *am* fond of you.
RHETT: Fond of me?
SCARLETT: Well, if I said I was madly in love with you, you'd *know* I was lying.

---

[10]My focus on gender has superseded an extended race/class analysis, but I am not suggesting that race and class are unimportant categories in the film, particularly as they could be applied to Scarlett's relationships to Mammy and Prissy as well as to the African American males and lower-class Euroamericans around her. Certainly the racism and classism of the film's perspective — not just that depicted in it from Scarlett's era — have been legitimate sources of objection and critical opposition, and part of the general ambivalence toward the film that I believe merely adds to its notoriety.

Whether or not her candor renders Scarlett likable, it reflects the reality that marriage, for women, has been the designated route to economic stability. When Scarlett confronts viewers with this truth, she tears through the thin lining of the romantic myth to expose a thick and less attractive layer of necessary materialism.

Unfortunately for Rhett, he accepts Scarlett's terms and embarks upon his own lost cause. His loving commitment to her is truly a "fatal attraction" because he is simultaneously drawn both to those qualities in her he cannot conquer *and* to the idea of conquering them. Further, if those qualities are male then the enterprise becomes as much a contest between masculinities as between male and female, perhaps rendering victory all the more essential to Rhett. While he repeatedly and successfully uses force, his real aim is Scarlett's willing and total submission. Indeed what Rhett wants — even specifies in his departing monologue — is a "little girl" like deceased daughter Bonnie, whom he can "pet" and "spoil." The comparison is meaningful, for his speech reveals that no difference exists in his mind between the husband-wife and father-daughter relation, the key dynamic of which is again male control and female powerlessness.

The confusion of gender identity and roles within the character of Scarlett has generated commentary on the novel also. Both Anne Edwards and Elizabeth Fox-Genovese, for example, have noted parallels between Margaret Mitchell and Scarlett in apparent sexual/gender "confusion."[11] Fox-Genovese stated that such "ambivalence" reaches "schizophrenic proportions" in Mitchell's "play with transsexual identifications."[12] In addition, both writers have linked this confusion to Mitchell's era (b. 1900) and the phenomenon of the "new woman" of her adulthood.[13]

Conspicuously absent in the critical literature, however, is specific reference to homosexuality, itself a relatively new concept in the age of the "New Woman." Am I trying to bring Scarlett (and/or Mitchell) into the lesbian fold? Yes and no. "Lesbian," we are discovering, is a complicated word and as dependent for its meaning on the complex interactions of cultural structures, institutions, and attitudes as on simplistic notions of who seems to desire whom. Christina Simmons, for example, examined the "fear of lesbianism" in the 1920s and 1930s (Mitchell's era, it should be noted) and assigned a symbolic as well as literal (sexual) meaning to the lesbian identity: ". . . lesbianism represented women's autonomy in various forms — feminism, careers, refusal to marry, failure to adjust to marital sexuality."[14] Scarlett, of course, thinks she loves and desires men (Ashley, Rhett) though at times she appears incapable of

---

[11] Edwards, *Road,* 54, 72.

[12] Fox-Genovese, "Scarlett O'Hara," 400, 408.

[13] Fox-Genovese, "Scarlett O'Hara," passim; Edwards, *Road,* 72–73.

[14] Christina Simmons, "Companionate Marriage and the Lesbian Threat," *Frontiers,* vol. 4, no. 3, p. 58, and see her notes. The latter failure, incidentally, is attributed to Mitchell by Edwards in *Road,* 117.

loving anyone but herself. Here the options available to a woman of her time, place, and personality must be considered. When she does not respond positively to Melanie's affection (as when Melanie calls them "two sisters"), Scarlett denies herself a potential intimate friendship and in so doing leaves herself the choices of either heterosexual marriage or standing alone — the perennial dichotomy in a heterosexist society. At film's end, Scarlett is alone, all her marriages having failed (the others were loveless and passionless, after all). If viewers sympathetic to such sisterhood could set aside the myth, they might hope that Scarlett would set her sights on female companionship rather than on Rhett's. But this, of course, cannot be: as a representation of female autonomy, a lesbian in the political sense only, she is problematic enough for her audiences.[15]

A great strength of the film is the ending. Nothing less than the optimism 25 Scarlett evokes would be as attractive to an American audience, while her determination to face the future by returning to the past is equally attuned to the national mentality. The question of who or what triumphs at the end is sometimes raised and often answered in terms of an old/new dichotomy.[16] I say something older indeed prevails: the romantic myth in its personification, Scarlett.

This myth, as I have argued throughout, defines romance as male dominance and female submission. Additional traditions, such as that of rugged individualism and the American ambivalence over agrarian virtues versus urban and technological progress, serve to complicate further an already gendered situation because those traditions have been implicitly male-oriented. But Scarlett's apparent desire to get Rhett back verifies her femininity, and with it the myth; however ambiguous she has repeatedly appeared, however unacceptable she has been as a female in her self-serving individualism, she is redeemed at last by her belief that her happiness is rooted in emotional dependence on a man.

Just as the film's plot replicates power relationships rooted in gender, so does the history of its making and its reception, raising the issue of how many (and what kind of) "gazes" are responsible for the final product, not to mention the decades of commentary.[17] My reading suggests the film contains a complex mixture of male and female perspectives (as our society has defined them); however, in the end, in both the film (in the form of Scarlett's professed

---

[15] I have scratched only the surface of the topic of gender and sexuality and of the ongoing debate in queer theory over "social constructionism" vs. "essentialism." See Vicki L. Eaklor, "Learning from History: A Queer Problem," *Journal of Gay, Lesbian, and Bisexual Identity*, Vol. 3, No. 3 (July, 1998), 196–97, for a brief explanation.

[16] Jones, "Bad Little Girl," 115; Fox-Genovese, "Scarlett O'Hara," 397.

[17] The concept of a "male gaze" has been discussed in feminist art and film theory since the mid-1970s and refers to the predominantly male perspective that has informed visual productions. See Laura Mulvey, "Visual Pleasure and Narrative Cinema," *Screen*, 16 (1975), 6–18; and Ann E. Kaplan, *Women and Film: Both Sides of the Camera* (New York, 1983).

desire for Rhett) and its saga (in the reviews arguing love-it-as-entertainment/ hate-it-as-art), the male gaze wins. So far.

If the day comes when every institution is not dominated by masculine values and traits, when women's experiences are taken as seriously as men's, when portrayal of those experiences unhesitatingly is considered art, paradoxically *Gone with the Wind* will lose and gain status: Its role as purveyor of the romantic myth will be of historic interest only, while its astute exposure of women's dilemmas and choices will place it even more firmly inside that canon reserved for "great" films. In losing the tension that underlies its popularity, then, its status may actually shift from "popular" to "art" film and, also paradoxically, it may generate less discussion. But all this is speculation and anything could happen. "After all, tomorrow . . ."

READING THE TEXT

1. Why does Eaklor believe that viewers of *Gone with the Wind* have a "love/hate" relationship with the film?
2. Summarize in your own words how, in Eaklor's view, Scarlett O'Hara both embodies and subverts traditional female gender roles.
3. How does Rhett Butler represent male power?
4. How does Eaklor interpret the infamous rape scene?
5. According to Eaklor, what role does homosexuality play in the film?

READING THE SIGNS

1. Write an essay in which you respond to Eaklor's assertion that "Scarlett embodies masculine ideals housed in a female form" (para. 13). If you support this claim, be sure to advance evidence beyond that which she provides; if you oppose it, explain how her interpretations may be problematic.
2. Watch a video or DVD of *Gone with the Wind*, and support, refute, or modify Eaklor's claim that "Rhett and Ashley are not merely different: they represent opposite ends of the masculinity continuum as our society defines it" (para. 12).
3. Interview some fans of *Gone with the Wind*, focusing on their perception of gender roles in the film. Use your results as evidence to demonstrate, refute, or complicate Eaklor's claim that Americans have a "love/hate" relationship with the film.
4. Read or review Robert B. Ray's "The Thematic Paradigm" (p. 308), and then write an essay arguing whether you think Scarlett O'Hara can be considered a "hero" — and if so, specifying which type of hero, according to Ray's taxonomy.

JESSICA HAGEDORN

Asian Women in Film: No Joy, No Luck

Why do movies always seem to portray Asian women as tragic victims of history and fate? Jessica Hagedorn (b. 1949) asks in this essay, which originally appeared in Ms. *Even such movies as* The Joy Luck Club, *based on Amy Tan's breakthrough novel that elevated Asian American fiction to bestseller status, reinforce old stereotypes of the powerlessness of Asian and Asian American women. A screenwriter and novelist, Hagedorn calls for a different kind of storytelling that would show Asian women as powerful controllers of their own destinies. Hagedorn's publications include the novels* Dogeaters *(1990),* The Gangster of Love *(1996), and* Dream Jungle *(2001);* Danger and Beauty *(1993), a collection of poems;* Charlie Chan Is Dead: An Anthology of Contemporary Asian American Fiction *(1993); and* Fresh Kill *(1994), a screenplay.*

Pearl of the Orient. Whore. Geisha. Concubine. Whore. Hostess. Bar Girl. Mama-san. Whore. China Doll. Tokyo Rose. Whore. Butterfly. Whore. Miss Saigon. Whore. Dragon Lady. Lotus Blossom. Gook. Whore. Yellow Peril. Whore. Bangkok Bombshell. Whore. Hospitality Girl. Whore. Comfort Woman. Whore. Savage. Whore. Sultry. Whore. Faceless. Whore. Porcelain. Whore. Demure. Whore. Virgin. Whore. Mute. Whore. Model Minority. Whore. Victim. Whore. Woman Warrior. Whore. Mail-Order Bride. Whore. Mother. Wife. Lover. Daughter. Sister.

As I was growing up in the Philippines in the 1950s, my fertile imagination was colonized by thoroughly American fantasies. Yellowface variations on the exotic erotic loomed larger than life on the silver screen. I was mystified and enthralled by Hollywood's skewed representations of Asian women: sleek, evil goddesses with slanted eyes and cunning ways, or smiling, sarong-clad South Seas "maidens" with undulating hips, kinky black hair, and white skin darkened by makeup. Hardly any of the "Asian" characters were played by Asians. White actors like Sidney Toler and Warner Oland played "inscrutable Oriental detective" Charlie Chan with taped eyelids and a singsong, chop suey accent. Jennifer Jones was a Eurasian doctor swept up in a doomed "interracial romance" in *Love Is a Many Splendored Thing.* In my mother's youth, white actor Luise Rainer played the central role of the Patient Chinese Wife in the 1937 film adaptation of Pearl Buck's novel *The Good Earth.* Back then, not many thought to ask why; they were all too busy being grateful to see anyone in the movies remotely like themselves.

Cut to 1960: *The World of Suzie Wong,* another tragic East/West affair. I am now old enough to be impressed. Sexy, sassy Suzie (played by Nancy Kwan) works out of a bar patronized by white sailors, but doesn't seem bothered by any of it. For a hardworking girl turning nightly tricks to support her baby, she manages to parade an astonishing wardrobe in damn near every scene, down to matching handbags and shoes. The sailors are also strictly Hollywood, sanitized and not too menacing. Suzie and all the other prostitutes in this movie are cute, giggling, dancing sex machines with hearts of gold. William Holden plays an earnest, rather prim, Nice Guy painter seeking inspiration in The Other. Of course, Suzie falls madly in love with him. Typically, she tells him, "I not important," and "I'll be with you until you say — Suzie, go away." She also thinks being beaten by a man is a sign of true passion and is terribly disappointed when Mr. Nice Guy refuses to show his true feelings.

Next in Kwan's short-lived but memorable career was the kitschy 1961 musical *Flower Drum Song*, which, like *Suzie Wong*, is a thoroughly American commercial product. The female roles are typical of Hollywood musicals of the times: women are basically airheads, subservient to men. Kwan's counterpart is the Good Chinese Girl, played by Miyoshi Umeki, who was better playing the Loyal Japanese Girl in that other classic Hollywood tale of forbidden love, *Sayonara*. Remember? Umeki was so loyal, she committed double suicide with actor Red Buttons. I instinctively hated *Sayonara* when I first saw it as a child; now I understand why. Contrived tragic resolutions were the only way Hollywood got past the censors in those days. With one or two exceptions, somebody in these movies always had to die to pay for breaking racial and sexual taboos.

Until the recent onslaught of films by both Asian and Asian American filmmakers, Asian Pacific women have generally been perceived by Hollywood with a mixture of fascination, fear, and contempt. Most Hollywood movies either trivialize or exoticize us as people of color and as women. Our intelligence is underestimated, our humanity overlooked, and our diverse cultures treated as interchangeable. If we are "good," we are childlike, submissive, silent, and eager for sex (see France Nuyen's glowing performance as Liat in the film version of *South Pacific*) or else we are tragic victim types (see *Casualties of War*, Brian De Palma's graphic 1989 drama set in Vietnam). And if we are not silent, suffering doormats, we are demonized dragon ladies — cunning, deceitful, sexual provocateurs. Give me the demonic any day — Anna May Wong as a villain slithering around in a slinky gown is at least gratifying to watch, neither servile nor passive. And she steals the show from Marlene Dietrich in Josef von Sternberg's *Shanghai Express*. From the 1920s through the 1930s, Wong was our only female "star." But even she was trapped in limited roles, in what filmmaker Renee Tajima has called the dragon lady/lotus blossom dichotomy.

Cut to 1985: There is a scene toward the end of the terribly dishonest but weirdly compelling Michael Cimino movie *Year of the Dragon* (cowritten by Oliver Stone) that is one of my favorite twisted movie moments of all time. If you ask a lot of my friends who've seen that movie (especially if they're Asian), it's one of their favorites too. The setting is a crowded Chinatown

Michelle Yeoh, *Tomorrow Never Dies*, 1997.

nightclub. There are two very young and very tough Jade Cobra gang girls in a shoot-out with Mickey Rourke, in the role of a demented Polish American cop who, in spite of being Mr. Ugly in the flesh — an arrogant, misogynistic bully devoid of any charm — wins the "good" Asian American anchorwoman in the film's absurd and implausible ending. This is a movie with an actual disclaimer as its lead-in, covering its ass in advance in response to anticipated complaints about "stereotypes."

My pleasure in the hard-edged power of the Chinatown gang girls in *Year of the Dragon* is my small revenge, the answer to all those Suzie Wong "I want to be your slave" female characters. The Jade Cobra girls are mere background to the white male foreground/focus of Cimino's movie. But long after the movie has faded into video-rental heaven, the Jade Cobra girls remain defiant, fabulous images in my memory, flaunting tight metallic dresses and spiky cock's-comb hairdos streaked electric red and blue.

Mickey Rourke looks down with world-weary pity at the unnamed Jade Cobra girl (Doreen Chan) he's just shot who lies sprawled and bleeding on the street: "You look like you're gonna die, beautiful."

JADE COBRA GIRL: "Oh yeah? [blood gushing from her mouth] I'm proud of it."

ROURKE: "You are? You got anything you wanna tell me before you go, sweetheart?"

JADE COBRA GIRL: "Yeah. [pause] Fuck you."

Cut to 1993: I've been told that like many New Yorkers, I watch movies with the right side of my brain on perpetual overdrive. I admit to being grouchy and overcritical, suspicious of sentiment, and cynical. When a critic like Richard Corliss of *Time* magazine gushes about *The Joy Luck Club* being "a fourfold

Terms of Endearment," my gut instinct is to run the other way. I resent being told how to feel. I went to see the 1993 eight-handkerchief movie version of Amy Tan's bestseller with a group that included my ten-year-old daughter. I was caught between the sincere desire to be swept up by the turbulent mother-daughter sagas and my own stubborn resistance to being so obviously manipulated by the filmmakers. With every flashback came tragedy. The music soared; the voice-overs were solemn or wistful; tears, tears, and more tears flowed onscreen. Daughters were reverent; mothers carried dark secrets.

I was elated by the grandness and strength of the four mothers and the luminous actors who portrayed them, but I was uneasy with the passivity of the Asian American daughters. They seemed to exist solely as receptors for their mothers' amazing life stories. It's almost as if by assimilating so easily into American society, they had lost all sense of self.

In spite of my resistance, my eyes watered as the desperate mother played   10
by Kieu Chinh was forced to abandon her twin baby girls on a country road in war-torn China. (Kieu Chinh resembles my own mother and her twin sister, who suffered through the brutal Japanese occupation of the Philippines.) So far in this movie, an infant son had been deliberately drowned, a mother played by the gravely beautiful France Nuyen had gone catatonic with grief, a concubine had cut her flesh open to save her dying mother, an insecure daughter had been oppressed by her boorish Asian American husband, another insecure daughter had been left by her white husband, and so on. . . . The overall effect was numbing as far as I'm concerned, but a man sitting two rows in front of us broke down sobbing. A Chinese Filipino writer even more grouchy than me later complained, "Must ethnicity only be equated with suffering?"

Because change has been slow, *The Joy Luck Club* carries a lot of cultural baggage. It is a big-budget story about Chinese American women, directed by a Chinese American man, cowritten and coproduced by Chinese American women. That's a lot to be thankful for. And its box office success proves that an immigrant narrative told from female perspectives can have mass appeal. But my cynical side tells me that its success might mean only one thing in Hollywood: more weepy epics about Asian American mother-daughter relationships will be planned.

That the film finally got made was significant. By Hollywood standards (think white male; think money, money, money), a movie about Asian Americans even when adapted from a bestseller was a risky proposition. When I asked a producer I know about the film's rumored delays, he simply said, "It's still an *Asian* movie," surprised I had even asked. Equally interesting was director Wayne Wang's initial reluctance to be involved in the project; he told the *New York Times*, "I didn't want to do another Chinese movie."

Maybe he shouldn't have worried so much. After all, according to the media, the nineties are the decade of "Pacific Overtures" and East Asian chic. Madonna, the pop queen of shameless appropriation, cultivated Japanese high-tech style with her music video "Rain," while Janet Jackson faked kitschy orientalia in hers, titled "If." Critical attention was paid to movies from China,

Japan, and Vietnam. But that didn't mean an honest appraisal of women's lives. Even on the art house circuit, filmmakers who should know better took the easy way out. Takehiro Nakajima's 1992 film *Okoge* presents one of the more original film roles for women in recent years. In Japanese, "okoge" means the crust of rice that sticks to the bottom of the rice pot; in pejorative slang, it means fag hag. The way "okoge" is used in the film seems a reappropriation of the term; the portrait Nakajima creates of Sayoko, the so-called fag hag, is clearly an affectionate one. Sayoko is a quirky, self-assured woman in contemporary Tokyo who does voice-overs for cartoons, has a thing for Frida Kahlo paintings, and is drawn to a gentle young gay man named Goh. But the other women's roles are disappointing, stereotypical "hysterical females" and the movie itself turns conventional halfway through. Sayoko sacrifices herself to a macho brute Goh desires, who rapes her as images of Frida Kahlo paintings and her beloved Goh rising from the ocean flash before her. She gives birth to a baby boy and endures a terrible life of poverty with the abusive rapist. This sudden change from spunky survivor to helpless, victimized woman is baffling. Whatever happened to her job? Or that arty little apartment of hers? Didn't her Frida Kahlo obsession teach her anything?

Then there was Tiana Thi Thanh Nga's *From Hollywood to Hanoi,* a self-serving but fascinating documentary. Born in Vietnam to a privileged family that included an uncle who was defense minister in the Thieu government and an idolized father who served as press minister, Nga (a.k.a. Tiana) spent her adolescence in California. A former actor in martial arts movies and fitness teacher ("Karaticize with Tiana"), the vivacious Tiana decided to make a record of her journey back to Vietnam.

From Hollywood to Hanoi is at times unintentionally very funny. Tiana 15 includes a quick scene of herself dancing with a white man at the Metropole hotel in Hanoi, and breathlessly announces: "That's me doing the tango with Oliver Stone!" Then she listens sympathetically to a horrifying account of the My Lai massacre by one of its few female survivors. In another scene, Tiana cheerfully addresses a food vendor on the streets of Hanoi: "Your hairdo is so pretty." The unimpressed, poker-faced woman gives a brusque, deadpan reply: "You want to eat, or what?" Sometimes it is hard to tell the difference between Tiana Thi Thanh Nga and her Hollywood persona: the real Tiana still seems to be playing one of her B-movie roles, which are mainly fun because they're fantasy. The time was certainly right to explore postwar Vietnam from a Vietnamese woman's perspective; it's too bad this film was done by a Valley Girl.

Nineteen ninety-three also brought Tran Anh Hung's *The Scent of Green Papaya*, a different kind of Vietnamese memento — this is a look back at the peaceful, lush country of the director's childhood memories. The film opens in Saigon, in 1951. A willowy ten-year-old girl named Mui comes to work for a troubled family headed by a melancholy musician and his kind, stoic wife. The men of this bourgeois household are idle, pampered types who take naps while the women do all the work. Mui is male fantasy: she is a devoted servant, enduring acts of cruel mischief with patience and dignity; as an adult, she barely speaks. She scrubs floors, shines shoes, and cooks with loving care and never a complaint. When she is sent off to work for another wealthy musician, she ends up being impregnated by him. The movie ends as the camera closes in on Mui's contented face. Languid and precious, *The Scent of Green Papaya* is visually haunting, but it suffers from the director's colonial fantasy of women as docile, domestic creatures. Steeped in highbrow nostalgia, it's the arty Vietnamese version of *My Fair Lady* with the wealthy musician as Professor Higgins, teaching Mui to read and write.

And then there is Ang Lee's tepid 1993 hit, *The Wedding Banquet* — a clever culture-clash farce in which traditional Chinese values collide with contemporary American sexual mores. The somewhat formulaic plot goes like this: Wai-Tung, a yuppie landlord, lives with his white lover, Simon, in a chic Manhattan brownstone. Wai-Tung is an only child and his aging parents in Taiwan long for a grandchild to continue the family legacy. Enter Wei-Wei, an artist who lives in a grungy loft owned by Wai-Tung. She slugs tequila straight from the bottle as she paints and flirts boldly with her young, uptight landlord, who brushes her off. "It's my fate. I am always attracted to handsome gay men," she mutters. After this setup, the movie goes downhill, all edges blurred in a cozy nest of happy endings. In a refrain of Sayoko's plight in *Okoge*, a pregnant, suddenly complacent Wei-Wei gives in to family pressures — and never gets her life back.

"It takes a man to know what it is to be a real woman."

—Song Liling in *M. Butterfly*

Ironically, two gender-bending films in which men play men playing women reveal more about the mythology of the prized Asian woman and the superficial trappings of gender than most movies that star real women. The slow-moving *M. Butterfly* presents the ultimate object of Western male desire as the spy/opera

Anna May Wong.

diva Song Liling, a Suzie Wong/Lotus Blossom played by actor John Lone with a five o'clock shadow and bobbing Adam's apple. The best and most profound of these forays into cross-dressing is the spectacular melodrama *Farewell My Concubine*, directed by Chen Kaige. Banned in China, *Farewell My Concubine* shared the prize for Best Film at the 1993 Cannes Film Festival with Jane Campion's *The Piano*. Sweeping through 50 years of tumultuous history in China, the story revolves around the lives of two male Beijing Opera stars and the woman who marries one of them. The three characters make an unforgettable triangle, struggling over love, art, friendship, and politics against the bloody backdrop of cultural upheaval. They are as capable of casually betraying each other as they are of selfless, heroic acts. The androgynous Dieyi, doomed to play the same female role of concubine over and over again, is portrayed with great vulnerability, wit, and grace by male Hong Kong pop star Leslie Cheung. Dieyi competes with the prostitute Juxian (Gong Li) for the love of his childhood protector and fellow opera star, Duan Xiaolou (Zhang Fengyi).

Cheung's highly stylized performance as the classic concubine-ready-to-die-for-love in the opera within the movie is all about female artifice. His side-long glances, restrained passion, languid stance, small steps, and delicate, refined gestures say everything about what is considered desirable in Asian women — and are the antithesis of the feisty, outspoken woman played by Gong Li. The characters of Dieyi and Juxian both see suffering as part and parcel of love and life. Juxian matter-of-factly says to Duan Xiaolou before he agrees to marry her: "I'm used to hardship. If you take me in, I'll wait on you hand and foot. If you tire of me, I'll . . . kill myself. No big deal." It's an echo of Suzie Wong's servility, but the context is new. Even with her back to the wall, Juxian is not helpless or whiny. She attempts to manipulate a man while admitting to the harsh reality that is her life.

Dieyi and Juxian are the two sides of the truth of women's lives in most 20 Asian countries. Juxian in particular — wife and ex-prostitute — could be seen as a thankless and stereotypical role. But like the characters Gong Li has played in Chinese director Zhang Yimou's films, *Red Sorghum*, *Raise the Red Lantern*, and especially *The Story of Qiu Ju*, Juxian is tough, obstinate, sensual, clever, oafish, beautiful, infuriating, cowardly, heroic, and banal. Above all, she is resilient. Gong Li is one of the few Asian Pacific actors whose roles have been drawn with intelligence, honesty, and depth. Nevertheless, the characters she plays are limited by the possibilities that exist for real women in China.

"Let's face it. Women still don't mean shit in China," my friend Meeling reminds me. What she says so bluntly about her culture rings painfully true, but in less obvious fashion for me. In the Philippines, infant girls aren't drowned, nor were their feet bound to make them more desirable. But sons were and are cherished. To this day, men of the bourgeois class are coddled and prized, much like the spoiled men of the elite household in *The Scent of Green Papaya*. We do not have a geisha tradition like Japan, but physical beauty is overtreasured. Our daughters are protected virgins or primed as potential beauty queens. And many of us have bought into the image of the white man as our handsome savior: G.I. Joe.

Buzz magazine recently featured an article entitled "Asian Women/L.A. Men," a report on a popular hangout that caters to white men's fantasies of nubile Thai women. The lines between movies and real life are blurred. Male screenwriters and cinematographers flock to this bar-restaurant, where the waitresses are eager to "audition" for roles. Many of these men have been to Bangkok while working on film crews for Vietnam War movies. They've come back to L.A., but for them, the movie never ends. In this particular fantasy the boys play G.I. Joe on a rescue mission in the urban jungle, saving the whore from herself. "A scene has developed here, a kind of R-rated *Cheers*," author Alan Rifkin writes. "The waitresses audition for sitcoms. The customers date the waitresses or just keep score."

Colonization of the imagination is a two-way street. And being enshrined on a pedestal as someone's Pearl of the Orient fantasy doesn't seem so demeaning, at first; who wouldn't want to be worshipped? Perhaps that's why Asian women are the ultimate wet dream in most Hollywood movies; it's no secret how well we've been taught to play the role, to take care of our men. In Hollywood vehicles, we are objects of desire or derision; we exist to provide sex, color, and texture in what is essentially a white man's world. It is akin to what Toni Morrison calls "the Africanist presence" in literature. She writes: "Just as entertainers, through or by association with blackface, could render permissible topics that otherwise would have been taboo, so American writers were able to employ an imagined Africanist persona to articulate and imaginatively act out the forbidden in American culture." The same analogy could be made for the often titillating presence of Asian women in movies made by white men.

Movies are still the most seductive and powerful of artistic mediums, manipulating us with ease by a powerful combination of sound and image. In many ways, as females and Asians, as audiences or performers, we have learned to settle for less — to accept the fact that we are either decorative, invisible, or one-dimensional. When there are characters who look like us represented in a movie, we have also learned to view between the lines, or to add what is missing. For many of us, this way of watching has always been a necessity. We fill in the gaps. If a female character is presented as a mute, willowy beauty, we convince ourselves she is an ancestral ghost — so smart she doesn't have to speak at all. If she is a whore with a heart of gold, we claim her as a tough feminist icon. If she is a sexless, sanitized, boring nerd, we embrace her as role model for our daughters, rather than the tragic whore. And if she is presented as an utterly devoted saint suffering nobly in silence, we lie and say she is just like our mothers. Larger than life. Magical and insidious. A movie is never just a movie, after all.

READING THE TEXT

1. Summarize in your own words Hagedorn's view of the traditional images of Asian women as presented in American film.

2. What is the chronology of Asian women in film that Hagedorn presents, and why do you think she gives us a historical overview?

3. Why does Hagedorn say that the film *The Joy Luck Club* "carries a lot of cultural baggage" (para. 11)?

4. What sort of images of Asian women does Hagedorn imply that she would prefer to see?

READING THE SIGNS

1. Rent a videotape or DVD of *The Joy Luck Club* (or another film featuring Asian characters, such as *The Fast and the Furious*), and write an essay in which you support, refute, or modify Hagedorn's interpretation of the film.

2. In class, form teams and debate the proposition that Hollywood writers and directors have a social responsibility to avoid stereotyping ethnic characters. To develop your team's arguments, first brainstorm films that depict various ethnicities, and then discuss whether the portrayals are damaging or benign. You might also consult Michael Omi's "In Living Color: Race and American Culture" (p. 549).

3. Study a magazine that targets Asian American readers, such as *Transpacific* or *Yolk*. Then write an essay in which you consider the extent to which Asian women fit the stereotypes that Hagedorn describes, keeping in mind the magazine's intended readership (businessmen, twentysomethings of both sexes, and so forth).

4. Watch one of the gender-bending films Hagedorn mentions (such as *M. Butterfly*), and write your own analysis of the gender roles portrayed in the film. To develop your ideas, consult Aaron Devor's "Gender Role Behaviors and Attitudes" (p. 458).

MICHAEL PARENTI

Class and Virtue

In 1993, a movie called Indecent Proposal *presented a story in which a billionaire offers a newly poor middle-class woman a million dollars if she'll
sleep with him for one night. In Michael Parenti's (b. 1933) terms, what was
really indecent about the movie was the way it showed the woman falling in
love with the billionaire, thus making a romance out of a class outrage. But
the movie could get away with it, partly because Hollywood has always conditioned audiences to root for the ruling classes and to ignore the inequities
of class privilege. In this selection from* Make-Believe Media: The Politics
of Entertainment *(1992), Parenti argues that Hollywood has long been in
the business of representing the interests of the ruling classes. Whether it is
forgiving the classist behavior in* Pretty Woman *or glamorizing the lives of
the wealthy, Hollywood makes sure its audiences leave the theater thinking
you can't be too rich. Parenti is a writer who lectures widely at university
campuses around the country. His publications include* Power and the
Powerless *(1978),* Inventing Reality: The Politics of the News Media
(1986), Democracy for the Few *(1988),* Against Empire *(1995),* Dirty
Truths *(1996),* America Besieged *(1998), and* History as Mystery *(1999).*

Class and Virtue

The entertainment media present working people not only as unlettered and
uncouth but also as less desirable and less moral than other people. Conversely, virtue is more likely to be ascribed to those characters whose speech
and appearance are soundly middle- or upper-middle class.

Even a simple adventure story like *Treasure Island* (1934, 1950, 1972)
manifests this implicit class perspective. There are two groups of acquisitive
persons searching for a lost treasure. One, headed by a squire, has money
enough to hire a ship and crew. The other, led by the rascal Long John Silver,
has no money — so they sign up as part of the crew. The narrative implicitly
assumes from the beginning that the squire has a moral claim to the treasure,
while Long John Silver's gang does not. After all, it is the squire who puts up
the venture capital for the ship. Having no investment in the undertaking
other than their labor, Long John and his men, by definition, will be "stealing"
the treasure, while the squire will be "discovering" it.

To be sure, there are other differences. Long John's men are cutthroats.
The squire is not. Yet, one wonders if the difference between a bad pirate and
a good squire is itself not preeminently a matter of having the right amount of
disposable income. The squire is no less acquisitive than the conspirators. He
just does with money what they must achieve with cutlasses. The squire and

his associates dress in fine clothes, speak an educated diction, and drink brandy. Long John and his men dress slovenly, speak in guttural accents, and drink rum. From these indications alone, the viewer knows who are the good guys and who are the bad. Virtue is visually measured by one's approximation to proper class appearances.

Sometimes class contrasts are juxtaposed within one person, as in *The Three Faces of Eve* (1957), a movie about a woman who suffers from multiple personalities. When we first meet Eve (Joanne Woodward), she is a disturbed, strongly repressed, puritanically religious person, who speaks with a rural, poor-Southern accent. Her second personality is that of a wild, flirtatious woman who also speaks with a rural, poor-Southern accent. After much treatment by her psychiatrist, she is cured of these schizoid personalities and emerges with a healthy third one, the real Eve, a poised, self-possessed, pleasant woman. What is intriguing is that she now speaks with a cultivated, affluent, Smith College accent, free of any low-income regionalism or ruralism, much like Joanne Woodward herself. This transformation in class style and speech is used to indicate mental health without any awareness of the class bias thusly expressed.

Mental health is also the question in *A Woman under the Influence* (1974), the story of a disturbed woman who is married to a hard-hat husband. He cannot handle — and inadvertently contributes to — her emotional deterioration. She is victimized by a spouse who is nothing more than an insensitive, working-class bull in a china shop. One comes away convinced that every unstable woman needs a kinder, gentler, and above all, more *middle-class* hubby if she wishes to avoid a mental crack-up.

Class prototypes abound in the 1980s television series *The A-Team.* In each episode, a Vietnam-era commando unit helps an underdog, be it a Latino immigrant or a disabled veteran, by vanquishing some menacing force such as organized crime, a business competitor, or corrupt government officials. As always with the make-believe media, the A-Team does good work on an individualized rather than collectively organized basis, helping particular victims by thwarting particular villains. The A-Team's leaders are two white males of privileged background. The lowest ranking members of the team, who do none of the thinking nor the leading, are working-class palookas. They show they are good with their hands, both by punching out the bad guys and by doing the maintenance work on the team's flying vehicles and cars. One of them, "B.A." (bad ass), played by the African American Mr. T., is visceral, tough, and purposely bad-mannered toward those he doesn't like. He projects an image of crudeness and ignorance and is associated with the physical side of things. In sum, the team has a brain (the intelligent white leaders) and a body with its simpler physical functions (the working-class characters), a hierarchy that corresponds to the social structure itself.[1]

[1]Gina Marchetti, "Class, Ideology and Commercial Television: An Analysis of *The A-Team," Journal of Film and Video* 39, Spring 1987, pp. 19–28.

Sometimes class bigotry is interwoven with gender bigotry, as in *Pretty Woman* (1990). A dreamboat millionaire corporate raider finds himself all alone for an extended stay in Hollywood (his girlfriend is unwilling to join him), so he quickly recruits a beautiful prostitute as his playmate of the month. She is paid three thousand dollars a week to wait around his super-posh hotel penthouse ready to perform the usual services and accompany him to business dinners at top restaurants. As prostitution goes, it is a dream gig. But there is one cloud on the horizon. She is low-class. She doesn't know which fork to use at those CEO power feasts, and she's bothersomely fidgety, wears tacky clothes, chews gum, and, y'know, doesn't talk so good. But with some tips from the hotel manager, she proves to be a veritable Eliza Doolittle in her class metamorphosis. She dresses in proper attire, sticks the gum away forever, and starts picking the right utensils at dinner. She also figures out how to speak a little more like Joanne Woodward without the benefit of a multiple personality syndrome, and she develops the capacity to sit in a poised, wordless, empty-headed fashion, every inch the expensive female ornament.

She is still a prostitute but a classy one. It is enough of a distinction for the handsome young corporate raider. Having liked her because she was charmingly cheap, he now loves her all the more because she has real polish and is a more suitable companion. So suitable that he decides to do the right thing by her: set her up in an apartment so he can make regular visits at regular prices. But now she wants the better things in life, like marriage, a nice house, and, above all, a different occupation, one that would allow her to use less of herself. She is furious at him for treating her like, well, a prostitute. She decides to give up her profession and get a high-school diploma so that she might make a better life for herself — perhaps as a filing clerk or receptionist or some other of the entry-level jobs awaiting young women with high school diplomas.[2]

After the usual girl-breaks-off-with-boy scenes, the millionaire prince returns. It seems he can't concentrate on making money without her. He even abandons his cutthroat schemes and enters into a less lucrative but supposedly more productive, caring business venture with a struggling old-time entrepreneur. The bad capitalist is transformed into a good capitalist. He then carries off his ex-prostitute for a lifetime of bliss. The moral is a familiar one, updated for post-Reagan yuppiedom: A woman can escape from economic and gender exploitation by winning the love and career advantages offered by a rich male. Sexual allure goes only so far unless it develops a material base and becomes a class act.[3]

READING THE TEXT

1. According to Parenti, what characteristics are typically attributed to working-class and upper-class film characters?

[2]See the excellent review by Lydia Sargent, *Z Magazine*, April 1990, pp. 43–45.
[3]Ibid.

2. How does Parenti see the relationship between "class bigotry" and "gender bigotry" (para. 7) in *Pretty Woman*?

3. What relationship does Parenti see between mental health and class values in films?

READING THE SIGNS

1. Rent a DVD or videotape of *Wall Street,* and analyze the class issues that the movie raises. Alternately, watch an episode of *The Apprentice,* and perform the same sort of analysis.

2. Do you agree with Parenti's interpretation of *Pretty Woman*? Write an argumentative essay in which you defend, challenge, or complicate his reading of the film.

3. Read or review Aaron Devor's "Gender Role Behaviors and Attitudes" (p. 458). How would Devor explain the gender bigotry that Parenti finds in *Pretty Woman*?

4. Rent the 1954 film *On the Waterfront*, and watch it with your class. How are labor unions and working-class characters portrayed in that film? Does the film display the class bigotry that Parenti describes?

5. Read or review Michael Omi's "In Living Color: Race and American Culture" (p. 549). Then write a journal entry in which you create a category of cinematic racial bigotry that corresponds to Parenti's two categories of class and gender bigotry. What films that you have seen illustrate your new category?

VIVIAN C. SOBCHACK
The Postmorbid Condition

When Bonnie and Clyde *shuddered to a spectacular conclusion with the slow-motion machine-gunning of its main characters, the point was that in a society plagued by random and senseless violence Hollywood had a responsibility to make some kind of meaning out of it. But when Quentin Tarantino uses senseless violence for comic effect, the point, Vivian C. Sobchack (b. 1940) argues, is that there is no point at all, or rather, that the human body has lost its meaning in contemporary life and has become little more than a machine whose destruction is on a par with an exploding automobile. Offering a profound and disturbing explanation for the popularity of movies like* Pulp Fiction *and* Natural Born Killers, *Sobchack reveals the forces behind the dehumanization of Hollywood violence. A professor and associate dean in the School of Theater, Film, and Television at UCLA, Sobchack is the author of* Screening Space: The American Science Fiction Film *(1987),* Address of the Eye: A Phenomenology of Film Experience *(1991),* The Persistence of History: Cinema, Television, and the Modern Event *(1995),* Meta-Morphing: Visual Transformation and the Culture of Quick-Change *(1999), and* Carnal Thoughts: Embodiment and Moving Image Culture *(2004).*

In an essay I wrote twenty-five years ago, I argued that screen violence in American films of the late 1960s and early 1970s was new and formally different from earlier "classical" Hollywood representations of violence. This new interest in violence and its new formal treatment not only literally satisfied an intensified cultural desire for "close-up" knowledge about the material fragility of bodies, but also — and more important — made increasingly senseless violence in the "civil" sphere sensible and meaningful by stylizing and aestheticizing it, thus bringing intelligibility and order to both the individual and social body's increasingly random and chaotic destruction. Indeed, I argued that random and senseless violence was elevated to meaning in these then "new" movies, its "transcendence" achieved not only by being up there on the screen, but also through long lingering gazes at carnage and ballets of slow motion that conferred on violence a benediction and the grace of a cinematic "caress."

Today, most American films have more interest in the presence of violence than in its meaning. There are very few attempts to confer order or perform a benediction upon the random and senseless death, the body riddled with bullets, the laying waste of human flesh. (The application of such order, benediction, and transcendental purpose is, perhaps, one of the explicit achievements of Steven Spielberg's high-tech but emotionally anachronistic *Saving Private Ryan*, and it is no accident that its context is a morally intelligible

World War II.) Indeed, in today's films (and whatever happened started happening sometime in the 1980s), there is no transcendence of "senseless" violence: It just *is*. Thus, the camera no longer caresses it or transforms it into something with more significance than its given instance. Instead of caressing violence, the cinema has become increasingly *careless* about it: either merely nonchalant or deeply lacking in care. Unlike medical melodramas, those films that describe violent bodily destruction evoke no tears in the face of mortality and evidence no concern for the fragility of flesh. Samuel L. Jackson's violent role and religious monologues in Quentin Tarantino's *Pulp Fiction* notwithstanding, we see no grace or benediction attached to violence. Indeed, its very intensity seems diminished: we need noise and constant stimulation and quantity to make up for a lack of significant meaning.

Perhaps this change in attitude and treatment of violence is a function of our increasingly *technologized* view of the body and flesh. We see this view dramatized outside the theater in the practices and fantasies of "maintenance" and "repair" represented by the "fitness center" and cosmetic surgery. Inside the theater, we see it dramatized in the "special effects" allowed by new technological developments and in an increasingly hyperbolic and quantified treatment of violence and bodily damage that is as much about "more" as it is about violence. It seems to me that this quantitative move to "more" in relation to violence — more blood, more gore, more characters (they're really not people) blown up or blown away — began with the contemporary horror film, with "slasher" and "splatter" films that hyperbolized violence and its victims in terms of quantity rather than through exaggerations of form. Furthermore, unlike in the "New Hollywood" films of the late 1960s and 1970s (here one thinks of Peckinpah or Penn), excessive violence in these "low" genre films, while eliciting screams, also elicited laughter, too much becoming, indeed, "too much": incredible, a "gross-out," so "outrageous" and "over the top" that ironic reflexivity set in (for both films and audiences) and the mounting gore and dead bodies became expected — and funny. (Here *Scream* and its sequel are recent examples.)

This heightened sense of reflexivity and irony that emerges from quantities of violence, from "more," is not necessarily progressive nor does it lead to a "moral" agenda or a critique of violence. (By virtue of its excesses and its emphasis on quantity and despite his intention, Oliver Stone's *Natural Born Killers* is quite ambiguous in this regard.) Indeed, in its present moment, this heightened reflexivity and irony merely leads to a heightened sense of representation: that is, care for the film as experience and text, perhaps, but a lack of any real concern for the bodies blown away (or up) upon the screen. In recent "splatter" films, in Tarantino films like *Reservoir Dogs* and *Pulp Fiction*, and in quite a number of action thrillers, bodies are more carelessly *squandered* than carefully stylized. Except, of course, insofar as excess, and hyperbole, itself constitutes stylization. Thus, most of the violence we see on screen today suggests Grand Guignol rather than Jacobean tragedy. However, in our current cultural moment, tiredly described as "postmodern" but filled with new forms of violence like "road rage," the exaggeration and escalating quantification of violence and gore are a great deal less transgressive than they were — and a great deal more absurd. Thus, Tarantino has said on various occasions that he doesn't take violence "very seriously" and describes it as "funny" and "outrageous."

This hyperbolic escalation and quantification of violence also has become   5
quite common to the action picture and thriller, where the body count only exceeds the number of explosions and neither matters very much to anyone: here violence and the laying waste of bodies seems more "naturalized": that is, it regularly functions to fill up screen space and time in lieu of narrative complexity, and to make the central character look good by "virtue" of his mere survival (see, for example, *Payback*). Again, there seems no moral agenda or critique of violence here — only wisecracks and devaluation uttered out of the sides of a Bruce Willis–type mouth. Indeed, here is the careless violence and laconic commentary of comic books (where the panels crackle with zaps and bullets and explosions and the body count is all that counts).

On a more progressive note, I suppose it is possible to see this new excessive and careless treatment of violence on screen as a satiric form of what Russian literary theorist Mikhail Bakhtin has called "grotesque realism." That is, excessive representations of the body and its messier aspects might be read as containing critical and liberatory potential — this, not only because certain social taboos are broken, but also because these excessive representations of the grotesquerie of being embodied are less "allegorical" and fantastic than they are exaggerations of concrete conditions in the culture of which they are a part. In this regard, and particularly relevant to "indie" crime dramas and the action thriller (a good deal of it science-fictional), much has been written recently about the "crisis of the body" and a related "crisis of masculinity." Both of these crises are no longer of the *Bonnie and Clyde* or *Wild Bunch* variety: They are far too much inflected and informed by *technological* concerns and confusions and a new sense of the body as a technology, altered by technology, enabled by technology, and disabled by technology. Indeed, along with the Fordist assembly line and its increasing production of bodies consumed as they are violently "wasted" on the screen, comes the production of bodies as both technological *subjects* and *subjected to* technology: enhanced and extended, but also extinguished by Uzis, bombs, whatever the latest in firepower. Thus, we might argue, the excessive violence we see on the screen, the carelessness and devaluation of mere human flesh, is both a recognition of the high-tech, powerful, and uncontrollable subjects we (men, mostly) have become through technology — and an expression of the increasing frustration and rage at what seems a lack of agency and effectiveness as we have become increasingly controlled by and subject to technology.

This new quantification of and carelessness toward violence on the screen also points to other aspects of our contemporary cultural context. We have come both a long way and not so far from the assassins, serial killers, and madmen who made their mass presence visibly felt in the late 1960s and early 1970s. They, like the bodies wasted on the screen, have proliferated at

FIGURE 1   John Travolta and Samuel L. Jackson are buddies and professional killers in *Pulp Fiction*, which takes a cartoonish approach to graphic violence, using a character's exploding head as the basis for an extended comic sketch.

an increasingly faster and decreasingly surprising rate. They and the violence that accompanies them are now a common, omnipresent phenomenon of daily life — so much so that, to an unprecedented degree, we are resigned to living with them in what has become an increasingly uncivil society. "Senseless" and "random" violence pervades our lives and is barely remarkable or specific any longer — and while "road rage" and little children killed by stray bullets of gang bangers do elicit a moral *frisson*, for the most part we live in and suspect the absence of a moral context in this decade of extreme relativism. Violence, like "shit," happens — worth merely a bumper sticker nod that reconciles it with a general sense of helplessness (rather than despair).

No longer elevated through balletic treatment on narrative purpose, violence on the screen is sensed — indeed, appreciated — as senseless. But then so is life under the extremity of such technologized and uncivil conditions. Indeed, what has been called the "postmodern condition" might be more accurately thought of as the "postmortem condition." There's a kind of meta-sensibility at work here: life, death, and the movies are a "joke" or an "illusion" and everyone's in on it. Violence on the screen and in the culture is not related to a moral context, but to a proliferation of images, texts, and spectacle. And, given that we cannot contain or stop this careless proliferation, violence and death both on the street and in *Pulp Fiction* become reduced to the practical — and solvable — problem of cleanup.

Pain, too, drops out of the picture. The spasmodic twitching that ends *Bonnie and Clyde* has become truly lifeless. The bodies now subjected to violence are just "dummies": multiple surfaces devoid of subjectivity and gravity, "straw men," if you will. "Wasting" them doesn't mean much. Hence, the power (both appealing and off-putting) of those few films that remind us that bodily damage hurts, that violently wasting lives has grave consequences. Hence, the immense popularity of *Saving Private Ryan*, a movie in which the massive quantity of graphic physical damage and the violent "squandering" of bodies and lives is "redeemed" to social purpose and meaning, its senselessness made sensible by its (re)insertion in a clearly defined (and clearly past) moral context. Hence, also, the popular neglect of *Beloved* or *Affliction*, movies in which violence is represented "close up" as singularly felt: graphically linked to bodily pain and its destruction of subjectivity. In these films, violence is not dramatized quantitatively or technologically and thus becomes extremely difficult to watch: that is, even though an image, understood by one's own flesh as *real.*

I am not sure how to end this particular postmortem on my original essay. 10 I still can't watch the eyeball being slit in *Un Chien Andalou.* But, as with *Straw Dogs* and *The French Connection*, I could and did watch all the violence in *Pulp Fiction.* Nonetheless, there's been a qualitative change as well as a quantitative one: while I watched those earlier violent films compulsively, with some real need to know what they showed me, I watch the excesses of the current ones casually, aware they won't show me anything real that I don't already know.

READING THE TEXT

1. What was Sobchack's argument in the essay on screen violence that she wrote now thirty years ago?

2. How does contemporary screen violence differ from that of the 1960s and 1970s, according to Sobchack?

3. What does Sobchack mean by referring to "our increasingly *technologized* view of the body" (para. 3)?

4. In what ways do irony and satire contribute to the desensitizing of contemporary audiences in the face of extreme screen violence, according to Sobchack?

READING THE SIGNS

1. Media violence is one of the most controversial issues in current cultural politics. Referring to a selection of current violent films, write an essay arguing for or against the proposition that screen violence desensitizes viewers to the realities of violence.

2. Write an argumentative essay in which you support, refute, or modify Sobchack's claim that films such as *Beloved* fail to attract audiences because, unlike most violent films, they depict pain and violence as "*real*" (para. 9). To develop support for your position, interview acquaintances who watched such a film and those who chose to avoid it.

3. In class, stage a debate on the proposition that the film industry should restrict its depictions of violence.

4. Rent a video or DVD of *Rollerball*, *Starship Troopers*, *Kill Bill, Vol. 2*, or another violent film. To what extent does the film illustrate Sobchack's view that "we need noise and constant stimulation and quantity to make up for a lack of significant meaning" (para. 2)?

5. Rent a video or DVD of *Boyz N the Hood,* and analyze it semiotically. Use your observations as evidence for an essay in which you argue whether the film's violence is desensitizing, as Sobchack finds to be the case for most contemporary films, or whether it strikes the viewer as "real." How does the film's genre — gangster film — affect your interpretation of the violence? To develop your ideas, read or review Todd Boyd's "So You Wanna Be a Gangsta?" (p. 331).

6. In class, discuss the reasons many moviegoers find violence entertaining. What does the prevalence of violence say about modern American cultural values?

Reservoir Dogs

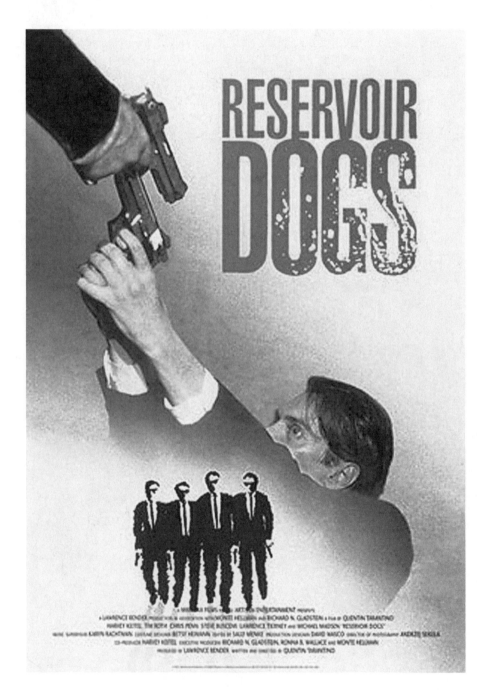

READING THE SIGNS

1. Based on the *Reservoir Dogs* poster, how would you characterize the subject matter of this film? Does the poster make you want to see the film? Why or why not? What is the effect of including one figure with part of his face obscured and the other with only his arm visible? What does the image of the four men at the bottom suggest? How do you interpret the splattering on the letters of the title?

2. Who, in your opinion, is the intended audience for this film? Why? What elements in this poster appeal to that intended audience?

3. A version of this poster includes the caption, "Four perfect killers. One perfect crime. Now all they have to fear is each other." In your opinion, is the ad more or less effective with this added text? Why or why not?

4. If you haven't seen *Reservoir Dogs*, rent it (though be warned that parts are quite violent). How well does this poster represent the film? If you had to design your own poster for this movie, what would it look like?

5

AMERICAN PARADOX

Culture and Contradiction in the U.S.A.

Janet-Gate

The 2004 half-time show for Super Bowl XXXVII was proceeding routinely enough, with two MTV stars providing the entertainment amidst a carefully choreographed musical extravaganza, when suddenly something went wrong. In the aftermath of the catastrophe, both of the stars insisted that there had been an accident — a "wardrobe malfunction" to be exact — but the damage had been done. Before you could say "Janet Jackson's breast," the nation had risen up in wrath. Anti-indecency legislation began to pour out of Washington D.C., Justin Timberlake pouted and apologized, Janet Jackson canceled an appearance or two, and Howard Stern decided that life would be easier on satellite radio.

As we write this introduction a year later, the dust is still settling on the Jackson-Timberlake matter. The fines for broadcast indecency continue to be raised. Righteous indignation continues to be a good attitude to take in the halls of Congress. But, somehow, the whole matter seems a little askew, because if you had watched the on-screen promotions for the half-time show for Super Bowl XXXVII prior to the actual event, you would have seen just about as much of Janet Jackson as you could see when her bustier came off. You can see about that much of many a star if you log on to the Yahoo! home page or look at a weather Web site. In fact, you can't look anywhere without seeing pretty much what so upset the nation at half-time.

So what's going on? On the one hand, Americans are using female sexuality to sell everything from CDs to Pepsi (Super Bowl XXXVI featured an intensely hyped Pepsi ad with Britney Spears) to pizza (a pizza ad broadcast during Super Bowl XXXVII featured an erotically prepped Jessica Simpson).

Exploring the Signs of American Contradictions

The Janet Jackson–Justin Timberlake "wardrobe malfunction" during the 2004 Super Bowl half-time show led to heightened sensitivity to supposedly offensive episodes in the media, with increased FCC monitoring of programming and with Congress increasing fines for indecency. In your journal, explore the consequences of these responses. Do you regard them as a contradiction between the need to protect audiences, especially children, on the one hand, and the constitutional guarantee of freedom of speech, on the other?

Plunging waist and necklines have been all the rage in everyday women's fashion for years. But the Timberlake-Jackson snafu struck a nerve that lies at the center of one of America's most profound contradictions.

That contradiction lies in the tension that stretches between America's Puritan roots and its capitalist ideology. From the Puritans we get our belief that sex is evil, something to be endured only on behalf of "family values"; from capitalism we get our everything-goes-when-it-comes-to-making-profits attitude. At Super Bowl XXXVII both of these traditions, usually kept in separate spheres, collided. On the one hand, there was the football game: America's favorite secular ritual that is cast as a celebration of the most traditional national values—not Puritanism precisely, but certainly wholesome athletic competition and family entertainment. On the other hand, there was the money: the $2 million-plus per half-minute advertising charges and the money CBS put up for the broadcast rights. With so much money on the line (the bottom line, not the goal line), the Super Bowl has to guarantee a large audience to its advertisers, and in recent years that has meant letting the kings of pop music, from Michael Jackson to U2 to Jacko's sister, handle the half-time show in MTV-inspired extravaganzas. But what is commonplace on MTV (and that's a lot raunchier than what happened at half-time) is still shocking to the American heartland, wherein the Super Bowl is still a symbol of traditionalism and family values. So it was really no surprise at all that something would go wrong. What was surprising was that it took so long for such a collision to happen.

The larger story here is the story of America's many contradictions, which are often much more profound than our family values versus capitalist values contest and which have exploded far more seriously. America was founded, for example, on universal principles of freedom and human equality, but slave owners helped write a constitution that guaranteed the rights of slaveholders. It took a civil war that killed over 650,000 people to settle the matter, the most terrible war in American history. Americans have also been among the most resource-voracious people in history, gobbling up and destroying much of what was an unspoiled continent when the nation was founded, and yet Americans also invented the environmentalist movement. Look at it this way: The country that gave the world Standard Oil is also the birthplace of the Sierra Club.

To the rest of the world, Americans look like crazy, mixed-up hypocrites, but we ourselves hardly notice it because we live our many contradictions in the texture of our cultural lives. These contradictions can make us look rather silly, as the Super Bowl XXXVII brouhaha did, but they also make us very interesting, certainly worthy of cultural analysis.

America's Five Big Contradictions

America presents enough cultural contradictions to fill an entire volume of analyses, but we'll look briefly here at five very basic ones that, at least in part, can help explain the notorious electoral division between "red" and "blue" states that David Brooks writes about in this chapter. One of those contradictions we have already looked at: America's curious dichotomy between cultural Puritanism and a capitalistic tendency to exploit erotic voyeurism on behalf of corporate profits. We inherit that Puritanism from the Puritans themselves, who founded the Massachusetts Bay Colony in the 1620s. Deeply repressive of any expression of human sexuality, Puritanism in America had become so striking by the nineteenth century that British visitors began to joke about finding the legs of American pianos draped in woolen stockings to avoid the exposure of a bare leg. It was this puritanical streak that caused the notorious filming of Elvis Presley from the waist up when he first performed on *The Ed Sullivan Show* in the 1950s (broadcasters objected to the King's vigorous pelvic gyrations). And it prompted a cultural backlash against such early rock 'n' rollers as Chuck Berry (arrested on a Mann Act violation), Little Richard (who performed in drag), and Jerry Lee Lewis (who married his thirteen-year-old cousin) that led to the popularization of such squeaky-clean performers as Pat Boone and Debbie Reynolds.

An America that once judicially banned James Joyce's classic novel *Ulysses* because it contained a brothel scene, a soliloquy on oral sex, and the "F" word now can transform a classic children's story like "The Cat in the Hat" into a movie filled with off-color humor, while selling to preteen girls revealing tops and trousers that might have once embarrassed a prostitute. Prime-time network TV programs like *Desperate Housewives* (which staged its own sexually revealing NFL stunt in 2004 on behalf of some free publicity) turn the asexual suburbs of the classic sitcoms upside down, while in the aftermath of such early reality TV hits as *Temptation Island* and *The Bachelor* it's hard to miss a steamy hot-tub scene somewhere when one turns on the television. And there's always the pornographic video that made Paris Hilton a household word rather than an ostracized exhibitionist.

The second American contradiction, described in detail in this chapter's reading by Jack Solomon, concerns our tendency to embrace simultaneously cultural populism and cultural elitism. That is to say, Americans at once value that democratic society "of the people, by the people, and for the people" that Abraham Lincoln so eloquently described in the Gettysburg Address, while at the same time we embrace an American dream that urges us to rise above the crowd to achieve elite status, power, and money. Thus, back in the eighteenth century, a French writer named St. Jean de Crèvecoeur could celebrate an American society that, unlike aristocratic Europe, did not contain large gaps between rich and poor; but at the same time, Americans can turn the television show *The Apprentice,* which stars a billionaire who made his start by inheriting millions, into a top TV hit, and subscribe to a magazine like *Fortune,* whose primary purpose is to let us know about who really has the bucks.

Next, America's tradition of self-reliant individualism is side by side with a tendency toward conformity that prompts us to be just like everybody else. Thus, where Ralph Waldo Emerson and Henry David Thoreau propounded the virtues of self-reliance in the nineteenth century, and Americans to this day tend to be suspicious of centralized governmental institutions that limit personal freedom, America is also the country that in the McCarthyite 1950s compelled its citizens to conform to a middle-class standard of conduct and appearance, threatening the odd individual who happened to grow a beard or refuse to wear a business suit with an accusation of being a communist. And even today in small-town America, individuals can experience enormous social pressures to join the same churches as their neighbors and, generally, to live the same sort of lives.

Paradoxically, when Americans do rebel against the forces of conformism, they tend to do so in ways that only reproduce the ways of conformity through mass consumption. That is, the consumer marketplace is filled with mass-produced goods and services whose advertisements promise that your individual uniqueness will be assured if you (like a few million other consumers) buy this or that product, as in the Reebok campaign that insisted that if you bought a shoe just like the shoes that millions of other consumers were buying, it would "let U be you."

A variant of this contradiction lies in the American tendency to insist on complete personal freedom while simultaneously embracing institutions of social order and control. This contradiction is shared by those on the political left and right alike; they just disagree on which personal freedoms and social

Discussing the Signs of American Contradictions

In class, discuss the results of the 2004 presidential and other recent national elections. Do you find in the results a fundamental divide between the values and political positions of the so-called blue and red states? If students hail from different states, compare the political climates in your home states; if most of the class comes from one state, consider whether your state has an internal red-blue divide. If you see differences in political attitudes, what are they, and who is aligned with which positions?

institutions they prefer. The right, for instance, passionately values personal gun ownership but forcefully opposes the right of individuals to marry whomever they please. Conversely, the left decries unrestricted gun ownership while it advocates gay marriage. The right embraces social institutions like the church and family, while the left prefers governmental social programs. Neither side always recognizes such contradictions, but in living them simultaneously both are strikingly American.

Then there is the cultural contradiction between American altruism (most dramatically embodied in the sacrifices made by New York City firefighters during the September 11 attacks on the World Trade Center) and the libertarianism that draws Americans to the novels of Ayn Rand and the politics of a sort of neo–Social Darwinism. We like to think of ourselves as a caring, charitable people, but we don't like welfare and we especially hate paying taxes. We like social services, but we don't like to make personal sacrifices to pay for them. If you happen to attend a public college, you know about this contradiction firsthand: Your tuition is going up because the people of your state will not pay higher taxes to support higher education, conveniently placing the burden on you.

Finally, there is the contradiction between America's materialistic adoration of money and possessions and its profound commitment to religion and spirituality. The same land that attracted John Smith to Jamestown in 1607 in search of instant and easy wealth also attracted the Pilgrims in 1620 in search of religious freedom, along with Puritans in search of a place to build a theocratic "city on a hill." The most consumer-oriented society in history, America is also a place where some 80 percent of the population claims to be religious. Perhaps nothing in America better exemplifies this contradiction than the American Christmas, which combines the rituals of Christianity with the rituals of rampant consumerism. Every year everyone complains about this, but no one does anything about it — which is probably a good thing because, with a quarter of the nation's retail sales taking place during the Christmas season, the economy would collapse if anything really were done.

What's Red and Blue and Mad All Over?

These contradictions, which have been part of the fabric of American culture from the nation's beginning, have recently been displayed on a grand scale in two successive presidential elections in which the country split almost exactly down the middle between what have come to be called the "red states" (roughly the South, the Midwest, and the noncoastal West) and the "blue states" (the East Coast north of Virginia, the Old Northwest, and the West Coast). Although these terms run the risk of overgeneralization, the red states still tend to embrace spiritual religiosity, a small-town version of communal conformity, social populism, and Puritanism, whereas the blue states tend to be more secular, anti-Puritan, and commercially oriented. A large proportion of red-state voters, for example, claimed that "moral values" (probably a euphemism for opposition to gay marriage) guided their votes, while coastal Hollywood and New York (from P Diddy to Michael Moore) rose up in force to endorse their vision of American society. Of course, folks in the red states can exemplify blue-state traits, and vice versa. But a general sense that these two electoral sections of the country are parting ways around a fundamental split of basic values continues to grow, profoundly worrying those who fear that the contradictions that once made us Americans are now dividing America (just as the country was once deeply divided over the contradiction between the ringing phrases of the Declaration of Independence and a Constitution that enabled the existence of human slavery).

Privatizing the Public Sphere

The contradictions we have surveyed thus far might be called ethical contradictions — that is, contradictions in our value systems. In recent years, however, a new American contradiction has emerged that might best be referred to as a lifestyle contradiction: It can be found in the emerging number of gated residential communities, the explosion of cell-phone ownership, the popularity of humongous SUVs, and the advent of the iPod. What all of these apparently unrelated phenomena have in common is their reflection of a new attitude toward the public sphere, one that, in effect, privatizes it through the creation of personalized lifestyle cocoons. Whenever someone retreats into a guard-gated neighborhood, or purchases a giant SUV because such cars are more likely to "prevail" over smaller vehicles in a traffic accident, or gabs on a cell phone while driving, dining in a restaurant, or sitting in class, one is effectively denying the existence of all those other people who share the same public space. Even the iPod, which enables you to personalize your own private musical playlist, creates a singular auditory realm that differs substantially from the shared realm of broadcast radio.

The contradiction here lies in the way that the inclusive embrace of America's official Latin slogan *e pluribus unum* ("in many, one") is transposed

Reading the Signs of American Contradictions on the Net

Despite the explosion in the number of media outlets in the last decade, critics have charged that the increased consolidation of media has in fact homogenized the mass media, with Americans paradoxically now having a narrower range of options available to them. Does the Internet — an environment that allows for blogs, chat rooms, discussion forums, and the like — manage to cut through this paradox? Or, with the rise of powerhouses like Amazon.com, AOL, and eBay, do you see signs of corporate control threatening the much-heralded democratic freedom that the Internet offers?

into an oppositional relationship between the private individual and the public commonweal. In the early 1960s, President John F. Kennedy thrilled Americans when he commanded, "Ask not what your country can do for you, ask what you can do for your country." It is hard to imagine such a slogan even being uttered today, much less revered, in an era when the lifestyle choices of more and more Americans signify a withdrawal from, mistrust of, and even hostility toward their fellow citizens.

The system in which the signs of American communal disaffection may be discerned can be expanded to include the types of entertainment that are especially popular today. As analyzed in our introduction to Chapter 3, the schadenfreude-ridden realm of reality TV, in which viewers take pleasure in the humiliation and discomfort of others, also signifies an increasingly atomized society. This is not an exclusively American phenomenon by any means, however, as similar signs of social decay are visible globally today. The causes of such social disaffection are quite complex and lie beyond the scope of this book — for certainly, popular culture is not the source of global alienation. But we may find the effects of this new contradiction reflected throughout popular culture, indicating once again how the apparently trivial circumstances of everyday life can be signifiers of serious social issues.

The Readings

David Brooks begins our survey of American contradictions with an ultimately optimistic exploration of the cultural divide that has made the terms "red America" and "blue America" household words. Anna Quindlen follows with a meditation on the tensions and promises inherent in American diversity and the struggle to live up to the national motto *e pluribus unum*. Gregg Easterbrook then looks at the paradox inherent in a spiritual nation founded on principles of self-denial as it launches into an era of hyperconsumerism. Jack Solomon's analysis of some of the fundamental mythologies that underlie American advertising highlights the contradiction between American populism and the elitism at the heart of the American dream, while Alfred Lubrano offers a personal reflection on what it was like to move from working-class commonality to the Ivy League elite. Next, Richard Corliss takes up the contradiction between America's evangelical traditions and its often irreverent popular culture, showing how a new synthesis between old opponents is now forming. Lucy R. Lippard's analysis of the "alternating current" in the American psyche oscillating between the country and the city illuminates one of America's oldest ideological paradoxes, while Mariah Burton Nelson critiques the cultural double standard that compels female athletes to be as concerned about their femininity as they are about winning. Randall Kennedy concludes the chapter with a provocative look at racial profiling, a law-enforcement practice rooted in the fundamental contradiction between the values declared in the Declaration of Independence and the realities of American history.

DAVID BROOKS
One Nation, Slightly Divisible

> *Red is red, and blue is blue, and never the twain shall meet — or so one might conclude after two consecutive presidential elections in which the American electorate divided decisively between so-called "red states" and "blue states." Shortly after the 2000 election, which first introduced the red state-blue state division, David Brooks went on the road (he didn't have to go far) to see whether Americans were so hopelessly culturally divided after all. He found that, while red America may have fewer Starbucks and Pottery Barn outlets than does blue America, the feared divide may not go so deep after all. Brooks (b. 1961) is a columnist for the* New York Times *and a commentator on* The NewsHour with Jim Lehrer. *This selection was first published in 2001 in the* Atlantic Monthly. *He is the author of* Bobos in Paradise: The New Upper Class and How They Got There *(2000) and* On Paradise Drive: How We Live Now (and Always Have) in the Future Tense *(2004).*

Sixty-five miles from where I am writing this sentence is a place with no Starbucks, no Pottery Barn, no Borders or Barnes & Noble. No blue *New York Times* delivery bags dot the driveways on Sunday mornings. In this place people don't complain that Woody Allen isn't as funny as he used to be, because they never thought he was funny. In this place you can go to a year's worth of dinner parties without hearing anyone quote an aperçu he first heard on *Charlie Rose*. The people here don't buy those little rear-window stickers when they go to a summer-vacation spot so that they can drive around with "MV" decals the rest of the year; for the most part they don't even go to Martha's Vineyard.

The place I'm talking about goes by different names. Some call it America. Others call it Middle America. It has also come to be known as Red America, in reference to the maps that were produced on the night of the 2000 presidential election. People in Blue America, which is my part of America, tend to live around big cities on the coasts. People in Red America tend to live on farms or in small towns or small cities far away from the coasts. Things are different there.

Everything that people in my neighborhood do without motors, the people in Red America do with motors. We sail; they powerboat. We cross-country ski; they snowmobile. We hike; they drive ATVs. We have vineyard tours; they have tractor pulls. When it comes to yard work, they have rider mowers; we have illegal aliens.

Different sorts of institutions dominate life in these two places. In Red America churches are everywhere. In Blue America Thai restaurants are everywhere. In Red America they have QVC, the Pro Bowlers Tour, and hunting. In Blue America we have NPR, Doris Kearns Goodwin, and socially conscious investing. In Red America the Wal-Marts are massive, with parking lots the size of state parks. In Blue America the stores are small but the markups are big. You'll rarely see a Christmas store in Blue America, but in Red America, even in July, you'll come upon stores selling fake Christmas trees, wreath-decorated napkins, Rudolph the Red-Nosed Reindeer collectible thimbles and spoons, and little snow-covered villages.

We in the coastal metro Blue areas read more books and attend more 5 plays than the people in the Red heartland. We're more sophisticated and cosmopolitan — just ask us about our alumni trips to China or Provence, or our interest in Buddhism. But don't ask us, please, what life in Red America is like. We don't know. We don't know who Tim LaHaye and Jerry B. Jenkins are, even though the novels they have co-written have sold about 40 million copies over the past few years. We don't know what James Dobson says on his radio program, which is listened to by millions. We don't know about Reba or Travis. We don't know what happens in mega-churches on Wednesday evenings, and some of us couldn't tell you the difference between a fundamentalist and an evangelical, let alone describe what it means to be a Pentecostal. Very few of us know what goes on in Branson, Missouri, even though it has seven million visitors a year, or could name even five NASCAR drivers, although stock-car races are the best-attended sporting events in the country. We don't know how to shoot or clean a rifle. We can't tell a military officer's rank by looking at his insignia. We don't know what soy beans look like when they're growing in a field.

All we know, or all we think we know, about Red America is that millions and millions of its people live quietly underneath flight patterns, many of them are racist and homophobic, and when you see them at highway rest stops, they're often really fat and their clothes are too tight.

And apparently we don't want to know any more than that. One can barely find any books at Amazon.com about what it is like to live in small-town America — or, at least, any books written by normal people who grew up in small towns, liked them, and stayed there. The few books that do exist were written either by people who left the heartland because they hated it (Bill Bryson's *The Lost Continent,* for example) or by urbanites who moved to Red America as part of some life-simplification plan (*Moving to a Small Town: A Guidebook for Moving from Urban to Rural America*; National Geographic's *Guide to Small Town Escapes*). Apparently no publishers or members of the Blue book-buying public are curious about Red America as seen through Red America's eyes.

Crossing the Meatloaf Line

Over the past several months, my interest piqued by those stark blocks of color on the election-night maps, I have every now and then left my home in

Montgomery County, Maryland, and driven sixty-five miles northwest to Franklin County, in south-central Pennsylvania. Montgomery County is one of the steaming-hot centers of the great espresso machine that is Blue America. It is just over the border from northwestern Washington, D.C., and it is full of upper-middle-class towns inhabited by lawyers, doctors, stockbrokers, and establishment journalists like me — towns like Chevy Chase, Potomac, and Bethesda (where I live). Its central artery is a burgeoning high-tech corridor with a multitude of sparkling new office parks housing technology companies such as United Information Systems and Sybase, and pioneering biotech firms such as Celera Genomics and Human Genome Sciences. When I drive to Franklin County, I take Route 270. After about forty-five minutes I pass a Cracker Barrel — Red America condensed into chain-restaurant form. I've crossed the Meatloaf Line; from here on there will be a lot fewer sun-dried-tomato concoctions on restaurant menus and a lot more meatloaf platters.

Franklin County is Red America. It's a rural county, about twenty-five miles west of Gettysburg, and it includes the towns of Waynesboro, Chambersburg, and Mercersburg. It was originally settled by the Scotch-Irish, and has plenty of Brethren and Mennonites along with a fast-growing population of evangelicals. The joke that Pennsylvanians tell about their state is that it has Philadelphia on one end, Pittsburgh on the other, and Alabama in the middle. Franklin County is in the Alabama part. It strikes me as I drive there that even though I am going north across the Mason-Dixon line, I feel as if I were going south. The local culture owes more to Nashville, Houston, and Daytona than to Washington, Philadelphia, or New York.

I shuttled back and forth between Franklin and Montgomery Counties 10 because the cultural differences between the two places are great, though the geographic distance is small. The two places are not perfect microcosms of Red and Blue America. The part of Montgomery County I am here describing is largely the Caucasian part. Moreover, Franklin County is in a Red part of a Blue state: overall, Pennsylvania went for Gore. And I went to Franklin County aware that there are tremendous differences within Red America, just as there are within Blue. Franklin County is quite different from, say, Scottsdale, Arizona, just as Bethesda is quite different from Oakland, California.

Nonetheless, the contrasts between the two counties leap out, and they are broadly suggestive of the sorts of contrasts that can be seen nationwide. When Blue America talks about social changes that convulsed society, it tends to mean the 1960s rise of the counterculture and feminism. When Red America talks about changes that convulsed society, it tends to mean World War II, which shook up old town establishments and led to a great surge of industry.

Red America makes social distinctions that Blue America doesn't. For example, in Franklin County there seems to be a distinction between those fiercely independent people who live in the hills and people who live in the valleys. I got a hint of the distinct and, to me, exotic hill culture when a hill dweller asked me why I thought hunting for squirrel and rabbit had gone out of fashion. I thought maybe it was just more fun to hunt something bigger. But he said, "McDonald's. It's cheaper to get a hamburger at McDonald's than to go out and get it yourself."

There also seems to be an important distinction between men who work outdoors and men who work indoors. The outdoor guys wear faded black T-shirts they once picked up at a Lynyrd Skynyrd concert and wrecked jeans that appear to be washed faithfully at least once a year. They've got wraparound NASCAR sunglasses, maybe a NAPA auto parts cap, and hair cut in a short wedge up front but flowing down over their shoulders in the back— a cut that is known as a mullet, which is sort of a cross between Van Halen's style and Kenny Rogers's, and is the ugliest hairdo since every hairdo in the seventies. The outdoor guys are heavily accessorized, and their accessories are meant to show how hard they work, so they will often have a gigantic wad of keys hanging from a belt loop, a tape measure strapped to the belt, a pocket knife on a string tucked into the front pants pocket, and a pager or a cell phone affixed to the hip, presumably in case some power lines go down somewhere and need emergency repair. Outdoor guys have a thing against sleeves. They work so hard that they've got to keep their arm muscles unencumbered and their armpit hair fully ventilated, so they either buy their shirts sleeveless or rip the sleeves off their T-shirts first thing, leaving bits of fringe hanging over their BAD TO THE BONE tattoos.

The guys who work indoors can't project this rugged proletarian image. It's simply not that romantic to be a bank-loan officer or a shift manager at the local distribution center. So the indoor guys adopt a look that a smart-ass, sneering Blue American might call Bible-academy casual—maybe Haggar slacks, which they bought at a dry-goods store best known for its appliance department, and a short-sleeved white Van Heusen shirt from the Bon-Ton. Their image projects not "I work hard" but "I'm a devoted family man." A lot of indoor guys have a sensitive New Age demeanor. When they talk about the days their kids were born, their eyes take on a soft Garth Brooks expression, and they tear up. They exaggerate how sinful they were before they were born again. On Saturdays they are patio masters, barbecuing on their gas grills in full Father's Day-apron regalia.

At first I thought the indoor guys were the faithful, reliable ones: the ones 15 who did well in school, whereas the outdoor guys were druggies. But after talking with several preachers in Franklin County, I learned that it's not that simple. Sometimes the guys who look like bikers are the most devoted community-service volunteers and church attendees.

The kinds of distinctions we make in Blue America are different. In my world the easiest way to categorize people is by headroom needs. People who went to business school or law school like a lot of headroom. They buy humongous sport-utility vehicles that practically have cathedral ceilings over the front seats. They live in homes the size of country clubs, with soaring entry atriums so high that they could practically fly a kite when they come through the front door. These big-headroom people tend to be predators: their jobs have them negotiating and competing all day. They spend small fortunes on dry cleaning. They grow animated when talking about how much they love their blackberries. They fill their enormous wall space with huge professional family portraits — Mom and Dad with their perfect kids (dressed in light-blue oxford shirts) laughing happily in an orchard somewhere.

Small-headroom people tend to have been liberal-arts majors, and they have liberal-arts jobs. They get passive-aggressive pleasure from demonstrating how modest and environmentally sensitive their living containers are. They hate people with SUVs, and feel virtuous driving around in their low-ceilinged little Hondas, which often display a RANDOM ACTS OF KINDNESS bumper sticker or one bearing an image of a fish with legs, along with the word "Darwin," just to show how intellectually superior to fundamentalist Christians they are.

Some of the biggest differences between Red and Blue America show up on statistical tables. Ethnic diversity is one. In Montgomery County 60 percent of the population is white, 15 percent is black, 12 percent is Hispanic, and 11 percent is Asian. In Franklin County 95 percent of the population is white. White people work the gas-station pumps and the 7-Eleven counters. (This is something one doesn't often see in my part of the country.) Although the nation is growing more diverse, it's doing so only in certain spots. According to an analysis of the 2000 census by Bill Frey, a demographer at the Milken Institute, well over half the counties in America are still at least 85 percent white.

Another big thing is that, according to 1990 census data, in Franklin County only 12 percent of the adults have college degrees and only 69 percent have high school diplomas. In Montgomery County 50 percent of the adults have college degrees and 91 percent have high school diplomas. The education gap extends to the children. At Walt Whitman High School, a public school in Bethesda, the average SAT scores are 601 verbal and 622 math, whereas the national average is 506 verbal and 514 math. In Franklin County, where people are quite proud of their schools, the average SAT scores at, for example, the Waynesboro area high school are 495 verbal and 480 math. More and more kids in Franklin County are going on to college, but it is hard to believe that their prospects will be as bright as those of the kids in Montgomery County and the rest of upscale Blue America.

Because the information age rewards education with money, it's not surprising that Montgomery County is much richer than Franklin County. According to some estimates, in Montgomery County 51 percent of households have annual incomes above $75,000, and the average household income is $100,365. In Franklin County only 16 percent of households have incomes above $75,000, and the average is $51,872.

A major employer in Montgomery County is the National Institutes of Health, which grows like a scientific boomtown in Bethesda. A major economic engine in Franklin County is the interstate highway Route 81. Trucking companies have gotten sick of fighting the congestion on Route 95, which runs up the Blue corridor along the northeast coast, so they move their stuff along 81, farther inland. Several new distribution centers have been built along 81 in Franklin County, and some of the workers who were laid off when their factories closed, several years ago, are now settling for $8.00 or $9.00 an hour loading boxes.

The two counties vote differently, of course — the differences, on a nationwide scale, were what led to those red-and-blue maps. Like upscale areas everywhere, from Silicon Valley to Chicago's North Shore to suburban Connecticut, Montgomery County supported the Democratic ticket in last year's presidential election, by a margin of 63 percent to 34 percent. Meanwhile, like almost all of rural America, Franklin County went Republican, by 67 percent to 30 percent.

However, other voting patterns sometimes obscure the Red-Blue cultural divide. For example, minority voters all over the country overwhelmingly supported the Democratic ticket last November. But — in many respects, at least — blacks and Hispanics in Red America are more traditionalist than blacks and Hispanics in Blue America, just as their white counterparts are. For example, the Pew Research Center for the People and the Press, in Washington, D.C., recently found that 45 percent of minority members in Red states agree with the statement "AIDS might be God's punishment for immoral sexual behavior," but only 31 percent of minority members in Blue states do. Similarly, 40 percent of minorities in Red states believe that school boards should have the right to fire homosexual teachers, but only 21 percent of minorities in Blue states do.

From Cracks to a Chasm?

These differences are so many and so stark that they lead to some pretty troubling questions: Are Americans any longer a common people? Do we have one national conversation and one national culture? Are we loyal to the same institutions and the same values? How do people on one side of the divide regard those on the other?

I went to Franklin County because I wanted to get a sense of how deep the divide really is, to see how people there live, and to gauge how different their lives are from those in my part of America. I spoke with ministers, journalists, teachers, community leaders, and pretty much anyone I ran across. I consulted with pollsters, demographers, and market-research firms. 25

Toward the end of my project the World Trade Center and the Pentagon were attacked. This put a new slant on my little investigation. In the days immediately following September 11 the evidence seemed clear that despite our differences, we are still a united people. American flags flew everywhere in Franklin County and in Montgomery County. Patriotism surged. Pollsters started to measure Americans' reactions to the events. Whatever questions they asked, the replies were near unanimous. Do you support a military response against terror? More than four fifths of Americans said yes. Do you support a military response even if it means thousands of U.S. casualties? More than three fifths said yes. There were no significant variations across geographic or demographic lines.

A sweeping feeling of solidarity was noticeable in every neighborhood, school, and workplace. Headlines blared, "A NATION UNITED" and "UNITED STATE." An attack had been made on the very epicenter of Blue America — downtown Manhattan. And in a flash all the jokes about and seeming hostility toward New Yorkers vanished, to be replaced by an outpouring of respect, support, and love. The old hostility came to seem merely a sort of sibling rivalry, which means nothing when the family itself is under threat.

But very soon there were hints that the solidarity was fraying. A few stray notes of dissent were sounded in the organs of Blue America. Susan Sontag wrote a sour piece in *The New Yorker* about how depressing it was to see what she considered to be a simplistically pro-American reaction to the attacks. At rallies on college campuses across the country speakers pointed out that America had been bombing other countries for years, and turnabout was fair play. On one NPR talk show I heard numerous callers express unease about what they saw as a crude us-versus-them mentality behind President Bush's rhetoric. Katha Pollitt wrote in *The Nation* that she would not permit her daughter to hang the American flag from the living-room window, because, she felt, it "stands for jingoism and vengeance and war." And there was evidence that among those with less-strident voices, too, differences were beginning to show. Polls revealed that people without a college education were far more confident than people with a college education that the military could defeat the terrorists. People in the South were far more eager than people in the rest of the country for an American counterattack to begin.

It started to seem likely that these cracks would widen once the American response got under way, when the focus would be not on firemen and rescue workers but on the Marines, the CIA, and the special-operations forces. If the war was protracted, the cracks could widen into a chasm, as they did during Vietnam. Red America, the home of patriotism and military service (there's a big military-recruitment center in downtown Chambersburg), would undoubtedly support the war effort, but would Blue America (there's a big gourmet dog bakery in downtown Bethesda) decide that a crude military response would only deepen animosities and make things worse?

A Cafeteria Nation

These differences in sensibility don't in themselves mean that America has 30 become a fundamentally divided nation. As the sociologist Seymour Martin Lipset pointed out in *The First New Nation* (1963), achievement and equality are the two rival themes running throughout American history. Most people, most places, and most epochs have tried to intertwine them in some way.

Moreover, after bouncing between Montgomery and Franklin Counties, I became convinced that a lot of our fear that America is split into rival camps arises from mistaken notions of how society is shaped. Some of us still carry the old Marxist categories in our heads. We think that society is like a layer cake, with the upper class on top. And, like Marx, we tend to assume that wherever there is class division there is conflict. Or else we have a sort of *Crossfire* model in our heads: where would people we meet sit if they were guests on that show?

But traveling back and forth between the two counties was not like crossing from one rival camp to another. It was like crossing a high school cafeteria. Remember high school? There were nerds, jocks, punks, bikers, techies, druggies, God Squadders, drama geeks, poets, and Dungeons & Dragons weirdoes. All these cliques were part of the same school: they had different sensibilities; sometimes they knew very little about the people in the other cliques; but the jocks knew there would always be nerds, and the nerds knew there would always be jocks. That's just the way life is.

And that's the way America is. We are not a divided nation. We are a cafeteria nation. We form cliques (call them communities, or market segments, or whatever), and when they get too big, we form subcliques. Some people even get together in churches that are "nondenominational" or in political groups that are "independent." These are cliques built around the supposed rejection of cliques.

We live our lives by migrating through the many different cliques associated with the activities we enjoy and the goals we have set for ourselves. Our freedom comes in the interstices; we can choose which set of standards to live by, and when.

We should remember that there is generally some distance between 35 cliques — a buffer zone that separates one set of aspirations from another. People who are happy within their cliques feel no great compulsion to go out and reform other cliques. The jocks don't try to change the nerds. David Rawley, [a] Greencastle minister . . . , has been to New York City only once in his life. "I was happy to get back home," he told me. "It's a planet I'm a little scared of. I have no desire to go back."

What unites the two Americas, then, is our mutual commitment to this way of life — to the idea that a person is not bound by his class, or by the religion of his fathers, but is free to build a plurality of connections for himself. We are participants in the same striving process, the same experimental journey. . . .

READING THE TEXT

1. Summarize in your own words the typical characteristics of red and blue America, as Brooks presents them.

2. What does Brooks mean by "the easiest way to categorize people [in blue America] is by headroom needs" (para. 16)?

3. What ethnic and economic patterns does Brooks see in red and blue America?

4. How do the September 11 attacks affect Brooks's view of the two Americas?

READING THE SIGNS

1. In class, form groups and debate whether Brooks could be accused of stereotyping Americans as well as whether he is identifying a fundamental contradiction in American culture.

2. Would Brooks characterize your community as red or blue? Provide specific details to demonstrate your position. If you believe your community escapes Brooks's dichotomy, explain why.

3. Brooks wrote this article in 2001. To what extent does the red-blue state divide still exist after the 2004 presidential election? If you believe that it remains, has the divide become larger or smaller? You might analyze media coverage of that election for evidence in support of your position.

4. In an analytic essay, write your response to Brooks's question, "Are Americans any longer a common people?" (para. 24). To develop your ideas, you might consult Anna Quindlen's "A Quilt of a Country" (p. 397) and the Introduction to Chapter 7, "Constructing Race: Readings in Multicultural Semiotics" (p. 541).

5. Write an essay assessing the validity of Brooks's analogy between America and a high school cafeteria (para. 32).

ANNA QUINDLEN
A Quilt of a Country

"This is a nation founded on a conundrum," Anna Quindlen (b. 1953) argues in this analysis of American cultural contradictions written in the wake of the September 11 terror attacks. Can a country that simultaneously embraces community and individualism, or ethnic cultural specificity and national cultural assimilation, possibly survive? America's contradictions have been tested before, most notably during the Civil War, and they are being tested again, but in the end, Quindlen suggests, this "quilt of a country" is built to endure. A prominent novelist and Pulitzer Prize–winning cultural commentator, Quindlen is the author of many books, including Object Lessons *(1991),* One True Thing *(1994),* A Short Guide to a Happy Life *(2000),* Blessings: A Novel *(2002), and* Loud and Clear *(2004). She is also a columnist for* Newsweek, *where this reading first appeared.*

America is an improbable idea. A mongrel nation built of ever-changing disparate parts, it is held together by a notion, the notion that all men are created equal, though everyone knows that most men consider themselves better than someone. "Of all the nations in the world, the United States was built in nobody's image," the historian Daniel Boorstin wrote. That's because it was built of bits and pieces that seem discordant, like the crazy quilts that have been one of its great folk art forms, velvet and calico and checks and brocades.

Out of many, one. That is the ideal.

The reality is often quite different, a great national striving consisting frequently of failure. Many of the oft-told stories of the most pluralistic nation on earth are stories not of tolerance, but of bigotry. Slavery and sweatshops, the burning of crosses and the ostracism of the other. Children learn in social studies class and in the news of the lynching of blacks, the denial of rights to women, the murders of gay men. It is difficult to know how to persuade them that this amounts to "crown thy good with brotherhood," that amid all the failures is something spectacularly successful. Perhaps they understand it at this moment, when enormous tragedy, as it so often does, demands a time of reflection on enormous blessings.

This is a nation founded on a conundrum, what Mario Cuomo has characterized as "community added to individualism." These two are our defining ideals; they are also in constant conflict. Historians today bemoan the ascendancy of a kind of prideful apartheid in America, saying that the clinging to ethnicity, in background and custom, has undermined the concept of unity. These historians must have forgotten the past, or have gilded it. The New York of my children is no more Balkanized, probably less so, than the Philadelphia of my father, in which Jewish boys would walk several blocks out of their way to avoid the Irish divide of Chester Avenue. (I was the product of a mixed marriage, across barely bridgeable lines: an Italian girl, an Irish boy. How quaint it seems now, how incendiary then.) The Brooklyn of Francie Nolan's famous tree, the Newark of which Portnoy complained, even the uninflected WASP suburbs of Cheever's characters: They are ghettos, pure and simple. Do the Cambodians and the Mexicans in California coexist less easily today than did the Irish and Italians of Massachusetts a century ago? You know the answer.

What is the point of this splintered whole? What is the point of a nation   5
in which Arab cabbies chauffeur Jewish passengers through the streets of New York — and in which Jewish cabbies chauffeur Arab passengers, too, and yet speak in theory of hatred, one for the other? What is the point of a nation in which one part seems to be always on the verge of fisticuffs with another, blacks and whites, gays and straights, left and right, Pole and Chinese and Puerto Rican and Slovenian? Other countries with such divisions have in fact divided into new nations with new names, but not this one, impossibly interwoven even in its hostilities.

Once these disparate parts were held together by a common enemy, by the fault lines of world wars and the electrified fence of communism. With the end of the cold war, there was the creeping concern that without a focus for hatred and distrust, a sense of national identity would evaporate, that the left side of the hyphen — African-American, Mexican-American, Irish-American — would overwhelm the right. And slow-growing domestic traumas like economic unrest and increasing crime seemed more likely to emphasize division than community. Today the citizens of the United States have come together once more because of armed conflict and enemy attack. Terrorism has led to devastation — and unity.

Yet even in 1994, the overwhelming majority of those surveyed by the National Opinion Research Center agreed with this statement: "The U.S. is a unique country that stands for something special in the world." One of the things that it stands for is this vexing notion that a great nation can consist entirely of refugees from other nations, that people of different, even warring religions and cultures can live, if not side by side, then on either side of the country's Chester Avenues. Faced with this diversity there is little point in trying to isolate anything remotely resembling a national character, but there are two strains of behavior that, however tenuously, abet the concept of unity.

There is that Calvinist undercurrent in the American psyche that loves the difficult, the demanding, that sees mastering the impossible, whether it be prairie or subway, as a test of character, and so glories in the struggle of this fractured coalescing. And there is a grudging fairness among the citizens of the United States that eventually leads most to admit that, no matter what the English-only advocates try to suggest, the new immigrants are not so different from our own parents or grandparents. Leonel Castillo, former director of the Immigration and Naturalization Service and himself the grandson of Mexican immigrants, once told the writer Studs Terkel proudly, "The old neighborhood Ma-Pa stores are still around. They are not Italian or Jewish or Eastern European any more. Ma and Pa are now Korean, Vietnamese, Iraqi, Jordanian, Latin American. They live in the store. They work seven days a week. Their kids are doing well in school. They're making it. Sound familiar?"

Tolerance is the word used most often when this kind of coexistence succeeds, but tolerance is a vanilla pudding word, standing for little more than the allowance of letting others live unremarked and unmolested. Pride seems excessive, given the American willingness to endlessly complain about them, them being whoever is new, different, unknown, or currently under suspicion. But patriotism is partly taking pride in this unlikely ability to throw all of us together in a country that across its length and breadth is as different as a dozen countries, and still be able to call it by one name. When photographs of the faces of all of those who died in the World Trade Center destruction are assembled in one place, it will be possible to trace in the skin color, the shape of the eyes and the noses, the texture of the hair, a map of the world. These are the representatives of a mongrel nation that somehow, at times like this, has one spirit. Like many improbable ideas, when it actually works, it's a wonder.

READING THE TEXT

1. Describe in your own words the "ideal" and "real" stories about the American ideal, according to Quindlen.

2. Why do you think Quindlen says that "historians must have forgotten the past, or have gilded it" (para. 4)?

3. Characterize Quindlen's tone and style throughout this selection, including her use of personal experience and rhetorical questions. What effect do these strategies have on the reader?

4. Why does Quindlen call "tolerance" a "vanilla pudding word" (para. 9)?

5. In the writer's view, how does the United States maintain unity despite its diversity?

READING THE SIGNS

1. In an argumentative essay, support, challenge, or complicate Quindlen's assertion that "tolerance is a vanilla pudding word" (para. 9).

2. Compare Quindlen's explanation of the meaning of tolerance with that described in the Introduction to Chapter 7. Which do you find more persuasive, and why?

3. Interview some friends or relatives about whether they agree or disagree with the National Opinion Research Center's statement: "The U.S. is a unique country that stands for something special in the world" (para. 7). Use your findings as the basis of an essay about the validity of this statement.

4. In an essay, support, oppose, or complicate Quindlen's claim: "Faced with this diversity there is little point in trying to isolate anything remotely resembling a national character" (para. 7).

GREGG EASTERBROOK
The Progress Paradox

When Hillary Rodham Clinton denounced a rampant American "materialism that undermines our spiritual centers" and then went on to purchase a $1.7 million home, she joined a long line of Americans who, as Gregg Easterbrook (b. 1953) points out, have stumbled over an enduring American contradiction between the spiritual tradition of embracing ascetic self-denial and the equally American tradition of going for the gold. In this analysis of American consumption gone wild, Easterbrook informs us of such consumer goods as the $10,000 Hermès "Kelly" handbag and the $2.7 million Patek Philippe Calibre 89 wristwatch. And while we are not all in the market for such items, Easterbrook suggests, we are inundated by so much information about the lifestyles of the rich and famous that we may suffer from a "catalog-induced anxiety" that drives us to spend too much for stuff ourselves. Is this what democracy is about? Easterbrook is a senior editor at the New Republic *and a contributing editor for the* Atlantic Monthly *and the* Washington Monthly. *He is the author of several books, including* A Moment on the Earth *(1995),* Tuesday Morning Quarterback *(2001),* The Here and Now *(2002), and* The Progress Paradox: How Life Gets Better While People Feel Worse *(2003), from which this selection is taken.*

In the year 2002 in the United States, it became fashionable for women to show their navels. Midriff-baring outfits were standard throughout the country for teen girls, and even some executive women wore to the office ensembles in which the top didn't quite connect with the skirt or pants. As the midriff became a public matter, some women felt their belly buttons didn't look right; certainly not flawless, like that of pop singer Britney Spears, who started the fad and who seemed to go bare-naveled even during snowstorms. The response? Plastic surgeons began offering a procedure that would make any belly button cute and symmetrical like Britney's. The goal was not health (some navel conditions do require correction for medical reasons) but looks. The cost ran about $5,000, paid by the patient, not insurance.[1] Cosmetic surgeons reported that navel touch-ups were a hot business,[2] partly because the procedure is painless and

---

[1] See "Navels, Nipples Get Attention at Surgeons' Offices," *Wall Street Journal*, August 1, 2002.

[2] Women's fashion in 2002 also favored the "perky" nipple visible through clothes, and though this effect can be obtained by not wearing a bra, most women aren't comfortable without bras, so alternatives were required. One was offered by a firm called BodyPerks, which sold discreet plastic aureole enhancers that could be slipped into the bra cup. BodyPerks

does not involve two weeks in seclusion waiting for the bruising to subside, often required by face-lifts and rhinoplasties.

While women were pushing the envelope on cosmetic surgical intervention — in addition to standard face-lifts, tucks, and breast augmentations, "Botox" injection for wrinkle-reduction became popular — men were hardly inactive. Procedures for men have been the biggest growth area in plastic surgery for about a decade, with male face-lifts and beer-belly reductions popular. Paralleling breast implantation, men have begun to purchase pectoral implants: silicon embedded along the chest muscles to give a man barrel pecs without hours spent in the gym. The ostensible point of most male cosmetic surgery is to make the patient look younger, though on many men a face-lift is so easily detected the true purpose must be to proclaim that the man can afford it. As a status marker, perhaps either one — either the simulacrum of youth or the broadcasting of possession of sufficient money to buy same — will do.

Perhaps your wants are not self-focused; let's say, focused instead on flora. So many Americans and Europeans love flowers, and have the leisure time and discretionary income in which to breed them, that the number of varieties is beginning to exceed the available supply of names. As Cynthia Crossen has written,[3] there are now in the world at least 100,000 named lily varieties and 14,000 named dahlias, most coming into existence recently.

Week's Roses of Upland, California, a flower-breeding firm, will let you name a new rose variety for $10,000. Most people choose to name the rose after themselves, and the buyers are not necessarily dilettantes but often typical middle-class people who save or even take out loans for the thrill of having a rose in their name, even if their flower must compete with thousands of other signature roses. For $75,000, Jackson & Perkins of Somis, California, another producer of hybrid flowers, will give a new rose variety the name of your choosing, fly you and a companion to Los Angeles for a weekend that includes a fine dinner with the company's plant-breeders and, once the new hybrid blooms, ship three hundred of them FedEx around the country to anyone you select, so that friends and family will smell the rose that bears your name. More than a hundred Jackson & Perkins rose varieties, named in this way and funded by rose-lovers at the cost of more than $7.5 million, now exist.[4]

---

advertised in women's magazines — "now also available in mocha," proclaimed one ad — and became a hot sales item after the one-track-mind heroines of the television show *Sex and the City* wore them for an episode and got lots of hot guy action. But BodyPerks don't work with swimsuits or once your clothes have fallen to the floor. Enter cosmetic surgery for the nipple, to insert an enhancing disk for that frisky look twenty-four-seven, or to correct imperfections, achieving symmetry and sex appeal. Nipple augmentation did not take off as much as navel improvement, but cosmetic surgeons reported decent business here, too, despite an $8,000-to-$10,000 price tag, again paid solely by the patient.

[3]See "Roses by Other Names," Cynthia Crossen, *Wall Street Journal*, June 29, 2001.

[4]My thanks to Anand Giriharadas for research on this point.

Augmented Britney-class navels, simulated barrel chests, $75,000 personal   5
roses—it would be easy to make fun of such things as runaway materialism.
But if what you want in life is a perfect midriff or a flower that bears your name,
and a physician's office or hybrid-plant laboratory can make your wish come
true, why not? You only live once.

To think that in the West today not just a landed elite, but millions of people
have the resources to choose to have their bodies surgically altered to seek visual perfection, while the medical profession possesses the knowledge to do
such things safely, is stunning when we ponder that it is only necessary to
step back three generations to reach the time when for most people anything
beyond a routine doctor's visit was a prohibitive expense, and in any event
physicians could do nothing about most basic conditions. By the same token,
for many centuries only the wealthy possessed the time, resources, and leisure
in which to breed and contemplate flowers; today, specialized flowers and
bulbs are a multibillion-dollar industry, as millions of people in the United
States and Europe produce private gardens with flowers more exquisite than
any a king might have strolled past in previous centuries. But to think that we
live in a world where millions of people, tens or even hundreds of millions,
can indulge themselves so immoderately.

Indeed, though the contemporary acquisition-oriented mode of Western
life exhibits many forms of immoderation that could be ridiculed, in a sense
the only unimpeachable objection to materialism is that everyone can't join
the merrymaking. In the United States one person in eight lives in poverty,
while most of the population suffers some form of money uncertainty.
Globally, more than a billion are destitute while another two billion, though
reasonably fed and clothed, will never know circumstances like Western suburban life. That everyone cannot have too much is a strong indictment of the
Western system. Most other complaints about modern materialism reduce,
by comparison, to various forms of covetousness and shouting against the
wind.

The catch is that there is no relationship between having a perfect navel
or named rose, or grand home or expensive car or any such item, and happiness. A perfect navel makes you look better; a large home allows daily life in
comfort; a fine car means you get where you are going; you might look good,
live grandly, travel in style, and still feel forlorn. We would be foolish to expect
possessions to make us happy, or an economic system to care about our emotional state. All any economic system will ever "care" about is the manufacture and distribution of the maximum volume of goods and services. Western
economics attains that goal, but the manufacture and distribution of the maximum volume of goods and services turns out to have comparatively little to
do with whether men and women are happy.

As ever more material things become available and fail to make us
happy, material abundance may even have the perverse effect of instilling
unhappiness—because it will never be possible to have everything that economics can create. Each year the world offers more alluring items to buy and

acquire, yet many find being deprived of material items "more cruel than possessing them was sweet, and people were unhappy to lose them without being happy to possess them." A summation of consumer dilemmas from Jean-Jacques Rousseau said this in 1754.[5] If you don't have the things of the world you are unhappy, but having the things of the world may do no service to your well-being.

The Revenge of the Plastic

That perhaps as many as five hundred million middle-class or above men and women of the Western world get more all the time and expect the stuff to make them happy may, in itself, explain much of contemporary discontent. If you expect the stuff to make you happy, you are sure to be unhappy. Your American Express card cannot buy you happiness but, paradoxically, it can buy you unhappiness: Call this "the revenge of the plastic." But let's set that aside for a moment to consider the stuff and the way we obtain it.

In case you're thinking of purchasing a wristwatch, the Patek Philippe Calibre 89 costs $2.7 million, as it is not only formed of gold and jewels but contains an internal gyroscope to compensate for tiny distortions in the earth's gravity, producing time readings accurate to the microsecond — which would be useful in case you're thinking of launching a space probe. Sales of the Calibre 89 are infrequent, but there is a waiting list for Patek Philippe models costing $45,000. Rolex watches that sell for around $6,000 are actually mass-marketed, offered in malls, advertised in *Time* and *Newsweek*. Most high-end watches are self-winding, so what to do if you own more than one? More than one means you can't wear each timepiece daily, providing the wrist motion on which a self-winding watch depends. What you do in that event is go to the Asprey & Garrard store on Fifth Avenue in New York City and put down $5,700 for a calfskin box in which six electrically powered wrists slowly rotate, winding your self-winding high-end watches.

Wild spending by the very rich, always a factor or else the world would not contain beautiful old manors and chateaus, in the contemporary era has taken on an almost comic air. In the 1970s, there were believed to be about 200 privately owned yachts longer than 100 feet in the world; today there are at least 5,000. A yacht of this length costs at least $10 million to purchase, plus at least $1 million annually for crew and upkeep. In 2000, one of the founders of the Blockbuster video-rental chain paid $56 million for an entire small island near the Bahamas. Its amenities included a manor home, four houses for guests or staff, powerplant, on-beach fitness center, and desalinization facility. Pop

[5]The quote is from Rousseau's *Second Discourse*, also called the *Discourse on the Origins and Basis of Inequality among Men*.

singer Barbara Mandrell in contrast was looking to sell her 27,000-square-foot residence; the property included a helicopter landing pad and handy indoor shooting range. Bill Gates has finally moved into his $53 million, 66,000-square-foot megahome, with three underground parking garages and a reception hallway itself larger than the entire typical American house. In this price-no-object ego indulgence, Gates probably feels lonely.

As spending by the rich is supposed to trickle down to others, the desire for wild spending has trickled down to the huge Western population that is not rich but is well off. At this writing there was a two-year waiting list for the Hermès "Kelly" handbag, which costs $10,000 and is barely distinguishable from far less expensive handbags. Barneys, a New York City department store, was at this writing selling crocodile-skin eyeglass holders for $255 and a $930 designer teapot. Sharper Image was selling a $1,590 robotic dog toy that "produces amazingly realistic movement." Mercedes and Volkswagen were offering cars list-priced at more than $200,000. Several auto manufacturers had begun to offer not just heated seats but chilled seats — air conditioning pipes run through them, so that the seat is cool to the touch in summertime. Ford's Expedition, a luxury SUV, was offering "power running boards." Press a button and servomotors make the running boards descend and swivel outward to form steps, helping passengers ascend into the huge vehicle. That's all well and good, but it's so inconvenient to have to push the button! When will they offer automatic power running boards?

Catalog-Induced Anxiety

High-end products can sell in numbers because 205,000 American households had incomes exceeding $1 million in 1999, according to the Internal Revenue Service. In the Gilded Era, the number of millionaires (by the income standards of the time) was perhaps a few hundred. Today's society produces so many very-well-off people that millionaires could populate the entire city of Rochester, New York, a remarkable thought.[6] And though, in the past, the typical person could only wonder what it might be like to be an Astor, today anyone can peruse the specifics of millionairehood. Television obsessively documents the lavish lives of the wealthy and glamorous; glossy-stock magazines such as *Architectural Digest* let you into their homes; catalogs for the most expensive things imaginable are readily available to anyone; the floor plan and elevations of Gates's megahome can be downloaded from the Web.

Ready viewing of lifestyle information about the rich creates, for some, a condition that might be called "catalog-induced anxiety." People can see, in agonizing detail, all the things they will never possess. Catalog-induced anxiety, 15

---

[6]Rochester's population is about 220,000.

whether from catalogs themselves or from other forms of public exposure of the lives of the rich or celebrated, may make what a typical person possesses seem paltry, even if the person is one of the many tens of millions of Americans and Europeans living well by objective standards and extremely well by the standards of human history.

As the desire for wild spending trickles down, ostentation about money becomes ever more common, and not just among surgeons and celebrities. In recent years, suburban communities have begun to suffer not only from the McMansion craze but from "house bloat," the building of huge homes on a block of average-sized houses. "Bloated" homes may come right up to the property setback line to achieve maximum mass; in addition to being a way to burn money, visually they scream "my house is bigger than yours!" Certain buyers find a bloated home on a block of average-sized houses more satisfying than a McMansion on a McMansion block, since the bloated home appears so much bigger than what's around it. Bloated homes often have pillared entrances and similar ostentatious touches. In 2001, Mamaroneck, New York, a bedroom community for Manhattan, enacted a statute limiting to seven thousand square feet the residences that could be built on the half-acre lots beneath the town's housing stock. Seven thousand square feet is three times the interior volume of the typical new American home, which itself is double the volume of the typical home just a generation ago. Builders protested that the Mamaroneck statute was unfair because there was already a backlog of buyers who wanted homes larger than seven thousand square feet. In 2000, *The Wall Street Journal* quoted an official of Toll Brothers, a leading builder of bloated homes, as saying, "We sell what nobody needs."[7]

In 2000, around the peak of the stock-market bubble, builders in the Hamptons, a favorite beach destination of Manhattanites, were offering not some but hundreds of new summer homes priced between $5 million and $8 million.[8] So many homes coming onto the market had maxed out on luxury features that driving the price up farther had become a sort of challenge, with one builder putting $25,000 worth of imported faucets into a single bathroom. Another challenge had arisen to see how much customers could drive up the price of add-ons. As recently as a decade ago, $200,000 was top dollar for a built-in swimming pool with all possible extras. By 2000, *The New York Times* reported, a Hamptons firm called Tortorella Swimming Pools was charging $1.5 million per pool and its order book was so full that the company was turning away business. One and a half million dollars buys a "themed pool" — Atlantis and Stonehenge were popular — with bridges, spa grottos, and theatrical lighting effects. The buyers are not movie stars or Hugh Hefner, rather

[7]See "Look at All Their Stuff," *Wall Street Journal*, January 7, 2000.
[8]See "Wowing Them with Excess in the Hamptons," *The New York Times*, July 18, 2000.

doctors and lawyers and investment bankers desperate to find a way to burn money. . . .

Of course, it is standard to denounce materialism in others while lusting for it ourselves. At the end of the 1990s, Hillary Rodham Clinton decried "a consumer-driven culture that promotes values that undermine democracy" and blasted "materialism that undermines our spiritual centers." Shortly thereafter, she bought a $1.7 million home and signed an $8 million book contract. As the novelist Daniel Akst has noted, Rodham Clinton thus joined the long line of commentators "bent on saving the rest of us from the horrors of consumption" while taking care to make themselves rich and comfy.

The line Clinton joined is long. In 1897, the great writer Edith Wharton published a book, *The Decoration of Houses*, arguing that people should live modestly, without pretense or shows of money. At the time, Wharton, one of America's first literary celebrities, herself lived in a thirty-five-room mansion called The Mount, where she was attended by ten full-time servants. Many figures in philosophy, religion, politics, and other fields have recommended that others pay no heed to material concerns, while being obsessed with the same things themselves. For example, the nineteenth-century philosopher Arthur Schopenhauer, who advised people to renounce their desires for popularity or status, nevertheless suffered intense, almost debilitating fits of depression over the fact that [philosopher G. W. F.] Hegel's public lectures drew larger crowds than his.[9]

In a way, denouncing the material desires of others while avidly pursuing acquisition for yourself is a rational strategy: If others actually do seek less, then by the rules of supply and demand, prices of the material things for which you are grasping will decline. Denouncing materialism by others while being desirous of worldly goods yourself may also, simply, be the public face versus the private thirst.[10] As James Twitchell, a professor at the University of Florida, has written, "No one ever rises to the defense of materialism" because to say that you covet worldly things is considered poor taste.[11] Yet almost everyone practices acquisitiveness in his or her own life. A small percentage of

20

[9]See *Beside Still Waters* by Gregg Easterbrook, New York: William Morrow, 1998.

[10]For amusing examples of simultaneous finger-wagging about materialism in others combined with shallow cravings by the writer, see *Consuming Desires: Consumption, Culture and the Pursuit of Happiness*, Roger Rosenblatt, editor, New York: Houghton Mifflin, 1999. The book is a collection of essays denouncing materialism, but numerous contributors essentially argue that everyone else should be deprived, though not them. The environmental activist Stephanie Mills, for example, stridently denounces sprawl and other people's desires for detached homes, then notes she owns the thirty acres around her home so that she doesn't have to be disturbed by seeing the comings and goings of neighbors. Thirty acres devoted solely to a single person's home! If everyone demanded this, the entire nation would need to be paved over. (Average home lot size in the United States is one-quarter of an acre.)

[11]See *Lead Us into Temptation* by James Twitchell, New York: Columbia University Press, 1999.

people genuinely do not care about what they accumulate, emphasizing the spiritual. But in the United States and European Union, this faction is a clear minority, while often those who call themselves spiritual or religious are the most voracious, insatiable acquirers. . . .

READING THE TEXT

1. According to Easterbrook, what is the significance of the increased popularity of elective plastic surgery among both men and women?
2. Characterize Easterbrook's tone in this essay. How does it affect the persuasiveness of his argument?
3. Summarize in your own words the central contradiction in Americans' habits as consumers that is the focus of Easterbrook's argument.
4. Describe what the author means by "the revenge of the plastic" (para. 10).
5. What is Easterbrook's view of those who denounce materialism?

READING THE SIGNS

1. While the great majority of college students do not have the disposable income of working adults, they are also immersed in American consumer culture. In your journal, reflect on your own habits of consumption and those of friends and acquaintances. Do you and those you know feel the urge to buy material possessions, whether they be clothing, CDs, or electronic gadgets? If so, to what extent do these possessions provide you with pleasure? If you disdain possessions, what response do you receive from others?
2. Analyze the advertising in magazines intended for economically comfortable readers, such as the *New Yorker* or *Forbes*. Use your observations to support an argument about the extent to which such publications encourage "runaway materialism" (para. 5).
3. Write an essay in which you support, oppose, or modify the proposition that the media's intense coverage of wealthy celebrities such as Martha Stewart, Donald Trump, and Paris Hilton works to intensify people's desire for material possessions.
4. Write a response to Easterbrook's claim that "material abundance may even have the perverse effect of instilling unhappiness" (para. 9).
5. Read or review Laurence Shames's "The More Factor" (p. 76), first published in 1989. Then, adopting Shames's perspective, write a response to Easterbrook's argument. Would Shames agree or disagree with Easterbrook's fundamental position that "runaway materialism" brings with it unhappiness?

"Leave Area Clean"

READING THE SIGNS

1. What contradictory impulses does this image bring to mind? Is litter an inevitable by-product of our consumption-oriented society?

2. The Web site **www.stoplittering.com**, featuring the slogan "Just Pick It Up," suggests that the problem of litter can be solved if everyone stopped to clean up a few pieces of litter each day. Do you think this idea might work? Would you be willing to give it a try? Can you think of a more effective method of preventing the kind of litter seen in this image? What are some trade-offs with your method? What, in your opinion, should be the penalty for littering?

JACK SOLOMON
Masters of Desire: The Culture of American Advertising

When the background music in a TV or radio automobile commercial is classical, you can be pretty certain that the ad is pitching a Lexus or a Mercedes. When it's country western, it's probably for Dodge or Chevy. English accents are popular in Jaguar ads, while a good western twang sure helps move pickup trucks. Whenever advertisers make use of status-oriented or common-folk-oriented cultural cues, they are playing on one of America's most fundamental contradictions, as Jack Solomon (b. 1954) explains in this cultural analysis of American advertising. The contradiction is between the simultaneous desire for social superiority (elitism) and social equality (populism) that lies at the heart of the American dream. And one way or another, it offers a good way to pitch a product. Solomon, a professor of English at California State University, Northridge, is the author of The Signs of Our Time *(1988), from which this selection is taken, and* Discourse and Reference in the Nuclear Age *(1988). He is also coeditor with Sonia Maasik of both* California Dreams and Realities *(2004) and this textbook.*

Amongst democratic nations, men easily attain a certain equality of condition; but they can never attain as much as they desire.

— ALEXIS DE TOCQUEVILLE

On May 10, 1831, a young French aristocrat named Alexis de Tocqueville arrived in New York City at the start of what would become one of the most famous visits to America in our history. He had come to observe firsthand the institutions of the freest, most egalitarian society of the age, but what he found was a paradox. For behind America's mythic promise of equal opportunity,

Tocqueville discovered a desire for *unequal* social rewards, a ferocious competition for privilege and distinction. As he wrote in his monumental study, *Democracy in America*:

> When all privileges of birth and fortune are abolished, when all professions are accessible to all, and a man's own energies may place him at the top of any one of them, an easy and unbounded career seems open to his ambition. . . . But this is an erroneous notion, which is corrected by daily experience. [For when] men are nearly alike, and all follow the same track, it is very difficult for any one individual to walk quick and cleave a way through the same throng which surrounds and presses him.

Yet walking quick and cleaving a way is precisely what Americans dream of. We Americans dream of rising above the crowd, of attaining a social summit beyond the reach of ordinary citizens. And therein lies the paradox.

The American dream, in other words, has two faces: the one communally egalitarian and the other competitively elitist. This contradiction is no accident; it is fundamental to the structure of American society. Even as America's great myth of equality celebrates the virtues of mom, apple pie, and the girl or boy next door, it also lures us to achieve social distinction, to rise above the crowd and bask alone in the glory. This land is your land and this land is my land, Woody Guthrie's populist anthem tells us, but we keep trying to increase the "my" at the expense of the "your." Rather than fostering contentment, the American dream breeds desire, a longing for a greater share of the pie. It is as if our society were a vast high-school football game, with the bulk of the participants noisily rooting in the stands while, deep down, each of them is wishing he or she could be the star quarterback or head cheerleader.

For the semiotician, the contradictory nature of the American myth of equality is nowhere written so clearly as in the signs that American advertisers use to manipulate us into buying their wares. "Manipulate" is the word here, not "persuade"; for advertising campaigns are not sources of product information, they are exercises in behavior modification. Appealing to our subconscious emotions rather than to our conscious intellects, advertisements are designed to exploit the discontentments fostered by the American dream, the constant desire for social success and the material rewards that accompany it. America's consumer economy runs on desire, and advertising stokes the engines by transforming common objects — from peanut butter to political candidates — into signs of all the things that Americans covet most.

But by semiotically reading the signs that advertising agencies manufac- 5 ture to stimulate consumption, we can plot the precise state of desire in the audiences to which they are addressed. Let's look at a representative sample of ads and what they say about the emotional climate of the country and the fast-changing trends of American life. Because ours is a highly diverse, pluralistic society, various advertisements may say different things depending on their intended audiences, but in every case they say something about America, about the status of our hopes, fears, desires, and beliefs.

We'll begin with two ad campaigns conducted by the same company that bear out Alexis de Tocqueville's observations about the contradictory nature of American society: General Motors' campaigns for its Cadillac and Chevrolet lines. First, consider an early magazine ad for the Cadillac Allanté. Appearing as a full-color, four-page insert in *Time*, the ad seems to say "I'm special — and so is this car" even before we've begun to read it. Rather than being printed on the ordinary, flimsy pages of the magazine, the Allanté spread appears on glossy coated stock. The unwritten message here is that an extraordinary car deserves an extraordinary advertisement, and that both car and ad are aimed at an extraordinary consumer, or at least one who wishes to appear extraordinary compared to his more ordinary fellow citizens.

Ads of this kind work by creating symbolic associations between their product and what is most coveted by the consumers to whom they are addressed. It is significant, then, that this ad insists that the Allanté is virtually an Italian rather than an American car, an automobile, as its copy runs, "Conceived and Commissioned by America's Luxury Car Leader — Cadillac" but "Designed and Handcrafted by Europe's Renowned Design Leader — Pininfarina, SpA, of Turin, Italy." This is not simply a piece of product information, it's a sign of the prestige that European luxury cars enjoy in today's automotive marketplace. Once the luxury car of choice for America's status drivers, Cadillac has fallen far behind its European competitors in the race for the prestige market. So the Allanté essentially represents Cadillac's decision, after years of resisting the trend toward European cars, to introduce its own European import — whose high cost is clearly printed on the last page of the ad. . . .

American companies manufacture status symbols because American consumers want them. As Alexis de Tocqueville recognized a century and a half ago, the competitive nature of democratic societies breeds a desire for social distinction, a yearning to rise above the crowd. But given the fact that those who do make it to the top in socially mobile societies have often risen from the lower ranks, they still look like everyone else. In the socially immobile societies of aristocratic Europe, generations of fixed social conditions produced subtle class signals. The accent of one's voice, the shape of one's nose, or even the set of one's chin immediately communicated social status. Aside from the nasal bray and uptilted head of the Boston Brahmin, Americans do not have any native sets of personal status signals. If it weren't for his Mercedes-Benz and Manhattan townhouse, the parvenu Wall Street millionaire often couldn't be distinguished from the man who tailors his suits. Hence, the demand for status symbols, for the objects that mark one off as a social success, is particularly strong in democratic nations — stronger even than in aristocratic societies, where the aristocrat so often looks and sounds different from everyone else.

Status symbols, then, are signs that identify their possessors' place in a social hierarchy, markers of rank and prestige. We can all think of any number of status symbols — Rolls-Royces, Beverly Hills mansions, even Shar Pei puppies (whose rareness and expense has rocketed them beyond Russian wolfhounds as status pets and has even inspired whole lines of wrinkle-faced stuffed toys) — but how do we know that something *is* a status symbol? The explanation is quite simple: When an object (or puppy!) either costs a lot of money or requires influential connections to possess, anyone who possesses it must also possess the necessary means and influence to acquire it. The object itself really doesn't matter, since it ultimately disappears behind the presumed social potency of its owner. Semiotically, what matters is the signal it sends, its value as a sign of power. One traditional sign of social distinction is owning a country estate and enjoying the peace and privacy that attend it. Advertisements for Mercedes-Benz, Jaguar, and Audi automobiles thus frequently feature drivers motoring quietly along a country road, presumably on their way to or from their country houses.

Advertisers have been quick to exploit the status signals that belong to body language as well. As Hegel observed in the early nineteenth century, it is an ancient aristocratic prerogative to be seen by the lower orders without having to look at them in return. Tilting his chin high in the air and gazing down at the world under hooded eyelids, the aristocrat invites observation while refusing to look back. We can find such a pose exploited in an advertisement for Cadillac Seville in which we see an elegantly dressed woman out for a drive with her husband in their new Cadillac. If we look closely at the woman's body language, we can see her glance inwardly with a satisfied smile on her face but not outward toward the camera that represents our gaze. She is glad to be seen by us in her Seville, but she isn't interested in looking at *us*!

Ads that are aimed at a broader market take the opposite approach. If the American dream encourages the desire to "arrive," to vault above the mass, it also fosters a desire to be popular, to "belong." Populist commercials accordingly transform products into signs of belonging, utilizing such common icons as country music, small-town life, family picnics, and farmyards. All of these icons are incorporated in GM's "Heartbeat of America" campaign for its Chevrolet line. Unlike the Seville commercial, the faces in the Chevy ads look straight at us and smile. Dress is casual; the mood upbeat. Quick camera cuts take us from rustic to suburban to urban scenes, creating an American montage filmed from sea to shining sea. We all "belong" in a Chevy.

Where price alone doesn't determine the market for a product, advertisers can go either way. Both Johnnie Walker and Jack Daniel's are better-grade whiskies, but where a Johnnie Walker ad appeals to the buyer who wants a mark of aristocratic distinction in his liquor, a Jack Daniel's ad emphasizes the down-home, egalitarian folksiness of its product. Johnnie Walker associates itself with such conventional status symbols as sable coats, Rolls-Royces, and black gold; Jack Daniel's gives us a Good Ol' Boy in overalls. In fact, Jack Daniel's Good Ol' Boy is an icon of backwoods independence, recalling the days of the moonshiner and the Whisky Rebellion of 1794. Evoking emotions quite at odds with those stimulated in Johnnie Walker ads, the advertisers of Jack Daniel's have chosen to transform their product into a sign of America's populist tradition. The fact that both ads successfully sell whisky is itself a sign of the dual nature of the American dream. . . .

Populist advertising is particularly effective in the face of foreign competition. When Americans feel threatened from the outside, they tend to circle the wagons and temporarily forget their class differences. In the face of the Japanese automotive "invasion," Chrysler runs populist commercials in which Lee Iacocca joins the simple folk who buy his cars as the jingle "Born in America" blares in the background. Seeking to capitalize on the popularity of Bruce Springsteen's *Born in the USA* album, these ads gloss over Springsteen's ironic lyrics in a vast display of flag-waving. Chevrolet's "Heartbeat of America" campaign attempts to woo American motorists away from Japanese automobiles by appealing to their patriotic sentiments.

The patriotic iconography of these campaigns also reflects the general cultural mood of the early to mid-1980s. After a period of national anguish in the wake of the Vietnam War and the Iran hostage crisis, America went on a patriotic binge. American athletic triumphs in the Lake Placid and Los Angeles Olympics introduced a sporting tone into the national celebration, often making international affairs appear like one great Olympiad in which America was always going for the gold. In response, advertisers began to do their own flag-waving.

The mood of advertising during this period was definitely upbeat. Even 15 deodorant commercials, which traditionally work on our self-doubts and fears of social rejection, jumped on the bandwagon. In the guilty sixties, we had ads like the "Ice Blue Secret" campaign with its connotations of guilt and shame. In the feel-good Reagan eighties, "Sure" deodorant commercials featured images of triumphant Americans throwing up their arms in victory to reveal — no wet marks! Deodorant commercials once had the moral echo of Nathaniel Hawthorne's guilt-ridden *The Scarlet Letter*; in the early eighties they had all the moral subtlety of *Rocky IV*, reflecting the emotions of a Vietnam-weary nation eager to embrace the imagery of America Triumphant. . . .

Live the Fantasy

By reading the signs of American advertising, we can conclude that America is a nation of fantasizers, often preferring the sign to the substance and easily enthralled by a veritable Fantasy Island of commercial illusions. Critics of Madison Avenue often complain that advertisers create consumer desire, but semioticians don't think the situation is that simple. Advertisers may give shape to consumer fantasies, but they need raw material to work with, the subconscious dreams and desires of the marketplace. As long as these desires remain unconscious, advertisers will be able to exploit them. But by bringing the fantasies to the surface, you can free yourself from advertising's often hypnotic grasp.

I can think of no company that has more successfully seized upon the subconscious fantasies of the American marketplace — indeed the world marketplace — than McDonald's. By no means the first nor the only hamburger chain in the United States, McDonald's emerged victorious in the "burger wars" by transforming hamburgers into signs of all that was desirable in American life. Other chains like Wendy's, Burger King, and Jack-In-The-Box continue to advertise and sell widely, but no company approaches McDonald's transformation of itself into a symbol of American culture.

McDonald's success can be traced to the precision of its advertising. Instead of broadcasting a single "one-size-fits-all" campaign at a time, McDonald's pitches its burgers simultaneously at different age groups, different classes, even different races (Budweiser beer, incidentally, has succeeded in the same way). For children, there is the Ronald McDonald campaign, which presents a fantasy world that has little to do with hamburgers in any rational sense but a great deal to do with the emotional desires of kids. Ronald McDonald and his friends are signs that recall the Muppets, *Sesame Street*, the circus, toys, storybook illustrations, even *Alice in Wonderland*. Such signs do not signify hamburgers. Rather, they are displayed in order to prompt in the child's mind an automatic association of fantasy, fun, and McDonald's.

The same approach is taken in ads aimed at older audiences — teens, adults, and senior citizens. In the teen-oriented ads we may catch a fleeting glimpse of a hamburger or two, but what we are really shown is a teenage fantasy: groups of hip and happy adolescents singing, dancing, and cavorting together. Fearing loneliness more than anything else, adolescents quickly respond to the group appeal of such commercials. "Eat a Big Mac," these ads say, "and you won't be stuck home alone on Saturday night."

To appeal to an older and more sophisticated audience no longer so 20 afraid of not belonging and more concerned with finding a place to go out to at night, McDonald's has designed the elaborate "Mac Tonight" commercials, which have for their backdrop a nightlit urban skyline and at their center a cabaret pianist with a moon-shaped head, a glad manner, and Blues Brothers shades. Such signs prompt an association of McDonald's with nightclubs and urban sophistication, persuading us that McDonald's is a place not only for breakfast or lunch but for dinner too, as if it were a popular off-Broadway nightspot, a place to see and be seen. Even the parody of Kurt Weill's "Mack the Knife" theme song that Mac the Pianist performs is a sign, a subtle signal to the sophisticated hamburger eater able to recognize the origin of the tune in Bertolt Brecht's *Threepenny Opera*.

For yet older customers, McDonald's has designed a commercial around the fact that it employs a large number of retirees and seniors. In one such ad, we see an elderly man leaving his pretty little cottage early in the morning to start work as "the new kid" at McDonald's, and then we watch him during his first day on the job. Of course he is a great success, outdoing everyone else with his energy and efficiency, and he returns home in the evening to a loving wife and a happy home. One would almost think that the ad was a kind of moving "help wanted" sign (indeed, McDonald's *was* hiring elderly employees at the time), but it's really just directed at consumers. Older viewers can see themselves wanted and appreciated in the ad — and perhaps be distracted from the rationally uncomfortable fact that many senior citizens take such jobs because of financial need and thus may be unlikely to own the sort of home that one sees in the commercial. But realism isn't the point here. This is fantasyland, a dream world promising instant gratification no matter what the facts of the matter may be.

Practically the only fantasy that McDonald's doesn't exploit is the fantasy of sex. This is understandable, given McDonald's desire to present itself as a family restaurant. But everywhere else, sexual fantasies, which have always had an important place in American advertising, are beginning to dominate the advertising scene. You expect sexual come-ons in ads for perfume or cosmetics or jewelry — after all, that's what they're selling — but for room deodorizers? In a magazine ad for Claire Burke home fragrances, for example, we see a well-dressed couple cavorting about their bedroom in what looks like a cheery preparation for sadomasochistic exercises. Jordache and Calvin Klein pitch blue jeans as props for teenage sexuality. The phallic appeal of automobiles, traditionally an implicit feature in automotive advertising, becomes quite explicit in a Dodge commercial that shifts back and forth from shots of a young man in an automobile to teasing glimpses of a woman — his date — as she dresses in her apartment.

The very language of today's advertisements is charged with sexuality. Products in the more innocent fifties were "new and improved," but everything in the eighties is "hot!" — as in "hot woman," or sexual heat. Cars are "hot." Movies are "hot." An ad for Valvoline pulses to the rhythm of a "heat wave, burning in my car." Sneakers get red hot in a magazine ad for Travel Fox athletic shoes in which we see male and female figures, clad only in Travel Fox shoes, apparently in the act of copulation — an ad that earned one of *Adweek*'s annual "badvertising" awards for shoddy advertising.

The sexual explicitness of contemporary advertising is a sign not so much of American sexual fantasies as of the lengths to which advertisers will go to get attention. Sex never fails as an attention-getter, and in a particularly competitive, and expensive, era for American marketing, advertisers like to bet on a sure thing. Ad people refer to the proliferation of TV, radio, newspaper, magazine, and billboard ads as "clutter," and nothing cuts through the clutter like sex.

By showing the flesh, advertisers work on the deepest, most coercive   25 human emotions of all. Much sexual coercion in advertising, however, is a sign of a desperate need to make certain that clients are getting their money's worth. The appearance of advertisements that refer directly to the prefabricated fantasies of Hollywood is a sign of a different sort of desperation: a desperation for ideas. With the rapid turnover of advertising campaigns mandated by the need to cut through the "clutter," advertisers may be hard pressed for new ad concepts, and so they are more and more frequently turning to already-established models. In the early 1980s, for instance, Pepsi-Cola ran a series of ads broadly alluding to Steven Spielberg's *E.T.* In one such ad, we see a young boy, who, like the hero of *E.T.*, witnesses an extraterrestrial visit. The boy is led to a soft-drink machine where he pauses to drink a can of Pepsi as the spaceship he's spotted flies off into the universe. The relationship between the ad and the movie, accordingly, is a parasitical one, with the ad taking its life from the creative body of the film. . . .

Madison Avenue has also framed ad campaigns around the cultural prestige of high-tech machinery. This is especially the case with sports cars, whose high-tech appeal is so powerful that some people apparently fantasize about *being* sports cars. At least, this is the conclusion one might draw from a Porsche commercial that asked its audience, "If you were a car, what kind of car would you be?" As a candy-red Porsche speeds along a rain-slick forest road, the ad's voice-over describes all the specifications you'd want to have if you *were* a sports car. "If you were a car," the commercial concludes, "you'd be a Porsche."

In his essay "Car Commercials and *Miami Vice*," Todd Gitlin explains the semiotic appeal of such ads as those in the Porsche campaign. Aired at the height of what may be called America's "myth of the entrepreneur," these commercials were aimed at young corporate managers who imaginatively identified with the "lone wolf" image of a Porsche speeding through the woods. Gitlin points out that such images cater to the fantasies of faceless corporate men who dream of entrepreneurial glory, of striking out on their own like John DeLorean and telling the boss to take his job and shove it. But as DeLorean's spectacular failure demonstrates, the life of the entrepreneur can be extremely risky. So rather than having to go it alone and take the risks that accompany entrepreneurial independence, the young executive can substitute fantasy for reality by climbing into his Porsche — or at least that's what Porsche's advertisers wanted him to believe.

But there is more at work in the Porsche ads than the fantasies of corporate America. Ever since Arthur C. Clarke and Stanley Kubrick teamed up to present us with HAL 9000, the demented computer of *2001: A Space Odyssey*, the American imagination has been obsessed with the melding of man and machine. First there was television's *Six Million Dollar Man*, and then movieland's *Star Wars*, *Blade Runner*, and *Robocop*, fantasy visions of a future dominated by machines. Androids haunt our imaginations as machines seize the initiative. *Time* magazine's "Man of the Year" for 1982 was a computer. Robot-built automobiles appeal to drivers who spend their days in front of computer screens — perhaps designing robots. When so much power and prestige is being given to high-tech machines, wouldn't you rather be a Porsche?

In short, the Porsche campaign is a sign of a new mythology that is emerging before our eyes, a myth of the machine, which is replacing the myth of the human. The iconic figure of the little tramp caught up in the cogs of industrial production in Charlie Chaplin's *Modern Times* signified a humanistic revulsion to the age of the machine. Human beings, such icons said, were superior to machines. Human values should come first in the moral order of things. But as Edith Milton suggests in her essay "The Track of the Mutant," we are now coming to believe that machines are superior to human beings, that mechanical nature is superior to human nature. Rather than being threatened by machines, we long to merge with them. *The Six Million Dollar Man* is one iconic figure in the new mythology; Harrison Ford's sexual coupling with an android is another. In such an age it should come as little wonder that computer-synthesized Max Headroom should be a commercial spokesman for Coca-Cola, or that Federal

Express should design a series of TV ads featuring mechanical-looking human beings revolving around strange and powerful machines.

Fear and Trembling in the Marketplace

While advertisers play on and reflect back at us our fantasies about everything   30
from fighter pilots to robots, they also play on darker imaginings. If dream and desire can be exploited in the quest for sales, so can nightmare and fear.

The nightmare equivalent of America's populist desire to "belong," for example, is the fear of not belonging, of social rejection, of being different. Advertisements for dandruff shampoos, mouthwashes, deodorants, and laundry detergents ("Ring around the Collar!") accordingly exploit such fears, bullying us into consumption. Although ads of this type are still around in the 1980s, they were particularly common in the fifties and early sixties, reflecting a society still reeling from the witch-hunts of the McCarthy years. When any sort of social eccentricity or difference could result in a public denunciation and the loss of one's job or even liberty, Americans were keen to conform and be like everyone else. No one wanted to be "guilty" of smelling bad or of having a dirty collar.

"Guilt" ads characteristically work by creating narrative situations in which someone is "accused" of some social "transgression," pronounced guilty, and then offered the sponsor's product as a means of returning to "innocence." Such ads, in essence, are parodies of ancient religious rituals of guilt and atonement, whereby sinning humanity is offered salvation through the agency of priest and church. In the world of advertising, a product takes the place of the priest, but the logic of the situation is quite similar.

In commercials for Wisk detergent, for example, we witness the drama of a hapless housewife and her husband as they are mocked by the jeering voices of children shouting "Ring around the Collar!" "Oh, those dirty rings!" the housewife groans in despair. It's as if she and her husband were being stoned by an angry crowd. But there's hope, there's help, there's Wisk. Cleansing her soul of sin as well as her husband's, the housewife launders his shirts with Wisk, and behold, his collars are clean. Product salvation is only as far as the supermarket. . . .

If guilt looks backward in time to past transgressions, fear, like desire, faces forward, trembling before the future. In the late 1980s, a new kind of fear commercial appeared, one whose narrative played on the worries of young corporate managers struggling up the ladder of success. Representing the nightmare equivalent of the elitist desire to "arrive," ads of this sort created images of failure, storylines of corporate defeat. In one ad for Apple computers, for example, a group of junior executives sits around a table with the boss as he asks each executive how long it will take his or her department to complete some publishing jobs. "Two or three days," answers one nervous executive. "A week, on overtime," a tight-lipped woman responds. But one young up-and-comer can have everything ready tomorrow, today, or yesterday, because his department uses a Macintosh desktop publishing system. Guess who'll get the next promotion?

For other markets, there are other fears. If McDonald's presents senior citi- 35
zens with bright fantasies of being useful and appreciated beyond retirement, companies like Secure Horizons dramatize senior citizens' fears of being caught short by a major illness. Running its ads in the wake of budgetary cuts in the Medicare system, Secure Horizons designed a series of commercials featuring a pleasant old man named Harry — who looks and sounds rather like Carroll O'Connor — who tells us the story of the scare he got during his wife's recent illness. Fearing that next time Medicare won't cover the bills, he has purchased supplemental health insurance from Secure Horizons and now securely tends his roof-top garden. . . .

The Future of an Illusion

There are some signs in the advertising world that Americans are getting fed up with fantasy advertisements and want to hear some straight talk. Weary of extravagant product claims and irrelevant associations, consumers trained by years of advertising to distrust what they hear seem to be developing an immunity to commercials. At least, this is the semiotic message I read in the "new realism" advertisements of the eighties, ads that attempt to convince you that what you're seeing is the real thing, that the ad is giving you the straight dope, not advertising hype.

You can recognize the "new realism" by its camera techniques. The light-ing is usually subdued to give the ad the effect of being filmed without studio lighting or special filters. The scene looks gray, as if the blinds were drawn. The camera shots are jerky and off-angle, often zooming in for sudden and unflattering close-ups, as if the cameraman were an amateur with a home video recorder. In a "realistic" ad for AT&T, for example, we are treated to a monologue by a plump stockbroker — his plumpness intended as a sign that he's for real and not just another actor — who tells us about the problems he's had with his phone system (not AT&T's) as the camera jerks around, generally filming him from below as if the cameraman couldn't quite fit his equipment into the crammed office and had to film the scene on his knees. "This is no fancy advertisement," the ad tries to convince us, "this is sincere."

An ad for Miller draft beer tries the same approach, re-creating the effect of an amateur videotape of a wedding celebration. Camera shots shift sud-denly from group to group. The picture jumps. Bodies are poorly framed. The color is washed out. Like the beer it is pushing, the ad is supposed to strike us as being "as real as it gets."

Such ads reflect a desire for reality in the marketplace, a weariness with Madison Avenue illusions. But there's no illusion like the illusion of reality. Every special technique that advertisers use to create their "reality effects" is, in fact, more unrealistic than the techniques of "illusory" ads. The world, in reality, doesn't jump around when you look at it. It doesn't appear in subdued gray tones. Our eyes don't have zoom lenses, and we don't look at things with our heads cocked to one side. The irony of the "new realism" is that it is more unrealistic, more artificial, than the ordinary run of television advertising.

But don't expect any truly realistic ads in the future, because a realistic 40 advertisement is a contradiction in terms. The logic of advertising is entirely semiotic: It substitutes signs for things, framed visions of consumer desire for the thing itself. The success of modern advertising, its penetration into every corner of American life, reflects a culture that has itself chosen illusion over reality. At a time when political candidates all have professional image-makers attached to their staffs, and the President of the United States can be an actor who once sold shirt collars, all the cultural signs are pointing to more illusions in our lives rather than fewer — a fecund breeding ground for the world of the advertiser.

READING THE TEXT

1. Describe in your own words the paradox of the American dream, as Solomon sees it.

2. In Solomon's view, why do status symbols work particularly well in manipulating American consumers?

3. What are " 'guilt' ads" (para. 32), according to Solomon, and how do they affect consumers?

4. Why, in Solomon's view, has McDonald's been so successful in its ad campaigns?

5. What relationship does Solomon see between the "new realism" (para. 37) of some ads and the paradoxes of the American dream?

READING THE SIGNS

1. The American political scene has changed since the late 1980s, when this selection was first published. In an analytic essay, argue whether you believe the contradiction between populism and elitism that Solomon describes still affects American advertising and media. Be sure to discuss specific media examples. To develop your ideas, consult Thomas Frank's "Countercultural Consumerism" (p. 136) and Gregg Easterbrook's "The Progress Paradox" (p. 400).

2. Read or review David Brooks's "One Nation, Slightly Divisible" (p. 388). In an essay, argue whether you see a correlation between Brooks's red state/blue state dichotomy and Solomon's populist-elitist paradox. Be sure to support your position with specific examples from the media or consumer culture.

3. Bring to class a general-interest magazine such as *Time,* and work in small groups to study the advertising. Do the ads tend to have an elitist or populist appeal? What relationship do you see between the appeal you identify and the magazine's target readership? Present your group's findings to the class.

4. In class, brainstorm a list of status symbols common in advertising today. Then discuss what groups they appeal to and why. Can you detect any patterns based on gender, ethnicity, or age?

5. In your college library, locate an issue of a popular magazine from an earlier decade, such as the 1930s or 1940s. Then write an essay in which you compare and contrast the advertising found in that early issue with the advertising in a current issue of the same publication. What similarities and differences do you find in the myths underlying the advertising, and what is their significance?

ALFRED LUBRANO
The Shock of Education: How College Corrupts

One of America's most fundamental contradictions lies at the heart of the American dream itself. That is, America's promise of social mobility compels those who begin at the bottom to leave behind their origins in order to succeed, which entails giving up a part of oneself and leaving one's home behind. It can be a wrenching transition, and in this reflection on what it means to achieve the dream, Alfred Lubrano describes the strain of moving between two worlds, relating both his own experiences moving from working-class Brooklyn to an Ivy League school and those of other working-class "straddlers" who moved into the middle class. The son of a bricklayer, Lubrano (b. 1956) is a journalist and National Public Radio commentator. He is the author of Limbo: Blue-Collar Roots, White-Collar Dreams *(2004), from which this selection is taken.*

College is where the Great Change begins. People start to question the blue-collar take on the world. Status dissonance, the sociologists call it. Questions arise: Are the guys accurate in saying people from such-and-such a race are really so bad? Was Mom right when she said nice girls don't put out? Suddenly, college opens up a world of ideas — a life of the mind — abstract and intangible. The core blue-collar values and goals — loyalty to family and friends, making money, marrying, and procreating — are supplanted by stuff you never talked about at home: personal fulfillment, societal obligation, the pursuit of knowledge for knowledge's sake, and on and on. One world opens and widens; another shrinks.

There's an excitement and a sadness to that. The child, say Sennett and Cobb, is deserting his past, betraying the parents he is rising above, an unavoidable result when you're trying to accomplish more with your life than merely earning a paycheck.[1] So much will change between parent and child, and between

---

[1]Richard Sennett and Jonathan Cobb, *The Hidden Injuries of Class* (New York: Alfred A. Knopf, 1972), 131.

peers, in the college years. "Every bit of learning takes you further from your parents," says Southwest Texas State University history professor Gregg Andrews, himself a Straddler. "I say this to all my freshmen to start preparing them." The best predictor of whether you're going to have problems with your family is the distance between your education and your parents', Jake Ryan says. You may soon find yourself with nothing to talk to your folks or friends about.

This is the dark part of the American story, the kind of thing we work to hide. Mobility means discomfort, because so much has to change; one can't allow for the satisfactions of stasis: You prick yourself and move, digging spurs into your own hide to get going, forcing yourself to forget the comforts of the barn. In this country, we speak grandly of this metamorphosis, never stopping to consider that for many class travelers with passports stamped for new territory, the trip is nothing less than a bridge burning.

Fighting Self-Doubt

When Columbia plucked me out of working-class Brooklyn, I was sure they had made a mistake, and I remained convinced of that throughout most of my time there. My high school was a gigantic (4,500 students) factory; we literally had gridlock in the halls between classes, kids belly to back between history and English class. A teacher once told me that if every one of the reliable corps of truant students actually decided to show up to class one day, the school could not hold us all. (We were unofficially nicknamed "the Italian Army." When our football guys played nearby New Utrecht, which boasted an equivalent ethnic demographic, kids dubbed the game the "Lasagna Bowl.") Lafayette High School roiled with restless boys and girls on their way to jobs in their parents' unions or to secretaries' desks. How could you move from that to an elite college?

At night, at home, the difference in the Columbia experiences my father and I were having was becoming more evident. The family still came together for dinner, despite our disparate days. We talked about general stuff, and I learned to self-censor. I'd seen how ideas could be upsetting, especially when wielded by a smarmy freshman who barely knew what he was talking about. No one wanted to hear how the world worked from some kid who was first learning to use his brain; it was as unsettling as riding in a car with a new driver. When he taught a course on Marx, Sackrey said he used to tell his students just before Thanksgiving break not to talk about "this stuff at the dinner table" or they'd mess up the holiday. Me mimicking my professors' thoughts on race, on people's struggle for equality, or on politics didn't add to the conviviality of the one nice hour in our day. So I learned to shut up.

After dinner, my father would flip on the TV in the living room. My mom would grab a book and join him. And I'd go looking for a quiet spot to study. In his autobiography, *Hunger of Memory: The Education of Richard Rodriguez*, the 5 brilliant Mexican-American Straddler, writer, and PBS commentator invokes British social scientist Richard Hoggart's "scholarship boys," finding pieces of himself in them. Working-class kids trying to advance in life, the scholarship boys learned to withdraw from the warm noise of the gathered family to isolate themselves with their books.[2] (Read primarily as a memoir of ethnicity and — most famously — an anti-affirmative action tract, the book is more genuinely a dissertation on class. At a sidewalk café in San Francisco, Rodriguez himself tells me how often his book is miscatalogued.) Up from the immigrant working class, Rodriguez says in our interview, the scholarship boy finds himself moving between two antithetical places: home and school. With the family, there is intimacy and emotion. At school, one learns to live with "lonely reason." Home life is in the now, Rodriguez says; school life exists on an altogether different plane, calm and reflective, with an eye toward the future.

The scholarship boy must learn to distance himself from the family circle in order to succeed academically, Rodriguez tells me. By doing this, he slowly loses his family. There's a brutality to education, he says, a rough and terrible disconnect. Rodriguez says he despised his parents' "shabbiness," their inability to speak English. "I hated that they didn't know what I was learning," he says. He thought of D. H. Lawrence's *Sons and Lovers*, and of Paul Morel, the coal miner's son. Lawrence is a model for Rodriguez, in a way. Rodriguez remembers the scene in which the son watches his father pick up his schoolbooks, his rough hands fingering the volumes that are the instruments separating the two men. Books were establishing a disharmony between the classroom and Rodriguez's house. Preoccupation with language and reading is an effeminacy not easily understood by workers. "It sears your soul to finally decide to talk like your teacher and not your father," Rodriguez says. "I'm not talking about anything less than the grammar of the heart."

Myself, I studied in the kitchen near the dishwasher because its white noise drowned out the television. As long as the wash cycle ran, I could not hear Mr. T and the A-Team win the day. I did not begrudge my father his one indulgence; there wasn't much else that could relax him. He was not a drinker. TV drained away the tumult and hazard of his Columbia day. My own room was too close to the living room. My brother's small room was too crowded for both of us to study in. You never went in your parents' bedroom without them in it, inviting you. When the dishes were clean and the kitchen again too quiet to beat back the living room noise, I'd go downstairs to my grandparents' apartment. If they were both watching the same TV show on the first floor, then the basement was free. Here was profound and almost disquieting silence. I could hear the house's systems rumble and shake: water whooshing through

---

[2]Richard Rodriguez, *Hunger of Memory: The Education of Richard Rodriguez* (New York: Bantam Books, 1983), 46. Rodriguez himself quotes from Richard Hoggart, *The Uses of Literacy* (London: Chatto and Windus, 1957), chap. 10.

pipes, the oil burner powering on and off, and the refrigerator humming with a loud efficiency. Down in the immaculate redwood-paneled kitchen/living room, which sometimes still smelled of the sausages and peppers my grandfather may have made that night (my grandparents cooked and ate in their basement, something that never seemed unusual to us), I was 90 minutes from my school and two floors below my family in a new place, underscoring my distance from anything known, heightening my sense of isolation — my limbo status. I read Homer, Shakespeare, and Molière down there. I wrote a paper on landscape imagery in Dante's *Inferno*. In my self-pitying, melodramatic teenager's mind, I thought I had been banished to a new, lonely rung of hell that Dante hadn't contemplated.

By 11 P.M., I'd go back upstairs. My mother would be in bed, my father asleep on his chair. I'd turn off the TV, which awakened my dad. He'd walk off to bed, and I'd study for a couple more hours. His alarm would go off before 5 A.M., and he'd already be at Columbia by the time I woke up at 6:30. That's how our Ivy League days ended and began. When my father was done with Columbia, he moved on to another job site. When I was done with Columbia, I was someone else. I'd say I got the better deal. But then, my father would tell you, that was always the plan. . . .

Macbeth and Other Foolishness

Middle-class kids are groomed for another life. They understand, says Patrick Finn, why reading *Macbeth* in high school could be important years down the road. Working-class kids see no such connection, understand no future life for which digesting Shakespeare might be of value. Very much in the now, working-class people are concerned with immediate needs. And bookish kids are seen as weak.

Various education studies have shown that schools help reinforce class. 10 Teachers treat the working class and the well-to-do differently, this work demonstrates, with the blue-collar kids getting less attention and respect. It's no secret, education experts insist, that schools in poorer areas tend to employ teachers who are less well-trained. In these schools, the curriculum is test-based and uncreative. Children are taught, essentially, to obey and fill in blanks. By fourth grade, many of the children are bored and alienated; nothing in school connects to their culture. Beyond that, many working-class children are resistant to schooling and uncooperative with teachers, experts say. They feel pressure from other working-class friends to not participate and are told that being educated is effeminate and irrelevant. Educators have long understood that minority children have these problems, says Finn. But they rarely understand or see that working-class white kids have similar difficulties. "So we're missing a whole bunch of people getting screwed by the education systems," he says.

In our conversations, Finn explains that language is a key to class. In a working-class home where conformity is the norm, all opinions are dictated by group consensus, by what the class says is so. There's one way to do everything, there's one way to look at the world. Since all opinions are shared, there's never a need to explain thought and behavior. You talk less. Language in such a home, Finn says, is implicit.

Things are different in a middle-class home. There, parents are more willing to take the time to explain to little Janey why it's not such a good idea to pour chocolate sauce on the dog. If Janey challenges a rule of the house, she's spoken to like an adult, or at least not like a plebe at some military school. (Working-class homes are, in fact, very much like the military, with parents barking orders, Straddlers tell me. It's that conformity thing again.) There is a variety of opinions in middle-class homes, which are more collaborative than conformist, Finn says. Middle-class people have a multiviewed take on the world. In such a home, where one needs to express numerous ideas and opinions, language is by necessity explicit.

When it's time to go to school, the trouble starts. The language of school — of the teachers and the books — is explicit. A child from a working-class home is at a huge disadvantage, Finn says, because he's used to a narrower world of expression and a smaller vocabulary of thought. It's little wonder that kids from working-class homes have lower reading scores and do less well on SATs than middle-class kids, Finn says.

In high school, my parents got me a tutor for the math part of the SATs, to bolster a lackluster PSAT score. That sort of thing happens all the time in middle-class neighborhoods. But we were setting precedent among our kind. Most kids I knew from the community were not taking the SATs, let alone worrying about their scores. If you're from the middle class, you do not feel out of place preparing for college. Parents and peers help groom you, encourage you, and delight in your progress. Of course, when you get to freshman year, the adjustments can be hard on anyone, middle-class and working-class kids alike. But imagine going through freshman orientation if your parents are ambivalent — or hostile — about your being there, and your friends aren't clear about what you're doing.

It was like that for my friend Rita Giordano, 45, also a journalist, also from 15 Brooklyn. Her world, like mine, was populated by people who thought going from 60th to 65th Streets was a long journey. So when Rita took sojourns into Greenwich Village by herself on Saturday mornings as a teenager, she made sure not to tell any of her friends. It was too oddball to have to explain. And she'd always come back in time to go shopping with everyone. She couldn't figure out why she responded to the artsy vibe of the Village; she was just aware that there were things going on beyond the neighborhood. When it came time for college, she picked Syracuse University because it was far away, a new world to explore. That bothered her friends, and she'd have to explain herself to them on trips back home. "What do you do up there?" they asked her. "Don't you get homesick?" Suddenly, things felt awkward among childhood friends who had always been able to talk. "It was confusing to come home and see people thinking that you're not doing what they're doing, which meant you're rejecting them," said Rita, a diminutive, sensitive woman with large, brown eyes. " 'Don't they see it's still me?' I wondered. I started feeling like, how do I coexist in these two worlds, college and home? I mean, I could talk to my girlfriends about what color gowns their bridesmaids would wear at their fantasy weddings. But things like ambition and existential questions about where you fit in the world and how you make your mark — we just didn't go there."

And to make matters more complicated, there was a guy. Rita's decision to go to Syracuse didn't sit well with the boyfriend who was probably always going to remain working class. "In true Brooklyn fashion, he and his friends decided one night they were going to drive 400 miles to Syracuse to bring me back, or whatever. But on the way up, they totaled the car and my boyfriend broke his leg. He never got up there, and after that, the idea of him bringing me to my senses dissipated."

Another Straddler, Loretta Stec, had a similar problem with a blue-collar lover left behind. Loretta, a slender 39-year-old English professor at San Francisco State University with delicate features and brown hair, needed to leave the commotion of drugs and friends' abortions and the repressed religious world of Perth Amboy, New Jersey, for the calm life of the mind offered by Boston College. The only problem was Barry. When Loretta was 17, she and Barry, an older construction worker, would ride motorcycles in toxic waste dumps. He was wild and fine — what every working-class girl would want. But Loretta knew life had to get better than Perth Amboy, so she went off to Boston. Barry and she still got together, though. They even worked on the same taping crew at a construction site during the summer between Loretta's freshman and sophomore years. But the differences between them were growing. All the guys on the job — Barry included — thought it was weird that Loretta would read the *New York Times* during lunch breaks. "What's with that chick?" people asked.

By the time Loretta returned to Boston for her second year, she knew she was in a far different place than Barry. The working class was not for her. Hanging around with this guy and doing construction forever — it sounded awful. "I was upwardly mobile, and I was not going to work on a construction crew anymore," Loretta says. She tried to break it off, but Barry roared up I-95 in a borrowed car to change her mind. Loretta lived in an old Victorian with middle-class roommates who had never met anyone like Barry. When he showed up with a barking Doberman in tow, she recalled he was screaming like Stanley Kowalski in *A Streetcar Named Desire* that he wanted Loretta back. The women became terrified. Loretta was able to calm first Barry, then her roommates. Afterward, the couple went to listen to some music. In a little place on campus, a guitar trio started performing a Rolling Stones song. Suddenly, Barry turned to Loretta and began scream-singing about wild horses not being able to drag him from her, really loud, trying to get her to see his resolve. "People were wondering who was this guy, what's his deal?" Loretta says. "It pointed out the clash between my new world and the old. You don't do stuff like that. It was embarrassing, upsetting, and confusing. I didn't want to hurt him. But I knew it wasn't going to work for me." They walked around campus, fighting about things coming to an end. At some point, she recalls, Barry noticed that a college student with a nicer car than his — Loretta can't remember exactly what it was — had parked behind his car, blocking him. Already ramped up, Barry had a fit and smashed a headlight of the fancy machine with a rock. There Loretta was, 100 feet from her campus Victorian, newly ensconced in a clean world of erudition and scholarship, far from the violence and swamps of central Jersey. Her bad-boy beau, once so appealing, was raving and breathing hard, trying to pull her away from the books, back down the turnpike to the working class.

"That was really the end of it," Loretta says. "I couldn't have a guy around who was going to act like that. He was wild and crazy and I was trying to make my way." Barry relented, and left Loretta alone. They lost touch, and Loretta later learned that Barry had died, the cause of death unknown to her. It was such a shock. . . .

READING THE TEXT

1. What is your response to Lubrano's title, and why do you think he chose it?
2. Summarize in your own words the difference between Lubrano's high school and college experiences.
3. What does Richard Rodriguez mean by "There's a brutality to education" (para. 6)?
4. Why did Lubrano avoid discussing his Columbia University experiences with his family?
5. How does child-rearing differ in blue-collar and middle-class families, according to Lubrano?

READING THE SIGNS

1. In your journal, reflect on the effects — positive or negative — that attending college has had on your relationship with your family and high school friends. How do you account for any changes that may have occurred?
2. In an argumentative essay, support, challenge, or complicate Gregg Andrews's statement that "every bit of learning takes you further from your parents" (para. 1).
3. Write a synthesis of the personal tales of Lubrano, Loretta Stec, and Rita Giordano. Then use your synthesis as the basis for an essay explaining how their collective experiences support Lubrano's position that "for many class travelers with passports stamped for new territory, the trip is nothing less than a bridge burning" (para. 2).

4. Interview students from both blue-collar and middle- or upper-class backgrounds about the effect that attending college has had on their relationships with their family and high school friends. Use your findings to support your assessment of Lubrano's position that college can create divisions between blue-collar students and their families but that it tends not to have that effect on other classes.

RICHARD CORLISS
The Gospel According to Spider-Man

"For decades, America has embraced a baffling contradiction," Richard Corliss writes in this Time *analysis published in 2004. "The majority of its people are churchgoing Christians, many of them evangelical. Yet its mainstream pop culture . . . is secular at best, often raw and irreligious." As often happens in the strange dialectics of history, however, antitheses can come to meet in a new synthesis, as they do in America when a religious pastor can offer a sermon entitled "Catwoman: Discovering My True Identity." As Corliss reports, this melding of religion and pop culture is no isolated event, and with the growing Christian rock music and Christian film industries, we can expect to see more such weddings of onetime antagonists in the future. A senior writer for* Time, *Corliss (b. 1944) is also the author of* Talking Pictures *and* Greta Garbo *(both 1974).*

The Congregation for today's service of the Journey, "a casual, contemporary, Christian church," fills the Promenade, a theater on upper Broadway in New York City. The Sunday-morning faithful — a few hundred strong — have come to hear the Journey's laid-back pastor, Nelson Searcy, give them the word. The word made film. Searcy, 32, who in jeans and a goatee looks like a way less Mephistophelian Charlie Sheen, is about to deliver the last of the church's eight-part God on Film series. The topic? "*Catwoman:* Discovering My True Identity."

Searcy points to a large screen at his right that shows other comic-book heroes with multiple identities. In his sermon, he alludes only vaguely to the Catwoman myth and gives the impression that he (like most other Americans) hasn't seen the Halle Berry version. But Searcy knows that a person tormented by questions of image and identity can find encouragement in the message of Genesis 1:27: "So God created people in his own image." That biblical quotation is projected on the screen, which also features an icon of a smiling cartoon Catwoman sporting purple tights, a feather boa, and a whip.

For decades, America has embraced a baffling contradiction. The majority of its people are churchgoing Christians, many of them evangelical. Yet its mainstream pop culture, especially film, is secular at best, often raw and irreligious. In many movies, piety is for wimps, and the clergy are depicted as oafs and predators. It's hard to see those two vibrant strains of society ever coexisting, learning from each other.

Yet the two are not only meeting; they're also sitting down and breaking bread together. The unearthly success of Mel Gibson's *The Passion of the Christ* helped movie execs recognize that fervent Christians, who spend hundreds of millions of dollars on religious books and music, are worth courting. Publicists hired by studios feed sermon ideas based on new movies to ministers. Meanwhile, Christians are increasingly borrowing from movies to drive home theological lessons. Clergy of all denominations have commandeered pulpits, publishing houses, and especially websites to spread the gospel of cinevangelism.

What's the biblical import of, say, *Spider-Man*? "Peter Parker gives us all   5
a chance to be heroic," says Erwin McManus, pastor of Mosaic, a Baptist-affiliated church in Los Angeles. "The problem is, we keep looking for radioactive spiders, but really it's God who changes us." What's the big idea behind *The Village*, according to the website movieministry.com? "Perfect love drives out fear." Behind *The Notebook*? "God can step in where science cannot." And, gulp, *Anchorman*? "What is love?" If your minister floated those notions recently, it may be because movieministry.com provides homilies for Sunday sermons. The website is a kind of Holy Ghostwriter.

By spicing Matthew and Mark with Ebert and Roeper, ministers can open a window to biblical teachings and a door to the very demographic that Hollywood studios know how to reach: young people.

"Film, especially for those under 35, is the medium through which we get our primary stories, our myths, our read on reality," says Robert K. Johnston, professor of theology and culture at the Fuller Theological Seminary and the author of the newly published *Finding God in the Movies: 33 Films of Reel Faith*. It was members of that generation, says Johnston, who "even if they loved God, were simply not going to church. Clergy are realizing that unless we reorient how we talk about our faith, we will lose the next generation." He sees movies as modern parables that connect to an audience that seeks not reason but emotional relevance. "As the culture has moved from a modern to a postmodern era, we have moved from wanting to understand truth rationally to understanding truth as it's embedded in story," he says.

The cinevangelists would say that the churches' appropriation of pop culture is nothing new. "Jesus also used stories," Johnston says. "In his day, parables were the equivalent of movies." Marc Newman, who runs movieministry.com, traces pop proselytizing back to the Apostle Paul. "In Acts there's a Scripture describing how he came to the Areopagus, the marketplace in Athens where people exchanged ideas. Paul speaks to the men of Athens and refers to their poets and their prophets. He used the things they knew as a way to reach out with the Gospel."

If Paul could cite Greek poets to the Greeks, then today's proselytizers will bring the church to moviegoers and, they hope, vice versa. "Today, with DVDs and the VCR, all of us can engage a movie text," Johnston says. "When a person in a worship congregation refers to *The Shawshank Redemption*, either people have seen it or they can rent it." In addition, 3,000-screen bookings and saturation marketing guarantee that a film that opens Friday will have been seen or at least talked about by Sunday morning.

Some conservative clergy prefer using the Bible, not *Bruce Almighty*, as the 10 text for a sermon. "It's not my cup of tea," says Jerry Falwell of movie-inspired sermons. But progressive Christians love plumbing the subtexts of comedies, satires, and action movies. Now, says Ted Baehr of movieguide.org, "a church group can highlight biblical teachings by using anything from *Dodgeball* to *Saved!* to *Kill Bill*."

Baehr, who grew up in Hollywood (his father was ranger Bob Allen in cowboy serials of the '30s), has put his Columbia University Film School education to use by giving a Christian take on current movies. "We try to teach people media wisdom. If Christians didn't believe in communications, they wouldn't believe that in the beginning was the word and the word was God and the word has a salutary effect within society."

But movies? From the beginning, they were considered, in the words of Catholic doctrine, an occasion of sin. The Catholic Legion of Decency was more notable for proscribing movies than promoting them. Some of the sterner Christian sects forbade filmgoing. And that was when Hollywood still produced religious films, from uplifting tales of jolly priests (Bing Crosby in *Going My Way*) and selfless sisters (Audrey Hepburn in *The Nun's Story*) to outright miracle plays like *The Song of Bernadette*, with Jennifer Jones as a French girl who had a vision at Lourdes.

By the '70s, the religious film had virtually disappeared. Today, *The Passion* aside, the genre exists only in niche markets: Mormon films (Ryan Little's *Saints and Soldiers*, Richard Dutcher's *God's Army*), well crafted and proudly square; and Rapture movies (*The Moment After, Caught in the Rapture*), which announce a personal and earthly apocalypse. Both types of film usually fly under the radar of studios, critics, and audiences.

Rarely, a Christian message is implicated in a Hollywood film. Steven Spielberg's *Close Encounters of the Third Kind*, in which an ordinary guy sees the light and travels far to make contact with extraterrestrials, was conceived by its original screenwriter, Paul Schrader, as Saul's transforming journey to become the Apostle Paul. *The Matrix* (the first one, not the sequels) was manna to hermeneuticians. In a recent Museum of Modern Art film series called "The Hidden God: Film and Faith," *Groundhog Day*, the Bill Murray comedy about a man who relives the same day over and over, was cited as a profound statement of faith, either Buddhist (rebirth), Jewish (acceptance), or Christian (redemption).

In the broadest sense, movies are getting more religious. According to Baehr, 15 only one film in 1985 (*The Trip to Bountiful*) had "positive Christian content," compared with 69 in 2003 (including *Finding Nemo*, *Spy Kids 3D* and *Master and Commander*). Of course, it all depends on what counts as Christian and who's doing the counting. What's irrefutable is the growing number of theocentric movie websites, most recently a sophisticated one launched in February by the magazine *Christianity Today*.

The clergy may see all this as a revival; Hollywood sees it as a customer bonanza. New Line Cinema reaches out to Christian groups with films — like *Secondhand Lions*, about a boy living with his two codgerly, kindly uncles — whose themes might resonate. Says Russell Schwartz, New Line's president of domestic marketing: "The thing about all special-interest groups — Christian, Jewish, whatever — is that they have to discover something relevant to their experience." Some studio bosses go further. Baehr says he talked with a mogul who told him, "We want to be seen as Christian friendly. We realize there's a big church audience out there, and we need to reach them."

"It's a vast, untapped market," says Jonathan Bock, a former sitcom writer (*Hangin' with Mr. Cooper*), whose Grace Hill Media helps sell Hollywood films to Christian tastemakers. He pitches media outlets like *Catholic Digest* and *The 700 Club* and has created sermons and Bible-study guides and marketed such movies as *The Lord of the Rings*, *Signs*, *The Rookie*, and, yes, *Elf*. "The ground was softened before *The Passion*," says Bock. "There are hundreds of Christian critics and Jewish writers and ministers who are writing about films." And millions of the faithful who see them. A July 2004 study by George Barna, the Gallup of born-again religion, shows that Christian Evangelicals are among the most frequent moviegoers. "Being a Christian used to mean you didn't go to Hollywood movies," says David Bruce, who runs the website hollywoodjesus.com. "Now it is seen as a missionary activity."

All this could just be the church's appropriation of Hollywood salesmanship: luring audiences with promises of a movie and some good talk, as the Journey's Searcy offered. Finding a Christian message in secular films like *Catwoman* and *Spider-Man* could be either a delusion or, as Jeffrey Overstreet, a critic for *Christianity Today* says, "a way of affirming that God's truth is inescapable and can be found even in the stories of people who don't believe in him."

Hollywood doesn't necessarily want to make Christian movies. It wants to make movies Christians think are Christian. Moviemakers are happy to be the money changers in the temple, even as preachers are thrilled that a discussion of — what, *Harold & Kumar Go to White Castle*? — can guarantee a full house on Sunday.

READING THE TEXT

1. What is the effect of Corliss's opening description of Nelson Searcy's sermon entitled "*Catwoman*: Discovering My True Identity"?

2. Describe in your own words the contradiction in American culture that the writer identifies.

3. Why do some viewers find Christian messages in films like *Spider-Man,* according to Corliss?

4. What conflicts does Corliss see in the religious attitudes toward popular culture?

5. How does Corliss use the history of popular culture to explain the current tendency of religion to engage with popular culture?

READING THE SIGNS

1. Write an essay in which you support, refute, or complicate Corliss's contention that films like *Spider-Man* enable religious groups to "open a window to biblical teachings and a door to the very demographic that Hollywood studios know how to reach: young people" (para. 6).

2. Taking Corliss's article into account, write your own explanation of the response to *The Passion of the Christ,* which was supported by many Christian groups and opposed both by some Christian and Jewish groups. Alternatively, interpret the response to another film or TV program that includes a spiritual dimension, such as *Touched by an Angel.*

3. Adopting the perspective of Nelson Searcy, write a response to Corliss's claim that Christian evangelicals' view of moviegoing as a "missionary activity . . . could just be the church's appropriation of Hollywood salesmanship" (paras. 17–18).

4. Write an argumentative response to Corliss's assertion that "Hollywood doesn't necessarily want to make Christian movies. It wants to make movies Christians think are Christian" (para. 19).

5. Visit **www.movieministry.com,** and assess the validity of Corliss's claim that "the Web site is a kind of Holy Ghostwriter" (para. 5).

LUCY R. LIPPARD
Alternating Currents

America's foundation as an agrarian nation seems a thing of the past now, with three-quarters of the population living in cities or suburbs. But as Lucy R. Lippard (b. 1937) indicates in this excerpt from The Lure of the Local: Senses of Place in a Multicentered Society *(1997), you can take an American out of the country, but you can't take the country out of America. Reflecting on the complex tensions between our urban realities and rural mythologies, Lippard meditates here on the role that space plays in the construction of personal and communal consciousness. An art critic and historian whose many books include* Get the Message? A Decade of Art for Social Change *(1984),* Mixed Blessings: New Art in a Multicultural America *(1990),* The Pink Glass Swan: Selected Feminist Essays on Art *(1995), and* White/Red Cesar Paternosto *(2000), Lippard has written as well for the* Village Voice, In These Times, *and* Z Magazine.

The U.S. population today is 75 percent urban/suburban, but there remains an emotional tension between city and country, an alternating current that pulls at most Americans at various times in their lives. If the city represents the high voltage of the new (or at least the novel) and the country represents the calming tradition of the old, we are always looking for ways to balance our needs for both. I lived in Manhattan for my first nine years and returned at age twenty-one for thirty-seven adult years. While my current addresses are rural, my local knowledge of cities is New York-based and New York-biased.

The city has been seen as a field of indifference to the rest of world, as a triumph of objective over subjective, male over female, culture over nature, materialism over spirituality and idealism.[1] The inherited rural kinship systems of ancient cities were replaced with civil communities, which in turn broke down with industrialization (or perhaps before, with the medieval plagues), when cities became increasingly impersonal. The idealized vision of the Puritans' "City on the Hill" (exposed and exemplary to those living "below") notwithstanding, most positive American mythologies depend on a rural context. During the nineteenth century, as the colonization of the countryside by capital accelerated, the Jeffersonian ideal of a nation of small towns and farmers waned. Ralph Waldo Emerson's ideal "City of the West" was an attempt to reconcile nature and civilization, intended as a human community with open gates and open arms. Instead, cities, aided by absentee landlords and proto-agribusiness, began to suck up country energy and resources. By 1880, urban

---

[1] Yi-Fu Tuan's *Topophilia* was an invaluable source for this section.

populations in the western United States were already growing at four times the rate of the countryside.

Herbert Gans observed in the late sixties that American society gives its allegiance to two poles — the micro-unit of the family and the macro-unit of the nation, while local community falls through the cracks. Today, one of those poles is collapsing: under half of eligible Americans voted in the 1996 presidential election.[2] This decline in participation in social policymaking can be seen as a product of a dehumanized urban ambience, the loss of a sense of local power in places where "neighborliness is often exhausted by a nod of the head."

The clichéd image of the cold, heartless city and the warm, cuddly heartland of small towns has long since been disproved. There is no Eden. But the sheer size of the metropolis can be intimidating as well as exhilarating and seems to belie communal intimacy. What, then, constitutes the lure of the local in this environment presumed to transcend any such effect? How do cities look and feel to those who live in them? And what are their relationships to the land they are built on, to the land people left to come to them?

Cities are enormously complex palimpsests of communal history and memory, a fact that tends to be obscured by their primary identities as sites of immediacy, money, power, and energy concentrated on the present and future. Many people come to the city to escape the "local," the isolation of rural life, the rigidity and constrictions of smaller towns.

> We who live here wear this corner of the city like a comfortable old coat, an extension of our personalities, threadbare yet retaining a beauty of its own. This is the intimacy of cities, made more precious and more secret by our knowledge that it is one of many cells or corners in a great city that is not so much a labyrinth as a web or a shawl. We wrap ourselves in the city as we journey through it. Muffled, we march, "like Juno in a cloud," drawing it around us like a cloak of many colours: a disguise, a refuge, an adventure, a home.
>
> — ELIZABETH WILSON

The urban ego is in fact parochial; New Yorkers (like Parisians or Bostonians) are among the most provincial people in the world. They are often as bound to their own neighborhoods and as ignorant of the rest of the city (aside from midtown) as any small towner. A city is a center plus the sum of its neighborhoods, a collage created by juxtaposing apples and oranges. When I first lived in New York I would sometimes take the subway to a stop I'd never been to and spend hours walking in new territory, foreign countries. It was always interesting even when it was boring. All those people, all those little rooms. What were they doing in there? What lives were being played out so near and yet so far from my own? I loved my own life and didn't envy the

---

[2]The League of Women Voters estimates that 49 percent of eligible voters did vote in 1996, some 6 percent less than 1992, but other groups put the figure much lower; I read somewhere that only 39 percent voted in 1992.

women closed behind those doors; but at the same time I pictured an intimacy, a reassuring monotony that I knew I had surrendered forever.

Women in particular come to the city to break away from family expectations, domestic confinement, or to escape boredom and past mistakes. Some thrive on the crowds and new anonymity; others spend the rest of their lives thinking that someday they'll go "home." My own experience reflects Elizabeth Wilson's contention that the disorder of the city is a woman's medium, implying that it allows us to slip through the cracks of order: "The city is 'masculine' in its triumphal scale, its towers and vistas and arid industrial regions; it is 'feminine' in its enclosing embrace, in its indeterminacy and labyrinthine uncenteredness. We might even go so far as to claim that urban life is actually based on this perpetual struggle between rigid routinized order and pleasurable anarchy, the male-female dichotomy."

Where the citydweller may revel in her daily anonymity and freedom from self within crowded spaces, she also struggles to find an emotional community that will offer the intimacy for which Americans pine, even after we have made the choices that make it less and less likely. In small towns, if you go to the store, you must be prepared for at least minimal social intercourse. In cities, you can go out and float in your own space for hours, expending no more than an occasional monosyllabic request for food or services. You don't even have to say please and thank you if you're in an area where you don't expect to be seen again or where you just want to burn your bridges. However, spaces take on the aura of your interactions in them. There is a hardwon median between idiotically artificial courtesy and complete, even hostile, disregard.

Urban experience, vast and elusive, epitomizes the multicentered experience that fuels such energies. I'd include the arts among them. "One of the most fascinating aspects of place in recent years is that it has become more homogenous in some ways" — through mass culture — "and more heterogeneous

Times Square, New York City, billboard ads at night.

in others" (through specialization and ghettoization), according to Sharon Zukin. The city is a social network, a web that entangles everyone who enters it, even the loneliest. Visually articulated by the syncretic cultures it contains, it is defined by a dialectic between the opinions of locals and of outsiders. Looking around in a city is visual overload (whereas looking around in a suburb tips the opposite end of the scale). Impressions are confused and even chaotic. Long-time residents rushing here and there often forget to look at their surroundings while newcomers and visitors get lost and overwhelmed.

The city is the site of delightful and terrifying encounters that could not 10 happen anywhere else. But each city is different, evoking different feelings in its residents and visitors, attractive to individuals at different moods of their lives. The light, the climate, the style, the materials, the flora and fauna (or lack thereof), the spaces and proportions, not to mention the demography and population, make cities and their neighborhoods unique. Cultural geographers have argued about whether the city is a series of reflections of "reality" held as images in the minds of its observers, or whether it is in itself a concrete representation, a collective work of art, a symbolic creation of those who inhabit it or those who control it.

Anne Spirn describes the city as an "infernal machine" with nobody coordinating it, nobody in charge, nobody taking responsibility or understanding the cumulative ecological effect of all the fragmented construction. Yet the city produces spaces and buildings, and even parks, that share its scale and impersonality. Class stratification is one component; especially in midtown New York, where the range of stores, restaurants, and modes of public transportation serves very different clients. Country estates may be inaccessible, and elite suburban neighborhoods guarded, but in cities, rich and poor occupy the same spaces. The habitats of the powerful and the powerless exist within tighter confines, side by side in sharp contrast. (As a child, I had a sitter who often detoured from our culturally determined route to Central Park; she took me to weddings in Fifth Avenue churches, as well as to a German bar in Yorkville where her boyfriend worked.) So long as we behave ourselves, any of us can loiter briefly outside the Plaza Hotel or Park Avenue apartment houses to glimpse the stomping grounds of the rich and famous, and the rich and famous must now and then drive through the Lower East Side or the South Bronx, or the outwardly colorless byways of Forest Hills or Sunnyside. . . .

Nature is fragmented and isolated in the city. Those who have no urge whatsoever to live in the country have houseplants to recall the existence of "nature," or to reassure themselves that nature can be or has been tamed: they go to parks to see trees. The more affluent have rooftop gardens, tiny designer back yards, and bucolic weekend retreats. The less affluent cultivate community gardens. Even those who love the city and can live there comfortably look for ways of escaping it periodically, either by the Fresh Air Fund, vacations or, for the more privileged, weekend homes featuring lawns, trees, and other simulacra of small town life — visited, but not committed to. In 1956, Marshall McLuhan wrote that the city was in fact a return to the simultaneity that governed tribal cultures, in which "all experience and all past lives were *now*."

From the Native American historical viewpoint, cities simply replaced civilization. Artist Jimmie Durham decries the deracination of civic centers from their
landscapes: "At one time New York was a city *on an island:* it was a city with a
location in the physical world. Unlike villages or settlements, cities always establish themselves *against* their environment. . . . Where are we? We are in the
European City. The United States is a political/cultural construction *against* the
American continent. . . . There have been many, but it is hard for us to imagine
a 'great sylvanization,' like a 'great civilization.' Civilizations, cities, build signs
and monuments by definition and are then recognized by their signs. The sign
of forest dwellers is the absence of monuments."

As soon as we move to a city, we search for our own center in it. In the
absence of valid communal centers, cities need artificial symbolic centers like
Saint Louis's Arch, Washington's Monument, or particularly obtrusive office
buildings that function (only) visually as the church spire once did, marking
the place where power is abstracted and institutionalized. Landmarks have to
be imposing and/or charged with celebrity status to claim attention. New
York's Chrysler and Empire State buildings are classic examples. Like earlier
skyscrapers, they were probably inspired to some extent by the "stateliness of
the American landscape."[3] [Then] they [were] outgrown but not outclassed by
the bland towers of the World Trade Center.[4] Giant complexes like Battery
Park City in Lower Manhattan, created by celebrity architects and usually
accompanied by large-scale, expensive public art, are "designer" objects "of
quality," veiling the reality of social polarization in "real life." Generating
ideological vibes of domination through spectacle, such control centers can be
seen, Darrel Crilley observes, "not as signs of enduring vitality, but as enormous and cautionary symbols of changes underway in the relationship
between property development and aesthetics."

> I view great cities as pestilential to the morals, the health and the liberties
> of man. True, they nourish some of the elegant arts, but the useful ones
> can thrive elsewhere, and less perfection in the others, with more health,
> virtue and freedom, would be my choice.
> — THOMAS JEFFERSON (in the midst of a yellow-fever epidemic)

The city's image remains negative, or Un-American, in opposition to the
"family values" purportedly nourished outside of these "dens of iniquity."
One reason for this bad press is that cities have traditionally been the homes
of the sinful arts. Marxists have noted that in order to maintain its dynamism,
capitalism must keep destroying and re-creating itself, whether through
planned obsolescence or a novelty-driven art market. For economic as well as
aesthetic and educational reasons, artists are attracted to change.

The city visibly illustrates the dialectic between the heterogenous market,   15
where everything is for sale, and the homogenous place, where people resist the

---

[3]*Cosmopolitan*, 1875, quoted in Gwendolyn Wright.
[4]This reading was first published in 1997. – Eds.

Antwane Wilson panhandles in Cleveland, Ohio, in 2002.

processes of defamiliarization and change. As new ideas and new money-making schemes pop up each day, the most imposing structures can prove short lived. The social cacophony of a big city multiplies exponentially with its diversity and excess of nervous energy. At the same time, the dissolution of its familiar landscapes has the same effect on its inhabitants as slower changes in the countryside. The rug is pulled out from under our sense of self when stores close or switch functions, when vacant lots appear or disappear, or when buildings are remodeled. Even when the changes are for the better, the ghosts remain.

WORKS CITED

Crilley, Darrel. "Megastructures and Urban Change: Aesthetics, Ideology, and Design." In Paul Knox, ed., *The Restless Urban Landscape*. Englewood Cliffs, N.J.: Prentice Hall, 1993.

Durham, Jimmie. *A Certain Lack of Coherence: Writings on Art and Cultural Politics*, ed. Jean Fisher. London: Kala Press, 1993.

Jefferson, Thomas. *Primary Documents,* no. 4, 1995.

McLuhan, Marshall. "The Media Fit the Battle of Jericho." *Explorations Six,* July 1956.

Spirn, Anne W. *The Granite Garden: Urban Nature and Human Design*. New York: Basic Books, 1984.

Tuan, Yi-Fu. *Topophilia: A Study of Environmental Perception, Attitudes and Values*. Englewood Cliffs, N.J.: Prentice Hall, 1974.

Wilson, Elizabeth. *The Sphinx in the City*. Berkeley: University of California Press, 1991.

Wright, Gwendolyn. *Building the Dream: A Social History of Housing in America*. New York: Pantheon Books, 1981.

Zukin, Sharon. *Landscapes of Power: From Detroit to Disney World*. Berkeley: University of California Press, 1991.

READING THE TEXT

1. Define in your own words the "alternating current," as Lippard puts it, "that pulls at most Americans at various times in their lives" (para. 1).

2. According to Lippard, what contrasting mythological significances do urban and rural areas have?

3. What role does nature play in the cityscape, in Lippard's view?

4. What are the assumptions underlying the common image of the city as "negative, or Un-American" (para. 14)?

5. Why does Lippard assert that women especially find freedom in city life?

READING THE SIGNS

1. Whether you live in a rural, suburban, or urban environment, reflect in your journal on Lippard's claim that most Americans feel torn between the country and the city at some point in their lives. Have you felt this "alternating current" (para. 1) yourself? Why or why not? If you have, in what way did you resolve the competing desires?

2. In "One Nation, Slightly Divisible" (p. 388), David Brooks claims that "people [who live] in Blue America . . . tend to live around big cities on the coasts. People in Red America tend to live on farms or in small towns or small cities far away from the coasts" (para. 2). Using Lippard's discussion of the mythologies of the city and country as a critical framework, write an essay in which you analyze each group's preferred place to live.

3. Today many Americans live neither in the city nor the country; they live in suburbs. Using Lippard's essay as a model, write your own analysis of the suburb's mythological significance.

4. If you live in a city, conduct a survey of local residents that addresses the "lure" that the urban life has for them. Use your results to formulate a response to Lippard's question: "What . . . constitutes the lure of the local in this environment presumed to transcend any such effect?" (para. 4).

5. Write an essay in which you evaluate the validity of Lippard's contention that women can feel more liberated in an urban environment than in a rural community.

MARIAH BURTON NELSON

I Won. I'm Sorry.

Athletic competition, when you come right down to it, is about winning, which is no problem for men, whose gender codes tell them that aggression and domination are admirable male traits. But "how can you win, if you're female?" Mariah Burton Nelson asks, when the same gender codes insist that women must be "feminine," "not aggressive, not victorious." And so women athletes, even when they do win, go out of their way to signal their femininity by dolling themselves up and smiling a lot. Beauty and vulnerability seem to be as important to today's female athlete as brawn and gold medals, Nelson complains, paradoxically contradicting the apparent feminist gains that women athletes have made in recent years. A former Stanford University and professional basketball player, Nelson (b. 1957) is the author of five books, including Embracing Victory *(1998),* The Unburdened Heart *(2000), and* We Are All Athletes *(2002). This piece originally appeared in* SELF *magazine.*

When Sylvia Plath's husband, Ted Hughes, published his first book of poems, Sylvia wrote to her mother: "I am so happy that HIS book is accepted FIRST. It will make it so much easier for me when mine is accepted. . . ."

After Sylvia killed herself, her mother published a collection of Sylvia's letters. In her explanatory notes, Aurelia Plath commented that from the time she was very young, Sylvia "catered to the male of any age so as to bolster his sense of superiority." In seventh grade, Aurelia Plath noted, Sylvia was pleased to finish second in a spelling contest. "It was nicer, she felt, to have a boy first."

How many women still collude in the myth of male superiority, believing it's "nicer" when boys and men finish first? How many of us achieve but only in a lesser, smaller, feminine way, a manner consciously or unconsciously designed to be as nonthreatening as possible?

Since I'm tall, women often talk to me about height. Short women tell me, "I've always wanted to be tall — but not as tall as you!" I find this amusing, but also curious. Why not? Why not be six-two?

Tall women tell me that they won't wear heels because they don't want to appear taller than their husbands or boyfriends, even by an inch. What are these women telling me — and their male companions? Why do women regulate their height in relation to men's height? Why is it still rare to see a woman who is taller than her husband?

Women want to be tall enough to feel elegant and attractive, like models. They want to feel respected and looked up to. But they don't want to be so tall that their height threatens men. They want to win — to achieve, to reach new heights — but without exceeding male heights.

How can you win, if you're female? Can you just do it? No. You have to play the femininity game. Femininity by definition is not large, not imposing, not competitive. Feminine women are not ruthless, not aggressive, not victorious. It's not feminine to have a killer instinct, to want with all your heart and soul to win — neither tennis matches nor elected office nor feminist victories such as abortion rights. It's not feminine to know exactly what you want, then go for it.

Femininity is about appearing beautiful and vulnerable and small. It's about winning male approval.

One downhill skier who asked not to be identified told me the following story: "I love male approval. Most women skiers do. We talk about it often. There's only one thing more satisfying than one of the top male skiers saying, 'Wow, you are a great skier. You rip. You're awesome.'

"But it's so fun leaving 99 percent of the world's guys in the dust — oops," 10 she laughs. "I try not to gloat. I've learned something: If I kick guys' butts and lord it over them, they don't like me. If, however, I kick guys' butts then act 'like a girl,' there is no problem. And I do mean girl, not woman. Nonthreatening."

Femininity is also about accommodating men, allowing them to feel bigger than and stronger than and superior to women; not emasculated by them.

Femininity is unhealthy, obviously. It would be unhealthy for men to act passive, dainty, obsessed with their physical appearance, and dedicated to bolstering the sense of superiority in the other gender, so it's unhealthy for women too. These days, some women are redefining femininity as strong, as athletic, as however a female happens to be, so that "feminine" becomes synonymous with "female." Other women reject both feminine and masculine terms and stereotypes, selecting from the entire range of human behaviors instead of limiting themselves to the "gender-appropriate" ones. These women smile only when they're happy, act angry when they're angry, dress how they want to. They cling to their self-respect and dignity like a life raft.

But most female winners play the femininity game to some extent, using femininity as a defense, a shield against accusations such as bitch, man-hater, lesbian. Feminine behavior and attire mitigate against the affront of female victory, soften the hard edges of winning. Women who want to win without losing male approval temper their victories with beauty, with softness, with smallness, with smiles.

In the fifties, at each of the Amateur Athletic Union's women's basketball championships, one of the players was crowned a beauty queen. (This still happens at Russian women's ice hockey tournaments.) Athletes in the All-American Girls Baseball League of the forties and fifties slid into base wearing skirts. In 1979, professional basketball players with the California Dreams were sent to John Robert Powers' charm school. Ed Temple, the legendary coach of the Tennessee State Tigerbelles, the team that produced Wilma Rudolph, Wyomia Tyus, Willye White, Madeline Manning, and countless other champions, enforced a dress code and stressed that his athletes should be "young ladies first, track girls second."

Serena Williams at Wimbledon.

Makeup, jewelry, dress, and demeanor were often dictated by the male 15
coaches and owners in these leagues, but to some extent the players played
along, understanding the tradeoff: in order to be "allowed" to compete, they
had to demonstrate that they were, despite their "masculine" strivings, real
("feminine") women.

Today, both men and women wear earrings, notes Felshin, "but the media
is still selling heterosexism and 'feminine' beauty. And if you listen carefully, in
almost every interview" female athletes still express apologetic behavior through
feminine dress, behavior, and values.

Florence Griffith-Joyner, Gail Devers, and other track stars of this modern era
dedicate considerable attention to portraying a feminine appearance. Basketball
star Lisa Leslie has received more attention for being a model than for leading
the Americans to Olympic victory. Steffi Graf posed in bikinis for the 1997 *Sports
Illustrated* swimsuit issue. In a Sears commercial, Olympic basketball players

apply lipstick, paint their toenails, rock babies, lounge in bed, and pose and dance in their underwear. Lisa Leslie says, "Everybody's allowed to be themselves. Me, for example, I'm very feminine."

In an Avon commercial, Jackie Joyner Kersee is shown running on a beach while the camera lingers on her buttocks and breasts. She tells us that she can bench-press 150 pounds and brags that she can jump farther than "all but 128 men." Then she says: "And I have red toenails." Words flash on the screen: "Just another Avon lady." Graf, Mary Pierce, Monica Seles, and Mary Jo Fernandez have all played in dresses. They are "so much more comfortable" than skirts, Fernandez explained. "You don't have to worry about the shirt coming up or the skirt being too tight. It's cooler, and it's so feminine."

"When I put on a dress I feel different—more feminine, more elegant, more ladylike—and that's nice," added Australia's Nicole Bradtke: "We're in a sport where we're throwing ourselves around, so it's a real asset to the game to be able to look pretty at the same time."

Athletes have become gorgeous, flirtatious, elegant, angelic, darling—and the skating commentators' favorite term: "vulnerable." Some think this is good news: proof that femininity and sports are compatible. "There doesn't have to be such a complete division between 'You're beautiful and sexy' and 'you're athletic and strong,'" says Linda Hanley, a pro beach volleyball player who also appeared in a bikini in the 1997 *Sports Illustrated* swimsuit issue.

Athletes and advertisers reassure viewers that women who compete are still willing to play the femininity game, to be cheerleaders. Don't worry about us, the commercials imply. We're winners but we'll still look pretty for you. We're acting in ways that only men used to act but we'll still act how you want women to act. We're not threatening. We're not lesbians. We're not ugly, not bad marriage material. We're strong but feminine. Linguists note that the word "but" negates the part of the sentence that precedes it.

There are some recent examples of the media emphasizing female power in an unambiguous way. "Women Muscle In," the *New York Times Magazine* proclaimed in a headline. The *Washington Post* wrote, "At Olympics, Women Show Their Strength." And a new genre of commercials protests that female athletes are NOT cheerleaders, and don't have to be. Olympic and pro basketball star Dawn Staley says in a Nike commercial that she plays basketball "for the competitiveness" of it. "I need some place to release it. It just builds up, and sports is a great outlet for it. I started out playing with the guys. I wasn't always accepted. You get criticized, like: 'You need to be in the kitchen. Go put on a skirt.' I just got mad and angry and went out to show them that I belong here as much as they do."

Other commercials tell us that women can compete like conquerors. A Nike ad called "Wolves" shows girls leaping and spiking volleyballs while a voice says, "They are not sisters. They are not classmates. They are not friends. They are not even the girls' team. They are a pack of wolves. Tend to your sheep." Though the athletes look serious, the message sounds absurd. When I show this commercial to audiences, they laugh. Still, the images do depict the power of the volleyball players: their intensity, their ability to pound the ball almost through the floor. The script gives the players (and viewers) permission not to be ladylike, not to worry about whether their toenails are red.

But in an American Basketball League commercial, the Philadelphia Rage's female basketball players are playing rough; their bodies collide. Maurice Chevalier sings, "Thank heaven for little girls." The tag line: "Thank heaven, they're on our side."

Doesn't all this talk about girls and ladies simply focus our attention on 25 femaleness, femininity, and ladylike behavior? The lady issue is always there in the equation: something to redefine, to rebel against. It's always present, like sneakers, so every time you hear the word *athlete* you also hear the word *lady*—or feminine, or unfeminine. It reminds me of a beer magazine ad from the eighties that featured a photo of Olympic track star Valerie Brisco-Hooks. "Funny, she doesn't look like the weaker sex," said the print. You could see her impressive muscles. Clearly the intent of the ad was to contrast an old stereotype with the reality of female strength and ability. But Brisco-Hooks was seated, her legs twisted pretzel style, arms covering her chest. But in that position, Brisco-Hooks didn't look very strong or able. In the line, "Funny, she doesn't look like the weaker sex," the most eye-catching words are funny, look, weaker, and sex. Looking at the pretzel that is Valerie, you begin to think that she looks funny. You think about weakness. And you think about sex.

When she was young, Nancy Kerrigan wanted to play ice hockey with her older brothers. Her mother told her, "You're a girl. Do girl things."

Figure skating is a girl thing. Athletes in sequins and "sheer illusion sleeves" glide and dance, their tiny skirts flapping in the breeze. They achieve, but without touching or pushing anyone else. They win, but without visible signs of sweat. They compete, but not directly. Their success is measured not by confrontation with an opponent, nor even by a clock or a scoreboard. Rather, they are judged as beauty contestants are judged: by a panel of people who interpret the success of the routines. Prettiness is mandatory. Petite and groomed and gracious, figure skaters—like cheerleaders, gymnasts, and aerobic dancers—camouflage their competitiveness with niceness and prettiness until it no longer seems male or aggressive or unseemly.

The most popular sport for high school and college women is basketball. More than a million fans shelled out an average of $15 per ticket in 1997, the inaugural summer of the Women's National Basketball Association. But the most televised women's sport is figure skating. In 1995 revenue from skating shows and competitions topped six hundred million dollars. In the seven months between October 1996 and March 1997, ABC, CBS, NBC, Fox, ESPN, TBS, and USA dedicated 162.5 hours of programming to figure skating, half of it in prime time. Kerrigan earns up to three hundred thousand dollars for a single performance.

Nearly 75 percent of the viewers of televised skating are women. The average age is between twenty-five and forty-five years old, with a household income of more than fifty thousand dollars. What are these women watching? What are they seeing? What's the appeal?

Like golf, tennis, and gymnastics, figure skating is an individual sport favored by white people from the upper classes. The skaters wear cosmetics, frozen smiles, and revealing dresses. Behind the scenes they lift weights and sweat like any serious athlete, but figure skating seems more dance than sport, more grace than guts, more art than athleticism. Figure skating allows women to compete like champions while dressed like cheerleaders.

In women's figure skating, smiling is part of "artistic expression." In the final round, if the competitors are of equal merit, artistry weighs more heavily than technique. Midori Ito, the best jumper in the history of women's skating, explained a weak showing at the 1995 world championships this way: "I wasn't 100 percent satisfied. . . . I probably wasn't smiling enough."

The media portray female figure skaters as "little girl dancers" or "fairy tale princesses" (NBC commentator John Tesh); as "elegant" (Dick Button); as "little angels" (Peggy Fleming); as "ice beauties" and "ladies who lutz" (*People* magazine). Commentators frame skaters as small, young, and decorative creatures, not superwomen but fairy-tale figments of someone's imagination.

After Kerrigan was assaulted by a member of Tonya Harding's entourage, she was featured on a *Sports Illustrated* cover crying "Why me?" When she recovered to win a silver medal at the Olympics that year, she became "America's sweetheart" and rich to boot. But the princess turned pumpkin shortly after midnight, as soon as the ball was over and she stopped smiling and started speaking. Growing impatient during the Olympic medal ceremony while everyone waited for Baiul, Kerrigan grumbled, "Oh, give me a break, she's just going to cry out there again. What's the difference?"

What were Kerrigan's crimes? She felt too old to cavort with cartoon characters. Isn't she? She expressed anger and disappointment — even bitterness and bad sportsmanship — about losing the gold. But wasn't she supposed to want to win? What happens to baseball players who, disappointed about a loss, hit each other or spit on umpires? What happens to basketball players and football players and hockey players who fight? Men can't tumble from a princess palace because we don't expect them to be princesses in the first place, only athletes.

Americans fell out of love with Kerrigan not because they couldn't adore an athlete who lacked grace in defeat, but because they couldn't adore a female athlete who lacked grace in defeat.

Female politicians, lawyers, and businesswomen of all ethnic groups also play the femininity game. Like tennis players in short dresses, working women seem to believe it's an asset to look pretty (but not too pretty) while throwing themselves around. The female apologetic is alive and well in corporate board rooms, where women say "I'm sorry, maybe someone else already stated this idea, but . . ." and smile while they say it.

When Newt Gingrich's mother revealed on television that Newt had referred to Hillary Clinton as a bitch, how did Hillary respond? She donned a pink suit and met with female reporters to ask how she could "soften her image." She seemed to think that her competitiveness was the problem and femininity the solution.

So if you want to be a winner and you're female, you'll feel pressured to play by special, female rules. Like men, you'll have to be smart and industrious, but in addition you'll have to be "like women": kind, nurturing, accommodating, nonthreatening, placating, pretty, and small. You'll have to smile. And not act angry. And wear skirts. Nail polish and makeup help, too.

READING THE TEXT

1. Summarize in your own words the contradictory messages about appropriate gender behavior that women athletes must contend with, according to Nelson.

2. Nelson begins her article with an anecdote about poet Sylvia Plath. How does this opening frame her argument about women in sports?

3. What is the "femininity game" (para. 7), in Nelson's view, and how do the media perpetuate it?

4. What sports are coded as "feminine," according to Nelson, and why?

READING THE SIGNS

1. Watch a women's sports event on television, such as an LPGA match, analyzing the behavior and appearance of the athletes. Use your observations as evidence in an essay in which you assess the validity of Nelson's claims about the contradictory gender role behaviors of female athletes.

2. If you are a female athlete, write a journal entry exploring whether you are pressured to act feminine and your responses to that pressure. If you are not a female athlete, reflect on the behavior and appearance of women athletes on your campus. Do you see signs that they are affected by the femininity game?

3. Obtain a copy of a magazine that focuses on women's sports, such as *Sports Illustrated Woman*. Analyze the articles and ads in the magazine, noting models' and athletes' clothing, physical appearance, and speech patterns. Using Nelson's argument as a critical framework, write an essay in which you analyze whether the magazine perpetuates traditional gender roles or presents sports as an avenue for female empowerment.

4. Interview women athletes at your campus about the extent to which they are pressured by the femininity game. Have they been accused of being lesbians or bitches simply because they are athletes? Do they feel pressure to be physically attractive or charming? Do you see any correlation between an athlete's sport and her responses? Use your observations as the basis of an argument about the influence of traditional gender roles on women's sports at your school.

RANDALL KENNEDY

Blind Spot

Racial profiling has been a hot-button issue in recent years, eliciting such sardonic condemnations as the claim that for many Americans it has become a crime to be caught "driving while black." Randall Kennedy (b. 1955), a professor of law at Harvard Law School, enters the controversy here from an unusual angle, finding a fundamental contradiction in the positions of both supporters and opponents of racial profiling. With supporters of racial profiling asserting the rights of the community over those of the individual, while at the same time endorsing the rights of the individual over those of the community when it comes to affirmative action, and opponents of racial profiling doing just the reverse, it is time, Kennedy suggests, for both sides to listen to what the other has to say. Kennedy is the author of Race, Crime, and the Law *(1997),* Nigger: The Strange Career of a Troublesome Word *(2002), and* Interracial Intimacies: Sex, Marriage, Identity, and Adoption *(2003). This selection originally appeared in the April 2002 issue of the* Atlantic Monthly.

What is one to think about "racial profiling"? Confusion abounds about what the term even means. It should be defined as the policy or practice of using race as a factor in selecting whom to place under special surveillance: if police officers at an airport decide to search Passenger A because he is twenty-five to forty years old, bought a first-class ticket with cash, is flying cross-country, and is apparently of Arab ancestry, Passenger A has been subjected to racial profiling. But officials often prefer to define racial profiling as being based *solely* on race; and in doing so they are often seeking to preserve their authority to act against a person *partly* on the basis of race. Civil-rights activists, too, often define racial profiling as solely race-based; but their aim is to arouse their followers and to portray law-enforcement officials in as menacing a light as possible.

The problem with defining racial profiling in the narrow manner of these strange bedfellows is that doing so obfuscates the real issue confronting Americans. Exceedingly few police officers, airport screeners, or other authorities charged with the task of foiling or apprehending criminals act solely on the basis of race. Many, however, act on the basis of intuition, using race along with other indicators (sex, age, patterns of past conduct) as a guide. The difficult question, then, is not whether the authorities ought to be allowed to act against individuals on the basis of race alone; almost everyone would disapprove of that. The difficult question is whether they ought to be allowed to use race *at all* in schemes of surveillance. If, indeed, it is used, the action amounts to racial discrimination. The extent of the discrimination may be relatively small when race is only one factor among many, but even a little racial discrimination should require lots of justification.

The key argument in favor of racial profiling, essentially, is that taking race into account enables the authorities to screen carefully and at less expense those sectors of the population that are more likely than others to contain the criminals for whom officials are searching. Proponents of this theory stress that resources for surveillance are scarce, that the dangers to be avoided are grave, and that reducing these dangers helps everyone — including, sometimes especially, those in the groups subjected to special scrutiny. Proponents also assert that it makes good sense to consider whiteness if the search is for Ku Klux Klan assassins, blackness if the search is for drug couriers in certain locales, and Arab nationality or ethnicity if the search is for agents of al Qaeda.

Some commentators embrace this position as if it were unassailable, but under U.S. law racial discrimination backed by state power is presumptively illicit. This means that supporters of racial profiling carry a heavy burden of persuasion. Opponents rightly argue, however, that not much rigorous empirical proof supports the idea of racial profiling as an effective tool of law enforcement. Opponents rightly contend, also, that alternatives to racial profiling have not been much studied or pursued. Stressing that racial profiling generates clear harm (for example, the fear, resentment, and alienation felt by innocent people in the profiled group), opponents of racial profiling sensibly question whether compromising our hard-earned principle of anti-discrimination is worth merely speculative gains in overall security.

A notable feature of this conflict is that champions of each position frequently embrace rhetoric, attitudes, and value systems that are completely at odds with those they adopt when confronting another controversial instance of racial discrimination — namely, affirmative action. Vocal supporters of racial profiling who trumpet the urgency of communal needs when discussing law enforcement all of a sudden become fanatical individualists when condemning affirmative action in college admissions and the labor market. Supporters of profiling, who are willing to impose what amounts to a racial tax on profiled groups, denounce as betrayals of "color blindness" programs that require racial diversity. A similar turnabout can be seen on the part of many of those who support affirmative action. Impatient with talk of communal needs in assessing racial profiling, they very often have no difficulty with subordinating the interests of individual white candidates to the purported good of the whole. Opposed to race consciousness in policing, they demand race consciousness in deciding whom to admit to college or select for a job.

The racial-profiling controversy — like the conflict over affirmative action — will not end soon. For one thing, in both cases many of the contestants are animated by decent but contending sentiments. Although exasperating, this is actually good for our society; and it would be even better if participants in the debates acknowledged the simple truth that their adversaries have something useful to say.

Which man looks guilty?

Which man looks guilty? If you picked the man on the right, you're wrong.

Wrong for judging people based on the color of their skin. Because if you

look closely, you'll see they're the same man. Unfortunately, racial stereo-

typing like this happens every day. On America's highways, police stop drivers

based on their skin color rather than for the way they are driving. For example,

in Florida 80% of those stopped and searched were black and Hispanic,

while they constituted only 5% of all drivers. These humiliating and illegal

searches are violations of the Constitution and must be fought. Help us defend

your rights. Support the ACLU. www.aclu.org **american civil liberties union**

READING THE TEXT

1. Summarize in your own words the contradiction Kennedy sees in the controversies over racial profiling and affirmative action.

2. Why does Kennedy say that definitions of racial profiling are marked by "confusion" (para. 1)?

3. Why do you think Kennedy calls opponents and supporters of racial profiling "strange bedfellows" (para. 2)?

4. Why does Kennedy think "the decent but contending sentiments" at the heart of the racial profiling controversy are "good for our society" (para. 6)?

READING THE SIGNS

1. Kennedy sees a contradiction between opposing racial profiling and promoting affirmative action. Write an essay in which you support, refute, or modify his stance.

2. Write a journal entry in which you reflect on an experience in which you believe you were singled out because of your appearance, ethnicity, gender, or other physically obvious characteristic. How did you respond at the time, and would you respond the same way today? Alternatively, write about a friend who had such an experience.

3. Write an essay in which you explore the relative claims of the rights of the individual and the rights of the community in modern American culture. To what extent do these claims reflect a fundamental contradiction in American social ideology?

4. In the debates over both racial profiling and affirmative action, the discussions tend to presume that determining ethnic identity is a simple matter. Read or review Jack Lopez's "Of Cholos and Surfers" (p. 597), Nell Bernstein's "Goin' Gangsta, Choosin' Cholita" (p. 604), and Melissa Algranati's "Being an Other" (p. 613), and write an essay in which you explore the implications that mixed-race backgrounds and cultural practices such as claiming may have for these debates.

WE'VE COME A LONG WAY, MAYBE

Gender Codes in American Culture

Babes in Boyland

It probably all began with *Charlie's Angels* — no, not the movie with Cameron Diaz but Aaron Spelling's hit from the 1970s that really put the "jiggle" into prime-time television. Then there was *Bay Watch* (also known as "Babe Watch"), and suddenly it wasn't Kansas anymore. Move over Donna Reed, June Lockhart, Lucille Ball, and Mary Tyler Moore, and make way for Pamela Anderson, Paris Hilton, Molly Sims, and Nicollette Sheridan — not to mention the exotic dancers on *The Sopranos*, the bikini-clad contestants on any number of reality dating programs, and the half-naked jungle girls on *Survivor* (yep, in the scorching sun of the tropics, what a gal really needs is her bikini top and her cut-off short shorts).

Meanwhile, on MTV and a concert stage near you, Britney Spears, Lil' Kim, Beyoncé, Jennifer Lopez, Christina Aguilera, and practically any contemporary diva you can think of can't seem to decide whether they are pop stars or porn stars, apparently hiring their costume designers from a pool of Frederick's of Hollywood rejects. Not to be outdone, American girls and women from their tweens to forties are lowering their necklines and waistbands, raising their blouse bottoms, and, sometimes, flaunting their thongs.

It seems odd, somehow, that more than thirty years after the women's movement so vigorously challenged the reduction of women to their value as sex objects American popular culture today appears to have regressed to one continuous peep show. As Victoria's Secret is shouted from the rooftops and breast-enhancement surgery becomes almost as common as dentistry, a curious signal is being sent today about the status of America's gender codes. The semiotic question is: What exactly is that signal telling us?

Interpreting American Gender Codes

Whether you have heard the term *gender code* before, you are already familiar with what it constitutes, because a gender code is a culturally constructed belief system that defines and dictates the appropriate roles and behavior for men and women in society. Whether you are a woman or a man, a gender code has been guiding your life since you were born. For example, a gender code impels parents to give their female children dolls (to prepare them for their adult lives as mothers) and to give their male children sports equipment, toy guns, and violent video games (to prepare them for the active and aggressive role that men are supposed to take in society). It is a gender code that tells girls that their primary concern should be with their appearance and with attracting boys, while telling boys that it's not their appearance that counts but how many times they "score." And it is a gender code that tells girls that they aren't good at math (one talking Barbie doll exclaimed just this), while leading boys to math-savvy careers in science and technology.

Since gender codes are often justified on the basis of appeals to the "natural" differences between the two sexes, they are especially difficult to contest, and those women and men who do challenge them are often denounced as being "unnatural." But one of the key arguments of the feminist movement as it emerged in the 1970s was that gender codes are socially, not naturally, constructed, and usually reflect cultural values rather than natural facts. Take, for example, the huge national controversy that erupted in the early 1990s when a young woman named Shannon Faulkner had to go all the way to the Supreme Court to gain entrance to the Citadel Military Academy. Although by that time women regularly were being admitted to academies like West Point, the Citadel's admissions policy maintained a lingering cultural belief that women don't really belong in the military. This belief continues to be encoded in the fact that women who are in the armed services are not allowed to serve in combat units (former Speaker of the House Newt Gingrich justified this ban by insisting that women couldn't fight in the field because they "got infections"—a classic

---

Exploring the Signs of Gender

In your journal, explore the expectations about gender roles that you grew up with. What gender norms were you taught by your family, either overtly or implicitly? Have you ever had any conflicts with your parents over "natural" gender roles? If so, how did you resolve them? Do you think your gender-related expectations today are the same as those you had when you were a child?

appeal to nature). By contesting the Citadel's admissions policy, Shannon Faulkner was, in effect, challenging a deeply held gender code, and the fuss made about the whole matter illustrates just how emotional such codes can be. When Faulkner finally won her court case and entered the Citadel, she was followed around by hordes of reporters (who carefully reported on everything from her pushup performance to her weight), and when she finally succumbed to the pressure and left, the campus erupted in an ecstatic celebration.

In the Faulkner incident, then, we find the gender code that holds that it is the role of men, not of women, to be warriors: Men are the protectors, women are the ones to be protected (women and children first, as they said on the *Titanic*). This code is reinforced by the traditional belief that men are the aggressive sex, while women are passive. In sexual matters, men, accordingly, are expected to be the pursuers (he calls), while women are the pursued (she waits by the phone). Men are measured by their intellects, personal wealth, or power; women are valued for their bodies, which are ever on display to the gaze of the male eye.

We could go on and on. Note, though, how in each case gender roles are arrayed across a system of binary oppositions (men are this, women are the opposite). Indeed, these oppositions are so deeply encoded in our culture that you may find yourself protesting that men *are* aggressive, women *are* passive, men (as the bestseller has it) *are* from Mars, women *are* from Venus. But the fact that these roles can be reversed—indeed, they are being reversed more and more often these days—shows that they reflect cultural values rather than natural facts.

Prefeminist or Postfeminist?

Since the traditional patriarchal gender code tells women that their role in life is to be sexually attractive to men, the rampant eroticization of the female body in contemporary fashion and entertainment would thus appear to be a reversion to the prefeminist era, a striking rejection of feminist goals and aspirations. But it may not be that simple because it is also the case that traditional gender codes insist that female sexuality must be tightly controlled by male masters, whereas for many women the confident display of their sexuality is actually empowering rather than degrading, a taking charge rather than a knuckling under—an attitude that was behind the immense popularity, among women, of the television hit *Sex and the City*.

This latter perspective reflects the point of view of what has come to be called *postfeminism*. Postfeminists, who regard themselves as representing an evolution within the feminist movement itself, have argued that being proud of her body and using it to get what she wants is part of a woman's empowerment, and so have applauded the new erotics as a gender code advance rather than a regression. More traditional feminists who are less persuaded by this position point out, however, that by focusing her attention on her body rather than her mind, the postfeminist woman is in some danger of subjecting herself to the tyranny of a youth-worshipping culture that will reject her once she is past the peak of her sexually appealing years. Besides, if men are not held to sometimes impossible standards of physical beauty (especially with regard to weight), why should women be? If a man can use his intelligence to get ahead, why shouldn't a woman?

So does the transformation of popular culture into a vast stage presenting eye candy for guys merit a feminist or postfeminist interpretation? There are passionate adherents on both sides of the question. There is no easy or right answer. Consider the facts. What is your interpretation?

The Myths of Gender

If you find yourself feeling uneasy when addressing such questions, you are not alone. For this uneasiness is rooted in the fact that our gender codes, like any cultural mythology, provide a framework through which we can understand and experience our world. If that framework is disrupted, our world suffers a dislocation and we feel threatened. You may think this isn't so, believing, for instance, that women shouldn't be in the military. If that's the case, ask yourself why you feel that way. If you're concerned about women getting unfair advantages in the feminist era (one reason some Americans rooted for the Citadel), wouldn't it seem that allowing them to share the dangerous duty of military combat would actually be the opposite of a privilege?

That many Americans, women as well as men, don't always see it this way shows just how durable our gender codes are. It thus is one of the major tasks of cultural semiotics to expose the outlines of gender myths to reveal just how deeply they influence our lives. Think of how these myths may shape your own behavior. Traditionally, for instance, the myths that govern courtship in America dictate that the man pays the expenses on a date and is responsible for all the logistics, even providing transportation and a destination. But there is no natural reason for this to be so; it's just a cultural expectation, one that has been changing for some time. Ask yourself: Who pays when you date? Who drives? Do you even care? Your answers will help you find your place in today's shifting terrain of gender myths.

In examining the gender myths that influence your own life, you should recognize the difference between the biological category of *sex* and the cultural category of *gender*. Your sex is determined by your chromosomes, but your gender goes beyond your sex to the roles that society has determined are appropriate for you. Your sex, in other words, is your birthright, but the roles you play in society are largely determined by your culture. In everyday life, however, this distinction between the natural category of sex and the

---

Discussing the Signs of Gender

Bring to class a magazine that targets one gender (such as *Maxim* or *Jane*). In small groups, study both the articles and the advertising in your sample magazines, focusing on the gender roles assumed for men and women. List the major roles on the board by magazine title. What patterns do you find? Do some magazines adhere to traditional roles, while others depart from them? How can you account for your findings?

---

cultural category of gender is blurred because socially determined gender roles are regarded as naturally dictated sexual necessities.

Even the standards of beauty that men as well as women are held to are culturally determined. The ideal medieval woman, for example, was short, slender, high-waisted, and small-breasted, and boasted a high, domed forehead whose effect she enhanced by shaving her hairline. By the Renaissance, she had filled out considerably, and in the paintings of Peter Paul Rubens could appear positively pudgy by contemporary standards (we even have an adjective, *Rubenesque*, for well-padded feminine beauty). More recently, we have seen a shift from the hourglass figures of the fifties to the aerobically muscled hard bodies of today. You may assume that this is it, the last stop, the one truly beautiful body, but stick around. Wait to see what's fashionable in bodies in the years to come.

Men, too, have seen their bodily ideals change over time. The ideal man of the eighteenth century, for example, was a rather heavyset fellow, rounded in appearance, and with a hint of a double chin, while today's ideal (especially in the corporate world) has square-hewn features and a jutting jaw (cleft if possible: Just look at some ads for business-oriented services to see what today's businessman wants to look like). Now think for a moment: What would you look like if you had the choice? Would you look like the ideal of the 1950s or 1960s? Would you be long and lean, or buff, courtesy of Nautilus?

Metrosexual or NASCAR Dad?

It is important to realize, then, that men, too, are controlled by gender codes. A successful man is expected to accumulate wealth and power in his middle years; when young, well, just think of the typical Big Man on Campus. Is he not likely to be an athlete (the warrior role on a school campus) and a sexual star? The Big Man on Campus who doesn't land a pro sports contract is likely to grow up into what is now called a NASCAR Dad — that is, a family man who, in binary relation to his wife the Soccer Mom, takes charge of his family and enjoys such traditionally male-coded activities as stock-car racing and watching professional sports. Something of a throwback to the benignly patriarchal dads of the 1950s, the NASCAR Dad offers one gender option to contemporary American men that is strikingly different from a second choice that has also appeared in recent years: the metrosexual.

The metrosexual is a straight guy who cares about such traditionally female-coded matters as personal grooming, fashion, and home decor, and he has been widely popularized in such programs as *Queer Eye for the Straight Guy*. Offering a way of modifying the old gender codes without breaking them, the metrosexual profile is especially attractive to unmarried urban males (whereas the NASCAR Dad typically is a suburbanite). It lets men toy with the rules without overthrowing them. But in other areas of contemporary popular culture the codes are not simply being modified; they're being bent quite out of shape.

Gender Bending

Probably the most deeply held gender codes in our culture are those that define our sexual orientation. So fundamental are such codes to our sense of personal and social identity that it is still somewhat controversial to analyze them. Surely, you may believe, sexual orientation is determined by nature. What has culture to do with it?

But a growing number of scholars engaged in gender studies are questioning the natural determination of sexual orientation. This is especially true for those involved in "queer theory," a movement that deliberately takes a once-pejorative term and subverts it to signify the dismantling of traditional gender norms. For such scholars, the categories of human sexuality, too, are social constructions, inscribing cultural rather than natural divisions. For example, what counts as homosexual behavior in American culture is not necessarily considered homosexual in other cultures, as could be seen when in the early 1980s many of the Haitian men who contracted AIDS denied being homosexual (they were bisexual), because in their cultural code bisexuality

Reading Gender on the Net

Use a search engine such as Yahoo! or Google to research what issues are considered "male" and "female" territory on the Internet. Focus your search on a comparison of specific topics, such as "men's rights" and "women's rights." Compare your findings with those of your classmates.

and homosexuality are clearly distinguished from each other, which they are not in the United States.

The most dramatic signs that America's codes governing sexual orientation are shifting can be seen not in the scholarly publications of queer theorists, however, but in the products of popular culture. With the mainstream success of such television programs as *Queer Eye for the Straight Guy* and *Will and Grace,* not to mention *Queer as Folk* and *The L Word,* it is evident that homosexuality is finally more or less out of the cultural closet and ready for prime time.

That doesn't mean there still isn't controversy when it comes to alternative sexualities. The national debate over gay marriage, which had such a powerful influence on the 2004 presidential election, continues as we write these words, and it is not likely to go away soon. The fact that you may have strong feelings about the matter is itself a signifier of the powerful hold our gender codes have on us. Taking us to the core of our sense of ourselves as individual and social beings, involving deeply held religious and moral beliefs, gender codes, like all cultural mythologies, are ultimately political in nature, calling for semiotic analyses that will take us far beyond the classroom.

The Readings

The chapter begins with Aaron Devor's analysis of gender roles and the ways in which men and women manipulate the signs by which we traditionally communicate our gender identity. Kevin Jennings follows with a personal memoir that chronicles his struggles with growing up gay in conflict with the traditional construction of male heterosexuality, while Sean Cahill enters the debate over gay marriage with a survey of case studies that support marriage equality in the United States, especially in the wake of the 9/11 catastrophe. Deborah Blum is next with an article suggesting that biology *does* play a role in gender identity and that we can best understand the gender gap by looking at both the cultural and the physiological determinants of human behavior. Ilana Fried offers a UCLA student's op-ed piece on the controversy over the president of Harvard University's remarks concerning women in science, followed by Naomi Wolf's indictment of the "beauty myth" that forces otherwise liberated women to feel trapped inside their own bodies. Joan Morgan then accuses hip-hop lyrics of intimidating and degrading black women. Deborah Tannen looks at the way that women are always "marked" in our society: No detail of a woman's appearance, from her hair to her shoes to her name, fails to send a gender-coded message about her, Tannen argues. James William Gibson's analysis of the warrior fantasies that have arisen in the wake of the Vietnam War and the rise of feminism sounds a warning note in the politics of gender identity, and Michael A. Messner explores the role that sport takes in the construction of masculine identity in America. Finally, Henry Jenkins concludes the chapter with an interpretation of professional wrestling as a kind of soap opera for working-class men.

AARON DEVOR

Gender Role Behaviors and Attitudes

"Boys will be boys, and girls will be girls": few of our cultural mythologies seem as natural as this one. But in this exploration of the gender signals that traditionally tell what a "boy" or "girl" is supposed to look and act like, Aaron Devor (b. 1951) shows how these signals are not "natural" at all but instead are cultural constructs. While the classic cues of masculinity — aggressive posture, self-confidence, a tough appearance — and the traditional signs of femininity — gentleness, passivity, strong nurturing instincts — are often considered "normal," Devor explains that they are by no means biological or psychological necessities. Indeed, he suggests, they can be richly mixed and varied, or to paraphrase the old Kinks song "Lola," "Boys can be girls and girls can be boys." Devor is associate dean of social sciences at the University of Victoria and author of Gender Blending: Confronting the Limits of Duality *(1989), from which this selection is excerpted, and* FTM: Female-to-Male Transsexuals in Society *(1997).*

Gender Role Behaviors and Attitudes

The clusters of social definitions used to identify persons by gender are collectively known as "femininity" and "masculinity." Masculine characteristics are used to identify persons as males, while feminine ones are used as signifiers for femaleness. People use femininity or masculinity to claim and communicate their membership in their assigned, or chosen, sex or gender. Others recognize our sex or gender more on the basis of these characteristics than on the basis of sex characteristics, which are usually largely covered by clothing in daily life.

These two clusters of attributes are most commonly seen as mirror images of one another with masculinity usually characterized by dominance and aggression, and femininity by passivity and submission. A more even-handed description of the social qualities subsumed by femininity and masculinity might be to label masculinity as generally concerned with egoistic dominance and femininity as striving for cooperation or communion.[1] Characterizing femininity and masculinity in such a way does not portray the two clusters of characteristics as being in a hierarchical relationship to one another

---

[1] Eleanor Maccoby, *Social Development: Psychological Growth and the Parent-Child Relationship* (New York: Harcourt, Brace, Jovanovich, 1980), p. 217. Egoistic dominance is a striving for superior rewards for oneself or a competitive striving to reduce the rewards for one's competitors even if such action will not increase one's own rewards. Persons who are motivated by desires for egoistic dominance not only wish the best for themselves but also wish to diminish the advantages of others whom they may perceive as competing with them.

but rather as being two different approaches to the same question, that question being centrally concerned with the goals, means, and use of power. Such an alternative conception of gender roles captures the hierarchical and competitive masculine thirst for power, which can, but need not, lead to aggression, and the feminine quest for harmony and communal well-being, which can, but need not, result in passivity and dependence.

Many activities and modes of expression are recognized by most members of society as feminine. Any of these can be, and often are, displayed by persons of either gender. In some cases, cross-gender behaviors are ignored by observers, and therefore do not compromise the integrity of a person's gender display. In other cases, they are labeled as inappropriate gender role behaviors. Although these behaviors are closely linked to sexual status in the minds and experiences of most people, research shows that dominant persons of either gender tend to use influence tactics and verbal styles usually associated with men and masculinity, while subordinate persons, of either gender, tend to use those considered to be the province of women.[2] Thus it seems likely that many aspects of masculinity and femininity are the result, rather than the cause, of status inequalities.

Popular conceptions of femininity and masculinity instead revolve around hierarchical appraisals of the "natural" roles of males and females. Members of both genders are believed to share many of the same human characteristics, although in different relative proportions; both males and females are popularly thought to be able to do many of the same things, but most activities are divided into suitable and unsuitable categories for each gender class. Persons who perform the activities considered appropriate for another gender will be expected to perform them poorly; if they succeed adequately, or even well, at their endeavors, they may be rewarded with ridicule or scorn for blurring the gender dividing line.

The patriarchal gender schema currently in use in mainstream North American society reserves highly valued attributes for males and actively supports the high evaluation of any characteristics which might inadvertently become associated with maleness. The ideology underlying the schema postulates that the cultural superiority of males is a natural outgrowth of the innate predisposition of males toward aggression and dominance, which is assumed to flow inevitably from evolutionary and biological sources. Female attributes are likewise postulated to find their source in innate predispositions acquired in the evolution of the species. Feminine characteristics are thought to be intrinsic to the female facility for childbirth and breastfeeding. Hence, it is popularly believed that the social position of females is biologically mandated to be intertwined with the care of children and a "natural" dependency on men for

---

[2]Judith Howard, Philip Blumstein, and Pepper Schwartz, "Sex, Power, and Influence Tactics in Intimate Relationships," *Journal of Personality and Social Psychology* 51 (1986), pp. 102–9; Peter Kollock, Philip Blumstein, and Pepper Schwartz, "Sex and Power in Interaction: Conversational Privileges and Duties," *American Sociological Review* 50 (1985), pp. 34–46.

the maintenance of mother-child units. Thus the goals of femininity and, by implication, of all biological females are presumed to revolve around heterosexuality and maternity.[3]

Femininity, according to this traditional formulation, "would result in warm and continued relationships with men, a sense of maternity, interest in caring for children, and the capacity to work productively and continuously in female occupations."[4] This recipe translates into a vast number of proscriptions and prescriptions. Warm and continued relations with men and an interest in maternity require that females be heterosexually oriented. A heterosexual orientation requires women to dress, move, speak, and act in ways that men will find attractive. As patriarchy has reserved active expressions of power as a masculine attribute, femininity must be expressed through modes of dress, movement, speech, and action which communicate weakness, dependency, ineffectualness, availability for sexual or emotional service, and sensitivity to the needs of others.

Some, but not all, of these modes of interrelation also serve the demands of maternity and many female job ghettos. In many cases, though, femininity is not particularly useful in maternity or employment. Both mothers and workers often need to be strong, independent, and effectual in order to do their jobs well. Thus femininity, as a role, is best suited to satisfying a masculine vision of heterosexual attractiveness.

Body postures and demeanors which communicate subordinate status and vulnerability to trespass through a message of "no threat" make people appear to be feminine. They demonstrate subordination through a minimizing of spatial use: People appear feminine when they keep their arms closer to their bodies, their legs closer together, and their torsos and heads less vertical than do masculine-looking individuals. People also look feminine when they point their toes inward and use their hands in small or childlike gestures. Other people also tend to stand closer to people they see as feminine, often invading their personal space, while people who make frequent appeasement gestures, such as smiling, also give the appearance of femininity. Perhaps as an outgrowth of a subordinate status and the need to avoid conflict with more socially powerful people, women tend to excel over men at the ability to correctly interpret, and effectively display, nonverbal communication cues.[5]

---

[3]Nancy Chodorow, *The Reproduction of Mothering: Psychoanalysis and the Reproduction of Mothering* (Berkeley: University of California Press, 1978), p. 134.

[4]Jon K. Meyer and John E. Hoopes, "The Gender Dysphoria Syndromes: A Position Statement on So-Called 'Transsexualism,'" *Plastic and Reconstructive Surgery* 54 (Oct. 1974), pp. 444–51.

[5]Erving Goffman, *Gender Advertisements* (New York: Harper Colophon Books, 1976); Judith A. Hall, *Non-Verbal Sex Differences: Communication Accuracy and Expressive Style* (Baltimore: Johns Hopkins University Press, 1984); Nancy M. Henley, *Body Politics: Power, Sex and Non-Verbal Communication* (Englewood Cliffs, N.J.: Prentice-Hall, 1979); Marianne Wex, *"Let's Take Back Our Space": "Female" and "Male" Body Language as a Result of Patriarchal Structures* (Berlin: Frauenliteraturverlag Hermine Fees, 1979).

Rearing children is work typically done by women, but not always.

Speech characterized by inflections, intonations, and phrases that convey nonaggression and subordinate status also make a speaker appear more feminine. Subordinate speakers who use more polite expressions and ask more questions in conversation seem more feminine. Speech characterized by sounds of higher frequencies are often interpreted by listeners as feminine, childlike, and ineffectual.[6] Feminine styles of dress likewise display subordinate status through greater restriction of the free movement of the body, greater exposure of the bare skin, and an emphasis on sexual characteristics. The more gender distinct the dress, the more this is the case.

Masculinity, like femininity, can be demonstrated through a wide variety 10 of cues. Pleck has argued that it is commonly expressed in North American society through the attainment of some level of proficiency at some, or all, of the following four main attitudes of masculinity. Persons who display success and high status in their social group, who exhibit "a manly air of toughness, confidence, and self-reliance" and "the aura of aggression, violence, and daring," and who conscientiously avoid anything associated with femininity are seen as exuding masculinity.[7] These requirements reflect the patriarchal ideology that masculinity results from an excess of testosterone, the assumption being that androgens supply a natural impetus toward aggression, which in turn impels males toward achievement and success. This vision of masculinity

[6]Karen L. Adams, "Sexism and the English Language: The Linguistic Implications of Being a Woman," in *Women: A Feminist Perspective*, 3rd ed., ed. Jo Freeman (Palo Alto, Calif.: Mayfield, 1984), pp. 478–91; Hall, pp. 37, 130–37.

[7]Joseph H. Pleck, *The Myth of Masculinity* (Cambridge, Mass.: MIT Press, 1981), p. 139.

also reflects the ideological stance that ideal maleness (masculinity) must remain untainted by female (feminine) pollutants.

Masculinity, then, requires of its actors that they organize themselves and their society in a hierarchical manner so as to be able to explicitly quantify the achievement of success. The achievement of high status in one's social group requires competitive and aggressive behavior from those who wish to obtain it. Competition which is motivated by a goal of individual achievement, or egoistic dominance, also requires of its participants a degree of emotional insensitivity to feelings of hurt and loss in defeated others, and a measure of emotional insularity to protect oneself from becoming vulnerable to manipulation by others. Such values lead those who subscribe to them to view feminine persons as "born losers" and to strive to eliminate any similarities to feminine people from their own personalities. In patriarchally organized societies, masculine values become the ideological structure of the society as a whole. Masculinity thus becomes "innately" valuable and femininity serves a contrapuntal function to delineate and magnify the hierarchical dominance of masculinity.

Body postures, speech patterns, and styles of dress which demonstrate and support the assumption of dominance and authority convey an impression of masculinity. Typical masculine body postures tend to be expansive and aggressive. People who hold their arms and hands in positions away from their bodies, and who stand, sit, or lie with their legs apart — thus maximizing the amount of space that they physically occupy — appear most physically masculine. Persons who communicate an air of authority or a readiness for aggression by standing erect and moving forcefully also tend to appear more masculine. Movements that are abrupt and stiff, communicating force and threat rather than flexibility and cooperation, make an actor look masculine. Masculinity can also be conveyed by stern or serious facial expressions that suggest minimal receptivity to the influence of others, a characteristic which is an important element in the attainment and maintenance of egoistic dominance.[8]

Speech and dress which likewise demonstrate or claim superior status are also seen as characteristically masculine behavior patterns. Masculine speech patterns display a tendency toward expansiveness similar to that found in masculine body postures. People who attempt to control the direction of conversations seem more masculine. Those who tend to speak more loudly, use less polite and more assertive forms, and tend to interrupt the conversations of others more often also communicate masculinity to others. Styles of dress which emphasize the size of upper body musculature, allow freedom of movement, and encourage an illusion of physical power and a look of easy physicality all suggest masculinity. Such appearances of strength and readiness to action serve to create or enhance an aura of aggressiveness and intimidation central to an appearance of masculinity. Expansive postures and gestures

[8]Goffman; Hall; Henley; Wex.

combine with these qualities to insinuate that a position of secure dominance is a masculine one.

Gender role characteristics reflect the ideological contentions underlying the dominant gender schema in North American society. That schema leads us to believe that female and male behaviors are the result of socially directed hormonal instructions which specify that females will want to have children and will therefore find themselves relatively helpless and dependent on males for support and protection. The schema claims that males are innately aggressive and competitive and therefore will dominate over females. The social hegemony of this ideology ensures that we are all raised to practice gender roles which will confirm this vision of the nature of the sexes. Fortunately, our training to gender roles is neither complete nor uniform. As a result, it is possible to point to multitudinous exceptions to, and variations on, these themes. Biological evidence is equivocal about the source of gender roles; psychological androgyny is a widely accepted concept. It seems most likely that gender roles are the result of systematic power imbalances based on gender discrimination.[9]

READING THE TEXT

1. List the characteristics that Devor describes as being traditional conceptions of "masculinity" and "femininity" (para. 1)

2. What relationship does Devor see between characteristics considered masculine and feminine?

3. How does Devor explain the cultural belief in the "superiority" (para. 5) of males?

4. How, according to Devor, do speech and dress communicate gender roles?

READING THE SIGNS

1. In small same-sex groups, brainstorm lists of traits that you consider masculine and feminine, and then have each group write its list on the board. Compare the lists produced by male and female groups. What patterns of differences or similarities do you see? To what extent do the traits presume a heterosexual orientation? How do you account for your results?

2. Study the speech patterns, styles of dress, and other nonverbal cues communicated by your friends during a social occasion, such as a party, trying not to reveal that you are observing them for an assignment. Then write an essay in which you analyze these cues used by your friends. To what extent do your friends enact the traditional gender codes Devor describes?

3. Study a popular magazine such as *Elle*, *Rolling Stone*, or *Maxim* for advertisements depicting men and women interacting with each other. Then write an essay in which you interpret the body postures of the models, using Devor's

[9]Howard, Blumstein, and Schwartz; Kollock, Blumstein, and Schwartz.

selection as your framework for analysis. How do males and females typically stand? To what extent do the models enact stereotypically masculine or feminine stances? To develop your essay, consult Steve Craig's "Men's Men and Women's Women" (p. 161) and Warren St. John's "Metrosexuals Come Out" (p. 174).

4. Devor argues that female fashion traditionally restricts body movement whereas male styles of dress commonly allow freedom of movement. In class, discuss whether this claim is still true today, being sure to consider a range of clothing types (such as athletic wear, corporate dress, party fashion, and so forth). To develop your ideas, consult Mariah Burton Nelson, "I Won. I'm Sorry." (p. 439).

KEVIN JENNINGS
American Dreams

When Ellen DeGeneres became the first television star to come out of the closet on prime-time TV, gay men and lesbians around the country celebrated what appeared to be a major step forward for one of America's most marginalized communities. But the firestorm of protest that also attended Ellen's coming-out equally demonstrated just how far homosexuals have to go before winning full acceptance into American society. In this personal narrative of what it means to grow up gay in America, Kevin Jennings (b. 1963) reveals the torment endured by a child forced to conceal his difference from everyone around him, especially his own parents. With years of self-denial and one suicide attempt behind him, Jennings shows how he eventually came to accept himself as he is and in so doing achieved his own version of the American dream. Jennings is founder and director of Gay, Lesbian, and Straight Education Network (GLSEN) and author (with Pat Shapiro) of Always My Child: A Parent's Guide to Understanding Your Gay, Lesbian, Bisexual, Transgendered, or Questioning Son or Daughter *(2003).*

When I was little, I honestly thought I would grow up to be the president. After all, I lived in a land of opportunity where anyone, with enough determination and hard work, could aspire to the highest office in the land. I planned to live out the American Dream.

I realized, however, that something was amiss from an early age. I grew up in the rural community of Lewisville, North Carolina, just outside the city of Winston-Salem. As you might guess from the city's name, Winston-Salem,

Winston-Salem makes its living from the tobacco industry: It was cigarettes that propelled local conglomerate RJR-Nabisco to its status as one of the world's largest multinational corporations. Somehow this rising tide of prosperity never lapped at our doors, and the Jennings family was a bitter family indeed. Poor whites descended from Confederate veterans, we eagerly sought out scapegoats for our inexplicable failure to "make it" in the land of opportunity. My uncles and cousins joined the Ku Klux Klan, while my father, a fundamentalist minister, used religion to excuse his prejudices — against blacks, against Jews, against Catholics, against Yankees, against Communists and liberals (basically the same thing, as far as he was concerned), and, of course, against gays. Somehow the golden rule of "Do unto others as you would have them do unto you" never made it into his gospel. Instead, I remember church services filled with outbursts of paranoia, as we were warned about the evils of those whom we (incorrectly) held responsible for our very real oppression. I grew up believing that there was a Communist plot undermining our nation, a Jewish conspiracy controlling the banks and the media, and that black men — whom I unselfconsciously referred to as "niggers" — spent their days plotting to rape white women. In case this seems like a history lesson on the Stone Age, please consider that I was born in 1963 and graduated from high school in 1981. Hardly the ancient past!

Seniors march for gay rights.

My father's profession as a traveling minister never left much money for luxuries like college tuition. Nevertheless, my mother was determined that I, her last chance, was going to make good on the Dream that had been denied to her and to my four older siblings — that one of her children would be the first member of our extended family ever to go to college. Not that it was going to be easy: my father died when I was eight, and my mother went to work at McDonald's (the only job she could get with her limited credentials). Every penny was watched carefully; dinner was often leftover quarter-pounders that she didn't have to pay for. I'm the only person I know who sees the Golden Arches, takes a bite, and thinks, "Mmm, just like Mom used to make!"

Throughout high school, I was determined to make it, determined to show my mother — and myself — that the American Dream really could come true. I worked hard and got ahead, earning a scholarship to Harvard after I had remade myself into the image of what I was told a successful person was like. Little did I realize at that point the price I was paying to fit in.

The first thing to go was any sign of my Southern heritage. As I came into   5 contact with mainstream America, through high school "gifted and talented" programs and, later, at college in Massachusetts, I began to realize that we Southerners were different. Our home-cooked meals — grits, turnip greens, red-eye gravy — never seemed to show up in frozen dinners, and if a character on television spoke with a Southern accent, that immediately identified him or her as stupid or as comic relief. As the lesbian writer Blanche Boyd put it:

> When television programs appeared, a dreadful truth came clear to me: Southerners were not normal people. We did not sound like normal people . . . [and] what we chose to talk about seemed peculiarly different also. I began to realize we were hicks. Television took away my faith in my surroundings. I didn't want to be a hick. I decided to go North, where people talked fast, walked fast, and acted cool. I practiced talking like the people on television. . . . I became desperate to leave the South.

Like Blanche Boyd, I deliberately erased my accent and aped the false monotone of television newscasters. I never invited college friends home to North Carolina for fear they might meet my family and realize they were worthless, ignorant hicks — which is how I'd come to view those whom I loved. I applied to colleges on the sole criterion that they not be in the South. I ran as far from Lewisville, North Carolina, as I could.

But there were some things about myself I could not escape from or change, no matter how hard I tried — among them the fact that I am gay.

I had always known I was gay, even before I had heard the word or knew what it meant. I remember that at age six or seven, the "adult" magazines that so fascinated my older brothers simply didn't interest me at all, and I somehow knew that I'd better hide this feeling from them. As I grew older and began to understand what my feelings meant, I recoiled in horror from myself. After all, my religious upbringing as a Southern Baptist had taught me that gay people were twisted perverts destined for a lifetime of eternal damnation.

Being as set as I was on achieving the American Dream, I was not about to accept the fact that I was gay. Here is where I paid the heaviest price for my Dream. I pursued what I thought was "normal" with a vengeance in high school, determined that, if the spirit was weak, the flesh would be more willing at the prospect of heterosexuality. I dated every girl I could literally get my hands on, earning a well-deserved reputation as a jerk who tried to see how far he could get on the first date. I attacked anyone who suggested that gay people might be entitled to some rights, too, and was the biggest teller of fag jokes at Radford High. But what I really hated was myself, and this I couldn't escape from, no matter how drunk or stoned I got, which I was doing on an almost daily basis by senior year.

That was also the year I fell in love for the first time, with another boy in my class. It turned out he was gay, too, and we made love one night in late May. I woke up the next morning and realized that it was true — I really was a fag after all. I spent that day trying to figure out how I was going to live the American Dream, which seemed impossible if I was homosexual. By nightfall I decided it *was* impossible, and without my Dream I couldn't see a reason why I'd want to be alive at all. I went to my family's medicine cabinet, took the new bottle of aspirin out, and proceeded to wash down 140 pills with a glass of gin. I remember the exact number — 140 — because I figured I could only get down about ten at one swallow, so I carefully counted out fourteen little stacks before I began. Thanks to a friend who got to me in time, I didn't die that night. My story has a happy ending — but a lot of them don't. Those moments of desperation helped me understand why one out of every three gay teens tries to commit suicide.

At Harvard, the most important lessons I learned had little to do with Latin American or European history, which were my majors. Instead, I learned the importance of taking control of my own destiny. I met a great professor who taught me that as long as I stayed in the closet, I was accepting the idea that there was something wrong with me, something that I needed to hide. After all, as my favorite bisexual, Eleanor Roosevelt, once said, "No one can make you feel inferior without your consent." By staying closeted, I was consenting to my own inferiority. I realized that for years, I had let a Dream — a beautiful, seductive, but ultimately false Dream — rule my life. I had agreed to pay its price, which was the rejection of my family, my culture, and eventually myself. I came to understand that the costs of the Dream far outweighed its rewards. I learned that true freedom would be mine only when I was able to make my own decisions about what I wanted out of life instead of accepting those thrust upon me by the Dream. Since I made that realization, I have followed my own path instead of the one I had been taught was "right" all my life.

Once I started down this new path, I began to make some discoveries about the society in which I was raised, and about its notions of right and wrong. I began to ask many questions, and the answers to these questions were not always pleasant. Why, for example, did my mother always earn less than men who did the same exact work? Why did I learn as a child that to cheat someone was to "Jew" them? Why was my brother ostracized when he fell in love with and later married a black woman? Why did everyone in my family work so hard and yet have so little? I realized that these inequalities were part of the game, the rules of which were such that gays, blacks, poor people, women, and many others would always lose to the wealthy white heterosexual Christian men who have won the Presidency forty-two out of forty-two times. Those odds — 100 percent — are pretty good ones to bet on. No, I discovered that true freedom could not be achieved by a Dream that calls on us to give up who we are in order to fit in and become "worthy" of power. Holding power means little if women have to become masculine "iron ladies" to get it, if Jews have to "Americanize" their names, if blacks have to learn to speak so-called Standard English (though we never acknowledge *whose* standard it is), or if gays and lesbians have to hide what everyone else gets to celebrate — the loves of their lives.

Real freedom will be ours when the people around us — and when we ourselves — accept that we, too, are "real" Americans, and that we shouldn't have to change to meet anyone else's standards. In 1924, at age twenty-two, the gay African-American poet Langston Hughes said it best, in his poem "I, Too":

> Tomorrow,
> I'll be at the table
> When company comes.
> Nobody'll dare
> Say to me,
> "Eat in the kitchen,"
> Then.
> Besides,
> They'll see how beautiful I am
> And be ashamed —
> I, too, am America.

By coming out as a gay man and demanding my freedom, I realize that I have done the most American thing of all. And while I have come a long way since the days when I dreamed of living in the White House, I have discovered that what I'm fighting for now is the very thing I thought I'd be fighting for if I ever became President — "liberty and justice for all."

READING THE TEXT

1. According to Jennings, how did his southern upbringing influence his goals for the future?

2. Why did Jennings feel he had to eschew his southern heritage?

3. In what ways did Jennings deny to himself his sexual orientation, and why did he do so?

4. In your own words, trace the evolution of Jennings's understanding of the American dream as he grew up.

5. What is the relationship between the excerpt from Langston Hughes's "I, Too" and Jennings's story?

READING THE SIGNS

1. In your journal, write your own account of how you responded to normative gender codes as a high school student. To what extent did you feel pressure to conform or to renounce traditional expectations — or to do both?

2. Jennings describes his early attempts to deny his sexual orientation. In class, discuss how other minority or underprivileged groups — ethnic minorities, women, the disabled — sometimes try to erase their identity. What social and cultural forces motivate such self-denial? Use the discussion as a springboard for an essay in which you explore why one might be motivated to do so.

3. In class, brainstorm two lists: films or TV shows that reinforce heterosexuality as normative and those that present homosexuality positively. Then compare your lists. What conclusions do you draw about popular culture's influence on American gender codes? To develop your ideas, consult Marisa Connolly, "Homosexuality on Television: The Heterosexualization of *Will and Grace*" (p. 287).

4. Compare and contrast Jennings's arrival at a confident sense of identity with that of Melissa Algranati ("Being an Other," p. 613). How do you explain any differences you observe?

SEAN CAHILL
The Case for Marriage Equality

It has been argued that gay marriage was the crucial issue on which the 2004 presidential election turned, but whether that was indeed the case, there is no denying that gay marriage continues to be a hot-button issue in American life. In this reading, Sean Cahill presents a case for gay marriage, profiling gay couples who were denied the benefits enjoyed by married couples in the aftermath of such personal catastrophes as the September 11 attacks on the World Trade Center. Cahill invites the reader to judge: Is this fair and just? Cahill is director of the National Gay and Lesbian Task Force Policy Institute and author of Same-Sex Marriage in the United States: Focus on the Facts *(2004), from which this selection is taken.*

Marriage aims to promote healthy families by protecting the economic and emotional interdependence of family members and giving priority to their bonds. Gay couples have the same needs as opposite-sex couples: same-sex couples are often emotionally and economically interdependent, sharing household and financial responsibilities, and they often raise children or take care of other family members together. Legal protection of partner relationships, which includes a comprehensive package of economic and social rights and responsibilities for couples and their children, provides families with security and peace of mind. A 2004 report by the U.S. General Accounting Office lists 1,138 ways in which marital relationships are given special treatment by the federal government.[1]

Two Stories

. . . The effects of being unable to marry are felt in families headed by same-sex couples throughout the country, in large and small ways. Being unable to marry has particularly devastating consequences when one partner dies. For the surviving partner, securing the basic right to the financial support the deceased partner contributed to their household — a right afforded to hetero-sexual couples through marriage — involves protracted battles with federal and state bureaucracies, at a time of great emotional strain, and often with little result.

LOIS MARRERO AND MICKIE MASHBURN

In July 2001, Lois Marrero, an officer in the Tampa, Florida, Police Depart-ment, was killed while trying to stop a bank robbery. Mickie Mashburn, Lois's partner of 11 years and a 17-year veteran of the Tampa Police Department, grieved with Lois's family, with whom she had been close for 18 years. The night Lois was killed, Lois's sister told interviewers, "We love Mickie; she is part of our family." Lois and Mickie lived publicly as a lesbian couple. They had been joined in a public commitment ceremony ten years earlier and lived together and took care of one another. They educated the Tampa police force about gay and lesbian issues. It was Lois's death, however, that made it clear that their relationship was not recognized in significant ways.

Although they had shared bills for years, Mickie was told she was not eli-gible for Lois's pension. She sued, but at the end of a bitter trial Lois's blood relatives took Lois's pension and left Mickie with nothing. "The money can't bring Lois back," Mickie says, "but we need to have this right for our relation-ships. No one else should go through what I have gone through. We need to be accepted like everyone else."[2] Had Mickie and Lois had the right to marry,

---

[1]General Accounting Office (2004, January 23). Report to Senate Majority Leader William Frist. GAO-04-353R. This represents an increase since 1997, when the GAO issued its first report that listed 1,049 federal laws and benefits that only married spouses can access. General Accounting Office (1997, January 31). *Tables of laws in the United States Code involving marital status, by category.* www.gao.gov/archive/1997/og97016.pdf. Accessed December 4, 2003.

[2]Adapted from a profile of Mickie Mashburn and Lois Marrero in Cahill, S., Ellen, M., and Tobias, S. (2002). *Family policy: Issues affecting gay, lesbian, bisexual and transgender families.* New York: Policy Institute of the National Gay and Lesbian Task Force. pp. 152–53.

they would have been able to protect their family and their right to inherit each other's pension in the event of an untimely death.

LARRY COURTNEY AND EUGENE CLARK

Larry Courtney and Eugene Clark moved together to New York from Washington, D.C., in 1988 so that Larry could accept a job offer. Larry and Eugene enjoyed life in New York. They reveled in the general acceptance of their gay relationship as a family unit. They entertained friends and family. They went to the theater. They went to some of the city's many gay bars. They vacationed together and spent holidays together with different family members or with friends. When Eugene's mother had a stroke in 1995, Eugene and Larry brought her from Washington to live with them in their small Manhattan apartment; they both nursed her and cared for her until she passed away in 1999. Eugene and Larry lived life as a married couple. In 1994, when it became legal, they registered in New York City as domestic partners, receiving a certificate that was as close to a marriage license as they would ever have.

On October 30, 2001, Eugene Clark and Larry Courtney would have celebrated 14 years as committed lifetime partners. On the morning of September 11, 2001, they got up early, had coffee together, and dressed for work. Eugene kissed Larry goodbye and said, "I'll see you tonight." He left a little earlier than usual so that he could vote in New York City's primary election before the polls got crowded. He then boarded the subway for the ride to his office at Aon Consulting on the 102nd floor of the South Tower of the World Trade Center.

At approximately 8:55 AM Larry arrived at his own office in midtown Manhattan to a voicemail message from Eugene that said, "Don't worry, the plane hit the other building. I'm OK. We are evacuating." At 9:03 AM a second hijacked plane hit the 86th floor of the South Tower. The building collapsed at 10:05 AM. Eugene did not come home.

After frantic searching of the streets and emergency rooms, and after posting his photograph along with the many others, Larry reported Eugene as a missing person at the Armory. He later filed an affidavit for a death certificate at the makeshift Family Center at Pier 94. Among a host of other paperwork Larry received in the mail were documents from Cambridge Integrated Services Group, Inc., for filing a workers' compensation claim. He sent the paperwork off and was summoned for a hearing in April 2002. At the hearing, Cambridge stated that Larry did not qualify for the benefits that Eugene's company had been paying for during his tenure because the couple did not fit the "legally married" criteria. The benefits could be paid to Eugene's surviving parent, his father. But Eugene had not seen or spoken to his father in over 20 years, and he had never spoken to Larry about him.

Larry decided to fight for his spousal rights and teamed up with the Lambda Legal Defense and Education Fund, which was advocating for many other surviving partners. They were ultimately successful, and New York State

Senate Bill S7685 became law on August 20, 2002. The bill designated domestic partners as spouses of victims of 9/11, due full spousal benefits from workers' compensation. The bill is restricted to the 9/11 attacks, however. It does not protect same-sex spouses who lose partners in other tragedies.[3]

Surviving Same-Sex Partners and the Aftermath of 9/11

Of the nearly 3,000 Americans and foreign nationals killed in the 9/11 terrorist   10
attacks in New York, Washington, D.C., and Pennsylvania, many were gay, lesbian, or bisexual individuals in long-term, committed relationships like Larry and Eugene's. Because these were high-profile atrocities of international significance, the tragic losses these gay couples suffered were prominent. In the weeks and months following 9/11, moderate Republicans such as New York Mayor Rudy Giuliani and Governor George Pataki backed equal treatment of same-sex surviving partners. So too did the American Red Cross, the United Way of New York, and the U.S. Congress, which passed the Mychal Judge Police and Fire Chaplains Public Safety Officers' Benefit Act, named for Father Mychal Judge, the New York Fire Department chaplain killed while administering last rites to firefighters killed at the World Trade Center. Signed into law by President Bush on June 24, 2002, the law grants a one-time federal benefit of $250,000 to any designated beneficiary recognized under the deceased's police officer's or firefighter's life insurance plan. Prior to the Judge Act, the federal benefit was given only to spouses, children, and parents of officers who died in the line of duty. The Judge Act was retroactive only to September 11, 2001 (and so partners of police officers and firefighters killed in the line of duty prior to this date, such as Mickie Mashburn, cannot benefit).

Peggy Neff, whose partner of 18 years, Sheila Hein, was killed at the Pentagon on September 11, 2001, received compensation from the September 11 Victims Compensation Fund in January 2003. She was the first same-sex survivor to ever receive such compensation from the federal government.[4] Neff's case was strong in that Hein's will named her as the beneficiary. As of June 2004, the fund had just completed its distribution of funds. It was unclear exactly how approximately 20 other same-sex surviving partners of people killed in 9/11 had been treated by the fund. According to Eric Ferrero of Lambda Legal, other gay partners were given funds. Sometimes they split the money with parents, siblings, and other members of the victim's family of origin.

[3]Adapted from a speech given by Larry Courtney at the National Gay and Lesbian Task Force Leadership Awards Deck Party, in Provincetown, Massachusetts, August 25, 2002.

[4]Dahir, M. (2003, March 4). A federal nod to gay partners: Will Peggy Neff's award from the federal Victim Compensation Fund help all same-sex couples win more legal recognition? *The Advocate*.

The compassion shown to same-sex surviving partners after 9/11 was decried and challenged by organizations with an anti-gay agenda:

Robert Knight, director of Concerned Women for America's Culture and Family Institute, accused surviving partners like Larry Courtney and the gay advocates who helped him of "trying to hijack the moral capital of marriage and apply it to their own relationships," which he characterized as "counterfeit marriage." Cybercast News Service — a right wing website that frequently quotes religious right, anti-gay activists — reported that Knight said that "family benefits were originally created to provide for a stay-at-home parent caring for a child, not for homosexual sex partners who usually both work."[5]

After the American Red Cross decided to provide services to gay surviving partners of 9/11 victims, CWA criticized the group's "broad and inclusive definition of family."[6] CWA's Culture and Family Institute also censured the 45 members of Congress who urged Attorney General John Ashcroft to adopt a federal policy similar to that promoted by Governor Pataki in New York state, claiming that lawmakers and "homosexual activists" were exploiting the tragedy "to ask Ashcroft to pave way for 'domestic partner' benefits."[7]

Focus on the Family's James Dobson said, "Pataki diluted the definition of 'family' by giving gay partners the same access to terrorist relief benefits that married couples have."[8] FOF also criticized Pataki's actions as advancing the "gay agenda."[9]

The Traditional Values Coalition's Lou Sheldon accused gay activists of "taking advantage" of the national tragedy to promote their agenda. Sheldon urged that relief assistance be "given on the basis and priority of one man and one woman in a marital relationship."[10] Such a policy would have also left out unmarried opposite-sex partners of 9/11 victims. "We don't devalue the loss of these innocent people," Sheldon insisted, "but we think this is not

---

[5]Johnson, J. (2001, October 22). Homosexuals seek survivor benefits intended for families. Cybercast News Service (CNSNews.com.). www.dadi.org/homogred.htm. Accessed February 9, 2004. Knight's use of the term *hijack* was particularly offensive in that he was describing efforts of gay partners to get help dealing with the grief of losing their loved ones in terrorist attacks caused by the hijacking of four jet aircraft.

[6]Concerned Women for America, quoted in People for the American Way Foundation (PFAWF) (2002). *Hostile climate: Report on anti-gay activity.* 8th edition. Washington, DC: Author. p. 33.

[7]The Culture and Family Institute of Concerned Women for America quoted in PFAWF (2002). p. 31.

[8]Dobson, J. (2002, January). Dr. Dobson's newsletter. Colorado Springs, CO: Focus on the Family. www.family.org/docstudy/newsletters/a0019238.html. Accessed February 9, 2004.

[9]Focus on the Family, quoted in PFAWF (2002). p. 31.

[10]Sheldon, quoted in PFAWF (2002). p. 33; Berkowitz, B. (2001, October 21). Religious right on the ropes. AlterNet. www.alternet.org/print.html?StoryID=11840. Accessed February 9, 2004.

the time to institutionalize such 'partnerships' and put them on the same level as marriage."[11]

Peter Sprigg of the Family Research Council also accused gays of "taking advantage of the grief and compassion that Americans do feel. . . . To redefine the family based on our grief over the losses that people may have experienced as a result of the terror attacks would be bad law and bad policy."[12]

Perhaps as a result of these objections, the initial interim regulations issued by the Department of Justice in December 2001 and the final regulations issued in March 2002 did not explicitly recognize same-sex partners, but instead left the states to determine who is eligible for victim's compensation under the federal fund.[13] However, most states do not provide any legal recognition to same-sex partners, even those in committed, long-term, or lifelong relationships. As of March 2002, when the September 11th Fund issued its final regulations, none of the three states where the attacks occurred — New York, Pennsylvania, and Virginia — afforded any recognition to same-sex partners of state residents.[14] . . .

READING THE TEXT

1. What effect do the stories of the deaths of Lois Marrero and Eugene Clark have on the reader?

2. According to Cahill, why were gay survivors of 9/11 victims ultimately able to receive spousal benefits while survivors of other tragedies are unable to do so?

3. Summarize in your own words the attitude that Robert Knight, director of Concerned Women for America's Culture and Family Institute, has toward same-sex marriage.

4. Describe the tone Cahill uses when he discusses same-sex couples and those who oppose recognizing such unions.

READING THE SIGNS

1. In class, brainstorm different patterns of family structure — two parents, single parent, extended family, unmarried adults without children, and so forth — thinking about your own family as well as the families of friends and acquaintances. Use your discussion as the basis for an essay in which you propose your own definition of family.

[11]Sheldon, quoted in PFAWF (2002). p. 33.
[12]Sprigg, quoted in PFAWF (2002). p. 33.
[13]PFAWF (2002). pp. 31–32.
[14]Human Rights Campaign (2001). *The state of the workplace for lesbian, gay, bisexual and transgender Americans 2001*. Washington, DC: Author; Human Rights Campaign (2002). *Domestic partner benefits*. Washington, DC: Author. www.hrc.org/worknet/dp/index.asp. Accessed November 2, 2002.

2. Write an argument supporting, opposing, or complicating the proposition that the gay partners of police officers slain in the line of duty be granted survivor's benefits.

3. Write a letter to Lou Sheldon in which you support, refute, or modify his belief that survivor's benefits should be " 'given on the basis and priority of one man and one woman in a marital relationship' " (para. 16).

4. Write an essay in which you respond to the proposition that the survivor's benefits allowed in the 9/11 attacks be extended to same-sex survivors of other tragedies.

5. Research the current status of attempts to legalize same-sex marriages, and use your findings as the basis of an argument supporting or opposing such unions.

DEBORAH BLUM

The Gender Blur: Where Does Biology End and Society Take Over?

There's an old argument over whether nature or nurture is more important in determining human behavior. Nowhere is this argument more intense than in gender studies, where proponents of the social construction of gender identities are currently exploring the many ways in which our upbringing shapes our behavior. But after watching her two-year-old son emphatically choose to play only with carnivorous dinosaur toys and disdainfully reject the "wimpy" vegetarian variety, Deborah Blum decided that nurture couldn't be all that there was to it. Exploring the role of biology in the determination of human behavior, Blum argues that both nature and nurture have to be taken into account if we are to understand gender differences. A Pulitzer Prize–winning professor of journalism at the University of Wisconsin at Madison, Blum is the author of several books, including Sex on the Brain: The Biological Differences between Men and Women *(1997) and* Love at Goon Park *(2002).*

I was raised in one of those university-based, liberal elite families that politicians like to ridicule. In my childhood, every human being — regardless of gender — was exactly alike under the skin, and I mean exactly, barring his or her different opportunities. My parents wasted no opportunity to bring this point home. One Christmas, I received a Barbie doll and a softball glove. Another brought a green enamel stove, which baked tiny cakes by the heat of a lightbulb, and also a set of steel-tipped darts and competition-quality dart-board. Did I mention the year of the chemistry set and the ballerina doll?

It wasn't until I became a parent — I should say, a parent of two boys — that I realized I had been fed a line and swallowed it like a sucker (barring the part about opportunities, which I still believe). This dawned on me during my older son's dinosaur phase, which began when he was about two-and-a-half. Oh, he loved dinosaurs, all right, but only the blood-swilling carnivores. Plant-eaters were wimps and losers, and he refused to wear a T-shirt marred by a picture of a stegosaur. I looked down at him one day, as he was snarling around my feet and doing his toddler best to gnaw off my right leg, and I thought: This goes a lot deeper than culture.

Raising children tends to bring on this kind of politically incorrect reaction. Another friend came to the same conclusion watching a son determinedly bite his breakfast toast into the shape of a pistol he hoped would blow away — or at least terrify — his younger brother. Once you get past the guilt part — Did I do this? Should I have bought him that plastic allosaur with the oversized teeth? — such revelations can lead you to consider the far more interesting field of gender biology, where the questions take a different shape: Does love of carnage begin in culture or genetics, and which drives which? Do the gender roles of our culture reflect an underlying biology, and, in turn, does the way we behave influence that biology?

The point I'm leading up to — through the example of my son's innocent love of predatory dinosaurs — is actually one of the most straightforward in this debate. One of the reasons we're so fascinated by childhood behaviors is that, as the old saying goes, the child becomes the man (or woman, of course). Most girls don't spend their preschool years snarling around the house and pretending to chew off their companion's legs. And they — mostly — don't grow up to be as aggressive as men. Do the ways that we amplify those early differences in childhood shape the adults we become? Absolutely. But it's worth exploring the starting place — the faint signal that somehow gets amplified.

"There's plenty of room in society to influence sex differences," says 5 Marc Breedlove, a behavioral endocrinologist at the University of California at Berkeley and a pioneer in defining how hormones can help build sexually different nervous systems. "Yes, we're born with predispositions, but it's society that amplifies them, exaggerates them. I believe that — except for the sex differences in aggression. Those [differences] are too massive to be explained simply by society."

Aggression does allow a straightforward look at the issue. Consider the following statistics: Crime reports in both the United States and Europe record between 10 and 15 robberies committed by men for every one by a woman. At one point, people argued that this was explained by size difference. Women weren't big enough to intimidate, but that would change, they predicted, with the availability of compact weapons. But just as little girls don't routinely make weapons out of toast, women — even criminal ones — don't seem drawn to weaponry in the same way that men are. Almost twice as many male thieves and robbers use guns as their female counterparts do.

Or you can look at more personal crimes: domestic partner murders. Three-fourths of men use guns in those killings; 50 percent of women do. Here's more from the domestic front: In conflicts in which a woman killed a man, he tended to be the one who had started the fight — in 51.8 percent of the cases, to be exact. When the man was the killer, he again was the likely first aggressor, and by an even more dramatic margin. In fights in which women died, they had started the argument only 12.5 percent of the time.

Enough. You can parade endless similar statistics but the point is this: Males are more aggressive, not just among humans but among almost all species on earth. Male chimpanzees, for instance, declare war on neighboring troops, and one of their strategies is a warning strike: They kill females and infants to terrorize and intimidate. In terms of simple, reproductive genetics, it's an advantage of males to be aggressive: You can muscle your way into dominance, winning more sexual encounters, more offspring, more genetic future. For the female — especially in a species like ours, with time for just one successful pregnancy a year — what's the genetic advantage in brawling?

Thus the issue becomes not whether there is a biologically influenced sex difference in aggression — the answer being a solid, technical "You betcha" — but rather how rigid that difference is. The best science, in my opinion, tends to align with basic common sense. We all know that there are extraordinarily gentle men and murderous women. Sex differences are always generalizations: they refer to a behavior, with some evolutionary rationale behind it. They never define, entirely, an individual. And that fact alone should tell us that there's always — even in the most biologically dominated traits — some flexibility, an instinctive ability to respond, for better and worse, to the world around us.

This is true even with physical characteristics that we've often assumed 10 are nailed down by genetics. Scientists now believe height, for instance, is only about 90 percent heritable. A person's genes might code for a six-foot-tall body, but malnutrition could literally cut that short. And there's also some evidence, in girls anyway, that children with stressful childhoods tend to become shorter adults. So while some factors are predetermined, there's evidence that the prototypical male/female body design can be readily altered.

It's a given that humans, like most other species — bananas, spiders, sharks, ducks, any rabbit you pull out of a hat — rely on two sexes for reproduction. So basic is that requirement that we have chromosomes whose primary purpose is to deliver the genes that order up a male or a female. All other chromosomes are numbered, but we label the sex chromosomes with the letters X and Y. We get one each from our mother and our father, and the basic combinations are these: XX makes female, XY makes male.

There are two important — and little known — points about these chromosomal matches. One is that even with this apparently precise system, there's nothing precise — or guaranteed — about the physical construction of male and female. The other point makes that possible. It appears that sex doesn't matter in the early stages of embryonic development. We are unisex at the point of conception.

If you examine an embryo at about six weeks, you see that it has the ability to develop in either direction. The fledgling embryo has two sets of ducts — Wolffian for male, Muellerian for female — an either/or structure, held in readiness for further development. If testosterone and other androgens are released by hormone-producing cells, then the Wolffian ducts develop into the channel that connects penis to testes, and the female ducts wither away.

Without testosterone, the embryo takes on a female form; the male ducts vanish and the Muellerian ducts expand into oviducts, uterus, and vagina. In other words, in humans, anyways (the opposite is true in birds), the female is the default sex. Back in the 1950s, the famed biologist Alfred Jost showed that if you castrate a male rabbit fetus, choking off testosterone, you produce a completely feminized rabbit.

We don't do these experiments in humans — for obvious reasons — but   15 there are naturally occurring instances that prove the same point. For instance: In the fetal testes are a group of cells, called Leydig cells, that make testosterone. In rare cases, the fetus doesn't make enough of these cells (a defect known as Leydig cell hypoplasia). In this circumstance we see the limited power of the XY chromosome. These boys have the right chromosomes and the right genes to be boys; they just don't grow a penis. Obstetricians and parents often think they see a baby girl, and these children are routinely raised as daughters. Usually, the "mistake" is caught about the time of puberty, when menstruation doesn't start. A doctor's examination shows the child to be internally male; there are usually small testes, often tucked within the abdomen. As the researchers put it, if the condition had been known from the beginning, "the sisters would have been born as brothers."

Just to emphasize how tricky all this body-building can get, there's a peculiar genetic defect that seems to be clustered by heredity in a small group of villages in the Dominican Republic. The result of the defect is a failure to produce an enzyme that concentrates testosterone, specifically for building the genitals. One obscure little enzyme only, but here's what happens without it: You get a boy with undescended testes and a penis so short and stubby that it resembles an oversized clitoris.

In the mountain villages of this Caribbean nation, people are used to it. The children are usually raised as "conditional" girls. At puberty, the secondary tide of androgens rises and is apparently enough to finish the construction project. The scrotum suddenly descends, the phallus grows, and the child develops a distinctly male body — narrow hips, muscular build, and even slight beard growth. At that point, the family shifts the child over from daughter to son. The dresses are thrown out. He begins to wear male clothes and starts dating girls. People in the Dominican Republic are so familiar with this condition that there's a colloquial name for it: *guevedoces*, meaning "eggs (or testes) at 12."

It's the comfort level with this slip-slide of sexual identity that's so remarkable and, I imagine, so comforting to the children involved. I'm positive that the sexual transition of these children is less traumatic than the abrupt awareness of the "sisters who would have been brothers." There's a message of tolerance there, well worth repeating, and there are some other key lessons too.

These defects are rare and don't alter the basic male-female division of our species. They do emphasize how fragile those divisions can be. Biology allows flexibility, room to change, to vary and grow. With that comes room for error as well. That it's possible to live with these genetic defects, that they don't merely kill us off, is a reminder that we, male and female alike, exist on a continuum of biological possibilities that can overlap and sustain either sex.

Marc Breedlove points out that the most difficult task may be separating 20 how the brain responds to hormones from how the brain responds to the *results* of hormones. Which brings us back, briefly, below the belt: In this context, the penis is just a result, the product of androgens at work before birth. "And after birth," says Breedlove, "virtually everyone who interacts with that individual will note that he has a penis, and will, in many instances, behave differently than if the individual was a female."

Do the ways that we amplify physical and behavioral differences in childhood shape who we become as adults? Absolutely. But to understand that, you have to understand the differences themselves — their beginning and the very real biochemistry that may lie behind them.

Here is a good place to focus on testosterone — a hormone that is both well-studied and generally underrated. First, however, I want to acknowledge that there are many other hormones and neurotransmitters that appear to influence behavior. Preliminary work shows that fetal boys are a little more active than fetal girls. It's pretty difficult to argue socialization at that point. There's a strong suspicion that testosterone may create the difference.

And there are a couple of relevant animal models to emphasize the point. Back in the 1960s, Robert Goy, a psychologist at the University of Wisconsin at Madison, first documented that young male monkeys play much more roughly than young females. Goy went on to show that if you manipulate testosterone level — raising it in females, damping it down in males — you can reverse those effects, creating sweet little male monkeys and rowdy young females.

Is testosterone the only factor at work here? I don't think so. But clearly we can argue a strong influence, and, interestingly, studies have found that girls with congenital adrenal hypoplasia — who run high in testosterone — tend to be far more fascinated by trucks and toy weaponry than most little girls are. They lean toward rough-and-tumble play, too. As it turns out, the strongest influence on this "abnormal" behavior is not parental disapproval, but the company of other little girls, who tone them down and direct them toward more routine girl games.

And that reinforces an early point: If there is indeed a biology to sex differ- 25 ences, we amplify it. At some point — when it is still up for debate — we gain a sense of our gender, and with it a sense of "gender-appropriate" behavior.

Some scientists argue for some evidence of gender awareness in infancy, perhaps by the age of 12 months. The consensus seems to be that full-blown "I'm a girl" or "I'm a boy" instincts arrive between the ages of 2 and 3. Research shows that if a family operates in a very traditional, Beaver Cleaver kind of environment, filled with awareness of and association with "proper" gender behaviors, the "boys do trucks, girls do dolls" attitude seems to come very early. If a child grows up in a less traditional family, with an emphasis on

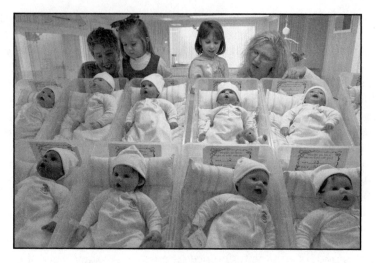

Girls and moms check out an American Girl doll fashion show in Staten Island, New York.

partnership and sharing — "We all do the dishes, Joshua" — children maintain a more flexible sense of gender roles until about age 6.

In this period, too, relationships between boys and girls tend to fall into remarkably strict lines. Interviews with children find that 3-year-olds say that about half their friendships are with the opposite sex. By the age of 5, that drops to 20 percent. By 7, almost no boys or girls have, or will admit to having, best friends of the opposite sex. They still hang out on the same playground, play on the same soccer teams. They may be friendly, but the real friendships tend to be boy-to-boy or girl-to-girl.

There's some interesting science that suggests that the space between boys and girls is a normal part of development; there are periods during which children may thrive and learn from hanging out with peers of the same sex. Do we, as parents, as a culture at large, reinforce such separations? Is the pope Catholic? One of my favorite studies looked at little boys who asked for toys. If they asked for a heavily armed action figure, they got the soldier about 70 percent of the time. If they asked for a "girl" toy, like a baby doll or a Barbie, their parents purchased it maybe 40 percent of the time. Name a child who won't figure out how to work *that* system.

How does all this fit together — toys and testosterone, biology and behavior, the development of the child into the adult, the way that men and women relate to one another?

Let me make a cautious statement about testosterone: It not only has 30 some body-building functions, it influences some behaviors as well. Let's make that a little less cautious: These behaviors include rowdy play, sex drive, competitiveness, and an in-your-face attitude. Males tend to have a higher baseline of testosterone than females — in our species, about seven to ten times as much — and therefore you would predict (correctly, I think) that all of those behaviors would be more generally found in men than in women.

But testosterone is also one of my favorite examples of how responsive biology is, how attuned it is to the way we live our lives. Testosterone, it turns out, rises in response to competition and threat. In the days of our ancestors, this might have been hand-to-hand combat or high-risk hunting endeavors. Today, scientists have measured testosterone rise in athletes preparing for a game, in chess players awaiting a match, in spectators following a soccer competition.

If a person — or even just a person's favored team — wins, testosterone continues to rise. It falls with a loss. (This also makes sense in an evolutionary perspective. If one was being clobbered with a club, it would be extremely unhelpful to have a hormone urging one to battle on.) Testosterone also rises in the competitive world of dating, settles down with a stable and supportive relationship, climbs again if the relationship starts to falter.

It's been known for years that men in high-stress professions — say, police work or corporate law — have higher testosterone levels than men in the ministry. It turns out that women in the same kind of strong-attitude professions have higher testosterone than women who choose to stay home. What I like about this is the chicken-or-egg aspect. If you argue that testosterone influenced the behavior of those women, which came first? Did they have high testosterone and choose the law? Or did they choose the law, and the competitive environment ratcheted them up on the androgen scale? Or could both be at work?

And, returning to children for a moment, there's an ongoing study by Pennsylvania researchers, tracking that question in adolescent girls, who are being encouraged by their parents to engage in competitive activities that were once for boys only. As they do so, the researchers are monitoring, regularly, two hormones: testosterone and cortisol, a stress hormone. Will these hormones rise in response to this new, more traditionally male environment? What if more girls choose the competitive path; more boys choose the other? Will female testosterone levels rise, male levels fall? Will that wonderful, unpredictable, flexible biology that we've been given allow a shift, so that one day, we will literally be far more alike?

We may not have answers to all those questions, but we can ask them, 35 and we can expect that the answers will come someday, because science clearly shows us that such possibilities exist. In this most important sense, sex differences offer us a paradox. It is only through exploring and understanding what makes us different that we can begin to understand what binds us together.

READING THE TEXT

1. What effect do Blum's opening personal-experience anecdotes have on the persuasiveness of her argument?

2. What evidence does Blum offer to support her contention that males are naturally more aggressive than females?

3. How does testosterone affect human behavior, according to Blum's research?

4. In Blum's view, how do the cultural choices that humans make, such as engaging in sports or other competitive activities, affect hormonal balances?

READING THE SIGNS

1. In your journal, reflect on the way your upbringing shaped your sense of appropriate gender behavior.

2. Blum's selection challenges the common cultural studies position that gender behavior is socially constructed. Write an essay in which you defend, qualify, or reject Blum's point of view. To develop your ideas, consult Aaron Devor's "Gender Role Behaviors and Attitudes" (p. 458) and Kevin Jennings's "American Dreams" (p. 464).

3. Write an essay describing how you would raise a boy to counteract his tendencies toward aggressive behavior. To develop your ideas, consult James William Gibson, "Warrior Dreams" (p. 504).

4. Visit the library and investigate recent research on the possible genetic basis for homosexuality. Then write an essay in which you extend Blum's argument for the biological basis of gendered behavior to sexual orientation.

ILANA FRIED

Don't Let Social Notions Curb Ability

In late 2004, Harvard University President Lawrence H. Summers stirred up a national controversy when he remarked that the scarcity of women in the sciences might be due to biological differences between the sexes. In the midst of the ensuing uproar challenging Summers's observation, Ilana Fried, an undergraduate at UCLA, wrote the following op-ed piece for the Daily Bruin, *arguing at once for not being too hard on Summers while calling for gender equality in all walks of life. Ilana Fried (b. 1985) is a history major at UCLA and a* Daily Bruin *columnist.*

This quarter, I'm taking two science classes. They're not necessarily difficult — but they're science classes. And, to put it mildly, science has never been my forte. Harvard President Lawrence H. Summers remarked last week that "innate differences" between men and women may render some females less qualified for the scientific and engineering worlds.

I wanted to know if Summers was a pure sexist, a misunderstood speaker, or a man with a valid point. Why, above all, is science so difficult for me?

The past week has proved quite a ride for Summers and his staff. It seems that journalists, academics, and politicians deride or defend him left and right. Summers issued an official apology stating, "I was wrong to have spoken in a way that has resulted in an unintended signal of discouragement to talented girls and women."

And letters have flooded papers, such as the *New York Times,* offering brazen, bold, even accusatory opinions. "As the president of Harvard," wrote David Ballantyne of North Carolina to the *Times,* "Summers should be media-savvy enough to realize that according to currently fashionable double standards, it is not advisable to make public statements claiming that men might be innately better at anything."

Summers has received an unprecedented level of attention. Some see his comments as unapologetically sexist. Others, like Ballantyne, see him as a victim of double standards. Personally, I don't think his speech was a very big deal — it was small fries.

But I do understand the implications and issues raised by his speech. Overall, Summers offered a less-than-politically correct remark and was harshly berated for doing so. But he didn't intend to offend anybody, and he didn't wish to spark national controversy.

At the very least, his speech directed attention toward some very important issues, namely, women in the science and technology sector.

I believe that women today still face real barriers in these worlds. As a young girl, I noticed these problems myself, in spite of the fact that I attended a single-sex school from kindergarten to eighth grade. At this school, I learned a lot about what was expected of me.

The majority of the students I studied with preferred history and English — not chemistry. Our only exception to the rule was, perhaps, sexual education. Essentially, the humanities seemed sympathetic and flexible. Science, on the other hand, remained logical, impersonal, and dependent upon awkward tools. These were all things we tried to avoid as young women. So, at the end of the day, science was unavoidably masculine.

But of course it wasn't that simple. Many of my all-female classmates enjoyed our science classes. And many scored very high marks in them. But all too commonly, these students downplayed their scientific abilities, explaining that they were only decent students — nothing exceptional.

There was a general feeling of discomfort in science class. It seemed that science was interesting and fun but just wasn't expected of us. So we gave very little back in return, only waiting for our photography and sewing electives later into the day.

Nobody told us we were unfit for science. But there was an unwritten understanding that it wasn't best for us.

This brings me back to my original question: Were we actually unqualified? In one sense, some may claim that we were. As the Harvard president hinted, men and women may have different brains.

According to the *Canadian Press,* "Women's brains are more densely packed than men's in the 'executive' portion of the brain, the area responsible for reason, judgment, memory and some emotion." Women also traditionally have a more-dominant left brain, which has been shown to process information linearly and sequentially.

Meanwhile, men typically employ the right brain, and "test better on spa- 15
tial tasks, target direct motor skills, spotting shapes embedded in complex diagrams, and mathematical reasoning," according to the *Encyclopedia of Educational Technology*. For example, men have been found to be more skilled in rotating an object in their head.

However, these innate differences just aren't enough. Women are making major strides in science, regardless of which brain hemisphere they supposedly employ, and they are forces to be reckoned with.

In 2003, I started my first year at UCLA. Happily, I found that while some departments, such as engineering, seemed predominantly male, others seemed refreshingly equal. I was pleased to see a plethora of female science and pre-med students.

And as a North Campus[1] loyal, it was great news to hear success stories from my South Campus counterparts, male and female.

Sometimes I wonder what Summers would have to say about them. How "innate" are their inabilities? Usually, I just like to think that they're all great scientists, regardless of their gender.

So here I am, taking two science classes, and, admittedly, I'm a bit nervous. 20
Sure, I'm a North Campus kid. I wasn't even a great science student in high school. But the more I think about my worries, the more I understand their socialized roots and meanings.

The truth is I was never encouraged (or discouraged) with respect to science. I was just lightly led to believe that maybe it wasn't the best for me. I think it's high time I changed my ways. There's no reason not to.

READING THE TEXT

1. Summarize in your own words Harvard President Lawrence H. Summers's position on women and science, according to Fried.

2. What is Fried's own academic background, and how does it inform her argument?

3. Explain in your own words what Fried means by writing that, in her all-female grade school, "there was an unwritten understanding that [science] wasn't best for us" (para. 12).

4. Examine Fried's consideration of arguments that are ultimately not her own. How does she address them, and how does that manner of address affect your perception of the persuasiveness of her argument?

---

[1]At UCLA, North Campus houses the humanities, arts, and social sciences, and South Campus is home to the sciences and engineering departments. –Eds.

READING THE SIGNS

1. In your journal, reflect on the extent to which you were encouraged to pursue science as a field of intellectual study. If you are female, did you find, like Fried, that the sciences tended to be "downplayed" (para. 10)? If you are male, did you feel encouraged to follow a scientific direction? Did you notice different academic preferences among students of the opposite gender? Did male or female students receive different treatment by teachers or counselors?

2. Research the responses, from both academics and the general public, to Summers's statements about women and science. Analyze those responses, tracking the extent to which they reflect a belief in either the biological or the cultural basis of the abilities of the two genders. Use your findings to support your own evaluation of the validity of those responses.

3. Study your college catalogue, and note the percentage of science professors, both tenured and untenured, who are women. Interview several of these professors about their experiences studying science, both before and during their college years. Use your results as the basis of an essay in which you assess Fried's assertion that "women today still face real barriers" in science and technology (para. 8). Alternatively, interview some female students who are studying in these fields.

4. Research Summers's original statements about women and science. Then write an essay in which you explain whether you "see his comments as unapologetically sexist," "see him as a victim of double standards" (para. 5), or have an alternative view.

5. Adopting the view of Deborah Blum ("The Gender Blur: Where Does Biology End and Society Take Over?" p. 475) *or* Aaron Devor ("Gender Role Behaviors and Attitudes," p. 458), write a response to Fried's article.

NAOMI WOLF
The Beauty Myth

Before Kate Moss there was Twiggy, and before Twiggy, well, women weren't expected to look so slim — not, at least, if we judge by Marilyn Monroe. And for Naomi Wolf (b. 1962), that's exactly the problem. Contemporary standards of feminine beauty have devolved to a point that can only be described as anorexic, and America's young women are paying the price through a near-epidemic of bulimia and anorexia. The most effective way to combat this epidemic, Wolf argues, is to show how what we call "beautiful" is a cultural myth that has been framed for certain purposes — essentially, Wolf believes, to keep women under control by imprisoning them in their bodies. A prominent figure in feminist and neofeminist circles, Wolf is the author of The Beauty Myth *(1991), from which this selection is excerpted;* Fire with Fire *(1993);* Promiscuities *(1997);* Misconceptions: Truth, Lies, and the Unexpected on the Journey to Motherhood *(2001); and* The Treehouse: Eccentric Wisdom from My Father on How to Live, Love, and See *(2005).*

At last, after a long silence, women took to the streets. In the two decades of radical action that followed the rebirth of feminism in the early 1970s, Western women gained legal and reproductive rights, pursued higher education, entered the trades and the professions, and overturned ancient and revered beliefs about their social role. A generation on, do women feel free?

The affluent, educated, liberated women of the First World, who can enjoy freedoms unavailable to any woman ever before, do not feel as free as they want to. And they can no longer restrict to the subconscious their sense that this lack of freedom has something to do with apparently frivolous issues, things that really should not matter. Many are ashamed to admit that such trivial concerns — to do with physical appearance, bodies, faces, hair, clothes — matter so much. But in spite of shame, guilt, and denial, more and more women are wondering if it isn't that they are entirely neurotic and alone but rather that something important is indeed at stake that has to do with the relationship between female liberation and female beauty.

The more legal and material hindrances women have broken through, the more strictly and heavily and cruelly images of female beauty have come to weigh upon us. Many women sense that women's collective progress has stalled; compared with the heady momentum of earlier days, there is a dispiriting climate of confusion, division, cynicism, and above all, exhaustion. After years of much struggle and little recognition, many older women feel burned out; after years of taking its light for granted, many younger women show little interest in touching new fire to the torch.

During the past decade, women breached the power structure; meanwhile, eating disorders rose exponentially and cosmetic surgery became the fastest-growing medical specialty. During the past five years, consumer spending doubled, pornography became the main media category, ahead of legitimate films and records combined, and thirty-three thousand American women told researchers that they would rather lose ten to fifteen pounds than achieve any other goal. More women have more money and power and scope and legal recognition than we have ever had before; but in terms of how we feel about ourselves *physically*, we may actually be worse off than our unliberated grandmothers. Recent research consistently shows that inside the majority of the West's controlled, attractive, successful working women, there is a secret "underlife" poisoning our freedom; infused with notions of beauty, it is a dark vein of self-hatred, physical obsessions, terror of aging, and dread of lost control.

It is no accident that so many potentially powerful women feel this way. 5 We are in the midst of a violent backlash against feminism that uses images of female beauty as a political weapon against women's advancement: the beauty myth. It is the modern version of a social reflex that has been in force since the Industrial Revolution. As women released themselves from the feminine mystique of domesticity, the beauty myth took over its lost ground, expanding as it waned to carry on its work of social control.

The contemporary backlash is so violent because the ideology of beauty is the last one remaining of the old feminine ideologies that still has the power to control those women whom second-wave feminism would have otherwise made relatively uncontrollable: It has grown stronger to take over the work of social coercion that myths about motherhood, domesticity, chastity, and passivity no longer can manage. It is seeking right now to undo psychologically and covertly all the good things that feminism did for women materially and overtly.

This counterforce is operating to checkmate the inheritance of feminism on every level in the lives of Western women. Feminism gave us laws against job discrimination based on gender; immediately case law evolved in Britain and the United States that institutionalized job discrimination based on women's appearances. Patriarchal religion declined; new religious dogma, using some of the mind-altering techniques of older cults and sects, arose around age and weight to functionally supplant traditional ritual. Feminists, inspired by Betty Friedan, broke the stranglehold on the women's popular press of advertisers for household products, who were promoting the feminine mystique; at once, the diet and skin care industries became the new cultural censors of women's intellectual space, and because of their pressure, the gaunt, youthful model supplanted the happy housewife as the arbiter of successful womanhood. The sexual revolution promoted the discovery of female sexuality; "beauty pornography" — which for the first time in women's history artificially links a commodified "beauty" directly and explicitly to sexuality — invaded the mainstream to undermine women's new and vulnerable sense of sexual self-worth. Reproductive rights gave Western women control over our own bodies; the weight of fashion models plummeted to 23 percent below that of ordinary women, eating disorders rose exponentially, and a mass neurosis was promoted that used food and weight to strip women of that sense of control. Women insisted on politicizing health; new technologies of invasive, potentially deadly "cosmetic" surgeries developed apace to re-exert old forms of medical control of women.

Every generation since about 1830 has had to fight its version of the beauty myth. "It is very little to me," said the suffragist Lucy Stone in 1855, "to have the right to vote, to own property, etcetera, if I may not keep my body, and its uses, in my absolute right." Eighty years later, after women had won the vote, and the first wave of the organized women's movement had subsided, Virginia Woolf wrote that it would still be decades before women could tell the truth about their bodies. In 1962, Betty Friedan quoted a young woman trapped in the Feminine Mystique: "Lately, I look in the mirror, and I'm so afraid that I'm going to look like my mother." Eight years after that, heralding the cataclysmic second wave of feminism, Germaine Greer described "the Stereotype": "To her belongs all that is beautiful, even the very word beauty itself . . . she is a doll . . . I'm sick of the masquerade." In spite of the great revolution of the second wave, we are not exempt. Now we can look out over ruined barricades: A revolution has come upon us and changed everything in its path, enough time has passed since then for babies to have grown into women, but there still remains a final right not fully claimed.

The beauty myth tells a story: The quality called "beauty" objectively and universally exists. Women must want to embody it and men must want to possess women who embody it. This embodiment is an imperative for women and not for men, which situation is necessary and natural because it is biological, sexual, and evolutionary: Strong men battle for beautiful women, and beautiful women are more reproductively successful. Women's beauty must correlate to their fertility, and since this system is based on sexual selection, it is inevitable and changeless.

None of this is true. "Beauty" is a currency system like the gold standard. 10 Like any economy, it is determined by politics, and in the modern age in the West it is the last, best belief system that keeps male dominance intact. In assigning value to women in a vertical hierarchy according to a culturally imposed physical standard, it is an expression of power relations in which women must unnaturally compete for resources that men have appropriated for themselves.

"Beauty" is not universal or changeless, though the West pretends that all ideals of female beauty stem from one Platonic Ideal Woman; the Maori admire a fat vulva, and the Padung, droopy breasts. Nor is "beauty" a function of evolution: Its ideals change at a pace far more rapid than that of the evolution of species, and Charles Darwin was himself unconvinced by his own explanation that "beauty" resulted from a "sexual selection" that deviated from the rule of natural selection; for women to compete with women through "beauty" is a reversal of the way in which natural selection affects all other mammals. Anthropology has overturned the notion that females must be "beautiful" to be selected to mate: Evelyn Reed, Elaine Morgan, and others have dismissed sociobiological assertions of innate male polygamy and female monogamy. Female higher primates are the sexual initiators; not only do they seek out and enjoy sex with many partners, but "every nonpregnant female takes her turn at being the most desirable of all her troop. And that cycle keeps turning as long as she lives." The inflamed pink sexual organs of primates are often cited by male sociobiologists as analogous to human arrangements relating to female "beauty," when in fact that is a universal, nonhierarchical female primate characteristic.

Nor has the beauty myth always been this way. Though the pairing of the older rich men with young, "beautiful" women is taken to be somehow inevitable, in the matriarchal Goddess religions that dominated the Mediterranean from about 25,000 B.C.E. to about 700 B.C.E., the situation was reversed: "In every culture, the Goddess has many lovers. . . . The clear pattern is of an older woman with a beautiful but expendable youth — Ishtar and Tammuz, Venus and Adonis, Cybele and Attis, Isis and Osiris . . . their only function the service of the divine 'womb.' " Nor is it something only women do and only men watch: among the Nigerian Wodaabes, the women hold economic power and the tribe is obsessed with male beauty; Wodaabe men spend hours together in elaborate makeup sessions, and compete — provocatively painted and dressed, with swaying hips and seductive expressions — in beauty contests judged by women. There is no legitimate historical or biological justification for the beauty myth; what it is doing to women today is a result of nothing more exalted than the need of today's power structure, economy, and culture to mount a counteroffensive against women.

If the beauty myth is not based on evolution, sex, gender, aesthetics, or God, on what is it based? It claims to be about intimacy and sex and life, a celebration of women. It is actually composed of emotional distance, politics, finance, and sexual repression. The beauty myth is not about women at all. It is about men's institutions and institutional power.

The qualities that a given period calls beautiful in women are merely symbols of the female behavior that that period considers desirable: *The beauty myth is always actually prescribing behavior and not appearance.* Competition between women has been made part of the myth so that women will be divided from one another. Youth and (until recently) virginity have been "beautiful" in women since they stand for experiential and sexual ignorance. Aging in women is "unbeautiful" since women grow more powerful with time, and since the links between generations of women must always be newly broken: Older women fear young ones, young women fear old, and the beauty myth truncates for all the female life span. Most urgently, women's identity must be premised upon our "beauty" so that we will remain vulnerable to outside approval, carrying the vital sensitive organ of self-esteem exposed to the air.

Though there has, of course, been a beauty myth in some form for as long as there has been patriarchy, the beauty myth in its modern form is a fairly recent invention. The myth flourishes when material constraints on women are dangerously loosened. Before the Industrial Revolution, the average woman could not have had the same feelings about "beauty" that modern women do who experience the myth as continual comparison to a mass-disseminated physical ideal. Before the development of technologies of mass production — daguerreotypes, photographs, etc. — an ordinary woman was exposed to few such images outside the Church. Since the family was a productive unit and women's work complemented men's, the value of women who were not aristocrats or prostitutes lay in their work skills, economic shrewdness, physical strength, and fertility. Physical attraction, obviously, played its part; but "beauty" as we understand it was not, for ordinary women, a serious issue in the marriage marketplace. The beauty myth in its modern form gained ground after the upheavals of industrialization, as the work unit of the family was destroyed, and urbanization and the emerging factory system demanded what social engineers of the time termed the "separate sphere" of domesticity, which supported the new labor category of the "breadwinner" who left home for the workplace during the day. The middle class expanded, the standards of living and of literacy rose, the size of families shrank; a new class of literate, idle women developed, on whose submission to enforced domesticity the

At the beauty parlor: a "trivial" concern?

evolving system of industrial capitalism depended. Most of our assumptions about the way women have always thought about "beauty" date from no earlier than the 1830s, when the cult of domesticity was first consolidated and the beauty index invented.

For the first time new technologies could reproduce — in fashion plates, daguerreotypes, tintypes, and rotogravures — images of how women should look. In the 1840s the first nude photographs of prostitutes were taken; advertisements using images of "beautiful" women first appeared in mid-century. Copies of classical artworks, postcards of society beauties and royal mistresses, Currier and Ives prints, and porcelain figurines flooded the separate sphere to which middle-class women were confined.

Since the Industrial Revolution, middle-class Western women have been controlled by ideals and stereotypes as much as by material constraints. This situation, unique to this group, means that analyses that trace "cultural conspiracies" are uniquely plausible in relation to them. The rise of the beauty myth was just one of several emerging social fictions that masqueraded as natural components of the feminine sphere, the better to enclose those women inside it. Other such fictions arose contemporaneously: a version of childhood that required continual maternal supervision; a concept of female biology that required middle-class women to act out the roles of hysterics and hypochondriacs; a conviction that respectable women were sexually anesthetic; and a definition of women's work that occupied them with repetitive, time-consuming, and painstaking tasks such as needlepoint and lacemaking. All such Victorian inventions as these served a double function — that is, though they were encouraged as a means to expend female energy and intelligence in harmless ways, women often used them to express genuine creativity and passion.

But in spite of middle-class women's creativity with fashion and embroidery and child rearing, and, a century later, with the role of the suburban housewife that devolved from these social fictions, the fictions' main purpose was served: During a century and a half of unprecedented feminist agitation, they effectively counteracted middle-class women's dangerous new leisure, literacy, and relative freedom from material constraints.

Though these time- and mind-consuming fictions about women's natural role adapted themselves to resurface in the postwar Feminine Mystique, when the second wave of the women's movement took apart what women's magazines had portrayed as the "romance," "science," and "adventure" of homemaking and suburban family life, they temporarily failed. The cloying domestic fiction of "togetherness" lost its meaning and middle-class women walked out of their front doors in masses.

So the fictions simply transformed themselves once more: Since the women's movement had successfully taken apart most other necessary fictions of femininity, all the work of social control once spread out over the whole network of these fictions had to be reassigned to the only strand left intact, which action consequently strengthened it a hundredfold. This reimposed onto liberated women's faces and bodies all the limitations, taboos, and punishments of the repressive laws, religious injunctions, and reproductive enslavement that no longer carried sufficient force. Inexhaustible but ephemeral beauty work took over from inexhaustible but ephemeral housework. As the economy, law, religion, sexual mores, education, and culture were forcibly opened up to include women more fairly, a private reality colonized female consciousness. By using ideas about "beauty," it reconstructed an alternative female world with its own laws, economy, religion, sexuality, education, and culture, each element as repressive as any that had gone before.

Since middle-class Western women can best be weakened psychologically now that we are stronger materially, the beauty myth, as it has resurfaced in the last generation, has had to draw on more technological sophistication and reactionary fervor than ever before. The modern arsenal of the myth is a dissemination of millions of images of the current ideal; although this barrage is generally seen as a collective sexual fantasy, there is in fact little that is sexual about it. It is summoned out of political fear on the part of male-dominated institutions threatened by women's freedom, and it exploits female guilt and apprehension about our own liberation — latent fears that we might be going too far. This frantic aggregation of imagery is a collective reactionary hallucination willed into being by both men and women stunned and disoriented by the rapidity with which gender relations have been transformed: a bulwark of reassurance against the flood of change. The mass depiction of the modern woman as a "beauty" is a contradiction: Where modern women are growing, moving, and expressing their individuality, as the myth has it, "beauty" is by definition inert, timeless, and generic. That this hallucination is necessary and deliberate is evident in the way "beauty" so directly contradicts women's real situation.

And the unconscious hallucination grows ever more influential and pervasive because of what is now conscious market manipulation: powerful industries — the $33-billion-a-year diet industry, the $20-billion cosmetics industry, the $300-million cosmetic surgery industry, and the $7-billion pornography industry — have arisen from the capital made out of unconscious anxieties, and are in turn able, through their influence on mass culture, to use, stimulate, and reinforce the hallucination in a rising economic spiral.

This is not a conspiracy theory; it doesn't have to be. Societies tell themselves necessary fictions in the same way that individuals and families do. Henrik Ibsen called them "vital lies," and psychologist Daniel Goleman describes them working the same way on the social level that they do within families: "The collusion is maintained by directing attention away from the fearsome fact, or by repackaging its meaning in an acceptable format." The costs of these social blind spots, he writes, are destructive communal illusions. Possibilities for women have become so open-ended that they threaten to destabilize the institutions on which a male-dominated culture has depended, and a collective panic reaction on the part of both sexes has forced a demand for counter-images.

The resulting hallucination materializes, for women, as something all too real. No longer just an idea, it becomes three-dimensional, incorporating within itself how women live and how they do not live: It becomes the Iron Maiden. The original Iron Maiden was a medieval German instrument of torture, a body-shaped casket painted with the limbs and features of a lovely, smiling young woman. The unlucky victim was slowly enclosed inside her; the lid fell shut to immobilize the victim, who died either of starvation or, less cruelly, of the metal spikes embedded in her interior. The modern hallucination in which women are trapped or trap themselves is similarly rigid, cruel, and euphemistically painted. Contemporary culture directs attention to imagery of the Iron Maiden, while censoring real women's faces and bodies.

Why does the social order feel the need to defend itself by evading the fact 25 of real women, our faces and voices and bodies, and reducing the meaning of women to these formulaic and endlessly reproduced "beautiful" images? Though unconscious personal anxieties can be a powerful force in the creation of a vital lie, economic necessity practically guarantees it. An economy that depends on slavery needs to promote images of slaves that "justify" the institution of slavery. Western economics are absolutely dependent now on the continued underpayment of women. An ideology that makes women feel "worth less" was urgently needed to counteract the way feminism had begun to make us feel worth more. This does not require a conspiracy; merely an atmosphere. The contemporary economy depends right now on the representation of women within the beauty myth. Economist John Kenneth Galbraith offers an economic explanation for "the persistence of the view of homemaking as a 'higher calling'": the concept of women as naturally trapped within the Feminine Mystique, he feels, "has been forced on us by popular sociology, by magazines, and by fiction to disguise the fact that woman in her role of consumer has been essential to the development of our industrial society. . . . Behavior that is essential for economic reasons is transformed into a social virtue." As soon as a woman's primary social value could no longer be defined as the attainment of virtuous domesticity, the beauty myth redefined it as the attainment of virtuous beauty. It did so to substitute both a new consumer imperative and a new justification for economic unfairness in the workplace where the old ones had lost their hold over newly liberated women.

Another hallucination arose to accompany that of the Iron Maiden: The caricature of the Ugly Feminist was resurrected to dog the steps of the women's movement. The caricature is unoriginal; it was coined to ridicule the feminists of the nineteenth century. Lucy Stone herself, whom supporters saw as "a prototype of womanly grace . . . fresh and fair as the morning," was derided by detractors with "the usual report" about Victorian feminists: "a big masculine woman, wearing boots, smoking a cigar, swearing like a trooper." As Betty Friedan put it presciently in 1960, even before the savage revamping of that old caricature: "The unpleasant image of feminists today resembles less the feminists themselves than the image fostered by the interests who so bitterly opposed the vote for women in state after state." Thirty years on, her conclusion is more true than ever: That resurrected caricature, which sought to punish women for their public acts by going after their private sense of self, became the paradigm for new limits placed on aspiring women everywhere. After the success of the women's movement's second wave, the beauty myth was perfected to checkmate power at every level in individual women's lives.

The modern neuroses of life in the female body spread to woman after woman at epidemic rates. The myth is undermining — slowly, imperceptibly, without our being aware of the real forces of erosion — the ground women have gained through long, hard, honorable struggle.

The beauty myth of the present is more insidious than any mystique of femininity yet: A century ago, Nora slammed the door of the doll's house; a generation ago, women turned their backs on the consumer heaven of the isolated multi-applianced home; but where women are trapped today, there is no door to slam. The contemporary ravages of the beauty backlash are destroying women physically and depleting us psychologically. If we are to free ourselves from the dead weight that has once again been made out of femaleness, it is not ballots or lobbyists or placards that women will need first; it is a new way to see.

READING THE TEXT

1. What is the "secret 'underlife' poisoning" (para. 4) modern women's lives, according to Wolf?
2. Summarize in your own words what Wolf means by "the beauty myth" (para. 5).
3. What relationship does Wolf see between the beauty myth and feminism?
4. How has the beauty myth replaced the myth of "virtuous domesticity" (para. 25), in Wolf's opinion?
5. What does Wolf see as the significance of the Iron Maiden, both historically and today?

READING THE SIGNS

1. Discuss in your journal your attitudes toward your body. To what extent have your attitudes been shaped by contemporary standards of physical attractiveness for your gender?
2. Visit a local art museum (or an online collection of such a museum), and study the different ways in which women's bodies are represented. How do the images reflect the history of the beauty myth that Wolf presents? Use your findings to support an analytical essay about how women are represented in art.
3. Bring to class a women's magazine such as *Elle* or *Cosmopolitan,* and in small groups examine the ways in which both advertising and fashion displays portray women. Discuss what the ideal image of female beauty is in your publications.
4. Write an essay in which you support, challenge, or qualify Wolf's belief that the beauty myth constitutes an "Iron Maiden" (para. 24) that torments the lives of modern women. Develop your ideas by consulting Mariah Burton Nelson, "I Won. I'm Sorry." (p. 439).
5. Wolf does not discuss whether men are bound by their own version of the beauty myth. In class, form teams, and debate whether men are as trapped by standards of ideal physical attractiveness as women. To develop your ideas, consult Warren St. John's "Metrosexuals Come Out" (p. 174), Mariah Burton Nelson's "I Won. I'm Sorry." (p. 439), and James William Gibson's "Warrior Dreams" (p. 504).

"Hey Bud"

READING THE SIGNS

1. What are your initial impressions of this sign? To whom is it directed?

2. To what does the word *Bud* refer? The word *cans*? The word *our*?

3. Describe the facial expressions and body language of the models in this image. How do they compare to those of a typical model in a beer advertisement? How do the models' facial expressions and body language serve the purpose of both types of ads?

4. Do you think this is an effective ad? Explain your answer.

JOAN MORGAN

Sex, Lies, and Videos

Hip-hop culture is widely viewed as the expression of black pride, and even defiance, but in this opinion piece written for Essence *in 2002, Joan Morgan points out that the parade of skinny white, Asian, Latina, or light-skinned black women who appear in typical rap videos can be hard on black girls and women who don't look like that. A fan of hip-hop herself, Morgan thinks "it's time to set some standards" that protect African American children. Morgan (b. 1964) is editor-at-large for* Essence *and author of* When Chickenheads Come Home to Roost *(1999).*

It was the timbre of her voice that haunted me. It was soft and tinged with defeat. "I can't watch rap videos anymore," said the former fan who spoke to me from the University of Massachusetts audience I was addressing that day. "They make me feel bad about myself. Even when the images aren't bordering on pornographic, the girls in them are always skinny, White, Asian, or Latino — anything but Black. Or if a dancer is Black, then she's extremely light-skinned." She herself was pretty and thick with skin the color of milk chocolate.

This young woman's alienation and frustration resonated through the crowd of college-age women. "If this is who is considered beautiful by our men, where does that leave me?" was a common remark. For the next hour or so, the discussion I was supposed to be facilitating on the role of women in hip-hop turned into a lengthy discourse on why so many die-hard female fans had finally given up.

It wasn't as if I couldn't empathize. Remaining a hip-hop loyalist these days is a formidable task with a questionable payoff. Rap music has journeyed from the South Bronx underground to Corporate America, as 70 percent of hip-hop consumers are now White. For many artists, the shift in the market has meant adopting mainstream values, resulting in the proliferation of thin, White and light images of women. When you couple that with a visual aesthetic that relies heavily on T&A and crotch shots, suffice it to say the average rap video taps into just about every insecurity and erroneous belief about sensuality related to Black women. Especially troubling is the unavoidable message that shaking our half-naked asses in front of a man is the only way we have to secure male affection.

Fewer than five years ago, the discussion I had at the university would have been very different. To be sure, sexism in hip-hop would have been part of it, but there also would've been lively debates over freedom of speech, Latifah's Afrofemme regality versus the punanny politics of Lil' Kim, and the deliciously guilty pleasure of discarding feminist principles for a few hours of booty-shaking hedonistic abandon. Now we could no longer get past the sense of degradation most young women feel while watching rap videos.

Several of them raised concerns about how those images affect younger 5
girls. One expressed dismay at seeing her 5-year-old niece (who watches
videos with her twentysomething mom, mind you) provocatively winding to
the ridiculously infectious hook of Nas's "Oochie Wally" in which a woman
sings, "He really, really turned me out. He really, really got to gut me. He
really, really made me scream and shout." Another shared her futile attempts
to quell her pubescent 12-year-old cousin's fear that her emerging hips and
breasts were making her "too fat" to wear the designer gear that defines her
ghetto-fabulous aspirations.

These stories echo the frustrations of so many other women I know. A principal at a New York public junior-high school has to send her female students
home repeatedly for "coming to school in the hooker wear they see in these
videos." She's concerned for their safety, and she's afraid they'll get picked up
for soliciting. My friend Irene Prince, the mother of a 14-year-old girl, laments:
"The problem with rap is that the images of cool women they present are
always degrading to girls. They get to be only one thing — toys for boys. I don't
want my daughter modeling herself after that."

Certainly there is little question that the majority of Black girls are ill-
equipped to handle this onslaught of sexually degrading content. Although Black
girls continue to have a more positive body image than many of their White
counterparts, our young women are developing eating disorders at a greater rate
than previously, according to the U.S. Department of Health and Human Services
Office on Women's Health. And with thin, scantily clad video vixens informing
their notion of an aesthetic ideal, 90 percent of those affected with eating disorders are adolescent and young adult females. Combine these factors with the
reality that father figures are absent from so many of our homes, and it is easy to
see why Black girls are likely to think that wearing little to nothing and competing with women for sexual attention is the only way to secure male interest.

But for all the attention the half-dressed hoochie may get, what rap videos
don't portray is that without financial independence, education, ambition, intelligence, spirituality and love, punanny alone ain't all that powerful. In fact, it's
easily replaceable and inexhaustible in supply. As my girlfriend Irene said to
me, "In rap videos, there is no self. Girls become body parts and nothing more."

As women, we cannot abdicate the responsibility we have to our children. As
female hip-hop fans, we can no longer afford to buy into the music's most clichéd
disclaimer — that rap's content is intended for mature audiences. True, it is a parent's role to monitor what his or her children are watching, but there's also no
denying that the current generation is essentially parenting itself. Sixty-two percent of our children are being raised without the benefit of both parents in the
home, and many of them without the benefit of extended family. Indeed, in a
great number of homes, television is the babysitter. It really does take a village,
y'all, and in the absence of parental figures, we gotta parent one another's kids.

It's time to set some standards. Instead of resigning ourselves to being at 10
the mercy of the media, we have to recognize our power to have an impact
on it. Individual acts of resistance — banning cable from our homes, refusing

to buy CDs with misogynistic content — are simply not enough. In the late eighties, MTV was besieged with complaints that its videos were too full of content inappropriate for younger kids. Viewers collectively issued an effective ultimatum: "Clean it up, or we ban you from our homes."

MTV responded accordingly by blurring any suggestions of nudity, gang insignias, or drugs and refusing to play rap videos with hard-core content. Yet when media giant Viacom bought BET, it let the station air programming that it would never allow on MTV. Evidently it wasn't acceptable to air near-pornographic images for the young, largely White audience of MTV, but it was fine to dump them on the young, largely Black BET audience. And why is that? Because we aren't complaining.

It's up to us to identify these videos for what they are — adult content that shouldn't be shown in prime time. If White America can determine what's too toxic for their children, we can, too. Every parent, college student, female hip-hop fan and journalist who has spoken to me about the disturbing content of videos should also put his or her objections down in an e-mail or letter. Send it off to every station that plays these videos, and demand that they be put on after 9:00 P.M. If the response isn't favorable, we should join forces with our peers, colleagues, community leaders, and congregations to threaten a boycott of not only the station but also its advertisers. I bet we would see immediate changes then. We would see, perhaps, a space where our girls can enjoy the music they love, without risking their self-esteem and souls in the process.

READING THE TEXT

1. To what features of hip-hop videos does Morgan particularly object?

2. How has hip-hop evolved, according to Morgan, and how does she feel about changes in the genre?

3. What does Morgan see as the differences in the portrayals of white and African American women in hip-hop and pop music?

4. In your own words describe Morgan's solution to the problem of misogyny in hip-hop.

READING THE SIGNS

1. Conduct a random survey of female hip-hop fans, inquiring about their attitudes toward hip-hip music and videos. Use your findings as the basis of an essay assessing the validity of Morgan's claim that most young women feel a "sense of degradation . . . while watching rap videos" (para. 4).

2. Watch some recent hip-hop videos, and analyze the images of women they present. To what extent do the women follow the pattern — of being thin, light-skinned, and scantily clad — that Morgan describes?

3. Survey a broad array of images of women in popular culture — you can look to advertising, other musical genres than hip-hop, film, and TV — and analyze how women are represented. Then write an essay in which you argue whether Morgan's objections to hip-hop's depiction of women can be applied to other

media as well. To develop your ideas, consult Andre Mayer, "The New Sexual Stone Age" (p. 284).

4. Watch videos of several female hip-hop artists, and analyze their representation of women. To what extent do they duplicate the patterns Morgan describes? To develop your ideas, consult Gwendolyn Pough, "Women, Rap, Wreck" (p. 275).

5. Write an essay in which you support, refute, or complicate Morgan's claim that hip-hop has "adopt[ed] mainstream values" (para. 3).

DEBORAH TANNEN
There Is No Unmarked Woman

If you use the pronoun "s/he" when writing, or write "women and men" rather than "men and women," you are not just writing words: You are making a statement that may "mark" you as being a "feminist." In this analysis of the way everything a woman does marks her in some way or other—from writing and speaking to the way she dresses and styles her hair—Deborah Tannen (b. 1945) reveals the asymmetrical nature of gender semiotics in our culture. Wearing makeup or not wearing makeup sends a signal about a woman, whereas a man without makeup sends no signal at all. Tannen's analysis shows how what men do is implicitly considered the norm in society, and so is relatively neutral, while women's difference inevitably marks them, "because there is no unmarked woman." University Professor in Linguistics at Georgetown University, Tannen is the author of many books, including the best-selling You Just Don't Understand: Women and Men in Conversation *(1986),* Talking from 9 to 5 *(1994),* Gender and Discourse *(1994),* The Argument Culture *(1998), and* I Only Say This Because I Love You: How the Way We Talk Can Make or Break Family Relationships throughout Our Lives *(2001).*

Some years ago I was at a small working conference of four women and eight men. Instead of concentrating on the discussion I found myself looking at the three other women at the table, thinking how each had a different style and how each style was coherent.

One woman had dark brown hair in a classic style, a cross between Cleopatra and Plain Jane. The severity of her straight hair was softened by wavy bangs and ends that turned under. Because she was beautiful, the effect was more Cleopatra than plain.

The second woman was older, full of dignity and composure. Her hair was cut in a fashionable style that left her with only one eye, thanks to a side part that let a curtain of hair fall across half her face. As she looked down to read her prepared paper, the hair robbed her of bifocal vision and created a barrier between her and the listeners.

The third woman's hair was wild, a frosted blond avalanche falling over and beyond her shoulders. When she spoke she frequently tossed her head, calling attention to her hair and away from her lecture.

Then there was makeup. The first woman wore facial cover that made her [5] skin smooth and pale, a black line under each eye and mascara that darkened already dark lashes. The second wore only a light gloss on her lips and a hint of shadow on her eyes. The third had blue bands under her eyes, dark blue shadow, mascara, bright red lipstick, and rouge; her fingernails flashed red.

I considered the clothes each woman had worn during the three days of the conference: In the first case, man-tailored suits in primary colors with solid-color blouses. In the second, casual but stylish black T-shirts, a floppy collarless jacket and baggy slacks or a skirt in neutral colors. The third wore a sexy jumpsuit; tight sleeveless jersey and tight yellow slacks; a dress with gaping armholes and an indulged tendency to fall off one shoulder.

Shoes? No. 1 wore string sandals with medium heels; No. 2, sensible, comfortable walking shoes; No. 3, pumps with spike heels. You can fill in the jewelry, scarves, shawls, sweaters — or lack of them.

As I amused myself finding coherence in these styles, I suddenly wondered why I was scrutinizing only the women. I scanned the eight men at the table. And then I knew why I wasn't studying them. The men's styles were unmarked.

The term "marked" is a staple of linguistic theory. It refers to the way language alters the base meaning of a word by adding a linguistic particle that has no meaning on its own. The unmarked form of a word carries the meaning that goes without saying — what you think of when you're not thinking anything special.

The unmarked tense of verbs in English is the present — for example, *visit*. [10] To indicate past, you mark the verb by adding *ed* to yield *visited*. For future, you add a word: *will visit*. Nouns are presumed to be singular until marked for plural, typically by adding *s* or *es*, so *visit* becomes *visits* and *dish* becomes *dishes*.

The unmarked forms of most English words also convey "male." Being male is the unmarked case. Endings like *ess* and *ette* mark words as "female." Unfortunately, they also tend to mark them for frivolousness. Would you feel safe entrusting your life to a doctorette? Alfre Woodard, who was an Oscar nominee for best supporting actress, says she identifies herself as an actor because "actresses worry about eyelashes and cellulite, and women who are actors worry about the characters we are playing." Gender markers pick up extra meanings that reflect common associations with the female gender: not quite serious, often sexual.

Each of the women at the conference had to make decisions about hair, clothing, makeup, and accessories, and each decision carried meaning. Every style available to us was marked. The men in our group had made decisions, too, but the range from which they chose was incomparably narrower. Men can choose styles that are marked, but they don't have to, and in this group none did. Unlike the women, they had the option of being unmarked.

Take the men's hair styles. There was no marine crew cut or oily longish hair falling into eyes, no asymmetrical, two-tiered construction to swirl over a bald top. One man was unabashedly bald; the others had hair of standard length, parted on one side, in natural shades of brown or gray or graying. Their hair obstructed no views, left little to toss or push back or run fingers through and, consequently, needed and attracted no attention. A few men had beards. In a business setting, beards might be marked. In this academic gathering, they weren't.

There could have been a cowboy shirt with string tie or a three-piece suit or a necklaced hippie in jeans. But there wasn't. All eight men wore brown or blue slacks and nondescript shirts of light colors. No man wore sandals or boots; their shoes were dark, closed, comfortable, and flat. In short, unmarked.

Although no man wore makeup, you couldn't say the men didn't wear 15 makeup in the sense that you could say a woman didn't wear makeup. For men, no makeup is unmarked.

I asked myself what style we women could have adopted that would have been unmarked, like the men's. The answer was none. There is no unmarked woman.

There is no woman's hairstyle that can be called standard, that says nothing about her. The range of women's hairstyles is staggering, but a woman whose hair has no particular style is perceived as not caring about how she looks, which can disqualify her from many positions, and will subtly diminish her as a person in the eyes of some.

Women must choose between attractive shoes and comfortable shoes. When our group made an unexpected trek, the woman who wore flat, laced shoes arrived first. Last to arrive was the woman in spike heels, shoes in hand and a handful of men around her.

If a woman's clothing is tight or revealing (in other words, sexy), it sends a message — an intended one of wanting to be attractive, but also a possibly unintended one of availability. If her clothes are not sexy, that too sends a message, lent meaning by the knowledge that they could have been. There are thousands of cosmetic products from which women can choose and myriad ways of applying them. Yet no makeup at all is anything but unmarked. Some men see it as a hostile refusal to please them.

Women can't even fill out a form without telling stories about themselves. 20 Most forms give four titles to choose from. "Mr." carries no meaning other than that the respondent is male. But a woman who checks "Mrs." or "Miss" communicates not only whether she has been married but also whether she has conservative tastes in forms of address — and probably other conservative values as well. Checking "Ms." declines to let on about marriage (checking "Mr." declines nothing since nothing was asked), but it also marks her as either liberated or rebellious, depending on the observer's attitudes and assumptions.

I sometimes try to duck these variously marked choices by giving my title as "Dr." — and in so doing risk marking myself as either uppity (hence sarcastic

responses like "Excuse *me*!") or an overachiever (hence reactions of congratu-
latory surprise like "Good for you!").

All married women's surnames are marked. If a woman takes her husband's
name, she announces to the world that she is married and has traditional values.
To some it will indicate that she is less herself, more identified by her husband's
identity. If she does not take her husband's name, this too is marked, seen
as worthy of comment: She has *done* something; she has "kept her own name."
A man is never said to have "kept his own name" because it never occurs to anyone that he might have given it up. For him using his own name is unmarked.

A married woman who wants to have her cake and eat it too may use her
surname plus his, with or without a hyphen. But this too announces her marital
status and often results in a tongue-tying string. In a list (Harvey O'Donovan,
Jonathan Feldman, Stephanie Woodbury McGillicutty), the woman's multiple
name stands out. It is marked.

I have never been inclined toward biological explanations of gender differences in language, but I was intrigued to see Ralph Fasold bring biological
phenomena to bear on the question of linguistic marking in his book *The Socio-
linguistics of Language*. Fasold stresses that language and culture are particularly
unfair in treating women as the marked case because biologically it is the male
that is marked. While two X chromosomes make a female, two Y chromosomes
make nothing. Like the linguistic markers *s*, *es*, or *ess*, the Y chromosome doesn't
"mean" anything unless it is attached to a root form — an X chromosome.

Developing this idea elsewhere Fasold points out that girls are born with fully   25
female bodies, while boys are born with modified female bodies. He invites men
who doubt this to lift up their shirts and contemplate why they have nipples.

In his book, Fasold notes "a wide range of facts which demonstrates that
female is the unmarked sex." For example, he observes that there are a few
species that produce only females, like the whiptail lizard. Thanks to partheno-
genesis, they have no trouble having as many daughters as they like. There
are no species, however, that produce only males. This is no surprise, since
any such species would become extinct in its first generation.

Fasold is also intrigued by species that produce individuals not involved
in reproduction, like honeybees and leaf-cutter ants. Reproduction is handled
by the queen and a relatively few males; the workers are sterile females.
"Since they do not reproduce," Fasold said, "there is no reason for them to be
one sex or the other, so they default, so to speak, to female."

Fasold ends his discussion of these matters by pointing out that if language
reflected biology, grammar books would direct us to use "she" to include males
and females and "he" only for specifically male referents. But they don't.
They tell us that "he" means "he or she," and that "she" is used only if the referent is specifically female. This use of "he" as the sex-indefinite pronoun is
an innovation introduced into English by grammarians in the eighteenth and
nineteenth centuries, according to Peter Mühlhäusler and Rom Harré in *Pro-
nouns and People*. From at least about 1500, the correct sex-indefinite pronoun was "they," as it still is in casual spoken English. In other words, the
female was declared by grammarians to be the marked case.

Writing this article may mark me not as a writer, not as a linguist, not as an analyst of human behavior, but as a feminist — which will have positive or negative, but in any case powerful, connotations for readers. Yet I doubt that anyone reading Ralph Fasold's book would put that label on him.

I discovered the markedness inherent in the very topic of gender after 30 writing a book on differences in conversational style based on geographical region, ethnicity, class, age, and gender. When I was interviewed, the vast majority of journalists wanted to talk about the differences between women and men. While I thought I was simply describing what I observed — something I had learned to do as a researcher — merely mentioning women and men marked me as a feminist for some.

When I wrote a book devoted to gender differences in ways of speaking, I sent the manuscript to five male colleagues, asking them to alert me to any interpretation, phrasing, or wording that might seem unfairly negative toward men. Even so, when the book came out, I encountered responses like that of the television talk show host who, after interviewing me, turned to the audience and asked if they thought I was male-bashing.

Leaping upon a poor fellow who affably nodded in agreement, she made him stand and asked, "Did what she say accurately describe you?" "Oh, yes," he answered. "That's me exactly." "And what she said about women — does that sound like your wife?" "Oh yes," he responded. "That's her exactly." "Then why do you think she's male-bashing?" He answered, with disarming honesty, "Because she's a woman and she's saying things about men."

To say anything about women and men without marking oneself as either feminist or anti-feminist, male-basher or apologist for men seems as impossible for a woman as trying to get dressed in the morning without inviting interpretations of her character.

Sitting at the conference table musing on these matters, I felt sad to think that we women didn't have the freedom to be unmarked that the men sitting next to us had. Some days you just want to get dressed and go about your business. But if you're a woman, you can't, because there is no unmarked woman.

READING THE TEXT

1. Explain in your own words what Tannen means by "marked" (para. 9).

2. Why does Tannen say that men have the option of being "unmarked" (para. 9)?

3. What significance does Tannen see in Ralph Fasold's biological explanations of linguistic gender differences?

READING THE SIGNS

1. Do you agree with Tannen's assumption that men have the luxury of remaining "unmarked" (para. 9) in society? Do you think it's possible to be purely unmarked? To develop your essay, you might interview some men, particularly those who elect to have an unconventional appearance, and read James William Gibson's "Warrior Dreams" (p. 504).

2. In class, survey the extent to which the males and females in your class are "marked" or "unmarked," in Tannen's terms, studying such signs as clothing and hairstyle. Do the males tend to have unmarked styles, while the women tend to send a message by their choices? Discuss the results of your survey, and reflect on the validity of Tannen's claims.

3. Interview at least five women who are married, and ask them about their choice of names: Did they keep their "own" name, adopt their husband's, or opt for a hyphenated version? What signals do they want to send about their identity through their names? Use the results of your interviews to write a reflective essay on how our names function as signs, particularly as gender-related signs.

4. What would an unmarked appearance for women be like? Write a speculative essay in which you imagine the features of an unmarked female appearance. If you have difficulty imagining such an appearance, try to explain why.

JAMES WILLIAM GIBSON
Warrior Dreams

> *If you think that Rambo was a joke, James William Gibson has news for you: His popularity was a symptom of an identity crisis that has afflicted American men since the advent of feminism and the U.S. defeat in Vietnam more than a quarter of a century ago. Feeling unmanned by a war lost and by the rewriting of gender codes in the wake of the sexual revolution, millions of American men, as Gibson puts it, "began to dream, to fantasize about the powers and features of another kind of man who could retake and reorder the world." Such fantasy warriors include Rambo, Dirty Harry, and Jack Ryan, fictional role models for the gun-toting legions of a new paramilitary subculture that is quite real, and growing. Paintball, anyone? Gibson (b. 1951) is professor of sociology at California State University, Long Beach, and author of* The Perfect War: Technowar in Vietnam *(1986) and* Warrior Dreams: Paramilitary Culture in Post-Vietnam America *(1994), from which this selection is excerpted.*

We couldn't see them, but we could hear their bugles sound the call. The Communist battalions were organizing for a predawn assault. Captain Kokalis smiled wickedly; he'd been through this before. A "human wave" assault composed of thousands of enemy soldiers was headed our way. The captain ordered the remaining soldiers in his command to check their .30- and .50-caliber machine guns. Earlier in the night, the demolitions squad attached to our unit had planted mines and explosive charges for hundreds of meters in front of our position.

And then it began. At a thousand meters, the soldiers emerged screaming from the gray-blue fog. "Fire!" yelled Captain Kokalis. The gun crews opened up with short bursts of three to seven rounds; their bullets struck meat. Everywhere I could see, clusters of Communist troops were falling by the second. But the wave still surged forward. At five hundred meters, Kokalis passed the word to his gunners to increase their rate of fire to longer strings of ten to twenty rounds. Sergeant Donovan, the demolitions squad leader, began to reap the harvest from the night's planting. Massive explosions ripped through the Communist troops. Fire and smoke blasted into the dawn sky. It was as if the human wave had hit a submerged reef; as the dying fell, wide gaps appeared in the line where casualties could no longer be replaced.

But still they kept coming, hundreds of men, each and every one bent on taking the American position and wiping us out. As the Communists reached one hundred meters, Kokalis gave one more command. Every machine gun in our platoon went to its maximum rate of sustained full-automatic frenzy, sounding like chain saws that just keep cutting and cutting.

And then it was over. The attack subsided into a flat sea of Communist dead. No Americans had been killed or wounded. We were happy to be alive, proud of our victory. We only wondered if our ears would ever stop ringing and if we would ever again smell anything other than the bittersweet aroma of burning gunpowder. . . .

Although an astonishing triumph was achieved that day, no historian will ever find a record of this battle in the hundreds of volumes and thousands of official reports written about the Korean or Vietnam wars. Nor was the blood spilt part of a covert operation in Afghanistan or some unnamed country in Africa, Asia, or Latin America.   5

No, this battle was fought inside the United States, a few miles north of Las Vegas, in September 1986. It was a purely *imaginary* battle, a dream of victory staged as part of the *Soldier of Fortune* magazine's annual convention. The audience of several hundred men, women, and children, together with reporters and a camera crew from *CBS News,* sat in bleachers behind half a dozen medium and heavy machine guns owned by civilians. Peter G. Kokalis, *SOF*'s firearms editor, set the scene for the audience and asked them to imagine that the sandy brushland of the Desert Sportsman Rifle and Pistol Club was really a killing zone for incoming Communist troops. Kokalis was a seasoned storyteller; he'd given this performance before. When the fantasy battle was over, the fans went wild with applause. Kokalis picked up a microphone, praised Donovan (another *SOF* staff member) — "He was responsible for that whole damn Communist bunker that went up" — and told the parents in the audience to buy "claymores [antipersonnel land mines] and other good shit for the kids." A marvelous actor who knew what his audience wanted, Kokalis sneered, "Did you get that, CBS, on your videocam? Screw you knee-jerk liberals."[1]

The shoot-out and victory over Communist forces conducted at the Desert Sportsman Rifle and Pistol Club was but one battle in a cultural or imaginary "New War" that had been going on since the late 1960s and early 1970s. The bitter controversies surrounding the Vietnam War had discredited the old American ideal of the masculine warrior hero for much of the public. But in 1971, when Clint Eastwood made the transition from playing cowboys in old *Rawhide* reruns and spaghetti westerns to portraying San Francisco police detective Harry Callahan in *Dirty Harry,* the warrior hero returned in full force. His backup arrived in 1974 when Charles Bronson appeared in *Death Wish,* the story of a mild-mannered, middle-aged architect in New York City who, after his wife is murdered and his daughter is raped and driven insane, finds new meaning in life through an endless war of revenge against street punks.

In the 1980s, Rambo and his friends made their assault. The experience of John Rambo, a former Green Beret, was the paradigmatic story of the decade. In *First Blood* (1982), he burns down a small Oregon town while suffering hallucinatory flashbacks to his service in Vietnam. Three years later, in *Rambo: First Blood, Part 2,* he is taken off a prison chain gang by his former commanding officer in Vietnam and asked to perform a special reconnaissance mission to find suspected American POWs in Laos, in exchange for a Presidential pardon. His only question: "Do we get to win this time?" And indeed, Rambo does win. Betrayed by the CIA bureaucrat in charge of the mission, Rambo fights the Russians and Vietnamese by himself and brings the POWs back home.

Hundreds of similar films celebrating the victory of good men over bad through armed combat were made during the late 1970s and 1980s. Many were directed by major Hollywood directors and starred well-known actors. Elaborate special effects and exotic film locations added tens of millions to production costs. And for every large-budget film, there were scores of cheaper formula films employing lesser-known actors and production crews. Often these "action-adventure" films had only brief theatrical releases in major markets. Instead, they made their money in smaller cities and towns, in sales to Europe and the Third World, and most of all, in the sale of videocassettes to rental stores. Movie producers could even turn a profit on "video-only" releases; action-adventure films were the largest category of video rentals in the 1980s.

At the same time, Tom Clancy became a star in the publishing world. His book *The Hunt for Red October* (1984) told the story of the Soviet Navy's most erudite submarine commander, Captain Markus Ramius, and his effort to defect

10

---

[1]Peter G. Kokalis, speaking at the *Soldier of Fortune* firepower demonstration at the Desert Sportsman Rifle and Pistol Club, Las Vegas, Nev., September 20, 1986.

to the United States with the Soviets' premier missile-firing submarine. *Red Storm Rising* (1986) followed, an epic of World War III framed as a high-tech conventional war against the Soviet Union. Clancy's novels all featured Jack Ryan, Ph.D., a former Marine captain in Vietnam turned academic naval historian who returns to duty as a CIA analyst and repeatedly stumbles into life-and-death struggles in which the fate of the world rests on his prowess. All were bestsellers.

President Reagan, Secretary of the Navy John Lehman, and many other high officials applauded Clancy and his hero. Soon the author had a multimillion-dollar contract for a whole series of novels, movie deals with Paramount, and a new part-time job as a foreign-policy expert writing op-ed pieces for the *Washington Post*, the *Los Angeles Times*, and other influential newspapers around the country. His success motivated dozens of authors, mostly active-duty or retired military men, to take up the genre. The "technothriller" was born.

At a slightly lower level in the literary establishment, the same publishing houses that marketed women's romance novels on grocery and drugstore paperback racks rapidly expanded their collections of pulp fiction for men. Most were written like hard-core pornography, except that inch-by-inch descriptions of penises entering vaginas were replaced by equally graphic portrayals of bullets, grenade fragments, and knives shredding flesh: "He tried to grab the handle of the commando knife, but the terrorist pushed down on the butt, raised the point and yanked the knife upward through the muscle tissue and guts. It ripped intestines, spilling blood and gore."[2] A minimum of 20 but sometimes as many as 120 such graphically described killings occurred in each 200- to 250-page paperback. Most series came out four times a year with domestic print runs of 60,000 to 250,000 copies. More than a dozen different comic books with titles like *Punisher*, *Vigilante*, and *Scout* followed suit with clones of the novels.

Along with the novels and comics came a new kind of periodical which replaced the older adventure magazines for men, such as *True* and *Argosy*, that had folded in the 1960s. Robert K. Brown, a former captain in the U.S. Army Special Forces during the Vietnam War, founded *Soldier of Fortune: The Journal of Professional Adventurers* in the spring of 1975, just before the fall of Saigon. *SOF*'s position was explicit from the start: the independent warrior must step in to fill the dangerous void created by the American failure in Vietnam. By the mid-1980s *SOF* was reaching 35,000 subscribers, had newsstand sales of another 150,000, and was being passed around to at least twice as many readers.[3]

---

[2]Gar Wilson, *The Fury Bombs*, vol. 5 of *Phoenix Force* (Toronto: Worldwide Library, 1983), 30.

[3]*SOF* regularly hired the firm of Starch, Inra, Hopper to study their readership. A condensed version of their 1986 report, from which these figures were taken, was made available to the press at the September 1986 *SOF* convention in Las Vegas.

Half a dozen new warrior magazines soon entered the market. Some, like *Eagle*, *New Breed*, and *Gung-Ho*, tried to copy the *SOF* editorial package — a strategy that ultimately failed. But most developed their own particular pitch. *Combat Handguns* focused on pistols for would-be gunfighters. *American Survival Guide* advertised and reviewed everything needed for "the good life" after the end of civilization (except birth control devices — too many Mormon subscribers, the editor said), while *S.W.A.T.* found its way to men who idealized these elite police teams and who were worried about home defense against "multiple intruders."

During the same period, sales of military weapons took off. Colt offered 15 two semiautomatic versions of the M16 used by U.S. soldiers in Vietnam (a full-size rifle and a shorter-barreled carbine with collapsible stock). European armories exported their latest products, accompanied by sophisticated advertising campaigns in *SOF* and the more mainstream gun magazines. Israeli Defense Industries put a longer, 16-inch barrel on the Uzi submachine gun (to make it legal) and sold it as a semiautomatic carbine. And the Communist countries of Eastern Europe, together with the People's Republic of China, jumped into the market with the devil's own favorite hardware, the infamous AK47. The AK sold in the United States was the semiautomatic version of the assault rifle used by the victorious Communists in Vietnam and by all kinds of radical movements and terrorist organizations around the world. It retailed for $300 to $400, half the price of an Uzi or an AR-15; complete with three 30-round magazines, cleaning kit, and bayonet, it was truly a bargain.

To feed these hungry guns, munitions manufacturers packaged new "generic" brands of military ammo at discount prices, often selling them in cases of 500 or 1,000 rounds. New lines of aftermarket accessories offered parts for full-automatic conversions, improved flash-hiders, scopes, folding stocks, and scores of other goodies. In 1989, the U.S. Bureau of Alcohol, Tobacco and Firearms (ATF) estimated that two to three million military-style rifles had been sold in this country since the Vietnam War. The Bureau released these figures in response to the public outcry over a series of mass murders committed by psychotics armed with assault rifles.

But the Bureau's statistics tell only part of the story. In less than two decades, millions of American men had purchased combat rifles, pistols, and shotguns and begun training to fight their own personal wars. Elite combat shooting schools teaching the most modern techniques and often costing $500 to over $1,000 in tuition alone were attended not only by soldiers and police but by increasing numbers of civilians as well. Hundreds of new indoor pistol-shooting ranges opened for business in old warehouses and shopping malls around the country, locations ideal for city dwellers and suburbanites.

A new game of "tag" blurred the line between play and actual violence: men got the opportunity to hunt and shoot other men without killing them or risking death themselves. The National Survival Game was invented in 1981 by two old friends, one a screenwriter for the weight-lifting sagas that gave

Arnold Schwarzenegger his first starring roles, and the other a former member of the Army's Long Range Reconnaissance Patrol (LRRP) in Vietnam.[4] Later called paintball because it utilized guns firing balls of watercolor paint, by 1987 the game was being played by at least fifty thousand people (mostly men) each weekend on both outdoor and indoor battlefields scattered across the nation. Players wore hard-plastic face masks intended to resemble those of ancient tribal warriors and dressed from head to toe in camouflage clothes imported by specialty stores from military outfitters around the world. The object of the game was to capture the opposing team's flag, inflicting the highest possible body count along the way.

One major park out in the Mojave Desert seventy miles southeast of Los Angeles was named Sat Cong Village. *Sat Cong* is a slang Vietnamese phrase meaning "Kill Communists" that had been popularized by the CIA as part of its psychological-warfare program. Sat Cong Village employed an attractive Asian woman to rent the guns, sell the paintballs, and collect the twenty-dollar entrance fee. Players had their choice of playing fields: Vietnam, Cambodia, or Nicaragua. On the Nicaragua field, the owner built a full-size facsimile of the crashed C-47 cargo plane contracted by Lieutenant Colonel Oliver North to supply the Contras. The scene even had three parachutes hanging from trees; the only thing missing was the sole survivor of the crash, Eugene Hasenfus.

The 1980s, then, saw the emergence of a highly energized culture of war and the 20 warrior. For all its varied manifestations, a few common features stood out. The New War culture was not so much military as paramilitary. The new warrior hero was only occasionally portrayed as a member of a conventional military or law enforcement unit; typically, he fought alone or with a small, elite group of fellow warriors. Moreover, by separating the warrior from his traditional state-sanctioned occupations — policeman or soldier — the New War culture presented the warrior roles as the ideal identity for *all* men. Bankers, professors, factory workers, and postal clerks could all transcend their regular stations in life and prepare for heroic battle against the enemies of society.

To many people, this new fascination with warriors and weapons seemed a terribly bad joke. The major newspapers and magazines that arbitrate what is to be taken seriously in American society scoffed at the attempts to resurrect the warrior hero. Movie critics were particularly disdainful of Stallone's Rambo films. *Rambo: First Blood, Part 2* was called "narcissistic jingoism" by *The New Yorker* and "hare-brained" by the *Wall Street Journal*. The *Washington Post* even intoned that "Sly's body looks fine. Now can't you come up with a workout for his soul?"

But in dismissing Rambo so quickly and contemptuously, commentators failed to notice the true significance of the emerging paramilitary culture. They missed the fact that quite a few people were not writing Rambo off as a

[4]Lionel Atwill, *Survival Game: Airgun National Manual* (New London, N.H.: The National Survival Game, Inc., 1987), 22–30.

complete joke; behind the Indian bandanna, necklace, and bulging muscles, a new culture hero affirmed such traditional American values as self-reliance, honesty, courage, and concern for fellow citizens. Rambo was a worker and a former enlisted man, not a smooth-talking professional. That so many seemingly well-to-do, sophisticated liberals hated him for both his politics and his uncouthness only added to his glory. Further, in their emphasis on Stallone's clownishness the commentators failed to see not only how widespread paramilitary culture had become but also its relation to the historical moment in which it arose.

Indeed, paramilitary culture can be understood only when it is placed in relation to the Vietnam War. America's failure to win that war was a truly profound blow. The nation's long, proud tradition of military victories, from the Revolutionary War through the century-long battles against the Indians to World Wars I and II, had finally come to an end. Politically, the defeat in Vietnam meant that the post–World War II era of overwhelming American political and military power in international affairs, the era that in 1945 *Time* magazine publisher Henry Luce had prophesied would be the "American Century," was over after only thirty years. No longer could U.S. diplomacy wield the big stick of military intervention as a ready threat—a significant part of the American public would no longer support such interventions, and the rest of the world knew it.

Moreover, besides eroding U.S. influence internationally, the defeat had subtle but serious effects on the American psyche. America has always celebrated war and the warrior. Our long, unbroken record of military victories has been crucially important both to the national identity and to the personal identity of many Americans—particularly men. The historian Richard Slotkin locates a primary "cultural archetype" of the nation in the story of a heroic warrior whose victories over the enemy symbolically affirm the country's fundamental goodness and power; we win our wars because, morally, we deserve to win. Clearly, the archetypal pattern Slotkin calls "regeneration through violence" was broken with the defeat in Vietnam.[5] The result was a massive disjunction in American culture, a crisis of self-image: If Americans were no longer winners, then who were they?

This disruption of cultural identity was amplified by other social transfor-   25
mations. During the 1960s, the civil rights and ethnic pride movements won many victories in their challenges to racial oppression. Also, during the 1970s and 1980s, the United States experienced massive waves of immigration from Mexico, Central America, Vietnam, Cambodia, Korea, and Taiwan. Whites, no longer secure in their power abroad, also lost their unquestionable dominance at home; for the first time, many began to feel that they too were just another hyphenated ethnic group, the Anglo-Americans.

Extraordinary economic changes also marked the 1970s and 1980s. U.S. manufacturing strength declined substantially; staggering trade deficits with

[5]Richard Slotkin, *Regeneration through Violence: The Mythology of the American Frontier, 1660–1860* (Middletown, Conn.: Wesleyan University Press, 1973).

other countries and the chronic federal budget deficits shifted the United States from creditor to debtor nation. The post–World War II American Dream— which promised a combination of technological progress and social reforms, together with high employment rates, rising wages, widespread home own- ership, and ever increasing consumer options—no longer seemed a likely prospect for the great majority. At the same time, the rise in crime rates, par- ticularly because of drug abuse and its accompanying violence, made people feel more powerless than ever.

While the public world dominated by men seemed to come apart, the pri- vate world of family life also felt the shocks. The feminist movement chal- lenged formerly exclusive male domains, not only in the labor market and in many areas of political and social life but in the home as well. Customary male behavior was no longer acceptable in either private relationships or pub- lic policy. Feminism was widely experienced by men as a profound threat to their identity. Men had to change, but to what? No one knew for sure what a "good man" was anymore.

It is hardly surprising, then, that American men—lacking confidence in the government and the economy, troubled by the changing relations between the sexes, uncertain of their identity or their future—began to *dream*, to fanta- size about the powers and features of another kind of man who could retake and reorder the world. And the hero of all these dreams was the paramilitary warrior. In the New War he fights the battles of Vietnam a thousand times, each time winning decisively. Terrorists and drug dealers are blasted into oblivion. Illegal aliens inside the United States and the hordes of nonwhites in the Third World are returned by force to their proper place. Women are revealed as dan- gerous temptresses who have to be mastered, avoided, or terminated.

Obviously these dreams represented a flight from the present and a rejec- tion and denial of events of the preceding twenty years. But they also indicated a more profound and severe distress. The whole modern world was damned as unacceptable. Unable to find a rational way to face the tasks of rebuilding soci- ety and reinventing themselves, men instead sought refuge in myths from both America's frontier past and ancient times. Indeed, the fundamental narratives that shape paramilitary culture and its New War fantasies are often nothing but reinterpretations or reworkings of archaic warrior myths.

In ancient societies, the most important stories a people told about them- selves concerned how the physical universe came into existence, how their ancestors first came to live in this universe, and how the gods, the universe, and society were related to one another. These cosmogonic, or creation, myths frequently posit a violent conflict between the good forces of order and the evil forces dedicated to the perpetuation of primordial chaos.[6] After the war in which the gods defeat the evil ones, they establish the "sacred order," in which all of the society's most important values are fully embodied. Some 30

[6]Mircea Eliade, *Myth and Reality*, trans. Willard R. Trask (New York: Harper and Row, 1963).

creation myths focus primarily on the sacred order and on the deeds of the gods and goddesses in paradise. Other myths, however, focus on the battles between the heroes and villains that lead up to the founding.[7] In these myths it is war and the warrior that are most sacred. American paramilitary culture borrows from both kinds of stories, but mostly from this second, more violent, type.

In either case, the presence, if not the outright predominance, of archaic male myths at the moment of crisis indicates just how far American men jumped psychically when faced with the declining power of their identities and organizations. The always-precarious balance in modern society between secular institutions and ways of thinking on the one hand and older patterns of belief informed by myth and ritual on the other tilted decisively in the direction of myth. The crisis revealed that at some deep, unconscious level these ancient male creation myths live on in the psyche of many men and that the images and tales from this mythic world of warriors and war still shape men's fantasies about who they are as men, their commitments to each other and to women, and their relationships to society and the state.

READING THE TEXT

1. How, according to Gibson, did the American defeat in Vietnam lead to the construction of a new kind of "warrior" (para. 20) identity for men?

2. Outline how popular culture helped to shape the warrior image, in Gibson's view.

3. What role does Gibson believe the women's movement played in constructing a new male identity?

4. Explain in your own words how today's "warrior dreams" relate to ancient mythologies.

5. Why does Gibson believe that the Rambo character should be taken seriously?

READING THE SIGNS

1. Read or review the following selection by Michael A. Messner, "Power at Play: Sport and Gender Relations." Then compare Messner's argument about the role of sports in the construction of male identity with Gibson's analysis of warrior dreams.

2. Gibson suggests that the warrior fantasies found throughout political and popular culture have dangerous real-world implications. Write a critical essay in which you support, complicate, or challenge this suggestion. As you develop your argument, consider such incidents as the 1999 Columbine High School massacre and the 2005 massacre in Red Lake, Minnesota, both committed by teenage boys.

[7]Richard Stivers, *Evil in Modern Myth and Ritual* (Athens: University of Georgia Press, 1982).

3. Using Gibson's argument as your critical framework, write an analysis of the attractions of professional wrestling as described in Henry Jenkins's " 'Never Trust a Snake': WWF Wrestling as Masculine Melodrama" (p. 524).

4. In class, brainstorm current films, TV shows, and videogames that are targeted to a male audience. Then discuss the extent to which the warrior dreams that Gibson describes still influence popular culture.

MICHAEL A. MESSNER
Power at Play: Sport and Gender Relations

Every little boy should play Little League, right? Sports help to build character, right? Perhaps, but according to Michael A. Messner (b. 1952), the games men play are more than that: They are rituals designed to maintain the ideology and values of a competitive and hierarchical culture. Because masculine identity is rooted in the need to win, athletic competition, according to Messner, causes "men to experience their own bodies as machines . . . and to see other people's bodies as objects of their power and domination." Author of Power at Play: Sports and the Problem of Masculinity *(1992), from which this selection is excerpted, Messner is a professor and chair of the department of sociology at the University of Southern California. He is also coeditor of* Men's Lives *(1995) and* Sport, Men, and the Gender Order: Critical Feminist Perspectives *(1990) and coauthor of* Sex, Violence, and Power in Sports: Rethinking Masculinity *(1994). He is, most recently, the author of* Taking the Field: Women, Men, and Sports *(2002),* Paradoxes of Youth and Sport *(2002), and* Men's Lives *(2004).*

The closer we come to uncovering some form of exemplary masculinity, a masculinity which is solid and sure of itself, the clearer it becomes that masculinity is structured through contradiction: the more it asserts itself, the more it calls itself into question.

— LYNN SEGAL, *Slow Motion*

In 1973, conservative writer George Gilder, later to become a central theorist of the antifeminist family policies of the Reagan administration, was among the first to sound the alarm that the contemporary explosion of female athletic participation might threaten the very fabric of civilization. "Sports," Gilder wrote, "are possibly the single most important male rite in modern society." The woman athlete "reduces the game from a religious male rite to a mere physical exercise, with some treacherous danger of psychic effect."

Athletic performance, for males, embodies "an ideal of beauty and truth," while women's participation represents a "disgusting perversion" of this truth.[1] In 1986, over a decade later, a similar view was expressed by John Carroll in a respected academic journal. Carroll lauded the masculine "virtue and grace" of sport, and defended it against its critics, especially feminists. He concluded that in order to preserve sport's "naturally conserving and creating" tendencies, especially in the realms of "the moral and the religious, . . . women should once again be prohibited from sport: They are the true defenders of the humanist values that emanate from the household, the values of tenderness, nurture and compassion, and this most important role must not be confused by the military and political values inherent in sport. Likewise, sport should not be muzzled by humanist values: it is the living arena for the great virtue of manliness."[2]

The key to Gilder's and Carroll's chest-beating about the importance of maintaining sport as a "male rite" is their neo-Victorian belief that male-female biological differences predispose men to aggressively dominate public life, while females are naturally suited to serve as the nurturant guardians of home and hearth. As Gilder put it, "The tendency to bond with other males in intensely purposeful and dangerous activity is said to come from the collective demands of pursuing large animals. The female body, on the other hand, more closely resembles the body of nonhunting primates. A woman throws, for example, very like a male chimpanzee."[3] This perspective ignores a wealth of historical, anthropological, and biological data that suggest that the equation of males with domination of public life and females with the care of the domestic sphere is a cultural and historical construction.[4] In fact, Gilder's and Carroll's belief that sport, *a socially constructed institution*, is needed to sustain male-female difference contradicts their assumption that these differences are "natural." As R. W. Connell has argued, social practices that exaggerate male-female difference (such as dress, adornment, and sport) "are part of a continuing effort to sustain a social definition of gender, an effort that is necessary precisely *because the biological logic . . . cannot sustain the gender categories.*"[5]

[1] G. Gilder, *Sexual Suicide* (New York: Bantam Books, 1973), pp. 216, 218.

[2] J. Carroll, "Sport: Virtue and Grace," *Theory, Culture and Society* 3 (1986), pp. 91–98. Jennifer Hargreaves delivers a brilliant feminist rebuttal to Carroll's masculinist defense of sport in the same issue of the journal. See J. Hargreaves, "Where's the Virtue? Where's the Grace? A Discussion of the Social Production of Gender through Sport," pp. 109–21.

[3] G. Gilder, p. 221.

[4] For a critical overview of the biological research on male-female difference, see A. Fausto-Sterling, *Myths of Gender: Biological Theories about Men and Women* (New York: Basic Books, 1985). For an overview of the historical basis of male domination, see R. Lee and R. Daly, "Man's Domination and Woman's Oppression: The Question of Origins," in M. Kaufman, ed., *Beyond Patriarchy: Essays by Men on Pleasure, Power, and Change* (Toronto: Oxford University Press, 1987), pp. 30–44.

[5] R. W. Connell, *Gender and Power* (Stanford: Stanford University Press, 1987), p. 81 (emphasis in original text).

Indeed, I must argue against the view that sees sport as a natural realm within which some essence of masculinity unfolds. Rather, sport is a social institution that, in its dominant forms, was created by and for men. It should not be surprising, then, that my research with male athletes reveals an affinity between the institution of sport and men's developing identities. As the young males in my study became committed to athletic careers, the gendered values of the institution of sport made it extremely unlikely that they would construct anything but the kinds of personalities and relationships that were consistent with the dominant values and power relations of the larger gender order. The competitive hierarchy of athletic careers encouraged the development of masculine identities based on very narrow definitions of public success. Homophobia and misogyny were the key bonding agents among male athletes, serving to construct a masculine personality that disparaged anything considered "feminine" in women, in other men, or in oneself. The fact that winning was premised on physical power, strength, discipline, and willingness to take, ignore, or deaden pain inclined men to experience their own bodies as machines, as instruments of power and domination — and to see other peoples' bodies as objects of their power and domination. . . .

The Costs of Athletic Masculinity

As boys, the men in my study were initially attracted to playing sport because it was a primary means to connect with other people — especially fathers, brothers, and male peers. But as these young males became committed to athletic careers, their identities became directly tied to continued public success. Increasingly, it was not just "being there with the guys" but beating the other guys that mattered most. As their need for connection with others became defined more abstractly, through their relationships with "the crowd," their actual relationships with other people tended to become distorted. Other individuals were increasingly likely to be viewed as (male) objects to be defeated or (female) objects to be manipulated and sexually conquered. As a result, the socially learned means through which they constructed their identities (public achievement within competitive hierarchies) did not deliver what was most craved and needed: intimate connection and unity with other people. More often than not, athletic careers have exacerbated existing insecurities and ambivalences in young men's developing identities, thus further diminishing their capacity for intimate relationships with others.

In addition to relational costs, many athletes — especially those in "combat sports" such as football — paid a heavy price in terms of health. While the successful operation of the male body-as-weapon may have led, for a time, to victories on the athletic field, it also led to injuries and other health problems that lasted far beyond the end of the athletic career.

It is extremely unlikely that a public illumination of the relational and health costs paid by male athletes will lead to a widespread rejection of sport by young males. There are three reasons for this. First, the continued affinity between sport and developing masculine identities suggests that many boys will continue to be attracted to athletic careers for the same reasons they have in the past. Second, since the successful athlete often basks in the limelight of public adoration, the relational costs of athletic masculinity are often not apparent until after the athletic career ends, and he suddenly loses his connection to the crowd. Third, though athletes may recognize the present and future health costs of their athletic careers, they are likely to view them as dues willingly paid. In short, there is a neat enough fit between the psychological and emotional tendencies of young males and the institution of sport that these costs — if they are recognized at all — will be considered "necessary evils," the price men pay for the promise of "being on top."[6]

Competing Masculinities

Boys' emerging identities may influence them to be attracted to sport, but they nevertheless tend to experience athletic careers differently, based upon variations in class, race, and sexual orientation. Despite their similarities, boys and young men bring different problems, anxieties, hopes, and dreams to their athletic experiences, and thus tend to draw different meanings from, and make different choices about, their athletic careers.

RACE, CLASS, AND THE CONSTRUCTION OF ATHLETIC MASCULINITY

My interviews reveal that within a social context stratified by class and by race, the choice to pursue — or not to pursue — an athletic career is determined by the individual's rational assessment of the available means to construct a respected masculine identity. White middle-class men were likely to reject athletic careers and shift their masculine strivings to education and nonsport careers. Conversely, men from poor and blue-collar backgrounds, especially blacks, often perceived athletic careers to be their best chance

---

[6]Indeed, "men's liberationists" of the 1970s were overly optimistic in believing that a public illumination of the "costs of masculinity" would induce men to "reject the male role." See, for instance, W. Farrell, *The Liberated Man* (New York: Bantam Books, 1975); J. Nichols, *Men's Liberation: A New Definition of Masculinity* (New York: Penguin Books, 1975). These men's liberationists underestimated the extent to which the costs of masculinity are linked to the promise of power and privilege. One commentator went so far as to argue that the privileges of masculinity were a "myth" perpetrated by women to keep men in destructive success-object roles. See H. Goldberg, *The Hazards of Being Male: Surviving the Myth of Masculine Privilege* (New York: Signet, 1976). For more recent discussions of the need to analyze both the "costs" and the "privileges" of dominant conceptions of masculinity, see M. E. Kann, "The Costs of Being on Top," *Journal of the National Association for Women Deans, Administrators, and Counselors* 49 (1986): 29–37; and M. A. Messner, "Men Studying Masculinity: Some Epistemological Questions in Sport Sociology," *Sociology of Sport Journal* 7 (1990): 136–53.

for success in the public sphere. For nearly all of the men from lower-class backgrounds, the status and respect that they received through sport was temporary — it did not translate into upward mobility.

One might conclude from this that the United States should adopt a public policy of encouraging young lower-class black males to "just say no" to sport. This strategy would be doomed to failure, because poor young black men's decisions to pursue athletic careers can be viewed as rational, given the constraints that they continue to face. Despite the increased number of black role models in nonsport professions, employment opportunities for young black males actually deteriorated in the 1980s, and nonathletic opportunities in higher education also declined. By 1985, blacks constituted 14 percent of the college-aged (18–24 years) U.S. population, but as a proportion of students in four-year colleges and universities, they had dropped to 8 percent. By contrast, black men constituted 49 percent of male college basketball players, and 61 percent of male basketball players in institutions that grant athletic scholarships.[7] For young black men, then, organized sport appears to be more likely to get them to college than their own efforts in nonathletic activities.

In addition to viewing athletic careers as an arena for career success, there is considerable evidence that black male athletes have used sport as a cultural space within which to forge a uniquely expressive style of masculinity, a "cool pose." As Richard Majors puts it,   10

> Due to structural limitations, a black man may be impotent in the intellectual, political, and corporate world, but he can nevertheless display a potent personal style from the pulpit, in entertainment, and in athletic competition, with a verve that borders on the spectacular. Through the virtuosity of a performance, he tips the socially imbalanced scales in his favor and sends the subliminal message: "See me, touch me, hear me, but, white man, you can't copy me!"[8]

In particular, black men have put their "stamp" on the game of basketball. There is considerable pride in U.S. black communities in the fact that black men have come to dominate the higher levels of basketball — and in the expressive style with which they have come to do so. The often aggressive "cool pose" of black male athletes can thus be interpreted as a form of masculinity that symbolically challenges the class constraints and the institutionalized racism that so many young black males face.

---

[7] W. J. Wilson and K. M. Neckerman, "Poverty and Family Structure: The Widening Gap between Evidence and Public Policy Issues," in S. H. Danzinger and D. H. Weinberg, eds., *Fighting Poverty* (Cambridge: Harvard University Press, 1986), pp. 232–59; F. J. Berghorn et al., "Racial Participation in Men's and Women's Intercollegiate Basketball: Continuity and Change, 1958–1985." *Sociology of Sport Journal* 5 (1988), 107–24.

[8] R. Majors, "'Cool Pose': Black Masculinity and Sports," in M. A. Messner and D. F. Sabo, *Sport, Men, and the Gender Order: Critical Feminist Perspectives* (Champaign, Ill.: Human Kinetics Publishers, 1990), p. 111.

SEXUAL ORIENTATION AND THE CONSTRUCTION OF ATHLETIC MASCULINITY

Until very recently, it was widely believed that gay men did not play organized sports. Nongay people tended to stereotype gay men as "too effeminate" to be athletic. This belief revealed a confusion between sexual orientation and gender. We now know that there is no neat fit between how "masculine" or "feminine" a man is, and whether or not he is sexually attracted to women, to men, to both, or to neither.[9] Interestingly, some gay writers also believed that gay men were not active in sport. For instance, Dennis Altman wrote in 1982 that most gay men were not interested in sport, since they tended to reject the sexual repression, homophobia, and misogyny that are built into the sportsworld.[10]

The belief that gay men are not interested or involved in sport has proven to be wrong. People who made this assumption were observing the overtly masculine and heterosexual culture of sport and then falsely concluding that all of the people within that culture must be heterosexual. My interview with Mike T. and biographies of gay athletes such as David Kopay suggest that young gay males are often attracted to sport because they are just as concerned as heterosexual boys and young men with constructing masculine identities.[11] Indeed, a young closeted gay male like Mike T. may view the projection of an unambiguous masculinity as even more critical than his nongay counterparts do. As Mike told me, "There are a *lot* of gay men in sports," but they are almost all closeted and thus not visible to public view.

As Mike's story illustrates, gay male athletes often share similar motivations and experiences with nongay athletes. This suggests that as long as gay athletes stay closeted, they are contributing to the construction of culturally dominant conceptions of masculinity. However, Brian Pronger's recent research suggests that many gay male athletes experience organized sport in unique ways. In particular, Pronger's interviews with gay male athletes indicate that they have a "paradoxical" relationship to the male athletic culture. Though the institution itself is built largely on the denial (or sublimation) of any erotic bond between men, Pronger argues, many (but not all) gay athletes experience life in the locker room, as well as the excitement of athletic competition, as highly erotic. Since their secret desires (and, at times, secret actions) run counter to the heterosexist culture of the male locker room, closeted gay male athletes develop ironic sensibilities about themselves, their bodies, and the sporting activity itself.[12] Gay men are sexually oppressed through sport, Pronger argues, but the ironic ways they often redefine the athletic context

---

[9]See S. Kleinberg, "The New Masculinity of Gay Men, and Beyond," in Kaufman, *Beyond Patriarchy,* pp. 120–38.

[10]D. Altman, *The Homosexualization of America* (Boston: Beacon Press, 1982).

[11]See D. Kopay and P. D. Young, *The Dave Kopay Story* (New York: Arbor House, 1977).

[12]B. Pronger, "Gay Jocks: A Phenomenology of Gay Men in Athletics," in Messner and Sabo, *Sport, Men, and the Gender Order,* pp. 141–52; and *The Arena of Masculinity: Sports, Homosexuality, and the Meaning of Sex* (New York: St. Martin's Press, 1990).

can be interpreted as a form of resistance with the potential to undermine and transform the heterosexist culture of sport.

THE LIMITS OF MASCULINE RESISTANCES

Men's experience of athletic careers — and the meanings they assign to these   15
experiences — are contextualized by class, race, and sexual orientation. My research, and that of other social scientists, suggests that black male athletes construct and draw on an expressive and "cool" masculinity in order to resist racial oppression. Gay male athletes sometimes construct and draw on an "ironic" masculinity in order to resist sexual oppression. In other words, poor, black, and gay men have often found sport to be an arena in which they can build a masculinity that is, in some ways, resistant to the oppressions they face within hierarchies of intermale dominance.

But how real is the challenge these resistant masculinities pose to the role that sport has historically played in perpetuating existing differences and inequalities? A feminist perspective reveals the limited extent to which we can interpret black and gay athletic masculinities as liberating. Through a feminist lens, we can see that in adopting as their expressive vehicle many of the dominant aspects of athletic masculinity (narrow definitions of public success; aggressive, sometimes violent competition; glorification of the athletic male body-as-machine; verbal misogyny and homophobia), poor, black, and gay male athletes contribute to the continued subordination of women, as well as to the circumscription of their own relationships and development.

Tim Carrigan, Bob Connell, and John Lee assert that rather than undermining social inequality, men's struggles within class, racial, and sexual hierarchies of intermale dominance serve to reinforce men's global subordination of women. Although strains caused by differences and inequalities among men represent potential avenues for social change, ultimately, "the fissuring of the categories 'men' and 'women' is one of the central facts about a patriarchal power and the way it works. In the case of men, the crucial division is between hegemonic masculinity and various subordinated masculinities."[13] Hegemonic masculinity is thus defined in relation to various subordinated masculinities as well as in relation to femininities. This is a key insight for the contemporary meaning of sport. Utilizing the concept of "multiple masculinities," we can begin to understand how race, class, age, and sexual hierarchies among men help to construct and legitimize men's overall power and privilege over women. In addition, the false promise of sharing in the fruits of hegemonic masculinity often ties black, working-class, or gay men into their marginalized and subordinate status. For instance, my research suggests that while black men's development of "cool pose" within sport can be interpreted as creative resistance against one form of social domination (racism), it also

[13]T. Carrigan, B. Connell, and J. Lee, "Hard and Heavy: Toward a New Sociology of Masculinity," *Theory and Society* 14 (1985): 551–603.

demonstrates the limits of an agency that adopts other forms of social domination (athletic masculinity) as its vehicle.

My research also suggests how homophobia within athletic masculine cultures tends to lock men — whether gay or not — into narrowly defined heterosexual identities and relationships. Within the athletic context, homophobia is closely linked with misogyny in ways that ultimately serve to bond men together as superior to women. Given the extremely oppressive levels of homophobia within organized sport, it is understandable why the vast majority of gay male athletes would decide to remain closeted. But the public construction of a heterosexual/masculine status requires that a closeted gay athlete actively participate in (or at the very least, tolerate) the ongoing group expressions of homophobia and misogyny — what Mike T. called "locker room garbage." Thus, though he may feel a sense of irony, and may even confidentially express that sense of irony to gay male friends or to researchers, the public face that the closeted gay male athlete presents to the world is really no different from that of his nongay teammates. As long as he is successful in this public presentation-of-self as heterosexual/masculine, he will continue to contribute to (and benefit from) men's power over women.

SPORT IN GAY COMMUNITIES

The fissuring of the category "men," then, as it is played out within the dominant institution of sport, does little to threaten — indeed, may be a central mechanism in — the reconstruction of existing class, racial, sexual, and gender inequalities.[14] Nevertheless, since the outset of the gay liberation movement in the early 1970s, organized sport has become an integral part of developing gay and lesbian communities. The ways that "gay" sports have been defined and organized are sometimes different — even radically different — than the dominant institution of sport in society.

The most public sign of the growing interest in athletics in gay communities was the rapid growth and popularity of bodybuilding among many young, urban gay men in the 1970s and early 1980s. The meanings of gay male bodybuilding are multiple and contradictory.[15] On the one hand, gay male

[14]One potentially important, but largely unexplored, fissure among men is that between athletes and nonathletes. There are tens of millions of boys who do *not* pursue athletic careers. Many boys dislike sport. Others may yearn to be athletes, but may not have the body size, strength, physical capabilities, coordination, emotional predisposition, or health that is necessary to successfully compete in sports. What happens to these boys and young men? What kinds of adult masculine identities and relationships do they eventually develop? Does the fact of not having been an athlete play any significant role in their masculine identities, goals, self-images, and relationships? The answers to these questions, of course, lie outside the purview of my study. But they are key to understanding the contemporary role that sport plays in constructions of gender.

[15]For interesting discussions of bodybuilding, gender, and sexuality, see B. Glassner, *Bodies: Why We Look the Way We Do (and How We Feel about It)* (New York: G. P. Putnam's Sons, 1988); A. M. Klein, "Little Big Man: Hustling, Gender Narcissism, and Homophobia in Bodybuilding," in Messner and Sabo, *Sport, Men, and the Gender Order,* pp. 127–40.

bodybuilding overtly eroticizes the muscular male body, thus potentially disrupting the tendency of sport to eroticize male bodies under the guise of aggression and competition. On the other hand, the building of muscular bodies is often motivated by a conscious need by gay men to prove to the world that they are "real men." Gay bodybuilding thus undermines cultural stereotypes of homosexual men as "nelly," effeminate, and womanlike. But it also tends to adopt and promote a very conventional equation of masculinity with physical strength and muscularity.[16] In effect, then, as gay bodybuilders attempt to sever the cultural link between masculinity and heterosexuality, they uncritically affirm a conventional dichotomization of masculinity/male vs. femininity/female.

By contrast, some gay athletes have initiated alternative athletic institutions that aim to challenge conventional views of sexuality and gender. Originally Mike T. had gone into sport to prove that he was "male," and cover up the fact that he was gay. When his career as an Olympic athlete finally ended, he came out publicly, and soon was a very active member of the San Francisco Bay Area gay community. He rekindled his interest in the arts and dance. He also remained very active in athletics, and he increasingly imagined how wonderful it would be to blend the beauty and exhilaration of sport, as he had experienced it, with the emergent, liberating values of the feminist, gay, and lesbian communities of which he was a part. In 1982, his dream became a reality, as 1,300 athletes from twelve different nations gathered in San Francisco to participate in the first ever Gay Games.[17]

Though many of the events in the Gay Games are "conventional" sports (track and field, swimming, etc.), and a number of "serious athletes" compete

[16]Alan Klein's research revealed that nongay male bodybuilders are also commonly motivated by a need to make a public statement with their muscular bodies that they are indeed "masculine." To the nongay bodybuilder, muscles are the ultimate sign of heterosexual masculinity. But, ironically, as one nongay male bodybuilder put it, "We're everything the U.S. is supposed to stand for: strength, determination, everything to be admired. But it's not the girls that like us, it's the fags!" Interestingly, Klein found that many male bodybuilders who defined themselves as "straight" (including the one quoted above) made a living by prostituting themselves to gay men. See Klein, "Little Big Man," p. 135.

For a thought-provoking feminist analysis of the contradictory relationship between gay male sexuality and masculinity, see T. Edwards, "Beyond Sex and Gender: Masculinity, Homosexuality, and Social Theory," in J. Hearn and D. Morgan, eds., *Men, Masculinities, and Social Theory* (London: Unwin Hyman, 1990), pp. 110–23.

[17]The Gay Games were originally called the "Gay Olympics," but the U.S. Olympic Committee went to court to see that the word "Olympics" was not used to denote this event. Despite the existence of "Police Olympics," "Special Olympics," "Senior Olympics," "Xerox Olympics," "Armenian Olympics," even "Crab Cooking Olympics," the U.S.O.C. chose to enforce their control legally over the term "Olympics" when it came to the "Gay Olympics." For further discussion of the politics of the Gay Games, see M. A. Messner, "Gay Athletes and the Gay Games: An Interview with Tom Waddell," *M: Gentle Men for Gender Justice* 13 (1984): 13–14.

in the events, overall the Games reflect a value system and a vision based on feminist and gay liberationist ideals of equality and universal participation. As Mike T. said,

> You don't win by beating someone else. We defined winning as doing your very best. That way, everyone is a winner. And we have age-group competition, so all ages are involved. We have parity: If there's a men's sport, there's a women's sport to complement it. And we go out and recruit in Third World and minority areas. All of these people are gonna get together for a week, they're gonna march in together, they're gonna hold hands, and they'll say, "Jesus Christ! This is wonderful!" There's this *discovery*: "I had no idea women were such fun!" and, "God! Blacks are okay — I didn't do anything to offend him, and we became *friends*!" and, "God, that guy over there is in his sixties, and I had no *idea* they were so sexually *active*!" — [laughs].

This emphasis on bridging differences, overcoming prejudices, and building relationships definitely enhanced the athletic experience for one participant I interviewed. This man said that he loved to swim, and even loved to compete, because it "pushed" him to swim "a whole lot better." Yet in past competitions, he had always come in last place. As he put it, "The Gay Games were just wonderful in many respects. One of them was that people who came in second, or third, and *last* got standing ovations from the crowd — the crowd genuinely recognized the thrill of giving a damn good shot, regardless of where you came in, and gave support to that. Among the competitors, there was a whole lot of joking and supportiveness."

In 1986, 3,482 athletes participated in Gay Games II in San Francisco. In 1990, at Gay Games III in Vancouver, 7,200 athletes continued the vision of building, partly through sport, an "exemplary community" that eliminates sexism, homophobia, and racism. Mike T. described what the Gay Games mean to him:

> To me, it's one of those steps in a thousand-mile journey to try and raise consciousness and enlighten people — *not* just people outside the gay community, but within the gay community as well, [because] we're just as racist, ageist, nationalistic, and chauvinistic as anybody else. Maybe it's simplistic to some people, you know, but why does it have to be complicated? Put people in a position where they can experience this process of discovery, and here it is! I just hope that this is something that'll take hold and a lot of people will get the idea.

The Gay Games represent a radical break from past and current conceptions of the role of sport in society. But they do not represent a major challenge to sport as an institution. Alternative athletic venues like the Gay Games, since they exist outside of the dominant sports institution, do not directly confront or change the dominant structure. On the other hand, these experiments are valuable in terms of demonstrating the fact that alternative value systems and structures are possible.[18]

READING THE TEXT

1. Why, in Messner's view, did conservatives such as George Gilder and John Carroll want to prohibit women from competing in athletic competitions?
2. What does Messner mean when he writes that "sport is a social institution that . . . was created by and for men" (para. 3)?
3. What roles do class, race, and sexual orientation play in the construction of athletic masculinity, according to Messner?
4. In what ways, according to Messner, do the Gay Games differ from the Olympic Games?

READING THE SIGNS

1. In your journal, explore what athletic participation, whether in organized sports such as Little League or in informal activities such as jogging or hiking, has meant to you. Do you believe such participation has shaped your attitudes about gender roles? If you haven't participated much in sports, what is your attitude toward athletic competition?
2. Write an argumentative essay challenging or supporting George Gilder's position that the female athlete "reduces the game from a religious male rite to a mere physical exercise, with some treacherous danger of psychic effect" (para. 1).
3. In class, outline the racial and gender coding of professional sports. Which ethnicities dominate which sports? In which sports have women received social acceptance? Then discuss the reasons for the ethnic and gender patterns you have found.
4. Study a magazine such as *Sports Illustrated,* and write an essay in which you explain the extent to which the magazine perpetuates the traditional attitudes about gender roles that Messner claims sports encourage.
5. In class, form mixed-gender teams and debate Messner's contention that sports encourage homophobia and misogyny. To develop your ideas, consult Mariah Burton Nelson, "I Won. I'm Sorry." (p. 439), and the following essay by Henry Jenkins, " 'Never Trust a Snake': WWF Wrestling as Masculine Melodrama."

[18]During the 1982 Gay Games in San Francisco, the major local newspapers tended to cover the Games mostly in the "lifestyle" sections of the paper, not in the sports pages. Alternative sports demonstrate the difficulties of attempting to change sport in the absence of larger institutional transformations. For instance, the European sport of korfball was developed explicitly as a sex-egalitarian sport. The rules of korfball aim to neutralize male-female biological differences that may translate into different levels of ability. But recent research shows that old patterns show up, even among the relatively "enlightened" korfball players. Korfball league officials are more likely to be male than female. More important, the more "key" roles within the game appear to be dominated by men, while women are partially marginalized. See D. Summerfield and A. White, "Korfball: A Model of Egalitarianism?" *Sociology of Sport Journal* 6 (1989): 144–51.

HENRY JENKINS

"Never Trust a Snake": WWF Wrestling as Masculine Melodrama

When Big Boss Man goes up against Repo Man, he is not only filling a slot in the World Wrestling Federation lineup: He's providing cathartic relief for every working-class Joe who's ever had his truck repossessed, Henry Jenkins (b. 1958) suggests in this social analysis of the WWF (now known as the WWE, or World Wrestling Entertainment). Falling further and further behind in a postindustrial economy, working-class men turn to professional wrestling for fantasies of empowerment. And the WWF gladly complies, offering elaborately staged "morality plays" that can make a man feel like, well, a man *again in a world in which physical might always makes right. Think of it as a muscle-bound soap opera. The director of the comparative media studies program at MIT, Jenkins is the editor of* The Children's Culture Reader *(1998) and the coeditor of* Classical Hollywood Comedy *(with Kristine B. Karnick, 1995),* Science Fiction Audiences *(with John Tulloch, 1995),* From Barbie to Mortal Kombat *(with Justine Cassell, 1998),* Hop on Pop: The Politics and Pleasures of Popular Culture *(with Tara McPherson and Jane Shattuc, 2002),* Rethinking Media Change *(with David Thorburn, 2003), and* Democracy and New Media *(with David Thorburn, 2003).*

See, your problem is that you're looking at this as a *wrestling* battle — two guys getting into the ring together to see who's the better athlete. But it goes so much deeper than that. Yes, wrestling's involved. Yes, we're going to pound each other's flesh, slam each other's bodies and hurt each other really bad. But there's more at stake than just wrestling, my man. There's a morality play. Randy Savage thinks he represents the light of righteousness. But, you know, it takes an awful lot of light to illuminate a dark kingdom.

— JAKE "THE SNAKE" ROBERTS[1]

There are people who think that wrestling is an ignoble sport. Wrestling is not a sport, it is a spectacle, and it is no more ignoble to attend a wrestled performance of Suffering than a performance of the sorrows of Arnolphe or Andromaque.

— ROLAND BARTHES[2]

Like World Wrestling Federation superstar Jake "the Snake" Roberts, Roland Barthes saw wrestling as a "morality play," a curious hybrid of sports and

---

[1]"WWF Interview: A Talk with Jake 'the Snake' Roberts," *WWF Magazine,* February 1992, p. 17.

[2]Roland Barthes, "The World of Wrestling," in Susan Sontag, ed., *A Barthes Reader* (New York: Hill and Wang, 1982), p. 23.

theater. For Barthes, wrestling was at once a "spectacle of excess," evoking the pleasure of grandiloquent gestures and violent contact, and a lower form of tragedy, where issues of morality, ethics, and politics were staged. Wrestling enthusiasts have no interest in seeing a fair fight but rather hope for a satisfying restaging of the ageless struggle between the "perfect bastard" and the suffering hero.[3] What wrestling offers its spectators, Barthes tells us, is a story of treachery and revenge, "the intolerable spectacle of powerlessness" and the exhilaration of the hero's victorious return from near-collapse. Wrestling, like conventional melodrama, externalizes emotion, mapping it onto the combatants' bodies and transforming their physical competition into a search for a moral order. Restraint or subtlety has little place in such a world. Everything that matters must be displayed, publicly, unambiguously, and mercilessly.

Barthes's account focuses entirely upon the one-on-one match as an isolated event within which each gesture must be instantly legible apart from any larger context of expectations and associations: "One must always understand everything on the spot."[4] Barthes could not have predicted how this focus upon the discrete event or the isolated gesture would be transformed through the narrative mechanisms of television. On television, where wrestling comes with a cast of continuing characters, no single match is self-enclosed; rather, personal conflicts unfold across a number of fights, interviews, and enacted encounters. Television wrestling offers its viewers complexly plotted, ongoing narratives of professional ambition, personal suffering, friendship and alliance, betrayal and reversal of fortune. Matches still offer their share of acrobatic spectacle, snake handling, fire eating, and colorful costumes. They are, as such, immediately accessible to the casual viewer, yet they reward the informed spectator for whom each body slam and double-arm suplex bears specific narrative consequences. A demand for closure is satisfied at the level of individual events, but those matches are always contained within a larger narrative trajectory which is itself fluid and open.

The WWF broadcast provides us with multiple sources of identification, multiple protagonists locked in their own moral struggles against the forces of evil. The proliferation of champion titles — the WWF World Champion belt, the Million Dollar belt, the Tag Team champion belt, the Intercontinental champion belt — allows for multiple lines of narrative development, each centering around its own cluster of affiliations and antagonisms. The resolution of one title competition at a major event does little to stabilize the program universe, since there are always more belts to be won and lost, and in any case, each match can always be followed by a rematch which reopens old issues. Outcomes may be inconclusive because of count-outs or disqualifications, requiring future rematches. Accidents may result in surprising shifts in

[3]Ibid., p. 25.
[4]Ibid., p. 29.

moral and paradigmatic alignment. Good guys betray their comrades and form uneasy alliances with the forces of evil; rule-breakers undergo redemption after suffering crushing defeats.

The economic rationale for this constant "buildup" and deferral of narrative interests is obvious. The World Wrestling Federation (WWF) knows how to use its five weekly television series and its glossy monthly magazine to ensure subscription to its four annual pay-per-view events and occasional pay-per-view specials.[5] Enigmas are raised during the free broadcasts which will be resolved only for a paying audience. Much of the weekly broadcast consists of interviews with the wrestlers about their forthcoming bouts, staged scenes providing background on their antagonisms, and in-the-ring encounters between WWF stars and sparring partners which provide a backdrop for speculations about forthcoming plot developments. Read cynically, the broadcast consists purely of commercial exploitation. Yet this promotion also has important aesthetic consequences, heightening the melodramatic dimensions of the staged fights and transforming televised wrestling into a form of serial fiction for men. . . .

Playing with Our Feelings

Norbert Elias and Eric Dunning's pathbreaking study *The Quest for Excitement:*   5
Sport and Leisure in the Civilizing Process invites us to reconsider the affective dimensions of athletic competition. According to their account, modern civilization demands restraint on instinctive and affective experience, a process of repression and sublimation which they call the "civilizing process." Elias has spent much of his intellectual life tracing the gradual process by which Western civilization has intensified its demands for bodily and emotional control, rejecting the emotional volatility and bodily abandon that characterized Europe during the Middle Ages:

> Social survival and success in these [contemporary] societies depend . . . on a reliable armour, not too strong and not too weak, of individual self-restraint. In such societies, there is only a comparatively limited scope for the show of strong feelings, of strong antipathies towards and dislike of other people, let alone of hot anger, wild hatred or the urge to hit someone over the head.[6]

[5]For useful background on the historical development of television wrestling, as well as for an alternative reading of its narrative structures, see Michael R. Ball, *Professional Wrestling as Ritual Drama in American Popular Culture* (Lewiston: Edwin Mellen Press, 1990). For a performance-centered account of WWF Wrestling, see Sharon Mazer, "The Doggie Doggie World of Professional Wrestling," *The Drama Review*, Winter 1990, pp. 96–122.

[6]Norbert Elias and Eric Dunning, *The Quest for Excitement: Sport and Leisure in the Civilizing Process* (New York: Basil Blackwell, 1986), p. 41.

Such feelings do not disappear, but they are contained by social expectations:

> To see grown-up men and women shaken by tears and abandon themselves to their bitter sorrow in public . . . or beat each other savagely under the impact of their violent excitement [experiences more common during the Middle Ages] has ceased to be regarded as normal. It is usually a matter of embarrassment for the onlooker and often a matter of shame or regret for those who have allowed themselves to be carried away by their excitement.[7]

What is at stake here is not the intensity of feeling but our discomfort about its spectacular display. Emotion may be strongly felt, but it must be rendered invisible, private, personal; emotion must not be allowed to have a decisive impact upon social interactions. Emotional openness is read as a sign of vulnerability, while emotional restraint is the marker of social integration. Leaders are to master emotions rather than to be mastered by them. Yet, as Elias writes, "We do not stop feeling. We only prevent or delay our acting in accordance with it."[8] Elias traces the process by which this emotional control has moved from being outwardly imposed by rules of conduct to an internalized and largely unconscious aspect of our personalities. The totality of this restraint exacts its own social costs, creating psychic tensions which somehow must be redirected and released within socially approved limitations.

Sports, he argues, constitute one of many institutions which society creates for the production and expression of affective excitement.[9] Sports must somehow reconcile two contradictory functions — "the pleasurable de-controlling of human feelings, the full evocation of an enjoyable excitement on the one hand and on the other the maintenance of a set of checks to keep the pleasantly de-controlled emotions under control."[10] These two functions are never fully resolved, resulting in occasional hooliganism as excitement outstrips social control. Yet the conventionality of sports and the removal of the real-world consequences of physical combat (in short, sport's status as adult play) facilitate a controlled and sanctioned release from ordinary affective restraints. The ability to resolve conflicts through a prespecified moment of arbitrary closure delimits the spectator's emotional experience. Perhaps most important, sports offer a shared emotional experience, one which reasserts the desirability of belonging to a community.

Elias and Dunning are sensitive to the class implications of this argument: the "civilizing process" began at the center of "court society" with the aristocracy and spread outward to merchants wishing access to the realms of social and economic power and to the servants who must become unintrusive

[7]Ibid., pp. 64–65.
[8]Ibid., p. 111.
[9]Ibid., p. 49.
[10]Ibid.

participants in their masters' lives. Elias and Dunning argue that these class distinctions still surface in the very different forms of emotional display tolerated at the legitimate theater (which provides an emotional outlet for bourgeois spectators) and the sports arena (which provides a space for working-class excitement): the theater audience is to "be moved without moving," to restrain emotional display until the conclusion, when it may be indicated through their applause; while for the sports audience, "motion and emotion are intimately linked," and emotional display is immediate and uncensored.[11] These same distinctions separate upper-class sports (tennis, polo, golf) which allow minimal emotional expression from lower-class sports (boxing, wrestling, soccer) which demand more overt affective display. Of course, such spectacles also allow the possibility for upper- or middle-class patrons to "slum it," to adopt working-class attitudes and sensibilities while engaging with the earthy spectacle of the wrestling match. They can play at being working-class (with working-class norms experienced as a remasculinization of yuppie minds and bodies), can imagine themselves as down to earth, with the people, safe in the knowledge that they can go back to the office the next morning without too much embarrassment at what is a ritualized release of repressed emotions.

Oddly absent from their account is any acknowledgment of the gender-specificity of the rules governing emotional display. Social conventions have traditionally restricted the public expression of sorrow or affection by men and of anger or laughter by women. Men stereotypically learn to translate their softer feelings into physical aggressiveness, while women convert their rage into the shedding of tears. Such a culture provides gender-specific spaces for emotional release which are consistent with dominant constructions of masculinity and femininity — melodrama (and its various manifestations in soap opera or romance) for women, sports for men. Elias and Dunning's emphasis upon the affective dimensions of sports allows us to more accurately (albeit schematically) map the similarities and differences between sports and melodrama. Melodrama links female affect to domesticity, sentimentality, and vulnerability, while sports links male affect to physical prowess, competition, and mastery. Melodrama explores the concerns of the private sphere, sports those of the public. Melodrama announces its fictional status, while sports claims for itself the status of reality. Melodrama allows for the shedding of tears, while sports solicits shouts, cheers, and boos. Crying, a characteristically feminine form of emotional display, embodies internalized emotion; tears are quiet and passive. Shouting, the preferred outlet for male affect, embodies externalized emotion; it is aggressive and noisy. Women cry from a position of emotional (and often social) vulnerability; men shout from a position of physical and social strength (however illusory).

WWF wrestling, as a form which bridges the gap between sport and melodrama, allows for the spectacle of male physical prowess (a display which is

[11] Ibid., p. 50.

greeted by shouts and boos) but also for the exploration of the emotional and moral life of its combatants. WWF wrestling focuses on both the public and the private, links nonfictional forms with fictional content, and embeds the competitive dimensions of sports within a larger narrative framework which emphasizes the personal consequences of that competition. The "sports entertainment" of WWF wrestling adopts the narrative and thematic structures implicit within traditional sports and heightens them to ensure the maximum emotional impact. At the same time, WWF wrestling adopts the personal, social, and moral conflicts that characterized nineteenth-century theatrical melodrama and enacts them in terms of physical combat between male athletes. In doing so, it foregrounds aspects of masculine mythology which have a particular significance for its predominantly working-class male audience — the experience of vulnerability, the possibilities of male trust and intimacy, and the populist myth of the national community. . . .

Might Makes Right

Within traditional sports, competition is impersonal, the product of prescribed 10
rules which assign competitors on the basis of their standings or on some pre-specified form of rotation. Rivalries do, of course, arise within this system and are the stuff of the daily sports page, but many games do not carry this added affective significance. Within the WWF, however, all competition depends upon intense rivalry. Each fight requires the creation of a social and moral opposition and often stems from a personal grievance. Irwin R. Schyster (IRS) falsely accuses the Big Boss Man's mother of tax evasion and threatens to throw her in jail. Sid Justice betrays Hulk Hogan's friendship, turning his back on his tag team partner in the middle of a major match and allowing him to be beaten to a pulp by his opponents, Ric Flair and the Undertaker. Fisticuffs break out between Bret Hart and his brother, "Rocket," during a special "Family Feud" match which awakens long-simmering sibling rivalries. Such offenses require retribution within a world which sees trial by combat as the preferred means of resolving all disputes. Someone has to "pay" for these outrages, and the exacting of payment will occur in the squared ring.

The core myth of WWF wrestling is a fascistic one: ultimately, might makes right; moral authority is linked directly to the possession of physical strength, while evil operates through stealth or craftiness (mental rather than physical sources of power). The appeal of such a myth to a working-class audience should be obvious. In the realm of their everyday experience, strength often gets subordinated into alienated labor. Powerful bodies become the means of their economic exploitation rather than a resource for bettering their lot. In WWF wrestling, physical strength reemerges as a tool for personal empowerment, a means of striking back against personal and moral injustices. Valerie Walkerdine argues that the *Rocky* films, which display a similar appeal, offer "fantasies of omnipotence, heroism and salvation . . . a counterpoint to the experience of oppression and powerlessness."[12] Images of fighting, Walkerdine argues, embody "a class-specific and gendered use of the body," which ennobles the physical skills possessed by the working-class spectator: "Physical violence is presented as the only way open to those whose lot is manual and not intellectual labor. . . . The fantasy of the fighter is the fantasy of a working-class male omnipotence over the forces of humiliating oppression which mutilate and break the body in manual labor."[13]

A central concern within wrestling, then, is how physical strength can ensure triumph over one's abusers, how one can rise from defeat and regain dignity through hand-to-hand combat. Bad guys cheat to win. They manipulate the system and step outside the rules. They use deception, misdirection, subterfuge, and trickery. Rarely do they win fairly. They smuggle weapons into the ring to attack their opponents while their managers distract the referees. They unwrap the turnbuckle pads and slam their foes' heads into metal posts. They adopt choke holds to suffocate them or zap them with cattle prods. Million Dollar Man purposefully focuses his force upon Roddy Piper's wounded knee, doing everything he can to injure him permanently. Such atrocities require rematches to ensure justice; the underdog heroes return next month and, through sheer determination and willpower, battle their antagonists into submission.

Such plots allow for the serialization of the WWF narrative, forestalling its resolution, intensifying its emotional impact. Yet at the same time, the individual match must be made narratively satisfying on its own terms, and so, in practice, such injustices do not stand. Even though the match is over and its official outcome determined, the hero shoves the referee aside and, with renewed energy, bests his opponent in a fair (if nonbonding) fight. Whatever the outcome, most fights end with the protagonist standing proudly in the center of the ring, while his badly beaten antagonist retreats shamefully to his dressing room. Justice triumphs both in the long run and in the short run. For the casual viewer, it is the immediate presentation of triumphant innocence that matters, that satisfactorily resolves the drama. Yet for the WWF fan, what matters is the ultimate pursuit of justice as it unfolds through the complexly intertwined stories of the many different wrestlers.

Body Doubles

Melodramatic wrestling allows working-class men to confront their own feelings of vulnerability, their own frustrations at a world which promises them patriarchal authority but which is experienced through relations of economic

---

[12]Valerie Walkerdine, "Video Replay: Families, Films and Fantasy," in Victor Burgin, James Donald, and Cora Kaplan, eds., *Formations of Fantasy* (London: Methuen, 1986), pp. 172–74.
[13]Ibid., p. 173.

subordination. Gender identities are most rigidly policed in working-class male culture, since unable to act *as* men, they are forced to act *like* men, with a failure to assume the proper role the source of added humiliation. WWF wrestling offers a utopian alternative to this situation, allowing a movement from victimization toward mastery. Such a scenario requires both the creation and the constant rearticulation of moral distinctions. Morality is defined, first and foremost, through personal antagonisms. As Christine Gledhill has written of traditional melodrama, "Innocence and villainy construct each other: while the villain is necessary to the production and revelation of innocence, innocence defines the boundaries of the forbidden which the villain breaks."[14] In the most aesthetically pleasing and emotionally gripping matches, these personal antagonisms reflect much deeper mythological oppositions — the struggles between rich and poor, white and black, urban and rural, America and the world. Each character stands for something, draws symbolic meaning by borrowing stereotypes already in broader circulation. An important role played by color commentary is to inscribe and reinscribe the basic mythic oppositions at play within a given match. Here, the moral dualism of masculine melodrama finds its voice through the exchanges between two announcers, one (Mean Jean Okerlund) articulating the protagonist's virtues, the other (Bobby "the Brain" Heenan) justifying the rule-breaker's transgressions.

Wrestlers are often cast as doppelgängers, similar yet morally opposite figures. Consider, for example, how *WWF Magazine* characterizes a contest between the evil Mountie and the heroic Big Boss Man: "In conflict are Big Boss Man's and the Mountie's personal philosophies: the enforcement of the law vs. taking the law into one's own hands, the nightstick vs. the cattle prod, weakening a foe with the spike slam vs. disabling him with the nerve-crushing carotid control technique."[15] The Canadian Mountie stands on one page, dressed in his bright red uniform, clutching his cattle prod and snarling. The former Georgia prison guard, Big Boss Man, stands on the other, dressed in his pale blue uniform, clutching an open pair of handcuffs, with a look of quiet earnestness. At this moment the two opponents seem to be made for each other, as if no other possible contest could bear so much meaning, though the Big Boss Man and the Mountie will pair off against other challengers in the next major event.

The most successful wrestlers are those who provoke immediate emotional commitments (either positive or negative) and are open to constant rearticulation, who can be fit into a number of different conflicts and retain semiotic value. Hulk Hogan may stand as the defender of freedom in his feud

[14]Christine Gledhill, "The Melodramatic Field: An Investigation," in Christine Gledhill, ed., *Home Is Where the Heart Is: Studies in Melodrama and the Woman's Film* (London: BFI, 1987), p. 21.

[15]Keith Elliot Greenberg, "One Step Too Far: Boss Man and Mountie Clash over Meaning of Justice," *WWF Magazine*, May 1991, p. 40.

with Sgt. Slaughter, as innocence betrayed by an ambitious friend in his contest against Sid Justice, and as an aging athlete confronting and overcoming the threat of death in his battle with the Undertaker. Big Boss Man may defend the interests of the economically depressed against the Repo Man, make the streets safe from the Nasty Boys, and assert honest law enforcement in the face of the Mountie's bad example.

The introduction of new characters requires their careful integration into the WWF's moral universe before their first match can be fought. We need to know where they will stand in relation to the other protagonists and antagonists. The arrival of Tatanka on the WWF roster was preceded by a series of segments showing the Native American hero visiting the tribal elders, undergoing rites of initiation, explaining the meaning of his haircut, makeup, costume, and war shout. His ridicule by the fashion-minded Rick "the Model" Martel introduced his first antagonism and ensured the viewer's recognition of his essential goodness.

Much of the weekly broadcasts centers on the manufacturing of these moral distinctions and the creation of these basic antagonisms. A classic example might be the breakup of the Rockers. A series of accidents and minor disagreements sparked a public showdown on Brutus "the Barber" Beefcake's Barber Shop, a special program segment. Shawn Michaels appeared at the interview, dressed in black leather and wearing sunglasses (already adopting iconography signaling his shift toward the dark side). After a pretense of reconciliation and a series of clips reviewing their past together, Michaels shoved his partner, Marty Jannetty, through the barber-shop window, amid Brutus's impotent protests.[16] The decision to feature the two team members as independent combatants required the creation of moral difference, while the disintegration of their partnership fit perfectly within the program's familiar doppelgänger structure. *WWF Magazine* portrayed the events in terms of the biblical story of Cain and Abel, as the rivalry of two "brothers":

> [The Rockers] were as close as brothers. They did everything together, in and out of the ring. But Michaels grew jealous of Jannetty and became impatient to succeed. While Jannetty was content to bide his time, work to steadily improve with the knowledge that championships don't come easily in the WWF, Michaels decided he wanted it all now—and all for himself.[17]

If an earlier profile had questioned whether the two had "separate identities," this reporter has no trouble making moral distinctions between the patient

---

[16]Brutus was injured in a motorcycle accident several years ago and had his skull reconstructed; he is no longer able to fight but has come to represent the voice of aged wisdom within the WWF universe. Brutus constantly articulates the values of fairness and loyalty in the face of their abuse by the rule-breaking characters, pushing for reconciliations that might resolve old feuds, and watching as these disputes erupt and destroy his barber shop.

[17]"The Mark of Cain: Shawn Michaels Betrays His Tag Team Brother," *WWF Magazine*, March 1992, p. 41.

Jannetty and the impatient Michaels, the self-sacrificing Jannetty and the self-centered Michaels. Subsequent broadcasts would link Michaels professionally and romantically with Sensational Sherri, a woman whose seductive charms have been the downfall of many WWF champs. As a manager, Sherri is noted for her habit of smuggling foreign objects to ringside in her purse and interfering in the matches to ensure her man's victory. Sherri, who had previously been romantically involved with Million Dollar Man Ted Dibiase, announced that she would use her "Teddy Bear's" money to back Michaels's solo career, linking his betrayal of his partner to her own greedy and adulterous impulses. All of these plot twists differentiate Jannetty and Michaels, aligning spectator identification with the morally superior partner. Michaels's paramount moral failing is his all-consuming ambition, his desire to dominate rather than work alongside his long-time partner.

The Rockers' story points to the contradictory status of personal advancement within the WWF narrative: these stories hinge upon fantasies of upward mobility, yet ambition is just as often regarded in negative terms, as ultimately corrupting. Such a view of ambition reflects the experience of people who have worked hard all of their lives without much advancement and therefore remain profoundly suspicious of those on top. Wrestling speaks to those who recognize that upward mobility often has little to do with personal merit and a lot to do with a willingness to stomp on those who get in your way. Virtue, in the WWF moral universe, is often defined by a willingness to temper ambition through personal loyalties, through affiliation with others, while vice comes from putting self-interest ahead of everything else. This distrust of self-gain was vividly illustrated during a bout between Rowdy Roddy Piper and Bret "the Hitman" Hart at the 1992 Wrestlemania. This competition uncharacteristically centered on two good guys. As a result, most viewers suspected that one fighter would ultimately be driven to base conduct by personal desire for the Intercontinental Championship belt. Such speculations were encouraged by ambiguous signs from the combatants during "buildup" interviews and exploited during the match through a number of gestures which indicate moral indecision: Rowdy stood ready to club Hart with an illegal foreign object; the camera cut repeatedly to close-ups of his face as he struggled with his conscience before casting the object aside and continuing a fair fight. In the end, however, the two long-time friends embraced each other as Piper congratulated Hart on a more or less fairly won fight. The program situated this bout as a sharp contrast to the feud between Hulk Hogan and Sid Justice, the major attraction at this pay-per-view event. Their budding friendship had been totally destroyed by Justice's overriding desire to dominate the WWF: "I'm gonna crack the head of somebody big in the WWF. . . . No longer is this Farmboy from Arkansas gonna take a back seat to anybody."[18] Rowdy and Hart value their friendship over their ambition; Justice lets nothing stand in the way of his quest for power.

[18]"WWF Superstars Talk about Wrestlemania," *WWF Magazine*, March 1992, p. 18.

Perfect Bastards

WWF wrestlers are not rounded characters; the spectacle has little room for   20
the novelistic, and here the form may push the melodramatic imagination to
its logical extremes. WWF wrestlers experience no internal conflicts which
might blur their moral distinctiveness. Rather, they often display the "undivid-
edness" that Robert Heilman sees as a defining aspect of nineteenth-century
melodramatic characters:

> [The melodramatic character displays] oneness of feeling as competitor,
> crusader, aggressor; as defender, counterattacker, fighter for survival; he
> may be assertive or compelled, questing or resistant, obsessed or desper-
> ate; he may triumph or lose, be victor or victim, exert pressure or be
> pressed. Always he is undivided, unperplexed by alternatives, untorn by di-
> vergent impulses; all of his strength or weakness faces in one direction.[19]

The WWF athletes sketch their moral failings in broad profile: The Mountie
pounds on his chest and roars, "I am the Mountie," convinced that no one can
contest his superiority, yet as soon as the match gets rough, he slides under
the ropes and tries to hide behind his scrawny manager. The Million Dollar
Man shoves hundred-dollar bills into the mouths of his defeated opponents,
while Sherri paints her face with gilded dollar signs to mark her possession by
the highest bidder. Ravishing Rick Rude wears pictures of his opponents on
his arse, relishing his own vulgarity. Virtue similarly displays itself without fear
of misrecognition. Hacksaw Jim Duggan clutches an American flag in one
hand and a two-by-four in the other.

The need for a constant recombination of a fixed number of characters
requires occasional shifts in moral allegiances (as occurred with the breakup
of the Rockers). Characters may undergo redemption or seduction, but these
shifts typically occur quickly and without much ambiguity. There is rarely any
lingering doubt or moral fence-straddling. Such characters are good one week
and evil the next. Jake "the Snake" Roberts, a long-time hero — albeit one who
enjoys his distance from the other protagonists — uncharacteristically offered
to help the Ultimate Warrior prepare for his fight against the Undertaker. Their
grim preparations unfolded over several weeks, with Jake forcing the Warrior
to undergo progressively more twisted rituals — locking him into a coffin, bury-
ing him alive — until finally Jake shoved him into a room full of venomous
snakes. Bitten by Jake's cobra, Lucifer, the Ultimate Warrior staggered toward
his friend, who simply brushed him aside. As the camera pulled back to show
the Undertaker standing side by side with Jake, the turncoat laughed, "Never
trust a snake." From that moment forward, Jake was portrayed as totally evil,
Barthes's perfect bastard. Jake attacks Macho Man Randy Savage's bride, Elizabeth, on their wedding day and terrorizes the couple every chance he gets.

[19]Robert Bechtold Heilman, *The Iceman, the Arsonist and the Troubled Agent: Tragedy and
Melodrama on the Modern Stage* (Seattle: University of Washington Press, 1973), p. 53.

The program provides no motivation for such outrages, though commentary both in the broadcasts and in the pages of the wrestling magazines constantly invites such speculation: "What makes Jake hate Savage and his bride so fiercely? Why does he get his jollies — as he admits — from tormenting her?" What Peter Brooks said about the villains of traditional melodrama holds equally well here: "Evil in the world of melodrama does not need justification; it exists, simply. . . . And the less it is adequately motivated, the more this evil appears simply volitional, the product of pure will."[20] Jake is evil because he is a snake; it's in his character and nothing can change him, even though in this case, less than a year ago, Jake was as essentially good as he is now totally demented. We know Jake is evil without redemption, because he tells us so, over and over:

> I'm not really sure I have any soul at all. . . . Once I get involved in something — no matter how demented, no matter how treacherous, no matter how far off the mark it is from normal standards — I never back down. I just keep on going, deeper and deeper into the blackness, far past the point where any sensible person would venture. You see, a person with a conscience — a person with a soul — would be frightened by the sordid world I frequent. But Jake the Snake isn't scared at all. To tell you the truth, I can't get enough of it.[21]

Jake recognizes and acknowledges his villainy; he names it publicly and unrepentantly.

Peter Brooks sees such a process of "self-nomination" as an essential feature of the melodramatic imagination: "Nothing is spared because nothing is left unsaid; the characters stand on stage and utter the unspeakable, give voice to their deepest feelings, dramatize through their heightened and polarized words and gestures the whole lesson of their relationship."[22] The soliloquy, that stock device of the traditional melodrama, is alive and well in WWF wrestling. Wrestlers look directly into the audience and shove their fists toward the camera; they proclaim their personal credos and describe their sufferings. Tag team partners repeat their dedication to each other and their plans to dominate their challengers. Villains profess their evil intentions and vow to perform various forms of mayhem upon their opponents. Their rhetoric is excessively metaphoric, transforming every fight into a life-and-death struggle. Much as nineteenth-century theatrical melodrama used denotative music to define the characters' moral stances, the wrestlers' entry into the arena is preceded by theme songs which encapsulate their personalities. Hulk's song describes him as "a real American hero" who "fights for the rights of every man." The Million Dollar Man's jingle proclaims his compelling interest in "money, money, money," while Jake's song repeats "trust me, trust me, trust me."

---

[20]Brooks, p. 34.
[21]"WWF Interview: A Talk with Jake 'the Snake' Roberts," p. 17.
[22]Brooks, p. 4.

This public declaration ensures the constant moral legibility of the WWF narrative and thereby maximizes the audience's own emotional response. Spectators come to the arena or turn on the program to express intense emotion — to cheer the hero, to boo and jeer the villain — without moral ambiguity or emotional complexity. (Wrestling fans sometimes choose to root for the villains, taking pleasure in their self-conscious inversion of the WWF's moral universe, yet even this perverse pleasure requires moral legibility.) Operating within a world of absolutes, WWF wrestlers wear their hearts on their sleeves (or, in Ravishing Rick Rude's case, on the seat of their pants) and project their emotions from every inch of their bodies. Much as in classic melodrama, external actions reveal internal states; moral disagreements demand physical expressions. As Brooks writes, "Emotions are given a full acting-out, a full representation before our eyes. . . . Nothing is *under*stated, all is *over*stated."[23] The Million Dollar Man cowers, covering his face and retreating, crawling on hands and knees backward across the ring. Sherri shouts at the top of her ample lungs and pounds the floor with her high-heel shoe. Rowdy Roddy Piper gets his dander up and charges into the ring. With a burst of furious energy, he swings madly at his opponents, forcing them to scatter right and left. Roddy spits in the Million Dollar Man's eyes, flings his sweaty shirt in his face, or grabs Sherri, rips off her dress, throws her over his knee, and spanks her. Such characters embody the shameful spectacle of emotional display, acting as focal points for the audience's own expression of otherwise repressed affect.

Invincible Victims

Fans eagerly anticipate these excessive gestures as the most appropriate means of conveying the characters' moral attitudes. Through a process of simplification, the wrestler's body has been reduced to a series of iconic surfaces and stock attitudes. We know not only how the performer is apt to respond to a given situation but what bodily means will be adopted to express that response. Wrestlers perform less with their eyes and hands than with their arms and legs and with their deep, resounding voices. Earthquake's bass rumble and Roddy's fiery outbursts, Ric Flair's vicious laughter and Macho Man's red-faced indignation are "too much" for the small screen, yet they articulate feelings that are too intense to be contained.

This process of simplification and exaggeration transforms the wrestlers into cartoonish figures who may slam each other's heads into iron steps, throw each other onto wooden floors, smash each other with steel chairs, land with their full weight on the other's prone stomach, and emerge without a scratch, ready to fight again. Moral conflict will continue unabated; no defeat can be final within a world where the characters are omnipotent. If traditional melodrama

[23]Ibid., p. 41.

foregrounded long-suffering women's endurance of whatever injustices the world might throw against them, WWF wrestling centers around male victims who ultimately refuse to accept any more abuse and fight back against the aggressors.

Such a scenario allows men to acknowledge their own vulnerability, safe in the knowledge that their masculine potency will ultimately be restored and that they will be strong enough to overcome the forces which subordinate them. Hulk Hogan has perfected the image of the martyred hero who somehow captures victory from the closing jaws of defeat. Badly beaten in a fight, Hulk lies in a crumpled heap. The referee lifts his limp arms up, once, twice, ready to call the fight, when the crowd begins to clap and stomp. The mighty hero rises slowly, painfully to his feet, rejuvenated by the crowd's response. Blood streams through his blond hair and drips across his face, but he whips it aside with a broad swing of his mighty arms. Hulk turns to face his now-terrified assailant.

"Seeing Is Believing"

Such broad theatricality cuts against wrestling's tradition of pseudorealism; the programs' formats mimic the structures and visual style of nonfiction television, of sports coverage, news broadcasts, and talk shows. The fiction is, of course, that all of this fighting is authentic, spontaneous, unscripted. The WWF narrative preserves that illusion at all costs. There is no stepping outside the fiction, no acknowledgment of the production process or the act of authorship. When the performers are featured in *WWF Magazine*, they are profiled in character. Story segments are told in the form of late-breaking news reports or framed as interviews. The commentators are taken by surprise, interrupted by seemingly unplanned occurrences. During one broadcast, Jake the Snake captured Macho Man, dragging him into the ring. Jake tied him to the ropes and menaced him with a cobra which sprang and bit him on the forearm. The camera was jostled from side to side by people racing to Macho's assistance and panned abruptly trying to follow his hysterical wife as she ran in horror to ringside. A reaction shot shows a child in the audience reduced to tears by this brutal spectacle. Yet, at the same time, the camera refused to show us an image "too shocking" for broadcast. Macho Man's arm and the snake's gaping mouth were censored, blocked by white bars, not unlike the blue dot that covered the witness's face at the William Kennedy Smith rape trial that same week. (A few weeks later, the "uncensored" footage was at last shown, during a prime-time broadcast, so that viewers could see "what really happened.") The plot lines are thus told through public moments where a camera could plausibly be present, though such moments allow us insight into the characters' private motivations.

As Ric Flair often asserted during his brief stay in the WWF, "Pictures don't lie; seeing is believing," and yet it is precisely seeing and not believing that is a central pleasure in watching television wrestling. What audiences see is completely "unbelievable," as ring commentators frequently proclaim — unbelievable because these human bodies are unnaturally proportioned and monstrously large, because these figures who leap through the air seem to defy all natural laws, and, most important, because these characters participate within the corny and timeworn plots of the nineteenth-century melodrama. The pleasure comes in seeing what cannot be believed, yet is constantly asserted to us as undeniably true. Fans elbow each other in the ribs, "Look how fake," taking great pride in their ability to see through a deception that was never intended to convince.

Such campy self-acknowledgment may be part of what makes male spec-   30 tators' affective engagement with this melodramatic form safe and acceptable within a traditionally masculine culture which otherwise backs away from overt emotional display. Whenever the emotions become too intense, there is always a way of pulling back, laughing at what might otherwise provoke tears. WWF wrestling, at another level, provokes authentic pain and rage, particularly when it embraces populist myths of economic exploitation and class solidarity, feeds a hunger for homosocial bonding, or speaks to utopian fantasies of empowerment. The gap between the campy and the earnest reception of wrestling may reflect the double role which Elias and Dunning ascribe to traditional sports: the need to allow for the de-controlling of powerful affects while at the same time regulating their expression and ensuring their ultimate containment. The melodramatic aspects are what trigger emotional release, while the campy aspects contain it within safe bounds. The plots of wrestling cut close to the bone, inciting racial and class antagonisms that rarely surface this overtly elsewhere in popular culture, while comic exaggeration ensures that such images can never fully be taken seriously.

READING THE TEXT

1. What are the similarities between Roland Barthes's and Jake "the Snake" Roberts's attitudes toward professional wrestling?
2. What is the "core myth" (para. 11) of the WWF, according to Jenkins? What evidence does he give for his contention?
3. How does professional wrestling allow "working-class men to confront their own feelings of vulnerability" (para. 14)?
4. How does the WWF maintain its fiction that its contests are "authentic, spontaneous, unscripted" (para. 28)?
5. In what sense is the WWF a source of melodrama for men, according to Jenkins?

READING THE SIGNS

1. Watch some WWF or WWE contests, and write an analysis interpreting the viewer fantasies to which they appeal.

2. Read or review Michael A. Messner's "Power at Play: Sport and Gender Relations" (p. 513), and write an essay analyzing the ways in which the WWF reinforces traditional masculine gender codes. To develop your ideas, consult Aaron Devor's "Gender Role Behaviors and Attitudes" (p. 458).

3. Write a journal entry describing your attraction to WWF events if you are a fan. Conversely, explain why you never watch the WWF if you are not a fan.

4. For many fans of the WWF, the attraction is campy irony rather than literal belief. Write an essay comparing and contrasting the social class differences that divide those fans who believe in the fictions of the WWF and those who don't. For a discussion of camp, consult Andy Medhurst's "Batman, Deviance, and Camp" (p. 753).

5. Write an essay in which you explore the extent to which Jenkins's claim that sports "reasserts the desirability of belonging to a community" (para. 6) is valid. Be sure to use as evidence sports other than wrestling.

7

CONSTRUCTING RACE

Readings in Multicultural Semiotics

Michael Jordan. Michael Jackson. Miles Davis. Duke Ellington. Ella Fitzgerald. Oprah Winfrey. Whitney Houston. Serena Williams. Venus Williams. Tiger Woods. Tupac Shakur. Barry Bonds. Bill Cosby. Eddie Murphy. Will Smith. Denzel Washington. Muhammad Ali. Shaquille O'Neal. Naomi Campbell. Halle Berry. Mariah Carey. Alicia Keys. Usher. Beyoncé.

The list could go on, of course, but in naming just this partial roster of African American popular cultural superstars we mean to point to a multicultural phenomenon that can make one think twice about what is meant by the words *dominant culture*. For while Caucasians remain the dominant ethnic group in America, and European culture remains our dominant culture, when it comes to popular culture, African Americans enjoy an especially prominent status. Indeed, given that African Americans are the originators of America's most popular musical forms today — hip-hop, rock 'n' roll, and jazz — and are the stars of America's most popular professional sports, it is impossible to imagine modern culture without them. You may even object that our brief list of African American icons is too short to do justice to their place in the current cultural pantheon.

It has not always been this way, of course. Jazz was once denounced as "jungle music" by white critics, and rock 'n' roll was regarded as the "devil's music." Black athletes were barred from participation in mainstream professional sports (the Harlem Globetrotters were created because blacks weren't allowed in the early NBA), and black actors often had to accept demeaning roles to get any work in Hollywood at all (think of *Amos 'n' Andy* or of Prissy in *Gone with the Wind*). Even today, the National Association for the Advancement of Colored People (NAACP) can point every year to a new television season that once again underrepresents African Americans.

Still, when it comes to popular culture, the multicultural nature of American society is especially striking. Multiculturalism refers to that scholarly, political, and educational movement that contests the traditional monocultural perspective on America. That perspective regards American culture as a product of European history, the extension of a tradition that began in Greece and Rome and that was brought to America by the English. Multiculturalists challenge that perspective by exploring the contributions of such historically marginalized Americans as Africans, Asians, Latins, and Native Americans in the creation of American culture. And nowhere has this contribution been more prominent than in the realm of popular culture.

Interpreting Multicultural Semiotics

Until recently, the multicultural nature of American popular culture has been most visible in binary terms: that is, black and white. But with the emerging Ñ generation, whose pop superstars include Ricky Martin, Marc Anthony, Jennifer Lopez, and Penélope Cruz, along with the increasing number of Dominican stars in professional baseball, the Latino and Latina contribution to popular culture is no longer in the shadows. The Asian contribution, which has tended to be restricted to a certain stereotyping of Asians as experts in the martial arts, includes such performers as Bruce Lee and Jackie Chan (who, to be precise, is not an American), but as one of the fastest-growing demographic groups in America, Asians will continue to increase their presence in popular culture. Native Americans, for their part, are still struggling with a dominant cultural tendency either to view them through the eye of a gunsight (the most common perspective of mid-century cinema and TV) or to sentimentalize them as New Age Noble Savages (consider Oliver Stone's use of Native American characters in *The Doors* and *Natural Born Killers*). But as multicultural awareness continues to grow, the roster of Native American popular cultural stars will certainly go well beyond Buffy Ste. Marie.

The special place that African Americans enjoy in popular culture was underscored in 2001 with the making of *Ali*, a movie that brought together two of the defining icons of contemporary American popular culture: Muhammad Ali and Will Smith. Commanding what was then the highest box-office gross ever for a Christmas Day release, the movie was a potent signifier of the way that, at least within popular culture, the racial polarities of American history are receding. Once, Muhammad Ali was an outlaw, whose change of name and religion, along with his high-profile refusal to be drafted into the armed services, made him a symbol of racial resistance. In his famous showdown with Joe Frazier — the historic "thrilla in Manila" — he was widely regarded as black America's champion in a confrontation in which he denounced his opponent as an Uncle Tom in the service of white America — an aspersion that it took Ali

Alicia Keys performing at Radio City Music Hall.

thirty years to apologize for to the wounded Frazier. But now, Muhammad Ali is a national symbol like Martin Luther King Jr. Indeed, in the wake of the September 11, 2001, attacks, he was asked to make a public service address, to be broadcast throughout the Islamic world, explaining that America's war on terrorism is not a war on Islam.

As a cultural signifier, *Ali* can be related to Spike Lee's *Malcolm X*, a film that also marked the culmination of a historical process by which a symbol of racial resistance has been transformed into a national hero who has even been

---

Exploring the Signs of Race

In your journal, reflect on the question, "Who are you?" How does your ethnicity contribute to your sense of self? Are there other factors that contribute to your identity? If so, what are they, and how do they relate to your ethnicity? If you don't perceive yourself in ethnic terms, why do you think that's the case?

---

featured on his own postage stamp. Such an association can show us how *Ali*'s release is no isolated event: It is a signifier of a change in American cultural relations that has seen the emergence of black heroes who are as important as such traditional heroes as George Washington and Abraham Lincoln. Indeed, a related signifier in this context is the fact that both Washington's and Lincoln's birthdays, once celebrated as separate national holidays, have been consolidated into a single, somewhat anonymous Presidents' Day.

The careers of the actors who played Ali and Malcolm X in these two films are also culturally significant. Before Denzel Washington was picked to play Malcolm X in Lee's movie, he had already established himself as one of Hollywood's leading men. By playing Malcolm X, one of the most powerful symbols in African American history, Washington, who was certainly aware of the historic mantle that was being cast across his shoulders, fully emerged as another such icon. A later signifier of Washington's iconic status was his portrayal of a corrupt cop in *Training Day*. Prior to this film, Washington always played the good guy. By playing Alonzo in *Training Day*, Washington demonstrated not only that he could play villains as well as heroes but that his place in pop culture was so secure that he could be cast as a bad guy without exacerbating sensitivities to negative stereotyping. At a time when Hollywood is trying to live down a history of portraying black men as criminals and callous womanizers, few black actors can safely be cast in such roles. But Denzel Washington's heroic status ensured that his casting in this role would be seen as a star branching out and not as a denigrating stereotype.

Will Smith's role as Muhammad Ali, for its part, is semiotically related to Washington's Malcolm X. For by the time he took this role, Smith, too, had become one of Hollywood's leading men. By playing Ali — indeed, as *Entertainment Weekly* has noted, by *becoming* Ali — Smith signified his ascension into the ranks of certified cultural icons. Interestingly, Smith began his career as a rapper, before rap had fully crossed over to become young America's favorite form of musical entertainment; moved to prime-time TV in *The Fresh Prince of Bel Air*; and then turned to Hollywood in such films as *Men in Black* and *Wild Wild West*. Playing Ali, then, gave Smith a chance not only to aim for full cultural superstardom but also to become involved, at least imaginatively, in professional sports, a career move that, in effect, placed him in a starring role in all four of America's leading entertainment venues.

Who Are We?

Whether in the realm of popular or political culture, multicultural semiotics always involves the question of cultural identity, because from the semiotic point of view, value systems and mythologies are culturally constructed. To put this another way, *what* you value depends on *who* you are. So, ask yourself a simple question: "Who am I?" Ask a classmate, "Who are you?" What's the answer? Did your classmate give her name? Did you? Or did each of you answer differently? Did you say "I am an American"? Or did you say "I am an African American," or an "Asian American," or a "Latino," or a "Native American"? Would you answer "I am a European American" or a "Jewish American"? How-ever you answered the question, can you say why you answered as you did?

To ask how you identify yourself and why you do so is to probe further into the semiotics of race and culture in America's multicultural society. Some of you may believe that there is a right answer to our question, that it is es-sential that all Americans think of themselves as *Americans* first and fore-most. Others of you may believe just as strongly that your ethnic and cultural identity comes first. In either case, your beliefs reflect a worldview, or cultural mythology, that guides you in your most fundamental thoughts about your identity. Let's look at those myths for a moment.

Say that you feel that all American citizens should view themselves sim-ply as Americans. If so, your feelings reflect a basic cultural mythology best known as the myth of the American "melting pot." This is the belief that America offers all its citizens the opportunity to blend together into one har-monious whole that will erase the many differences among us on behalf of a new, distinctly American, identity. This belief has led many immigrants to seek to assimilate into what they perceive as the dominant American culture, shedding the specific cultural characteristics that may distinguish them from what they see as the American norm. And it is a belief that stands behind some of the most generous impulses in our culture — at least ideally.

Discussing the Signs of Race

Demographers predict that, by the middle of the twenty-first century, America will no longer have any racial or ethnic majority population. In class, discuss what effects this may have on Americans' sense of this country's history, culture, and identity.

But what if you don't buy this belief? What if, as far as you are concerned, you're proud to belong to a different community, one that differs from the basically Anglo-Saxon culture that has become the dominant and normative culture for assimilation? Or what if you and your people have found that you were never really allowed to blend in anyway, that in spite of the promise, the melting pot was never meant for you? If so, how does the myth of the melting pot look to you? Does it look the same as it would to someone who never had any trouble assimilating, or never needed to, because he or she already belonged to the dominant culture?

To see that the myth of the melting pot looks different depending on who is looking at it is to see why it is so precious to some Americans and so irrelevant to others. It is to realize again the fundamental semiotic precept that our social values are culturally determined rather than inscribed in the marble of absolute truth. This may be difficult to accept, especially if you and your classmates all come from the same culture and hence all hold the same values. But if you know people who are different, you might want to ask them how the myth of the melting pot looks from their perspective. Does it look like an ideal that our nation should strive to achieve? Or does it look like an invitation to cultural submission? It all depends on who's looking.

The failure to recognize that different people view the melting pot differently is one of the major sources of racial misunderstanding and, thus, conflict in America today. On the one hand, we need to realize that many Americans, particularly nonwhites, have felt excluded from full economic and cultural participation in American life and may deeply resent the view that we all should just see ourselves as Americans. But on the other hand, we also need to realize that many of today's Americans descend from non–Anglo-Saxon European immigrants who embraced the image of the melting pot, prospered, and passed their gratitude on to their descendants. For such Americans, the myth of the melting pot appears to be so benevolent that it doesn't seem right to attack it. A debate that acknowledges the historical reasons for this difference in viewpoint has a better chance to result in some consensus than one that presumes that one side's affection for the melting pot is "racist" or that the other's resentment is "petty" or "un-American."

Reading Race on the Net

Many Internet sites are devoted to the culture of a particular ethnicity, such as Afronet (http://www.afronet.com). Visit several such sites, and survey the breadth of information available about different ethnic groups. To what extent can a researcher learn about various ethnicities on the Net? Is there any information that you wish would appear on the Net but could not find? Do you find any material problematic?

Such a recognition is difficult to achieve, of course, because of the way that cultural worldviews tend to present themselves in absolute terms. We don't look at our belief systems and say "this is our belief system"; we say "this is the truth." All cultures do this. Even the way cultures form their sense of identity involves a certain reliance on absolutes by assuming that their culture is normative, the right way to be. It's not just Anglo-Saxon America, in other words, that presumes its centrality in the order of things. We can see how groups of people implicitly believe in their privileged place in the world by looking at the names with which they identify themselves. Take the members of the largest Native American tribe in the United States. To the rest of the world, they are known as the Navajos. This is not the name the Navajos use among themselves, however, for the word *Navajo* does not come from their language. In all likelihood, the name was given to them by neighboring Pueblo Indians, for whom the term *Navahu* means "large area of cultivated lands." But in the language of the Navajo, which is quite different from that of the Pueblo, they are not the people of the tilled fields. They are, quite simply, the People, the most common English translation of the word *diné*, the name by which the Navajo know themselves.

Or take the Hmong of Southeast Asia. *Hmong* simply means "person," and so to say "I am a Hmong" implicitly states "I am a person." And even the names of such different nations as Ireland and Iran harbor an ancient sense of normative "peoplehood," for both names are derived from the word *Aryan*, which itself once bore the simple meaning "the people." To be sure, when someone says "I am diné," or "I am Hmong," or "I am Irish," he or she does not mean "I am a human being and the rest of you aren't." Nonetheless, we find inscribed within the unconscious history of these ancient tribal names the trace of a belief found within many a tribal name: the sense that one's own tribe comes first in the order of things.

The Readings

This chapter looks at the social construction of racial identity in America, beginning with Michael Omi's survey of how race works as a sign in popular American culture. Leon E. Wynter follows with a historical analysis of how, beginning with Michael Jackson's *Thriller*, African American popular culture crossed over from the cultural margin to the center — of both entertainment and brand imaging. Benjamin DeMott indicts Hollywood's tendency to mask the grim realities of America's racial history behind "happy faced" images of black-white friendship and solidarity, while Paul C. Taylor analyzes white performers who excel in black-identified cultural activities like basketball and the blues. An excerpt from Angeline F. Price's Web site devoted to describing the stereotyped images of "white trash" that are disseminated through the American popular media follows. Next, Jack Lopez offers a personal memoir of what it is like to be a wannabe surfer in the Mexican American community of East Los Angeles, while Nell Bernstein reports on the phenomenon of "claiming" — white teens choosing to identify themselves with nonwhite ethnic groups. An autobiographical reflection by bell hooks on her childhood preference for "brown" dolls over white follows, after which Melissa Algranati offers a college student's perspective on what it's like to be a Puerto Rican-Egyptian-American Jew in a country that demands clear ethnic identifications. Fan Shen concludes the chapter with an analysis of the role that his Chinese heritage has played in his experience both as a student and as a professor of freshman composition.

MICHAEL OMI

In Living Color: Race and American Culture

Though many like to think that racism in America is a thing of the past, Michael Omi argues that racism is a pervasive feature in our lives, one that is both overt and inferential. Using race as a sign by which we judge a person's character, inferential racism invokes deep-rooted stereotypes, and as Omi shows in his survey of American film, television, and music, our popular culture is hardly immune from such stereotyping. Indeed, when ostensibly "progressive" programs like Saturday Night Live *can win the National Ethnic Coalition of Organizations' "Platinum Pit Award" for racist stereotyping in television, and shock jocks such as Howard Stern command big audiences and salaries, one can see popular culture has a way to go before it becomes colorblind. The author of* Racial Formation in the United States: From the 1960s to the 1980s *(with Howard Winant, 1986, 1994), Omi is a professor of comparative ethnic studies at the University of California, Berkeley. His most recent project is a survey of antiracist organizations and initiatives.*

In February 1987, Assistant Attorney General William Bradford Reynolds, the nation's chief civil rights enforcer, declared that the recent death of a black man in Howard Beach, New York, and the Ku Klux Klan attack on civil rights marchers in Forsyth County, Georgia, were "isolated" racial incidences. He emphasized that the places where racial conflict could potentially flare up were "far fewer now than ever before in our history," and concluded that such a diminishment of racism stood as "a powerful testament to how far we have come in the civil rights struggle."[1]

Events in the months following his remarks raise the question as to whether we have come quite so far. They suggest that dramatic instances of racial tension and violence merely constitute the surface manifestations of a deeper racial organization of American society — a system of inequality which has shaped, and in turn been shaped by, our popular culture.

In March, the NAACP released a report on blacks in the record industry entitled "The Discordant Sound of Music." It found that despite the revenues generated by black performers, blacks remain "grossly underrepresented" in the business, marketing, and A&R (Artists and Repertoire) departments of major record labels. In addition, few blacks are employed as managers, agents, concert promoters, distributors, and retailers. The report concluded that:

---

[1]Reynolds's remarks were made at a conference on equal opportunity held by the bar association in Orlando, Florida. *The San Francisco Chronicle* (7 February 1987).

> The record industry is overwhelmingly segregated and discrimination is rampant. No other industry in America so openly classifies its operations on a racial basis. At every level of the industry, beginning with the separation of black artists into a special category, barriers exist that severely limit opportunities for blacks.[2]

Decades after the passage of civil rights legislation and the affirmation of the principle of "equal opportunity," patterns of racial segregation and exclusion, it seems, continue to characterize the production of popular music.

The enduring logic of Jim Crow is also present in professional sports. In April, Al Campanis, vice president of player personnel for the Los Angeles Dodgers, explained to Ted Koppel on ABC's *Nightline* about the paucity of blacks in baseball front offices and as managers. "I truly believe," Campanis said, "that [blacks] may not have some of the necessities to be, let's say, a field manager or perhaps a general manager." When pressed for a reason, Campanis offered an explanation which had little to do with the structure of opportunity of institutional discrimination within professional sports:

> [W]hy are black men or black people not good swimmers? Because they don't have the buoyancy. . . . They are gifted with great musculature and various other things. They're fleet of foot. And this is why there are a lot of black major league ballplayers. Now as far as having the background to become club presidents, or presidents of a bank, I don't know.[3]

Black exclusion from the front office, therefore, was justified on the basis of biological "difference."

The issue of race, of course, is not confined to the institutional arrange-   5
ments of popular culture production. Since popular culture deals with the symbolic realm of social life, the images which it creates, represents, and disseminates contribute to the overall racial climate. They become the subject of analysis and political scrutiny. In August, the National Ethnic Coalition of Organizations bestowed the "Golden Pit Awards" on television programs, commercials, and movies that were deemed offensive to racial and ethnic groups. *Saturday Night Live*, regarded by many media critics as a politically "progressive" show, was singled out for the "Platinum Pit Award" for its comedy skit "Ching Chang" which depicted a Chinese storeowner and his family in a derogatory manner.[4]

These examples highlight the *overt* manifestations of racism in popular culture — institutional forms of discrimination which keep racial minorities out of the production and organization of popular culture, and the crude racial

---

[2]Economic Development Department of the NAACP, "The Discordant Sound of Music (A Report on the Record Industry)," (Baltimore, Maryland: The NAACP, 1987), pp. 16–17.

[3]Campanis's remarks on *Nightline* were reprinted in *The San Francisco Chronicle* (April 9, 1987).

[4]Ellen Wulfhorst, "TV Stereotyping: It's the 'Pits,' " *The San Francisco Chronicle* (August 24, 1987).

caricatures by which these groups are portrayed. Yet racism in popular culture is often conveyed in a variety of implicit, and at times invisible, ways. Political theorist Stuart Hall makes an important distinction between *overt* racism, the elaboration of an explicitly racist argument, policy, or view, and *inferential* racism which refers to "those apparently naturalized representations of events and situations relating to race, whether 'factual' or 'fictional,' which have racist premises and propositions inscribed in them as a set of *unquestioned assumptions*." He argues that inferential racism is more widespread, common, and indeed insidious since "it is largely *invisible* even to those who formulate the world in its terms."[5]

Race itself is a slippery social concept which is paradoxically both "obvious" and "invisible." In our society, one of the first things we notice about people when we encounter them (along with their sex/gender) is their *race*. We utilize race to provide clues about *who* a person is and *how* we should relate to her/him. Our perception of race determines our "presentation of *self*," distinctions in status, and appropriate modes of conduct in daily and institutional life. This process is often unconscious; we tend to operate off of an unexamined set of *racial beliefs*.

Racial beliefs account for and explain variations in "human nature." Differences in skin color and other obvious physical characteristics supposedly provide visible clues to more substantive differences lurking underneath. Among other qualities, temperament, sexuality, intelligence, and artistic and athletic ability are presumed to be fixed and discernible from the palpable mark of race. Such diverse questions as our confidence and trust in others (as salespeople, neighbors, media figures); our sexual preferences and romantic images; our tastes in music, film, dance, or sports; indeed our very ways of walking and talking are ineluctably shaped by notions of race.

Ideas about race, therefore, have become "common sense" — a way of comprehending, explaining, and acting in the world. This is made painfully obvious when someone disrupts our common sense understandings. An encounter with someone who is, for example, racially "mixed" or of a racial/ethnic group we are unfamiliar with becomes a source of discomfort for us, and momentarily creates a crisis of racial meaning. We also become disoriented when people do not act "black," "Latino," or indeed "white." The content of such stereotypes reveals a series of unsubstantiated beliefs about who these groups are, what they are like, and how they behave.

The existence of such racial consciousness should hardly be surprising. 10 Even prior to the inception of the republic, the United States was a society shaped by racial conflict. The establishment of the Southern plantation economy, Western expansion, and the emergence of the labor movement, among other significant historical developments, have all involved conflicts over the definition and nature of the *color line*. The historical results have been distinct

[5]Stuart Hall, "The Whites of Their Eyes: Racist Ideologies and the Media," in George Bridges and Rosalind Brunt, eds., *Silver Linings* (London: Lawrence and Wishart, 1981), pp. 36–37.

and different groups have encountered unique forms of racial oppression — Native Americans faced genocide, blacks were subjected to slavery, Mexicans were invaded and colonized, and Asians faced exclusion. What is common to the experiences of these groups is that their particular "fate" was linked to historically specific ideas about the significance and meaning of race.[6] Whites defined them as separate "species," ones inferior to Northern European cultural stocks, and thereby rationalized the conditions of their subordination in the economy, in political life, and in the realm of culture.

A crucial dimension of racial oppression in the United States is the elaboration of an ideology of difference or "otherness." This involves defining "us" (i.e., white Americans) in opposition to "them," an important task when distinct racial groups are first encountered, or in historically specific periods where preexisting racial boundaries are threatened or crumbling.

Political struggles over the very definition of who an "American" is illustrate this process. The Naturalization Law of 1790 declared that only free *white* immigrants could qualify, reflecting the initial desire among Congress to create and maintain a racially homogeneous society. The extension of eligibility to all racial groups has been a long and protracted process. Japanese, for example, were finally eligible to become naturalized citizens after the passage of the Walter-McCarran Act of 1952. The ideological residue of these restrictions in naturalization and citizenship laws is the equation within popular parlance of the term "American" with "white," while other "Americans" are described as black, Mexican, "Oriental," etc.

Popular culture has been an important realm within which racial ideologies have been created, reproduced, and sustained. Such ideologies provide a framework of symbols, concepts, and images through which we understand, interpret, and represent aspects of our "racial" existence.

Race has often formed the central themes of American popular culture. Historian W. L. Rose notes that it is a "curious coincidence" that four of the "most popular reading-viewing events in all American history" have in some manner dealt with race, specifically black/white relations in the south.[7] Harriet Beecher Stowe's *Uncle Tom's Cabin*, Thomas Ryan Dixon's *The Clansman* (the inspiration for D. W. Griffith's *The Birth of a Nation*), Margaret Mitchell's *Gone with the Wind* (as a book and film), and Alex Haley's *Roots* (as a book and television miniseries), each appeared at a critical juncture in American race relations and helped to shape new understandings of race.

Emerging social definitions of race and the "real American" were reflected   15 in American popular culture of the nineteenth century. Racial and ethnic stereotypes were shaped and reinforced in the newspapers, magazines, and pulp fiction of the period. But the evolution and ever-increasing sophistication of

[6]For an excellent survey of racial beliefs see Thomas F. Gossett, *Race: The History of an Idea in America* (New York: Shocken Books, 1965).

[7]W. L. Rose, *Race and Region in American Historical Fiction: Four Episodes in Popular Culture* (Oxford: Clarendon Press, 1979).

visual mass communications throughout the twentieth century provided, and continue to provide, the most dramatic means by which racial images are generated and reproduced.

Film and television have been notorious in disseminating images of racial minorities which establish for audiences what these groups look like, how they behave, and, in essence, "who they are." The power of the media lies not only in their ability to reflect the dominant racial ideology, but in their capacity to shape that ideology in the first place. D. W. Griffith's aforementioned epic *Birth of a Nation*, a sympathetic treatment of the rise of the Ku Klux Klan during Reconstruction, helped to generate, consolidate, and "nationalize" images of blacks which had been more disparate (more regionally specific, for example) prior to the film's appearance.[8]

In television and film, the necessity to define characters in the briefest and most condensed manner has led to the perpetuation of racial caricatures, as racial stereotypes serve as shorthand for scriptwriters, directors, and actors. Television's tendency to address the "lowest common denominator" in order to render programs "familiar" to an enormous and diverse audience leads it regularly to assign and reassign racial characteristics to particular groups, both minority and majority.

Many of the earliest American films deal with racial and ethnic "difference." The large influx of "new immigrants" at the turn of the century led to a proliferation of negative images of Jews, Italians, and Irish which were assimilated and adapted by such films as Thomas Edison's *Cohen's Advertising Scheme* (1904). Based on an old vaudeville routine, the film featured a scheming Jewish merchant, aggressively hawking his wares. Though stereotypes of these groups persist to this day,[9] by the 1940s many of the earlier ethnic stereotypes had disappeared from Hollywood. But, as historian Michael Winston observes, the "outsiders" of the 1890s remained: "the ever-popular Indian of the Westerns; the inscrutable or sinister Oriental; the sly, but colorful Mexican; and the clowning or submissive Negro."[10]

In many respects the "Western" as a genre has been paradigmatic in establishing images of racial minorities in film and television. The classic scenario involves the encircled wagon train or surrounded fort from which whites bravely fight off fierce bands of Native American Indians. The point of reference and viewer identification lies with those huddled within the circle — the representatives of "civilization" who valiantly attempt to ward off the

[8]Melanie Martindale-Sikes, "Nationalizing 'Nigger' Imagery Through *Birth of a Nation*," paper prepared for the 73rd Annual Meeting of the American Sociological Association (September 4–8, 1978) in San Francisco.

[9]For a discussion of Italian, Irish, Jewish, Slavic, and German stereotypes in film, see Randall M. Miller, ed., *The Kaleidoscopic Lens: How Hollywood Views Ethnic Groups* (Englewood, N.J.: Jerome S. Ozer, 1980).

[10]Michael R. Winston, "Racial Consciousness and the Evolution of Mass Communications in the United States," *Daedalus*, vol. III, No. 4 (Fall 1982).

forces of barbarism. In the classic Western, as writer Tom Engelhardt observes, "the viewer is forced behind the barrel of a repeating rifle and it is from that position, through its gun sights, that he receives a picture history of Western colonialism and imperialism."[11]

Westerns have indeed become the prototype for European and American [20] excursions throughout the Third World. The cast of characters may change, but the story remains the same. The "humanity" of whites is contrasted with the brutality and treachery of nonwhites; brave (i.e., white) souls are pitted against the merciless hordes in conflicts ranging from Indians against the British Lancers to Zulus against the Boers. What Stuart Hall refers to as the imperializing "white eye" provides the framework for these films, lurking outside the frame and yet seeing and positioning everything within; it is "the unmarked position from which . . . 'observations' are made and from which, alone, they make sense."[12]

Our "common sense" assumptions about race and racial minorities in the United States are both generated and reflected in the stereotypes presented by the visual media. In the crudest sense, it could be said that such stereotypes underscore white "superiority" by reinforcing the traits, habits, and predispositions of nonwhites which demonstrate their "inferiority." Yet a more careful assessment of racial stereotypes reveals intriguing trends and seemingly contradictory themes.

While all racial minorities have been portrayed as "less than human," there are significant differences in the images of different groups. Specific racial minority groups, in spite of their often interchangeable presence in films steeped in the "Western" paradigm, have distinct and often unique qualities assigned to them. Latinos are portrayed as being prone toward violent outbursts of anger; blacks as physically strong, but dim-witted; while Asians are seen as sneaky and cunningly evil. Such differences are crucial to observe and analyze. Race in the United States is not reducible to black/white relations. These differences are significant for a broader understanding of the patterns of race in America, and the unique experience of specific racial minority groups.

It is somewhat ironic that *real* differences which exist within a racially defined minority group are minimized, distorted, or obliterated by the media. "All Asians look alike," the saying goes, and indeed there has been little or no attention given to the vast differences which exist between, say, the Chinese and Japanese with respect to food, dress, language, and culture. This blurring within popular culture has given us supposedly Chinese characters who wear kimonos; it is also the reason why the fast-food restaurant McDonald's can offer "Shanghai McNuggets" with teriyaki sauce. Other groups suffer a similar fate. Professor Gretchen Bataille and Charles Silet find the cinematic Native American of the Northeast wearing the clothing of the Plains Indians, while living in the dwellings of Southwestern tribes:

---

[11] Tom Engelhardt, "Ambush at Kamikaze Pass," in Emma Gee, ed., *Counterpoint: Perspectives on Asian America* (Los Angeles: Asian American Studies Center, UCLA, 1976), p. 270.
[12] Hall, "Whites of Their Eyes," p. 38.

> The movie men did what thousands of years of social evolution could not
> do, even what the threat of the encroaching white man could not do;
> Hollywood produced the homogenized Native American, devoid of tribal
> characteristics or regional differences.[13]

The need to paint in broad racial strokes has thus rendered "internal" differences invisible. This has been exacerbated by the tendency for screenwriters
to "invent" mythical Asian, Latin American, and African countries. Ostensibly
done to avoid offending particular nations and peoples, such a subterfuge reinforces the notion that all the countries and cultures of a specific region are
the same. European countries retain their distinctiveness, while the Third
World is presented as one homogeneous mass riddled with poverty and governed by ruthless and corrupt regimes.

While rendering specific groups in a monolithic fashion, the popular cultural imagination simultaneously reveals a compelling need to distinguish and
articulate "bad" and "good" variants of particular racial groups and individuals.
Thus each stereotypic image is filled with contradictions: The bloodthirsty Indian
is tempered with the image of the noble savage; the *bandido* exists along with
the loyal sidekick; and Fu Manchu is offset by Charlie Chan. The existence of
such contradictions, however, does not negate the one-dimensionality of these
images, nor does it challenge the explicit subservient role of racial minorities.
Even the "good" person of color usually exists as a foil in novels and films to underscore the intelligence, courage, and virility of the white male hero.

Another important, perhaps central, dimension of racial minority stereo- 25
types is sex/gender differentiation. The connection between race and sex has
traditionally been an explosive and controversial one. For most of American
history, sexual and marital relations between whites and nonwhites were
forbidden by social custom and by legal restrictions. It was not until 1967, for
example, that the U.S. Supreme Court ruled that antimiscegenation laws were
unconstitutional. Beginning in the 1920s, the notorious Hays Office, Hollywood's attempt at self-censorship, prohibited scenes and subjects which dealt
with miscegenation. The prohibition, however, was not evenly applied in practice. White men could seduce racial minority women, but white women were
not to be romantically or sexually linked to racial minority men.

Women of color were sometimes treated as exotic sex objects. The sultry
Latin temptress — such as Dolores Del Rio and Lupe Velez — invariably had
boyfriends who were white North Americans; their Latino suitors were portrayed as being unable to keep up with the Anglo-American competition.
From Mary Pickford as Cho-Cho San in *Madame Butterfly* (1915) to Nancy
Kwan in *The World of Suzie Wong* (1961), Asian women have often been seen
as the gracious "geisha girl" or the prostitute with a "heart of gold," willing to
do anything to please her man.

---

[13]Gretchen Bataille and Charles Silet, "The Entertaining Anachronism: Indians in American Film," in Randall M. Miller, ed., *Kaleidoscopic Lens*, p. 40.

By contrast, Asian men, whether cast in the role of villain, servant, side-kick, or kung fu master, are seen as asexual or, at least, romantically undesirable. As Asian American studies professor Elaine Kim notes, even a hero such as Bruce Lee played characters whose "single-minded focus on perfecting his fighting skills precludes all other interests, including an interest in women, friendship, or a social life."[14]

The shifting trajectory of black images over time reveals an interesting dynamic with respect to sex and gender. The black male characters in *The Birth of a Nation* were clearly presented as sexual threats to "white womanhood." For decades afterwards, however, Hollywood consciously avoided portraying black men as assertive or sexually aggressive in order to minimize controversy. Black men were instead cast as comic, harmless, and nonthreatening figures exemplified by such stars as Bill "Bojangles" Robinson, Stepin Fetchit, and Eddie "Rochester" Anderson. Black women, by contrast, were divided into two broad character types based on color categories. Dark black women such as Hattie McDaniel and Louise Beavers were cast as "dowdy, frumpy, dumpy, overweight mammy figures"; while those "close to the white ideal," such as Lena Horne and Dorothy Dandridge, became "Hollywood's treasured mulattoes" in roles emphasizing the tragedy of being of mixed blood.[15]

It was not until the early 1970s that tough, aggressive, sexually assertive black characters, both male and female, appeared. The "blaxploitation" films of the period provided new heroes (e.g., *Shaft*, *Superfly*, *Coffy*, and *Cleopatra Jones*) in sharp contrast to the submissive and subservient images of the past. Unfortunately, most of these films were shoddy productions which did little to create more enduring "positive" images of blacks, either male or female.

In contemporary television and film, there is a tendency to present and equate racial minority groups and individuals with specific social problems. Blacks are associated with drugs and urban crime, Latinos with "illegal" immigration, while Native Americans cope with alcoholism and tribal conflicts. Rarely do we see racial minorities "out of character," in situations removed from the stereotypic arenas in which scriptwriters have traditionally embedded them. Nearly the only time we see young Asians and Latinos of either sex, for example, is when they are members of youth gangs, as *Boulevard Nights* (1979), *Year of the Dragon* (1985), and countless TV cop shows can attest to.

Racial minority actors have continually bemoaned the fact that the roles assigned them on stage and screen are often one-dimensional and imbued with stereotypic assumptions. In theater, the movement toward "blind casting" (i.e., casting actors for roles without regard to race) is a progressive step, but it remains to be seen whether large numbers of audiences can suspend their "beliefs" and deal with a Latino King Lear or an Asian Stanley Kowalski.

[14]Elaine Kim, "Asian Americans and American Popular Culture" in Hyung-Chan Kim, ed., *Dictionary of Asian American History* (New York: Greenwood Press, 1986), p. 107.

[15]Donald Bogle, "A Familiar Plot (A Look at the History of Blacks in American Movies)," *The Crisis*, Vol. 90, No. 1 (January 1983), p. 15.

By contrast, white actors are allowed to play anybody. Though the use of white actors to play blacks in "black face" is clearly unacceptable in the contemporary period, white actors continue to portray Asian, Latino, and Native American characters on stage and screen.

Scores of Charlie Chan films, for example, have been made with white leads (the last one was the 1981 *Charlie Chan and the Curse of the Dragon Queen*). Roland Winters, who played Chan in six features, was once asked to explain the logic of casting a white man in the role of Charlie Chan: "The only thing I can think of is, if you want to cast a homosexual in a show, and you get a homosexual, it'll be awful. It won't be funny . . . and maybe there's something there."[16]

Such a comment reveals an interesting aspect about myth and reality in popular culture. Michael Winston argues that stereotypic images in the visual media were not originally conceived as representations of reality, nor were they initially understood to be "real" by audiences. They were, he suggests, ways of "coding and rationalizing" the racial hierarchy and interracial behavior. Over time, however, "a complex interactive relationship between myth and reality developed, so that images originally understood to be unreal, through constant repetition began to *seem* real."[17]

Such a process consolidated, among other things, our "common sense" understandings of what we think various groups should look like. Such presumptions have led to tragicomical results. Latinos auditioning for a role in a television soap opera, for example, did not fit the Hollywood image of "real Mexicans" and had their faces bronzed with powder before filming because they looked too white. Model Aurora Garza said, "I'm a real Mexican and very dark anyway. I'm even darker right now because I have a tan. But they kept wanting to make my face darker and darker."[18]

Historically in Hollywood, the fact of having "dark skin" made an actor or 35 actress potentially adaptable for numerous "racial" roles. Actress Lupe Velez once commented that she had portrayed "Chinese, Eskimos, Japs, squaws, Hindus, Swedes, Malays, and Japanese."[19] Dorothy Dandridge, who was the first black woman teamed romantically with white actors, presented a quandary for studio executives who weren't sure what race and nationality to make her. They debated whether she should be a "foreigner," an island girl, or a West Indian.[20] Ironically, what they refused to entertain as a possibility was to present her as what she really was, a black American woman.

The importance of race in popular culture is not restricted to the visual media. In popular music, race and race consciousness have defined, and continue to

---

[16]Frank Chin, "Confessions of the Chinatown Cowboy," *Bulletin of Concerned Asian Scholars*, Vol. 4, No. 3 (Fall 1972).

[17]Winston, "Racial Consciousness," p. 176.

[18]*The San Francisco Chronicle*, September 21, 1984.

[19]Quoted in Allen L. Woll, "Bandits and Lovers: Hispanic Images in American Film," in Miller, ed., *Kaleidoscopic Lens*, p. 60.

[20]Bogle, "Familiar Plot," p. 17.

define, formats, musical communities, and tastes. In the mid-1950s, the secretary of the North Alabama White Citizens Council declared that "Rock and roll is a means of pulling the white man down to the level of the Negro."[21] While rock may no longer be popularly regarded as a racially subversive musical form, the very genres of contemporary popular music remain, in essence, thinly veiled racial categories. "R & B" (Rhythm and Blues) and "soul" music are clearly references to *black* music, while Country & Western or heavy metal music are viewed, in the popular imagination, as *white* music. Black performers who want to break out of this artistic ghettoization must "cross over," a contemporary form of "passing" in which their music is seen as acceptable to white audiences.

The airwaves themselves are segregated. The designation "urban contemporary" is merely radio lingo for a "black" musical format. Such categorization affects playlists, advertising accounts, and shares of the listening market. On cable television, black music videos rarely receive airplay on MTV, but are confined instead to the more marginal BET (Black Entertainment Television) network.

In spite of such segregation, many performing artists have been able to garner a racially diverse group of fans. And yet, racially integrated concert audiences are extremely rare. Curiously, this "perverse phenomenon" of racially homogeneous crowds takes place despite the color of the performer. Lionel Richie's concert audiences, for example, are virtually all-white, while Teena Marie's are all-black.[22]

Racial symbols and images are omnipresent in popular culture. Commonplace household objects such as cookie jars, salt and pepper shakers, and ashtrays have frequently been designed and fashioned in the form of racial caricatures. Sociologist Steve Dublin in an analysis of these objects found that former tasks of domestic service were symbolically transferred onto these commodities.[23] An Aunt Jemima–type character, for example, is used to hold a roll of paper towels, her outstretched hands supporting the item to be dispensed. "Sprinkle Plenty," a sprinkle bottle in the shape of an Asian man, was used to wet clothes in preparation for ironing. Simple commodities, the household implements which help us perform everyday tasks, may reveal, therefore, a deep structure of racial meaning.

A crucial dimension for discerning the meaning of particular stereotypes and   40 images is the *situation context* for the creation and consumption of popular culture. For example, the setting in which "racist" jokes are told determines the function of humor. Jokes about blacks where the teller and audience are black constitute a form of self-awareness; they allow blacks to cope and "take the edge

[21]Dave Marsh and Kevin Stein, *The Book of Rock Lists* (New York: Dell Publishing Co., 1981), p. 8.

[22]*Rock & Roll Confidential*, No. 44 (February 1987), p. 2.

[23]Steven C. Dublin, "Symbolic Slavery: Black Representations in Popular Culture," *Social Problems*, Vol. 34, No. 2 (April 1987).

off" of oppressive aspects of the social order which they commonly confront. The meaning of these same jokes, however, is dramatically transformed when told across the "color line." If a white, or even black, person tells these jokes to a white audience, it will, despite its "purely" humorous intent, serve to reinforce stereotypes and rationalize the existing relations of racial inequality.

Concepts of race and racial images are both overt and implicit within popular culture — the organization of cultural production, the products themselves, and the manner in which they are consumed are deeply structured by race. Particular racial meanings, stereotypes, and myths can change, but the presence of a *system* of racial meanings and stereotypes, of racial ideology, seems to be an enduring aspect of American popular culture.

The era of Reaganism and the overall rightward drift of American politics and culture has added a new twist to the question of racial images and meanings. Increasingly, the problem for racial minorities is not that of misportrayal, but of "invisibility." Instead of celebrating racial and cultural diversity, we are witnessing an attempt by the right to define, once again, who the "real" American is, and what "correct" American values, mores, and political beliefs are. In such a context, racial minorities are no longer the focus of sustained media attention; when they do appear, they are cast as colored versions of essentially "white" characters.

The possibilities for change — for transforming racial stereotypes and challenging institutional inequities — nonetheless exist. Historically, strategies have involved the mobilization of political pressure against an offending institution(s). In the late 1950s, for instance, "Nigger Hair" tobacco changed its name to "Bigger Hare" due to concerted NAACP pressure on the manufacturer. In the early 1970s, Asian American community groups successfully fought NBC's attempt to resurrect Charlie Chan as a television series with white actor Ross Martin. Amidst the furor generated by Al Campanis's remarks cited at the beginning of this essay, Jesse Jackson suggested that a boycott of major league games be initiated in order to push for a restructuring of hiring and promotion practices.

Partially in response to such action, Baseball Commissioner Peter Ueberroth announced plans in June 1987 to help put more racial minorities in management roles. "The challenge we have," Ueberroth said, "is to manage change without losing tradition."[24] The problem with respect to the issue of race and popular culture, however, is that the *tradition* itself may need to be thoroughly examined, its "common sense" assumptions unearthed and challenged, and its racial images contested and transformed.

READING THE TEXT

1. Describe in your own words the difference between "overt" and "inferential" racism (para. 6).

[24]*The San Francisco Chronicle* (June 13, 1987).

2. Why, according to Omi, is popular culture so powerful in shaping America's attitudes toward race?

3. What relationship does Omi see between gender and racial stereotypes?

4. How did race relations change in America during the 1980s, in Omi's view?

READING THE SIGNS

1. In class, brainstorm on the blackboard stereotypes, both positive and negative, attributed to specific racial groups. Then discuss the possible sources of these stereotypes. In what ways have they been perpetuated in popular culture, including film, TV, advertising, music, and consumer products? What does your discussion reveal about popular culture's influence on our most basic ways of seeing the world?

2. Watch a DVD or video of *Malcolm X* or another film that addresses race relations, such as *Mi Familia*. Using Omi's essay as your critical framework, write an essay in which you explore how this film may reflect or redefine American attitudes toward racial identity and race relations.

3. Study an issue of a magazine targeted to a specific ethnic readership, such as *Ebony* or *Yolk*, analyzing both its articles and its advertising. Then write an essay in which you explore the extent to which the magazine accurately reflects that ethnicity or, in Omi's words, appeals to readers as "colored versions of essentially 'white' characters" (para. 42).

4. Omi claims that "television and film [tend] to present and equate racial minority groups and individuals with specific social problems" (para. 30). In class, brainstorm a list of films and TV shows with characters who are ethnic minorities; pick one example and watch it. Does Omi's claim apply to that example, or does it demonstrate different patterns of racial representation? To develop your analysis, consult Benjamin DeMott, "Put on a Happy Face: Masking the Differences between Blacks and Whites" (p. 567).

LEON E. WYNTER
Marketing in Color

For all of their impact on American popular culture, black entertainers and athletes still had to play second fiddle to their white counterparts until the 1980s, when pop stars like Michael Jackson and sports stars like Michael Jordan helped propel black celebrities into the forefront of American popular culture. This cultural reversal was accompanied by a marketing revolution, Leon E. Wynter (b. 1953) observes in this analysis of the racial transformation of American consumer culture. Wynter created and wrote the "Business and Race" column for the Wall Street Journal *for ten years and is a regular contributor to National Public Radio. He is the author of* American Skin: Pop Culture, Big Business, and the End of White America *(2002), from which this selection is taken.*

In the spring of 1999, shortly after securing the freedom of three American soldiers captured by the Yugoslavian Army during the NATO miniwar on Yugoslavia over Kosovo, the Reverend Jesse Jackson paid a call on the headquarters of PepsiCo in the bucolic New York suburb of Purchase. Still basking in the glow of his latest freelance foreign policy coup, Jackson's mission was to press top executives to throw more corporate-securities-underwriting work toward certain black- and minority-owned firms. With a small entourage in tow, Jackson's very presence in the mostly empty halls of the secluded corporate campus caused a bigger stir than most anybody in the well-starched head office of the perennial number-two cola maker could remember. It remained for one older employee, a black maintenance man, to put the pageantry of the sales call into context.

"'This is the most excitement since the day Don King came up here,'" said Pepsi marketing executive Maurice Cox, quoting the maintenance man's words. Indeed, everyone involved with selling Pepsi seemed to remember the fall 1983 day when the already-legendary, if not infamous, boxing promoter's humongous white stretch limousine, "big — like the kind they have today, only it was back then," parked on the cobblestone path before Pepsi's executive suite. The day Don King brought Pepsi the then-outrageous proposal of a $5 million sponsorship deal for the twenty-three-year-old "soul singer" Michael Jackson and his brothers was memorable enough to merit a chapter, just two years later, in Pepsi president Roger Enrico's 1986 book on the 1980s cola wars.

> Many important personages have come to Pepsico headquarters . . . none of them made the entrance King did. A land yacht of a limo pulled up, and out stepped this man in a white fur coat that had to cost as much as the car. King's pearly gray hair had been freshly electrocuted and was reaching the sky. Around King's neck was a blindingly shiny necklace, on

which hung his logo, a crown with "DON" on top, just in case you might forget he is the king.

Such a man did not come quickly through the halls.

"Hi, everybody, I'm Don King," he told one and all.[1]

Enshrining the moment was the least Enrico could do, because his decision to take a deal that only Don King would think of proposing to a *Fortune* 100 firm back then fixed the word *legendary* before the former PepsiCo chairman's name and secured his place in marketing history. It was a meeting that no one doing marketing at Coke's Atlanta headquarters would forget, either. For decades Pepsi had been desperate to gain a marketing edge over Coke. Enrico, who had just become president of the Pepsi-Cola division, was determined to do whatever it took to pull Coke, still the most hallowed American brand name, down to earth. Beyond the theatrics of the messenger, Don King's message was that Michael Jackson was about to shatter previously shatterproof barriers between black entertainers and mainstream popular culture. But even King's bombast failed to anticipate the financial records Jackson would also break along the way on the strength of the *Thriller* album. Released early in 1983, it had already topped the charts with nearly 10 million copies sold by the time King came to Pepsi. *Thriller* went on to quadruple that number and became the biggest-selling album in history. Guinness actually held the presses on the 1984 edition of the *World Records* book (a first in itself) to include *Thriller* as the top seller of all time, passing Carole King's 1970 *Tapestry*, when the industry-shaking album had still hit only 25 million in sales. The $5 million sponsorship deal Pepsi announced in December 1983 was also a Guinness record; it lasted until Jackson signed a $15 million personal endorsement deal with Pepsi two years later.

The awards, concert attendance, television ratings, and the like connected with Jackson during the mid-1980s, summed up by the term *Michaelmania*, could make up a book by themselves. So could the impact of the "Jackson phenomenon," as it was also called, on the very foundations of media-driven commercial culture. It spawned an orgy of "who is he and who are we as a society" journalistic navel-gazing not seen over a performing act since the Beatles landed in the States in 1964. In one week in March 1984, culture critics at both *Time* magazine and the *Washington Post* vainly exhausted more than six thousand words trying to plumb the connection between the Jackson persona and our collective psyche. Writing right after Jackson took eight out of a possible ten awards at the 1984 Grammys (another record) and searching for meaning, the authors seemed to be drowning in the sea of statistics (1 million albums sold per week for over twenty-four weeks and still counting), in the flood of celebrity swells (Jane Fonda, Elizabeth Taylor, Katharine Hepburn, Brooke Shields, Steven Spielberg) attached to the Jackson tide, and in the wave of historical icon comparisons (Babe Ruth, Al Jolson, Elvis, Howard Hughes, the Beatles).

[1] Roger Enrico and Jesse Kornbluth, *The Other Boy Blinked: How Pepsi Won the Cola Wars* (New York: Bantam Books, 1986).

All they really knew for sure was what the *Post*'s Richard Harrington [5] asserted:

> The combined evidence of the bottom line, the hard listen and the long view is difficult to resist: Jackson is the biggest thing since the Beatles. He is the hottest single phenomenon since Elvis Presley. He just may be the most popular black singer ever.[2]

And still they missed it.

Harrington was to the point in noting that the breathtakingly styled music of *Thriller* wasn't a breakthrough in itself, and that "Michael Jackson is far more popular than influential (again more like Elvis, rather than the Beatles)." But *Time*'s Jay Cocks came closer to the pith of the moment in observing that

> *Thriller* brought black music back to mainstream radio, from which it had been effectively banished after restrictive "special-format program-ming" was introduced in the mid-'70s. Listeners could put more carbona-tion in their pop and cut their heavy-metal diet with a dose of the fleetest soul around. "No doubt about it," says composer-arranger Quincy Jones, who produced *Off the Wall* and *Thriller* with Jackson. "He's taken us right up there where we belong. Black music had to play second fiddle for a long time, but its spirit is the whole motor of pop. Michael has connected with every soul in the world."[3]

But neither analysis detected the fault lines deep in the crust of popular cul-ture that happened to intersect with the frail black performer's mercurial rise. Michael Jackson the earthquake struck where the emerging entertainment-information economy met the mother-seam of color at the core of American popular culture. At the epicenter, on the surface, was the thing called pop.

Pop, as a music-industry (as opposed to musical) category, had always been a euphemism for *white* until Michael unleashed "the power of *Thriller*." For example, Chuck Berry, for all his classic hit songs and unimpeachable claim to rock and roll's paternity, landed only one number-one pop single in his career, and that was at the end, with the novelty tune "My Dingaling" in 1972. In the 1960s and 1970s, the biggest Motown acts, the Bacharach-David-produced Dionne Warwick hits, and a few black bands like Earth, Wind and Fire garnered black performers their first significant "crossover" spots on the pop charts, but most black acts could aspire only to *Billboard*'s rhythm-and-blues chart.[4] As part of the Jackson Five, Michael Jackson had been one of the exceptions to the in-dustry practices that limited black access to the pop charts. Between 1970 and 1976, the group had landed seven singles in the pop top ten.

---

[2]Richard Harrington, "WHO IS HE? Somewhere over the Rainbow with the Enigma of the '80s," *Washington Post*, March 18, 1984.

[3]Jay Cocks, "Why He's a Thriller: Michael Jackson's Songs, Steps and Sexy Aura Set a Flashy Beat for the Decade," *Time*, March 19, 1984.

[4]In 1982, in a bow to nascent political correctness, *Billboard* renamed the rhythm-and blues chart the "black music" chart.

Yet for nonwhite performers, even holding precious slots on the pop charts did not a pop star make. Until *Thriller* the unofficial "King" or "Queen of Pop" had always been white, no matter how many records a black artist sold or how much airplay it got.

American pop, as it turned out, is more than an industry chart. True pop   10
icon status, at the very top, is a state of grace that approaches divine right over one's consumer-subjects in the marketplace. It's a cross between being royalty and being in the top management of mainstream affinity, complete with rituals of respect, ceremonies of adoration, and titles. Pop is what Elvis was after he stopped his initial blues shouting and let Colonel Parker make him the perfect (but not too perfect) heartthrob for white teenage girls as the 1950s became the 1960s. He was the "King." Pop is the firm Sinatra controlled before Elvis, and for many Americans over a certain age, he remained the "Chairman" until the day he died. By the time your parents could be seen nodding in agreement with their peers that "I Want to Hold Your Hand" was really classically inspired, it was the Beatles, one of whom (Paul McCartney) was actually knighted by the queen. Pop is the universal white blue-collar factory that Bruce Springsteen ran in the late 1970s and into the 1980s. He was "the Boss."

To be sure, there were titles enough to go around in the marginal kingdoms of R&B and soul and gospel and Latin music: Aretha Franklin — Queen, James Brown — Godfather, Celia Cruz — Queen of Salsa, and so on. Still, no nonwhites needed to apply for mainstream pop music honorifics as the 1970s became the 1980s. Ditto, with a few notable exceptions, pop positions in television, movies, and (significantly) fashion and style. Bill Cosby, Coke's primary general-market pitchman in the 1970s, also sold well for Jell-O and Ford. O. J. Simpson broke entirely new ground for retired black professional athletes with his ubiquitous Hertz commercials. But neither man would be recognized or recognizable as a pop icon until the early 1990s, and not just because they had yet to star in their respective hit television shows. Until Michael Jackson and *Thriller*, marketers simply assumed that no matter how successful a nonwhite performer might be, whiteness was an indispensable requirement for the exaggerated state of mass identification that constitutes "pop stardom."

Then Roger Enrico bet the farm on Michael Jackson and *Thriller* — and won.

As the 1980s began, the business of whiteness-centered pop was, as usual, lurching between cyclical feast and famine. But by the decade's end, the same forces that brought *Thriller*'s eruption would move whiteness from indispensable to merely useful in the business of pop, *permanently*, while raising the influence, the reach, and most important, the aggregate profitability of pop entertainment to unimagined heights. By 1990 America's collective pop culture, bonded to the cutting edge of a revolution in telecommunications and information technology, had assumed the lead role in the world's most powerful global economy. Think about it: In 1980 the business of pop could not have imagined the multidimensional marketing star power of Michael Jackson, Michael Jordan, Whitney Houston, or Eddie Murphy. It hadn't seen the platinum branding of predominantly nonwhite professional basketball, football, and baseball or the "Nike-ization" of marketing that attended it. It hadn't even seen a hint of the multibillion-dollar music-fashion-style-literature industry called hip-hop. In other words, in 1980 American commercial popular culture hadn't seen nothing yet.

By the late 1980s, what began with the specific case of Michael Jackson's crossover from the *Billboard* rhythm-and-blues chart to the pop chart had become a much broader and yet diffuse phenomenon whose substance was hard to pin down and whose political authority was negligible. Color was weaving through music, sports, television, movies, news media, and literature in a bold band that had never been seen before. It was the sixty-three-year-old Miss America color line broken four times in one decade. (Okay, Suzette Charles was only runner-up to Vanessa Williams until Williams was forced to abdicate, but she still wore the crown.) It was double takes on top of double takes at what people of color could almost routinely be seen doing or be heard saying on television. It was that megawatt moment at the 1990 MTV awards when Madonna, flanked by her black backup singers, snapped her fingers three times while describing the letter Z in the air with that just-so flick of the wrist, and the dismissive gesture crossed over from sisters in "the hood" to the world at the speed of light, without a word uttered in any language but soul.

But most of all it was selling. By the end of the 1980s a potent new distillation of commercial popular culture was everywhere on the rise: modern brand marketing. At the same time that nonwhite singers, athletes, writers, actors, and others crossed racial lines into the mainstream culture, the lines separating sport, singing, dance, drama, writing, fashion, journalism, and comedy began to blur into a larger phenomenon called "infotainment." Every once-discrete form of popular entertainment and information culture, and much high culture too, began boiling down to the common denominator of logos, labels, icons, and celebrities, four plural nouns that in turn boil down to just one thing: brands. By something more than coincidence, nonwhite individuals in general and urban- (read: black-, Hispanic-, or Asian-) identified cultural forms in particular became basic, and sometimes indispensable, elements in establishing or building brands.

READING THE TEXT

1. What is the purpose behind beginning the essay with the anecdote about Jesse Jackson?
2. What does Wynter mean by "an orgy of 'who is he and who are we as a society' journalistic navel-gazing" (para. 4)?

3. What does Wynter see as the long-term significance of the success of *Thriller*?

4. Why does Wynter believe the media "missed" the real implications of Michael Jackson's success?

READING THE SIGNS

1. In class, brainstorm a list of pop artists whom you consider icons. Then study the class list, and write your own essay evaluating Wynter's claim in paragraph 10: "True pop icon status, at the very top, is a state of grace that approaches divine right over one's consumer-subjects in the marketplace." To develop your analysis, conduct an online survey of the endorsement deals that stars on the class list have arranged and evaluate their potency in the consumer market.

2. This selection ends with a broad assertion: "nonwhite individuals in general and urban- (read: black-, Hispanic-, or Asian-) identified cultural forms in particular became basic, and sometimes indispensable, elements in establishing or building brands" (para. 15). Write an essay in which you provide details that demonstrate, refute, or complicate this general statement. Base your essay on an analysis of specific brands and their ad campaigns.

3. In class, discuss Wynter's style and tone. Do you see his writing as productively dramatic or overly hyperbolic, and what effect does your response have on the persuasiveness of his argument?

4. Write an exploratory essay in which you present your own definition of what counts as pop in today's culture. You might base your essay on a random survey of people from varying ethnicities, genders, and age groups, to glean their viewpoints.

5. Assuming Wynter's perspective, write a response to Michael Omi's argument in "In Living Color: Race and American Culture" (p. 549). Do you think Wynter would concur with Omi's argument, or do you think he would modify or update it?

6. Wynter writes, "To be sure, there were titles enough to go around in the marginal kingdoms of R&B and soul and gospel and Latin music" (para. 11). Research the status of such music in the 1960s and 1970s, and write an essay in which you support, refute, or complicate his depiction of such genres as "marginal."

BENJAMIN DeMOTT

Put on a Happy Face: Masking the Differences between Blacks and Whites

By looking at the movies, you'd think that race relations in the United States were in splendid shape. Just look at Danny Glover and Mel Gibson in the Lethal Weapon *movies, or consider* Driving Miss Daisy. *But according to Benjamin DeMott (1924–2005), things are not so rosy. In fact, DeMott argues in this essay that Hollywood has effectively concealed the true state of American racial politics behind a pleasing façade of black and white happy-faces, and so has inadvertently worked to distract movie audiences from the pressing need to improve our racial climate. A writer whose interests include the media and American racial and class politics, DeMott's books include* Created Equal: Reading and Writing about Class in America *(1985),* The Imperial Middle: Why Americans Can't Think Straight about Class *(1990),* The Trouble with Friendship: Why Americans Can't Think Straight about Race *(1995),* Killer Woman Blues: Why Americans Can't Think Straight about Gender and Power *(2000), and* Junk Politics: The Trashing of the American Mind *(2004).*

At the movies these days, questions about racial injustice have been amicably resolved. Watch *Pulp Fiction* or *Congo* or *A Little Princess* or any other recent film in which both blacks and whites are primary characters and you can, if you want, forget about race. Whites and blacks greet one another on the screen with loving candor, revealing their common humanity. In *Pulp Fiction*, an armed black mobster (played by Samuel L. Jackson) looks deep into the eyes of an armed white thief in the middle of a holdup (played by Tim Roth) and shares his version of God's word in Ezekiel, whereupon the two men lay aside their weapons, both more or less redeemed. The moment inverts an earlier scene in which a white boxer (played by Bruce Willis) risks his life to save another black mobster (played by Ving Rhames), who is being sexually tortured as a prelude to his execution.

Pulp Fiction (gross through July [1995]: $107 million) is one of a series of films suggesting that the beast of American racism is tamed and harmless. Close to the start of *Die Hard with a Vengeance* (gross through July [1995]: $95 million) the camera finds a white man wearing sandwich boards on the corner of Amsterdam Avenue and 138th Street in Harlem. The boards carry a horrific legend: I HATE NIGGERS. A group of young blacks approach the man with murderous intent, bearing guns and knives. They are figures straight out of a national nightmare — ugly, enraged, terrifying. No problem. A black man, again played by Jackson, appears and rescues the white man, played by Willis. The black man and white man come to know each other well. In time the white man declares flatly to the black, "I need you more than you need me." A moment later he charges the black with being a racist — with not liking whites as much as the white man likes blacks — and the two talk frankly about their racial prejudices. Near the end of the film, the men have grown so close that each volunteers to die for the other.

Pulp Fiction and *Die Hard with a Vengeance* follow the pattern of *Lethal Weapon 1, 2,* and *3*, the Danny Glover/Mel Gibson buddy vehicles that collectively grossed $357 million, and *White Men Can't Jump*, which, in the year of the L.A. riots, grossed $76 million. In *White Men Can't Jump*, a white dropout, played by Woody Harrelson, ekes out a living on black-dominated basketball courts in Los Angeles. He's arrogant and aggressive but never in danger because he has a black protector and friend, played by Wesley Snipes. At the movie's end, the white, flying above the hoop like a stereotypical black player, scores the winning basket in a two-on-two pickup game on an alley-oop pass from his black chum, whereupon the two men fall into each other's arms in joy. Later, the black friend agrees to find work for the white at the store he manages.

WHITE (helpless): I gotta get a job. Can you get me a job?
BLACK (affectionately teasing): Got any references?
WHITE (shy grin): You.

Such dialogue is the stuff of romance. What's dreamed of and gained is a place where whites are unafraid of blacks, where blacks ask for and need nothing from whites, and where the sameness of the races creates a common fund of sweet content.[1] The details of the dream matter less than the force that makes it come true for both races, eliminating the constraints of objective reality and redistributing resources, status, and capabilities. That cleansing social force supersedes political and economic fact or policy; that force, improbably enough, is friendship.

Watching the beaming white men who know how to jump, we do well to   5
remind ourselves of what the camera shot leaves out. Black infants die in America at twice the rate of white infants. (Despite the increased numbers of middle-class blacks, the rates are diverging, with black rates actually rising.)

---

[1] I could go on with examples of movies that deliver the good news of friendship: *Regarding Henry, Driving Miss Daisy, Forrest Gump, The Shawshank Redemption, Philadelphia, The Last Boy Scout, 48 Hours I–II, Rising Sun, Iron Eagle I–II, Rudy, Sister Act, Hearts of Dixie, Betrayed, The Power of One, White Nights, Clara's Heart, Doc Hollywood, Cool Runnings, Places in the Heart, Trading Places, Fried Green Tomatoes, Q & A, Platoon, A Mother's Courage: The Mary Thomas Story, The Unforgiven, The Air Up There, The Pelican Brief, Losing Isaiah, Smoke, Searching for Bobby Fischer, An Officer and a Gentleman, Speed,* etc.

One out of every two black children lives below the poverty line (as compared with one out of seven white children). Nearly four times as many black families exist below the poverty line as white families. More than 50 percent of African American families have incomes below $25,000. Among black youths under age twenty, death by murder occurs nearly ten times as often as among whites. Over 60 percent of births to black mothers occur out of wedlock, more than four times the rate for white mothers. The net worth of the typical white household is ten times that of the typical black household. In many states, five to ten times as many blacks as whites age eighteen to thirty are in prison.

The good news at the movies obscures the bad news in the streets and confirms the Supreme Court's . . . decisions on busing, affirmative action, and redistricting. Like the plot of *White Men Can't Jump*, the Court postulates the existence of a society no longer troubled by racism. Because black-white friendship is now understood to be the rule, there is no need for integrated schools or a congressional Black Caucus or affirmative action. The Congress and state governors can guiltlessly cut welfare, food assistance, fuel assistance, Head Start, housing money, fellowship money, vaccine money. Justice Anthony Kennedy can declare, speaking for the Supreme Court majority last June [1995], that creating a world of genuine equality and sameness requires only that "our political system and our society cleanse themselves . . . of discrimination."

The deep logic runs as follows: *Yesterday white people didn't like black people, and accordingly suffered guilt, knowing that the dislike was racist and knowing also that as moral persons they would have to atone for the guilt. They would have to ante up for welfare and Head Start and halfway houses and free vaccine and midnight basketball and summer jobs for schoolkids and graduate fellowships for promising scholars and craft-union apprenticeships and so on, endlessly. A considerable and wasteful expense. But at length came the realization that by ending dislike or hatred it would be possible to end guilt, which in turn would mean an end to redress: no more wasteful ransom money. There would be but one requirement: the regular production and continuous showing forth of evidence indisputably proving that hatred has totally vanished from the land.*

I cannot tell the reader how much I would like to believe in this sunshine world. After the theater lights brighten and I've found coins for a black beggar on the way to my car and am driving home through downtown Springfield, Massachusetts, the world invented by *Die Hard with a Vengeance* and America's highest court gives way only slowly to the familiar urban vision in my windshield — homeless blacks on trash-strewn streets, black prostitutes staked out on a corner, and signs of a not very furtive drug trade. I know perfectly well that most African Americans don't commit crimes or live in alleys. I also know that for somebody like myself, downtown Springfield in the late evening is not a good place to be.

The movies reflect the larger dynamic of wish and dream. Day after day the nation's corporate ministries of culture churn out images of racial harmony. Millions awaken each morning to the friendly sight of Katie Couric nudging a perky elbow into good buddy Bryant Gumbel's side. My mailbox and millions of demographically similar others are choked with flyers from companies (Wal-Mart, Victoria's Secret) bent on publicizing both their wares and their social bona fides by displaying black and white models at cordial ease with one another. A torrent of goodwill messages about race arrives daily — revelations of corporate largesse, commercials, news features, TV specials, all proclaiming that whites like me feel strongly positive impulses of friendship for blacks and that those same admirable impulses are effectively eradicating racial differences, rendering blacks and whites the same. BellSouth TV commercials present children singing "I am the keeper of the world" — first a white child, then a black child, then a white child, then a black child. Because Dow Chemical likes black America, it recruits young black college grads for its research division and dramatizes, in TV commercials, their tearful-joyful partings from home. ("Son, show 'em what you got," says a black lad's father.) American Express shows an elegant black couple and an elegant white couple sitting together in a theater, happy in one another's company. (The couples share the box with an oversized Gold Card.) During the evening news I watch a black mom offer Robitussin to a miserably coughing white mom. Here's *People* magazine promoting itself under a photo of John Lee Hooker, the black bluesman. "We're these kinds of people, too," *People* claims in the caption. In [a recent] production of *Hamlet* on Broadway, Horatio [was] played by a black actor. On *The 700 Club*, Pat Robertson joshes Ben Kinchlow, his black sidekick, about Ben's far-out ties.

What counts here is not the saccharine clumsiness of the interchanges 10 but the bulk of them — the ceaseless, self-validating gestures of friendship, the humming, buzzing background theme: *All decent Americans extend the hand of friendship to African Americans; nothing but nothing is more auspicious for the African American future than this extended hand.* Faith in the miracle cure of racism by change-of-heart turns out to be so familiar as to have become unnoticeable. And yes, the faith has its benign aspect. Even as they nudge me and others toward belief in magic (instant pals and no-money-down equality), the images and messages of devoted relationships between blacks and whites do exert a humanizing influence.

Nonetheless, through these same images and messages the comfortable majority tells itself a fatuous untruth. Promoting the fantasy of painless answers, inspiring groundless self-approval among whites, joining the Supreme Court in treating "cleansing" as *inevitable,* the new orthodoxy of friendship incites culture-wide evasion, justifies one political step backward after another, and greases the skids along which, tomorrow, welfare block grants will slide into state highway-resurfacing budgets. Whites are part of the solution, says this orthodoxy, if we break out of the prison of our skin color, say hello, as equals, one-on-one, to a black stranger, and make a black friend. We're part of the problem if we have an aversion to black people or are frightened of them, or if we feel that the more distance we put between them and us the better, or if we're in the habit of asserting our superiority rather than acknowledging our common humanity. Thus we shift the problem away from politics — from black experience and the history of slavery — and perceive it as a matter of the suspicion and fear found within the white heart; solving the problem asks no more of us than that we work on ourselves, scrubbing off the dirt of ill will.

The approach miniaturizes, personalizes, and moralizes; it removes the large and complex dilemmas of race from the public sphere. It tempts audiences to see history as irrelevant and to regard feelings as decisive — to believe that the fate of black Americans is shaped mainly by events occurring in the hearts and minds of the privileged. And let's be frank: the orthodoxy of friendship feels *nice*. It practically *consecrates* self-flattery. The "good" Bill Clinton who attends black churches and talks with likable ease to fellow worshipers was campaigning when Los Angeles rioted in '92. "White Americans," he said, "are gripped by the isolation of their own experience. Too many still simply have no friends of other races and do not know any differently." Few black youths of working age in South-Central L.A. had been near enough to the idea of a job even to think of looking for work before the Rodney King verdict, but the problem, according to Clinton, was that whites need black friends.

Most of the country's leading voices of journalistic conscience (editorial writers, television anchorpersons, syndicated columnists) roundly endorse the doctrine of black-white friendship as a means of redressing the inequalities between the races. Roger Rosenblatt, editor of the *Columbia Journalism Review* and an especially deft supplier of warm and fuzzy sentiment, published an essay in *Family Circle* arguing that white friendship and sympathy for blacks simultaneously make power differentials vanish and create interracial identity between us, one by one. The author finds his *exemplum* in an episode revealing the personal sensitivity, to injured blacks, of one of his children.

"When our oldest child, Carl, was in high school," he writes, "he and two black friends were standing on a street corner in New York City one spring evening, trying to hail a taxi. The three boys were dressed decently and were doing nothing wild or threatening. Still, no taxi would pick them up. If a driver spotted Carl first, he might slow down, but he would take off again when he saw the others. Carl's two companions were familiar with this sort of abuse. Carl, who had never observed it firsthand before, burned with anger and embarrassment that he was the color of a world that would so mistreat his friends."

Rosenblatt notes that when his son "was applying to colleges, he wrote his essay on that taxi incident with his two black friends. . . . He was able to articulate what he could not say at the time — how ashamed and impotent he

15

felt. He also wrote of the power of their friendship, which has lasted to this day and has carried all three young men into the country that belongs to them. To all of us."

In this homily white sympathy begets interracial sameness in several ways. The three classmates are said to react identically to the cabdrivers' snub; i.e., they feel humiliated. "[Carl] could not find the words to express his humiliation and his friends *would* not express theirs."

The anger that inspires the younger Rosenblatt's college-admission essay on racism is seen as identical with black anger. Friendship brings the classmates together as joint, equal owners of the land of their birth ("the country that belongs to [all of] them"). And Rosenblatt supplies a still larger vision of essential black-white sameness near the end of his essay: "Our proper hearts tell the truth," he declares, "which is that we are all in the same boat, rich and poor, black and white. We are helpless, wicked, heroic, terrified, and we need one another. We need to give rides to one another."

Thus do acts of private piety substitute for public policy while the possibility of urgent political action disappears into a sentimental haze. "If we're looking for a formula to ease the tensions between the races," Rosenblatt observes, then we should "attack the disintegration of the black community" and "the desperation of the poor." Without overtly mocking civil rights activists who look toward the political arena "to erase the tensions," Rosenblatt alludes to them in a throwaway manner, implying that properly adjusted whites look elsewhere, that there was a time for politicking for "equal rights" but we've passed through it. Now is a time in which we should listen to our hearts at moments of epiphany and allow sympathy to work its wizardry, cleansing and floating us, blacks and whites "all in the same boat," on a mystical undercurrent of the New Age.

Blacks themselves aren't necessarily proof against this theme, as witness a recent essay by James Alan McPherson in the Harvard journal *Reconstruction*. McPherson, who received the 1977 Pulitzer Prize for fiction for his collection of stories *Elbow Room,* says that "the only possible steps, the safest steps . . . small ones" in the movement "toward a universal culture" will be those built not on "ideologies and formulas and programs" but on experiences of personal connectedness.

"Just this past spring," he writes, "when I was leaving a restaurant after [20] taking a [white] former student to dinner, a black [woman on the sidewalk] said to my friend, in a rasping voice, 'Hello, girlfriend. Have you got anything to spare?' " The person speaking was a female crack addict with a child who was also addicted. "But," writes McPherson, when the addict made her pitch to his dinner companion, "I saw in my friend's face an understanding and sympathy and a shining which transcended race and class. Her face reflected one human soul's connection with another. The magnetic field between the two women was charged with spiritual energy."

The writer points the path to progress through interpersonal gestures by people who "insist on remaining human, and having human responses. . . .

Perhaps the best that can be done, now, is the offering of understanding and support to the few out of many who are capable of such gestures, rather than devising another plan to engineer the many into one."

The elevated vocabulary ("soul," "spiritual") beatifies the impulse to turn away from the real-life agenda of actions capable of reducing racial injustice. Wherever that impulse dominates, the rhetoric of racial sameness thrives, diminishing historical catastrophes affecting millions over centuries and inflating the significance of tremors of tenderness briefly troubling the heart or conscience of a single individual — the boy waiting for a cab, the woman leaving the restaurant. People forget the theoretically unforgettable — the caste history of American blacks, the connection between no schools for longer than a century and bad school performance now, between hateful social attitudes and zero employment opportunities, between minority anguish and majority fear.

How could this way of seeing have become conventional so swiftly? How did the dogmas of instant equality insinuate themselves so effortlessly into courts and mass audiences alike? How can a white man like myself, who taught Southern blacks in the 1960s, find himself seduced — as I have been more than once — by the orthodoxy of friendship? In the civil rights era, the experience for many millions of Americans was one of discovery. A hitherto unimagined continent of human reality and history came into view, inducing genuine concern and at least a temporary setting aside of self-importance. I remember with utter clarity what I felt at Mary Holmes College in West Point, Mississippi, when a black student of mine was killed by tailgating rednecks; my fellow tutors and I were overwhelmed with how shamefully wrong a wrong could be. For a time, we were released from the prisons of moral weakness and ambiguity. In the year or two that followed — the mid-Sixties — the notion that some humans are more human than others, whites more human than blacks, appeared to have been overturned. The next step seemed obvious: society would have to admit that when one race deprives another of its humanity for centuries, those who have done the depriving are obligated to do what they can to restore the humanity of the deprived. The obligation clearly entailed the mounting of comprehensive *long-term* programs of developmental assistance — not guilt-money handouts — for nearly the entire black population. The path forward was unavoidable.

It was avoided. Shortly after the award of civil rights and the institution, in 1966, of limited preferential treatment to remedy employment and educational discrimination against African Americans, a measure of economic progress for blacks did appear in census reports. Not much, but enough to stimulate glowing tales of universal black advance and to launch the good-news barrage that continues to this day (headline in the *New York Times*, June 18, 1995: "Moving on Up: The Greening of America's Black Middle Class").

After Ronald Reagan was elected to his first term, the new dogma of 25 black-white sameness found ideological support in the form of criticism of so-called coddling. Liberal activists of both races were berated by critics of both races for fostering an allegedly enfeebling psychology of dependency that discouraged African Americans from committing themselves to individual self-development. In 1988, the charge was passionately voiced in an essay in these pages, "I'm Black, You're White, Who's Innocent?" by Shelby Steele, who attributed the difference between black rates of advance and those of other minority groups to white folks' pampering. Most blacks, Steele claimed, could make it on their own — as voluntary immigrants have done — were they not held back by devitalizing programs that presented them, to themselves and others, as somehow dissimilar to and weaker than other Americans. This argument was all-in-the-same-boatism in a different key; the claim remained that progress depends upon recognition of black-white sameness. Let us see through superficial differences to the underlying, equally distributed gift for success. Let us teach ourselves — in the words of the Garth Brooks tune — to ignore "the color of skin" and "look for . . . the beauty within."

Still further support for the policy once known as "do-nothingism" came from points-of-light barkers, who held that a little something might perhaps be done *if* accompanied by enough publicity. Nearly every broadcaster and publisher in America moves a bale of reportage on pro bono efforts by white Americans to speed the advance of black Americans. Example: McDonald's and the National Basketball Association distribute balloons when they announce they are addressing the dropout problem with an annual "Stay in School" scheme that gives schoolkids who don't miss a January school day a ticket to an all-star exhibition. The publicity strengthens the idea that these initiatives will nullify the social context — the city I see through my windshield. Reports of white philanthropy suggest that the troubles of this block and the next should be understood as phenomena in transition. The condition of American blacks need not be read as the fixed, unchanging consequence of generations of bottom-caste existence. Edging discreetly past a beggar posted near the entrance to Zabar's or H&H Bagels, or, while walking the dog, stepping politely around black men asleep on the sidewalk, we need not see ourselves and our fellows as uncaring accomplices in the acts of social injustice.

Yet more powerful has been the ceaseless assault, over the past generation, on our knowledge of the historical situation of black Americans. On the face of things it seems improbable that the cumulative weight of documented historical injury to African Americans could ever be lightly assessed. Gifted black writers continue to show, in scene after scene — in their studies of middle-class blacks interacting with whites — how historical realities shape the lives of their black characters. In *Killer of Sheep*, the brilliant black filmmaker Charles Burnett dramatizes the daily encounters that suck poor blacks into will-lessness and contempt for white fairy tales of interracial harmony; he quickens his historical themes with images of faceless black meat processors gutting undifferentiated, unchoosing animal life. Here, say these images, as though talking back to Clarence Thomas, here is a basic level of black life unchanged over generations. Where there's work, it's miserably paid and ugly. Space allotments at home and at work cramp body and mind. Positive expectation withers in infancy. People fall into the habit of jeering at aspiration as though at the bidding of physical law. Obstacles at every hand prevent people from loving and being loved in decent ways, prevent children from believing their parents, prevent parents from believing they themselves know anything worth knowing. The only true self, now as in the long past, is the one mocked by one's own race. "Shit on you, nigger," says a voice in *Killer of Sheep*. "Nothing you say matters a good goddamn."

For whites, these words produce guilt, and for blacks, I can only assume, pain and despair. The audience for tragedy remains small, while at the multiplex the popular enthusiasm for historical romance remains constant and vast. During the last two decades, the entertainment industry has conducted a siege on the pertinent past, systematically excising knowledge of the consequences of the historical exploitation of African Americans. Factitious renderings of the American past blur the outlines of black-white conflict, redefine the ground of black grievances for the purpose of diminishing the grievances, restage black life in accordance with the illusory conventions of American success mythology, and present the operative influences on race history as the same as those implied to be pivotal in *White Men Can't Jump* or a Bell-South advertisement.

Although there was scant popular awareness of it at the time (1977), the television miniseries *Roots* introduced the figure of the Unscathed Slave. To an enthralled audience of more than 80 million the series intimated that the damage resulting from generations of birth-ascribed, semianimal status was largely temporary, that slavery was a product of motiveless malignity on the social margins rather than of respectable rationality, and that the ultimate significance of the institution lay in the demonstration, by freed slaves, that no force on earth can best the energies of American Individualism. ("Much like the Waltons confronting the depression," writes historian Eric Foner, a widely respected authority on American slavery, "the family in *Roots* neither seeks nor requires outside help; individual or family effort is always sufficient.") Ken Burns's much applauded PBS documentary *The Civil War* (1990) went even further than *Roots* in downscaling black injury; the series treated slavery, birth-ascribed inferiority, and the centuries-old denial of dignity as matters of slight consequence. (By "implicitly denying the brutal reality of slavery," writes historian Jeanie Attie, Burns's programs crossed "a dangerous moral threshold." To a group of historians who asked him why slavery had been so slighted, Burns said that any discussion of slavery "would have been lengthy and boring.")

Mass media treatments of the civil rights protest years carried forward 30 the process, contributing to the "positive" erasure of difference. Big-budget films like *Mississippi Burning,* together with an array of TV biographical specials on Dr. Martin Luther King and others, presented the long-running struggle between disenfranchised blacks and the majority white culture as a heartwarming episode of interracial unity; the speed and caringness of white response to the oppression of blacks demonstrated that broadscale race conflict or race difference was inconceivable.

A consciousness that ingests either a part or the whole of this revisionism loses touch with the two fundamental truths of race in America; namely, that because of what happened in the past, blacks and whites cannot yet be the same; and that because what happened in the past was no mere matter of ill will or insult but the outcome of an established caste structure that has only very recently begun to be dismantled, it is not reparable by one-on-one goodwill. The word "slavery" comes to induce stock responses with no vital sense of a grinding devastation of mind visited upon generation after generation. Hoodwinked by the orthodoxy of friendship, the nation either ignores the past, summons for it a detached, correct "compassion," or gazes at it as though it were a set of aesthetic conventions, like twisted trees and fragmented rocks in nineteenth-century picturesque painting — lifeless phenomena without bearing on the present. The chance of striking through the mask of corporate-underwritten, feel-good, ahistorical racism grows daily more remote. The trade-off — whites promise friendship, blacks accept the status quo — begins to seem like a good deal.

Cosseted by Hollywood's magic lantern and soothed by press releases from Washington and the American Enterprise Institute, we should never forget what we see and hear for ourselves. Broken out by race, the results of every social tabulation from unemployment to life expectancy add up to a chronicle of atrocity. The history of black America fully explains — to anyone who approaches it honestly — how the disaster happened and why neither guilt money nor lectures on personal responsibility can, in and of themselves, repair the damage. The vision of friendship and sympathy placing blacks and whites "all in the same boat," rendering them equally able to do each other favors, "to give rides to one another," is a smiling but monstrous lie.

READING THE TEXT

1. How does DeMott view current race relations in America, and how have recent Hollywood films presented a distorted view of those relations?

2. How, in DeMott's view, do films represent the wish fulfillment of mainstream America?

3. What does DeMott see as the social effect of fantasy-laden images of happy race relations?

4. What does DeMott mean when he says that "acts of private piety substitute for public policy while the possibility of urgent political action disappears into a sentimental haze" (para. 18)?

5. How does DeMott interpret the depiction of slavery in productions such as *Roots* and *The Civil War*?

READING THE SIGNS

1. Watch a video or DVD of one of the films that DeMott discusses in his essay. Then write your own analysis of the race relations depicted in the film. To what extent do you find his claim that the film sugarcoats race relations to be valid? Alternatively, watch a more recent film and discuss whether you see evidence of the sugarcoating DeMott decries.

2. DeMott focuses on black-white relations in this essay. In class, discuss how other ethnicities, such as Latinos or Asian Americans, fit his argument. To develop your ideas, consult the introduction to this chapter.

3. DeMott is critical of the unrealistic portrayal of race relations in film. In your journal, explore whether you believe this lack of realism has a positive or negative impact on Americans' attitudes toward race.

4. DeMott contends that the same unrealistic friendships between the races appear in product catalogues and advertising. Select a favorite catalogue or magazine, and study the models populating the pages. Then write an essay in which you support, refute, or modify his contention.

5. If you were to produce a film that depicts current race relations in America, what sort of film would you create? Write a creative essay describing your film idea, then share it with your classmates.

PAUL C. TAYLOR

Funky White Boys and Honorary Soul Sisters

Can white boys really sing the blues? Or is Eric Clapton just a wannabe who's never paid his dues? For some black critics, the only way that Clapton, and other white performers of black cultural forms, could pay their dues would be to become black, but Paul C. Taylor (b. 1967) isn't so sure. Reflecting on his own youthful identification with white musicians and athletes whose mastery of black cultural activities qualified them for membership in what he called "the Funky White Boys Club," Taylor explains why many blacks are uncomfortable with funky white boys (and honorary white soul sisters). Taylor is an associate professor of philo-sophy at Temple University. He is the author of Race: A Philosophical Introduction *(2004).*

Question: What do Stevie Ray Vaughan, Larry Bird, and Phil Woods have in common? Answer: All were charter members of a club that I created when I was growing up. They didn't know this, of course; and the existence of the club says at least as much about me as it does about its members. It speaks, for example, to the existence of an impulse that found expression in other ways — in, for example, the all-star bands that I imagined to unite the likes of Louis Armstrong and Wynton Marsalis, Bird and Branford Marsalis; as well as in my attachment to comic books like *The Justice League of America*, featuring super-groups composed of heroes who otherwise flew solo. But the club I cre-ated wasn't just about me and my need to foster cooperation among my idols and heroes. It was also about something that its members had in common, a commonality indicated by the name they collectively bore: The Funky White Boys Club.

One became eligible for admission to the FWB by being a white person who excelled in a cultural practice that might plausibly be considered part of, or disproportionately shaped by or linked to, black culture. So the late blues-man Vaughan gained entry for his faithful extension of the guitar artistry of Albert King and Jimi Hendrix, Woods was honored for his reverent appropria-tion of Charlie Parker, and Larry Bird got in just because he was so damn *good* at basketball, never mind his stereotypically "white" playing style and over-whelmingly white team (tellingly, the *Celtics* of Boston). Creating the FWB was my way of marking and celebrating what seemed to me that most anomalous of circumstances: the existence of white people who violated the core assump-tions of commonsense racial logic and dared to do things white people weren't supposed to be capable of.

Eventually noticing that the FWB was indeed a boys club, I created a com-panion female group and inducted Bonnie Raitt and Martina Navratilova as charter members. But due either to a dearth of imagination or a loss of interest, I neglected to name the female group and soon neglected the whole project. That may have been the year when video killed the radio star and MTV was born, giving me more pleasantly mind-numbing ways to spend my time.

The clubs languished in the depths of my memory until fairly recently, when an article in *Vibe* magazine called them to my attention once again.[1] The article was an update on the R&B singer/bassist Teena Marie, a white woman who at one time was the protégée of Rick James. (James is the man who gave us — and, unfortunately, M. C. Hammer — the song "Superfreak" and then acted out the song in a series of encounters with the law. Luckily his, well, eccentricities form no part of our story here and won't be mentioned again.) The text of the piece was arrayed around a series of moody photographs of Marie, one of which bore the caption "honorary soul sister." When I saw this my mind made one of those instant and unmotivated associations that keep psychoanalysts in business and I realized that that should have been the name of the female funky white boys: the honorary soul sisters.

I found the name appropriate not only because, as I then remembered, 5 Marie was one of the early members of the group, but also because the title laid bare the curious nature of the venture I'd undertaken all those years ago, exposing assumptions that the expression "funky white boys" leaves submerged. Why is Teena Marie only an *honorary* soul sister? Why can't she be a real one? Clearly the answer lies in the other title. According to the dominant assumptions of commonsense racial logic, white boys aren't *supposed* to be funky, and white women aren't supposed to be soulful. Teena Marie is just honorary because she's white, and Stevie Ray Vaughan was funky despite being white. There is rather widespread agreement on these assumptions, as evidenced by the frequency with which one still encounters references to the stereotypical white person without rhythm. But it's much less clear what's behind the assumptions. Just what does race have to do with being soulful?

The *Vibe* article inspired these sorts of questions for me because I read it shortly after concluding an unsatisfactory print debate with another philosopher on a related topic, the question of whether white people can play the blues.[2] His position was that they can, despite claims to the contrary; my position was, and is, that *of course* they can, and that perhaps we'd be better served by looking into the motivation one might have for claiming the contrary. That debate put me in the habit of examining issues of race, culture, and authenticity, so I started to wonder about my youthful conviction that Stevie Ray Vaughan's status as a bluesman was merely honorary. In effect, the issue we'd pursued in the earlier debate was focused and narrowed into this question: What was I doing in those younger days when I created the clubs?

---

[1]Chuck Eddy, "Teena in Wonderland," *Vibe* magazine, November 1994.
[2]" . . . So Black and Blue: Response to Rudinow," *Journal of Aesthetics and Art Criticism* 53:3, 313–16, 1995.

Or: What is it about Teena Marie's whiteness that makes her only an *honorary* soul sister?

I'd like to share my thoughts on that topic, as well as on one other. I want to consider also what we should say about the urge to create Funky White Boys clubs. Is it a simple and indefensible racist impulse, relying on essentialist notions of racial characteristics and traits? Or is it something else?

1. Metaphysical Nationalism and the FWB

My clubs started with some rough but fairly reliable generalizations about race and culture. Here's one: By and large, black people tend to participate jointly in distinctive forms of life. This is a claim that sociology can bear out and that history can explain. More important, it is a claim that is neither contradicted nor undermined by the remarkable variety of lives and styles that black people can inhabit. People always say that no two snowflakes are alike, but if they had nothing in common we wouldn't call them both snowflakes. Both are tiny bits of crystalized water, a fact which is prior to all of the very real differences between them. They differ widely within a certain sphere of commonality: there is unity underlying the diversity. The same is true of black people — by which I mean "African-descended peoples in the Americas." Or, alternatively, to paraphrase a definition from W. E. B. Du Bois, "those people who would have had to ride the Jim Crow car in Georgia had they been there in 1940."[3]

By and large, black people speak or at least understand cognate cultural and experiential languages, whatever our many regional, political, religious, ethnic, or individual differences. This is what struck me as a youth. I knew that my black friends differed from my white friends, that they listened to different music and ate different foods and spoke differently: I had seen it and heard it myself. I knew they aspired to different styles of play on the basketball court after school; I knew that this Bud Powell fellow I'd started listening to was playing in a way that my white piano teachers never mentioned, much less demonstrated.

Knowing these things I drew a conclusion: white people who do things the way we do must have a special status, because most white people don't, or can't. And this conclusion led me to another rough but reliable generalization: By and large, white people are unable to participate in or appreciate black cultural practices. So in the same way that John Turturro's character in Spike Lee's *Do the Right Thing* exempts Magic Johnson and Prince from blackness because they're somehow special, my young mind exempted from whiteness the white people who could participate in black culture. They became honorary black folk, almost. No longer just white boys, but *funky* white boys.

---

[3]See W. E. B. Du Bois, *Dusk of Dawn* (1940; New Brunswick: Transaction Press, 1984), 153.

Now, rough but reliable generalizations may suffer one of two fates when stored in an active and curious mind. On the one hand, they may be complicated by additional conditions and have the limits of their reliability precisely marked. This is what happened in my case. When I learned about class differences within and across races, about regional cultural variation and so forth, I realized that whatever I said about The Race was going to be riddled with exceptions and conditions except at a very lofty level of abstraction, and that whatever I said was going to have to answer to the evidence of history and sociology.

On the other hand, the generalizations may be rigidified into necessary truths and the observations which motivate them rendered inevitable. This happens to the points I started with when they are taken up into the framework of a certain kind of cultural nationalism. Cultural nationalism is in part the view that all black people participate in a common form of life, that we share a disposition to enjoy and create the same cultural forms, the same modes of speech and movement, expression and performance. For a cultural nationalist, the possibility of both a vibrant black community and a sane, settled individual black identity rest principally upon one thing: the existence of a coherent, identifiable, *distinct* set of black cultural practices. For the nationalist, "black English" and "black art" and "black music" have to be meaningful expressions, marking some important boundaries. And the behaviors inside the boundaries have to add up to a distinctive culture.

So far the nationalist position is consistent with the mindset that motivated my clubs. But a truly committed nationalist goes farther. A committed nationalist on the model of Molefi Asante hardens my rough generalizations into metaphysical and ethical principles in his search for something deeper and more reliable than the contingencies of history to underwrite the unity of black culture. The metaphysical principle is *essentialism*, which in this context entails that *it is of the nature* of black people, completely apart from considerations of history and sociology, to produce certain forms of life. The list of adjectives used in describing that life ought to be familiar. We favor rhythm over melody, it says; organic unities over dualist bifurcations, blues scales over Greek modes, improvisation over scripting, and so forth and so on. On this view black people naturally and *necessarily* gravitate toward certain cultural forms simply because that's what it is to be black.

The ethical principle has to do with *authenticity*, and like the metaphysical principle from which it follows, hardens a rough generalization into dogma. The generalization, you'll recall, was that white people tend not to be able to participate in or enjoy black cultural practices. Essentialism rigidifies this generalization about how capacities *tend* to be distributed into an airtight claim of necessity, the claim that all black people and only black people can participate in black culture because black cultural practices express the nature of black people. The authenticity principle takes the claim about capacity, about what certain people *can* do, and turns it into a claim about permission, about what certain people *may* do. Not only, it turns out, are white people not able to take part in black culture; they are not even allowed to try. (Perhaps this is the sort of slip that English teachers are trying to help us avoid with their fussiness about the distinction between "may" and "can.")

There is another element to the ethics of committed nationalism, the idea 15 of racial *obligation*. This idea follows also from a plausible generalization, this time the point that if the people who created a culture don't maintain it by continued participation, chances are it will die out. The committed nationalist takes this simple point and turns it into a moral imperative. Black people, he argues, should participate in their culture; those who don't are shirking an obligation to the race. As an added incentive, the nationalist I have in mind is likely to point out that the moral error of opting out of the culture carries with it the prospect of psychological ruin, as the unscrupulous negro loses touch with her true identity and, on Asante's version of this account, "loses her center." The notion of cultural-racial obligation provides some additional support for the exclusionary rhetoric of authenticity: white people are in the same position with regard to their own culture, facing the same psychological and moral dangers, and so should worry about their own ways of life instead of dabbling elsewhere. Instead of interfering with our culture they should be contributing to their own.

Let's get clear on the plausible claims behind (way behind) what I've been calling committed cultural nationalism. For one thing, there are regularities in the practices of black diaspora cultures. For another, it does seem to be a good thing for black people to participate in these cultures, good, that is, for both the people and the practices. The individual participants are able to draw existential sustenance from and take shelter in the symbolic and meaningful practices of their cultures, while the cultures themselves are able to persist and proliferate. (Although in this age of pluralism and global consumer culture there is less danger of a cultural form dying out if its original participants neglect it. Blues music, for example, is more likely to die out these days if white people start to neglect it, since many blacks have already consigned it to the dustbin of history.) The difficulty with committed cultural nationalism is that it tries to find some otherworldly support for these plausible ideas.

In particular, this nationalism tries to find some basis for black cultural continuity that's deeper than culture, than history, than the empirical striving and effort of concrete human beings, and as a result culture turns out not to be very important after all. Perhaps a better name for the view would be *metaphysical nationalism,* because it requires invoking an elaborate and unnecessary metaphysical apparatus to make sense of perfectly natural facts. Sociology, anthropology, history, and politics are more than adequate to account for the continuities that interest the nationalist. We just don't *need* to conjure up an elaborate metaphysics to explain the extent to which black people are, culturally and otherwise, *a* people. To do so is a bit like using an atom bomb to kill a housefly. But questions of explanatory adequacy aside, it is simply more interesting to point out the concrete, historical linkages that connect santeria to West Africa, King Sunny Ade to James Brown, than to trace them all to a single transhistorical essence. It is far more impressive for people to remember their roots themselves and create *themselves* despite the fetters of oppression and forced forgetfulness than it is for them to serve as the vehicles of a transcendent racial essence.

As we saw above, metaphysical nationalism also provides an ontological grounding for racial exclusivism, for the claim that all and *only* black people can participate in black culture. From this perspective Teena Marie is an honorary soul sister because she gets close to the core styles and conventions of R&B. The same holds true for Stevie Ray Vaughan and blues performance. But these performers will never be more than honorary because they're not truly expressing their deepest essences. That is to say, to participate truly and fully in the practice is to express the essence that manifests itself in the practice, and white people simply don't have the essence to express. On this view Vaughan is just imitating Albert King; Phil Woods is just imitating Charlie Parker. And if you listen closely, some people say, you can tell the difference. Never mind that white performers in black idioms or styles are not always mimics, or the possibility that any alleged categorical difference between white and black performances may simply be an overzealous interpretation of stylistic differences between individual performers. And never mind that we could account for any discernible categorical difference that *did* arise by referring to culture, to the lower probability that a white person will be socialized into the communities where the conventions of performance are taught and learned.

As we also saw above, the ethical dimensions of metaphysical nationalism can lead to an exclusivist posture by supporting the claim that even if white people can participate in black styles, they *shouldn't* do so. From this perspective Teena Marie is honorary because she's treading on what is by rights someone else's cultural turf. The honor of (almost-) soul sister status is extended as a grant of permission, and participation without it is immoral. But the frailty of nationalist metaphysics undermines this point as well. Without the metaphysics that link the racial essence to its cultural manifestation there is no reason to assume that the boundaries of culture and the boundaries of race are coextensive. Without the metaphysics there is no reason not to let Bonnie Raitt or Eric Clapton carry on the blues aspect of black culture. And even apart from the historical and sociological considerations I've mentioned above, there seems to be little reason to accept the metaphysics of racial essences. That is, on the evidence of the biological sciences alone, evidence that has been steadily mounting for some time, especially in this century, the idea that race membership as a matter of physiology somehow carries with it interesting moral and cultural traits seems to be a pernicious fiction.

Blues legend Stevie Ray Vaughan.

2. Aesthetics Instead of Authenticity

I want to distance both my present self and my thirteen-year-old self from 20
metaphysical nationalism and its excesses. All those years ago I hadn't yet
thought out the possible theoretical extensions of the commonsense racial
logic I'd accepted. Having done so now, I reject them. Metaphysical nationalism is too timid and narrow; it downplays the wonderful diversity and creativity of African diaspora cultures — with an "s" — and of the concrete, historically located people who've created reggae, R&B, hard bop, and hip-hop. And
worst of all for our present purposes, it stands in the way of explaining how
we can reasonably make judgments like the ones behind the title of "honorary

soul sister." The metaphysical nationalist approach makes these judgments just as inappropriate and ungrounded as any other racist exclusion. Either whites are just naturally incapable or black culture is just naturally off limits.

But having rejected the metaphysical/ethical route to racial exclusivism, I need to offer some other motivation for the urge that led to my imagined clubs. I do this not just to defend myself (although that's always fun) but also, and more importantly, because I want to displace and decenter the dialectic of essentialism-cum-racism. That is, I want to mark off a conceptual space within which we can examine assertions like "white people can't play the blues" without recourse to the vocabularies of essentialism *or* racism. I want us to be able to say something more interesting about the roots of these assertions than that the speaker is a racial essentialist and therefore a racist. This is important to me because I think relatively few of the people who make or presuppose assertions of the sort I have in mind are essentialists or racists. I don't think the FWB was a racist venture, nor do I think that of *Vibe* magazine's decision to use the expression "honorary soul sister." Luckily, there is a way to understand what I was up to, what the *Vibe* magazine people were up to, without slipping into the paralogisms of racial essences. There is a way to explain the urge to withhold or confer the status of funkiness and soulfulness without relying on the bare fact of race.

The approach I have in mind proceeds from yet another plausible and probably familiar idea, especially familiar when it comes to black music, that I'll call *the Elvis Effect*. When white participation in traditionally black avenues of cultural production produces feelings of unease, this is the Elvis Effect. I could as easily call it the Benny Goodman, the Dave Brubeck, or the Vanilla Ice effect, because all follow the same pattern. Black people participate almost exclusively in a cultural practice, mostly untouched by the interest, interference, or acclaim of the white community. A white person finds his or her way into the practice, becomes proficient, and is "discovered" by the white community. The community embraces the practice, but only in the person of the white "pioneer" who introduced it. It snaps up his records or copies his arrangements (or flocks to get cornrows, or lets its jeans sag around its knees), all the while oblivious to the fact that the true pioneers are probably still toiling in obscurity and poverty, and that the black community has probably moved on to something else that has yet to be "discovered."

Of course my brief description of phenomena that produce the Elvis Effect is a crude and over-simple rendering of complex historical events. For one thing it overlooks issues like the extent to which "white" country music and "black" blues grow from common southern roots that grew into people like Elvis as naturally as it did into, say, Muddy Waters; for another, it passes completely over the role of white record companies in preserving and promulgating black musical culture. But it isn't too crude to make the point. How else can we explain the fact that Benny Goodman gets movies made about him, gigs at Carnegie Hall, and the title of the king of swing, while we're still waiting for the movies — the *big* movies — about Duke Ellington and Fletcher

Henderson? How else can we account for the fact that Maynard Ferguson and Chet Baker could, decades ago, beat out Dizzy Gillespie, Miles, *and* Clifford Brown in *Downbeat* polls for best trumpeter? (Baker, maybe. But Ferguson?) How else can we explain the phenomenal sales of Vanilla Ice and New Kids on the Block, not to mention Dave Koz?

The Elvis Effect isn't hard to explain. When we talk about black music in the twentieth century we're talking about commodities, market phenomena, so the relative weakness of black consumer power, as a function both of community size and individual wealth and income, is certainly a factor. And then there's the industrial side, the cynical marketing side, of the music business, which gave us Terence Trent D'Arby in much the same way that it gave us Vanilla Ice (the relative merits of each I'll leave up to you). But the most important factor is *the historically racist trajectory* of white American appetites for cultural commodities. That's why in the early days of the blues-based pop styles (soul, rock, and R&B) black musicians often heard their songs on the radio being covered by white performers, or found their pictures effaced from their own album covers to avoid repulsing white consumers. (Both of which are well rendered in Robert Townsend's film, *The Five Heartbeats.*) That's why the Beatles and the rest of the 1960s British invaders were surprised that no one here seemed to understand the homegrown roots of this new rock and roll: that's why we need Eric Clapton to explain Muddy Waters to us — or one reason, anyway. It is too easy for too many people here to assume that nothing of cultural value can come from black folks, or to concede the point but limit the damage by treating the black origins as raw material to be refined by sophisticated whites.

The Elvis Effect is not new. I've just given the name to a phenomenon 25 with which we're all familiar. I bring it up now to make two points. The first is that the familiarity of the Elvis Effect allows it to provide a backdrop for the experience of art in traditionally black idioms. The second is that this backdrop, and the way it mediates the aesthetic experience, can explain what I've been calling the funky white boys urge, the impulse to distinguish white contributions to traditionally black cultural practices.

When I talk about an aesthetic experience I mean an event, the collection of related perceptions and appraisals that emerges from a certain kind of interaction between an observer and an object. On some conceptions of aesthetic experience, like the one John Dewey articulates in his book, *Art as Experience*, the aesthetic experience is more appropriately considered the work of art than the art object itself. The aesthetic experience brings the object to life in what you do with the sounds D'Angelo has recorded for you, what you do with the figures and hues that Picasso has kindly left you — and what they do with, and to, you.

The art object, the painting or the recorded sounds or the novel, is the focus of an aesthetic experience, which — and here we reach the crucial point — works very much like an experience of visual perception and recognition. When you focus your eyes on something, all around the central point of clarity you see a vast fringe that's fuzzy and out of focus. You usually don't notice this fringe, this periphery; that is, after all, what being focused means. But the fringe is there, and it is essential to the coherence of what you see. If you didn't have peripheral vision the objects in plain sight would seem disconnected and isolated, floating free from the rest of the world. Much like this perceptual fringe there is a theoretical fringe that helps us make sense of the sensations that arise from the encounter with the object. The sensations become organized into an experience of a certain *kind* of object, say, a cow, only if you have the concept "cow" available in your cognitive repertoire. Otherwise you've simply encountered a big, smelly beast that makes weird sounds. Perhaps more clearly, you can experience something as a baseball bat only if the right theoretical background is in place to support your perceptual encounter with the stick of wood. If it isn't, if, say, you're from a pre-industrial culture and don't know how to distinguish a baseball from Bisquick, then you've simply encountered a funny stick.

The experience of an artwork follows the same pattern. The work itself is surrounded by a vast range of peripheral experience which stretches out and makes connections with the rest of the world. You may not think about this fringe, this backdrop to experience, but without it the art object doesn't make sense as the kind of thing it's supposed to be, and it can't contribute to the right kind of aesthetic experience. Unless one internalizes the conventions of western painterly representation, one will see only splashes of paint where an art critic sees angels or receding horizons or bowls of fruit. And unless one understands that the conventions of artistic practice undergird the experience of painterly representation, one treats the painting as nothing more than a *picture* when it is so much more, a commentary on a tradition, a manipulation and rejection of themes and approaches created and perfected over time. Unless one can read these in the work, see them along with the work, the work remains opaque. This history is the fringe, the penumbra that makes the experience coherent and complete.

Similarly, unless we appreciate the narrative of the development of jazz composition and improvisation, Ornette Coleman sounds like he never quite finished learning how to play the saxophone. But when we know the history, when we can notice the periphery of the experience, we can hear his interpretation and critique of the techniques of jazz performance. Or: until you can hear the echoes of Marvin Gaye and Prince and southern gospel *and* hip-hop on D'Angelo's album *Brown Sugar*, until you feel the incredible syncretism of the church organ grounded by a thundering jeep beat on the song "Higher," you'll miss the point and miss out on the most satisfying aspects of the experiences promised by encounters with the album — which, incidentally, is precisely what some hip-hop obsessed reviewers did before the album's sales showed them that maybe this guy was onto something.

My claim here is that the Elvis Effect can serve as the periphery for the 30 reception and experience of white performances in black expressive traditions.

In the same way that knowing a bit of art history changes the way we appreciate, the way we *see*, a painting, knowing the historically racist trajectory of white American appetites for cultural commodities can change the way one hears Eric Clapton — or the Canadian dancehall dj Snow. Knowledge of the historically racist trajectory of white American appetites for cultural commodities can erect affective obstacles to the reception and enjoyment of otherwise impeccable arrangements of sounds; that knowledge can interfere with and frustrate the pattern of response that would otherwise attend the perception of the music, just as knowing a little more about the context for Picasso's work can and should frustrate the pattern of response that would otherwise lead one to say "my little sister can do *that*."

My point is that the urge to keep Teena Marie at arm's length, to invite her in conditionally as an honorary participant, can be an aesthetic response rather than a moral or a metaphysical one. It can proceed from the realization that "I've heard of Eric Clapton only because he's white," the realization that the dollars I spend on a ticket to his show or to buy his CD will fuel the machine which perhaps without racist intent produces racist outcomes: the realization that if I participate in this process, I'll be partially responsible for the next sister who toils in poverty while the white woman with her style gets the big record deal.

3. Conclusion

What, then, does race have to do with funkiness and soulfulness? Simply this: Race is the principal dynamic in a historical drama that shapes the possibilities for aesthetic experience of traditionally black cultural practices. Less concisely but more simply: Most of us share or are at least acquainted with a cluster of moderately plausible intuitions linking race to cultural production. I've been concerned here with three in particular. One says that there is something answering to the title "black culture," or that there are some things answering to that title. Another says that it is good for black people to perpetuate these cultures. And the last says that white people are either unwilling or unable to participate in these cultures, and that the ones who are willing and who are able differ somehow from the rest. These intuitions, when ossified into a metaphysical nationalism, can support a project something like my honorary soul sisters club, but a project predicated on the view that white people have neither the proper nature nor the moral standing to participate in black culture. This approach can lead to the urge to create funky white boys clubs, but it does so while leaving the undeniable fact of white participation utterly inexplicable, making black and white participants immoral and neurotic, and subordinating history to the dictates of a transcendent racial essence. I've explained these consequences of metaphysical nationalism already, so I'll introduce one more for good measure: it plays into the hands of racism. After all, even if the metaphysical nationalist denies that she's a racist, she has given plenty of ammunition to the white racist. While she's saying that the black essence is linked to rhythm and the like, the white racist can say "You're right, we don't have rhythm; our essence is concerned with other things, like rationality and cognitive powers."

I propose avoiding, instead of inviting, this debate with the racist. Instead of invoking nationalist metaphysics, let's take history and culture seriously. On the view I propose, the three plausible intuitions regarding the existence and worth of black culture and the relation between white participants and the culture are joined by a fourth, which says that white participation tends to exploit and thereby to imperil black culture and its main proponents. This intuition leads to the Elvis Effect, and recognizing that fact enables us to link the other intuitions to the funky white boys club impulse *without* inciting the racist or engaging in an act of metaphysical conjuring. History reports that the fate of black expressive innovation has too often been cooptation without compensation, and it supports the prediction that white participation portends dilution, commercialization, and decay for the culture. Awareness of this history seeps into the reception of white performances and makes a qualitative difference in the aesthetic experience — it seeps in, incidentally, not to distract but to inform, the way the history of painting informs one's appreciation of Picasso's *Les Demoiselles D'Avignon*.

This appeal to what we might call a problematized aesthetic response motivates the claim that Stevie Ray Vaughan and Stan Getz are merely honorary. The background to the aesthetic experience is such that what would otherwise be heard as a blues performance is instead experienced as the performance of an honorary bluesman. Teena Marie is honorary not because she lacks the right nature or the moral entitlement to participate in the culture of black music, but because the listener's encounter with the sounds that Marie produces is complicated by the background of commonsense theory that informs the perception and recognition of the sounds.

Some disclaimers are in order. First of all, I am not claiming that the way 35 to understand my particular adolescent urge to designate funky white boys and honorary soul sisters proceeded from an awareness of the historically racist trajectory of white cultural consumption. In the same way that my FWB project didn't rise to the level of definiteness necessary to become metaphysical nationalism, it certainly wasn't definite or politically astute enough to be motivated by the Elvis Effect. It was simply what it was: a youthful effort to occupy an idle mind by following out the consequences of certain familiar and prominent generalizations about race and culture. I am claiming, however, that just as my FWB-urge was neither racist nor essentialist, other similar positions can be neither racist nor essentialist, and that one way to account for such positions is by appeal to the Elvis Effect and the long shadow it can cast over aesthetic experiences.

Second, I don't mean to endorse the claim that white people can only be honorary participants in black culture. I mean only to explain it, or some versions of it. My aim has been to point out only that one can make such claims without being a racist or an essentialist, largely on the basis of certain rough but plausible generalizations about race and culture. Of course, such claims and generalizations are much less plausible now than they were even ten years ago, now that hip-hop culture has penetrated into the deepest and palest recesses of America. And, as it happens, they weren't terribly plausible even then, standing as they did in a tense relationship to the long history of white contribution to and participation in allegedly "black" forms like blues and jazz. But their validity aside, the claims and generalizations are familiar, and as such can be expected to serve as the backdrop to aesthetic experience.

I have a final comment about one of those generalizations, the one concerning what I've labeled "the Elvis Effect." Focusing on the racism of the processes by which black cultural forms have historically found their way into the broader culture moves us past the dialectic of essentialism and authenticity. It shows that there may be concrete political concerns that make racial solidarity an attractive mode of political and cultural practice. It reminds us that anything validly claiming the title "black culture" comes from the concrete strivings of black people rather than from some essence outside of culture. And it reminds us that the strivings of those people take place not in the sociological and historical vacuum often assumed in discussions of racial justice, but in the context of a rich historical drama that is shaped by power relations, by economics and politics. Furthermore, linking judgments like the ones behind the FWB to the background material of economics, history, and politics reminds us that aesthetic experience has a context, one that is as much cultural and political as it is theoretical and art-historical.

READING THE TEXT

1. What were the criteria for inclusion in Taylor's "Funky White Boys Club" (para. 1)?
2. Why did *Vibe* call Teena Marie an "honorary soul sister" (para. 4) rather than a real one?
3. What is the difference between "cultural nationalism" (para. 16) and "metaphysical nationalism" (para. 17)?
4. Define the "Elvis Effect" (para. 22) in your own words.

READING THE SIGNS

1. Conduct a class debate on whether whites can be authentic performers of African American cultural activities. Be sure to base your arguments on the work of specific artists and performers.
2. Taylor suggests that metaphysical nationalism "plays into the hands of racism" (para. 32) and thus rejects it. Write an essay in which you argue your position on racial exclusivity in popular entertainment and sports.

3. As rap and hip-hop gain mainstream acceptance, more white performers are adopting their styles and rhythms. Write an essay comparing the history of rap and hip-hop with that of rock 'n' roll. To what extent do you think history will repeat itself?

4. Write an essay arguing for or against the value of preserving one's biological ethnic heritage. To develop your ideas, consult Nell Bernstein ("Goin' Gangsta, Choosin' Cholita," p. 604), bell hooks ("Baby," p. 610), or Jack Lopez ("Of Cholos and Surfers," p. 597).

ANGELINE F. PRICE
Working Class Whites

> *Over the years, American popular culture has worked — not always successfully and sometimes fitfully — to rid itself of the racial stereotyping that has so marred its history. But one group of Americans, Angeline F. Price believes, has not benefited from this repudiation of negative stereotyping: working-class whites, especially those in the South. So Price has set up a Web site to analyze and document the ways in which "white trash" continue to be subject to distortion and disrespect in the mass media. We present here a selection from that site, the rest of which can be viewed at http://xroads.virginia.edu/ ~ MA97/price/intro.htm. Price is the Web center director for Allegiance Technologies.*

"One class gets the sugar and the other gets the shit" (Fussell, 25), and in American society the "other" is invariably poverty stricken and powerless. Classism is at the core of the problem. The hatred of the poor is an evil secret of America, hidden by the ingrained myths of "liberty and justice for all." Americans are taught to believe in a classless, equal opportunity society. Yet, the facts of poverty, illiteracy, and ignorance are hard to ignore, and the reality is that some people have advantages over other people depending on which family they are born into. Therefore, when wealthy people confront the poor, a sense of guilt and superiority merge into the reactionary fear that has manifested itself as racism and classism through the centuries. Sut Lovingood, an anti-hero of Southwestern humor, may have put it best when he said of the genteel class, "they are powerful feard ove low things, low ways, an' low pepil" (Cook, 8).

The working class white has always been an ideal candidate for this role in society, and mainstream society has revealed their fright. As Jim Goad explains in his Redneck Manifesto, the "redneck" stereotype is especially fitting because it fills all the scapegoat requirements: biological differences — inbred, less intelligent, unattractive; geographic and regional differences — trailer parks, rural South, hillbilly; economic differences — poor, sick, lazy, dirty; cultural differences — fundamentalist, superstitious, loud, kin networks; and moral differences — trashy, racist, violent (Goad, 76).

Representations of working class whites in the popular media are responsible for the dissemination of "white trash" as well as "good country folk" stereotypes in society. The working class white, placed in these two distinct roles, serves as a personified id and superego for the collective psyche of America, particularly of middle and upper class whites.

The "white trash" portrayal represents the little devil on one shoulder — embodying racism, ignorance, violence, filth, and base desires. He operates outside of societal boundaries with an emphasis on the "id's" instinct and primalism. The "good country folk" portrayal represents the little angel on the other side — embodying simplicity, loyalty, faith in religion and humanity, and a connection to family and community. This "superego" maintains moral absolutes in a world where such ideals no longer belong.

Society has not chosen one to be the representative model, but instead ⁵ *uses* (and I mean that in the harshest sense) this dichotomy to fulfill its own desires on either end of the spectrum. As "id," the working class white is burdened with all the crimes and guilt of the white race over time. This allows the audience to feel justifiable hatred toward a group which they can demonize and thereby release guilt and aggression unto — while hating what is worst within themselves. As "superego," the working class white is used to nostalgize and idealize the desire for a simpler life. Thus enabling the audience to reassure itself of qualities they hope are best within themselves in a kind, moral world. These images reappear over time and in many forms of media. They are considered for their impact on public perception and treatment of working class whites.

Modern day experience with white trash stereotypes is, as with most modern cultural phenomena, disseminated through movies and television. The images society has created fall into two conflicting categories. Most often the working class white is a whisky-drinking, abusive, violently racist, uneducated, macho, close-minded, dirty, fat, insensitive, monster-truck-show-watching hunter who is better laughed at than associated with. Yet in rare instances, one encounters the poor white as honest, hard-working, honorable, simple, loyal, God-fearing, and patriotic. And here exists the dichotomy of white trash versus good country folk.

American society has used the working class white to alternately allay its fear of faltering morality or to bolster its confidence in the correctness of the modern lifestyle. Examples of this tendency occur in the typecasting of working class whites in television series as well as film. Stemming from the disillusionment of Vietnam, Watergate, and other corruptions of the time, we can trace a movement of "good country folk" in the television shows of the

In Appalachia, 1984.

seventies. Programs like *The Andy Griffith Show* and *The Waltons* provided a simple, honest way of life that appealed to viewers as an escape from the cynicism and the loss of moral absolutes that was becoming prevalent in society. Once again, America turned to the South as the appropriate setting for such nostalgia.

At around the same time, we also have popular Southern sitcoms like *The Dukes of Hazzard* and *The Beverly Hillbillies* playing on the more typical stereotype of uneducated, criminal (Duke brothers' constant battles with the corrupt Boss Hogg) characters with substandard eating habits and speech patterns. We also find sexy yet innocent women protected by their families with Daisy and Ellie May. *The Beverly Hillbillies* proves that even when poor whites stumble upon money, they retain their low class ways, and are useful only for the purposes of humor. *The Dukes of Hazzard* gives a solid continuation of redneck stereotypes, tempered with the idea that the Dukes are "never meanin' no harm" as the theme song implies.

The use of violence in film and writing is often a hallmark of social passion. During the 1930s there was a movement to expose the brutality of the lives of working class whites. Yet often the attempts to give aid were actually forms of condescension and control. That is commonly the effect of the literature and case studies of the time. John Ford's film adaptation of *The Grapes of Wrath* is the strongest example of dignified poor white media portrayal. Henry Fonda and Jane Darwell, echoing the themes of Southern agrarianism, are rural saints attacked by the forces of modern, capitalistic society.

In recent years, the popularity of poor white imagery has come in two 10 forms. One is the simple, idiotic portrayal in the humorous sketches of Jeff Foxworthy (a middle to upper class actor — not a redneck) and the brass

The television show *The Beverly Hill-billies*, about a poor Ozark family that strikes it rich and moves to Beverly Hills, ran from 1962 to 1971.

unorthodoxy of Roseanne, or the dark and perverse killer in movies like *Deliverance* or *Sling Blade*. Though the complex and human character in *Sling Blade* is much easier to accept than the sodomizing mountain man in *Deliverance*, both characters portray a warped sense of morality that is equated to their Southern, poor white upbringing. The father of the killer in *Sling Blade* is shown surrounded by religious iconography, and he and his wife blatantly use religion to justify their horrific treatment of the child and the murder of an unwanted baby that is born to them. The depth of ignorance necessary to explain the characters' behavior is only fitting in the environment of the poor white. Filled with domestic violence and dark secrets, the Southern small town setting ensures that such events would not take place in any other context.

Deliverance may be the most well-known and damaging film centered around poor whites, in this case "hillbillies." *Deliverance* embodies all the fear of urban modern America concerning what is most primitive and dangerous in the character of man. The conflict is between modern mainstream capitalist America and the lurking potential of evil in mankind . . . an evil which has been left behind to remain only in those mountaineers most remote and ignorant of civilization. In the film, urban macho man takes on the raw brutality of nature and its inhabitants with no respect and pays the price. The punishment is one of male on male rape by the embodiment of poor white trash, confirming mainstream America's fear of the poverty-stricken savage.

The view from inside the working class is much more complex. The working class white is operating off his own cultural, family, and individual biases; yet coupled with these are the pervasive, historically assumed ideas that violence, racism, and fundamentalism are somehow inherent in his class. Even if

John Steinbeck's novel *The Grapes of Wrath* (1939) was made into a movie starring Henry Fonda.

one becomes aware of the layers of identification applied to oneself, and most people do not, a battle against your own heritage is difficult at best, and usually impossible. The class to which we are born, in which our family circulates and our formative years are spent, is the guiding principle with which we view other groups and their cultural beliefs within our life experience.

Films that show poor whites as violent people who attack wealthy citified whites allow the rich to justify their treatment of "white trash" by portraying the poor whites as racist, criminal, and uneducated. This allows other typically marginalized groups to join upper class whites against the "white trash." This justifies upper class stereotyping of poor whites and serves to aid in relieving upper class white guilt over treatment of "others" in the past.

The hatred and condescension of the poor seems to be the last available method of prejudice in our society. Just as Americans have made an effort to educate, understand, and alter the treatment of marginalized groups and alternate cultures within our society, we have held on to poor whites as a group to demean. Making assumptions about groups of any sort on societal and biased definitions is flawed in any situation. As with other groups, there must be an effort taken to use an open mind and individual code to ascribe merit to those in our world.

WORKS CITED

Cook, Sylvia Jenkins. *From Tobacco Road to Route 66: The Southern Poor in Fiction.* Chapel Hill: University of North Carolina Press, 1976.

Fussell, Paul. *Class.* New York: Simon & Schuster, 1983.

Goad, Jim. *The Redneck Manifesto.* New York: Simon & Schuster, 1997.

READING THE TEXT

1. Explain in your own words Price's definitions of "white trash" and "good country folk."

2. What is the logic behind Price's analogies between white trash and the id and between good country folk and the superego?

3. Summarize in your own words the evolution of cinematic depictions of poor whites from the 1970s to more recent years.

4. What does Price mean by "a battle against your own heritage is difficult at best, and usually impossible" (para. 12)?

READING THE SIGNS

1. Watch a recent movie that has working-class white characters, and analyze it according to the stereotypes that Price describes. Do you find depictions of "white trash" or "good country folk," or do the characters have traits that Price does not discuss?

2. At your school's media library, watch an episode of one of the TV shows Price mentions, such as *The Dukes of Hazzard* or *The Beverly Hillbillies*, or watch one of the films she describes. Then write your own analysis of its portrayal of the characters. Is the portrayal hostile or affectionate toward working-class white characters?

3. Write a reflective essay responding to Price's assertion: "The hatred and condescension of the poor seems to be the last available method of prejudice in our society" (para. 14). Support your essay with reference to current popular entertainment.

4. In class, discuss why the "white trash" stereotype persists, even in an age of heightened sensitivity about racial stereotyping. Use the class discussion as a springboard for an essay proposing your own explanation for this phenomenon.

5. Compare and contrast Price's argument about how class is depicted in the media with that of Michael Parenti in "Class and Virtue" (p. 368). How do you account for any differences you discern?

JACK LOPEZ
Of Cholos and Surfers

*If you want to be a surfer, L.A.'s the place to be, but things can get com-
plicated if you come from East Los Angeles, which is not only miles from
the beach but is also the home turf for many a cholo street gangster who
may not look kindly on a Mexican American kid carrying a copy of*
Surfer Quarterly *and wearing Bermuda shorts. This is exactly what happened to Jack Lopez (b. 1950), as he tells it in this memoir of growing up
Latino in the 1960s — but not to worry, the beach and the barrio are not
mutually exclusive, and, in the end, Lopez was able to have "the best of
both worlds." A professor of English at California State University,
Northridge, Lopez is a short-story writer and essayist whose books
include* Cholos and Surfers: A Latino Family Album *(1998) and* Snapping
Lines *(2001).*

The only store around that had this new magazine was a Food Giant on Vermont Avenue, just off Imperial. *Surfer Quarterly*, it was then called. Now it's
Surfer Magazine and they've celebrated their thirtieth anniversary. Sheldon
made the discovery by chance when he'd gone shopping with his mother,
who needed something found only at Food Giant. Normally we didn't go that
far east to shop; we went west toward Crenshaw, to the nicer part of town.

We all wanted to be surfers, in fact called ourselves surfers even though
we never made it to the beach, though it was less than ten miles away. One of
the ways you could become a surfer was to own an issue of *Surfer Quarterly*.
Since there had been only one prior issue, I was hot to get the new one. To be
a surfer you also had to wear baggy shorts, large Penney's Towncraft T-shirts,
and go barefoot, no matter how much the hot sidewalks burned your soles.

That summer in the early sixties I was doing all sorts of odd jobs around
the house for my parents: weeding, painting the eaves, baby-sitting during the
daytime. I was earning money so that I could buy Lenny Muelich's surfboard,
another way to be a surfer. It was a Velzy-Jacobs, ten feet six inches long,
twenty-four inches wide, and it had the coolest red oval decal. Lenny was my
across-the-street neighbor, two years older than I, the kid who'd taught me
the facts of life, the kid who'd taught me how to wrestle, the kid who'd played
army with me when we were children, still playing in the dirt.

Now we no longer saw much of each other, though he still looked out for
me. A strange thing happened to Lenny the previous school year. He grew.
Like the Green Giant or something. He was over six feet tall and the older
guys would let him hang out with them. So Lenny had become sort of a hood,
wearing huge Sir Guy wool shirts, baggy khaki pants with the cuffs rolled, and
French-toed black shoes. He drank wine, even getting drunk in the daytime

with his hoodlum friends. Lenny was now respected, feared, even, by some of the parents, and no longer needed or desired to own a surfboard — he was going in the opposite direction. There were two distinct paths in my neighborhood: hood or surfer.

I was entering junior high school in a month, and my best friends were Sheldon Cohen and Tom Gheridelli. They lived by Morningside Heights, and their fathers were the only ones to work, and their houses were more expensive than mine, and they'd both been surfers before I'd aspired toward such a life. Sheldon and Tom wore their hair long, constantly cranking their heads back to keep their bangs out of their eyes. They were thirteen years old. I was twelve. My parents wouldn't let hair grow over my ears no matter how much I argued with them. But I was the one buying a surfboard. Lenny was holding it for me. My parents would match any money I saved over the summer.

Yet *Surfer Quarterly* was more tangible since it only cost one dollar. Lenny's Velzy Jacobs was forty-five dollars, quite a large sum for the time. The issue then became one of how to obtain the object of desire. The Food Giant on Vermont was reachable by bike, but I was no longer allowed to ride up there. Not since my older brother had gone to the Southside Theatre one Saturday and had seen a boy get knifed because he wasn't colored. Vermont was a tough area, though some of the kids I went to school with lived up there and they weren't any different from us. Yet none of them wished to be surfers, I don't think.

What was needed was for me to include my father in the negotiation. I wasn't allowed to ride my bike to Vermont, I reasoned with him. Therefore, he should drive me. He agreed with me and that was that. Except I had to wait until the following Friday when he didn't have to work.

My father was a printer by trade. He worked the graveyard shift. I watched my younger brother and sister during the day (my older brother, who was fifteen years old, was around in case anything of consequence should arise, but we mostly left him alone) until my mother returned from work — Reaganomics had hit my family decades before the rest of the country. Watching my younger sister and brother consisted of keeping them quiet so my father could sleep.

In the late afternoons I'd go to Sportsman's Park, where I'd virtually grown up. I made the all-stars in baseball, basketball, and football. Our first opponent on the path to the city championships was always Will Rogers Park in Watts. Sheldon and Tom and I had been on the same teams. Sometimes I'd see them in the afternoons before we'd all have to return home for dinner. We'd pore over Sheldon's issue of *Surfer* while sitting in the bleachers next to the baseball diamond. If it was too hot we'd go in the wading pool, though we were getting too old for that scene, since mostly women and kids used it.

When Friday afternoon arrived and my father had showered and my mother had returned from work, I reminded my father of our agreement. We drove the neighborhood streets up to Vermont, passing Washington High

School, Normandie Avenue, Woodcrest Elementary School, and so on. We spoke mostly of me. Was I looking forward to attending Henry Clay Junior High? Would I still be in accelerated classes? My teachers and the principal had talked with my parents about my skipping a grade but my parents said no.

Just as my father had exhausted his repertoire of school questions, we arrived at the Food Giant. After parking in the back lot, we entered the store and made for the liquor section, where the magazines were housed. I stood in front of the rack, butterflies of expectation overtaking my stomach while my father bought himself some beer. I knew immediately when I found the magazine. It looked like a square of water was floating in the air. An ocean-blue cover of a huge wave completely engulfing a surfer with the headline BANZAI PIPELINE. I held the magazine with great reverence, as if I were holding something of spiritual value, which it was.

"Is that it?" my father asked. He held a quart of Hamm's in each hand, his Friday night allotment.

"Yes." I beamed.

At the counter my father took the magazine from me, leafing through it much too casually, I thought. I could see the bulging veins in his powerful forearms, and saw too the solid bumps that were his biceps.

"Looks like a crazy thing to do," he said, finally placing the magazine on the counter next to the beer. My father, the practical provider, the person whose closet was pristine for lack of clothes — although the ones he did own were stylish, yet not expensive. This was why he drank beer from quart bottles — it was cheaper that way. I know now how difficult it must have been raising four children on the hourly wages my parents made.

The man at the counter rang up the purchases, stopping for a moment to look at the *Surfer*. He smiled.

"*¿Eres mexicano?*" my father asked him.

"*Sí', ¿cómo no?*" the man answered.

Then my father and the store clerk began poking fun at my magazine in Spanish, nothing too mean, but ranking it as silly adolescent nonsense.

When we got back in the car I asked my father why he always asked certain people if they were Mexican. He only asked men who obviously were, thus knowing in advance their answers. He shrugged his shoulders and said he didn't know. It was a way of initiating conversation, he said. Well, it was embarrassing for me, I told him. Because I held the magazine in my lap, I let my father off the hook. It was more important that I give it a quick thumb-through as we drove home. The *Surfer* was far more interesting for me as a twelve-year-old than larger issues of race.

I spent the entire Friday evening holed up in my room, poring over the magazine, not even interested in eating popcorn or watching *77 Sunset Strip*, our familial Friday-night ritual. By the next morning I had almost memorized every photo caption and their sequence. I spoke with Sheldon on the phone and he and Tom were meeting me later at Sportsman's Park. I did my chores in a self-absorbed trance, waiting for the time when I could share my treasure with my friends. My mother made me eat lunch before I was finally able to leave.

Walking the long walk along Western Avenue toward Century and glancing at the photos in the magazine, I didn't pay attention to the cholo whom I passed on the sidewalk. I should have been more aware, but was too preoccupied. So there I was, in a street confrontation before I knew what had happened.

"You a surfer?" he said with disdain. He said it the way you start to say *chocolate. Ch*, like in *choc — churfer*. But that didn't quite capture it, either.

I stopped and turned to face him. He wore a wool watch cap pulled down onto his eyebrows, a long Sir Guy wool shirt with the top button buttoned and all the rest unbuttoned, khaki pants so long they were frayed at the bottoms and so baggy I couldn't see his shoes. I wore Bermuda shorts and a large Towncraft T-shirt. I was barefoot. My parents wouldn't let hair grow over my ears. Cholo meets surfer. Not a good thing. As he clenched his fists I saw a black cross tattooed onto the fleshy part of his hand.

His question was *not* like my father's. My father, I now sensed, wanted a   25 common bond upon which to get closer to strangers. This guy was Mexican American, and he wanted to fight me because I wore the outfit of a surfer.

I rolled the magazine in a futile attempt to hide it, but the cholo viewed this action as an escalation with a perceived weapon. It wasn't that I was overly afraid of him, though fear can work to your advantage if used correctly. I was big for my age, athletic, and had been in many fights. The problem was this: I was hurrying off to see my friends, to share something important with them, walking on a summer day, and I didn't feel like rolling on the ground with some stranger because *he'd* decided we must do so. Why did he get to dictate when or where you would fight? There was another consideration, one more utilitarian: Who knew what sort of weapons he had under all that baggy clothing? A rattail comb, at the least. More likely a knife, because in those days guns weren't that common.

At Woodcrest Elementary School there was a recently arrived Dutch Indonesian immigrant population. One of the most vicious fights I had ever seen was the one when Victor VerHagen fought his own cousin. And the toughest fight I'd ever been in was against Julio, something during a baseball game. There must be some element of self-loathing that propels us to fight those of our own ethnicity with a particular ferocity.

Just before the cholo was going to initiate the fight, I said, "I'm Mexican." American of Mexican descent, actually.

He seemed unable to process this new information. How could someone be Mexican and dress like a surfer? He looked at me again, this time seeing beyond the clothes I wore. He nodded slightly.

This revelation, this recognition verbalized, molded me in the years to   30 come. A surfer with a peeled nose and a Karmann Ghia with surf racks driving down Whittier Boulevard in East L.A. to visit my grandparents. The charmed life of a surfer in the midst of cholos.

When I began attending junior high school, there was a boy nicknamed Niño, who limped around the school yard one day. I discovered the reason for his limp when I went to the bathroom and he had a rifle pointed at boys and was taking their money. I fell in love with a girl named Shirley Pelland, the younger sister of a local surfboard maker. I saw her in her brother's shop after school, but she had no idea I loved her. That fall the gang escalation in my neighborhood became so pronounced my parents decided to move. We sold our house very quickly and moved to Huntington Beach, and none of us could sleep at night for the quiet. We were surrounded by cornfields and strawberry fields and tomato fields. As a bribe for our sudden move my parents chipped in much more than matching funds so I could buy Lenny Muelich's surfboard. I almost drowned in the big waves of a late-autumn south swell, the first time I went out on the Velzy-Jacobs. But later, after I'd surfed for a few years, I expertly rode the waves next to the pier, surfing with new friends.

But I've got ahead of myself. I must return to the cholo who is about to attack. But there isn't any more to tell about the incident. We didn't fight that summer's day over thirty years ago. In fact, I never fought another of my own race and don't know if this was a conscious decision or if circumstances dictated it. As luck would have it, I fought only a few more times during my adolescence and did so only when attacked.

My father's question, which he'd asked numerous people so long ago, taught me these things: The reason he had to ask was because he and my mother had left the safe confines of their Boyle Heights upbringing. They had thrust themselves and their children into what was called at the time the melting pot of Los Angeles. They bought the post–World War II American dream of assimilation. I was a pioneer in the sociological sense that I had no distinct ethnic piece of geography on which my pride and honor depended. Cast adrift in the city streets. Something gained, something lost. I couldn't return to my ethnic neighborhood, but I could be a surfer. And I didn't have to fight for ethnic pride over my city street. The neighborhood kids did, however, stick together, though this was not based upon race. It was a necessity. The older guys would step forward to protect the younger ones. That was how it was done.

The most important thing I learned was that I could do just about anything I wished, within reason. I could be a surfer, if I chose, and even cholos would respect my decision. During my adolescence I went to my grandparents' house for all the holidays. They lived in East Los Angeles. When I was old enough to drive I went on my own, sometimes with a girlfriend. I was able to observe my Los Angeles Mexican heritage, taking a date to the *placita* for Easter service and then having lunch at Olvera Street. An Orange County girl who had no idea this part of Los Angeles existed. I was lucky; I got the best of both worlds.

READING THE TEXT

1. What symbolic significance did being a surfer have for Lopez and his friends?
2. How did Lopez's attitude toward his Mexican heritage compare with that of his father, and how do you explain any difference?
3. Why does the cholo object to Lopez's surfer clothing?
4. How did Lopez eventually reconcile his surfer and his Mexican American identities?
5. Characterize Lopez's tone and persona in this selection. How do they affect your response as a reader?

READING THE SIGNS

1. In your journal, write your own account of how, in your childhood, you developed a sense of ethnic identity. Use Lopez's article as a model that pinpoints concrete, specific events as being significant.
2. Compare and contrast Lopez's development of a sense of ethnic identity with that of Melissa Algranati in "Being an Other" (p. 613). How can you account for any differences you see?
3. A generational gap separated Lopez's and his father's attitudes toward assimilation. Interview several friends, preferably of different ethnicities, and their parents about their sense of ethnic identity. Write an essay in which you explore the extent to which one's age can influence one's attitudes toward ethnicity.
4. In class, discuss the extent to which your community is characterized by "distinct ethnic piece[s] of geography" (para. 33). Do people of different ethnicities interact frequently? Or do people tend to associate primarily with those of the same background? Use your discussion as the basis of an essay in which you evaluate the race relations in your community, taking care to suggest causes for the patterns that you see.

JIM WHITMER

Four Teens

READING THE SIGNS

1. Describe Whitmer's photograph. What is taking place? How would you characterize the attitudes of the four youths in this photo? Examine them one by one. You might comment on their facial and body expressions, for instance.

2. What do you think is the relationship among these four youths? What evidence do you have for your answers? Assume that the photographer has deliberately placed each subject in the photograph. Speculate on the motives of his placement and the effect he has achieved.

3. How would you characterize the clothing, hair, and jewelry — the styles — of the figures in the photo? That is, what do their styles say about them? Would you be willing to adopt their styles? Why or why not?

NELL BERNSTEIN

Goin' Gangsta, Choosin' Cholita

> *Ever wonder about wannabes — white suburban teenagers who dress and act like nonwhite inner-city gangsters? In this report on the phenomenon of "claiming," Nell Bernstein (b. 1965) probes some of the feelings and motives of teens who are "goin' gangsta" or "choosin' cholita" — kids who try on a racial identity not their own. Their reasons may surprise you. Bernstein is editor of* YO!, *a San Francisco area journal of teen life published by the Pacific News Service, and she has published in* Glamour, Woman's Day, Salon, *and* Mother Jones.

Her lipstick is dark, the lip liner even darker, nearly black. In baggy pants, a blue plaid Pendleton, her bangs pulled back tight off her forehead, 15-year-old April is a perfect cholita, a Mexican gangsta girl.

But April Miller is Anglo. "And I don't like it!" she complains. "I'd rather be Mexican."

April's father wanders into the family room of their home in San Leandro, California, a suburb near Oakland. "Hey, cholita," he teases. "Go get a suntan. We'll put you in a barrio and see how much you like it."

A large, sandy-haired man with "April" tattooed on one arm and "Kelly" — the name of his older daughter — on the other, Miller spent 21 years working in a San Leandro glass factory that shut down and moved to Mexico a couple of years ago. He recently got a job in another factory, but he expects NAFTA to swallow that one, too.

"Sooner or later we'll all get nailed," he says. "Just another stab in the back of the American middle class." 5

Later, April gets her revenge: "Hey, Mr. White Man's Last Stand," she teases. "Wait till you see how well I manage my welfare check. You'll be asking me for money."

A once almost exclusively white, now increasingly Latin and black working-class suburb, San Leandro borders on predominantly black East Oakland. For decades, the boundary was strictly policed and practically impermeable. In 1970 April Miller's hometown was 97 percent white. By 1990 San Leandro was 65 percent white, 6 percent black, 15 percent Hispanic, and 13 percent Asian or Pacific Islander. With minorities moving into suburbs in growing numbers and cities becoming ever more diverse, the boundary between city and suburb is dissolving, and suburban teenagers are changing with the times.

In April's bedroom, her past and present selves lie in layers, the pink walls of girlhood almost obscured, Guns N' Roses and Pearl Jam posters overlaid by rappers Paris and Ice Cube. "I don't have a big enough attitude to be a black girl," says April, explaining her current choice of ethnic identification.

What matters is that she thinks the choice is hers. For April and her friends, identity is not a matter of where you come from, what you were born into, what color your skin is. It's what you wear, the music you listen to, the words you use — everything to which you pledge allegiance, no matter how fleetingly.

The hybridization of American teens has become talk show fodder, with 10 "wiggers" — white kids who dress and talk "black" — appearing on TV in full gangsta regalia. In Indiana a group of white high school girls raised a national stir when they triggered an imitation race war at their virtually all-white high school last fall simply by dressing "black."

In many parts of the country, it's television and radio, not neighbors, that introduce teens to the allure of ethnic difference. But in California, which demographers predict will be the first state with no racial majority by the year 2000, the influences are more immediate. The California public schools are the most diverse in the country: 42 percent white, 36 percent Hispanic, 9 percent black, 8 percent Asian.

Sometimes young people fight over their differences. Students at virtually any school in the Bay Area can recount the details of at least one "race riot" in which a conflict between individuals escalated into a battle between their clans. More often, though, teens would rather join than fight. Adolescence, after all, is the period when you're most inclined to mimic the power closest at hand, from stealing your older sister's clothes to copying the ruling clique at school.

White skaters and Mexican would-be gangbangers listen to gangsta rap and call each other "nigga" as a term of endearment; white girls sometimes affect Spanish accents; blond cheerleaders claim Cherokee ancestors.

"Claiming" is the central concept here. A Vietnamese teen in Hayward, another Oakland suburb, "claims" Oakland — and by implication blackness — because he lived there as a child. A law-abiding white kid "claims" a Mexican gang he says he hangs with. A brown-skinned girl with a Mexican father and a white mother "claims" her Mexican side, while her fair-skinned sister "claims" white. The word comes up over and over, as if identity were territory, the self a kind of turf.

At a restaurant in a minimall in Hayward, Nicole Huffstutler, 13, sits with her 15 friends and describes herself as "Indian, German, French, Welsh, and, um . . . American": "If somebody says anything like 'Yeah, you're just a peckerwood,' I'll walk up and I'll say 'white pride!' 'Cause I'm proud of my race, and I wouldn't wanna be any other race."

"Claiming" white has become a matter of principle for Heather, too, who says she's "sick of the majority looking at us like we're less than them." (Hayward schools were 51 percent white in 1990, down from 77 percent in 1980, and whites are now the minority in many schools.)

Asked if she knows that nonwhites have not traditionally been referred to as "the majority" in America, Heather gets exasperated: "I hear that all the time, every day. They say, 'Well, you guys controlled us for many years, and it's time for us to control you.' Every day."

When Jennifer Vargas — a small, brown-skinned girl in purple jeans who quietly eats her salad while Heather talks — softly announces that she's "mostly Mexican," she gets in trouble with her friends.

"No, you're not!" scolds Heather.

"I'm mostly Indian and Mexican," Jennifer continues flatly. "I'm very little . . . I'm mostly . . ."

"Your mom's white!" Nicole reminds her sharply. "She has blond hair."

"That's what I mean," Nicole adds. "People think that white is a bad thing. They think that white is a bad race. So she's trying to claim more Mexican than white."

"I have very little white in me," Jennifer repeats. "I have mostly my dad's side, 'cause I look like him and stuff. And most of my friends think that me and my brother and sister aren't related, 'cause they look more like my mom."

"But you guys are all the same race, you just look different," Nicole insists. She stops eating and frowns. "OK, you're half and half each what your parents have. So you're equal as your brother and sister, you just look different. And you should be proud of what you are — every little piece and bit of what you are. Even if you were Afghan or whatever, you should be proud of it."

Will Mosley, Heather's 17-year-old brother, says he and his friends listen to rap groups like Compton's Most Wanted, NWA, and Above the Law because they "sing about life" — that is, what happens in Oakland, Los Angeles, anyplace but where Will is sitting today, an empty Round Table Pizza in a mini-mall.

"No matter what race you are," Will says, "if you live like we do, then that's the kind of music you like."

And how do they live?

"We don't live bad or anything," Will admits. "We live in a pretty good neighborhood, there's no violence or crime. I was just . . . we're just city people, I guess."

Will and his friend Adolfo Garcia, 16, say they've outgrown trying to be something they're not. "When I was 11 or 12," Will says, "I thought I was becoming a big gangsta and stuff. Because I liked that music, and thought it was the coolest, I wanted to become that. I wore big clothes, like you wear in jail. But then I kind of woke up. I looked at myself and thought, 'Who am I trying to be?'"

They may have outgrown blatant mimicry, but Will and his friends remain convinced that they can live in a suburban tract house with a well-kept lawn on a tree-lined street in "not a bad neighborhood" and still call themselves "city" people on the basis of musical tastes. "City" for these young people means crime, graffiti, drugs. The kids are law-abiding, but these activities connote what Will admiringly calls "action." With pride in his voice, Will predicts that "in a couple of years, Hayward will be like Oakland. It's starting to get more known, because of crime and things. I think it'll be bigger, more things happening, more crime, more graffiti, stealing cars."

"That's good," chimes in 15-year-old Matt Jenkins, whose new beeper — an item that once connoted gangsta chic but now means little more than an active social life — goes off periodically. "More fun."

The three young men imagine with disdain life in a gangsta-free zone. "Too bland, too boring," Adolfo says. "You have to have something going on. You can't just have everyday life."

"Mowing your lawn," Matt sneers.

"Like Beaver Cleaver's house," Adolfo adds. "It's too clean out here."

Not only white kids believe that identity is a matter of choice or taste, or 35 that the power of "claiming" can transcend ethnicity. The Manor Park Locos — a group of mostly Mexican-Americans who hang out in San Leandro's Manor Park — say they descend from the Manor Lords, tough white guys who ruled the neighborhood a generation ago.

They "are like our . . . uncles and dads, the older generation," says Jesse Martinez, 14. "We're what they were when they were around, except we're Mexican."

"There's three generations," says Oso, Jesse's younger brother. "There's Manor Lords, Manor Park Locos, and Manor Park Pee Wees." The Pee Wees consist mainly of the Locos' younger brothers, eager kids who circle the older boys on bikes and brag about "punking people."

Unlike Will Mosley, the Locos find little glamour in city life. They survey the changing suburban landscape and see not "action" or "more fun" but frightening decline. Though most of them are not yet 18, the Locos are already nostalgic, longing for a Beaver Cleaver past that white kids who mimic them would scoff at.

Walking through nearly empty Manor Park, with its eucalyptus stands, its softball diamond and tennis courts, Jesse's friend Alex, the only Asian in the group, waves his arms in a gesture of futility. "A few years ago, every bench was filled," he says. "Now no one comes here. I guess it's because of everything that's going on. My parents paid a lot for this house, and I want it to be nice for them. I just hope this doesn't turn into Oakland."

Glancing across the park at April Miller's street, Jesse says he knows what 40 the white cholitas are about. "It's not a racial thing," he explains. "It's just all the most popular people out here are Mexican. We're just the gangstas that everyone knows. I guess those girls wanna be known."

Not every young Californian embraces the new racial hybridism. Andrea Jones, 20, an African American who grew up in the Bay Area suburbs of Union City and Hayward, is unimpressed by what she sees mainly as shallow mimicry. "It's full of posers out here," she says. "When *Boyz N the Hood* came out on video, it was sold out for weeks. The boys all wanna be black, the girls all wanna be Mexican. It's the glamour."

Driving down the quiet, shaded streets of her old neighborhood in Union City, Andrea spots two white preteen boys in Raiders jackets and hugely baggy pants strutting erratically down the empty sidewalk. "Look at them," she says. "Dislocated."

She knows why. "In a lot of these schools out here, it's hard being white," she says. "I don't think these kids were prepared for the backlash that is going on, all the pride now in people of color's ethnicity, and our boldness with it. They have nothing like that, no identity, nothing they can say they're proud of.

"So they latch onto their great-grandmother who's a Cherokee, or they take on the most stereotypical aspects of being black or Mexican. It's beautiful to appreciate different aspects of other people's culture — that's like the dream of what the 21st century should be. But to garnish yourself with pop culture stereotypes just to blend — that's really sad."

Roland Krevocheza, 18, graduated last year from Arroyo High School in   45 San Leandro. He is Mexican on his mother's side, Eastern European on his father's. In the new hierarchies, it may be mixed kids like Roland who have the hardest time finding their place, even as their numbers grow. (One in five marriages in California is between people of different races.) They can always be called "wannabes," no matter what they claim.

"I'll state all my nationalities," Roland says. But he takes a greater interest in his father's side, his Ukrainian, Romanian, and Czech ancestors. "It's more unique," he explains. "Mexican culture is all around me. We eat Mexican food all the time, I hear stories from my grandmother. I see the low-riders and stuff. I'm already part of it. I'm not trying to be; I am."

His darker-skinned brother "says he's not proud to be white," Roland adds. "He calls me 'Mr. Nazi.'" In the room the two share, the American flags and the reproduction of the Bill of Rights are Roland's; the Public Enemy poster belongs to his brother.

Roland has good reason to mistrust gangsta attitudes. In his junior year in high school, he was one of several Arroyo students who were beaten up outside the school at lunchtime by a group of Samoans who came in cars from Oakland. Roland wound up with a split lip, a concussion, and a broken tailbone. Later he was told that the assault was "gang-related" — that the Samoans were beating up anyone wearing red.

"Rappers, I don't like them," Roland says. "I think they're a bad influence on kids. It makes kids think they're all tough and bad."

Those who, like Roland, dismiss the gangsta and cholo styles as affecta-   50 tions can point to the fact that several companies market overpriced knockoffs of "ghetto wear" targeted at teens.

But there's also something going on out here that transcends adolescent faddishness and pop culture exoticism. When white kids call their parents "racist" for nagging them about their baggy pants; when they learn Spanish to talk to their boyfriends; when Mexican-American boys feel themselves descended in spirit from white "uncles"; when children of mixed marriages insist that they are whatever race they say they are, all of them are more than just confused.

They're inching toward what Andrea Jones calls "the dream of what the 21st century should be." In the ever more diverse communities of Northern California, they're also facing the complicated reality of what their 21st century will be.

Meanwhile, in the living room of the Miller family's San Leandro home, the argument continues unabated. "You don't know what you are," April's father has told her more than once. But she just keeps on telling him he doesn't know what time it is.

READING THE TEXT

1. How do teens like April Miller define their identity, according to Bernstein?
2. Describe in your own words what "claiming" (para. 14) an ethnic identity means. Why do so many teens "claim" a new ethnicity, according to Bernstein?
3. What relationship does Bernstein see between claiming and the mass media?
4. What does being white mean to many of the kids who claim a nonwhite identity?
5. What does the city signify to the young people whom Bernstein describes?

READING THE SIGNS

1. In class, stage a conversation between April Miller and her father on her adoption of a Mexican identity, with April defending her choice and her father repudiating it.
2. Write an essay in which you support, challenge, or modify Andrea Jones's assumption that it is media-generated "glamour" that prompts young people to claim a new ethnic identity. Be sure to support your argument with evidence, such as specific pop culture personalities.
3. Write an argumentative essay in which you explain whether the claiming fad is an expression of racial tolerance or racial stereotyping.
4. Bernstein describes teens claiming the identities of ethnic minorities, but she provides few instances of claiming a white identity. In an essay, propose your own explanation for this pattern. To develop your ideas, consult Angeline F. Price, "Working Class Whites" (p. 591).
5. Assuming the perspective of Jack Lopez in "Of Cholos and Surfers" (p. 597), write an analysis of the social and cultural pressures that prompt these teens' desire to "claim" an ethnicity. Do they desire to "have the best of both worlds," as Lopez does, or are other forces at work?

BELL HOOKS
Baby

Dolls are among the oldest of toys, traditionally given to little girls to help model their future behavior as wives and mothers. But what is a child to think about a doll that isn't of her own race? This dilemma is faced by millions of American girls who aren't white when they are given dolls like white Barbie. Faced with a similar dilemma as a little girl when given a Barbie doll, bell hooks (b. 1952) describes in this personal reminiscence how she chose to give her loyalty instead to a brown doll named Baby, who looked a lot more like her. bell hooks (the pen name of Gloria Watkins) is Distinguished Professor of English at City College of New York and the author of numerous books of cultural criticism, including Black Looks: Race and Representation *(1992);* Killing Rage: Ending Racism *(1995);* Bone Black *(1996), from which this selection is taken;* All about Love: New Visions *(2001);* Communion: The Female Search for Love *(2002);* Plantation Culture *(2005); and* A Woman's Mourning Song *(2005).*

We learn early that it is important for a woman to marry. We are always marrying our dolls to someone. He of course is always invisible, that is until they made the Ken doll to go with Barbie. One of us has been given a Barbie doll for Christmas. Her skin is not white white but almost brown from the tan they have painted on her. We know she is white because of her blond hair. The newest Barbie is bald, with many wigs of all different colors. We spend hours dressing and undressing her, pretending she is going somewhere important. We want to make new clothes for her. We want to buy the outfits made just for her that we see in the store but they are too expensive. Some of them cost as much as real clothes for real people. Barbie is anything but real, that is why we like her. She never does housework, washes dishes, or has children to care for. She is free to spend all day dreaming about the Kens of the world. Mama laughs when we tell her there should be more than one Ken for Barbie, there should be Joe, Sam, Charlie, men in all shapes and sizes. We do not think that Barbie should have a girlfriend. We know that Barbie was born to be alone — that the fantasy woman, the soap opera girl, the girl of *True Confessions*, the Miss America girl was born to be alone. We know that she is not us.

My favorite doll is brown, brown like light milk chocolate. She is a baby doll and I give her a baby doll name, Baby. She is almost the same size as a real baby. She comes with no clothes, only a pink diaper, fastened with tiny gold pins and a plastic bottle. She has a red mouth the color of lipstick slightly open so that we can stick the bottle in it. We fill the bottle with water

"I did not want a white doll to play with."

and wait for it to come through the tiny hole in Baby's bottom. We make her many new diapers, but we are soon bored with changing them. We lose the bottle and Baby can no longer drink. We still love her. She is the only doll we will not destroy. We have lost Barbie. We have broken the leg of another doll. We have cracked open the head of an antique doll to see what makes the crying sound. The little thing inside is not interesting. We are sorry but nothing can be done — not even mama can put the pieces together again. She tells us that if this is the way we intend to treat our babies she hopes we do not have any. She laughs at our careless parenting. Sometimes she takes a minute to show us the right thing to do. She too is terribly fond of Baby. She says that she looks so much like a real newborn. Once she came upstairs, saw Baby under the covers, and wanted to know who had brought the real baby from downstairs.

She loves to tell the story of how Baby was born. She tells us that I, her problem child, decided out of nowhere that I did not want a white doll to play with, I demanded a brown doll, one that would look like me. Only grown-ups think that the things children say come out of nowhere. We know they come from the deepest parts of ourselves. Deep within myself I had begun to worry that all this loving care we gave to the pink and white flesh-colored dolls meant that somewhere left high on the shelves were boxes of unwanted, unloved brown dolls covered in dust. I thought that they would remain there forever, orphaned and alone, unless someone began to want them, to want to give them love and care, to want them more than anything. At first they ignored my wanting. They complained. They pointed out that white dolls were easier to find, cheaper. They never said where they found Baby but I know. She was always there high on the shelf, covered in dust — waiting.

READING THE TEXT

1. What does hooks mean when she says "we know that Barbie was born to be alone" (para. 1)?
2. Why did Baby receive more care and protection than other dolls and toys that were in her family?
3. What is the purpose of giving little girls dolls, according to hooks?
4. Describe hooks's style and and personal voice in this selection. How do they affect your response to her ideas?

READING THE SIGNS

1. If you played with dolls as a child, reflect in your journal on the extent to which the ethnicity of the dolls made a difference to you.
2. Visit a toy store, and study the ethnic identities of the dolls you see there. How many ethnicities are represented? How do you account for your observations?
3. Investigate the ethnic patterns in other forms of children's entertainment and play, such as Saturday morning TV cartoons or video games. Then write an essay analyzing the racial ideologies you discover. To develop your ideas, consult Michael Omi's "In Living Color: Race and American Culture" (p. 549).
4. Write an essay in which you propose your own argument about how dolls, board games, and other forms of play work to construct gender roles for both boys and girls, using as your evidence specific examples of toys and games. To develop your ideas, consult Aaron Devor's "Gender Role Behaviors and Attitudes" (p. 458), Deborah Blum's "The Gender Blur: Where Does Biology End and Society Take Over?" (p. 475), and Emily Prager's "Our Barbies, Ourselves" (p. 769).

MELISSA ALGRANATI
Being an Other

In a country as obsessed with racial identification as America is, Melissa Algranati poses a dilemma. As she puts it, "there are not too many Puerto Rican, Egyptian Jews out there," so the only category left for her on the census form is "other." In this personal essay, Algranati tells the story of how she came to be an "other," a saga of two immigrant families from different continents who eventually came together in a "marriage that only a country like America could create." Algranati is a graduate of the State University of New York at Binghamton and has a master's degree from Columbia University. She is a staff writer for www.studio2b.org.

Throughout my whole life, people have mistaken me for other ethnic backgrounds rather than for what I really am. I learned at a young age that there are not too many Puerto Rican, Egyptian Jews out there. For most of my life I have been living in two worlds, and at the same time I have been living in neither. When I was young I did not realize that I was unique, because my family brought me up with a healthy balance of Puerto Rican and Sephardic customs. It was not until I took the standardized PSAT exam that I was confronted with the question: "Who am I?" I remember the feeling of confusion as I struggled to find the right answer. I was faced with a bad multiple-choice question in which there was only supposed to be one right answer, but more than one answer seemed to be correct. I did not understand how a country built on the concept of diversity could forget about its most diverse group, inter-ethnic children. I felt lost in a world of classification. The only way for me to take pride in who I am was to proclaim myself as an other, yet that leaves out so much. As a product of a marriage only a country like America could create, I would now try to help people understand what it is like to be a member of the most underrepresented group in the country, the "others."

My father, Jacques Algranati, was born in Alexandria, Egypt. As a Sephardic Jew, my father was a minority in a predominantly Arab world. Although in the minority, socially my father was a member of the upper middle class and lived a very comfortable life. As a result of strong French influence in the Middle Eastern Jewish world, my father attended a French private school. Since Arabic was the language of the lower class, the Algranati family spoke French as their first language. My whole family is polyglot, speaking languages from the traditional Sephardic tongue of Ladino to Turkish and Greek. My grandfather spoke seven languages. Basically, my father grew up in a close-knit Sephardic community surrounded by family and friends.

However, in 1960 my father's world came to a halt when he was faced with persecution on an institutional level. As a result of the Egyptian-Israeli

An extended American family.

conflict, in 1956 an edict was issued forcing all foreign-born citizens and Jews out of Egypt. Although my father was a native-born citizen of the country, because of a very strong anti-Jewish sentiment, his citizenship meant nothing. So in 1960 when my family got their exit visas, as Jews had done since the time of the Inquisition, they packed up and left the country as one large family group.

Unable to take many possessions or much money with them, my father's family, like many Egyptian Jews, immigrated to France. They proceeded to France because they had family who were able to sponsor them. Also, once in France my family hoped to be able to receive a visa to America much sooner, since French immigration quotas to the United States were much higher than those in Egypt. Once in France my family relied on the generosity of a Jewish organization, the United Jewish Appeal. For nine months my father lived in a hotel sponsored by the United Jewish Appeal and attended French school until the family was granted a visa to the United States.

Since my father's oldest brother came to the United States first with his wife, they were able to sponsor the rest of the family's passage over. The Algranati family eventually settled in Forest Hills, Queens. Like most immigrants, my family settled in a neighborhood filled with immigrants of the same background. Once in the United States, my father rejoined many of his old friends from Egypt, since most Egyptian Jewish refugees followed a similar immigration path. At the age of fourteen my father and his group of   5 friends were once again forced to adjust to life in a new country, but this time they had to learn a new language in order to survive. Like many of his friends, my father was forced to leave the comforts and luxuries of his world for the hardships of a new world. But as he eloquently puts it, once his family and friends were forced to leave, there was really nothing to stay for.

Like my father, my mother is also an immigrant; however my parents come from very different parts of the world. Born in Maniti, Puerto Rico, my mom spent the first five years of her life in a small town outside of San Juan. Since my grandfather had attended private school in the United States when he was younger, he was relatively proficient in English. Like many immigrants, my grandfather came to the United States first, in order to help establish the family. After securing a job and an apartment, he sent for my grandmother, and three weeks later my mother and her fourteen-year-old sister came.

Puerto Ricans are different from many other people who come to this country, in the sense that legally they are not considered immigrants. Because Puerto Rico is a commonwealth of the United States, Puerto Ricans are granted automatic U.S. citizenship. So unlike most, from the day my mother and her family stepped on U.S. soil they were considered citizens. The only problem was that the difference in language and social status led "real" Americans not to consider them citizens.

As a result of this unique status, my mother faced many hardships in this new country. From the day my mother entered first grade, her process of Americanization had begun. Her identity was transformed. She went from being Maria Louisa Pinto to becoming Mary L. Pinto. Not only was my mother given a new name when she began school, but a new language was forced upon her as well. Confronted by an Irish teacher, Mrs. Walsh, who was determined to Americanize her, my mother began her uphill battle with the English language. Even until this day my mother recalls her traumatic experience when she learned how to pronounce the word "run":

"Repeat after me, run."

"Rrrrrrrrrun." 10

"No, Mary, run."

"Rrrrrrrrrun."

No matter how hard my mother tried she could not stop rolling her "r's." After several similar exchanges Mrs. Walsh, with a look of anger on her face, grabbed my mother's cheeks in her hand and squeezed as she repeated in a stern voice, "RUN!" Suffice it to say my mother learned how to speak English without a Spanish accent. It was because of these experiences that my mother made sure the only language spoken in the house or to me and my sister was English. My parents never wanted their children to experience the pain my mother went through just to learn how to say the word "run."

My mother was confronted with discrimination not only from American society but also from her community. While in the United States, my mother lived in a predominantly Spanish community. On first coming to this country her family lived in a tenement in the Bronx. At the age of twelve my mother was once more uprooted and moved to the projects on the Lower East Side. As one of the first families in a predominantly Jewish building, it was a step up for her family.

It was not her environment that posed the biggest conflict for her; it was her appearance. My mother is what people call a "white Hispanic." With her blond hair and blue eyes my mother was taken for everything but a Puerto Rican. Once my mother perfected her English, no one suspected her ethnicity unless she told them. Since she was raised to be above the ghetto, never picking up typical "Hispanic mannerisms," she was able to exist in American society with very little difficulty. Because of a very strong and protective mother and the positive influence and assistance received from the Henry Street Settlement, my mother was able to escape the ghetto. As a result of organizations like Henry Street, my mother was given opportunities such as fresh air camps and jobs in good areas of the city, where she was able to rise above the drugs, alcohol, and violence that consumed so many of her peers.

As a result of her appearance and her upbringing, my mother left her people and the ghetto to enter American society. It was here as an attractive "white" female that my mother and father's two very different worlds merged. My parents, both working on Wall Street at the time, were introduced by a mutual friend. Since both had developed a rather liberal view, the differences in their backgrounds did not seem to be a major factor. After a year of dating my parents decided to get engaged.

Although they were from two different worlds, their engagement seemed to bring them together. Growing up in the midst of the Jewish community of the Lower East Side, my mother was constantly influenced by the beauty of Judaism. Therefore, since my mother never had much connection with Catholicism and had never been baptized, she decided to convert to Judaism and raise her children as Jews. The beauty of the conversion was that no one in my father's family forced her to convert; they accepted her whether she converted or not. As for my mother's family, they too had no real objections to the wedding or conversion. To them the only thing that mattered was that my father was a nice guy who made my mom happy. The most amusing part of the union of these two different families came when they tried to communicate. My father's family is descended from Spanish Jewry where many of them spoke an old Castilian-style Spanish, while my mother's family spoke a very modern Caribbean-style Spanish. To watch them try to communicate in any language other than English was like watching a session of the United Nations.

It was this new world, that of Puerto Rican Jewry, my parents created for me and my sister, Danielle. Resembling both my parents, having my mother's coloring with my father's features, I have often been mistaken for various ethnicities. Possessing light hair and blue eyes, I am generally perceived as the "all-American" girl. Occasionally I have been mistaken for Italian since my last name, Algranati, although Sephardic, has a very Italian flair to it. I have basically lived a chameleon-like existence for most of my life.

15

As a result of my "otherness," I have gained "acceptance" in many different crowds. From this acceptance I have learned the harsh reality behind my "otherness." I will never forget the time I learned about how the parents of one of my Asian friends perceived me. From very early on, I gained acceptance with the parents of one of my Korean friends. Not only did they respect me as a person and a student, but her father even went so far as to consider me like "one of his daughters." I will always remember how I felt when I heard they made one of their daughters cancel a party because she had invited Hispanics. Even when my friend pointed out that I, the one they loved, was Hispanic they refused to accept it. Even today to them, I will always be Jewish and not Puerto Rican because to them it is unacceptable to "love" a Puerto Rican.

Regardless of community, Jewish or Puerto Rican, I am always confronted   20 by bigots. Often I am forced to sit in silence while friends utter in ignorance stereotypical responses like: "It was probably some spic who stole it," or "You're just like a Jew, always cheap."

For the past three years I have worked on the Lower East Side of Manhattan at the Henry Street Settlement. Basically my mother wanted me to support the organization that helped her get out of the ghetto. Unlike when my mother was there, the population is mostly black and Hispanic. So one day during work I had one of my fellow workers say to me "that is such a collegian white thing to say." I responded by saying that his assumption was only partially correct and asked him if he considered Puerto Rican to be white. Of course he doubted I was any part Hispanic until he met my cousin who "looks" Puerto Rican. At times like these I really feel for my mother, because I know how it feels not to be recognized by society for who you are.

Throughout my life I do not think I have really felt completely a part of any group. I have gone through phases of hanging out with different crowds trying in a sense to find myself. Basically, I have kept my life diverse by attending both Catholic-sponsored camps and Hebrew school at the same time. Similar to my parents, my main goal is to live within American society. I choose my battles carefully. By being diverse I have learned that in a society that is obsessed with classification the only way I will find my place is within myself. Unfortunately, society has not come to terms with a fast-growing population, the "others." Therefore when asked the infamous question: "Who are you?" I respond with a smile, "a Puerto Rican Egyptian Jew." Contrary to what society may think, I know that I am somebody.

READING THE TEXT

1. Summarize in your own words why Algranati feels like one of the "others" (para. 1).

2. How did the childhood experiences of Algranati's parents differ?

3. How does physical appearance affect strangers' perceptions of ethnic identity, according to Algranati?

4. Why does Algranati say she has never "really felt completely a part of any group" (para. 22)?

READING THE SIGNS

1. In your journal, reflect on your answer to the question "Who am I?"

2. Write an essay in which you defend or oppose the practice of asking individuals to identify their ethnicity in official documents such as census forms and school applications.

3. Algranati's background includes racial, cultural, and religious differences. Write an essay explaining how you would identify yourself if you were in her shoes.

4. Do you think Algranati would be sympathetic or hostile toward people who "try on" different ethnic identities? Writing as if you were Algranati, write a letter to one of the teens who "claims" a new ethnic identity in Nell Bernstein's "Goin' Gangsta, Choosin' Cholita" (p. 604).

5. In class, brainstorm names of biracial actors, musicians, or models. Then discuss the extent to which the mass media presume that people fit neatly into ethnic categories. What is the effect of such a presumption?

FAN SHEN

The Classroom and the Wider Culture: Identity as a Key to Learning English Composition

> *Writing conventions involve more cultural presuppositions and mythologies than we ordinarily recognize. Take the current practice of using the first-person singular pronoun "I" when writing an essay. Such a convention presumes an individualistic worldview, which can appear very strange to someone coming from a communal culture, as Fan Shen relates in this analysis of the relation between culture and composition. Hailing from the People's Republic of China, where the group comes before the individual in social consciousness, Shen describes what it was like to move to the United States and have to learn a whole new worldview to master the writing conventions that he himself now teaches as a professor of English at Rochester Community and Technical College. A writer as well as a teacher, Shen has translated three books from English into Chinese and has written numerous articles for both English and Chinese publications. His latest book is his autobiography,* Gang of One: Memoirs of a Red Guard *(2004).*

One day in June 1975, when I walked into the aircraft factory where I was working as an electrician, I saw many large-letter posters on the walls and many people parading around the workshops shouting slogans like "Down with the word 'I'!" and "Trust in masses and the Party!" I then remembered that a new political campaign called "Against Individualism" was scheduled to begin that day. Ten years later, I got back my first English composition paper at the University of Nebraska–Lincoln. The professor's first comments were: "Why did you always use 'we' instead of 'I'?" and "Your paper would be stronger if you eliminated some sentences in the passive voice." The clashes between my Chinese background and the requirements of English composition had begun. At the center of this mental struggle, which has lasted several years and is still not completely over, is the prolonged, uphill battle to recapture "myself."

In this paper I will try to describe and explore this experience of reconciling my Chinese identity with an English identity dictated by the rules of English composition. I want to show how my cultural background shaped—and shapes—my approaches to my writing in English and how writing in English redefined—and redefines—my *ideological* and *logical* identities. By "ideological identity" I mean the system of values that I acquired (consciously and unconsciously) from my social and cultural background. And by "logical identity" I mean the natural (or Oriental) way I organize and express my thoughts in writing. Both had to be modified or redefined in learning English

619

composition. Becoming aware of the process of redefinition of these different identities is a mode of learning that has helped me in my efforts to write in English, and, I hope, will be of help to teachers of English composition in this country. In presenting my case for this view, I will use examples from both my composition courses and literature courses, for I believe that writing papers for both kinds of courses contributed to the development of my "English identity." Although what I will describe is based on personal experience, many Chinese students whom I talked to said that they had had the same or similar experiences in their initial stages of learning to write in English.

Identity of the Self: Ideological and Cultural

Starting with the first English paper I wrote, I found that learning to compose in English is not an isolated classroom activity, but a social and cultural experience. The rules of English composition encapsulate values that are absent in, or sometimes contradictory to, the values of other societies (in my case, China). Therefore, learning the rules of English composition is, to a certain extent, learning the values of Anglo-American society. In writing classes in the United States I found that I had to reprogram my mind, to redefine some of the basic concepts and values that I had about myself, about society, and about the universe, values that had been imprinted and reinforced in my mind by my cultural background, and that had been part of me all my life.

Rule number one in English composition is: Be yourself. (More than one composition instructor has told me, "Just write what *you* think.") The values behind this rule, it seems to me, are based on the principle of protecting and promoting individuality (and private property) in this country. The instruction was probably crystal clear to students raised on these values, but, as a guideline of composition, it was not very clear or useful to me when I first heard it. First of all, the image or meaning that I attached to the word "I" or "myself" was, as I found out, different from that of my English teacher. In China, "I" is always subordinated to "We" — be it the working class, the Party, the country, or some other collective body. Both political pressure and literary tradition require that "I" be somewhat hidden or buried in writings and speeches; presenting the "self" too obviously would give people the impression of being disrespectful of the Communist Party in political writings and boastful in scholarly writings. The word "I" has often been identified with another "bad" word, "individualism," which has become a synonym for selfishness in China. For a long time the words "self" and "individualism" have had negative connotations in my mind, and the negative force of the words naturally extended to the field of literary studies. As a result, even if I had brilliant ideas, the "I" in my papers always had to show some modesty by not competing with or trying to stand above the names of ancient and modern authoritative figures. Appealing to Mao or other Marxist authorities became the required way (as well as the most "forceful" or "persuasive" way) to prove one's point in written discourse. I remember that in China I had even committed what I can call "reversed plagiarism" — here, I suppose it would be called "forgery" — when I was in middle school: willfully attributing some of my thoughts to "experts" when I needed some arguments but could not find a suitable quotation from a literary or political "giant."

Now, in America, I had to learn to accept the words "I" and "self" as something glorious (as Whitman did), or at least something not to be ashamed of or embarrassed about. It was the first and probably biggest step I took into English composition and critical writing. Acting upon my professor's suggestion, I intentionally tried to show my "individuality" and to "glorify" "I" in my papers by using as many "I's" as possible — "I think," "I believe," "I see" — and deliberately cut out quotations from authorities. It was rather painful to hand in such "pompous" (I mean immodest) papers to my instructors. But to an extent it worked. After a while I became more comfortable with only "the shadow of myself." I felt more at ease to put down *my* thoughts without looking over my shoulder to worry about the attitudes of my teachers or the reactions of the Party secretaries, and to speak out as "bluntly" and "immodestly" as my American instructors demanded.

But writing many "I's" was only the beginning of the process of redefining myself. Speaking of redefining myself is, in an important sense, speaking of redefining the word "I." By such a redefinition I mean not only the change in how I envisioned myself, but also the change in how *I* perceived the world. The old "I" used to embody only one set of values, but now it had to embody multiple sets of values. To be truly "myself," which I knew was a key to my success in learning English composition, meant *not to be my Chinese self* at all. That is to say, when I write in English I have to wrestle with and abandon (at least temporarily) the whole system of ideology which previously defined me in myself. I had to forget Marxist doctrines (even though I do not see myself as a Marxist by choice) and the Party lines imprinted in my mind and familiarize myself with a system of capitalist/bourgeois values. I had to put aside an ideology of collectivism and adopt the values of individualism. In composition as well as in literature classes, I had to make a fundamental adjustment: If I used to examine society and literary materials through the microscopes of Marxist dialectical materialism and historical materialism, I now had to learn to look through the microscopes the other way around, i.e., to learn to look at and understand the world from the point of view of "idealism." (I must add here that there are American professors who use a Marxist approach in their teaching.)

The word "idealism," which affects my view of both myself and the universe, is loaded with social connotations, and can serve as a good example of how redefining a key word can be a pivotal part of redefining my ideological identity as a whole.

To me, idealism is the philosophical foundation of the dictum of English composition: "Be yourself." In order to write good English, I knew that I had to be myself, which actually meant not to be my Chinese self. It meant that I had to create an English self and be *that* self. And to be that English self, I felt, I had to understand and accept idealism the way a Westerner does. That is to say, I had to accept the way a Westerner sees himself in relation to the universe and society. On the one hand, I knew a lot about idealism. But on the other hand, I knew nothing about it. I mean I knew a lot about idealism through the propaganda and objections of its opponent, Marxism, but I knew little about it from its own point of view. When I thought of the word "materialism"—which is a major part of Marxism and in China has repeatedly been "shown" to be the absolute truth—there were always positive connotations, and words like "right," "true," etc., flashed in my mind. On the other hand, the word "idealism" always came to me with the dark connotations that surround words like "absurd," "illogical," "wrong," etc. In China "idealism" is depicted as a ferocious and ridiculous enemy of Marxist philosophy. Idealism, as the simplified definition imprinted in my mind had it, is the view that the material world does not exist; that all that exists is the mind and its ideas. It is just the opposite of Marxist dialectical materialism which sees the mind as a product of the material world. It is not too difficult to see that idealism, with its idea that mind is of primary importance, provides a philosophical foundation for the Western emphasis on the value of individual human minds, and hence individual human beings. Therefore, my final acceptance of myself as of primary importance—an importance that overshadowed that of authority figures in English composition—was, I decided, dependent on an acceptance of idealism.

My struggle with idealism came mainly from my efforts to understand and to write about works such as Coleridge's *Biographia Literaria* and Emerson's "Over-Soul." For a long time I was frustrated and puzzled by the idealism expressed by Coleridge and Emerson—given their ideas, such as "I think, therefore I am" (Coleridge obviously borrowed from Descartes) and "the transparent eyeball" (Emerson's view of himself)—because in my mind, drenched as it was in dialectical materialism, there was always a little voice whispering in my ear "You are, therefore you think." I could not see how human consciousness, which is not material, could create apples and trees. My intellectual conscience refused to let me believe that the human mind is the primary world and the material world secondary. Finally, I had to imagine that I was looking at a world with my head upside down. When I imagined that I was in a new body (born with the head upside down) it was easier to forget biases imprinted in my subconsciousness about idealism, the mind, and my former self. Starting from scratch, the new inverted self—which I called my "English Self" and into which I have transformed myself—could understand and *accept*, with ease, idealism as "the truth" and "himself" (i.e., my English Self) as the "creator" of the world.

Here is how I created my new "English Self." I played a "game" similar to   10 ones played by mental therapists. First I made a list of (simplified) features about writing associated with my old identity (the Chinese Self), both ideological and logical, and then beside the first list I added a column of features about writing associated with my new identity (the English Self). After that I pictured myself getting out of my old identity, the timid, humble, modest Chinese "I," and creeping into my new identity (often in the form of a new skin or a mask), the confident, assertive, and aggressive English "I." The new "Self" helped me to remember and accept the different rules of Chinese and English composition and the values that underpin these rules. In a sense, creating an English Self is a way of reconciling my old cultural values with the new values required by English writing, without losing the former.

An interesting structural but not material parallel to my experiences in this regard has been well described by Min-zhan Lu in her important article, "From Silence to Words: Writing as Struggle" (*College English* 49 [April 1987]: 437–48). Min-zhan Lu talks about struggles between two selves, an open self and a secret self, and between two discourses, a mainstream Marxist discourse and a bourgeois discourse her parents wanted her to learn. But her struggle was different from mine. Her Chinese self was severely constrained and suppressed by mainstream cultural discourse, but never interfused with it. Her experiences, then, were not representative of those of the majority of the younger generation who, like me, were brought up on only one discourse. I came to English composition as a Chinese person, in the fullest sense of the term, with a Chinese identity already fully formed.

Identity of the Mind: Illogical and Alogical

In learning to write in English, besides wrestling with a different ideological system, I found that I had to wrestle with a logical system very different from the blueprint of logic at the back of my mind. By "logical system" I mean two things: the Chinese way of thinking I used to approach my theme or topic in written discourse, and the Chinese critical/logical way to develop a theme or topic. By English rules, the first is illogical, for it is the opposite of the English way of approaching a topic; the second is alogical (nonlogical), for it mainly uses mental pictures instead of words as a critical vehicle.

THE ILLOGICAL PATTERN

In English composition, an essential rule for the logical organization of a piece of writing is the use of a "topic sentence." In Chinese composition, "from surface to core" is an essential rule, a rule which means that one ought to reach a topic gradually and "systematically" instead of "abruptly."

The concept of a topic sentence, it seems to me, is symbolic of the values of a busy people in an industrialized society, rushing to get things done, hoping to attract and satisfy the busy reader very quickly. Thinking back, I realized that I did not fully understand the virtue of the concept until my life began to rush at the speed of everyone else's in this country. Chinese composition, on the other hand, seems to embody the values of a leisurely paced rural society whose inhabitants have the time to chew and taste a topic slowly. In Chinese composition, an introduction explaining how and why one chooses this topic is not only acceptable, but often regarded as necessary. It arouses the reader's interest in the topic little by little (and this is seen as a virtue of composition) and gives him/her a sense of refinement. The famous Robert B. Kaplan "noodles" contrasting a spiral Oriental thought process with a straight-line Western approach ("Cultural Thought Patterns in Inter-Cultural Education," *Readings on English as a Second Language*, Ed. Kenneth Croft, 2nd ed., Winthrop, 1980, 403–10) may be too simplistic to capture the preferred pattern of writing in English, but I think they still express some truth about Oriental writing. A Chinese writer often clears the surrounding bushes before attacking the real target. This bush-clearing pattern in Chinese writing goes back two thousand years to Kong Fuzi (Confucius). Before doing anything, Kong says in his *Luen Yu (Analects)*, one first needs to call things by their proper names (expressed by his phrase "Zheng Ming" 正名). In other words, before touching one's main thesis, one should first state the "conditions" of composition: how, why, and when the piece is being composed. All of this will serve as a proper foundation on which to build the "house" of the piece. In the two thousand years after Kong, this principle of composition was gradually formalized (especially through the formal essays required by imperial examinations) and became known as "Ba Gu," or the eight-legged essay. The logic of Chinese composition, exemplified by the eight-legged essay, is like the peeling of an onion: Layer after layer is removed until the reader finally arrives at the central point, the core.

Ba Gu still influences modern Chinese writing. Carolyn Matalene has an   15
excellent discussion of this logical (or illogical) structure and its influence on her Chinese students' efforts to write in English ("Contrastive Rhetoric: An American Writing Teacher in China," *College English* 47 [November 1985]: 789–808). A recent Chinese textbook for composition lists six essential steps (factors) for writing a narrative essay, steps to be taken in this order: time, place, character, event, cause, and consequence (*Yuwen Jichu Zhishi Liushi Jiang* [*Sixty Lessons on the Basics of the Chinese Language*], Ed. Beijing Research Institute of Education, Beijing Publishing House, 1981, 525–609). Most Chinese students (including me) are taught to follow this sequence in composition.

The straightforward approach to composition in English seemed to me, at first, illogical. One could not jump to the topic. One had to walk step by step to reach the topic. In several of my early papers I found that the Chinese approach — the bush-clearing approach — persisted, and I had considerable difficulty writing (and in fact understanding) topic sentences. In what I deemed to be topic sentences, I grudgingly gave out themes. Today, those papers look to me like Chinese papers with forced or false English openings. For example, in a narrative paper on a trip to New York, I wrote the forced/false topic sentence, "A trip to New York in winter is boring." In the next few paragraphs, I talked about the weather, the people who went with me, and so on, before I talked about what I learned from the trip. My real thesis was that one could always learn something even on a boring trip.

THE ALOGICAL PATTERN

In learning English composition, I found that there was yet another cultural blueprint affecting my logical thinking. I found from my early papers that very often I was unconsciously under the influence of a Chinese critical approach called the creation of "yijing," which is totally non-Western. The direct translation of the word "yijing" is: yi, "mind or consciousness," and jing, "environment." An ancient approach which has existed in China for many centuries and is still the subject of much discussion, yijing is a complicated concept that defies a universal definition. But most critics in China nowadays seem to agree on one point, that yijing is the critical approach that separates Chinese literature and criticism from Western literature and criticism. Roughly speaking, yijing is the process of creating a pictorial environment while reading a piece of literature. Many critics in China believe that yijing is a creative process of inducing oneself, while reading a piece of literature or looking at a piece of art, to create mental pictures, in order to reach a unity of nature, the author, and the reader. Therefore, it is by its very nature both creative and critical. According to the theory, this nonverbal, pictorial process leads directly to a higher ground of beauty and morality. Almost all critics in China agree that yijing is not a process of logical thinking — it is not a process of moving from the premises of an argument to its conclusion, which is the foundation of Western criticism. According to yijing, the process of criticizing a piece of art or literary work has to involve the process of creation on the reader's part. In yijing, verbal thoughts and pictorial thoughts are one. Thinking is conducted largely in pictures and then "transcribed" into words. (Ezra Pound once tried to capture the creative aspect of yijing in poems such as "In a Station of the Metro." He also tried to capture the critical aspect of it in his theory of imagism and vorticism, even though he did not know the term "yijing.") One characteristic of the yijing approach to criticism, therefore, is that it often includes a description of the created mental pictures on the part of the reader/critic and his/her mental attempt to bridge (unite) the literary work, the pictures, with ultimate beauty and peace.

In looking back at my critical papers for various classes, I discovered that I unconsciously used the approach of yijing, especially in some of my earlier papers when I seemed not yet to have been in the grip of Western logical critical approaches. I wrote, for instance, an essay entitled "Wordsworth's Sound and Imagination: The Snowdon Episode." In the major part of the essay I described the pictures that flashed in my mind while I was reading passages in Wordsworth's long poem, *The Prelude*.

> I saw three climbers (myself among them) winding up the mountain in silence "at the dead of night," absorbed in their "private thoughts." The

sky was full of blocks of clouds of different colors, freely changing their shapes, like oily pigments disturbed in a bucket of water. All of a sudden, the moonlight broke the darkness "like a flash," lighting up the mountain tops. Under the "naked moon," the band saw a vast sea of mist and vapor, a silent ocean. Then the silence was abruptly broken, and we heard the "roaring of waters, torrents, streams / Innumerable, roaring with one voice" from a "blue chasm," a fracture in the vapor of the sea. It was a joyful revelation of divine truth to the human mind: the bright, "naked" moon sheds the light of "higher reasons" and "spiritual love" upon us; the vast ocean of mist looked like a thin curtain through which we vaguely saw the infinity of nature beyond; and the sounds of roaring waters coming out of the chasm of vapor cast us into the boundless spring of imagination from the depth of the human heart. Evoked by the divine light from above, the human spring of imagination is joined by the natural spring and becomes a sustaining source of energy, feeding "upon infinity" while transcending infinity at the same time. . . .

Here I was describing my own experience more than Wordsworth's. The picture described by the poet is taken over and developed by the reader. The imagination of the author and the imagination of the reader are thus joined together. There was no "because" or "therefore" in the paper. There was little *logic*. And I thought it was (and it is) criticism. This seems to me a typical (but simplified) example of the yijing approach. (Incidentally, the instructor, a kind professor, found the paper interesting, though a bit "strange.")

I am not saying that such a pattern of "alogical" thinking is wrong — in fact some English instructors find it interesting and acceptable — but it is very non-Western. Since I was in this country to learn the English language and English literature, I had to abandon Chinese "pictorial logic," and to learn Western "verbal logic."

If I Had to Start Again

The change is profound: Through my understanding of new meanings of 20 words like "individualism," "idealism," and "I," I began to accept the underlying concepts and values of American writing, and by learning to use "topic sentences" I began to accept a new logic. Thus, when I write papers in English, I am able to obey all the general rules of English composition. In doing this I feel that I am writing through, with, and because of a new identity. I welcome the change, for it has added a new dimension to me and to my view of the world. I am not saying that I have entirely lost my Chinese identity. In fact I feel that I will never lose it. Any time I write in Chinese, I resume my old identity, and obey the rules of Chinese composition such as "Make the 'I' modest," and "Beat around the bush before attacking the central topic." It is necessary for me to have such a Chinese identity in order to write authentic Chinese. (I have seen people who, after learning to write in English, use

English logic and sentence patterning to write Chinese. They produce very awkward Chinese texts.) But when I write in English, I imagine myself slipping into a new "skin," and I let the "I" behave much more aggressively and knock the topic right on the head. Being conscious of these different identities has helped me to reconcile different systems of values and logic, and has played a pivotal role in my learning to compose in English.

Looking back, I realize that the process of learning to write in English is in fact a process of creating and defining a new identity and balancing it with the old identity. The process of learning English composition would have been easier if I had realized this earlier and consciously sought to compare the two different identities required by the two writing systems from two different cultures. It is fine and perhaps even necessary for American composition teachers to teach about topic sentences, paragraphs, the use of punctuation, documentation, and so on, but can anyone design exercises sensitive to the ideological and logical differences that students like me experience — and design them so they can be introduced at an early stage of an English composition class? As I pointed out earlier, the traditional advice "Just be yourself" is not clear and helpful to students from Korea, China, Vietnam, or India. From "Be yourself" we are likely to hear either "Forget your cultural habit of writing" or "Write as you would write in your own language." But neither of the two is what the instructor meant or what we want to do. It would be helpful if he or she pointed out the different cultural/ideological connotations of the word "I," the connotations that exist in a group-centered culture and an individual-centered culture. To sharpen the contrast, it might be useful to design papers on topics like "The Individual vs. The Group: China vs. America" or "Different 'I's' in Different Cultures."

Carolyn Matalene mentioned in her article (789) an incident concerning American businessmen who presented their Chinese hosts with gifts of cheddar cheese, not knowing that the Chinese generally do not like cheese. Liking cheddar cheese may not be essential to writing English prose, but being truly accustomed to the social norms that stand behind ideas such as the English "I" and the logical pattern of English composition — call it "compositional cheddar cheese" — is essential to writing in English. Matalene does not provide an "elixir" to help her Chinese students like English "compositional cheese," but rather recommends, as do I, that composition teachers not be afraid to give foreign students English "cheese," but to make sure to hand it out slowly, sympathetically, and fully realizing that it tastes very peculiar in the mouths of those used to a very different cuisine.

READING THE TEXT

1. Why does Shen say English composition is "a social and cultural experience" (para. 3)?
2. What are the differences between Western and Chinese views of the self, according to Shen?

3. What does Shen mean by the "yijing" (para. 17) approach to writing?

4. In a paragraph, summarize the process by which Shen learned to write English composition essays.

READING THE SIGNS

1. In your journal, brainstorm ways in which you were brought up either to assert your individuality or to subordinate yourself to group interests (you might consider involvement in school or sports activities). Then stand back, and consider your brainstormed list. To what extent were you raised with a "Western" concept of self? How do your ethnic background and gender affect your sense of self-identity?

2. Compare and contrast Shen's experience in his composition class with your own experiences. How do ethnicity and gender shape a writer's experiences?

3. In class, discuss the extent to which your classes, including your writing class, assume either Western or Chinese styles of learning and discourse. Then write an essay describing the results of your discussion, using the "yijing" approach that Shen discusses.

4. Has anything you have learned in your writing class felt "foreign" to you? Write a list, as Shen did, that names features about writing that come "naturally" to you, and then list those that seem "unnatural." Study your lists. Which features seem culturally determined, and which seem linked to your own personality and way of thinking? Can you make this distinction? How can these lists help you as a writer?

POPULAR SPACES

Interpreting the Built Environment

The Territorial Imperative

Space. When most of us think about it, if we think about it at all, we think of emptiness, of the nowhere through which we must pass to get somewhere, of sheer distance, or of the starlit reaches of the universe. Time may be money, but space is, well, nothingness, or little more than the empty hollow in which we find ourselves.

And yet, in spite of its apparent blankness, space isn't empty at all, because the spaces in which we conduct our everyday lives are filled with meanings, with visible and invisible codes that govern the way we move and that tell us, quite literally, where we may and may not go and what we may do when we get there. Consider an ordinary street. You may walk down it, but you need to stick to the side (or sidewalk if there is one), and it's best to stay to the right if there's any oncoming foot traffic. If private houses are on the street, you may approach the front door, but you're not supposed to cut through the yard, and you're certainly not allowed to enter without permission. You may enter the public space of a store, shopping center, or post office, but you might need to pay to enter a museum, and you will need to pass through a security checkpoint if you are entering a courthouse or an airline terminal.

The spaces created by the built environment are not the only ones shot through with written and unwritten rules. Take your personal space: What rules govern it? Ask yourself: How close will you allow someone to get to you? It depends on who it is, doesn't it? Friends can get close, and lovers closer indeed, but what happens when someone who is neither intrudes into those spaces that are reserved only for your closest acquaintances? How does your home signal to others the rules you wish to set for maintaining your personal space?

The spaces of everyday life, both public and private, personal and architectural, are, in short, packed with complex codes that we violate or ignore at our peril. These codes all originate in the way that human beings define their *territories*. A territory is a space that has been given meaning through having been claimed by an individual or group of individuals. Unclaimed, unmarked space is socially meaningless, but put up a building or a fence, and the uncircumscribed landscape becomes a bounded territory, a human habitat with its own rules for permitted and unpermitted behavior. Anyone unaware of those rules can't survive for long in human society.

Human beings, of course, are not alone in living under the territorial imperative. Many animal species mark their territories and so transform empty space into codified environments. Where humans are different is in the complexity of their territorial codes, and, more profoundly, in the way that culture has intervened to produce them. To put this another way, the territorial imperative is ours by nature, but the actual codes that govern our territories are socially constructed and thus differ from culture to culture.

To see this, one need only look at the varied ways in which different cultures inscribe space with rules for behavior. Take the way we define the permitted distance between two people who are speaking to one another. The spatial codes of Mediterranean culture, for example, allow you to get very close to the person you are talking to, while those of traditional English society call for quite a generous setback — which is why the English seem cold and standoffish to Italians and why Italians seem "pushy" or intrusive to the English. Or consider the codes that govern the way you should enter a private home. In traditional Japanese society, the polite move is to take your shoes off first. But how would it look if you do so as you enter a typical American home?

Because the human environment is socially constructed, it is semiotic through and through and thus open to cultural interpretation. By interpreting the spatial rules that govern a culture, you can learn a great deal about that culture. Sometimes what you will learn is not especially earth-shaking (that Italians and the English differ on the rules for proper speaking distance, for instance). But often interpreting spatial codes, especially of the built environment, can be eye opening, particularly because public spaces can reflect and reinforce a culture's political ideology and power structure. It is no accident, for example, that the distinctive architecture of Imperial Rome was designed to reflect and convey the massive power of a society that thrived through military conquest. Buildings like the Roman Coliseum and Forum expressed the might of an empire that stretched from North Africa to Britain. While Americans have copied Roman design in their own political architecture (the Capitol Building in Washington, D.C., is Roman in essence), twentieth-century America's contributions to architectural history include the shopping mall and the office tower, buildings that reflect the values of a capitalist society devoted to business and consumption rather than military conquest and empire building.

A culture's spatial codes can reflect its gender codes as well. Consider how in America we tend to regard the private, domestic space of the home as being essentially feminine (if you think not, consider how Martha Stewart targets female consumers or how magazines like *Better Homes and Gardens* are still largely women's publications), while the more public space of a business office is considered to be essentially masculine. Such a division reproduces a cultural ideology that still, after some thirty years of feminist activism, sees the domestic realm as primarily a woman's environment, while men belong in the corporate "jungle," fighting it out with other men for supremacy and power.

The organization of a business office reflects such an ideology of power relations through its distribution of space. Hierarchically patriarchal in its spatial organization, the business office rewards the winner of the fight — the company CEO — with the largest office, the biggest desk, and the best views. Ordinary office workers have to make do with cubicles — nonoffices that spatially communicate their subordinate status in the corporate hierarchy. You could see this pattern rather realistically parodied in the Mike Judge movie *Office Space*, but anyone who has ever worked in a modern office already knows all about the semiotics of the cubicle.

The home, in contrast, is considered a matriarchal space and so reflects the essentially nonhierarchical nature of traditional women's culture (though we should point out that patriarchal privilege intrudes into the domestic space of the home by way of the "master" bedroom, which, as the space where the man of the house sleeps, is usually larger and more luxurious than the other bedrooms in the house). And perhaps no other room in the modern American home better exemplifies the nonhierarchical nature of matriarchal space than the kitchen. Once a place reserved almost exclusively for women, or for servants in richer households, the contemporary kitchen is a space where the whole family can gather together more or less as equals. It is significant, then, that modern homebuyers often regard the size of a home's kitchen as a crucial factor in deciding whether to purchase a house — the bigger, the better. Could this be a sign of a cultural desire, among men as well as women, for a space that is marked by cooperation rather than competition? Or is the size of one's kitchen just another status symbol? Think it over. We'll let you decide.

Home, Home on the Range

Space is of particular importance to Americans, who have made it a part of their national character. From the very beginning of the European settlement of what would become the United States, the availability of land, of open space ("open," of course, to a European: the Native Americans whose territory it was didn't consider the land open), has been critical in the shaping of American identity. Whether officially inscribed in the nineteenth-century

The home as work space.

notion of Manifest Destiny or simply reflected in a national tendency for itchy-footedness — the restless need to pull up stakes now and then and go on the road — the American desire for an open frontier has never ceased. Indeed, the "open road," which has been celebrated in such literary classics as Walt Whitman's "Song of the Open Road" and Jack Kerouac's *On the Road* (1957), is one of America's most evocative public symbols. Now that the real frontier has long been settled and closed to further free wandering, Americans have turned to a new electronic "frontier" that is often called, not coincidentally, the "information superhighway."

The American attitude toward space is especially reflected in our preferred housing patterns. Middle-class Europeans tend to live in urban apartments. If they can afford one, a European family may own a country villa, but most have their primary residences in cities. Americans, on the other hand, prefer to live in single-family houses, usually situated in residential suburbs, complete with their own yards and grounds. Those yards, especially when covered with a lawn, are essentially symbolic remnants of the pastures and prairies that once beckoned to restless Americans from the frontier. The frontier has long since disappeared, but its ghost still lingers on the suburban lawn, crabgrass and all.

So important to Americans is the notion of frontier spaciousness that we even give it a moral value. City dwellers are still considered to be somehow less American than country folk (note how we speak of the agricultural Midwest as the American "heartland": this refers not only to the geographic location of the midwestern states but to its national significance as the spiritual center of the nation), and the city itself is still often regarded as a corrupt space where you may work or entertain yourself but from which you flee back to the more "wholesome" spaces of a suburb. This national moral preference for rural open space over the tighter spaces of the city was made explicit in Thomas Jefferson's stated hope that America would remain a nation of small farmers and would not repeat the urban experience of Europe; it continues today in populist political movements that demonize the city (and those who live in it) while celebrating the virtues of country life. Thus, while today America is, despite Jefferson's hopes, largely an urban nation, our ideology is still essentially rural, tied to a vanished frontier that lingers on in our dreams and desires.

Interpreting Popular Spaces

Let's say that you are assigned a paper in which you are to analyze the cultural significance of a public space of your choosing, and you decide to interpret a shopping mall. How would you go about it? You might well begin by visiting one. Now, look around you: What do you see, and who do you see? You will want to answer both of these questions carefully because the answers you come up with will comprise the heart of your analysis.

Let's begin with who you see. Do you see a lot of teenagers? It will be likely that you do. Now ask yourself what they are doing. Are they shopping, or are they walking around in groups and generally hanging out? Some of the teens will be shopping (we'll get back to them, and other shoppers, in a moment), but many, if not most, will probably just be hanging around. Your next question is, "Why here?"

To answer that question, you need to consider some alternatives, some different places where teens can hang out. There are many such places, and we'll

---

Exploring the Signs of Public Space

In your journal, reflect on your use of public space for recreational or entertainment purposes. Where do you spend most of your time? In fully public parks (include both urban and wilderness parks in your consideration)? Or in commercial spaces such as theme parks or shopping malls? Do you spend time in public libraries or in bookstores such as Borders or Barnes & Noble? In which sort of public spaces do you feel more comfortable, and what is it about the spaces that makes you feel this way?

---

leave most of them to you to identify and consider, but for the moment we'll look at one alternative: a public park. That would be different, and, what is more, public parks are designed for relaxation, recreation, and socializing. But if you hung out in shopping malls yourself, did you ever consider a park instead?

It is likely that you didn't. Now ask yourself why. Most probably your answer would include one or more of the following responses, depending on where you grew up. If it was in a large city, you may have considered the local parks to be too dangerous (New York's Central Park, a popular teen hangout, may be an exception here), or there may not have been any parks convenient for the purpose. If you grew up in a suburb, there probably weren't any public parks anyway, beyond a few rather sterile squares of lawn with play equipment designed for young children. And if you spent your hanging-out years in a small town or village, the town center was probably too dull.

All of these possible responses (and any other ones that you may come up with) point to larger cultural issues. Let's look at them one by one. Say that the parks in your city are simply too dangerous for hanging out, that they have been allowed to decay and are now the territories of street gangs, drug dealers, and the homeless. That, of course, isn't what they were built for. America's urban parks are supposed to provide a kind of public garden for city dwellers who otherwise would have little or no access to the pleasures of nature. They are spaces in which all classes of society can gather on terms of relative equality and were once the sites of such public entertainments as band and orchestral concerts. To some extent, urban parks are still used for such purposes, but less and less so in America's most hard-pressed cities, where the public gardens are becoming public nuisances. At the same time, few, if any, parks are being built today on the scale of such urban gardens as San Francisco's Golden Gate Park, the Boston Common, or New York's Central Park, as whatever land is still left for development is reserved for office towers, shopping centers, and condominiums. When new public spaces are developed, as in Baltimore's Harbor Place, they are often tied to commercial projects that favor upscale consumers over the inner-city residents that they frequently displace. Now ask yourself: What shift in values does this neglect of public park construction in favor of commercial development reflect?

But maybe you live in a suburb and the state of the local park isn't an issue. There might not even be any public parks in your neighborhood. So you will have a different set of questions to ask. First, why do you (or your family) live in a suburb? After answering that, ask why your suburb has so few public parks, if any. Are there any substitutes for a park? Does your apartment or condominium complex have recreational facilities, including swimming pools and gyms, reserved for the residents? Do your parents belong to a country club, or do you live in a gated community that has its own exclusive park? Or is your family's yard all the park you need?

The answers to these questions all point to a cultural meaning, from the reasons America has changed from being an urban society (as it was in the 1930s and 1940s) to a suburban society (as it increasingly has been since World War II), to the ways in which spaces tied to private property rights are replacing public parks as places of recreation. These are facts that can be associated with some of your conclusions about America's current attitude toward its urban centers, because there is a relation between suburbanization, commercialization, and privatization, on the one hand, and the decay of such public spaces as the urban park, on the other. Can you describe that relation?

Maybe you don't think any of this applies to you because you come from a small town that is neither urban nor suburban. Fine, so ask where teens hang out in your community. Do they choose the town center if a nice new mall has gone up on the interstate? If they are at all typical, it is likely that they will prefer the new mall. Why?

The answer seems obvious — because there's more to do at the mall. And there is. A lot more. The same answer could be given by someone from the city or the suburbs. But let's continue to look at what teens are doing at the mall, and, while we're at it, let's now include another group that tends to hang out in modern shopping malls, spending more time sitting and strolling than actually shopping: senior citizens.

Whether teen or senior, we can observe, a lot of people at the mall are using it *as if it were a public park*. Just look at the place. See any park benches, sidewalk-style cafés, trees (artificial or real), even running water? If your local mall is like most contemporary malls, it includes some, if not all, of these features, as well as others that make it resemble, well, what? A public park, right? Which is exactly the way that many of its patrons — who are not, incidentally, spending a lot of money — treat it. It would seem, then, that Americans have not lost the knack of enjoying public parks; it's just that they are looking elsewhere for them and finding them simulated at the local shopping mall. What might this mean?

To answer that question, you should consider what the mall is there for in the first place. It isn't there for the public good, you know. And it isn't owned by the public. Shopping malls are designed and built by corporate interests whose purpose is to make money. Though they resemble, or even actively

---

Discussing the Signs of Public Space

Discuss in class the spatial organization of your college or university campus. In what ways does your campus environment encourage—or discourage—communal relations among students, both for socializing and for studying? What styles of learning does classroom space encourage? For instance, are most classrooms large lecture halls or small seminar rooms? Can chairs and desks be moved to facilitate small group work? What message does the campus's architectural style send? Is it monumental and imposing? Cozy and supportive? Sterile and impersonal? Boastful?

---

simulate, nonprofit public spaces like parks, they are not really public; rather, they are quasi-public commercial spaces that wish to attract people into them as potential consumers. And one way of doing that is to offer the kind of park experience that the public sector is increasingly failing to offer.

Do you see a pattern emerging here? How might you characterize a society that is investing less and less of its resources in public parks and more and more in what are essentially private parks under corporate control? What does such a society value? What is it losing interest in?

But, you may object, you don't have to spend any money at the mall, and, since anyone can enter and use the facilities, isn't this awfully generous on the part of the private companies that own the malls? Doesn't it save the public sector a lot of money on park construction? A fair enough objection, but consider: Is it true that anyone at all can really use the mall? Private security patrols are hired to discourage some entrants. And while people are allowed to visit the mall without spending much or any money, malls are not really designed with generosity in mind. As we've just mentioned, the simulated parks found in many modern shopping malls were constructed with the intention of drawing people into the mall. After all, you can't sell anything without having foot traffic. But that's only the beginning, because simulating parks is just the tip of the iceberg when it comes to ways in which shopping malls are designed to encourage consumption. For while the mall does offer a parklike experience to the nonshopping public, the whole structure of the contemporary shopping center, from its spatial arrangement to the "themes" around which modern malls are designed, is addressed to the shopper.

To "read" this address, you can turn from asking *who* you see at the mall to *what*. We've already considered the parklike settings, so let's turn to some other features likely to appear in modern malls.

In the past two decades, two "thematic" styles have tended to dominate mall construction and design. The first, which was especially popular in the

1980s, is the so-called birdcage or atrium mall — like Chicago's Water Tower Place, Houston's Galleria, and Toronto's Eaton Centre (or probably a mall near you). The second, which has been popular more recently, especially in large urban areas, is the so-called streetwalk, such as Santa Monica's Third Street Promenade and Miami Beach's Lincoln Road Mall. An analysis of these two kinds of mall can reveal a great deal about the ways in which malls are designed to stimulate consumption and so, in effect, pay for themselves. Let's start with the birdcage mall.

Birdcage malls tend to be towers of glass and steel, with vaulting skylights, rocketing glassed-in elevators, cascading stairways, and aerial sidewalks. Though they are often set in urban centers and feature parklike attractions, they tend to shut the real city out by providing no views to the outside save what can be seen of the sky through the skylights. Indeed, with their sprawling food courts and parklike plazas — often filled with carnival-like attractions (especially at Christmastime) — they can look like a mixture of urban park and theme park all rolled into one. So, as always in a semiotic analysis, we need to ask why.

To answer this, consider why birdcage malls would want to shut out any view of the city streets on which they are set. That's not too hard to answer: Many inner cities today are pretty rundown and so can be threatening to the kind of shoppers malls want to attract — middle-class consumers with money to spend. So the birdcage mall insulates them from the grittier realities of the street while offering some of the pleasures of an urban park in a simulated and sanitized form. That's why you're likely to find trees and park benches, fountains and sidewalk cafés, in a birdcage mall. Now, what about the theme park ambience?

To answer this question, just ask yourself how you feel when you enter a real theme park, such as Disney World. Don't you feel like you're on some

Reading the Signs of Virtual Space on the Net

With the much-celebrated invention of "virtual space," the Internet has the potential to alter our conceptions and experience of space. Visiting a library, for example, once meant traveling to a large public building; now, with the Internet, you can visit most public and university libraries without leaving your home. Test the effect of this change by visiting online several libraries from around the world, perhaps by conducting a search for information related to a current assignment, and then visit in person your campus library. Then, in a reflective essay, consider the effect that the Internet has on your behavior as a student and on your sense of space. Does the Internet expand your sense of the world or, conversely, shrink it?

sort of vacation, happily suspended from the cares of everyday life? Now ask how you spend money in a theme park. Won't you purchase as a souvenir some otherwise useless object that, in other circumstances, you would regard as badly overpriced? Or a snack whose cost might equal the price of several dinners at home? That at least is what most people do when visiting theme parks, because the whole point of the visit is to stop worrying about things like money and just have fun, something that usually translates into a bout of free spending.

How does that explain why birdcage malls are designed to look like theme parks? Are those products you're buying needed purchases or souvenirs? The mall's design is intended to make you forget the difference.

The spatial design of a birdcage mall not only makes you want to spend money; it also controls your itinerary as you walk from one shop to another. Have you ever wondered why it is so difficult to find a stairway that will take you where you want to go in a birdcage mall? That's because the stairways aren't designed to take you where you want: They're designed to take you where the mall designers want, which means past as many shops as possible before you get to your destination. This effect is especially pronounced in the layout of an IKEA furniture warehouse: Visit one if there's one nearby and check it out. Isn't it almost impossible to get out of the store once you've entered it without having to walk past every display in the place? And there's so much nice stuff: Won't you be likely to end up buying something you weren't even looking for?

Streetwalks are different. For one thing, they aren't enclosed. For another, they tend to be as linear as the streets they are set on. And they don't resemble theme parks. But that doesn't make them innocent; streetwalks simply work a different strategy in getting you to buy.

To decode a streetwalk mall, it is useful to consider where it is situated. Usually a streetwalk is located in an area that has been reclaimed from urban blight. Ironically, streetwalk malls often rise on the same streets that once were part of a city's central business district but that decayed as middle-class consumers drifted to the suburbs (and to outlying shopping malls), leaving empty and boarded-up storefronts in their wake, along with a few struggling businesses catering mostly to the poor. As the street is resurrected (or, rather, gentrified) in a streetwalk development, the original look and feel of a nineteenth-century urban business district is often simulated — complete with turn-of-the-century-style streetlamps, brownstone shopfronts, and cobbled streets — but the resulting experience is not authentically urban. For one thing, to make room for the upscale emporia and cappuccino bars that streetwalk malls feature, the lingering businesses that served the poor have to be forced out — usually through the agency of rapidly rising rents. At the same time, to make certain that the clientele that the streetwalk wants to attract — usually younger, affluent consumers — don't feel threatened, private security patrols are hired to keep out the sorts of people who might make the streetwalk experience, well, a little too genuine, people like the homeless and street gang members who are very much a part of authentic urban experience these days.

So there's something a little ironic about the streetwalk, isn't there? Designed to re-create an authentic urban shopping experience and so attract shoppers who are tired of the simulations of birdcage and other enclosed malls, the streetwalk creates its own set of simulations. Indeed, as has been made explicit at Universal City's City Walk shopping mall in Los Angeles, which you pay to enter after parking your car underground so you can shop on a "city street" that has no cars on it, the streetwalk is essentially an urban theme park.

You're now ready to write your analysis. After sifting through all of your observations, and all of the questions and answers that stem from them, you can construct a thesis around the patterns you have discovered. We have seen how the modern shopping mall has replaced the public park as a place to gather and socialize in America, and we have also seen how two contemporary mall styles seek to simulate an urban shopping experience by taking the city out of the city, and so, essentially, turn that experience into a commodity itself that can be consumed as the entertainments at a theme park are consumed. These patterns can be differentially related to America's traditional preference for rural space over urban space — hinting, perhaps, at a certain reversal, or at least modification, of our past attitudes toward the city in the last twenty-five years. Which of the two styles of mall characterizes the mall you plan to analyze? Or does your mall use different architectural codes to prompt consumers to buy? We'll leave it to you to put all the pieces together to see what they might mean.

The Readings

Malcolm Gladwell begins this chapter with a startling revelation of the elaborate research that underlies the design of retail spaces, showing how the most innocent-looking display may be planned in response to detailed studies of the behavior and psychology of the shopping public. Susan Willis follows with an analytical report on what she found during her visit to the synthetic utopia of Disney World. Karen Karbo then offers a personal and poignant reminiscence on the significance of the family dining room. Barrie B. Greenbie's analysis of the codes that pervade residential neighborhoods explains why our domestic spaces look the way they do, while Rina Swentzell offers a cultural comparison of a traditional Native American pueblo community and the European American school that was imposed upon it. C. Carney Strange and James H. Banning then analyze the ways in which the spatial design of a university can affect the education and behavior that take place there, and Daphne Spain describes the gender hierarchies encoded in a typical office space. Finally, Camilo José Vergara concludes the chapter with an exploration of the urban ghetto, conducted with both his camera and his pen.

MALCOLM GLADWELL
The Science of Shopping

Ever wonder why the season's hottest new styles at stores like the Gap are usually displayed on the right at least fifteen paces in from the front entrance? It's because that's where shoppers are most likely to see them as they enter the store, gear down from the walking pace of a mall corridor, and adjust to the shop's spatial environment. Ever wonder how shop managers know this sort of thing? It's because, as Malcolm Gladwell (b. 1963) reports here, they hire consultants like Paco Underhill, a "retail anthropologist" and "urban geographer" whose studies (often aided by hidden cameras) of shopping behavior have become valuable guides to store managers looking for the best ways to move the goods. Does this feel just a little Orwellian? Read on. A staff writer for the New Yorker, *in which this selection first appeared, Gladwell has also written* The Tipping Point *(2000) and* Blink: The Power of Thinking without Thinking *(2005).*

Human beings walk the way they drive, which is to say that Americans tend to keep to the right when they stroll down shopping-mall concourses or city sidewalks. This is why in a well-designed airport travellers drifting toward their gate will always find the fast-food restaurants on their left and the gift shops on their right: people will readily cross a lane of pedestrian traffic to satisfy their hunger but rarely to make an impulse buy of a T-shirt or a magazine. This is also why Paco Underhill tells his retail clients to make sure that their window displays are canted, preferably to both sides but especially to the left, so that a potential shopper approaching the store on the inside of the sidewalk — the shopper, that is, with the least impeded view of the store window — can see the display from at least twenty-five feet away.

Of course, a lot depends on how fast the potential shopper is walking. Paco, in his previous life, as an urban geographer in Manhattan, spent a great deal of time thinking about walking speeds as he listened in on the great debates of the nineteen-seventies over whether the traffic lights in midtown should be timed to facilitate the movement of cars or to facilitate the movement of pedestrians and so break up the big platoons that move down Manhattan sidewalks. He knows that the faster you walk the more your peripheral vision narrows, so you become unable to pick up visual cues as quickly as someone who is just ambling along. He knows, too, that people who walk fast take a surprising amount of time to slow down — just as it takes a good stretch of road to change gears with a stick-shift automobile. On the basis of his research, Paco estimates the human downshift period to be anywhere from twelve to twenty-five feet, so if you own a store, he says, you never want to be next door to a bank: potential shoppers speed up when they walk past a bank (since there's nothing to look at), and by the time they slow down they've walked right past your business. The downshift factor also means that when potential shoppers enter a store it's going to take them from five to fifteen paces to adjust to the light and refocus and gear down from walking speed to shopping speed — particularly if they've just had to navigate a treacherous parking lot or hurry to make the light at Fifty-seventh and Fifth.

Paco calls that area inside the door the Decompression Zone, and something he tells clients over and over again is never, *ever* put anything of value in that zone — not shopping baskets or tie racks or big promotional displays — because no one is going to see it. Paco believes that, as a rule of thumb, customer interaction with any product or promotional display in the Decompression Zone will increase at least thirty per cent once it's moved to the back edge of the zone, and even more if it's placed to the right, because another of the fundamental rules of how human beings shop is that upon entering a store — whether it's Nordstrom or K Mart, Tiffany or the Gap — the shopper invariably and reflexively turns to the right. Paco believes in the existence of the Invariant Right because he has actually verified it. He has put cameras in stores trained directly on the doorway, and if you go to his office, just above Union Square, where videocassettes and boxes of Super-eight film from all his work over the years are stacked in plastic Tupperware containers practically up to the ceiling, he can show you reel upon reel of grainy entryway video — customers striding in the door, downshifting, refocusing, and then, again and again, making that little half turn.

Paco Underhill is a tall man in his mid-forties, partly bald, with a neatly trimmed beard and an engaging, almost goofy manner. He wears baggy khakis and shirts open at the collar, and generally looks like the academic he might have been if he hadn't been captivated, twenty years ago, by the ideas of the urban anthropologist William Whyte. It was Whyte who pioneered the use of time-lapse photography as a tool of urban planning, putting cameras in parks and the plazas in front of office buildings in midtown Manhattan, in order to determine what distinguished a public space that worked from one that didn't. As a Columbia undergraduate, in 1974, Paco heard a lecture on Whyte's work and, he recalls, left the room "walking on air." He immediately read everything Whyte had written. He emptied his bank account to buy cameras and film and make his own home movie, about a pedestrian mall in Poughkeepsie. He took his "little exercise" to Whyte's advocacy group, the Project for Public Spaces, and was offered a job. Soon, however, it dawned on Paco that Whyte's ideas could be taken a step further — that the same techniques he used to establish why a plaza worked or didn't work could also be used to determine why a store worked or didn't work. Thus was born the field of retail anthropology, and, not long afterward, Paco founded Envirosell, which in just over fifteen years has counselled some of the most familiar names in American retailing, from Levi Strauss to Kinney, Starbucks, McDonald's, Blockbuster, Apple Computer, AT&T, and a number of upscale retailers that Paco would rather not name.

When Paco gets an assignment, he and his staff set up a series of video- ₅
cameras throughout the test store and then back the cameras up with Envirosell staffers — trackers, as they're known — armed with clipboards. Where
the cameras go and how many trackers Paco deploys depends on exactly what
the store wants to know about its shoppers. Typically, though, he might use six
cameras and two or three trackers, and let the study run for two or three days,
so that at the end he would have pages and pages of carefully annotated tracking sheets and anywhere from a hundred to five hundred hours of film. These
days, given the expansion of his business, he might tape fifteen thousand
hours in a year, and, given that he has been in operation since the late seventies, he now has well over a hundred thousand hours of tape in his library.

Even in the best of times, this would be a valuable archive. But today, with
the retail business in crisis, it is a gold mine. The time per visit that the average
American spends in a shopping mall was sixty-six minutes last year — down
from seventy-two minutes in 1992 — and is the lowest number ever recorded.
The amount of selling space per American shopper is now more than double
what it was in the mid-seventies, meaning that profit margins have never
been narrower, and the costs of starting a retail business — and of failing —
have never been higher. In the past few years, countless dazzling new retailing temples have been built along Fifth and Madison Avenues — Barneys,
Calvin Klein, Armani, Valentino, Banana Republic, Prada, Chanel, NikeTown,
and on and on — but it is an explosion of growth based on no more than a
hunch, a hopeful multimillion-dollar gamble that the way to break through is
to provide the shopper with spectacle and more spectacle. "The arrogance is
gone," Millard Drexler, the president and C.E.O. of the Gap, told me. "Arrogance makes failure. Once you think you know the answer, it's almost always
over." In such a competitive environment, retailers don't just want to know
how shoppers behave in their stores. They *have* to know. And who better to
ask than Paco Underhill, who in the past decade and a half has analyzed tens
of thousands of hours of shopping videotape and, as a result, probably knows
more about the strange habits and quirks of the species *Emptor americanus*
than anyone else alive?

Paco is considered the originator, for example, of what is known in the trade as
the butt-brush theory — or, as Paco calls it, more delicately, *le facteur bousculade* —
which holds that the likelihood of a woman's being converted from a browser
to a buyer is inversely proportional to the likelihood of her being brushed on
her behind while she's examining merchandise. Touch — or brush or bump or
jostle — a woman on the behind when she has stopped to look at an item, and
she will bolt. Actually, calling this a theory is something of a misnomer, because
Paco doesn't offer any explanation for why women react that way, aside from
venturing that they are "more sensitive back there." It's really an observation,
based on repeated and close analysis of his videotape library, that Paco has
transformed into a retailing commandment: a women's product that requires
extensive examination should never be placed in a narrow aisle.

Paco approaches the problem of the Invariant Right the same way. Some retail thinkers see this as a subject crying out for interpretation and speculation. The design guru Joseph Weishar, for example, argues, in his magisterial *Design for Effective Selling Space*, that the Invariant Right is a function of the fact that we "absorb and digest information in the left part of the brain" and "assimilate and logically use this information in the right half," the result being that we scan the store from left to right and then fix on an object to the right "essentially at a 45 degree angle from the point that we enter." When I asked Paco about this interpretation, he shrugged, and said he thought the reason was simply that most people are right-handed. Uncovering the fundamentals of "why" is clearly not a pursuit that engages him much. He is not a theoretician but an empiricist, and for him the important thing is that in amassing his huge library of in-store time-lapse photography he has gained enough hard evidence to know how often and under what circumstances the Invariant Right is expressed and how to take advantage of it.

What Paco likes are facts. They come tumbling out when he talks, and, because he speaks with a slight hesitation — lingering over the first syllable in, for example, "re-tail" or "de-sign" — he draws you in, and you find yourself truly hanging on his words. "We have reached a historic point in American history," he told me in our very first conversation. "Men, for the first time, have begun to buy their own underwear." He then paused to let the comment sink in, so that I could absorb its implications, before he elaborated: "Which means that we have to *totally* rethink the way we sell that product." In the parlance of Hollywood scriptwriters, the best endings must be surprising and yet inevitable; and the best of Paco's pronouncements take the same shape. It would never have occurred to me to wonder about the increasingly critical role played by touching — or, as Paco calls it, petting — clothes in the course of making the decision to buy them. But then I went to the Gap and to Banana Republic and saw people touching, and fondling and, one after another, buying shirts and sweaters laid out on big wooden tables, and what Paco told me — which was no doubt based on what he had seen on his videotapes — made perfect sense: that the reason the Gap and Banana Republic have tables is not merely that sweaters and shirts look better there, or that tables fit into the warm and relaxing residential feeling that the Gap and Banana Republic are trying to create in their stores, but that tables invite — indeed, symbolize — touching. "Where do we eat?" Paco asks. "We eat, we pick up food, on tables."

Paco produces for his clients a series of carefully detailed studies, totalling 10 forty to a hundred and fifty pages, filled with product-by-product breakdowns and bright-colored charts and graphs. In one recent case, he was asked by a major clothing retailer to analyze the first of a new chain of stores that the firm planned to open. One of the things the client wanted to know was how successful the store was in drawing people into its depths, since the chances that shoppers will buy something are directly related to how long they spend shopping, and how long they spend shopping is directly related to how deep

Sports apparel for sale at a NikeTown store in Chicago.

they get pulled into the store. For this reason, a supermarket will often put dairy products on one side, meat at the back, and fresh produce on the other side, so that the typical shopper can't just do a drive-by but has to make an entire circuit of the store, and be tempted by everything the supermarket has to offer. In the case of the new clothing store, Paco found that ninety-one percent of all shoppers penetrated as deep as what he called Zone 4, meaning more than three-quarters of the way in, well past the accessories and shirt racks and belts in the front, and little short of the far wall, with the changing rooms and the pants stacked on shelves. Paco regarded this as an extraordinary figure, particularly for a long, narrow store like this one, where it is not unusual for the rate of penetration past, say, Zone 3 to be under fifty percent. But that didn't mean the store was perfect — far from it. For Paco, all kinds of questions remained.

Purchasers, for example, spent an average of eleven minutes and twenty-seven seconds in the store, nonpurchasers two minutes and thirty-six seconds. It wasn't that the nonpurchasers just cruised in and out: in those two minutes and thirty-six seconds, they went deep into the store and examined an average of 3.42 items. So why didn't they buy? What, exactly, happened to cause some browsers to buy and other browsers to walk out the door?

Then, there was the issue of the number of products examined. The purchasers were looking at an average of 4.81 items but buying only 1.33 items. Paco found this statistic deeply disturbing. As the retail market grows more cutthroat, store owners have come to realize that it's all but impossible to increase the number of customers coming in, and have concentrated instead on getting the customers they do have to buy more. Paco thinks that if you can sell someone a pair of pants you must also be able to sell that person a belt, or a pair of socks, or a pair of underpants, or even do what the Gap does so well: sell a person a complete outfit. To Paco, the figure 1.33 suggested that the store was doing something very wrong, and one day when I visited him in his office he sat me down in front of one of his many VCRs to see how he looked for the 1.33 culprit.

It should be said that sitting next to Paco is a rather strange experience. "My mother says that I'm the best-paid spy in America," he told me. He laughed, but he wasn't entirely joking. As a child, Paco had a nearly debilitating stammer, and, he says, "since I was never that comfortable talking I always relied on my eyes to understand things." That much is obvious from the first moment you meet him: Paco is one of those people who look right at you, soaking up every nuance and detail. It isn't a hostile gaze, because Paco isn't hostile at all. He has a big smile, and he'll call you "chief" and use your first name a lot and generally act as if he knew you well. But that's the awkward thing: He has looked at you so closely that you're sure he does know you well, and you, meanwhile, hardly know him at all.

This kind of asymmetry is even more pronounced when you watch his shopping videos with him, because every movement or gesture means something to Paco — he has spent his adult life deconstructing the shopping experience — but nothing to the outsider, or, at least, not at first. Paco had to keep stopping the video to get me to see things through his eyes before I began to understand. In one sequence, for example, a camera mounted high on the wall outside the changing rooms documented a man and a woman shopping for a pair of pants for what appeared to be their daughter, a girl in her midteens. The tapes are soundless, but the basic steps of the shopping dance are so familiar to Paco that, once I'd grasped the general idea, he was able to provide a running commentary on what was being said and thought. There is the girl emerging from the changing room wearing her first pair. There she is glancing at her reflection in the mirror, then turning to see herself from the back. There is the mother looking on. There is the father — or, as fathers are known in the trade, the "wallet carrier" — stepping forward and pulling up the jeans. There's the girl trying on another pair. There's the primp again. The twirl. The mother. The wallet carrier. And then again, with another pair. The full sequence lasted twenty minutes, and at the end came the take-home lesson, for which Paco called in one of his colleagues, Tom Moseman, who had supervised the project.

"This is a very critical moment," Tom, a young, intense man wearing little 15 round glasses, said, and he pulled up a chair next to mine. "She's saying, 'I don't know whether I should wear a belt.' Now here's the salesclerk. The girl says to him, 'I need a belt,' and he says, 'Take mine.' Now there he is taking her back to the full-length mirror."

A moment later, the girl returns, clearly happy with the purchase. She wants the jeans. The wallet carrier turns to her, and then gestures to the salesclerk. The wallet carrier is telling his daughter to give back the belt. The girl gives back the belt. Tom stops the tape. He's leaning forward now, a finger jabbing at the screen. Beside me, Paco is shaking his head. I don't get it — at least, not at first — and so Tom replays that last segment. The wallet carrier tells the girl to give back the belt. She gives back the belt. And then, finally, it dawns on me why this store has an average purchase number of only 1.33. "Don't you see?" Tom said. "*She wanted the belt.* A great opportunity to make an add-on sale . . . *lost!*"

Should we be afraid of Paco Underhill? One of the fundamental anxieties of the American consumer, after all, has always been that beneath the pleasure and the frivolity of the shopping experience runs an undercurrent of manipulation, and that anxiety has rarely seemed more justified than today. The practice of prying into the minds and habits of American consumers is now a multibillion-dollar business. Every time a product is pulled across a supermarket checkout scanner, information is recorded, assembled, and sold to a market-research firm for analysis. There are companies that put tiny cameras inside frozen-food cases in supermarket aisles; market-research firms that feed census data and behavioral statistics into algorithms and come out with complicated maps of the American consumer; anthropologists who sift through the garbage of carefully targeted households to analyze their true consumption patterns; and endless rounds of highly organized focus groups and questionnaire takers and phone surveyors. That some people are now tracking our every shopping move with video cameras seems in many respects the last straw: Paco's movies are, after all, creepy. They look like the surveillance videos taken during convenience-store holdups — hazy and soundless and slightly warped by the angle of the lens. When you watch them, you find yourself waiting for something bad to happen, for someone to shoplift or pull a gun on a cashier.

The more time you spend with Paco's videos, though, the less scary they seem. After an hour or so, it's no longer clear whether simply by watching people shop — and analyzing their every move — you can learn how to control them. The shopper that emerges from the videos is not pliable or manipulable. The screen shows people filtering in and out of stores, petting and moving on, abandoning their merchandise because checkout lines are too long, or leaving a store empty-handed because they couldn't fit their stroller into the aisle between two shirt racks. Paco's shoppers are fickle and headstrong, and are quite unwilling to buy anything unless conditions are perfect — unless the belt is presented at *exactly* the right moment. His theories of the butt-brush and petting and the Decompression Zone and the Invariant Right seek not to make shoppers conform to the desires of sellers but to make sellers conform to the desires of shoppers. What Paco is teaching his clients is a kind of slavish devotion to the shopper's every whim. He is teaching them humility.

READING THE TEXT

1. Summarize in your own words the ways that retailers use spatial design to affect the behavior and buying habits of consumers.

2. What is Gladwell's tone in this selection, and what does it reveal about his attitude toward the retail industry's manipulation of customers?

3. What is the effect on the reader of Gladwell's description of Paco Underhill's appearance and background?

4. Why does Paco Underhill's mother say that he is "the best-paid spy in America" (para. 13)?

READING THE SIGNS

1. Visit a local store or supermarket, and study the spatial design. How many of the design strategies that Gladwell describes do you observe, and how do they affect customers' behavior? Use your observations as the basis for an essay interpreting the store's spatial design. To develop your ideas further, consult Anne Norton's "The Signs of Shopping" (p. 83).

2. In class, form teams and debate the proposition that the surveillance of consumers by retail anthropologists is manipulative and unethical.

3. Visit the Web site of a major retailer (such as **www.abercrombieandfitch.com** or **www.thegap.com**). How is the retailer's online "store" designed to encourage consuming behavior?

4. Write an essay in response to Gladwell's question: "Should we be afraid of Paco Underhill?" (para. 17).

SUSAN WILLIS

Disney World: Public Use / Private State

If your idea of heaven is a place where you need only relax and wait for someone to take care of your every comfort and amusement, and where no unexpected surprises can crop up and destroy your enjoyment, then Disney World is for you. For Susan Willis (b. 1946), on the other hand, such a thoroughly programmed environment falls a good deal short of paradise. In this essay, she explains why. Could it be that Disney World is just another "brave new world"? A professor of English at Duke University, Willis specializes in minority literature and cultural studies and is the author of Specifying: Black Women Writing the American Experience *(1987) and* A Primer for Daily Life *(1991). She is also one of four coauthors of* Inside the Mouse: Work and Play at Disney World *(1995), from which this selection is taken.*

At Disney World, the erasure of spontaneity is so great that spontaneity itself has been programmed. On the "Jungle Cruise" khaki-clad tour guides teasingly engage the visitors with their banter, whose apparent spontaneity has been carefully scripted and painstakingly rehearsed. Nothing is left to the imagination or the unforeseen. Even the paths and walkways represent the programmed assimilation of the spontaneous. According to published reports, there were no established walkways laid down for the opening-day crowds at Disneyland.[1] Rather, the Disney Imagineers waited to see where people would walk, then paved over their spontaneous footpaths to make prescribed routes.

The erasure of spontaneity has largely to do with the totality of the built and themed environment. Visitors are inducted into the park's program, their every need predefined and presented to them as a packaged routine and set of choices. "I'm not used to having everything done for me." This is how my companion at Disney World reacted when she checked into a Disney resort hotel and found that she, her suitcase, and her credit card had been turned into the scripted components of a highly orchestrated program. My companion later remarked that while she found it odd not to have to take care of everything herself (as she normally does in order to accomplish her daily tasks), she found it "liberating" to just fall into the proper pattern, knowing that nothing could arise that hadn't already been factored into the system. I have heard my companion's remarks reiterated by many visitors to the park

---

[1]Scott Bukatman, "There's Always Tomorrowland: Disney and the Hypercinematic Experience." *October* 57 (Summer 1991), pp. 55–78.

Magic Kingdom, Disney World.

with whom I've talked. Most describe feeling "freed up" ("I didn't have to worry about my kids," "I didn't have to think about anything") by the experience of relinquishing control over the complex problem-solving thoughts and operations that otherwise define their lives. Many visitors suspend daily perceptions and judgments altogether, and treat the wonderland environment as more real than real. I saw this happen one morning when walking to breakfast at my Disney resort hotel. Two small children were stooped over a small snake that had crawled out onto the sun-warmed path. "Don't worry, it's rubber," remarked their mother. Clearly only Audio-Animatronic simulacra of the real world can inhabit Disney World. A real snake is an impossibility.

In fact, the entire natural world is subsumed by the primacy of the artificial. The next morning I stepped outside at the end of an early morning shower. The humid atmosphere held the combination of sun and rain. "Oh! Did they turn the sprinklers on?" This is the way my next-door neighbor greeted the day as she emerged from her hotel room. The Disney environment puts visitors inside the world that Philip K. Dick depicted in *Do Androids Dream of Electric Sheep?* — where all animal life has been exterminated, but replaced by the production of simulacra, so real in appearance that people have difficulty recalling that real animals no longer exist. The marvelous effect of science fiction is produced out of a dislocation between two worlds, which the reader apprehends as an estrangement, but the characters inside the novel cannot grasp because they have only the one world: the world of simulacra. The effect of the marvelous cannot be achieved unless the artificial environment is perceived through the retained memory of everyday reality. Total absorption into the Disney environment cancels the possibility for the marvelous and leaves the visitor with the banality of a park-wide sprinkler system. No muggers, no rain, no ants, and no snakes.

Amusement is the commodified negation of play. What is play but the spontaneous coming together of activity and imagination, rendered more pleasurable by the addition of friends? At Disney World, the world's most highly developed private property "state" devoted to amusement, play is all but eliminated by the absolute domination of program over spontaneity. Every ride runs to computerized schedule. There is no possibility of an awful thrill, like being stuck at the top of a ferris wheel. Order prevails particularly in the queues for the rides that zigzag dutifully on a prescribed path created out of stanchions and ropes; and the visitor's assimilation into the queue does not catapult him or her into another universe, as it would if Jorge Luis Borges fabricated the program. The Disney labyrinth is a banal extension of the ride's point of embarkation, which extends into the ride as a hyper-themed continuation of the queue. The "Backstage Movie Tour" has done away with the distinction between the ride and its queue by condemning the visitor to a two-and-a-half-hour-long pedagogical queue that preaches the process of movie production. Guests are mercilessly herded through sound stages and conveyed across endless back lots where one sees the ranch-style houses used in TV commercials and a few wrecked cars from movie chase scenes. Happily, there are a few discreet exit doors, bail-out points for parents with bored children. Even Main Street dictates programmed amusement because it is not a street but a conduit, albeit laden with commodity distractions, that conveys the visitor to the Magic Kingdom's other zones where more queues, rides, and commodities distinguish themselves on the basis of their themes. All historical and cultural references are merely ingredients for decor. Every expectation is met programmatically and in conformity with theme. Mickey as Sorcerer's Apprentice does not appear in the Wild West or the exotic worlds of Jungle and Adventure, the niches for Davy Crockett and Indiana Jones. Just imagine the chaos, a park-wide short circuit, that the mixing of themed ingredients might produce. Amusement areas are identified by a "look," by characters in costume, by the goods on sale: What place — i.e., product — is Snow White promoting if she's arm in arm with an astronaut? The utopian intermingling of thematic opportunities such as occurred at the finale of the movie *Who Framed Roger Rabbit?*, with Warner and Disney "toons" breaking their copyrighted species separation to cavort with each other and the human actors, will not happen at Disney World.

However, now that the costumed embodiment of Roger Rabbit has taken 5 up residence at Disney World, he, too, can expect to have a properly assigned niche in the spectacular Disney parade of characters. These have been augmented with a host of other Disney/Lucas/Spielberg creations, including Michael Jackson of "Captain EO" and C3PO and R2D2 of *Star Wars*, as well as Disney buyouts such as Jim Henson's Muppets and the Saturday morning cartoon heroes, the Teenage Mutant Ninja Turtles. The Disney Corporation's acquisition of the stock-in-trade of popular culture icons facilitates a belief commonly held by young children that every popular childhood figure "lives" at Disney World. In the utopian imagination of children, Disney World may well be a never-ending version of the finale to *Roger Rabbit* where every product of the imagination lives in community. In reality, the products (of adult imaginations) live to sell, to be consumed, to multiply.

What's most interesting about Disney World is what's not there. Intimacy is not in the program even though the architecture includes several secluded nooks, gazebos, and patios. During my five-day stay, I saw only one kiss — and this a husbandly peck on the cheek. Eruptions of imaginative play are just as rare. During the same five-day visit, I observed only one such incident even though there were probably fifty thousand children in the park. What's curious about what's not at Disney is that there is no way of knowing what's not there until an aberrant event occurs and provokes the remembrance of the social forms and behaviors that have been left out. This was the case with the episode of spontaneous play. Until I saw real play, I didn't realize that it was missing. The incident stood out against a humdrum background of uniform amusement: hundreds of kids being pushed from attraction to attraction in their strollers, hundreds more waiting dutifully in the queues or marching about in family groups — all of them abstaining from the loud, jostling, teasing, and rivalrous behaviors that would otherwise characterize many of their activities. Out of this homogenous "amused" mass, two kids snagged a huge sombrero each from an open-air stall at the foot of the Mexico Pavilion's Aztec temple stairway and began their impromptu version of the Mexican hat dance up and down the steps. Their play was clearly counterproductive as it took up most of the stairway, making it difficult for visitors to enter the pavilion. Play negated the function of the stairs as conduit into the attraction. The kids abandoned themselves to their fun, while all around them, the great mass of visitors purposefully kept their activities in line with Disney World's prescribed functions. Everyone but the dancers seemed to have accepted the park's unwritten motto: "If you pay, you shouldn't play." To get your money's worth, you have to do everything and do it in the prescribed manner. Free play is gratuitous and therefore a waste of the family's leisure time expenditure.

Conformity with the park's program upholds the Disney value system. Purposeful consumption — while it costs the consumer a great deal — affirms the value of the consumer. "Don't forget, we drove twenty hours to get here." This is how one father admonished his young son who was squirming about on the floor of EPCOT's Independence Hall, waiting for the amusement to begin. The child's wanton and impatient waste of time was seen as a waste of the family's investment in its amusement. If a family is to realize the value of its leisure time consumptions, then every member must function as a proper consumer.

The success of Disney World as an amusement park has largely to do with the way its use of programming meshes with the economics of consumption as a value system. In a world wholly predicated on consumption, the dominant order need not proscribe those activities that run counter to consumption, such as free play and squirming, because the consuming public largely polices itself against gratuitous acts which would interfere with the production of consumption as a value. Conformity with the practice of consumption is so widespread and deep at Disney World that occasional manifestations of boredom or spontaneity do not influence the compulsively correct behavior of others. Independence Hall did not give way to a seething mass of squirming youngsters even though all had to sit through a twenty-minute wait. Nor did other children on the margins of the hat dance fling themselves into the fun. Such infectious behavior would have indicated communally defined social relations or the desire for such social relations. Outside of Disney World in places of public use, infectious behavior is common. One child squirming about on the library floor breeds others; siblings chasing each other around in a supermarket draw others; one child mischievously poking at a public fountain attracts others; kids freeloading rides on a department store escalator can draw a crowd. These playful, impertinent acts indicate an imperfect mesh between programmed environment and the value system of consumption. Consumers may occasionally reclaim the social, particularly the child consumer who has not yet been fully and properly socialized to accept individuation as the bottom line in the consumer system of value. As an economic factor, the individual exists to maximize consumption — and therefore profits — across the broad mass of consumers. This is the economic maxim most cherished by the fast-food industry, where every burger and order of fries is individually packaged and consumed to preclude consumer pooling and sharing.

At Disney World the basic social unit is the family. This was made particularly clear to me because as a single visitor conducting research, I presented a problem at the point of embarkation for each of the rides. "How many in your group?" "One." The lone occupant of a conveyance invariably constructed to hold the various numerical breakdowns of the nuclear family (two, three, or four) is an anomaly. Perhaps the most family-affirming aspect of Disney World is the way the queues serve as a place where family members negotiate who will ride with whom. Will Mom and Dad separate themselves so as to accompany their two kids on a two-person ride? Will an older sibling assume the responsibility for a younger brother or sister? Every ride asks the family to evaluate each of its member's needs for security and independence. This is probably the only situation in a family's visit to Disney World where the social relations of family materialize as practice. Otherwise and throughout a family's stay, the family as nexus for social relations is subsumed by the primary definition of family as the basic unit of consumption. In consumer society at large, each of us is an atomized consumer. Families are composed of autonomous, individuated consumers, each satisfying his or her age- and gender-differentiated taste in the music, video, food, and pleasure marketplace. In contrast, Disney World puts the family back together. Even teens are integrated in their families and are seldom seen roaming the park in teen groups as they might in shopping malls.

Families at Disney World present themselves as families, like the one I 10 saw one morning on my way to breakfast at a Disney resort hotel: father, mother, and three children small to large, each wearing identical blue Mickey Mouse T-shirts and shorts. As I walked past them, I overheard the middle child say, "We looked better yesterday — in white." Immediately, I envisioned the family in yesterday's matching outfits, and wondered if they had bought identical ensembles for every day of their stay.

All expressions of mass culture include contradictory utopian impulses, which may be buried or depicted in distorted form, but nevertheless generate much of the satisfaction of mass cultural commodities (whether the consumer recognizes them as utopian or not). While the ideology of the family has long functioned to promote conservative — even reactionary — political and social agendas, the structure of the family as a social unit signifies communality rather than individuality and can give impetus to utopian longings for communally defined relations in society at large. However, when the family buys into the look of a family, and appraises itself on the basis of its look ("We looked better yesterday"), it becomes a walking, talking commodity, a packaged unit of consumption stamped with the Mickey logo of approval. The theoretical question that this family poses for me is not whether its representation of itself as family includes utopian possibilities (because it does), but whether such impulses can be expressed and communicated in ways not accessible to commodification.

In its identical dress, the family represents itself as capitalism's version of a democratized unit of consumption. Differences and inequalities among family members are reduced to distinctions in age and size. We have all had occasion to experience the doppelgänger effect in the presence of identical twins who choose (or whose families enforce) identical dress. Whether chosen or imposed, identical twins who practice the art of same dress have the possibility of confounding or subverting social order. In contrast, the heterogeneous family whose members choose to dress identically affirms conformity with social order. The family has cloned itself as a multiple, but identical consumer, thus enabling the maximization of consumption. It is a microcosmic representation of free market democracy where the range of choices is restricted to the series of objects already on the shelf. In this system there is no radical choice. Even the minority of visitors who choose to wear their Rolling Stones and Grateful Dead T-shirts give the impression of having felt constrained not to wear a Disney logo.

Actually, Disney has invented a category of negative consumer choices for those individuals who wish to express nonconformity. This I discovered as I prepared to depart for my Disney research trip, when my daughter Cassie (fifteen years old and "cool" to the max) warned me, "Don't buy me any of that Disney paraphernalia." As it turned out, she was happy to get a pair of boxer shorts emblazoned with the leering images of Disney's villains: two evil queens, the Big Bad Wolf, and Captain Hook. Every area of Disney World includes a Disney Villains Shop, a chain store for bad-guy merchandise. Visitors who harbor anti-Disney sentiments can express their cultural politics by consuming the negative Disney line. There is no possibility of an anticonsumption at Disney World. All visitors are, by definition, consumers, their status conferred with the price of admission.

At Disney World even memories are commodities. How the visitor will remember his or her experience of the park has been programmed and indicated by the thousands of "Kodak Picture Spot" signposts. These position the photographer so as to capture the best views of each and every attraction, so that even the most inept family members can bring home perfect postcardlike photos. To return home from a trip to Disney World with a collection of haphazardly photographed environments or idiosyncratic family shots is tantamount to collecting bad memories. A family album comprised of pictureperfect photo-site images, on the other hand, constitutes the grand narrative of the family's trip to Disney World, the one that can be offered as testimony to money well spent. Meanwhile, all those embarrassing photos, the ones not programmed by the "Picture Spots," that depict babies with ice cream all over their faces or toddlers who burst into tears rather than smiles at the sight of those big-headed costumed characters that crop up all over the park — these are the images that are best left forgotten.

The other commodified form of memory is the souvenir. As long as there 15 has been tourism there have also been souvenirs: objects marketed to concretize the visitor's experience of another place. From a certain point of view, religious pilgrimage includes aspects of tourism, particularly when the culmination of pilgrimage is the acquisition of a transportable relic. Indeed, secular mass culture often imitates the forms and practices of popular religious culture. For many Americans today who make pilgrimages to Graceland and bring home a mass-produced piece of Presley memorabilia, culture and religion collide and mesh.

Of course, the desire to translate meaningful moments into concrete objects need not take commodified form. In Toni Morrison's *Song of Solomon*, Pilate, a larger-than-life earth mother if there ever was one, spent her early vagabondage gathering a stone from every place she visited. Similarly, I know of mountain climbers who mark their ascents by bringing a rock back from each peak they climb. Like Pilate's stones, these tend to be nondescript and embody personal remembrances available only to the collector. In contrast, the commodity souvenir enunciates a single meaning to everyone: "I was there. I bought something." Unlike the souvenirs I remember having seen as a child, seashells painted with seascapes and the name of some picturesque resort town, most souvenirs today are printed with logos (like the Hard Rock Café T-shirt), or renderings of copyrighted material (all the Disney merchandise). The purchase of such a souvenir allows the consumer the illusion of participating in the enterprise as a whole, attaining a piece of the action. This is the consumerist version of small-time buying on the stock exchange. We all

trade in logos — buy them, wear them, eat them, and make them the containers of our dreams and memories. Similarly, we may all buy into capital with
the purchase of public stock. These consumerist activities give the illusion of
democratic participation while denying access to real corporate control which
remains intact and autonomous, notwithstanding the mass diffusion of its
logos and stock on the public market. Indeed the manipulation of public
stock initiated during the Reagan administration, which has facilitated one
leveraged buyout after another, gives the lie to whatever wistful remnants of
democratic ownership one might once have attached to the notion of "public" stocks.

Disney World is logoland. The merchandise, the costumes, the scenery — all is
either stamped with the Disney logo or covered by copyright legislation. In
fact, it is impossible to photograph at Disney World without running the risk
of infringing a Disney copyright. A family photo in front of Sleeping Beauty's
Castle is apt to include dozens of infringements: the castle itself, Uncle
Harry's "Goofy" T-shirt, the kids' Donald and Mickey hats, maybe a costumed
Chip 'n Dale in the background. The only thing that saves the average family
from a lawsuit is that most don't use their vacation photos as a means for
making profit. I suspect the staff of "America's Funniest Home Videos" systematically eliminates all family videos shot at Disney World; otherwise prize
winners might find themselves having to negotiate the legal difference between
prize and profit, and in a larger sense, public use versus private property. As
an interesting note, Michael Sorkin, in a recent essay on Disneyland, chose a
photo of "[t]he sky above Disney World [as a] substitute for an image of the
place itself." Calling Disney World "the first copyrighted urban environment,"
Sorkin goes on to stress the "litigiousness" of the Disney Corporation.[2] It
may be that *Design Quarterly*, where Sorkin published his essay, pays its contributors, thus disqualifying them from "fair use" interpretations of copyright
policy.
    Logos have become so much a part of our cultural baggage that we hardly
notice them. Actually they are the cultural capital of corporations. Pierre Bourdieu invented the notion of cultural capital with reference to individuals. In a
nutshell, cultural capital represents the sum total of a person's ability to buy
into and trade in the culture. This is circumscribed by the economics of class
and, in turn, functions as a means for designating an individual's social standing. Hence people with higher levels of education who distinguish themselves
with upscale or trendy consumptions have more cultural capital and can command greater privilege and authority than those who, as Bourdieu put it, are
stuck defining themselves by the consumption of necessity. There are no cultural objects or practices that do not constitute capital, no reserves of culture
that escape value. Everything that constitutes one's cultural life is a commodity and can be reckoned in terms of capital logic.

[2]Michael Sorkin, "See You in Disneyland," *Design Quarterly* (Winter 1992), pp. 5–13.

In the United States today there is little difference between persons and corporations. Indeed, corporations enjoy many of the legal rights extended to individuals. The market system and its private property state are "peopled" by corporations, which trade in, accumulate, and hoard up logos. These are the cultural signifiers produced by corporations, the impoverished imagery of a wholly rationalized entity. Logos are commodities in the abstract, but they are not so abstracted as to have transcended value. Corporations with lots of logos, particularly upscale, high-tech logos, command more cultural capital than corporations with fewer, more humble logos.

In late twentieth-century America, the cultural capital of corporations has [20] replaced many of the human forms of cultural capital. As we buy, wear, and eat logos, we become the henchmen and admen of the corporations, defining ourselves with respect to the social standing of the various corporations. Some would say that this is a new form of tribalism, that in sporting corporate logos we ritualize and humanize them, we redefine the cultural capital of the corporations in human social terms. I would say that a state where culture is indistinguishable from logo and where the practice of culture risks infringement of private property is a state that values the corporate over the human.

While at Disney World, I managed to stow away on the behind-the-scenes tour reserved for groups of corporate conventioneers. I had heard about this tour from a friend who is also researching Disney and whose account of underground passageways, conduits for armies of workers and all the necessary materials and services that enable the park to function, had elevated the tour to mythic proportions in my imagination.

But very little of the behind-the-scenes tour was surprising. There was no magic, just a highly rational system built on the compartmentalization of all productive functions and its ensuing division of labor, both aimed at the creation of maximum efficiency. However, instances do arise when the rational infrastructure comes into contradiction with the onstage (park-wide) theatricalized image that the visitor expects to consume. Such is the case with the system that sucks trash collected at street level through unseen pneumatic tubes that transect the backstage area, finally depositing the trash in Disney's own giant compactor site. To the consumer's eyes, trash is never a problem at Disney World. After all, everyone dutifully uses the containers marked "trash," and what little manages to fall to the ground (generally popcorn) is immediately swept up by the French Foreign Legion trash brigade. For the consumer, there is no trash beyond its onstage collection. But there will soon be a problem as environmental pressure groups press Disney to recycle. As my companion on the backstage tour put it, "Why is there no recycling at Disney World — after all, many of the middle-class visitors to the park are already sorting and recycling trash in their homes?" To this the Disney guide pointed out that there is recycling, backstage: bins for workers to toss their Coke cans and other bins for office workers to deposit papers. But recycling onstage would break the magic of themed authenticity. After all, the "real" Cinderella's Castle was not equipped with recycling bins, nor did the denizens of

Main Street, U.S.A., circa 1910, foresee the problem of trash. To maintain the image, Disney problem solvers are discussing hiring a minimum-wage workforce to rake, sort, and recycle the trash on back lots that the environmentally aware visitor will never see.

While I have been describing the backstage area as banal, the tour through it was not uneventful. Indeed there was one incident that underscored for me the dramatic collision between people's expectations of public use and the highly controlled nature of Disney's private domain. As I mentioned, the backstage tour took us to the behind-the-scenes staging area for the minute-by-minute servicing of the park and hoopla of its mass spectacles such as firework displays, light shows, and parades. We happened to be in the backstage area just as the parade down Main Street was coming to an end. Elaborate floats and costumed characters descended a ramp behind Cinderella's Castle and began to disassemble before our eyes. The floats were alive with big-headed characters, clambering off the superstructures and out of their heavy, perspiration-drenched costumes. Several "beheaded" characters revealed stocky young men gulping down Gatorade. They walked toward our tour group, bloated Donald and bandy-legged Chip from the neck down, carrying their huge costume heads, while their real heads emerged pea-sized and aberrantly human.

We had been warned *not* to take pictures during the backstage tour, but one of our group, apparently carried away by the spectacle, could not resist. She managed to shoot a couple of photos of the disassembled characters before being approached by one of the tour guides. As if caught in a spy movie, the would-be photographer pried open her camera and ripped out the whole roll of film. The entire tour group stood in stunned amazement; not, I think, at the immediate presence of surveillance, but at the woman's dramatic response. In a situation where control is so omnipresent and conformity with control is taken for granted, any sudden gesture or dramatic response is a surprise.

At the close of the tour, my companion and I lingered behind the rest of the group to talk with our tour guides. As a professional photographer, my companion wanted to know if there is a "normal" procedure for disarming behind-the-scenes photographic spies. The guide explained that the prescribed practice is to impound the cameras, process the film, remove the illicit photos, and return the camera, remaining photos, and complimentary film to the perpetrator. When questioned further, the guide went on to elaborate the Disney rationale for control over the image: the "magic" would be broken if photos of disassembled characters circulated in the public sphere; children might suffer irreparable psychic trauma at the sight of a "beheaded" Mickey; Disney exercises control over the image to safeguard childhood fantasies.

What Disney employees refer to as the "magic" of Disney World has actually to do with the ability to produce fetishized consumptions. The unbroken seamlessness of Disney World, its totality as a consumable artifact, cannot tolerate the revelation of the real work that produces the commodity. There would be no magic if the public should see the entire cast of magicians in various stages of disassembly and fatigue. That selected individuals are permitted to witness the backstage labor facilitates the word-of-mouth affirmation of the tremendous organizational feat that produces Disney World. The interdiction against photography eliminates the possibility of discontinuity at the level of image. There are no images to compete with the copyright-perfect onstage images displayed for public consumption. It's not accidental that our tour guide underscored the fact that Disney costumes are tightly controlled. The character costumes are made at only one production site and this site supplies the costumes used at Tokyo's Disneyland and EuroDisney. There can be no culturally influenced variations on the Disney models. Control over the image ensures the replication of Disney worldwide. The prohibition against photographing disassembled characters is motivated by the same phobia of industrial espionage that runs rampant throughout the high-tech information industry. The woman in our tour group who ripped open her camera and destroyed her film may not have been wrong in acting out a spy melodrama. Her photos of the disassembled costumes might have revealed the manner of their production — rendering them accessible to non-Disney replication. At Disney World, the magic that resides in the integrity of childhood fantasy is inextricably linked to the fetishism of the commodity and the absolute control over private property as it is registered in the copyrighted image.

As I see it, the individual's right to imagine and to give expression to unique ways of seeing is at stake in struggles against private property. Mickey Mouse, notwithstanding his corporate copyright, exists in our common culture. He is the site for the enactment of childhood wishes and fantasies, for early conceptualizations and renderings of the body, a being who can be imagined as both self and other. If culture is held as private property, then there can be only one correct version of Mickey Mouse, whose logo-like image is the cancellation of creativity. But the multiplicity of quirky versions of Mickey Mouse that children draw can stand as a graphic question to us as adults: Who, indeed, owns Mickey Mouse?

What most distinguishes Disney World from any other amusement park is the way its spatial organization, defined by autonomous "worlds" and wholly themed environments, combines with the homogeneity of its visitors (predominantly white, middle-class families) to produce a sense of community. While Disney World includes an underlying utopian impulse, this is articulated with nostalgia for a small-town, small-business America (Main Street, U.S.A.), and the fantasy of a controllable corporatist world (EPCOT). The illusion of community is enhanced by the longing for community that many visitors bring to the park, which they may feel is unavailable to them in their own careers, daily lives, and neighborhoods, thanks in large part to the systematic erosion of the public sector throughout the Reagan and Bush administrations. In the last decade the inroads of private, for-profit enterprise in areas previously defined by public control, and the hostile aggression of tax backlash coupled with "me first" attitudes have largely defeated the possibility of community in our homes and cities.

Whenever I visit Disney World, I invariably overhear other visitors making comparisons between Disney World and their home towns. They stare out over EPCOT's lake and wonder why developers back home don't produce similar aesthetic spectacles. They talk about botched, abandoned, and misconceived development projects that have wrecked their local landscapes. Others see Disney World as an oasis of social tranquility and security in comparison to their patrolled, but nonetheless deteriorating, maybe even perilous neighborhoods. A[n] essay in *Time* captured some of these sentiments: "Do you see anybody [at Disney World] lying on the street or begging for money? Do you see anyone jumping on your car and wanting to clean your windshield — and when you say no, they get abusive?"[3]

Comments such as these do more than betray the class anxiety of the 30 middle strata. They poignantly express the inability of this group to make distinctions between what necessarily constitutes the public and the private sectors. Do visitors forget that they pay a daily use fee (upwards of $150 for a four-day stay) just to be a citizen of Disney World (not to mention the $100 per night hotel bill)? Maybe so — and maybe it's precisely *forgetting* that visitors pay for.

If there is any distinction to be made between Disney World and our local shopping malls, it would have to do with Disney's successful exclusion of all factors that might put the lie to its uniform social fabric. The occasional Hispanic mother who arrives with extended family and illegal bologna sandwiches is an anomaly. So too is the first-generation Cubana who buys a year-round pass to Disney's nightspot, Pleasure Island, in hopes of meeting a rich and marriageable British tourist. These women testify to the presence of Orlando, Disney World's marginalized "Sister City," whose overflowing cheap labor force and overcrowded and under-funded public institutions are the unseen real world upon which Disney's world depends.

READING THE TEXT

1. In Willis's view, how does Disney World create an artificial, programmed environment, and why does it do this?

2. What does Willis mean when she claims that "amusement is the commodified negation of play" (para. 4)?

3. Why does Willis believe that a theme park such as Disney World "puts the family back together" (para. 9)?

4. How does Disney World appeal to nonconformists?

5. Summarize in your own words Willis's interpretation of the "magic" of Disney World.

[3]"Fantasy's Reality," *Time*, 27 May 1991, p. 54.

READING THE SIGNS

1. In class, brainstorm a list of Disney products, characters, and movies, and then discuss the impact of the Disney corporation on American consumer life.

2. In an argumentative essay, defend, refute, or modify Willis's assumption that Disney World is too controlling in its "processing" of visitors. If you prefer, you can focus on any other Disney park you may have visited. You may want to refresh your memory of the park by visiting the Disney Web site at www.disney.go.com.

3. Visit a local theme park, and study whether it controls the consumer habits of its visitors as Willis claims Disney World does. Then write an essay in which you analyze your park's control over consumer behavior.

4. Willis concludes by suggesting a comparison between Disney World and shopping malls. In an essay, compare and contrast the ways that Disney World and a local mall you have visited control consumer spending habits. To develop your ideas, consult Anne Norton's "The Signs of Shopping" (p. 83) and Malcolm Gladwell's "The Science of Shopping" (p. 642).

5. Write an essay in which you describe how you would design a new theme park for the twenty-first century. What themes would you emphasize? What activities and amenities would you provide, and what would they look like? What messages would they communicate to visitors? Be sure to explain your choices.

KAREN KARBO
The Dining Room

> *Real estate agents usually feature the number of bedrooms a house has,
> or the view from the deck, but we all know that, for better or for worse,
> the family dining room is where the action is. And in this memoir, writ-
> ten in an unusual second-person form, of a life begun in Southern Cali-
> fornia, Karen Karbo (b. 1956) focuses on the role her family's dining
> rooms have had in her life. Here is where "your father never knows what
> to say" and "you are not allowed to leave anything on the table." At once
> funny and tragic, Karbo's memories assume a near-universal dimension
> for just about anyone who has grown up in the United States. A corre-
> spondent for* Outside *magazine, Karbo is the author of* Big Girl in the
> Middle *(with Gabrielle Reece, 1997),* Motherhood Made a Man Out of
> Me *(2000),* Generation EX: Tales from the Second Wives Club *(2001),
> and* The Stuff of Life: A Daughter's Memoir *(2004).*

You live with your parents in an apartment building called the Something
Arms in Sherman Oaks, a sun-blasted suburb of Los Angeles. The building is
standard Sun Belt issue, white stucco flecked with gold, a rectangular swimming pool with no diving board, a panel of mailboxes just inside the front
gate. You live in an upstairs apartment overlooking the Dumpsters. Your dining-
room table is a card table, your dining room is the kitchen side of the living
room. They are just starting out, your parents. It is 1962.

Every stuffy apartment has a kid or two in it. All you need to go swimming is one adult sitting poolside. It is usually a mother. It is usually your
mother, who can't swim herself, who is allergic to the sun, but has an itch,
always, to be out of the apartment. She is a woman with itches, your mother.
Days before she dies she will admit as much. She will tell you she was born in
the wrong time. She will tell you she should have been you.

One afternoon, when you are five or six, you are showing your mother
how you can swim the entire length of the pool without coming up for air.
Your mother is sitting on a chaise, drinking a beer and clipping articles about
decorating from *Family Circle.* You go under and she is watching you from
over the rim of her glass. When you come up you find her talking to Bernie
the mailman. She is making him laugh with a story about how, in her high
school Senior Will, she bequeathed her thick copper-colored hair to every girl
in the school. How she got on to this subject, you will never know. It is part of
what your mother calls the Gift of Gab, something, along with your mother's
fine hair, you failed to inherit.

The dining-room table, the card table, is the only table in the apartment.
Your mother sews at this table, hemming large squares of floral fabric in the

earth tones of the era — brown, gold, avocado — tablecloths for this very table. You learn cursive writing at this table, your pencil marks pocked and wobbly from writing on the squishy vinyl surface.

At parent-teacher conferences, Mrs. Warnack, your first-grade teacher, 5 tells your mother that your writing resembles the hand of Mrs. Warnack's maiden aunt.

You ask your mother, What's maiden? Your mother says it's what happens when a girl winds up old and unloved.

Mrs. Warnack also tells your mother that while she enjoys having you in class, you need to learn self-control.

You ask your mother, What's self-control? Your mother says not having it is how a girl winds up old and unloved.

When your parents have saved up enough for a down payment, they move to a house in the suburbs, a tract house on the border of Whittier and La Habra, also the border of Los Angeles County and Orange County.

One side of the street has sidewalks but no streetlights (Orange County), the 10 other side has streetlights but no sidewalks (Los Angeles County). Your mother trains you to always say you live in Whittier, on account of it is the hometown of President Nixon, whom your mother worked to help elect. It also has a college, from which President Nixon graduated. La Habra has a lot of Mexicans. Not that we're better than Them, says your mother, but we're Whittier people.

In Whittier, you have a real dining-room table. Your mother calls it a dining-room suite. The suite is made of some heavy wood, ashy brown with little black flecks. The table comes with a couple of leaves, stretching it to seat about eight hundred. The style is Mediterranean, with six matching chairs and a sideboard that, your mother says, nearly gave the furniture delivery man a hernia. She is proud of this fact, her expensive dining-room suite bringing a man to his knees, literally. Now, she says, she can Entertain.

Entertaining means Parties. Your mother likes the minor holidays, Saint Patrick's Day, Memorial Day. One Halloween, the dining-room table is covered with a black paper tablecloth, orange crepe paper streamers twist away from the chandelier, not crystal, but cut glass, bought on time from a furniture store next to the Polar Palace, where you sometimes go ice skating, hoping someone will ask you to skate. Your mother has spent the last two days making Sweet and Sour Meatballs, liver pâté, and a lot of other grown-up food. The night of the party she is dressed in red leotards, black felt tail, and horns.

You ask your mother, Are you a devil, or what?

Your mother says, *The* Devil, sweetheart.

The Whittier dining room is still the kitchen side of the living room, but 15 the living room is bigger than in the Sherman Oaks apartment. It is Fancy. It has burnt orange shag carpeting. On the windows facing the patio are gold brocade curtains that are tied back with thick gold cords with tassels. You like to tickle the dog's nose with the tassel, making him sneeze.

You are not allowed to leave anything on the table. You do your homework on the Formica breakfast bar in the kitchen, where your handwriting improves, and where you eat breakfast and dinner six days a week on all non-Holidays and all non–Other Special Occasions.

The Other Special Occasions include Sunday dinner, birthday dinners, graduation dinners, and the few times you have a boy over to dinner. You can count the number of times you have a boy over to dinner on one hand. You can count the number of boys you actually like who come to dinner on one finger.

Jeff is the summer of eighth grade going into ninth. He is perfect because he is one of three boys in the ninth grade who is taller than you. Together, you make tie-dye T-shirts and make out in the pool when your mother is out at the A&P. Jeff introduces you to hickeys and shoplifting. He knows the meaning of all the lyrics on the soundtrack of *Hair*.

Jeff has hair to his shoulders, streaked with auburn from the sun. Your mother says she doesn't like it, it makes him a hippy pot-smoking flower child, but once you saw her hold it back for him while he was leaning to get a drink of water from the tap at the sink. When you do this you are told to get a glass.

Another time your mother chases Jeff around the kitchen, trying to put his hair in pigtails, while you take pictures with your Instamatic. After you get the pictures back your mother says you shouldn't have taken pictures. You humiliated him. 20

When Jeff eats over, it is always in the dining room. Having what your mother calls a beau is a Special Occasion. You are never sure if Jeff is your beau or just your friend, and neither is Jeff. You worry, because according to your mother, he has to be one or the other. If he kisses you, he is a beau. But what if he also talks about other girls he has kissed? Other *boys* he has kissed? You ask your mother. She says, Just don't let him touch you above your knees or below your shoulders. That's for after you're married. You ask her this while she is sewing you a halter dress, backless, pink gingham. Sexy, you think, but you're not quite sure.

Dinner in the dining room always has beef in it. It is always white, green, and brown — potatoes, vegetables, and the beef. Or it's something that takes forever to cook. Beef Stroganoff, something that needs to simmer. There are Pop 'n' Fresh rolls in a basket, coddled in a cloth napkin that matches the Linen. The Linen is not bought at a department store.

The last time Jeff has dinner at your house he has already found a new girl that he likes, a girl one grade older who, it is rumored, Puts Out. You don't Put Out, you've obeyed your mother. Of all the things you must do to make a boy like you, Putting Out, the one thing he would like you to do above all others, is exactly the thing you must never do. Your mother says it's a little like holding a dog treat just above the dog's nose, so he can smell it but never quite reach it. You say, Yeah, but am I the treat or the person holding the treat? Both, says your mother.

No matter where your family eats, your father never knows what to say. He is an engineer. He can rebuild a sports car from the lug nuts up, but has trouble with simple conversation. No problem, usually, because your mother does all the talking. All the planning, all the shopping, all the cooking, all the table setting, all the serving. On the last night Jeff has dinner at your house, the last night he kisses you, although you will hold a torch for him well into college, where he becomes an art major and the lover of a man ten years his senior, your father attempts a joke.

"What's a wild goose?"   25

"I don't know, Dad, what's a wild goose?"

"About this much off center." He holds up his thumb and forefinger, displaying an invisible inch.

Jeff goes har-har-har. Phony? You can't tell. You don't get it. Jeff is sitting across from you. You catch his eye, mouth the words "I don't get it." He rolls his eyes. He mouths something back, he spells something, three letters, a-s-s, partly cupping his hand. You struggle to understand.

You ask your mother, What does an ass have to do with a goose?

Jeff rounds his shoulders, collapsing in on himself like a Halloween pump- 30
kin past its prime. Your mother has a laugh like a machine gun. Your father blushes, mute.

At your birthday dinner, a few months later, there is a present at your place, beside your crystal water glass: *How to Get a Teenage Boy and What to Do with Him When You Get Him*. Not let your father tell jokes, you think, although that seems to be the least of your problems.

When your mother gets the itch to remodel, she has the living room extended to make a real dining room. There are now two steps up and a sliding glass door leading out to the patio. The construction guys arrive a little after seven in the morning and sometimes stay until dinner. Sometimes, you come home from swim team in the afternoon to find the main construction guy having a beer with your mother.

In 1971 there is a huge earthquake, one that will make world news. Most earthquakes are like train rides, but this one feels as if you're standing on a carpet that's being shaken out by unseen hands. You and your mother lunge for the door between the kitchen and the dining room at the same time. You stand there, you two, wedged shoulder to shoulder in the door frame, looking out the sliding glass door, watching while the surface of the swimming pool gathers itself into a tidal wave. You watch while the water slops over the side of the pool, runs down the patio, and sloshes against the sliding glass door, where it seeps beneath the door, drenching the burnt orange shag. Your mother, not a native Californian, worries to the point of insomnia about mildew for weeks. Once, getting up in the middle of the night to use the bathroom, you catch her in her olive green quilted bathrobe, down on her hands and knees, sniffing the carpet.

Senior year, you and most of your friends are not invited to the prom. The Cool Crowd, the soshes, has decided that the prom is only for losers, and as you are in the Second Coolest Crowd, you decide the same thing. You are relieved, since, as your mother says, There is no one Decent on the horizon anyway.

The one boy who she has decided is Decent is Steve, the older brother of 35
one of your friends. Steve has already graduated and gone away to college in Colorado. Your mother buys you special stationery so you can write him letters

at his dorm. Steve has had the same girlfriend for years, but she has a terminal disease, so there is hope for you. Steve actually answers your letters. He addresses you Hey Foxy! Your mother put you on Dr. Stillman's diet, hardboiled eggs and dietetic Jell-O, for when Steve comes home for the summer.

In the meantime, your mother decides you should host a dinner party the night of the prom. She will let each of your guests have a glass of Chablis if you help her plan the menu. You know what this means: cooking. Your mother has forbidden you to take typing in school because, she says, you are destined for Greater things. You secretly feel the same way about cooking.

You and your mother have a fight. You are not going to help plan the menu. You want to know why you can't just eat *food*, why does it always have to be a menu. You don't give a shit about one measly glass of Chablis, you use that word, *shit*. She slaps you across the face. You surprise yourself by slapping her right back. Your fingers leave stripes on her cheek. You say you don't want a dinner party. You say if she's so hot to have a dinner party, she should have one for her own friends and leave yours alone. She says you're an ingrate. You wail, Stop prosecuting me! Your mother's anger dissolves, diluted by amusement.

It's *persecuting*, she says. You're not as smart as you think you are, she says, and I thank the dear Lord for that.

You don't help with the menu, but get your glass of wine anyway. The afternoon of the prom is warm, the evening rose-colored. Even in this stupid suburb (you already know that Whittier, La Habra, whatever you want to call it is a place made for leaving) the evening smells of orange blossoms and possibilities, the kind of evening that, for the rest of your life, for reasons you will never understand, makes you ache. What you will understand is that this kind of evening also made your mother ache, and that's why she cooked.

You have seven friends over. You wear your pink gingham halter dress. Your mother had made lasagna, which she calls la-zag-na, thinking she's funny, a tossed green salad, garlic bread, and Dutch Chocolate Whip 'n' Chill for dessert. You eat off her bone china, use her silver service, then pile into her car, a 1964 Ford Galaxy convertible. You drink sloe gin and 7-Up, you cruise Whittier Boulevard, then cruise the high school, you get so drunk you throw up over the side of your mother's car. You take the car through the all-night, do-it-yourself car wash, spraying chunks of ricotta cheese off the side of the car. You vow to get out of Whittier, La Habra, whatever you want to call it, and never come back.

You go to college, a private college in Los Angeles, thirty minutes away in light traffic. At college, there are many Decent boys on the horizon. More Our Ilk, says your mother.

Your mother keeps track of your boyfriends by their fathers' professions. Mr. Golden West Broadcasting has a father who's the head of production there. Mr. Sunkist's father is vice president. There is also a Mr. Neurosurgeon.

When you talk to your mother on the phone she says, I can't keep your boyfriends straight! She always wants you to bring them home for dinner. You don't, because you can't. Mainly because Mr. Golden West Broadcasting, Mr. Sunkist, and Mr. Neurosurgeon are not your boyfriends. They are boys you know from a class or they are the boyfriends of your new sorority sisters. You pretend they are yours, because you know hearing about them will make your mother happy, and she is.

You should have known something was up when no one was invited to Thanksgiving. Thanksgiving is your mother's favorite holiday. It required days of menu-planning and shopping, getting up in pre-dawn darkness to put in the turkey. It required inviting Family, who drank more than they ate, and were sent stumbling to their cars with paper plates bowed with leftovers.

But this year, it is just you and your father and your mother. Your mother isn't feeling well. She has one of her headaches. She sits at her usual place at the head of the table, trying to slide a mound of stuffing onto her fork, then working to bring the fork to her mouth. She makes it look as difficult as a party trick. If you were either a child or an adult, you would notice that she is not right. But you are seventeen, and only have eyes for yourself.

Twenty minutes after you arrive at your dorm your father calls to tell you what he couldn't bring himself to tell you at the dining-room table: in a week, your mother will have exploratory brain surgery.

You ask your father, Will she be okay?

Your father says, Of course.

After the surgery, the surgeon comes out in his greens. He looks at you, but he talks to your father. The surgeon says, "How old is she?"

Your mother doesn't die right away, but her personality does. The tumor was shaped like a plate of spaghetti minus the plate. To remove as much of it as possible, they needed to take a goodly amount of healthy brain tissue. *Goodly* is the surgeon's word. You ask your father, in the car on the way home, What does he mean by goodly? A sound comes out of your father, like someone gasping for air.

Your mother comes home from the hospital. She stops cooking, but she refuses to stop smoking. You do not have Friday classes, so you come home every weekend on Thursday afternoon. You come home every Thursday afternoon to find her sitting in the kitchen, at the Formica breakfast bar, trying to get the cigarette to stay between her fingers. She wraps a rubber band around the top of her index and middle fingers to keep them closed.

You drive her to chemo on Friday. Afterward, you stop for a box of glazed doughnuts, her lunch. She sits at the dining-room table while you tell her about your boyfriends. It doesn't matter that this is not an Occasion. The way you make it sound, a marriage proposal is just around the corner.

You do have a date with a boy from your oceanography class. He is Mr. Head Lettuce; his father owns a corporate farm in Bakersfield. You don't tell your mother about Mr. Head Lettuce. You don't know why. You have the feeling she won't understand that his father isn't a hick with manure beneath his fingernails; also, you make Mr. Head Lettuce cry, telling him how your mother is dying, only she doesn't really know it. She knows it, then she forgets it.

You and Mr. Head Lettuce stand in line for six hours to see *The Exorcist*. It gives you a lot of time to talk.

You tell him how, just last week, your mother told you she wanted Fun 55
Mom put on her headstone. You were sitting at the dining-room table. She was
eating her glazed doughnuts straight from the box, flecks of glaze on her chin.

Your mother says, Aren't I the Funnest Mom you know?

You say, You are.

Your mother says, Don't humor me because I look like a plucked chicken.
Do I look like a plucked chicken?

In the first days after her surgery, your mother gamely bought a wardrobe
of turbans, all in shades of orange — apricot, squash, and tangerine. Now, she
doesn't bother. Her hair is gone. On one side of her head is the scar, scabby, a
rusty croquet wicket. Scratching it has become a bad habit, something she
does when she isn't smoking or eating.

Mr. Head Lettuce whispers, Are you close to her, your mother I mean?   60

You say, I don't know. Sure.

You mean, Yes. You mean, No. You mean, N/A. It's like asking if your left
leg is close to your right leg.

You never go out with Mr. Head Lettuce again. No one is touching you
above your knees or below your shoulders. Your mother should be relieved,
but you know this is not what she had in mind. No one is touching you at all.

Then, a miracle happens.

Suddenly, there is a Boy, Mr. Orthodontist from Palos Verdes. His name is 65
also Jeff. You meet him at a fraternity mixer and you hear through the
grapevine that he is going to ask you out, and — this is the miracle — the
grapevine was right, he does ask you out. He asks you out for the night of your
eighteenth birthday.

You are expected home for your birthday, which falls on a Saturday that
year. You come home in the afternoon to find the dining-room table already set.
The gold brocade curtains are open, sun filters through the dark pink bougainvil-
lea that covers the trellis over the patio. The table is covered with a gold tablecloth, the cut crystal is out, two glasses at each place, one for water, one for
wine.

At your place, oddly, there is a stack of identical envelopes. Birthday cards
that came in the mail? You don't think you know that many people.

Your mother shuffles in with another card for the pile. She is supposed to
be getting better, your mother, but something in you knows that you don't get
better from this; the most you can hope for is not getting worse.

You flip through the cards, recognizing her palsied handwriting on each
envelope. You and your mother understand what has happened at the same
moment. Apparently, she couldn't remember whether she'd gotten you a
card or not.

Your mother says, They are all from me.   70

Dinner is prime rib with baked potato. Sour cream and chives, only your
mother brings out Cool Whip and chives. You look at your father over the table.
He will not meet your gaze. He slices open his potato, then leaves it empty. Your
mother bypasses her potato, spooning Cool Whip directly into her mouth.

You, like your mother, are a woman with itches. Suddenly, you itch to get away. Away from this dining-room table, away from this tract house, this suburb, this life. You stand up, in the middle of your birthday dinner and say, I have a date. I have to go.

Your father says, Your mother worked for a week on this meal.

Your mother says, Let her go.

It is the last thing your mother ever says to you.   75

You date Mr. Orthodontist twice, then set him up with a sorority sister he eventually marries. Six days after your birthday, your father calls, crying incoherently — you think it's an obscene phone call — to say that your mother has gone into a coma. She lives like that for a day and a night. A month after your mother's death, your father sells her dining-room suite. You note he sells it at a loss.

READING THE TEXT

1. Karbo uses the second-person address ("you") in this selection, even though, as a memoir, it describes her own experiences. How does the second person affect your reading of this selection?

2. Karbo elects to capitalize some words that normally do not require capitalization (for instance, "Entertain," "Fancy"). What message does she communicate by using such capitalization?

3. Characterize Karbo's and her mother's relationships to the male characters, including Karbo's father, her boyfriends, and visitors to the house. How do they compare?

4. Why you think Karbo's father sells the dining-room suite after her mother dies?

5. In class, write on the board passages from "The Dining Room" you find humorous. Discuss why you think Karbo includes such humor and its effect on the reader.

READING THE SIGNS

1. Write an essay in which you analyze the ways in which the various dining tables and rooms that Karbo describes symbolize her relationship with her mother. What connection do you see in the differences in physical spaces and in the evolution of the daughter-mother relationship as Karbo grows up?

2. Karbo describes her mother from her point of view. Study the selection, looking for clues that would allow you to infer her mother's attitudes throughout the piece. Then try some role-playing: Assume the role of Karbo's mother, and write her remembrance of the dining rooms that this selection describes.

3. In a journal entry, write a memoir of a physical place, whether in your own home or elsewhere, that symbolizes your relationship with family members or others important in your life.

4. Chart Karbo's characterization of her mother before and after she develops a brain tumor. How does that characterization evolve, both in content and in tone? Use your observations as evidence for a stylistic analysis of this selection.

RICHARD HUTCHINGS

Argument at Dinner

READING THE SIGNS

1. What evidence in the photo supports the idea that this group of people is a family? How would you characterize their relationships? What event is taking place?

2. Assume that this scene has been staged for the camera. Why has the photographer chosen to position the people as they are? Describe how each character contributes to the overall effect of the scene.

3. Write a scene in which you imagine dialogue for the characters in the photograph.

BARRIE B. GREENBIE
Home Space: Fences and Neighbors

Your home is a complex semiotic signaling system, presenting your, and your family's, "social face to the world," as the late Barrie B. Greenbie (1920–1998) writes in this selection from his book Spaces: Dimensions of the Human Landscape *(1981). Indeed, the walls, doors, yards, and gates of your home constitute a set of rules defining for visitors the boundaries of your personal territory and what behaviors are permitted within it. Greenbie's books include* Design for Diversity *(1976),* Space and Spirit in Modern Japan *(1988), and* The Hole in the Heart Land: An American Mystery *(1996).*

Each of us resides in the center of a personal universe. Our most important boundary is our own skin; the most significant "home" for any of us is within our own bodies, for that is where all experience of whatever larger environments we may encounter resides. Our awareness of the multifold hierarchies of space that constitute our world radiates from that center, like the ripples formed by a butterfly on the surface of a pond, intersecting and reverberating with those of other things and beings.

The newborn infant is apparently quite unaware of boundaries, even that of its own skin. Its own needs and sensations *are* its world. But as children learn to cope with separateness from others in space, they also learn to perceive and to manipulate external objects to form various sets of boundaries within which they can feel secure. Other human beings become part of an increasingly complex environment, and physical structures take on new possibilities for shaping and controlling relations with other people. The very small child thinks of things and spaces in terms of "me"; the older child begins to think more and more in terms of "we." "My house" becomes "our house."

The psychoanalyst Carl Jung placed great emphasis on the house as a symbol of self, and many others have elaborated this idea.[1] Of course Jung considered "self" both in a social as well as individual sense, and in fact the concept of *self* has no meaning except in the context of *others*. Most of us share our houses with some sort of family group during most of our lives, and while parts of an adequately sized house may belong primarily to one or another individual, the boundaries of the home are usually those of a cluster

---

[1] Carl G. Jung, *Memories, Dreams and Reflections* (London: Fontana Library Series, 1969). For an exceptionally good summary and elaboration, see Clare Cooper, "The House as Symbol of the Self," in *Designing for Human Behavior*, ed. J. Lang et al. (Stroudsburg, Pa.: Dowden, Hutchinson and Ross, 1974).

of selves which form a domestic unit. Even people who by choice or circumstance live alone express in their homes the images and traditions formed at one time in a family group.

The architects Kent C. Bloomer and Charles W. Moore view buildings as the projection into space of our awareness of our own bodies. Fundamental and obvious as this relationship might seem, it has been to a great extent ignored in contemporary architecture. A major exception to the rule is the single-family home. Bloomer and Moore sum up the personal situation very well in their book *Body, Memory, and Architecture*:

> One tell-tale sign remains, in modern America, of a world based not on a Cartesian abstraction, but on our sense of ourselves extended beyond the boundaries of our bodies to the world around: that is the single-family house, free-standing like ourselves, with a face and a back, a hearth (like a heart) and a chimney, an attic full of recollections of *up*, and a basement harboring implications of *down*.[2]

Many North American tract houses fit this characterization less ade-   5
quately than they might. But whatever the deficiencies of domestic and other kinds of contemporary architecture may be, they are as nothing compared to the shortcomings of most urban design. A good deal of excellent literature exists on the requirements of interior personal and family space. Far less thought is given to the out-of-doors relationships of one living space to another. This book will focus on the hierarchical structures that extend from the "skin" of the family home to the street and beyond.

As with the living body, the crucial elements of the building are the openings, through which life-giving exchanges take place with the outside world. The poet refers to the eyes as the windows of the soul; the architect should view windows as the eyes of the life within the house. The doors permit the exchanges and cohabitings that support and renew that life. The life of the home is of mind and spirit as well as body, a fact that so much mass housing, especially "public" housing, has overlooked.

The way human beings present the walls of their abodes to the world around them bears the same relation to family identity as clothing, hair style, and makeup do to the individuality of the person. In Amsterdam, Holland, the eighteenth-century houses of the burghers traditionally had elaborately decorated gables called *halsgevel* which were the personal emblems of each family. The forms and shapes, the symbols and meanings we put forth and read back from the facades of our homes are expressions of our individual personalities combined with those of our class, culture, and time. The often deplored "look-alike houses" of North American suburbs are as much a function of the physical and social mobility of the modern middle class as of mass taste and mass

---

[2]Kent C. Bloomer and Charles W. Moore, *Body, Memory, and Architecture* (New Haven and London: Yale University Press, 1977), p. 1.

production. Houses that are really lived in for long do not look alike, any more than do the people who live in them.

The openings in the walls enclosing a space make the difference between a boundary and a barrier, between an enclave and a prison. As the house walls present our social face to the world, so they let the world come in to us. The important thing in both cases is the degree of control we exercise in the interchange. The environmental psychologist Irwin Altman considers all privacy as a matter of regulating interaction with other people.[3] He distinguishes between "desired levels of privacy" and "achieved levels of privacy." In his model, if we desire less privacy than we have, we are lonely; if we desire more privacy, we feel crowded. This simple formula seems very useful when it comes to laying out and designing all aspects of the man-made landscape, but particularly that encompassing the home. Of course, we interact not only with other human beings but with the elements of nonhuman nature, and these too the walls serve to regulate. Windows of our houses let in air and sunlight; they also let in cold and wind. They reveal to us the events and forms of life outside; in the country the shade of trees and the sounds of birds, in town the moon and stars and the shapes of other people's houses. The landscape seen from the window is not the same as that seen from the street outside; the difference is precisely that one is revealed through an opening that is framed and that may be closed at will. Especially in the city, the activities of others may impinge on us too urgently for comfort. Indeed, for modern city dwellers the problems caused by unwanted interactions with other human beings are usually far more severe than those dealing with predators and weather, which historically has been a main function of shelter.

In the public places of towns and cities we are largely on our own as individuals; we exercise control over others to the extent of our position in the "absolute hierarchy," which is based on personal capacities derived from social or economic status, physical or psychological strength, or simply the possession of knowledge, that is, being "street-wise." If we do not rely on these, then we must rely on laws created and enforced by persons who do have such dominant characteristics in one way or another: the police, judges, and legislators. The implicit authority that derives from personal territory is a function almost entirely of ownership or possession of a particular piece of space. This authority, which home turf gives to all of us who are not homeless, is the most basic of human rights. It is recognized, at least in principle, by law in almost all societies, as suggested by the saying "a man's home is his castle." In a world which appears increasingly out of control to the ordinary citizen, the home at least still offers a bastion where every man can be king and every woman queen.

---

[3]Irwin Altman, *The Environment and Social Behavior* (Monterey, Cal.: Brooks Cole, 1975), pp. 5–31.

If this authority is confined to the spaces enclosed by building walls, feelings 10 of influence over, and responsibility for, the larger public landscape are likely to be seriously diminished. If this authority extends outward in relative degree through transition zones into the public street, the street is much more likely to be an attractive, secure, and civilized place. The degree to which the rise of crime in American cities and in the cities of many other countries is related to their spatial design can only be guessed at. But at least one student of the subject, the architect Oscar Newman, has made a convincing case that the relationship in public housing is very strong. His observations, supported by data which have been the subject of some controversy, suggest that where large apartment buildings provide transitional spaces, which are perceived by residents and visitors alike to be under the proprietorship and surveillance of the occupants of the adjacent units, robbery, muggings, and all forms of street crime are greatly reduced. Newman calls such space "defensible space."[4] The unfortunate realities of life in contemporary cities, especially in the pluralistic United States, make the term vividly appropriate. But it puts an unduly negative emphasis on the universal relationship between fences and neighbors.

Where crime is not a problem the existence of transition zones and the sense of enclave appear to be related strongly to a general sense of "community" and to the maintenance and general attractiveness of a residential area. A number of studies have shown that the degree to which residents of various types of housing know their neighbors is significantly less on through streets than on dead-end, or cul-de-sac, streets.[5] While the shape, size, location, and degree of enclosure by fences or shrubs and trees will vary considerably with the style and period of the place, as well as with the culture of the residents, the structuring of transitional spaces between private and public places, allowing for different degrees of publicness and privateness, is important to all. The greater the degree of diversity in the outlook and life-style of neighbors, the more important such structuring becomes. Adequate spatial organization of the urban landscape is the prerequisite for social and cultural diversity. Expanding clusters of fences and gateways, of openings and closings, can give coherent and legible form to complex social behavior.

The transitional spaces between the house and the street have two different but related aspects. One is the transition between the inside and the outside of the home envelope, the "here" and "there" polarity that governs all human experience. This occurs first in the relation of the rooms to the house, and then in terms of house to yard, yard to street space, street to neighborhood, and so on. These establish the boundaries or extensions of "skin" between us and the material environment. The second aspect of transitional space involves the continuum between private and public. For those

[4]Oscar Newman, *Defensible Space* (New York: Macmillan Co., 1972).
[5]The relation of neighboring to street pattern is especially well described in John B. Lansing et al., *Planned Residential Environments* (Ann Arbor: University of Michigan, 1970). Interestingly, this study was done for a highway department.

who seek surcease from interminable interactions with our own kind, the most important aspect may be the transition between oneself and nonhuman nature; windows may look out over small walled gardens or distant views of mountains or sea. For those who find stimulation and creative satisfaction mainly in human interactions, the important transition between inside and outside, between our personal here and the larger there, may be in terms of the private built environment of our house or apartment and the built environment of the urban scene. Probably most of us seek some measure of both, but the proportions and priorities vary widely. Creative urban design will maximize free choice in all directions. Thus, we can look at transitional space as being between one level of physical enclosure and another, and simultaneously as being between one level of social enclosure and another. On the one hand it establishes a relationship between interior and exterior architecture, on the other between private and public life.

The egalitarian attitudes of American culture have led many people to think of fences entirely in terms of exclusion, of keeping something or somebody out. But more constructively, they should be viewed in terms of inclusion, of protecting something within. J. B. Jackson has stated it especially well, defining a boundary as "that which binds together."[6] Apart from weather and serious crime situations, that something to be protected from within is largely psychological. It makes a difference whether we view the fence in terms of an intruder or visitor (photo 1), or as lord of our own domain (photo 2). Only the chronically homeless should see fences per se as exclusionary.

Aesthetically, fences provide form and texture in the urban landscape. Kinesthetically, they define the path space and serve as guides to our body orienting sense. The environmental psychologist J. J. Gibson has defined what he calls the "haptic system," a combination of the several tactile senses with information from our own muscles as we move. Bloomer and Moore, in their discussion of *Body, Memory, and Architecture*, have used the word *haptic* to describe that mentally extended sense of touch which comes about through the total experience of living and acting in a space.[7] While Gibson distinguishes between the haptic system and the visual system, what we see is in fact blended with conscious and unconscious memories of what we have literally *felt* in past associations with the scene before us. Therefore it is appropriate to use the term *haptic* in connection with visual experience, as Bloomer and Moore have done, and as I will do throughout this book. But it is important to remember that it applies to seen objects which at one time or another have been touched and acted upon. For example, we cannot visualize a stairway as a stairway unless at one time or another we have climbed a

---

[6]Ervin H. Zube, ed., *Landscapes: Selected Writings of J. B. Jackson* (Amherst: University of Massachusetts Press, 1970), p. 70.

[7]The concept of *haptic* is well developed for design purposes in Bloomer and Moore, *Body, Memory, and Architecture*, chap. 4. The source of the word is in J. J. Gibson, *The Perception of the Visual World* (Boston: Houghton Mifflin, 1950), pp. 97–98.

PHOTO 1

PHOTO 2

stair. If we have never done so, it will be merely an abstract form. Strictly speaking, only the astronauts who have walked on the moon can have haptic associations with that object, which has for so long been visualized in different ways. If the moon has haptic meaning for the rest of us, it is only because we associate it in our minds with something like a marble or the face of a man. Actually, because we have no physical, haptic associations with it, we can imagine it to be anything we want. Because we experience our earthly environment with all our senses, including smell and sound, the haptic system puts us in imaginative physical contact with places and objects we once touched but now only see, hear, or smell. . . .

The concept of haptic experience is particularly important in considering 15 fences because not only do they have texture in themselves (the pickets in photo 3) which we can reach out and feel, but they define the kinds of spaces through which we have at one time or another moved. In the human landscape, fences of the type shown permit us visually to enter spaces which we cannot, ought not, or wish not to enter physically; such fences enable us to experience vicariously other people's life space without involving ourselves with them or they with us. *The essence of civilized life is sharing space with others without intruding or being intruded upon.* All sorts of social conventions assist in this endeavor. Fences are high among them. Hold a hand over the shadow in the lower part of photo 1 and the scene becomes one of a tranquil domestic yard. When the hand is removed, the human form of the shadow immediately suggests an intruder. The shadow is even more menacing than an actual figure would be, for reasons that are beyond the scope of this book. The point here is that the fence creates a permeable boundary which controls but does not isolate.

The variety and aesthetic richness of fence designs in various landscape compositions, old and new, here and there, the world over, is limitless. At their best they rival any design form of which the human race is capable. Architecture has been called the mother of the arts. Surely, then, landscape architecture is the father of the arts. Perhaps the terms should be reversed to allow for "mother earth." In any case, both begin by confirming the boundaries of living space.

Photo 4 shows a group of houses quite typical of new suburban developments throughout North America, although the larger landscape in this case is quite special. These are essentially boxes, sitting on, rather than in, a generally undifferentiated space, the emptiness of which is only increased by contrast

PHOTO 3

PHOTO 4

PHOTO 5

with the visually rich environment beyond. Real estate merchants call these buildings "Cape Cod" houses. Photo 5 shows a real Cape Cod house. It is on Cape Cod. It occupies a place, not merely a space. In time, of course, the scene in photo 4 will also become a place because the people who live in it will make it one. The trees will grow, shrubs and flowers will emerge, and, depending on the local culture, fences may appear. One way or another the void between the walls of the houses will become elaborated into transitional subspaces, defining both the family yards and the community street. Photo 6 presents a similar house but a very different environment. Although it will take no prizes in landscape architecture, it provides a living space outside as well as in. The prototype of contemporary subdivisions was Levittown, Long Island. Photo 7 shows it as it appeared when newly constructed just after World War II. Today the bleak rows of look-alike "Cape Cod" houses have been transformed into a varied and sensually rich environment, full of interesting yard spaces and individual details. Photo 8 was taken in 1976. In the intervening thirty years, not only had the street trees grown, but shrubs had been planted, extensions added, and yards defined, each in its way expressing as well as enclosing a unique personality. Unfortunately the physical and social landscape around these now pleasant streets has not developed in the same way, and reportedly Levittown residents have been leaving for more secure, if not necessarily greener, pastures.

In the hierarchy of spaces between internal rooms and the street, a most important area is the threshold, which traditionally has been enhanced by some sort of porch. The porch is transitional, structurally as well as spatially, between inside and outside, offering shelter overhead and a raised floor below, but open to the sides. The feeling of being outdoors under a sheltering roof is quite a different spatial experience from that of being outside, exposed to the sky. Most animals, when approaching an open place, stop at the edge of the woods or whatever environment has sheltered them, a phenomenon well known to cat owners, who are forced to let summer flies or winter winds inside while pussy pauses between the jamb and the open door. Environmental sociologists and psychologists, and some landscape architects, are well aware of the tendency of human beings to congregate at the edges of an open

PHOTO 6

PHOTO 7

PHOTO 8

space rather than in the center. Most of us feel much more relaxed with a wall at our backs. These impulses had obvious evolutionary survival value. The feeling of pleasant security given by an overhead roof or canopy very likely originated in the arboreal environment of our primate ancestors, and of course there is a present basis for it in the protection it offers from rain or excessive sun while we enjoy the feeling of being out-of-doors. A terrace or deck without a roof also enables us to be out in the landscape but above it, securely connected to our house. The porch on the street or approach side offers an extension of the built living space out into the social environment, and generally it is also a welcoming transitional area for visitors. On the porch one shares one's house with nonfamily members in a way that is much less intimate than inviting them inside. It is a much more pleasant way of dealing with salesmen, canvassers, and neighborly conversations, especially when the house is not in shape for visitors. Aesthetically, the porch presents to the person entering a visible architectural space rather than the sometimes forbidding side of a perforated box. Porches, porticoes, terraces, colonnades are as important to architecture as fenestration and as important to urban design as fences. When we think of the Acropolis in Athens we immediately visualize the Parthenon, which functionally is a portico surrounding a comparatively insignificant interior space. The Greeks, blessed with a benign climate, seemed to like to look outward from their buildings. Perhaps the most famous porch in the world is the Porch of the Caryatids on the Erechtheum, near the Parthenon. It is just as memorable as the Parthenon though not as typical.

The "capes" and "ranches" and "split-levels" packaged by the building business since World War II in American suburbia do have the free-standing quality described by Bloomer and Moore. But, at least when they are new, they are usually short on porches as well as defined front yard space. They really are boxes; one is either inside or out, with the consequences for our sense of privacy and publicness discussed above. Builders and developers will argue that porches are no longer put on houses because people do not seek to have them there. Fashion is often illogical and capricious, and the relationship of behavior to environment is rarely clear-cut. It is often hard to know if a given phenomenon is a cause or an effect. In contrast, most vernacular houses of the world do have porches of one sort or another, even the most primitive of them. Until World War II, most American houses did, too, and a great deal of socializing in towns and cities occurred in them. The "piazza" usually had a hammock and several chairs, and relaxing there, with or without visitors, permitted a pleasant relation to the life of the community which was not as private as being indoors and not as public as being on the street. One could enjoy the presence and casual company of neighbors and even strangers without any more involvement than one wished. For children, particularly, porches were fine play areas, and much visiting took place in rain or shine, with considerably less strain on adults inside. Older readers may recall the days when one of the ways of controlling the sexual behavior of adolescents was the convention of turning the front porch over to young people when they were courting. There is a limit to what is likely to take place on a front porch (even today), and as a result a very effective but indirect form of chaperonage took place. At present, some veranda socializing continues in older towns and the more stable older neighborhoods of cities, but the automobile has certainly changed things to a great extent.

In contemporary North American towns and suburbs, especially those inhab- 20
ited by the middle classes, probably the most important yard spaces are not

in front but in back.[8] As we turn the streets over to our children and our auto-mobiles, adult socializing turns to the rear, and I found in one study that this is true also in older working-class areas where houses still have front porches. The term *backyard* used to imply a utility area where tools were stored and clothes were dried and children went or were sent. Now the backyard is the first to acquire fences, trees, shrubbery. The porch has been traded for the "patio." The sense of security, pleasure, and pride that human beings find in a piece of private landscape, away from the street, occurs on all levels of scale and affluence, and one can safely conclude that it is found the world over in all climes and times. Where space is adequate, the public urban landscape is greatly enhanced if backyard gardens can flow around side yards and are par-tially visible from the street without being too accessible.

However, in our increasingly crowded and resource hungry world, space is less and less available for such purposes. In attempting to cope with such a world, some planners and architects treat the desire for a single-family home on its own plot of land, no matter how small, as irrational and therefore dis-missible, as they do so many other social and psychological realities. Irrational it may be, but dismissible it is not. Failure to consider the human "territorial imperative" has created at least as much hell on the domestic urban scene of most industrialized countries as it has on the international one. If we must learn to live on less acreage, as skyrocketing land prices and dwindling energy supplies suggest we must, the problem is to understand the spatial relation-ships involved so as to maintain the essentials at increased densities. . . .

READING THE TEXT

1. Explain in your own words why Greenbie claims that "the structuring of tran-sitional spaces between private and public places, allowing for different degrees of publicness and privateness, is important to all" (para. 11).

2. Why does Greenbie see fences as inclusive structural features, not exclusive ones?

3. What does psychologist J. J. Gibson mean by "haptic system" (para. 14)?

4. Explain what Greenbie means when he contrasts houses that sit "on" space with those that are "in" the landscape.

5. What significance does Greenbie ascribe to thresholds, porches, and other entranceways, on the one hand, and to backyards, on the other?

6. What does architect Oscar Newman mean by "defensible space" (para. 10)?

[8]For a further discussion of the meaning of yards to North Americans, see J. B. Jackson, "Ghosts at the Door," *Landscape* 1, no. 1 (1951): 3–4, and Roger L. Welsch, "Front Door, Back Door," *Natural History* 88, no. 6 (1979): 76–82. For a more comprehensive anthropological view of front–back relationships, see Amos Rapoport, *Human Aspects of Urban Form* (New York: Pergamon Press, 1977).

READING THE SIGNS

1. Using this selection as your critical framework, write a semiotic analysis of your own home (or, alternatively, a friend's home). In what ways does it function as a symbol of your and your family's identity? To develop your ideas, read or review Joan Kron's "The Semiotics of Home Decor" (p. 109).

2. Visit the residential neighborhood closest to your college campus, and analyze it in Greenbie's terms. To what extent do homes have transitional spaces that invite a sense of community? Be sure to support your argument with analyses of specific properties.

3. Study a dormitory on your campus, and write an essay analyzing its spatial design. Does it work to create a sense of community, or does it have so much "defensible space" that residents feel alienated from each other?

4. Both Greenbie and Malcolm Gladwell ("The Science of Shopping," p. 642) discuss the effect of transitional zones (in residential buildings and retail spaces, respectively) on human behavior. Compare and contrast their discussions of these zones. How do you account for any differences you might observe?

5. Write your own analysis of the suburban developments shown in photos 4–8. To what extent do you agree with Greenbie's judgments of them?

6. Write an essay supporting, challenging, or complicating Greenbie's assertion: *"The essence of civilized life is sharing space with others without intruding or being intruded upon"* (para. 15). To develop your ideas, consider the experiential differences in living in apartments, dormitories, suburban homes, farms, and other sorts communities. Also consult Lucy R. Lippard's "Alternating Currents" (p. 432) and Camilo José Vergara's "The Ghetto Cityscape" (p. 714).

RINA SWENTZELL

Conflicting Landscape Values:
The Santa Clara Pueblo and Day School

For the European American builders of the Bureau of Indian Affairs day school for the Santa Clara Pueblo community, a building was a kind of triumph over nature, a way of organizing and controlling space for specifically human purposes. For the Pueblo Indians who were compelled to go to school there, a building must exist in a harmonious relationship with the land it is on to reflect the larger bond between human beings and the earth. Thus, the effect of educating Pueblo children in a European building, as Rina Swentzell (b. 1939) suggests in this selection, is, at best, to confuse them, and, at worst, to destroy the traditional basis of their culture. The results, Swentzell reveals, are not heartening. Trained in architecture and American studies, Swentzell actively promotes the traditional Pueblo way of life as well as environmental communication through architecture.

Two very different relationships to the land are represented by the Santa Clara Pueblo, in New Mexico and the Bureau of Indian Affairs (BIA) day school established next to it. These relationships reflect the divergent worldviews of two cultures, as well as their differing methods and content of education.

Pueblo people believe that the primary and most important relationship for humans is with the land, the natural environment, and the cosmos, which in the pueblo world are synonymous. Humans exist within the cosmos and are an integral part of the functioning of the earth community.

The mystical nature of the land, the earth, is recognized and honored. Direct contact and interaction with the land, the natural environment, is sought. In the pueblo, there are no manipulated outdoor areas that serve to distinguish humans from nature. There are no outdoor areas that attest to human control over nature, no areas where nature is domesticated.

Santa Clara, where I was born, is a typical Tewa pueblo with myths that connect it to the nearby prehistoric sites and that also inextricably weave the human place into a union with the land whence the people emerged. The people dwell at the center, around the *nansipu*, the "emergence place" or "breathing place." The breath flows through the center as it does through other breathing places in the low hills and far mountains. These symbolic places remind the people of the vital, breathing earth and their specific locations are where the people can feel the strongest connection to the flow of energy, or the creation of the universe. The plants, rocks, land, and people

Santa Clara Pueblo, 1879. Photo by J. K. Hillers. Courtesy Smithsonian Institution, National Anthropological Archives.

are part of an entity that is sacred because it breathes the creative energy of the universe.

The physical location of Santa Clara Pueblo is of great importance — the Rio Grande snakes along the east of the pueblo; the mysterious Black Mesa, where the mask whippers emerge, is to the south; the surrounding low hills contain shrines and special ceremonial areas; and the far mountains define the valley where humans live. 5

This world, for me as a child, was very comfortable and secure because it gave a sense of containment. We roamed in the fields and nearby hills. At an early age we learned an intimacy with the natural environment and other living creatures. We learned of their connectedness to rocks, plants, and other animals through physical interaction and verbal communication. We gained tremendous confidence and an unquestioning sense of belonging within the natural ordering of the cosmos. Learning happened easily. It was about living. In fact, the word for learning in Tewa is *haa-pu-weh*, which translates as "to have breath." To breathe or to be alive is to learn.

Within the pueblo, outdoor and indoor spaces flowed freely and were hardly distinguishable. One moved in bare feet from interior dirt floors enclosed by mud walls to the well-packed dirt smoothness of the pueblo plaza. In this movement, all senses were utilized. Each of the various dirt surfaces (interior walls, outdoor walls, plaza floor) was touched, smelled, and tasted. Special

Kiva at Santa Clara Pueblo, 1930. Photo by Fayette W. Van Zile. Courtesy Smithsonian Institution, National Anthropological Archives.

rocks were carried in the mouth so that their energy would flow into us. Everything was touchable, knowable, and accessible.

There was consistency in that world because the colors, textures, and movements of the natural landscape were reflected everywhere in the human-made landscape. Reflection on the cosmos was encouraged. Separation of natural and human-made spaces was minimal, so conscious beautification of either outdoor or indoor spaces was not necessary. Landscaping — bringing in trees, shrubs, and grass for aesthetic reasons — was thought to be totally unnecessary. The mobility of humans and animals was accepted, but the mobility of plants rooted in their earth places was inconceivable.

The pueblo plaza was almost always full. People cooked outdoors, husked corn, dried food, and sat in the sun. The scale of the pueblo plaza was such that I never felt lost in it even when I was the only person there.

The form and organization of the pueblo house reinforced the sense of security and importance of place. One sat on and played on the center of the world (the *nansipu*) and thereby derived a sense of significance. Houses were climbed on, jumped on, slept on, and cooked on. They were not material symbols of wealth but were rather, in Thoreau's terminology, a most direct and elegantly simple expression of meeting the human need for shelter.

Construction methods and materials were uncomplicated. The most direct methods were combined with the most accessible materials. Everyone participated, without exception — children, men, women, and elders. Anybody could build a house or any necessary structure. Designers and architects were unnecessary since there was no conscious aesthetic striving or stylistic interest.

Crucial elements of the house interiors were the low ceilings; rounded and hand-plastered walls; small, dark areas; tiny, sparse windows, and doors; and multiple-use rooms. All interior spaces were shared by everybody, as were the exterior spaces. The need for individual privacy was not important enough to affect the plan of pueblo houses. Privacy was viewed in a different way; it was carried around within the individual and walls and physical space were not needed to defend it. Sharing was crucial.

Within the house, as without, spirits moved freely. Members of families were sometimes buried in the dirt floor and their spirits became a part of the house environment. Besides those spirits there were others who had special connections with the house structure because they assisted in its construction or because they were born or died in it. Since houses survived many generations, the spirits were many. Houses were blessed with a special ceremony similar to the ritual performed for a baby at birth. There was also an easy acceptance of the deterioration of a house. Houses, like people's bodies, came from and went back into the earth.

Santa Clara Pueblo: view from roof of Pueblo Church, 1899. Photo by Vroman. Courtesy Smithsonian Institution, National Anthropological Archives.

Santa Clara Pueblo: view from roof of Pueblo Church, 1899. Photo by Vromen. Courtesy Smithsonian Institution, National Anthropological Archives.

Evolution of the Santa Clara Pueblo from traditional form (top left) to recent years (bottom). Drawing by Rina Swentzell.

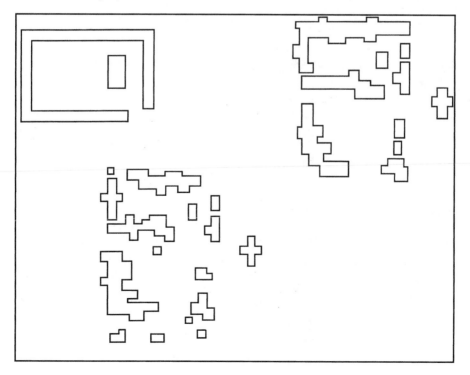

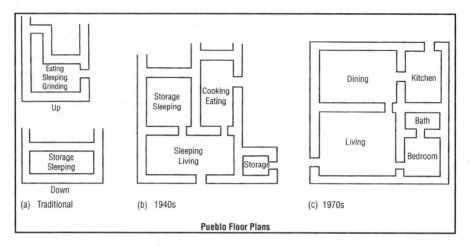

Typical pueblo interior room arrangements: (a) traditional, (b) 1940s, (c) 1970s.
Drawing by Rina Swentzell.

Ideas that characterize the pueblo human-made and natural environments, then, are that humans and nature are inseparable, that human environments emulate and reflect the cosmos, that creative energy flows through
the natural environment (of which every aspect, including rocks, trees, clouds,
and people, is alive), and that aesthetics and the cosmos are synonymous.

How Western Education Shaped the BIA Day School Landscape

"The goal, from the beginning of attempts at formal education of the American Indian, has been not so much to educate him as to change him."[1]

Santa Clara Day School was introduced to such a world in the early 1890s
during the BIA's golden age of constructing schools for Native Americans. In
the very early years of European settlement in America, various religious
groups attempted to civilize and Christianize Native Americans. In 1832, that
responsibility was assumed by the Commissioner of Indian Affairs and the
focus narrowed to civilizing Native Americans.

From 1890 to 1928, the goal was to assimilate Native Americans; the
tactics were dissolving their social structure through Western education and
destroying their land base. After 1928, when an influential government
study asked for "a change in point of view" in how Native Americans should
be educated, programs in bilingual education, adult basic education, training
of Native American teachers, Native American culture, and in-service teacher

[1]Committee on Labor and Public Welfare, *Indian Education: A National Tragedy—A National
Challenge* (Washington: U.S. Government Printing Office, 1969), 10.

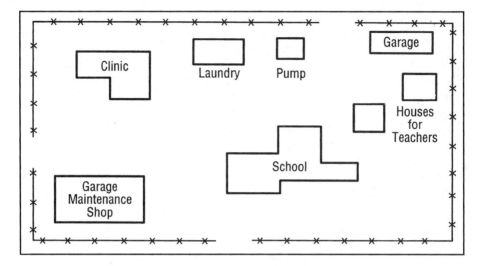

Santa Clara Bureau of Indian Affairs school grounds: plan. Drawing by Rina Swentzell.

training were initiated across the country. But these programs were halted almost as quickly, and certainly before the ideas reached the Santa Clara Day School.

The years after 1944 saw a new determination to terminate Native American reservations and abolish the special relationships between Native Americans and the federal government, relationships that had been guaranteed by centuries of law and treaties.[2] It was during this time, from 1945 to 1951, that I attended Santa Clara Pueblo Day School.

The government school grounds and buildings, built during the 1920s, not only reflected that attitude of changing and civilizing Native Americans but also characterized the general Western European attitude of human control that seems to stem from the Renaissance glorification of human capabilities. Everything had to be changed to make it accord with the Western way of thinking and being. The BIA school compounds reflected a foreign worldview that opposed the pueblo world and its physical organization.

At Santa Clara, the BIA school complex was located a quarter of a mile 20 from the center of the pueblo and had a barbed-wire fence around its periphery. That fence defined the complex and effectively kept the two worlds separate. The cattle guards and the double-stiled ladders built over the fence provided the only openings into the compound. They kept out both animals and old people. All large rocks and natural trees had been removed a long time before I was a student and there were but a few foreign elm trees in the barren, isolated landscape.

[2]Ibid., 13.

The loss of trust that occurred when people moved from the pueblo to the school setting was most striking. Within the pueblo, preschool-aged children were allowed enormous freedom of activity and choice; to a great extent they were trusted as capable of being in charge of themselves. This liberal assumption created its own self-fulfilling prophecy. Since pueblo children were expected to care for themselves in an adequate, responsible way, they generally did.

But within the BIA school, there was a different attitude: The overall atmosphere was one of skepticism. The fence was an expression of the lack of respect and trust in others. Although the formal reason given for the fence was that it kept out animals, everyone in the pueblo knew its purpose was also to keep people out. It was unsettling to know that other people had to protect themselves physically from community.

As the school grounds were separated from the life and environment around them, so were the various structures located within the compound separate from each other. There were separate laundry and shower buildings — as part of the civilizing effort, everybody, including adults, was supposed to take showers. Also included in the compound were a health clinic, a maintenance shop, the main school building, and small separate houses for the teachers. All of them were scattered seemingly randomly in the approximately five-acre compound.

Within the school building, children were grouped into rooms according to grade level. Inside the various classrooms, the divisions continued. Those who could read well were separated from those who could not. Individual desks and mats were assigned. Individual achievement was praised. Concentration on the individual, or the parts, which has become the hallmark of modern American society, was strongly emphasized. This was in contrast to the holistic concepts of the pueblo, which emphasized togetherness and cooperation and which were expressed in connected and multiple-function structures.

The floor plan of the school was efficient and designed to create an aspi-   25
ration of moving up — the good old American attitude of upward mobility — from one room and grade level to the next. The move, however, was always disappointing because there were expectations that something special would happen in the next room, but it never did. The whole system had a way of making people unhappy with the present situation. Again, this was totally foreign to pueblo thinking, which worked toward a settling into the earth and, consequently, into being more satisfied with the moment and the present.

Inside the schoolhouse the ceilings were very high. The proportions of the rooms were discomforting — the walls were very tall relative to the small floor space. The Catholic church in the pueblo also had high ceilings, for Spanish priests sought to maximize both interior and exterior height in the missions they built. But in the church there was no sense of overhead, top-heavy space.

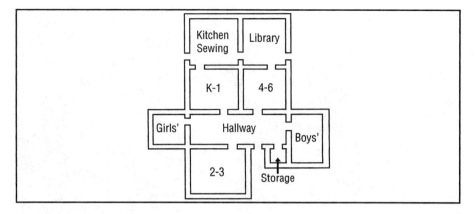

Santa Clara Pueblo Day School: plan. Drawing by Rina Swentzell.

It had heavy, soft walls at eye level to balance its height, as well as dark interiors that made the height less obvious.

Although there were plenty of buildings on the school grounds, it seemed that there were never enough people to make the spaces within the grounds feel comfortable. Everything seemed at a distance. The message was, Don't touch, don't interact. The exterior formality of the structures, as well as the materials used, discouraged climbing on them, scratching them, tasting them, or otherwise affecting them. There was no way to be part of the place, the buildings, or the lives of teachers who lived there.

The creation of artificial play areas on the school grounds within the pueblo context and community was ironic. The total environment (natural as well as human-created) was included in the pueblo world of play. Play and work were barely distinguishable. Every activity was something to be done and done as well as possible; the relaxation or joy that play gives was to be found in submerging oneself in the activity at hand.

Play and work were distinguished from one another in the BIA school, and specific time was assigned for both. There were recesses from work, yet play was constantly supervised so that the children could not discover the world for themselves. Every possible danger was guarded against. Lack of trust was evident in the playground as opposed to the pueblo setting, where we roamed the fields and hills.

It was apparent that the Anglo teachers preferred indoor and human-made spaces over the outdoors, and they tried to instill this preference in us. In the pueblo, the outdoors was unquestionably preferred. 30

The saddest aspect of the entire school complex was the ground. There was no centering, no thought, no respect given to the ground. The native plants and rocks had been disturbed a long time ago and the land had lost all the variety one finds in small places created by bushes, rocks or rises, and falls

Buildings at the BIA school were constructed with pitched roofs, which were foreign to the Pueblo residents. Photo by Rina Swentzell.

of the ground. The ground has been scraped and leveled, and metal play equipment was set upon it. It was also a gray color, which was puzzling because the ground in the pueblo plaza, only a quarter of a mile away, was a warm brown.

The sensation of being in the pueblo was very different from that of being on the school grounds. The pueblo plaza had soulfulness. It was endowed with spirit. The emergence place of the people from the underground was located within the plaza and the breath of the cosmos flowed in and out of it. The land, the ground, breathed there; it was alive. The school grounds were imbued with sadness because the spirit of the place, the land, was not recognized. Nothing flowed naturally. The vitality of the school came from faraway worlds, from lands described in books. Appreciation of the immediate landscape was impossible.

The Legacy of Conflicting Landscape Values

The pueblo and the school grounds were imbued with different cultural values, attitudes, and perceptions, and the students who moved from one setting to the other were deeply affected by those differences.

The school was part of a world that was whole unto itself, and its orientation toward the future, time assignments, specialized buildings, artificial playgrounds, and overall concern with segmentation were elements of a conscious worldview that was not concerned with harmony and acceptance of spirituality in the landscape.

The government did not come to Santa Clara Pueblo out of inner kindness 35
or benevolence. Rather, the government was dealing with Native Americans
in what it considered to be the most efficient manner. This efficiency, which
was so apparent in the structures, took away human interaction and dignity.
We had to give ourselves totally to this order.

BIA authoritarianism assured the absence of any human-to-human or
human-to-nature interaction. The monumental structures and sterile outdoor
spaces in no manner stimulated the community to enter and exchange communications at any time or at any level of equality. In that people-proof environment, the natural curiosity that children have about their world was dulled
and respect for teachers far exceeded respect for the larger forces in the
world.

Santa Clara Day School was a typical American school of its era — isolated
and authoritatively emphatic. Its visual landscape read accordingly with the
surrounding fence, the barren land, and the tall, pitched-roof structures scattered within the compound.

But the longest-lasting impact may not be visual. The two physical settings taught different types of behavior to pueblo children. Consequently, lack
of confidence and feelings of inadequacy have become characteristic traits of
children who lived in the pueblo and went to the BIA school.

READING THE TEXT

1. Summarize in your own words the Pueblo community's relationship to the
   land.
2. In class, list on the board the typical architectural features of a Pueblo village.
   Then discuss how those features reflect the Pueblo worldview. What underlying cultural values, in other words, are expressed in Pueblo building and community design?
3. List the architectural features of the BIA day school. How does this list
   compare with your list of the Pueblo's traditionally preferred architectural
   design?
4. Summarize in your own words the traditional Pueblo and the BIA methods of
   education.
5. Swentzell reveals that she grew up in the Santa Clara Pueblo. In what ways
   does her inclusion of personal experience affect the persuasiveness of her
   argument?

READING THE SIGNS

1. Study the physical design of your composition classroom. Does it have mov-
   able chairs, or are the seats bolted to the floor? Does the design enable small
   group work to occur, or is it more conducive to lectures? Of what materials is
   the furniture constructed? Use the details of your observations as evidence for
   an essay in which you argue whether the room's physical layout enhances

or impedes learning as your instructor has designed the course. To develop your ideas, consult C. Carney Strange and James H. Banning, "Educating by Design" (p. 699).

2. Write an essay in which you argue to what extent the BIA day school architecture reflects the American myth of Manifest Destiny — the belief that it was God's plan that Anglo Americans should dominate North America from the Atlantic to the Pacific oceans. You might consult a history textbook or the Internet for an overview of this belief.

3. Both Swentzell and Fan Shen ("The Classroom and the Wider Culture: Identity as a Key to Learning English Composition," p. 619) describe non-Western approaches to education. Study the two selections, noting the educational methods that the authors describe as non-Western. Write an argumentative essay in which you evaluate those methods. To what extent would American education benefit from including approaches it traditionally has not emphasized?

4. Swentzell describes Pueblo educational philosophy as valuing hands-on learning that could stimulate students' curiosity about the world around them. In class, debate whether you believe that philosophy could benefit education at the university level. Use your class discussion as a springboard for your own argumentative essay about this question.

C. CARNEY STRANGE AND JAMES H. BANNING
Educating by Design

A college campus isn't just a collection of buildings separated by walk-ways, lawns, and trees: It is a planned environment whose dimensions and design assist in the functioning of the campus as a whole. In this description of the educational logic of campus design, C. Carney Strange and James H. Banning show how every building, from the admissions office to the library, helps or hinders the college experience. C. Carney Strange (b. 1947), a professor of education at Bowling Green State University, and James H. Banning (b. 1938), a professor of education at Colorado State University, are coauthors of Educating by Design: Creating Campus Learning Environments That Work *(2001), from which this selection is taken.*

Scenario: The Campus Visit

The Carter family — Joe, Dorothy, and son Eric — picked up their rental car after landing at Mountain International Airport and started on the forty-mile trip to Mid-Rocky University (MRU). The occasion for their visit was twofold: to attend Dorothy's niece's graduation later in the day and to visit the admissions office for a campus tour as Eric is thinking about attending MRU.

They found the interstate to MRU without a problem. As they approached the community of Redville, the home of MRU, they began to look for signs directing them to the university campus. The first sign indicated that the next three exits would lead to the university stadium. While discussing the question of whether the university stadium exit would be the same as the university exit, they missed the first exit. The first exit went by so quickly, that when the second exit came up they decided to take it. At the top of the exit ramp the sign indicated that the stadium was to the left. After going several miles without any additional signage, they discovered that they were in an area that resembled a university. On further inspection at the next stoplight, they noticed a faint Mid-Rocky University sign embedded in a concrete pillar. They also saw a directional sign with the word *Visitor* on it. They appeared to be in luck and faithfully followed the next three visitor signs assuming that they would lead to the admissions office, a welcome or information center, or at least to a visitors' parking lot. But after obeying four directional signs they found themselves at a dead-end in front of the university's power plant.

After asking a few people for additional directions, they backtracked and eventually found a visitors' parking lot. After examining MRU's you-are-here map (located in a faculty parking lot), they discovered the admissions office was at least nearby. After being confused by the sign outside the admissions building, they finally entered to find the admission office located on the second floor of the building. At the top of the two flights of steps they were not at all sure they had found the correct admissions office because the signage seemed to suggest that it was admissions for the university's graduate school. They were correct, however, and so they acquired the needed information about MRU, a college catalogue, and the admissions application material.

Next on the Carters' agenda was a quick self-guided campus tour. They wandered through several buildings just to get a feel for the campus. They noted that the buildings, while showing some age, were well kept and that there was very little litter around the grounds or inside the buildings. Dorothy, a professor herself at a large land-grant university on the East Coast, peeked into several classrooms. She found what she had become all too familiar with — large classrooms with the seats bolted down in rows with an elevated lectern some distance from the first row of students. In the Education building she did notice a carpeted classroom with moveable chairs, tables, and several pieces of visual aid equipment. This was what she was hoping to find, since MRU was marketing itself as "a learning university with a college feel." Finding only one such classroom, she remained a bit skeptical about the marketing slogan.

After a quick tour of the academic buildings, the Carters asked for directions to the student union. Finding the student union was relatively simple; it was in the center of campus and almost every sidewalk eventually led to the plaza in front of the building. The student union was busy with activity but looked well maintained with little trash or signs of abuse. In fact, it was obvious that a renovation project had just been completed. The decor was oak and mauve, and most of the "institutional" stainless steel and plastic had been removed. From a table in a quiet corner of the food court, a pleasant lagoon could be seen with geese swimming near the shore. Just west of the lagoon was a nice rolling landscape with a few pines and old elm trees marking the area in a rather stately manner. 5

On the way out of the building, Eric asked a passing student how far it was to walk to the stadium. The student responded with a polite laugh and indicated that the stadium was five or six miles from campus and there was no direct walking route. It now seemed to the Carters that it was a bit of luck on their part that they did not try to find the university by following highway signs to the stadium.

After checking into the local motel and grabbing a fast bite to eat, it was time to find the field house for the graduation ceremonies. The ceremonies went smoothly despite what seemed to be an unusual amount of rowdiness. But Dorothy and Joe just passed it off, lamenting the need to reintroduce civility as subject matter for university and college curricula. By evening's end, they had accomplished their goals. Their niece was pleased that they were able to attend her graduation, and the campus visit, though frustrating at times, did expose Eric to Mid-Rocky University.

The Carter family's experiences in this scenario are common to all who visit, study, or work on a college or university campus. This scenario also illustrates just how complex and important the physical design and spaces of these institutions and their environs are in terms of how individuals interact with them. . . .

From the view of prospective college students, the physical features are often among the most important factors in creating a critical first impression of an institution (Sturner, 1973; Thelin & Yankovich, 1987). The basic layout of the campus, open spaces and shaded lawns (Griffith, 1994), the accessibility and cleanliness of parking lots, interior color schemes, the shape and design of a residence hall or classroom building, a library or gallery, an impressive fitness center, and even the weather on the day of a campus visit all shape initial attitudes in subtle ways (Stern, 1986). In a firsthand study of campus life on twenty-nine different college campuses, Boyer (1987) observed:

> Little wonder that when we asked students what influenced them most during their visit to a campus, about half mentioned "the friendliness of students we met." But it was the buildings, the trees, the walkways, and the well-kept lawns that overwhelmingly won out. The appearance of the campus is, by far, the most influential characteristic during campus visits, and we gained the distinct impression that when it comes to recruiting students, the director of buildings and grounds may be more important than the academic dean. [p. 17]

It is clear that the campus physical environment is an important feature that influences students' attraction to and satisfaction with a particular institution. What then is the nature of that influence, and how does the campus physical environment shape specific behavior? . . .

How the Physical Environment Communicates Nonverbally

The complexity surrounding campus physical environments and the influence of their designs and spaces becomes clearer when the nature of that influence and how the features of various campus environments impact specific behaviors are considered. Whether natural or synthetic, the physical aspects of any campus environment offer many possibilities for human response, rendering some behaviors more probable than others. It is the nature of this influence to be both functional and symbolic. An admissions office located on a second floor is functional in that its design is capable of allowing the duties and activities of the admissions office to be carried out, but the location also sends out messages or symbolizes various possibilities. For example, the symbolic message of a second-floor location may communicate that the institution does not give serious consideration to the users of the service nor their needs for accessibility and convenience. Or the message may be that the institution does not see this function as an important aspect of its mission. Perhaps the second-floor location also indicates that the university is without the necessary funds to relocate the office. The symbolic view of campus environments suggests that they can potentially convey all of these messages, depending of course on the meaning people ascribe to them.

It is this link between the functional and symbolic aspects of campus physical environments that leads to an understanding of how campus physical environments impact behavior. Rapaport (1982) suggested that the important link between function and symbol in the physical environment is nonverbal communication. He noted, "Since environments apparently provide cues for behavior, but do not do it verbally, it follows that they must represent a form of nonverbal behavior" (p. 50). Nonverbal communication incorporates "those messages expressed by other than linguistic means" (Adler & Towne, 1987, p. 188). Cues from the physical environment naturally fall into this category. Rapaport (1982) states: "environments are more than just inhibiting, facilitating, or even catalytic; they not only remind, they also predict and describe" (p. 77). The environment "thus communicates, through a whole set of cues, the most appropriate choices to be made: the cues are meant to elicit appropriate emotions, interpretations, behaviors, and transactions by setting up the appropriate situations and contexts" (Rapaport, pp. 80–81).

The functional aspects of campus physical environments are designed and built, but the function of designing and building creates nonverbal messages that users of the campus environment then read. For example, if the campus decides to make a curb wheelchair accessible by molding some asphalt to the curb, instead of installing proper curb cuts, such an adaptation might be technically functional, but it may also encode messages of "not caring enough to do it correctly," "not valuing the user," or just "responding minimally to needs of the physically challenged." When the student in a wheelchair rolls up to the makeshift curb, the decoded message may reveal that "the institution doesn't care about me; I am not valued." On the other hand, if the curb cut is correctly designed and constructed, the encoded and decoded messages may strike a different tone, conveying a sense that "the institution cared enough to do it correctly." Consequently the person concludes: "I feel valued" and "You care about me." Again, both adaptations are functional, but they are quite different in their symbolic messages. The functionality of the campus physical environment not only affords and constrains certain activities, but it also communicates important nonverbal, symbolic messages.

The research supporting the nonverbal communications link between the physical environment and behavior is well established. For example, it has been shown that the attractiveness of a room influences positive affect and the energy level of those working in the room (Maslow & Mintz, 1956). Low lighting, soft music, and comfortable seats encourage people to spend more time in a restaurant or bar (Sommer, 1978); the artifacts on the walls of a student room can reflect messages about the student's adjustment to the university (Hansen & Altman, 1976).

Mehrabian's (1981) work adds another important element to the conceptual link between the physical environment and nonverbal communication, pointing out that nonverbal messages are often seen as more truthful than verbal or written messages. The nonverbal messages of the physical environment may sometimes contradict those given verbally. For example, the visitors' signs in the opening scenario, although intended to say "Welcome," in fact, communicated to the Carter family a nonverbal "Not Welcome!" message. While the campus president may speak about the open posture of the campus and welcome ethnic minorities, the presence of defamatory graffiti on buildings may suggest just the opposite. Double messages have strong impact, and when a person on campus perceives an inconsistency between the verbal and nonverbal, or between the language and the nonlanguage message, the nonverbal often becomes most believable (Eckman, 1985). For example, Dorothy Carter, in the opening scenario, had a difficult time believing the slogan "a learning university with a college feel" due to the restrictive physical designs of the classrooms she observed. To paraphrase Anderson's (1971) quote attributed to Sir Kenneth Clark: "If one had to say which was telling the truth about the school, a speech by the principal or the actual school building, classrooms, and material he or she was responsible for providing, one should believe the building" (p. 291). Mehrabian and Wiener (1967), Mehrabian (1981), and Birdwhistell (1970) all suggest that the emotional impact of communication is primarily carried by the nonverbal component of communications. If a picture is worth a thousand words, viewing the campus physical environment not only leads to a more truthful picture but perhaps to a far more complete one as well. . . .

CAMPUS PHYSICAL ENVIRONMENTS AS BEHAVIOR SETTINGS

Behavior settings (Barker, 1968) are the social and physical situations in which 15 human behavior occurs (Wicker, 1984). The college campus is a classic behavior setting, composed of essentially two parts: the human or social aspects of the setting and the nonhuman component or physical aspects. For example, on the college campus, as students, faculty, and staff interact, they do so within a physical environment including many nonhuman components such as pathways, parking lots, activity fields, statuary, artwork, and buildings, presenting a myriad of designs that vary in size, color, and arrangement. It is the transactional (or mutually influential) relationship between the human and nonhuman elements in the behavior setting that shapes behavior. The essence of this behavior setting impact was captured by Barker and Wright (1951) when they concluded from their observations that the behaviors of children could be predicted more accurately from knowing the situation (behavior setting) the children were in than from knowing individual characteristics of the children (Wicker, 1984). The behavior setting can function like a nonverbal mnemonic device (Rapaport, 1982) where encoded messages in the physical component of the behavioral setting serve to remind participants what behaviors are expected. For example, an athletic field house is a behavior setting. The seating, props, cheerleaders, and decor are all cues that loud and rowdy sports event behaviors are not only appropriate but expected in such a place. The rowdiness the Carter family observed during MRU's commencement ceremony might prompt consideration of a redesign of the behavior setting or a change to an alternative venue.

At more than a few campuses, the Carters' concern about rowdiness in the opening scenario is also shared by faculty and administrators. Many of the institutions experiencing rowdiness during graduation exercises often hold their ceremonies in an athletic field house. Students are sometimes seated in the same arrangement as when they attend a basketball game and are most often grouped into departments and colleges, which encourages a team identity. The cues related to sporting events are usually visible, including basketball backboards, hoops, scoreboards, and time clocks. In many cases the banners of previous victories and accomplishments are hanging from the rafters as well. With such reminders from the behavior setting, sporting behaviors, rather than commencement behaviors, are cued. It is the encoded messages of the behavior setting that remind students that yelling, cheering, and rowdy behavior are presumed appropriate for that particular setting. Improvement in student decorum can usually be made by removing as many of the sporting cues as possible and replacing them with cues associated with convocation. For example, the use of plants and flowers, seating arrangements on the floor of the field house rather than in the bleachers, use of classical music, and use of light, carpet, and other textured surfaces to soften the atmosphere can also send different messages about the importance of such events. These cues do not determine the behavior, but they may increase the probability of a more desirable outcome, in this case, a reduction of rowdy behavior.

Another important aspect of the behavior setting is the sometimes supportive or sometimes antagonistic relationship between human and nonhuman components. Physical features can set broad limits on the phenomena that can occur in a setting, making some behaviors more or less likely than others — a concept labeled "intersystems congruence" (Michelson, 1970, p. 25). For example, in a classroom it would be difficult to form small group discussions to increase communication skills if all the chairs were bolted to the floor in straight rows. On the other hand, by having moveable chairs or cushions, the physical aspects of the classroom setting would be supportive of the desired behavior. When the physical and behavioral aspects of a setting are compatible, a synomorphic relationship is said to exist (Wicker, 1984). In other words, the physical structures and designs of the setting allow participants to do what they desire, while participants in turn take full advantage of the possibilities of the setting. Apparent between the human and nonhuman components is a mutuality of support. Common sense and experience suggest that when the physical environment of a campus, building, or classroom supports the desired behavior, better outcomes result. From the behavior setting point of view, campus designs and spaces do not merely create a functional space, mood, or atmosphere, they facilitate certain behaviors (Wicker, 1984).

Proxemics.   Other concepts underscoring the importance of the nonverbal communications occurring within a behavior setting are found in the study of the social implications of use of physical space, or proxemics. Hall (1996) provided the pioneering work on how humans use space in their everyday life. Important to the understanding of proxemics is the concept of spatial zones, which refers to the distances people tend to establish between themselves and others when they engage in social interaction. Four distinct zones or distances have been described in the literature: intimate (0 to 1.5 feet), used for relationships like comforting; personal (1.5 to 4 feet), used for everyday conversations with friends; social (4 to 12 feet), used for impersonal and business-type conversations; and public (more than 12 feet), used for formal presentations to a group. The social and psychological aspects of physical space also communicate messages to the inhabitants of campus physical environments. If a student walks into a classroom and the teaching podium is 20 feet away from the first row of chairs, then a distinct message regarding the formal nature of the upcoming classroom experience is communicated very clearly. It was this same cue about the formality of the classroom in the opening scenario that raised questions in Dorothy Carter's mind about the promotion of a "college feel" to Mid-Rocky University. On the other hand, a simple couch located in a secluded space in the student union will signal the possibility for intimate social interaction. . . .

Designing for Student Learning and Development

College and university environments are places with a special purpose: student learning. Student learning and development embrace complex goals, requiring the input and coordination of all aspects of campus environments, including their physical design and space. Banning and Cunard (1986) noted that, among the many methods employed to foster student learning and development, the use of the physical environment is perhaps the least understood and the most neglected. The physical environment, however, can contribute to college student learning and development in two important ways. First, the actual features of the physical environment can encourage or discourage the processes of learning and development. Second, the process of designing campus physical environments can also promote the acquisition of skills important to the process of learning and developing.

Physical features of a campus environment can hinder or promote learning. For example, the entrance to a college library can communicate a warm welcome or not, depending on its design. To not enter a library and not use its many resources would likely have a negative impact on the intellectual growth of students. So too might entering a library to discover that the wayfinding aspects of the building are so confusing that they contribute to unnecessary levels of frustration and stress. Under these conditions, students gain less information and knowledge. With a more inviting entrance design and less intimidating wayfinding, the probability of becoming engaged in intellectual activities is increased.

Once a student is encouraged to enter by the design of the campus building, then an array of influences is both possible and probable. For example, the proxemics associated with seating arrangements in a lounge area in a student center can either promote or inhibit social interaction. The physical artifact messages of support or nonsupport can take many forms, signaling a sense of belonging, a feeling of being welcomed, a sense of safety, and a sense of role, worth, and value (Banning & Bartels, 1993). Such messages enhance or detract from students' ability to cope with college stress. For example, consider the contrast between a poster in the campus union advertising an upcoming gay, lesbian, bisexual, and transgendered awareness week as compared to the unfortunate homophobic graffiti found in many campus restrooms. Consider also a student wheelchair user anticipating the excitement of an on-campus event but who cannot find an accessible entrance to the sponsoring facility. Processes of growth and development can be readily hindered by such undeserved stress.

In addition to the direct impact of symbols and designs, participant involvement in the processes of designing and building campus spaces might also contribute to significant learning opportunities. As noted in Banning and Cunard (1986), "students who participate meaningfully in a design or redesign effort become involved in complex analytical behavior, participate in leadership positions, engage in significant oral and written communications skills, and work within the give and take of group settings" (p. 3). Participation of all users in the design process increases the probability of eliminating negative and unintended nonverbal messages. In fact, the likelihood that a campus design will meet the needs of the community may be a direct function of the extent to which community members participate in the design process. It is clear that they can assist in illuminating these complex issues of function and meaning, the effects of behavior settings, proxemics, wayfinding, and the power of nonverbal communications in artifacts and traces.

WORKS CITED

Adler, R., & Towne, N. (1987). *Looking out–looking in*. Austin, TX: Holt, Rinehart and Winston.

Anderson, P. (1971). The school as an organic teaching aid. In R. McClure (Ed.), *National Society for the Study of Education yearbook, Part 1. The curriculum: Retrospect and prospect*. Chicago: University of Chicago Press.

Banning, J. H., & Bartels, S. (1993). A taxonomy for physical artifacts: Understanding campus multiculturalism. *The Campus Ecologist, 11*(3), 2–3.

Banning, J. H., & Cunard, M. (1986). The physical environment supports student development. *The Campus Ecologist, 4*(1), 1–3.

Barker, R. (1968). *Ecological psychology*. Palo Alto, CA: Stanford University Press.

Barker, R., & Wright, H. (1951). *One boy's day*. New York: HarperCollins.

Birdwhistell, R. (1970). *Kinesics and context*. Philadelphia: University of Pennsylvania Press.

Boyer, E. (1987). *College: The undergraduate experience in America*. New York: Harper-Collins.

Eckman, P. (1985). *Telling lies: Clues to deceit in marketplace, politics, and marriage*. New York: Norton.

Griffith, J. C. (1994). Open space preservation: An imperative for quality campus environments. *Journal of Higher Education, 65*, 645–69.

Hall, E. T. (1996). *The hidden dimension*. New York: Anchor Books.

Hansen, W. B., & Altman, I. (1976). Decorating personal places: A descriptive analysis. *Environment and Behavior, 8*, 491–505.

Maslow, A. H., & Mintz, N. (1956). Effects of those aesthetic surroundings: Initial effects of those aesthetic surroundings upon perceiving "energy" and "well-being" in faces. *Journal of Psychology, 41*, 247–54.

Mehrabian, A. (1981). *Silent messages* (2nd ed.). Belmont, CA: Wadsworth.

Mehrabian, A., & Wiener, M. (1967). Decoding of inconsistent communications. *Journal of Personality and Social Psychology, 6*, 109–14.

Michelson, W. (1970). *Man and his urban environment: A sociological approach*. Reading, MA: Addison-Wesley.

Rapaport, A. (1982). *The meaning of the built environment*. Thousand Oaks, CA: Sage.

Sommer, R. (1978). *Personal space: The behavioral basis of design*. Englewood Cliffs, NJ: Prentice Hall.

Stern, R. A. (1986). *Pride of place: Building the American dream*. New York: Houghton Mifflin.

Sturner, W. F. (1973). The college environment. In D. W. Vermilye (Ed.), *The future in the making* (pp. 71–86). San Francisco: Jossey-Bass.

Thelin, J. R., & Yankovich, J. (1987). Bricks and mortar: Architecture and the study of higher education. In J. C. Smart (Ed.), *Higher education: Handbook of theory and research, Vol. 3* (pp. 57–83). New York: Agathon Press.

Wicker, A. W. (1984). *An introduction to ecological psychology*. Cambridge University Press.

READING THE TEXT

1. What do the authors mean when they claim that physical aspects of campus design have "both functional and symbolic" (para. 10) influences?

2. Summarize in your own words the various ways a campus's physical environment can affect human behavior.

3. Describe in your own words a "behavior setting" (para. 15). According to the authors, how does an athletic stadium operate as such a setting?

4. In what ways can learning be affected by campus design, in the authors' view?

5. Why do Strange and Banning begin with the story of the visit by a prospective student and his family to a college campus?

READING THE SIGNS

1. In your journal, reflect on your own first visit to your college or university campus. How did it compare with that of the Carter family?

2. Study your writing course's syllabus, and discuss with your instructor and classmates the course goals and the rationale behind the various in-class activities. Then write an analysis of the room in which your composition class meets. To what extent does its layout and design enable or frustrate the kind of learning that is the course goal?

3. Working in teams, conduct an in-depth analysis of the physical environment on your campus. Each team should focus on a particular set of details: verbal messages such as signs, physical layout of classrooms, or library accessibility, for example. Have the teams present their findings to the class. What conclusions do you draw about whether your school's physical environment encourages student learning?

4. Strange and Banning conclude by advocating that users participate in the process of designing campus buildings. Working in groups, select one building or space on your campus that you consider unsuccessful and analyze its shortcomings. Then propose a redesign of the building, explaining how your changes would enable it to meet the campus community's needs more successfully.

DAPHNE SPAIN

Spatial Segregation and Gender Stratification in the Workplace

> *In the spatial hierarchy of the American workplace, having a private office all to yourself is one of the most visible signifiers of status within the organization. But as Daphne Spain reveals, the spatial arrangement of the ordinary workplace is often a marker of gender relations as well. With most women working in "open-floor" (such as secretarial) occupations, and most men frequently enjoying "closed-door" (or managerial) positions, a certain level of gender segregation is to be found in the typical American workplace. Analyzing the social implications of this stratification of working space, Spain shows how the architecture of the workplace not only reflects but reinforces exist-ing gender hierarchies. Spain teaches in the School of Architecture at the University of Virginia and is the author of* Gendered Spaces *(1992), from which this selection is taken, and* How Women Saved the City *(2001). She is also coauthor, with Suzanne M. Bianchi, of* Balanc-ing Act: Motherhood, Marriage, and Employment among American Women *(1996).*

To what extent do women and men who work in different occupations also work in different spaces? Baran and Teegarden (1987, 206) propose that occupational segregation in the insurance industry is "tantamount to spatial segregation by gender" since managers are overwhelmingly male and clerical staff are predominantly female. This essay examines the spatial conditions of women's work and men's work and proposes that working women and men come into daily contact with one another very infrequently. Further, women's jobs can be classified as "open floor," but men's jobs are more likely to be "closed door." That is, women work in a more public environment with less control of their space than men. This lack of spatial control both reflects and contributes to women's lower occupational status by limiting opportunities for the transfer of knowledge from men to women.

It bears repeating that my argument concerning space and status deals with structural workplace arrangements of women as a group and men as a group, *not* with occupational mobility for individual men and women. Extraordinary people always escape the statistical norm and experience up-ward mobility under a variety of circumstances. The emphasis here is on the ways in which workplaces are structured to provide different spatial arrange-ments for the typical working woman and the typical working man and how those arrangements contribute to gender stratification. . . .

Typical Women's Work: "Open-Floor Jobs"

A significant proportion of women are employed in just three occupations: teaching, nursing, and secretarial work. In 1990 these three categories alone accounted for 16.5 million women, or 31 percent of all women in the labor force (U.S. Department of Labor 1991, 163, 183). Aside from being concentrated in occupations that bring them primarily into contact with other women, women are also concentrated spatially in jobs that limit their access to knowledge. The work of elementary schoolteachers, for example, brings them into daily contact with children, but with few other adults. When not dealing with patients, nurses spend their time in a lounge separate from the doctors' lounge. Nursing and teaching share common spatial characteristics with the third major "women's job" — that of secretary.

Secretarial/clerical work is the single largest job category for American women. In 1990, 14.9 million women, or more than one of every four employed women, were classified as "administrative support, including clerical"; 98 percent of all secretaries are female (U.S. Department of Labor 1991, 163, 183). Secretarial and clerical occupations account for over three-quarters of this category and epitomize the typical "woman's job." It is similar to teaching and nursing in terms of the spatial context in which it occurs.

Two spatial aspects of secretarial work operate to reduce women's status. 5 One is the concentration of many women together in one place (the secretarial "pool") that removes them from observation of and/or input into the decision-making processes of the organization. Those decisions occur behind the "closed doors" of the managers' offices. Second, paradoxically, is the very public nature of the space in which secretaries work. The lack of privacy, repeated interruptions, and potential for surveillance contribute to an inability to turn valuable knowledge into human capital that might advance careers or improve women's salaries relative to men's.

Like teachers and nurses, secretaries process knowledge, but seldom in a way beneficial to their own status. In fact, secretaries may wield considerable informal power in an organization, because they control the information flow. Management, however, has very clear expectations about how secretaries are to handle office information. Drawing from their successful experience with grid theory, business consultants Robert Blake, Jane Mouton, and Artie Stockton have outlined the ideal boss-secretary relationship for effective office teamwork. In the first chapter of *The Secretary Grid*, an American Management Association publication, the following advice is offered:

> The secretary's position at the center of the information network raises the issue of privileged communications and how best to handle it. Privileged communication is information the secretary is not free to divulge, no matter how helpful it might be to others. And the key to handling it is the answer to the question "Who owns the information?" The answer is, "The boss does." . . . The secretary's position with regard to this information is that of the hotel desk clerk to the contents of the safety deposit

box that stores the guest's valuables. She doesn't own it, but she knows what it is and what is in it. The root of the word *secretary* is, after all, *secret*: something kept from the knowledge of others. (Blake, Mouton, and Stockton 1983, 4–5; emphasis in original)

In other words, secretaries are paid *not* to use their knowledge for personal gain, but only for their employers' gain. The workplace arrangements that separate secretaries from managers within the same office reinforce status differences by exposing the secretary mainly to other secretaries bound by the same rules of confidentiality. Lack of access to and interaction with managers inherently limits the status women can achieve within the organization.

The executive secretary is an exception to the rule of gendered spatial segregation in the workplace. The executive secretary may have her own office, and she has access to more aspects of the managerial process than other secretaries. According to another American Management Association publication titled *The Successful Secretary*: "Probably no person gets to observe and see management principles in operation on a more practical basis than an executive secretary. She is privy to nearly every decision the executive makes. She has the opportunity to witness the gathering of information and the elements that are considered before major decisions are made and implemented" (Belker 1981, 191).

Yet instructions to the successful executive secretary suggest that those with the closest access to power are subject to the strictest guidelines regarding confidentiality. When physical barriers are breached and secretaries spend a great deal of time with the managers, rules governing the secretary's use of information become more important. The executive secretary is cautioned to hide shorthand notes, remove partially typed letters from the typewriter, lock files, and personally deliver interoffice memos to prevent unauthorized persons from gaining confidential information from the boss's office (Belker 1981, 66).

The executive secretary has access to substantial information about the company, but the highest compliment that can be paid her is that she does not divulge it to anyone or use it for personal gain. Comparing the importance of confidentiality to the seal of the confessional, Belker counsels secretaries that "the importance of confidentiality can't be over-emphasized. Your company can be involved in some delicate business matters or negotiations, and the wrong thing leaked to the wrong person could have an adverse effect on the result. . . . Years ago, executive secretaries were sometimes referred to as confidential secretaries. It's a shame that title fell out of popular usage, because it's an accurate description of the job" (Belker 1981, 73–74). 10

Typical Men's Work: "Closed-Door Jobs"

The largest occupational category for men is that of manager. In 1990, 8.9 million men were classified as "executive, administrative, and managerial." This group constituted 14 percent of all employed men (U.S. Department of

Labor 1991, 163, 183). Thus, more than one in ten men works in a supervisory position.

Spatial arrangements in the workplace reinforce these status distinctions, partially by providing more "closed door" potential to managers than to those they supervise. Although sales and production supervisors may circulate among their employees, their higher status within the organization is reflected by the private offices to which they can withdraw. The expectation is that privacy is required for making decisions that affect the organization. Rather than sharing this privacy, the secretary is often in charge of "gate-keeping" — protecting the boss from interruptions.

Just as there are professional manuals for the successful secretary, there are also numerous guidelines for the aspiring manager. Harry Levinson's widely read *Executive* (1981) (a revision of his 1968 *The Exceptional Executive*) stresses the importance of managerial knowledge of the entire organization. A survey of large American companies asking presidents about suitable qualities in their successors revealed the following profile: "A desirable successor is a person with a general knowledge and an understanding of the whole organization, capable of fitting specialized contributions into profitable patterns. . . . The person needs a wide range of liberal arts knowledge together with a fundamental knowledge of business. . . . A leader will be able to view the business in global historical and technical perspective. Such a perspective is itself the basis for the most important requisite, what one might call 'feel' — a certain intuitive sensitivity for the right action and for handling relationships with people" (Levinson 1981, 136).

The importance of knowledge is stressed repeatedly in this description. The successful manager needs knowledge of the organization, of liberal arts, and of business in general. But equally important is the intuitive ability to carry out actions. This "feel" is not truly intuitive, of course, but is developed through observation and emulation of successful executives. Levinson identifies managerial leadership as "an art to be cultivated and developed," which is why it cannot be learned by the book; rather, "it must be learned in a relationship, through identification with a teacher" (Levinson 1981, 145).

Because the transfer of knowledge and the ability to use it are so crucial 15 to leadership, Levinson devotes a chapter to "The Executive as Teacher." He advises that there is no prescription an executive can follow in acting as a teacher. The best strategy is the "shine and show them" approach — the manager carries out the duties of office as effectively as possible and thereby demonstrates to subordinates how decisions are made. There are no formal conditions under which teaching takes place; it is incorporated as part of the routine of the business day. In Levinson's words, "The process of example-setting goes on all the time. Executives behave in certain ways, sizing up problems, considering the resources . . . that can be utilized to meet them, and making decisions about procedure. Subordinates, likewise, watch what they are doing and how they do it" (Levinson 1981, 154).

Just as in the ceremonial men's huts of nonindustrial societies, constant contact between elders and initiates is necessary for the transmission of knowledge. Levinson implies that it should be frequent contact to transfer most effectively formal and informal knowledge. Such frequent and significant contact is missing from the interaction between managers and secretaries. Given the spatial distance between the closed doors of managers and the open floors of secretaries, it is highly unlikely that sufficient contact between the two groups could occur for secretaries to alter their positions within the organization.

In addition to giving subordinates an opportunity to learn from the boss, spatial proximity provides opportunities for subordinates to be seen by the boss. This opportunity has been labeled "visiposure" by the author of *Routes to the Executive Suite* (Jennings 1971, 113). A combination of "visibility" and "exposure," visiposure refers to the opportunity to "see and be seen by the right people" (Jennings 1971, 113). Jennings counsels the rising executive that "the abilities to see and copy those who can influence his career and to keep himself in view of those who might promote him are all-important to success." The ultimate form of visiposure is for the subordinate's manager to be seen by the right managers as well. Such "serial visiposure" is the "sine qua non of fast upward mobility" and is facilitated by face-to-face interaction among several levels of managers and subordinates (Jennings 1971, 113–14).

Both Levinson and Jennings acknowledge the importance of physical proximity to achieving power within an organization, yet neither pursues the assumptions underlying the transactions they discuss — that is, the spatial context within which such interactions occur. To the extent women are segregated from men, the transfer of knowledge — with the potential for improving women's status — is limited.

Office Design and Gender Stratification

Contemporary office design clearly reflects the spatial segregation separating women and men. Secretaries (almost all of whom are women) and managers (nearly two-thirds of whom are men) have designated areas assigned within the organization. . . .

Privacy can be a scarce resource in the modern office. Empirical studies 20 have shown that privacy in the office involves "the ability to control access to one's self or group, particularly the ability to *limit others' access to one's workspace*" (Sundstrom 1986, 178; emphasis added). Business executives commonly define privacy as the ability to control information and space. In other words, privacy is connected in people's minds with the spatial reinforcement of secrecy. Studies of executives, managers, technicians, and clerical employees have found a high correlation between enclosure of the work space (walls and doors) and perceptions of privacy; the greater the privacy, the greater the satisfaction with work. Employees perceive spatial control as a resource in the workplace that affects their job satisfaction and performance (Sundstrom, Burt, and Kemp 1980; Sundstrom 1986).

Not surprisingly, higher status within an organization is accompanied by greater control of space. In the Sundstrom study, most secretaries (75 percent) reported sharing an office; about one-half (55 percent) of bookkeepers and accountants shared an office; and only 18 percent of managers and administrators shared space. Secretaries had the least physical separation from other workers, while executives had the most (Sundstrom 1986, 184).

Two aspects of the work environment are striking when the spatial features of the workplaces for secretaries and executives are compared: the low number of walls or partitions surrounding secretaries (an average of 2.1), compared with executives (an average of 3.5), and the greater surveillance that accompanies the public space of secretaries. Three-quarters of all secretaries were visible to their supervisors, compared with only one-tenth of executives. As one would expect given the physical description of their respective offices, executives report the greatest sense of privacy and secretaries the least (Sundstrom 1986, 185). Doors do not necessarily have to be closed or locked in order to convey the message of differential power; they merely have to be available for closing and be seen as controlled at the executive's discretion (Steele 1986, 46).

The spatial distribution of employees in an office highlights the complex ways in which spatial segregation contributes to gender stratification. Workers obviously are not assigned space on the basis of sex, but on the basis of their positions within the organization. Theoretically, managers have the most complex jobs and secretaries have the least complex, yet research on secretaries and managers with equal degrees of office enclosure suggests that women's space is still considered more public than men's space. Sundstrom found that "in the workspaces with equivalent enclosure — private offices — [respondents] showed differential ratings of privacy, with lowest ratings by secretaries. This could reflect social norms. Secretaries have low ranks, and co-workers or visitors may feel free to walk unannounced into their workspaces. However, they may knock respectfully at the entrance of the workspaces of managers. . . . *Perhaps a private office is more private when occupied by a manager than when occupied by a secretary*" (Sundstrom 1986, 191; emphasis added). This passage suggests that even walls and a door do not insure privacy for the typical working woman in the same way they do for the typical working man. Features that should allow control of workspace do not operate for secretaries as they do for managers.

WORKS CITED

Baran, Barbara, and Suzanne Teegarden. 1987. "Women's Labor in the Office of the Future: A Case Study of the Insurance Industry." In *Women, Households, and the Economy*, edited by Lourdes Beneria and Catharine R. Stimpson, pp. 201–24. New Brunswick, N.J.: Rutgers University Press.
Belker, Loren. 1981. *The Successful Secretary*. New York: American Management Association.

Blake, Robert, Jane S. Mouton, and Artie Stockton. 1983. *The Secretary Grid*. New York: American Management Association.

Jennings, Eugene Emerson. 1971. *Routes to the Executive Suite*. New York: McGraw-Hill.

Levinson, Harry. 1981. *Executive*. Cambridge: Harvard University Press.

Steele, Fritz. 1986. "The Dynamics of Power and Influence in Workplace Design and Management." In *Behavioral Issues in Office Design*, edited by Jean D. Wineman, pp. 43–64. New York: Van Nostrand Reinhold.

Sundstrom, Eric. 1986. "Privacy in the Office." In *Behavioral Issues in Office Design*, edited by Jean Wineman, pp. 177–202. New York: Van Nostrand Reinhold.

Sundstrom, Eric, Robert Burt, and Douglas Kemp. 1980. "Privacy at Work: Architectural Correlates of Job Satisfaction and Job Performance." *Academy of Management Journal* 23 (March): 101–17.

U.S. Department of Labor. 1991. *Employment and Earnings* 38 (January). Washington, D.C.: Bureau of Labor Statistics.

READING THE TEXT

1. Summarize in your own words how traditional office design can be considered " 'tantamount to spatial segregation by gender' " (para. 1).

2. Define the differences between "open-floor" and "closed-door" (para. 1) jobs. What are the spatial arrangements that signal those differences?

3. According to Spain, how is the executive secretary "an exception to the rule of gendered spatial segregation in the workplace" (para. 8)?

4. In Spain's view, how does office design restrict or enhance the privacy of employees?

READING THE SIGNS

1. In class, form small groups and design an office space that is not hierarchically organized. Have the groups present the design to the class, explaining the reasoning behind their design choices.

2. If you work in an office environment, write an analysis of the spatial design of your workplace. To what extent does it follow the gendered patterns that Spain describes? Alternatively, survey the faculty or staff offices at your college or university. Do they reflect Spain's analysis?

3. Interview at least five women about their jobs and work environments. To what extent do their experiences support Spain's claim that "women are . . . concentrated spatially in jobs that limit their access to knowledge" (para. 3)?

4. Write a letter to business consultants Robert Blake, Jane Mouton, and Artie Stockton in which you respond to their description of the ideal boss-secretary relationship, published in the American Management Association's *The Secretary Grid* (para. 6).

CAMILO JOSÉ VERGARA
The Ghetto Cityscape

What happens when a society abandons its central-city residential dis-
tricts (better known as urban ghettos) to the forces of poverty and decay?
Usually those who take an interest in these matters focus on the people
left behind in such neighborhoods, but Camilo José Vergara (b. 1944)
feels that something has been left out of the sociology of urban poverty:
an examination of the ghetto environment itself and its effects on
the people who live there. So packing camera and notebook, Vergara
has spent years visiting the places that much of America would like to
forget — the "green ghettos," the "institutional ghettos," and the "new
immigrant ghettos," as he defines them — that lie beyond the gaze of
most Americans. A photographer, Vergara has written for many publica-
tions, including the New York Times, *the* Nation, *the* Atlantic, *and*
Architectural Record. *His books include* Silent Cities: The Evolution of
the American Cemetery *(with Kenneth T. Jackson, 1989);* The New
American Ghetto *(1995), from which this selection is taken;* Unexpected Chicagoland *(with Timothy J. Samuelson, 2001); and* Subway
Memories *(2004).*

If you were among the nearly eleven thousand people who lived in two-story
row houses in North Camden in the 1960s, you could walk to work at Ester-
brook Pen, at Knox Gelatin, at RCA, or at J. R. Evans Leather. You could shop
on Broadway, a busy three-mile-long commercial thoroughfare, nicknamed
the "Street of Lights" because of its five first-run movie theaters with their
bright neon signs.

After J. R. Evans Leather was abandoned and almost completely demol-
ished, its smokestack stood alone in a vast field by the Delaware River, a symbol
of the demise of industry in Camden. Hundreds of row houses — once counted
among the best ordinary urban dwellings in America — have been scooped up
by bulldozers, their debris carted to a dump in Delaware. Walking along North
Camden's narrow streets, one passes entire blocks without a single structure,
the empty land crisscrossed by footpaths. The scattered dwellings that remain
are faced with iron bars, so that they resemble cages.

With nearly half of its overwhelmingly Latino population on some form of
public assistance, this once thriving working-class neighborhood is now the
poorest urban community in New Jersey. In 1986, former mayor Alfred Pierce
called Camden a reservation for the destitute. The north section of the city
has become the drug center for South Jersey, and it hosts a large state prison.

North Camden is not unique. Since the riots of the 1960s, American
cities have experienced profound transformations, best revealed in the spatial

restructuring of their ghettos and in the emergence of new urban forms. During the past decade, however, the "underclass" and homelessness have dominated the study of urban poverty. Meanwhile, the power of the physical surroundings to shape lives, to mirror people's existence, and to symbolize social relations has been ignored. When scholars from across the political spectrum discuss the factors that account for the persistence of poverty, they fail to consider its living environments. And when prescribing solutions, they overlook the very elements that define the new ghettos: the ruins and the semi-ruins; the medical, warehousing, and behavior-modification institutions; the various NIMBYs, fortresses, and walls; and, not least, the bitterness and anger resulting from living in these places.

Dismissing the value of information received through sight, taste, and   5 smell, or through the emotional overtones in an informant's voice, or from the sensation of moving through the spaces studied, has led to the creation of constructs without character, individuality, or a sense of place. And although the limitations of statistical data — particularly when dealing with very poor populations — are widely acknowledged, our great dependency on numbers is fiercely defended. Other approaches are dismissed as impressionistic, anecdotal, as poetry, or "windshield surveys."

Yet today's ghettos are diverse, rich in public and private responses to the environment, in expressions of cultural identity, and in reminders of history. These communities are uncharted territory; to be understood, their forms need to be identified, described, inventoried, and mapped.

An examination of scores of ghettos across the nation reveals three types: "green ghettos," characterized by depopulation, vacant land overgrown by nature, and ruins; "institutional ghettos," publicly financed places of confinement designed mainly for the native-born; and "new immigrant ghettos," deriving their character from an influx of immigrants, mainly Latino and West Indian. Some of these communities have continued to lose population; others have emerged where a quarter-century ago there were white ethnic blue-collar neighborhoods; and sections of older ghettos have remained stable, working neighborhoods or have been rebuilt.

The Green Ghetto: Return to Wilderness?

Green ghettos, where little has been done to counter the effect of disinvestment, abandonment, depopulation, and dependency, are the leftovers of a society. Best exemplified by North Camden, Detroit's East Side, Chicago's Lawndale, and East St. Louis in Illinois, they are expanding outward to include poor suburbs of large cities such as Robbins, Illinois, and are even found in small cities such as Benton Harbor, Michigan.

Residents, remembering the businesses that moved to suburban malls, the closed factories, the fires, complain of living in a threatening place bereft of jobs and stores and neglected by City Hall. In many sections of these ghettos, pheasants and rabbits have regained the space once occupied by humans, yet these are not wilderness retreats in the heart of the city. "Nothing but weeds are growing there" is a frequent complaint about vacant lots, expressing no mere distaste for the vegetation, but moral outrage at the neglect that produces these anomalies. Plants grow wildly on and around the vestiges of the former International Harvester Component Plant in West Pullman, Chicago. Derelict industrial buildings here and in other ghettos have long ago been stripped of anything of value. Large parcels of land lie unkempt or paved over, subtracted from the life of the city. Contradicting a long-held vision of our country as a place of endless progress, ruins, once unforeseen, are now ignored.

Institutional Ghettos: The New Poorhouses

In New York City, Newark, and Chicago, large and expensive habitats — institutional ghettos — have been created for the weakest and most vulnerable members of our society. Institution by institution, facility by facility, these environments have been assembled in the most drug-infested and destitute parts of cities. They are the complex poorhouses of the twenty-first century, places to store a growing marginal population officially certified as "not employable." Residents are selected from the entire population of the municipality for their lack of money or home, for their addictions, for their diseases and other afflictions. Nonresidents come to these institutions to pick up medications, surplus food, used clothes; to get counseling or training; or to do a stint in prison. Other visitors buy drugs and sex. 10

Sterling Street, Newark, 1980.

As Greg Turner, the manager of a day shelter on the Near West Side of Chicago, puts it: "They say, 'Let's get them off the streets and put them together in groups.' It is like the zoo: we are going to put the birds over here; we are going to put the reptiles over there; we are going to put the buffalo over here; we are going to put the seals by the pool. It is doing nothing to work with the root of the problem, just like they do nothing to work with the children, to teach them things so they don't grow up and become more homeless people or substance abusers."

Although the need for individual components — for instance, a homeless shelter or a waste incinerator — may be subject to public debate, the overall consequences of creating such "campuses" of institutions are dismissed. The most important barrier to their growth is the cost to the taxpayers of building and maintaining them.

Such sections of the city are not neighborhoods. The streets surrounding Lincoln Park in south Newark, for example, an area that includes landmark houses, grand public buildings, and a once-elegant hotel, were chosen by two drug treatment programs because six of its large mansions would provide inexpensive housing for a residential treatment program. On the northwest corner of the park, a shelter for battered women just opened in another mansion, and a block north in a former garage is a men's shelter and soup kitchen. The largest structures overlooking the park, the hotel and a former federal office building, house the elderly, who fear going out by themselves. No children play in the park; no parents come home from work. This is a no-man's-land devoted to the contradictory goals of selling drugs and getting high, on the one hand, and becoming clean and employed on the other.

Sterling Street replaced by a parking lot, 1994.

New Immigrant Ghettos: Dynamic and Fluid

In other parts of New York and Chicago a community of recent immigrants is growing up, but this type of ghetto is most visible in South Central Los Angeles and Compton, where the built environment is more intimate than in older ghettos, the physical structures are more adaptable, and it is easier for newcomers to imprint their identity. Here paint goes a long way to transform the appearance of the street.

The new immigrant ghettos are characterized by tiny offices providing 15 services such as driving instruction, insurance, and immigration assistance; by stores that sell imported beer, produce, and canned goods; and by restaurants offering home cooking. Notable are the businesses that reflect the busy exchange between the local population and their native country: money transfers, travel agencies, even funeral homes that arrange to have bodies shipped home.

To get by, most residents are forced to resort to exploitative jobs paying minimum wage or less and usually lacking health benefits. For housing they crowd together in small, badly maintained apartments, in cinder-block garages, or in trailers.

Not being eligible for public or city-owned housing may in the long run prove to be a blessing for the newcomers. Although forced to pay high rents, immigrants tend to concentrate in neighborhoods that are part of the urban economy, thus avoiding the extreme social disorganization, isolation, and violence that characterize other types of ghettos. Because of the huge influx of young people with expectations that life will be better for their children and grandchildren, these ghettos are more dynamic and fluid, resembling the foreign-born communities of a century ago.

READING THE TEXT

1. Why does Vergara see North Camden, New Jersey, as exemplary of city life?
2. According to Vergara, what realities of city life have scholars overlooked, and what explanation does he give for their oversights?
3. Summarize in your own words the three categories of cityscape that Vergara proposes.

READING THE SIGNS

1. If you live in or near an inner-city area, analyze it in terms of the three categories Vergara proposes in this selection. Which category does it best fit, and why? If it doesn't fit any of Vergara's categories, propose one of your own, and explain why that category best fits your area.
2. Adopting Vergara's perspective, write a response to Lucy R. Lippard ("Alternating Currents," p. 432) in which you critique her analysis of city life. Consider both her interpretations and the scope of her selection.

3. In a reflective essay, discuss the symbolic meaning of nature in urban life. In addition to Vergara's selection, read or review Lucy R. Lippard's "Alternating Currents" (p. 432) and Rina Swentzell's "Conflicting Landscape Values: The Santa Clara Pueblo and Day School" (p. 685).

4. In an argumentative essay, support, challenge, or modify Vergara's suggestion that "the power of the physical surroundings to shape lives, to mirror people's existence, and to symbolize social relations" (para. 4) is at least equivalent to that of economic conditions. To develop your ideas, consult Barrie B. Greenbie's "Home Space: Fences and Neighbors" (p. 672).

AMERICAN ICONS

The Mythic Characters of Popular Culture

Where Have All the Icons Gone?

Where have you gone, Darryl Strawberry? No, wait, that doesn't sound right. The song said "Joe DiMaggio," and what Paul Simon was getting at in his classic musical theme to *The Graduate* was that something heroic was vanishing from American life, that the great popular icons of the past weren't being replaced. And Darryl Strawberry, like DiMaggio a lean, smooth, power-hitting outfielder who ended his career with the Yankees, might have been a modern baseball icon himself had he not gotten into so much drug trouble. Well, there's always Barry Bonds, baseball's single-season home run record holder and probable all-time home run leader. Except, isn't some sort of cloud involving anabolic steroids hanging over the man?

It isn't a good time for sports heroes, whose performance and pay may be better than ever, but whose images aren't doing so well. The fact of the matter is that it isn't such a good time for most American icons these days. Michael Jackson was in court for four months in 2005, Martha Stewart was on probation after a five-month jail stay, and Madonna's getting stale. Perhaps that explains the emergence in recent years of new kinds of American icons, figures magnified to larger-than-life proportions not because they really are larger than life but precisely because they aren't outstanding at all. Such "icons" include Donald Trump, Jessica Simpson, and the Hilton sisters, figures whose outsized popularity seems to rest on a peculiar combination of fascination and contempt, making them, in effect, anti-icons.

If you look around, you'll find a lot of anti-icons these days, many (if not most) of them on reality TV. They include Ozzy Osbourne (a second-class rock icon if he was ever any sort of icon at all) and his family, who have become the family that everyone loves to laugh at and feel superior to. In the realm of fictional anti-icons, we have the whole Simpson clan whose idiotic dysfunctionality, especially Homer's, can make anyone feel smooth and sophisticated. The anti-icons also include Ryan Seacrest, the disk jockey and *American Idol* host whom no one would ever mistake for an idol in his own right, and the growing list of *Survivor* "all stars" whose claim to fame involves a knack for stabbing other people in the back.

Such a proliferation of anti-icons marks a profound difference in the system of popular American icons, a difference that points to a striking change in America's mood. That so many anti-icons are contemptible, and that their contemptibility is part of their appeal, suggests not only a deep cultural cynicism that rejects the possibility of genuine heroic stature but also a nagging disappointment, a feeling that life isn't delivering what was promised, leading to a desire to be able to feel that at least one is a better person than the idiots on TV. This cynicism may well have its roots in the debacles of the Vietnam War and the Watergate scandal, which brought about the demise of political icons, and in the broken promises of the media, which, through the fantasies of television and the movies, have long represented lives that are far more exciting than anything an ordinary person can ever experience. And then there is advertising, which promises everything but delivers only credit-card debt. In reaction, Americans are embracing anti-icons whom they at once can identify with ("I'm as pretty as she is, and I can party, too") and despise ("what a creep" or "what a dope").

Perhaps the creation of what might be called an interactive society also has something to do with the anti-icon phenomenon. With so many opportunities to interact with others (even Web-savvy celebrities) on the Internet, along with the chance to become television figures themselves through the auspices of reality TV, Americans may be losing their sense of the aura that traditionally surrounds those icons who are truly larger than life. "No man is a hero to his valet," the old adage has it, and in an interactive world in which we are all promised a chance to participate directly in our popular culture, perhaps we are becoming valets of sorts, developing an affinity for anti-icons who are more like us — warts and all — rather than soaring far above us.

The Way We Were

The emergence of the anti-icon, at least for the time being, compels us to reassess the entire place of icons in our society. Traditionally, a culture's icons include those figures who have been mythologized into larger-than-life symbols that capture our imagination by embodying our deepest values and desires. An icon is not simply a popular figure or celebrity (though he or she often is in our entertainment culture); an icon is also someone, or something, that has a

---

Exploring the Signs of American Characters

Children's television is filled with characters, from Winnie the Pooh to G.I. Joe, from the Muppets to the Mighty Morphin Power Rangers. Choose a character with whom you grew up, and explore in your journal what role that character played in your life. Did you simply watch the character on TV, or did you play-act games with it? Did you ever buy — or want to buy — any products related to that character? Why? Does that character mean anything to you today?

---

meaning, a cultural significance that goes beyond any particular qualities he, she, or it might have.

In many ways, an icon is like a hero, but while heroes can become icons, their fame and significance are usually more fleeting. For example, when we wrote the fourth edition of this book, the men and women of the New York City Fire and Police Departments had become instant heroes in the wake of the 9/11 attacks on the World Trade Center. For a short time, they even became icons, with FDNY caps and tee shirts appearing everywhere in a national celebration of what then appeared to be a return to a more traditional sort of cultural symbol after years of ever-increasing celebrity worship. But the brief day of the 9/11 icons is long past. They are still heroes but lack that mythic aura that distinguishes the icon from the hero. To illustrate that aura we can look at two American icons who weren't heroic at all but who shine among the brightest of our iconic stars.

Forever Elvis

Let's start with Elvis Presley, who is one of America's most popular and enduring cultural icons, a man who, more in death than in life, has become the object of an almost cultlike veneration. Though his significance is not precisely the same to everyone, his cultural status is such that Paul Simon could make him a symbol for American life in his 1980s hit "Graceland," and the word *Elvis* has seemed to assume a life of its own. But what is it that has enabled this humble southern truck driver to become such a potent American icon? What does Elvis mean to us?

The fact that Elvis Presley began his adult life as a humble southern truck driver is an important part of his iconic significance. After all, in his rise to the peak of early rock 'n' roll stardom, Elvis exemplified, in an especially glamorous way, the mythic promise of the American dream. Few American mythologies are more important to us than this one, and Elvis Presley's life has been particularly inspiring to those rural and small-town southern working-class youth who can most closely identify with it. (The identification of working-class fans from New Jersey with Bruce Springsteen is a closely related phenomenon: Indeed, Springsteen's nickname, the Boss, is a signifier of his cultural connection to the King.)

But that is not the end of Elvis Presley's iconic significance, not by a long shot. After all, a lot of other figures in the entertainment world have exemplified the American dream, but none quite stands up to Elvis. There is something different about Elvis, a difference that helps explain just what is so special about him.

That difference lies, in part, in his pioneering role in the invention of rock 'n' roll. It is important to note in this regard, however, that Elvis Presley did not actually invent rock 'n' roll. The credit for that has been given to such figures as Chuck Berry, Bill Haley, and Carl Perkins. Nor was Elvis alone in popularizing the new music, though he became its biggest star. What made Presley so special had less to do with the music than with what the music signified, and to see what that was we need only consider such well-known historical facts as the one that his performances were so sexually suggestive that when he first appeared on *The Ed Sullivan Show* he was filmed from the waist up.

Bumping and grinding to the beat, Elvis Presley brought to the stage the raw sexual energy that lay at the heart of the blues, boogie, and bop — those African American musical forms that Chuck Berry combined with country music in his invention of rock music. It was this sexual energy, combined with the racist climate of the Jim Crow South, that caused rock 'n' roll to be denounced as the devil's music and that led to a musical segregation in which rhythm and blues, with all of its original sexual energy intact, was socially marginalized as "black music." Meanwhile rock, often in a sanitized form, came to be appropriated by such squeaky-clean white performers as Pat Boone, Ricky Nelson, and Connie Francis.

But sex was too important a part of rock's essential appeal to be so neatly suppressed, and while, in the segregated America of the 1950s, a black performer could not deliver it, a white boy who "sounded black" could. By making sex such an explicit part of his act, Elvis Presley, in effect, released the erotic energies of a generation that was gearing up for a sexual revolution.

In doing so, Elvis became a kind of modern Dionysus. The mythic center of a cult that swept through Greece over two thousand years ago, Dionysus was a godlike figure — usually depicted as a young man — whose rituals included the violent release of sexual energy. Dionysus has since become an enduring symbol of sexual expression, an archetypal figure whose universal appeal has been reflected in American popular culture through such male sex symbols as Rudolph Valentino and Elvis Presley, men who are not simply good-looking or sexy but who seem to embody sexuality itself.

Indeed, Dionysus offers us a clue into the origin of all those stories about Elvis's "survival." That is, part of the cult of Dionysus included his ritual murder, but he always came back to life, refusing to die. Now think of Elvis's death, and all those funny denials, the rumors: that he did not really die, that he is working as a grocery checkout clerk in Minneapolis, that he was just spotted at the 7 Eleven down the street. Refusing to stay dead, Elvis completes his mythic circuit, becoming archetypal through the never-dying, ever-potent figure of Dionysus. Such a man can never die.

Like a Candle in the Wind

If all this sounds like a lot for one man to symbolize, don't worry. Elvis isn't America's only sex symbol, nor even its most prominent. That honor belongs to Marilyn Monroe.

In many ways, the iconic significance of Marilyn Monroe resembles that of Elvis. The rise of factory worker Norma Jean to superstardom, for example, also exemplifies the American dream in its gaudiest aspects. And like Elvis, Marilyn functions as a potent sex symbol in a society ever on the lookout for sex symbols. Again like Elvis, Marilyn died young and thus enjoys the legendary status of those other popular American characters who died early (have you seen her with Elvis and James Dean in that poster where they are all sitting together at a fifties-style coffee shop counter?). And, of course, like Elvis, Marilyn has her own postage stamp. But still Marilyn Monroe is different. She's no female Dionysus, for example. Her appeal is more subtle than that, less violent and ecstatic. But it has proven just as enduring.

So what does Marilyn Monroe mean to you? Is she just another sex symbol? But then, why do some women still identify with her today, women who can hardly be said to be sexists in their response to her? And men too: Is the enduring popularity of Marilyn Monroe among American men simply a sexual thing? Why is she such a popular icon among gays?

As you ponder such questions, you might consider the system of American sex symbols to which Marilyn Monroe belongs. Each decade seems to have its dominant figure. In the 1930s, for example, there was Jean Harlow, a platinum-blond sex goddess who is best remembered through a photograph in which she is posed lying seductively on a bearskin rug. In the 1940s, there

---

Discussing the Signs of American Characters

In class, brainstorm a list of your favorite pop cultural icons. Then analyze your list. What mythological significance can you attach to the characters on your list? Do any rival the stature of an Elvis or a Marilyn? If so, what's their appeal; if not, why do you think they don't? What does the list say about the class's collective interests, concerns, and values?

Marilyn Monroe and Joe DiMaggio.

was Rita Hayworth, whose most famous image shows her posed crouching in her lingerie on a bed. But then there's Monroe in *The Seven Year Itch*, playing a gentle if airheaded sex toy who displays her sexuality without fully being aware of it. Probably her most famous image comes from that film, when an updraft of air blows her skirts around her waist as she walks over a subway vent. She laughs as she tries to hold her skirts down. And that's how she's most often remembered, laughing and innocent, even vulnerable.

Now consider the difference between these three images: Harlow's and Hayworth's seductive, challenging poses, and Monroe's childlike laughter and vulnerability. It's that laughter and that innocence that set Monroe apart, the vulnerability that distinguishes her from the other sex goddesses of American popular culture. As the song goes, Marilyn is remembered "like a candle in the wind," as a fragile flame unable to endure the gales of popular attention. What can you make of that vulnerability, of the way that Marilyn signifies today more as a victim of her own fame than as a sex symbol? Does this indicate any uneasiness on America's part about its tendency to worship, and so sometimes destroy, its entertainers?

Pitching the Product

By analyzing such cultural icons as Elvis Presley and Marilyn Monroe — real people who came to embody their society's most basic desires — we can thus learn a great deal about American culture. But there are many other kinds of American icons — from political icons like Abraham Lincoln and Martin Luther King Jr., to scientific icons like Albert Einstein — who represent the best

---

Reading Characters on the Net

One important component in American popular culture is the cult of the celebrity. What role has the Internet played in fostering a celebrity's status? Select a celebrity who interests you, and visit the Web sites, both official and fan-sponsored, associated with that person. How does the official site construct an image for the celebrity, and how does it create a community of fans? In what ways are the fan-generated sites responses to the celebrity's image?

---

in a culture. The trouble is that such icons are getting harder to find. For one thing, many of them — like Thomas Jefferson, and, to a lesser extent, George Washington — are being pulled off their pedestals. And for another, they are getting crowded out by another kind of cultural character, one that is constructed not from the stuff of America's social and political history but from its nature as a consumer culture. For these icons, whether they are real-life people or pure inventions, are constructed for one purpose: to pitch the product

Note, for example, how whenever anyone achieves widespread popularity, or even notoriety, in America, the measure of their success is made by how many product endorsements they get. Tiger Woods is the current king of the endorsers, while Lance Armstrong, with his record-breaking Tour de France triumphs, has substantially expanded his endorsement portfolio. Conversely, when NBA icon Kobe Bryant was hauled into court on a sexual assault charge, commentators immediately speculated on his endorsement contracts losses.

Wherever you look, you can find such commercial icons, and some of them aren't even real. How much beer has Louie the Lizard sold, and what were Joe Camel's sales figures before antismoking legislation forced him to "retire"? How many flashlights has the Energizer Bunny lit up? And how's the Taco Bell chihuahua doing? Advertisers are constantly creating such figures to appeal to specifically targeted markets (Joe Camel, for instance, was accused of being created to sell cigarettes to children), and they often become much admired in their own right (Spuds MacKenzie was quite a hero in the late 1980s).

That so many of America's cultural icons have been subsumed, or even created, to serve commercial interests is a sign of just how profoundly America has embraced the values of a consumer culture. And few icons have been left out of the consumer stampede. Martin Luther King Jr. has been appropriated for a telecommunications pitch, and Albert Einstein's image has been splashed across more ad campaigns than we can count. For their part, George Washington and Abraham Lincoln are the names of sales events. Very little, it seems, is too sacred not to be used for commercial purposes. Or is it that consumerism itself has become sacred?

Back to the Future

And herein lies what may be the most profound significance of America's contemporary iconic system. Dominated by celebrities from the sports and entertainment postindustrial complex (please forgive our word coinage here, but nothing else quite expresses it), America's roster of icons points to a society that is forever celebrating its own consumer-driven popular culture. Neglecting or even forgetting those icons from the past who were nation builders (like George Washington and Benjamin Franklin) or symbols of especially admirable character or consciousness (when the authors of this book were in school, Henry David Thoreau and John Muir were such icons), we have turned to icons created by the culture industry for the purpose of securing profits. It was virtually inevitable that a society so devoted to entertainment should enshrine its entertainers in its iconic pantheon. But perhaps this is why, in the end, the anti-icon has recently appeared: Deep down, perhaps, Americans recognize that entertainers are not the worthiest of cultural symbols, and so we are coming to raise up the anti-iconic entertainer as a paradoxical signifier of both our worship and our disdain.

The Readings

Jake Brennan begins this chapter with a caustic look at those celebrities, or anti-icons, whose claims to fame are both mystifying and a bit irritating, but who continue to inhabit the pop cultural horizon. Michael Eric Dyson follows with an interpretation of the cultural significance of Michael Jordan, an icon whose claim to fame is not a bit mystifying. Gary Engle follows with an analysis of the original Superman, a cartoon hero who, Engle argues, is very much a symbol of the American way. Andy Medhurst's interpretation of Batman from a gay perspective provides some clues as to why Robin was excluded from Tim Burton's *Batman*. Emily Prager and Gary Cross come next with analyses of two of America's favorite characters, Barbie and G.I. Joe — iconic toys who continue to shape American childhoods. Mark Caldwell takes a look at Martha Stewart — before her trial, imprisonment, and release — and her not uncontroversial role as an icon of American domesticity, and Jenny Lyn Bader concludes the chapter with a nostalgic essay on the place of heroes within her own generation — twenty- and thirtysomethings who have seen the old heroes topple and who wonder whether America has room for any new ones.

JAKE BRENNAN

Celebrities Who Aren't Really Celebrities

When William Hung became an overnight sensation due to his excruciating performance on American Idol, *he joined a long and growing line of anti-icons in contemporary American popular culture who, Jake Brennan believes, "aren't really celebrities" at all. From Kato Kaelin to Monica Lewinsky, a lot of ordinary people are being plucked out of obscurity for instant, if fleeting, fame. Such is the power of a media-obsessed, media-driven culture, but as Brennan asks, can anyone explain why Zsa Zsa Gabor became famous? Brennan is a lifestyle commentator for AskMen.com, where this article first appeared.*

Why are some people famous? This question has confounded critics since Zsa Zsa Gabor's third facelift. A much simpler, related question is: Do you need talent to make it? If Rupert Jee from *The Late Show with David Letterman* is any indication, apparently not.

What Rupert's getting is exposure. Exposure is good, but it hardly guarantees long-term success. It turns out you need some kind of talent to secure a future in the entertainment world. Who knew? Actually, not even talent will do the trick, as people's tastes change faster than a politician's expression when caught, mid-enjoyment, with a "professional."

One of the only ways to get attention consistently is to shock people in new and "interesting" ways. See, you can't spell "infamous" without spelling "famous" — people often get the two confused, as any sort of recognition is now considered desirable by the truly vacuous in our society.

Why Do We Care?

But why are we interested in such non-celebrities? Well, it's a way for we normal folk to live vicariously through other people. From *Survivor*, for example, we get to learn how people might react if we tell them how we *really* feel, deep down, about the freckles on their feet. Another equally cromulent theory is that we want our faces to stand out among the ever-growing crowd because the world's population is exploding.

Whatever the reason, the word "celebrity" comes from the Latin *celeber*,   5
meaning "to celebrate, honor, frequent," as in "this person's talent is to be celebrated." So tell me, why would I want to celebrate or honor (I don't even want to think about "frequent") Rupert Jee? Because he's average? I think I've got that angle covered myself, thanks.

Could it be that the term celebrity is suffering from overuse? Could it be that I, one lone writer, am powerless to stop the pseudo-celebrity deluge, and am therefore simply left to analyze it? Huh, could be.

The History of the Phenomenon

Among the many shrewd observations Andy Warhol can be credited for (and probably his most famous, speaking of fame . . .) is his statement, "in the future, everybody will be famous for 15 minutes." The crack was as much a commentary on how easy it was becoming to get noticed by the media, as it was on how such recognition was increasingly desired by the media's audience — Joe and Jane Average. And so the vicious media circle was set in motion.

What the Average family forgot along the way was that the people claiming media attention merited (originally, at least) our attention for some talent or newsworthy exploit. But somewhere along the way exploits turned into stunts, talent started to include a marked lack thereof, and reality television was born.

From *Survivor* to *Fear Factor*, reality TV is part of the problem.

Reality TV started innocently enough with game shows that put real people 10 on the spot — often, ironically, alongside celebrity has-beens. Take a look at today's *Hollywood Squares* and tell me the last time you saw Nipsey Russell or Jamie Farr using their "talent" anywhere else. Maybe it was this hodgepodge of former talent and Joe Averages that kicked this whole cult-of-celebrity deal into high gear. Think about it: who in their right mind isn't aspiring to be the next Martin Mull or Charo?

Fast forward to the 21st century and you've got game shows on 'roids, and called, of all things, "reality programming." Gee, and I thought that referred to the news. Anyway, on one channel people are starving and cat fighting on an island, on the next they're confronting their fears in unthinkably disgusting ways for, like, 40 bucks ("Ooh, did he just vomit, or is that just the pureed maggot bath getting a little ripe?" "I don't know, Bob. Let's see if we can get a tighter shot!").

Types of Smell-ebrity?

It turns out there are more than a few kinds of instant celebrities. What does it say about our society that the talentless and the merely banal among us can be subdivided further than that?

For better or worse, there are the one-hit wonders who never seem to go away; the obviously talentless, or *smell-ebrities* (they're famous because they stink); the celebrities by association; and those who seem to just stumble upon fame like Paris Hilton on a dance floor.

ONE-HIT WONDERS

This category comprises those who were trying to leave their mark with their talent, but only ended up doing so once. They're forever only known for that accomplishment, and try to ride it as long as they can.

A bar for such astronauts (they're not quite stars) would be frequented by Mark Hamill ([who] played Luke Skywalker in the original *Star Wars* trilogy), Ray Jay Johnson ("now you can call me Ray, and you can call me Jay . . ." Shut up already!), and Philip Seymour Hoffman's former child star character in the cinematic hit, *Along Came Polly*.

The phenomenon was well parodied on *The Simpsons* when Bart knocked over the set of Krusty the Klown's show, turned to the camera and said, "I didn't do it." He quickly became the "I didn't do it" boy, with figurines, lunchboxes . . . everything, actually, that Bart himself has in our three-dimensional world. Luckily for Bart, though — and for us — the writers behind him have a little more up their sleeves than does the perennially 10-year-old slacker they create.

Many who fall into this category find their fleeting fame intoxicating (often literally). The more resourceful parlay their one hit into something more. This is where Ernest, that ugly plumber or electrician or whatever the hell he was, comes in. This guy stretched one commercial into something like nine (too many) movies: *Ernest Goes to Camp, Ernest Goes to the Proctologist*, etc.

STINKERS

Two words: William Hung. From his rendition of Ricky Martin's "She Bangs" on *American Idol* that had cats mewling and tearing up furniture across the continent, this guy has made quite an impression, appearing on *The Ellen DeGeneres Show*, opening sporting events with his gift of song, and even boasting his own fan Web site.

There are many more nobodies, from Paris to Steve-O. In fact, many reality show contestants fall into this category: the only thing that qualifies them to be on TV is that they're real (and real average). David Letterman has also been fond of creating such faux-celebrities: Sirajul and Mujibur are good sports and all, but smooth they ain't. Oh, and did I mention Rupert Jee?

And even an event as lofty as the Olympic Games has seen its share, thanks to its at times bizarre qualifying quotas. The Jamaican bobsled team and Britain's bespectacled ski jumping phenom Eddie the Eagle are but two examples.

Anyone who does something controversial for publicity could also fall into this category. The accidental-on purpose release of the Paris Hilton sex tape has humiliated her all the way to the bank. The poor darlin'!

And on that note, let's not forget the entire crew from *Jackass* (Johnny Knoxville, Steve-O et al.). These guys are merely putting together an organized version of what a lot of "guys" were thinking of doing — and actually doing — at age 12. I guess this is them getting points for organization, then.

STUMBLERS

Whereas the smell-ebrities seek out fame for their incompetence, some people suddenly find themselves in the media spotlight. I'm talking about the Kato Kaelins, the Joey Buttafuocos, and the John Wayne Bobbitts of this world. There's also Abe Zapruder, who shot the famous home video of John F. Kennedy's assassination. This kind of fame often falls upon people involved in court cases. Not to be confused with . . .

(IN)FAMOUS BY ASSOCIATION

Here I'm thinking of Monica Lewinsky (and Linda Tripp), Shoshanna Lonstein (who used to date Jerry Seinfeld), and Cris Judd (who used to be married to J.Lo). We're talking all the Baldwins except Alec, we're talking Zsa Zsa Gabor. And can I get a "woo-woo" for Golden Globe–nominated actor (what?) Frank Stallone, Sly's brother?

Some of these folks have made deft transitions (Lewinsky), others, not so   25 much (Tripp). Interestingly, even "legitimately" famous people use this method to their advantage. Brad Pitt and Jennifer Aniston were set up by their publicists, and I'm not thinking Penelope Cruz was exactly reluctant to shack up with Tommy.

Media-Made Non-Celebrities

There's a whole industry out there based on building up and tearing down such folk. Ever heard of the *New York Post*'s Page Six? How about *Entertainment Tonight* or *Extra*? They "made" Nicole Richie (who incidentally happens to have a famous dad).

The problem (or one of the many problems, rather) with all this is that people believe misinformation — especially in this Internet age, when there are no publishers vetting the veracity of Internet factoids. I mean, how do you know these are even really my opinions? But seriously, rumors can create and destroy these people in an instant, many of whom have not been preparing themselves for the glare of the media spotlight their entire life.

What Happens Next?

The harsh reality is that many of these has-beens don't enjoy the downhill as much as the climb up. After fame, reality seems so mundane. The adjustment is tough. But do I feel sorry for these people? The stumblers and some of the one-hit wonders, sure, sometimes. But the smell-ebrities and fame associates, nuh-uh. I mean, compare Gary Coleman (cute little Arnold from *Diff'rent Strokes*) to Linda Tripp, and you tell me where your soft spot is.

How Do You Know You're Through?

There are a few telltale signs that your time has come:

- You're asked to do a late-night infomercial
- For women, you depend on a *Playboy* spread to revive your career (e.g., Nancy Sinatra, etc. ad infinitum)
- You're invited to appear on *Celebrity Mole* (e.g., Stephen Baldwin)
- You call up journalists for interviews, not the other way around
- People keep saying to you, "Man, I thought you were dead!"

That's a Wrap

There are all sorts of different egos out there, each seeking the amount of   30
fame they need to "get by." But remember that real celebs don't play to the
paparazzi and are still sought by them, while non-celebrities love the attention because they know they need the exposure to stay alive. Actual celebrities support themselves with their talent, not some sideshow bastardization
of it.

If you fall in the spotlight, enjoy your 15 minutes of fame while you can.
Save the dough it brings you for a rainy day. Trust me, there will be many.

READING THE TEXT

1. Summarize in your own words Brennan's response to his question, "Why are some people famous?" (para. 1).
2. What does Brennan mean by "non-celebrity" and "smell-ebrity"?
3. How has reality TV contributed to the explosion of "non-celebrities"?
4. Characterize Brennan's tone and style. How does it contribute to the persua-siveness of his argument?

READING THE SIGNS

1. Watch a program such as *The Late Show with David Letterman* or *Entertain-ment Tonight*, and evaluate Brennan's claim that such shows contribute to the creation of noncelebrities.
2. In class, brainstorm a list of current "one-hit wonders" (para. 14). Then analyze your list: Why is it that these people have caught the public's eye? What does their success, however fleeting, say about American cultural values?
3. Adopting the perspective of Jenny Lyn Bader in "Larger Than Life" (p. 784), critique the noncelebrity trend that Brennan describes. How do you think Bader might explain it?

4. Write an essay defending, refuting, or modifying Brennan's claim that we are interested in noncelebrities because "it's a way for we normal folk to live vicariously through other people" (para. 4).

5. Write an essay in which you assess the validity of Brennan's distinction between real celebrities and noncelebrities. Can you draw a clear line between the two categories? Be sure to base your discussion on the status of specific famous people.

MICHAEL ERIC DYSON

Be Like Mike? Michael Jordan and the Pedagogy of Desire

It's hard to keep up with Michael Jordan. Not only is it impossible to beat him on the court, but you can't even figure out what to call him these days. A former NBA megastar? Well, he's retired twice and has now come back for the second time, which is an appropriate addition to the legend that Michael Eric Dyson (b. 1958) analyzes in this selection. Situating Jordan within the context of American social and cultural history, Dyson shows what basketball, and everything that goes with it, means in America, especially for African American youth. And it isn't just air time. A professor of religious studies at the University of Pennsylvania, Dyson is author of Reflecting Black: African-American Cultural Criticism *(1993), from which this essay is taken;* Making Malcolm: The Myth and Meaning of Malcolm X *(1995);* Between God and Gangsta Rap: Bearing Witness to Black Culture *(1996);* Holler If You Hear Me: Searching for Tupac Shakur *(2001);* Word Is Bond: The Tradition of Testimony *(2005);* Is Bill Cosby Right? *(2005);* Pride: The Seven Deadly Sins *(2005); and* Mercy, Mercy Me: The Art, Loves and Demons of Marvin Gaye *(2005).*

Michael Jordan is perhaps the best, and best-known, athlete in the world today. He has attained unparalleled cultural status because of his extraordinary physical gifts, his marketing as an icon of race-transcending American athletic and moral excellence, and his mastery of a sport that has become the metaphoric center of black cultural imagination. But the Olympian sum of Jordan's cultural meaning is greater than the fluent parts of his persona as athlete, family man, and marketing creation. There is hardly cultural precedence for the character of his unique fame, which has blurred the line between private and public, between personality and celebrity, and between substance and symbol. Michael Jordan stands at the breach between perception and intuition, his cultural meaning perennially deferred from closure because his career symbolizes possibility itself, gathering into its unfolding narrative the shattered remnants of previous incarnations of fame and yet transcending their reach.

Jordan has been called "the new DiMaggio" (Boers 1990, 30) and "Elvis in high-tops," indications of the herculean cultural heroism he has come to embody. There is even a religious element to the near worship of Jordan as a cultural icon of invincibility, as he has been called a "savior of sorts," "basketball's high priest" (Bradley 1991–92, 60), and "more popular than Jesus," except with "better endorsement deals" (Vancil 1992, 51). But the quickly developing cultural canonization of Michael Jordan provokes reflection about the contradictory uses to which Jordan's body is put as a seminal cultural text and ambiguous symbol of fantasy, and the avenues of agency and resistance available especially to black youth who make symbolic investment in Jordan's body as a means of cultural and personal possibility, creativity, and desire.

I understand Jordan in the broadest sense of the term to be a public pedagogue, a figure of estimable public moral authority whose career educates us about productive and disenabling forms of knowledge, desire, interest, consumption, and culture in three spheres: the culture of athletics that thrives on skill and performance; the specific expression of elements of African American culture; and the market forces and processes of commodification expressed by, and produced in, advanced capitalism. By probing these dimensions of Jordan's cultural importance, we may gain a clearer understanding of his function in American society.

Athletic activity has shaped and reflected important sectors of American society. First, it produced communities of common athletic interest organized around the development of highly skilled performance. The development of norms of athletic excellence evidenced in sports activities cemented communities of participants who valorized rigorous sorts of physical discipline in preparation for athletic competition and in expressing the highest degree of athletic skill. Second, it produced potent subcultures that inculcated in their participants norms of individual and team accomplishment. Such norms tapped into the bipolar structures of competition and cooperation that pervade American culture. Third, it provided a means of reinscribing Western frontier myths of exploration and discovery-as-conquest onto a vital sphere of American culture. Sports activities can be viewed in part as the attempt to symbolically ritualize and metaphorically extend the ongoing quest for mastery of environment and vanquishing of opponents within the limits of physical contest.

Fourth, athletic activity has served to reinforce habits and virtues centered in collective pursuit of communal goals that are intimately connected to the common good, usually characterized within athletic circles as "team spirit." The culture of sport has physically captured and athletically articulated the mores, folkways, and dominant visions of American society, and at its best it

5

has been conceived as a means of symbolically embracing and equitably pursuing the just, the good, the true, and the beautiful. And finally, the culture of athletics has provided an acceptable and widely accessible means of white male bonding. For much of its history, American sports activity has reflected white patriarchal privilege, and it has been rigidly defined and socially shaped by rules that restricted the equitable participation of women and people of color.

Black participation in sports in mainstream society, therefore, is a relatively recent phenomenon. Of course, there have existed venerable traditions of black sports, such as the Negro (baseball) Leagues, which countered the exclusion of black bodies from white sports. The prohibition of athletic activity by black men in mainstream society severely limited publicly acceptable forms of displaying black physical prowess, an issue that had been politicized during slavery and whose legacy extended into the middle of the twentieth century. Hence, the potentially superior physical prowess of black men, validated for many by the long tradition of slave labor that built American society, helped reinforce racist arguments about the racial regimentation of social space and the denigration of the black body as an inappropriate presence in traditions of American sport.

Coupled with this fear of superior black physical prowess was the notion that inferior black intelligence limited the ability of blacks to perform excellently in those sports activities that required mental concentration and agility. These two forces — the presumed lack of sophisticated black cognitive skills and the fear of superior black physical prowess — restricted black sports participation to thriving but financially handicapped subcultures of black athletic activity. Later, of course, the physical prowess of the black body would be acknowledged and exploited as a supremely fertile zone of profit as mainstream athletic society literally cashed in on the symbolic danger of black sports excellence.

Because of its marginalized status within the regime of American sports, black athletic activity often acquired a social significance that transcended the internal dimensions of game, sport, and skill. Black sport became an arena not only for testing the limits of physical endurance and forms of athletic excellence — while reproducing or repudiating ideals of American justice, goodness, truth, and beauty — but it also became a way of ritualizing racial achievement against socially imposed barriers to cultural performance.

In short, black sport activity often acquired a heroic dimension, as viewed in the careers of figures such as Joe Louis, Jackie Robinson, Althea Gibson, Wilma Rudolph, Muhammad Ali, and Arthur Ashe. Black sports heroes transcended the narrow boundaries of specific sports activities and garnered importance as icons of cultural excellence, symbolic figures who embodied social possibilities of success denied to other people of color. But they also captured and catalyzed the black cultural fetishization of sport as a means of expressing black cultural style, as a means of valorizing craft as a marker of racial and self-expression, and as a means of pursuing social and economic mobility.

It is this culture of black athletics, created against the background of social ₁₀ and historical forces that shaped American athletic activity, that helped produce Jordan and help explain the craft that he practices. Craft is the honing of skill by the application of discipline, time, talent, and energy toward the realization of a particular cultural or personal goal. American folk cultures are pervaded by craft, from the production of cultural artifacts that express particular ethnic histories and traditions to the development of styles of life and work that reflect and symbolize a community's values, virtues, and goals. Michael Jordan's skills within basketball are clearly phenomenal, but his game can only be sufficiently explained by understanding its link to the fusion of African American cultural norms and practices, and the idealization of skill and performance that characterize important aspects of American sport. I will identify three defining characteristics of Jordan's game that reflect the influence of African American culture on his style of play.

First, Jordan's style of basketball reflects the *will to spontaneity*. I mean here the way in which historical accidence is transformed into cultural advantage, and the way acts of apparently random occurrence are spontaneously and imaginatively employed by Africans and African Americans in a variety of forms of cultural expression. When examining Jordan's game, this feature of African American culture clearly functions in his unpredictable eruptions of basketball creativity. It was apparent, for instance, during game two of the National Basketball Association 1991 championship series between Jordan's Chicago Bulls and the Los Angeles Lakers, in a shot that even Jordan ranked in his all-time top ten (McCallum 1991, 32). Jordan made a drive toward the lane, gesturing with his hands and body that he was about to complete a patent Jordan dunk shot with his right hand. But when he spied defender Sam Perkins slipping over to oppose his shot, he switched the ball in midair to his left hand to make an underhanded scoop shot instead, which immediately became known as the "levitation" shot. Such improvisation, a staple of the will to spontaneity, allows Jordan to expand his vocabulary of athletic spectacle, which is the stimulation of a desire to bear witness to the revelation of truth and beauty compressed into acts of athletic creativity.

Second, Jordan's game reflects the *stylization of the performed self*. This is the creation and projection of a sport persona that is an identifying mark of diverse African American creative enterprises, from the complexly layered jazz experimentation of John Coltrane, the trickstering and signifying comedic routines of Richard Pryor, and the rhetorical ripostes and oral significations of rapper Kool Moe Dee. Jordan's whole game persona is a graphic depiction of the performed self as flying acrobat, resulting in his famous moniker "Air Jordan." Jordan's performed self is rife with the language of physical expressiveness: head moving, arms extending, hands waving, tongue wagging, and legs spreading.

He has also developed a resourceful repertoire of dazzling dunk shots that further express his performed self and that have garnered him a special niche within the folklore of the game: the cradle jam, rock-a-baby, kiss the rim, lean in, and the tomahawk. In Jordan's game, the stylization of a performed self has allowed him to create a distinct sports persona that has athletic as well as economic consequences, while mastering sophisticated levels of physical expression and redefining the possibilities of athletic achievement within basketball.

Finally, there is the subversion of perceived limits through the use of *edifying deception*, which in Jordan's case centers around the space/time continuum. This moment in African American cultural practice is the ability to flout widely understood boundaries through mesmerization and alchemy, a subversion of common perceptions of the culturally or physically possible through the creative and deceptive manipulation of appearance. Jordan is perhaps most famous for his alleged "hang time," the uncanny ability to remain suspended in midair longer than other basketball players while executing his stunning array of improvised moves. But Jordan's "hang time" is technically a misnomer and can be more accurately attributed to Jordan's skillful athletic deception, his acrobatic leaping ability, and his intellectual toughness in projecting an aura of uniqueness around his craft than to his defiance of gravity and the laws of physics.

No human being, including Michael Jordan, can successfully defy the law 15 of gravity and achieve relatively sustained altitude without the benefit of machines. As Douglas Kirkpatrick points out, the equation for altitude is $1/2g \times t2 = VO \times t$ ("How Does Michael Fly?"). However, Jordan appears to hang by *stylistically* relativizing the fixed coordinates of space and time through the skillful management and manipulation of his body in midair. For basketball players, hang time is the velocity and speed with which a player takes off combined with the path the player's center of gravity follows on the way up. At the peak of a player's vertical jump, the velocity and speed is close to, or at, zero; hanging motionless in the air is the work of masterful skill and illusion ("How Does Michael Fly?"). Michael Jordan, through the consummate skill and style of his game, only appears to be hanging in space for more than the one second that human beings are capable of remaining airborne.

But the African American aspects of Jordan's game are indissolubly linked to the culture of consumption and the commodification of black culture.[1] Because of Jordan's supreme mastery of basketball, his squeaky-clean image, and his youthful vigor in pursuit of the American Dream, he has become, along with Bill Cosby, the quintessential pitchman in American society. Even his highly publicized troubles with gambling, his refusal to visit the White House after the Bulls' championship season, and a book that purports to expose the underside of his heroic myth have barely tarnished his All-American

---

[1] I do not mean here a theory of commodification that does not accentuate the forms of agency that can function even within restrictive and hegemonic cultural practices. Rather, I think that, contrary to elitist and overly pessimistic Frankfurt School readings of the spectacle of commodity within mass cultures, common people can exercise "everyday forms of resistance" to hegemonic forms of cultural knowledge and practice. For an explication of the function of everyday forms of resistance, see Scott, *Domination and the Arts of Resistance*.

image.[2] Jordan eats Wheaties, drives Chevrolets, wears Hanes, drinks Coca-Cola, consumes McDonald's, guzzles Gatorade, and, of course, wears Nikes. He and his shrewd handlers have successfully produced, packaged, marketed, and distributed his image and commodified his symbolic worth, transforming cultural capital into cash, influence, prestige, status, and wealth. To that degree, at least, Jordan repudiates the sorry tradition of the black athlete as the naif who loses his money to piranha-like financial wizards, investors, and hangers-on. He represents the new-age athletic entrepreneur who understands that American sport is ensconced in the cultural practices associated with business, and that it demands particular forms of intelligence, perception, and representation to prevent abuse and maximize profit.

From the very beginning of his professional career, Jordan was consciously marketed by his agency Pro-Serv as a peripatetic vehicle of American fantasies of capital accumulation and material consumption tied to Jordan's personal modesty and moral probity. In so doing, they skillfully avoided attaching to Jordan the image of questionable ethics and lethal excess that plagued inside traders and corporate raiders on Wall Street during the mid-eighties, as Jordan began to emerge as a cultural icon. But Jordan is also the symbol of the spectacle-laden black athletic body as the site of commodified black cultural imagination. Ironically, the black male body, which has been historically viewed as threatening and inappropriate in American society (and remains so outside of sports and entertainment), is made an object of white desires to domesticate and dilute its more ominous and subversive uses, even symbolically reducing Jordan's body to dead meat (McDonald's McJordan hamburger), which can be consumed and expelled as waste.

Jordan's body is also the screen upon which are projected black desires to emulate his athletic excellence and replicate his entry into reaches of unimaginable wealth and fame. But there is more than vicarious substitution and the projection of fantasy onto Jordan's body that is occurring in the circulation and reproduction of black cultural desire. There is also the creative use of desire and fantasy by young blacks to counter, and capitulate to, the forces of cultural dominance that attempt to reduce the black body to a commodity and text that is employed for entertainment, titillation, or financial gain. Simply said, there is no easy correlation between the commodification of black youth culture and the evidences of a completely dominated consciousness.

Even within the dominant cultural practices that seek to turn the black body into pure profit, disruptions of capital are embodied, for instance, in messages circulated in black communities by public moralists who criticize the exploitation of black cultural creativity by casual footwear companies. In short, there are instances of both black complicity and resistance in the

---

[2]For a critical look at Jordan behind the myth, see Smith, *The Jordan Rules*.

commodification of black cultural imagination, and the ideological criticism of exploitative cultural practices must always be linked to the language of possibility and agency in rendering a complex picture of the black cultural situation. As Henry Giroux observes:

> The power of complicity and the complicity of power are not exhausted simply by registering how people are positioned and located through the production of particular ideologies structured through particular discourses. . . . It is important to see that an overreliance on ideology critique has limited our ability to understand how people actively participate in the dominant culture through processes of accommodation, negotiation, and even resistance. (Giroux 1992, 194–95)

In making judgments about the various uses of the black body, especially Jordan's symbolic corporeality, we must specify how both consent and opposition to exploitation are often signaled in expressions of cultural creativity.

In examining his reactions to the racial ordering of athletic and cultural 20 life, the ominous specificity of the black body creates anxieties for Jordan. His encounters with the limits of culturally mediated symbols of race and racial identity have occasionally mocked his desire to live beyond race, to be "neither black nor white" (Patton 1986, 52), to be "viewed as a person" (Vancil 1992, 57). While Jordan chafes under indictment by black critics who claim that he is not "black enough," he has perhaps not clearly understood the differences between enabling versions of human experience that transcend the exclusive gaze of race and disenabling visions of human community that seek race neutrality.

The former is the attempt to expand the perimeters of human experience beyond racial determinism, to nuance and deepen our understanding of the constituent elements of racial identity, and to understand how race, along with class, gender, geography, and sexual preference, shape and constrain human experience. The latter is the belief in an intangible, amorphous, nonhistorical, and raceless category of "person," existing in a zone beyond not simply the negative consequences of race, but beyond the specific patterns of cultural and racial identity that constitute and help shape human experience. Jordan's unclarity is consequential, weighing heavily on his apolitical bearing and his refusal to acknowledge the public character of his private beliefs about American society and the responsibility of his role as a public pedagogue.

Indeed it is the potency of black cultural expressions that not only have helped influence his style of play, but have also made the sneaker industry he lucratively participates in a multi-billion-dollar business. Michael Jordan has helped seize upon the commercial consequences of black cultural preoccupation with style and the commodification of the black juvenile imagination at the site of the sneaker. At the juncture of the sneaker, a host of cultural, political, and economic forces and meanings meet, collide, shatter, and are reassembled to symbolize the situation of contemporary black culture.

The sneaker reflects at once the projection and stylization of black urban realities linked in our contemporary historical moment to rap culture and the underground political economy of crack, and reigns as the universal icon for the culture of consumption. The sneaker symbolizes the ingenious manner in which black cultural nuances of cool, hip, and chic have influenced the broader American cultural landscape. It was black street culture that influenced sneaker companies' aggressive invasion of the black juvenile market in taking advantage of the increasing amounts of disposable income of young black men as a result of legitimate and illegitimate forms of work.

Problematically, though, the sneaker also epitomizes the worst features of the social production of desire and represents the ways in which moral energies of social conscience about material values are drained by the messages of undisciplined acquisitiveness promoted by corporate dimensions of the culture of consumption. These messages, of rapacious consumerism supported by cultural and personal narcissism, are articulated on Wall Street and are related to the expanding inner-city juvenocracy, where young black men rule over black urban space in the culture of crack and illicit criminal activity, fed by desires to "live large" and to reproduce capitalism's excesses on their own terrain. Also, sneaker companies make significant sums of money from the illicit gains of drug dealers.

Moreover, while sneaker companies have exploited black cultural expressions of cool, hip, chic, and style, they rarely benefit the people who both consume the largest quantity of products and whose culture redefined the sneaker companies' raison d'être. This situation is more severely compounded by the presence of spokespeople like Jordan, Spike Lee, and Bo Jackson, who are either ineffectual or defensive about or indifferent to the lethal consequences (especially in urban black-on-black violence over sneaker company products) of black juvenile acquisition of products that these figures have helped make culturally desirable and economically marketable.

Basketball is the metaphoric center of black juvenile culture, a major means by which even temporary forms of cultural and personal transcendence of personal limits are experienced. Michael Jordan is at the center of this black athletic culture, the supreme symbol of black cultural creativity in a society of diminishing tolerance for the black youth whose fascination with Jordan has helped sustain him. But Jordan is also the iconic fixture of broader segments of American society, who see in him the ideal figure: a black man of extraordinary genius on the court and before the cameras, who by virtue of his magical skills and godlike talents symbolizes the meaning of human possibility, while refusing to root it in the specific forms of culture and race in which it must inevitably make sense or fade to ultimate irrelevance.

Jordan also represents the contradictory impulses of the contemporary culture of consumption, where the black athletic body is deified, reified, and rearticulated within the narrow meanings of capital and commodity. But there is both resistance and consent to the exploitation of black bodies in Jordan's explicit cultural symbolism, as he provides brilliant glimpses of black culture's ingenuity of improvisation as a means of cultural expression and survival. It is also partially this element of black culture that has created in American society a desire to dream Jordan, to "be like Mike."

This pedagogy of desire that Jordan embodies, although at points immobilized by its depoliticized cultural contexts, is nevertheless a remarkable achievement in contemporary American culture: a six-foot-six American man of obvious African descent is the dominant presence and central cause of athletic fantasy in a sport that twenty years ago was denigrated as a black man's game and hence deemed unworthy of wide attention or support. Jordan is therefore the bearer of meanings about black culture larger than his individual life, the symbol of a pedagogy of style, presence, and desire that is immediately communicated by the sight of his black body before it can be contravened by reflection.

In the final analysis, his big black body — graceful and powerful, elegant and dark — symbolizes the possibilities of other black bodies to remain safe long enough to survive within the limited but significant sphere of sport, since Jordan's achievements have furthered the cultural acceptance of at least the athletic black body. In that sense, Jordan's powerful cultural capital has not been exhausted by narrow understandings of his symbolic absorption by the demands of capital and consumption. His body is still the symbolic carrier of racial and cultural desires to fly beyond limits and obstacles, a fluid metaphor of mobility and ascent to heights of excellence secured by genius and industry. It is this power to embody the often conflicting desires of so many that makes Michael Jordan a supremely instructive figure for our times.

WORKS CITED

Boers, Terry. "Getting Better All the Time." *Inside Sports*, May 1990, pp. 30–33.
Bradley, Michael. "Air Everything." *Basketball Forecast*, 1991–92, pp. 60–67.
Giroux, Henry. *Border Crossings: Cultural Workers and the Politics of Education*. New York: Routledge, 1992.
"How Does Michael Fly?" *Chicago Tribune*, February 27, 1990, p. 28.
McCallum, Jack. "His Highness." *Sports Illustrated*, June 17, 1991, pp. 28–33.
Patton, Paul. "The Selling of Michael Jordan." *New York Times Magazine*, November 9, 1986, pp. 48–58.
Scott, James. *Domination and the Arts of Resistance*. New Haven, Conn.: Yale University Press, 1990.
Smith, Sam. *The Jordan Rules*. New York: Simon and Schuster, 1992.
Vancil, Mark. "*Playboy* Interview: Michael Jordan." *Playboy*, May 1992, pp. 51–64.

READING THE TEXT

1. What does Dyson mean by the term "public pedagogue" (para. 3)?

2. What social forces have caused black athletes to assume "a heroic dimension" (para. 9) in American life, according to Dyson?

3. What evidence does Dyson provide to show that Jordan's skills express African American "cultural norms and practices" (para. 10)?

4. What connection does Dyson make between Jordan's athletic skills and America's "culture of consumption" (para. 16)?

5. Why, in Dyson's view, was Jordan especially effective in promoting the sneaker industry?

READING THE SIGNS

1. Dyson observes that some critics have complained that Jordan is not "black enough" (para. 20). Write an essay in which you support or oppose this criticism, being sure to discuss the underlying assumptions about the role of a hero or role model.

2. Write an argumentative essay in response to the proposition that basketball is primarily a black form of cultural expression. To develop your ideas, read or review Paul C. Taylor's "Funky White Boys and Honorary Soul Sisters" (p. 578).

3. In class, brainstorm athletic heroes, both male and female. Then discuss the reasons these athletes appeal to the public. Use the class discussion as a basis for an essay in which you analyze why Americans so often turn to athletes for heroes and role models.

4. Write an essay in which you support or refute Dyson's contention that "the culture of athletics has provided an acceptable and widely accessible means of white male bonding" (para. 5). To develop your ideas, consult Michael A. Messner, "Power at Play: Sport and Gender Relations" (p. 513).

GARY ENGLE

What Makes Superman So Darned American?

Since his initial appearance in a June 1938 comic book, and through countless more radio serials, books, toys, Web sites, video games, movies, and television shows — including his latest incarnation in the hit WB show Smallville — Superman has fought for "truth, justice, and the American way." In this semiotic analysis of the enduring appeal of Superman, Gary Engle (b. 1947) argues why the Man of Steel — whom Engle views as the ultimate immigrant — has dominated the pantheon of American characters for so many years. Of all our heroes, Engle claims, Superman alone "achieves truly mythic stature, interweaving a pattern of beliefs, literary conventions, and cultural traditions of the American people more powerfully and more accessibly than any other cultural symbol of the twentieth century, perhaps of any period in our history." A specialist in popular culture, Engle is an associate professor of English at Cleveland State University. In addition to over two hundred magazine and journal articles, he has written The Grotesque Essence: Plays from the American Minstrel Stage *(1978).*

When I was young I spent a lot of time arguing with myself about who would win in a fight between John Wayne and Superman. On days when I wore my cowboy hat and cap guns, I knew the Duke would win because of his pronounced superiority in the all-important matter of swagger. There were days, though, when a frayed army blanket tied cape-fashion around my neck signalled a young man's need to believe there could be no end to the potency of his being. Then the Man of Steel was the odds-on favorite to knock the Duke for a cosmic loop. My greatest childhood problem was that the question could never be resolved because no such battle could ever take place. I mean, how would a fight start between the only two Americans who never started anything, who always fought only to defend their rights and the American way?

Now that I'm older and able to look with reason on the mysteries of childhood, I've finally resolved the dilemma. John Wayne was the best older brother any kid could ever hope to have, but he was no Superman.

Superman is *the* great American hero. We are a nation rich with legendary figures. But among the Davy Crocketts and Paul Bunyans and Mike Finks and Pecos Bills and all the rest who speak for various regional identities in the pantheon of American folklore, only Superman achieves truly mythic stature, interweaving a pattern of beliefs, literary conventions, and cultural traditions of the American people more powerfully and more accessibly than any other cultural symbol of the twentieth century, perhaps of any period in our history.

The core of the American myth in *Superman* consists of a few basic facts that remain unchanged throughout the infinitely varied ways in which the myth is told — facts with which everyone is familiar, however marginal their knowledge of the story. Superman is an orphan rocketed to Earth when his native planet Krypton explodes; he lands near Smallville and is adopted by Jonathan and Martha Kent, who inculcate in him their American middle-class ethic; as an adult he migrates to Metropolis where he defends America — no, the world! no, the Universe! — from all evil and harm while playing a romantic game in which, as Clark Kent, he hopelessly pursues Lois Lane, who hopelessly pursues Superman, who remains aloof until such time as Lois proves worthy of him by falling in love with his feigned identity as a weakling. That's it. Every narrative thread in the mythology, each one of the thousands of plots in the fifty-year stream of comics and films and TV shows, all the tales involving the demigods of the Superman pantheon — Superboy, Supergirl, even Krypto the Superdog — every single one reinforces by never contradicting this basic set of facts. That's the myth, and that's where one looks to understand America.

It is impossible to imagine Superman being as popular as he is and   5
speaking as deeply to the American character were he not an immigrant and an orphan. Immigration, of course, is the overwhelming fact in American history. Except for the Indians, all Americans have an immediate sense of their origins elsewhere. No nation on Earth has so deeply embedded in its social consciousness the imagery of passage from one social identity to another: the *Mayflower* of the New England separatists, the slave ships from Africa and the subsequent underground railroads toward freedom in the North, the sailing ships and steamers running shuttles across two oceans in the nineteenth century, the freedom airlifts in the twentieth. Somehow the picture just isn't complete without Superman's rocketship.

Like the peoples of the nation whose values he defends, Superman is an alien, but not just any alien. He's the consummate and totally uncompromised alien, an immigrant whose visible difference from the norm is underscored by his decision to wear a costume of bold primary colors so tight as to be his very skin. Moreover, Superman the alien is real. He stands out among the hosts of comic book characters (Batman is a good example) for whom the superhero role is like a mask assumed when needed, a costume worn over their real identities as normal Americans. Superman's powers — strength, mobility, x-ray vision and the like — are the comic-book equivalents of ethnic characteristics, and they protect and preserve the vitality of the foster community in which he lives in the same way that immigrant ethnicity has sustained American culture linguistically, artistically, economically, politically, and spiritually. The myth of Superman asserts with total confidence and a childlike innocence the value of the immigrant in American culture.

From this nation's beginnings Americans have looked for ways of coming to terms with the immigrant experience. This is why, for example, so much of American literature and popular culture deals with the theme of dislocation,

"*The* great American hero": A collector of Superman memorabilia poses with his finds, Fountain Valley, California.

generally focused in characters devoted or doomed to constant physical movement. Daniel Boone became an American legend in part as a result of apocryphal stories that he moved every time his neighbors got close enough for him to see the smoke of their cabin fires. James Fenimore Cooper's Natty Bumppo spent the five long novels of the Leatherstocking saga drifting ever westward, like the pioneers who were his spiritual offspring, from the Mohawk valley of upstate New York to the Great Plains where he died. Huck Finn sailed through the moral heart of America on a raft. Melville's Ishmael, Wister's Virginian, Shane, Gatsby, the entire Lost Generation, Steinbeck's Okies, Little Orphan Annie, a thousand fiddlefooted cowboy heroes of dime novels and films and television — all in motion, searching for the American dream or stubbornly refusing to give up their innocence by growing old, all symptomatic of a national sense of rootlessness stemming from an identity founded on the experience of immigration.

Individual mobility is an integral part of America's dreamwork. Is it any wonder, then, that our greatest hero can take to the air at will? Superman's ability to fly does more than place him in a tradition of mythic figures going back to the Greek messenger god Hermes or Zetes the flying Argonaut. It makes him an exemplar in the American dream. Take away a young man's wheels and you take away his manhood. Jack Kerouac and Charles Kuralt go on the road; William Least Heat Moon looks for himself in a van exploring the veins of America in its system of blue highways; legions of gray-haired retirees turn Air Stream trailers and Winnebagos into proof positive that you can, in the end, take it with you. On a human scale, the American need to keep moving suggests a neurotic aimlessness under the surface of adventure.

But take the human restraints off, let Superman fly unencumbered when and wherever he will, and the meaning of mobility in the American consciousness begins to reveal itself. Superman's incredible speed allows him to be as close to everywhere at once as it is physically possible to be. Displacement is, therefore, impossible. His sense of self is not dispersed by his life's migration but rather enhanced by all the universe that he is able to occupy. What American, whether an immigrant in spirit or in fact, could resist the appeal of one with such an ironclad immunity to the anxiety of dislocation?

In America, physical dislocation serves as a symbol of social and psychological movement. When our immigrant ancestors arrived on America's shores they hit the ground running, some to homestead on the Great Plains, others to claw their way up the socioeconomic ladder in coastal ghettos. Upward mobility, westward migration, Sunbelt relocation — the wisdom in America is that people don't, can't, mustn't end up where they begin. This belief has the moral force of religious doctrine. Thus the American identity is ordered around the psychological experience of forsaking or losing the past for the opportunity of reinventing oneself in the future. This makes the orphan a potent symbol of the American character. Orphans aren't merely free to reinvent themselves. They are obliged to do so.

When Superman reinvents himself, he becomes the bumbling Clark Kent, 10 a figure as immobile as Superman is mobile, as weak as his alter ego is strong. Over the years commentators have been fond of stressing how Clark Kent provides an illusory image of wimpiness onto which children can project their insecurities about their own potential (and, hopefully, equally illusory) weaknesses. But I think the role of Clark Kent is far more complex than that.

During my childhood, Kent contributed nothing to my love for the Man of Steel. If left to contemplate him for too long, I found myself changing from cape back into cowboy hat and guns. John Wayne, at least, was no sissy that I could ever see. Of course, in all the Westerns that the Duke came to stand for in my mind, there were elements that left me as confused as the paradox between Kent and Superman. For example, I could never seem to figure out why cowboys so often fell in love when there were obviously better options: horses to ride, guns to shoot, outlaws to chase, and savages to kill. Even on the days when I became John Wayne, I could fall victim to a never-articulated anxiety about the potential for poor judgment in my cowboy heroes. Then, I generally drifted back into a worship of Superman. With him, at least, the mysterious communion of opposites was honest and on the surface of things.

What disturbed me as a child is what I now think makes the myth of Superman so appealing to an immigrant sensibility. The shape-shifting between Clark Kent and Superman is the means by which this mid-twentieth-century, urban story — like the pastoral, nineteenth-century Western before it — addresses in dramatic terms the theme of cultural assimilation.

At its most basic level, the Western was an imaginative record of the American experience of westward migration and settlement. By bringing the forces of civilization and savagery together on a mythical frontier, the Western addressed the problem of conflict between apparently mutually exclusive identities and explored options for negotiating between them. In terms that a boy could comprehend, the myth explored the dilemma of assimilation — marry the school marm and start wearing Eastern clothes or saddle up and drift further westward with the boys.

The Western was never a myth of stark moral simplicity. Pioneers fled civilization by migrating west, but their purpose in the wilderness was to rebuild civilization. So civilization was both good and bad, what Americans fled from and journeyed toward. A similar moral ambiguity rested at the heart of the wilderness. It was an Eden in which innocence could be achieved through spiritual rebirth, but it was also the anarchic force that most directly threatened the civilized values America wanted to impose on the frontier. So the dilemma arose: In negotiating between civilization and the wilderness, between the old order and the new, between the identity the pioneers carried with them from wherever they came and the identity they sought to invent, Americans faced an impossible choice. Either they pushed into the New World wilderness and forsook the ideals that motivated them or they clung to their origins and polluted Eden.

The myth of the Western responded to this dilemma by inventing the idea 15 of the frontier in which civilized ideals embodied in the institutions of family, church, law, and education are revitalized by the virtues of savagery: independence, self-reliance, personal honor, sympathy with nature, and ethical uses of violence. In effect, the mythical frontier represented an attempt to embody the perfect degree of assimilation in which both the old and new identities came together, if not in a single self-image, then at least in idealized relationships, like the symbolic marriage of reformed cowboy and displaced school marm that ended Owen Wister's prototypical *The Virginian,* or the mystical masculine bonding between representatives of an ascendant and a vanishing America — Natty Bumppo and Chingachgook, the Lone Ranger and Tonto. On the Western frontier, both the old and new identities equally mattered.

As powerful a myth as the Western was, however, there were certain limits to its ability to speak directly to an increasingly common twentieth-century immigrant sensibility. First, it was pastoral. Its imagery of dusty frontier towns and breathtaking mountainous desolation spoke most affectingly to those who conceived of the American dream in terms of the nineteenth-century immigrant experience of rural settlement. As the twentieth century wore on, more immigrants were, like Superman, moving from rural or small-town backgrounds to metropolitan environments. Moreover, the Western was historical, often elegiacally so. Underlying the air of celebration in even the most epic and romantic of Westerns — the films of John Ford, say, in which John Wayne stood tall for all that any good American boy could ever want to be — was an awareness that the frontier was less a place than a state of mind represented in historic terms by a fleeting moment glimpsed imperfectly in the rapid wave of westward migration and settlement. Implicitly, then, whatever balance of past and future identities the frontier could offer was itself tenuous or illusory.

Twentieth-century immigrants, particularly the Eastern European Jews who came to America after 1880 and who settled in the industrial and mercantile centers of the Northeast — cities like Cleveland where Jerry Siegel and Joe Shuster grew up and created Superman — could be entertained by the Western, but they developed a separate literary tradition that addressed the theme of assimilation in terms closer to their personal experience. In this tradition issues were clear-cut: Clinging to an Old World identity meant isolation in ghettos, confrontation with a prejudiced mainstream culture, second-class social status, and impoverishment. On the other hand, forsaking the past in favor of total absorption into the mainstream, while it could result in socioeconomic progress, meant a loss of the religious, linguistic, even culinary traditions that provided a foundation for psychological well-being. Such loss was particularly tragic for the Jews because of the fundamental role played by history in Jewish culture.

Writers who worked in this tradition — Abraham Cahan, Daniel Fuchs, Henry Roth, and Delmore Schwartz, among others — generally found little reason to view the experience of assimilation with joy or optimism. Typical of the tradition was Cahan's early novel *Yekl*, on which Joan Micklin Silver's film *Hester Street* was based. A young married couple, Jake and Gitl, clash over his need to be absorbed as quickly as possible into the American mainstream and her obsessive preservation of their Russian-Jewish heritage. In symbolic terms, their confrontation is as simple as their choice of headgear — a derby for him, a babushka for her. That the story ends with their divorce, even in the context of their gradual movement toward mutual understanding of one another's point of view, suggests the divisive nature of the pressures at work in the immigrant communities.

Where the pressures were perhaps most keenly felt was in the schools. Educational theory of the period stressed the benefits of rapid assimilation. In the first decades of this century, for example, New York schools flatly rejected bilingual education — a common response to the plight of non–English-speaking immigrants even today — and there were conscientious efforts to indoctrinate the children of immigrants with American values, often at the expense of traditions within the ethnic community. What resulted was a generational rift in which children were openly embarrassed by and even contemptuous of their parents' values, setting a pattern in American life in which second-generation immigrants migrate psychologically if not physically from their parents, leaving it up to the third generation and beyond to rediscover their ethnic roots.

Under such circumstances, finding a believable and inspiring balance 20 between the old identity and the new, like that implicit in the myth of the frontier, was next to impossible. The images and characters that did emerge from the immigrant communities were often comic. Seen over and over in the fiction and popular theater of the day was the figure of the *yiddische Yankee*, a jingoistic optimist who spoke heavily accented American slang, talked baseball like an addict without understanding the game, and dressed like a Broadway dandy on a budget — in short, one who didn't understand

America well enough to distinguish between image and substance and who paid for the mistake by becoming the butt of a style of comedy bordering on pathos. So engrained was this stereotype in popular culture that it echoes today in TV situation comedy. . . .

Throughout American popular culture between 1880 and the Second World War the story was the same. Oxlike Swedish farmers, German brewers, Jewish merchants, corrupt Irish ward healers, Italian gangsters — there was a parade of images that reflected in terms often comic, sometimes tragic, the humiliation, pain, and cultural insecurity of people in a state of transition. Even in the comics, a medium intimately connected with immigrant culture, there simply was no image that presented a blending of identities in the assimilation process in a way that stressed pride, self-confidence, integrity, and psychological well-being. None, that is, until Superman.

The brilliant stroke in the conception of Superman — the sine qua non that makes the whole myth work — is the fact that he has two identities. The myth simply wouldn't work without Clark Kent, mild-mannered newspaper reporter and later, as the myth evolved, bland TV newsman. Adopting the white-bread image of a wimp is first and foremost a moral act for the Man of Steel. He does it to protect his parents from nefarious sorts who might use them to gain an edge over the powerful alien. Moreover, Kent adds to Superman's powers the moral guidance of a Smallville upbringing. It is Jonathan Kent, fans remember, who instructs the alien that his powers must always be used for good. Thus does the myth add a mainstream white Anglo-Saxon Protestant ingredient to the American stew. Clark Kent is the clearest stereotype of a self-effacing, hesitant, doubting, middle-class weakling ever invented. He is the epitome of visible invisibility, someone whose extraordinary ordinariness makes him disappear in a crowd. In a phrase, he is the consummate figure of total cultural assimilation, and significantly, he is not real. Implicit in this is the notion that mainstream cultural norms, however useful, are illusions.

Though a disguise, Kent is necessary for the myth to work. This uniquely American hero has two identities, one based on where he comes from in life's journey, one on where he is going. One is real, one an illusion, and both are necessary for the myth of balance in the assimilation process to be complete. Superman's powers make the hero capable of saving humanity; Kent's total immersion in the American heartland makes him want to do it. The result is an improvement on the Western: an optimistic myth of assimilation but with an urban, technocratic setting.

One must never underestimate the importance to a myth of the most minute elements which do not change over time and by which we recognize the story. Take Superman's cape, for example. When Joe Shuster inked the first Superman stories, in the early thirties when he was still a student at Cleveland's Glenville High School, Superman was strictly beefcake in tights, looking more like a circus acrobat than the ultimate Man of Steel. By June of 1938 when *Action Comics* no. 1 was issued, the image had been altered to include a cape, ostensibly to make flight easier to render in the pictures. But it wasn't the cape of Victorian melodrama and adventure fiction, the kind worn with a clasp around the neck. In fact, one is hard-pressed to find any precedent in popular culture for the kind of cape Superman wears. His emerges in a seamless line from either side of the front yoke of his tunic. It is a veritable growth from behind his pectorals and hangs, when he stands at ease, in a line that doesn't so much drape his shoulders as stand apart from them and echo their curve, like an angel's wings.

In light of this graphic detail, it seems hardly coincidental that Super- 25 man's real, Kryptonic name is Kal-El, an apparent neologism by George Lowther, the author who novelized the comic strip in 1942. In Hebrew, *el* can be both root and affix. As a root, it is the masculine singular word for God. Angels in Hebrew mythology are called *benei Elohim* (literally, sons of the Gods), or *Elyonim* (higher beings). As an affix, *el* is most often translated as "of God," as in the plenitude of Old Testament given names: Ishma-el, Dani-el, Ezeki-el, Samu-el, etc. It is also a common form for named angels in most Semitic mythologies: Israf-el, Aza-el, Uri-el, Yo-el, Rapha-el, Gabri-el and — the one perhaps most like Superman — Micha-el, the warrior angel and Satan's principal adversary.

The morpheme *Kal* bears a linguistic relation to two Hebrew roots. The first, *kal*, means "with lightness" or "swiftness" (faster than a speeding bullet in Hebrew?). It also bears a connection to the root *hal*, where *h* is the guttural *ch* of *chutzpah*. *Hal* translates roughly as "everything" or "all." *Kal-el*, then, can be read as "all that is God," or perhaps more in the spirit of the myth of Superman, "all that God is." And while we're at it, *Kent* is a form of the Hebrew *kana*. In its *k-n-t* form, the word appears in the Bible, meaning "I have found a son."

I'm suggesting that Superman raises the American immigrant experience to the level of religious myth. And why not? He's not just some immigrant from across the waters like all our ancestors, but a real alien, an extraterrestrial, a visitor from heaven if you will, which fact lends an element of the supernatural to the myth. America has no national religious icons nor any pilgrimage shrines. The idea of a patron saint is ludicrous in a nation whose Founding Fathers wrote into the founding documents the fundamental if not eternal separation of church and state. America, though, is pretty much as religious as other industrialized countries. It's just that our tradition of religious diversity precludes the nation's religious character from being embodied in objects or persons recognizably religious, for such are immediately identified by their attachment to specific sectarian traditions and thus contradict the eclecticism of the American religious spirit.

In America, cultural icons that manage to tap the national religious spirit are of necessity secular on the surface and sufficiently generalized to incorporate the diversity of American religious traditions. Superman doesn't have to be seen as an angel to be appreciated, but in the absence of a tradition of national religious iconography, he can serve as a safe, nonsectarian focus for essentially religious sentiments, particularly among the young.

In the last analysis, Superman is like nothing so much as an American boy's fantasy of a messiah. He is the male, heroic match for the Statue of Liberty, come like an immigrant from heaven to deliver humankind by sacrificing himself in the service of others. He protects the weak and defends truth and justice and all the other moral virtues inherent in the Judeo-Christian tradition, remaining ever vigilant and ever chaste. What purer or stronger vision could there possibly be for a child? Now that I put my mind to it, I see that John Wayne never had a chance.

READING THE TEXT

1. Why does Superman's status as "an immigrant and an orphan" (para. 5) make him deeply American, according to Engle?
2. What is the significance of Superman's ability to fly?
3. Why does Engle see physical dislocation as being so typically American?
4. What is the significance of Superman's two identities, in Engle's view?

READING THE SIGNS

1. Interview three classmates or friends whose families are immigrants to this country. Then compare their experience with that of the mythological character Superman. To what extent does the Superman character reflect real-life immigrant experience? What does his story leave out? Try to account for any differences you may find.
2. Do you agree with Engle's suggestion "that Superman raises the American immigrant experience to the level of religious myth" (para. 27)?
3. How would Superman fit the definitions of hero that Robert B. Ray outlines in "The Thematic Paradigm" (p. 308)?
4. Engle only briefly discusses the fact that Superman happens to be both male and Caucasian. What is the significance of the character's gender and race? How do you think they may have influenced Superman's status as an American mythological hero? For a discussion of race and gender, consult Michael Omi's "In Living Color: Race and American Culture" (p. 549) and Aaron Devor's "Gender Role Behaviors and Attitudes" (p. 458).
5. Watch an episode of *Smallville* or one of the *Superman* movies, and write an essay in which you explore whether — and why — the depiction of this character either perpetuates or alters his mythological status.

ANDY MEDHURST

Batman, Deviance, and Camp

Have you ever wondered what happened to Robin in the recent Batman movies? In this analysis of the history of Batman, excerpted from The Many Lives of the Batman *(1991), Andy Medhurst (b. 1959) explains why Robin had to disappear. Arguing that Batman has been "re-heterosexualized" in the wake of the insinuatingly homoerotic TV series of the 1960s, Medhurst indicts the homophobia of Batfans whose "Bat-Platonic Ideal of how Batman should really be" holds no place for the "camped crusader." Medhurst teaches media studies, popular culture, and lesbian and gay studies at the University of Sussex, England. He is the author of* A National Joke: Popular Comedy and English Cultural Identities *(2004). He has also coedited, with Sally Munt,* Lesbian and Gay Studies: A Critical Introduction *(1997), and, with Joanne Lacey,* The Representation Reader *(2004).*

Only someone ignorant of the fundamentals of psychiatry and of the psychopathology of sex can fail to realize a subtle atmosphere of homoeroticism which pervades the adventure of the mature "Batman" and his young friend "Robin."

— FREDRIC WERTHAM[1]

It's embarrassing to be solemn and treatise-like about Camp. One runs the risk of having, oneself, produced a very inferior piece of Camp.

— SUSAN SONTAG[2]

I'm not sure how qualified I am to write this essay. Batman hasn't been particularly important in my life since I was seven years old. Back then he was crucial, paramount, unmissable as I sat twice weekly to watch the latest episode on TV. Pure pleasure, except for the annoying fact that my parents didn't seem to appreciate the thrills on offer. Worse than that, they actually laughed. How could anyone laugh when the Dynamic Duo were about to be turned into Frostie Freezies (pineapple for the Caped Crusader, lime for his chum) by the evil Mr. Freeze?

Batman and I drifted apart after those early days. Every now and then I'd see a repeated episode and I soon began to understand and share that once infuriating parental hilarity, but this aside I hardly thought about the man in the cape at all. I knew about the subculture of comic freaks, and the new and

[1]Fredric Wertham, *Seduction of the Innocent* (London: Museum Press, 1955), p. 190.
[2]Susan Sontag, "Notes on Camp," in *A Susan Sontag Reader* (Harmondsworth: Penguin Books), p. 106.

alarmingly pretentious phrase "graphic novel" made itself known to me, but I still regarded (with the confidence of distant ignorance) such texts as violent, macho, adolescent and, well, silly.

That's when the warning bells rang. The word "silly" reeks of the complacent condescension that has at various times been bestowed on all the cultural forms that matter most to me (Hollywood musicals, British melodramas, pop music, soap operas), so what right had I to apply it to someone else's part of the popular cultural playground? I had to rethink my disdain, and 1989 has been a very good year in which to do so, because in terms of popular culture 1989 has been the Year of the Bat.

This essay, then, is not written by a devotee of Batman, someone steeped in every last twist of the mythology. I come to these texts as an interested outsider, armed with a particular perspective. That perspective is homosexuality, and what I want to try and do here is to offer a gay reading of the whole Batbusiness. It has no pretension to definitiveness, I don't presume to speak for all gay people everywhere. I'm male, white, British, thirty years old (at the time of writing) and all of those factors need to be taken into account. Nonetheless, I'd argue that Batman is especially interesting to gay audiences for three reasons.

Firstly, he was one of the first fictional characters to be attacked on the grounds of presumed homosexuality, by Fredric Wertham in his book *Seduction of the Innocent*. Secondly, the 1960s TV series was and remains a touchstone of camp (a banal attempt to define the meaning of camp might well start with "like the sixties' *Batman* series"). Thirdly, as a recurring hero figure for the last fifty years, Batman merits analysis as a notably successful construction of masculinity. 5

Nightmare on Psychiatry Street: Freddy's Obsession

Seduction of the Innocent is an extraordinary book. It is a gripping, flamboyant melodrama masquerading as social psychology. Fredric Wertham is, like Senator McCarthy,[3] like Batman, a crusader, a man with a mission, an evangelist. He wants to save the youth of America from its own worst impulses, from its id, from comic books. His attack on comic books is founded on an astonishingly crude stimulus-and-response model of reading, in which the child (the child, for Wertham, seems an unusually innocent, blank slate waiting to be written on) reads, absorbs, and feels compelled to copy, if only in fantasy terms, the content of the comics. It is a model, in other words, which takes for granted extreme audience passivity.

This is not the place to go into a detailed refutation of Wertham's work, besides which such a refutation has already been done in Martin Barker's

---

[3]**Senator McCarthy** United States Senator Joseph R. McCarthy (1908–1957), who in the 1950s hunted and persecuted suspected Communists and Communist sympathizers.–EDS.

excellent *A Haunt of Fears*.[4] The central point of audience passivity needs stressing, however, because it is crucial to the celebrated passage where Wertham points his shrill, witch-hunting finger at the Dynamic Duo and cries "queer."

Such language is not present on the page, of course, but in some ways *Seduction of the Innocent* (a film title crying out for either D. W. Griffith or Cecil B. DeMille) would be easier to stomach if it were. Instead, Wertham writes with anguished concern about the potential harm that Batman might do to vulnerable children, innocents who might be turned into deviants. He employs what was then conventional psychiatric wisdom about the idea of homosexuality as a "phase":

> Many pre-adolescent boys pass through a phase of disdain for girls. Some comic books tend to fix that attitude and instill the idea that girls are only good for being banged around or used as decoys. A homoerotic attitude is also suggested by the presentation of masculine, bad, witch-like or violent women. In such comics women are depicted in a definitely anti-erotic light, while the young male heroes have pronounced erotic overtones. The muscular male supertype, whose primary sex characteristics are usually well emphasized, is in the setting of certain stories the object of homoerotic sexual curiosity and stimulation.[5]

The implications of this are breathtaking. Homosexuality, for Wertham, is synonymous with misogyny. Men love other men because they hate women. The sight of women being "banged around" is liable to appeal to repressed homoerotic desires (this, I think, would be news to the thousands of women who are systematically physically abused by heterosexual men). Women who do not conform to existing stereotypes of femininity are another incitement to homosexuality.

Having mapped out his terms of reference, Wertham goes on to peel the 10
lid from Wayne Manor:

> Sometimes Batman ends up in bed injured and young Robin is shown sitting next to him. At home they lead an idyllic life. They are Bruce Wayne and "Dick" Grayson. Bruce Wayne is described as a "socialite" and the official relationship is that Dick is Bruce's ward. They live in sumptuous quarters, with beautiful flowers in large vases, and have a butler, Alfred. Batman is sometimes shown in a dressing gown. . . . It is like a wish dream of two homosexuals living together. Sometimes they are shown on a couch, Bruce reclining and Dick sitting next to him, jacket off, collar open, and his hand on his friend's arm.[6]

So, Wertham's assumptions of homosexuality are fabricated out of his interpretation of certain visual signs. To avoid being thought queer by Wertham,

---

[4]Martin Barker, *A Haunt of Fears* (London: Pluto Press, 1984).
[5]Wertham, p. 188.
[6]Wertham, p. 190.

Bruce and Dick should have done the following: Never show concern if the other is hurt, live in a shack, only have ugly flowers in small vases, call the butler "Chip" or "Joe" if you have to have one at all, never share a couch, keep your collar buttoned up, keep your jacket on, and never, ever wear a dressing gown. After all, didn't Noel Coward[7] wear a dressing gown?

Wertham is easy to mock, but the identification of homosexuals through dress codes has a long history.[8] Moreover, such codes originate as semiotic systems adopted by gay people themselves, as a way of signalling the otherwise invisible fact of sexual preference. There is a difference, though, between sporting the secret symbols of a subculture if you form part of that subculture and the elephantine spot-the-homo routine that Wertham performs.

Bat-fans have always responded angrily to Wertham's accusation. One calls it "one of the most incredible charges . . . unfounded rumours . . . sly sneers"[9] and the general response has been to reassert the masculinity of the two heroes, mixed with a little indignation: "If they had been actual men they could have won a libel suit."[10] This seems to me not only to miss the point, but also to *reinforce* Wertham's homophobia — it is only possible to win a libel suit over an "accusation" of homosexuality in a culture where homosexuality is deemed categorically inferior to heterosexuality.

Thus the rush to "protect" Batman and Robin from Wertham is simply the other side to the coin of his bigotry. It may reject Wertham, cast him in the role of dirty-minded old man, but its view of homosexuality is identical. Mark Cotta Vaz thus describes the imputed homosexual relationship as "licentious" while claiming that in fact Bruce Wayne "regularly squired the most beautiful women in Gotham City and presumably had a healthy sex life."[11] Licentious versus healthy — Dr. Wertham himself could not have bettered this homophobic opposition.

Despite the passions aroused on both sides (or rather the two facets of 15 the same side), there is something comic at the heart of this dispute. It is, simply, that Bruce and Dick are *not* real people but fictional constructions, and hence to squabble over their "real" sex life is to take things a little too far. What is at stake here is the question of reading, of what readers do with the raw material that they are given. Readers are at liberty to construct whatever fantasy lives they like with the characters of the fiction they read (within the

---

[7]**Noel Coward** (1899–1973) British playwright, actor, and composer known for witty, sophisticated comedies.–EDS.

[8]See, for example, the newspaper stories on "how to spot" homosexuals printed in Britain in the fifties and sixties, and discussed in Jeffrey Weeks, *Coming Out: Homosexual Politics in Britain* (London: Quartet, 1979).

[9]Phrases taken from Chapters 5 and 6 of Mark Cotta Vaz, *Tales of the Dark Knight: Batman's First Fifty Years* (London: Futura, 1989).

[10]Les Daniels, *Comix: A History of Comic Books in America* (New York: Bonanza Books, 1971), p. 87.

[11]Cotta Vaz, pp. 47 and 53.

limits of generic and narrative credibility, that is). This returns us to the unfortunate patients of Dr. Wertham:

> One young homosexual during psychotherapy brought us a copy of *Detective* comic, with a Batman story. He pointed out a picture of "The Home of Bruce and Dick," a house beautifully landscaped, warmly lighted and showing the devoted pair side by side, looking out a picture window. When he was eight this boy had realized from fantasies about comic book pictures that he was aroused by men. At the age of ten or eleven, "I found my liking, my sexual desires, in comic books. I think I put myself in the position of Robin. I did want to have relations with Batman . . . I remember the first time I came across the page mentioning the 'secret batcave.' The thought of Batman and Robin living together and possibly having sex relations came to my mind. . . ."[12]

Wertham quotes this to shock us, to impel us to tear the pages of *Detective* away before little Tommy grows up and moves to Greenwich Village, but reading it as a gay man today I find it rather moving and also highly recognizable.

What this anonymous gay man did was to practice that form of bricolage[13] which Richard Dyer has identified as a characteristic reading strategy of gay audiences.[14] Denied even the remotest possibility of supportive images of homosexuality within the dominant heterosexual culture, gay people have had to fashion what we could out of the imageries of dominance, to snatch illicit meanings from the fabric of normality, to undertake a corrupt decoding for the purposes of satisfying marginalized desires.[15] This may not be as necessary as it once was, given the greater visibility of gay representations, but it is still an important practice. Wertham's patient evokes in me an admiration, that in a period of American history even more homophobic than most, there he was, raiding the citadels of masculinity, weaving fantasies of oppositional desire. What effect the dread Wertham had on him is hard to predict, but I profoundly hope that he wasn't "cured."

It wasn't only Batman who was subjected to Dr. Doom's bizarre ideas about human sexuality. Hence:

> The homosexual connotation of the Wonder Woman type of story is psychologically unmistakable. . . . For boys, Wonder Woman is a frightening image. For girls she is a morbid ideal. Where Batman is anti-feminine, the attractive Wonder Woman and her counterparts are definitely anti-masculine. Wonder Woman has her own female following. . . . Her

---

[12]Wertham, p. 192.

[13]**bricolage** A new object created by reassembling bits and pieces of other objects; here, gay-identified readings produced from classic texts.–EDS.

[14]Richard Dyer, ed., *Gays and Film*, 2nd edition (New York: Zoetrope, 1984), p. 1.

[15]See Richard Dyer, "Judy Garland and Gay Men," in Dyer, *Heavenly Bodies* (London: BFI, 1987), and Claire Whitaker, "Hollywood Transformed: Interviews with Lesbian Viewers," in Peter Steven, ed., *Jump Cut: Hollywood, Politics and Counter-Cinema* (Toronto: Between the Lines, 1985).

followers are the "Holiday girls," i.e. the holiday girls, the gay party girls, the gay girls.[16]

Just how much elision can be covered with one "i.e."? Wertham's view of homosexuality is not, at least, inconsistent. Strong, admirable women will turn little girls into dykes — such a heroine can only be seen as a "morbid ideal."

Crazed as Wertham's ideas were, their effectiveness is not in doubt. The mid-fifties saw a moral panic about the assumed dangers of comic books. In the United States companies were driven out of business, careers wrecked, and the Comics Code introduced. This had distinct shades of the Hays Code[17] that had been brought in to clamp down on Hollywood in the 1930s, and under its jurisdiction comics opted for the bland, the safe, and the reactionary. In Britain there was government legislation to prohibit the importing of American comics, as the comics panic slotted neatly into a whole series of anxieties about the effects on British youth of American popular culture.[18]

And in all of this, what happened to Batman? He turned into Fred MacMurray from *My Three Sons*. He lost any remaining edge of the shadowy vigilante of his earliest years, and became an upholder of the most stifling small-town American values. Batwoman and Batgirl appeared (June Allyson and Bat-Gidget) to take away any lingering doubts about the Dynamic Duo's sex lives. A 1963 story called "The Great Clayface-Joker Feud" has some especially choice examples of the new, squeaky-clean sexuality of the assembled Bats. 20

Batgirl says to Robin, "I can hardly wait to get into my Batgirl costume again! Won't it be terrific if we could go on a crime case together like the last time? (sigh)." Robin replies, "It sure would, Betty (sigh)." The elder Bats look on approvingly. Batgirl is Batwoman's niece — to make her a daughter would have implied that Batwoman had had (gulp) sexual intercourse, and that would never do. This is the era of Troy Donohue and Pat Boone,[19] and Batman as ever serves as a cultural thermometer, taking the temperature of the times.

The Clayface/Joker business is wrapped up (the villains of this period are wacky conjurors, nothing more, with no menace or violence about them) and the episode concludes with another tableau of terrifying heterosexual contentment. "Oh Robin," simpers Batgirl, "I'm afraid you'll just have to hold me! I'm still so shaky after fighting Clayface . . . and you're so strong!" Robin: "Gosh Batgirl, it was swell of you to calm me down when I was worried about Batman tackling Clayface alone." (One feels a distinct Wertham influence here: If Robin shows concern about Batman, wheel on a supportive female,

---

[16]Wertham, pp. 192–93.

[17]**Hays Code** The 1930 Motion Picture Production Code, which described in detail what was morally acceptable in films.–EDS.

[18]See Barker.

[19]**Troy Donohue and Pat Boone** Clean-cut, all-American-boy stars from the 1950s and 1960s.–EDS.

the very opposite of a "morbid ideal," to minister in a suitably self-effacing way.) Batwoman here seizes her chance and tackles Batman: "You look worried about Clayface, Batman . . . so why don't you follow Robin's example and let me soothe you?" Batman can only reply "Gulp."

Gulp indeed. While it's easy simply to laugh at strips like these, knowing as we do the way in which such straight-faced material would be mercilessly shredded by the sixties' TV series, they do reveal the retreat into coziness forced on comics by the Wertham onslaught and its repercussions. There no doubt were still subversive readers of *Batman*, erasing Batgirl on her every preposterous appearance and reworking the Duo's capers to leave some room for homoerotic speculation, but such a reading would have had to work so much harder than before. The *Batman* of this era was such a closed text, so immune to polysemic interpretation, that its interest today is only as a symptom — or, more productively, as camp. "The Great Clayface-Joker Feud" may have been published in 1963, but in every other respect it is a fifties' text. If the 1960s began for the world in general with the Beatles, the 1960s for Batman began with the TV series in 1966. If the Caped Crusader had been all but Werthamed out of existence, he was about to be camped back into life.

The Camped Crusader and the Boys Wondered

Trying to define "camp" is like attempting to sit in the corner of a circular room. It can't be done, which only adds to the quixotic appeal of the attempt. Try these:

> To be camp is to present oneself as being committed to the marginal with a commitment greater than the marginal merits.[20]
>
> Camp sees everything in quotation marks. It's not a lamp but a "lamp"; not a woman but a "woman." . . . It is the farthest extension, in sensibility, of the metaphor of life as theatre.[21]
>
> Camp is . . . a way of poking fun at the whole cosmology of restrictive sex roles and sexual identifications which our society uses to oppress its women and repress its men.[22]
>
> Camp was and is a way for gay men to re-imagine the world around them . . . by exaggerating, stylizing and remaking what is usually thought to be average or normal.[23]
>
> Camp was a prison for an illegal minority; now it is a holiday for consenting adults.[24]

[20]Mark Booth, *Camp* (London: Quartet, 1983), p. 18.

[21]Sontag, p. 109.

[22]Jack Babuscio, "Camp and the Gay Sensibility," in Dyer, ed., *Gays and Film*, p. 46.

[23]Michael Bronski, *Culture Clash: The Making of Gay Sensibility* (Boston: South End Press), p. 42.

[24]Philip Core, *Camp: The Lie That Tells the Truth* (London: Plexus), p. 7.

All true, in their way, but all inadequate. The problem with camp is that it   25
is primarily an experiential rather than an analytical discourse. Camp is a set
of attitudes, a gallery of snapshots, an inventory of postures, a modus vivendi,
a shop-full of frocks, an arch of eyebrows, a great big pink butterfly that just
won't be pinned down. Camp is primarily an adjective, occasionally a verb,
but never anything as prosaic, as earthbound, as a noun.

Yet if I propose to use this adjective as a way of describing one or more of
the guises of Batman, I need to arrive at some sort of working definition. So,
for the purposes of this analysis, I intend the term "camp" to refer to a playful, knowing, self-reflexive theatricality. *Batman*, the sixties' TV series, was
nothing if not knowing. It employed the codes of camp in an unusually public
and heavily signaled way. This makes it different from those people or texts
who are taken up by camp audiences without ever consciously putting camp
into practice. The difference may be very briefly spelled out by reference to Hollywood films. If *Mildred Pierce*[25] and *The Letter*[26] were taken up *as* camp,
teased by primarily gay male audiences into yielding meaning not intended
by their makers, then *Whatever Happened to Baby Jane?*[27] is a piece of self-
conscious camp, capitalizing on certain attitudinal and stylistic tendencies
known to exist in audiences. *Baby Jane* is also, significantly, a 1960s' film, and
the 1960s were the decade in which camp swished out of the ghetto and up
into the scarcely prepared mainstream.

A number of key events and texts reinforced this. Susan Sontag wrote her
Notes on Camp, which remains the starting point for researchers even now. Pop
Art[28] was in vogue (and in *Vogue*) and whatever the more elevated claims of
Lichtenstein,[29] Warhol,[30] and the rest, their artworks were on one level a new
inflection of camp. The growing intellectual respectability of pop music displayed very clearly that the old barriers that once rigidly separated high and
low culture were no longer in force. The James Bond films, and even more so
their successors like *Modesty Blaise*, popularized a dry, self-mocking wit that
makes up one part of the multifaceted diamond of camp. And on television
there were *The Avengers, The Man from UNCLE, Thunderbirds*, and *Batman*.

---

[25]*Mildred Pierce* 1945 murder mystery film that traces the fortunes of a homemaker
who breaks with her husband.–Eds.

[26]*The Letter* 1940 murder movie whose ending was changed to satisfy moral standards
of the time.–Eds.

[27]*Whatever Happened to Baby Jane?* Macabre 1962 film about a former child movie
star living in an old Hollywood mansion.–Eds.

[28]**Pop Art** Art movement, begun in the 1950s, that borrowed images and symbols from
popular culture, particularly from commercial products and mass media, as a critique of traditional fine art.–Eds.

[29]**Lichtenstein** Roy Lichtenstein (1923–1997), American artist at the center of the Pop
Art movement, best known for melodramatic comic-book scenes.–Eds.

[30]**Warhol** Andy Warhol (1930?–1987), pioneering Pop artist known for reproducing stereotyped images of famous people, such as Marilyn Monroe, and of commercial products,
such as Campbell's Soup cans.–Eds.

To quote the inevitable Sontag, "The whole point of Camp is to dethrone the serious. . . . More precisely, Camp involves a new, more complex relation to 'the serious.' One can be serious about the frivolous, frivolous about the serious."[31]

The problem with Batman in those terms is that there was never anything truly serious to begin with (unless one swallows that whole portentous Dark Knight charade, more of which in the next section). Batman in its comic book form had, unwittingly, always been camp—it was serious (the tone, the moral homilies) about the frivolous (a man in a stupid suit). He was camp in the way that classic Hollywood was camp, but what the sixties' TV series and film did was to overlay this "innocent" camp with a thick layer of ironic distance, the self-mockery version of camp. And given the long associations of camp with the homosexual male subculture, Batman was a particular gift on the grounds of his relationship with Robin. As George Melly put it, "The real Batman series were beautiful because of their unselfconscious absurdity. The remakes, too, at first worked on a double level. Over the absorbed children's heads we winked and nudged, but in the end what were we laughing at? The fact they didn't know that Batman had it off with Robin."[32]

It was as if Wertham's fears were being vindicated at last, but his 1950s' bigot's anguish had been supplanted by a self-consciously hip 1960s' playfulness. What adult audiences laughed at in the sixties' *Batman* was a camped-up version of the fifties they had just left behind.

Batman's lessons in good citizenship ("We'd like to feel that our efforts may help every youngster to grow up into an honest, useful citizen"[33]) were another part of the character ripe for ridiculing deconstruction—"Let's go, Robin, we've set another youth on the road to a brighter tomorrow" (the episode "It's How You Play the Game"). Everything the Adam West Batman said was a parody of seriousness, and how could it be otherwise? How could anyone take genuinely seriously the words of a man dressed like that?

The Batman/Robin relationship is never referred to directly; more fun can be had by presenting it "straight," in other words, screamingly camp. Wertham's reading of the Dubious Duo had been so extensively aired as to pass into the general consciousness (in George Melly's words, "We all knew Robin and Batman were pouves"[34]), it was part of the fabric of *Batman*, and the makers of the TV series proceeded accordingly.

Consider the Duo's encounter with Marsha, Queen of Diamonds. The threat she embodies is nothing less than heterosexuality itself, the deadliest threat to the domestic bliss of the Bat-couple. She is even about to marry Batman before Alfred intervenes to save the day. He and Batman flee the church,

---

[31]Sontag, p. 116.

[32]George Melly, *Revolt into Style: The Pop Arts in the 50s and 60s* (Oxford: Oxford University Press, 1989 [first published 1970]), p. 193.

[33]"The Batman Says," *Batman #3* (1940), quoted in Cotta Vaz, p. 15.

[34]Melly, p. 192.

but have to do so in the already decorated Batmobile, festooned with wedding paraphernalia including a large "Just Married" sign. "We'll have to drive it as it is," says Batman, while somewhere in the audience a Dr. Wertham takes feverish notes. Robin, Commissioner Gordon, and Chief O'Hara have all been drugged with Marsha's "Cupid Dart," but it is of course the Boy Wonder who Batman saves first. The dart, he tells Robin, "contains some secret ingredient by which your sense and your will were affected," and it isn't hard to read that ingredient as heterosexual desire, since its result, seen in the previous episode, was to turn Robin into Marsha's slobbering slave.

We can tell with relief now, though, as Robin is "back in fighting form" (with impeccable timing, Batman clasps Robin's shoulder on the word "fighting"). Marsha has one last attempt to destroy the duo, but naturally she fails. The female temptress, the seductress, the enchantress must be vanquished. None of this is in the least subtle (Marsha's cat, for example, is called Circe) but this type of mass-market camp can't afford the luxury of subtlety. The threat of heterosexuality is similarly mobilized in the 1966 feature film, where it is Bruce Wayne's infatuation with Kitka (Catwoman in disguise) that causes all manner of problems.

A more interesting employment of camp comes in the episodes where the Duo battle the Black Widow, played by Tallulah Bankhead. The major camp coup here, of course, is the casting. Bankhead was one of the supreme icons of camp, one of its goddesses: "Too intelligent not to be self-conscious, too ambitious to bother about her self-consciousness, too insecure ever to be content, but too arrogant ever to admit insecurity, Tallulah personified camp."[35]

A heady claim, but perhaps justified, because the Black Widow episodes are, against stiff competition, the campiest slices of Batman of them all. The stories about Bankhead are legendary — the time when on finding no toilet paper in her cubicle she slipped a ten dollar bill under the partition and asked the woman next door for two fives, or her whispered remark to a priest conducting a particularly elaborate service and swinging a censor of smoking incense, "Darling, I love the drag, but your purse is on fire" — and casting her in *Batman* was the final demonstration of the series' commitment to camp.

The plot is unremarkable, the usual Bat-shenanigans; the pleasure lies in the detail. Details like the elderly Bankhead crammed into her Super-Villainess costume, or like the way in which (through a plot detail I won't go into) she impersonates Robin, so we see Burt Ward miming to Bankhead's voice, giving the unforgettable image of Robin flirting with burly traffic cops. Best of all, and Bankhead isn't even in this scene but the thrill of having her involved clearly spurred the writer to new heights of camp, Batman has to sing a song to break free of the Black Widow's spell. Does he choose to sing "God Bless America"? Nothing so rugged. He clutches a flower to his Bat chest and sings Gilbert and Sullivan's "I'm Just a Little Buttercup." It is this single

[35]Core, p. 25.

image, more than any other, that prevents me from taking the post–Adam West Dark Knight at all seriously.

The fundamental camp trick which the series pulls is to make the comics speak. What was acceptable on the page, in speech balloons, stands revealed as ridiculous once given audible voice. The famous visualized sound effects (URKKK! KA-SPLOOSH!) that are for many the fondest memory of the series work along similar lines. Camp often makes its point by transposing the codes of one cultural form into the inappropriate codes of another. It thrives on mischievous incongruity.

The incongruities, the absurdities, the sheer ludicrousness of Batman were brought out so well by the sixties' version that for some audiences there will never be another credible approach. I have to include myself here. I've recently read widely in postsixties Bat-lore, and I can appreciate what the writers and artists are trying to do, but my Batman will always be Adam West. It's impossible to be somber or pompous about Batman because if you try the ghost of West will come Bat-climbing into your mind, fortune cookie wisdom on his lips and keen young Dick by his side. It's significant, I think, that the letters I received from the editors of this book began "Dear Bat-Contributor."[36] Writers preparing chapters about James Joyce or Ingmar Bergman do not, I suspect, receive analogous greetings. To deny the large camp component of Batman is to blind oneself to one of the richest parts of his history.

Is There Bat-Life after Bat-Camp?

The international success of the Adam West incarnation left Batman high and dry. The camping around had been fun while it lasted, but it hadn't lasted very long. Most camp humor has a relatively short life span, new targets are always needed, and the camp aspect of Batman had been squeezed dry. The mass public had moved on to other heroes, other genres, other acres of merchandising, but there was still a hard Bat-core of fans to satisfy. Where could the Bat go next? Clearly there was no possibility of returning to the caped Eisenhower, the benevolent patriarch of the 1950s. That option had been well and truly closed down by the TV show. Batman needed to be given his dignity back, and this entailed a return to his roots.

This, in any case, is the official version. For the unreconstructed devotee of the Batman (that is, people who insist on giving him the definite article before the name), the West years had been hell — a tricksy travesty, an effeminizing of the cowled avenger. There's a scene in *Midnight Cowboy* where Dustin Hoffman tells Jon Voight that the only audience liable to be receptive to his cowboy clothes are gay men looking for rough trade. Voight is appalled — "You

40

---

[36]This essay originally appeared in an anthology, *The Many Lives of the Batman: Critical Approaches to a Superhero and His Media.*–EDS.

mean to tell me John Wayne was a fag?" (quoted, roughly, from memory). This outrage, this horror at shattered illusions, comes close to encapsulating the loathing and dread the campy Batman has received from the old guard of Gotham City and the younger born-again Bat-fans.

So what has happened since the 1960s has been the painstaking rehetero-sexualization of Batman. I apologize for coining such a clumsy word, but no other quite gets the sense that I mean. This strategy has worked, too, for large audiences, reaching its peak with the 1989 film. To watch this and then come home to see a video of the 1966 movie is to grasp how complete the transformation has been. What I want to do in this section is to trace some of the crucial moments in that change, written from the standpoint of someone still unashamedly committed to Bat-camp.

If one wants to take Batman as a Real Man, the biggest stumbling block has always been Robin. There have been disingenuous claims that "Batman and Robin had a blood-brother closeness. Theirs was a spiritual intimacy forged from the stress of countless battles fought side by side"[37] (one can imagine what Tallulah Bankhead might say to *that*), but we know otherwise. The Wertham lobby and the acolytes of camp alike have ensured that any Batman/Robin relationship is guaranteed to bring on the sniggers. Besides which, in the late 1960s, Robin was getting to be a big boy, too big for any shreds of credibility to attach themselves to all that father-son smokescreen. So in 1969 Dick Grayson was packed off to college and the Bat was solitary once more.

This was a shrewd move. It's impossible to conceive of the recent, obsessive, sturm-und-drang Batman with a chirpy little Robin getting in the way.[38] A text of the disturbing power of *The Killing Joke*[39] could not have functioned with Robin to rupture the grim dualism of its Batman/Joker struggle. There was, however, a post–Dick Robin, but he was killed off by fans in that infamous telephone poll.[40]

It's intriguing to speculate how much latent (or blatant) homophobia lay 45 behind that vote. Did the fans decide to kill off Jason Todd so as to redeem Batman for unproblematic heterosexuality? Impossible to say. There are other factors to take into account, such as Jason's apparent failure to live up to the expectations of what a Robin should be like. The sequence of issues in which Jason/Robin died, *A Death in the Family*, is worth looking at in some detail,

---

[37]Cotta Vaz, p. 53.

[38]A female Robin is introduced in the *Dark Knight Returns* series, which, while raising interesting questions about the sexuality of Batman, which I don't here have the space to address, seems significant in that the Dark Knight cannot run the risk of reader speculation that a traditionally male Robin might provoke.

[39]***The Killing Joke*** Graphic novel by Alan Moore, Brian Bolland, and John Higgins (New York: DC Comics 1988).–Eds.

[40]**telephone poll** In a 1988 issue of the *Batman* comic, a "post-Dick Robin," Jason Todd, was badly injured in an explosion, and readers were allowed to phone the publisher to vote on whether he should be allowed to survive.–Eds.

however, in order to see whether the camp connotations of Bruce and Dick had been fully purged.

The depressing answer is that they had. This is very much the Batman of the 1980s, his endless feud with the Joker this time uneasily stretched over a framework involving the Middle East and Ethiopia. Little to be camp about there, though the presence of the Joker guarantees a quota of sick jokes. The sickest of all is the introduction of the Ayatollah Khomeini, a real and important political figure, into this fantasy world of THUNK! and THER-ACKK! and grown men dressed as bats. (As someone who lived in the part of England from which Reagan's planes took off on their murderous mission to bomb Libya, I fail to see the humor in this cartoon version of American foreign policy: It's too near the real thing.)

Jason dies at the Joker's hands because he becomes involved in a search for his own origins, a clear parallel to Batman's endless returns to *his* Oedipal scenario. Families, in the Bat-mythology, are dark and troubled things, one more reason why the introduction of the fifties versions of Batwoman and Batgirl seemed so inappropriate. This applies only to real, biological families, though; the true familial bond is between Batman and Robin, hence the title of these issues. Whether one chooses to read Robin as Batman's ward (official version), son (approved fantasy), or lover (forbidden fantasy), the sense of loss at his death is bound to be devastating. Batman finds Robin's body and, in the time-honored tradition of Hollywood cinema, is at least able to give him a loving embrace. Good guys hug their dead buddies, only queers smooch when still alive.

If the word "camp" is applied at all to the eighties' Batman, it is a label for the Joker. This sly displacement is the cleverest method yet devised of preserving Bat-heterosexuality. The play that the texts regularly make with the concept of Batman and the Joker as mirror images now takes a new twist. The Joker is Batman's "bad twin," and part of that badness is, increasingly, an implied homosexuality. This is certainly present in the 1989 film, a generally glum and portentous affair except for Jack Nicholson's Joker, a characterization enacted with venomous camp. The only moment when this dour film comes to life is when the Joker and his gang raid the Art Gallery, spraying the paintings and generally camping up a storm.

The film strives and strains to make us forget the Adam West Batman, to the point of giving us Vicki Vale as Bruce Wayne's lover, and certainly Michael Keaton's existential agonizing (variations on the theme of why-did-I-have-to-be-a-Bat) is a world away from West's gleeful subversion of truth, justice and the American Way. This is the same species of Batman celebrated by Frank Miller: "If your only memory of Batman is that of Adam West and Burt Ward exchanging camped-out quips while clobbering slumming guest-stars Vincent Price and Cesar Romero, I hope this book will come as a surprise. . . . For me, Batman was never funny. . . ."[41]

41 Frank Miller, "Introduction," *Batman: Year One* (London: Titan, 1988).

The most recent linkage of the Joker with homosexuality comes in   50
Arkham Asylum, the darkest image of the Bat-world yet. Here the Joker has
become a parody of a screaming queen, calling Batman "honey pie," given to
exclamations like "oooh!" (one of the oldest homophobic clichés in the book),
and pinching Batman's behind with the advice, "Loosen up, tight ass." He
also, having no doubt read his Wertham, follows the pinching by asking,
"What's the matter? Have I touched a nerve? How is the Boy Wonder? Started
shaving yet?" The Bat-response is unequivocal: "Take your filthy hands off
me. . . . Filthy degenerate!"

Arkham Asylum is a highly complex reworking of certain key aspects of
the mythology, of which the sexual tension between Batman and the Joker is
only one small part. Nonetheless the Joker's question "Have I touched a
nerve?" seems a crucial one, as revealed by the homophobic ferocity of Batman's reply. After all, the dominant cultural construction of gay men at the
end of the 1980s is as plague carriers, and the word "degenerate" is not far
removed from some of the labels affixed to us in the age of AIDS.

Batman: Is He or Isn't He?

The one constant factor through all of the transformations of Batman has
been the devotion of his admirers. They will defend him against what they
see as negative interpretations, and they carry around in their heads a kind of
essence of batness, a Bat-Platonic Ideal of how Batman should really be. The
Titan Books reissue of key comics from the 1970s each carry a preface by a
noted fan, and most of them contain claims such as "This, I feel, is Batman as
he was meant to be."[42]

Where a negative construction is specifically targeted, no prizes for guess-
ing which one it is: "you . . . are probably also fond of the TV show he appeared
in. But then maybe you prefer Elvis Presley's Vegas years or the later Jerry
Lewis movies over their early stuff . . . for me, the definitive Batman was then
and always will be the one portrayed in these pages."[43]

The sixties' TV show remains anathema to the serious Bat-fan precisely
because it heaps ridicule on the very notion of a serious Batman. *Batman* the
series revealed the man in the cape as a pompous fool, an embodiment of
superseded ethics, and a closet queen. As Marsha, Queen of Diamonds, put it,
"Oh Batman, darling, you're so divinely square." Perhaps the enormous success of the 1989 film will help to advance the cause of the rival Bat-archetype,
the grim, vengeful Dark Knight whose heterosexuality is rarely called into
question (his humorlessness, fondness for violence, and obsessive monoma-
nia seem to me exemplary qualities for a heterosexual man). The answer,
surely, is that they needn't be mutually exclusive.

[42]Kim Newman, "Introduction," *Batman: The Demon Awakes* (London: Titan, 1989).
[43]Jonathan Ross, "Introduction," *Batman: Vow from the Grave* (London: Titan, 1989).

If I might be permitted a rather camp comparison, each generation has 55
its definitive Hamlet, so why not the same for Batman? I'm prepared to admit
the validity, for some people, of the swooping eighties' vigilante, so why are
they so concerned to trash my sixties' camped crusader? Why do they insist
so vehemently that Adam West was a faggy aberration, a blot on the otherwise impeccably butch Bat-landscape? What *are* they trying to hide?

If I had a suspicious frame of mind, I might think that they were protesting too much, that maybe Dr. Wertham was on to something when he targeted these narratives as incitements to homosexual fantasy. And if I want
Batman to be gay, then, for me, he is. After all, outside of the minds of his
writers and readers, he doesn't really exist.

READING THE TEXT

1. Summarize the objections that Fredric Wertham makes to Batman in *Seduction of the Innocent*.

2. In a paragraph, write your own explanation of what Medhurst means by "camp" (para. 24).

3. What evidence does Medhurst supply to demonstrate that Batman is a gay character?

4. Explain what Medhurst means by his closing comments: "And if I want Batman to be gay, then, for me, he is. After all, outside the minds of his writers and readers, he doesn't really exist" (para. 56).

READING THE SIGNS

1. Do you agree with Medhurst's argument that the Batman and Robin duo were really a covert gay couple? Write an essay supporting or challenging his position, being sure to study his evidence closely. You may want to visit your school's media library to find file tapes of old *Batman* shows, or read contemporary reviews of *Batman*, to gather evidence for your essay.

2. Check your college library for a copy of Fredric Wertham's *Seduction of the Innocent*. Then write your own critique of Wertham's attack on Batman.

3. Buy a few copies of the current *Batman* comic book, and write an essay in which you explain Batman's current sexual orientation.

4. Visit your college library and obtain a copy of Susan Sontag's "Notes on Camp" (included in Sontag's collections *Against Interpretation* and *The Susan Sontag Reader*). How would Sontag interpret the character of Batman?

Mr. Clean

READING THE SIGNS

1. What particular product does this advertisement promote? What argument does it make in the text at the lower left? How persuasive is this ad, in your opinion? How do the images contribute to the effectiveness of the ad?

2. Describe "Mr. Clean." (For additional images of Mr. Clean — including the Mr. Clean action figure — log onto **www.mrclean.com**.) What physical characteristics make him a good pitchman for a cleaning product?

3. What is the significance of the text "Go Ahead. Make My Spray"? Why would the makers of Mr. Clean want to include this text when advertising their product? Do you think its use is effective? Why or why not?

EMILY PRAGER
Our Barbies, Ourselves

Little girls throughout America should know that Barbie is not drawn to scale. In this tongue-in-cheek essay on the role Barbie has played in her life, Emily Prager (b. 1952) reveals the damaging effect of a doll that establishes such an impossible standard of physical perfection for little girls — and for little boys who grow up expecting their girlfriends to look like Barbie. When not contemplating what Barbie has done to her, Prager is a columnist with the New York Times *and an essayist and fiction writer who has published for the* National Lampoon, *the* Village Voice, *and* Penthouse, *among other magazines. Her books include a work of historical fiction for children,* World War II Resistance Stories; *a book of humor,* The Official I Hate Videogames Handbook; *and works of fiction such as* Clea and Zeus Divorce *(1987) and* Eve's Tattoo *(1991). Her most recent book is* Wuhu Diary: On Taking My Adopted Daughter Back to Her Hometown in China *(2001).*

I read an astounding obituary in the *New York Times* not too long ago. It concerned the death of one Jack Ryan. A former husband of Zsa Zsa Gabor, it said, Mr. Ryan had been an inventor and designer during his lifetime. A man of eclectic creativity, he designed Sparrow and Hawk missiles when he worked for the Raytheon Company, and, the notice said, when he consulted for Mattel he designed Barbie.

If Barbie was designed by a man, suddenly a lot of things made sense to me, things I'd wondered about for years. I used to look at Barbie and wonder, What's wrong with this picture? What kind of woman designed this doll? Let's be honest: Barbie looks like someone who got her start at the Playboy Mansion. She could be a regular guest on *The Howard Stern Show*. It is a fact of Barbie's design that her breasts are so out of proportion to the rest of her body that if she were a human woman, she'd fall flat on her face.

If it's true that a woman didn't design Barbie, you don't know how much saner that makes me feel. Of course, that doesn't ameliorate the damage. There are millions of women who are subliminally sure that a thirty-nine-inch bust and a twenty-three-inch waist are the epitome of lovability. Could this account for the popularity of breast implant surgery?

I don't mean to step on anyone's toes here. I loved my Barbie. Secretly, I still believe that neon pink and turquoise blue are the only colors in which to decorate a duplex condo. And like many others of my generation, I've never married, simply because I cannot find a man who looks as good in clam diggers as Ken.

The question that comes to mind is, of course, Did Mr. Ryan design Barbie   5 as a weapon? Because it *is* odd that Barbie appeared about the same time in my consciousness as the feminist movement — a time when women sought equality and small breasts were king. Or is Barbie the dream date of weapons designers? Or perhaps it's simpler than that: Perhaps Barbie is Zsa Zsa if she were eleven inches tall. No matter what, my discovery of Jack Ryan confirms what I have always felt: There is something indescribably masculine about Barbie — dare I say it, phallic. For all her giant breasts and high-heeled feet, she lacks a certain softness. If you asked a little girl what kind of doll she wanted for Christmas, I just don't think she'd reply, "Please, Santa, I want a hard-body."

On the other hand, you could say that Barbie, in feminist terms, is definitely her own person. With her condos and fashion plazas and pools and beauty salons, she is definitely a liberated woman, a gal on the move. And she has always been sexual, even totemic. Before Barbie, American dolls were flat-footed and breastless, and ineffably dignified. They were created in the image

"A gal on the move": Barbie with Ken.

of little girls or babies. Madame Alexander was the queen of doll makers in the fifties, and her dollies looked like Elizabeth Taylor in *National Velvet*. They represented the kind of girls who looked perfect in jodhpurs, whose hair was never out of place, who grew up to be Jackie Kennedy — before she married Onassis. Her dolls' boyfriends were figments of the imagination, figments with large portfolios and three-piece suits and presidential aspirations, figments who could keep dolly in the style to which little girls of the fifties were programmed to become accustomed, a style that spasmed with the sixties and the appearance of Barbie. And perhaps what accounts for Barbie's vast popularity is that she was also a sixties woman: into free love and fun colors, anticlass, and possessed of real, molded boyfriend, Ken, with whom she could chant a mantra.

But there were problems with Ken. I always felt weird about him. He had no genitals, and, even at age ten, I found that ominous. I mean, here was Barbie with these humongous breasts, and that was OK with the toy company. And then, there was Ken with that truncated, unidentifiable lump at his groin. I sensed injustice at work. Why, I wondered, was Barbie designed with such obvious sexual equipment and Ken not? Why was his treated as if it were more mysterious than hers? Did the fact that it was treated as such indicate that somehow his equipment, his essential maleness, was considered more powerful than hers, more worthy of the dignity of concealment? And if the issue in the mind of the toy company was obscenity and its possible damage to children, I still object. How do they think I felt, knowing that no matter how many water beds they slept in, or hot tubs they romped in, or swimming pools they lounged by under the stars, Barbie and Ken could never make love? No matter how much sexuality Barbie possessed, she would never turn Ken on. He would be forever withholding, forever detached. There was a loneliness about Barbie's situation that was always disturbing. And twenty-five years later, movies and videos are still filled with topless women and covered men. As if we're all trapped in Barbie's world and can never escape.

God, it certainly has cheered me up to think that Barbie was designed by Jack Ryan. . . .

READING THE TEXT

1. Why does Prager say "a lot of things made sense" (para. 2) to her after she learned Barbie was designed by a man?

2. What is Prager's attitude toward Ken?

3. How do Madame Alexander dolls differ from Barbies?

READING THE SIGNS

1. Bring a toy to class and, in same-sex groups, discuss its semiotic significance; you may want to focus particularly on how the toys may be intended for one gender or another. Then have each group select one toy and present your interpretation of it to the whole class. What gender-related patterns do you find in the presentations?

2. Think of a toy you played with as a child, and write a semiotic interpretation of it, using Prager's essay as a model. Be sure to consider differences between your childhood response to the toy and your current response.

3. Did you have a Barbie doll when you were a child? If so, write a journal entry in which you explore what the doll meant to you when you were young and how Prager's essay has caused you to rethink your attitudes.

4. Consider how Jack Ryan, the creator of Barbie, would defend his design. Write a letter, as if you were Ryan, addressed to Prager in which you justify Barbie's appearance and refute Prager's analysis.

5. Barbie can be seen as embodying not only America's traditional gender roles but also its consumerist ethos. Visit a toy store or an online shopping site to learn about the "accessories" one can buy for Barbie. Then write an essay exploring the extent to which Barbie illustrates the "hunger for more" described by Laurence Shames in "The More Factor" (p. 76). Develop your ideas by consulting Gregg Easterbrook's "The Progress Paradox" (p. 400).

GARY CROSS

Barbie, G.I. Joe, and Play in the 1960s

Toys aren't only toys. For as Gary Cross observes in this excerpt from Kids' Stuff: Toys and the Changing World of American Childhood *(1997), toys are signifiers of the shifting terrain of American culture and belief. So it is revealing that Barbie, who was designed to be the ultimate consumer, has stayed that way for more than forty years, while G.I. Joe mutated from an ordinary infantryman into a high-tech action-adventure hero and finally disappeared. Consumption, it seems, never goes out of style, but not everything we consume stays in fashion. So who says that toys aren't signs of our times? Cross is a professor of history at Pennsylvania State University who specializes in analyzing the roles that toys play in the shaping of American childhood. He is the author of several books, including* Time and Money: The Making of Consumer Culture *(1993),* Technology and American Society: A History *(with Rick Szostak, 1995), and* An All-Consuming Century *(2000).*

Television and the new business climate in the toy industry alone did not transform the meaning of play. Toys were changing because American society was changing. By looking at the two most important trend-setting toys we can find clues to these changes. Much has been written about Barbie and G.I. Joe as icons of popular culture. But Barbie and G.I. Joe were also toys, and like other toys they were mostly given to children by adults.

Barbie began her career as a stiff plastic dress-up figure. Ruth Handler often claimed that she invented Barbie to fill a void in girls' play. Girls wanted a less cumbersome and more fun version of the fashion paper doll. In using paper dolls as a model Mattel was in effect redirecting doll play away from the friendship and nurturing themes of the companion and baby dolls that had predominated since the 1900s. In the nineteenth century paper dolls were used to display the latest styles and to portray royalty and famous actresses, especially in magazines devoted to fashion. They were associated with an adult world of quasi-aristocratic consumption. They had little to do with domestic or friendship themes. Paper dolls and their focus on fashion were an important part of girls' play in the first half of the twentieth century, but they were only a minor part of the toy business.[1]

Mattel, however, put fashion doll play at the center of the industry. The idea of making the paper fashion doll three dimensional was hardly new. Even the association of doll play with consumption was not innovative. It had been built into the concepts of dolls from Patsy to Toni. But Barbie was not a child doll dressed in children's fashions. Rather Barbie was in the shape of a young woman with very long legs and an exaggerated hourglass figure. She looked neither like the little girl who owned her nor like the little girl's mother. She was neither a baby, a child, nor a mother but a liberated teenager, almost a young woman. Handler admitted that even in this her creation was not so original. She "borrowed" the look from a German dress-up doll she and her daughter Barbara had noticed on a vacation in Switzerland. But she marketed it on a grand scale at a perfect point in the history of American childhood: at the end of the 1950s.[2]

Barbie was an early rebel against the domesticity that dominated the lives of baby-boom mothers. It may not be surprising that some of the first generation of Barbie owners became feminists in the late 1960s and 1970s. The revolt against, at least, the momism of the feminine mystique was played out with Barbie, who never cared for babies or children. But Mattel's doll was also an autonomous teenager with no visible ties to parents in a time when the earliest of the baby-boom generation were just entering their teens. This crop of teenagers, coming of age in a more affluent United States, had more choices than their parents had had and were freer of adult control. To the eight-year-old of 1960, Barbie represented a hoped-for future of teenage freedom. It was this attraction of Barbie that long survived the maturation of the baby-boom generation. It is also not surprising that when Mattel market-tested Barbie it found that mothers were not nearly so positive about the doll

---

[1] Ruth Handler, *Dream Doll* (Stamford, Conn.: Longmeadow Press, 1994), chs. 4–5; Rebecca Harnmell, "To Educate and Amuse: Paper Dolls and Toys, 1640–1900" (M.A. thesis, University of Delaware, 1988, University Microforms International, Ann Arbor, 1989).

[2] Handler, *Dream Doll;* A. Glen Mandeville, *Doll Fashion Anthology and Price Guide,* 4th ed. (Cumberland, Md.: Hobby House, 1993), 1–33; K. Westenhouser, *The Story of Barbie* (Paducah, Ky.: Collector Books, 1994), 5–15; Billy Boy, *Barbie: Her Life and Times* (New York: Crown, 1987), 17–28, 40–44.

The Hasbro Toy Company runs a "fun lab," shown here, in order to evaluate how children respond to toys.

as were their daughters. Mothers recognized that this doll was a break from the tradition of nurturing and companion play and that girls apparently welcomed it.

Despite all this, Barbie hardly "taught" girls to shed female stereotypes. 5 Rather she prompted them to associate the freedom of being an adult with carefree consumption. With her breasts and slender waist, Barbie came literally to embody the little girl's image of what it meant to be grown up. At the same time, in her contemporary fashions, she represented the up-to-date. Barbie did not invite children to be Mommy, nor was she the child's friend in a secret garden of caring and sharing. She was what the little girl was not and, even more important, what her mother was not. She was a fashion model with a large wardrobe designed to attract attention. Instead of teaching girls how to diaper a baby or use floor cleaners, Barbie play was an education in consumption — going to the hairdresser and shopping for that perfect evening gown for the big dance. Even when she had a job (model, stewardess, or later even a doctor), her work and life had nothing to do with the jobs of most women. Barbie was never a cashier at Wal-Mart or a homemaker.

If Barbie taught that freedom meant consumption, the Barbie line was designed to maximize parents' real spending. Playing consumer required that Barbie have a constantly changing wardrobe of coordinated clothing and accessories. Clothing sets were often much more expensive than the "hook," the doll itself. The first Barbie advertising brochure featured, for example, a Barbie-Q Outfit, Suburban Shopper, Picnic Set (with fishing pole), Evening

Splendor (complete with strapless sheath), and even a Wedding Day Set. By the early 1960s Barbie had play environments, for example the Barbie Fashion Shop and Barbie's Dream House.[3]

Barbie's glamour required constant purchases of dolls and accessories. Playing grown up meant that Barbie had to have a boy friend, Ken (introduced in 1961). Because Barbie seemed to be six to seven years older than her owners, Mattel introduced in 1964 a little sister, Skipper, with whom the children could identify. Naturally Skipper developed her own entourage of "friends." In 1975 Mattel carried the transition doll to its logical conclusion with "Growing Up Skipper." Six-year-olds could mechanically reenact their growing-up fantasy: when her arm was rotated, Skipper grew taller and developed breasts.

Barbie also needed "friends" to shop and have fun with. Mattel manufactured an endless array of Midge, Francie, and Stacey dolls, all "sold separately." Like Barbie's clothing, they changed with the times. While Midge (1963) was the "freckled-faced and impish" girl next door, Francie (1966) and Stacey (1968) reflected the impact of English styles and music in the age of the Beatles. In 1968 Christie, a black friend for Barbie, was introduced, reflecting changing American race relations. Ken vanished suddenly in 1969 (apparently too stodgy an image to fit the long-haired Vietnam era) only to reappear two years later looking much more husky and hip.[4]

Mattel tapped into a young girl's fantasy life to create a demand for possessions. Company researchers watched girls play and noted that they enjoyed hair and dress-up games as well as acting out shopping, travel, and dating. They designed accessories to provide props for these play activities. And if the child did not immediately know what the story lines were to be, Mattel provided them on the back of the packages.

Barbie's impact on the traditional doll industry was enormous. Only 60 10 doll companies remained in 1969 of the more than 200 that existed when Barbie appeared in 1959. Barbie helped reduce the share of baby dolls from 80 percent of dolls in 1959 to only 38 percent in 1975. Barbie's success inevitably prompted much imitation. Ideal produced Tammy (who conceded the existence of parents with Mom and Dad dolls). American Character offered Tressy, with "hair that really grows." Topper's Penny Brite and the "perfectly proportioned" Tina of Ross Products were others. None survived long in a field dominated by Barbie.[5]

Mattel succeeded [in] keeping successive generations of little girls wanting Barbie and not some other fashion doll. Ruth Handler resisted the temptation

---

[3]Mattel, "Barbie, Teen-Age Fashion Model," "Barbie, Teen-Age Fashion Model, and Ken, Barbie's Boy Friend (He's a Doll)," "Exclusive Fashions by Mattel," book 3 (Hawthorne, Calif.: Mattel, 1958, 1960, 1963). All in the Strong Museum.

[4]"The Origins of the Barbie Doll (and Her 'Family')," Mattel Press Kit, Please Touch Museum, Toy Fair Collection (hereafter TFC), Box 5.

[5]"Inside the Doll Market," *Toys*, March 1975, 23–25.

to give Barbie a fixed personality or even a "look." Handler liked to say this allowed girls to imagine what Barbie was really like. But from a marketing standpoint this made Barbie a fixture, even a "clothes hanger," upon which accessories could be draped. Partly because she came first, Barbie became the trademark fashion doll. All others were imitations. And Barbie never grew old or out of date as did the dolls made in the image of ephemeral glamour queens like Farrah Fawcett-Majors. Barbie was the eternal star — despite her changeable hair and skin color. Barbie was still Barbie.

Mattel even succeeded in persuading little girls to "trade in" their old Barbies for a discount on a new look in 1967. Adults found this strange — voluntarily parting with a "loved" doll. But the girls saw it differently: they were simply trading in an old model for a new, much as their parents traded in their flashy 1959 Chevys for the more sedate look of 1960s models. Barbie's environment — clothes, hair, playsets, and friends — changed with adult fashion. But Barbie's face and shape remained a constant symbol of growing up. Thus Mattel created that elusive and contradictory prize — an ephemeral classic — and in doing so reshaped the play of American girls. A doll that mothers at first disliked became the doll that mothers had to give to their daughters.[6]

Hasbro's G.I. Joe mirrored the success of Barbie by becoming a perennial fad. It achieved this feat, at first, not by challenging expectations of fathers as Barbie broke with the doll culture of mothers, but by affirming the values and experiences of many fathers. Like so many other contemporary toys, G.I. Joe was inspired by a TV series, an action-adventure show, *The Lieutenant* (1963), that was supposed to appeal to adult men. But the program failed even before the toy appeared. G.I. Joe was not tied to any specific media personality or story. He represented the average soldier, evoking memories of fathers' experience in World War II and the Korean War. The original G.I. Joe of 1964 shared with Barbie the critical feature of being a dress-up doll, although marketed as "America's Moveable Fighting Man." At twelve inches, half an inch taller than Barbie, G.I. Joe was suitable for costuming in the uniforms of the four American military services (sold separately). Again like Barbie, G.I. Joe was accessorized. Hasbro adopted what was often called the "razor and razor blade" principle of marketing. Once the boy had the doll he needed accessories — multiple sets of uniforms, jeeps, tents, and weaponry.[7]

Still, Joe was not simply a boys' version of Barbie. The obvious historical precedent was the cast-metal soldier, very different from the paper doll. Miniature soldiers had been part of boy's play for centuries. The object was to

---

[6]Billy Boy, *Barbie*, 92; Mandeville, *Fashion Anthology*, 41–43, 69–71; Ron Goulart, *The Assault on Childhood* (Los Angeles: Sherbourne, 1969), 26.

[7]"Fact Sheet: Hasbro's G.I. Joe, A Real American Hero," Hasbro Press Kit, Feb. 1993, TFC, Box 3; Susan Manos and Paris Manos, *Collectible Male Action Figures* (Paducah, Ky.: Collector Books, 1990), 8–9.

reenact the drama of present and past battles. G.I. Joe added to this traditional game by giving boys articulated figures with a man's shape and musculature. The Joes were a major improvement over cheap and impersonal plastic soldiers that stood on bases. Joe took the play beyond the traditional deployment of infantry, cannon, and cavalry. Detailed "Manuals," accompanying the doll, marched "Joe through basic training up to combat readiness," showing the boy how to pose his toy to crouch in a trench or throw a grenade. Joe changed war games from the pleasure of acting the general — arranging soldiers and weapons on a field of battle — to playing the soldier, the G.I. whom the boy dressed and posed. This probably made war play far more appealing to young children because they could identify with the individual soldier. Joe may have contributed to the decline of other forms of boys' play, at least temporarily, insofar as erector sets almost disappeared and Tinkertoys and Lincoln Logs were relegated to preschoolers in the G.I. Joe era.[8]

Nevertheless, the early G.I. Joe did not challenge traditional war play as 15 Barbie displaced baby doll and companion doll play. G.I. Joe's success was based on a boy's identity with the all-male world of heroic action aided by modern military equipment and gadgetry. The play was conventional, featuring males bonding in adventure. This was a womanless world. Boys rejected the idea of a female nurse when it was introduced to the G.I. Joe line in 1965. These boys could play war the way their fathers might have fought it in World War II or in Korea. And they could dress their Joes in battle gear similar to that worn by conscripted uncles or older brothers serving their two-year stints in the army of the mid-1960s. The object was not the clash of enemies (as would be the case with later action figures). Even though boys made their Joe dolls fight each other, Hasbro offered soldiers from only one side. The point was to imitate the real world of adults in the military. G.I. Joe still connected fathers with sons.

Again in contrast to Barbie, G.I. Joe went through major changes. By 1967 as the Vietnam war heated up and adults such as Benjamin Spock attacked war toys, sales decreased. Beginning in 1970 Hasbro responded by transforming the "fighting" Joes into an "Adventure Team." Joes searched for sunken treasure and captured wild animals. As the Vietnam war wound down to its bitter end in 1975, it was awkward to sell military toys glorifying contemporary jungle warfare. While veterans of World War II and even Korea might enjoy giving their sons toys that memorialized their own youth, the situation for fathers who had reached manhood during the Vietnam era was very different. Most of these men wanted to forget the Vietnam war (whether they fought in it or opposed it), not to give their sons toys recalling this military disaster or any real war.

In 1976, with the Vietnam War in the past, G.I. Joe became "Super Joe" and shrank to eight inches (because of higher costs for plastic). He no longer

---

[8]"G.I. Joe, Action Soldiers: America's Moveable Fighting Man" (Pawtucket, R.I.: Hasbro, 1964), Strong Museum.

could be dressed. He returned to the role of a fighter, but he did not rejoin the ranks of enlisted men. He no longer was part of a world that fathers, uncles, or older brothers had ever experienced. Instead he was a high-tech hero, no longer connected to a troublesome reality. His laser beams and rocket command vehicles helped him fight off aliens, the Intruders. Added to his team was Bullet Man, the first of a long line of superhumans. The object of play was to pit good guys against bad guys, not to imitate real military life. But even these changes could not save Joe. From 1978 to 1981 the "Great American Hero" disappeared from store shelves to be pushed aside by an even more fantasyful line of toys based on George Lucas's *Star Wars*.[9]

With Barbie little girls combined growing up with feminine consumerism. This gave Barbie a permanent aisle of hot-pink packages in every serious toy store. G.I. Joe began as a celebration of an all-male world of realistic combat. But Joe encountered deeper contradictions in the 1960s than did Barbie and was forced to flee into fantasy. Still, both toys became models for toy play and consumption that still prevail today. They did so by breaking away from the worlds of parents.

READING THE TEXT

1. According to Cross, how was the creation of Barbie related to the "fashion paper doll" (para. 2)?

2. How did Barbie assist, in Cross's words, in the "revolt against . . . the momism of the feminine mystique" (para. 4)?

3. Why did the G.I. Joe doll undergo more profound design changes in its history than did Barbie?

4. In Cross's view, what were the ingredients for the G. I. Joe doll's success?

READING THE SIGNS

1. What sort of doll would you design for girls or boys? Sketch your proposed doll, and write an essay explaining the rationale for your design. Share your sketch with the class.

2. Visit a toy store, and study the action-adventure dolls that are now available. Then write an essay in which you analyze the extent to which the dolls reflect the "warrior dreams" that James William Gibson describes ("Warrior Dreams," p. 504).

3. Write an essay in which you explain your own view of how toys and games socialize children to cultural norms and expectations. To develop your ideas, read or review bell hooks's "Baby" (p. 610) and Emily Prager's "Our Barbies, Ourselves" (p. 769).

[9]Manos and Manos, *Male Action Figures*, 20–33, 38–43; Vincent Santelmo, *The Official 30th Anniversary Salute to G.I. Joe* (Iola, Wis.: Kreuse, 1994), 17–18, 66–72, 75–97, 325, 343, 412–13.

4. Divide the blackboard into two sections: male and female. Have the class write on the board, in the gender-appropriate section, the name of a favorite childhood toy. Then study the results. Do you find any gender patterns? How many of the toys could be classified as "gender-neutral"?

MARK CALDWELL
The Assault on Martha Stewart

You might think that a felony conviction and a jail sentence would imperil anyone's iconic status, but you'd be wrong. "Martha's job is to be a cultural icon," a fan Web site proclaims, ensuring that the diva of domesticity will maintain, as Mark Caldwell (b. 1946) puts it, her "institutional status." If you've ever turned to Martha Stewart to learn whether the toilet paper flap should hang over or under the roll, Caldwell's analysis of her rise to fame is a must-read. Caldwell teaches at Fordham University and is the author of The Last Crusade *(1988) and* A Short History of Rudeness *(1999), from which this selection is taken.*

Martha Stewart began her ascent to fame as a Connecticut caterer. But by 1990 she had become an institution, both a national symbol of the epidemic American infatuation with gracious living and the scapegoat of a nascent backlash. Miss Manners, at present probably our most influential etiquette authority, has a widely syndicated newspaper column and a number of books in general circulation. But Martha Stewart represents an altogether different order of fame, with dozens of titles in print, her own monthly magazine, *Martha Stewart Living*, a daily syndicated half-hour TV program, an interactive World Wide Web site, a mail-order shopping service, an eponymous home products department in Kmart stores, even an umbrella corporation with a suitable business-octopus name: Martha Stewart Living Omnimedia, Inc.

Stewart is only the most visible figure in a thriving lifestyle industry that churns out books, magazines, and exemplars of every other medium from television to CD-ROMs. It has mirrored the growth of retail chains like Crate and Barrel, Pottery Barn, the Gap, and Williams-Sonoma, which sell the trappings of designer-anointed home life in mall outlets and mail-order catalogues. Stewart stands out because of her relentless drive; also because her audience is so large and devoted. She has even achieved the dubious apotheosis of academic attention (a cultural studies anthology is in the works, to be titled *The Martha Stewart Collection*.[1] And, in the culminating proof of her ascent to institutional status, she recently provoked a best-selling unauthorized biography, Jerry Oppenheimer's *Martha Stewart — Just Desserts*. Both her popularity and the negative reaction it has inspired warrant a closer look.

Oppenheimer dwells relentlessly on what he sees as Stewart's pathological ambition and cutthroat business competitiveness, but — hostile though his portrait is — he never questions the sincerity of her dedication to raising the aesthetic tone of American domestic life. Stewart has a reputation for fussy and expensive elegance, but her interests span cooking, gardening, decorating, entertaining, even family relations and finance. And her dominant theme is not costly luxury, but rather studious care — taking pains to make one's daily life pleasant, artful, dignified. The acutest pleasure, in Stewart's world, lies not in buying elegance (though she offers multiple shopping opportunities), but in achieving it through skill and thoughtfulness. In early 1997, she and Kmart inaugurated a new "Everyday" collection, cornerstone of a design-it-yourself department for the budget-minded devotee of good taste. There are no carriage-trade pretensions in these store displays, no attempts to ape the moneyed ambiance of expensive retail stores like Bergdorf Goodman or ABC Carpet and Home.

At Kmart, a near-life-sized cardboard Martha stands at the main entrance, directing customers to the home furnishings department. At the Astor Square branch in Manhattan (a recent immigrant from the suburbs), in the fall of 1997, Martha Stewart Everyday abutted a pre-Halloween display of plastic pumpkins, Reese's Peanut Butter cups, vinyl trash cans, and zebra-stripped polyester rugs. Stewart's wares were well made, subdued in color, simply designed, and unpretentious: a line of trademarked paints, some terrycloth bathrobes (modeled by Stewart with a matching towel wrapped around her head), table linens, bedsheets. Amidst it all stood a TV monitor reeling out a promotional video loop in which Stewart, smiling and husky voiced, touted her merchandise: not, however, with a hard sell, but a characteristic emphasis on technique. "Our fitted sheets," Stewart purred, "have extra-deep pockets. . . . Do you know the secret of folding a fitted sheet? I learned this from my mom. . . ."[2]

Martha Stewart Living, her monthly magazine, conjures a colorful yet gauzy panorama of amiable, sun-dappled home life, a blend of casual, sentimental, and elegant. Longer established home life magazines like *Architectural Digest* or *House Beautiful* tend to embody their visions of the lush life in detailed spreads of aggressively "done" rooms and distinctive, almost always expensive houses, more or less exhaustively documented in photographs, often accompanied by floor plans and replete with tips about where to buy the furniture and accessories pictured. Artful touches, often contributed by a stylist, suggest human occupancy — a just-this-side-of-slovenly heap of books

5

---

[1] This project, to be undertaken by Linda Robertson and Jodi Dean of Hobart & William Smith Colleges, was announced in a September 15, 1997, posting in the online magazine *Slate*.

[2] Transcribed at Kmart, 8th Street and Broadway, New York, September 25, 1997.

and magazines on the night stand, or a dining-room table with candles ablaze and one chair casually pulled aside, as if drawing the reader to fantasize himself into the scene. With Stewart, it's usually not the design concept that draws the reader or viewer in, but rather Stewart's presence, sometimes in a photo but always hovering in the text and offering hints about how to create an atmosphere of elegance. Her advice is on the whole heavier on labor than expense: instructions for how to make miniature hamburgers for parties, or for donning dust mask and rubber gloves to color linen napkins with natural dyes like fustic and madder root (two projects included in the September 1997 issue of *Martha Stewart Living*). Her message is that beyond a merely passable way of doing things glimmers a classy and distinguished way, discoverable if one pursues it with the dedicated perfectionism of the artist.

Stationery, for example. The undiscriminating may buy it off the drug or convenience store shelf; the more ambitious may splurge on the expensive formal letter papers ready boxed at a stationery store; the still more *raffiné* can have them printed or engraved. But all these upward increments in taste leave one short of the Stewart standard.

> Martha Stewart looked for years for just the right emblem for her stationery. Last year, she found an image she liked: a cornucopia engraved onto the frontispiece of a rare seventeenth-century book called *Worlidge's Husbandry*. She brought it to Joy Lewis, who recognized the drawing as a banknote-style engraving. Lewis hired a retired employee of the bureau that engraves United States banknotes to re-create the design. Martha's monogram was blind-embossed, or impressed onto the paper without color, in classic Roman type. The cornucopia was engraved and inked in "van Dyck Brown," the color black fades to after a hundred years.[3]

Snobbery and materialism? That has certainly become a major theme in the attack on Martha Stewart that began in the early 1990s. Oppenheimer's *Just Desserts*, for example, juxtaposes Stewart's unremarkable Polish American childhood in Nutley, New Jersey, against her supposed pretensions, implying that the determination with which she climbed out of it and her obsession with style constitute an attempt to hide sordid beginnings, break out of the humble sphere she belongs in by right, and elbow her way in among the wealthy elite.

But this exaggerates Stewart's snobbery and ignores her attentiveness to the hard work behind good taste. The distinguishing characteristic of her stationery, after all, lies not in its cost but rather in the ingenuity and painstaking research that went into its design, as well as in its rejection of the mass-produced. And nowhere does Stewart try to conceal either her lower-middle-class origins, or painful events in her adult life, like her 1990 divorce.[4] Indeed, she writes quite candidly about them in the "Letter from Martha" that opens,

---

[3]*Martha Stewart Living* (May 1996), p. 118.
[4]See Jerry Oppenheimer, *Martha Stewart—Just Desserts: The Unauthorized Biography* (New York: Morrow, 1997), p. 318.

and the "Remembering" column that closes, every issue of *Martha Stewart Living*. In one such column, she recalls a childhood memory of her family poring longingly through Sears and Montgomery Ward catalogues,[5] which at the time seemed the utmost reach of upward-aspiring fantasy. Oppenheimer, with an air of having discovered a closely guarded secret, reveals that Stewart's parents shopped at Two Guys from Harrison, a now defunct and decidedly low-rent New Jersey discount outlet; but Stewart herself has reminisced almost nostalgically about Two Guys in "Remembering."[6] Stewart's agenda seems not to imitate upper-class manner, but rather to *separate* the art of civilized living from class; to relocate it . . . from a sense of belonging to a particular status group to a schooling in good taste that anybody might acquire with thought and careful study.

Stewart's stationery is described — and readers seem to take it — not as a possession to drool jealously over but rather as an illustration of the forethought, care, and discrimination everyday life deserves. When Stewart photographs a house, she usually emphasizes not the likely-to-be-intimidating whole, but rather a nook, a corner in the garden, a space small and intimate enough for anyone to imitate no matter how unprepossessing the property or how unexceptional one's means. Her locations exude a leisure and luxury that encourage imitation, and don't remove the reader to an envying distance. Like Emily Post before her, Stewart tries to universalize rather than restrict the accomplishments of class. Post's difficulty lay in never being quite able to explain or decide who the "Best People" were, even though she believed in their existence. Stewart, however, represents a contemporary effort to solve this difficulty. Her criterion for admission among the Best People is a readily learnable ability to appreciate and create what she likes to call "Good Things," an approach more apt to break down social barriers than fortify them. One recent feature in *Martha Stewart Living* covered an impeccable soul-food luncheon served in a Harlem apartment.[7] Good taste and an appreciation for "Good Things" are, as Stewart presents them, meant to cross cultural, ethnic, and class lines, becoming accessible to everybody everywhere.

The democratizing of good taste has been decried: Pottery Barn, for 10 example, has been taxed by critics for offering mass-produced good design at bargain prices to mail-order customers in the hinterlands as well as to well-heeled urbanites. The implication — rather unflattering to design considered as a serious pursuit — is that a beautiful object loses its aesthetic value as soon as it gains wide appreciation. Beauty, in other words, is a quality conferred by an elite rather than created by an artist, and the patina vanishes as soon as the masses admire it. Stewart, I suspect, would disagree. Do her critics mistrust her because she encourages snobbery or because she undercuts it?

[5]*Martha Stewart Living* (June 1996), p. 156.
[6]*Martha Stewart Living* (September 1997), p. 216.
[7]*Martha Stewart Living* (May 1996), p. 104.

READING THE TEXT

1. What evidence does Caldwell provide to demonstrate Martha Stewart's status as an icon of the "lifestyle industry" (para. 2)?

2. What are the ingredients of Stewart's appeal to the consumers who turn to her for advice on domestic design, according to Caldwell?

3. What does Caldwell suggest is the basis for the criticism that Stewart encourages snobbery and materialism?

4. Explain in your own words what Caldwell means by the "democratizing of good taste" (para. 10).

READING THE SIGNS

1. Buy an issue of *Martha Stewart Living*, and analyze the text, the photographs, and the advertising. Use your observations as evidence for an essay in which you evaluate whether the magazine does "cross cultural, ethnic, and class lines" (para. 9).

2. Interview some fans of Martha Stewart's empire, asking them about their attraction to her products and the ways in which they use them. Do they, for instance, follow her instructions on making their own decorative objects? Did their attitudes toward Stewart change after her felony conviction? Use your results to formulate an argument about whether Stewart's appeal really is the "democratizing of good taste" (para. 10).

3. Visit a Martha Stewart display in a local KMart store, and study the layout and marketing features of this part of the store. Write a semiotic analysis of the display, focusing on how its design works to encourage consumption and to create brand loyalty. To develop your ideas, consult Anne Norton's "The Signs of Shopping" (p. 83) and Malcolm Gladwell's "The Science of Shopping" (p. 642).

4. Consult "The Progress Paradox" by Gregg Easterbrook (p. 400), and write an essay in which you argue whether the Martha Stewart empire and similar companies contribute to the pattern he describes: "material abundance may even have the perverse effect of instilling unhappiness" (para. 9).

JENNY LYN BADER

Larger Than Life

Do you have any heroes? Or does the very concept of heroism seem passé in today's irony-rich, self-conscious era? In this essay that first appeared in Next: Young American Writers on the New Generation *(1994), Jenny Lyn Bader (b. 1968) surveys the role of heroes for her generation, comparing her point of view with those of past generations. Maybe heroes are obsolete, Bader suggests; maybe we'd just be better off with role models who, while not providing the commanding presence of the full-fledged hero, can at least provide some guidance to an often confused Generation X. A New York–based playwright, Bader has published numerous essays on language and culture, specializing in artistic, spiritual, and moral issues. She is coauthor of* He Meant, She Meant: The Definitive Male-Female Dictionary *(1997).*

When my grandmother was young, she would sometimes spot the emperor Franz Josef riding down the cobbled roads of the Austro-Hungarian Empire.

She came of age so long ago that the few surviving photographs are colored cream and chestnut. Early on, she saw cars replace horses and carriages. When she got older, she marveled at the first televisions. Near the end of her life, she grew accustomed to remote control and could spot prime ministers on color TV. By the time she died, the world was freshly populated by gadgetry and myth. Her generation bore witness to the rise of new machinery created by visionaries. My generation has seen machinery break down and visionaries come under fire.

As children, we enjoyed collecting visionaries, the way we collected toys or baseball cards. When I was a kid, I first met Patrick Henry and Eleanor Roosevelt, Abraham Lincoln and Albert Einstein. They could always be summoned by the imagination and so were never late for play dates. I thought heroes figured in any decent childhood. I knew their stats.

Nathan Hale. Nelson Mandela. Heroes have guts.

Michelangelo. Shakespeare. Heroes have imagination. 5

They fight. Alexander the Great. Joan of Arc.

They fight for what they believe in. Susan B. Anthony. Martin Luther King.

Heroes overcome massive obstacles. Beethoven, while deaf, still managed to carry an unforgettable tune. Homer, while blind, never failed to give an excellent description. Helen Keller, both deaf and blind, still spoke to the world. FDR, despite his polio, became president. Moses, despite his speech impediment, held productive discussions with God.

They inspire three-hour movies. They make us weepy. They do the right thing while enduring attractive amounts of suffering. They tend to be

784

self-employed. They are often killed off. They sense the future. They lead lives that make us question our own. They are our ideals, but not our friends.

They don't have to be real. Some of them live in books and legends. They don't have to be famous. There are lower-profile heroes who get resurrected by ambitious biographers. There are collective heroes: firefighters and astronauts, unsung homemakers, persecuted peoples. There are those whose names we can't remember, only their deeds: "you know, that woman who swam the English Channel," "the guy who died running the first marathon," "the student who threw himself in front of the tank at Tiananmen Square." There are those whose names we'll never find out: the anonymous benefactor, the masked man, the undercover agent, the inventor of the wheel, the unknown soldier. The one who did the thing so gutsy and terrific that no one will ever know what it was.

Unlike icons (Marilyn, Elvis) heroes are not only sexy but noble, too. Unlike idols (Gretzky, Streisand), who vary from fan to fan, they are almost universally beloved. Unlike icons and idols, heroes lack irony. And unlike icons and idols, heroes are no longer in style.

As centuries end, so do visions of faith — maybe because the faithful get nervous as the double zeroes approach and question what they've been worshipping. Kings and queens got roughed up at the end of the eighteenth century; God took a beating at the end of the nineteenth; and as the twentieth century draws to a close, outstanding human beings are the casualties of the moment. In the 1970s and 1980s, Americans started feeling queasy about heroism. Those of us born in the sixties found ourselves on the cusp of that change. A sweep of new beliefs, priorities, and headlines has conspired to take our pantheon away from us.

Members of my generation believed in heroes when they were younger but now find themselves grasping for them. Even the word *hero* sounds awkward. I find myself embarrassed to ask people who their heroes are, because the word just doesn't trip off the tongue. My friend Katrin sounded irritated when I asked for hers. She said, "Oh, Jesus. . . . Do people still have heroes?"

We don't. Certainly not in the traditional sense of adoring perfect people. Frequently not at all. "I'm sort of intrigued by the fact that I don't have heroes right off the top of my head," said a colleague, Peter. "Can I get back to you?"

Some of us are more upset about this than others. It's easy to tell which of us miss the heroic age. We are moved by schmaltzy political speeches, we warm up to stories of pets saving their owners, we even get misty-eyed watching the Olympics. We mope when model citizens fail us. My college roommate, Linda, remembers a seventh-grade class called "Heroes and She-roes." The first assignment was to write about a personal hero or she-ro. "I came home," Linda told me, "and cried and cried because I didn't have one. . . . Carter had screwed up in Iran and given the malaise speech. Gerald Ford was a nothing and Nixon was evil. My parents told me to write about Jane Fonda the political activist and I just kept crying."

Not everyone feels sentimental about it. A twentyish émigré raised in the former Soviet Union told me: "It's kind of anticlimactic to look for heroes when you've been brought up in a culture that insists on so many heroes. . . . What do you want me to say? Lenin? Trotsky?" Even though I grew up in the relatively propaganda-free United States, I understood. The America of my childhood insisted on heroes, too.

Of all the myths I happily ate for breakfast, the most powerful one was our story of revolution. I sang about it as early as kindergarten and read about it long after. The story goes, a few guys in wigs skipped town on some grumpy church leaders and spurned a loopy king to branch out on their own. The children who hear the story realize they don't have to believe in old-fangled clergy or a rusty crown — but they had better believe in those guys with the wigs.

I sure did. I loved a set of books known as the "Meet" series: *Meet George Washington, Meet Andrew Jackson, Meet the Men Who Sailed the Seas*, and many more. I remember one picture of an inspired Thomas Jefferson, his auburn ponytail tied in a black ribbon, penning words with a feather as a battle of banners and cannon fire raged behind him.

A favorite "Meet" book starred Christopher Columbus. His resistance to the flat-earth society of his day was engrossing, especially to a kid like me who had trouble trying new foods let alone seeking new land masses. I identified with his yearning for a new world and his difficulty with finding investors. Standing up to the king and queen of Spain was like convincing your parents to let you do stuff they thought was idiotic. Now, my allowance was only thirty-five cents a week, but that didn't mean I wasn't going to ask for three ships at some later date.

This is pretty embarrassing: I adored those guys. The ones in the white 20 powder and ponytails, the voluptuous hats, the little breeches and cuffs. They were funny-looking, but lovable. They did outrageous things without asking for permission. They invented the pursuit of happiness.

I had a special fondness for Ben Franklin, statesman and eccentric inventor. Inventions, like heroes, made me feel as though I lived in a dull era. If I'd grown up at the end of the nineteenth century, I could have spoken on early telephones. A few decades later, I could have heard the new sounds of radio. In the sixties, I could have watched black-and-white TVs graduate to color.

Instead, I saw my colorful heroes demoted to black and white. Mostly white. By the time I finished high school, it was no longer hip to look up to the paternalistic dead white males who launched our country, kept slaves and mistresses, and massacred native peoples. Suddenly they weren't visionaries but oppressors, or worse — objects. Samuel Adams became a beer, John Hancock became a building, and the rest of the guys in wigs were knocked off one by one, in a whodunit that couldn't be explained away by the fact of growing up.

The flag-waving of my youth, epitomized by America's bicentennial, was a more loving homage than I know today. The year 1976 rolled in while Washington was still reeling from Saigon, but the irony was lost on me and my second-grade classmates. The idea of losing seemed miles away. We celebrated July Fourth with wide eyes and patriotic parties. Grown-ups had yet to tell themselves (so why should they tell us?) that the young nation on its birthday had suffered a tragic defeat.

Historians soon filled us in about that loss, and of others. Discovering America was nothing compared to discovering the flaws of its discoverers, now cast as imperialist sleaze, racist and sexist and genocidal. All things heroic — human potential, spiritual fervor, moral resplendence — soon became suspect. With the possible exception of bodybuilding, epic qualities went out of fashion. Some will remember 1992 as the year Superman died. Literally, the writers and illustrators at D.C. Comics decided the guy was too old to keep leaping buildings and rescuing an aging damsel in distress. When rumors circulated that he would be resurrected, readers protested via calls to radio shows, letters to editors, and complaints to stores that they were in no mood for such an event.

A monster named Doomsday killed Superman, overcoming him not with Kryptonite but with brute force. Who killed the others? I blame improved modes of character assassination, media hype artists, and scholars. The experts told me that Columbus had destroyed cultures and ravaged the environment. They also broke the news that the cowboys had brazenly taken land that wasn't theirs. In a way, I'm glad I didn't know that earlier; dressing up as a cowgirl for Halloween wouldn't have felt right. In a more urgent way, I wish I had known it then so I wouldn't have had to learn it later.

Just fifteen years after America's bicentennial came Columbus's quincentennial, when several towns canceled their annual parades in protest of his sins. Soon other festivities started to feel funny. When my aunt served corn pudding last Thanksgiving, my cousin took a spoonful, then said drily that the dish was made in honor of the Indians who taught us to use corn before we eliminated them. Uncomfortable chuckles followed. Actually, neither "we" nor my personal ancestors had come to America in time to kill any Native Americans. Yet the holiday put us in the same boat with the pilgrims and anchored us in the white man's domain.

I am fascinated by how we become "we" and "they." It's as if siding with the establishment is the Alka-Seltzer that helps us stomach the past. To swallow history lessons, we turn into "we": one nation under God of proud but remorseful Indian killers. We also identify with people who look like us. For example, white northerners studying the Civil War identify both with white slaveholders and with northern abolitionists, aligning with both race and place. Transsexuals empathize with men and women. Immigrants identify with their homeland and their adopted country. Historians proposing a black Athena and a black Jesus have inspired more of such bonding.

I'll admit that these empathies can be empowering. I always understood the idea of feeling stranded by unlikely role models but never emotionally grasped it until I watched Penny Marshall's movie *A League of Their Own*. For the first time, I appreciated why so many women complain that sports bore them. I had enjoyed baseball before but never as intensely as I enjoyed the games in that film. The players were people like me. Lori Petty, petite, chirpy, wearing a skirt, commanded the pitcher's mound with such aplomb that I was moved. There's something to be said for identifying with people who remind us of ourselves, though Thomas Jefferson and Lori Petty look more like each other than either of them looks like me. I'll never know if I would've read the "Meet" books with more zeal if they'd described our founding mothers. I liked them as they were.

Despite the thrill of dames batting something on the big screen besides their eyelashes, the fixation on look-alike idols is disturbing for those who get left out. In the movie *White Men Can't Jump*, Wesley Snipes tells Woody Harrelson not to listen to Jimi Hendrix, because "White people can't hear Jimi." Does this joke imply that black people can't hear Mozart? That I can admire Geena Davis's batting but never appreciate Carlton Fisk? Besides dividing us from one another, these emotional allegiances divide us from potential heroes too, causing us to empathize with, say, General Custer and his last stand instead of with Sitting Bull and the victorious Sioux.

Rejecting heroes for having the wrong ethnic credentials or sex organs 30 says less about our multicultural vision than our lack of imagination. By focusing on what we are instead of who we can become, by typecasting and miscasting our ideals — that's how we become "we" and "they." If heroes are those we'd like to emulate, it does make sense that they resemble us. But the focus on physical resemblance seems limited and racist.

Heroes should be judged on their deeds, and there are those with plenty in common heroically but not much in terms of ethnicity, nationality, or gender. Just look at Harriet Tubman and Moses; George Washington and Simón Bolivar; Mahatma Gandhi and Martin Luther King; Murasaki and Milton; Cicero and Ann Richards. Real paragons transcend nationality. It didn't matter to me that Robin Hood was English — as long as he did good, he was as American as a barbecue. It didn't matter to Queen Isabella that Columbus was Italian as long as he sailed for Spain and sprinkled her flags about. The British epic warrior Beowulf was actually Swedish. Both the German hero Etzel and the Scandinavian hero Atli were really Attila, king of the Huns. With all this borrowing going on, we shouldn't have to check the passports of our luminaries; the idea that we can be like them not literally but spiritually is what's uplifting in the first place.

The idea that we can never be like them has led to what I call jealousy journalism. You know, we're not remotely heroic so let's tear down anyone who is. It's become hard to remember which papers are tabloids. Tell-all articles promise us the "real story" — implying that greatness can't be real. The safe thing about *Meet George Washington* was that you couldn't actually meet him. Today's stories and pictures bring us closer. And actually meeting your heroes isn't the best idea. Who wants to learn that a favorite saint is really just an egomaniac with a publicist?

Media maestros have not only knocked public figures off their pedestals, they've also lowered heroism standards by idealizing just about everyone.

Oprah, Geraldo, and the rest turn their guests into heroes of the afternoon because they overcame abusive roommates, childhood disfigurement, deranged spouses, multiple genitalia, cheerleading practice, or zany sexual predilections. In under an hour, a studio audience can hear their epic sagas told.

While TV and magazine producers helped lead heroes to their graves, the academic community gave the final push. Just as my peers and I made our way through college, curriculum reformers were promoting "P.C." agendas at the expense of humanistic absolutes. Scholars invented their own tabloidism, investigating and maligning both dead professors and trusty historical figures. Even literary theory helped, when deconstructionists made it trendy to look for questions instead of answers, for circular logic instead of linear sense, for defects, contradictions, and the ironic instead of meaning, absolutes, and the heroic.

It was the generations that preceded ours who killed off our heroes. And 35 like everyone who crucified a superstar, these people thought they were doing a good thing. The professors and journalists consciously moved in a positive direction — toward greater tolerance, openness, and realism — eliminating our inspirations in the process. The death of an era of hero worship was not the result of the cynical, clinical materialism too often identified with my generation. It was the side effect of a complicated cultural surgery, of an operation that may have been necessary and that many prescribed.

So with the best of intentions, these storytellers destroyed bedtime stories. Which is too bad for the kids, because stories make great teachers. Children glean by example. You can't tell a child "Be ingenious," or "Do productive things." You can tell them, "This Paul Revere person jumped on a horse at midnight, rode wildly through the dark, figured out where the mean British troops were coming to attack the warm, fuzzy, sweet, great-looking colonists, and sent messages by code, igniting our fight for freedom," and they'll get the idea. America's rugged values come gift wrapped in the frontier tales of Paul Bunyan, Daniel Boone, Davy Crockett — fables of independence and natural resources. Kids understand that Johnny Appleseed or Laura Ingalls Wilder would never need a Cuisinart. Pioneer and prairie stories convey the fun of roughing it, showing kids how to be self-reliant, or at least less spoiled.

Children catch on to the idea of imitating qualities, not literal feats. After returning his storybook to the shelf, little Billy doesn't look around for a dragon to slay. Far-off stories capture the imagination in an abstract but compelling way, different from, say, the more immediate action-adventure flick. After watching a James Bond film festival, I might fantasize about killing the five people in front of me on line at the supermarket, while legends are remote enough that Columbus might inspire one to be original, but not necessarily to study Portuguese or enlist in the navy. In tales about conquerors and cavaliers, I first flirted with the idea of ideas.

Even Saturday-morning cartoons served me as parables, when I woke up early enough to watch the classy Superfriends do good deeds. Sure, the gender ratio between Wonder Woman and the gaggle of men in capes seemed unfair, but I was rapt. I wonder whether I glued myself to my television and my high expectations with too much trust, and helped to set my own heroes up for a fall.

Some heroes have literally been sentenced to death by their own follow-ers. *Batman* subscribers, for example, were responsible for getting rid of Bat-man's sidekick, Robin. At the end of one issue, the Joker threatened to kill the Boy Wonder, and readers could decide whether Robin lived or died by calling one of two "900" numbers. The public voted overwhelmingly for his murder. I understand the impulse of those who dialed for death. At a certain point, eter-nal invincibility grows as dull and predictable as wearing a yellow cape and red tights every day of the year. It's not human. We get fed up.

My generation helped to kill off heroism as teenagers, with our language. 40 We used heroic words that once described brave deeds — *excellent, amazing, awesome* — to describe a good slice of pizza or a sunny day. In our everyday speech, *bad* meant good. *Hot* meant cool. In the sarcastic slang of street gangs in Los Angeles, *hero* currently means traitor, specifically someone who snitches on a graffiti artist.

Even those of us who lived by them helped shatter our own myths, which wasn't all negative. We discovered that even the superhero meets his match. Every Achilles needs a podiatrist. Every rhapsodically handsome leader has a mistress or a moment of moral ambiguity. We injected a dose of reality into our expectations. We even saw a viable presidential candidate under a heap of slung mud, a few imperfections, an alleged tryst or two.

We're used to trysts in a way our elders aren't. Our parents and grandpar-ents behave as if they miss the good old days when adulterers wore letter sweaters. They feign shock at the extramarital exploits of Thomas Jefferson, Frank Sinatra, JFK, Princess Di. Their hero worship is a romance that falters when beloved knights end up unfaithful to their own spouses. People my age aren't amazed by betrayal. We are suspicious of shining armor. Even so, tabloid sales escalate when a Lancelot gives in to temptation — maybe because the jerk who cheats on you somehow becomes more attractive. Other genera-tions have gossiped many of our heroes into philanderers. The presumptuous hero who breaks your heart is the most compelling reason not to get involved in the first place.

Seeing your legends discredited is like ending a romance with someone you loved but ultimately didn't like. However much you longed to trust that per-son, it just makes more sense not to. Why pine away for an aloof godlet who proves unstable, erratic, and a rotten lover besides? It's sad to give up fantasies but mature to trade them in for healthier relationships grounded in reality.

We require a new pantheon: a set of heroes upon whom we can rely, who will not desert us when the winds change, and whom we will not desert. It's unsettling, if not downright depressing, to go through life embarrassed about the identity of one's childhood idols.

Maybe we should stick to role models instead. Heroes have become 45 quaint, as old-fashioned as gas-guzzlers — and as unwieldy, requiring too

Heroes for today: caps for sale in New York following September 11.

much investment and energy. Role models are more like compact cars, less glam and room but easier to handle. They take up less parking space in the imagination. Role models have a certain degree of consciousness about their job. The cast members of *Beverly Hills 90210*, for example, have acknowledged that they serve as role models for adolescents, and their characters behave accordingly: they refrain from committing major crimes; they overcome inclinations toward substance abuse; they see through adult hypocrisy; and any misdemeanors they do perpetrate are punished. For moral mediators we could do better, but at least the prime-time writing staff is aware of the burden of having teen groupies.

Heroes don't have the luxury of staff writers or the opportunity to endorse designer jeans. Hercules can't go on *Nightline* and pledge to stop taking steroids. Prometheus can't get a presidential pardon. Columbus won't have a chance to weep to Barbara Walters that he didn't mean to endanger leatherback turtles or monk seals or the tribes of the Lucayas. Elizabeth I never wrote a bestseller about how she did it her way.

Role models can go on talk shows, or even host them. Role models may live next door. While a hero might be a courageous head of state, a saint, a leader of armies, a role model might be someone who put in a three-day presidential bid, your local minister, your boss. They don't need their planes to go down in flames to earn respect. Role models have a job, accomplishment, or hairstyle worth emulating.

Rather than encompassing that vast kit and caboodle of ideals, role models can perform a little neat division of labor. One could wish to give orders like Norman Schwarzkopf but perform psychoanalysis like Lucy Van Pelt, to chair a round-table meeting as well as King Arthur but negotiate as well as Queen Esther,[1] to eat like Orson Welles but look like Helen of Troy, and so forth. It was General Schwarzkopf, the most tangible military hero for anyone my age, who vied instead for role-model status by claiming on the cover of his book: *It Doesn't Take a Hero.* With this title he modestly implies that anyone with some smarts and élan could strategize and storm as well as he has.

Role models are admirable individuals who haven't given up their lives or livelihoods and may even have a few hangups. They don't have to be prone to excessive self-sacrifice. They don't go on hunger strikes; they diet. They are therefore more likely than heroes to be free for lunch, and they are oftener still alive.

Heroism is a living thing for many of my contemporaries. In my informal 50 poll, I not only heard sob stories about the decline of heroes, I also discovered something surprising: the ascent of parents. While the founding fathers may be passé, actual mothers, fathers, grands, and great-grands are undeniably "in." An overwhelming number of those I polled named their household forebears as those they most admired. By choosing their own relatives as ideals, people in their twenties have replaced impersonal heroes with the most personal role models of all. Members of my purportedly lost generation have not only realized that it's time to stop believing in Santa Claus, they have chosen to believe instead in their families — the actual tooth fairy, the real Mr. and Mrs. Claus. They have stopped needing the folks from the North Pole, the guys with the wigs, the studs and studettes in tights and capes.

In a way it bodes well that Superman and the rest could be killed or reported missing. They were needed to quash the most villainous folks of all: insane communists bearing nuclear weapons, heinous war criminals, monsters named Doomsday. The good news about Superman bleeding to death was that Doomsday died in the struggle.

If the good guys are gone, so is the world that divides down the middle into good guys and bad guys. A world without heroes is a rigorous, demanding place, where things don't boil down to black and white but are rich with shades of gray; where faith in lofty, dead personages can be replaced by faith in ourselves and one another; where we must summon the strength to imagine a five-dimensional future in colors not yet invented. My generation grew up to see our world shift, so it's up to us to steer a course between naiveté and nihilism, to reshape vintage stories, to create stories of spirit without apologies.

I've heard a few. There was one about the woman who taught Shakespeare to inner-city fourth graders in Chicago who were previously thought to be retarded or hopeless. There was a college groundskeeper and night watchman, a black man with a seventh-grade education, who became a contracts expert, wrote poetry and memoirs, and invested his salary so wisely that he

---

[1] **Queen Esther** Jewish heroine of the biblical Book of Esther. —EDS.

bequeathed 450 acres of mountainous parkland to the university when he died. There was the motorcyclist who slid under an eighteen-wheeler at full speed, survived his physical therapy only to wind up in a plane crash, recovered, and as a disfigured quadriplegic started a business, got happily married, and ran for public office; his campaign button bore a caption that said "Send me to Congress and I won't be just another pretty face. . . ."

When asked for her heroes, a colleague of mine spoke of her great-grandmother, a woman whose husband left her with three kids in Galicia, near Poland, and went to the United States. He meant to send for her, but the First World War broke out. When she made it to America, her husband soon died, and she supported her family; at one point she even ran a nightclub. According to the great-granddaughter, "When she was ninety she would tell me she was going to volunteer at the hospital. I would ask how and she'd say, 'Oh, I just go over there to read to the old folks.' The 'old folks' were probably seventy. She was a great lady."

My grandmother saved her family, too, in the next great war. She did not 55 live to see the age of the fax, but she did see something remarkable in her time, more remarkable even than the emperor riding down the street: she saw him walking down the street. I used to ask her, "Did you really see the emperor Franz Josef walking down the street?"

She would say, "Ya. Walking down the street." I would laugh, and though she'd repeat it to amuse me, she did not see what was so funny. To me, the emperor was someone you met in history books, not on the streets of Vienna. He was larger than life, a surprising pedestrian. He was probably just getting some air, but he was also laying the groundwork for my nostalgia of that time when it would be natural for him to take an evening stroll, when those who were larger than life roamed cobblestones.

Today, life is larger.

READING THE TEXT

1. Why do you think Bader begins and ends her essay with an anecdote regarding her grandmother, and what effect does that anecdote have on the reader?
2. How does Bader define *hero, icon,* and *role model,* and what is her attitude toward each?
3. What are the heroes and myths that Bader grew up with, and how does she feel about them now?
4. In your own words, explain Bader's attitude toward political correctness.
5. How does Bader characterize her generation of twentysomethings?

READING THE SIGNS

1. In your journal, brainstorm a list of heroes whom you admired as a child, and then compare your list with the traditional heroes whom Bader mentions. How do you account for any differences or similarities?

2. Write an argumentative essay that supports, challenges, or modifies Bader's contention that her generation needs role models, not heroes.

3. In class, discuss how a writer might, as Bader suggests, "reshape vintage stories, . . . create stories of spirit without apologies" (para. 52). Then, in a creative essay, write your own "story of spirit."

4. In class, brainstorm a list of traditional American heroes, and then discuss whether they have lost their luster and, if so, why.

5. Assume Bader's perspective on heroes, and write an analytic essay in which you explain why Michael Jordan remains an admirable figure. To develop your ideas, consult Michael Eric Dyson's "Be Like Mike? Michael Jordan and the Pedagogy of Desire" (p. 734).

6. In class, discuss the extent to which the September 11, 2001, attacks altered Americans' conceptions of heroism. Use the discussion as the basis of an essay in which you propose your own definition of what constitutes a hero today.

GLOSSARY

archetype (n.)   A recurring character type or plot pattern found in literature, mythology, and popular culture. Sea monsters like Jonah's whale and Moby Dick are archetypes, as are stories that involve long sea journeys or descents into the underworld.

canon (n.)   Books or works that are considered essential to a literary tradition, as the plays of Shakespeare are part of the canon of English literature.

class (n.)   A group of related objects or people. Those who share the same economic status in a society are said to be of the same social class: for example, working class, middle class, upper class. Members of a social class tend to share the same interests and political viewpoints.

code (n.)   A system of **signs** or values that assigns meanings to the elements that belong to it. Thus, a traffic code defines a red light as a "stop" signal and a green light as a "go," while a fashion code determines whether an article of clothing is stylish. To *decode* a system is to figure out its meanings, as in interpreting the tattooing and body-piercing fads.

connotation (n.)   The meaning suggested by a word, as opposed to its objective reference, or **denotation**. Thus, the word *flag* might connote (or suggest) feelings of patriotism, while it literally denotes (or refers to) a pennantlike object.

consumption (n.)   The use of products and services, as opposed to their production. A *consumer culture* is one that consumes more than it produces. As a consumer culture, for example, America uses more goods such as TV sets and stereos than it manufactures, which results in a trade deficit with those *producer cultures* (such as Japan) with which America trades.

context (n.)   The environment in which a **sign** can be interpreted. In the context of a college classroom, for example, tee shirts, jeans, and sneakers are interpreted as ordinary casual dress. Wearing the same outfit in the context of a job interview at IBM would be interpreted as meaning that you're not serious about wanting the job.

cultural studies (n.)   The academic study of ordinary, everyday culture rather than **high culture**. See also **culture; culture industry; mass culture; popular culture**.

culture (n.)   The overall system of values and traditions shared by a group of people. Not exactly synonymous with *society*, which can include numerous cultures within its boundaries, a culture encompasses the worldviews of those who belong to it. Thus, the United States, which is a **multicultural** society, includes the differing worldviews of people of African, Asian, Native American, and European descent. See also **cultural studies; culture industry; high culture; mass culture; popular culture**.

culture industry (n.)   The commercial forces behind the production of **mass culture** or entertainment. See also **culture; cultural studies; high culture; mass culture; popular culture**.

denotation (n.)   The particular object or class of objects to which a word refers. Contrast with **connotation**.

discourse (n.)   The words, concepts, and presuppositions that constitute the knowledge and understanding of a particular community, often academic or professional.

dominant culture (n.)   The group within a **multicultural** society whose traditions, values, and beliefs are held to be normative, as the European tradition is the dominant culture in the United States.

Eurocentric (adj.)   Related to a worldview founded on the traditions and history of European culture, usually at the expense of non-European cultures.

function (n.)   The utility of an object, as opposed to its cultural meaning. Spandex or lycra shorts, for example, have a functional value for cyclists because they're lightweight and aerodynamic. On the other hand, such shorts have become a general fashion item for both men and women because of their cultural meaning, not their function. Many noncyclists wear spandex to project an image of hard-bodied fitness, sexiness, or just plain trendiness, for instance.

gender (n.)   One's sexual identity and the roles that follow from it, as determined by the norms of one's culture rather than by biology or genetics. The assumption that women should be foremost in the nurturing of children is a gender norm; the fact that only women can give birth is a biological phenomenon.

hacker (n.)   A person who "breaks into" another person's or an institution's computer system without permission, either for entertainment or criminal purposes.

high culture (n.)   The products of the elite arts, including classical music, literature, drama, opera, painting, and sculpture. See also **cultural studies; culture; culture industry; mass culture; popular culture**.

icon (n.), **iconic** (adj.)   In **semiotics**, a **sign** that visibly resembles its referent, as a photograph looks like the thing it represents. More broadly, an icon is someone (often a celebrity) who enjoys a commanding or representative place in popular culture. Michael Jackson and Madonna are music video icons. Contrast with **symbol**.

ideology (n.)   The beliefs, interests, and values that determine one's interpretations or judgments and that are often associated with one's social class. For example, in the ideology of modern business, a business is designed to produce profits, not social benefits.

image (n.)   Literally, a pictorial representation; more generally, the identity that one projects to others through such things as clothing, grooming, speech, and behavior.

Internet (n.)   An electronic network, originally developed for military purposes, that links millions of computers around the world. Also called the *Net, World Wide Web,* or *Web.*

mass culture (n.)   A subset of **popular culture** that includes the popular entertainments that are commercially produced for widespread consumption. See also **cultural studies; culture; culture industry; high culture**.

mass media (n. pl.)   The means of communication, often controlled by the **culture industry**, that include newspapers, popular magazines, radio, television, film, and the Internet.

multiculturalism (n.), **multicultural** (adj.)   In American education, the movement to incorporate the traditions, history, and beliefs of the United States' non-European cultures into a traditionally *monocultural* (or single-culture) curriculum dominated by European thought and history.

mythology (n.)   The overall framework of values and beliefs incorporated in a given cultural system or worldview. Any given belief within such a structure — like the belief that "a woman's place is in the home" — is called a *myth.*

politics (n.)   Essentially, the practice of promoting one's interests in a competitive social environment. Not restricted to electioneering; there may be office politics, classroom politics, academic politics, and sexual politics.

popular culture (n.)   That segment of a **culture** that incorporates the activities of everyday life, including the consumption of consumer goods and the production and enjoyment of mass-produced entertainments. See also **cultural studies; culture industry; high culture; mass culture**.

postmodernism (n.), **postmodern** (adj.)   The worldview behind contemporary literature, art, music, architecture, and philosophy that rejects traditional attempts to make meaning out of human history and experience. For the *postmodern* artist, art does not attempt to create new explanatory myths or **symbols** but rather recycles or repeats existing images, as does the art of Andy Warhol.

semiotics (n.)   In short, the study of **signs**. Synonymous with *semiology*, semiotics is concerned with both the theory and practice of interpreting linguistic, cultural, and behavioral sign systems. One who practices *semiotic analysis* is called a *semiotician* or *semiologist*.

sign (n.)   Anything that bears a meaning. Words, objects, images, and forms of behavior are all signs whose meanings are determined by the particular **codes**, or **systems**, in which they appear.

symbol (n.), **symbolic** (adj.)   A **sign**, according to semiotician C. S. Peirce, whose significance is arbitrary. The meaning of the word *bear*, for example, is arbitrarily determined by those who use it. Contrast with **icon**.

system (n.)   The **code**, or network, within which a **sign** functions and so achieves its meaning through its associational and differential relations with other signs. The English language is a sign system, as is a fashion code.

text (n.)   A complex of **signs**, which may be linguistic, imagistic, behavioral, or musical, that can be read or interpreted.

virtual reality (n.)   A simulated world that is created using computer technology.

Acknowledgments (continued from page iv)

Melissa Algranati. "Being an Other." From *Becoming American, Becoming Ethnic: College Students Explore Their Roots*, edited by Thomas Dublin. Copyright © 1996 by Melissa Algranati. Reprinted by permission of the author.

Jenny Lyn Bader. "Larger Than Life." From *Next: Young American Writers of the New Generation*, edited by Eric Liu. Copyright © 1994 by Jenny Lyn Bader. Reprinted by permission of the William Morris Agency as agents for the author.

Nell Bernstein. "Goin' Gangsta, Choosin' Cholita." Copyright © 1995 by Nell Bernstein. First published in *The Utne Reader*, March–April 1995. Reprinted by permission of the author.

Deborah Blum. Excerpt from *The Gender Blur: Where Does Biology End and Society Take Over?* by Deborah Blum. Copyright © 1997 by Deborah Blum. Reprinted by permission of International Creative Management, Inc.

Todd Boyd. "So You Wanna Be a Gangsta?" From *Am I Black Enough for You?* by Todd Edward Boyd, pp. 82–103. Copyright © 1997 by Indiana University Press. Reprinted by permission of the publisher.

Jake Brennan. "Celebrities Who Aren't Really Celebrities." From www.askman.com. Reprinted by permission of the author.

David Brooks. "One Nation, Slightly Divisible." From *The Atlantic Monthly*, December 2001. Copyright © 2001 by David Brooks. Reprinted by permission of the author.

Sean Cahill. "The Case for Marriage Equality." From *Same-Sex Marriage in the United States* by Sean Cahill. Copyright © 2004 by Lexington Books. Reprinted with the permission of the publisher.

Mark Caldwell. "The Assault on Martha Stewart." From *A Short History of Rudeness* by Mark Caldwell. Copyright © 1999 by Mark Caldwell. Reprinted by permission of St. Martin's Press, LLC.

Marisa Connolly. "Homosexuality on Television: The Heterosexualization of *Will and Grace*." From www.gnovis.georgetown.edu. Georgetown University's online peer-reviewed journal of Communication, Culture, and Technology, Volume 3, Fall 2003, gnovis.georgetown.edu. Reprinted by permission of the author.

Richard Corliss. "The Gospel According to *Spider-Man*." From *Time*, August 16, 2004. Copyright © 2005 Time, Inc. Reprinted by permission.

Steve Craig. "Men's Men and Women's Women:" From *Issues and Effects of Mass Communication: Other Voices* by Steve Craig. Reprinted with the permission of the author.

Anita Creamer. "Reality TV Meets Plastic Surgery: An Ugly Shame." From *The Sacramento Bee*, April 18, 2005. Copyright © 2005, The Sacramento Bee. Reprinted with permission.

Gary Cross. "Barbie, G.I. Joe, and Play in the 1960s." From *Kids' Stuff: Toys and the Changing World of American Childhood* by Gary Cross, pp. 171–77. Copyright © 1997 by the President and Fellows of Harvard College. Reprinted by permission of the publisher.

Fred Davis. "Blue Jeans." From *Fashion, Culture, and Identity* by Fred Davis. Copyright © 1992 by Fred Davis. First appeared in *Qualitative Sociology* 12, No. 4 (Winter 1989). Reprinted with permission of The University of Chicago Press.

Benjamin DeMott. "Put on a Happy Face: Masking the Differences between Blacks and Whites." Copyright © 1995 by *Harper's Magazine*. All rights reserved. Reproduced from the September issue by special permission.

David Denby. "High-School Confidential: Notes on Teen Movies." First published in *The New Yorker*, May 31, 1999. Copyright © 1999 by David Denby. Reprinted with the permission of the author.

Aaron Devor. "Gender Role Behaviors and Attitudes." From *Gender Blending: Confronting the Limits of Duality* by Holly Devor. Copyright © 1989 by Indiana University Press. Reprinted with permission of the publisher.

Susan Douglas. "Signs of Intelligent Life on TV." Appeared in May–June 1995 issue of *Ms. Magazine*. Copyright © 1995 by *Ms. Magazine*. Reprinted by permission of *Ms. Magazine* and the author.

Michael Eric Dyson. "Be Like Mike? Michael Jordan and the Pedagogy of Desire." From *Cultural Studies*, vol 6, 1993. Reprinted by permission of Taylor & Francis Ltd. www.tandf.co.uk.

Laurence Shames. "The More Factor." From *The Hunger for More* by Laurence Shames. Copyright © 1989 by Laurence Shames. Published by Times Books, a division of Random House, Inc. Reprinted with permission of the Stuart Krichevsky Agency, Inc.

Fan Shen. "The Classroom and the Wider Culture: Identity as a Key to Learning English Composition." From *College Composition and Communication 40*, December 1989. Copyright © 1989 by the National Council of Teachers of English. Reprinted with permission.

Vivian C. Sobchack. "The Postmorbid Condition." An excerpt from "The Violent Dance: A Personal Memoir of Death in the Movies" (pp. 119–24), from *Screening Violence*, ed. Stephen Prince. Reprinted by permission of the author.

Jack Solomon. "Masters of Desire: The Culture of American Advertising." From *The Signs of Our Time* by Jack Fisher Solomon. Used by permission of Jeremy P. Tarcher, an imprint of Penguin Group (USA) Inc.

Daphne Spain. "Spatial Segregation and Gender Stratification in the Workplace." From *Gendered Spaces* by Daphne Spain. Copyright © 1992 by the University of North Carolina Press. Used by permission of the publisher.

Steven D. Stark. "*The Oprah Winfrey Show* and the Talk-Show Furor." From *Glued to the Set: The Sixty Television Shows and Events That Made Us What We Are* by Steven D. Stark. Copyright © 1997 by Steven D. Stark. Reprinted with the permission of The Free Press, a Division of Simon & Schuster Adult Publishing Group. All rights reserved.

Gloria Steinem. "Sex, Lies, and Advertising." From *Ms. Magazine*, July/August 1990. Copyright © 1990 Gloria Steinem. Updated in *Moving Beyond Words* by Gloria Steinem. © 1994 by Gloria Steinem. Reprinted with the permission of East Toledo Productions.

C. Carney Strange and James H. Banning. "Educating by Design." Originally titled: "Physical Environments: The Role of Design and Space," from *Educating by Design* by Strange and Banning. Copyright © 2001 by Jossey-Bass. Reprinted with permission of John Wiley & Sons, Inc.

Rina Swentzell. "Conflicting Landscape Values: The Santa Clara Pueblo and Day School." From *Understanding Ordinary Landscapes* by Groth and Brissi, pp. 56–66. Copyright © 1997 by Yale University Press. Reprinted by permission of Yale University Press.

Deborah Tannen. "There Is No Unmarked Woman." Originally titled "Marked Women, Unmarked Men," as published in *The New York Times*, June 20, 1993. Copyright © Deborah Tannen. Reprinted with permission by the author.

Paul C. Taylor. "Funky White Boys and Honorary Soul Sisters." First published in the *Michigan Quarterly Review*, (Spring 1997) vol 36: 2: 320–35. Copyright © 1997 Paul C. Taylor. Reprinted by permission of the author.

James B. Twitchell. "What We Are to Advertisers." From *Lead Us into Temptation: The Triumph of American Materialism* by James B. Twitchell. Copyright © 1999 by James B. Twitchell. Reprinted by permission of the author.

Camilo José Vergara. "The Ghetto Cityscape." From *The New American Ghetto* by Camilo José Vergara. Copyright © 1995 by Camilo José Vergara. Reprinted by permission of Rutgers University Press.

Susan Willis. "Disney World: Public Use / Private State." From pp. 180–98 in *Inside the Mouse: Work and Play at Disney World* by Susan Willis. Copyright © 1995, Duke University Press. Reprinted by permission of the publisher. All rights reserved.

Naomi Wolf. Excerpt from pp. 9–19 in *The Beauty Myth* by Naomi Wolf. Copyright © 1991 by Naomi Wolf. Reprinted by permission of HarperCollins Publishing Inc. William Morrow Inc.

Leon E. Wynter. "Marketing in Color." From *American Skin* by Leon Wynter. Copyright © 2002 by Leon Wynter. Reprinted by permission of the William Morris Agency, Inc. on behalf of the author.

ARTWORK

Introduction
Symphony orchestra, © Miro Vintoniv/Stock Boston.
Barnum & Bailey circus poster, courtesy of The Granger Collection, New York.

Woman with ipod, © Mario Tama/Getty Images.
Leave It to Beaver television still, © ABC/THE KOBAL COLLECTION.
Woman in VW beetle, courtesy Sonia Maasik.
Wizard of Oz film still, © MGM/THE KOBAL COLLECTION.
Casablanca film still, © WARNER BROS/THE KOBAL COLLECTION.
Elvis Presley in *Jail House Rock*, © MGM/THE KOBAL COLLECTION.
The Beatles on Ed Sullivan, © Bernard Gotfryd/Hulton Archive/Getty Images.
Saturday Night Fever film still, © PARAMOUNT/THE KOBAL COLLECTION.
Madonna performs, © Mike Segar/Reuters/Landov.
Britney Spears and snake, © Frank Micelotta/Getty Images.
Lee Jeans advertisement, Image courtesy of The Advertising Archives.
Chapter 1
Roz Chast Economy Doctor cartoon, © The New Yorker Collection 2001, Roz Chast from cartoonbank.com. All Rights Reserved.
Best Buy Christmas Shoppers, © AP Photo/Lincoln Journal Star, Ken Blackbird.
SUV bumpersticker, © AP Photo/Justin Sullivan.
Street in Lahore, Pakistan, © Sean Sprague/Stock Boston.
Chapter 2
Mind if I Smoke? billboard, © Theo Anderson/Independent Photographers Network (IPN).
Home Shopping Network television still, © Jeff Greenberg/PhotoEdit.
Star Wars cereal box, © Bill Freeman/PhotoEdit.
OnStar ad, courtesy of OnStar. Used by permission.
Sub-Zero ad, courtesy of Sub-Zero and New Yorker cartoonist Danny Shanahan. Used by permission.
Redwood Creek, courtesy of Redwood Creek/E.J. Gallo. Used by permission.
Phoenix Wealth, courtesy of The Phoenix Companies, Inc. Used by permission.
Symantec, courtesy of Symantec Corporation. Used by permission.
Nevada Tourism, courtesy of Nevada Commission on Tourism. Used by permission.
Cooper Tire, courtesy of Cooper Tire & Rubber Company and Chas Krider Photography. Used by permission.
Chapter 3
I Love Lucy film still, courtesy CBS Photo Archive/Hulton Archive/Getty Images.
American Idol finalists, © Robert Galbraith/Reuters/Landov.
Survivor television still, © Monty Brinton/CBS Photo Archive. CBS Broadcasting, Inc. All Rights Reserved.
The Apprentice banner at Trump Tower, © Nancy Kaszerman/ZUMA/Corbis.
Oprah Winfrey, © AP Photo/Ron Wurzer.
Salt 'n' Pepa perform, © David Corio.
Chapter 4
Hollywood Sign, © Robert Landau/CORBIS.
Row of Oscar Statues, © EuroStyle Graphics, photographersdirect.com.
Star Wars film still, courtesy of Photofest.
American Me film still, courtesy of Photofest.
Rhett and Scarlett in *Gone with the Wind*, © SELZNICK/MGM/THE KOBAL COLLECTION.
Michelle Yeoh in *Tomorrow Never Dies*, courtesy of Photofest.
Anna May Wong, courtesy of Photofest.
Pulp Fiction film still, courtesy of Photofest.
Chapter 5
Janet Jackson and Justin Timberlake perform at Super Bowl halftime, © AP Photo/Elise Amendola.
Leave Area Clean/pollution photo, © Royalty-Free/CORBIS.
Times Square, © Joel Gordon.
Panhandler on Cleveland sidewalk, © Alan Goldsmith/CORBIS.
Serena Williams, © AP Photo/Alastair Grant.
Which Man Looks Guilty? advertisement, © Bill Aron/PhotoEdit.

Chapter 6

Hennessy advertisement, "appropriately complex," appears by permission of Jas Hennessy & Co., France/Schieffelin & Somerset distributors.

Househusband greets working wife, © Geoff Manasse/Independent Photographers Network/IPN.

Seniors march for gay rights, © Joel Gordon.

Girls and mothers looking at newborn dolls, © Jeff Greenberg/The Image Works.

At the beauty parlor, © Joel Gordon.

"Hey Bud" advertisement, © Michael Newman/PhotoEdit.

Chapter 7

Crayola multi-cultural pack, © AP Photo/Douglas Healey.

Alicia Keys, © Robert Spencer/Retna.

Stevie Ray Vaughan, © Andrea Laubach/Retna.

Mother and son in Appalachia, © David Turnley/CORBIS.

Beverly Hillbillies television still, © CBS Photo Archive/Getty Images.

Chapter 8

Mall interior, © Mike Mazzaschi/Stock Boston.

The home as work space, © Stephen Simpson/Getty Images.

Disneyworld, © Dagmar Fabricius/Stock Boston.

Family argument at dinner, © Richard Hutchings/Photo Researchers.

Santa Clara Pueblo J.K. Hillers, 1879 courtesy of the Smithsonian Institution, National Anthropological Archives.

Santa Clara Pueblo Fayette W. Van Zile, 1930, courtesy of the Smithsonian Institution, National Anthropological Archives.

Santa Clara Pueblo Vroman, 1899 (Hillers), courtesy of the Smithsonian Institution, National Anthropological Archives.

Santa Clara Pueblo Vroman, 1899, courtesy of the Smithsonian Institution, National Anthropological Archives.

Drawings of layouts of Santa Clara appear by permission of Rina Swentzell.

Photo of BIA School at Santa Clara appears by permission of Rina Swentzell.

Camilo Jose Vergara, "Sterling Street, Newark, 1980." Copyright © 1995 by Camilo Jose Vergara. By permission of the author.

Camilo Jose Vergara, "Sterling Street replaced by parking lot, 1994." Copyright © 1995 by Camilo Jose Vergara. By permission of the author.

Niketown store interior, © Cathy Melloan Resources/PhotoEdit.

Photographs from Barrie Greenbie, *Spaces: Dimensions of the Human Landscape* © 1981 Yale University Press. Used by permission of Mrs. Vlasta Greenbie and Yale University Press.

Chapter 9

Elvis performs, © AP Photo.

Mr. Clean advertisement, Copyright © The Procter & Gamble Company. Used by permission.

Boy licking GI Joe doll, © Steven Rubin/The Image Works.

Ken giving Barbie an Oscar, © Topham/The Image Works.

Marilyn Monroe and Joe DiMaggio on their wedding day, courtesy The Kobal Collection.

Superman collector, © Michael Justice/The Image Works.

NYPD hats for sale at World Trade Center site, © Arnold Gold/New Haven Register/The Image Works.

Index of Authors and Titles